DICTIONARY OF HOLLAND OCCUPATIONAL CODES

Third Edition

Gary D. Gottfredson, PhD
John L. Holland, PhD

DICTIONARY OF HOLLAND OCCUPATIONAL CODES

Third Edition

Gary D. Gottfredson, PhD
John L. Holland, PhD

PAR Psychological Assessment Resources, Inc.

Library of Congress Cataloging-in-Publication Data

Gottfredson, Gary D.
　　Dictionary of Holland occupational codes / Gary D. Gottfredson,
John L. Holland. — 3rd ed.
　　　　　p.　cm.
　　Includes bibliographical references and index.
　　ISBN 0-911907-26-2
　　1. Occupations—United States—Classification. 2. Occupations—Classification.
3. Vocational guidance—United States.
I. Holland, John L. II. Title.
HB2595.G67 1996
331.7'0012—dc20　　　　　　　　　　　　　　　　　　　　　　　96-43949
　　　　　　　　　　　　　　　　　　　　　　　　　　　　　　　　　CIP

9 8 7 6 5　　　　　　　Reorder #3488 (1-800-331-TEST)　　　Printed in the U.S.A.

TABLE OF CONTENTS

Part 1: Introduction to Using Holland Codes

This volume applies the Holland environmental classification to seven of the most widely used occupational classifications and information sources in the United States. It makes Holland's theory of person–job congruence accessible to counselors, clients, and researchers who use or wish to use the voluminous amounts of occupational information collected by state and federal agencies.

Part 1 of this volume introduces Holland's (1985/1992) theory of vocational personalities and work environments and the typologies of persons and environments that are at its heart. The classification of work environments is highlighted in this introduction, and the description is drawn from the account provided by Gottfredson and Holland (1991). This theory is intended to explain career choice, satisfaction, and persistence. This section also introduces classifications developed by the U.S. Departments of Labor, Commerce, and Education for gathering and reporting employment and education statistics. These include the classification and definitions provided by the *Dictionary of Occupational Titles* (DOT; Employment and Training Administration, 1991a), the *Occupational Employment Statistics* system (OES; Bureau of Labor Statistics, 1995), the *Standard Occupational Classification* (SOC) *Manual* (Office of Federal Statistical Policy Standards,1980), the *Census Occupational Classification* (COC; Bureau of the Census, 1992), the *Classification of Instructional Programs* (CIP; National Center for Education Statistics, 1991), the *Guide for Occupational Exploration Classification* (GOE; Harrington & O'Shea, 1984; U.S. Department of Labor, 1979), and the *Occupational Outlook Handbook* (OOH; Bureau of Labor Statistics, 1996).

Part 2 provides a way for users of occupational information to go from an assessment of an individual's vocational interests or personality to occupational information accessible through the seven government classifications listed in the preceding paragraph. Part 3 provides a way to go from an occupational title used in any other classification to the Holland classification.

The theoretical origin and statistical development of the Holland codes are summarized in Part 4. This part describes how job analysis ratings of each DOT occupation were used to create a three-letter code. The development of this comprehensive classification also produced some valuable byproducts: a clearer knowledge of the distinguishing characteristics of each occupational category, the distribution of occupations among the categories, and more evidence of the validity of the classification.

The codes in this volume are the outcome of the fifth major attempt to extend the Holland classification to all occupations. Earlier attempts (Gottfredson & Holland, 1989; Gottfredson, Holland, & Ogawa, 1982; Holland, 1973; Viernstein, 1972) were helpful and led to this reorganization. Although the present classification is the most recent, the codes listed still should be regarded as useful approximations. The results of future research will eventually lead to another revision as the classification is improved in response to new data.

The extension of the earlier work to the current compendium of codes for new occupations and to more governmental classification systems is described in Part 5. Some applications of the Holland classification in research and practice are described in Part 6.

What Is the Classification? Two Parallel Typologies

The occupational–environmental typology is based on a theory of persons and work environments (Holland, 1985/1992). The theory uses a classification of persons to describe and explain individual differences and similarities, and a classification of work environments to describe and explain differences and similarities among positions and occupations. The theory uses both classifications and a small number of additional concepts to explain career choice and persistence, attraction and retention of workers, and job satisfaction and environmental compatibility.

Persons

People can be described by their degree of resemblance to six theoretical personality types labeled Realistic, Investigative, Artistic, Social, Enterprising, or Conventional. Each type is characterized by distinctive preferences, outlooks, competencies, and self-perceptions. In practical application, information about a person's preferences, outlooks, competencies, and self-estimates is used to assess the degree to which an individual resembles each of the six personality types. The Self-Directed Search (SDS; Holland, Powell, & Fritzsche, 1994) is the most direct implementation of the theory for classifying individuals, although a number of other inventories also aim to implement the theory.

The six personality types are briefly described in Table 1. These ideal personality types are used to describe the similarity of any particular individual to one or more of these stereotypical abstractions.

To apply the classification, *individuals* are described according to their degree of resemblance to the six ideal personality types. The SDS (Holland, Powell, & Fritzsche, 1994) or the Vocational Preference Inventory (VPI; Holland, 1985) can be used to assess the degree of resemblance of a person to the six personality types. The categories into which a person's expressed occupational aspirations or history of employment fall also can be used to estimate the resemblance of a person to the six ideal types.

Environments

The personality types are paralleled by six model environments that also are used to describe the resemblance of specific work environments to abstract models. The present volume focuses on the environmental typology. The salient features of the environmental models are summarized in Table 2.

Realistic. The Realistic model environment requires manual and mechanical competencies and interaction with machines, tools, and objects. It rewards the display of practical, mechanical, technical, and physical abilities. The Realistic model environment allows the expression of practical, productive, and concrete values and robust, adventurous, and risky personal styles. This environment demands and rewards conforming behavior and practical accomplishment. Occupations classified as Realistic tend to involve concrete and practical activity and the use of machines, tools, or materials.

Investigative. The Investigative model environment requires analytical, technical, scientific, and verbal competencies. It rewards the display of skepticism and persistence in problem solving, the achievement or documentation of new knowledge, or the understanding or solution of practical and technical problems. Occupations classified as Investigative tend to involve analytical or intellectual activity aimed at problem solving, trouble-shooting, or the creation and use of knowledge.

Artistic. The Artistic model environment requires innovation or creative ability. It rewards the display of imagination in artistic, literary, or musical accomplishments, and allows the expression of unconventional ideas or manners. Occupations classified as Artistic generally involve creative work in the arts: music, writing, performance, sculpture, or other relatively unstructured and intellectual endeavors.

Table 1
A Brief Description of the Holland Personality Typology

Attribute	Personality Type					
	Realistic	Investigative	Artistic	Social	Enterprising	Conventional
Preferences for activities and occupations	Manipulation of machines, tools and things	Exploration, understanding and prediction or control of natural and social phenomena	Literary, musical, or artistic activities	Helping, teaching, treating, counseling, or serving others through personal interaction	Persuading, manipulating, or directing others	Establishing or maintaining orderly routines, application of standards
Values	Material rewards for tangible accomplishments	Development or acquisition of knowledge	Creative expression of ideas, emotions or sentiments	Fostering the welfare of others, social service	Material accomplishment and social status	Material or financial accomplishment and power in social, business, or political arenas
Sees self as	Practical, conservative, and having manual and mechanical skills—lacking social skills	Analytical, intelligent, skeptical and having academic talent—lacking interpersonal skills	Open to experience, innovative, intellectual—lacking clerical or office skills	Empathic, patient, and having interpersonal skills —lacking mechanical ability	Having sales and persuasive ability —lacking scientific ability	Having technical skills in business or production—lacking artistic competencies
Others see as	Normal, frank	Asocial, intellectual	Unconventional, disorderly, creative	Nurturing, agreeable, extroverted	Energetic, gregarious	Careful, conforming
Avoids	Interaction with people	Persuasion or sales activities	Routines and conformity to established rules	Mechanical and technical activity	Scientific, intellectual, or abstruse topics	Ambiguous or unstructured undertakings

Table 2
A Brief Description of the Holland Environmental Typology

Attribute	Environmental Type					
	Realistic	Investigative	Artistic	Social	Enterprising	Conventional
Requires	Manual and mechanical competencies, interaction with machines, tools, and objects	Analytical, technical, scientific, and verbal competencies	Innovation or creative ability, emotionally expressive interaction with others	Interpersonal competencies, skill in mentoring, treating, healing, or teaching others	Skills in persuasion and manipulation of others	Clerical skills, skills in meeting precise standards for performance
Demands and rewards the display of	Conforming behavior, practical accomplishment	Skepticism and persistence in problem solving, documentation of new knowledge, understanding or solution of problems	Imagination in literary, artistic or musical accomplishment	Empathy, humanitarianism sociability, friendliness	Initiative in the pursuit of financial or material accomplishment; dominance; self-confidence	Organizational ability, conformity, dependability
Values or personal styles allowed expression	Practical, productive and concrete values; robust, risky, adventurous styles	Acquisition of knowledge through scholarship or investigation	Unconventional ideas or manners, aesthetic values	Concern for the welfare of others	Acquisitive or power-oriented styles, responsibility	Conventional outlook and concern for orderliness and routines
Occupations or other environments involve	Concrete, practical activity; use of machines, tools, materials	Analytical or intellectual activity aimed at trouble-shooting or creation and use of knowledge	Creative work in music, writing, performance, sculpture, or unstructured intellectual endeavors	Working with others in a helpful or facilitating way	Selling, leading, manipulating others to attain personal or organizational goals	Working with things, numbers, or machines to meet predictable organizational demands or specified standards
Sample occupations	Carpenter, truck operator	Psychologist, microbiologist	Musician, interior designer	Counselor, clergy member	Lawyer, retail store manager	Production editor, bookkeeper

Social. The Social model environment requires interpersonal competencies and skill in treating, healing, or teaching others. The Social environment allows the expression of empathy and humanitarianism. It rewards the expression of concern for the welfare of others. Occupations classified as Social typically involve working with people in a helpful or facilitative way.

Enterprising. The Enterprising model environment requires skills in the persuasion and manipulation of other people. It allows the expression of acquisitive or power-oriented personal styles. It rewards initiative in the pursuit of financial or material accomplishment. Occupations classified as Enterprising tend to involve working with people in a supervisory or persuasive way to achieve some organizational goal.

Conventional. The Conventional model environment requires clerical skills or skills in meeting precise standards for performance. It allows the expression of a conventional outlook and a concern for orderliness and routines. It rewards organizational ability, conformity, and dependability. Occupations classified as conventional typically involve working with things, numbers, or machines in an orderly way to meet the regular and predictable demands of an organization or to meet specified standards.

Work environments are assessed or described according to their degree of resemblance to the six ideal environmental types. Several methods are used to assess the degree of resemblance of a position or occupation to the model environments. Occupations were originally classified according to the inventoried interests of persons employed in or aspiring to them (Holland, 1973). More recently, occupations were classified by using job analysis data developed by the U.S. Employment Service to produce the forerunner of the present volume (Gottfredson & Holland, 1989). The Position Classification Inventory (PCI; Gottfredson & Holland, 1991)—a structured job analysis inventory—is the most recent method for identifying occupations according to the theoretical classification. It is the method that most directly applies the theoretical formulations to implement the classification.

Any particular occupational environment will show a profile of resemblance to the six ideal types. For example, the PCI profile for experimental psychologist shown in Figure 1 implies that this occupation most resembles the Investigative environmental model, followed by Artistic. This profile is based on job descriptions by 10 incumbents. In most applications, a one- to three-letter code describes the types an environment most resembles. By convention, the first letter denotes the environmental model resembled most, the second letter denotes the type next most closely resembled, and so on. By the use of two- or three-letter codes, the six main categories are divided into a larger number of subcategories.

Some environmental models are more closely related than others; similarly, certain personality types are more closely related than others. These degrees of resemblance are summarized by the hexagonal arrangement in Figure 2. Theoretically, distances on the hexagonal model are inversely proportional to the resemblances among the types. For example, a Realistic occupation is more closely related to a Conventional or an Investigative occupation than it is to a Social occupation. Environments opposite each other on the hexagon are most distinct from one another. The Realistic environment often involves work with machines or tools, whereas the Social environment involves work with people rather than tools or machines. The Investigative environment requires skepticism and analytical skill, whereas the Enterprising environment requires persuasiveness and other social skills. The Artistic environment requires creativity, whereas the Conventional environment rewards orderliness and the application of established rules or standards for performance.

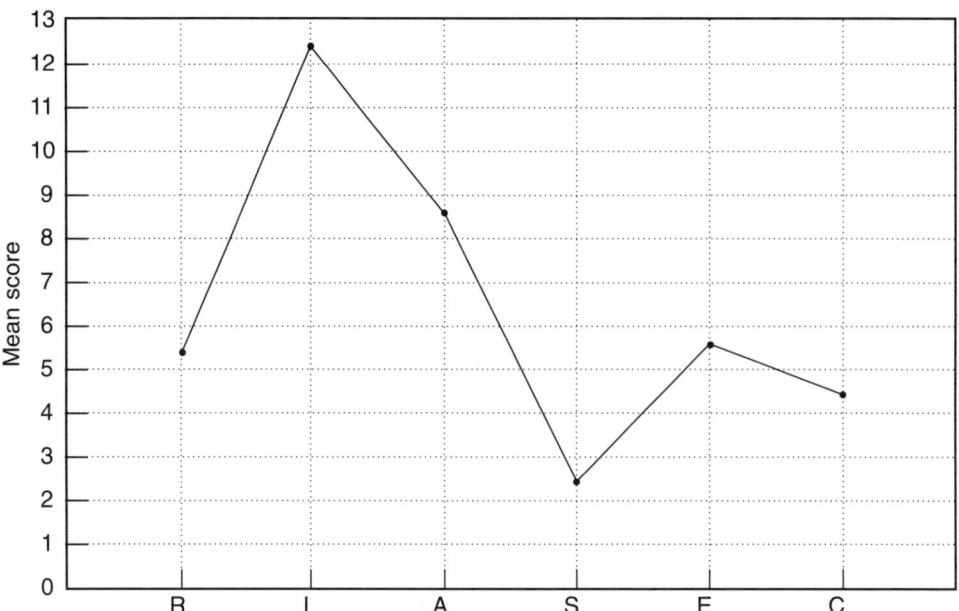

Figure 1. Position Classification Inventory profile, experimental psychologist. Job descriptions were provided by 10 incumbents. Data are from *Position Classification Inventory professional manual* (p. 49), by G. D. Gottfredson and J. L. Holland, 1991, Odessa, FL: Psychological Assessment Resources, Inc. Copyright 1991 by Psychological Assessment Resources, Inc. Adapted with permission.

Level of Complexity

A distinguishing feature of occupations is the level of complexity they involve. Some occupations make great and varied cognitive demands on workers, and other jobs are simple to perform and require little special preparation. Similarly, individual differences in ability distinguish those who quickly learn to perform complex jobs well and those who require more time to acquire skilled performance of complex jobs. Accordingly, it is useful to supplement the classification of both people and occupations according to level of complexity.

It has been possible to measure a large number of specific and more general abilities on which individuals differ. Because specific and general abilities are usually substantially correlated with each other, it also is useful to summarize a great deal of information about individual differences using measures of general ability. Similarly, job analysts have traditionally assessed the worker trait requirements of occupations using a large number of specific demands. Because the specific cognitive and skilled performance demands of occupations are usually highly correlated with each other, it is possible to summarize a large amount of information about differences among occupations by using a general measure of complexity.

Person–Environment Interactions

Individuals seek and remain in congruent environments; and environments recruit, retain, and reward congruent people. Congruence is assessed according to the degree of match between the vocational personality of an individual and the environmental type of an occupation or position. A person who most resembles the Realistic type and works in an occupation that most resembles the Realistic environmental model is most congruent, and a Realistic person who works in a Social environment is least congruent. Intermediate distances according to the hexagon imply intermediate degrees of congruence.

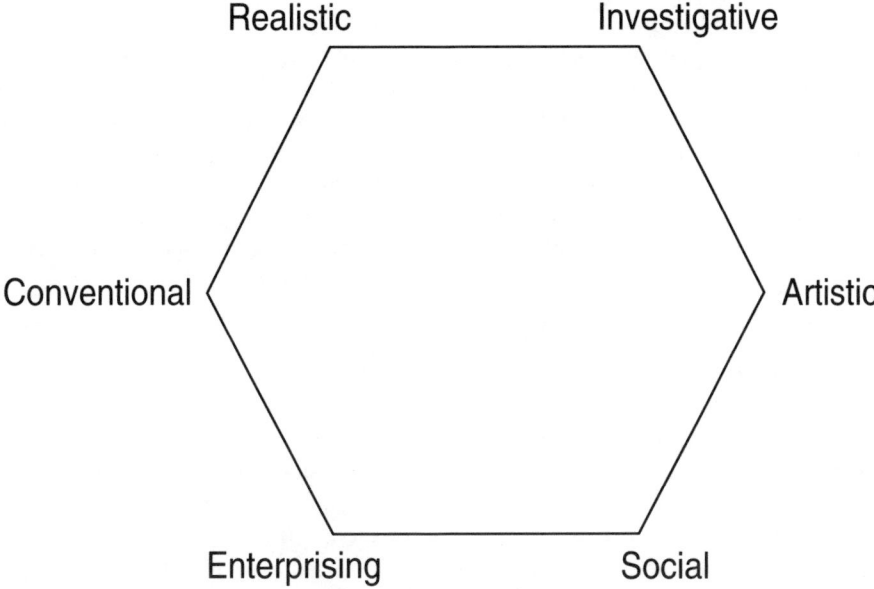

Figure 2. A hexagon summarizing relations among environmental and personality types.

Other things being equal, people are expected to seek, to be satisfied in, and to remain in congruent environments. For example, a person who most resembles the Investigative type according to an SDS assessment would be expected to seek and remain in Investigative jobs. In contrast, an Investigative individual is expected to avoid, to be dissatisfied in, and to leave an Enterprising environment. These outcomes are expected because an Investigative environment provides opportunities for the expression of and rewards for analytical competencies and a skeptical outlook, whereas an Enterprising environment fails to reward these personal characteristics and instead requires confidence and persuasive ability.

Other things being equal, people seek, are selected for, and remain in occupations that roughly match their level of general ability to the level of complexity required by the work. For example, a person with a high level of general ability will find it easy to acquire the skills needed to perform complex work. In contrast, individuals who lack high levels of general ability seldom enter or persist in jobs characterized by high levels of complexity.

Other Classifications and Data Sources

The principal aim of this volume is to link the Holland occupational classification to occupational information organized using other important classifications. This section briefly describes these classifications and notes their applications.

Dictionary of Occupational Titles

The premier reference resource on occupations in the United States economy has been the DOT which has gone through multiple editions—the most recently printed edition being the fourth (Employment and Training Administration, 1991a). This monumental compendium provides structured and highly disciplined descriptions of over 12,000 specific occupations. Of equal importance, the job analysts of the Employment and Training Administration's field centers have produced a massive body of data on 12,741 occupations by employing the job analysis methods described in the *Handbook for Analyzing Jobs* (Employment and Training Administration, 1972, 1991b). These data form an invaluable resource for counselors and others who assist persons with vocational exploration, job searches, or a need to cope with a disability. Vocational professionals have long used the printed versions of the DOT as a source of job information their clients can understand. These information sources also are important for researchers.

The following illustrates an entry in the DOT:

005.167-014 DRAINAGE-DESIGN COORDINATOR (waterworks)

> Plans, designs, and coordinates construction of drainage systems in irrigation district, based on knowledge of soils, slope of land, and availability and economic use of existing drainage canals: Requests engineering surveys and soil tests to determine surface profile, types of soil, and characteristics such as salinity, water table, and areas of subnormal crop growth. Studies data and sketches scale drawing of tile and open ditch drains for area, using triangles, scales, dividers, and other drawing instruments. Indicates depth, spacing, and size of tilling for crop area leading to district drainage canals. Considers drainage cost to improve fertility, at least cost to farmer and district. Recommends deepening of drainage canals when field excavation prevents gravity flow, or provides for installation of sumps and electric pumps to drain low areas. Arranges for sale to farmers of district approved drainage materials, such as concrete wells and pipes. Determines need for securing easements and right-of-way deeds for district drainage structures. Inspects completed systems to determine that installation conforms to plan.

GOE: 05.01.03   STRENGTH: S   GED: R5 M5 L4   SVP: 8   DLU: 77

A DOT definition provides an account of the main activities performed by workers in an occupation; the special knowledge, methods, materials, and tools used; and people with whom a worker interacts. The nine-digit code itself conveys a great deal of information to a practiced user. The first digit conveys information about primary occupational category ranging roughly from low level to high level work. The second and third digits identify the division and relatively homogeneous group the occupation represents. For example, occupations with the first three digits "215" are Payroll, Timekeeping, and Duty Roster Clerks.

The middle three digits in a DOT code convey information about the level of complexity of an occupational incumbent's involvement with data, people, and things. A *low* number for data (4th digit) represents a *high* level of complexity of involvement with people. A *low number for people* (5th digit) represents a *high* level of complexity of involvement with people. And a *low number for things* (6th digit) represents a *high* level of complexity of involvement with things. The data-people-things part of the DOT code number is interpreted as follows (Employment and Training Administration, 1991a):

DATA (4th Digit)	PEOPLE (5th Digit)	THINGS (6th Digit)
0 Synthesizing	0 Mentoring	0 Setting Up
1 Coordinating	1 Negotiating	1 Precision Working
2 Analyzing	2 Instructing	2 Operating-Controlling
3 Compiling	3 Supervising	3 Driving-Operating
4 Computing	4 Diverting	4 Manipulating
5 Copying	5 Persuading	5 Tending
6 Comparing	6 Speaking-Signalling	6 Feeding-Offbearing
	7 Serving	7 Handling
	8 Taking Instructions-Helping	

The final three digits of the DOT code number simply give each occupation a unique number. Beyond this they carry no information. Following the body of the DOT definition is a "trailer" which contains information about the classification of the occupation in the GOE, the strength required of incumbents, the level of educational development required, and specific vocational preparation needed to become proficient. For more details, see the explanations in the DOT.

Occupational Employment Statistics System

The Bureau of Labor Statistics (BLS) uses the OES classification as a basis for developing national information on occupational employment, including projections of employment. The OES is also used by State Employment Security Agencies to conduct surveys of industries and occupations that provide information about employment and wages. In addition to the national information on employment, wages, and projections using the OES, state-specific information is usually available from the research sections of State Employment Security Agencies.

An important product developed using the OES is the OOH (Bureau of Labor Statistics, 1996a). The OOH is a career exploration reference book and CD-ROM (Bureau of Labor Statistics, 1996b) resource that interprets government job analysis, wage, and employment forecast information in a form that is easily used by young people and adults. The Occupational Outlook Division of the Bureau of Labor Statistics formulates descriptions of work in most career areas and supplements information available from other sources with information gathered from trade associations, professional societies, unions, industrial organizations, and government agencies.

Each entry in the OOH describes the nature of the work; working conditions; numbers of persons employed; training, other qualifications, and opportunities for advancement; employment outlook; earnings; and sources of additional information about the career area.

Standard Occupational Classification

The SOC was developed by the U.S. Office of Federal Statistical Policy and Standards to provide a uniform method of classifying occupations for agencies of the federal government, so that comparable data can be generated by those agencies and by professional associations and labor unions. The classification is intended to cover "all occupations in which work is performed for pay or profit, including work performed in family-operated enterprises where direct remuneration may not be made to family members" (Office of Federal Statistical Policy and Standards, 1980). The SOC provided a structure for the development of the two most recent Census occupational classifications as well as the OES classification.

Census Classification of Occupations

The 1990 Census Occupational Classification (U.S. Bureau of the Census, 1992) is closely related to the SOC. The census is the most comprehensive periodic source of information about the U.S. population, its employment and earnings by occupation, and other social and economic data.

Classification of Instructional Programs

The CIP (National Center for Education Statistics, 1991) is used by the U.S. Department of Education for surveys and collection of information about institutions' educational program offerings, enrollments, and completions. It also has special research applications, such as the analysis of information from transcripts in the National Longitudinal Study of the high school class of 1972 (which have been coded using the CIP). The CIP also is the basis of government statistics on such things as the number of bachelor's degrees conferred by discipline (National Center for Education Statistics, 1994).

Guide for Occupational Exploration

The GOE (Employment and Training Administration, 1979) was developed to help vocational counselors and those they assist explore occupations by grouping together DOT occupational titles judged to be similar in terms of the interest areas measured by the Employment Service's interest inventory (Droege & Hawk, 1977). Although it is no longer available from the Government Printing Office, a version of the GOE edited by Harrington and O'Shea (1984) is available from distributors of reprinted government documents.

The first two digits of the 6-digit GOE codes provide information about interest groupings using the Employment and Training Administration's 12 groups:

01   Artistic. Interest in creative expression of feelings or ideas.

02   Scientific. Interest in discovering, collecting, and analyzing information about the natural world, and in applying scientific research findings to problems in medicine, the life sciences, and the natural sciences.

03   Plants and Animals. Interest in working with plants and animals, usually outdoors.

04   Protective. Interest in using authority to protect people and property.

05   Mechanical. Interest in applying mechanical principles to practical situations by use of machines or hand tools.

06   Industrial. Interest in repetitive, concrete, organized activities done in a factory setting.

07   Business Detail. Interest in organized, clearly defined activities requiring accuracy and attention to details, primarily in an office setting.

08   Selling. Interest in bringing others to a particular point of view by personal persuasion, using sales and promotional techniques.

09   Accommodating. Interest in catering to the wishes and needs of others, usually on a one-to-one basis.

10   Humanitarian. Interest in helping others with their mental, spiritual, social, physical, or vocational needs.

11   Leading and Influencing. Interest in leading and influencing others by using high-level verbal or numerical abilities.

12   Physical Performing. Interest in physical activities performed before an audience.

The Indexes

Most of this book is made up of indexes that translate the occupational classifications described earlier into the Holland environmental classification. These indexes are of two types: (a) *classified indexes* that organize occupations, instructional programs, or occupational groups by grouping occupations representing a specific Holland type together, and (b) *alphabetical indexes* that list occupations, instructional programs, and occupational groups in alphabetical order.

Classified Indexes

Each of the six classified indexes in Part 2 places related or similar occupations together. This is accomplished by using the Holland occupational classification (HOC) as the primary organizing tool and by using the level of complexity (Cx) as a supplementary classification tool.

Realistic (R) occupations are listed first, followed by Investigative (I), Artistic (A), Social (S), Enterprising (E), and Conventional (C) occupations. Within each major category (R, I, A, S, E, and C), Holland subcategories also are organized in RIASEC order. That is, RI precedes RA and RS, and so forth.

Within each three-letter Holland category, occupations are listed in descending order of level of complexity. Occupations involving the most complex work are listed first. Occupations classified in the same three-letter Holland category and at the same complexity level are listed in alphabetical order.

The first column (headed "HOC") provides a three-letter Holland code for each occupation.

The second column (headed "Cx") shows the estimated complexity level.

The third column lists the occupational title as it is used in each source occupational classification. For the DOT occupations, the industry designation used in the DOT together with the title is also provided. Users should know that each occupation may also be found in a number of other industries although only one is listed.

In each classified index, the fourth column (headed by an acronym indicating the source occupational classification) indicates the occupational code assigned to each occupation in the original classification being mapped into the Holland classification (e.g., DOT, OES, or Census).

Key to Abbreviations Used in the Indexes

Abbreviation	*Example*	*Interpretation*
DOT	003.161-018	a *Dictionary of Occupational Titles* 9-digit code
OES	22105	an *Occupational Employment Statistics* 5-digit code
SOC	1625	a *Standard Occupational Classification* 4-digit code
COC	184	a *Census Occupational Classification* 3-digit code
CIP	13.0402	a *Classification of Instructional Programs* 6-digit code
GOE	07.02.03	a *Guide for Occupational Exploration* 6-digit subgroup code
HOC	RIA	a 3-letter Holland Occupational Code
Cx	68	a 2-digit code for the occupation's level of complexity

---

Alphabetical Indexes

Alphabetical listings of occupations in each of the systems translated into the Holland classification are provided in Part 3. For each of these systems, users can locate a title as they would in a dictionary to determine the Holland code. Part 3 uses the same abbreviations applied in Part 2.

Using the Indexes

Counselors and clients can use the classified indexes to search for all occupations or instructional programs suggested by a person's Holland code obtained using the SDS or the VPI. In addition, the alphabetical indexes (Part 3) provide ready access to the Holland code for any occupational title, subgroup, or instructional program used in the DOT, OES classification, SOC, COC, CIP, GOE, or OOH. Because this volume offers complete and rapid exploration of all occupations and instructional programs, clients should find taking the SDS or VPI a more helpful experience.

Search for Related Categories

When using this book to search for occupations that match your vocational interest assessment (your Holland code), do not limit your search to occupations that exactly match your three-letter code. Explore occupations that match other arrangements of the letters of your code, especially occupations matching the first two letters of your code in either order.

Clients should explore several permutations of their three-letter codes. Although most clients will find many occupations whose codes precisely match their SDS or VPI assessment results, they should be urged to expand their career exploration to include closely related codes.

One of the most common misuses of the classification in counseling and guidance applications occurs when clients are led to focus solely on the three-letter code that exactly matches the three-letter code from their personal inventory results. A person whose SDS assessment produces a code of SIA should be directed to search all occupations listed under SIA in this classification, as well as IAS, ISA, SAI, AIS, and ASI occupations.

Occasionally, a client's SDS or VPI assessment produces a three-letter code for which there are no corresponding occupations or instructional programs. Such a client should be directed to broaden his or her search of occupations by examining all occupations in the major category corresponding to the first letter of the Holland code and occupations matching all two-letter permutations of the Holland code.

Some Interpretations and Cautions

Several cautions are important in making interpretations of any occupational information. Experienced counselors have long recognized the following points, but it is important to emphasize them for new users of the classification system.

1. The categories in the classification are not distinct—black or white, all or none. Even a casual review of the classifications in Part 2 will reveal that the six main categories blend together at the edges. For example, CR occupations in the Conventional category resemble RC occupations in the Realistic category. In general, occupations involving less complexity are less clearly identifiable as belonging to any major group than are occupations entailing more complexity. Therefore, the distinctions among low level occupations are somewhat blurred.

2. The average person has well developed ideas about many occupations (O'Dowd & Beardslee, 1967). Although many occupational perceptions have a moderate degree of validity, some perceptions form inaccurate stereotypes. The categories in the Holland classification appear to have undergone similar mistaken stereotyping (e.g., "Realistic jobs never require paper work, Conventional jobs never involve tools, Investigative jobs never require artistic judgment"). It is more accurate to think of the main categories in the Holland classification as bands or rings that blend into each other than to view the categories as six separate bins.

3. A person does not resemble one type and no other. An occupation does not fit into one main category and no other. For these reasons, the number of possible occupations or positions that are congruent with a particular person is large. When the levels of resemblance also are taken into account, this outcome is easily understood. Some people resemble two or three theoretical types to the same degree, and some occupations resemble two or more occupational groups to the same degree. Further, the codes assigned to a few occupations shift from one study to the next. "Police officer" is a good example. S, E, and R are the main categories suggested by divergent data at different times, so that one study suggests RSE and another suggests SRE. "Engineer" is another occupation for which I and R are the codes usually suggested by interest inventory data, but the positions of I and R change from study to study—even for the same engineering specialty.

4. A variety of people are found successfully working within any single occupation, but people resembling some types are found more frequently than others (see Holland & Holland, 1977; or Holland, Powell, & Fritzsche, 1994, pp. 20-21). For example, most counselors have codes that include S, A, and E, but a few have codes of C or R. In short, all occupations tolerate a range of types, but some types appear to cope more successfully with an occupation's demands than do others. See Holland's theory for a more complete explanation of person-environment fit (Holland, 1985/1992) .

5. The specific positions or jobs subsumed by a single occupational title also are sometimes varied. But when an occupational classification has been carefully composed by grouping similar work together, work done by different individuals in different specific positions tends to be similar. Nevertheless, some occupations appear more homogeneous than others. For example, most counselors' jobs are clearly dominated by social activities with artistic and enterprising activities somewhat less salient. Job analysis seldom suggests anything but "Social" for the primary classification for counselor. Other occupations, such as Musical Instrument Repairer, are more difficult to classify because job analysis information implies that this occupation involves activities characterized by several occupational models. See the Position Classification Inventory Manual (Gottfredson & Holland, 1991) for more information about heterogeneity within occupations.

7. Most occupations do not resemble a single environmental type and no other. This is why three letters have been listed for all occupations and instructional programs in the

classified indexes. Nevertheless, some occupations have a strong resemblance to one type and much weaker resemblance to other types. Sometimes the ordering of letters beyond the first letter is essentially arbitrary because there is little evidence of strong links to more than one type. This occurs most often with occupations with low complexity levels. For low level occupations, the second and third letters listed may not be particularly meaningful.

Some Frequently Asked Questions

Does this classification supersede all earlier versions of the Holland classification? Yes—when in doubt, use this one.

Will the Occupations Finder be changed? Yes, when the SDS is revised, the most up-to-date information will be used for the Occupations Finder codes.

Is this revision of codes ever going to end? I'm tired of revising my occupational information files. It is unlikely that revisions will cease. Occupations evolve and the nature of information about the work involved changes over time. Information about occupations will always be imperfect due to errors in sampling, limitations in occupational analyses, and changes in job content over time. Therefore, codes will always be approximations or estimates, but the empirically derived estimates in this volume are the best we can produce at this time. This revision also provides Holland codes for groupings made by other classifications such as the CIP and GOE subgroups that have not heretofore been available.

Can I use these codes with other interest inventories besides the SDS and VPI? This volume is intended for use with the SDS or the VPI, and it will be most compatible with these inventories. The codes are expected to be compatible with other inventories, but no empirical tests of compatibility have been made.

In the past, codes based on the interests of males using either norms or raw scores from various inventories have been very similar. In contrast, codes based on the inventoried interests of women using sex-based norms or "balanced" scales sometimes produce codes that are at variance with the codes produced by raw scores. They also are at variance with the codes based on the occupational analysis data presented here. Efforts to erase sex differences (Cronbach, 1984), to the extent that they are successful, restrict the domain of interests measured to those that show limited sex differences or distort scores by inflating interest scores in some areas and deflating scores in others. In short, these codes should be compatible with other inventories for males, but may be compatible for females only with inventories reporting raw score profiles or profiles based on pooled norms. Users of inventories using sex-based norms or balanced scales should conduct new research or regard their applications as experimental when using these codes.

Don't occupational codes and codes for fields of training vary from region to region and from institution to institution? Yes. And sometimes they vary from sample to sample. If you have been collecting PCI, SDS, or VPI data to create a local classification, you should continue to do so. Your data will usually be most valid for your situation. Most institutions do not have carefully developed and comprehensive data. This volume supplements what institutions can do for themselves.

What should I do when I find an occupation with a code that seems strange or in error? Locate and read the DOT definition or the definition used in another classification. Look at the job analysis ratings in published volumes (Employment and Training Administration, 1981, 1982, 1986, 1991a) or, if you have the technical resources, review the data archives developed by the Employment and Training Administration.

In some cases, the title assigned to an occupational group may not convey an accurate impression of the work's content to most readers or may involve a misclassification of a detailed occupation in a particular system. For example, the CIP title "Design and Visual Communications" (500401) has been assigned a Holland code of RIE, which looks wrong. Scrutiny of the DOT occupations related to this CIP code according to the crosswalk between DOT and CIP prepared by the Department of Education (National Crosswalk Service Center, 1993) shows that only two occupations are "related." One of these is "Faculty Member, College and University" (090.227-010) and the second is "Decorator" (298.381-101). As explained in Part 5, a link to faculty member in the CIP crosswalk was disregarded in developing Holland codes because the link was too general to be useful. The related DOT occupation of "Decorator" describes the job of a worker who "Prepares and installs decorations and displays from blueprints or drawings for trade and industrial shows…Constructs portable installations, according to specifications, using wood working power tools" (Employment and Training Administration, 1991b, p. 236). Possibly the Education Department analysts made an error assigning this DOT code as related, or possibly not. In any event, the RIE code assigned here is consistent with the underlying data.

Another example is provided by the Holland code of SCR assigned to the OES title, "Computer Support Specialist" (25104). The three detailed DOT occupations related to this OES title in the crosswalk prepared by Bureau of Labor Statistics (BLS) analysts are "User Support Analyst Supervisor" (032.132-010, ESC), "User Support Analyst" (032.262-010, CSI), and "Microcomputer Support Specialist" (039.264-010, RSI). All three related occupations involve helping people, although the OES title may not convey this feature of these occupations to many people.

Careful review should clarify most apparent misclassifications—the occupational title itself does not always convey an accurate picture of the occupation.

Also, review occupations with the identical code at about the same complexity level. For example, if you are in doubt about an RIE occupation, look at other RIE occupations at a similar level to clarify for yourself the conceptual meaning of the category involved. Review Part 4 for additional insights into the distinctions among the categories.

If persons knowledgeable about the occupation are available, have them complete PCIs to describe it. This is a direct way to classify any occupation according to the typology. When the job is analyzed directly, you do not need to know how it is classified according to the DOT or other classification system.

Finally, exercise circumspection in taking the codes listed here at face value. They are based on fallible data and data that may be based on a small number of job analyses.

What should I do when I cannot find a code for a specific occupational title in the alphabetized indexes? All occupational titles in the DOT, SOC, and the other source classifications are included in these indexes. Any title, however, may have a number of synonyms.

Try finding a synonymous title or transposing the words in the title. For example, "Newspaper Editor" may be found under "Editor, Newspaper." Finally, consult the DOT for alternate titles that are listed under defined titles. Be creative and persistent in your search; try to think of more general or more specific alternatives for a given title.

What should I tell a client who wants to pursue an artistic career and looks like a CES according to the SDS? Stimulate the client to examine how he or she will use the CES interests, values, and competencies in an occupation dominated by Artistic types and tasks. Explore with the client the origin of the Artistic aspiration—what it means to him or her. Such exploration may reveal that the client can explain such a choice and that the explanation is backed by personal and other evidence, or that the client recognizes the aspiration as a fantasy which may easily be relinquished. As an alternative, have the client describe a desired artistic occupation using the PCI. This may reveal an unusual understanding of what the occupation entails.

Whatever happens, help the client explore both A and CES options.

If the client has an undifferentiated (flat) profile of SDS or VPI scores, explore the possibility that the person may lack well articulated interests in any area. People with flat profiles may require more assistance.

Why are there DOT codes in this Dictionary that are not in my copy of the DOT? The 1977 edition of the DOT (Employment and Training Administration) listed 12,099 titles. As new jobs were analyzed, the Employment and Training Administration issued *Supplements* (1982-1986), and it also made minor changes in titles for a few DOT codes. For example "Teacher, Handicapped" was changed to "Teacher, Handicapped Student" in the published 1991 Edition of the DOT. More recently, the Employment and Training Division changed this title again to "Teacher, Physically Impaired." Similarly the title "Nuclear Medical Technologist" was changed to "Nuclear Medicine Technologist." Updated titles are listed in this *Dictionary*.

In other cases, the job analysts changed the code assigned to a title without changing the title. For example, the 1977 Edition code for "Dental Assistant" was listed as 079.371-010, and the code has subsequently been revised to 079.361-018. This implies a somewhat higher level of involvement with people than did the published code. And sometimes both the code number and title changed, as in the change from "Director, Preschool" (092.137-010) to "Director, Day Care Center" (092.167-010). The most recent data are contained here, and the information is sometimes more recent than in the most recent published version of the DOT.

For a few occupations, the Department of Labor assigned the same DOT code to work positions related to different Holland types. The most striking instances of this practice occurred for college faculty: Faculty from distinct subjects were assigned a single nine-digit DOT code. The present *Dictionary* provides separate codes for faculty in various fields.

Part 2: From Holland Codes to Occupations

From Holland Codes to the Dictionary of Occupational Titles Occupations

HOC	Cx	Title	DOT
RIA	67	Television Technician (radio-tv broad.)	194.062-010
RIA	57	Internal Carver (plastic prod.)	754.381-010
RIA	57	Treater (petrol. refin.)	549.362-014
RIA	55	Relief-Map Modeler (any industry)	777.381-042
RIA	54	Decorator (glass mfg.; glass products)	740.381-010
RIA	54	Lighting-Equipment Operator (amuse. & rec.)	962.381-014
RIS	76	Electronics-Design Engineer (profess. & kin.)	003.061-034
RIS	73	Mechanical Engineer (profess. & kin.)	007.061-014
RIS	71	Electrical-Design Engineer (profess. & kin.)	003.061-018
RIS	71	Electronics-Research Engineer (profess. & kin.)	003.061-038
RIS	71	Tool Designer (profess. & kin.)	007.061-026
RIS	71	Tool-Designer Apprentice (profess. & kin.)	007.061-030
RIS	70	Forester (profess. & kin.)	040.167-010
RIS	70	Weight Analyst (profess. & kin.)	020.167-030
RIS	69	Inspector, Elevators (government ser.)	168.167-038
RIS	69	Well-Logging Captain, Mud Analysis (petrol. & gas)	010.131-010
RIS	67	Appraiser (any industry)	191.287-010
RIS	67	Nuclear Medicine Technologist (medical ser.)	078.361-018
RIS	66	Assayer (profess. & kin.)	022.281-010
RIS	66	Field Engineer (radio-tv broad.)	193.262-018
RIS	65	Malt-Specifications-Control Assistant (beverage)	022.261-014
RIS	64	Color Developer (paper & pulp)	530.261-010
RIS	64	Development Mechanic (aircraft mfg.)	693.261-014
RIS	64	Model Maker (aircraft mfg.)	693.261-018
RIS	63	Farmer, General (agriculture)	421.161-010
RIS	62	Avionics Technician (aircraft mfg.; air trans.)	823.261-026
RIS	62	Custom Ski Maker (toy-sport equip.)	732.281-010
RIS	62	Electronic-Production-Line-Maintenance Mechanic (electron. comp.)	629.261-022
RIS	62	Electronics Mechanic (any industry)	828.261-022
RIS	62	Electronics-Mechanic Apprentice (any industry)	828.261-026
RIS	62	Engine Tester (aircraft mfg.; air trans.)	621.261-014
RIS	62	Helicopter Pilot (any industry)	196.263-038
RIS	62	Machinist, Experimental (machine shop)	600.260-022
RIS	62	Supervisor, Electronic Controls Repairer (engine-turbine)	828.131-010
RIS	61	Data Communications Technician (any industry)	823.261-030
RIS	61	Embalmer (personal ser.)	338.371-014
RIS	61	Embalmer Apprentice (personal ser.)	338.371-010
RIS	61	Gunsmith, Ballistics Laboratory (ordnance)	609.260-010
RIS	61	Landscape Gardener (agriculture)	408.161-010
RIS	60	Biological Photographer (profess. & kin.)	143.362-010
RIS	60	Electrician, Aircraft (aircraft mfg.; air trans.)	825.261-018
RIS	60	Experimental Mechanic (motor-bicycles)	600.260-014
RIS	60	Metallurgical Technician (profess. & kin.)	011.261-010
RIS	60	Model Maker I (jewelry-silver.)	700.281-018
RIS	60	Paramedic (medical ser.)	079.364-026
RIS	60	Prospector (any industry)	024.284-010
RIS	60	Radiation-Therapy Technologist (medical ser.)	078.361-034

Part 2: From Holland Codes to Occupations

From Holland Codes to the Dictionary of Occupational Titles Occupations

HOC	Cx	Title	DOT
RIS	60	Seed Analyst (profess. & kin.)	040.361-014
RIS	60	Test Technician (agric. equip.)	019.261-022
RIS	60	Transformer Tester (utilities)	724.281-010
RIS	59	Cabinetmaker (woodworking)	660.280-010
RIS	59	Cabinetmaker Apprentice (woodworking)	660.280-014
RIS	59	Conservator, Artifacts (profess. & kin.)	055.381-010
RIS	59	Exhaust Equipment Operator (electron. comp.)	599.382-014
RIS	59	Fire-Fighting-Equipment Specialist (government ser.)	638.281-010
RIS	59	Machine Try-Out Setter (machine tools)	600.360-010
RIS	59	Pattern Marker I (woodworking)	761.381-022
RIS	59	Sample Maker, Appliances (house. appl.; light. fix.)	600.280-054
RIS	59	Supervisor, Knitting II (knitting)	685.130-010
RIS	59	Welding Technician (profess. & kin.)	011.261-014
RIS	58	Elevator Repairer (any industry)	825.281-030
RIS	58	Elevator-Repairer Apprentice (any industry)	825.281-034
RIS	58	Industrial-Gas Servicer (utilities)	637.261-022
RIS	58	Multi-Operation-Forming-Machine Setter (any industry)	616.260-014
RIS	58	Optician Apprentice, Dispensing (optical goods; retail trade)	299.361-014
RIS	58	Optician, Dispensing (optical goods; retail trade)	299.361-010
RIS	58	Radiographer (any industry)	199.361-010
RIS	58	Radioisotope-Production Operator (profess. & kin.)	015.362-022
RIS	58	Surface-Plate Finisher (stonework)	775.281-010
RIS	58	Tube Rebuilder (electron. comp.)	725.381-010
RIS	57	Batch-and-Furnace Operator (glass mfg.)	572.382-010
RIS	57	Blower and Compressor Assembler (machinery mfg.)	801.361-010
RIS	57	Floor-Covering Layer (railroad equip.)	622.381-026
RIS	57	Honey Grader-and-Blender (food prep., n.e.c.)	520.361-010
RIS	57	Inset Cutter (fabrication, n.e.c.)	739.381-038
RIS	57	Inspector (forging)	612.261-010
RIS	57	Maintenance Mechanic (leather mfg.)	629.280-010
RIS	57	Model Maker, Fluorescent Lighting (light. fix.)	723.361-010
RIS	57	Ornamental-Iron Worker (construction)	809.381-022
RIS	57	Ornamental-Iron-Worker Apprentice (construction)	809.381-026
RIS	57	Patternmaker, Plastics (plastic prod.)	754.381-014
RIS	57	Plant Propagator (agriculture)	405.361-010
RIS	57	Pump Erector (construction)	637.281-010
RIS	57	Pumper (petrol. refin.)	549.360-010
RIS	57	Salvage Inspector (railroad equip.)	622.381-038
RIS	57	Section Leader, Screen Printing (textile)	652.260-010
RIS	57	Substation Operator (utilities)	952.362-026
RIS	57	Substation Operator Apprentice (utilities)	952.362-030
RIS	57	Tank Erector (construction)	860.381-070
RIS	57	Transmission Tester (tel. & tel.)	822.361-026
RIS	56	Carpenter, Rough (construction)	860.381-042
RIS	56	Compounder, Flavorings (beverage)	529.381-010
RIS	56	Crystal Machining Coordinator (electron. comp.)	679.362-010
RIS	56	Die Finisher (machine shop)	601.381-010
RIS	56	Gun Examiner (ordnance)	736.281-010

HOC	Cx	Title	DOT
RIS	56	Model Maker, Fiberglass (concrete prod.)	777.381-010
RIS	56	Oil-Well-Service Operator (petrol. & gas)	939.462-010
RIS	56	Photoengraving Proofer (print. & pub.)	971.381-038
RIS	56	Photoengraving-Proofer Apprentice (print. & pub.)	971.381-040
RIS	56	Private-Branch-Exchange Installer (tel. & tel.)	822.381-018
RIS	56	Repairer, Welding, Brazing, and Burning Machines (welding)	626.361-010
RIS	56	Saw Maker (cutlery-hrdwr.)	601.381-034
RIS	56	Siderographer (print. & pub.)	979.381-030
RIS	56	Stoker Erector-and-Servicer (any industry)	637.281-014
RIS	56	Yeast-Culture Developer (beverage)	022.381-010
RIS	55	Hood Maker (tex. prod., n.e.c.)	804.481-010
RIS	55	Multi-Operation-Forming-Machine Operator I (any industry)	616.360-026
RIS	54	Balancer, Scale (office machines)	710.381-014
RIS	54	Flame-Hardening-Machine Setter (heat treating)	504.380-010
RIS	54	Gardener, Special Effects and Instruction Models (motion picture; museums)	406.381-010
RIS	54	Stonecutter, Hand (stonework)	771.381-014
RIS	54	Welder Apprentice, Arc (welding)	810.384-010
RIS	54	Welder, Arc (welding)	810.384-014
RIS	53	Boat-Oar Maker (woodworking)	761.381-010
RIS	53	Firer, Kiln (pottery & porc.)	573.662-010
RIS	53	Streetcar Repairer (railroad equip.)	807.381-026
RIS	53	Tenoner Operator (woodworking)	669.382-018
RIS	52	Cloth Printer (any industry)	652.382-010
RIS	52	Envelope-Folding-Machine Adjuster (paper goods)	641.380-010
RIS	52	New-Car Get-Ready Mechanic (automotive ser.; retail trade)	806.361-026
RIS	52	Survival-Equipment Repairer (government ser.)	739.381-054
RIS	50	Furnace Operator (nonfer. metal; smelt. & refin.)	512.362-014
RIS	50	Measurer (retail trade)	869.367-014
RIS	50	Punch-Press Operator, Automatic (any industry)	615.482-026
RIS	49	Bullet-Slug-Casting-Machine Operator (ordnance)	502.382-010
RIS	49	Mixer Operator I (chemical)	550.382-018
RIS	49	Pipe Cutter (mfd. bldgs.)	862.682-010
RIS	49	Screwdown Operator (steel & rel.)	613.382-018
RIS	49	Wood-Turning-Lathe Operator (woodworking)	664.382-014
RIS	48	Heat Treater II (heat treating)	504.682-018
RIS	48	Jointer Operator (woodworking)	665.682-042
RIS	48	Pocket Cutter (woodworking)	667.482-014
RIS	48	Rotary-Shear Operator (any industry)	615.482-030
RIS	48	Stove-Carriage Operator (fabrication, n.e.c.)	590.662-022
RIS	48	Temperer (heat treating)	504.682-026
RIS	47	Coke-Crusher Operator (steel & rel.)	544.662-010
RIS	47	Cupola Tender (foundry)	512.662-010
RIS	47	Dinkey Operator (any industry)	919.663-014
RIS	47	Hoop Maker, Machine (wood. container)	619.682-030
RIS	47	Hydro-Sprayer Operator (agriculture)	408.662-010

Part 2: From Holland Codes to Occupations

From Holland Codes to the Dictionary of Occupational Titles Occupations

HOC	Cx	Title	DOT
RIS	47	Lamber (agriculture)	410.364-010
RIS	47	Operating Engineer (construction; mine & quarry)	859.683-010
RIS	47	Operating-Engineer Apprentice (construction; mine & quarry)	859.683-014
RIS	47	Punch-Press Operator III (any industry)	615.682-014
RIS	47	Resaw Operator (woodworking)	667.682-058
RIS	47	Slitter-Scorer-Cut-Off Operator (paper goods)	649.682-038
RIS	47	Stevedore I (water trans.)	911.663-014
RIS	47	Upsetter (forging)	611.662-010
RIS	46	Stopping Builder (mine & quarry)	869.684-058
RIS	45	Log-Truck Driver (logging)	904.683-010
RIE	77	Geologist, Petroleum (petrol. & gas)	024.061-022
RIE	77	Ordnance Engineer (chemical; ordnance)	019.061-022
RIE	76	Field-Service Engineer (aircraft mfg.)	002.167-014
RIE	76	Induction-Coordination Power Engineer (utilities)	003.167-038
RIE	76	Petroleum Engineer (petrol. & gas)	010.061-018
RIE	76	Protection Engineer (utilities)	003.167-054
RIE	76	Standards Engineer (profess. & kin.)	012.061-018
RIE	76	Stress Analyst (aircraft mfg.)	002.061-030
RIE	75	Mechanical-Design Engineer, Facilities (profess. & kin.)	007.061-018
RIE	74	Faculty Member, College or University, Engineering (education)	090.227-010
RIE	74	Mining Engineer (mine & quarry)	010.061-014
RIE	71	Aeronautical Test Engineer (aircraft mfg.)	002.061-018
RIE	71	Automotive Engineer (auto. mfg.)	007.061-010
RIE	71	Chemical-Test Engineer (profess. & kin.)	008.061-026
RIE	71	Commercial Engineer (radio-tv broad.)	003.187-014
RIE	71	Electronics Engineer (profess. & kin.)	003.061-030
RIE	71	Flight-Operations Inspector (government ser.)	196.163-010
RIE	70	Customer-Equipment Engineer (tel. & tel.)	003.187-018
RIE	70	Distribution-Field Engineer (utilities)	003.167-014
RIE	70	Engineer-in-Charge, Transmitter (radio-tv broad.)	003.167-034
RIE	70	Plant Engineer (profess. & kin.)	007.167-014
RIE	69	Controller, Remotely-Piloted Vehicle (aircraft mfg.)	196.263-026
RIE	69	Drainage-Design Coordinator (waterworks)	005.167-014
RIE	69	Estimator and Drafter (utilities)	019.261-014
RIE	69	Facilities Planner (any industry)	019.261-018
RIE	69	Facilities-Flight-Check Pilot (government ser.)	196.263-034
RIE	68	Admeasurer (government ser.)	169.284-010
RIE	68	Oceanographer, Assistant (military ser.)	025.267-010
RIE	68	Quality Control Technician (profess. & kin.)	012.261-014
RIE	67	Airplane Pilot, Commercial (air trans.)	196.263-014
RIE	67	Auto-Design Checker (auto. mfg.)	017.261-010
RIE	67	Drafter, Directional Survey (petrol. & gas)	010.281-010
RIE	67	Drafter, Geophysical (petrol. & gas)	010.281-018
RIE	67	Test Pilot (aircraft mfg.)	196.263-042
RIE	66	Detailer (profess. & kin.)	017.261-018
RIE	66	Detailer, Furniture (profess. & kin.)	017.261-022

HOC	Cx	Title	DOT
RIE	66	Die Designer (machine shop)	007.161-010
RIE	66	Die-Designer Apprentice (machine shop)	007.161-014
RIE	66	Drafter, Castings (profess. & kin.)	007.261-014
RIE	66	Electrical Technician (profess. & kin.)	003.161-010
RIE	66	Executive Pilot (any industry)	196.263-030
RIE	66	Field Service Engineer (profess. & kin.)	828.261-014
RIE	66	Flight Engineer (air trans.)	621.261-018
RIE	66	Inspector, Air-Carrier (government ser.)	168.264-010
RIE	66	Inspector, Industrial Waste (government ser.)	168.267-054
RIE	66	Inspector, Missile (aircraft mfg.)	806.261-038
RIE	66	Observer, Seismic Prospecting (petrol. & gas)	010.161-018
RIE	66	Scientific Glass Blower (glass products)	006.261-010
RIE	65	Airplane Pilot, Photogrammetry (business ser.)	196.263-018
RIE	65	Drafter, Automotive Design Layout (auto. mfg.)	017.281-026
RIE	65	Engineering Model Maker (inst. & app.; office machines)	693.260-018
RIE	65	Inspector, Tool (machine shop)	601.281-022
RIE	65	Observer, Gravity Prospecting (petrol. & gas)	010.261-018
RIE	64	Drafter, Detail (profess. & kin.)	017.261-030
RIE	64	Electromechanical Technician (inst. & app.)	710.281-018
RIE	64	Field Engineer, Specialist (petrol. & gas)	010.261-010
RIE	64	Inspector, Material Disposition (aircraft mfg.)	806.261-034
RIE	64	Patternmaker, Plaster (aircraft mfg.)	777.281-018
RIE	64	Proof Technician (ordnance)	199.171-010
RIE	64	Radioactivity-Instrument Maintenance Technician (petrol. & gas)	828.281-022
RIE	64	Research Mechanic (aircraft mfg.)	002.261-014
RIE	64	Shoe-Lay-Out Planner (boot & shoe)	012.187-014
RIE	64	Spectroscopist (profess. & kin.)	011.281-014
RIE	64	Wind Tunnel Mechanic (aircraft mfg.)	869.261-026
RIE	63	Conservation Technician (museums)	102.261-010
RIE	63	Designer and Patternmaker (boot & shoe)	788.281-010
RIE	63	Drafter, Cartographic (profess. & kin.)	018.261-010
RIE	63	Drafter, Landscape (profess. & kin.)	001.261-014
RIE	63	Drafter, Oil and Gas (petrol. & gas; petrol. refin.)	017.281-030
RIE	63	Electrician (construction)	824.261-010
RIE	63	Electrician, Research (aircraft mfg.)	726.261-014
RIE	63	Electronic-Sales-and-Service Technician (profess. & kin.)	828.251-010
RIE	63	Experimental-Box Tester (wood. container)	761.281-014
RIE	63	Film Laboratory Technician I (motion picture)	976.381-010
RIE	63	Fluid-Power Mechanic (any industry)	600.281-010
RIE	63	Identification Officer (government ser.)	377.264-010
RIE	63	Inspector, Aircraft Launching and Arresting Systems (government ser.)	806.264-014
RIE	63	Laboratory Assistant (petrol. & gas)	024.381-010
RIE	63	Observer, Electrical Prospecting (petrol. & gas)	010.261-014
RIE	63	Relay Technician (utilities)	821.261-018
RIE	63	Reptile Farmer (agriculture)	413.161-014
RIE	63	Technical Operator (petrol. & gas)	930.167-010
RIE	63	Tool-and-Die Maker (machine shop)	601.260-010

Part 2: From Holland Codes to Occupations

From Holland Codes to the Dictionary of Occupational Titles Occupations

HOC	Cx	Title	DOT
RIE	63	Tool-and-Die-Maker Apprentice (machine shop)	601.260-014
RIE	63	Well-Logging Operator, Mud Analysis (petrol. & gas)	010.281-022
RIE	62	Carver, Hand (woodworking)	761.281-010
RIE	62	Die Maker, Bench, Stamping (machine shop)	601.281-010
RIE	62	Electrician, Locomotive (railroad equip.)	825.281-026
RIE	62	Inspector, Outside Production (aircraft mfg.)	806.261-042
RIE	62	Inspector, Plastics and Composites (aircraft mfg.)	806.261-046
RIE	62	Lay-Out Worker I (any industry)	809.281-010
RIE	62	Machinist (machine shop)	600.280-022
RIE	62	Machinist Apprentice (machine shop)	600.280-026
RIE	62	Patternmaker Apprentice, Wood (foundry)	661.281-018
RIE	62	Patternmaker, Envelope (paper goods)	649.361-010
RIE	62	Patternmaker, Wood (foundry)	661.281-022
RIE	62	Pilot, Submersible (any industry)	029.383-010
RIE	62	Poultry Breeder (agriculture)	411.161-014
RIE	62	Rocket-Motor Mechanic (aircraft mfg.)	693.261-022
RIE	62	Test-Engine Operator (petrol. refin.)	029.261-018
RIE	62	Tester (petrol. refin.)	029.261-022
RIE	61	Aircraft-Armament Mechanic (government ser.)	632.261-010
RIE	61	Die Maker, Stamping (machine shop)	601.280-010
RIE	61	Electrical-Discharge-Machine Set-up Operator (machine shop)	609.380-010
RIE	61	Electrical-Instrument Repairer (any industry)	729.281-026
RIE	61	Experimental Aircraft Mechanic (aircraft mfg.)	621.261-022
RIE	61	Farmer, Fruit Crops, Bush and Vine (agriculture)	403.161-014
RIE	61	Field-Map Editor (profess. & kin.)	018.262-010
RIE	61	Fire-Control Mechanic (government ser.)	632.261-014
RIE	61	Gunsmith (any industry)	632.281-010
RIE	61	Inspector, Gauge and Instrument (machine shop)	601.281-018
RIE	61	Lay-Out Worker (machine shop)	600.281-018
RIE	61	Machinist, Motion-Picture Equipment (motion picture; photo. appar.)	714.281-018
RIE	61	Milling-Machine Set-up Operator I (machine shop)	605.280-010
RIE	61	Optician (optical goods)	716.280-018
RIE	61	Patternmaker (furniture)	709.381-034
RIE	61	Pharmacist Assistant (military ser.)	074.381-010
RIE	61	Photographic Equipment Technician (photo. appar.)	714.281-022
RIE	61	Prosthetics Technician (protective dev.)	712.381-038
RIE	61	Tester, Rocket Motor (aircraft mfg.)	806.261-022
RIE	61	Tool Maker (machine shop)	601.280-042
RIE	61	Tool-Maker Apprentice (machine shop)	601.280-058
RIE	61	Weather Observer (profess. & kin.)	025.267-014
RIE	60	Airframe-and-Power-Plant Mechanic (aircraft mfg.; air trans.)	621.281-014
RIE	60	Airframe-and-Power-Plant-Mechanic Apprentice (air trans.)	621.281-018
RIE	60	Biomedical Equipment Technician (profess. & kin.)	019.261-010
RIE	60	Blaster (any industry)	859.261-010
RIE	60	Brass-Wind-Instrument Maker (musical inst.)	730.381-018

Dictionary of Holland Occupational Codes

HOC	Cx	Title	DOT
RIE	60	Brazing-Machine Setter (welding)	813.360-010
RIE	60	Decorator (any industry)	298.381-010
RIE	60	Die Maker (print. & pub.)	979.281-010
RIE	60	Engine-Lathe Set-up Operator, Tool (machine shop)	604.280-010
RIE	60	Instrument Inspector (aircraft mfg.; air trans.)	722.381-014
RIE	60	Lay-Out Inspector (machine shop)	600.281-014
RIE	60	Meteorological-Equipment Repairer (any industry)	823.281-018
RIE	60	Mock-Up Builder (aircraft mfg.)	693.361-014
RIE	60	Mold Maker, Die-Casting and Plastic Molding (machine shop)	601.280-030
RIE	60	Optical-Instrument Assembler (optical goods)	711.381-010
RIE	60	Patternmaker Apprentice, Metal (foundry)	600.280-046
RIE	60	Patternmaker, Metal (foundry)	600.280-050
RIE	60	Patternmaker, Metal, Bench (foundry)	693.281-018
RIE	60	Plastics Fabricator (aircraft mfg.; plastic prod.)	754.381-018
RIE	60	Precision Assembler (aircraft mfg.)	806.381-082
RIE	60	Rocket-Engine-Component Mechanic (aircraft mfg.)	621.281-030
RIE	60	Spring-Manufacturing Set-up Technician (clock & watch)	619.280-018
RIE	60	Template Maker, Extrusion Die (machine shop)	601.280-038
RIE	60	Test Equipment Mechanic (aircraft mfg.)	710.361-014
RIE	60	Test-Engine Evaluator (petrol. refin.)	010.261-026
RIE	60	Turret-Lathe Set-up Operator, Tool (machine shop)	604.280-022
RIE	60	Welder, Experimental (welding)	819.281-022
RIE	59	Aircraft Mechanic, Electrical and Radio (aircraft mfg.)	825.381-010
RIE	59	Assembly Technician (office machines)	633.261-010
RIE	59	Boring-Machine Set-up Operator, Jig (machine shop)	606.280-010
RIE	59	Boring-Mill Set-up Operator, Horizontal (machine shop)	606.280-014
RIE	59	Bottle-House Quality-Control Technician (beverage)	029.361-010
RIE	59	Chucking-Machine Set-up Operator (machine shop)	604.380-010
RIE	59	Chucking-Machine Set-up Operator, Multiple Spindle, Vertical (machine shop)	604.380-014
RIE	59	Die Maker, Trim (machine shop)	601.280-014
RIE	59	Die Maker, Wire Drawing (machine shop)	601.280-018
RIE	59	Electric-Meter Tester (utilities)	821.381-010
RIE	59	Electronic Masking System Operator (print. & pub.)	972.282-018
RIE	59	Electronics Inspector (comm. equip.; electron. comp.; inst. & app.)	726.381-010
RIE	59	Embroidery Patternmaker (retail trade; wholesale tr.)	782.361-014
RIE	59	Engraver, Picture (print. & pub.)	979.281-018
RIE	59	Experimental Assembler (any industry)	739.381-026
RIE	59	Farmer, Cash Grain (agriculture)	401.161-010
RIE	59	Field Artillery Operations Specialist (military ser.)	378.367-014
RIE	59	Gear-Cutting-Machine Set-up Operator, Tool (machine shop)	602.280-010
RIE	59	Grinder Operator, Tool (machine shop)	603.280-018
RIE	59	Grinder Set-up Operator, Jig (machine shop)	603.280-026
RIE	59	Grinder Set-up Operator, Universal (machine shop)	603.280-030
RIE	59	Harpsichord Maker (musical inst.)	730.281-034
RIE	59	Horticultural-Specialty Grower, Field (agriculture)	405.161-014

HOC	Cx	Title	DOT
RIE	59	Inspector, Chief (utilities)	956.267-010
RIE	59	Inspector, Precision Assembly (aircraft mfg.)	806.281-026
RIE	59	Inspector, Railroad (government ser.)	168.287-018
RIE	59	Instrument Maker (any industry)	600.280-010
RIE	59	Instrument Mechanic, Weapons System (inst. & app.)	711.281-014
RIE	59	Instrument-Maker Apprentice (any industry)	600.280-018
RIE	59	Internal-Combustion-Engine Inspector (engine-turbine)	806.261-010
RIE	59	Jig-Boring Machine Operator, Numerical Control (machine shop)	606.382-014
RIE	59	Job Printer (print. & pub.)	973.381-018
RIE	59	Job-Printer Apprentice (print. & pub.)	973.381-022
RIE	59	Laboratory Technician (auto. mfg.)	019.261-030
RIE	59	Line Installer, Street Railway (r.r. trans.)	821.361-022
RIE	59	Machine Builder (machinery mfg.; machine tools)	600.281-022
RIE	59	Machine Setter (machine shop)	600.360-014
RIE	59	Machine Setter (clock & watch)	600.380-022
RIE	59	Maintenance Machinist (machine shop)	600.280-042
RIE	59	Maintenance Mechanic, Telephone (any industry)	822.281-018
RIE	59	Milling-Machine Set-up Operator II (machine shop)	605.282-010
RIE	59	Needlemaker (button & notion)	619.280-010
RIE	59	Overhauler (textile)	628.261-010
RIE	59	Patternmaker (fabrication, n.e.c.)	772.381-014
RIE	59	Pipe Fitter (ship-boat mfg.)	862.261-010
RIE	59	Plastic-Fixture Builder (machine shop)	601.381-030
RIE	59	Profiling-Machine Set-up Operator, Tool (machine shop)	605.280-018
RIE	59	Relay Tester (utilities)	729.281-038
RIE	59	Screw-Machine Set-up Operator, Multiple Spindle (machine shop)	604.280-014
RIE	59	Shot-Peening Operator (aircraft mfg.)	617.280-010
RIE	59	Spring Coiling Machine Setter (metal prod., n.e.c.)	616.260-018
RIE	59	Supervisor, Asbestos-Cement Sheet (nonmet. min.)	679.130-018
RIE	59	Tap-and-Die-Maker Technician (clock & watch)	601.280-034
RIE	59	Template Maker (any industry)	601.381-038
RIE	59	Tool-Machine Set-up Operator (machine shop)	601.280-054
RIE	59	Torsion Spring Coiling Machine Setter (metal prod., n.e.c.)	616.260-022
RIE	59	Turret-Lathe Set-up Operator (machine shop)	604.380-026
RIE	59	Unattended-Ground-Sensor Specialist (military ser.)	378.382-018
RIE	59	Welder Setter, Resistance Machine (welding)	812.360-010
RIE	58	Aircraft Body Repairer (air trans.)	807.261-010
RIE	58	Alteration Tailor (garment; personal ser.; retail trade)	785.261-010
RIE	58	Automotive-Maintenance-Equipment Servicer (any industry)	620.281-018
RIE	58	Bakery-Machine Mechanic (bakery products)	629.281-010
RIE	58	Bricklayer Apprentice (construction)	861.381-022
RIE	58	Cable Television Installer (radio-tv broad.)	821.281-010
RIE	58	Carbide Operator (machine shop)	601.380-010
RIE	58	Die Maker (paper goods)	739.381-018
RIE	58	Die Sinker (machine shop)	601.280-022
RIE	58	Die-Maker Apprentice (paper goods)	739.381-022

Dictionary of Holland Occupational Codes

HOC	Cx	Title	DOT
RIE	58	Die-Try-Out Worker, Stamping (machine shop)	601.281-014
RIE	58	Drill-Press Set-up Operator, Multiple Spindle (machine shop)	606.380-010
RIE	58	Drill-Press Set-up Operator, Radial (machine shop)	606.380-014
RIE	58	Drill-Press Set-up Operator, Radial, Tool (machine shop)	606.380-018
RIE	58	Electric-Motor Repairer (any industry)	721.281-018
RIE	58	Electrician (ship-boat mfg.)	825.381-030
RIE	58	Electrician, Automotive (automotive ser.)	825.281-022
RIE	58	Electrotyper (print. & pub.)	974.381-010
RIE	58	Electrotyper Apprentice (print. & pub.)	974.381-014
RIE	58	Engine Repairer, Service (engine-turbine)	625.281-018
RIE	58	Engine-Lathe Set-up Operator (machine shop)	604.380-018
RIE	58	Engraver, Hand, Hard Metals (engraving)	704.381-026
RIE	58	Etcher Apprentice, Photoengraving (print. & pub.)	971.381-010
RIE	58	Etcher, Photoengraving (print. & pub.)	971.381-014
RIE	58	Fitter I (any industry)	801.261-014
RIE	58	Gas-Appliance Servicer (any industry)	637.261-018
RIE	58	Grinder Operator, External, Tool (machine shop)	603.280-010
RIE	58	Grinder Operator, Surface, Tool (machine shop)	603.280-014
RIE	58	Grinder Set-up Operator, Internal (machine shop)	603.280-022
RIE	58	Hydroelectric-Machinery Mechanic (utilities)	631.261-010
RIE	58	Inside-Meter Tester (utilities)	729.281-034
RIE	58	Inspector, Precision (optical goods)	716.381-010
RIE	58	Instrument Repairer (tel. & tel.)	722.281-010
RIE	58	Instrument-Maker and Repairer (petrol. & gas)	600.280-014
RIE	58	Lead Burner (welding)	819.281-010
RIE	58	Lead-Burner Apprentice (welding)	819.281-014
RIE	58	Machine Set-up Operator (machine shop)	600.380-018
RIE	58	Machinist Apprentice, Automotive (automotive ser.)	600.280-030
RIE	58	Machinist Apprentice, Outside (ship-boat mfg.)	623.281-022
RIE	58	Machinist, Automotive (automotive ser.)	600.280-034
RIE	58	Machinist, Outside (ship-boat mfg.)	623.281-030
RIE	58	Maintenance Mechanic (construction; petrol. & gas; pipe lines)	620.281-046
RIE	58	Maintenance Mechanic, Compressed-Gas Plant (chemical)	630.261-010
RIE	58	Mock-Up Builder (vehicles, n.e.c.)	693.381-018
RIE	58	Model Maker (clock & watch)	693.380-010
RIE	58	Outboard-Motor Mechanic (engine-turbine; ship-boat mfg.)	623.281-042
RIE	58	Parts Salvager (any industry)	638.281-026
RIE	58	Photoengraver (print. & pub.)	971.381-022
RIE	58	Photoengraver Apprentice (print. & pub.)	971.381-026
RIE	58	Photographer, Photoengraving (electron. comp.; print. & pub.)	971.382-014
RIE	58	Planer Set-up Operator, Tool (machine shop)	605.282-014
RIE	58	Planer-Type-Milling-Machine Set-up Operator (machine shop)	605.282-018
RIE	58	Pneumatic-Tool Repairer (any industry)	630.281-010
RIE	58	Precision-Lens Grinder (optical goods)	716.382-018
RIE	58	Precision-Lens-Grinder Apprentice (optical goods)	716.382-022

HOC	Cx	Title	DOT
RIE	58	Profiling-Machine Set-up Operator I (machine shop)	605.280-014
RIE	58	Quarry Supervisor, Dimension Stone (mine & quarry)	930.134-010
RIE	58	Roller, Primary Mill (steel & rel.)	613.362-014
RIE	58	Rubberizing Mechanic (any industry)	630.281-030
RIE	58	Screw-Machine Set-up Operator, Single Spindle (machine shop)	604.280-018
RIE	58	Screw-Machine Set-up Operator, Swiss-Type (clock & watch)	604.260-010
RIE	58	Signal Maintainer (r.r. trans.)	822.281-026
RIE	58	Spring Maker (metal prod., n.e.c.)	616.280-010
RIE	58	Supervisor, Parachute Manufacturing (tex. prod., n.e.c.)	789.132-026
RIE	58	Tailor Apprentice, Alteration (garment; personal ser.; retail trade)	785.261-018
RIE	58	Technical Testing Engineer (motion picture)	194.381-010
RIE	58	Technician, Plant and Maintenance (radio-tv broad.)	822.281-030
RIE	58	Test Driver II (auto. mfg.)	806.283-010
RIE	58	Tool Maker, Bench (machine shop)	601.281-026
RIE	58	Tool-Grinder Operator (machine shop)	603.280-038
RIE	58	Transformer Assembler I (elec. equip.)	820.381-014
RIE	58	Wind-Generating-Electric-Power Installer (construction; utilities)	821.381-018
RIE	57	Acid-Tank Liner (construction)	861.381-010
RIE	57	Airborne Sensor Specialist (military ser.)	378.382-010
RIE	57	Almond-Paste Mixer (sugar & conf.)	529.361-010
RIE	57	Assembler, Aircraft, Structures and Surfaces (aircraft mfg.)	806.381-026
RIE	57	Assembler, Photographic Equipment (photo. appar.)	714.381-010
RIE	57	Assembler-Installer, General (aircraft mfg.)	806.361-014
RIE	57	Balancing-Machine Set-up Worker (any industry)	809.382-010
RIE	57	Calibrator (inst. & app.)	710.381-034
RIE	57	Calibrator, Barometers (inst. & app.)	710.381-042
RIE	57	Carpenter, Mold (brick & tile; concrete prod.)	860.381-034
RIE	57	Cellophane-Casting-Machine Repairer (plastic prod.)	629.281-014
RIE	57	Chronometer Assembler and Adjuster (clock & watch)	715.381-038
RIE	57	Cruiser (forestry; logging)	459.387-010
RIE	57	Cutting-Machine Fixer (textile)	585.380-010
RIE	57	Cylinder-Press Operator (print. & pub.)	651.362-010
RIE	57	Cylinder-Press-Operator Apprentice (print. & pub.)	651.362-014
RIE	57	Deep Submergence Vehicle Crewmember (military ser.)	623.281-014
RIE	57	Die Maker (jewelry-silver.)	601.381-014
RIE	57	Die Setter (forging)	612.360-010
RIE	57	Die-Casting-Machine Setter (foundry)	514.360-010
RIE	57	Die-Maker Apprentice (jewelry-silver.)	601.381-022
RIE	57	Document Restorer (profess. & kin.)	979.361-010
RIE	57	Dry-Cell Tester (elec. equip.)	727.381-018
RIE	57	Electric-Meter Repairer (utilities)	729.281-014
RIE	57	Electric-Meter-Repairer Apprentice (utilities)	729.281-018
RIE	57	Electrical and Radio Mock-Up Mechanic (aircraft mfg.)	693.381-026
RIE	57	Electrogalvanizing-Machine Operator (electroplating)	500.362-010
RIE	57	Electromedical-Equipment Repairer (any industry)	729.281-030

HOC	Cx	Title	DOT
RIE	57	Elevator Constructor (construction)	825.361-010
RIE	57	Engine Repairer, Production (engine-turbine)	625.381-010
RIE	57	Firesetter (elec. equip.; electron. comp.; inst. & app.)	692.360-018
RIE	57	Furniture-Upholsterer Apprentice (any industry)	780.381-022
RIE	57	Gas-Regulator Repairer (petrol. refin.; pipe lines; utilities)	710.381-026
RIE	57	Gear Inspector (machine shop)	602.362-010
RIE	57	Gear-Cutting-Machine Set-up Operator (machine shop)	602.380-010
RIE	57	Grinder Machine Setter (machine shop)	603.380-010
RIE	57	Grinder Set-up Operator, Gear, Tool (machine shop)	602.360-010
RIE	57	Hardener (clock & watch)	504.382-010
RIE	57	Heat Treater I (heat treating)	504.382-014
RIE	57	Heat-Treater Apprentice (heat treating)	504.382-018
RIE	57	High-Energy-Forming Equipment Operator (aircraft mfg.)	619.380-010
RIE	57	Honing-Machine Set-up Operator, Tool (machine shop)	603.382-022
RIE	57	Inspector of Dredging (water trans.)	850.387-010
RIE	57	Inspector, Photographic Equipment (photo. appar.)	714.381-014
RIE	57	Job Setter, Honing (machine shop)	603.280-034
RIE	57	Knitter Mechanic (knitting)	685.360-010
RIE	57	Last-Model Maker (wood prod., n.e.c.)	761.381-018
RIE	57	Lathe Operator, Numerical Control (machine shop)	604.362-010
RIE	57	Location-and-Measurement Technician (clock & watch)	715.381-078
RIE	57	Machine Setter (any industry)	616.360-022
RIE	57	Machine Setter (woodworking)	669.280-010
RIE	57	Mail-Processing-Equipment Mechanic (government ser.)	633.261-014
RIE	57	Metal Sprayer, Machined Parts (any industry)	505.380-010
RIE	57	Milking-System Installer (agric. equip.; retail trade)	809.381-018
RIE	57	Mine-Car Repairer (mine & quarry)	622.381-030
RIE	57	Model Maker, Scale (office machines)	710.361-010
RIE	57	Molder (aircraft mfg.; concrete prod.; foundry)	518.361-010
RIE	57	Molder Apprentice (aircraft mfg.; concrete prod.; foundry)	518.361-014
RIE	57	Molder, Sweep (foundry)	518.361-018
RIE	57	Oil-Field Equipment Mechanic (petrol. & gas)	629.381-014
RIE	57	Operating-Table Assembler (furniture)	706.381-026
RIE	57	Patternmaker (stonework)	703.381-010
RIE	57	Patternmaker (engraving)	751.381-010
RIE	57	Photographic-Plate Maker (electron. comp.)	714.381-018
RIE	57	Plaster Molder I (foundry)	777.381-034
RIE	57	Plaster-Pattern Caster (machine tools)	777.381-038
RIE	57	Plastic Tool Maker (machine shop)	601.381-026
RIE	57	Plater (electroplating)	500.380-010
RIE	57	Plater Apprentice (electroplating)	500.380-014
RIE	57	Polymerization-Kettle Operator (plastic-synth.)	558.382-050
RIE	57	Processor, Solid Propellant (chemical)	590.464-010
RIE	57	Prototype-Deicer Assembler (rubber goods)	759.261-010
RIE	57	Pumper-Gauger (chemical; petrol. refin.; pipe lines)	914.382-014
RIE	57	Pumper-Gauger Apprentice (chemical; petrol. refin.; pipe lines)	914.382-018
RIE	57	Rotary-Head-Milling-Machine Set-up Operator (machine shop)	605.382-030

HOC	Cx	Title	DOT
RIE	57	Router Set-up Operator, Numerical Control (machine shop)	605.360-010
RIE	57	Sample Stitcher (garment)	785.361-018
RIE	57	Setter, Automatic-Spinning Lathe (any industry)	604.360-010
RIE	57	Shaper Set-up Operator, Tool (machine shop)	605.382-038
RIE	57	Shipfitter (ship-boat mfg.)	806.381-046
RIE	57	Shipfitter Apprentice (ship-boat mfg.)	806.381-050
RIE	57	Shoemaker, Custom (boot & shoe)	788.381-014
RIE	57	Shop Tailor (garment; retail trade)	785.361-022
RIE	57	Shop Tailor Apprentice (garment; retail trade)	785.361-026
RIE	57	Special Effects Specialist (amuse. & rec.; motion picture; radio-tv broad.)	962.281-018
RIE	57	Spinner, Hand (any industry)	619.362-018
RIE	57	Spinner, Hydraulic (any industry)	619.362-022
RIE	57	Stencil Cutter (railroad equip.)	970.381-038
RIE	57	Storage Battery Inspector and Tester (elec. equip.)	727.381-022
RIE	57	Stripper, Lithographic II (print. & pub.)	972.381-022
RIE	57	Tape-Recorder Repairer (any industry)	720.281-014
RIE	57	Taximeter Repairer (automotive ser.)	710.281-038
RIE	57	Tester, Motors and Controls (elec. equip.)	721.281-030
RIE	57	Thread Inspector (petrol. & gas)	862.381-038
RIE	57	Tracer (construction; stonework)	779.381-022
RIE	57	Turbine Operator (utilities)	952.362-042
RIE	57	Web-Press Operator (print. & pub.)	651.362-030
RIE	57	Web-Press-Operator Apprentice (print. & pub.)	651.362-034
RIE	57	Welder Setter, Electron-Beam Machine (welding)	815.380-010
RIE	57	Welder-Fitter (welding)	819.361-010
RIE	57	Welder-Fitter Apprentice (welding)	819.361-014
RIE	57	Welding-Machine Operator, Electron Beam (welding)	815.382-010
RIE	57	Well-Drill Operator (construction)	859.362-010
RIE	57	Wire-Mesh-Filter Fabricator (metal prod., n.e.c.)	709.381-046
RIE	56	Assembler, Internal Combustion Engine (engine-turbine)	806.481-014
RIE	56	Assembler, Tubing (aircraft mfg.)	806.381-034
RIE	56	Aviation Support Equipment Repairer (military ser.)	639.281-010
RIE	56	Blacksmith (forging)	610.381-010
RIE	56	Blacksmith Apprentice (forging)	610.381-014
RIE	56	Boilermaker Fitter (struct. metal)	805.361-014
RIE	56	Chaser (jewelry-silver.)	704.381-010
RIE	56	Confectionery Cooker (sugar & conf.)	526.382-014
RIE	56	Distillation Operator (chemical)	552.462-010
RIE	56	Ear-Mold Laboratory Technician (plastic prod.)	777.361-010
RIE	56	Engraver, Machine (print. & pub.)	979.382-014
RIE	56	Final Inspector, Motorcycles (motor-bicycles)	806.281-018
RIE	56	Form Builder (construction)	860.381-046
RIE	56	Four-Slide-Machine Operator I (any industry)	619.382-018
RIE	56	Four-Slide-Machine Setter (any industry)	616.380-010
RIE	56	Fuel-Injection Servicer (any industry)	625.281-022
RIE	56	Gas-Main Fitter (utilities)	862.361-014
RIE	56	Gear-Shaver Set-up Operator (machine shop)	602.382-030
RIE	56	Governor Assembler, Hydraulic (elec. equip.)	721.381-018

HOC	Cx	Title	DOT
RIE	56	Grinder Set-up Operator (machine shop)	603.382-034
RIE	56	Inspector, Metal Can (tinware)	709.367-010
RIE	56	Inspector, Typewriter Assembly and Parts (office machines)	706.381-022
RIE	56	Last-Pattern Grader (wood prod., n.e.c.)	693.382-010
RIE	56	Lay-Out Worker (jewelry-silver.)	700.381-026
RIE	56	Meter Repairer (any industry)	710.281-034
RIE	56	Miner (construction)	850.381-010
RIE	56	Panelboard Operator (mine & quarry; smelt. & refin.)	939.362-014
RIE	56	Photoengraving Finisher (print. & pub.)	971.381-030
RIE	56	Photoengraving Printer (print. & pub.)	971.381-034
RIE	56	Photographer Apprentice, Lithographic (print. & pub.)	972.382-010
RIE	56	Photographer, Lithographic (print. & pub.)	972.382-014
RIE	56	Plasterer, Molding (concrete prod.; construction)	842.361-026
RIE	56	Plate Finisher (print. & pub.)	659.360-010
RIE	56	Power-Transformer Repairer (utilities)	821.361-034
RIE	56	Recovery Operator (paper & pulp)	552.362-018
RIE	56	Router Operator (any industry)	605.382-034
RIE	56	Saw Filer (any industry)	701.381-014
RIE	56	Screw-Machine Set-up Operator (machine shop)	604.380-022
RIE	56	Shear Setter (any industry)	615.380-010
RIE	56	Stereotyper (print. & pub.)	974.382-014
RIE	56	Stereotyper Apprentice (print. & pub.)	974.382-010
RIE	56	Street-Light Repairer (utilities)	729.381-018
RIE	56	Switchboard Operator (chemical)	952.362-038
RIE	56	Welding-Machine Operator, Arc (welding)	810.382-010
RIE	56	Wool Sorter (textile)	589.387-014
RIE	56	Yard Inspector (ship-boat mfg.)	869.281-018
RIE	55	Automotive Technician, Exhaust Emissions (government ser.)	620.281-014
RIE	55	Diagrammer and Seamer (carpet & rug)	789.484-010
RIE	55	Fermentation Operator (beverage)	522.382-014
RIE	55	Forming-Machine Adjuster (glass mfg.)	629.281-026
RIE	55	Gear Hobber Set-up Operator (machine shop)	602.382-010
RIE	55	Gear-Generator Set-up Operator, Spiral Bevel (machine shop)	602.382-014
RIE	55	Gear-Generator Set-up Operator, Straight Bevel (machine shop)	602.382-018
RIE	55	Gear-Milling-Machine Set-up Operator (machine shop)	602.382-022
RIE	55	Gear-Shaper Set-up Operator (machine shop)	602.382-026
RIE	55	Inspector (plastic prod.; plastic-synth.)	559.381-010
RIE	55	Linotype Operator (print. & pub.)	650.582-010
RIE	55	Metal-Spraying-Machine Operator, Automatic I (any industry)	505.382-010
RIE	55	Miner I (mine & quarry)	939.281-010
RIE	55	Missile Facilities Repairer (military ser.)	828.281-018
RIE	55	Platen-Press Operator (print. & pub.)	651.362-018
RIE	55	Platen-Press-Operator Apprentice (print. & pub.)	651.362-022
RIE	55	Preservation Inspector, Marine Equipment (government ser.)	929.367-010

HOC	Cx	Title	DOT
RIE	55	Propulsion-Motor-and-Generator Repairer (automotive ser.)	721.281-026
RIE	55	Pulp-and-Paper Tester (paper & pulp)	539.364-010
RIE	55	Screen Maker, Textile (textile)	971.381-046
RIE	55	Smoking-Pipe Maker (fabrication, n.e.c.)	761.381-030
RIE	55	Target Aircraft Technician (military ser.)	378.281-010
RIE	55	Threading-Machine Setter (machine shop)	609.380-014
RIE	55	Vehicle-Fuel-Systems Converter (automotive ser.)	620.281-070
RIE	55	Watch Assembler (clock & watch)	715.381-094
RIE	54	Assembler, Watch Train (clock & watch)	715.381-014
RIE	54	Chemical-Etching Processor (aircraft mfg.)	704.381-014
RIE	54	Color Matcher (leather mfg.; plastic-synth.; tex. prod., n.e.c.)	550.381-010
RIE	54	Duplicator-Punch Operator (any industry)	615.482-014
RIE	54	Electric-Motor-Control Assembler (elec. equip.)	721.381-014
RIE	54	Extrusion-Press Adjuster (elec. equip.)	614.380-010
RIE	54	Film Inspector (photofinishing)	976.362-010
RIE	54	Firer, Locomotive (r.r. trans.)	910.363-010
RIE	54	Fuel-System-Maintenance Worker (any industry)	638.381-010
RIE	54	Gear Repairer (water trans.)	623.381-010
RIE	54	Gear-Lapping-Machine Operator (machine shop)	602.482-010
RIE	54	Harp-Action Assembler (musical inst.)	730.381-030
RIE	54	Industrial-Gas Fitter (utilities)	862.381-014
RIE	54	Inspector, Cold Working (ordnance)	612.384-010
RIE	54	Machine Setter (button & notion)	690.380-010
RIE	54	Machinist Apprentice, Wood (woodworking)	669.380-010
RIE	54	Machinist, Wood (woodworking)	669.380-014
RIE	54	Marble Setter (construction)	861.381-030
RIE	54	Microfiche Duplicator (business ser.)	976.381-014
RIE	54	Model-and-Mold Maker (brick & tile)	777.381-014
RIE	54	Mold Setter (inst. & app.; office machines; plastic prod.; recording)	556.380-010
RIE	54	Motion-Picture Projectionist (amuse. & rec.; motion picture)	960.362-010
RIE	54	Motorcycle Repairer (automotive ser.)	620.281-054
RIE	54	Oil Boiler (tex. prod., n.e.c.)	543.362-010
RIE	54	Pipe Tester (petrol. & gas)	930.382-014
RIE	54	Plate Setter, Flexographic Press (print. & pub.)	659.381-010
RIE	54	Quality Technician, Fiberglass (glass mfg.)	579.384-014
RIE	54	Reproduction Technician (any industry)	976.361-010
RIE	54	Roll-Forming-Machine Set-up Mechanic (any industry)	613.360-010
RIE	54	Setter, Cold-Rolling Machine (machine shop)	617.682-022
RIE	54	Sign Erector I (fabrication, n.e.c.)	869.381-026
RIE	54	Sound Technician (any industry)	829.281-022
RIE	54	Stonecutter Apprentice, Hand (stonework)	771.381-010
RIE	54	Straight-Pin-Making-Machine Operator (button & notion)	609.482-014
RIE	54	Tinter (paint & varnish)	550.381-014
RIE	54	Treating Inspector (wood prod., n.e.c.)	569.367-010
RIE	54	Truck-Body Builder (auto. mfg.; automotive ser.)	807.281-010

HOC	Cx	Title	DOT
RIE	54	Turret-Punch-Press Operator (any industry)	615.482-038
RIE	53	Autoclave Operator I (chemical)	553.382-010
RIE	53	Automobile-Body Repairer (automotive ser.)	807.381-010
RIE	53	Belt-Press Operator I (rubber goods)	553.362-010
RIE	53	Blocker, Metal Base (print. & pub.)	974.682-010
RIE	53	Bow Maker, Custom (toy-sport equip.)	732.381-010
RIE	53	Bulk-Station Operator (petrol. & gas)	570.362-010
RIE	53	Coater Operator (any industry)	509.382-010
RIE	53	Fabricator-Assembler, Metal Products (any industry)	809.381-010
RIE	53	Fruit-Buying Grader (can. & preserv.; wholesale tr.)	529.387-018
RIE	53	Heater II (steel & rel.)	542.362-010
RIE	53	Mailing-Machine Operator (print. & pub.)	208.462-010
RIE	53	Major-Assembly Inspector (agric. equip.)	801.381-018
RIE	53	Oil-Recovery-Unit Operator (petrol. refin.)	549.382-014
RIE	53	Opener-Verifier-Packer, Customs (government ser.)	168.387-010
RIE	53	Pharmaceutical Operator (pharmaceut.)	559.382-042
RIE	53	Player-Piano Technician (musical inst.)	730.381-050
RIE	53	Printer (print. & pub.)	979.382-018
RIE	53	Profiling-Machine Set-up Operator II (machine shop)	605.382-026
RIE	53	Punch-Press Setter (any industry)	619.380-014
RIE	53	Quality-Control Tester (paper goods; plastic-synth.)	559.367-010
RIE	53	Roll-Forming-Machine Operator I (any industry)	617.482-018
RIE	53	Roller Repairer (textile)	979.381-026
RIE	53	Stencil Cutter (stonework)	771.281-010
RIE	53	Supervisor, Finishing Department (nonmet. min.)	679.137-010
RIE	53	Tester, Compressed Gases (chemical)	549.364-010
RIE	53	Thermal-Cutting-Machine Operator (welding)	816.482-010
RIE	53	Vinegar Maker (food prep., n.e.c.)	522.382-038
RIE	53	Well Puller (petrol. & gas)	930.382-030
RIE	52	Aircraft Launch and Recovery Technician (military ser.)	912.682-010
RIE	52	Brazing-Machine Operator (welding)	813.382-014
RIE	52	Buffing-Machine Operator (any industry)	603.382-010
RIE	52	Chemical Preparer (chemical; electron. comp.)	550.685-030
RIE	52	Desulfurizer Operator (steel & rel.)	541.362-010
RIE	52	Draw-Bench Operator (any industry)	614.682-010
RIE	52	Hydroelectric-Machinery-Mechanic Helper (utilities)	631.364-010
RIE	52	Machine Set-up Operator, Paper Goods (paper goods)	649.380-010
RIE	52	Paint-Sprayer Operator, Automatic (any industry)	599.382-010
RIE	52	Press Setter (nonfer. metal; steel & rel.)	617.480-014
RIE	52	Safety-Pin-Assembling-Machine Operator (button & notion)	616.482-010
RIE	52	Welding-Machine Operator, Thermit (welding)	815.682-014
RIE	52	Yard Engineer (r.r. trans.)	910.363-018
RIE	51	Brake Coupler, Road Freight (r.r. trans.)	910.367-010
RIE	51	Brazer, Furnace (welding)	813.482-010
RIE	51	Broaching-Machine Set-up Operator (machine shop)	605.382-010
RIE	51	Bus Driver, Day-Haul or Farm Charter (agriculture)	913.363-010
RIE	51	Carpet Cutter (retail trade)	929.381-010
RIE	51	Center-Machine Operator (sugar & conf.)	520.682-014

HOC	Cx	Title	DOT
RIE	51	Clean-Out Driller (petrol. & gas)	930.363-010
RIE	51	Cloth-Shrinking Tester (textile)	587.384-010
RIE	51	Coating-Machine Operator I (tex. prod., n.e.c.)	584.382-010
RIE	51	Color-Printer Operator (photofinishing)	976.382-014
RIE	51	Contour-Band-Saw Operator, Vertical (machine shop)	607.382-010
RIE	51	Embosser (print. & pub.)	659.382-010
RIE	51	Fixture Repairer-Fabricator (any industry)	630.384-010
RIE	51	Granulator-Machine Operator (pharmaceut.)	559.382-026
RIE	51	Iron-Plastic Bullet Maker (ordnance)	590.365-010
RIE	51	Leather Grader (glove & mit.)	784.387-014
RIE	51	Line Tender, Flakeboard (wood prod., n.e.c.)	569.382-010
RIE	51	Mortising-Machine Operator (woodworking)	665.482-014
RIE	51	Operator, Catalyst Concentration (plastic-synth.)	550.382-026
RIE	51	Oxygen-Furnace Operator (steel & rel.)	512.382-010
RIE	51	Rafter-Cutting-Machine Operator (mfd. bldgs.)	669.382-014
RIE	51	Repairer, Heavy (auto. mfg.)	620.381-022
RIE	51	Router Operator (stonework)	676.462-010
RIE	51	Sailor, Pleasure Craft (water trans.)	911.664-014
RIE	51	Saturator Operator (chemical; steel & rel.)	558.362-018
RIE	51	Stone-Lathe Operator (stonework)	674.662-010
RIE	51	Supply Controller (concrete prod.)	570.382-018
RIE	51	Swing-Type-Lathe Operator (woodworking)	664.382-010
RIE	51	Taxi Driver (motor trans.)	913.463-018
RIE	51	Waxing-Machine Operator (paper goods)	534.482-010
RIE	51	Welder Apprentice, Gas (welding)	811.684-010
RIE	51	Welding-Machine Operator, Electroslag (welding)	815.382-014
RIE	50	Benzene-Washer Operator (chemical; steel & rel.)	551.682-010
RIE	50	Brazer, Induction (welding)	813.382-010
RIE	50	Buckshot-Swage Operator (ordnance)	612.682-010
RIE	50	Color Maker (tex. prod., n.e.c.)	550.382-014
RIE	50	Cuprous-Chloride Operator (chemical)	558.382-034
RIE	50	Drilling-Machine Operator (mine & quarry)	930.482-010
RIE	50	Electrode Turner-and-Finisher (elec. equip.)	692.682-034
RIE	50	Extruder Operator (forging)	614.482-014
RIE	50	Flash-Drier Operator (chemical)	553.462-010
RIE	50	Forging-Press Operator I (forging)	611.482-010
RIE	50	Metal Sprayer, Corrosion Prevention (any industry)	843.482-010
RIE	50	Mixing-Machine Operator (any industry)	550.382-022
RIE	50	New-Car Inspector (motor trans.)	919.363-010
RIE	50	Plastics-Spreading-Machine Operator (plastic-synth.)	554.382-014
RIE	50	Poultry Inseminator (agriculture)	411.384-010
RIE	50	Printer, Plastic (plastic prod.; tex. prod., n.e.c.)	651.382-026
RIE	50	Proof-Technician Helper (ordnance)	736.387-014
RIE	50	Quality Assurance Monitor (auto. mfg.)	806.367-018
RIE	50	Saturation-Equipment Operator (fabrication, n.e.c.)	582.665-022
RIE	50	Setter, Molding-and-Coremaking Machines (foundry)	518.380-010
RIE	50	Soda-Column Operator (chemical)	558.382-054
RIE	50	Stock Cutter (saw. & plan.)	667.482-018
RIE	50	Stone Grader (stonework)	670.384-010

HOC	Cx	Title	DOT
RIE	50	Tire Builder, Automobile (rubber tire)	750.384-010
RIE	50	Tractor-Trailer-Truck Driver (any industry)	904.383-010
RIE	50	Weigher-Bulker (chemical)	550.582-014
RIE	49	Blood Tester, Fowl (agriculture)	411.364-010
RIE	49	Calender Operator (rubber goods; rubber tire)	554.362-010
RIE	49	Calender Operator (fabrication, n.e.c.)	590.682-010
RIE	49	Cell Repairer (chemical)	826.384-010
RIE	49	Clay-Stain Mixer (brick & tile)	773.487-010
RIE	49	Coal-Equipment Operator (utilities)	921.683-022
RIE	49	Construction Worker I (construction)	869.664-014
RIE	49	Die-Casting-Machine Operator I (foundry)	514.382-010
RIE	49	Driller, Machine (construction; mine & quarry)	930.382-010
RIE	49	Dry-Press Operator (brick & tile)	575.662-010
RIE	49	Fitter, Ventilated Rib (ordnance)	736.381-014
RIE	49	Frame Straightener (motor-bicycles)	807.484-010
RIE	49	Header (wood prod., n.e.c.)	665.682-014
RIE	49	Inspector (boot & shoe)	788.384-010
RIE	49	Lock-Corner-Machine Operator (woodworking)	665.382-014
RIE	49	Metal Control Worker (foundry)	512.487-010
RIE	49	Milk Driver (dairy products)	905.483-010
RIE	49	Pile-Driver Operator (construction)	859.682-018
RIE	49	Planer, Stone (stonework)	675.682-018
RIE	49	Pottery-Machine Operator (pottery & porc.)	774.382-010
RIE	49	Roof-Cement-and-Paint Maker (build. mat., n.e.c.; nonmet. min.)	550.382-030
RIE	49	Rubber and Plastics Worker (military ser.)	891.684-014
RIE	49	Solderer-Assembler (welding)	813.684-014
RIE	49	Stock Grader (woodworking)	667.382-010
RIE	49	Stonecutter, Machine (stonework)	677.682-022
RIE	49	Timber-Sizer Operator (saw. & plan.)	665.482-018
RIE	49	Tin Recovery Worker (smelt. & refin.)	512.382-018
RIE	49	Wire Drawer (nonfer. metal)	614.382-010
RIE	49	Wood-Carving-Machine Operator (woodworking)	665.382-018
RIE	48	Arch-Cushion-Skiving-Machine Operator (rubber goods)	690.682-010
RIE	48	Belly Builder (musical inst.)	730.684-018
RIE	48	Beveling-and-Edging-Machine Operator (glass mfg.; glass products)	673.682-014
RIE	48	Buffing-Machine Operator, Silverware (jewelry-silver.)	603.682-010
RIE	48	Capsule-Filling-Machine Operator (pharmaceut.)	559.682-010
RIE	48	Carbon-Coater-Machine Operator (pen & pencil)	534.682-014
RIE	48	Casting-Machine Operator, Automatic (elec. equip.)	502.482-014
RIE	48	Chemical Compounder (chemical)	559.682-018
RIE	48	Coloring Checker (jewelry-silver.)	735.587-010
RIE	48	Dado Operator (woodworking)	669.382-010
RIE	48	Expansion-Joint Builder (rubber goods)	759.664-014
RIE	48	Farm-Machine Operator (agriculture)	409.683-010
RIE	48	Final Inspector (boot & shoe)	753.687-018
RIE	48	Flexographic-Press Operator (paper goods; print. & pub.)	651.682-010
RIE	48	Forming-Roll Operator I (any industry)	617.482-014

Part 2: From Holland Codes to Occupations

From Holland Codes to the Dictionary of Occupational Titles Occupations

HOC	Cx	Title	DOT
RIE	48	Furnace Operator (smelt. & refin.)	513.462-010
RIE	48	Honing-Machine Operator, Production (machine shop)	603.482-034
RIE	48	Hose Maker (rubber goods)	752.684-030
RIE	48	Impregnating-Tank Operator (any industry)	599.685-046
RIE	48	Lozenge Maker (sugar & conf.)	529.682-026
RIE	48	Miter Grinder Operator (glass mfg.; glass products)	673.682-026
RIE	48	Motorboat Operator (any industry)	911.663-010
RIE	48	Powder Blender and Pourer (chemical)	550.485-022
RIE	48	Redeye Gunner (military ser.)	378.682-010
RIE	48	Rock-Drill Operator II (construction)	850.662-014
RIE	48	Roll Grinder (rubber reclaim.)	629.682-010
RIE	48	Sandblaster, Stone (stonework)	673.382-010
RIE	48	Sandblaster, Stone Apprentice (stonework)	673.382-014
RIE	48	Silvering Applicator (glass products)	574.582-010
RIE	48	Tracer-Powder Blender (chemical)	550.585-042
RIE	48	Treating-Plant Operator (wood prod., n.e.c.)	563.662-010
RIE	47	Abrasive Grader (optical goods)	570.682-010
RIE	47	Angle Shear Operator (any industry)	615.482-010
RIE	47	Appliance Repairer (house. appl.)	723.584-010
RIE	47	Bellows Filler (inst. & app.)	710.684-014
RIE	47	Box-Folding-Machine Operator (paper goods)	649.682-010
RIE	47	Brazer, Resistance (welding)	813.682-010
RIE	47	Casting-Wheel Operator (smelt. & refin.)	514.682-010
RIE	47	Cell Tester (chemical)	558.584-010
RIE	47	Channeling-Machine Runner (mine & quarry)	930.383-010
RIE	47	Combiner Operator (paper & pulp; paper goods)	534.682-026
RIE	47	Console Assembler (musical inst.)	730.684-030
RIE	47	Cut-and-Print-Machine Operator (ordnance)	659.682-010
RIE	47	Cut-Off-Saw Operator, Metal (machine shop)	607.682-010
RIE	47	Cutting-Machine Operator (print. & pub.)	640.682-018
RIE	47	Draw-Bench Operator (nonfer. metal; steel & rel.)	614.482-010
RIE	47	Drier Operator (mine & quarry)	543.682-014
RIE	47	Dry-Charge-Process Attendant (elec. equip.)	590.685-026
RIE	47	Foundation-Drill Operator (construction)	859.682-014
RIE	47	Head Sawyer (saw. & plan.)	667.662-010
RIE	47	Heater (forging)	619.682-022
RIE	47	High-Density Finishing Operator (wood prod., n.e.c.)	539.562-010
RIE	47	Horticultural Worker I (agriculture)	405.684-014
RIE	47	Hostler (motor trans.)	909.663-010
RIE	47	Hostler (r.r. trans.)	910.683-010
RIE	47	Laborer, Car Barn (r.r. trans.)	910.583-010
RIE	47	Loading-Machine Operator (mine & quarry)	932.683-014
RIE	47	Machine Molder (foundry)	518.682-010
RIE	47	Mixing-Machine Tender (chemical; pharmaceut.)	550.685-090
RIE	47	Motor Operator (r.r. trans.)	910.683-014
RIE	47	Multiple-Drum Sander (woodworking)	662.682-014
RIE	47	Pack-Room Operator (plastic-synth.)	559.684-010
RIE	47	Planer Operator (woodworking)	665.682-022
RIE	47	Plant Operator (concrete prod.; construction)	570.682-014

Part 2: From Holland Codes to Occupations

From Holland Codes to the Dictionary of Occupational Titles Occupations

HOC	Cx	Title	DOT
RIE	47	Pot Builder (chemical)	826.684-022
RIE	47	Prefitter, Doors (woodworking)	666.582-010
RIE	47	Press Operator, Hardboard (wood prod., n.e.c.)	569.682-014
RIE	47	Roller-Machine Operator (metal prod., n.e.c.)	611.482-014
RIE	47	Router Operator (woodworking)	665.682-030
RIE	47	Scalper Operator (nonfer. metal)	605.682-022
RIE	47	Shaper Operator (woodworking)	665.682-034
RIE	47	Shell-Machine Operator (chemical)	649.682-030
RIE	47	Shuttle-Car Operator (mine & quarry)	932.683-022
RIE	47	Slab-Depiler Operator (steel & rel.)	504.665-010
RIE	47	Sprayer, Hand (agriculture)	408.684-014
RIE	47	Stone Layout Marker (stonework)	670.587-010
RIE	47	Stranding-Machine Operator (elec. equip.; light. fix.; metal prod., n.e.c.; nonfer. metal)	616.682-034
RIE	47	Stroke-Belt-Sander Operator (woodworking)	662.682-018
RIE	47	Tablet-Making-Machine Operator (paper goods)	649.682-042
RIE	47	Thinner (paint & varnish)	550.585-038
RIE	47	Track-Moving-Machine Operator (construction; mine & quarry)	910.663-010
RIE	47	Wastewater-Treatment-Plant Attendant (sanitary ser.)	955.585-010
RIE	46	Brine Maker I (chemical)	550.685-018
RIE	46	Caser, Shoe Parts (boot & shoe)	788.687-026
RIE	46	Catalyst-Recovery Operator (chemical)	551.685-022
RIE	46	Curb-Machine Operator (construction)	853.683-010
RIE	46	Door-Machine Operator (steel & rel.)	519.663-010
RIE	46	Drill-Press Set-up Operator, Single Spindle (machine shop)	606.682-018
RIE	46	Elevating-Grader Operator (construction)	850.663-014
RIE	46	Fence-Making Machine Operator (metal prod., n.e.c.)	616.582-010
RIE	46	Form-Grader Operator (construction)	850.683-022
RIE	46	Growth-Media Mixer, Mushroom (agriculture)	405.683-014
RIE	46	Lye Treater (chemical; soap & rel.)	551.685-094
RIE	46	Pigment Furnace Tender (chemical)	553.685-086
RIE	46	Pipe-Wrapping-Machine Operator (construction; pipe lines)	862.682-014
RIE	46	Profile-Shaper Operator, Automatic (woodworking)	665.682-026
RIE	46	Scraper Operator (construction)	850.683-038
RIE	46	Stock-Patch Sawyer (woodworking)	667.682-082
RIE	46	Track-Surfacing-Machine Operator (construction)	910.683-018
RIE	46	Yard Worker (agriculture)	929.583-010
RIE	45	Aligner, Barrel and Receiver (ordnance)	736.684-010
RIE	45	Broaching-Machine Operator, Production (machine shop)	605.682-014
RIE	45	Door Assembler (mfd. bldgs.; vehicles, n.e.c.)	806.684-050
RIE	45	Filling-Machine Set-up Mechanic (food prep., n.e.c.)	920.680-010
RIE	45	Hooker Inspector (textile)	689.685-078
RIE	45	Line-Service Attendant (air trans.)	912.687-010
RIE	45	Log Marker (logging; millwork-plywood)	454.687-018
RIE	45	Mixer I (tex. prod., n.e.c.)	550.685-074
RIE	45	Ordnance Truck Installation Mechanic (ordnance)	806.684-098

Part 2: From Holland Codes to Occupations

From Holland Codes to the Dictionary of Occupational Titles Occupations

HOC	Cx	Title	DOT
RIE	45	Road-Mixer Operator (construction)	859.683-026
RIE	45	Roll Operator (plastic-synth.)	554.682-018
RIE	45	Roller-Print Tender (print. & pub.)	971.685-010
RIE	45	Rotary-Screen-Printing-Machine Operator (textile)	652.582-014
RIE	45	Torch-Straightener-and-Heater (any industry)	709.684-086
RIE	44	Garbage Collector Driver (motor trans.)	905.663-010
RIE	44	Gum-Scoring-Machine Operator (sugar & conf.)	520.682-022
RIE	44	Heater-Planer Operator (construction)	853.683-014
RIE	44	Joint-Cleaning-and-Grooving-Machine Operator (construction)	853.683-018
RIE	44	Mill Attendant I (chemical)	555.565-010
RIE	44	Painter, Touch-Up (any industry)	749.684-038
RIE	44	Painter, Tumbling Barrel (any industry)	599.685-070
RIE	44	Stamper, Machine (pottery & porc.)	652.682-022
RIE	44	Tree-Shear Operator (logging)	454.683-010
RIE	44	Utility-Tractor Operator (construction)	850.683-046
RIE	44	Veneer-Lathe Operator (millwork-plywood)	664.662-010
RIE	43	Dump-Truck Driver (any industry)	902.683-010
RIE	43	Mill Helper (nonfer. metal)	502.684-014
RIE	43	Mixer (paint & varnish)	550.685-078
RIE	43	Water-Truck Driver II (construction; petrol. & gas)	905.683-010
RIE	42	Cut-Off Saw Tender, Metal (machine shop)	607.685-010
RIE	42	Furnace-and-Wash-Equipment Operator (ordnance)	503.685-026
RIE	42	Heat Welder, Plastics (plastic prod.)	553.684-010
RIE	42	Mixer II (chemical)	737.687-090
RIE	42	Singer (textile)	585.685-106
RIE	41	Crusher Operator (concrete prod.)	570.685-018
RIE	41	Laborer, Poultry Farm (agriculture)	411.687-018
RIE	41	Porcelain-Enamel Repairer (any industry)	741.684-030
RIE	41	String Laster (boot & shoe)	690.685-406
RIE	41	Utility Bag Assembler (leather prod.)	783.684-030
RIE	40	Belt Sander, Stone (stonework)	673.666-010
RIE	40	Beveler (nonmet. min.)	673.685-022
RIE	40	Laborer, General (paint & varnish)	559.685-110
RIE	40	Ski-Top Trimmer (plastic prod.)	690.685-370
RIE	40	Splitter Tender (saw. & plan.)	663.685-038
RIE	40	Stable Attendant (any industry)	410.674-022
RIC	72	Optical Engineer (profess. & kin.)	019.061-018
RIC	70	Heat-Transfer Technician (profess. & kin.)	007.181-010
RIC	68	Instrumentation Technician (profess. & kin.)	003.261-010
RIC	68	Optomechanical Technician (optical goods; photo. appar.)	007.161-030
RIC	68	Parking Analyst (government ser.)	199.261-014
RIC	66	Civil Engineering Technician (profess. & kin.)	005.261-014
RIC	66	Hog-Confinement-System Manager (agriculture)	410.161-022
RIC	66	Solar-Energy-Systems Designer (profess. & kin.)	007.161-038
RIC	66	Special Procedures Technologist, Cardiac Catheterization (medical ser.)	078.362-050
RIC	66	Special Procedures Technologist, Magnetic Resonance Imaging (MRI) (medical ser.)	078.362-058

HOC	Cx	Title	DOT
RIC	64	Machine Repairer, Maintenance (any industry)	638.261-030
RIC	64	Radio Station Operator (aircraft mfg.)	193.262-026
RIC	63	Fastener Technologist (nut & bolt)	612.260-010
RIC	63	Quality Assurance Analyst (profess. & kin.)	033.262-010
RIC	62	Inspector, Assemblies and Installations (aircraft mfg.)	806.261-030
RIC	62	Tool Builder (aircraft mfg.)	693.281-030
RIC	61	Crystal Growing Technician (electron. comp.)	590.262-010
RIC	60	Carpenter, Prototype (ship-boat mfg.)	806.281-058
RIC	60	Laboratory Technician, Pharmaceutical (pharmaceut.)	559.361-010
RIC	60	Laboratory Tester (any industry)	029.261-010
RIC	60	Maintenance Repairer, Industrial (any industry)	899.261-014
RIC	59	Grinder Set-up Operator, Thread Tool (machine shop)	603.260-010
RIC	59	Metal Fabricator (any industry)	619.361-014
RIC	59	Metal-Fabricator Apprentice (any industry)	619.361-018
RIC	59	Operational Test Mechanic (aircraft mfg.)	806.261-050
RIC	59	Ornamental-Metal Worker (metal prod., n.e.c.)	619.260-014
RIC	59	Stripper, Lithographic I (print. & pub.)	972.281-022
RIC	59	Tank Calibrator (business ser.)	229.387-014
RIC	58	Film Flat Inspector (print. & pub.)	972.284-010
RIC	58	Hot-Cell Technician (profess. & kin.)	015.362-018
RIC	58	Inspector, Electromechanical (inst. & app.)	729.361-010
RIC	58	Scanner (profess. & kin.)	015.384-010
RIC	58	Smoke Tester (smelt. & refin.)	012.281-010
RIC	57	Assembler and Tester, Electronics (office machines)	710.281-010
RIC	57	Camera Operator, Animation (motion picture)	143.382-010
RIC	57	Evaporator Operator I (chemical)	553.382-018
RIC	57	Patternmaker (furniture; garment; tex. prod., n.e.c.)	781.361-014
RIC	57	Tester (profess. & kin.)	011.361-010
RIC	55	Inspector, Processing (aircraft mfg.)	806.381-074
RIC	55	Vector Control Assistant (government ser.)	049.364-014
RIC	54	Automobile-Service-Station Mechanic (automotive ser.)	620.261-030
RIC	54	Crystal Grower (comm. equip.; electron. comp.)	590.382-014
RIC	54	Quality Control Inspector (sugar & conf.)	529.367-034
RIC	54	Rim-Fire-Priming Tool Setter (ordnance)	632.380-022
RIC	52	Dye-Lab Technician (knitting)	582.384-010
RIC	51	Painter, Electrostatic (any industry)	599.682-010
RIC	51	Sewer-Line Repairer (sanitary ser.)	869.664-018
RIC	50	Assembler I (office machines)	706.684-014
RIC	50	Pulverizer-Mill Operator (rubber goods; rubber reclaim.)	555.382-010
RIC	49	Sampler (mine & quarry)	579.484-010
RIC	48	Chemical Operator II (chemical)	558.685-062
RIC	48	Roll-Sheeting Cutter (tex. prod., n.e.c.)	699.682-026
RIC	47	Sign Writer, Machine (any industry)	659.682-026
RIC	46	Embosser (leather mfg.; leather prod.)	690.682-030
RIC	46	Sprayer Operator (smelt. & refin.)	505.682-010
RIC	46	Trimmer (plastic prod.)	690.482-014
RIC	42	Picker Tender (textile)	680.685-074
RAI	58	Concrete Sculptor (concrete prod.)	777.281-010

Part 2: From Holland Codes to Occupations

From Holland Codes to the Dictionary of Occupational Titles Occupations

HOC	Cx	Title	DOT
RAS	56	Cook Apprentice, Pastry (hotel & rest.)	313.381-018
RAS	56	Cook, Pastry (hotel & rest.)	313.381-026
RAS	49	Ice-Cream Chef (hotel & rest.)	313.381-034
RAE	61	Clay Modeler (any industry)	779.281-010
RAE	59	Bonsai Culturist (agriculture)	405.161-010
RAE	59	Model Maker (pottery & porc.)	777.281-014
RAE	58	Chef De Froid (hotel & rest.)	313.281-010
RAE	57	Cartoon Designer (tex. prod., n.e.c.)	781.381-010
RAE	57	Painter, Sign (any industry)	970.381-026
RAE	57	Sound-Effects Technician (radio-tv broad.)	962.281-014
RAE	56	Piano Technician (any industry)	730.281-038
RAE	55	Glass Decorator (glass mfg.; glass products)	775.381-014
RAE	52	Decorator, Mannequin (fabrication, n.e.c.)	970.381-014
RAC	49	Painter (button & notion)	740.381-018
RSI	67	Inspector, Boiler (profess. & kin.)	168.167-026
RSI	65	Data Communications Analyst (profess. & kin.)	031.262-010
RSI	63	Farmer, Diversified Crops (agriculture)	407.161-010
RSI	61	Armorer Technician (museums)	109.281-010
RSI	61	Bridge Inspector (r.r. trans.)	869.287-010
RSI	61	Microcomputer Support Specialist (profess. & kin.)	039.264-010
RSI	61	Orthoptist (medical ser.)	079.371-014
RSI	61	Ultrasound Technologist (medical ser.)	078.364-010
RSI	60	Pollution-Control Technician (profess. & kin.)	029.261-014
RSI	59	Livestock Rancher (agriculture)	410.161-018
RSI	59	Supervisor, Roller Shop (textile)	979.131-014
RSI	58	Complaint Inspector (utilities)	829.261-010
RSI	58	Designer (protective dev.)	712.281-014
RSI	58	Diesel-Engine Tester (engine-turbine)	625.261-010
RSI	58	Final Tester (elec. equip.)	721.261-014
RSI	58	Heat-Treat Inspector (heat treating)	504.281-010
RSI	58	Line Maintainer (any industry)	821.261-014
RSI	57	Baker, Second (hotel & rest.)	313.361-010
RSI	57	Display Maker (fabrication, n.e.c.)	739.361-010
RSI	57	Emergency Medical Technician (medical ser.)	079.374-010
RSI	57	Furnace-Combustion Analyst (glass mfg.)	572.360-010
RSI	57	Pinsetter Adjuster, Automatic (toy-sport equip.)	829.381-010
RSI	57	Stock Maker, Custom (ordnance)	761.381-038
RSI	57	Switchboard Operator (utilities)	952.362-034
RSI	56	Rigger (radio-tv broad.)	823.281-022
RSI	56	Slitter Service and Setter (tinware)	615.280-010
RSI	56	Tank Builder and Erector (construction)	860.381-066
RSI	55	Carpet-Loom Fixer (carpet & rug)	683.260-014
RSI	55	Etcher, Hand (print. & pub.)	971.261-010
RSI	55	Make-Up Arranger (print. & pub.)	973.381-026
RSI	55	Primer-Charging Tool Setter (ordnance)	694.360-010
RSI	54	Biological Aide (agriculture)	049.364-018

Part 2: From Holland Codes to Occupations

From Holland Codes to the Dictionary of Occupational Titles Occupations

HOC	Cx	Title	DOT
RSI	54	Brake Operator I (any industry)	617.360-010
RSI	54	Carbonation Equipment Operator (sugar & conf.)	529.582-010
RSI	53	Ballpoint-Pen-Assembly-Machine Operator (pen & pencil)	692.382-010
RSI	53	Control Operator (smelt. & refin.)	511.482-010
RSI	53	Fixer, Boarding Room (knitting)	580.380-010
RSI	53	Glass-Bulb-Machine Adjuster (glass mfg.)	575.360-010
RSI	53	Pickler, Continuous Pickling Line (any industry)	503.362-010
RSI	52	Guide Setter (steel & rel.)	613.361-010
RSI	51	Brazer, Assembler (welding)	813.684-010
RSI	51	Pantograph Setter (print. & pub.)	979.380-010
RSI	51	Spider Assembler (elec. equip.)	721.684-026
RSI	51	Tanner, Rotary Drum, Continuous Process (leather mfg.)	582.482-014
RSI	50	Harness Builder (textile)	683.380-010
RSI	49	Printer-Slotter Operator (paper goods)	659.662-010
RSI	48	Slitting-Machine Operator I (any industry)	699.682-030
RSI	47	Ambulance Driver (medical ser.)	913.683-010
RSI	47	Assembler, Unit (struct. metal)	809.681-010
RSI	46	Inspector-Repairer, Sandstone (stonework)	779.684-030
RSI	46	Locomotive-Crane Operator (any industry)	921.663-038
RSI	46	Tire-Regrooving-Machine Operator (automotive ser.)	690.662-010
RSI	44	Roller Maker (print. & pub.)	759.664-018
RSA	59	Model Maker (toy-sport equip.)	731.280-010
RSE	65	Field-Mechanical-Meter Tester (petrol. refin.; pipe lines; utilities)	953.281-010
RSE	65	Supervisor, Motor Vehicle Assembly (auto. mfg.)	806.134-010
RSE	64	Orthotist (medical ser.)	078.261-018
RSE	64	Prosthetist (medical ser.)	078.261-022
RSE	64	Transmitter Operator (radio-tv broad.)	193.262-038
RSE	63	Field-Service Engineer (photo. appar.)	826.261-010
RSE	63	Supervisor, Avionics Shop (air trans.)	823.131-018
RSE	63	Supervisor, Major Appliance Assembly (house. appl.)	827.131-014
RSE	63	Supervisor, Radio Interference (electron. comp.)	823.131-022
RSE	62	Wildlife Control Agent (government ser.)	379.267-010
RSE	61	Airport Electrician (air trans.)	824.281-010
RSE	61	Diamond Expert (jewelry-silver.)	770.267-010
RSE	61	Electrical Supervisor (petrol. & gas)	826.131-010
RSE	61	Glass-Cut-Off Supervisor (glass mfg.)	677.131-010
RSE	61	Oil-Well-Services Supervisor (petrol. & gas)	939.132-014
RSE	61	Orthotics Assistant (medical ser.)	078.361-022
RSE	61	Permanent-Mold Supervisor (foundry; nonfer. metal)	514.130-010
RSE	61	Prosthetics Assistant (medical ser.)	078.361-026
RSE	61	Supervisor, Boilermaking (struct. metal)	805.131-010
RSE	61	Supervisor, Electrical Assemblies (elec. equip.; machinery mfg.)	826.131-014
RSE	61	Supervisor, Natural-Gas-Field Processing (petrol. & gas; pipe lines)	549.131-010
RSE	61	Supervisor, Production (petrol. & gas)	939.131-014

Part 2: From Holland Codes to Occupations

From Holland Codes to the Dictionary of Occupational Titles Occupations

HOC	Cx	Title	DOT
RSE	60	Electrician, Substation (utilities)	820.261-018
RSE	60	Gamma-Facilities Operator (profess. & kin.)	015.362-014
RSE	60	Harp Maker (musical inst.)	730.281-030
RSE	60	Hydraulic-Pressure-Auto-Frettage-Machine-Operator Supervisor (ordnance)	619.130-010
RSE	60	Instructor, Decorating (pottery & porc.)	740.221-010
RSE	60	Knitting-Machine Fixer, Head (knitting)	689.130-018
RSE	60	Rerecording Mixer (motion picture; radio-tv broad.)	194.362-014
RSE	60	Supervisor (stonework)	679.130-010
RSE	60	Supervisor, Blooming Mill (steel & rel.)	613.130-010
RSE	60	Supervisor, Carding (textile)	680.130-010
RSE	60	Supervisor, Farm-Equipment Maintenance (agric. equip.)	624.131-010
RSE	60	Supervisor, Glycerin (soap & rel.)	559.132-098
RSE	60	Supervisor, Model Making (clock & watch)	693.130-010
RSE	60	Supervisor, Plastics Fabrication (boot & shoe; inst. & app.; plastic prod.; plastic-synth.)	556.130-010
RSE	60	Supervisor, Sanding (woodworking)	662.132-010
RSE	60	Supervisor, Toy Parts Former (toy-sport equip.)	692.130-034
RSE	60	Trouble Shooter II (utilities)	821.261-026
RSE	59	Boilermaker Apprentice (struct. metal)	805.261-010
RSE	59	Boilermaker I (struct. metal)	805.261-014
RSE	59	Cable Installer-Repairer (utilities)	821.361-010
RSE	59	Chief Operator (chemical)	558.260-010
RSE	59	Cutting Supervisor (glass products)	775.134-010
RSE	59	Dental-Equipment Installer and Servicer (wholesale tr.)	829.261-014
RSE	59	Electric-Motor-and-Generator Assembler (elec. equip.)	820.361-014
RSE	59	Electric-Track-Switch Maintainer (r.r. trans.)	825.261-010
RSE	59	Electronic-Organ Technician (any industry)	828.261-010
RSE	59	Final Inspector, Truck Trailer (auto. mfg.)	806.361-018
RSE	59	Heating-Plant Superintendent (any industry)	959.131-010
RSE	59	House-Mover Supervisor (construction)	869.131-022
RSE	59	Immigration Inspector (government ser.)	168.167-022
RSE	59	Inspector, Furniture and Bedding (government ser.)	168.267-046
RSE	59	Machinist Supervisor, Outside (ship-boat mfg.)	623.131-010
RSE	59	Mechanical Technician, Laboratory (clock & watch)	715.261-010
RSE	59	Ornamental-Metal-Worker Apprentice (metal prod., n.e.c.)	619.260-010
RSE	59	Pattern-Grader Supervisor (wood prod., n.e.c.)	693.132-010
RSE	59	Photographic-Equipment-Maintenance Technician (photo. appar.)	714.281-026
RSE	59	Pipe-Fitter Supervisor (ship-boat mfg.)	862.131-014
RSE	59	Sous Chef (hotel & rest.)	313.131-026
RSE	59	Supervisor I (nonmet. min.)	779.131-010
RSE	59	Supervisor, Aluminum Boat Assembly (ship-boat mfg.)	806.131-010
RSE	59	Supervisor, Briar Shop (fabrication, n.e.c.)	761.130-010
RSE	59	Supervisor, Burning, Forming, and Assembly (elec. equip.)	727.130-010
RSE	59	Supervisor, Component Assembler (mfd. bldgs.)	762.134-010
RSE	59	Supervisor, Electronics Production (comm. equip.; electron. comp.; office machines)	726.130-010
RSE	59	Supervisor, Electrotyping and Stereotyping (print. & pub.)	974.131-010

Dictionary of Holland Occupational Codes

HOC	Cx	Title	DOT
RSE	59	Supervisor, Lead Refinery (smelt. & refin.)	519.130-018
RSE	59	Supervisor, Ornamental Ironworking (construction)	809.131-014
RSE	59	Supervisor, Pattern Marking (garment)	781.131-010
RSE	59	Supervisor, Pipe Finishing (steel & rel.)	619.130-038
RSE	59	Supervisor, Pipeline Maintenance (pipe lines)	869.134-018
RSE	59	Supervisor, Quality Control (furniture)	763.134-010
RSE	59	Supervisor, Salvage (petrol. refin.)	929.131-010
RSE	59	Supervisor, Sawmill (saw. & plan.)	669.130-026
RSE	59	Supervisor, Scouring Pads (nonmet. min.)	759.135-010
RSE	59	Supervisor, Screen Making (textile)	971.131-014
RSE	59	Supervisor, Vacuum Metalizing (any industry)	505.130-014
RSE	59	Tnt-Line Supervisor (chemical)	559.131-018
RSE	59	Utility Supervisor, Boat and Plant (ship-boat mfg.)	899.131-022
RSE	58	Automobile-Repair-Service Estimator (automotive ser.)	620.261-018
RSE	58	Bricklayer (construction)	861.381-018
RSE	58	Candy Maker (sugar & conf.)	529.361-014
RSE	58	Coppersmith (ship-boat mfg.)	862.281-010
RSE	58	Coppersmith Apprentice (ship-boat mfg.)	862.281-014
RSE	58	Electrical-Appliance Servicer (any industry)	827.261-010
RSE	58	Electrical-Appliance-Servicer Apprentice (any industry)	827.261-014
RSE	58	Electrician Apprentice (ship-boat mfg.)	825.381-034
RSE	58	Machinist Apprentice, Marine Engine (ship-boat mfg.)	623.281-018
RSE	58	Machinist, Marine Engine (ship-boat mfg.)	623.281-026
RSE	58	Numerical Control Machine Set-up Operator (machine shop)	609.360-010
RSE	58	Set-up Mechanic, Coil-Winding Machines (elec. equip.)	724.360-010
RSE	58	Substation Inspector (utilities)	952.261-010
RSE	58	Supervisor, Asbestos Pipe (nonmet. min.)	679.130-014
RSE	58	Supervisor, Engine Assembly (engine-turbine)	806.130-010
RSE	58	Supervisor, Finishing (glass mfg.)	775.130-010
RSE	58	Supervisor, Fireworks Assembly (chemical)	737.131-010
RSE	58	Supervisor, Paste Plant (steel & rel.)	549.132-026
RSE	58	Supervisor, Reactor Fueling (chemical)	929.132-010
RSE	58	Supervisor, Rigger (ship-boat mfg.)	806.131-030
RSE	57	Boiler Operator (any industry)	950.382-010
RSE	57	Cable Tester (tel. & tel.)	822.361-010
RSE	57	Cotton Classer (agriculture; textile)	429.387-010
RSE	57	Electric-Motor Analyst (any industry)	721.261-010
RSE	57	Equipment Installer (tel. & tel.)	822.381-010
RSE	57	Equipment Installer (any industry)	828.381-010
RSE	57	Fur-Storage Clerk (retail trade)	369.367-010
RSE	57	Gas-Compressor Operator (any industry)	950.382-014
RSE	57	Inspector (office machines)	710.384-014
RSE	57	Line Installer-Repairer (tel. & tel.)	822.381-014
RSE	57	Pipe Fitter, Diesel Engine I (engine-turbine)	862.361-018
RSE	57	Poultry Farmer (agriculture)	411.161-018
RSE	57	Spring Inspector I (metal prod., n.e.c.)	616.361-010
RSE	57	Supervisor, Automatic Machines (clock & watch)	609.130-022
RSE	57	Supervisor, Grinding and Spraying (struct. metal)	809.134-010

Part 2: From Holland Codes to Occupations

From Holland Codes to the Dictionary of Occupational Titles Occupations

HOC	Cx	Title	DOT
RSE	57	Telegraph-Plant Maintainer (tel. & tel.)	822.381-022
RSE	57	Turbine-Blade Assembler (engine-turbine)	600.380-026
RSE	57	Voltage Tester (utilities)	821.381-014
RSE	56	Accordion Repairer (any industry)	730.281-014
RSE	56	Aging-Department Supervisor (textile)	582.132-010
RSE	56	Automobile Tester (automotive ser.)	620.261-014
RSE	56	Automobile-Mechanic Apprentice (automotive ser.)	620.261-012
RSE	56	Bench-Molder Apprentice (jewelry-silver.)	518.381-010
RSE	56	Card Grinder (nonmet. min.; textile)	680.380-010
RSE	56	Central-Office Installer (tel. & tel.)	822.361-014
RSE	56	Communications Technician (education)	962.362-010
RSE	56	Cook (hotel & rest.)	313.361-014
RSE	56	Cook Apprentice (hotel & rest.)	313.361-018
RSE	56	Custom-Feed-Mill Operator (grain-feed mills)	529.132-010
RSE	56	Deck Engineer (water trans.)	623.281-010
RSE	56	Electronic Equipment Repairer (comm. equip.; electron. comp.)	726.381-014
RSE	56	Glass-Ribbon-Machine Operator (glass mfg.)	575.362-014
RSE	56	Group Leader, Printed Circuit Board Quality Control (electron. comp.)	726.361-018
RSE	56	House Mover (construction)	869.261-010
RSE	56	Molder, Bench (jewelry-silver.)	518.381-022
RSE	56	Powder-Line Repairer (chemical)	629.261-018
RSE	56	Print Controller (photofinishing)	976.360-010
RSE	56	Quilter Fixer (tex. prod., n.e.c.)	689.260-014
RSE	56	Roll Operator I (any industry)	619.362-014
RSE	56	Screen-Printing-Equipment Setter (paper goods)	979.360-010
RSE	56	Supervisor, Cigar-Making Machine (tobacco)	529.132-034
RSE	56	Supervisor, Cloth Winding (tex. prod., n.e.c.)	689.130-022
RSE	56	Supervisor, Fish Bait Processing (toy-sport equip.)	550.132-014
RSE	56	Supervisor, Forming Department II (glass mfg.)	579.130-022
RSE	56	Supervisor, Pulp House (sugar & conf.)	529.130-030
RSE	56	Supervisor, Ride Assembly (amuse. & rec.)	801.131-018
RSE	56	Traffic Sergeant (government ser.)	375.137-026
RSE	55	Assembly-Machine-Set-up Mechanic (elec. equip.)	692.360-010
RSE	55	Automotive-Generator-and-Starter Repairer (automotive ser.)	721.281-010
RSE	55	Canvas Worker (ship-boat mfg.; tex. prod., n.e.c.)	739.381-010
RSE	55	Canvas-Worker Apprentice (ship-boat mfg.; tex. prod., n.e.c.)	739.381-014
RSE	55	Cook, Specialty, Foreign Food (hotel & rest.)	313.361-030
RSE	55	Gamekeeper (agriculture)	169.171-010
RSE	55	Loom Fixer (narrow fabrics; nonmet. min.; textile)	683.260-018
RSE	55	Monument Setter (construction)	861.361-014
RSE	55	Paperhanger (construction)	841.381-010
RSE	55	Proofsheet Corrector (print. & pub.)	973.381-030
RSE	55	Service Restorer, Emergency (r.r. trans.)	821.261-022
RSE	55	State-Highway Police Officer (government ser.)	375.263-018
RSE	55	Supervisor, Stitching Department (tex. prod., n.e.c.)	787.132-018

HOC	Cx	Title	DOT
RSE	54	Audio-Video Repairer (any industry)	729.281-010
RSE	54	Baker (bakery products)	526.381-010
RSE	54	Baker Apprentice (bakery products)	526.381-014
RSE	54	Blaster (mine & quarry)	931.261-010
RSE	54	Coin-Machine-Service Repairer (svc. ind. mach.)	639.281-014
RSE	54	Dressmaker (any industry)	785.361-010
RSE	54	Farm-Machinery Set-up Mechanic (agric. equip.)	624.381-018
RSE	54	Figure Refinisher and Repairer (retail trade)	739.381-034
RSE	54	Machine-Clothing Replacer (paper & pulp)	629.361-010
RSE	54	Neon-Sign Servicer (fabrication, n.e.c.)	824.281-018
RSE	54	Patternmaker (hat & cap)	784.361-010
RSE	54	Projection Printer (photofinishing)	976.381-018
RSE	54	Pump Mechanic (paper & pulp)	629.281-034
RSE	54	Spikemaking Supervisor (steel & rel.)	612.130-010
RSE	54	Stonemason (construction)	861.381-038
RSE	54	Stonemason Apprentice (construction)	861.381-042
RSE	54	Switchboard Operator Assistant (utilities)	952.367-014
RSE	54	Tile Setter (construction)	861.381-054
RSE	54	Tile Setter Apprentice (construction)	861.381-058
RSE	53	Assembler (clock & watch)	715.381-010
RSE	53	Cake Tester (grain-feed mills)	526.381-022
RSE	53	Cargo Checker (water trans.)	222.367-010
RSE	53	Induction-Machine Setter (heat treating)	504.380-014
RSE	53	Inspector and Tester (agric. equip.)	624.361-010
RSE	53	Loom Starter (textile)	683.360-014
RSE	53	Mold Stamper and Repairer (rubber tire)	709.381-026
RSE	53	Needle-Loom Setter (tex. prod., n.e.c.)	689.360-010
RSE	53	Oriental-Rug Repairer (any industry)	782.381-014
RSE	53	Press Operator, Heavy Duty (any industry)	617.260-010
RSE	53	Purification Operator II (chemical)	551.362-010
RSE	53	Saddle Maker (leather prod.)	783.381-026
RSE	53	Set-up Mechanic (pen & pencil)	692.380-010
RSE	53	Shooter, Seismograph (petrol. & gas)	931.361-018
RSE	53	Speed Operator (steel & rel.)	613.362-022
RSE	53	Steeple Jack (construction)	869.381-030
RSE	53	Triple-Air-Valve Tester (railroad equip.)	622.382-010
RSE	53	Wardrobe-Specialty Worker (motion picture; radio-tv broad.)	969.381-010
RSE	52	Baker, Test (grain-feed mills)	526.381-018
RSE	52	Battery Maintainer, Large Emergency Storage (utilities)	820.381-010
RSE	52	Carburetor Mechanic (automotive ser.)	620.281-034
RSE	52	Cook (domestic ser.)	305.281-010
RSE	52	Cook, Kettle (beverage; can. & preserv.; grain-feed mills)	526.381-026
RSE	52	Cook, Station (water trans.)	315.361-022
RSE	52	Drophammer Operator (aircraft mfg.; forging)	610.362-010
RSE	52	Electrical-Appliance Repairer (any industry)	723.381-010
RSE	52	Fabricator, Industrial Furnace (machinery mfg.)	826.381-010
RSE	52	First Helper (steel & rel.)	512.362-010
RSE	52	Furniture Finisher (woodworking)	763.381-010

From Holland Codes to the Dictionary of Occupational Titles Occupations

HOC	Cx	Title	DOT
RSE	52	Furniture-Finisher Apprentice (woodworking)	763.381-014
RSE	52	Mannequin-Mold Maker (fabrication, n.e.c.)	739.381-046
RSE	52	Mortuary Beautician (personal ser.)	339.361-010
RSE	52	Organ-Pipe Maker, Metal (musical inst.)	709.381-030
RSE	52	Refrigerator Tester (svc. ind. mach.)	827.384-010
RSE	52	Robotic Machine Operator (aircraft mfg.)	606.382-026
RSE	52	Tower Operator (r.r. trans.)	910.362-010
RSE	52	Tuner, Percussion (musical inst.)	730.381-058
RSE	52	Wig Maker (fabrication, n.e.c.)	739.381-058
RSE	51	Aerospace Physiological Technician (military ser.)	199.682-010
RSE	51	Balancing-Machine Operator (any industry)	609.462-010
RSE	51	Bleacher, Pulp (paper & pulp)	533.362-010
RSE	51	Cigarette-and-Filter Chief Inspector (tobacco)	529.367-010
RSE	51	Drier Operator I (plastic-synth.)	559.562-010
RSE	51	Furnace Operator (nonfer. metal)	613.462-014
RSE	51	Magazine Keeper (clerical)	222.367-038
RSE	51	Mechanical Oxidizer (fabrication, n.e.c.)	590.662-014
RSE	51	Miller, Wet Process (grain-feed mills)	521.662-010
RSE	51	Refrigeration Unit Repairer (svc. ind. mach.)	637.381-014
RSE	51	Roving Sizer (textile)	680.367-010
RSE	51	Slitting-Machine Operator II (any industry)	615.662-010
RSE	51	Welding-Rod Coater (elec. equip.)	505.382-014
RSE	50	Assembler I (ordnance)	736.381-010
RSE	50	Automatic-Wheel-Line Operator (machine shop)	609.682-010
RSE	50	Baker (hotel & rest.)	313.381-010
RSE	50	Barrel-Endshake Adjuster (clock & watch)	715.381-030
RSE	50	Bell Spinner (musical inst.)	619.682-010
RSE	50	Carbon-and-Graphite-Brush-Machine Operator (elec. equip.)	692.482-010
RSE	50	Catalytic-Converter Operator (chemical)	558.362-010
RSE	50	Coating-Machine Operator (sugar & conf.)	524.382-010
RSE	50	Cook, School Cafeteria (hotel & rest.)	313.381-030
RSE	50	Cook, Short Order (hotel & rest.)	313.374-014
RSE	50	Core Winding Operator (paper & pulp)	640.682-014
RSE	50	Cupola Operator, Insulation (nonmet. min.)	579.382-014
RSE	50	Deputy Sheriff, Grand Jury (government ser.)	377.363-010
RSE	50	Diffuser Operator (sugar & conf.)	523.562-010
RSE	50	Drier Operator (sugar & conf.)	529.682-022
RSE	50	Finishing-Area Operator (plastic-synth.)	559.362-014
RSE	50	Fire-Extinguisher Repairer (any industry)	709.384-010
RSE	50	Flanging-Roll Operator (any industry)	619.362-010
RSE	50	Furnace Operator (foundry; steel & rel.)	512.362-018
RSE	50	Garde Manager (hotel & rest.)	313.361-034
RSE	50	Glass-Bulb-Machine Former, Tubular Stock (glass mfg.)	575.382-018
RSE	50	Glazier (construction)	865.381-010
RSE	50	Glazier Apprentice (construction)	865.381-014
RSE	50	Goldbeater (metal prod., n.e.c.)	700.381-018
RSE	50	Horseshoer (agriculture)	418.381-010
RSE	50	Household-Appliance Installer (any industry)	827.661-010

HOC	Cx	Title	DOT
RSE	50	Inspection Clerk (fabrication, n.e.c.)	739.587-010
RSE	50	Jig Builder (wood. container)	761.381-014
RSE	50	Lamp-Shade Sewer (fabrication, n.e.c.)	787.381-010
RSE	50	Luggage Repairer (any industry)	365.361-010
RSE	50	Luster Applicator (glass mfg.; glass products)	740.381-014
RSE	50	Mannequin Wig Maker (fabrication, n.e.c.)	739.381-042
RSE	50	Molder (optical goods)	575.381-010
RSE	50	Multi-Operation-Machine Operator (any industry)	612.462-010
RSE	50	Nitrator Operator (chemical)	558.382-046
RSE	50	Painter (construction)	840.381-010
RSE	50	Pie Maker (hotel & rest.)	313.361-038
RSE	50	Primer-Inserting-Machine Adjuster (ordnance)	632.360-018
RSE	50	Shoe Repairer (personal ser.)	365.361-014
RSE	50	Sign Erector-and-Repairer (fabrication, n.e.c.)	869.361-018
RSE	50	Solderer (jewelry-silver.)	700.381-050
RSE	50	Steel-Die Printer (print. & pub.)	651.382-030
RSE	50	Stock Checker I (ordnance)	761.381-034
RSE	50	Stock Clerk (retail trade)	299.367-014
RSE	50	Tracer-Bullet-Charging-Machine Operator (ordnance)	694.382-014
RSE	49	Arch-Support Technician (protective dev.)	712.381-010
RSE	49	Automobile-Radiator Mechanic (automotive ser.)	620.381-010
RSE	49	Brick-and-Tile-Making-Machine Operator (brick & tile)	575.382-010
RSE	49	Calender Operator, Four-Roll (plastic prod.; rubber goods; rubber tire)	554.662-010
RSE	49	Carbide-Powder Processor (machine shop)	510.465-010
RSE	49	Centrifugal-Casting-Machine Operator III (foundry)	514.562-010
RSE	49	Coffee Roaster (food prep., n.e.c.)	523.682-014
RSE	49	Conche Operator (sugar & conf.)	526.382-010
RSE	49	Continuous-Absorption-Process Operator (sugar & conf.)	521.362-010
RSE	49	Cook, Barbecue (hotel & rest.)	313.381-022
RSE	49	Cook, Specialty (hotel & rest.)	313.361-026
RSE	49	Fuel Attendant (any industry)	953.362-010
RSE	49	Gas-Meter Checker (utilities)	953.367-014
RSE	49	Grinder Operator (grain-feed mills)	521.682-026
RSE	49	Gun-Perforator Loader (petrol. & gas)	931.384-010
RSE	49	Harp Regulator (musical inst.)	730.381-026
RSE	49	Linseed-Oil Refiner (oils & grease)	559.382-030
RSE	49	Meat Cutter (retail trade; wholesale tr.)	316.684-018
RSE	49	Meat-Cutter Apprentice (retail trade; wholesale tr.)	316.684-022
RSE	49	Newspaper-Delivery Driver (wholesale tr.)	292.363-010
RSE	49	Orthopedic Assistant (medical ser.)	078.664-010
RSE	49	Pig-Machine Operator (steel & rel.)	514.362-010
RSE	49	Putty Tinter-Maker (paint & varnish)	559.482-014
RSE	49	Rotor Casting-Machine Operator (elec. equip.)	502.482-018
RSE	49	Waste-Disposal Attendant (any industry)	955.383-010
RSE	48	Baker, Pizza (hotel & rest.)	313.381-014
RSE	48	Blast-Furnace Keeper (steel & rel.)	502.664-010
RSE	48	Butcher, Meat (hotel & rest.)	316.681-010
RSE	48	Clay-Structure Builder and Servicer (glass mfg.)	579.664-010

HOC	Cx	Title	DOT
RSE	48	Cocoa-Bean Roaster I (sugar & conf.)	523.362-010
RSE	48	Core-Drill Operator (any industry)	930.682-010
RSE	48	Corrugator Operator (paper goods)	641.562-010
RSE	48	Dog Groomer (personal ser.)	418.674-010
RSE	48	Dynamite-Packing-Machine Operator (chemical)	692.662-010
RSE	48	Farm worker, Field Crop I (agriculture)	404.663-010
RSE	48	Fur Nailer (fur goods)	783.684-014
RSE	48	Gelatin-Dynamite-Packing Operator (chemical)	692.662-014
RSE	48	Gilder (any industry)	749.381-010
RSE	48	Heating-and-Air-Conditioning Installer-Servicer Helper (construction)	637.664-010
RSE	48	Irish-Moss Operator (chemical)	529.382-030
RSE	48	Mobile-Home-Lot Utility Worker (retail trade)	899.484-010
RSE	48	Partition-Assembly-Machine Operator (any industry)	649.582-010
RSE	48	Rolling-Mill Operator (nonfer. metal)	613.462-018
RSE	48	Steel Pourer (steel & rel.)	502.664-014
RSE	48	Transferrer (print. & pub.)	972.381-026
RSE	48	Turner (pottery & porc.)	774.684-038
RSE	48	Weaver, Hand Loom (carpet & rug; textile)	683.684-030
RSE	48	Wirer, Cable (comm. equip.; elec. equip.)	729.381-022
RSE	47	Animal Keeper (amuse. & rec.)	412.674-010
RSE	47	Binding Cutter, Synthetic Cloth (tex. prod., n.e.c.)	699.682-010
RSE	47	Blanket-Winder Operator (paper goods)	641.682-010
RSE	47	Boat Rigger (retail trade; ship-boat mfg.)	806.464-010
RSE	47	Cell Maker (chemical)	844.681-010
RSE	47	Coater (textile)	584.682-010
RSE	47	Compression-Molding-Machine Operator (elec. equip.; plastic prod.)	556.682-014
RSE	47	Continuous-Mining-Machine Operator (mine & quarry)	930.683-010
RSE	47	Corrugator Operator (plastic-synth.)	556.665-014
RSE	47	Cutter (glove & mit.; tex. prod., n.e.c.)	699.682-014
RSE	47	Drier Tender (smelt. & refin.)	511.565-014
RSE	47	Drum Drier (grain-feed mills)	523.682-026
RSE	47	Farm worker, Livestock (agriculture)	410.664-010
RSE	47	Fence Erector (construction)	869.684-022
RSE	47	Forming-Machine Operator (button & notion)	559.665-022
RSE	47	Machine-Tank Operator (wood. container)	667.662-014
RSE	47	Manipulator (steel & rel.)	613.682-010
RSE	47	Marine Railway Operator (ship-boat mfg.)	921.662-022
RSE	47	Neon-Tube Pumper (fabrication, n.e.c.)	824.684-010
RSE	47	Painter, Rug Touch-Up (laundry & rel.)	364.381-010
RSE	47	Paraffin-Plant Operator (petrol. refin.)	541.682-010
RSE	47	Powder-Truck Driver (ordnance)	903.683-014
RSE	47	Redrying-Machine Operator (tobacco)	522.662-014
RSE	47	Roaster, Grain (grain-feed mills)	523.585-034
RSE	47	Rocket-Test-Fire Worker (ordnance)	806.384-022
RSE	47	Screen Repairer, Crusher (mine & quarry)	630.684-030
RSE	47	Sealer (office machines)	710.684-038
RSE	47	Septic-Tank Installer (construction)	851.663-010

HOC	Cx	Title	DOT
RSE	47	Shrink-Pit Operator (ordnance)	619.662-010
RSE	47	Starter (amuse. & rec.)	153.667-010
RSE	47	Supplies Packer (any industry)	919.687-022
RSE	47	Tag-Press Operator (paper goods)	649.682-046
RSE	47	Tank Tender (smelt. & refin.)	509.685-054
RSE	47	Thermometer Maker (inst. & app.)	710.681-026
RSE	47	Tongue-and-Groove-Machine Operator (woodworking)	669.662-018
RSE	47	Tube-Machine Operator (paper goods)	641.662-014
RSE	47	Variety-Saw Operator (woodworking)	667.682-086
RSE	47	Wallpaper Printer I (paper goods)	652.662-014
RSE	46	Boiler House Inspector (any industry)	805.667-010
RSE	46	Cemetery Worker (real estate)	406.684-010
RSE	46	Hat Maker (hat & cap)	784.684-042
RSE	46	Mechanical-Shovel Operator (mine & quarry)	932.683-018
RSE	46	Printer (glass products)	979.681-014
RSE	46	Reeling-Machine Operator (steel & rel.)	613.682-014
RSE	46	Scagliola Mechanic (nonmet. min.)	556.484-010
RSE	45	Anode Rebuilder (smelt. & refin.)	630.684-010
RSE	45	Box-Sealing-Machine Operator (paper goods)	641.662-010
RSE	45	Brine-Well Operator (chemical)	559.685-026
RSE	45	Charcoal Burner, Beehive Kiln (chemical)	563.682-010
RSE	45	Core-Cutter and Reamer (paper goods)	649.685-026
RSE	45	Cylinder Filler (chemical)	559.565-010
RSE	45	Dextrine Mixer (grain-feed mills)	523.682-018
RSE	45	Die-Cutting-Machine Operator, Automatic (tex. prod., n.e.c.; textile)	686.462-010
RSE	45	Explosives-Truck Driver (ordnance)	903.683-010
RSE	45	Finish-Machine Tender (pottery & porc.)	673.685-058
RSE	45	Glaze Maker (brick & tile; pottery & porc.)	570.685-098
RSE	45	Hide Inspector (leather mfg.)	783.687-018
RSE	45	House Worker, General (domestic ser.)	301.474-010
RSE	45	Icing Mixer (bakery products)	520.685-114
RSE	45	Kiln Operator, Malt House (beverage)	523.682-030
RSE	45	Leather Worker (leather prod.)	783.684-026
RSE	45	Locker-Plant Attendant (retail trade; wholesale tr.)	922.684-010
RSE	45	Portable Sawyer (railroad equip.)	899.684-030
RSE	45	Repairer, Finished Metal (any industry)	809.684-034
RSE	45	Silk-Screen Repairer (any industry)	979.684-038
RSE	45	Strapping-Machine Operator (wood. container)	692.682-058
RSE	45	Test-Department Helper (comm. equip.; elec. equip.)	729.664-010
RSE	45	Tree Trimmer (tel. & tel.; utilities)	408.664-010
RSE	45	Wax Bleacher (chemical)	551.685-158
RSE	44	Candy Puller (sugar & conf.)	520.685-046
RSE	44	Car-Dumper Operator (beverage)	921.662-010
RSE	44	Glazing Operator, Black Powder (chemical)	550.686-022
RSE	44	Hydraulic Press Operator (construction)	616.662-010
RSE	44	Molding-Machine Operator (toy-sport equip.)	575.682-014
RSE	44	Ordnance-Artificer Helper (government ser.)	632.684-010
RSE	44	Railroad-Car-Truck Builder (railroad equip.)	806.684-114

Part 2: From Holland Codes to Occupations

From Holland Codes to the Dictionary of Occupational Titles Occupations

HOC	Cx	Title	DOT
RSE	44	Repairer, Assembled Wood Products (woodworking)	769.684-038
RSE	44	Riveter (railroad equip.)	800.684-010
RSE	44	Steam-Tank Operator (nonmet. min.)	573.683-010
RSE	44	Tank-Car Inspector (chemical)	622.684-022
RSE	44	Tobacco Curer (agriculture)	523.682-038
RSE	44	Utility Worker, Roller Shop (textile)	628.684-034
RSE	44	Veneer-Slicing-Machine Operator (millwork-plywood)	663.682-018
RSE	43	Jinrikisha Driver (amuse. & rec.)	349.477-010
RSE	43	Laundry-Tub Maker (concrete prod.)	575.684-034
RSE	43	Tool Repairer (smelt. & refin.)	519.684-026
RSE	43	Wallpaper Inspector (paper goods)	652.687-042
RSE	42	General Worker, Lithographic (print. & pub.)	979.687-034
RSE	42	Powder Loader (mine & quarry)	931.667-010
RSE	42	Rug Inspector (laundry & rel.)	369.687-030
RSE	42	Ski Repairer, Production (toy-sport equip.)	732.684-118
RSE	42	Slot Router (furniture)	763.684-066
RSE	42	Yarn Examiner (glass mfg.; plastic-synth.; textile)	681.687-030
RSE	41	Compounder (chemical)	550.685-050
RSE	41	Drier Operator I (chemical)	553.665-026
RSE	41	Field Hauler (agriculture)	409.683-014
RSE	41	Flyer (amuse. & rec.; radio-tv broad.)	962.687-018
RSE	41	Globe Mounter (print. & pub.)	795.684-018
RSE	41	Helper, Electrical (utilities)	821.667-010
RSE	41	Laborer, Solder Making (nonfer. metal)	519.667-014
RSE	41	Lead-Burner Helper (elec. equip.)	727.687-070
RSE	41	Liquor-Bridge-Operator Helper (sugar & conf.)	521.687-078
RSE	41	Machine Helper (any industry)	619.687-014
RSE	41	Pneumatic-Hoist Operator (construction; mfd. bldgs.)	921.663-046
RSE	41	Polisher (glass mfg.; glass products)	775.684-058
RSE	41	Press Operator (brick & tile)	575.682-018
RSE	41	Spice Mixer (food prep., n.e.c.)	520.585-026
RSE	41	Stove Refinisher (any industry)	749.684-046
RSE	40	Assembler, Lay-Ups (toy-sport equip.)	677.685-014
RSE	40	Floor Service Worker, Spring (automotive ser.)	807.684-022
RSE	40	Heddle Cleaner, Machine (textile)	689.685-070
RSE	40	Jogger (print. & pub.)	651.686-018
RSE	40	Laborer (fabrication, n.e.c.)	590.687-010
RSE	40	Laborer, Hot-Plate Plywood Press (millwork-plywood)	569.686-026
RSE	40	Laborer, Salvage (any industry)	929.687-022
RSE	40	Lumber Handler (woodworking)	922.687-070
RSE	40	Metal-Fabricating-Shop Helper (any industry)	619.686-022
RSE	40	Scrapper (paper goods)	794.687-050
RSE	40	Steam-Conditioner Operator (tobacco)	522.685-094
RSE	40	Stock Checker, Apparel (retail trade)	299.667-014
RSE	40	Vacuum-Tank Tender (textile)	689.665-018
RSE	39	Cleaner, Industrial (any industry)	381.687-018
RSE	39	Hull and Deck Remover (ship-boat mfg.)	809.667-010
RSE	39	Rigger Helper (any industry)	921.687-026
RSE	39	Sheep Shearer (agriculture)	410.684-014

Part 2: From Holland Codes to Occupations

From Holland Codes to the Dictionary of Occupational Titles Occupations

HOC	Cx	Title	DOT
RSE	38	Beam Racker (textile)	681.686-010
RSE	38	Breaker (glass products)	779.687-010
RSE	38	Cake-Press-Operator Helper (plastic-synth.)	556.686-010
RSE	38	Casting-Wheel-Operator Helper (smelt. & refin.)	514.667-010
RSE	38	Chain Offbearer (saw. & plan.)	669.686-018
RSE	38	Chemical-Compounder Helper (chemical)	550.687-010
RSE	38	Cloth Framer (textile)	689.687-026
RSE	38	Color Dipper (textile)	652.687-014
RSE	38	Dynamite Reclaimer (chemical)	551.687-018
RSE	38	Forge Helper (forging)	619.686-034
RSE	38	Laborer, Shipyard (ship-boat mfg.)	809.687-022
RSE	38	Laborer, Tin Can (tinware)	709.686-010
RSE	38	Thermal Cutter, Hand II (welding)	816.684-010
RSE	38	Upholstery Cleaner (furniture)	780.687-058
RSE	38	Utility Worker, Forge (forging)	612.684-010
RSE	38	Wallpaper-Printer Helper (paper goods)	652.687-050
RSE	38	Wax-Pattern Coater (foundry)	518.687-022
RSE	37	Oil-Burner-Servicer-and-Installer Helper (any industry)	862.687-022
RSE	37	Wharf Tender (steel & rel.)	542.667-010
RSE	35	Offal Icer, Poultry (meat products)	525.687-054
RSC	60	Line Inspector (tel. & tel.)	822.267-010
RSC	59	Assembler, Mining Machinery (machinery mfg.)	801.261-010
RSC	59	Compositor Apprentice (print. & pub.)	973.381-014
RSC	59	Electrician Supervisor (ship-boat mfg.)	825.131-010
RSC	59	Electrician, Radio (any industry)	823.281-014
RSC	59	Radiotelephone Operator (any industry)	193.262-034
RSC	59	Supervisor, Photoengraving (print. & pub.)	971.131-010
RSC	59	Supervisor, Shuttle Veneering (woodworking)	669.130-038
RSC	58	Mechanical Inspector (petrol. refin.)	549.261-010
RSC	58	Orthotics Technician (protective dev.)	712.381-034
RSC	58	Radio Interference Investigator (electron. comp.)	823.261-014
RSC	57	Carpenter Inspector (any industry)	860.261-010
RSC	57	Electric-Organ Inspector and Repairer (musical inst.)	730.281-018
RSC	57	Liquefaction-and-Regasification-Plant Operator (utilities)	953.362-014
RSC	57	Molder, Punch (aircraft mfg.)	502.381-014
RSC	57	Quality-Control Inspector (cutlery-hrdwr.)	701.261-010
RSC	57	Supervisor, Framing Mill (wood prod., n.e.c.)	669.130-018
RSC	56	Cable Assembler and Swager (aircraft mfg.)	806.381-042
RSC	55	Engraver, Rubber (pen & pencil)	733.381-010
RSC	55	Pipe-Organ Tuner and Repairer (any industry)	730.361-014
RSC	55	Rubber-Stamp Maker (pen & pencil)	733.381-014
RSC	53	Color Matcher (knitting)	582.261-010
RSC	53	Control-Panel Operator (petrol. refin.)	546.382-010
RSC	53	Final Inspector, Paper (paper & pulp)	539.367-010
RSC	53	Flame-Annealing-Machine Setter (heat treating)	504.360-010
RSC	53	Rigger (any industry)	921.260-010
RSC	53	Silversmith II (jewelry-silver.)	700.281-022
RSC	52	Feeder-Switchboard Operator (utilities)	952.362-014

Part 2: From Holland Codes to Occupations

From Holland Codes to the Dictionary of Occupational Titles Occupations

HOC	Cx	Title	DOT
RSC	52	Tobacco Blender (retail trade)	790.381-010
RSC	52	Valve Repairer (chemical)	630.381-030
RSC	51	Lock Operator (water trans.)	911.362-010
RSC	51	Power-Driven-Brush Maker (fabrication, n.e.c.)	692.682-050
RSC	50	Clip-Loading-Machine Adjuster (ordnance)	694.362-010
RSC	50	Flat Clothier (textile)	628.382-010
RSC	50	Salad Maker (water trans.)	317.384-010
RSC	49	Bench Hand (jewelry-silver.)	735.381-010
RSC	49	Conductor (r.r. trans.)	910.667-014
RSC	49	Farm-Equipment Mechanic II (agric. equip.)	624.381-014
RSC	49	Kiln Burner (brick & tile)	573.682-010
RSC	49	Mixing-Roll Operator (fabrication, n.e.c.)	590.662-018
RSC	49	Spike-Machine Operator (steel & rel.)	612.662-010
RSC	49	Striper, Hand (any industry)	740.484-010
RSC	49	Upper-Leather Sorter (boot & shoe)	788.387-010
RSC	49	Wet-Mix Operator (chemical)	558.382-058
RSC	48	Armored-Car Guard and Driver (business ser.)	372.563-010
RSC	48	Bicycle Repairer (any industry)	639.681-010
RSC	48	Brazer, Controlled Atmospheric Furnace (welding)	813.685-010
RSC	48	Classifier Operator (smelt. & refin.)	511.562-010
RSC	48	Felting-Machine Operator (tex. prod., n.e.c.)	586.662-010
RSC	48	Glass Grinder (glass products)	775.684-030
RSC	48	Ironworker-Machine Operator (any industry)	615.482-018
RSC	48	Needle-Loom Operator (tex. prod., n.e.c.)	689.662-010
RSC	48	Oil-Pipe-Inspector Helper (petrol. & gas)	930.364-010
RSC	48	Spinner (sugar & conf.)	520.682-030
RSC	48	Steam-Drier Tender (carpet & rug)	581.685-058
RSC	48	Tank-Farm Attendant (chemical)	559.665-038
RSC	47	Autoclave Operator (textile)	587.682-010
RSC	47	Blender II (chemical)	550.665-010
RSC	47	Bullet-Casting Operator (ordnance)	502.682-010
RSC	47	Chair Upholsterer (furniture)	780.684-034
RSC	47	Chocolate Temperer (sugar & conf.)	523.682-010
RSC	47	Cocoa-Powder-Mixer Operator (sugar & conf.)	520.685-074
RSC	47	Cut-Off-Saw Operator I (woodworking)	667.682-022
RSC	47	Cutter Operator (any industry)	699.682-018
RSC	47	Finishing-Machine Operator (narrow fabrics)	582.682-010
RSC	47	Forging-Roll Operator (forging)	612.682-014
RSC	47	Glass Finisher (glass products)	775.684-026
RSC	47	Ion-Exchange Operator (pharmaceut.)	558.685-038
RSC	47	Lead-Press Operator (nonfer. metal)	691.382-014
RSC	47	Mail Handler (government ser.)	209.687-014
RSC	47	Maintenance Mechanic Helper (construction; petrol. & gas; pipe lines)	620.664-014
RSC	47	Operator, Prefinish (millwork-plywood)	562.685-018
RSC	47	Planishing-Press Operator (plastic-synth.)	690.682-058
RSC	47	Rigger (logging)	921.664-014
RSC	47	Seamless-Tube Roller (steel & rel.)	619.682-042
RSC	47	Tower Erector Helper (construction; utilities)	821.684-014

HOC	Cx	Title	DOT
RSC	47	Welder, Tack (welding)	810.684-010
RSC	46	Acrobatic Rigger (amuse. & rec.)	962.684-010
RSC	46	Cage Maker (concrete prod.)	709.684-030
RSC	46	Cake-Press Operator (plastic-synth.)	556.665-010
RSC	46	Drawing-In-Machine Tender (textile)	683.682-018
RSC	46	Engraver, Rubber (print. & pub.)	979.581-010
RSC	46	Mobile-Lounge Driver (motor trans.)	913.663-014
RSC	46	Nitroglycerin Neutralizer (chemical)	558.685-050
RSC	46	Refining-Machine Operator (oils & grease)	529.685-198
RSC	46	Stave-Log-Cut-Off Saw Operator (saw. & plan.)	667.682-078
RSC	46	Stripe Matcher (knitting)	689.662-014
RSC	46	Template Maker, Track (any industry)	809.484-014
RSC	46	Truss Assembler (millwork-plywood)	762.684-062
RSC	46	Vacuum-Conditioner Operator (tobacco)	522.685-102
RSC	45	Branner-Machine Tender (galvanizing)	509.685-014
RSC	45	Butler, Second (domestic ser.)	309.674-010
RSC	45	Chip Tuner (musical inst.)	730.684-026
RSC	45	Cooper (wood. container)	764.684-022
RSC	45	Irradiated-Fuel Handler (chemical)	921.663-034
RSC	45	Kettle Tender I (smelt. & refin.)	519.685-022
RSC	45	Knit-Goods Washer (knitting)	582.685-094
RSC	45	Lacquer Maker (paint & varnish)	559.682-030
RSC	45	Press Operator (plastic prod.)	690.682-062
RSC	45	Roof Assembler I (mfd. bldgs.)	869.684-042
RSC	45	Router Operator, Hand (aircraft mfg.; railroad equip.)	806.684-150
RSC	45	Rug Cutter (carpet & rug)	686.662-010
RSC	45	Sanitary Landfill Operator (sanitary ser.)	955.463-010
RSC	45	Sider (mfd. bldgs.)	860.684-014
RSC	45	Sounder (any industry)	911.667-018
RSC	45	Wax Blender (fabrication, n.e.c.)	550.585-046
RSC	44	Bottom-Precipitator Operator (smelt. & refin.)	511.664-010
RSC	44	Brake-Lining Finisher, Asbestos (nonmet. min.)	579.665-010
RSC	44	Depositing-Machine Operator (bakery products)	524.682-010
RSC	44	Dubbing-Machine Operator (motion picture; radio-tv broad.)	962.665-010
RSC	44	Radial-Arm-Saw Operator (woodworking)	667.682-054
RSC	44	Silverer (glass products)	574.684-014
RSC	44	Sizing-Machine-and-Drier Operator (tex. prod., n.e.c.)	582.665-026
RSC	44	Weigher, Alloy (nonfer. metal)	509.687-022
RSC	43	Bench Carpenter (woodworking)	760.684-010
RSC	43	Gatherer (glass mfg.)	575.684-026
RSC	43	Quarry Plug-and-Feather Driller (mine & quarry)	930.684-022
RSC	43	Stone-Mill Operator (paint & varnish)	555.682-022
RSC	43	Stripping-Shovel Operator (mine & quarry)	850.663-026
RSC	42	Coater Helper (textile)	584.665-010
RSC	42	Excavator (any industry)	850.684-010
RSC	42	Glass-Cutter Helper (any industry)	775.687-018
RSC	42	Winder Operator (fabrication, n.e.c.)	590.665-018
RSC	41	Bed Setter (stonework)	679.664-010

HOC to DOT

Part 2: From Holland Codes to Occupations

From Holland Codes to the Dictionary of Occupational Titles Occupations

HOC	Cx	Title	DOT
RSC	41	Counting-Machine Operator (paper goods)	649.685-030
RSC	41	Shipwright Helper (ship-boat mfg.)	860.664-018
RSC	41	Slitting-Machine-Operator Helper I (any industry)	699.587-010
RSC	41	Weigher and Mixer (chemical)	550.685-122
RSC	40	Card Tender (nonmet. min.; textile)	680.685-018
RSC	40	Dross Skimmer (smelt. & refin.)	519.683-010
RSC	40	Form-Tamper Operator (construction)	869.683-010
RSC	40	Polishing-Wheel Setter (any industry)	776.684-014
RSC	39	Clamper (woodworking)	669.685-030
RSC	39	Inspector III (furniture)	739.687-110
RSC	39	Primer Charger (ordnance)	737.687-102
RSC	39	Tool Grinder II (any industry)	603.664-010
RSC	38	Cutter, Wet Machine (paper & pulp)	539.686-010
RSC	38	Screen Printer Helper (any industry)	979.687-022
RSC	38	Stand-In (motion picture; radio-tv broad.)	961.667-014
RSC	36	Telephone-Directory Deliverer (business ser.)	230.667-014
REI	71	Materials Engineer (profess. & kin.)	019.061-014
REI	71	Safety Engineer, Mines (mine & quarry)	010.061-026
REI	70	Superintendent, Generating Plant (utilities)	184.167-166
REI	70	Test Engineer, Mechanical Equipment (profess. & kin.)	007.161-034
REI	68	Pilot, Ship (water trans.)	197.133-026
REI	68	Teacher, Industrial Arts (education)	091.221-010
REI	68	Traffic Technician (government ser.)	199.267-030
REI	67	Production Planner (profess. & kin.)	012.167-050
REI	66	General Supervisor (any industry)	183.167-018
REI	66	Tooling Coordinator, Production Engineering (aircraft mfg.)	169.167-054
REI	65	Inspector, Set-up and Lay-Out (machine shop)	601.261-010
REI	64	Inspector, Optical Instrument (optical goods)	711.281-010
REI	64	Supervisor, Power-Reactor (chemical)	509.130-014
REI	63	Access Coordinator, Cable Television (radio-tv broad.)	194.122-010
REI	63	Electrician Apprentice (construction)	824.261-014
REI	63	Farmer, Field Crop (agriculture)	404.161-010
REI	63	Farmer, Vegetable (agriculture)	402.161-010
REI	63	Gemologist (jewelry-silver.)	199.281-010
REI	63	Master, Passenger Barge (water trans.)	197.163-014
REI	63	Master, Yacht (water trans.)	197.133-014
REI	63	Ordnance Artificer (government ser.)	632.261-018
REI	63	Road Supervisor of Engines (r.r. trans.)	910.137-034
REI	63	Sales Representative, Aircraft (retail trade; wholesale tr.)	273.253-010
REI	63	Supervisor, Mine (mine & quarry)	181.167-018
REI	63	Tugboat Captain (water trans.)	197.133-030
REI	62	Delineator (profess. & kin.)	970.281-014
REI	62	Furrier (fur goods)	783.261-010
REI	62	Guide, Alpine (personal ser.)	353.164-010
REI	62	Horticultural-Specialty Grower, Inside (agriculture)	405.161-018
REI	62	Parts Cataloger (any industry)	229.267-010
REI	62	Turbine Operator, Head (utilities)	952.137-022

HOC	Cx	Title	DOT
REI	61	Farmer, Tree-Fruit-and-Nut Crops (agriculture)	403.161-010
REI	61	Filing-and-Polishing Supervisor (ordnance)	603.137-010
REI	61	Fine Arts Packer (museums)	102.367-010
REI	61	Inspector, Agricultural Commodities (government ser.)	168.287-010
REI	61	Machinery Erector (engine-turbine; machinery mfg.)	638.261-014
REI	61	Mate, Fishing Vessel (fishing & hunt.)	197.133-018
REI	61	Optician (optical goods; retail trade)	716.280-014
REI	61	Optician Apprentice (optical goods; retail trade)	716.280-010
REI	61	Powerhouse Mechanic (utilities)	631.261-014
REI	61	Powerhouse-Mechanic Apprentice (utilities)	631.261-018
REI	61	Rail-Flaw-Detector Operator (r.r. trans.)	910.263-010
REI	61	Supervisor, Inspection and Testing (elec. equip.)	721.131-014
REI	61	Supervisory Wastewater-Treatment-Plant Operator (sanitary ser.)	955.130-010
REI	61	X-Ray-Equipment Tester (any industry)	729.281-046
REI	60	Bus Inspector (automotive ser.)	620.281-030
REI	60	Experimental-Rocket-Sled Mechanic (aircraft mfg.)	825.281-038
REI	60	Maintenance Supervisor, Fire-Fighting-Equipment (government ser.)	638.131-018
REI	60	Patternmaker, Sample (cutlery-hrdwr.)	693.281-022
REI	60	Prop Maker (amuse. & rec.; motion picture)	962.281-010
REI	60	Sales-Service Representative, Milking Machines (retail trade)	299.251-010
REI	60	Salvage Engineer (machinery mfg.)	600.131-014
REI	60	Supervisor, CD-Area (chemical)	559.132-070
REI	60	Supervisor, Cell-Efficiency (chemical)	558.134-018
REI	60	Supervisor, Hot-Dip Plating (galvanizing)	501.137-010
REI	60	Supervisor, Hot-Dip-Tinning (steel & rel.)	501.130-010
REI	60	Supervisor, Shearing (any industry)	615.132-010
REI	60	Supervisor, Tree-Fruit-and-Nut Farming (agriculture)	403.131-010
REI	59	Assembler, Steam-and-Gas Turbine (engine-turbine)	600.261-010
REI	59	Carpenter, Maintenance (any industry)	860.281-010
REI	59	Experimental Mechanic, Electrical (motor-bicycles)	806.281-014
REI	59	Fretted-Instrument Repairer (any industry)	730.281-026
REI	59	Heavy Forger (forging)	612.361-010
REI	59	Instrument Technician (utilities)	710.281-030
REI	59	Instrument-Technician Apprentice (utilities)	710.281-042
REI	59	Lead-Section Supervisor (ordnance)	619.132-010
REI	59	Machine Fixer (carpet & rug)	628.281-010
REI	59	Maintenance Mechanic (any industry)	638.281-014
REI	59	Model Maker, Wood (any industry)	661.380-010
REI	59	Sheet-Metal Worker (any industry)	804.281-010
REI	59	Sheet-Metal-Worker Apprentice (any industry)	804.281-014
REI	59	Stationary Engineer (any industry)	950.382-026
REI	59	Stationary-Engineer Apprentice (any industry)	950.382-030
REI	59	Street-Openings Inspector (utilities)	859.267-010
REI	59	Suction-Dredge-Pipeline-Placing Supervisor (construction)	862.134-010
REI	59	Supervisor, Beam Department (leather mfg.)	589.134-010
REI	59	Supervisor, Bottle-House Cleaners (beverage)	529.132-022

HOC	Cx	Title	DOT
REI	59	Supervisor, Brine (chemical)	558.134-010
REI	59	Supervisor, Cell Room (chemical)	558.134-014
REI	59	Supervisor, Coremaker (paper & pulp)	640.132-010
REI	59	Supervisor, Grinding (any industry)	603.130-010
REI	59	Supervisor, Hydrochloric Area (chemical)	558.134-022
REI	59	Supervisor, Manufactured Buildings (mfd. bldgs.; vehicles, n.e.c.)	869.131-030
REI	59	Supervisor, Merchant-Mill Rolling and Finishing (steel & rel.)	613.130-014
REI	59	Supervisor, Metal Fabricating (any industry)	809.130-014
REI	59	Supervisor, Metal Hanging (mfd. bldgs.)	809.134-014
REI	59	Supervisor, Meter Shop (waterworks)	710.131-030
REI	59	Supervisor, Mold Shop (pottery & porc.)	777.131-010
REI	59	Supervisor, Net Making (toy-sport equip.)	789.132-022
REI	59	Supervisor, Paper Products (paper goods)	649.130-010
REI	59	Supervisor, Plastic Sheets (plastic prod.)	557.130-014
REI	59	Supervisor, Soaking Pits (steel & rel.)	509.132-010
REI	59	Supervisor, Specialty Manufacturing (steel & rel.)	616.130-014
REI	59	Supervisor, Steffen House (sugar & conf.)	529.132-086
REI	59	Supervisor, Tunnel Heading (construction)	859.137-018
REI	59	Technician, Submarine Cable Equipment (tel. & tel.)	822.281-034
REI	59	Tugboat Mate (water trans.)	197.133-034
REI	59	Watch Repairer (clock & watch)	715.281-010
REI	59	Watch Repairer Apprentice (clock & watch)	715.281-014
REI	59	Weld Inspector I (welding)	819.281-018
REI	58	Aircraft Mechanic, Rigging and Controls (aircraft mfg.)	806.381-018
REI	58	Assembler, Ground Support Equipment (aircraft mfg.)	809.261-010
REI	58	Carpenter, Ship (ship-boat mfg.)	860.281-014
REI	58	Dairy-Equipment Repairer (dairy products)	629.281-018
REI	58	Dental-Laboratory Technician (protective dev.)	712.381-018
REI	58	Dental-Laboratory-Technician Apprentice (protective dev.)	712.381-022
REI	58	Diamond Selector (jewelry-silver.)	770.281-010
REI	58	Diesel Mechanic (any industry)	625.281-010
REI	58	Diesel-Mechanic Apprentice (any industry)	625.281-014
REI	58	Filter-Plant Supervisor (smelt. & refin.)	511.135-010
REI	58	Fur Farmer (agriculture)	410.161-014
REI	58	Furnace Installer-and-Repairer, Hot Air (any industry)	869.281-010
REI	58	Game-Bird Farmer (agriculture)	412.161-010
REI	58	Logging-Equipment Mechanic (logging)	620.281-042
REI	58	Machinist Apprentice, Linotype (print. & pub.)	627.261-018
REI	58	Machinist, Linotype (print. & pub.)	627.261-022
REI	58	Mill Platform Supervisor (sugar & conf.)	521.132-010
REI	58	Repairer (smelt. & refin.)	630.281-026
REI	58	Service Mechanic, Compressed-Gas Equipment (chemical)	630.281-034
REI	58	Snow-Removing Supervisor (government ser.)	955.137-010
REI	58	Still Operator II (beverage)	522.382-026
REI	58	Supervisor, Cold Rolling (steel & rel.)	619.130-018
REI	58	Supervisor, Finishing-and-Shipping (steel & rel.)	619.132-026
REI	58	Supervisor, Sewer Maintenance (government ser.)	851.137-014

HOC	Cx	Title	DOT
REI	58	Tractor Mechanic (automotive ser.)	620.281-058
REI	58	Wastewater-Treatment-Plant Operator (sanitary ser.)	955.362-010
REI	58	Woods Boss (logging)	459.137-010
REI	57	Aircraft Mechanic, Armament (aircraft mfg.)	806.361-030
REI	57	Aircraft Mechanic, Environmental Control System (aircraft mfg.)	806.381-014
REI	57	Boiler (soap & rel.)	553.382-014
REI	57	Car Repairer, Pullman (r.r. trans.)	622.381-018
REI	57	Contour Wire Specialist, Denture (protective dev.)	712.381-014
REI	57	Corrosion-Control Fitter (pipe lines; utilities)	820.361-010
REI	57	Diesel-Engine Erector (engine-turbine)	625.361-010
REI	57	Dynamometer Tester, Engine (auto. mfg.)	806.281-010
REI	57	Electric-Motor Assembler and Tester (any industry)	721.281-014
REI	57	Electric-Tool Repairer (any industry)	729.281-022
REI	57	Fancy-Wire Drawer (jewelry-silver.)	700.381-014
REI	57	Forester Aide (forestry)	452.364-010
REI	57	House Repairer (construction)	869.381-010
REI	57	In-Flight Refueling System Repairer (military ser.)	829.281-018
REI	57	Inspector III (ordnance)	737.367-010
REI	57	Jewel-Bearing Maker (clock & watch)	770.381-030
REI	57	Liquor Blender (beverage)	522.382-018
REI	57	Lithographic Platemaker (print. & pub.)	972.381-010
REI	57	Lithographic-Plate-Maker Apprentice (print. & pub.)	972.381-014
REI	57	Maintenance Mechanic, Engine (water trans.)	623.281-034
REI	57	Model Maker II (jewelry-silver.)	709.381-018
REI	57	Model-Maker Apprentice (jewelry-silver.)	709.381-022
REI	57	Museum Technician (museums)	102.381-010
REI	57	Outboard-Motor Tester (engine-turbine)	623.261-014
REI	57	Packaging Supervisor (any industry)	920.132-010
REI	57	Plumber (construction)	862.381-030
REI	57	Plumber Apprentice (construction)	862.381-034
REI	57	Police Officer, Identification and Records (government ser.)	375.384-010
REI	57	Pump Servicer (any industry)	630.281-018
REI	57	Radio Mechanic (any industry)	823.261-018
REI	57	Refrigerating Engineer (any industry)	950.362-014
REI	57	Repeat Chief (print. & pub.)	970.361-014
REI	57	Repeat-Photocomposing-Machine Operator (print. & pub.)	971.382-018
REI	57	Section Leader and Machine Setter (textile)	689.260-018
REI	57	Set-up Mechanic, Automatic Line (pen & pencil)	692.380-014
REI	57	Steam Service Inspector (utilities)	862.361-022
REI	57	Stripper (print. & pub.)	971.381-050
REI	57	Stripper Apprentice (print. & pub.)	971.381-054
REI	57	Stucco Mason (construction)	842.381-014
REI	57	Television-and-Radio Repairer (any industry)	720.281-018
REI	57	Tin Roller, Hot Mill (steel & rel.)	613.360-018
REI	57	Treatment-Plant Mechanic (waterworks)	630.281-038
REI	57	Washing-and-Screening Plant Supervisor (construction)	570.132-018
REI	56	Automatic-Door Mechanic (construction)	829.281-010

HOC	Cx	Title	DOT
REI	56	Barge Captain (water trans.)	911.137-010
REI	56	Canal-Equipment Mechanic (waterworks)	899.281-010
REI	56	Casing-In-Line Setter (print. & pub.)	653.360-010
REI	56	Conduit Mechanic (construction; utilities)	869.361-010
REI	56	Construction-Equipment Mechanic (construction)	620.261-022
REI	56	Drill-Press Operator, Numerical Control (machine shop)	606.362-010
REI	56	Engraver, Seals (pen & pencil)	704.381-034
REI	56	Fabric-Machine Operator I (furniture)	616.362-010
REI	56	Fumigator (business ser.)	383.361-010
REI	56	Gas-Engine Repairer (any industry)	625.281-026
REI	56	Glass Bender (fabrication, n.e.c.)	772.381-010
REI	56	Glaze Supervisor (brick & tile)	574.130-010
REI	56	Inspector, Floor (machine shop)	609.361-010
REI	56	Knitting-Machine Fixer (knitting)	689.260-026
REI	56	Laboratory-Equipment Installer (construction)	869.381-014
REI	56	Lay-Out Technician (optical goods)	716.381-014
REI	56	Light Technician (motion picture; radio-tv broad.)	962.362-014
REI	56	Load Checker (utilities)	952.367-010
REI	56	Machining-and-Assembly Supervisor (elec. equip.)	619.131-010
REI	56	Molder, Pattern (foundry)	693.381-022
REI	56	Power-Saw Mechanic (any industry)	625.281-030
REI	56	Pressure Controller (utilities)	953.362-018
REI	56	Pyridine Operator (steel & rel.)	552.382-010
REI	56	Safe-and-Vault Service Mechanic (business ser.; wholesale tr.)	869.381-022
REI	56	Supervisor, Split Leather Department (leather mfg.)	589.130-030
REI	56	Swatch Checker (textile)	683.260-022
REI	56	Tree Surgeon (agriculture)	408.181-010
REI	56	Worm Grower (agriculture)	413.161-018
REI	55	Armor Reconnaissance Specialist (military ser.)	378.363-010
REI	55	Bricklayer (brick & tile)	861.381-014
REI	55	Burner Operator (chemical)	558.382-014
REI	55	Chemical Operator III (chemical)	559.382-018
REI	55	Crude-Oil Treater (petrol. & gas)	541.382-014
REI	55	Defensive Fire Control Systems Operator (military ser.)	378.382-014
REI	55	Ditch Rider (waterworks)	954.362-010
REI	55	Dyer (laundry & rel.)	364.361-010
REI	55	Expedition Supervisor (fishing & hunt.)	461.134-010
REI	55	Fire Chief's Aide (government ser.)	373.363-010
REI	55	Fire Inspector (any industry)	373.367-010
REI	55	Fur Sorter (fur goods)	783.384-010
REI	55	Inspector, Exhaust Emissions (auto. mfg.)	806.364-010
REI	55	Lathe Operator, Contact Lens (optical goods)	716.382-010
REI	55	Lead Operator (smelt. & refin.)	630.381-018
REI	55	Magneto Repairer (any industry)	721.281-022
REI	55	Miller, Head, Wet Process (grain-feed mills)	629.261-014
REI	55	Model Builder (furniture)	709.381-014
REI	55	Numerical Control Machine Operator (machine shop)	609.362-010
REI	55	Pipe Coverer and Insulator (ship-boat mfg.)	863.381-014

Part 2: From Holland Codes to Occupations

From Holland Codes to the Dictionary of Occupational Titles Occupations

HOC	Cx	Title	DOT
REI	55	Private-Branch-Exchange Repairer (tel. & tel.)	822.281-022
REI	55	Radio Repairer (any industry)	720.281-010
REI	55	Section-Plotter Operator (petrol. & gas)	194.382-010
REI	55	Sketch Maker II (print. & pub.)	972.381-018
REI	55	Structural-Steel Worker (construction)	801.361-014
REI	55	Structural-Steel-Worker Apprentice (construction)	801.361-018
REI	55	Supervisor, Covering and Lining (fabrication, n.e.c.)	780.134-010
REI	55	Supervisor, Garment Manufacturing (garment)	786.132-010
REI	55	Ware Tester (glass mfg.)	579.384-018
REI	55	Water-Quality Tester (paper & pulp)	539.367-014
REI	55	Yardage Estimator (garment)	221.484-010
REI	54	Assembler, Aircraft Power Plant (aircraft mfg.)	806.381-022
REI	54	Bench Hand (furniture)	706.381-014
REI	54	Bonding-Machine Setter (textile)	589.360-010
REI	54	Bricklayer, Firebrick and Refractory Tile (construction)	861.381-026
REI	54	Building-Equipment Inspector (utilities)	956.387-010
REI	54	Buttermaker (dairy products)	529.362-010
REI	54	Carpet Layer (retail trade)	864.381-010
REI	54	Cell Tender (chemical)	558.382-026
REI	54	Decontaminator (any industry)	199.384-010
REI	54	Draper (motion picture; radio-tv broad.)	962.381-010
REI	54	Electric-Golf-Cart Repairer (amuse. & rec.; automotive ser.)	620.261-026
REI	54	Final Assembler (office machines)	706.381-018
REI	54	Finishing Inspector (elec. equip.)	729.387-018
REI	54	Inspector (steel & rel.)	619.381-010
REI	54	Inspector, Eyeglass (optical goods)	713.384-014
REI	54	Inspector, Returned Materials (auto. mfg.)	806.384-014
REI	54	Lens-Mold Setter (optical goods)	713.381-010
REI	54	Link-and-Link-Knitting-Machine Operator (knitting)	685.380-010
REI	54	Lithograph-Press Operator, Tinware (tinware)	651.382-014
REI	54	Load-Out Supervisor (mine & quarry)	921.133-014
REI	54	Log Grader (logging; saw. & plan.)	455.367-010
REI	54	Loom Changer (textile)	683.360-010
REI	54	Natural-Gas-Treating-Unit Operator (petrol. & gas)	549.382-010
REI	54	Operator, Automated Process (electron. comp.)	590.382-010
REI	54	Oxygen-Plant Operator (chemical)	552.362-014
REI	54	Pantograph-Machine Set-up Operator (machine shop)	605.382-022
REI	54	Pattern Grader-Cutter (garment)	781.381-022
REI	54	Precipitator Supervisor (smelt. & refin.; steel & rel.)	511.132-010
REI	54	Precision-Lens Centerer and Edger (optical goods)	716.462-010
REI	54	Precision-Lens Generator (optical goods)	716.682-014
REI	54	Product Tester, Fiberglass (textile)	589.384-010
REI	54	Property Custodian (motion picture)	222.387-042
REI	54	Prospecting Driller (petrol. & gas)	930.382-018
REI	54	Refined-Syrup Operator (sugar & conf.)	520.485-022
REI	54	Repairer, Typewriter (office machines)	706.381-030
REI	54	Rotogravure-Press Operator (print. & pub.)	651.362-026
REI	54	Shipping and Receiving Clerk (clerical)	222.387-050

From Holland Codes to the Dictionary of Occupational Titles Occupations

HOC	Cx	Title	DOT
REI	54	Shot Dropper (ordnance)	502.362-010
REI	54	Sprinkler-Irrigation-Equipment Mechanic (agric. equip.)	624.361-014
REI	54	Stone Setter (jewelry-silver.; optical goods)	700.381-054
REI	54	Stone-Setter Apprentice (jewelry-silver.; optical goods)	700.381-058
REI	54	Supervisor, Fence Manufacture (metal prod., n.e.c.)	617.130-014
REI	54	Tower Operator (soap & rel.)	559.362-034
REI	54	Transformer Repairer (any industry)	724.381-018
REI	53	Absorption Operator (chemical)	551.382-010
REI	53	Aquatic Performer (amuse. & rec.)	159.347-014
REI	53	Ballpoint Pen Cartridge Tester (pen & pencil)	733.281-010
REI	53	Boatbuilder Apprentice, Wood (ship-boat mfg.)	860.361-014
REI	53	Boatbuilder, Wood (ship-boat mfg.)	860.361-010
REI	53	Bowling-Ball Grader and Marker (toy-sport equip.)	732.381-014
REI	53	Buffing-Line Set-up Worker (any industry)	603.360-010
REI	53	Caustic Operator (paper & pulp)	558.485-010
REI	53	Concrete-Stone Finisher (concrete prod.)	844.461-010
REI	53	Cylinder-Machine Operator (paper & pulp; wood prod., n.e.c.)	539.362-010
REI	53	Dairy-Processing-Equipment Operator (dairy products)	529.382-018
REI	53	Deburrer, Strip (clock & watch)	603.482-010
REI	53	Engraver, Pantograph I (engraving)	704.382-010
REI	53	Fish Farmer (fishing & hunt.)	446.161-010
REI	53	Forming-Machine Operator (glass mfg.)	575.382-014
REI	53	Fourdrinier-Machine Operator (paper & pulp; paper goods)	539.362-014
REI	53	Gas-Engine Operator (any industry)	950.382-018
REI	53	Glass-Rolling-Machine Operator (glass mfg.)	575.382-022
REI	53	Grinder, Gear (machine shop)	602.382-034
REI	53	Grinder, Hardboard (wood prod., n.e.c.)	569.682-010
REI	53	Hat-Block Maker (woodworking)	661.381-010
REI	53	Head Inspector (wood. container)	764.387-010
REI	53	Hydraulic-Press Servicer (ordnance)	626.381-018
REI	53	Inspector, Magnetic Particle and Penetrant (any industry)	709.364-010
REI	53	Instrument-Repairer Helper (any industry)	710.384-018
REI	53	Kettle Operator (plastic-synth.)	558.382-042
REI	53	Matrix-Bath Attendant (recording)	500.384-014
REI	53	Miller, Distillery (beverage)	521.362-014
REI	53	Paleontological Helper (profess. & kin.)	024.364-010
REI	53	Photostat Operator (any industry)	976.382-022
REI	53	Profile-Grinder Technician (clock & watch)	601.482-010
REI	53	Quality-Control Inspector (rubber tire)	750.367-010
REI	53	Rotary Driller (petrol. & gas)	930.382-026
REI	53	Screw-Machine Operator, Swiss-Type (clock & watch)	604.682-010
REI	53	Shear-Grinder Operator (textile)	628.382-014
REI	53	Shellfish Grower (fishing & hunt.)	446.161-014
REI	53	Soap Maker (soap & rel.)	559.382-054
REI	53	Solutions Operator (plastic-synth.)	550.382-034
REI	53	Specialties Operator (chemical)	559.582-014
REI	53	Subassembler (machinery mfg.)	706.381-038
REI	53	Terrazzo Worker (construction)	861.381-046

HOC	Cx	Title	DOT
REI	53	Terrazzo-Worker Apprentice (construction)	861.381-050
REI	53	Thermostat Repairer (inst. & app.)	710.381-050
REI	53	Thread-Milling-Machine Set-up Operator (machine shop)	605.382-042
REI	53	Tire Adjuster (retail trade)	241.367-034
REI	53	Tire Technician (rubber tire)	750.382-010
REI	53	Turbine Subassembler (engine-turbine)	706.381-042
REI	53	Vacuum Cleaner Repairer (any industry)	723.381-014
REI	53	Varnish Maker (paint & varnish)	553.382-022
REI	53	Water-Treatment-Plant Operator (waterworks)	954.382-014
REI	52	Acid Extractor (steel & rel.)	558.382-010
REI	52	Assembler, Aluminum Boats (ship-boat mfg.)	806.481-010
REI	52	Blow-up Operator (sugar & conf.)	529.485-014
REI	52	Body-Maker-Machine Setter (tinware)	616.360-010
REI	52	Brilliandeer-Lopper (jewelry-silver.)	770.261-010
REI	52	Buttermaker, Continuous Churn (dairy products)	529.382-010
REI	52	Casting-Machine Operator (machinery mfg.; print. & pub.)	654.382-010
REI	52	Catalyst Operator, Gasoline (chemical)	559.382-014
REI	52	Clarifying-Plant Operator (textile)	955.382-010
REI	52	Concrete-Stone Fabricator (concrete prod.)	575.461-010
REI	52	Engraver, Tire Mold (machine shop)	605.382-014
REI	52	Exterminator, Termite (business ser.)	383.364-010
REI	52	Fireworks Display Specialist (chemical)	969.664-010
REI	52	Grease Maker (petrol. refin.)	549.682-010
REI	52	Lapping-Machine Set-up Operator (machine shop)	603.382-026
REI	52	Lay-out Worker II (any industry)	809.381-014
REI	52	Melter Operator (sugar & conf.)	523.382-018
REI	52	Novelty Maker II (dairy products)	529.482-018
REI	52	Paint-Roller-Cover-Machine Setter (fabrication, n.e.c.)	692.682-046
REI	52	Perishable-Fruit Inspector (wholesale tr.)	910.387-010
REI	52	Precision-Lens Polisher (optical goods)	716.682-018
REI	52	Pumper (any industry)	914.682-010
REI	52	Railroad-Car Letterer (r.r. trans.)	845.681-010
REI	52	Sampler (oils & grease)	529.387-034
REI	52	Screw-Machine Operator, Multiple Spindle (machine shop)	604.382-010
REI	52	Smoke Jumper (forestry)	452.364-014
REI	52	Straightener, Hand (any industry)	709.484-014
REI	52	Tab-Card-Press Operator (print. & pub.)	651.382-034
REI	52	Type-Casting Machine Operator (print. & pub.)	654.582-010
REI	52	Welding-Machine Operator, Friction (welding)	814.382-010
REI	52	Welding-Machine Operator, Gas (welding)	811.482-010
REI	52	Wire-Frame-Lamp-Shade Maker (fabrication, n.e.c.)	709.684-098
REI	51	Artificial Inseminator (agriculture)	418.384-010
REI	51	Awning Maker-and-Installer (furniture; retail trade)	869.481-010
REI	51	Battery Tester (elec. equip.)	727.384-010
REI	51	Clerk-of-Scales (amuse. & rec.)	153.467-010
REI	51	Cloth-Finishing-Range Operator, Chief (textile)	589.562-010
REI	51	Coater (pharmaceut.)	554.382-010
REI	51	Color Checker, Roving or Yarn (textile)	582.387-010
REI	51	Color Weigher (fabrication, n.e.c.)	590.487-010

HOC	Cx	Title	DOT
REI	51	Die Barber (machine shop)	705.381-010
REI	51	Extrusion-Press Operator I (elec. equip.)	614.482-018
REI	51	Final Finisher, Forging Dies (machine shop)	705.484-014
REI	51	Final Inspector (glass products)	779.387-010
REI	51	Hardness Inspector (heat treating)	504.387-010
REI	51	Honing-Machine Set-up Operator (machine shop)	603.382-018
REI	51	Identification Clerk (government ser.)	209.362-022
REI	51	Inspector II (fabrication, n.e.c.)	590.367-010
REI	51	Inspector, Grain Mill Products (grain-feed mills)	529.387-026
REI	51	Irrigation System Installer (construction)	851.383-010
REI	51	Job Setter, Spline-Rolling Machine (machine shop)	617.480-010
REI	51	Keyseating-Machine Set-up Operator (machine shop)	605.382-018
REI	51	Lens Polisher, Hand (optical goods)	716.681-018
REI	51	Log Scaler (logging; millwork-plywood; paper & pulp; saw. & plan.)	455.487-010
REI	51	Make-Up Operator (chemical)	559.382-034
REI	51	Molasses and Caramel Operator (grain-feed mills)	526.382-022
REI	51	Novelty Maker I (dairy products)	529.482-014
REI	51	Paper-Coating-Machine Operator (photo. appar.)	534.582-010
REI	51	Plater, Barrel (electroplating)	500.362-014
REI	51	Pressure-Test Operator (ordnance)	737.387-018
REI	51	Pulp Grinder and Blender (paper & pulp; wood prod., n.e.c.)	530.682-010
REI	51	Quality-Control Technician (can. & preserv.; food prep., n.e.c.)	529.387-030
REI	51	Roll Tender (chemical)	559.362-030
REI	51	Screw-Machine Operator, Single Spindle (machine shop)	604.382-014
REI	51	Shipping Checker (clerical)	222.687-030
REI	51	Syrup Maker (beverage)	520.485-026
REI	51	Thermal Cutter, Hand I (welding)	816.464-010
REI	51	Underwater Hunter-Trapper (fishing & hunt.)	461.664-010
REI	51	Wad-Compressor Operator-Adjuster (ordnance)	535.482-010
REI	51	Welder, Gas (welding)	811.684-014
REI	51	Whipped-Topping Finisher (oils & grease)	529.682-034
REI	51	Winding Inspector (house. appl.)	729.384-022
REI	50	Arc Cutter (welding)	816.364-010
REI	50	Battery Repairer (any industry)	727.381-014
REI	50	Beadworker (fabrication, n.e.c.)	789.381-010
REI	50	Blending-Plant Operator (oils & grease)	520.682-010
REI	50	Blocker and Cutter, Contact Lens (optical goods)	716.681-010
REI	50	Boring-Machine Operator (woodworking)	666.382-010
REI	50	Bow Maker, Production (toy-sport equip.)	732.684-038
REI	50	Brick Tester (brick & tile)	579.384-010
REI	50	Calender Operator, Insulation Board (wood prod., n.e.c.)	539.482-010
REI	50	Cheesemaker Helper (dairy products)	529.682-014
REI	50	Colorer, Hides and Skins (leather mfg.)	582.482-010
REI	50	Contact-Acid-Plant Operator (chemical)	558.585-018
REI	50	Cook, Syrup Maker (beverage)	526.682-018
REI	50	Dough-Mixer Operator (bakery products)	520.462-010

HOC	Cx	Title	DOT
REI	50	Dry-Kiln Operator (brick & tile)	573.362-010
REI	50	Dyer (chemical)	554.384-010
REI	50	Filer, Finish (ordnance)	705.481-010
REI	50	Fulling-Machine Operator (tex. prod., n.e.c.)	586.382-010
REI	50	Glass Grinder, Laboratory Apparatus (glass products; inst. & app.)	775.382-010
REI	50	Hydrogenation Operator (oils & grease)	529.382-026
REI	50	Impregnating-Machine Operator (metal prod., n.e.c.)	590.362-014
REI	50	Inspector, Surgical Garment (protective dev.)	712.487-010
REI	50	Instrument-Technician Helper (utilities)	710.684-030
REI	50	Jig Fitter (machinery mfg.)	801.684-010
REI	50	Latex-Ribbon-Machine Operator (rubber goods)	559.682-034
REI	50	Liquid-Sugar Melter (sugar & conf.)	520.382-014
REI	50	Lithographic-Proofer Apprentice (print. & pub.)	651.582-014
REI	50	Machine Operator, Centrifugal-Control Switches (elec. equip.)	609.682-022
REI	50	Mat Tester (nonmet. min.)	579.387-010
REI	50	Mill Operator (brick & tile; pottery & porc.)	570.382-010
REI	50	Pasting-Machine Operator (elec. equip.)	505.482-010
REI	50	Percussion-Instrument Repairer (any industry)	730.381-042
REI	50	Plaster Mixer, Machine (concrete prod.)	570.382-014
REI	50	Platform Attendant (food prep., n.e.c.)	299.377-010
REI	50	Polystyrene-Bead Molder (plastic prod.)	556.382-018
REI	50	Printing-Roller Polisher (machine shop)	603.382-030
REI	50	Proof-Press Operator (print. & pub.)	651.582-010
REI	50	Pulp-Refiner Operator (paper & pulp)	530.382-010
REI	50	Pulper, Synthetic Soil Blocks (paper & pulp)	530.582-010
REI	50	Quality-Control Inspector (recording)	194.387-010
REI	50	Quality-Control Technician (svc. ind. mach.)	637.684-014
REI	50	Roll-Threader Operator (nut & bolt)	619.462-010
REI	50	Rotary-Kiln Operator (cement; chemical; mine & quarry)	573.382-010
REI	50	Slurry Mixer (ordnance)	539.362-018
REI	50	Slurry-Control Tender (smelt. & refin.)	510.465-014
REI	50	Starchmaker (grain-feed mills)	520.485-030
REI	50	Stretcher-Leveler Operator (nonfer. metal)	619.582-010
REI	50	Sweeper-Brush Maker, Machine (fabrication, n.e.c.)	692.682-066
REI	50	Tower Helper (chemical)	558.385-014
REI	50	Zinc-Plating-Machine Operator (electroplating)	500.485-010
REI	49	Alum-Plant Operator (chemical)	559.362-010
REI	49	Ball-Truing-Machine Operator (toy-sport equip.)	690.682-014
REI	49	Cathode Maker (chemical)	554.585-010
REI	49	Clay Maker (brick & tile; pottery & porc.)	570.482-010
REI	49	Decorating-Equipment Setter (glass mfg.; glass products)	652.380-010
REI	49	Dental-Amalgam Processor (nonfer. metal)	509.382-014
REI	49	Dry-Pan Charger (brick & tile)	570.683-010
REI	49	Electrician (mfd. bldgs.)	824.681-010
REI	49	Embossing-Press Operator, Molded Goods (fabrication, n.e.c.)	690.682-034
REI	49	Extruder Operator (plastic prod.; plastic-synth.)	557.382-010

HOC	Cx	Title	DOT
REI	49	Filer, Hand, Tool (machine shop)	705.484-010
REI	49	Final Inspector (auto. mfg.)	806.687-018
REI	49	Flavor Room Worker (dairy products)	529.685-130
REI	49	Glue Maker, Bone (chemical)	559.382-022
REI	49	Head Sawyer, Automatic (paper & pulp; saw. & plan.)	667.682-034
REI	49	Heat-Treating Bluer (heat treating)	504.682-022
REI	49	Hose Inspector and Patcher (rubber goods)	759.364-010
REI	49	Injection-Molding-Machine Operator (plastic prod.)	556.382-014
REI	49	Inspector II (pottery & porc.)	774.384-010
REI	49	Inspector, Paper Products (paper goods)	649.367-010
REI	49	Inspector, Poising (clock & watch)	715.384-018
REI	49	Kettle Operator I (chemical)	558.382-038
REI	49	Lime-Kiln Operator (concrete prod.)	573.462-010
REI	49	Linter-Saw Sharpener (oils & grease)	603.682-018
REI	49	Noodle-Press Operator (food prep., n.e.c.)	520.662-010
REI	49	Repairer, Welding Equipment (welding)	626.384-010
REI	49	Scouring-Train Operator (carpet & rug; textile)	589.662-010
REI	49	Scuba Diver (any industry)	379.384-010
REI	49	Shale Planer Operator (mine & quarry)	930.663-010
REI	49	Strip Roller (metal prod., n.e.c.)	613.682-022
REI	49	Tapper Operator (nut & bolt)	606.682-022
REI	49	Tester, Regulator (protective dev.; toy-sport equip.)	710.387-010
REI	49	Weigh-Tank Operator (oils & grease)	529.485-026
REI	49	Welding-Machine Operator, Ultrasonic (welding)	814.682-010
REI	48	Anodizer (any industry)	500.682-010
REI	48	Aquarist (amuse. & rec.)	449.674-010
REI	48	Awning Hanger (construction; retail trade; tex. prod., n.e.c.)	869.484-010
REI	48	Bellows Tester (inst. & app.)	710.687-014
REI	48	Blocker II (print. & pub.)	971.684-010
REI	48	Boat Outfitter (ship-boat mfg.)	806.684-146
REI	48	Centrifugal Operator (grain-feed mills; sugar & conf.)	521.682-010
REI	48	Chamfering-Machine Operator I (ordnance)	606.685-014
REI	48	Coagulating-Bath Mixer (plastic-synth.)	550.684-010
REI	48	Concrete-Fence Builder (construction)	869.681-010
REI	48	Contour Grinder (stonework)	675.682-010
REI	48	Curer, Foam Rubber (rubber goods)	553.682-014
REI	48	Developer (photofinishing)	976.681-010
REI	48	Double-End-Trimmer-and-Boring-Machine Operator (furniture)	669.682-038
REI	48	Dowel-Machine Operator (woodworking)	665.682-010
REI	48	Etcher (engraving)	704.684-010
REI	48	Farm worker, Fruit I (agriculture)	403.683-010
REI	48	Glass Cutter, Hand (optical goods)	716.681-014
REI	48	Grinding-Wheel Inspector (nonmet. min.)	776.487-010
REI	48	Humidifier Operator (wood prod., n.e.c.)	562.682-010
REI	48	Metal Hanger (mfd. bldgs.; vehicles, n.e.c.)	809.684-030
REI	48	Miller, Wood Flour (woodworking)	564.682-018
REI	48	Molasses Preparer (food prep., n.e.c.)	522.685-078

Dictionary of Holland Occupational Codes

HOC	Cx	Title	DOT
REI	48	Mold Setter (elec. equip.)	502.684-018
REI	48	Neutralizer (grain-feed mills)	522.685-082
REI	48	Ruling-Machine Set-up Operator (paper goods; print. & pub.)	659.682-022
REI	48	Silo Operator (tobacco)	529.682-030
REI	48	Silver-Solution Mixer (chemical)	550.684-026
REI	48	Stone Driller (stonework)	676.682-014
REI	48	Stone Polisher, Machine (stonework)	673.382-018
REI	48	Stone Polisher, Machine Apprentice (stonework)	673.382-022
REI	48	Tanning-Solution Maker (chemical)	550.682-014
REI	48	Vault Worker (business ser.)	222.587-058
REI	48	Wash Helper (chemical)	559.665-042
REI	47	Anode Builder (chemical)	826.684-010
REI	47	Babbitter (machine shop)	709.684-022
REI	47	Beveler (glass mfg.; glass products)	775.684-010
REI	47	Broth Mixer (bakery products)	520.585-014
REI	47	Calender-Machine Operator (nonmet. min.)	583.585-010
REI	47	Calendering-Machine Operator (knitting)	580.485-010
REI	47	Carbon Printer (print. & pub.)	979.684-010
REI	47	Carpenter II (mfd. bldgs.)	860.681-010
REI	47	Cell Changer (chemical)	826.684-014
REI	47	Circular Sawyer, Stone (stonework)	677.462-010
REI	47	Coating-Machine Operator (paper & pulp; paper goods)	534.682-018
REI	47	Coating-Machine Operator, Hardboard (paper goods; wood prod., n.e.c.)	534.682-022
REI	47	Compounder (pharmaceut.; soap & rel.)	550.685-046
REI	47	Convolute-Tube Winder (paper goods)	640.682-010
REI	47	Coper, Hand (stonework)	771.384-010
REI	47	Cylinder-Die-Machine Operator (paper goods)	649.682-014
REI	47	Dock Hand (air trans.)	919.683-010
REI	47	Dye-Range Operator, Cloth (textile)	582.582-010
REI	47	Dynamite-Cartridge Crimper (chemical)	692.685-078
REI	47	Embosser Operator (paper goods)	649.682-022
REI	47	Embroidery-Machine Operator (any industry)	787.682-022
REI	47	Farm worker, Rice (agriculture)	401.683-014
REI	47	Fretted-Instrument Inspector (musical inst.)	730.684-034
REI	47	Grinder-Chipper I (any industry)	705.684-030
REI	47	Harness Puller (textile)	683.684-018
REI	47	Hide Splitter (leather mfg.)	690.580-010
REI	47	Horizontal-Earth-Boring-Machine Operator (construction)	850.662-010
REI	47	Inspector, Glass or Mirror (glass products)	779.687-022
REI	47	Installer-Inspector, Final (vehicles, n.e.c.)	806.684-066
REI	47	Kettle Worker (soap & rel.)	553.685-070
REI	47	Last Remodeler-Repairer (boot & shoe; wood prod., n.e.c.)	739.684-106
REI	47	Lawn-Service Worker (agriculture)	408.684-010
REI	47	Lawn-Sprinkler Installer (construction)	869.684-030
REI	47	Liquor-Bridge Operator (sugar & conf.)	521.565-010
REI	47	Livestock-Yard Attendant (any industry)	410.674-018
REI	47	Metal-Finish Inspector (furniture)	703.687-018

HOC	Cx	Title	DOT
REI	47	Mixer Operator (sugar & conf.)	520.685-150
REI	47	Morgue Attendant (medical ser.)	355.667-010
REI	47	Mud Boss (smelt. & refin.)	519.585-014
REI	47	Package-Dyeing-Machine Operator (textile)	582.685-102
REI	47	Photographer Helper (any industry)	976.667-010
REI	47	Planer Operator (elec. equip.)	675.682-014
REI	47	Plastic Duplicator (machine tools)	754.684-038
REI	47	Pneumatic-Jack Operator (petrol. & gas)	939.682-014
REI	47	Polishing-Machine Operator (any industry)	603.682-026
REI	47	Rail-Tractor Operator (steel & rel.)	919.683-018
REI	47	Receiver, Fermenting Cellars (beverage)	522.662-010
REI	47	Service Representative (utilities; waterworks)	959.574-010
REI	47	Shellfish Dredge Operator (fishing & hunt.)	446.663-010
REI	47	Size Maker (paper & pulp)	550.682-010
REI	47	Spiral-Tube Winder (paper goods)	640.682-022
REI	47	Spring Fitter (metal prod., n.e.c.)	709.684-078
REI	47	Spring Former, Machine (metal prod., n.e.c.)	617.482-022
REI	47	Stock-Parts Inspector (furniture)	763.684-070
REI	47	Straightening-Press Operator II (any industry)	617.482-026
REI	47	Tin-Whiz-Machine Operator (textile)	582.685-154
REI	47	Track Repairer (r.r. trans.)	910.684-014
REI	47	Type-Rolling-Machine Operator (office machines)	619.382-022
REI	47	Water Regulator and Valve Repairer (waterworks)	862.684-030
REI	47	Water-Meter Installer (waterworks)	954.564-010
REI	47	Wire Sawyer (stonework)	677.462-014
REI	47	Wood Grinder Operator (paper & pulp)	530.662-014
REI	46	Assembler, Camper (vehicles, n.e.c.)	806.684-018
REI	46	Assembler, Wire-Mesh Gate (metal prod., n.e.c.)	801.384-010
REI	46	Bed Rubber (stonework)	673.685-014
REI	46	Chucking-Machine Operator (woodworking)	665.382-010
REI	46	Cloth Examiner, Machine (textile)	689.685-038
REI	46	Cooling-Pipe Inspector (construction)	862.687-010
REI	46	Drier Operator (chemical; pharmaceut.)	553.685-042
REI	46	Drill Operator, Automatic (glass products)	676.682-010
REI	46	Film-Casting Operator (plastic-synth.)	559.682-022
REI	46	Furnace Operator (elec. equip.)	543.682-018
REI	46	Furniture Assembler-and-Installer (retail trade)	739.684-082
REI	46	Last Trimmer (wood prod., n.e.c.)	669.682-054
REI	46	Mat Inspector (concrete prod.)	575.687-022
REI	46	Miller II (chemical)	555.682-010
REI	46	Print Inspector (pottery & porc.)	774.687-018
REI	46	Pumper, Brewery (beverage)	914.665-014
REI	46	Rock Splitter (stonework)	771.684-010
REI	46	Roof Fitter (railroad equip.)	806.684-126
REI	46	Rug Setter, Axminster (carpet & rug)	681.682-018
REI	46	Saw Setter (stonework)	701.684-022
REI	46	Scrap Handler (any industry)	509.685-050
REI	46	Seed-Yeast Operator (food prep., n.e.c.)	522.685-090
REI	46	Static Balancer (any industry)	724.384-014

HOC	Cx	Title	DOT
REI	46	Trimming Assembler (furniture)	780.684-114
REI	45	Barrel-Rib Matting-Machine Operator (ordnance)	605.682-010
REI	45	Binder Technician (glass mfg.)	550.585-010
REI	45	Cloth-Finishing-Range Tender (textile)	589.685-026
REI	45	Composition Mixer (fabrication, n.e.c.)	550.665-014
REI	45	Deckhand (water trans.)	911.687-022
REI	45	Farm worker, Grain I (agriculture)	401.683-010
REI	45	Form Maker, Plaster (plastic prod.)	777.684-010
REI	45	Gas-Appliance-Servicer Helper (any industry)	637.684-010
REI	45	Inspector (paper & pulp)	649.487-010
REI	45	Lead Caster (elec. equip.)	502.684-010
REI	45	Linen-Room Attendant (hotel & rest.; medical ser.)	222.387-030
REI	45	Marine Oiler (water trans.)	911.584-010
REI	45	MVA-Reactor Operator (chemical)	558.685-046
REI	45	Pellet-Press Operator (chemical)	555.685-042
REI	45	Repairer, Pens and Pencils (pen & pencil)	733.384-010
REI	45	Rewinder Operator (paper goods)	640.685-058
REI	45	Road-Oiling-Truck Driver (construction)	853.663-018
REI	45	Roofing-Machine Operator (build. mat., n.e.c.)	554.682-022
REI	45	Rope-Maker, Ropewalk (tex. prod., n.e.c.)	681.682-014
REI	45	Rubber Liner (machinery mfg.)	759.684-050
REI	45	Sand-Mill Grinder (paint & varnish)	555.682-018
REI	45	Sewer-Pipe Cleaner (business ser.)	899.664-014
REI	45	Silver Spray Worker (recording)	500.684-022
REI	45	Sizing-Machine Operator (ordnance)	649.582-014
REI	45	Skiff Operator (fishing & hunt.)	441.683-010
REI	45	Soda-Room Operator (beverage)	559.682-046
REI	45	Steel-Shot-Header Operator (ordnance)	611.682-010
REI	45	Transfer-Table Operator (railroad equip.; r.r. trans.)	910.683-022
REI	45	Washer, Machine (laundry & rel.)	361.665-010
REI	45	Wort Extractor (dairy products)	526.485-010
REI	44	Amalgamator (smelt. & refin.)	511.685-010
REI	44	Antitank Assault Gunner (military ser.)	378.464-010
REI	44	Arbor-Press Operator I (any industry)	616.682-010
REI	44	Assembler (wood. container)	762.684-010
REI	44	Automatic Pattern Edger (glass products)	673.682-010
REI	44	Casket Assembler, Metal (fabrication, n.e.c.)	809.684-014
REI	44	Concrete-Mixing-Truck Driver (construction)	900.683-010
REI	44	Concrete-Paving-Machine Operator (construction)	853.663-014
REI	44	Cook (meat products)	526.685-010
REI	44	Desizing-Machine Operator, Head-End (textile)	582.685-046
REI	44	Drier, Belt Conveyor (food prep., n.e.c.)	529.485-018
REI	44	Dust-Collector Attendant (mine & quarry)	511.685-022
REI	44	Extrusion-Press Operator II (elec. equip.)	614.685-014
REI	44	Folding-Machine Operator (paper goods)	649.685-046
REI	44	Forging-Press Operator II (forging)	611.685-010
REI	44	Hat-Forming-Machine Operator (hat & cap)	586.685-030
REI	44	Lock Tender II (construction)	850.663-018
REI	44	Log Sorter (logging)	455.684-010

HOC	Cx	Title	DOT
REI	44	Mixer, Wet Pour (concrete prod.)	579.682-010
REI	44	Mold Laminator (concrete prod.; ship-boat mfg.)	806.684-086
REI	44	Molder, Hand (brick & tile; elec. equip.)	575.684-042
REI	44	Ordinary Seaman (water trans.)	911.687-030
REI	44	Pond Tender (chemical)	939.685-010
REI	44	Roller I (sugar & conf.)	520.684-014
REI	44	Screen-Printing-Machine Operator (textile)	652.682-018
REI	44	Sink Cutter (stonework)	677.682-018
REI	44	Tip Inserter (woodworking)	669.682-066
REI	44	Tire Buffer (automotive ser.)	690.685-422
REI	44	Tractor-Mechanic Helper (automotive ser.)	620.684-030
REI	43	Boil-Off-Machine Operator, Cloth (textile)	582.685-022
REI	43	Boring-Machine Operator, Production (machine shop)	606.685-010
REI	43	Fish-Cake Maker (food prep., n.e.c.)	529.685-122
REI	43	Flame Channeler (construction; mine & quarry)	930.684-010
REI	43	Inspector, Shells (ordnance)	737.687-066
REI	43	Production Hardener (heat treating)	504.685-026
REI	43	Rubber-Mill Tender (plastic-synth.; rubber goods; rubber reclaim.; rubber tire)	550.685-102
REI	43	Spray-Machine Operator (brick & tile; pottery & porc.)	574.682-014
REI	43	Stone Polisher, Hand (stonework)	775.664-010
REI	43	Utility Worker, Extrusion (nonfer. metal)	691.685-030
REI	42	Automobile-Mechanic Helper (automotive ser.)	620.684-014
REI	42	Batter-Out (pottery & porc.)	575.684-010
REI	42	Boom-Conveyor Operator (any industry)	921.683-014
REI	42	Calcine-Furnace Tender (paint & varnish)	553.685-030
REI	42	Centrifuge Operator (dairy products)	521.685-042
REI	42	Centrifuge Operator (oils & grease)	521.685-050
REI	42	Circular-Sawyer Helper (stonework)	677.486-010
REI	42	Clean-Out-Driller Helper (petrol. & gas)	930.664-014
REI	42	Crusher Tender (any industry)	570.685-022
REI	42	Die Cleaner (food prep., n.e.c.)	529.687-062
REI	42	Dock Hand (ship-boat mfg.)	891.684-010
REI	42	Felt Carbonizer (tex. prod., n.e.c.)	586.687-010
REI	42	Ferryboat-Operator Helper (water trans.)	911.667-010
REI	42	Framer (wood prod., n.e.c.)	666.684-010
REI	42	Inspector I (fabrication, n.e.c.)	739.687-106
REI	42	Laundry Operator (laundry & rel.)	369.684-014
REI	42	Lead-Nitrate Processor (chemical)	558.585-030
REI	42	Loader, Malt House (beverage)	921.682-010
REI	42	Matrix Inspector (machinery mfg.)	654.687-010
REI	42	Pole Framer (utilities; wood prod., n.e.c.)	959.684-010
REI	42	Polisher (jewelry-silver.)	700.687-058
REI	42	Precipitate Washer (chemical)	551.685-110
REI	42	Presser, All-Around (laundry & rel.)	363.682-014
REI	42	Punch-Press Operator II (any industry)	615.685-030
REI	42	Rafter (logging)	455.664-010
REI	42	Restrictive-Preparation Operator (ordnance)	559.685-154
REI	42	Screener-and-Blender Operator (steel & rel.)	549.685-026

Part 2: From Holland Codes to Occupations

From Holland Codes to the Dictionary of Occupational Titles Occupations

HOC	Cx	Title	DOT
REI	42	Snag Grinder (foundry)	705.684-074
REI	42	Wire-Border Assembler (furniture)	780.685-018
REI	42	Wood-Web-Weaving-Machine Operator (furniture)	692.685-262
REI	42	Wool-Fleece Sorter (agriculture)	410.687-026
REI	41	Bag-Machine Operator (paper goods)	649.685-014
REI	41	Belt-Builder Helper (rubber goods)	759.684-018
REI	41	Bench Grinder (any industry)	705.684-010
REI	41	Change-House Attendant (any industry)	358.687-010
REI	41	Cheese Cutter (dairy products)	529.585-010
REI	41	Christmas-Tree Grader (forestry)	451.687-014
REI	41	Cooler Room Worker (meat products)	525.687-022
REI	41	Corduroy-Brusher Operator (textile)	585.685-034
REI	41	Creping-Machine-Operator Helper (paper goods)	534.687-014
REI	41	Cullet Crusher-and-Washer (glass mfg.)	570.685-026
REI	41	Cylinder-Press Feeder (print. & pub.)	651.686-010
REI	41	Deckhand, Fishing Vessel (fishing & hunt.)	449.667-010
REI	41	Driller Helper (construction; mine & quarry)	930.666-010
REI	41	Dry Cleaner, Hand (laundry & rel.)	362.684-010
REI	41	Dye-Reel-Operator Helper (textile)	582.686-014
REI	41	Edger-Machine Operator (stonework)	673.682-018
REI	41	End Stapler (wood. container)	669.685-054
REI	41	Equipment Cleaner (any industry)	599.684-010
REI	41	Feather Separator (tex. prod., n.e.c.)	589.685-054
REI	41	Filter-Press Tender, Head (grain-feed mills)	521.665-018
REI	41	Fisher, Spear (fishing & hunt.)	443.684-010
REI	41	Flour Blender (grain-feed mills)	520.685-106
REI	41	Food-Service Driver (hotel & rest.)	906.683-010
REI	41	Furnace Helper (heat treating)	504.686-014
REI	41	Handle Maker (pottery & porc.)	575.684-030
REI	41	Head Trimmer (meat products)	525.684-034
REI	41	Heavy-Forger Helper (forging)	612.687-014
REI	41	Hot-Top Liner (steel & rel.)	709.684-046
REI	41	Hydraulic-Boom Operator (smelt. & refin.)	921.683-046
REI	41	Jet Handler (plastic-synth.)	557.684-010
REI	41	Kapok-and-Cotton-Machine Operator (tex. prod., n.e.c.)	689.685-082
REI	41	Kiln-Transfer Operator (woodworking)	569.683-010
REI	41	Laborer, Chemical Processing (chemical)	559.687-050
REI	41	Laborer, General (steel & rel.)	509.687-026
REI	41	Material Handler (any industry)	929.687-030
REI	41	Miller Helper, Distillery (beverage)	521.687-082
REI	41	Paint Mixer, Hand (any industry)	550.684-018
REI	41	Patch Driller (fabrication, n.e.c.)	739.687-142
REI	41	Pelter (agriculture)	410.687-018
REI	41	Picker (saw. & plan.)	669.687-022
REI	41	Pig-Machine-Operator Helper (steel & rel.)	514.667-014
REI	41	Plater, Hot Dip (galvanizing)	501.685-010
REI	41	Polisher (button & notion)	599.685-078
REI	41	Powerhouse Helper (chemical)	550.685-098
REI	41	Roller-Machine Operator (leather mfg.)	583.685-094

Part 2: From Holland Codes to Occupations

From Holland Codes to the Dictionary of Occupational Titles Occupations

HOC	Cx	Title	DOT
REI	41	Sand-Cutter Operator (foundry)	570.683-014
REI	41	Sandblaster (any industry)	503.687-010
REI	41	Scratcher Tender (fabrication, n.e.c.)	555.685-050
REI	41	Screener Operator (any industry)	599.685-082
REI	41	Second Helper (steel & rel.)	512.684-010
REI	41	Second-Floor Operator (plastic-synth.)	557.685-022
REI	41	Separator Tender II (grain-feed mills)	521.685-290
REI	41	Shellfish-Bed Worker (fishing & hunt.)	446.684-014
REI	41	Skiving-Machine Operator (ordnance)	664.682-018
REI	41	Soaker, Hides (meat products)	582.685-134
REI	41	Sponge Buffer (plastic prod.)	690.685-390
REI	41	Squeezer Operator (wood. container)	669.685-082
REI	41	Stave-Log-Ripsaw Operator (saw. & plan.)	667.685-058
REI	41	Stiffener (hat & cap)	589.687-038
REI	41	Stone Rougher (optical goods)	673.685-074
REI	41	Switch Tender (r.r. trans.)	910.667-026
REI	41	Tank Cleaner (any industry)	891.687-022
REI	41	Thermoscrew Operator (can. & preserv.)	526.685-058
REI	41	Third Helper (steel & rel.)	512.687-014
REI	41	Timber-Framer Helper (mine & quarry)	869.687-042
REI	41	Tire Repairer (automotive ser.)	915.684-010
REI	41	Transfer Controller (saw. & plan.)	921.682-022
REI	41	Trim-Machine Operator (ordnance)	609.685-026
REI	41	Tube Drawer (nonfer. metal; steel & rel.)	614.685-022
REI	41	Upholsterer Helper (any industry)	780.687-054
REI	41	Votator-Machine Operator (meat products; oils & grease)	529.685-250
REI	41	Washing-Machine Operator (any industry)	599.685-118
REI	41	Water-Filter Cleaner (waterworks)	954.587-010
REI	41	Wire-Coating Operator, Metal (galvanizing)	501.485-010
REI	40	Assembler, Finger Buffs (tex. prod., n.e.c.)	739.685-010
REI	40	Automatic-Machine Attendant (paper goods)	649.685-010
REI	40	Band-Saw Operator (meat products)	525.685-010
REI	40	Band-Saw Operator (wood. container)	667.685-010
REI	40	Binder Selector (tobacco)	521.687-018
REI	40	Bowl Turner (fabrication, n.e.c.)	664.684-010
REI	40	Brine-Tank Tender (dairy products)	529.685-030
REI	40	Calender-Let-Off Helper (rubber goods; rubber tire)	554.686-014
REI	40	Carton Marker, Machine (boot & shoe; garment)	652.685-018
REI	40	Carton-Forming-Machine Tender (paper goods)	641.685-026
REI	40	Cement-Boat-and-Barge Loader (cement)	921.665-010
REI	40	Coating-Machine-Operator Helper (fabrication, n.e.c.)	590.686-010
REI	40	Cocoa-Bean Cleaner (sugar & conf.)	521.685-066
REI	40	Coiler (tex. prod., n.e.c.)	681.685-034
REI	40	Continuous-Linter-Drier Operator (chemical)	553.685-034
REI	40	Cover Stripper (paper goods)	641.685-034
REI	40	Crossband Layer (millwork-plywood)	762.687-026
REI	40	Crusher Tender (fabrication, n.e.c.)	555.685-022
REI	40	Cut-Off Sawyer, Log (paper & pulp; saw. & plan.)	667.685-034
REI	40	Cylinder-Sander Operator (woodworking)	662.685-014

Dictionary of Holland Occupational Codes

From Holland Codes to the Dictionary of Occupational Titles Occupations

HOC	Cx	Title	DOT
REI	40	Definer (button & notion)	599.685-022
REI	40	Dip-Lube Operator (ordnance)	503.685-014
REI	40	Distillery Worker, General (beverage)	529.687-066
REI	40	Driller, Hand (any industry)	809.684-018
REI	40	Dumper (any industry)	921.667-018
REI	40	Electrode-Cleaning-Machine Operator (elec. equip.)	559.685-062
REI	40	Excelsior-Machine Tender (saw. & plan.)	663.685-014
REI	40	Feather Mixer (tex. prod., n.e.c.)	589.685-050
REI	40	Feed Blender (grain-feed mills)	520.685-094
REI	40	Feed Grinder (grain-feed mills)	521.685-122
REI	40	Filter-Screen Cleaner (beverage)	521.687-054
REI	40	Fish-Liver Sorter (can. & preserv.; fishing & hunt.)	521.687-062
REI	40	Fish-Machine Feeder (can. & preserv.)	521.686-034
REI	40	Fisher, Pot (fishing & hunt.)	441.684-014
REI	40	Foam-Machine Operator (plastic prod.; plastic-synth.)	559.685-078
REI	40	Freight-Car Cleaner, Delta System (r.r. trans.)	910.687-022
REI	40	Fuel-House Attendant (saw. & plan.)	951.686-010
REI	40	Furnace Cleaner (any industry)	891.687-014
REI	40	Green-Chain Offbearer (millwork-plywood)	663.686-018
REI	40	Hide Puller (meat products)	525.685-022
REI	40	Irrigator, Gravity Flow (agriculture)	409.687-014
REI	40	Kelp Cutter (fishing & hunt.)	447.687-022
REI	40	Kettle Tender (sugar & conf.)	520.685-118
REI	40	Kettle Tender (beverage)	526.665-014
REI	40	Kiln Drawer (brick & tile)	929.687-014
REI	40	Laborer (meat products)	529.687-130
REI	40	Laborer, General (smelt. & refin.)	519.687-026
REI	40	Laundry Worker I (any industry)	361.684-014
REI	40	Leather Softener (boot & shoe)	788.687-090
REI	40	Liner Reroll Tender (rubber goods; rubber tire)	554.685-022
REI	40	Log Marker (logging)	455.687-010
REI	40	Milled-Rubber Tender (rubber goods; rubber tire)	553.685-078
REI	40	Mixing-Machine Operator (fabrication, n.e.c.)	680.685-066
REI	40	Molder-Machine Tender (nonmet. min.)	575.685-062
REI	40	Mottler-Machine Feeder (fabrication, n.e.c.)	550.686-034
REI	40	Oiling-Machine Operator (paper & pulp; paper goods)	534.685-018
REI	40	Painter, Spray II (any industry)	741.687-018
REI	40	Polishing-Machine-Operator Helper (any industry)	603.686-010
REI	40	Poultry-Picking Machine Tender (meat products)	525.685-026
REI	40	Pug-Mill-Operator Helper (brick & tile; pottery & porc.)	570.685-074
REI	40	Rack-Room Worker (beverage)	920.665-014
REI	40	Raw-Cheese Worker (dairy products)	529.686-078
REI	40	Riveting-Machine Operator (furniture)	616.685-058
REI	40	Rug Cleaner (carpet & rug)	689.687-066
REI	40	Scutcher Tender (textile)	589.685-090
REI	40	Sewage-Disposal Worker (sanitary ser.)	955.687-010
REI	40	Spice Cleaner (food prep., n.e.c.)	521.685-322
REI	40	Splitter Operator (stonework)	677.685-042
REI	40	Spout Worker (smelt. & refin.)	514.667-018

HOC	Cx	Title	DOT
REI	40	Spray-Painting-Machine Operator (any industry)	741.685-010
REI	40	Strand-and-Binder Controller (nonmet. min.)	680.685-106
REI	40	Tailings-Dam Laborer (smelt. & refin.)	511.687-026
REI	40	Tip Stretcher (hat & cap)	580.685-062
REI	40	Tumbler Tender (knitting)	581.685-062
REI	40	Utility Worker, Woolen Mill (textile)	689.686-050
REI	40	Warp Coiler (textile)	582.686-038
REI	40	Wash-House Worker (beverage)	529.685-254
REI	40	Yeast Pusher (beverage)	522.665-014
REI	39	Briner (can. & preserv.)	522.687-014
REI	39	Cleaner II (any industry)	919.687-014
REI	39	Farm-Machine Tender (agriculture)	409.685-010
REI	39	Fish-Egg Packer (can. & preserv.)	529.687-086
REI	39	Hot-Top-Liner Helper (steel & rel.)	709.687-018
REI	39	Ice Cutter (food prep., n.e.c.)	529.685-150
REI	39	Laborer, Wharf (can. & preserv.)	922.687-062
REI	39	Miller (cement)	570.685-046
REI	39	Rotary-Cutter Operator (rubber goods)	551.585-022
REI	39	Sheller II (can. & preserv.)	521.685-294
REI	39	Stone-Driller Helper (stonework)	676.686-010
REI	38	Bath-Mix Operator (plastic-synth.)	552.685-018
REI	38	Case-Loader Operator (beverage)	920.685-042
REI	38	Caster (pottery & porc.)	575.684-014
REI	38	Char Puller (grain-feed mills; sugar & conf.)	521.687-030
REI	38	Cooker Tender (oils & grease)	553.665-022
REI	38	Dust-Mill Operator (tex. prod., n.e.c.)	581.686-030
REI	38	Feed Weigher (grain-feed mills)	920.685-058
REI	38	Finisher Operator (can. & preserv.)	521.685-142
REI	38	Fisher, Terrapin (fishing & hunt.)	441.684-018
REI	38	Grinder (plastic prod.; plastic-synth.)	555.685-026
REI	38	Hair Clipper, Power (leather mfg.)	789.684-022
REI	38	Hair-Spinning-Machine Operator (leather mfg.)	689.686-030
REI	38	Hasher Operator (meat products)	521.685-170
REI	38	Hide Handler (meat products; oils & grease)	525.687-038
REI	38	Laborer (petrol. & gas)	939.687-018
REI	38	Shaker Washer (grain-feed mills)	521.687-114
REI	38	Shredder Tender (chemical)	555.665-010
REI	38	Spinning-Machine Tender (tex. prod., n.e.c.)	681.685-110
REI	38	Spreader (hat & cap)	581.687-022
REI	38	Washing-Machine Loader-and-Puller (laundry & rel.)	361.686-010
REI	37	Butcher, Fish (can. & preserv.)	525.684-014
REI	37	Compound Filler (chemical)	550.686-014
REI	37	Crab Butcher (can. & preserv.)	525.684-022
REI	37	Fruit-Press Operator (beverage; can. & preserv.)	521.685-146
REI	37	Naphthalene-Operator Helper (steel & rel.)	551.687-026
REI	37	Pond Worker (millwork-plywood; paper & pulp; saw. & plan.)	921.686-022
REI	36	Drying-Oven Attendant (hat & cap)	581.686-022
REI	35	Christmas-Tree Farm Worker (forestry)	451.687-010

HOC	Cx	Title	DOT
REA	62	Supervisor, Fitting (any industry)	801.131-014
REA	61	Manager, Marine Service (ship-boat mfg.)	187.167-130
REA	61	Supervisor, Diamond Finishing (jewelry-silver.)	770.131-014
REA	59	Dye-House Supervisor (leather mfg.)	582.131-010
REA	59	Machine-Adjuster Leader (ordnance)	619.137-010
REA	58	Cellar Supervisor (beverage)	529.131-010
REA	58	Cook, Chief (water trans.)	315.131-010
REA	58	Dot Etcher (print. & pub.)	972.281-010
REA	58	Dot Etcher Apprentice (print. & pub.)	972.281-018
REA	57	Wrecking Supervisor (construction)	869.137-014
REA	56	Model Maker (auto. mfg.)	693.380-014
REA	56	Model-and-Mold Maker, Plaster (concrete prod.)	777.381-018
REA	55	Aerialist (amuse. & rec.)	159.247-014
REA	55	Supervisor, Livestock-Yard (any industry)	410.134-010
REA	55	Supervisor, Soakers (beverage)	529.132-082
REA	55	Wood Grinder, Head (paper & pulp)	530.132-022
REA	54	Ammonia-Still Operator (steel & rel.)	559.382-010
REA	52	Thrower (pottery & porc.)	774.381-010
REA	51	Automatic-Window-Seat-and-Top-Lift Repairer (automotive ser.)	825.381-014
REA	51	Carbon-Furnace Operator (smelt. & refin.)	543.562-010
REA	51	Dental Ceramist Assistant (protective dev.)	712.664-010
REA	51	Letterer (profess. & kin.)	970.661-014
REA	50	Engraver (glass products)	775.381-010
REA	50	Grade Checker (construction)	850.467-010
REA	48	Locomotive Operator Helper (r.r. trans.)	910.367-022
REA	47	Ben-Day Artist (print. & pub.)	970.681-010
REA	47	Supercalender Operator (paper & pulp)	534.682-038
REA	46	Chain Repairer (carpet & rug)	683.684-010
REA	46	Pattern-Lease Inspector (textile)	683.384-010
REA	45	Huller Operator (grain-feed mills)	521.682-030
REA	45	Motor-Grader Operator (construction)	850.663-022
REA	44	Boat Patcher, Plastic (ship-boat mfg.)	807.684-014
REA	44	Pole-Peeling-Machine Operator (saw. & plan.; wood prod., n.e.c.)	663.682-014
REA	44	Press Tender (food prep., n.e.c.)	520.685-186
REA	44	Rendering-Equipment Tender (meat products)	529.685-202
REA	43	Airplane-Pilot Helper (agriculture)	409.667-010
REA	41	Exerciser, Horse (amuse. & rec.)	153.674-010
REA	40	Dust Box Worker (build. mat., n.e.c.)	574.667-010
RES	69	Radiological-Equipment Specialist (inst. & app.)	719.261-014
RES	67	Maintenance-Mechanic Supervisor (any industry)	638.131-022
RES	67	Supervisor, Mold Making (glass mfg.)	609.131-014
RES	65	Dispatcher, Radioactive-Waste-Disposal (chemical)	955.167-010
RES	65	Field-Service Representative (aircraft mfg.)	621.221-010
RES	65	Machine-Assembler Supervisor (machinery mfg.)	638.131-014
RES	65	Manager, Handicraft-or-Hobby Shop (amuse. & rec.)	187.161-014
RES	65	Superintendent, Building (any industry)	187.167-190
RES	65	Supervisor, Telephone Information (motor trans.)	237.137-010

Part 2: From Holland Codes to Occupations

From Holland Codes to the Dictionary of Occupational Titles Occupations

HOC	Cx	Title	DOT
RES	64	Automated Equipment Engineer-Technician (machinery mfg.)	638.261-010
RES	64	Logging-Operations Inspector (forestry; logging)	168.267-070
RES	64	Supervisor, Liquefaction-and-Regasification (utilities)	953.132-010
RES	63	Airplane Inspector (air trans.)	621.261-010
RES	63	Distilling-Department Supervisor (beverage)	522.131-010
RES	63	Electrician Supervisor, Substation (utilities)	820.131-010
RES	63	Fish and Game Warden (government ser.)	379.167-010
RES	63	Fishing-Tool Technician, Oil Well (petrol. & gas)	930.261-010
RES	63	Inspection Supervisor (chemical; nonfer. metal)	709.137-010
RES	63	Instructor, Watch Assembly (clock & watch)	715.221-010
RES	63	Line Supervisor (utilities)	821.131-014
RES	63	Machine-Shop Supervisor, Tool (machine shop)	600.130-010
RES	63	Powerhouse-Mechanic Supervisor (utilities)	631.131-010
RES	63	Railroad-Construction Director (r.r. trans.)	182.167-018
RES	63	Service Supervisor III (utilities)	184.167-126
RES	63	Supervisor, Chocolate-and-Cocoa Processing (sugar & conf.)	529.130-014
RES	63	Supervisor, Instrument Maintenance (any industry)	710.131-014
RES	63	Supervisor, Instrument Mechanics (utilities)	710.131-018
RES	63	Supervisor, Mold Shop (glass mfg.)	609.131-018
RES	63	Tool-and-Die Supervisor (machine shop)	601.130-010
RES	62	Cabinetmaker, Supervisor (woodworking)	660.130-010
RES	62	Compressor-Station Engineer, Chief (pipe lines)	914.132-010
RES	62	Custom Tailor (garment; personal ser.; retail trade)	785.261-014
RES	62	Electrical-Installation Supervisor (utilities)	821.131-010
RES	62	Electrician Apprentice, Powerhouse (utilities)	820.261-010
RES	62	Electrician, Powerhouse (utilities)	820.261-014
RES	62	Electronics Assembler, Developmental (any industry)	726.261-010
RES	62	Engine-Testing Supervisor (engine-turbine)	625.131-010
RES	62	Equipment Inspector (tel. & tel.)	822.261-014
RES	62	Fire Captain (government ser.)	373.134-010
RES	62	Gauger, Chief (petrol. & gas; petrol. refin.; pipe lines)	914.134-010
RES	62	Grease Maker, Head (petrol. refin.)	549.132-010
RES	62	Inspection Supervisor (machine shop)	609.131-010
RES	62	Instructor (boot & shoe)	788.222-010
RES	62	Senior Technician, Controls (pipe lines)	828.261-018
RES	62	Service Supervisor II (utilities)	821.131-018
RES	62	Station Engineer, Chief (pipe lines)	914.132-014
RES	62	Supervisor, Engine-Repair (engine-turbine)	625.131-014
RES	62	Supervisor, Field Pipelines (pipe lines)	914.132-022
RES	62	Supervisor, Furrier Shop (fur goods)	783.131-010
RES	62	Supervisor, Metalizing (any industry)	505.130-010
RES	62	Supervisor, Roofing Plant (build. mat., n.e.c.)	590.130-018
RES	62	Surface Supervisor (mine & quarry)	932.132-014
RES	62	Tailor Apprentice, Custom (garment; personal ser.; retail trade)	785.261-022
RES	62	Wireworker Supervisor (utilities)	821.131-026
RES	61	Artillery-Maintenance Supervisor (ordnance)	632.131-010

HOC	Cx	Title	DOT
RES	61	Elevator Examiner-and-Adjuster (any industry)	825.261-014
RES	61	Floor Supervisor, Endless-Belt-Weaving Department (narrow fabrics)	683.130-010
RES	61	Lock Maintenance Supervisor (construction)	899.131-014
RES	61	Loft Worker, Head (ship-boat mfg.)	661.131-010
RES	61	Machine-Shop Supervisor, Production (machine shop)	609.130-010
RES	61	Pattern-Chain Maker Supervisor (textile)	683.132-010
RES	61	Power-Reactor Operator (utilities)	952.362-022
RES	61	Refinery Operator (petrol. refin.)	549.260-010
RES	61	Steam-Distribution Supervisor (utilities)	862.137-014
RES	61	Supercharger-Repair Supervisor (air trans.)	621.131-010
RES	61	Supervisor (plumbing-heat.)	609.130-018
RES	61	Supervisor (struct. metal)	617.130-010
RES	61	Supervisor I (chemical)	559.132-054
RES	61	Supervisor, Carpenters (construction)	860.131-018
RES	61	Supervisor, Electrical Repair and Telephone Line Maintenance (utilities)	829.131-022
RES	61	Supervisor, Hot-Wound Spring Production (metal prod., n.e.c.)	619.130-026
RES	61	Supervisor, Joiners (ship-boat mfg.)	860.131-022
RES	61	Supervisor, Preparation Department (textile)	681.130-010
RES	61	Supervisor, Typesetting (print. & pub.)	650.132-010
RES	61	Supervisor, Wet Room (paper & pulp)	539.130-014
RES	61	Treating-Plant Supervisor (wood prod., n.e.c.)	561.131-010
RES	61	Welding Supervisor (welding)	819.131-014
RES	60	Accident-Prevention-Squad Police Officer (government ser.)	375.263-010
RES	60	Artificial-Plastic-Eye Maker (optical goods)	713.261-014
RES	60	Bakery-Machine-Mechanic Supervisor (bakery products)	629.131-010
RES	60	Control-Panel Tester (elec. equip.)	827.381-010
RES	60	Embroidery Supervisor (tex. prod., n.e.c.)	689.130-010
RES	60	Experimental Mechanic, Outboard Motors (engine-turbine)	623.261-010
RES	60	Fretted-Instrument Maker, Hand (musical inst.)	730.281-022
RES	60	Loom-Fixer Supervisor (narrow fabrics)	683.130-014
RES	60	Millwright (any industry)	638.281-018
RES	60	Millwright Apprentice (any industry)	638.281-022
RES	60	Model Maker, Firearms (ordnance)	600.260-018
RES	60	Power-Plant Operator (utilities)	952.382-018
RES	60	Production Supervisor (any industry)	699.130-010
RES	60	Refrigerating Engineer, Head (any industry)	950.131-010
RES	60	Shrink-Pit Supervisor (ordnance)	619.131-018
RES	60	Supervisor (electroplating)	500.131-010
RES	60	Supervisor (boot & shoe)	788.131-010
RES	60	Supervisor, Assembly (pen & pencil)	733.137-010
RES	60	Supervisor, Carbon-Paper-Coating (pen & pencil)	534.137-010
RES	60	Supervisor, Diversified Crops (agriculture)	407.131-010
RES	60	Supervisor, Dried Yeast (food prep., n.e.c.)	529.132-042
RES	60	Supervisor, Evaporator (chemical)	559.137-026
RES	60	Supervisor, Hardboard (wood prod., n.e.c.)	539.130-010

Part 2: From Holland Codes to Occupations

From Holland Codes to the Dictionary of Occupational Titles Occupations

HOC	Cx	Title	DOT
RES	60	Supervisor, Horticultural-Specialty Farming (agriculture)	405.131-010
RES	60	Supervisor, Insulation (nonmet. min.)	590.130-014
RES	60	Supervisor, Jewelry Department (jewelry-silver.)	700.131-018
RES	60	Supervisor, Machine Setter (any industry)	619.130-034
RES	60	Supervisor, Natural-Gas Plant (petrol. refin.)	542.130-010
RES	60	Supervisor, Nutritional Yeast (food prep., n.e.c.)	529.132-078
RES	60	Supervisor, Picking Crew (agriculture)	409.131-010
RES	60	Supervisor, Pipe Joints (brick & tile)	590.134-010
RES	60	Supervisor, Press Room (print. & pub.)	651.130-010
RES	60	Supervisor, Printing-Shop (print. & pub.)	979.130-014
RES	60	Supervisor, Pumping Station (waterworks)	954.130-010
RES	60	Supervisor, Punch-and-Assembly Department (elec. equip.)	619.130-042
RES	60	Supervisor, Railroad Car Repair (railroad equip.)	622.131-010
RES	60	Supervisor, Roundhouse (railroad equip.)	622.131-014
RES	60	Supervisor, Specialty Food Products (can. & preserv.; meat products)	529.137-062
RES	60	Supervisor, Spinning (textile)	682.130-010
RES	60	Supervisor, Structural Rolling-and-Finishing (steel & rel.)	613.130-018
RES	60	Supervisor, Toy Assembly (toy-sport equip.)	731.131-010
RES	60	Supervisor, Wheel Shop (railroad equip.)	622.131-018
RES	60	Track-Laying Supervisor (construction)	869.134-022
RES	60	Weave-Room Supervisor (carpet & rug)	683.130-018
RES	60	Weaving Supervisor (nonmet. min.; textile)	683.130-022
RES	59	Accordion Maker (musical inst.)	730.281-010
RES	59	Air-Conditioning Installer-Servicer, Window Unit (construction)	637.261-010
RES	59	Alumina-Plant Supervisor (smelt. & refin.)	511.130-010
RES	59	Artificial-Glass-Eye Maker (optical goods)	713.261-010
RES	59	Audio Operator (radio-tv broad.)	194.262-010
RES	59	Automatic-Equipment Technician (tel. & tel.)	822.281-010
RES	59	Automotive-Tire-Testing Supervisor (ordnance)	736.131-010
RES	59	Bakery Supervisor (bakery products)	526.131-010
RES	59	Braid-Pattern Setter (narrow fabrics)	683.260-010
RES	59	Brush-Fabrication Supervisor (fabrication, n.e.c.)	692.130-010
RES	59	Cabin-Equipment Supervisor (air trans.)	869.131-010
RES	59	Cable Supervisor (construction; tel. & tel.; utilities)	829.131-010
RES	59	Carpenter-Labor Supervisor (construction)	860.137-010
RES	59	Chemical-Processing Supervisor (pharmaceut.)	559.130-010
RES	59	Chimney Supervisor, Brick (construction)	861.131-014
RES	59	Clearing Supervisor (construction)	869.133-010
RES	59	Cloth-Grader Supervisor (textile)	689.134-010
RES	59	Coal-Yard Supervisor (any industry)	921.137-010
RES	59	Composing-Room Machinist (print. & pub.)	627.261-010
RES	59	Concreting Supervisor (construction)	869.131-014
RES	59	Crusher Supervisor (smelt. & refin.)	515.132-010
RES	59	Dock Supervisor (ship-boat mfg.)	891.131-010
RES	59	Electric-Distribution Checker (construction; utilities)	824.281-014
RES	59	Electric-Meter Installer I (utilities)	821.361-014

HOC	Cx	Title	DOT
RES	59	Electrician Supervisor (any industry)	829.131-014
RES	59	Elevator-Constructor Supervisor (construction)	825.131-014
RES	59	Engineer (water trans.)	197.130-010
RES	59	Engraving Supervisor (engraving)	704.131-010
RES	59	Field Supervisor, Oil-Well Services (petrol. & gas)	930.131-010
RES	59	Field-Assembly Supervisor (mfd. bldgs.)	869.131-018
RES	59	Finishing Supervisor (elec. equip.)	692.130-014
RES	59	Finishing-Area Supervisor (plastic-synth.)	559.132-022
RES	59	Forge-Shop Supervisor (forging)	612.131-010
RES	59	Foundry Supervisor (foundry)	519.131-010
RES	59	Guide, Hunting and Fishing (amuse. & rec.)	353.161-010
RES	59	Heat-Treat Supervisor (heat treating)	504.131-010
RES	59	Inspection Supervisor I (ordnance)	736.131-018
RES	59	Installation Superintendent, Pin-Setting Machine (construction)	829.131-018
RES	59	Kitchen Steward/Stewardess (hotel & rest.)	318.137-010
RES	59	Labor-Crew Supervisor (construction; utilities)	899.131-010
RES	59	Laboratory Supervisor (machine shop)	706.131-010
RES	59	Lock Tender, Chief Operator (water trans.)	911.131-014
RES	59	Loft Worker (ship-boat mfg.)	661.281-010
RES	59	Loft Worker Apprentice (ship-boat mfg.)	661.281-014
RES	59	Machinist Apprentice, Composing Room (print. & pub.)	627.261-014
RES	59	Mains-and-Service Supervisor (utilities)	862.137-010
RES	59	Maintenance Inspector (tel. & tel.)	822.261-018
RES	59	Manufacturer's Service Representative (machinery mfg.; machine tools)	638.261-018
RES	59	Mechanical-Maintenance Supervisor (any industry)	638.131-026
RES	59	Mill-Labor Supervisor (smelt. & refin.)	519.131-014
RES	59	Mortician Investigator (government ser.)	168.267-078
RES	59	Nitroglycerin Supervisor (chemical)	559.132-038
RES	59	Oil-Field Equipment Mechanic Supervisor (petrol. & gas)	629.131-014
RES	59	Pattern-Shop Supervisor (foundry)	693.131-010
RES	59	Pipe-Fitter Supervisor (construction)	862.131-010
RES	59	Pipe-Organ Builder (musical inst.)	730.281-042
RES	59	Plumber Supervisor (construction)	862.131-018
RES	59	Pot-Lining Supervisor (smelt. & refin.)	519.134-010
RES	59	Pot-Room Supervisor (smelt. & refin.)	512.135-010
RES	59	Powder-and-Primer-Canning Leader (ordnance)	737.137-014
RES	59	Press-Hand Supervisor (jewelry-silver.)	615.130-010
RES	59	Process-Area Supervisor (plastic-synth.)	559.132-042
RES	59	Pump-Servicer Supervisor (any industry)	630.131-010
RES	59	Quality-Control Supervisor (plastic-synth.)	559.131-014
RES	59	Refrigeration Mechanic (any industry)	637.261-026
RES	59	Regulator Inspector (utilities)	820.361-018
RES	59	Rigging Supervisor (construction)	921.130-010
RES	59	Scale Assembly Set-up Worker (office machines)	710.360-010
RES	59	Screw Supervisor (clock & watch)	609.130-014
RES	59	Shipwright (ship-boat mfg.)	860.381-058
RES	59	Shipwright Apprentice (ship-boat mfg.)	860.381-062

HOC	Cx	Title	DOT
RES	59	Shop Supervisor (struct. metal)	619.131-014
RES	59	Stationary-Engineer Supervisor (any industry)	950.131-014
RES	59	Substation Operator, Chief (utilities)	952.131-010
RES	59	Supervisor (cutlery-hrdwr.)	615.130-014
RES	59	Supervisor (nut & bolt)	616.130-010
RES	59	Supervisor (nonfer. metal)	691.130-010
RES	59	Supervisor (jewelry-silver.)	700.130-010
RES	59	Supervisor (jewelry-silver.; plastic prod.)	700.131-010
RES	59	Supervisor (metal prod., n.e.c.)	700.131-014
RES	59	Supervisor (clock & watch)	715.131-010
RES	59	Supervisor (musical inst.)	730.131-010
RES	59	Supervisor I (button & notion)	692.130-018
RES	59	Supervisor II (nonmet. min.)	579.132-010
RES	59	Supervisor VI (tex. prod., n.e.c.)	589.132-010
RES	59	Supervisor, Adjustable-Steel-Joist-Setting (construction)	869.134-014
RES	59	Supervisor, Aluminum Fabrication (ship-boat mfg.)	619.130-014
RES	59	Supervisor, Assembly Department (struct. metal)	809.130-010
RES	59	Supervisor, Assembly Room (furniture)	669.130-010
RES	59	Supervisor, Assembly Room (fabrication, n.e.c.)	739.134-010
RES	59	Supervisor, Bindery (print. & pub.)	653.131-010
RES	59	Supervisor, Bit and Shank Department (fabrication, n.e.c.)	739.130-010
RES	59	Supervisor, Blast Furnace (smelt. & refin.)	512.132-022
RES	59	Supervisor, Bleach (chemical)	559.137-018
RES	59	Supervisor, Board Mill (concrete prod.)	579.130-010
RES	59	Supervisor, Boatbuilders, Wood (ship-boat mfg.)	860.131-014
RES	59	Supervisor, Boiler Repair (any industry)	805.137-010
RES	59	Supervisor, Brineyard (can. & preserv.)	522.134-010
RES	59	Supervisor, Canal-Equipment Maintenance (waterworks)	899.130-010
RES	59	Supervisor, Carton and Can Supply (beverage)	920.132-014
RES	59	Supervisor, Casting-and-Pasting (elec. equip.)	502.130-010
RES	59	Supervisor, Cell Operation (smelt. & refin.)	519.132-018
RES	59	Supervisor, Cereal (grain-feed mills)	529.132-030
RES	59	Supervisor, Clay Shop (pottery & porc.)	774.130-010
RES	59	Supervisor, Coating (photo. appar.)	534.130-010
RES	59	Supervisor, Concrete Block Plant (concrete prod.)	579.130-014
RES	59	Supervisor, Concrete Pipe Plant (concrete prod.)	579.130-018
RES	59	Supervisor, Concrete-Stone Finishing (concrete prod.)	775.131-010
RES	59	Supervisor, Continuous-Weld-Pipe Mill (steel & rel.)	619.130-022
RES	59	Supervisor, Curing Room (tobacco)	529.137-038
RES	59	Supervisor, Cutting-and-Sewing Department (furniture)	780.131-010
RES	59	Supervisor, Dairy Processing (dairy products)	529.131-014
RES	59	Supervisor, Die Casting (foundry; smelt. & refin.)	514.130-014
RES	59	Supervisor, Drawing (nonfer. metal; steel & rel.)	614.132-010
RES	59	Supervisor, Dry-Wall Application (construction)	842.131-010
RES	59	Supervisor, Engraving (pen & pencil)	704.131-014
RES	59	Supervisor, Erection Shop (railroad equip.)	806.131-022
RES	59	Supervisor, Esters-and-Emulsifiers (chemical)	559.132-086
RES	59	Supervisor, Extruding Department (plastic prod.)	557.130-010
RES	59	Supervisor, Extrusion (forging)	614.132-014

HOC	Cx	Title	DOT
RES	59	Supervisor, Fabrication and Assembly (toy-sport equip.)	809.131-010
RES	59	Supervisor, Fabrication Department (light. fix.)	723.132-010
RES	59	Supervisor, Fertilizer Processing (chemical)	559.130-014
RES	59	Supervisor, Forming Department I (glass mfg.)	575.130-018
RES	59	Supervisor, Fur Dressing (leather mfg.)	589.130-022
RES	59	Supervisor, Furnace Process (chemical)	559.132-094
RES	59	Supervisor, Gear Repair (water trans.)	623.131-014
RES	59	Supervisor, Glazing Department (textile)	582.130-010
RES	59	Supervisor, Green End Department (millwork-plywood)	663.132-010
RES	59	Supervisor, Hot-Strip Mill (steel & rel.)	613.132-010
RES	59	Supervisor, Insecticide (chemical)	559.132-102
RES	59	Supervisor, Instrument Assembly (electron. comp.; inst. & app.)	710.131-038
RES	59	Supervisor, Insulation (construction)	863.134-014
RES	59	Supervisor, Labor Gang (any industry)	899.133-010
RES	59	Supervisor, Landscape (museums; waterworks)	406.134-014
RES	59	Supervisor, Last-Model Department (wood prod., n.e.c.)	761.131-010
RES	59	Supervisor, Lathing (construction)	842.131-014
RES	59	Supervisor, Line Department (r.r. trans.)	825.137-010
RES	59	Supervisor, Liquefaction (chemical)	559.132-106
RES	59	Supervisor, Liquid Yeast (food prep., n.e.c.)	529.132-066
RES	59	Supervisor, Litharge (paint & varnish)	559.132-110
RES	59	Supervisor, Marble (construction)	861.131-022
RES	59	Supervisor, Melt House (sugar & conf.)	522.130-010
RES	59	Supervisor, Metal Cans (tinware)	703.132-010
RES	59	Supervisor, Mill House (grain-feed mills)	529.132-074
RES	59	Supervisor, Mold Yard (steel & rel.)	519.137-010
RES	59	Supervisor, Packing (boot & shoe)	788.137-010
RES	59	Supervisor, Paint Roller Covers (fabrication, n.e.c.)	692.130-030
RES	59	Supervisor, Paper Machine (paper & pulp)	539.132-010
RES	59	Supervisor, Pile Driving (construction)	859.137-014
RES	59	Supervisor, Plastics (toy-sport equip.)	556.130-014
RES	59	Supervisor, Plate Heating, Rolling, and Finishing (steel & rel.)	619.132-030
RES	59	Supervisor, Plating and Point Assembly (pen & pencil)	733.130-010
RES	59	Supervisor, Precast and Prestressed Concrete (concrete prod.)	575.131-014
RES	59	Supervisor, Processing (chemical)	551.130-010
RES	59	Supervisor, Record Press (recording)	559.130-018
RES	59	Supervisor, Refining (chemical)	559.132-126
RES	59	Supervisor, Reinforced-Steel-Placing (construction)	801.134-010
RES	59	Supervisor, Reverberatory Furnace (smelt. & refin.)	519.130-022
RES	59	Supervisor, Rice Milling (grain-feed mills)	521.131-010
RES	59	Supervisor, Right-of-Way Maintenance (utilities)	859.133-010
RES	59	Supervisor, Roll Shop (steel & rel.)	604.130-010
RES	59	Supervisor, Roving Department (textile)	689.130-026
RES	59	Supervisor, Sandblaster (ship-boat mfg.)	503.137-010
RES	59	Supervisor, Sheet Manufacturing (smelt. & refin.)	500.132-010
RES	59	Supervisor, Shipfitters (ship-boat mfg.)	806.131-034

Part 2: From Holland Codes to Occupations

From Holland Codes to the Dictionary of Occupational Titles Occupations

HOC	Cx	Title	DOT
RES	59	Supervisor, Shop (petrol. & gas)	710.131-034
RES	59	Supervisor, Sintering Plant (smelt. & refin.)	519.130-026
RES	59	Supervisor, Slitting-and-Shipping (plastic-synth.)	690.130-014
RES	59	Supervisor, Spinning and Winding (plastic-synth.)	689.130-038
RES	59	Supervisor, Spring Production (metal prod., n.e.c.)	616.130-018
RES	59	Supervisor, Spring-Up (furniture)	780.134-014
RES	59	Supervisor, Steel Division (furniture)	616.130-022
RES	59	Supervisor, Structural-Steel Erection (construction)	809.131-018
RES	59	Supervisor, Tank Cleaning (water trans.)	891.137-018
RES	59	Supervisor, Tea and Spice (food prep., n.e.c.)	529.132-102
RES	59	Supervisor, Terrazzo (construction)	861.131-026
RES	59	Supervisor, Thermostatic Controls (inst. & app.)	710.131-042
RES	59	Supervisor, Tumbling and Rolling (clock & watch)	715.131-030
RES	59	Supervisor, Uranium Processing (smelt. & refin.)	519.130-030
RES	59	Supervisor, Vat House (chemical; leather mfg.)	582.132-022
RES	59	Supervisor, Webbing (tex. prod., n.e.c.)	789.137-014
RES	59	Supervisor, Winding and Twisting Department (textile)	681.130-014
RES	59	Supervisor, Wire-Rope Fabrication (metal prod., n.e.c.)	691.130-014
RES	59	Tapper Supervisor (smelt. & refin.)	514.134-010
RES	59	Utilities-and-Maintenance Supervisor (any industry)	899.131-018
RES	59	Violin Maker, Hand (musical inst.)	730.281-046
RES	59	Water-and-Sewer-Systems Supervisor (waterworks)	862.137-018
RES	59	Well Puller, Head (petrol. & gas)	939.131-018
RES	59	Yard Supervisor (woodworking)	929.133-010
RES	58	Animal Breeder (agriculture)	410.161-010
RES	58	Animal Trainer (amuse. & rec.)	159.224-010
RES	58	Automotive-Tire Tester (ordnance)	736.367-010
RES	58	Beekeeper (agriculture)	413.161-010
RES	58	Cash-Register Servicer (any industry)	633.281-010
RES	58	Cheesemaker (dairy products)	529.361-018
RES	58	Crane-Crew Supervisor (any industry)	921.133-010
RES	58	Dictating-Transcribing-Machine Servicer (any industry)	633.281-014
RES	58	Diver (any industry)	899.261-010
RES	58	Electrician (water trans.)	825.281-014
RES	58	Farm-Equipment Mechanic I (agric. equip.)	624.281-010
RES	58	Farm-Equipment-Mechanic Apprentice (agric. equip.)	624.281-014
RES	58	Field Service Technician, Poultry (agriculture)	411.267-010
RES	58	Forge-Shop-Machine Repairer (forging)	626.261-010
RES	58	Gasket Supervisor (wood prod., n.e.c.)	569.130-010
RES	58	Glaze Supervisor (pottery & porc.)	574.132-010
RES	58	Glued Wood Tester (woodworking)	762.384-010
RES	58	Greenskeeper I (any industry)	406.137-010
RES	58	Hearing-Aid Repairer (inst. & app.)	719.381-014
RES	58	Heating-and-Air-Conditioning Installer-Servicer (construction)	637.261-014
RES	58	Inspection Supervisor II (ordnance)	737.134-010
RES	58	Line Repairer (utilities)	821.361-026
RES	58	Locomotive Inspector (railroad equip.)	622.281-010
RES	58	Material-Handling Supervisor (any industry)	921.133-018

HOC	Cx	Title	DOT
RES	58	Mechanic, Industrial Truck (any industry)	620.281-050
RES	58	Mechanical-Test Technician (inst. & app.)	869.261-014
RES	58	Metal-Control Coordinator (nonfer. metal)	222.167-010
RES	58	Mold Maker I (jewelry-silver.)	700.381-034
RES	58	Mold-Maker Apprentice (jewelry-silver.)	700.381-038
RES	58	Motorboat Mechanic (engine-turbine; ship-boat mfg.)	623.281-038
RES	58	Office-Machine Servicer (any industry)	633.281-018
RES	58	Office-Machine-Servicer Apprentice (any industry)	633.281-022
RES	58	Orthodontic Band Maker (protective dev.)	712.381-026
RES	58	Patternmaker (metal prod., n.e.c.)	693.281-014
RES	58	Pipeline Construction Inspector (construction)	869.367-018
RES	58	Press Supervisor (brick & tile)	575.130-010
RES	58	Reclamation Supervisor (nonfer. metal)	512.132-014
RES	58	Remelt-Furnace Expediter (nonfer. metal)	512.132-018
RES	58	Roofing Supervisor (construction)	866.131-010
RES	58	Salesperson, Electric Motors (retail trade; wholesale tr.)	271.354-010
RES	58	Scale Mechanic (any industry)	633.281-026
RES	58	Scanner Operator (print. & pub.)	972.282-010
RES	58	Shell-Shop Supervisor (ordnance)	619.132-018
RES	58	Statistical-Machine Servicer (any industry)	633.281-030
RES	58	Supervisor (rubber reclaim.)	559.132-058
RES	58	Supervisor (toy-sport equip.)	732.130-010
RES	58	Supervisor II (fabrication, n.e.c.)	739.131-014
RES	58	Supervisor II (tex. prod., n.e.c.)	789.134-010
RES	58	Supervisor VI (nonmet. min.)	692.130-022
RES	58	Supervisor, Blast-Furnace-Auxiliaries (steel & rel.)	519.132-014
RES	58	Supervisor, Brew House (beverage)	529.132-026
RES	58	Supervisor, Cleaning (beverage; can. & preserv.; dairy products; food prep., n.e.c.)	699.137-010
RES	58	Supervisor, Concrete-Stone Fabricating (concrete prod.)	575.131-010
RES	58	Supervisor, Cook Room (can. & preserv.)	529.132-038
RES	58	Supervisor, Cooperage Shop (wood. container)	764.134-010
RES	58	Supervisor, Fabrication (wood prod., n.e.c.)	769.130-010
RES	58	Supervisor, Feed House (grain-feed mills)	529.132-050
RES	58	Supervisor, Felling-Bucking (logging)	454.134-010
RES	58	Supervisor, Fertilizer (chemical)	559.132-090
RES	58	Supervisor, Filtration (sugar & conf.)	529.130-022
RES	58	Supervisor, Fish Hatchery (fishing & hunt.)	446.134-010
RES	58	Supervisor, Line (any industry)	619.130-030
RES	58	Supervisor, Lump Room (tobacco)	520.137-010
RES	58	Supervisor, Matrix (recording)	500.134-010
RES	58	Supervisor, Mill (tex. prod., n.e.c.)	589.130-026
RES	58	Supervisor, Nut Processing (can. & preserv.)	529.130-026
RES	58	Supervisor, Packing (sugar & conf.)	920.130-010
RES	58	Supervisor, Paste Mixing (chemical)	550.137-014
RES	58	Supervisor, Pleating (tex. prod., n.e.c.)	583.137-010
RES	58	Supervisor, Refining (sugar & conf.)	529.130-034
RES	58	Supervisor, Rocket Propellant Plant (ordnance)	559.137-046
RES	58	Supervisor, Scrap Preparation (steel & rel.)	519.137-014

HOC	Cx	Title	DOT
RES	58	Supervisor, Soft Sugar (sugar & conf.)	529.130-038
RES	58	Supervisor, Solder Making (nonfer. metal)	519.132-022
RES	58	Supervisor, Sugar Refinery (grain-feed mills)	529.132-094
RES	58	Supervisor, Tank Storage (beverage)	529.132-098
RES	58	Supervisor, Tile-and-Mottle (fabrication, n.e.c.)	559.130-022
RES	58	Supervisor, Wash House (beverage)	529.132-106
RES	58	Supervisor, Weaving (carpet & rug)	689.130-030
RES	58	Supervisor, Whipped Topping (dairy products)	529.137-066
RES	58	Supervisor, White Sugar (sugar & conf.)	529.130-042
RES	58	Supervisor, Wood Room (paper & pulp)	530.132-018
RES	58	Testing-and-Regulating Technician (tel. & tel.)	822.261-026
RES	58	Tool Pusher (petrol. & gas)	930.130-010
RES	57	Anode-Crew Supervisor (smelt. & refin.)	630.134-010
RES	57	Baker, Head (hotel & rest.)	313.131-010
RES	57	Boat Repairer (ship-boat mfg.)	807.361-014
RES	57	Boilerhouse Mechanic (any industry)	805.361-010
RES	57	Box Tender (plastic-synth.)	689.280-010
RES	57	Car Repairer (railroad equip.)	622.381-014
RES	57	Car-Repairer Apprentice (railroad equip.)	622.381-022
RES	57	Chocolate-Production-Machine Operator (sugar & conf.)	529.382-014
RES	57	Clothing-Pattern Preparer (garment)	781.287-010
RES	57	Controller Repairer-and-Tester (railroad equip.)	825.381-018
RES	57	Dredge Operator Supervisor (mine & quarry)	939.132-010
RES	57	Electrical Inspector (aircraft mfg.; air trans.)	825.381-026
RES	57	Fixture Maker (light. fix.)	600.380-010
RES	57	Forming-Machine Upkeep Mechanic (glass mfg.)	575.380-010
RES	57	Gas-Meter Prover (utilities)	710.281-022
RES	57	House Builder (construction)	869.281-014
RES	57	Inspector, Motors and Generators (elec. equip.)	721.361-010
RES	57	Maintenance Repairer, Building (any industry)	899.381-010
RES	57	Mechanical-Unit Repairer (automotive ser.; railroad equip.)	620.381-018
RES	57	Motor-Room Controller (utilities)	820.662-010
RES	57	Pipe-Organ Installer (musical inst.)	730.381-046
RES	57	Protective-Signal Repairer (business ser.)	822.361-022
RES	57	Public-Address Servicer (any industry)	823.261-010
RES	57	Railroad Wheels and Axle Inspector (railroad equip.)	622.381-034
RES	57	Refinery Operator (grain-feed mills)	521.362-018
RES	57	Refrigeration Mechanic (svc. ind. mach.)	827.361-014
RES	57	Repairer (mine & quarry)	630.281-022
RES	57	Rotary-Rig Engine Operator (petrol. & gas)	950.382-022
RES	57	Sail-Lay-Out Worker (tex. prod., n.e.c.)	781.381-030
RES	57	Sewing-Machine Repairer (any industry)	639.281-018
RES	57	Shop Estimator (automotive ser.)	807.267-010
RES	57	Spring Repairer, Hand (automotive ser.)	619.380-018
RES	57	Supervisor, Alteration Workroom (retail trade)	785.131-010
RES	57	Supervisor, Assembly Stock (clerical)	222.137-042
RES	57	Supervisor, Field-Crop Farming (agriculture)	404.131-010
RES	57	Supervisor, Open-Hearth Stockyard (steel & rel.)	922.137-022
RES	57	Supervisor, Pig-Machine (steel & rel.)	514.137-010

HOC	Cx	Title	DOT
RES	57	Supervisor, Quilting (textile)	689.134-022
RES	57	Well-Point Pumping Supervisor (construction)	862.132-010
RES	56	Acoustical Carpenter (construction)	860.381-010
RES	56	Automobile Racer (amuse. & rec.)	153.243-010
RES	56	Boatswain (water trans.)	911.131-010
RES	56	Brake Repairer (automotive ser.)	620.281-026
RES	56	Card Clothier (textile)	628.381-010
RES	56	Carpenter, Railcar (railroad equip.)	860.381-038
RES	56	Casting Repairer (any industry)	619.281-010
RES	56	CD-Reactor Operator, Head (chemical)	558.362-014
RES	56	Chain Maker, Hand (jewelry-silver.)	700.381-010
RES	56	Cocoa-Bean Roaster II (sugar & conf.)	523.380-010
RES	56	Compounder (petrol. refin.)	540.382-010
RES	56	Door-Closer Mechanic (any industry)	630.381-014
RES	56	Drier Operator (food prep., n.e.c.)	523.362-014
RES	56	Electric-Motor Fitter (railroad equip.)	721.381-010
RES	56	Electrical-Equipment Tester (aircraft mfg.)	729.381-010
RES	56	Former, Hand (any industry)	619.361-010
RES	56	Furnace Installer (utilities)	862.361-010
RES	56	Gas-Welding-Equipment Mechanic (any industry)	626.381-014
RES	56	Gem Cutter (jewelry-silver.)	770.281-014
RES	56	Inspector (hotel & rest.)	321.137-014
RES	56	Inspector I (nonfer. metal)	619.364-010
RES	56	Line Erector (construction; utilities)	821.361-018
RES	56	Line-Erector Apprentice (construction; utilities)	821.361-030
RES	56	Loom Setter, Wire Weaving (metal prod., n.e.c.)	616.360-014
RES	56	Machine Assembler (machinery mfg.)	638.361-010
RES	56	Mechanic, Endless Track Vehicle (automotive ser.)	620.381-014
RES	56	Milling-Machine Set-up Operator, Numerical Control (machine shop)	605.380-010
RES	56	MVA-Reactor Operator, Head (chemical)	559.362-022
RES	56	Oil Pumper (petrol. & gas)	914.382-010
RES	56	Packaging Technician (paper goods)	739.281-010
RES	56	Paster Supervisor (brick & tile)	773.131-010
RES	56	Pipe Fitter, Diesel Engine II (engine-turbine)	862.381-022
RES	56	Pneumatic-Tube Repairer (any industry)	630.281-014
RES	56	Pumper, Head (petrol. & gas)	914.382-022
RES	56	Recording Engineer (radio-tv broad.; recording)	194.362-010
RES	56	Retoucher, Photoengraving (print. & pub.)	970.381-030
RES	56	Rigger (ship-boat mfg.)	806.261-014
RES	56	Rigger Apprentice (ship-boat mfg.)	806.261-018
RES	56	Rougher (steel & rel.)	613.362-018
RES	56	Section Leader and Machine Setter, Polishing (textile)	689.260-022
RES	56	Slab-Conditioner Supervisor (nonfer. metal)	609.132-010
RES	56	Soaping-Department Supervisor (textile)	582.132-014
RES	56	Street-Light Servicer (utilities)	824.381-010
RES	56	Supervisor (sugar & conf.)	920.137-018
RES	56	Supervisor III (button & notion)	690.130-010
RES	56	Supervisor IV (tex. prod., n.e.c.)	789.132-010

HOC	Cx	Title	DOT
RES	56	Supervisor, Abattoir (meat products)	525.131-010
RES	56	Supervisor, Cellars (beverage)	914.132-018
RES	56	Supervisor, Cemetery Workers (real estate)	406.134-010
RES	56	Supervisor, Conditioning Yard (steel & rel.)	619.134-010
RES	56	Supervisor, Cured Meats (meat products)	525.132-010
RES	56	Supervisor, Harvesting (chemical)	939.137-022
RES	56	Supervisor, Log Sorting (logging; millwork-plywood)	455.134-010
RES	56	Supervisor, Maintenance (chemical)	382.137-010
RES	56	Supervisor, Mirror Fabrication (glass products)	679.137-014
RES	56	Supervisor, Pit-and-Auxiliaries (steel & rel.)	514.137-014
RES	56	Supervisor, Poultry Farm (agriculture)	411.131-010
RES	56	Supervisor, Printing and Stamping (jewelry-silver.; leather prod.)	652.130-014
RES	56	Supervisor, Shuttle Fitting (woodworking)	669.130-030
RES	56	Supervisor, Shuttle Preparation (woodworking)	669.130-034
RES	56	Supervisor, Tank House (meat products)	525.132-014
RES	56	Supervisor, Vegetable Farming (agriculture)	402.131-010
RES	56	Supervisor, Vine-Fruit Farming (agriculture)	403.131-014
RES	56	Treating Engineer (wood prod., n.e.c.)	561.362-010
RES	55	Air-Conditioning Mechanic (automotive ser.)	620.281-010
RES	55	Assembler and Wirer, Industrial Equipment (elec. equip.; machinery mfg.)	826.361-010
RES	55	Bindery-Machine Setter (print. & pub.)	653.360-018
RES	55	Cargo Agent (air trans.)	248.367-018
RES	55	Carpenter, Bridge (r.r. trans.)	860.381-030
RES	55	Concentrator Operator (smelt. & refin.)	511.462-010
RES	55	Dry-Starch Operator (grain-feed mills)	520.362-014
RES	55	Embossing Toolsetter (ordnance)	616.260-010
RES	55	Finishing Supervisor, Plastic Sheets (plastic-synth.)	554.137-010
RES	55	Fitter (machine shop)	801.381-014
RES	55	Fur Dresser (leather mfg.)	589.361-010
RES	55	Hook Tender (logging)	921.131-010
RES	55	In-Flight Refueling Operator (military ser.)	912.662-010
RES	55	Incoming-Freight Clerk (water trans.)	248.362-010
RES	55	Inspector, Wire (metal prod., n.e.c.; nonfer. metal)	691.367-010
RES	55	Irrigator, Head (agriculture)	409.137-010
RES	55	Jockey (amuse. & rec.)	153.244-010
RES	55	Joiner (ship-boat mfg.)	860.381-050
RES	55	Joiner Apprentice (ship-boat mfg.)	860.381-054
RES	55	Line-Up Examiner (print. & pub.)	979.381-014
RES	55	Locomotive Engineer (r.r. trans.)	910.363-014
RES	55	Machine Fixer (textile)	689.260-010
RES	55	Organ-Pipe Voicer (musical inst.)	730.381-038
RES	55	Repairer I (chemical)	630.261-018
RES	55	Rug Dyer I (laundry & rel.)	364.361-014
RES	55	Sheet-Mill Supervisor (nonfer. metal)	619.132-014
RES	55	Smoke Jumper Supervisor (forestry)	452.134-010
RES	55	Sorting Supervisor (brick & tile)	920.137-014
RES	55	Supervisor, Fish Processing (can. & preserv.)	525.134-010

HOC	Cx	Title	DOT
RES	55	Supervisor, Laundry (laundry & rel.)	361.137-010
RES	55	Supervisor, Mattress and Boxsprings (furniture)	780.137-010
RES	55	Supervisor, Mold Cleaning and Storage (glass mfg.)	579.137-018
RES	55	Supervisor, Pipe Manufacture (fabrication, n.e.c.)	739.137-018
RES	55	Supervisor, Poultry Processing (meat products)	525.134-014
RES	55	Supervisor, Riprap Placing (construction)	850.137-018
RES	55	Supervisor, Shellfish Farming (fishing & hunt.)	446.133-010
RES	55	Supervisor, Stock Ranch (agriculture)	410.131-022
RES	55	Tower Erector (construction; utilities)	821.361-038
RES	55	Welder Apprentice, Combination (welding)	819.384-014
RES	55	Welder, Combination (welding)	819.384-010
RES	54	Automobile Upholsterer (automotive ser.)	780.381-010
RES	54	Automobile-Upholsterer Apprentice (automotive ser.)	780.381-014
RES	54	Blender (petrol. refin.)	540.462-010
RES	54	Boilermaker II (struct. metal)	805.381-010
RES	54	Camp Tender (agriculture)	410.137-010
RES	54	Circulating Process Inspector (elec. equip.)	829.361-018
RES	54	Coating-Machine Operator (galvanizing)	501.362-010
RES	54	Digester Operator (paper & pulp; paper goods)	532.362-010
RES	54	Drapery and Upholstery Measurer (retail trade)	299.364-010
RES	54	Dry-Starch Operator, Automatic (grain-feed mills)	529.362-014
RES	54	Electronics Utility Worker (comm. equip.; electron. comp.)	726.364-018
RES	54	Energy-Conservation Representative (utilities)	959.367-018
RES	54	Fire Fighter (any industry)	373.364-010
RES	54	Instructor, Weaving (textile)	683.222-010
RES	54	Lift-Slab Operator (construction)	869.662-010
RES	54	Maintenance Mechanic (grain-feed mills)	629.281-030
RES	54	Material Inspector (wood. container)	764.387-014
RES	54	Nail-Making-Machine Setter (steel & rel.)	616.460-010
RES	54	Oven-Equipment Repairer (steel & rel.)	630.261-014
RES	54	Painter Apprentice, Shipyard (ship-boat mfg.)	840.381-014
RES	54	Painter, Shipyard (ship-boat mfg.)	840.381-018
RES	54	Plant Operator, Furnace Process (chemical)	559.362-026
RES	54	Service-Unit Operator, Oil Well (petrol. & gas)	930.361-010
RES	54	Sizer, Machine (optical goods)	716.360-010
RES	54	Slipcover Cutter (retail trade; tex. prod., n.e.c.)	780.381-034
RES	54	Spray-Gun Repairer (any industry)	630.381-026
RES	54	Storekeeper (water trans.)	222.387-062
RES	54	Supervisor III (nonmet. min.)	575.130-014
RES	54	Supervisor, Corncob Pipe Manufacturing (fabrication, n.e.c.)	739.132-010
RES	54	Violin Repairer (any industry)	730.281-050
RES	54	Wire Weaver, Cloth (metal prod., n.e.c.)	616.382-014
RES	53	Assembler, Metal Building (construction)	801.381-010
RES	53	Automobile-Body Customizer (automotive ser.)	807.361-010
RES	53	Bell Maker (musical inst.)	730.381-014
RES	53	Coal Pipeline Operator (pipe lines)	914.362-010
RES	53	Color Maker (chemical)	550.382-010
RES	53	Cook, Railroad (r.r. trans.)	315.381-018

HOC	Cx	Title	DOT
RES	53	Corset Fitter (retail trade)	782.361-010
RES	53	Dial Maker (clock & watch)	715.381-046
RES	53	Die Polisher (nonfer. metal)	601.381-018
RES	53	Floor Layer (construction; retail trade)	864.481-010
RES	53	Floor-Layer Apprentice (construction; retail trade)	864.481-014
RES	53	Gas-Meter Installer (utilities)	953.364-010
RES	53	Harness Maker (leather prod.; retail trade)	783.381-018
RES	53	Inspector IV (ordnance)	559.387-010
RES	53	Lead Operator, Automatic Vulcanizing (rubber goods)	690.362-010
RES	53	Motorcycle Racer (amuse. & rec.)	153.243-014
RES	53	Panel-Machine Setter (paper goods)	640.360-010
RES	53	Perforator Operator, Oil Well (petrol. & gas)	931.382-010
RES	53	Pipe Installer (construction; utilities)	869.381-018
RES	53	Power Operator (tel. & tel.)	952.382-014
RES	53	Prescription Clerk, Lens-and-Frames (optical goods)	222.367-050
RES	53	Rope-Machine Setter (tex. prod., n.e.c.)	681.380-010
RES	53	Rubber Tester (rubber goods; rubber tire)	559.381-014
RES	53	Rug Repairer (laundry & rel.)	782.381-018
RES	53	Service Mechanic (auto. mfg.)	807.381-022
RES	53	Set-up Mechanic, Crown Assembly Machine (any industry)	692.362-010
RES	53	Soft-Tile Setter (construction; retail trade)	861.381-034
RES	53	Sorter-Pricer (nonprofit org.)	222.387-054
RES	53	Souvenir and Novelty Maker (metal prod., n.e.c.)	739.381-050
RES	53	Spotter (machine tools)	770.381-042
RES	53	Stencil Maker (carpet & rug)	979.381-038
RES	53	Sugar Boiler (sugar & conf.)	522.382-034
RES	53	Supervisor, Edging (glass products)	673.130-010
RES	53	Swaging-Machine Adjuster (ordnance)	617.360-014
RES	53	Syrup Mixer (grain-feed mills)	529.462-010
RES	53	Test Driver I (auto. mfg.)	806.283-014
RES	53	Tool-Crib Attendant (clerical)	222.367-062
RES	53	Transmission Mechanic (automotive ser.)	620.281-062
RES	53	Trawl Net Maker (tex. prod., n.e.c.)	789.381-018
RES	53	Wardrobe Supervisor (amuse. & rec.)	346.361-010
RES	53	Welder-Assembler (machinery mfg.)	819.381-010
RES	53	Welding-Machine Operator, Resistance (welding)	812.682-010
RES	52	Air-Conditioning-Unit Tester (svc. ind. mach.)	827.361-010
RES	52	Airplane Coverer (aircraft mfg.; air trans.)	849.381-010
RES	52	Airport Attendant (air trans.)	912.364-010
RES	52	Arch-Cushion-Press Operator (rubber goods)	556.362-010
RES	52	Assembler, Metal Bonding (aircraft mfg.)	806.384-030
RES	52	Automobile-Seat-Cover-and-Convertible-Top Installer (automotive ser.)	780.384-010
RES	52	Auxiliary-Equipment Operator (utilities)	952.362-010
RES	52	Bench Hand (bakery products)	520.384-010
RES	52	Blocker I (print. & pub.)	979.682-010
RES	52	Bookbinder (print. & pub.)	977.381-010
RES	52	Bookbinder Apprentice (print. & pub.)	977.381-014

HOC	Cx	Title	DOT
RES	52	Brush-Machine Setter (fabrication, n.e.c.)	692.360-014
RES	52	Butcher Apprentice (meat products)	525.381-010
RES	52	Butcher, All-Round (meat products)	525.381-014
RES	52	Car-Wash Supervisor (automotive ser.)	915.137-010
RES	52	Cement Mason (construction)	844.364-010
RES	52	Cement-Mason Apprentice (construction)	844.364-014
RES	52	Clamper (print. & pub.)	979.382-010
RES	52	Conveyor-Maintenance Mechanic (any industry)	630.381-010
RES	52	Cook (any industry)	315.361-010
RES	52	Diver (amuse. & rec.)	349.247-010
RES	52	Feed-Research Aide (agriculture)	049.364-010
RES	52	Finisher (steel & rel.)	613.382-014
RES	52	Fur Cutter (fur goods)	783.381-010
RES	52	Golf-Club Head Former (toy-sport equip.)	732.381-018
RES	52	Golf-Club Repairer (toy-sport equip.)	732.381-022
RES	52	Heater I (steel & rel.)	613.362-010
RES	52	Hydrometer Calibrator (inst. & app.)	710.381-030
RES	52	Laundry-Machine Mechanic (laundry & rel.)	629.261-010
RES	52	Nickel-Plant Operator (smelt. & refin.)	519.362-010
RES	52	Oil-Burner-Servicer-and-Installer (any industry)	862.281-018
RES	52	Plasterer (construction)	842.361-018
RES	52	Plasterer Apprentice (construction)	842.361-022
RES	52	Pneumatic-Tool Operator (ship-boat mfg.)	809.381-030
RES	52	Pump Installer (any industry)	630.684-018
RES	52	Railroad-Car Inspector (r.r. trans.)	910.387-014
RES	52	Recorder (steel & rel.)	221.367-050
RES	52	Reed Maker (machinery mfg.)	709.381-038
RES	52	Ring Maker (jewelry-silver.)	700.381-042
RES	52	Rodeo Performer (amuse. & rec.)	159.344-014
RES	52	Second Cook and Baker (water trans.)	315.381-026
RES	52	Sewing-Machine Assembler (machinery mfg.)	706.381-034
RES	52	Shooter (petrol. & gas)	931.361-014
RES	52	Tank-House Operator (smelt. & refin.)	519.362-014
RES	52	Tester, Electronic Scale (office machines)	710.381-046
RES	52	Timber Framer (mine & quarry)	869.381-034
RES	52	Upholsterer, Limousine and Hearse (auto. mfg.)	780.381-026
RES	52	Wirer (office machines)	729.281-042
RES	51	Assembler II (office machines)	710.381-010
RES	51	Assembly Repairer (agric. equip.)	624.381-010
RES	51	Auger Press Operator, Manual Control (brick & tile)	575.462-010
RES	51	Automated Cutting Machine Operator (aircraft mfg.)	699.362-010
RES	51	Automobile-Service-Station Attendant (automotive ser.)	915.467-010
RES	51	Battery Inspector (railroad equip.; r.r. trans.)	829.684-010
RES	51	Boat-Rental Clerk (amuse. & rec.)	295.467-014
RES	51	Case-Finishing-Machine Adjuster (ordnance)	626.381-010
RES	51	Chemical Mixer (photofinishing)	550.485-010
RES	51	Coal Washer (mine & quarry)	541.382-010
RES	51	Cottage-Cheese Maker (dairy products)	522.382-010
RES	51	Deep Submergence Vehicle Operator (military ser.)	911.263-010

HOC	Cx	Title	DOT
RES	51	Electric-Motor Winder (elec. equip.)	721.484-010
RES	51	Field-Ring Assembler (elec. equip.)	721.484-014
RES	51	Forming-Process Worker (elec. equip.)	590.362-010
RES	51	Fur-Repair Inspector (retail trade)	783.387-010
RES	51	Furnace Operator (chemical)	558.482-010
RES	51	Gas-Leak Inspector (pipe lines; utilities)	953.367-010
RES	51	Glass-Ribbon-Machine-Operator Assistant (glass mfg.)	575.365-010
RES	51	Grinder Set-up Operator, Centerless (machine shop)	603.382-014
RES	51	Gun-Repair Clerk (ordnance)	222.387-022
RES	51	Lapper, Hand, Tool (machine shop)	705.481-014
RES	51	Load-Test Mechanic (aircraft mfg.)	929.382-010
RES	51	Lock Assembler (furniture)	706.684-070
RES	51	Maple-Syrup Maker (food prep., n.e.c.)	523.382-014
RES	51	Masseur/Masseuse (personal ser.)	334.374-010
RES	51	Monomer-Purification Operator (chemical)	552.362-010
RES	51	Optical-Element Coater (optical goods)	716.382-014
RES	51	Poultry Tender (agriculture)	411.364-014
RES	51	Repairer, Handtools (cutlery-hrdwr.)	701.381-010
RES	51	Sampler, First (smelt. & refin.)	619.682-038
RES	51	Shoe-Repair Supervisor (personal ser.)	365.131-010
RES	51	Sterile-Products Processor (pharmaceut.)	559.682-054
RES	51	Trim-Machine Adjuster (ordnance)	609.280-010
RES	51	Tunnel-Kiln Operator (brick & tile)	573.382-018
RES	51	Utility Worker, Line Assembly (auto. mfg.)	806.367-010
RES	51	Wool-Fleece Grader (agriculture)	589.687-054
RES	50	Ager Operator (plastic-synth.)	553.482-010
RES	50	Alodize-Machine Operator (nonfer. metal)	509.462-010
RES	50	Assistant-Press Operator (print. & pub.)	651.585-010
RES	50	Back Tender, Paper Machine (paper & pulp)	534.662-010
RES	50	Beater Engineer (paper & pulp; tex. prod., n.e.c.)	530.662-010
RES	50	Beveler (stonework)	771.484-010
RES	50	Bus Driver (motor trans.)	913.463-010
RES	50	Coating-and-Embossing-Unit Operator (tex. prod., n.e.c.; textile)	583.682-010
RES	50	Coke Loader (steel & rel.)	921.563-010
RES	50	Compo Caster (wood prod., n.e.c.)	769.381-010
RES	50	Controls Operator, Molded Goods (fabrication, n.e.c.)	590.662-010
RES	50	Cook, Mess (water trans.)	315.371-010
RES	50	Cook, Third (water trans.)	315.381-022
RES	50	Denture-Model Maker (protective dev.)	712.684-046
RES	50	Drapery Hanger (retail trade)	869.484-014
RES	50	Driller-and-Reamer, Automatic (musical inst.)	606.382-010
RES	50	Electric-Organ Assembler and Checker (musical inst.)	730.381-022
RES	50	Engraver I (print. & pub.)	979.381-010
RES	50	Fabricator, Shower Doors and Panels (struct. metal)	739.381-030
RES	50	Ferryboat Operator (water trans.)	911.363-010
RES	50	Final Inspector (musical inst.)	730.367-010
RES	50	Fire Fighter, Crash, Fire, and Rescue (air trans.)	373.663-010
RES	50	Flatware Maker (jewelry-silver.)	700.682-010

Dictionary of Holland Occupational Codes

From Holland Codes to the Dictionary of Occupational Titles Occupations

HOC	Cx	Title	DOT
RES	50	Foundation Maker (fabrication, n.e.c.)	739.384-014
RES	50	Fur Finisher (fur goods)	783.381-014
RES	50	Furnace Operator (petrol. refin.)	542.562-010
RES	50	Gelatin Maker, Utility (chemical)	529.382-022
RES	50	Hairspring Truer (clock & watch)	715.381-058
RES	50	Hairspring Vibrator (clock & watch)	715.381-062
RES	50	Hammersmith (jewelry-silver.)	700.381-022
RES	50	Horse-Race Timer (amuse. & rec.)	153.367-014
RES	50	Inspector and Sorter (leather mfg.)	589.387-010
RES	50	Installer (mfd. bldgs.; vehicles, n.e.c.)	869.684-026
RES	50	Locket Maker (jewelry-silver.)	700.381-030
RES	50	Lubrication-Equipment Servicer (any industry)	630.381-022
RES	50	Meat Dresser (agriculture)	525.664-010
RES	50	Microphone-Boom Operator (motion picture; radio-tv broad.)	962.384-010
RES	50	Mold Stamper (machine shop)	709.684-054
RES	50	Nut Former (nut & bolt)	612.462-014
RES	50	Pearl Restorer (jewelry-silver.)	735.381-014
RES	50	Pipe-and-Tank Fabricator (wood. container)	669.380-018
RES	50	Plate Grainer (print. & pub.)	972.682-010
RES	50	Plate-Grainer Apprentice (print. & pub.)	972.682-014
RES	50	Register Repairer (r.r. trans.)	710.681-018
RES	50	Rigging Slinger (logging)	921.364-010
RES	50	Roll-Tube Setter (steel & rel.)	613.360-014
RES	50	Roller Engraver, Hand (print. & pub.)	979.681-018
RES	50	Rug Measurer (laundry & rel.; retail trade)	369.367-014
RES	50	Sawyer, Optical Glass (optical goods)	677.382-014
RES	50	Ski Maker, Wood (toy-sport equip.)	761.381-026
RES	50	Slasher Tender (textile)	582.562-010
RES	50	Soft-Sugar Operator, Head (sugar & conf.)	521.565-018
RES	50	Spring Former, Hand (metal prod., n.e.c.)	709.381-042
RES	50	Stroboscope Operator (textile)	689.364-010
RES	50	Threading-Machine Operator (machine shop)	604.682-014
RES	50	Tool Grinder I (any industry)	701.381-018
RES	50	Training Technician (can. & preserv.)	522.264-010
RES	50	Turbine Attendant (utilities)	952.567-010
RES	50	Vulcanized-Fiber-Unit Operator (paper goods)	539.565-010
RES	50	Welder, Explosion (welding)	814.684-010
RES	50	Yardage-Control Operator, Forming (glass mfg.)	575.662-014
RES	49	Able Seaman (water trans.)	911.364-010
RES	49	Abrasive-Coating-Machine Operator (nonmet. min.)	574.462-010
RES	49	Awning-Frame Maker (tex. prod., n.e.c.)	809.484-010
RES	49	Battery Recharger (elec. equip.)	727.381-010
RES	49	Blocker and Polisher, Gold Wheel (clock & watch)	715.381-034
RES	49	Calciner, Gypsum (concrete prod.)	579.382-010
RES	49	Cheese Grader (dairy products)	529.387-010
RES	49	Chlorinator Operator (chemical)	558.382-030
RES	49	Coil Connector (elec. equip.)	721.684-018
RES	49	Commutator Assembler (elec. equip.)	724.684-030

HOC	Cx	Title	DOT
RES	49	Cook (fishing & hunt.)	315.381-010
RES	49	Depositing-Machine Operator (sugar & conf.)	529.682-018
RES	49	Distributing Clerk (clerical)	222.587-018
RES	49	Dry Cleaner (laundry & rel.)	362.382-014
RES	49	Dry-Cleaner Apprentice (laundry & rel.)	362.382-010
RES	49	Dry-Placer-Machine Operator (mine & quarry)	939.382-010
RES	49	Electric-Cell Tender (chemical)	558.565-014
RES	49	Embossing-Press Operator (print. & pub.)	659.682-014
RES	49	Embossing-Press-Operator Apprentice (print. & pub.)	659.682-018
RES	49	Enrobing-Machine Operator (bakery products; sugar & conf.)	524.382-014
RES	49	Faller I (logging)	454.384-010
RES	49	Fermentation Operator (chemical)	558.682-018
RES	49	Folding-Machine Operator (print. & pub.)	653.382-010
RES	49	Frame Repairer (motor-bicycles)	807.381-018
RES	49	Freezer Operator (dairy products)	529.482-010
RES	49	Industrial-Gas-Servicer Helper (utilities)	637.384-010
RES	49	Inspector (mfd. bldgs.)	869.687-038
RES	49	Inspector I (ordnance)	737.387-014
RES	49	Inspector II (concrete prod.)	579.664-014
RES	49	Jacquard-Plate Maker (knitting)	685.381-010
RES	49	Janitor (any industry)	382.664-010
RES	49	Lens Mounter II (optical goods)	713.681-010
RES	49	Metal-Bonding Crib Attendant (chemical)	550.564-010
RES	49	Metal-Bonding Press Operator (aircraft mfg.)	553.382-026
RES	49	Mixer Operator, Hot Metal (steel & rel.)	509.362-010
RES	49	Mold Maker II (jewelry-silver.)	777.381-022
RES	49	Parking-Meter Servicer (government ser.)	710.384-026
RES	49	Piercing-Machine Operator (nonfer. metal)	613.482-014
RES	49	Print-Line Operator (furniture; wood prod., n.e.c.)	652.662-018
RES	49	Repairer, Manufactured Buildings (mfd. bldgs.; vehicles, n.e.c.)	869.384-010
RES	49	Scraper, Hand (machine shop)	705.384-010
RES	49	Shredding-Floor-Equipment Operator (plastic-synth.)	559.382-050
RES	49	Slaughterer, Religious Ritual (meat products)	525.361-010
RES	49	Spotter II (laundry & rel.)	362.381-010
RES	49	Straight-Line-Press Setter (ordnance)	616.360-034
RES	49	Top Polisher (stonework)	673.662-010
RES	49	Trimmer Operator (nut & bolt)	619.462-014
RES	49	Trouble Shooter I (utilities)	952.364-010
RES	49	Tube Bender, Brass-Wind Instruments (musical inst.)	617.382-010
RES	49	Utility Worker (mfd. bldgs.; vehicles, n.e.c.)	869.684-074
RES	49	Van Driver (motor trans.)	905.663-018
RES	48	Asbestos-Wire Finisher (nonfer. metal)	691.682-010
RES	48	Assembly Inspector (agric. equip.)	706.361-014
RES	48	Baggage Checker (air trans.; motor trans.)	357.477-010
RES	48	Bone-Char Kiln Operator (grain-feed mills)	523.662-010
RES	48	Cloth Grader (textile)	689.387-010
RES	48	Coin-Counter-and-Wrapper (clerical)	217.585-010

HOC	Cx	Title	DOT
RES	48	Coke Burner (steel & rel.)	543.682-010
RES	48	Composition-Roll Maker and Cutter (rubber goods)	559.482-010
RES	48	Cook, Dog-and-Cat Food (meat products)	526.682-014
RES	48	Crook Operator (musical inst.)	609.682-018
RES	48	Dissolver Operator (chemical)	558.682-014
RES	48	Edger, Automatic (saw. & plan.)	667.682-026
RES	48	Effervescent-Salts Compounder (pharmaceut.)	559.685-058
RES	48	Farm worker, Diversified Crops I (agriculture)	407.663-010
RES	48	Farm worker, General I (agriculture)	421.683-010
RES	48	Film Developer (motion picture; photofinishing)	976.382-018
RES	48	Firer, Marine (water trans.)	951.685-018
RES	48	Grader, Meat (meat products)	525.387-010
RES	48	Hair Preparer (fabrication, n.e.c.)	739.384-018
RES	48	Hairspring Assembler (clock & watch)	715.381-054
RES	48	High Rigger (amuse. & rec.; radio-tv broad.)	962.664-010
RES	48	Inker (print. & pub.)	659.667-010
RES	48	Inspector, Dials (clock & watch)	715.687-066
RES	48	Ion-Exchange Operator (chemical)	558.685-034
RES	48	Keyboard-Action Assembler (musical inst.)	730.684-042
RES	48	Lay-Out Worker (mfd. bldgs.)	869.684-034
RES	48	Leacher (smelt. & refin.)	511.582-010
RES	48	Mixer, Whipped Topping (food prep., n.e.c.)	520.385-010
RES	48	Mixer-and-Blender (food prep., n.e.c.)	520.685-154
RES	48	Motorcycle Subassembler (motor-bicycles)	806.684-094
RES	48	Mud-Plant Operator (petrol. & gas)	930.685-010
RES	48	Offset-Duplicating-Machine Operator (clerical)	207.682-018
RES	48	Packer, Denture (protective dev.)	712.684-034
RES	48	Painter Helper, Sign (any industry)	970.664-010
RES	48	Percolator Operator (grain-feed mills)	523.682-034
RES	48	Polisher (any industry)	705.684-058
RES	48	Polisher Apprentice (any industry)	705.684-066
RES	48	Pot Firer (chemical)	553.582-014
RES	48	Pulley-Mortiser Operator (woodworking)	666.482-010
RES	48	Raw-Silk Grader (textile)	689.687-062
RES	48	Refining-Machine Operator (sugar & conf.)	521.682-034
RES	48	Roll Builder (steel & rel.)	801.664-018
RES	48	Sorting-Grapple Operator (logging)	921.683-066
RES	48	Stone Grader (mine & quarry)	679.567-010
RES	48	Stone Repairer (stonework)	779.684-058
RES	48	Stove Tender (steel & rel.)	512.382-014
RES	48	Strong-Nitric Operator (chemical)	559.682-062
RES	48	Timing Adjuster (clock & watch)	715.681-010
RES	48	Wheelwright (automotive ser.)	706.381-046
RES	48	Wire-Wrapping-Machine Operator (office machines)	692.662-022
RES	48	Yard Coupler (r.r. trans.)	910.664-010
RES	48	Yarding Engineer (logging)	921.663-066
RES	47	Abrasive Mixer (nonmet. min.)	570.485-010
RES	47	Acid Maker (paper & pulp)	559.662-010
RES	47	Air-Compressor Operator (any industry)	950.685-010

HOC	Cx	Title	DOT
RES	47	Air-Drier-Machine Operator (paper & pulp)	534.682-010
RES	47	Airframe-and-Power-Plant-Mechanic Helper (aircraft mfg.; air trans.)	621.684-010
RES	47	Aluminum-Hydroxide-Process Operator (chemical; pharmaceut.)	559.685-014
RES	47	Asbestos Removal Worker (construction)	869.684-082
RES	47	Assembler (mfd. bldgs.; vehicles, n.e.c.)	869.684-010
RES	47	Assembler, Production Line (photo. appar.)	714.684-010
RES	47	Batch-Still Operator I (chemical)	552.685-014
RES	47	Batter Scaler (bakery products)	526.682-010
RES	47	Black-Ash-Burner Operator (paper & pulp)	553.682-010
RES	47	Bleach-Liquor Maker (paper & pulp)	550.662-010
RES	47	Boiler Reliner, Plastic Block (foundry)	849.484-010
RES	47	Brake Operator II (any industry)	619.685-026
RES	47	Casting-Room Operator (plastic-synth.)	556.585-010
RES	47	Centrifuge Operator (sugar & conf.)	529.682-010
RES	47	Chemical Mixer (textile)	550.585-018
RES	47	Chocolate Molder, Machine (sugar & conf.)	529.685-054
RES	47	Cocoa-Press Operator (sugar & conf.)	521.682-014
RES	47	Cracker-and-Cookie-Machine Operator (bakery products)	520.682-034
RES	47	Crimping-Machine Operator (any industry)	616.682-022
RES	47	Crutcher (soap & rel.)	550.685-054
RES	47	Cutter, Machine I (any industry)	781.684-014
RES	47	Dewaterer Operator (smelt. & refin.)	511.565-010
RES	47	Die Mounter (paper goods)	659.684-010
RES	47	Distiller II (chemical)	552.682-014
RES	47	Dragline Operator (any industry)	850.683-018
RES	47	Drier Operator II (chemical)	553.582-010
RES	47	Extractor-Plant Operator (chemical; oils & grease)	559.665-018
RES	47	Extruder Operator (grain-feed mills)	520.682-018
RES	47	Extrusion Bender (ship-boat mfg.)	804.684-014
RES	47	Farm worker, Bulbs (agriculture)	405.683-010
RES	47	Film Laboratory Technician II (motion picture)	976.685-018
RES	47	Final Inspector, Shuttle (woodworking)	769.684-022
RES	47	Firer, High Pressure (any industry)	951.685-010
RES	47	Fireworks Maker (chemical)	737.684-018
RES	47	Fisher, Diving (fishing & hunt.)	443.664-010
RES	47	Flusher (chemical)	559.682-026
RES	47	Frame-Table Operator (wood prod., n.e.c.)	669.662-014
RES	47	Fur Blender (leather mfg.)	783.681-010
RES	47	Fur Cleaner (laundry & rel.)	362.684-014
RES	47	Gas-Leak Inspector Helper (pipe lines; utilities)	953.667-010
RES	47	Gas-Mask Inspector (protective dev.)	712.687-022
RES	47	Grip (amuse. & rec.; radio-tv broad.)	962.684-014
RES	47	Grip (motion picture; radio-tv broad.)	962.687-022
RES	47	Hatter (laundry & rel.)	369.384-010
RES	47	Humidifier Attendant (textile; tobacco)	950.485-010
RES	47	Hydraulic-Pressure-Auto-Frettage-Machine Operator (ordnance)	694.682-014

HOC	Cx	Title	DOT
RES	47	Hydro-Pneumatic Tester (any industry)	862.687-018
RES	47	Inspector (chemical)	709.687-022
RES	47	Inspector, Golf Ball (toy-sport equip.)	732.567-010
RES	47	Inspector, Toys (toy-sport equip.)	731.687-022
RES	47	Lead Burner, Machine (elec. equip.)	727.662-010
RES	47	Leather Cutter (leather prod.)	783.684-022
RES	47	Lime-Kiln Operator (paper & pulp)	559.685-118
RES	47	Malt Roaster (beverage)	526.682-026
RES	47	Mirror-Finishing-Machine Operator (jewelry-silver.)	603.682-022
RES	47	Mixing-Machine Operator (plastic prod.; plastic-synth.)	550.685-134
RES	47	Mold Finisher (machine shop)	705.684-038
RES	47	Mold Maker (pottery & porc.)	777.684-018
RES	47	Muffler Installer (automotive ser.)	807.664-010
RES	47	Net Repairer (fishing & hunt.)	449.664-010
RES	47	Nicking-Machine Operator (cutlery-hrdwr.)	609.682-026
RES	47	Opaquer (protective dev.)	712.684-030
RES	47	Optical-Glass Silverer (optical goods)	574.484-010
RES	47	Paraffin-Plant-Sweater Operator (petrol. refin.)	543.682-022
RES	47	Plate Molder (pen & pencil; print. & pub.)	556.582-010
RES	47	Platen-Press Operator (paper goods)	649.682-026
RES	47	Pony Edger (saw. & plan.)	667.682-050
RES	47	Powder Worker, TNT (ordnance)	737.684-030
RES	47	Refiner (protective dev.)	712.684-038
RES	47	Repairer II (chemical)	630.684-026
RES	47	Repairer, General (auto. mfg.)	806.684-118
RES	47	Repairer, Switchgear (comm. equip.; elec. equip.)	729.684-038
RES	47	Screen-and-Cyclone Repairer (mine & quarry)	630.664-014
RES	47	Slime-Plant Operator I (smelt. & refin.)	510.685-030
RES	47	Smoke and Flame Specialist (military ser.)	378.682-014
RES	47	Spar-Machine Operator (wood prod., n.e.c.)	664.682-022
RES	47	Spindle Carver (woodworking)	761.682-018
RES	47	Sponge-Press Operator (rubber goods)	559.682-050
RES	47	Spray-Drier Operator (brick & tile)	573.382-014
RES	47	Squeak, Rattle, and Leak Repairer (automotive ser.)	620.364-010
RES	47	Steak Sauce Maker (can. & preserv.)	529.484-010
RES	47	Still Operator (agriculture; can. & preserv.)	522.685-098
RES	47	Stock Fitter (boot & shoe)	788.685-018
RES	47	Stock Sheets Cleaner-Inspector (glass products)	779.687-034
RES	47	Stretch-Machine Operator (plastic prod.)	559.682-058
RES	47	Taper (construction; mfd. bldgs.)	842.664-010
RES	47	Tire-Fabric-Impregnating-Range Operator, Chief (tex. prod., n.e.c.)	589.662-014
RES	47	Tool Dresser (any industry)	601.682-010
RES	47	Used-Car Renovator (retail trade)	620.684-034
RES	47	Utility Worker, Film Processing (photofinishing)	976.685-030
RES	47	Valve Grinder (machine shop)	706.684-098
RES	46	Aluminum-Pool Installer (construction)	809.664-010
RES	46	Blending-Machine Operator (dairy products)	522.685-010
RES	46	Boilermaker Helper II (struct. metal)	805.664-010

HOC to DOT

HOC	Cx	Title	DOT
RES	46	Bomb Loader (ordnance)	737.684-014
RES	46	Cage Maker, Machine (concrete prod.)	616.682-018
RES	46	Caster (nonfer. metal)	502.482-010
RES	46	Centrifugal-Station Operator, Automatic (sugar & conf.)	521.585-010
RES	46	Cobbler (boot & shoe)	788.381-010
RES	46	Cooker, Process Cheese (dairy products)	526.665-010
RES	46	Cremator (personal ser.)	359.685-010
RES	46	Dry-Wall Sprayer (mfd. bldgs.)	842.684-010
RES	46	Dye Weigher (any industry)	550.684-014
RES	46	Fiberglass Laminator (ship-boat mfg.; vehicles, n.e.c.)	806.684-054
RES	46	Fish Hatchery Worker (fishing & hunt.)	446.684-010
RES	46	Golf-Club Facer (toy-sport equip.)	761.684-010
RES	46	Kettle Operator (beverage)	522.682-010
RES	46	Maintenance-Repairer Helper, Industrial (any industry)	899.684-022
RES	46	Marshal (amuse. & rec.)	153.384-010
RES	46	Mat-Machine Operator (nonmet. min.)	579.662-010
RES	46	Mixer Tender, Board (concrete prod.)	570.685-062
RES	46	Pan Helper (chemical)	551.585-018
RES	46	Pantographer (print. & pub.)	979.382-022
RES	46	Pipeliner (pipe lines)	899.684-026
RES	46	Plaster Maker (nonmet. min.)	779.684-046
RES	46	Reinforcing-Metal Worker (construction)	801.684-026
RES	46	Retort-or-Condenser Press Operator (brick & tile)	575.382-026
RES	46	Roller Varnisher (print. & pub.)	979.682-022
RES	46	Shaft Mechanic (mine & quarry)	899.684-034
RES	46	Shake Sawyer (saw. & plan.)	667.682-070
RES	46	Smoker (meat products)	525.682-010
RES	46	Steel-Pourer Helper (steel & rel.)	502.664-018
RES	46	Still-Operator Helper (chemical)	552.685-030
RES	46	Stripping-Shovel Oiler (mine & quarry)	850.684-018
RES	46	Table Operator (nonfer. metal; steel & rel.)	613.682-026
RES	46	Tinning-Machine Set-up Operator (print. & pub.)	653.682-022
RES	46	Tone Cabinet Assembler (musical inst.)	730.684-090
RES	46	Trailer Assembler II (auto. mfg.)	806.684-082
RES	46	Trapper, Animal (fishing & hunt.)	461.684-014
RES	46	Vacuum Caster (foundry)	514.582-010
RES	46	Wicker Worker (furniture)	763.684-078
RES	46	Wire-Rope-Sling Maker (metal prod., n.e.c.)	709.684-102
RES	45	Automobile Wrecker (wholesale tr.)	620.684-010
RES	45	Barrel Straightener I (ordnance)	736.684-026
RES	45	Bonding-Machine Tender (textile)	589.665-010
RES	45	Car Trimmer (railroad equip.)	806.684-046
RES	45	Char-Filter-Tank Tender, Head (grain-feed mills)	521.665-010
RES	45	Chipping-Machine Operator (wood prod., n.e.c.)	564.682-010
RES	45	Clay Roaster (petrol. refin.)	573.685-014
RES	45	Concrete Rubber (concrete prod.)	844.684-010
RES	45	Corner-Trimmer Operator (wood. container)	667.682-018
RES	45	Cowpuncher (agriculture)	410.674-014
RES	45	Enameler (plumbing-heat.)	509.684-010

HOC	Cx	Title	DOT
RES	45	Exterminator (business ser.)	389.684-010
RES	45	Ferryboat Operator, Cable (water trans.)	911.664-010
RES	45	Film Printer (motion picture)	976.682-010
RES	45	Floor Winder (textile)	681.685-050
RES	45	Forming-Machine Tender (glass mfg.)	575.685-038
RES	45	Heater Helper (steel & rel.)	613.685-014
RES	45	Kettle Tender, Platinum and Palladium (smelt. & refin.)	511.685-034
RES	45	Mender (carpet & rug; textile)	782.684-042
RES	45	Metal-Bed Assembler (furniture)	706.684-082
RES	45	Motorcycle Assembler (motor-bicycles)	806.684-090
RES	45	Nut Roaster (can. & preserv.)	529.685-174
RES	45	Offset-Duplicating-Machine Operator (print. & pub.)	651.682-014
RES	45	Painter, Airbrush (any industry)	741.684-018
RES	45	Panel-Lay-Up Worker (woodworking)	761.684-018
RES	45	Plaster-Die Maker (pottery & porc.)	774.684-026
RES	45	Plodder Operator (soap & rel.)	556.682-018
RES	45	Pot Liner (smelt. & refin.)	519.664-014
RES	45	Predatory-Animal Hunter (fishing & hunt.)	461.661-010
RES	45	Pug-Mill Operator (smelt. & refin.)	510.685-022
RES	45	Repairer Helper (smelt. & refin.)	630.664-010
RES	45	Retort Operator (can. & preserv.)	526.682-034
RES	45	Rigger (construction)	869.683-014
RES	45	Rigger Helper (ship-boat mfg.)	806.684-122
RES	45	Scraper-Loader Operator (mine & quarry)	921.663-050
RES	45	Shield Runner (construction)	850.682-010
RES	45	Slitter-Creaser-Slotter Operator (paper goods)	649.682-034
RES	45	Tower-Excavator Operator (construction)	850.683-042
RES	45	Utility Worker, Merchant Mill (steel & rel.)	801.664-014
RES	45	Weigher-and-Crusher (smelt. & refin.)	515.567-010
RES	45	Weld Inspector II (welding)	819.687-010
RES	45	Wet Inspector, Optical Glass (optical goods)	716.687-034
RES	44	Assembler, Deck and Hull (ship-boat mfg.)	806.684-022
RES	44	Automobile-Accessories Installer (automotive ser.)	806.684-038
RES	44	Barrel-Lathe Operator, Inside (wood. container)	664.682-010
RES	44	Base-Draw Operator (ordnance)	504.685-010
RES	44	Bite-Block Maker (protective dev.)	712.684-014
RES	44	Blocker, Hand (optical goods)	716.684-010
RES	44	Boiler-Room Helper (any industry)	950.685-014
RES	44	Briquetter Operator (chemical)	559.685-030
RES	44	Cager (mine & quarry)	939.667-010
RES	44	Camouflage Specialist (military ser.)	378.684-010
RES	44	Casket Liner (fabrication, n.e.c.)	780.684-030
RES	44	Centrifugal-Drier Operator (chemical)	551.685-026
RES	44	Chauffeur (domestic ser.)	359.673-010
RES	44	Chauffeur, Funeral Car (personal ser.)	359.673-014
RES	44	Construction-Equipment-Mechanic Helper (construction)	620.664-010
RES	44	Core-Drill-Operator Helper (any industry)	930.687-014
RES	44	Crusher Setter (mine & quarry)	933.664-010
RES	44	Density Control Puncher (motion picture)	976.684-010

HOC	Cx	Title	DOT
RES	44	Derrick Operator (any industry)	921.663-022
RES	44	Digger (fabrication, n.e.c.)	739.687-070
RES	44	Ditcher Operator (r.r. trans.)	850.683-014
RES	44	Dividing-Machine Operator (bakery products)	520.685-086
RES	44	Doughnut Maker (bakery products)	526.684-010
RES	44	Driver-Utility Worker (auto. mfg.; automotive ser.)	919.663-018
RES	44	Earth-Boring-Machine Operator (construction; utilities)	859.682-010
RES	44	Extruding-Press Operator (ordnance)	614.685-010
RES	44	Firer, Kiln (sugar & conf.)	523.685-078
RES	44	Firer, Low Pressure (any industry)	951.685-014
RES	44	Flaking-Roll Operator (grain-feed mills)	520.685-102
RES	44	Forming-Machine Upkeep-Mechanic Helper (glass mfg.)	575.687-014
RES	44	Installer, Movable Bulkhead (railroad equip.)	806.684-074
RES	44	Lay-Out-Machine Operator (tex. prod., n.e.c.)	781.684-034
RES	44	Logging-Tractor Operator (forestry; logging; saw. & plan.)	929.663-010
RES	44	Lozenge-Dough Mixer (sugar & conf.)	520.685-122
RES	44	Mixer I (chemical)	559.665-026
RES	44	Molding Sander (woodworking)	662.682-010
RES	44	Mouthpiece Maker (musical inst.)	730.685-014
RES	44	Nitrocellulose Operator (chemical)	553.684-014
RES	44	Noodle Maker (food prep., n.e.c.)	529.385-010
RES	44	Odd-Shoe Examiner (boot & shoe)	788.667-010
RES	44	Oven Tender (bakery products)	526.685-030
RES	44	Oven Tender (paint & varnish)	553.685-082
RES	44	Paint Mixer, Machine (any industry)	550.485-018
RES	44	Pasteurizer (oils & grease)	523.585-026
RES	44	Pickling Solution Maker (meat products)	522.485-010
RES	44	Pie Maker, Machine (bakery products)	526.685-038
RES	44	Plugging-Machine Operator (woodworking)	669.682-062
RES	44	Powder-Mill Operator (sugar & conf.)	521.585-018
RES	44	Press-Machine Operator (fabrication, n.e.c.)	590.665-014
RES	44	Riveter, Pneumatic (any industry)	800.684-014
RES	44	Sand Mixer, Machine (foundry)	570.682-018
RES	44	Splash-Line Operator (fabrication, n.e.c.)	559.665-034
RES	44	Table Tender (smelt. & refin.)	511.685-062
RES	44	Table-Top Tile Setter (brick & tile)	763.684-074
RES	44	Tare Weigher (meat products; sugar & conf.; tobacco)	221.587-034
RES	44	Temperature Regulator, Pyrometer (foundry)	512.667-010
RES	44	Tester, Convertible Sofa Bedspring (furniture)	780.684-110
RES	44	Tile Sorter (brick & tile)	573.687-038
RES	44	Tow-Truck Operator (automotive ser.)	919.663-026
RES	44	Vacuum-Drier Tender (chemical)	553.685-106
RES	44	Vault Custodian (laundry & rel.)	369.587-010
RES	44	Vendor (amuse. & rec.)	291.457-022
RES	44	Weigher and Grader (chemical)	559.567-014
RES	43	Asphalt-Paving-Machine Operator (construction)	853.663-010
RES	43	Blanching-Machine Operator (can. & preserv.)	523.685-014
RES	43	Blast-Furnace-Keeper Helper (steel & rel.)	502.687-010
RES	43	Caster (nonmet. min.)	575.684-018

HOC	Cx	Title	DOT
RES	43	Curing-Bin Operator (grain-feed mills)	522.685-038
RES	43	Dehydrator Tender (can. & preserv.)	523.685-054
RES	43	Deodorizer (chemical)	522.685-046
RES	43	Electroformer (electroplating)	500.684-010
RES	43	Finisher (wood. container)	749.684-026
RES	43	Fisher, Net (fishing & hunt.)	441.684-010
RES	43	Fisher, Weir (fishing & hunt.)	441.684-022
RES	43	Fun-House Operator (amuse. & rec.)	342.665-010
RES	43	Gluer (woodworking)	762.687-034
RES	43	Graves Registration Specialist (military ser.)	355.687-014
RES	43	Heat Reader (forging)	612.687-010
RES	43	Helper, Metal Bonding (aircraft mfg.)	806.687-022
RES	43	Inspector, Filter Tip (tobacco)	529.667-010
RES	43	Lubrication Servicer (automotive ser.)	915.687-018
RES	43	Metal Fabricator Helper (any industry)	619.685-066
RES	43	Mixer Operator (chemical; electron. comp.)	550.685-082
RES	43	Ornamental-Metal-Worker Helper (metal prod., n.e.c.)	619.484-010
RES	43	Oven Operator (grain-feed mills)	526.585-010
RES	43	Overlay Plastician (ship-boat mfg.)	806.684-106
RES	43	Photographic-Machine Operator (clerical)	207.685-018
RES	43	Pickle Pumper (meat products)	522.685-086
RES	43	Porter, Marina (water trans.)	329.677-010
RES	43	Power-Shovel Operator (any industry)	850.683-030
RES	43	Reducing-Salon Attendant (personal ser.)	359.567-010
RES	43	Rug-Frame Mounter (carpet & rug)	687.464-010
RES	43	Silica-Filter Operator (beverage)	521.582-010
RES	43	Ski Molder (toy-sport equip.)	732.684-114
RES	43	Sorter Operator (saw. & plan.)	921.685-054
RES	43	Spar-Machine-Operator Helper (wood prod., n.e.c.)	664.685-030
RES	43	Spring-Repairer Helper, Hand (automotive ser.)	620.584-010
RES	43	Sterilizer Operator (dairy products)	523.685-114
RES	43	Straight-Line Edger (glass mfg.; glass products)	673.685-078
RES	43	Tire Recapper (automotive ser.)	750.685-014
RES	43	Tube Bender, Hand I (any industry)	709.684-090
RES	43	Wire Charger (elec. equip.)	614.586-010
RES	42	Automobile-Bumper Straightener (automotive ser.)	807.684-010
RES	42	Block-Making-Machine Operator (concrete prod.)	575.685-014
RES	42	Burn-Out Tender, Lace (tex. prod., n.e.c.)	589.685-018
RES	42	Button Grader (button & notion)	734.687-038
RES	42	Candle Molder, Machine (fabrication, n.e.c.)	692.685-038
RES	42	Carpet-Layer Helper (retail trade)	864.687-010
RES	42	Centrifugal-Casting-Machine Operator I (foundry)	514.685-010
RES	42	Child-Care Attendant, School (personal ser.)	355.674-010
RES	42	Clamp-Jig Assembler (woodworking)	762.687-022
RES	42	Cloth Examiner, Hand (textile)	781.687-014
RES	42	Cloth Shader (garment; textile)	582.685-026
RES	42	Coating-Mixer Tender (paper & pulp)	530.685-010
RES	42	Combat Surveillance and Target Acquisition Crewmember (military ser.)	378.687-010

HOC	Cx	Title	DOT
RES	42	Cooker (grain-feed mills)	526.685-022
RES	42	Cooler Tender (sugar & conf.)	520.585-018
RES	42	Cooper Helper (wood. container)	764.687-050
RES	42	Covering-Machine-Operator Helper (textile)	681.685-042
RES	42	Drier Tender (can. & preserv.)	523.685-066
RES	42	Edge Setter (boot & shoe)	690.685-146
RES	42	Examiner (print. & pub.)	979.687-010
RES	42	Extractor Operator (tex. prod., n.e.c.)	582.685-062
RES	42	Felt Hanger (build. mat., n.e.c.)	549.686-014
RES	42	Frit-Mixer-and-Burner (brick & tile; pottery & porc.)	579.685-014
RES	42	Furniture Cleaner (laundry & rel.)	362.684-022
RES	42	Fuse Maker (chemical)	559.685-094
RES	42	Gas-Pumping-Station Helper (utilities)	953.684-010
RES	42	Glue-Mill Operator (chemical)	559.685-098
RES	42	Grain Drier (beverage)	523.685-086
RES	42	Grain-Wafer-Machine Operator (bakery products)	523.685-094
RES	42	Grinder-Chipper II (any industry)	809.684-026
RES	42	Hat-Stock-Laminating-Machine Operator (hat & cap)	584.685-026
RES	42	Infantry Indirect Fire Crewmember (military ser.)	378.684-022
RES	42	Inspector, Aluminum Boat (ship-boat mfg.)	806.687-026
RES	42	Jet-Dyeing-Machine Tender (textile)	582.685-090
RES	42	Laborer, Landscape (agriculture)	408.687-014
RES	42	Laminator, Hand (furniture)	763.684-050
RES	42	Laminator, Preforms (plastic prod.)	754.684-050
RES	42	Latexer (carpet & rug)	584.684-010
RES	42	Lens Examiner (optical goods)	716.687-022
RES	42	Line Mover (railroad equip.)	921.664-010
RES	42	Linseed-Oil-Press Tender (oils & grease)	559.685-122
RES	42	Loader (mfd. bldgs.)	921.687-018
RES	42	Locker-Room Attendant (personal ser.)	358.677-014
RES	42	Logger, All-Round (logging)	454.684-018
RES	42	Metal-Spraying-Machine Operator, Automatic II (any industry)	505.685-014
RES	42	Mixer, Chili Powder (food prep., n.e.c.)	520.685-158
RES	42	Mixing-Machine Operator (food prep., n.e.c.)	520.665-014
RES	42	Pad Maker (textile)	589.687-030
RES	42	Pipe Changer (mine & quarry)	891.564-010
RES	42	Pipe-Smoker-Machine Operator (fabrication, n.e.c.)	739.687-150
RES	42	Plugger (steel & rel.)	613.687-010
RES	42	Popcorn-Candy Maker (sugar & conf.)	526.685-042
RES	42	Pretzel Cooker (bakery products)	526.685-054
RES	42	Printing-Roller Handler (textile)	652.385-010
RES	42	Round-Up-Ring Hand (concrete prod.)	579.587-010
RES	42	Service-Mechanic Helper, Compressed-Gas Equipment (chemical)	630.664-018
RES	42	Shoe-Repairer Helper (personal ser.)	365.674-010
RES	42	Sorter (brick & tile)	573.687-034
RES	42	Stubber (retail trade)	222.687-034
RES	42	Supply Clerk (personal ser.)	339.687-010

HOC	Cx	Title	DOT
RES	42	Towel Inspector (textile)	652.686-042
RES	42	Woodenware Assembler (woodworking)	762.687-070
RES	42	Yard Worker (domestic ser.)	301.687-018
RES	41	Amphibian Crewmember (military ser.)	378.683-010
RES	41	Assembler (pen & pencil)	733.685-010
RES	41	Assembler, Bicycle I (motor-bicycles)	806.684-014
RES	41	Assembler, Garment Form (fabrication, n.e.c.)	739.687-022
RES	41	Awning-Hanger Helper (construction; retail trade; tex. prod., n.e.c.)	869.687-010
RES	41	Back Washer (textile)	582.685-010
RES	41	Baker Helper (hotel & rest.)	313.684-010
RES	41	Bale-Tie-Machine Operator (metal prod., n.e.c.)	616.682-014
RES	41	Banding-Machine Operator (ordnance)	619.685-018
RES	41	Barker Operator (millwork-plywood)	663.682-010
RES	41	Barrel-Lathe Operator, Outside (wood. container)	664.682-014
RES	41	Bindery Worker (paper goods)	649.685-018
RES	41	Blacksmith Helper (forging)	610.684-010
RES	41	Blow-Pit Operator (paper & pulp)	533.665-010
RES	41	Board-Liner Operator (wood. container)	641.685-014
RES	41	Bottom Maker (steel & rel.)	509.687-010
RES	41	Bottomer I (mine & quarry)	932.667-010
RES	41	Bowling-Ball Molder (toy-sport equip.)	556.685-018
RES	41	Branding-Machine Tender (rubber goods)	690.685-042
RES	41	Bricklayer Helper, Firebrick and Refractory Tile (construction)	861.687-010
RES	41	Capacitor-Pack-Press Operator (elec. equip.)	726.684-010
RES	41	Carbon-Paper Interleafer (pen & pencil)	640.685-018
RES	41	Caretaker (domestic ser.)	301.687-010
RES	41	Case-Making-Machine Operator (print. & pub.)	653.685-018
RES	41	Casting-Machine-Service Operator (plastic-synth.)	559.687-018
RES	41	Catcher (steel & rel.)	613.686-010
RES	41	Char-Filter-Operator Helper (sugar & conf.)	521.687-034
RES	41	Cherry-Picker Operator (construction)	921.663-014
RES	41	Cleaner, Laboratory Equipment (any industry)	381.687-022
RES	41	Cloth Doffer (textile)	689.686-058
RES	41	Cloth-Bolt Bander (textile)	920.587-010
RES	41	Coating-Machine Operator (pen & pencil)	692.685-054
RES	41	Cocoa-Bean-Roaster Helper (sugar & conf.)	523.666-010
RES	41	Coil Assembler, Machine (furniture)	616.685-018
RES	41	Conditioner Tender (textile)	587.685-022
RES	41	Cook Helper, Pastry (hotel & rest.)	313.687-010
RES	41	Corn-Press Operator (food prep., n.e.c.)	529.685-078
RES	41	Corrugator-Operator Helper (paper goods)	641.686-018
RES	41	Crimp Setter (textile)	680.685-026
RES	41	Derrick Worker, Well Service (petrol. & gas)	930.683-018
RES	41	Die Tripper (brick & tile)	575.665-014
RES	41	Dropper, Fermenting Cellar (beverage)	522.685-054
RES	41	Extruding-Machine Operator (tex. prod., n.e.c.)	557.565-010
RES	41	Farm Worker, Dairy (agriculture)	410.684-010

Part 2: From Holland Codes to Occupations

From Holland Codes to the Dictionary of Occupational Titles Occupations

HOC	Cx	Title	DOT
RES	41	Field Artillery Crewmember (military ser.)	378.684-018
RES	41	Fig Caprifier (agriculture)	403.687-014
RES	41	Filter Operator (beverage; sugar & conf.)	521.685-126
RES	41	Finisher (plastic-synth.)	554.586-010
RES	41	Fitter Helper (any industry)	801.687-014
RES	41	Flame-Hardening-Machine Operator (heat treating)	504.685-014
RES	41	Flatcar Whacker (saw. & plan.)	807.667-010
RES	41	Floor Worker, Well Service (petrol. & gas)	930.684-014
RES	41	Force-Variation Equipment Tender (rubber tire)	690.685-182
RES	41	Frame-Table-Operator Helper (wood prod., n.e.c.)	669.685-058
RES	41	Frazer (fabrication, n.e.c.)	664.685-022
RES	41	Gill-Box Tender (textile)	680.685-058
RES	41	Glaze Handler (brick & tile)	571.685-014
RES	41	Graining-Press Operator (chemical)	557.682-010
RES	41	Hair-Boiler Operator (leather mfg.)	582.685-086
RES	41	Handle-Machine Operator (paper goods)	649.685-050
RES	41	Harness-and-Bag Inspector (tex. prod., n.e.c.)	789.687-086
RES	41	Hogshead Opener (tobacco)	920.687-102
RES	41	Honeycomb Decapper (food prep., n.e.c.)	521.687-070
RES	41	Hose Wrapper (rubber goods)	759.684-038
RES	41	Hose-Coupling Joiner (rubber goods)	759.687-014
RES	41	Infantry Weapons Crewmember (military ser.)	378.684-026
RES	41	Installer, Metal Flooring (railroad equip.)	806.684-070
RES	41	Kiln-Burner Helper (brick & tile)	573.687-026
RES	41	Laborer (pharmaceut.)	559.686-022
RES	41	Laborer, Ammunition Assembly I (ordnance)	737.687-070
RES	41	Laborer, Construction or Leak Gang (utilities)	862.684-014
RES	41	Laborer, Petroleum Refinery (petrol. refin.)	549.687-018
RES	41	Laborer, Powerhouse (utilities)	952.665-010
RES	41	Laborer, Starch Factory (grain-feed mills)	529.685-154
RES	41	Lace-Paper-Machine Operator (paper goods)	649.685-058
RES	41	Lathe Spotter (millwork-plywood)	663.686-022
RES	41	Launderer, Hand (laundry & rel.)	361.684-010
RES	41	Lead Handler (ordnance)	599.687-018
RES	41	Lens-Molding-Equipment Operator (glass mfg.)	575.685-054
RES	41	Liner Replacer (mine & quarry; smelt. & refin.)	801.664-010
RES	41	Liner-Machine Operator (paper goods)	641.685-058
RES	41	Linker (meat products)	529.687-150
RES	41	Loom Changeover Operator (carpet & rug)	683.687-030
RES	41	Machine Helper (welding)	819.666-010
RES	41	Matchbook Assembler (fabrication, n.e.c.)	649.685-074
RES	41	Melt-House Drag Operator (sugar & conf.)	529.687-158
RES	41	Mercury Washer (chemical)	551.685-098
RES	41	Mill Hand, Plate Mill (steel & rel.)	613.667-014
RES	41	Mold Closer (foundry)	518.684-018
RES	41	Mold Filler, Plastic Dolls (toy-sport equip.)	731.687-026
RES	41	Mold Parter (plastic-synth.)	556.587-010
RES	41	Mold-Insert Changer (boot & shoe)	753.687-034
RES	41	Molder, Pipe Covering (plastic prod.)	556.665-018

HOC	Cx	Title	DOT
RES	41	Mottler Operator (fabrication, n.e.c.)	550.665-022
RES	41	Packager, Hand (any industry)	920.587-018
RES	41	Painter Helper, Spray (any industry)	741.687-014
RES	41	Paper-Cup-Machine Operator (paper goods)	649.685-078
RES	41	Parachute Folder (tex. prod., n.e.c.)	789.684-034
RES	41	Pasting Inspector (brick & tile)	773.687-010
RES	41	Patch Finisher (textile)	582.684-010
RES	41	Peanut-Butter Maker (can. & preserv.; food prep., n.e.c.)	529.685-178
RES	41	Plastic-Joint Maker (brick & tile)	590.687-014
RES	41	Press Helper (plastic prod.)	651.586-010
RES	41	Presser (glass mfg.)	575.685-074
RES	41	Refrigeration-Mechanic Helper (any industry)	637.687-014
RES	41	Rodding-Anode Worker (smelt. & refin.)	519.687-034
RES	41	Roller (ship-boat mfg.)	806.687-046
RES	41	Rolling-Machine Operator (sugar & conf.)	520.685-198
RES	41	Rubber (personal ser.)	334.677-010
RES	41	Salvager Helper (petrol. refin.)	709.687-034
RES	41	Scarf Gluer (millwork-plywood)	762.684-054
RES	41	Scrap Baller (nonfer. metal; steel & rel.)	509.685-046
RES	41	Screen Tender, Chips (paper & pulp)	533.685-026
RES	41	Sensitized-Paper Tester (photo. appar.)	714.667-010
RES	41	Sexton (nonprofit org.)	389.667-010
RES	41	Signaler (construction)	869.667-014
RES	41	Sizer (textile)	582.687-026
RES	41	Slasher-Tender Helper (textile)	582.686-026
RES	41	Spot Picker, Molded Goods (fabrication, n.e.c.)	739.667-010
RES	41	Spout Tender I (chemical)	932.664-014
RES	41	Spring Assembler (metal prod., n.e.c.)	706.684-090
RES	41	Spring Salvage Worker (metal prod., n.e.c.)	610.684-014
RES	41	Squeegee Tender (rubber tire)	750.685-010
RES	41	Stave Jointer (wood. container)	665.685-030
RES	41	Steam-Press Tender I (rubber goods)	553.665-046
RES	41	Steel-Post Installer (utilities)	821.687-010
RES	41	Stitch-Bonding-Machine Tender (textile)	689.685-126
RES	41	Stitcher Operator (paper goods)	649.685-114
RES	41	Stopper Maker (steel & rel.)	519.684-022
RES	41	Streetcar-Repairer Helper (railroad equip.)	807.687-014
RES	41	Sugar Drier (grain-feed mills)	523.665-010
RES	41	Tailer (mine & quarry)	930.666-014
RES	41	Taper Operator (paper goods)	649.685-126
RES	41	Tie Inspector (saw. & plan.)	669.687-026
RES	41	Tie-Up Worker (office machines)	710.687-034
RES	41	Transfer-Table Operator Helper (railroad equip.; r.r. trans.)	910.667-030
RES	41	Tree Cutter (agriculture; logging)	454.684-026
RES	41	Tubing-Machine Operator (nonfer. metal; steel & rel.)	613.685-030
RES	41	Tubular-Splitting-Machine Tender (knitting)	686.685-070
RES	41	Utility Worker, Cloth Printing (textile)	652.586-010
RES	41	Van-Driver Helper (motor trans.)	905.687-014
RES	41	Vulcan Crewmember (military ser.)	378.663-010

HOC	Cx	Title	DOT
RES	41	Washer-and-Crusher Tender (mine & quarry)	939.685-014
RES	41	Weaver, Axminster (carpet & rug)	683.685-038
RES	41	Wet-and-Dry-Sugar-Bin Operator (sugar & conf.)	529.665-018
RES	41	Wire-Weaver Helper (metal prod., n.e.c.)	616.687-014
RES	41	Wood Hacker (fabrication, n.e.c.; paper & pulp)	569.687-026
RES	41	Wrapper Operator (metal prod., n.e.c.)	706.684-110
RES	40	Air-and-Water Filler (wood. container)	764.687-010
RES	40	Animal Eviscerator (meat products)	525.687-010
RES	40	Assembler Helper, Internal Combustion Engine (engine-turbine)	801.687-010
RES	40	Assembler, Wet Wash (laundry & rel.)	361.687-010
RES	40	Attendant, Campground (amuse. & rec.)	329.683-010
RES	40	Bagger (retail trade)	920.687-014
RES	40	Balloon Dipper (rubber goods)	599.687-010
RES	40	Beater-and-Pulper Feeder (paper & pulp; tex. prod., n.e.c.)	530.686-010
RES	40	Beveling-and-Edging-Machine-Operator Helper (glass mfg.; glass products)	673.686-010
RES	40	Blanket Washer (smelt. & refin.)	511.687-010
RES	40	Blanket-Winder Helper (paper goods)	641.686-010
RES	40	Block-Breaker Operator (chemical)	555.686-010
RES	40	Boat-Loader Helper (water trans.)	911.687-010
RES	40	Boilermaker Helper I (struct. metal)	805.687-010
RES	40	Bottom-Hole-Pressure-Recording-Operator Helper (petrol. & gas)	930.687-010
RES	40	Box-Blank-Machine-Operator Helper (wood. container)	669.686-014
RES	40	Brake-Lining-Finisher Helper, Asbestos (nonmet. min.)	579.687-010
RES	40	Cager Operator (can. & preserv.)	921.685-018
RES	40	Calender-Operator Helper (rubber goods; rubber tire)	554.686-018
RES	40	Car Icer (food prep., n.e.c.; meat products)	910.687-018
RES	40	Carbon Setter (smelt. & refin.)	519.667-010
RES	40	Carton-Forming-Machine Helper (any industry)	641.686-014
RES	40	Casting-Machine-Operator Helper (elec. equip.)	502.686-010
RES	40	Cell Preparer (plastic-synth.)	556.687-014
RES	40	Chain Saw Operator (chemical; logging; millwork-plywood)	454.687-010
RES	40	Char-Dust Cleaner and Salvager (sugar & conf.)	529.687-038
RES	40	Circus Laborer (amuse. & rec.)	969.687-010
RES	40	Cleaner (mfd. bldgs.)	869.687-018
RES	40	Cloth Tearer (garment)	781.687-018
RES	40	Cold-Press Loader (cutlery-hrdwr.)	701.687-018
RES	40	Company Laborer (mine & quarry)	939.687-014
RES	40	Compressor Operator II (chemical)	559.685-038
RES	40	Construction Worker II (construction)	869.687-026
RES	40	Contact-Acid-Plant-Operator Helper (chemical)	559.687-026
RES	40	Cook Helper (hotel & rest.)	317.687-010
RES	40	Counter-Supply Worker (hotel & rest.)	319.687-010
RES	40	Cutter, Banana Room (wholesale tr.)	929.687-010
RES	40	Cutting-Machine-Tender Helper (any industry)	690.686-030
RES	40	Cylinder-Die-Machine Helper (paper goods)	649.686-018

HOC	Cx	Title	DOT
RES	40	Day Worker (domestic ser.)	301.687-014
RES	40	Demolition Specialist (ordnance)	737.687-034
RES	40	Devulcanizer Charger (rubber reclaim.)	558.666-010
RES	40	Distillation-Operator Helper (chemical)	552.687-010
RES	40	Drier Operator V (chemical)	553.686-026
RES	40	Dry Curer (meat products)	525.687-026
RES	40	Dyer (woodworking)	562.687-010
RES	40	Dynamite-Packing-Machine Feeder (chemical)	692.686-038
RES	40	Edger-Machine Helper (stonework)	673.686-018
RES	40	Elastic-Tape Inserter (garment)	782.687-022
RES	40	Elevator Operator, Freight (any industry)	921.683-038
RES	40	Embossing-Machine Tender (paper goods)	649.685-038
RES	40	Expansion Envelope Maker, Hand (paper goods)	794.684-018
RES	40	Extractor Operator (chemical; oils & grease)	551.685-054
RES	40	Film Loader (motion picture)	962.687-014
RES	40	Filter Washer (chemical)	559.687-042
RES	40	Floor Attendant (glass mfg.)	579.687-018
RES	40	Forest Worker (forestry)	452.687-010
RES	40	Foundry Worker, General (foundry)	519.687-022
RES	40	Furnace-Installer-and-Repairer Helper, Hot Air (any industry)	869.687-030
RES	40	Gluer and Slicer, Hand (paper goods)	794.687-030
RES	40	Goods Layer (textile)	781.687-038
RES	40	Ground Mixer (chemical)	550.685-066
RES	40	Gum Puller (sugar & conf.)	520.687-038
RES	40	Hatch Tender (water trans.)	911.667-014
RES	40	Header (wood. container)	764.687-058
RES	40	Hoop-Maker Helper, Machine (wood. container)	619.686-014
RES	40	Installer, Door Furring (railroad equip.)	806.687-034
RES	40	Laborer, Airport Maintenance (air trans.)	899.687-014
RES	40	Laborer, Ammunition Assembly II (ordnance)	737.687-074
RES	40	Laborer, Aquatic Life (fishing & hunt.)	446.687-014
RES	40	Laborer, Canvas Shop (tex. prod., n.e.c.)	789.687-090
RES	40	Laborer, General (nonfer. metal)	519.686-010
RES	40	Laborer, General (machine shop)	609.684-014
RES	40	Laborer, Pipelines (pipe lines)	914.687-010
RES	40	Laborer, Stores (any industry)	922.687-058
RES	40	Laborer, Wood-Preserving Plant (wood prod., n.e.c.)	561.686-010
RES	40	Leasing-Machine Tender (textile)	681.685-054
RES	40	Liner-Machine-Operator Helper (paper goods)	641.686-022
RES	40	Loader, Magazine Grinder (paper & pulp)	530.686-014
RES	40	Loom-Winder Tender (textile)	681.685-062
RES	40	Lumber Straightener (saw. & plan.)	669.687-018
RES	40	Machine Helper (tex. prod., n.e.c.)	586.686-022
RES	40	Magnesium-Mill Operator (nonfer. metal)	607.686-010
RES	40	Miller (mine & quarry)	570.685-038
RES	40	Mold Cleaner (rubber goods)	556.687-018
RES	40	Molder, Inflated Ball (toy-sport equip.)	732.687-054
RES	40	Molder, Wax Ball (toy-sport equip.)	732.687-058

Part 2: From Holland Codes to Occupations

From Holland Codes to the Dictionary of Occupational Titles Occupations

HOC	Cx	Title	DOT
RES	40	Nitroglycerin Distributor (chemical)	559.664-010
RES	40	Nut-Process Helper (can. & preserv.)	529.486-010
RES	40	Opener Tender (textile)	680.685-070
RES	40	Packer, Agricultural Produce (agriculture)	920.687-134
RES	40	Packing-Floor Worker (tobacco)	920.686-026
RES	40	Pitch Filler (any industry)	619.687-018
RES	40	Plate-Take-Out Worker (elec. equip.)	500.687-010
RES	40	Plow-and-Boring-Machine Tender (woodworking)	665.685-018
RES	40	Porter, Sample Case (wholesale tr.)	299.687-010
RES	40	Printer-Slotter Helper (paper goods)	659.686-014
RES	40	Pulp-Press Tender (paper & pulp)	532.685-026
RES	40	Pulverizer (chemical)	555.685-046
RES	40	Reduction-Furnace-Operator Helper (chemical; oils & grease)	559.686-038
RES	40	Reeler (build. mat., n.e.c.)	549.685-022
RES	40	Reeler (woodworking)	769.684-034
RES	40	Ribbon Cutter (narrow fabrics)	781.687-050
RES	40	Rounding-Machine Tender (pen & pencil)	663.685-026
RES	40	Rubber-Cutting-Machine Tender (rubber goods)	690.685-342
RES	40	Sand Filler (mine & quarry)	939.687-034
RES	40	Scorer Helper (paper goods)	641.686-030
RES	40	Scrap Sorter (nonfer. metal)	509.686-018
RES	40	Screen-Printing-Machine-Operator Helper (textile)	652.686-038
RES	40	Shear-Grinder-Operator Helper (textile)	628.687-014
RES	40	Shore Hand, Dredge or Barge (construction; mine & quarry)	939.667-018
RES	40	Skein-Yarn-Dyer Helper (textile)	582.686-022
RES	40	Sliver-Lap-Machine Tender (textile)	680.685-094
RES	40	Softball Core Molder (toy-sport equip.)	732.687-070
RES	40	Sorting-Machine Operator (can. & preserv.)	521.685-318
RES	40	Spray-Machine Loader (brick & tile; pottery & porc.)	574.686-010
RES	40	Spring Coverer (furniture)	780.687-038
RES	40	Stacking-Machine Operator II (any industry)	739.685-038
RES	40	Stainer (fabrication, n.e.c.)	739.687-174
RES	40	Steam Cleaner (automotive ser.)	915.687-026
RES	40	Steel-Plate Caulker (any industry)	843.684-010
RES	40	Stopper-Maker Helper (steel & rel.)	519.687-038
RES	40	Stranding-Machine-Operator Helper (nonfer. metal)	616.687-010
RES	40	Striper, Machine (motor-bicycles)	749.686-010
RES	40	Tapper (nonfer. metal; smelt. & refin.)	514.664-014
RES	40	Threading-Machine Feeder, Automatic I (machine shop)	604.666-010
RES	40	Tower Attendant (paper & pulp)	559.666-010
RES	40	Truck-Driver Helper (any industry)	905.687-010
RES	40	Veneer-Stock Layer (millwork-plywood)	762.687-066
RES	40	Venetian-Blind Cleaner and Repairer (any industry)	739.687-198
RES	40	Welder Helper (welding)	819.687-014
RES	40	Wheel Assembler (mfd. bldgs.; vehicles, n.e.c.)	809.684-038
RES	40	Woodworking-Shop Hand (woodworking)	769.687-054
RES	39	Almond-Cutting-Machine Tender (can. & preserv.)	521.685-018

From Holland Codes to the Dictionary of Occupational Titles Occupations

HOC	Cx	Title	DOT
RES	39	Ball-Fringe-Machine Operator (tex. prod., n.e.c.)	689.685-010
RES	39	Barrel-Assembler Helper (wood. container)	669.685-010
RES	39	Block-Splitter Operator (paper & pulp)	663.685-010
RES	39	Boat-Hoist-Operator Helper (retail trade)	921.667-010
RES	39	Bobbin-Winder Tender (glass mfg.)	619.685-022
RES	39	Bottom-Hoop Driver (wood. container)	669.685-022
RES	39	Box-Spring Maker II (furniture)	780.684-022
RES	39	Canvas Shrinker (textile)	587.687-010
RES	39	Caser (petrol. & gas)	930.664-010
RES	39	Caster Helper (jewelry-silver.)	700.687-022
RES	39	Chaser (logging)	921.667-014
RES	39	Chip Washer (beverage)	522.686-010
RES	39	Cigarette-Making-Machine-Hopper Feeder (tobacco)	529.686-018
RES	39	Cleaner, Window (any industry)	389.687-014
RES	39	Cloth Feeder (textile)	589.686-014
RES	39	Coal Trimmer (water trans.)	911.687-018
RES	39	Conditioner-Tumbler Operator (laundry & rel.)	361.685-010
RES	39	Conveyor Loader I (meat products)	525.687-018
RES	39	Corner Former (wood. container)	617.685-014
RES	39	Crusher Operator (sugar & conf.)	521.685-090
RES	39	Distresser (furniture)	763.687-018
RES	39	Dry-Kiln Operator Helper (brick & tile)	573.687-014
RES	39	Dyer Helper (laundry & rel.)	364.687-010
RES	39	Fabric Normalizer (rubber goods)	559.685-066
RES	39	Faller II (logging)	454.684-014
RES	39	Feather-Drying-Machine Operator (tex. prod., n.e.c.)	581.686-034
RES	39	Filler Room Attendant (tobacco)	522.687-022
RES	39	Forming-Roll Operator II (any industry)	619.685-046
RES	39	Fur Glazer (fur goods)	369.684-010
RES	39	Furnace Helper (chemical)	558.686-010
RES	39	Icer, Machine (bakery products)	524.685-034
RES	39	Injection-Molding-Machine Offbearer (musical inst.)	690.686-042
RES	39	Jewel-Hole Cornerer (clock & watch)	770.684-014
RES	39	Laborer (toy-sport equip.)	732.687-030
RES	39	Laborer, Prestressed Concrete (concrete prod.)	575.687-018
RES	39	Last Putter-Away (boot & shoe; rubber goods)	922.687-066
RES	39	Lithographed-Plate Inspector (tinware)	651.687-010
RES	39	Loading-Shovel Oiler (mine & quarry)	932.667-014
RES	39	Lumber Sorter (woodworking)	922.687-074
RES	39	Machine Feeder, Raw Stock (tex. prod., n.e.c.; textile)	680.686-018
RES	39	Mash-Filter-Cloth Changer (beverage)	529.667-014
RES	39	Milk-Powder Grinder (dairy products)	521.685-222
RES	39	Mixing-Machine Feeder (chemical)	550.686-030
RES	39	Mixing-Machine Operator (can. & preserv.)	520.685-166
RES	39	Molder, Foam Rubber (rubber goods)	556.685-046
RES	39	Multiple-Drum-Sander Helper (woodworking)	662.686-014
RES	39	Offbearer, Sewer Pipe (brick & tile)	579.686-026
RES	39	Patcher Helper (steel & rel.)	861.687-014
RES	39	Porcelain-Enamel Laborer (any industry)	509.687-014

HOC	Cx	Title	DOT
RES	39	Poultry-Dressing Worker (meat products)	525.687-082
RES	39	Repairer, Shoe Sticks (rubber goods)	619.685-074
RES	39	Riveter Helper (any industry)	800.687-010
RES	39	Roof-Cement-and-Paint-Maker Helper (build. mat., n.e.c.; nonmet. min.)	550.686-038
RES	39	Rug-Cleaner Helper (laundry & rel.)	362.686-014
RES	39	Rug-Dyer Helper (laundry & rel.)	364.687-014
RES	39	Salvager (utilities)	729.687-030
RES	39	Sanding-Machine Operator (sugar & conf.)	524.665-010
RES	39	Setter Helper (brick & tile)	573.687-030
RES	39	Sheep Herder (agriculture)	410.687-022
RES	39	Shell-Sieve Operator (ordnance)	694.585-010
RES	39	Spin-Table Operator (toy-sport equip.)	732.687-074
RES	39	Stitch-Bonding-Machine-Tender Helper (textile)	689.686-042
RES	39	Sucker-Machine Operator (sugar & conf.)	529.685-234
RES	39	Veneer-Clipper Helper (millwork-plywood)	663.686-030
RES	38	Acid Dumper (elec. equip.)	727.687-010
RES	38	Automobile-Body-Repairer Helper (automotive ser.)	807.687-010
RES	38	Backing-In-Machine Tender (fabrication, n.e.c.)	590.685-010
RES	38	Baling-Machine Tender (any industry)	920.685-010
RES	38	Barrel-Charrer Helper (wood. container)	764.687-034
RES	38	Barrel-Raiser Helper (wood. container)	764.687-038
RES	38	Binder-and-Wrapper Packer (tobacco)	922.687-014
RES	38	Blow-Pit Helper (paper & pulp)	533.686-010
RES	38	Bowling-Ball-Mold Assembler (toy-sport equip.)	556.687-010
RES	38	Break-Off Worker (millwork-plywood)	663.686-014
RES	38	Breaking-Machine Operator (sugar & conf.)	521.685-034
RES	38	Briquette-Machine-Operator Helper (fabrication, n.e.c.)	549.686-010
RES	38	Brush Maker, Machine (fabrication, n.e.c.)	739.685-014
RES	38	Busher (nonmet. min.)	502.687-014
RES	38	Calcine Furnace Loader (paint & varnish)	553.486-010
RES	38	Carrier Packer (protective dev.)	920.687-066
RES	38	Casting-House Worker (nonfer. metal)	514.687-014
RES	38	Cell Cleaner (chemical)	559.687-022
RES	38	Cell Stripper (plastic-synth.)	556.686-014
RES	38	Centrifuge Operator (paint & varnish)	551.685-034
RES	38	Channel Installer (wood. container)	764.687-046
RES	38	Clipper (boot & shoe)	753.687-010
RES	38	Coffee Weigher (food prep., n.e.c.)	529.687-046
RES	38	Coil Binder (nonfer. metal)	619.687-010
RES	38	Column Precaster (mfd. bldgs.)	869.667-010
RES	38	Cone Treater (paper goods)	534.687-010
RES	38	Crate Liner (furniture)	920.687-078
RES	38	Crate Opener (furniture)	929.685-010
RES	38	Crutcher Helper (soap & rel.)	550.686-018
RES	38	Cutter-Operator Helper (mine & quarry)	930.687-018
RES	38	Dolly Pusher (radio-tv broad.)	962.687-010
RES	38	Door Core Assembler (woodworking)	762.687-030
RES	38	Draw-Bench-Operator Helper (nonfer. metal; steel & rel.)	614.686-010

HOC	Cx	Title	DOT
RES	38	Dresser (boot & shoe)	788.687-038
RES	38	Drum Loader and Unloader (beverage)	522.685-058
RES	38	Dry-Cleaner Helper (laundry & rel.)	362.686-010
RES	38	Etcher Helper, Hand (print. & pub.)	971.687-010
RES	38	Extractor-Operator Helper (chemical)	552.686-010
RES	38	Feather-Curling-Machine Operator (tex. prod., n.e.c.)	589.686-018
RES	38	Fleece Tier (agriculture)	410.687-010
RES	38	Folder (laundry & rel.)	369.687-018
RES	38	Forest-Fire Fighter (forestry)	452.687-014
RES	38	Forest-Products Gatherer (agriculture; forestry)	453.687-010
RES	38	Gluing-Machine Offbearer (woodworking)	569.686-022
RES	38	Handle Assembler (woodworking)	762.687-042
RES	38	Hardware Assembler (woodworking)	762.684-046
RES	38	Head-Machine Feeder (meat products)	525.686-018
RES	38	Hogshead Cooper I (wood. container)	764.684-026
RES	38	Hogshead Cooper II (wood. container)	764.687-070
RES	38	Hogshead Cooper III (wood. container)	764.687-074
RES	38	Horticultural Worker II (agriculture)	405.687-014
RES	38	Hose Cutter, Machine (rubber goods)	751.686-010
RES	38	Hose-Tubing Backer (rubber goods)	559.686-018
RES	38	Installer (museums)	922.687-050
RES	38	Kitchen Helper (hotel & rest.)	318.687-010
RES	38	Knock-Up Assembler (woodworking)	762.687-050
RES	38	Laborer, Boot and Shoe (boot & shoe)	788.687-066
RES	38	Laborer, General (brick & tile)	579.667-010
RES	38	Laborer, General (plastic prod.)	754.687-010
RES	38	Laborer, Gold Leaf (metal prod., n.e.c.)	700.687-038
RES	38	Laborer, Pie Bakery (bakery products)	529.686-054
RES	38	Lines Tender (water trans.)	911.687-026
RES	38	Lining Inserter (toy-sport equip.)	732.687-042
RES	38	Loader-Unloader, Screen-Printing Machine (textile)	652.686-022
RES	38	Long-Goods Helper, Machine (food prep., n.e.c.)	529.686-062
RES	38	Mattress Stripper (furniture)	780.687-026
RES	38	Mold Presser (tobacco)	790.687-022
RES	38	Molder, Meat (meat products)	520.685-174
RES	38	Molding-Machine Tender (pen & pencil)	570.685-066
RES	38	Packer, Insulation (nonmet. min.)	579.685-038
RES	38	Padding Gluer (furniture)	780.687-034
RES	38	Paint Pourer (fabrication, n.e.c.)	652.687-022
RES	38	Painter, Embossed or Impressed Lettering (any industry)	740.687-018
RES	38	Paper-Processing-Machine Helper (paper & pulp; paper goods)	534.686-010
RES	38	Power-Chisel Operator (cutlery-hrdwr.)	701.687-030
RES	38	Press Operator (oils & grease)	551.685-114
RES	38	Prizer (tobacco)	920.687-142
RES	38	Pumper Helper (any industry)	914.687-018
RES	38	Quarry Worker (mine & quarry)	939.667-014
RES	38	Reeler (paper goods)	640.685-054
RES	38	Reverser (toy-sport equip.)	732.687-066

Part 2: From Holland Codes to Occupations

From Holland Codes to the Dictionary of Occupational Titles Occupations

HOC	Cx	Title	DOT
RES	38	Roll Finisher (paper & pulp)	920.685-090
RES	38	Shaper, Baseball Glove (toy-sport equip.)	732.684-106
RES	38	Shingle Packer (saw. & plan.)	920.687-158
RES	38	Shuttle Spotter (woodworking)	664.685-026
RES	38	Sizing-Machine Tender (pen & pencil)	662.685-030
RES	38	Skinning-Machine Feeder (meat products)	525.686-022
RES	38	Slitter-Creaser-Slotter Helper (paper goods)	649.686-030
RES	38	Slunk-Skin Curer (meat products)	525.687-106
RES	38	Smoked Meat Preparer (meat products)	525.587-014
RES	38	Soap Grinder (soap & rel.)	555.685-062
RES	38	Spreader I (any industry)	781.687-058
RES	38	Stapler, Hand (furniture)	780.687-042
RES	38	Steamer-Blocker (hat & cap; knitting)	784.684-070
RES	38	Sterilizer (beverage)	920.687-182
RES	38	Stevedore II (water trans.)	922.687-090
RES	38	Stitching-Machine Operator (wood. container)	669.685-086
RES	38	Stripper (furniture)	749.687-030
RES	38	Target Trimmer (toy-sport equip.)	732.687-078
RES	38	Tester-Operator Helper (nonfer. metal)	614.686-014
RES	38	Tobacco-Cloth Reclaimer (tex. prod., n.e.c.)	589.686-050
RES	38	Top-Dyeing-Machine Loader (tex. prod., n.e.c.; textile)	582.686-030
RES	38	Tufter, Hand (furniture)	780.687-050
RES	38	Tumbler Operator (laundry & rel.)	369.685-034
RES	38	Veneer-Jointer Offbearer (millwork-plywood)	665.686-022
RES	38	Wire-Winding-Machine Operator (wood. container)	619.685-090
RES	38	Wool Sacker (agriculture)	920.687-198
RES	38	Wrapping-Machine Operator (paper goods)	641.685-098
RES	37	Apron Cleaner (nonmet. min.)	680.687-010
RES	37	Back Feeder, Plywood Layup Line (millwork-plywood)	569.686-010
RES	37	Blower Feeder, Dyed Raw Stock (textile)	581.686-010
RES	37	Bobbin Cleaner, Hand (textile)	689.687-014
RES	37	Bull-Gang Worker (tobacco)	922.687-026
RES	37	Cake Puller (oils & grease)	521.686-014
RES	37	Calender Feeder (rubber goods)	554.686-010
RES	37	Calender-Wind-Up Helper (rubber goods; rubber tire)	554.686-022
RES	37	Can Doffer (textile)	680.686-010
RES	37	Carton-Counter Feeder (tobacco)	921.686-010
RES	37	CD-Mixer Helper (rubber reclaim.)	553.686-014
RES	37	Cell Plasterer (smelt. & refin.)	519.687-010
RES	37	Cementer, Hand (boot & shoe)	788.687-030
RES	37	Choke Setter (logging)	921.687-014
RES	37	Clipper and Turner (furniture)	780.687-014
RES	37	Color Strainer (textile)	550.687-014
RES	37	Compound-Coating-Machine Offbearer (tinware)	509.666-010
RES	37	Deckhand (chemical)	553.686-022
RES	37	Drier Feeder (rubber reclaim.)	559.686-014
RES	37	Drier-Operator Helper (rubber reclaim.)	553.686-030
RES	37	Drying-Unit-Felting-Machine-Operator Helper (tex. prod., n.e.c.)	581.687-018

Part 2: From Holland Codes to Occupations

From Holland Codes to the Dictionary of Occupational Titles Occupations

HOC	Cx	Title	DOT
RES	37	Dust Puller (smelt. & refin.)	519.687-014
RES	37	Edge-Banding-Machine Offbearer (furniture; millwork-plywood)	762.686-010
RES	37	Exterminator Helper, Termite (business ser.)	383.687-010
RES	37	Farm worker, Grain II (agriculture)	401.687-010
RES	37	Feed-In Worker (grain-feed mills)	929.686-022
RES	37	Feed-Mixer Helper (grain-feed mills)	520.686-018
RES	37	Feeder-Catcher, Tobacco (tobacco)	529.686-038
RES	37	Fish Chopper, Gang Knife (can. & preserv.)	521.687-058
RES	37	Frame Hand (tex. prod., n.e.c.)	689.687-046
RES	37	Gambreler (meat products)	525.687-030
RES	37	Gambreler Helper (meat products)	525.687-034
RES	37	Grizzly Worker (mine & quarry; smelt. & refin.)	933.687-010
RES	37	Hardener Helper (clock & watch)	504.686-018
RES	37	Hassock Maker (tex. prod., n.e.c.)	780.687-018
RES	37	Hide Trimmer (meat products; oils & grease)	525.687-046
RES	37	Hopper Feeder (ordnance)	619.686-018
RES	37	House-Mover Helper (construction)	869.687-034
RES	37	Laborer, Brush Clearing (any industry)	459.687-010
RES	37	Meat Grinder (meat products)	521.685-214
RES	37	Mirror-Machine Feeder (glass products)	579.686-022
RES	37	Oilseed-Meat Presser (oils & grease)	521.685-242
RES	37	Paper Stripper (paper goods; print. & pub.)	922.687-078
RES	37	Pipe Stripper (concrete prod.)	575.687-026
RES	37	Plug Shaper, Machine (tobacco)	520.686-034
RES	37	Pneumatic Jacketer (nonfer. metal)	691.667-010
RES	37	Pole-Peeling-Machine-Operator Helper (wood prod., n.e.c.)	665.686-010
RES	37	Press Puller (grain-feed mills)	529.687-170
RES	37	Processor Helper (grain-feed mills)	521.686-050
RES	37	Pulp Piler (logging)	922.687-082
RES	37	Rack Loader I (tobacco)	529.686-074
RES	37	Renovator-Machine Operator (tex. prod., n.e.c.)	589.685-082
RES	37	Retort Unloader (chemical)	569.686-034
RES	37	Rubber Cutter (rubber goods; rubber tire)	559.685-158
RES	37	Shactor Helper (meat products)	525.687-090
RES	37	Shredded-Filler Hopper-Feeder (tobacco)	529.687-182
RES	37	Smoke-Room Operator (hat & cap)	784.687-066
RES	37	Soap Chipper (soap & rel.)	555.686-014
RES	37	Spike-Machine Heater (steel & rel.)	619.686-026
RES	37	Splitting-Machine-Operator Helper (stonework)	677.666-010
RES	37	Spreader (plastic-synth.)	554.687-010
RES	37	Steamer (tex. prod., n.e.c.)	789.687-170
RES	37	Stunner, Animal (meat products)	525.687-114
RES	37	Sugar-Chipper-Machine Operator (grain-feed mills)	521.685-354
RES	37	Syrup-Mixer Assistant (grain-feed mills)	520.687-058
RES	37	Tipple Tender (grain-feed mills)	521.685-366
RES	37	Tuber-Machine-Operator Helper (rubber goods; rubber tire)	690.686-070
RES	37	Wharf Worker (water trans.)	921.667-026
RES	36	Barrel Drainer (wood. container)	764.687-018

Part 2: From Holland Codes to Occupations

From Holland Codes to the Dictionary of Occupational Titles Occupations

HOC	Cx	Title	DOT
RES	36	Blender Laborer (tobacco)	520.687-010
RES	36	Box Bender (paper goods)	641.687-010
RES	36	Buzzsaw-Operator Helper (any industry)	667.687-010
RES	36	Car Pincher (steel & rel.)	922.687-034
RES	36	Chopper (chemical)	564.687-010
RES	36	Cotton Washer (plastic-synth.)	559.687-030
RES	36	Cut-In Worker (grain-feed mills)	521.686-030
RES	36	Filler-Block Inserter-Remover (furniture)	652.687-018
RES	36	Garbage Collector (motor trans.)	955.687-022
RES	36	Icer (wholesale tr.)	922.687-046
RES	36	Laborer, Syrup Machine (grain-feed mills)	521.687-074
RES	36	Press Bucker (any industry)	920.686-042
RES	36	Print-Line Feeder (furniture)	652.686-026
RES	36	Taker-Off, Hemp Fiber (tex. prod., n.e.c.)	589.686-046
RES	36	Washer (pen & pencil)	733.687-078
RES	35	Automatic Stacker (tinware)	619.686-010
RES	35	Barrel Filler I (beverage)	522.687-010
RES	35	Bolt Loader (saw. & plan.)	922.687-022
RES	35	Can Filler (tobacco)	922.687-030
RES	35	Dye-House Worker (leather mfg.)	582.686-010
RES	35	Electric-Fork Operator (agriculture)	921.685-042
RES	35	Filler Spreader (tobacco)	521.687-046
RES	35	Fish Drier (can. & preserv.)	523.687-014
RES	35	Inner-Tube Inserter (rubber tire)	750.687-010
RES	35	Seed Cutter (agriculture)	404.686-010
RES	35	Seedling Puller (forestry)	451.687-018
RES	35	Shaver (laundry & rel.)	362.687-018
RES	35	Sole Scraper (boot & shoe)	788.687-134
RES	35	Tapper, Hand (ordnance)	737.687-134
REC	68	Marine Surveyor (profess. & kin.)	014.167-010
REC	66	Manager, Orchard (agriculture)	180.167-066
REC	65	Millwright Supervisor (any industry)	638.131-030
REC	62	Construction Inspector (construction)	182.267-010
REC	61	Manager, Aerial Planting and Cultivation (agriculture)	180.167-062
REC	60	Inspector, Fabrication (aircraft mfg.)	806.361-022
REC	60	Jewel Supervisor (clock & watch)	770.131-010
REC	59	Cell-Feed-Department Supervisor (smelt. & refin.)	519.130-010
REC	59	Estimator, Jewelry (jewelry-silver.)	221.387-022
REC	59	Felt-Goods Supervisor, Needle Process (tex. prod., n.e.c.)	689.130-014
REC	59	Oil-Pipe Inspector (petrol. & gas)	930.267-010
REC	59	Steel-Pan-Form-Placing Supervisor (construction)	869.131-026
REC	59	Supervisor, Grease Refining (oils & grease)	553.132-010
REC	59	Supervisor, Lubrication (any industry)	699.131-010
REC	59	Supervisor, Pipelines (petrol. & gas)	862.131-022
REC	59	Supervisor, Swimming-Pool Maintenance (construction)	869.131-038
REC	59	Tankage Supervisor (construction)	869.131-034
REC	58	Dental Ceramist (protective dev.)	712.381-042
REC	58	Jeweler (jewelry-silver.)	700.281-010

HOC	Cx	Title	DOT
REC	58	Jeweler Apprentice (jewelry-silver.)	700.281-014
REC	58	Tune-Up Mechanic (automotive ser.)	620.281-066
REC	57	Final Inspector (clock & watch)	715.381-050
REC	57	Formation-Testing Operator (petrol. & gas)	930.261-014
REC	57	Locksmith (any industry)	709.281-010
REC	57	Locksmith Apprentice (any industry)	709.281-014
REC	57	Quarry Supervisor, Open Pit (mine & quarry)	939.131-010
REC	56	Cable Television Line Technician (radio-tv broad.)	821.261-010
REC	56	Engineer, Exhauster (steel & rel.)	950.362-010
REC	56	Lead Worker, Wafer Polishing (electron. comp.)	673.364-010
REC	56	Supervisor, Doping (construction)	843.134-010
REC	55	Aircraft-Shipping Checker (aircraft mfg.)	222.387-010
REC	55	Cigarette Tester (tobacco)	529.387-014
REC	55	Gas-Meter Mechanic I (utilities)	710.381-022
REC	55	Inspector, Insulation (nonfer. metal)	691.387-010
REC	55	Job Setter (electron. comp.)	616.380-014
REC	55	Material Clerk (clerical)	222.387-034
REC	55	Pin-Game-Machine Inspector (svc. ind. mach.)	729.381-014
REC	55	Sound Ranging Crewmember (military ser.)	378.362-010
REC	55	Wheel Inspector (r.r. trans.)	806.387-014
REC	54	Bead Maker (jewelry-silver.)	770.381-010
REC	54	Bonded Structures Repairer (aircraft mfg.)	807.381-014
REC	54	Cable Maintainer (utilities)	952.464-010
REC	54	Cargo Inspector (petrol. refin.; pipe lines)	549.387-010
REC	54	Drapery and Upholstery Estimator (retail trade)	299.387-010
REC	54	Gas-Pumping-Station Operator (utilities)	953.382-010
REC	54	Inspector, Watch Parts (clock & watch)	715.384-022
REC	54	Pharmacy Technician (medical ser.)	074.382-010
REC	54	Quality-Control Technician (beverage)	529.367-022
REC	54	Reconnaissance Crewmember (military ser.)	378.367-030
REC	54	Returned-Telephone-Equipment Appraiser (comm. equip.)	222.387-046
REC	54	Small-Engine Mechanic (any industry)	625.281-034
REC	54	Supervisor, Research Dairy Farm (agriculture)	410.134-022
REC	54	Weed Inspector (agriculture)	408.381-014
REC	54	Wharfinger (water trans.)	184.387-010
REC	53	Artillery or Naval Gunfire Observer (military ser.)	378.367-010
REC	53	Chronometer-Balance-and-Hairspring Assembler (clock & watch)	715.381-042
REC	53	Cistern-Room Operator (beverage)	520.382-010
REC	53	Facility Examiner (tel. & tel.)	959.367-014
REC	53	Gauger (beverage)	529.387-022
REC	53	Inspector, Fibrous Wallboard (wood prod., n.e.c.)	539.487-010
REC	53	Inspector, Packaging Materials (pharmaceut.)	920.387-010
REC	53	Kiln Operator (woodworking)	563.382-010
REC	53	Liquefaction-Plant Operator (chemical)	559.362-018
REC	53	Pattern Chart-Writer (paper goods)	789.381-014
REC	53	Recordist (motion picture)	962.382-010
REC	53	Rotary Derrick Operator (petrol. & gas)	930.382-022
REC	53	Special Tester (tobacco)	529.487-010

HOC	Cx	Title	DOT
REC	52	Calciner Operator (mine & quarry; smelt. & refin.)	513.362-010
REC	52	Conveyor Operator, Pneumatic System (food prep., n.e.c.)	921.382-010
REC	52	Deicer Tester (rubber goods)	729.387-014
REC	52	Green Inspector (elec. equip.)	726.367-010
REC	52	House-Piping Inspector (utilities)	953.367-018
REC	52	Inspector I (concrete prod.)	779.387-014
REC	52	Inspector, Watch Assembly (clock & watch)	715.381-070
REC	52	Loading-Unit Tool-Setter (ordnance)	632.380-014
REC	52	Luggage Maker (leather prod.)	783.381-022
REC	52	Molding-Machine Operator (sugar & conf.)	520.682-026
REC	52	Pallet-Stone Inserter (clock & watch)	715.381-082
REC	52	Pallet-Stone Positioner (clock & watch)	715.381-086
REC	52	Refinery Operator Helper (petrol. refin.)	542.362-014
REC	52	Roofer (construction)	866.381-010
REC	52	Roofer Apprentice (construction)	866.381-014
REC	52	Sample Maker I (jewelry-silver.)	700.381-046
REC	52	Smoking-Pipe Repairer (any industry)	739.484-018
REC	52	Truckload Checker (construction)	222.367-066
REC	51	Coagulation Operator (plastic-synth.)	559.582-010
REC	51	Cylinder Inspector-and-Tester (chemical)	953.387-010
REC	51	Engine Dispatcher (r.r. trans.)	910.367-018
REC	51	Evaporator Operator (can. & preserv.; dairy products; sugar & conf.)	521.382-010
REC	51	Frame Wirer (tel. & tel.)	822.684-010
REC	51	Furnace-Stock Inspector (elec. equip.)	559.364-010
REC	51	Galley Stripper (print. & pub.)	973.681-010
REC	51	Insulation-Worker Apprentice (construction)	863.364-010
REC	51	Knife Operator (concrete prod.)	579.382-018
REC	51	Lathe Winder (metal prod., n.e.c.)	619.482-010
REC	51	Masher (beverage)	522.482-010
REC	51	Phonograph-Needle-Tip Maker (comm. equip.)	770.382-014
REC	51	Pinsetter Mechanic, Automatic (any industry)	638.261-022
REC	51	Pump Operator, Byproducts (steel & rel.)	541.362-014
REC	51	Roadability-Machine Operator (auto. mfg.)	806.383-010
REC	51	Screwhead Polisher (clock & watch)	715.381-090
REC	51	Separator Operator (grain-feed mills)	521.382-014
REC	51	Sight Mounter (ordnance)	736.481-010
REC	50	Bootmaker, Hand (rubber goods)	753.381-010
REC	50	Caster (jewelry-silver.)	502.381-010
REC	50	Composition-Stone Applicator (construction)	861.361-010
REC	50	Compound Mixer (tinware)	509.485-010
REC	50	Crew Leader, Gluing (millwork-plywood)	569.565-010
REC	50	Cryolite-Recovery Operator (smelt. & refin.)	511.482-014
REC	50	Diamond Cleaver (jewelry-silver.)	770.381-014
REC	50	Dumper-Bailer Operator (petrol. & gas)	931.684-010
REC	50	Engine Turner (jewelry-silver.)	704.381-018
REC	50	Foiling-Machine Adjuster (ordnance)	629.381-010
REC	50	Gas Treater (any industry)	546.385-010
REC	50	Gear-Sorting-and-Inspecting Machine Operator (machine shop)	602.362-014

HOC	Cx	Title	DOT
REC	50	Inspector, Automatic Typewriter (office machines)	706.387-010
REC	50	Inspector, Hairspring I (clock & watch)	715.381-066
REC	50	Manometer Technician (smelt. & refin.)	519.387-010
REC	50	Matrix Plater (recording)	500.384-010
REC	50	Pump-Station Operator, Waterworks (waterworks)	954.382-010
REC	50	Zinc-Chloride Operator (smelt. & refin.)	511.385-010
REC	49	Banking Pin Adjuster (clock & watch)	715.381-018
REC	49	Barrel-Bridge Assembler (clock & watch)	715.381-026
REC	49	Coating-Machine Operator (fabrication, n.e.c.)	590.685-014
REC	49	Collet Maker (clock & watch)	609.682-014
REC	49	Converter Operator (grain-feed mills)	526.382-018
REC	49	Dredge Operator (construction; mine & quarry)	850.663-010
REC	49	Drier Operator (utilities)	543.382-010
REC	49	Farm worker, Vegetable I (agriculture)	402.663-010
REC	49	Gas-Regulator-Repairer Helper (petrol. refin.; pipe lines; utilities)	710.384-010
REC	49	Head-Saw Operator, Insulation Board (wood prod., n.e.c.)	677.682-010
REC	49	Log-Cut-Off Sawyer, Automatic (saw. & plan.)	667.682-090
REC	49	Mica Splitter (mine & quarry)	779.681-010
REC	49	Skin-Lap Bonder (aircraft mfg.)	806.684-130
REC	49	Sugar Controller (sugar & conf.)	529.565-010
REC	49	Thermometer Tester (inst. & app.)	710.384-030
REC	49	Utility Operator I (chemical)	559.682-066
REC	49	Watershed Tender (waterworks)	954.382-018
REC	49	Wink-Cutter Operator (rubber goods)	557.382-014
REC	49	Wire Drawer (clock & watch)	614.382-014
REC	48	Balloon Maker (rubber goods)	752.684-010
REC	48	Box-Blank-Machine Operator (wood. container)	669.662-010
REC	48	Bullet-Assembly-Press Setter-Operator (ordnance)	694.682-010
REC	48	Coin Collector (business ser.)	292.483-010
REC	48	Cook (chemical)	553.665-018
REC	48	Diamond Sizer and Sorter (clock & watch; jewelry-silver.)	770.687-014
REC	48	Draper (garment; knitting)	781.684-026
REC	48	Electric-Meter Installer II (utilities)	821.684-010
REC	48	Felt-Cutting-Machine Operator (tex. prod., n.e.c.)	686.682-018
REC	48	Filtration Operator, Polyethylene Catalyst (chemical)	551.562-010
REC	48	Finish Opener, Jewel Hole (clock & watch)	673.682-022
REC	48	Germination Worker (beverage)	522.585-014
REC	48	Hardness Tester (mine & quarry)	519.585-010
REC	48	Kettle Operator (smelt. & refin.)	519.685-018
REC	48	Knife Setter (sugar & conf.)	638.684-014
REC	48	Laminating-Machine Operator (knitting; textile)	584.682-014
REC	48	Potline Monitor (smelt. & refin.)	512.467-010
REC	48	Powered Bridge Specialist (military ser.)	378.683-014
REC	48	Recovery Operator (smelt. & refin.)	519.582-010
REC	48	Set-up Worker (clock & watch)	715.660-010
REC	48	Silk-Screen Cutter (any industry)	979.681-022
REC	48	Tank Assembler (wood. container)	764.684-030
REC	48	Tank Tender (sugar & conf.)	529.585-014

Part 2: From Holland Codes to Occupations

From Holland Codes to the Dictionary of Occupational Titles Occupations

HOC	Cx	Title	DOT
REC	47	Basin Operator (waterworks)	954.385-010
REC	47	Bellows Maker (photo. appar.)	714.684-014
REC	47	Boat Loader I (water trans.)	911.364-014
REC	47	Braider Operator (nonfer. metal)	691.682-014
REC	47	Briquette-Machine Operator (fabrication, n.e.c.)	549.662-010
REC	47	Bulldozer Operator I (any industry)	850.683-010
REC	47	Carbon Cutter (elec. equip.)	677.685-018
REC	47	Casket Inspector (fabrication, n.e.c.)	739.387-010
REC	47	Causticiser (paper & pulp)	558.382-018
REC	47	Decker Operator (paper & pulp)	533.682-010
REC	47	Dial Maker (office machines)	710.684-018
REC	47	Distiller I (chemical)	552.682-010
REC	47	Drill-Press Operator, Acoustical Tile (wood prod., n.e.c.)	649.682-018
REC	47	Drip Pumper (pipe lines; utilities)	953.583-010
REC	47	Equipment Cleaner-and-Tester (smelt. & refin.)	630.584-010
REC	47	Fermenter Operator (pharmaceut.)	559.685-070
REC	47	Filter Operator (grain-feed mills)	521.682-018
REC	47	Filter Tender (grain-feed mills)	522.665-010
REC	47	Final Inspector, Movement Assembly (clock & watch)	715.684-094
REC	47	Formula Weigher (pen & pencil)	559.685-082
REC	47	Gas Charger (svc. ind. mach.)	827.485-010
REC	47	Inspector, Timing (clock & watch)	715.685-034
REC	47	Inspector, Woodwind Instruments (musical inst.)	730.684-038
REC	47	Lathe Hand (jewelry-silver.)	700.682-014
REC	47	Mailer (print. & pub.)	222.587-030
REC	47	Map-and-Chart Mounter (print. & pub.)	979.684-022
REC	47	Milk-Receiver, Tank Truck (dairy products)	222.485-010
REC	47	Molder, Machine (pharmaceut.)	556.685-050
REC	47	Outfitter, Cabin (ship-boat mfg.)	806.684-102
REC	47	Painter, Mirror (glass products)	741.684-022
REC	47	Papier Mache Molder (fabrication, n.e.c.)	794.684-026
REC	47	Plaster Molder II (foundry)	518.484-010
REC	47	Plastics Worker (aircraft mfg.)	754.684-042
REC	47	Profiler, Hand (clock & watch)	715.685-054
REC	47	Purification Operator I (chemical)	551.685-122
REC	47	Safety Inspector, Truck (automotive ser.; motor trans.)	919.687-018
REC	47	Shuttle Inspector (woodworking)	769.684-046
REC	47	Sinter Feeder (steel & rel.)	513.685-010
REC	47	Spinner (jewelry-silver.)	700.684-074
REC	47	Still Operator (build. mat., n.e.c.)	543.682-026
REC	47	Tooth Polisher (clock & watch)	715.682-026
REC	47	V-Belt Curer (rubber goods)	553.682-026
REC	47	Ventilator (fabrication, n.e.c.)	739.384-022
REC	47	Wash-Mill Operator (chemical)	559.485-010
REC	46	Adjuster (furniture)	709.684-010
REC	46	Air-Conditioning-Coil Assembler (svc. ind. mach.)	706.684-010
REC	46	Ankle-Patch Molder (boot & shoe)	692.682-010
REC	46	Beam-Dyer Operator (textile)	582.685-014
REC	46	Brine Maker I (can. & preserv.)	522.685-018

HOC	Cx	Title	DOT
REC	46	Chauffeur (any industry)	913.663-010
REC	46	Chemical-Strength Tester (textile)	582.587-010
REC	46	Chucking-and-Sawing-Machine Operator (woodworking)	669.682-026
REC	46	Crater (any industry)	920.684-010
REC	46	Foam-Gun Operator (plastic prod.)	741.684-014
REC	46	Freezing-Machine Operator (pharmaceut.)	559.685-090
REC	46	Grinder-Mill Operator (smelt. & refin.)	519.485-010
REC	46	Gunner (grain-feed mills)	523.382-010
REC	46	Inspector, Multifocal Lens (optical goods)	716.687-018
REC	46	Leather Cleaner (laundry & rel.)	362.684-026
REC	46	Lens-Blank Gauger (optical goods)	716.687-026
REC	46	Liquid-Sugar Fortifier (sugar & conf.)	520.585-022
REC	46	Millwright Helper (any industry)	638.484-010
REC	46	Platen Builder-Up (print. & pub.)	651.384-010
REC	46	Pleating-Machine Operator (any industry)	583.685-082
REC	46	Shrimp-Peeling-Machine Operator (can. & preserv.)	521.682-038
REC	46	Sketch Maker I (print. & pub.)	979.381-034
REC	46	Sliding-Joint Maker (musical inst.)	730.684-078
REC	46	Spreader, Machine (any industry)	781.685-010
REC	46	Tapper, Balance-Wheel Screw Hole (clock & watch)	715.682-022
REC	46	Ticket Taker, Ferryboat (water trans.)	911.677-010
REC	46	Toy-Electric-Train Repairer (retail trade)	731.684-022
REC	46	Warp-Dyeing-Vat Tender (textile)	582.685-158
REC	46	Yeast-Fermentation Attendant (food prep., n.e.c.)	522.685-110
REC	45	Assembler, Surgical Garment (protective dev.)	712.684-010
REC	45	Blocker (laundry & rel.)	363.684-010
REC	45	Carpet Cutter I (carpet & rug)	781.684-010
REC	45	Chiller Tender (meat products)	523.585-014
REC	45	Core Checker (foundry)	518.687-010
REC	45	Cotton Baler (agriculture)	920.685-114
REC	45	Dog Bather (personal ser.)	418.677-010
REC	45	Dust Collector, Ore Crushing (smelt. & refin.)	511.682-010
REC	45	Dye-Tank Tender (tex. prod., n.e.c.)	582.685-054
REC	45	Finger-Grip-Machine Operator (glass products)	673.685-054
REC	45	Foxing-Cutting-Machine Operator, Automatic (boot & shoe)	690.682-038
REC	45	Glass Tinter (glass products)	840.684-010
REC	45	Glass-Lined Tank Repairer (beverage)	779.684-026
REC	45	Handler (pottery & porc.)	774.684-022
REC	45	Jacquard-Loom Weaver (textile)	683.662-010
REC	45	Kettle Tender II (smelt. & refin.)	511.685-030
REC	45	Lockstitch-Sewing-Machine Operator, Complete Garment (garment)	786.682-174
REC	45	Milk Receiver (dairy products)	222.585-010
REC	45	Miller, Head, Assistant, Wet Process (grain-feed mills)	629.684-014
REC	45	Poacher Operator (chemical)	551.685-106
REC	45	Pulp-Drier Firer (sugar & conf.)	523.585-030
REC	45	Refractory-Grinder Operator (brick & tile)	677.682-014
REC	45	Refrigerator Glazier (svc. ind. mach.)	865.684-022

HOC to DOT

HOC	Cx	Title	DOT
REC	45	Riveter, Hydraulic (any industry)	800.662-010
REC	45	Router (print. & pub.)	979.682-026
REC	45	Salt Washer (chemical)	551.685-126
REC	45	Sampler-Tester (nonmet. min.)	579.585-010
REC	45	Screen Operator (smelt. & refin.)	511.685-050
REC	45	Shear Operator II (any industry)	615.685-034
REC	45	Shell Assembler (ordnance)	737.684-038
REC	45	Silk Finisher (laundry & rel.)	363.681-010
REC	45	Slime-Plant Operator II (smelt. & refin.)	511.685-054
REC	45	Swimming-Pool Servicer (any industry)	891.684-018
REC	45	Tank-Truck Driver (petrol. refin.; retail trade; wholesale tr.)	903.683-018
REC	45	Truck-Crane Operator (any industry)	921.663-062
REC	45	Wharf Attendant (amuse. & rec.)	342.667-010
REC	44	Appliance Assembler, Line (house. appl.; svc. ind. mach.)	827.684-010
REC	44	Band-Machine Operator (rubber goods)	690.685-030
REC	44	Bias-Cutting-Machine Operator (tex. prod., n.e.c.)	686.682-014
REC	44	Bindery Worker (print. & pub.)	653.685-010
REC	44	Carbonizer (textile)	581.585-010
REC	44	Cell-Tender Helper (chemical)	558.685-022
REC	44	Cement Fittings Maker (concrete prod.)	779.684-010
REC	44	Checker, Bakery Products (bakery products)	222.487-010
REC	44	Cloth Inspector (knitting)	685.687-010
REC	44	Crystallizer Operator (sugar & conf.)	523.585-018
REC	44	Cutting-Machine Operator (sugar & conf.)	521.685-102
REC	44	Devulcanizer Tender (rubber reclaim.)	558.585-026
REC	44	Drier, Short Goods (food prep., n.e.c.)	523.587-010
REC	44	Driver Helper, Sales Route (retail trade; wholesale tr.)	292.667-010
REC	44	Dust Sampler (mine & quarry)	939.585-010
REC	44	Dye-Reel Operator (textile)	582.665-014
REC	44	Final-Dressing Cutter (meat products)	525.684-026
REC	44	Grader, Green Meat (meat products)	529.687-106
REC	44	Graphite Pan-Drier Tender (nonmet. min.)	549.685-014
REC	44	Hardener (hat & cap)	784.684-034
REC	44	Hat Blocker (laundry & rel.)	363.684-014
REC	44	Jigger (textile)	582.665-018
REC	44	Lock Installer (furniture)	706.684-078
REC	44	Mannequin Sander and Finisher (fabrication, n.e.c.)	739.684-122
REC	44	Musical-String Maker (musical inst.)	730.684-050
REC	44	Neutralizer (soap & rel.)	558.585-034
REC	44	Overlock-Machine Operator, Complete Garment (garment)	786.682-198
REC	44	Pressure-Tank Operator (chemical)	523.385-010
REC	44	Riveter, Portable Pinch (any industry)	800.682-010
REC	44	Screen Tender (paper & pulp)	533.685-022
REC	44	Sewing Machine Operator (leather prod.)	783.682-014
REC	44	Shingle Trimmer (saw. & plan.)	667.685-050
REC	44	Stave-Saw Operator (wood. container)	667.685-062
REC	44	Steam-Oven Operator (can. & preserv.)	526.382-026
REC	44	Tank Crewmember (military ser.)	378.683-018
REC	44	Utility Operator (garment)	786.682-262

HOC to DOT

HOC	Cx	Title	DOT
REC	44	Waist Pleater (tex. prod., n.e.c.)	583.684-014
REC	44	Wood Caulker (ship-boat mfg.)	843.384-010
REC	44	Yarn-Mercerizer Operator II (textile)	584.685-058
REC	43	Barrel-Dedenting-Machine Operator (beverage)	617.682-010
REC	43	Blocker (clock & watch)	715.684-034
REC	43	Browning Processor (ordnance)	505.685-010
REC	43	Button-Cutting-Machine Operator (button & notion)	734.384-010
REC	43	Compounder, Cork (wood prod., n.e.c.)	560.587-010
REC	43	Compressed-Gas-Plant Worker (chemical)	549.587-010
REC	43	Counter, Hand (paper goods)	794.687-018
REC	43	Cracking-and-Fanning-Machine Operator (sugar & conf.)	521.385-010
REC	43	Crystallizer Operator (grain-feed mills)	523.685-050
REC	43	Decating-Machine Operator (textile)	582.685-042
REC	43	Deliverer, Car Rental (automotive ser.; retail trade)	919.663-010
REC	43	Dethistler Operator (can. & preserv.)	521.685-106
REC	43	Dowel-Inserting-Machine Operator (woodworking)	669.682-042
REC	43	Drier, Long Goods (food prep., n.e.c.)	523.585-022
REC	43	Dry-House Tender (ordnance)	559.585-010
REC	43	Electroless Plater (any industry)	505.684-010
REC	43	Finisher (pottery & porc.)	774.684-018
REC	43	Finisher, Fiberglass Boat Parts (ship-boat mfg.)	809.684-022
REC	43	Flaker Operator (chemical; smelt. & refin.)	559.685-074
REC	43	Fresh-Work Inspector (tobacco)	529.687-090
REC	43	Gas-Mask Assembler (protective dev.)	712.684-022
REC	43	Gluing-Machine Operator (woodworking)	569.685-046
REC	43	Grain-Drier Operator (grain-feed mills)	523.685-090
REC	43	Inspector (hat & cap)	784.387-010
REC	43	Kiln-Furniture Caster (pottery & porc.)	579.684-018
REC	43	Lime-Sludge Mixer (paper & pulp)	550.585-026
REC	43	Mercury Purifier (chemical)	551.585-014
REC	43	Metal Sprayer, Production (any industry)	505.684-014
REC	43	Mill-and-Coal-Transport Operator (utilities)	544.665-010
REC	43	Mixer Operator Helper, Hot Metal (steel & rel.)	509.566-010
REC	43	Pad-Extractor Tender (knitting)	589.485-010
REC	43	Photograph Finisher (photofinishing)	976.487-010
REC	43	Pickler (can. & preserv.)	522.684-010
REC	43	Pickler Helper, Continuous Pickling Line (any industry)	503.686-010
REC	43	Spiral Runner (mine & quarry)	934.685-022
REC	43	Venetian-Blind Assembler (furniture; retail trade)	739.684-166
REC	43	Wet-Machine Tender (paper & pulp)	539.685-030
REC	42	Air-Conditioning Installer-Servicer Helper, Window Unit (construction)	637.687-010
REC	42	Almond Huller (can. & preserv.)	521.685-010
REC	42	Arrowsmith (toy-sport equip.)	732.684-010
REC	42	Assembler, Mechanical Pencils and Ballpoint Pens (pen & pencil)	733.687-014
REC	42	Autoclave Operator (knitting)	587.585-010
REC	42	Battery-Parts Assembler (elec. equip.)	727.687-038
REC	42	Beaming Inspector (leather mfg.)	585.687-010

HOC	Cx	Title	DOT
REC	42	Bender, Machine (paper goods)	641.685-010
REC	42	Blanket-Cutting-Machine Operator (tex. prod., n.e.c.)	689.585-010
REC	42	Bleach-Range Operator (textile)	582.685-018
REC	42	Blocker (glass mfg.; glass products)	673.685-026
REC	42	Blocker, Hand I (hat & cap)	580.684-010
REC	42	Book Repairer (any industry)	977.684-010
REC	42	Braiding-Machine Tender (rubber goods)	692.665-010
REC	42	Buckle-Frame Shaper (button & notion)	692.685-034
REC	42	Buffing-and-Polishing-Wheel Repairer (any industry)	739.684-030
REC	42	Bullet-Assembly-Press Operator (ordnance)	694.685-014
REC	42	Cannery Worker (can. & preserv.)	529.686-014
REC	42	Case Packer and Sealer (tobacco)	920.685-038
REC	42	Casket Coverer (fabrication, n.e.c.)	780.684-026
REC	42	Caster (plastic prod.)	754.684-022
REC	42	Cementer and Folder, Machine (boot & shoe)	690.685-070
REC	42	Chamfering-Machine Operator II (ordnance)	606.685-018
REC	42	Chick Sexer (agriculture)	411.687-014
REC	42	Chimney Sweep (any industry)	891.687-010
REC	42	Cigarette-Making-Machine Operator (tobacco)	529.685-066
REC	42	Cleaner-Touch-up Worker (office machines)	706.587-010
REC	42	Clip-Bolter and Wrapper (metal prod., n.e.c.)	709.684-038
REC	42	Cloth-Finishing-Range Operator (textile)	589.665-014
REC	42	Cloth-Shrinking-Machine Operator (textile)	587.685-018
REC	42	Cooker, Meal (oils & grease)	523.685-034
REC	42	Corn Cooker (food prep., n.e.c.)	522.685-034
REC	42	Coverer, Looseleaf Binder (print. & pub.)	795.687-010
REC	42	Crabber (textile)	582.685-038
REC	42	Cuprous-Chloride Helper (chemical)	558.585-022
REC	42	Deburrer, Machine (clock & watch)	715.685-018
REC	42	Dipping-Machine Operator (rubber goods)	556.685-034
REC	42	Display-Screen Fabricator (electron. comp.)	725.685-010
REC	42	Dough-Brake-Machine Operator (bakery products)	520.685-090
REC	42	Draw-Frame Tender (tex. prod., n.e.c.)	680.685-034
REC	42	Drier Attendant (can. & preserv.; grain-feed mills)	523.685-058
REC	42	Dyer Helper (hat & cap)	589.685-042
REC	42	Edger, Hand (glass mfg.; glass products)	775.684-014
REC	42	Electrician Helper, Automotive (automotive ser.)	825.684-010
REC	42	Electrifier Operator (textile)	585.685-042
REC	42	Extruder-Operator Helper (plastic prod.; plastic-synth.)	557.564-010
REC	42	Felt-Strip Finisher (tex. prod., n.e.c.)	586.685-018
REC	42	Filtering-Machine Tender (grain-feed mills)	521.685-138
REC	42	Finisher, Brush (fabrication, n.e.c.)	739.684-062
REC	42	Fish Smoker (can. & preserv.)	522.685-066
REC	42	Fish-Net Stringer (tex. prod., n.e.c.)	782.684-026
REC	42	Food Mixer (grain-feed mills)	520.687-034
REC	42	Foxing Painter (rubber goods)	584.685-022
REC	42	Garage Servicer, Industrial (any industry)	915.687-014
REC	42	Grainer, Machine (any industry)	652.686-014
REC	42	Grinder Operator (chemical)	555.685-034

HOC	Cx	Title	DOT
REC	42	Hardening-Machine Operator (hat & cap)	586.685-026
REC	42	Heat-Treater Helper (heat treating)	504.685-018
REC	42	Hide Inspector (meat products)	525.687-042
REC	42	Honey Processor (food prep., n.e.c.)	522.685-070
REC	42	Hop Weigher (beverage)	520.687-042
REC	42	Ice Maker (food prep., n.e.c.)	523.685-102
REC	42	Inspector and Tester (struct. metal)	809.687-018
REC	42	Inspector II (furniture)	780.687-022
REC	42	Inspector, Canned Food Reconditioning (can. & preserv.)	529.687-118
REC	42	Inspector, Clip-On Sunglasses (optical goods)	713.667-010
REC	42	Inspector, Eyeglass Frames (optical goods)	713.687-022
REC	42	Irrigator, Valve Pipe (agriculture)	409.684-010
REC	42	Jig Builder (metal prod., n.e.c.)	761.684-014
REC	42	Knife-Machine Operator (textile)	584.685-030
REC	42	Laborer, Electroplating (electroplating)	500.686-010
REC	42	Laborer, Grinding and Polishing (any industry)	705.687-014
REC	42	Lane-Marker Installer (construction)	859.684-010
REC	42	Lathe Sander (woodworking)	761.682-010
REC	42	Legend Maker (fabrication, n.e.c.)	979.684-018
REC	42	Level-Vial Inspector-and-Tester (cutlery-hrdwr.)	701.687-026
REC	42	Lime Slaker (concrete prod.)	570.685-034
REC	42	Maintenance-Mechanic Helper (any industry)	638.684-018
REC	42	Mash Grinder (dairy products)	520.685-130
REC	42	Mess Attendant (water trans.)	350.677-010
REC	42	Metal-Washing-Machine Operator (svc. ind. mach.)	503.685-034
REC	42	Molder, Lead Ingot (ordnance)	502.685-010
REC	42	Mop Maker (tex. prod., n.e.c.)	739.685-026
REC	42	Motorboat-Mechanic Helper (engine-turbine; ship-boat mfg.)	623.684-010
REC	42	Odd-Piece Checker (knitting)	221.587-018
REC	42	Oven Operator (fabrication, n.e.c.)	590.665-010
REC	42	Paster (brick & tile)	773.684-014
REC	42	Patcher (woodworking)	769.684-030
REC	42	Pattern Marker II (woodworking)	761.684-022
REC	42	Pinsetter-Mechanic Helper (any industry)	829.667-014
REC	42	Plate Gauger (print. & pub.)	979.687-018
REC	42	Power-Press Tender (any industry)	617.685-026
REC	42	Precast Molder (concrete prod.)	579.685-042
REC	42	Preservative Filler, Machine (can. & preserv.)	529.685-190
REC	42	Printer, Floor Covering (fabrication, n.e.c.)	652.685-066
REC	42	Roving-Weight Gauger (textile)	680.687-018
REC	42	Rug-Drying-Machine Operator (carpet & rug)	581.685-050
REC	42	Sampler (elec. equip.)	549.587-018
REC	42	Sandblast Operator (ordnance)	503.685-038
REC	42	Sausage Mixer (meat products)	520.685-206
REC	42	Screen Printer (any industry)	979.684-034
REC	42	Screen Tender (paper & pulp; wood prod., n.e.c.)	534.665-010
REC	42	Scrubbing-Machine Operator (tex. prod., n.e.c.)	582.685-122
REC	42	Sealing-and-Canceling-Machine Operator (clerical)	208.685-026

HOC	Cx	Title	DOT
REC	42	Shaker Tender (steel & rel.)	541.665-010
REC	42	Shrinking-Machine Operator (hat & cap)	586.685-034
REC	42	Skein-Yarn Dyer (textile)	582.685-130
REC	42	Slime-Plant-Operator Helper (smelt. & refin.)	511.685-058
REC	42	Spooling-Machine Operator (metal prod., n.e.c.; nonfer. metal)	691.685-026
REC	42	Spray-Gun-Repairer Helper (any industry)	630.684-034
REC	42	Stacker (leather prod.)	222.587-046
REC	42	Staining-Machine Operator (tex. prod., n.e.c.)	582.685-142
REC	42	Strip-Tank Tender (ordnance)	503.685-046
REC	42	Substation-Operator Helper (utilities)	952.687-014
REC	42	Tablet-Machine Operator (dairy products)	529.685-238
REC	42	Tank Pumper, Panelboard (beverage)	529.685-242
REC	42	Tank-House-Operator Helper (smelt. & refin.)	519.565-014
REC	42	Terrazzo-Tile Maker (brick & tile)	575.684-046
REC	42	Thermal Molder (rubber goods)	553.585-022
REC	42	Tipple Operator (saw. & plan.)	921.662-026
REC	42	Tipple Tender (millwork-plywood)	669.685-090
REC	42	Tire Builder (automotive ser.)	750.684-022
REC	42	Tire Vulcanizer (automotive ser.)	750.684-038
REC	42	Transfer Operator (paper & pulp)	921.685-066
REC	42	Tray-Casting-Machine Operator (dairy products)	520.685-218
REC	42	Trommel Tender (smelt. & refin.)	511.685-066
REC	42	Truer, Pinion and Wheel (clock & watch)	715.684-194
REC	42	Tube Assembler, Cathode Ray (electron. comp.)	725.684-022
REC	42	Tube Sorter (rubber reclaim.)	559.687-066
REC	42	Vacuum-Pan Operator II (chemical)	551.685-154
REC	42	Wafer-Machine Operator (bakery products)	526.685-066
REC	42	Washer (plastic-synth.)	582.685-162
REC	42	Winery Worker (beverage)	521.685-370
REC	42	Wire Drawer (jewelry-silver.)	735.687-042
REC	42	Wire-Drawing-Machine Tender (nonfer. metal)	614.685-026
REC	42	Yardage-Control Clerk (carpet & rug)	221.587-050
REC	41	Alodize-Machine Helper (nonfer. metal)	509.685-010
REC	41	Armature-Winder Helper, Repair (any industry)	721.684-010
REC	41	Assembler, Insulation and Flooring (ship-boat mfg.)	806.684-026
REC	41	Assembler, Motor Vehicle (auto. mfg.)	806.684-010
REC	41	Bagger (plastic prod.)	553.685-014
REC	41	Band Cutter (rubber goods)	690.685-026
REC	41	Barrel Raiser (wood. container)	764.684-018
REC	41	Bead Preparer (rubber goods)	692.685-022
REC	41	Bead-Machine Operator (hat & cap)	583.686-010
REC	41	Beamer (textile)	681.585-010
REC	41	Bedder (pottery & porc.)	573.687-010
REC	41	Belting-and-Webbing Inspector (narrow fabrics)	683.487-010
REC	41	Bench Worker (optical goods)	713.684-018
REC	41	Bending-Machine Operator II (any industry)	617.685-010
REC	41	Billposter (any industry)	299.667-010
REC	41	Bleach-Boiler Filler (paper & pulp)	533.685-010

HOC	Cx	Title	DOT
REC	41	Blender-Conveyor Operator (dairy products)	529.685-022
REC	41	Blocker (narrow fabrics; nonmet. min.)	689.685-014
REC	41	Bolter (grain-feed mills)	521.685-030
REC	41	Boner, Meat (meat products)	525.684-010
REC	41	Book-Sewing-Machine Operator I (print. & pub.)	653.685-014
REC	41	Bottom Wheeler (boot & shoe)	788.684-030
REC	41	Box-Spring Maker I (furniture)	780.684-018
REC	41	Braille-Duplicating-Machine Operator (print. & pub.)	207.685-010
REC	41	Brine Maker II (chemical)	551.687-014
REC	41	Broom Bundler (fabrication, n.e.c.)	692.685-030
REC	41	Bucket Chucker (wood. container)	664.685-014
REC	41	Buffer, Machine (leather mfg.)	585.685-018
REC	41	Buffing-Wheel Former, Automatic (tex. prod., n.e.c.)	689.685-034
REC	41	Burring-Machine Operator (nut & bolt)	615.685-010
REC	41	Button-and-Buckle Maker (any industry)	734.687-046
REC	41	Button-Facing-Machine Operator (button & notion)	690.685-066
REC	41	Canvas Repairer (any industry)	782.684-010
REC	41	Car Dropper (mine & quarry)	932.683-010
REC	41	Car Scrubber (railroad equip.)	845.684-010
REC	41	Car-Wash Attendant, Automatic (automotive ser.)	915.667-010
REC	41	Caustic Operator (plastic-synth.)	554.684-010
REC	41	Clam Sorter (fishing & hunt.)	446.687-010
REC	41	Clarifier-Operator Helper (smelt. & refin.)	511.667-010
REC	41	Clean-Rice Grader and Reel Tender (grain-feed mills)	521.685-062
REC	41	Cleaner (ordnance)	503.684-010
REC	41	Cloth Folder, Hand (tex. prod., n.e.c.; textile)	589.687-014
REC	41	Cloth-Doubling-and-Winding-Machine Operator (textile)	689.685-050
REC	41	Cloth-Stock Sorter (tex. prod., n.e.c.; textile)	789.687-034
REC	41	Cloth-Washer Operator (textile)	582.685-030
REC	41	Coating-Machine Operator II (tex. prod., n.e.c.)	584.685-018
REC	41	Comb-Machine Operator (fabrication, n.e.c.)	640.685-022
REC	41	Combat Rifle Crewmember (military ser.)	378.684-014
REC	41	Cooker, Casing (tobacco)	520.685-082
REC	41	Copy-Lathe Tender (woodworking)	664.685-018
REC	41	Core Feeder, Plywood Layup Line (millwork-plywood)	569.685-018
REC	41	Core Shaper (toy-sport equip.)	692.685-058
REC	41	Core-Composer Feeder (millwork-plywood)	669.685-038
REC	41	Coremaker, Machine III (foundry)	518.685-022
REC	41	Coremaker, Pipe (foundry)	518.684-014
REC	41	Cosmetics Presser (pharmaceut.)	556.685-026
REC	41	Crimping-Machine Operator (textile)	680.685-030
REC	41	Curtain-Stretcher Assembler (woodworking)	762.684-030
REC	41	Cut-Off-Saw Operator, Pipe Blanks (nonmet. min.)	677.685-026
REC	41	Debubblizer (plastic-synth.)	553.585-010
REC	41	Dehydrating-Press Operator (chemical; plastic-synth.)	551.685-046
REC	41	Deoiling-Machine and Pasteurizing-Machine Operator (beverage)	529.685-094
REC	41	Digester-Operator Helper (paper & pulp; paper goods)	532.686-010
REC	41	Doffer (textile)	689.686-022

HOC	Cx	Title	DOT
REC	41	Door Assembler I (woodworking)	762.684-034
REC	41	Drier Operator III (plastic-synth.)	581.685-018
REC	41	Dual-Hose Cementer (rubber goods)	690.685-134
REC	41	Duct Maker (construction; mfd. bldgs.)	809.687-010
REC	41	Dump Operator (any industry)	921.685-038
REC	41	Edge Burnisher, Uppers (boot & shoe)	690.685-138
REC	41	Embosser (boot & shoe)	690.685-158
REC	41	Expeller Operator (grain-feed mills; oils & grease)	529.685-106
REC	41	Extractor Operator (textile)	581.685-042
REC	41	Fabric Stretcher (furniture)	709.667-010
REC	41	Fabric-Lay-Out Worker (textile)	589.687-022
REC	41	Fabric-Machine Operator II (furniture)	616.685-022
REC	41	Filler Shredder, Machine (tobacco)	529.685-110
REC	41	Filter-Press Operator (any industry)	551.685-082
REC	41	Filter-Tank Operator (chemical)	551.585-010
REC	41	Fireworks Assembler (chemical)	737.587-014
REC	41	Fisher, Line (fishing & hunt.)	442.684-010
REC	41	Floorworker, Lasting (boot & shoe)	788.687-046
REC	41	Folder, Hand (paper goods)	794.687-022
REC	41	Folding-Machine Operator (knitting; textile)	589.685-058
REC	41	Folding-Machine Operator (textile)	689.585-014
REC	41	Forepart Laster (boot & shoe)	690.685-186
REC	41	Gas-and-Oil Servicer (motor trans.)	915.587-010
REC	41	Gas-Meter-Installer Helper (utilities)	953.687-010
REC	41	Glove Cleaner, Hand (laundry & rel.)	362.687-010
REC	41	Glove Turner (glove & mit.)	784.687-038
REC	41	Granulator Operator (sugar & conf.)	523.685-098
REC	41	Greaser Operator (hat & cap)	582.685-082
REC	41	Green-Coffee Blender (food prep., n.e.c.)	520.685-110
REC	41	Grinding-Machine Operator, Automatic (button & notion)	690.685-194
REC	41	Hammer-Mill Operator (smelt. & refin.)	515.687-010
REC	41	Hammer-Mill Operator (nonmet. min.)	570.685-030
REC	41	Hat-Blocking-Machine Operator I (hat & cap)	580.685-026
REC	41	Heating-Element Winder (elec. equip.; house. appl.)	723.685-010
REC	41	Hot-Room Attendant (personal ser.)	335.677-014
REC	41	Hothouse Worker (chemical)	549.687-014
REC	41	Inserting-Machine Operator (clerical)	208.685-018
REC	41	Insulation-Power-Unit Tender (construction; retail trade; wholesale tr.)	863.685-010
REC	41	Irrigator, Sprinkling System (agriculture)	409.685-014
REC	41	Jammer Operator (logging)	921.683-054
REC	41	Jewel-Corner-Brushing-Machine Operator (clock & watch)	770.685-026
REC	41	Knitting-Machine Operator Helper (knitting)	685.686-014
REC	41	Laborer, Tanbark (logging)	454.687-014
REC	41	Lacer (toy-sport equip.)	732.687-034
REC	41	Lacquer-Dipping-Machine Operator (button & notion)	509.685-034
REC	41	Last Repairer (boot & shoe; wood prod., n.e.c.)	739.684-110
REC	41	Last Scourer (wood prod., n.e.c.)	662.685-018
REC	41	Latex Spooler (rubber goods)	559.685-114

HOC to DOT

Part 2: From Holland Codes to Occupations

From Holland Codes to the Dictionary of Occupational Titles Occupations

HOC	Cx	Title	DOT
REC	41	Laundry-Machine Tender (tex. prod., n.e.c.)	589.685-066
REC	41	Leaf Coverer (smelt. & refin.)	519.684-014
REC	41	Lever Tender (forging)	612.685-010
REC	41	Light Air Defense Artillery Crewmember (military ser.)	378.684-030
REC	41	Liquor-Grinding-Mill Operator (sugar & conf.)	521.685-202
REC	41	Lubricating-Machine Tender (ordnance)	509.685-038
REC	41	Mangler (knitting)	583.685-070
REC	41	Marker, Hand (boot & shoe)	788.584-014
REC	41	Masker (any industry)	749.687-018
REC	41	Masking-Machine Feeder (plastic-synth.)	920.586-010
REC	41	Mat Puncher (rubber goods)	690.685-286
REC	41	Miner, Placer (mine & quarry)	939.684-014
REC	41	Mixer (hat & cap)	680.685-062
REC	41	Molder, Toilet Products (pharmaceut.)	556.687-022
REC	41	Nailing-Machine Operator (any industry)	669.682-058
REC	41	Offset-Press Operator II (print. & pub.)	651.685-018
REC	41	Oil Dipper (woodworking)	769.684-026
REC	41	Parachute Marker (tex. prod., n.e.c.)	789.587-018
REC	41	Patcher (steel & rel.)	861.684-014
REC	41	Pattern Gater (foundry)	801.684-014
REC	41	Pearl-Glue Operator (chemical)	550.685-094
REC	41	Pilling-Machine Operator (plastic prod.; plastic-synth.)	556.685-058
REC	41	Plate Worker (paper & pulp)	535.685-010
REC	41	Plywood-Scarfer Tender (millwork-plywood)	665.685-022
REC	41	Polymerization-Oven Operator (plastic-synth.)	556.585-014
REC	41	Porter (air trans.; motor trans.; r.r. trans.)	357.677-010
REC	41	Poultry Debeaker (agriculture)	411.687-026
REC	41	Presser, Form (any industry)	363.685-018
REC	41	Print-Shop Helper (print. & pub.)	979.684-026
REC	41	Progressive Assembler and Fitter (agric. equip.)	801.684-022
REC	41	Project-Crew Worker (any industry)	891.687-018
REC	41	Pump Tender, Cement Based Materials (concrete prod.; construction)	849.665-010
REC	41	Reclamation Kettle Tender, Metal (smelt. & refin.)	512.685-022
REC	41	Refractory Mixer (steel & rel.)	570.685-078
REC	41	Road-Roller Operator (construction)	859.683-030
REC	41	Rod-and-Tube Straightener (plastic-synth.)	559.587-010
REC	41	Roller Operator (hat & cap)	580.685-046
REC	41	Rolling-Down-Machine Operator (knitting; textile)	589.685-086
REC	41	Rolling-Mill-Operator Helper (nonfer. metal)	613.685-026
REC	41	Rope Maker, Machine (nonmet. min.)	681.685-082
REC	41	Rotary-Furnace Tender (chemical)	553.685-094
REC	41	Rough-Rice Tender (grain-feed mills)	521.685-274
REC	41	Sagger Preparer (pottery & porc.)	570.685-086
REC	41	Sand Plant Attendant (concrete prod.; mine & quarry)	934.685-014
REC	41	Sandwich-Machine Operator (dairy products)	529.685-210
REC	41	Sheepskin Pickler (meat products)	582.685-126
REC	41	Shirring-Machine Operator, Automatic (tex. prod., n.e.c.)	787.685-038
REC	41	Silver Stripper, Machine (glass products)	579.685-054

HOC	Cx	Title	DOT
REC	41	Sizer, Hand (hat & cap)	784.684-054
REC	41	Slicing-Machine Tender (furniture)	663.685-034
REC	41	Soft Crab Shedder (fishing & hunt.)	446.684-018
REC	41	Solderer, Barrel Ribs (ordnance)	736.684-038
REC	41	Spice Miller (food prep., n.e.c.)	521.685-326
REC	41	Splicing-Machine Operator (tex. prod., n.e.c.)	689.682-018
REC	41	Splitting-Machine Operator (rubber goods; rubber reclaim.)	690.685-386
REC	41	Sprayer, Machine (leather mfg.)	599.685-094
REC	41	Stacker-and-Sorter Operator (saw. & plan.)	921.682-018
REC	41	Stapling-Machine Operator (any industry)	692.685-202
REC	41	Steamer Tender (textile)	582.685-146
REC	41	Stock Shaper (ordnance)	761.684-046
REC	41	Stone Splitter (concrete prod.)	677.685-050
REC	41	Stove-Bottom Worker (fabrication, n.e.c.)	590.667-010
REC	41	Strand-Forming-Machine Operator (tex. prod., n.e.c.)	681.685-118
REC	41	Street-Sweeper Operator (government ser.)	919.683-022
REC	41	Sulfate Drier-Machine Operator (steel & rel.)	551.685-142
REC	41	Sweet-Goods-Machine Operator (bakery products)	520.685-214
REC	41	Synthetic-Filament Extruder (plastic-synth.)	557.565-014
REC	41	Tank Cleaner (paint & varnish)	559.684-022
REC	41	Taper, Machine (fabrication, n.e.c.)	692.685-214
REC	41	Tarring-Machine Operator (tex. prod., n.e.c.)	584.685-046
REC	41	Tetryl-Screen Operator (chemical)	551.685-146
REC	41	Tree-Surgeon Helper II (agriculture)	408.687-018
REC	41	Tubber (jewelry-silver.)	599.685-098
REC	41	Tumbler Operator (rubber goods)	553.585-026
REC	41	Tumbler Operator (any industry)	599.685-110
REC	41	Turner (fabrication, n.e.c.)	669.685-094
REC	41	Turning-Sander Tender (woodworking)	662.685-038
REC	41	Twisting-Machine Operator (any industry)	619.485-014
REC	41	Vacuum-Pan Operator I (chemical)	551.685-150
REC	41	Warp-Tension Tester (textile)	683.687-034
REC	41	Washer, Machine (any industry)	599.685-114
REC	41	Welt Wheeler (boot & shoe)	690.685-482
REC	41	Winding-Lathe Operator (ordnance)	619.685-086
REC	41	Work-Ticket Distributor (knitting)	221.667-010
REC	41	Wrapper-Hands Sprayer (tobacco)	522.687-042
REC	40	Abrasive-Mixer Helper (nonmet. min.)	570.686-014
REC	40	Air-Table Operator (mine & quarry)	549.685-010
REC	40	Assembler, Liquid Center (toy-sport equip.)	732.684-018
REC	40	Assembler, Ping-Pong Table (toy-sport equip.)	732.684-022
REC	40	Assembler-Arranger (fabrication, n.e.c.)	739.687-010
REC	40	Back Tender, Cloth Printing (textile)	652.685-010
REC	40	Bag-Machine-Operator Helper (paper goods)	649.686-010
REC	40	Baggage Handler (r.r. trans.)	910.687-010
REC	40	Baker Helper (bakery products)	526.686-010
REC	40	Baler (plastic-synth.)	690.685-022
REC	40	Banding-Machine Operator (furniture)	619.685-014
REC	40	Base-Filler Operator (toy-sport equip.)	732.685-010

Part 2: From Holland Codes to Occupations

From Holland Codes to the Dictionary of Occupational Titles Occupations

HOC	Cx	Title	DOT
REC	40	Batch Maker (nonfer. metal; steel & rel.)	515.685-010
REC	40	Batch Mixer (brick & tile)	570.687-010
REC	40	Blender-Machine Operator (oils & grease)	520.685-018
REC	40	Block-Press Operator (chemical)	556.685-014
REC	40	Bobbin Disker (glass mfg.)	734.687-022
REC	40	Boiling-Tub Operator (chemical)	551.685-014
REC	40	Bolter Helper (grain-feed mills)	521.686-010
REC	40	Bottle Packer (beverage)	920.685-026
REC	40	Box-Lining-Machine Feeder (paper goods)	641.685-018
REC	40	Brewery Cellar Worker (beverage)	522.685-014
REC	40	Brim Curler (hat & cap)	583.685-014
REC	40	Brush Operator (textile)	587.685-010
REC	40	Brusher, Machine (hat & cap)	587.685-014
REC	40	Bulk-Sealer Operator (plastic-synth.)	554.685-010
REC	40	Bull-Chain Operator (saw. & plan.)	921.685-014
REC	40	Bundle Tier and Labeler (saw. & plan.)	920.685-110
REC	40	Burner Tender (mine & quarry)	571.685-010
REC	40	Cable Puller (construction; utilities)	829.684-018
REC	40	Car Cooper (any industry)	910.687-014
REC	40	Car-Dumper-Operator Helper (beverage)	921.687-010
REC	40	Carcass Splitter (meat products)	525.684-018
REC	40	Carroting-Machine Operator (hat & cap)	586.685-010
REC	40	Carton-Forming-Machine Operator (any industry)	641.685-022
REC	40	Casting-Machine Operator (sugar & conf.)	520.685-062
REC	40	Centrifugal Spinner (concrete prod.)	575.664-010
REC	40	Char-Conveyor Tender (sugar & conf.)	529.685-050
REC	40	Chipper (chemical; paper & pulp; saw. & plan.)	564.685-014
REC	40	Clarifier (grain-feed mills; oils & grease)	521.685-054
REC	40	Clay Mixer (brick & tile)	570.685-014
REC	40	Cleaner III (any industry)	911.687-014
REC	40	Clinching-Machine Operator (elec. equip.)	616.685-014
REC	40	Coil-Rewind-Machine Operator (nonfer. metal)	619.685-030
REC	40	Coiler (protective dev.)	712.687-014
REC	40	Concrete-Pipe-Making-Machine Operator (concrete prod.)	575.665-010
REC	40	Conveyor Loader II (meat products)	525.686-014
REC	40	Conveyor Tender (any industry)	921.685-026
REC	40	Cook, Vacuum Kettle (can. & preserv.)	526.685-018
REC	40	Cooling-Machine Operator (beverage)	523.685-042
REC	40	Core Layer, Plywood Layup Line (millwork-plywood)	569.686-014
REC	40	Core Setter (foundry)	518.684-010
REC	40	Cork Grinder (toy-sport equip.)	662.685-010
REC	40	Corner Cutter (paper goods)	640.685-030
REC	40	Crayon-Sorting-Machine Feeder (pen & pencil)	929.686-018
REC	40	Crown-Assembly-Machine Operator (any industry)	692.685-062
REC	40	Cutch Cleaner (metal prod., n.e.c.)	700.687-030
REC	40	Cutter Helper (any industry)	781.687-022
REC	40	Cutter, Frozen Meat (can. & preserv.)	521.685-098
REC	40	Cutting-Machine Offbearer (tex. prod., n.e.c.)	689.686-018
REC	40	Cylinder Batcher (textile)	582.665-010

HOC	Cx	Title	DOT
REC	40	Dairy Helper (dairy products)	529.686-026
REC	40	Dehairing-Machine Tender (meat products)	525.685-018
REC	40	Design Printer, Balloon (rubber goods)	651.685-014
REC	40	Desk-Pen-Set Assembler (pen & pencil)	733.687-034
REC	40	Destaticizer Feeder (clock & watch)	715.686-010
REC	40	Dicer Operator (plastic-synth.)	690.685-130
REC	40	Dipper (rubber goods)	556.685-030
REC	40	Dipper (any industry)	599.685-026
REC	40	Dope-Dry-House Operator (chemical)	559.685-046
REC	40	Drapery-Head Former (retail trade)	781.684-030
REC	40	Drawer-In Helper, Hand (textile)	683.687-010
REC	40	Drawer-In, Stitch-Bonding Machine (textile)	689.684-014
REC	40	Drawing-Frame Tender (textile)	680.685-038
REC	40	Drier-and-Pulverizer Tender (chemical)	559.685-050
REC	40	Drying-Machine Operator, Package Yarns (textile)	581.685-026
REC	40	Dye-Weigher Helper (any industry)	550.687-018
REC	40	Ear-Muff Assembler (hat & cap)	784.687-022
REC	40	Enrobing-Machine Corder (sugar & conf.)	524.684-018
REC	40	Examiner (fabrication, n.e.c.)	739.687-082
REC	40	Feather Washer (tex. prod., n.e.c.)	582.685-066
REC	40	Filler (tex. prod., n.e.c.)	780.684-066
REC	40	Film Spooler (photo. appar.)	692.685-082
REC	40	Filter Helper (chemical)	551.685-074
REC	40	Filter-Press Tender (beverage)	521.685-130
REC	40	Final Assembler (garment)	789.687-046
REC	40	Fish Cleaner Machine Tender (can. & preserv.)	529.685-118
REC	40	Fish Packer (can. & preserv.)	920.687-086
REC	40	Fish-Bin Tender (can. & preserv.)	529.687-082
REC	40	Fishing-Line-Winding-Machine Operator (tex. prod., n.e.c.)	689.685-066
REC	40	Flocker (tex. prod., n.e.c.)	789.687-054
REC	40	Flower-Pot-Press Operator (pottery & porc.)	575.685-034
REC	40	Folding-Machine Feeder (paper goods)	641.685-050
REC	40	Folding-Machine Operator (clerical)	208.685-014
REC	40	Folding-Machine Operator (laundry & rel.)	369.686-010
REC	40	Folding-Machine Operator (garment)	583.685-042
REC	40	Frame Stripper (soap & rel.)	559.685-086
REC	40	Fringing-Machine Operator (knitting)	685.686-010
REC	40	Furnace Helper (chemical)	553.687-014
REC	40	Garland-Machine Operator (fabrication, n.e.c.)	692.685-090
REC	40	Garment Steamer (knitting)	582.685-078
REC	40	Glass Sander, Belt (glass products)	775.684-042
REC	40	Glass-Unloading-Equipment Tender (glass mfg.)	677.665-010
REC	40	Glove Pairer (glove & mit.)	784.687-034
REC	40	Glue-Spreading-Machine Operator (leather prod.)	584.665-014
REC	40	Gold Burnisher (pottery & porc.)	775.687-022
REC	40	Granulating-Machine Operator (tobacco)	521.685-158
REC	40	Gray-Cloth Tender, Printing (textile)	652.686-018
REC	40	Helper, Manufacturing (aircraft mfg.)	809.687-014
REC	40	Hooker-Laster (boot & shoe)	753.684-018

HOC	Cx	Title	DOT
REC	40	Hopper Attendant (sugar & conf.)	521.685-182
REC	40	Horizontal-Earth-Boring-Machine-Operator Helper (construction)	850.684-014
REC	40	Housecleaner (hotel & rest.)	323.687-018
REC	40	Hydraulic-Press Operator (knitting)	583.685-054
REC	40	Ice Cream Freezer Assistant (dairy products)	529.685-146
REC	40	Injection-Molding-Machine Tender (plastic prod.; recording; rubber goods)	556.685-038
REC	40	Inspector (elec. equip.)	727.687-062
REC	40	Irish-Moss Bleacher (fishing & hunt.)	447.687-014
REC	40	Kiln Drawer (pottery & porc.)	573.667-010
REC	40	Kiln Placer (pottery & porc.)	573.686-026
REC	40	Knotting-Machine Operator (paper goods)	649.685-054
REC	40	Label Drier (recording)	532.687-010
REC	40	Laborer, Cheesemaking (dairy products)	529.686-050
REC	40	Laborer, Concrete Plant (concrete prod.)	579.687-042
REC	40	Laborer, Shellfish Processing (can. & preserv.)	529.687-230
REC	40	Lagging-Machine Operator (nonfer. metal)	691.685-014
REC	40	Laster (boot & shoe)	753.684-022
REC	40	Laundry Worker II (any industry)	361.685-018
REC	40	Lease-Out Worker (textile)	683.684-022
REC	40	Line-Out Worker II (tobacco)	920.687-114
REC	40	Lingo Cleaner (textile)	683.687-026
REC	40	Log Cooker (wood. container)	562.665-010
REC	40	Machine Feeder (welding)	819.686-010
REC	40	Machine-Castings Plasterer (foundry)	519.687-030
REC	40	Marker (laundry & rel.)	369.687-026
REC	40	Marking-Machine Operator (knitting; tex. prod., n.e.c.)	652.685-050
REC	40	Mellowing-Machine Operator (hat & cap)	585.685-066
REC	40	Mica-Laminating-Machine Feeder (mine & quarry)	579.686-018
REC	40	Mixer (nonmet. min.)	570.685-050
REC	40	Mixer Operator II (chemical)	520.685-142
REC	40	Mop-Handle Assembler (tex. prod., n.e.c.)	739.687-122
REC	40	Mud-Mill Tender (smelt. & refin.)	519.685-026
REC	40	Mud-Mixer Operator (smelt. & refin.; steel & rel.)	570.685-070
REC	40	Multi-Operation-Forming-Machine Operator II (any industry)	616.685-042
REC	40	Munitions Handler (ordnance)	929.687-034
REC	40	Narrow-Fabric Calenderer (narrow fabrics)	583.685-074
REC	40	Noodle-Catalyst Maker (chemical)	559.685-126
REC	40	Novelty Worker (dairy products)	524.686-014
REC	40	Nut Steamer (can. & preserv.)	521.687-090
REC	40	Offal Separator (meat products)	525.684-038
REC	40	Order Filler, Linseed Oil (oils & grease)	920.686-022
REC	40	Packager, Machine (any industry)	920.685-078
REC	40	Packing-Machine Can Feeder (tobacco)	920.686-030
REC	40	Padding-Machine Operator (textile)	582.685-106
REC	40	Pager (machinery mfg.)	654.687-014
REC	40	Paint-Roller Covermaker (fabrication, n.e.c.)	739.684-142

Part 2: From Holland Codes to Occupations

From Holland Codes to the Dictionary of Occupational Titles Occupations

HOC	Cx	Title	DOT
REC	40	Panel-Machine Operator (paper goods)	640.685-038
REC	40	Patch-Machine Operator (paper goods)	641.685-066
REC	40	Photocopying-Machine Operator (clerical)	207.685-014
REC	40	Photostat-Operator Helper (any industry)	979.687-014
REC	40	Pin Maker (pottery & porc.)	575.686-018
REC	40	Plaster-Machine Tender (construction)	842.665-010
REC	40	Plating-Machine Operator (paper & pulp)	649.686-026
REC	40	Plug-Overwrap-Machine Tender (tobacco)	529.685-186
REC	40	Polishing-Pad Mounter (optical goods)	739.687-154
REC	40	Powder-Cutting Operator (chemical)	559.685-134
REC	40	Press Operator II (chemical)	551.685-118
REC	40	Press Operator, Pierce and Shave (clock & watch)	715.685-050
REC	40	Press Tender (rubber goods; rubber tire; toy-sport equip.)	556.685-066
REC	40	Presser, Buffing Wheel (tex. prod., n.e.c.)	583.685-090
REC	40	Printer, Floor Covering, Assistant (fabrication, n.e.c.)	652.687-038
REC	40	Rag-Cutting-Machine Feeder (paper & pulp; tex. prod., n.e.c.)	530.666-010
REC	40	Rawhide-Bone Roller (leather prod.)	789.684-042
REC	40	Reaming-Machine Tender (nonfer. metal)	606.685-034
REC	40	River (logging)	454.684-022
REC	40	Riveter (light. fix.)	616.685-054
REC	40	Rock-Dust Sprayer (mine & quarry)	939.687-026
REC	40	Roller-Leveler Operator (steel & rel.)	613.685-022
REC	40	Rolling-Machine Operator (textile)	585.685-078
REC	40	Rolling-Machine Operator (paper goods)	640.685-070
REC	40	Salvager (optical goods)	713.687-038
REC	40	Sawyer I (nonmet. min.)	677.686-010
REC	40	Scroll-Machine Operator (struct. metal)	616.685-062
REC	40	Scullion (water trans.)	318.687-014
REC	40	Sealing-Machine Operator (paper goods)	641.685-074
REC	40	Seed-Cleaner Operator (agriculture; oils & grease)	599.665-010
REC	40	Separator Operator, Shellfish Meats (can. & preserv.)	521.685-286
REC	40	Sewing-Machine Operator, Zipper (button & notion)	787.685-034
REC	40	Shake Backboard Notcher (saw. & plan.)	663.685-030
REC	40	Shaker Repairer (grain-feed mills)	769.664-010
REC	40	Shellfish-Processing-Machine Tender (can. & preserv.)	529.685-214
REC	40	Shipfitter Helper (ship-boat mfg.)	806.687-050
REC	40	Shot Bagger (ordnance)	920.687-170
REC	40	Sieve Maker (grain-feed mills)	529.684-018
REC	40	Singer (meat products)	525.687-098
REC	40	Sizer, Machine (hat & cap)	784.684-058
REC	40	Skeiner (narrow fabrics)	681.685-102
REC	40	Slide-Machine Tender (fabrication, n.e.c.)	641.685-078
REC	40	Slug-Press Operator (elec. equip.)	556.685-074
REC	40	Snuff-Box Finisher (tobacco)	920.687-174
REC	40	Spark-Plug Assembler (elec. equip.)	729.684-046
REC	40	Speed-Belt-Sander Tender (woodworking)	662.685-034
REC	40	Speeder Tender (textile)	681.685-106
REC	40	Spinning-Lathe Operator, Automatic (any industry)	619.685-082

HOC	Cx	Title	DOT
REC	40	Sponge Hooker (fishing & hunt.)	447.684-010
REC	40	Spooler Operator, Automatic (textile)	681.686-018
REC	40	Spooler, Sequins (plastic prod.)	920.686-046
REC	40	Spring Assembler (furniture)	780.684-098
REC	40	Stacker, Machine (woodworking)	569.685-066
REC	40	Stainer (leather prod.)	589.687-034
REC	40	Sticker, Animal (meat products)	525.684-050
REC	40	Stock Checker II (ordnance)	665.685-034
REC	40	Street-Light Cleaner (utilities)	952.667-010
REC	40	Stretcher (hat & cap)	580.685-054
REC	40	Strip Polisher (stonework)	673.685-082
REC	40	Stripper-Cutter, Machine (food prep., n.e.c.)	521.685-342
REC	40	Stuffing-Machine Operator (toy-sport equip.)	732.685-034
REC	40	Sunglass-Clip Attacher (optical goods)	713.687-042
REC	40	Sweatband-Cutting-Machine Operator (hat & cap)	690.686-062
REC	40	Tag-Machine Operator (paper goods)	649.685-118
REC	40	Taproom Attendant (amuse. & rec.)	312.677-010
REC	40	Taxi Servicer (motor trans.)	915.687-030
REC	40	Testing-Machine Operator (tinware)	703.685-014
REC	40	Threader (tex. prod., n.e.c.)	689.687-078
REC	40	Tie Presser (knitting)	789.687-178
REC	40	Tile-Power-Shear Operator (fabrication, n.e.c.)	692.685-222
REC	40	Traveler Changer (textile)	682.687-010
REC	40	Trimmer (mfd. bldgs.)	869.684-066
REC	40	Tripe Cooker (meat products)	526.685-062
REC	40	Tube Coater (metal prod., n.e.c.)	599.685-102
REC	40	Tube-Machine-Operator Helper (paper goods)	641.686-038
REC	40	Unleavened-Dough Mixer (bakery products)	520.685-226
REC	40	Varnish-Maker Helper (paint & varnish)	553.686-042
REC	40	Vulcanizer (boot & shoe)	690.685-4.2
REC	40	Washer (any industry)	599.687-030
REC	40	Washer, Hand (laundry & rel.)	361.687-030
REC	40	Waste Chopper (tex. prod., n.e.c.)	689.686-054
REC	40	Weld Inspector (elec. equip.)	724.685-014
REC	40	Wick-and-Base Assembler (fabrication, n.e.c.)	739.687-202
REC	40	Winder Helper (paper & pulp)	539.687-010
REC	40	Wire-Frame Dipper (button & notion)	734.684-026
REC	40	Wire-Winding-Machine Tender (rubber goods)	690.685-490
REC	40	Woodworking-Machine Feeder (woodworking)	669.686-030
REC	40	Woodworking-Machine Offbearer (woodworking)	669.686-034
REC	40	Wreath Machine Tender (button & notion)	739.685-058
REC	40	Wringer Operator (tobacco)	522.685-106
REC	40	Wringer Operator (chemical)	551.685-162
REC	40	Zipper Cutter (button & notion)	616.685-090
REC	39	Assembler, Bicycle II (motor-bicycles)	806.687-010
REC	39	Back-Strip-Machine Operator (boot & shoe)	690.685-018
REC	39	Bagger (knitting)	582.687-010
REC	39	Band Tumbler (rubber goods)	551.685-010
REC	39	Basting Puller (garment)	782.687-010

HOC	Cx	Title	DOT
REC	39	Battery-Container-Finishing Hand (elec. equip.)	727.687-034
REC	39	Beader (furniture)	739.687-034
REC	39	Beveling-Machine Operator (hat & cap)	690.686-010
REC	39	Bias-Machine-Operator Helper (rubber tire)	690.686-014
REC	39	Bin Cleaner (beverage; grain-feed mills)	529.687-014
REC	39	Bindery-Machine Feeder-Offbearer (print. & pub.)	653.686-026
REC	39	Blender (bakery products)	520.585-010
REC	39	Bobbin-Cleaning-Machine Operator (textile)	689.686-014
REC	39	Bottom Presser (boot & shoe)	690.685-034
REC	39	Brake-Lining Curer (nonmet. min.)	573.686-010
REC	39	Breaker Tender (steel & rel.)	544.685-010
REC	39	Brimer (metal prod., n.e.c.)	700.687-018
REC	39	Brown-Stock Washer (paper & pulp)	533.685-014
REC	39	Bucker (logging)	454.684-010
REC	39	Buffer, Automatic (boot & shoe)	690.685-050
REC	39	Bulker (tobacco)	522.687-018
REC	39	Bullet-Lubricating-Machine Operator (ordnance)	694.685-018
REC	39	Candle Molder, Hand (fabrication, n.e.c.)	739.687-054
REC	39	Candy Spreader (sugar & conf.)	520.687-022
REC	39	Chalk Cutter (pen & pencil)	733.687-022
REC	39	Channel Opener, Outsoles (boot & shoe)	690.685-082
REC	39	Charger-Operator Helper (steel & rel.)	504.686-010
REC	39	Chip-Bin Conveyor Tender (chemical; paper & pulp)	921.685-022
REC	39	Classifier (laundry & rel.)	361.687-014
REC	39	Cleaner (engraving)	704.687-010
REC	39	Cleaner and Preparer (elec. equip.)	721.687-010
REC	39	Cleat Feeder (wood. container)	669.687-010
REC	39	Clipper (any industry)	789.687-030
REC	39	Cloth-Shrinking-Machine-Operator Helper (textile)	587.686-010
REC	39	Coat-Hanger-Shaper-Machine Operator (woodworking)	669.685-034
REC	39	Compound Worker (recording)	559.686-010
REC	39	Cooker Cleaner (can. & preserv.)	529.687-054
REC	39	Corn Grinder (food prep., n.e.c.)	521.685-082
REC	39	Corn Popper (sugar & conf.)	526.685-026
REC	39	Custom-Feed-Mill-Operator Helper (grain-feed mills)	521.686-026
REC	39	Cutter II (fabrication, n.e.c.)	692.686-030
REC	39	Drier Tender I (oils & grease)	523.685-074
REC	39	Dry-Press-Operator Helper (brick & tile)	575.686-010
REC	39	Drying-Room Attendant (soap & rel.)	553.585-018
REC	39	Dye-Stand Loader (textile)	589.687-062
REC	39	Egg-Breaking-Machine Operator (can. & preserv.)	521.685-114
REC	39	Extractor-Machine Operator (can. & preserv.)	521.665-014
REC	39	Factory Helper (sugar & conf.)	529.686-034
REC	39	Farm worker, Diversified Crops II (agriculture)	407.687-010
REC	39	Farm worker, Field Crop II (agriculture)	404.687-010
REC	39	Farm worker, Fruit II (agriculture)	403.687-010
REC	39	Farm worker, Vegetable II (agriculture)	402.687-010
REC	39	Felting-Machine-Operator Helper (tex. prod., n.e.c.)	586.686-014
REC	39	Filter Changer (beverage)	521.687-050

Part 2: From Holland Codes to Occupations

From Holland Codes to the Dictionary of Occupational Titles Occupations

HOC	Cx	Title	DOT
REC	39	Fish Cleaner (can. & preserv.; fishing & hunt.)	525.684-030
REC	39	Flour-Blender Helper (grain-feed mills)	520.686-022
REC	39	Flumer I (sugar & conf.)	922.665-010
REC	39	Foiling-Machine Operator (ordnance)	692.685-086
REC	39	Folder (tex. prod., n.e.c.)	789.687-058
REC	39	Fur-Floor Worker (leather mfg.)	589.686-022
REC	39	Fusing-Machine Tender (garment; knitting)	583.685-046
REC	39	General Helper (food prep., n.e.c.)	522.686-014
REC	39	General Helper (sugar & conf.)	529.686-046
REC	39	Glove Former (glove & mit.; laundry & rel.)	363.687-010
REC	39	Glove Turner and Former, Automatic (glove & mit.)	583.686-018
REC	39	Goat Herder (agriculture)	410.687-014
REC	39	Grease-Refiner Operator (oils & grease)	551.685-086
REC	39	Hacker (brick & tile)	573.686-022
REC	39	Hat-Blocking-Machine Operator II (hat & cap)	580.685-030
REC	39	Honey Extractor (food prep., n.e.c.)	521.685-174
REC	39	Hot-Wort Settler (beverage)	521.685-186
REC	39	Ink Printer (jewelry-silver.; leather prod.; plastic prod.)	652.685-038
REC	39	Irish-Moss Gatherer (fishing & hunt.)	447.687-018
REC	39	Kiln Loader (beverage)	523.687-018
REC	39	Knock-Out Hand (plastic prod.)	754.684-034
REC	39	Lacer and Tier (elec. equip.)	724.687-010
REC	39	Laundry Laborer (laundry & rel.)	361.687-018
REC	39	Lead Former (pen & pencil)	575.685-050
REC	39	Leaf Conditioner (tobacco)	522.687-026
REC	39	Leaf-Conditioner Helper (tobacco)	522.687-030
REC	39	Loading-Machine-Operator Helper (mine & quarry)	939.686-010
REC	39	Loose-End Finder, Bobbin (knitting)	681.687-014
REC	39	Lowerator Operator (fabrication, n.e.c.)	922.686-014
REC	39	Mangle-Press Catcher (textile)	583.686-022
REC	39	Mash-Filter Operator (beverage)	521.565-014
REC	39	Mill Feeder (grain-feed mills)	520.685-134
REC	39	Mill-Operator Helper (any industry)	599.686-010
REC	39	Miller (beverage)	521.585-014
REC	39	Mix-Crusher Operator (elec. equip.)	544.585-010
REC	39	Mixer Operator (concrete prod.)	570.685-058
REC	39	Molder Helper (optical goods)	575.686-014
REC	39	Mosquito Sprayer (government ser.)	379.687-014
REC	39	Motor Polarizer (clock & watch)	715.687-090
REC	39	Mounter II (light. fix.)	692.685-126
REC	39	Neck Skewer (meat products)	525.687-050
REC	39	Needle-Punch-Machine-Operator Helper (textile)	689.686-034
REC	39	Nut-and-Bolt Assembler (nut & bolt)	929.587-010
REC	39	Order Runner (meat products)	525.687-058
REC	39	Paper-Bag-Press Operator (paper goods)	641.686-026
REC	39	Peanut Blancher (can. & preserv.)	521.685-246
REC	39	Plug Shaper, Hand (tobacco)	520.687-050
REC	39	Pointing-Machine Operator (plastic prod.; rubber goods)	690.685-310
REC	39	Pourer (fabrication, n.e.c.)	739.687-158

Part 2: From Holland Codes to Occupations

From Holland Codes to the Dictionary of Occupational Titles Occupations

HOC	Cx	Title	DOT
REC	39	Preparation-Room Worker (nonmet. min.)	570.686-018
REC	39	Press Feeder (knitting; textile)	583.686-030
REC	39	Press Hand (knitting)	583.687-010
REC	39	Press Machine Feeder (tobacco)	529.686-066
REC	39	Press Operator (rubber reclaim.)	559.685-138
REC	39	Presser, Automatic (laundry & rel.)	363.685-014
REC	39	Print Washer (photofinishing)	976.684-022
REC	39	Racker (clock & watch)	715.687-106
REC	39	Racker, Silk-Screen Printing (any industry)	659.687-014
REC	39	Raw-Stock-Machine Loader (textile)	582.686-018
REC	39	Roll Cutter (rubber goods)	690.685-322
REC	39	Roll Turner (knitting)	689.685-110
REC	39	Roller Cleaner (textile)	680.687-014
REC	39	Rouge Mixer (optical goods)	570.685-082
REC	39	Rug-Inspector Helper (tex. prod., n.e.c.)	589.686-038
REC	39	Sealer (fishing & hunt.)	461.684-010
REC	39	Shaker (hat & cap)	589.685-094
REC	39	Shaping-Machine Operator (plastic prod.)	690.685-354
REC	39	Shellacker (ordnance)	737.687-130
REC	39	Shoe Coverer (boot & shoe)	788.687-126
REC	39	Shrouder (meat products)	525.587-010
REC	39	Singer (narrow fabrics)	585.687-030
REC	39	Skein Winder (textile)	681.685-098
REC	39	Skein-Yarn Drier (textile)	581.685-054
REC	39	Skull Grinder (meat products)	521.687-130
REC	39	Sorter, Agricultural Produce (agriculture; can. & preserv.; wholesale tr.)	529.687-186
REC	39	Stenciler (any industry)	920.687-178
REC	39	Sumatra Opener (tobacco)	529.687-198
REC	39	Sweatband Flanger (hat & cap)	690.686-058
REC	39	Tape Coater (nonmet. min.)	692.685-210
REC	39	Toggle-Press Folder-and-Feeder (boot & shoe)	690.686-066
REC	39	Topper (knitting)	685.687-026
REC	39	Tray Drier (knitting)	581.686-038
REC	39	Trimmer, Hand (leather mfg.)	585.684-010
REC	39	Tube Handler (textile)	582.686-034
REC	39	Tube-Building-Machine Operator (rubber goods)	559.685-174
REC	39	Turner (can. & preserv.)	522.687-038
REC	39	Turner (any industry)	789.687-182
REC	39	Twisting-Machine Operator (comm. equip.; elec. equip.)	691.686-010
REC	39	Umbrella Finisher (fabrication, n.e.c.)	739.687-190
REC	39	Washer, Agricultural Produce (agriculture; can. & preserv.; sugar & conf.; wholesale tr.)	529.685-258
REC	39	Washroom Cleaner (sugar & conf.)	529.687-214
REC	39	Wood Handler (paper & pulp)	921.687-034
REC	38	Assembler (tex. prod., n.e.c.)	734.687-014
REC	38	Bag Cutter (tex. prod., n.e.c.)	789.687-010
REC	38	Bender, Hand (woodworking)	769.684-018
REC	38	Bleach Packer (chemical)	558.687-010

Part 2: From Holland Codes to Occupations

From Holland Codes to the Dictionary of Occupational Titles Occupations

HOC	Cx	Title	DOT
REC	38	Boat Buffer, Plastic (ship-boat mfg.)	849.684-010
REC	38	Bone Crusher (chemical)	555.685-014
REC	38	Bone-Char Operator (chemical)	553.686-010
REC	38	Border Measurer and Cutter (furniture)	780.687-010
REC	38	Box-Truck Washer (meat products)	529.687-018
REC	38	Brim Raiser (hat & cap)	784.687-010
REC	38	Cake Former (oils & grease)	520.685-038
REC	38	Cake Stripper (oils & grease)	520.685-042
REC	38	Can-Conveyor Feeder (food prep., n.e.c.)	529.685-046
REC	38	Casing Cleaner (meat products)	525.686-010
REC	38	Circle Edger (glass products)	673.685-038
REC	38	Cleaner (fabrication, n.e.c.)	739.687-058
REC	38	Clearance Cutter (clock & watch)	615.685-014
REC	38	Concrete-Vault Maker (concrete prod.)	579.684-010
REC	38	Continuous-Towel Roller (laundry & rel.)	361.685-014
REC	38	Corrugated-Fastener Driver (woodworking)	669.685-042
REC	38	Defective-Cigarette Slitter (tobacco)	529.685-090
REC	38	Distributor-Cleaner (tobacco)	529.687-070
REC	38	Drier Attendant (garment)	581.686-018
REC	38	Drying-Room Attendant (hat & cap)	581.687-014
REC	38	Dusting-and-Brushing-Machine Operator (rubber goods)	559.685-054
REC	38	Extractor Operator (any industry)	581.685-038
REC	38	Farm worker, General II (agriculture)	421.687-010
REC	38	Filter Cleaner (plastic-synth.)	559.687-038
REC	38	Flatwork Finisher (laundry & rel.)	363.686-010
REC	38	Flotation-Tender Helper (smelt. & refin.)	511.687-018
REC	38	Folding-Machine Tender (boot & shoe)	788.685-014
REC	38	Foot Worker (chemical)	934.687-010
REC	38	Foundry Laborer, Coreroom (foundry)	518.687-014
REC	38	Frame Trimmer II (wood prod., n.e.c.)	769.687-022
REC	38	Greens Tier (wholesale tr.)	920.687-094
REC	38	Hog Tender (woodworking)	564.685-018
REC	38	Hogshead Mat Assembler (wood. container)	764.687-082
REC	38	Hook Puller (narrow fabrics)	683.687-022
REC	38	Horseradish Maker (can. & preserv.)	529.685-142
REC	38	Kiln-Operator Helper (concrete prod.)	573.685-022
REC	38	Laborer, Concrete-Mixing Plant (construction)	579.665-014
REC	38	Lace-Roller Operator (leather prod.)	920.685-070
REC	38	Lamination Spinner (elec. equip.)	729.687-018
REC	38	Last Puller (boot & shoe)	788.687-086
REC	38	Linking-Machine Operator (meat products)	529.685-162
REC	38	Machine Cleaner (any industry)	699.687-014
REC	38	Mat Sewer (oils & grease)	529.687-154
REC	38	Matting-Press Tender (rubber goods)	556.685-042
REC	38	Mattress-Filling-Machine Tender (furniture)	780.685-010
REC	38	Mexican Food Maker, Hand (food prep., n.e.c.)	520.687-046
REC	38	Miller I (chemical)	570.685-042
REC	38	Molder, Shoe Parts (boot & shoe)	788.687-094
REC	38	Oyster Floater (fishing & hunt.)	449.687-010

From Holland Codes to the Dictionary of Occupational Titles Occupations

HOC	Cx	Title	DOT
REC	38	Packer-Fuser (chemical)	737.687-094
REC	38	Paraffin-Machine Operator (paper goods)	534.685-026
REC	38	Partition Assembler (wood. container)	762.687-054
REC	38	Picking-Machine Operator (any industry)	680.685-082
REC	38	Pickler (meat products)	522.687-034
REC	38	Polystyrene-Molding-Machine Tender (plastic prod.)	556.685-062
REC	38	Powderer (hat & cap)	784.687-058
REC	38	Press Operator (laundry & rel.)	363.685-010
REC	38	Presser, Hand (any industry)	363.684-018
REC	38	Production Helper (nonfer. metal)	691.687-010
REC	38	Punchboard-Filling-Machine Operator (paper goods)	649.685-094
REC	38	Putty Mixer and Applier (wood. container)	769.687-038
REC	38	Quilt Stuffer (tex. prod., n.e.c.)	789.687-130
REC	38	Rack Loader (fabrication, n.e.c.)	590.687-018
REC	38	Raw-Stock-Drier Tender (textile)	581.685-046
REC	38	Record-Changer Tester (comm. equip.)	720.687-014
REC	38	Roof-Truss-Machine Tender (mfd. bldgs.)	669.685-070
REC	38	Rug Cutter (fabrication, n.e.c.)	590.687-022
REC	38	Rug-Dry-Room Attendant (laundry & rel.)	369.685-026
REC	38	Sander, Hand (woodworking)	761.687-010
REC	38	Screen Handler (paper & pulp)	539.685-026
REC	38	Screen-Tender Helper (paper & pulp)	533.687-010
REC	38	Seam Steamer (garment)	789.687-166
REC	38	Shale Planer Operator Helper (mine & quarry)	930.667-010
REC	38	Shirt Presser (laundry & rel.)	363.685-026
REC	38	Shoe Turner (boot & shoe)	788.687-130
REC	38	Shot-Coat Tender (concrete prod.)	575.665-018
REC	38	Shuttle Hand (textile)	689.686-038
REC	38	Sieve-Grader Tender (can. & preserv.)	521.665-026
REC	38	Singer (hat & cap)	784.687-062
REC	38	Skin Lifter, Bacon (meat products)	521.687-126
REC	38	Slicing-Machine Tender (wood prod., n.e.c.)	663.686-026
REC	38	Spiral-Tube-Winder Helper (paper goods)	640.687-014
REC	38	Stamper (button & notion)	734.685-010
REC	38	Stave-Planer Tender (saw. & plan.)	665.686-014
REC	38	Steamer (meat products)	525.687-110
REC	38	Stone Cleaner (beverage)	529.687-190
REC	38	Stuffer (meat products)	520.685-210
REC	38	Swedger (jewelry-silver.)	735.687-038
REC	38	Sweet-Potato Disintegrator (can. & preserv.)	521.685-358
REC	38	Table-Cover Folder (tex. prod., n.e.c.)	920.687-186
REC	38	Tank Cleaner (chemical; plastic-synth.)	559.687-062
REC	38	Thread-Pulling-Machine Attendant (garment)	689.686-046
REC	38	Tip Bander (pen & pencil)	733.685-030
REC	38	Tire Mounter (fabrication, n.e.c.)	739.684-158
REC	38	Tube Cleaner (any industry)	891.687-030
REC	38	Tumbler Operator (chemical)	550.685-118
REC	38	Utility Worker (sugar & conf.)	529.686-086
REC	38	Washer (grain-feed mills)	529.687-210

HOC	Cx	Title	DOT
REC	38	Washer (clock & watch)	715.687-126
REC	38	Washroom Operator (sugar & conf.)	529.665-014
REC	38	Welt-Butter, Hand (boot & shoe)	788.687-162
REC	38	Wood-Heel Back-Liner (boot & shoe)	662.685-042
REC	38	Worm Picker (agriculture)	413.687-010
REC	37	Asbestos-Shingle Shearing-Machine Operator (nonmet. min.)	679.686-010
REC	37	Assembler (svc. ind. mach.)	731.687-010
REC	37	Bale Sewer (agriculture)	920.687-022
REC	37	Base Remover (light. fix.)	692.686-014
REC	37	Battery Stacker (elec. equip.)	727.687-030
REC	37	Blintze Roller (food prep., n.e.c.)	520.687-014
REC	37	Block Inspector (fabrication, n.e.c.)	739.687-038
REC	37	Bobbin Winder, Machine (boot & shoe)	681.685-022
REC	37	Bottom Bleacher (boot & shoe)	788.687-014
REC	37	Breaker-Up-Machine Operator (hat & cap)	589.685-014
REC	37	Broomcorn Seeder (fabrication, n.e.c.)	692.686-018
REC	37	Brusher (boot & shoe)	788.687-018
REC	37	Bundle Breaker (tex. prod., n.e.c.)	689.687-018
REC	37	Cake Wrapper (plastic-synth.)	589.687-010
REC	37	Casing-In-Line Feeder (print. & pub.)	653.686-010
REC	37	Casing-Running-Machine Tender (meat products)	525.685-014
REC	37	Cement Sprayer Helper, Nozzle (concrete prod.; construction)	844.687-010
REC	37	Chaser, Tar (steel & rel.)	549.687-010
REC	37	Clamper (pen & pencil)	733.687-026
REC	37	Cleaner, Commercial or Institutional (any industry)	381.687-014
REC	37	Cleaner, Wall (any industry)	381.687-026
REC	37	Cloth Sander (textile)	581.685-010
REC	37	Clothespin-Machine Operator (woodworking)	667.686-010
REC	37	Coffee-Roaster Helper (food prep., n.e.c.)	523.687-010
REC	37	Coke Drawer, Hand (steel & rel.)	543.687-010
REC	37	Cooker Loader (oils & grease)	921.685-030
REC	37	Cork-Pressing-Machine Operator (wood prod., n.e.c.)	569.686-018
REC	37	Cotton Tier (agriculture)	920.687-074
REC	37	Cutter, Hand III (any industry)	781.687-030
REC	37	Debrander (boot & shoe)	753.687-014
REC	37	Detacker (knitting; textile)	589.685-030
REC	37	Dipper (pen & pencil)	733.687-038
REC	37	Dipper and Drier (woodworking)	749.687-010
REC	37	Drier Operator (can. & preserv.)	523.685-062
REC	37	Drier-Operator Helper (chemical)	553.685-058
REC	37	Drum Attendant (leather mfg.; tex. prod., n.e.c.)	582.685-050
REC	37	Dulser (fishing & hunt.)	447.687-010
REC	37	Dust-Brush Assembler (house. appl.)	739.687-074
REC	37	Dyer (button & notion)	582.687-014
REC	37	Egg Breaker (any industry)	521.687-042
REC	37	Feather Renovator (laundry & rel.)	362.685-010
REC	37	Filler-Shredder Helper (tobacco)	529.687-078

HOC	Cx	Title	DOT
REC	37	First-Breaker Feeder (tex. prod., n.e.c.)	680.686-014
REC	37	Fish Bailer (fishing & hunt.)	914.685-010
REC	37	Flame Degreaser (automotive ser.)	503.685-022
REC	37	Folding-Machine Feeder (tex. prod., n.e.c.)	920.686-018
REC	37	Frame Feeder (chemical)	553.686-034
REC	37	Garment Turner (garment; knitting)	789.687-074
REC	37	General Helper (oils & grease)	529.687-094
REC	37	Gluten-Settling Tender (grain-feed mills)	521.685-150
REC	37	Greaser (ordnance)	736.687-010
REC	37	Harness Cleaner (textile)	699.687-010
REC	37	Hogshead Hooper (wood. container)	764.687-078
REC	37	Hoop Coiler (wood. container)	617.686-010
REC	37	Hopper Feeder (oils & grease)	551.686-018
REC	37	Keg Varnisher (wood. container)	749.687-014
REC	37	Laborer, Cook House (chemical)	551.687-022
REC	37	Laborer, General (motor trans.)	909.687-014
REC	37	Laborer, Tree Tapping (agriculture; forestry)	453.687-014
REC	37	Laborer, Vat House (chemical)	559.686-030
REC	37	Lacer I (boot & shoe)	788.687-070
REC	37	Latrine Cleaner (mine & quarry)	939.687-022
REC	37	Laundry-Bag-Punch Operator (paper goods)	649.685-062
REC	37	Leveler I (wood. container)	764.687-094
REC	37	Lining Scrubber (laundry & rel.)	362.687-014
REC	37	Machine Feeder (any industry)	699.686-010
REC	37	Meal-Grinder Tender (grain-feed mills)	521.685-210
REC	37	Mold Cleaner (toy-sport equip.)	732.687-046
REC	37	Mold Sheet Cleaner (metal prod., n.e.c.)	700.687-046
REC	37	Mold Stripper (toy-sport equip.)	732.687-050
REC	37	Molding-Machine-Operator Helper (sugar & conf.)	520.686-030
REC	37	Mud-Mixer Helper (steel & rel.)	549.687-022
REC	37	Odd Bundle Worker (tobacco)	529.687-166
REC	37	Opener (rubber goods)	559.686-034
REC	37	Opener II (hat & cap)	589.686-030
REC	37	Pad-Machine Feeder (saw. & plan.)	920.686-034
REC	37	Painter, Panel Edge (furniture)	740.687-022
REC	37	Peeled-Potato Inspector (food prep., n.e.c.)	521.687-094
REC	37	Pick Remover (textile)	689.687-058
REC	37	Picker (tobacco)	521.687-098
REC	37	Poultry Dresser (agriculture; meat products)	525.687-070
REC	37	Poultry Eviscerator (meat products)	525.687-074
REC	37	Poultry Killer (meat products)	525.684-042
REC	37	Press Operator, Meat (meat products)	520.685-182
REC	37	Presser, Handkerchief (laundry & rel.)	363.685-022
REC	37	Pulper Tender (can. & preserv.)	521.685-262
REC	37	Raker (carpet & rug)	789.687-138
REC	37	Rug-Sample Beveler (carpet & rug)	781.684-050
REC	37	Sample Washer (petrol. & gas)	939.687-030
REC	37	Screen Cleaner (wood prod., n.e.c.)	569.687-018
REC	37	Seedling Sorter (forestry)	451.687-022

HOC	Cx	Title	DOT
REC	37	Shackler (meat products)	525.687-086
REC	37	Shaker, Wearing Apparel (laundry & rel.)	361.687-026
REC	37	Shank-Piece Tacker (boot & shoe)	788.687-118
REC	37	Shaver (meat products)	525.687-094
REC	37	Sheet Turner (millwork-plywood)	762.687-062
REC	37	Slat Twister (furniture)	616.685-066
REC	37	Slat-Basket Maker Helper, Machine (wood. container)	669.686-026
REC	37	Slotter-Operator Helper (paper goods)	640.686-014
REC	37	Soda-Room Operator (plastic-synth.)	551.687-034
REC	37	Splicer (fabrication, n.e.c.)	692.687-010
REC	37	Splitter, Hand (button & notion)	734.687-086
REC	37	Spreader Operator, Automatic (tobacco)	529.685-222
REC	37	Stem-Dryer Maintainer (tobacco)	529.685-230
REC	37	Stripper (plastic prod.; rubber goods)	556.686-018
REC	37	Suction-Plate-Carrier Cleaner (tobacco)	529.687-194
REC	37	Sugar Presser (grain-feed mills)	521.685-350
REC	37	Suppository-Molding-Machine Operator (pharmaceut.)	556.686-022
REC	37	Tennis-Ball-Cover Cementer (toy-sport equip.)	795.687-030
REC	37	Tightening-Machine Operator (paper goods)	640.685-082
REC	37	Timber Packer (saw. & plan.)	922.687-094
REC	37	Trimmer, Meat (meat products)	525.684-054
REC	37	Tube Coverer (textile)	589.687-046
REC	37	Wax-Ball Knock-Out Worker (toy-sport equip.)	732.687-082
REC	37	Wet-Cotton Feeder (textile)	581.686-042
REC	37	Wrapping Machine Helper (tobacco)	529.687-222
REC	37	Wringer-Machine Operator (leather mfg.; tex. prod., n.e.c.)	589.685-098
REC	37	Yarn-Mercerizer-Operator Helper (textile)	584.686-010
REC	36	Almond Blancher, Hand (can. & preserv.)	521.687-010
REC	36	Bag Loader (ordnance)	737.687-014
REC	36	Band Salvager (agriculture)	929.686-014
REC	36	Belt Picker (mine & quarry)	939.687-010
REC	36	Bundles Hanger (tobacco)	529.686-010
REC	36	Carroting-Machine Offbearer (hat & cap)	586.686-010
REC	36	Cotton Puller (oils & grease)	521.686-022
REC	36	Drip-Box Tender (grain-feed mills)	521.687-038
REC	36	Dumper (chemical)	922.686-010
REC	36	Feather-Cutting-Machine Feeder (tex. prod., n.e.c.)	585.686-010
REC	36	Floor Worker (wood prod., n.e.c.)	739.687-098
REC	36	Flumer (grain-feed mills)	521.686-038
REC	36	Flumer II (sugar & conf.)	521.686-042
REC	36	Hammer Adjuster (clock & watch)	715.687-046
REC	36	Harvest Worker, Field Crop (agriculture)	404.687-014
REC	36	Hay Sorter (toy-sport equip.)	732.686-010
REC	36	Leather Coater (leather mfg.)	584.687-010
REC	36	Pallbearer (personal ser.)	359.687-010
REC	36	Picking-Table Worker (sugar & conf.)	521.687-102
REC	36	Pillow Cleaner (tex. prod., n.e.c.)	789.687-122
REC	36	Poultry Hanger (meat products)	525.687-078
REC	36	Print-Line Tailer (furniture)	652.686-030

Part 2: From Holland Codes to Occupations

From Holland Codes to the Dictionary of Occupational Titles Occupations

HOC	Cx	Title	DOT
REC	36	Snow Shoveler (government ser.)	955.687-014
REC	36	Steam-Tunnel Feeder (saw. & plan.)	562.686-010
REC	36	Straw-Hat-Washer Operator (hat & cap)	784.687-078
REC	36	Tin Stacker (tinware)	922.687-098
REC	36	Veneer-Drier Feeder (millwork-plywood)	563.686-014
REC	36	Washer, Carcass (meat products)	525.687-122
REC	36	Weeder-Thinner (agriculture)	409.687-018
REC	36	Wood-Pole Treater (wood prod., n.e.c.)	561.687-010
REC	36	Worm Packer (agriculture)	920.687-202
REC	36	Worm-Farm Laborer (agriculture)	413.687-014
REC	35	Automatic-Nailing-Machine Feeder (woodworking)	669.686-010
REC	35	Cherry Cutter (can. & preserv.)	524.687-010
REC	35	Compensator (paper goods)	640.685-026
REC	35	Ham-Rolling-Machine Operator (meat products)	529.685-138
REC	35	Ironer, Sock (laundry & rel.)	363.687-014
REC	35	Lacing-String Cutter (boot & shoe)	788.687-074
REC	35	Shaker (tobacco)	521.687-110
REC	35	Sleever (paper goods)	641.686-034
REC	35	Spool Maker (paper goods)	641.685-082
REC	35	Tree Planter (forestry)	452.687-018
REC	35	Trolley Cleaner (meat products)	529.687-206
RCI	71	Utilization Engineer (utilities)	007.061-034
RCI	66	Calibration Laboratory Technician (aircraft mfg.; electron. comp.)	019.281-010
RCI	65	Electrician, Maintenance (any industry)	829.261-018
RCI	64	Accelerator Operator (profess. & kin.)	015.362-010
RCI	64	Computerized Environmental Control Installer (electron. comp.)	828.281-026
RCI	64	Drafter, Architectural (profess. & kin.)	001.261-010
RCI	64	Estimator, Paperboard Boxes (paper goods)	221.362-018
RCI	64	Planetarium Technician (museums)	962.261-010
RCI	64	Repairer, Welding Systems and Equipment (welding)	626.261-014
RCI	63	Marquetry Worker (furniture)	761.281-018
RCI	62	Epitaxial Reactor Technician (electron. comp.)	590.282-010
RCI	62	Patternmaker (furniture)	661.280-010
RCI	62	Patternmaker, All-Around (foundry; plastic prod.)	693.280-014
RCI	62	Stereo-Plotter Operator (profess. & kin.)	018.281-010
RCI	62	Tool and Fixture Repairer (auto. mfg.)	601.281-030
RCI	60	Automotive-Cooling-System Diagnostic Technician (automotive ser.)	620.261-034
RCI	60	Deburring-and-Tooling-Machine Operator (office machines)	690.280-010
RCI	60	Electronic Equipment Set-up Operator (electron. comp.)	726.380-010
RCI	60	Laboratory Assistant, Metallurgical (steel & rel.)	011.261-022
RCI	60	Rotary-Engine Assembler (engine-turbine)	801.261-018
RCI	60	Swimming Pool Installer-and-Servicer (construction)	869.463-010
RCI	59	Hydraulic-Rubbish-Compactor Mechanic (sanitary ser.)	638.281-030
RCI	59	Service Technician, Computerized-Photofinishing Equipment (photofinishing)	714.281-030

Part 2: From Holland Codes to Occupations

From Holland Codes to the Dictionary of Occupational Titles Occupations

HOC	Cx	Title	DOT
RCI	59	Solar-Energy-System Installer (any industry)	637.261-030
RCI	58	Air and Hydronic Balancing Technician (any industry)	637.261-034
RCI	58	Construction Checker (utilities)	821.367-010
RCI	58	Furniture Restorer (museums)	763.380-010
RCI	58	Microelectronics Technician (electron. comp.)	590.362-022
RCI	58	Photo Mask Inspector (electron. comp.)	726.384-022
RCI	58	Poured-Concrete-Wall Technician (construction)	869.261-018
RCI	57	Assembler (tel. & tel.)	722.381-010
RCI	57	Assembler, Electromechanical (aircraft mfg.; electron.comp.; inst. & app.)	828.381-018
RCI	57	Autoclave Operator (aircraft mfg.)	553.362-014
RCI	57	Design Technician, Computer-Aided (electron. comp.)	003.362-010
RCI	57	Gravel Inspector (construction)	859.281-010
RCI	57	Hydraulic Repairer (any industry)	638.281-034
RCI	57	Inspector, Firearms (ordnance)	632.381-014
RCI	57	Nondestructive Tester (profess. & kin.)	011.261-018
RCI	57	Offset-Press Operator I (print. & pub.)	651.382-042
RCI	57	Offset-Press-Operator Apprentice (print. & pub.)	651.382-046
RCI	57	Quality-Control Tester (wood prod., n.e.c.)	569.384-010
RCI	57	Repairer, Recreational Vehicle (vehicles, n.e.c.)	869.261-022
RCI	57	Test Fixture Designer (electron. comp.)	726.364-014
RCI	57	Ultrasonic Tester (any industry)	739.281-014
RCI	56	Aircraft Mechanic, Plumbing and Hydraulics (aircraft mfg.)	806.381-066
RCI	56	Antenna Installer, Satellite Communications (any industry)	823.261-022
RCI	56	Automobile Mechanic (automotive ser.)	620.261-010
RCI	56	Blankmaker (glass mfg.)	579.382-022
RCI	56	Boring-Machine Operator (machine shop)	606.382-022
RCI	56	Custom Van Converter (auto. mfg.; automotive ser.)	806.381-070
RCI	56	Denture Waxer (protective dev.)	712.381-046
RCI	56	Extrusion-Die Repairer (nonfer. metal)	705.381-014
RCI	56	Installer, Electrical, Plumbing, Mechanical (ship-boat mfg.)	806.381-062
RCI	56	Quality Control Technician (concrete prod.)	579.364-010
RCI	56	Repairer, Gyroscope (inst. & app.)	710.381-054
RCI	56	Ski-Binding Fitter-and-Repairer (toy-sport equip.)	732.364-014
RCI	56	Supervisor, Research Kennel (agriculture)	418.137-014
RCI	56	Template Reproduction Technician (aircraft mfg.)	976.381-022
RCI	56	Tool Programmer, Numerical Control (electron. comp.)	609.262-010
RCI	56	Typing-Element-Machine Operator (office machines)	616.382-018
RCI	55	Bow Maker (musical inst.)	730.281-058
RCI	55	Die Maker, Electronic (machine shop)	601.381-042
RCI	55	Dye Automation Operator (textile)	582.362-014
RCI	55	Photo Mask Pattern Generator (electron. comp.)	976.382-038
RCI	55	Quality-Control Technician, Inked Ribbons (pen & pencil)	733.364-010
RCI	54	Auto-Body Repairer, Fiberglass (automotive ser.)	807.381-030
RCI	54	Block Maker (protective dev.)	719.381-018
RCI	54	Electrocardiograph Technician (medical ser.)	078.362-018
RCI	54	Epitaxial Reactor Operator (electron. comp.)	590.382-018

HOC	Cx	Title	DOT
RCI	54	Finisher, Denture (protective dev.)	712.381-050
RCI	54	Formula Clerk (textile)	221.367-090
RCI	54	Inspector, Receiving (aircraft mfg.; elec. equip.; electron. comp.)	222.384-010
RCI	54	Inventory Clerk (clerical)	222.387-026
RCI	54	Ion Implant Machine Operator (electron. comp.)	590.382-022
RCI	54	Monotype-Keyboard Operator (machinery mfg.; print. & pub.)	650.582-014
RCI	54	Numerical-Control Drill Operator, Printed Circuit Boards (electron. comp.)	606.382-018
RCI	54	Photo Mask Maker, Electron-Beam (electron. comp.)	972.382-018
RCI	54	Phototypesetter Operator (print. & pub.)	650.582-022
RCI	54	Process Controller (textile)	689.364-014
RCI	54	Proofer, Prepress (print. & pub.)	972.381-034
RCI	54	Upholsterer (aircraft mfg.)	780.384-014
RCI	53	Artificial-Foliage Arranger (retail trade)	899.364-014
RCI	53	Assistant Designer (garment)	781.361-010
RCI	53	Audiovisual Technician (any industry)	960.382-010
RCI	53	Custom-Leather-Products Maker (leather prod.)	783.361-010
RCI	53	Grader Marker (garment)	781.381-034
RCI	53	Incinerator Operator II (sanitary ser.)	955.362-014
RCI	53	Inspector, Assembly (furniture)	669.364-010
RCI	53	Inspector, Circuitry Negative (electron. comp.)	726.384-014
RCI	53	Mirror Installer (construction)	865.361-010
RCI	53	Production Technician, Semiconductor Processing Equipment (electron. comp.)	590.384-014
RCI	53	Setter, Juice Packaging Machines (can. & preserv.)	920.380-010
RCI	53	Step-and-Repeat Reduction Camera Operator (electron. comp.)	976.382-034
RCI	53	Tile Decorator (brick & tile)	773.381-010
RCI	53	Utility Operator (saw. & plan.)	669.682-070
RCI	52	Assembler, Subassembly (aircraft mfg.)	806.384-034
RCI	52	Code Inspector (government ser.)	168.367-018
RCI	52	Fingerprint Classifier (government ser.)	375.387-010
RCI	52	Health-Equipment Servicer (medical ser.)	359.363-010
RCI	52	Multi-Purpose Machine Operator (furniture)	669.382-022
RCI	52	Probe Test Equipment Technician, Semiconductor Wafers (electron. comp.)	729.360-010
RCI	52	Repairer, Probe Test Card, Semiconductor Wafers (electron. comp.)	726.361-022
RCI	52	Shotblast-Equipment Operator (foundry)	503.362-014
RCI	52	Switch Inspector (utilities)	952.381-010
RCI	51	Airport Utility Worker (air trans.)	912.663-010
RCI	51	Automatic Casting-Forging Machine Operator (forging)	611.682-014
RCI	51	Coordinate Measuring Equipment Operator (electron. comp.)	726.682-018
RCI	51	Coremaker (foundry)	518.381-014
RCI	51	Coremaker Apprentice (foundry)	518.381-018
RCI	51	Eddy-Current Inspector (steel & rel.)	619.381-014

HOC	Cx	Title	DOT
RCI	51	Egg Pasteurizer (agriculture)	529.682-038
RCI	51	Electrical Assembler (aircraft mfg.)	729.384-026
RCI	51	Inspector (pharmaceut.)	559.387-014
RCI	51	Insulation Worker (construction)	863.364-014
RCI	51	Laser-Beam-Trim Operator (electron. comp.)	726.682-010
RCI	51	Medical-Equipment Repairer (protective dev.; retail trade)	639.281-022
RCI	51	Photo Mask Processor (electron. comp.)	976.384-014
RCI	51	Photo Technician (electron. comp.)	976.384-010
RCI	51	Plant-Care Worker (agriculture)	408.364-010
RCI	51	Platemaker, Semiconductor Packages (electron. comp.)	972.384-014
RCI	51	Printed Circuit Board Component Tester, Chemical (electron. comp.)	726.684-074
RCI	51	Printed Circuit Board Component Tester, Pre-Assembly (electron. comp.)	726.684-078
RCI	51	Printed Circuit Board Inspector, Pre-Assembly (electron. comp.)	726.684-082
RCI	51	Processor, Instant Potato (food prep., n.e.c.)	523.382-022
RCI	51	Sample Clerk (plastic prod.)	222.387-066
RCI	51	Sewer-Line Photo-Inspector (sanitary ser.)	851.362-010
RCI	51	Sewing-Machine Tester (machinery mfg.)	709.382-010
RCI	51	Solar-Fabrication Technician (machine shop)	809.381-034
RCI	50	Brake Repairer, Railroad (r.r. trans.)	622.261-010
RCI	50	Inspector, Processing (sugar & conf.)	529.687-226
RCI	50	Knife Grinder (machine shop)	603.382-038
RCI	50	Numerical-Control Router Operator (aircraft mfg.; electron. comp.)	605.382-046
RCI	50	Pewter Caster (jewelry-silver.)	502.384-010
RCI	50	Rubber-Printing-Machine Operator (rubber goods)	652.462-010
RCI	50	Seed Core Operator (electron. comp.)	679.384-010
RCI	50	Skelp Processor (steel & rel.)	619.662-014
RCI	50	Turning Machine Set-up Operator (fabrication, n.e.c.)	669.382-026
RCI	49	Animal-Nursery Worker (amuse. & rec.; museums)	412.674-014
RCI	49	Crystal Grinder (electron. comp.)	673.382-026
RCI	49	Crystal Slicer (electron. comp.)	677.382-018
RCI	49	Diamond Driller (machine tools)	770.381-018
RCI	49	Extruding-Machine Operator (nonfer. metal)	691.382-010
RCI	49	Frame Repairer (furniture)	763.681-010
RCI	49	Inspector, Semiconductor Wafer Processing (electron. comp.)	726.384-018
RCI	49	Photographic Aligner, Semiconductor Wafers (electron. comp.)	976.382-030
RCI	49	Programming Equipment Operator (electron. comp.)	726.685-062
RCI	49	Quilting-Machine Operator (tex. prod., n.e.c.)	584.382-014
RCI	49	Rubber-Goods Cutter-Finisher (rubber goods)	690.680-010
RCI	49	Saw Operator (aircraft mfg.)	607.382-014
RCI	49	Surgical-Elastic Knitter, Hand Frame (protective dev.)	685.382-010
RCI	49	Tester, Wafer Substrate (electron. comp.)	726.684-106
RCI	49	Trimming Machine Set-up Operator (fabrication, n.e.c.)	664.382-018
RCI	49	Utility Worker, Production (pharmaceut.)	559.684-034

Part 2: From Holland Codes to Occupations

From Holland Codes to the Dictionary of Occupational Titles Occupations

HOC	Cx	Title	DOT
RCI	48	Assembler, Semiconductor (electron. comp.)	726.684-034
RCI	48	Case Hardener (heat treating)	504.682-014
RCI	48	Casket Assembler (fabrication, n.e.c.)	739.684-190
RCI	48	Diaper Machine Tender (protective dev.)	692.685-278
RCI	48	Die Set-up Operator, Printed Circuit Boards (electron. comp.)	699.380-010
RCI	48	Garden Worker (agriculture; museums)	406.684-018
RCI	48	Grader (woodworking)	669.687-030
RCI	48	Inspector I (furniture)	780.687-066
RCI	48	Inspector, Crystal (electron. comp.)	726.684-054
RCI	48	Inspector, Printed Circuit Boards (electron. comp.)	726.684-062
RCI	48	Running Rigger (ship-boat mfg.)	806.684-142
RCI	48	Sequencing-Machine Operator (electron. comp.)	726.382-010
RCI	47	Charge Preparation Technician (electron. comp.)	590.384-010
RCI	47	Instrument Assembler (inst. & app.)	710.684-046
RCI	47	Microfilm Processor (business ser.)	976.385-010
RCI	47	Plasma Etcher, Printed Circuit Boards (electron. comp.)	590.685-094
RCI	47	Trimmer Sawyer (saw. & plan.)	667.682-094
RCI	47	Wood-Fuel Pelletizer (fabrication, n.e.c.)	569.685-078
RCI	46	Assembler, Product (machine shop)	706.684-018
RCI	46	Balance-Bridge Assembler (clock & watch)	715.684-022
RCI	46	Carpet Sewer (carpet & rug; retail trade)	787.682-014
RCI	46	Dry-Cell-Assembly-Machine Tender (elec. equip.)	692.665-018
RCI	46	Inspector, Semiconductor Wafer (electron. comp.)	726.684-066
RCI	46	Metallization Equipment Tender, Semiconductors (comm. equip.; electron. comp.; inst. & app.)	590.685-086
RCI	46	Polishing Machine Tender (electron. comp.)	673.685-094
RCI	46	Screen-Machine Operator (tex. prod., n.e.c.)	559.682-070
RCI	46	Tablet-Making-Machine-Operator Helper (paper goods)	649.685-130
RCI	46	Test Fixture Assembler (electron. comp.)	726.684-098
RCI	45	Automatic Bandsaw Tender (furniture)	667.685-070
RCI	45	Car Blocker (any industry)	860.684-018
RCI	45	Card Grinder Helper (textile)	680.684-010
RCI	45	Coating Equipment Operator, Printed Circuit Boards (electron. comp.)	590.685-066
RCI	45	Flat Drier (tex. prod., n.e.c.)	581.685-078
RCI	45	Insulating-Machine Operator (nonfer. metal)	691.682-018
RCI	45	Lease Picker (textile)	689.684-018
RCI	45	Material Assembler (furniture)	781.684-066
RCI	45	Material Preparation Worker (electron. comp.)	590.684-030
RCI	45	Paint Stripper (petrol. refin.)	599.685-130
RCI	45	Plating Equipment Tender (electroplating)	500.685-014
RCI	45	Reworker, Printed Circuit Board (electron. comp.)	726.684-090
RCI	45	Rough Planer Tender (woodworking)	665.665-010
RCI	45	Router, Printed Circuit Boards (electron. comp.)	605.682-034
RCI	45	Solar-Energy-System-Installer Helper (any industry)	637.687-018
RCI	45	Splitting-Machine Operator (stonework)	677.685-046
RCI	45	Texturing-Machine Fixer (textile)	628.684-046
RCI	45	Tire Repairer (rubber tire)	750.681-010

Part 2: From Holland Codes to Occupations

From Holland Codes to the Dictionary of Occupational Titles Occupations

HOC	Cx	Title	DOT
RCI	45	Type-Proof Reproducer (machinery mfg.)	652.685-106
RCI	44	Band-Saw Operator (paper goods)	640.685-090
RCI	44	Boring-Machine Operator (furniture)	666.685-014
RCI	44	Diffusion Furnace Operator, Semiconductor Wafers (electron. comp.)	590.685-070
RCI	44	Plate Conditioner (steel & rel.)	819.664-010
RCI	44	Printed Circuit Board Assembler, Hand (comm. equip.; electron. comp.; inst. & app.; office machines)	726.684-070
RCI	44	Production-Machine Tender (auto. mfg.)	699.685-050
RCI	44	Saw Operator (electron. comp.)	726.682-026
RCI	44	Wire-Wrapping-Machine Operator (electron. comp.)	726.682-014
RCI	43	Brick Unloader Tender (brick & tile)	579.685-062
RCI	43	Briquette Operator (brick & tile)	579.685-066
RCI	43	Contact Printer, Printed Circuit Boards (electron. comp.)	976.684-030
RCI	43	Cut-Off-Machine Operator (steel & rel.)	619.685-094
RCI	43	Die Tester (electron. comp.)	726.685-030
RCI	43	Display Fabricator (fabrication, n.e.c.)	860.684-022
RCI	43	Inspector, Integrated Circuits (electron. comp.)	726.684-058
RCI	43	Laminator (wood prod., n.e.c.)	554.685-030
RCI	43	Pipe Stem Repairer (fabrication, n.e.c.)	739.684-186
RCI	43	Shaping Machine Tender (furniture)	665.685-046
RCI	43	Stripper-Etcher, Printed Circuit Boards (electron. comp.)	590.685-082
RCI	43	Tester, Semiconductor Packages (electron. comp.)	726.685-054
RCI	43	Tester, Semiconductor Wafers (electron. comp.)	726.684-102
RCI	42	Bander, Hand (any industry)	929.687-058
RCI	42	Battery Charger (any industry)	825.684-018
RCI	42	Black Oxide Coating Equipment Tender (electron. comp.)	501.685-018
RCI	42	Caster (brick & tile)	579.684-026
RCI	42	Cleaning Machine Tender, Semiconductor Wafers (electron. comp.)	590.685-062
RCI	42	Cotton Classer Aide (agriculture)	429.587-010
RCI	42	Developer, Printed Circuit Board Panels (electron. comp.)	976.685-034
RCI	42	Electroless Plater, Printed Circuit Board Panels (electron. comp.)	501.685-022
RCI	42	Etcher (electron. comp.)	590.685-078
RCI	42	Filling-Machine Operator (nonfer. metal)	699.685-038
RCI	42	Groover-and-Striper Operator (wood prod., n.e.c.)	669.685-102
RCI	42	Keymodule-Assembly-Machine Tender (office machines)	692.685-274
RCI	42	Loader-Demolder (furniture)	556.684-030
RCI	42	Palletizer (nonfer. metal)	929.687-054
RCI	42	Panel Cutter (furniture)	761.684-050
RCI	42	Plater, Printed Circuit Board Panels (electron. comp.)	500.684-026
RCI	42	Punch Press Operator (wood prod., n.e.c.)	669.685-106
RCI	42	Reflow Operator (electron. comp.)	726.685-038
RCI	42	Repairer, Kiln Car (brick & tile)	861.684-022
RCI	42	Roofing-Machine Tender (nonmet. min.)	590.685-098
RCI	42	Solder Deposit Operator (electron. comp.)	726.684-094
RCI	42	Taper, Printed Circuit Layout (electron. comp.)	017.684-010
RCI	42	Touch-Up Carver (fabrication, n.e.c.)	761.684-054

HOC	Cx	Title	DOT
RCI	42	Utility Tender, Carding (textile)	689.685-166
RCI	42	Wafer Cleaner (electron. comp.)	590.685-102
RCI	41	Beveler, Printed Circuit Boards (electron. comp.)	699.682-034
RCI	41	Bin Tripper Operator (steel & rel.)	922.665-014
RCI	41	Break-and-Load Operator (electron. comp.)	726.685-018
RCI	41	Cadmium Burner (chemical)	553.685-114
RCI	41	Cigar-Wrapper Tender, Automatic (tobacco)	529.685-286
RCI	41	Commissary Assistant (amuse. & rec.; museums)	412.687-010
RCI	41	Crystal Mounter (electron. comp.)	677.687-014
RCI	41	Die Attacher (electron. comp.)	726.684-042
RCI	41	Disc-Pad Grinder (nonmet. min.)	673.685-086
RCI	41	Etch Operator, Semiconductor Wafers (electron. comp.)	590.685-074
RCI	41	Helper, Shear Operator (steel & rel.)	615.687-010
RCI	41	Night-Patrol Inspector (fabrication, n.e.c.)	824.683-010
RCI	41	Oven-Press Tender I (nonmet. min.)	573.685-042
RCI	41	Oven-Press Tender II (nonmet. min.)	573.685-046
RCI	41	Photographic Processor, Semiconductor Wafers (electron. comp.)	976.685-038
RCI	41	Photoresist Laminator, Printed Circuit Board (electron. comp.)	554.685-034
RCI	41	Pinner, Printed Circuit Boards (electron. comp.)	699.685-046
RCI	41	Preassembler, Printed Circuit Board (electron. comp.)	726.687-038
RCI	41	Rod Tape Operator (electron. comp.)	726.685-042
RCI	41	Seed Pelleter (agriculture)	599.685-126
RCI	41	Sewing-Machine Operator, Paper Bags (paper goods)	787.685-054
RCI	41	Upholsterer, Assembly Line (furniture)	780.684-134
RCI	41	Utility Operator III (chemical)	549.685-042
RCI	41	Wafer Abrading Machine Tender (electron. comp.)	673.685-102
RCI	41	Wafer Mounter (electron. comp.)	726.685-058
RCI	41	Wave-Solder Offbearer (electron. comp.)	726.686-010
RCI	40	Bee Worker (agriculture)	413.687-018
RCI	40	Blending-Tank Tender Helper (can. & preserv.)	520.687-066
RCI	40	Briar-Wood Sorter (fabrication, n.e.c.)	769.687-058
RCI	40	Brush Loader and Handle Attacher (fabrication, n.e.c.)	739.687-206
RCI	40	Burner (brick & tile)	573.685-038
RCI	40	Can-Filling-and-Closing-Machine Tender (can. & preserv.)	529.685-282
RCI	40	Cubing-Machine Tender (concrete prod.)	920.685-106
RCI	40	Cut-Off-Saw Operator II (woodworking)	667.685-074
RCI	40	Cutter (brick & tile)	579.684-030
RCI	40	Fabricator, Artificial Breast (protective dev.)	712.684-042
RCI	40	Inspector I (pottery & porc.)	575.687-034
RCI	40	Inspector, Furniture Decals (furniture)	979.687-030
RCI	40	Laminator, Printed Circuit Boards (electron. comp.)	692.685-282
RCI	40	Lapper (textile)	689.687-090
RCI	40	Mixer (brick & tile)	579.685-074
RCI	40	Paint Trimmer, Pipe Bowls (fabrication, n.e.c.)	749.684-050
RCI	40	Radius Corner Machine Operator (glass products)	673.685-098
RCI	40	Repairer, Veneer Sheet (furniture)	769.684-058
RCI	40	Router Machine Operator (plastic prod.)	605.685-054

HOC	Cx	Title	DOT
RCI	40	Router Tender (furniture)	665.685-042
RCI	40	Saw Operator (brick & tile)	677.685-054
RCI	40	Sealer, Semiconductor Packages (electron. comp.)	726.687-042
RCI	40	Splicer (protective dev.)	759.684-070
RCI	40	Stitcher, Tape-Controlled Machine (boot & shoe)	690.685-494
RCI	40	Toe Puncher (knitting)	689.685-162
RCI	40	Trimmer, Printed Circuit Board Panels (electron. comp.)	699.685-054
RCI	40	Turning Lathe Tender (furniture)	664.685-034
RCI	40	Wire Brush Operator (fabrication, n.e.c.)	761.684-058
RCI	39	Deboner, Pet Food (can. & preserv.)	521.685-378
RCI	39	Deburrer, Printed Circuit Board Panels (electron. comp.)	603.686-014
RCI	39	Deflash and Wash Operator (electron. comp.)	726.685-022
RCI	39	Die Attaching Machine Tender (electron. comp.)	726.685-026
RCI	39	Disc-Pad Knockout Worker (nonmet. min.)	579.687-034
RCI	39	Disc-Pad-Plate Filler (nonmet. min.)	579.687-038
RCI	39	Electric Blanket Wirer (tex. prod., n.e.c.)	789.684-054
RCI	39	Etcher-Stripper, Semiconductor Wafers (electron. comp.)	590.684-026
RCI	39	Leak Tester, Semiconductor Packages (electron. comp.)	726.685-034
RCI	39	Loader, Semiconductor Dies (electron. comp.)	726.687-030
RCI	39	Marker Machine Attendant (glass mfg.)	579.685-070
RCI	39	Molder, Automobile Carpets (tex. prod., n.e.c.)	692.685-286
RCI	39	Offbearer, Pipe Smoking Machine (fabrication, n.e.c.)	563.686-018
RCI	39	Paster, Hat Lining (hat & cap)	692.686-070
RCI	39	Photo Mask Cleaner (electron. comp.)	590.684-034
RCI	39	Pipe Stem Aligner (fabrication, n.e.c.)	739.687-210
RCI	39	Scrubber Machine Tender (electron. comp.)	599.685-134
RCI	39	Tip-Out Worker (concrete prod.)	575.687-038
RCI	39	Wafer Breaker, Semiconductors (electron. comp.)	726.687-046
RCI	38	Blow-Molding-Machine Tender (toy-sport equip.)	556.685-086
RCI	38	Driller and Deburrer, Reflector (light. fix.)	676.686-014
RCI	38	Drum Cleaner (petrol. refin.)	599.687-034
RCI	38	Gluing-Machine Feeder (woodworking)	569.686-038
RCI	38	Press Offbearer (brick & tile)	579.686-030
RCI	38	Printing Screen Assembler (electron. comp.)	979.684-042
RCI	38	Rodding Machine Tender (furniture)	665.685-038
RCI	38	Spindle Repairer (textile)	628.684-042
RCI	38	Veneer-Taping-Machine Offbearer (millwork-plywood)	569.686-054
RCI	37	Disc-Pad Grinding Machine Feeder (nonmet. min.)	673.686-030
RCI	37	Glass-Cutting-Machine Feeder (glass products)	677.686-014
RCI	37	Hat Conditioner (hat & cap)	784.687-086
RCI	37	Scaling Machine Operator (can. & preserv.)	521.685-386
RCI	37	Sweatband Shaper (hat & cap)	784.687-090
RCI	37	Wood Scrap Handler (millwork-plywood)	564.686-010
RCI	36	Laminating-Machine Feeder (wood prod., n.e.c.)	569.686-042
RCI	36	Mold Filler (toy-sport equip.)	556.687-030
RCA	58	Glass Blower, Laboratory Apparatus (glass products; inst. & app.)	772.281-010
RCA	57	Airbrush Artist (profess. & kin.)	970.281-010

Part 2: From Holland Codes to Occupations

From Holland Codes to the Dictionary of Occupational Titles Occupations

HOC	Cx	Title	DOT
RCA	55	Photograph Retoucher (photofinishing)	970.281-018
RCA	47	Manugrapher (fabrication, n.e.c.)	970.681-022
RCA	46	Inker and Opaquer (motion picture)	970.681-018
RCS	66	Surveyor, Oil-Well Directional (petrol. & gas)	010.261-022
RCS	63	Aircraft-Photographic-Equipment Mechanic (photo. appar.)	714.281-010
RCS	63	Orthopedic-Boot-and-Shoe Designer and Maker (boot & shoe; protective dev.)	788.261-010
RCS	63	Sound Mixer (motion picture; radio-tv broad.; recording)	194.262-018
RCS	60	Instrument Repairer (any industry)	710.261-010
RCS	60	Radiation Monitor (profess. & kin.)	199.167-010
RCS	60	Reactor Operator, Test-and-Research (profess. & kin.)	015.362-026
RCS	60	Supervisor (office machines)	706.131-014
RCS	59	Compositor (print. & pub.)	973.381-010
RCS	59	Electroencephalographic Technologist (medical ser.)	078.362-022
RCS	59	Instrument Mechanic (any industry)	710.281-026
RCS	59	Safety Inspector (any industry)	168.264-014
RCS	59	Station Installer-and-Repairer (tel. & tel.)	822.261-022
RCS	59	Waste-Treatment Operator (chemical)	955.382-014
RCS	59	Watch Manufacturing Supervisor (clock & watch)	609.130-026
RCS	58	Drafter, Assistant (profess. & kin.)	017.281-018
RCS	58	Laboratory Technician, Artificial Breeding (agriculture)	040.361-010
RCS	57	Cable Splicer (construction; tel. & tel.; utilities)	829.361-010
RCS	57	Cable-Splicer Apprentice (construction; tel. & tel.; utilities)	829.361-014
RCS	57	Chemical-Radiation Technician (government ser.)	015.261-010
RCS	57	Diesel-Plant Operator (utilities)	952.382-010
RCS	57	Furniture Upholsterer (any industry)	780.381-018
RCS	57	Hydroelectric-Station Operator (utilities)	952.362-018
RCS	56	Biology Specimen Technician (profess. & kin.)	041.381-010
RCS	56	Form Designer (print. & pub.)	970.361-010
RCS	56	Hull Inspector (ship-boat mfg.)	806.264-010
RCS	56	Loading-Machine Tool-Setter (ordnance)	694.260-010
RCS	56	Machine Setter (nonmet. min.)	692.260-010
RCS	56	Protective-Signal Installer (business ser.)	822.361-018
RCS	56	Vibrator-Equipment Tester (machinery mfg.)	825.361-014
RCS	55	Engraving-Press Operator (print. & pub.)	651.382-010
RCS	55	Mash-Tub-Cooker Operator (beverage)	522.382-022
RCS	54	Artificial-Breeding Technician (agriculture)	418.384-014
RCS	54	Camera Operator, Title (motion picture)	976.382-010
RCS	54	Cylinder Grinder (print. & pub.)	500.381-010
RCS	54	Dry-Wall Applicator (construction)	842.361-030
RCS	54	Front-End Mechanic (automotive ser.)	620.281-038
RCS	54	Instant Print Operator (print. & pub.)	979.362-010
RCS	54	Parts Clerk (clerical)	222.367-042
RCS	54	Television Installer (any industry)	823.361-010
RCS	54	Trouble Locator, Test Desk (tel. & tel.)	822.361-030
RCS	54	Wind-Instrument Repairer (any industry)	730.281-054
RCS	54	Yield-Loss Inspector (grain-feed mills)	529.367-030
RCS	53	Carbon-Paper-Coating-Machine Setter (pen & pencil)	534.380-010

HOC	Cx	Title	DOT
RCS	53	Construction-and-Maintenance Inspector (petrol. refin.)	914.362-014
RCS	53	Fluoroscope Operator (nonfer. metal)	502.382-014
RCS	53	Installer, Interior Assemblies (aircraft mfg.)	806.381-078
RCS	53	Rubber-Goods Tester (elec. equip.; utilities)	759.381-010
RCS	53	Tape Transferrer (radio-tv broad.; recording)	194.382-014
RCS	53	Yeast Distiller (beverage)	522.362-010
RCS	52	Assembler (machinery mfg.)	706.361-010
RCS	52	Fish Roe Technician (can. & preserv.)	522.384-010
RCS	52	Fluid Jet Cutter Operator (aircraft mfg.)	699.382-010
RCS	52	Girdler (jewelry-silver.)	770.261-014
RCS	52	Hydraulic-Jack Adjuster (construction)	869.361-014
RCS	52	Lather (construction)	842.361-010
RCS	52	Lather Apprentice (construction)	842.361-014
RCS	52	Needle-Felt-Making-Machine Operator (tex. prod., n.e.c.)	689.362-010
RCS	52	Piano Tuner (any industry)	730.361-010
RCS	52	Sample Tester (chemical)	553.364-010
RCS	52	Sample-Taker Operator (petrol. & gas)	931.361-010
RCS	52	Tank Setter (petrol. & gas)	801.361-022
RCS	52	Trombone-Slide Assembler (musical inst.)	730.381-054
RCS	52	Upholsterer, Inside (furniture)	780.381-038
RCS	51	Bookmobile Driver (library)	249.363-010
RCS	51	Calender-Roll Press Operator (machinery mfg.)	692.462-010
RCS	51	Deicer Assembler, Electric (rubber goods)	739.684-050
RCS	51	Dough Mixer (bakery products)	520.685-234
RCS	51	Expediter Clerk (optical goods)	221.387-026
RCS	51	Flash-Drier Operator (grain-feed mills)	529.582-014
RCS	51	Frothing-Machine Operator (rubber goods)	550.362-010
RCS	51	Merchandise Distributor (retail trade)	219.367-018
RCS	51	Outsole Cutter, Automatic (rubber goods)	690.462-010
RCS	51	Process Inspector (ordnance)	736.381-018
RCS	51	Punch-Press Operator I (any industry)	615.382-010
RCS	50	Accordion Tuner (any industry)	730.381-010
RCS	50	Air-Compressor Mechanic (railroad equip.)	622.684-010
RCS	50	Air-Valve Repairer (railroad equip.)	622.381-010
RCS	50	Atomic-Fuel Assembler (chemical)	709.381-010
RCS	50	Barrel Assembler (clock & watch)	715.381-022
RCS	50	Charge-Machine Operator (chemical)	921.662-014
RCS	50	Coating-Machine Operator (carpet & rug; tex. prod., n.e.c.)	584.562-010
RCS	50	Cork Insulator, Refrigeration Plant (construction)	863.381-010
RCS	50	Drill-Press Operator, Printed Circuit Boards (electron. comp.)	676.382-010
RCS	50	Gauge-and-Weigh-Machine Adjuster (ordnance)	632.360-010
RCS	50	Glass Blower (glass mfg.)	772.381-022
RCS	50	Glass-Lathe Operator (electron. comp.)	674.382-010
RCS	50	Gun Synchronizer (ordnance)	632.381-010
RCS	50	Jewel Blocker and Sawyer (clock & watch)	770.381-026
RCS	50	Kick Press Setter (button & notion)	617.380-010
RCS	50	Metal-Reed Tuner (any industry)	730.381-034
RCS	50	Molder Operator (woodworking)	665.682-018

HOC	Cx	Title	DOT
RCS	50	Pad Hand (leather prod.)	780.381-030
RCS	50	Primer-Waterproofing-Machine Adjuster (ordnance)	632.380-018
RCS	50	Reed Repairer (textile)	628.484-010
RCS	50	Sheeter Operator (plastic-synth.)	690.382-010
RCS	50	Tank-Car Inspector (petrol. refin.)	910.384-010
RCS	50	Ware Finisher (glass mfg.)	772.381-018
RCS	50	Wave-Soldering Machine Operator (comm. equip.; electron. comp.; inst. & app.; office machines)	726.362-014
RCS	50	Wire Coiler (house. appl.)	724.362-010
RCS	50	Wool-and-Pelt Grader (meat products)	589.387-018
RCS	49	Aligner, Typewriter (office machines)	706.381-010
RCS	49	Autoclave Operator II (chemical)	709.682-010
RCS	49	Bending-Machine Operator I (any industry)	617.482-010
RCS	49	Blender (tobacco)	520.387-010
RCS	49	Bracelet and Brooch Maker (jewelry-silver.)	735.681-010
RCS	49	Case Preparer-and-Liner (ordnance)	509.384-010
RCS	49	Clicking-Machine Operator (boot & shoe; glove & mit.; leather prod.)	789.382-010
RCS	49	Crusher-and-Blender Operator (steel & rel.)	544.582-010
RCS	49	Fittings Finisher (plumbing-heat.)	619.382-014
RCS	49	Hammer Operator (aircraft mfg.)	617.382-014
RCS	49	Helper, Liquefaction-and-Regasification (utilities)	953.584-010
RCS	49	Hoist Operator (petrol. & gas)	932.363-010
RCS	49	Inspector (build. mat., n.e.c.)	549.367-010
RCS	49	Machine Setter-and-Repairer (plastic prod.)	690.380-014
RCS	49	Mill Operator, Rolls (any industry)	613.682-030
RCS	49	Mosaic Worker (glass products; nonmet. min.)	779.381-014
RCS	49	Operator, Cavity Pump (elec. equip.)	729.682-010
RCS	49	Patternmaker (glass products)	779.584-010
RCS	49	Plate Stacker, Machine (elec. equip.)	692.382-014
RCS	49	Salvage Worker (nonfer. metal)	619.387-010
RCS	49	Still-Pump Operator (petrol. refin.)	549.362-010
RCS	49	Switch Repairer (r.r. trans.)	622.684-018
RCS	49	Third-Rail Installer (r.r. trans.)	825.381-038
RCS	49	Twisting-Machine Operator (fabrication, n.e.c.)	692.682-070
RCS	49	Varnishing-Unit Tool Setter (ordnance)	632.380-026
RCS	48	Auxiliary-Equipment Tender (construction)	869.665-010
RCS	48	Bench-Shear Operator (furniture)	703.684-010
RCS	48	Cell Installer (chemical)	826.684-018
RCS	48	Centrifugal-Casting-Machine Tender (button & notion)	556.385-010
RCS	48	Chain Builder, Loom Control (textile)	683.381-010
RCS	48	Chip-Mixing-Machine Operator (wood prod., n.e.c.)	560.465-010
RCS	48	Clutch Rebuilder (automotive ser.)	620.684-022
RCS	48	Cutter Operator (mine & quarry)	930.683-014
RCS	48	Drawing-Kiln Operator (glass mfg.)	575.362-010
RCS	48	Drier Operator (can. & preserv.; dairy products)	523.682-022
RCS	48	Flying-Shear Operator (steel & rel.)	615.682-010
RCS	48	Fuller (textile)	586.682-010
RCS	48	Inspector II (ordnance)	737.687-054

HOC	Cx	Title	DOT
RCS	48	Inspector, Barrel Assembly (clock & watch)	715.684-114
RCS	48	Loading-Machine Adjuster (ordnance)	632.360-014
RCS	48	Maintenance Worker, Municipal (government ser.)	899.684-046
RCS	48	Measurer (struct. metal)	869.487-010
RCS	48	Observer Helper, Seismic Prospecting (petrol. & gas)	939.364-010
RCS	48	Photocomposing-Machine Operator (print. & pub.)	650.582-018
RCS	48	Printing-Machine Operator, Tape Rules (cutlery-hrdwr.)	652.662-010
RCS	48	Profile-Saw Operator (jewelry-silver.)	700.682-018
RCS	48	Proof Inspector (ordnance)	736.384-010
RCS	48	Pulverizing-and-Sifting Operator (chemical)	550.485-026
RCS	48	Rivet Heater (heat treating)	504.485-010
RCS	48	Spaghetti-Machine Operator (plastic prod.)	690.682-074
RCS	48	Stacking-Machine Operator I (any industry)	692.682-054
RCS	48	Stitching-Machine Operator (print. & pub.)	653.662-010
RCS	48	Tanning-Drum Operator (leather mfg.)	582.482-018
RCS	48	Transformer-Stock Clerk (utilities)	222.587-054
RCS	47	Ammonium-Nitrate Crystallizer (chemical)	553.685-010
RCS	47	Armature Bander (any industry)	724.684-010
RCS	47	Artificial-Candy Maker (fabrication, n.e.c.)	739.684-010
RCS	47	Assembler, Piano (musical inst.)	730.384-010
RCS	47	Barbed-Wire-Machine Operator (metal prod., n.e.c.)	616.382-010
RCS	47	Barrel Assembler (wood. container)	669.682-014
RCS	47	Batter Mixer (bakery products)	520.685-010
RCS	47	Bead-Forming-Machine Operator (rubber tire)	692.682-014
RCS	47	Billet Assembler (chemical)	614.684-010
RCS	47	Blueprinting-Machine Operator (any industry)	979.682-014
RCS	47	Bridge Operator, Slip (r.r. trans.)	919.682-010
RCS	47	Building Cleaner (any industry)	891.684-022
RCS	47	Candy-Maker Helper (sugar & conf.)	520.685-050
RCS	47	Capacitor Assembler (elec. equip.)	729.684-014
RCS	47	Carver (hotel & rest.)	316.661-010
RCS	47	Casting Operator (nonfer. metal)	514.662-010
RCS	47	Casting-and-Curing Operator (chemical)	559.682-014
RCS	47	Casting-Machine Operator (nonfer. metal)	502.682-014
RCS	47	Centrifugal-Casting-Machine Operator (jewelry-silver.)	502.682-018
RCS	47	Charger Operator (steel & rel.)	504.665-014
RCS	47	Chucking-and-Boring-Machine Operator (furniture)	669.682-022
RCS	47	Compressor (elec. equip.; pharmaceut.)	556.682-022
RCS	47	Coremaking-Machine Operator (elec. equip.)	692.682-030
RCS	47	Corner-Brace-Block-Machine Operator (furniture)	669.682-030
RCS	47	Cotton-Ball-Machine Tender (protective dev.)	580.685-022
RCS	47	Coupling-Machine Operator (steel & rel.)	619.682-014
RCS	47	Cracking-Unit Operator (plastic-synth.)	558.682-010
RCS	47	Drier Operator III (chemical)	553.685-050
RCS	47	Dry-Wall Applicator (construction; mfd. bldgs.)	842.684-014
RCS	47	Electrical-Line Splicer (petrol. & gas)	728.684-014
RCS	47	Embossing-Machine Operator (tex. prod., n.e.c.)	583.685-034
RCS	47	Embossing-Machine Operator (wood prod., n.e.c.)	669.682-046
RCS	47	Encapsulator (aircraft mfg.)	556.684-014

Part 2: From Holland Codes to Occupations

From Holland Codes to the Dictionary of Occupational Titles Occupations

HOC	Cx	Title	DOT
RCS	47	Finished-Stock Inspector (furniture)	763.687-026
RCS	47	Finisher, Hand (tex. prod., n.e.c.)	789.484-014
RCS	47	Fishing Accessories Maker (toy-sport equip.)	619.682-018
RCS	47	Flake-Cutter Operator (wood prod., n.e.c.)	564.682-014
RCS	47	Flesher (leather mfg.)	585.681-010
RCS	47	Gas-Check-Pad Maker (ordnance)	736.684-034
RCS	47	Grip Assembler (woodworking)	762.684-042
RCS	47	House Sitter (domestic ser.)	309.367-010
RCS	47	Hydraulic-Chair Assembler (furniture)	706.684-058
RCS	47	Hydraulic-Strainer Operator (plastic-synth.)	551.582-010
RCS	47	Incising-Machine Operator (wood prod., n.e.c.)	569.662-010
RCS	47	Knife Setter (saw. & plan.)	663.380-010
RCS	47	Lead Recoverer, Continuous-Naphtha-Treating Plant (petrol. refin.)	541.685-014
RCS	47	Leather Tooler (furniture)	763.684-054
RCS	47	Levers-Lace Machine Operator (tex. prod., n.e.c.)	683.682-026
RCS	47	Long-Wall Shear Operator (mine & quarry)	930.662-010
RCS	47	Mark-Up Designer (glass mfg.)	775.684-050
RCS	47	Mica Inspector (mine & quarry)	779.687-026
RCS	47	Monitor Car Operator (mine & quarry)	939.682-010
RCS	47	Nail-Assembly-Machine Operator (steel & rel.)	616.682-030
RCS	47	Oil-Well-Service-Operator Helper (petrol. & gas)	939.684-018
RCS	47	Ordering-Machine Operator (tobacco)	522.682-014
RCS	47	Overhead Crane Operator (any industry)	921.663-010
RCS	47	Paint Sprayer, Sandblaster (concrete prod.)	845.381-018
RCS	47	Painter, Stage Settings (motion picture)	840.681-010
RCS	47	Pantry Goods Maker (hotel & rest.)	317.684-014
RCS	47	Pen-and-Pencil Repairer (any industry)	733.684-014
RCS	47	Plate Former (elec. equip.)	500.684-018
RCS	47	Polisher (clock & watch)	715.682-018
RCS	47	Preform Plate Maker (ship-boat mfg.)	751.684-026
RCS	47	Primer-Powder Blender, Wet (chemical)	550.582-010
RCS	47	Profile Trimmer (jewelry-silver.)	607.682-014
RCS	47	Research Subject (any industry)	359.677-030
RCS	47	Ripsaw Operator (woodworking)	667.682-066
RCS	47	Rock-Drill Operator I (construction)	850.683-034
RCS	47	Roller-Mill Operator (paint & varnish)	555.682-014
RCS	47	Roofer Applicator (construction)	866.684-010
RCS	47	Rotary-Kiln Operator (smelt. & refin.)	513.682-010
RCS	47	Rougher Operator (steel & rel.)	613.662-014
RCS	47	Salvager (petrol. refin.)	709.684-070
RCS	47	Sawyer (plastic prod.; plastic-synth.)	690.482-010
RCS	47	Scarfing Machine Operator (steel & rel.)	816.682-010
RCS	47	Self-Sealing-Fuel-Tank Builder (rubber goods)	752.684-046
RCS	47	Shear Operator I (any industry)	615.682-018
RCS	47	Spindle Plumber (textile)	628.684-030
RCS	47	Top-Precipitator Operator (smelt. & refin.)	511.465-010
RCS	47	Trophy Assembler (jewelry-silver.)	735.684-018
RCS	47	Truck Driver, Heavy (any industry)	905.663-014

Dictionary of Holland Occupational Codes

HOC	Cx	Title	DOT
RCS	47	Veneer Jointer (millwork-plywood)	665.682-038
RCS	47	Wafer-Machine Operator (elec. equip.)	692.662-018
RCS	47	Warp-Knitting-Machine Operator (knitting)	685.665-018
RCS	47	Weaver, Bench Loom (metal prod., n.e.c.)	616.681-010
RCS	47	Wet-Plant Operator (smelt. & refin.)	519.665-018
RCS	46	Box Maker, Wood (wood. container)	760.684-014
RCS	46	Builder, Beam (mfd. bldgs.)	860.684-010
RCS	46	Car Inspector (railroad equip.)	910.667-010
RCS	46	Circular Saw Operator (construction)	869.682-010
RCS	46	Cloth-Mercerizer Operator (textile)	584.685-014
RCS	46	Color-Paste Mixer (textile)	550.685-038
RCS	46	Core-Drill Operator (construction)	869.682-014
RCS	46	Creping-Machine Operator (paper goods)	534.682-030
RCS	46	Diver Pumper (construction; fishing & hunt.)	899.682-010
RCS	46	Dry-End Operator (plastic-synth.)	559.665-014
RCS	46	Electric-Sign Assembler (fabrication, n.e.c.)	729.684-022
RCS	46	Grinder, Carbon Plant (smelt. & refin.)	544.565-010
RCS	46	Hoop Bender, Tank (wood. container)	619.682-026
RCS	46	Jacquard-Loom Weaver (narrow fabrics)	683.682-022
RCS	46	Joiner Helper (ship-boat mfg.)	860.664-014
RCS	46	Kiln Operator (smelt. & refin.)	513.565-010
RCS	46	Plater, Semiconductor Wafers and Components (electron. comp.)	500.684-030
RCS	46	Prop Attendant (amuse. & rec.)	962.684-022
RCS	46	Reamer, Hand (machine shop)	709.684-058
RCS	46	Reel Assembler (woodworking)	762.484-010
RCS	46	Roustabout (petrol. & gas)	869.684-046
RCS	46	Rug Cleaner, Hand (laundry & rel.)	369.384-014
RCS	46	Sampler (steel & rel.)	599.684-014
RCS	46	Tool Filer (pottery & porc.)	701.684-030
RCS	46	Truck Driver, Light (any industry)	906.683-022
RCS	46	Ultrasonic Tester (chemical)	709.687-054
RCS	46	Upholsterer, Outside (furniture)	780.684-118
RCS	46	Upholstery Repairer (furniture)	780.684-122
RCS	46	Utility Operator II (chemical)	709.684-094
RCS	46	Weaver, Narrow Fabrics (narrow fabrics; nonmet. min.)	683.682-046
RCS	46	Yard Worker, Used Building Materials (retail trade)	922.667-010
RCS	45	Agate Setter (office machines)	710.684-010
RCS	45	Carpet Weaver (carpet & rug)	683.682-010
RCS	45	Carpet Weaver, Jacquard Loom (carpet & rug)	683.682-014
RCS	45	Charging-Machine Operator (steel & rel.)	512.683-010
RCS	45	Coater (business ser.)	503.685-010
RCS	45	Cutter, Barrel Drum (tex. prod., n.e.c.)	690.682-026
RCS	45	Dipper (pottery & porc.)	774.684-014
RCS	45	Dresser Tender (textile)	681.682-010
RCS	45	Drier Tender (grain-feed mills)	523.685-070
RCS	45	Electrical-Appliance Preparer (any industry)	827.584-010
RCS	45	Equipment Monitor, Phototypesetting (print. & pub.)	650.682-010
RCS	45	Evaporator Operator II (chemical)	553.682-018

HOC	Cx	Title	DOT
RCS	45	Farm Worker, Poultry (agriculture)	411.584-010
RCS	45	Filling-and-Stapling-Machine Operator (fabrication, n.e.c.)	692.682-038
RCS	45	Finish Patcher (furniture)	763.684-034
RCS	45	Floor and Wall Applier, Liquid (construction)	864.684-010
RCS	45	Gift Wrapper (retail trade)	299.364-014
RCS	45	Grease Buffer (jewelry-silver.)	705.684-022
RCS	45	Harness Placer (textile)	683.680-010
RCS	45	Heel Breaster, Leather (boot & shoe)	690.682-042
RCS	45	Highway-Maintenance Worker (government ser.)	899.684-014
RCS	45	Hoist Operator (mine & quarry)	921.663-026
RCS	45	Hot-Die-Press Operator (boot & shoe)	690.682-050
RCS	45	Ingot Header (nonfer. metal; smelt. & refin.)	514.584-010
RCS	45	Inspector, General (any industry)	609.684-010
RCS	45	Laminating-Machine Operator (furniture)	692.685-106
RCS	45	Load Tester (metal prod., n.e.c.)	616.685-034
RCS	45	Log-Chipper Operator (logging)	564.662-010
RCS	45	Mattress Maker (furniture)	780.684-074
RCS	45	Nibbler Operator (any industry)	615.685-026
RCS	45	Pattern Wheel Maker (knitting)	685.684-010
RCS	45	Plumbing Assembler-Installer (mfd. bldgs.)	862.684-026
RCS	45	Plush Weaver (textile)	683.682-030
RCS	45	Precipitator II (smelt. & refin.)	511.685-042
RCS	45	Production Assembler (ordnance)	737.684-034
RCS	45	Production-Supply-Equipment Tender (food prep., n.e.c.)	921.685-050
RCS	45	Pump-Servicer Helper (any industry)	630.684-022
RCS	45	Recovery Operator (chemical)	558.682-022
RCS	45	Sinter-Machine Operator (smelt. & refin.; steel & rel.)	510.685-026
RCS	45	Sole-Conforming-Machine Operator (boot & shoe)	690.682-070
RCS	45	Spice Fumigator (food prep., n.e.c.)	529.685-218
RCS	45	Spring Tester I (metal prod., n.e.c.)	612.685-014
RCS	45	Springer (furniture)	780.684-106
RCS	45	Stitcher, Special Machine (boot & shoe)	690.682-078
RCS	45	Stone-Spreader Operator (construction)	853.663-022
RCS	45	Striper (paper goods)	651.682-018
RCS	45	Tester Operator (nonfer. metal)	614.684-014
RCS	45	Transformer Assembler II (elec. equip.)	820.684-010
RCS	45	Trimming-Machine Operator (button & notion)	690.682-090
RCS	45	V-Belt Builder (rubber goods)	759.684-066
RCS	45	Vacuum-Pan Operator III (chemical)	559.585-022
RCS	45	Veneer Stapler (ship-boat mfg.)	869.684-078
RCS	45	Weaver, Needle Loom (narrow fabrics)	683.665-010
RCS	45	Wet-End Operator I (plastic-synth.)	559.685-186
RCS	44	Animal-Ride Attendant (amuse. & rec.)	349.674-010
RCS	44	Annealer (heat treating)	504.682-010
RCS	44	Assembler-and-Gluer, Laminated Plastics (plastic prod.)	754.684-014
RCS	44	Bag Printer (print. & pub.)	651.685-010
RCS	44	Band-Saw Operator (tex. prod., n.e.c.)	686.682-010
RCS	44	Barrel Finisher (ordnance)	736.684-018

Part 2: From Holland Codes to Occupations

From Holland Codes to the Dictionary of Occupational Titles Occupations

HOC	Cx	Title	DOT
RCS	44	Binding Folder, Machine (boot & shoe)	788.684-018
RCS	44	Bone-Process Operator (chemical)	559.665-010
RCS	44	Bottom-Saw Operator (saw. & plan.)	667.682-014
RCS	44	Buffer I (any industry)	705.684-014
RCS	44	Carnallite-Plant Operator (smelt. & refin.)	519.484-010
RCS	44	Cigarette Inspector (tobacco)	529.567-010
RCS	44	Combining-Machine Operator (plastic-synth.)	554.685-018
RCS	44	Cutter Apprentice, Hand (any industry)	781.684-078
RCS	44	Cutter Operator (plastic-synth.)	555.585-010
RCS	44	Cutter, Hand I (any industry)	781.684-074
RCS	44	Dial Refinisher (clock & watch)	715.584-010
RCS	44	Drill-Press Operator (machine shop)	606.682-014
RCS	44	Fiberglass-Machine Operator (glass products)	574.682-010
RCS	44	Gauge Operator (fabrication, n.e.c.)	692.682-042
RCS	44	Glass Cutter (any industry)	775.684-022
RCS	44	Glass Installer (woodworking)	865.684-014
RCS	44	Hand Stamper (any industry)	709.684-042
RCS	44	Hoisting Engineer (any industry)	921.663-030
RCS	44	Jack Setter (mine & quarry)	939.684-010
RCS	44	Jigsaw Operator (woodworking)	667.682-042
RCS	44	Kiln Operator (steel & rel.)	509.565-010
RCS	44	Lead Burner (elec. equip.)	727.684-022
RCS	44	Packer (ordnance)	929.684-010
RCS	44	Paint-Brush Maker (fabrication, n.e.c.)	733.684-010
RCS	44	Paint-Spray Tender (glass products)	574.685-014
RCS	44	Press Operator, Carbon Blocks (smelt. & refin.)	514.682-014
RCS	44	Primer Expeditor and Drier (chemical)	553.385-014
RCS	44	Production-Machine Tender (nut & bolt)	619.365-010
RCS	44	Puncher (tex. prod., n.e.c.)	689.582-010
RCS	44	Quilting-Machine Operator (glove & mit.; tex. prod., n.e.c.)	689.685-106
RCS	44	Recording Studio Set-up Worker (recording)	962.664-014
RCS	44	Reinforcing-Steel-Machine Operator (construction)	859.683-022
RCS	44	Rope-Silica-Machine Operator (textile)	582.685-114
RCS	44	Rubber-Goods Repairer (any industry)	759.684-054
RCS	44	Sample Shoe Inspector and Reworker (boot & shoe)	788.684-098
RCS	44	Sawmill Worker (saw. & plan.)	667.687-018
RCS	44	Setter (brick & tile)	573.684-014
RCS	44	Shingle Sawyer (saw. & plan.)	667.485-010
RCS	44	Shotgun-Shell-Assembly-Machine Operator (ordnance)	694.385-010
RCS	44	Snuff-Container Inspector (tobacco)	920.667-014
RCS	44	Stock-Parts Fabricator (ship-boat mfg.)	769.684-050
RCS	44	Surveyor Helper (any industry)	869.567-010
RCS	44	Tractor-Crane Operator (any industry)	921.663-058
RCS	44	Trimmer (jewelry-silver.)	705.682-014
RCS	44	Water Tender (any industry)	599.685-122
RCS	44	Weaver, Tire Cord (tex. prod., n.e.c.)	683.682-050
RCS	43	Almond-Paste Molder (sugar & conf.)	520.684-010
RCS	43	Animal Caretaker (any industry)	410.674-010

HOC	Cx	Title	DOT
RCS	43	Calender Operator, Artificial Leather (tex. prod., n.e.c.)	584.685-010
RCS	43	Cutting-and-Printing-Machine Operator (tex. prod., n.e.c.)	652.685-022
RCS	43	Drier Operator VI (chemical)	553.685-118
RCS	43	Drier-and-Grinder Tender (mine & quarry)	579.685-010
RCS	43	Flux-Tube Attendant (nonfer. metal; smelt. & refin.)	519.687-018
RCS	43	Kiln-Operator Helper (smelt. & refin.)	513.587-010
RCS	43	Knurling-Machine Operator (ordnance)	604.685-018
RCS	43	Mixer (nonfer. metal; steel & rel.)	510.685-018
RCS	43	Mold Polisher (glass mfg.)	579.685-030
RCS	43	Needle-Loom Tender (tex. prod., n.e.c.)	689.685-090
RCS	43	Pump-Press Operator (paper & pulp)	539.685-022
RCS	43	Pumper Helper (petrol. refin.)	549.684-010
RCS	43	Roll-Up-Guider Operator (fabrication, n.e.c.)	590.685-050
RCS	43	Roving Winder, Fiberglass (textile)	681.485-010
RCS	43	Second Cutter (glass mfg.)	779.684-054
RCS	43	Stock Preparer (plastic prod.)	751.387-010
RCS	43	Tetryl-Dissolver Operator (chemical)	550.685-114
RCS	43	Trade Marker (fabrication, n.e.c.)	690.685-510
RCS	43	Veneer Grader (millwork-plywood)	569.687-034
RCS	43	Window Repairer (any industry)	899.684-042
RCS	43	Yard Worker (ship-boat mfg.)	921.683-086
RCS	42	Barley Steeper (beverage)	522.685-114
RCS	42	Belt Builder (rubber goods)	752.684-014
RCS	42	Blending-Machine Operator (textile)	680.685-010
RCS	42	Brush Material Preparer (fabrication, n.e.c.)	739.684-022
RCS	42	Casting-Operator Helper (nonfer. metal)	514.687-018
RCS	42	Checker-In (boot & shoe)	221.587-014
RCS	42	Cloth Trimmer, Machine (textile)	585.685-026
RCS	42	Cork Molder (wood prod., n.e.c.)	569.685-030
RCS	42	Cuff Cutter (glove & mit.)	686.685-018
RCS	42	Drill-Bit Sharpener (electron. comp.)	603.682-030
RCS	42	Filling-Machine Operator (pen & pencil)	733.685-014
RCS	42	Furnace Worker (elec. equip.)	543.666-010
RCS	42	Glass Cut-Off Tender (glass mfg.)	677.685-030
RCS	42	Glass Cutter, Oval or Circular (glass mfg.)	779.684-022
RCS	42	Gold Reclaimer (metal prod., n.e.c.)	709.685-010
RCS	42	Golf-Ball-Cover Treater (toy-sport equip.)	559.685-102
RCS	42	Golf-Club Weigher (toy-sport equip.)	732.587-014
RCS	42	Greaser (agric. equip.)	624.684-010
RCS	42	Impregnator (nonfer. metal; steel & rel.)	509.685-030
RCS	42	Impregnator-and-Drier Helper (elec. equip.; light. fix.)	599.685-050
RCS	42	Inspector, Fireworks (chemical)	737.687-062
RCS	42	Laboratory Helper (utilities)	821.564-010
RCS	42	Machinist Helper, Outside (ship-boat mfg.)	623.687-010
RCS	42	Magazine Repairer (print. & pub.)	653.685-022
RCS	42	Make-Up Operator Helper (chemical)	550.587-010
RCS	42	Marble Finisher (construction)	861.664-010
RCS	42	Mold Maker (smelt. & refin.)	518.664-010
RCS	42	Overhauler Helper (textile)	628.664-010

Part 2: From Holland Codes to Occupations

From Holland Codes to the Dictionary of Occupational Titles Occupations

HOC	Cx	Title	DOT
RCS	42	Pellet-Press Operator (ordnance)	694.685-034
RCS	42	Piano Case and Bench Assembler (musical inst.)	763.684-058
RCS	42	Piano Stringer (musical inst.)	730.684-054
RCS	42	Pipe Finisher (brick & tile)	779.684-042
RCS	42	Polysilicon Preparation Worker (electron. comp.)	590.684-038
RCS	42	Pot Tender (smelt. & refin.)	512.685-018
RCS	42	Primer Boxer (ordnance)	737.587-018
RCS	42	Priming-Mixture Carrier (ordnance)	922.587-010
RCS	42	Sample Cutter (furniture)	781.684-070
RCS	42	Sander (fabrication, n.e.c.)	761.684-030
RCS	42	Seal Mixer (elec. equip.)	540.687-010
RCS	42	Siding Stapler (millwork-plywood)	762.684-058
RCS	42	Silk-Screen Printer, Machine (any industry)	979.685-010
RCS	42	Slotter Operator (paper goods)	640.685-078
RCS	42	Staple-Processing-Machine Operator (textile)	680.585-014
RCS	42	Stripper and Taper (rubber goods)	899.684-038
RCS	42	Sweeping-Compound Blender (chemical)	550.685-110
RCS	42	Tire Groover (automotive ser.)	750.684-026
RCS	42	Tire Sorter (rubber tire)	750.687-022
RCS	42	Varnish Inspector (paint & varnish)	559.584-014
RCS	42	Weigher Operator (chemical)	559.687-070
RCS	42	Welder, Gun (welding)	810.664-010
RCS	42	Welder, Production Line (welding)	819.684-010
RCS	42	Wheel Lacer and Truer (motor-bicycles)	706.684-106
RCS	42	Winder (clock & watch)	715.687-130
RCS	41	Assembler (glove & mit.)	781.667-010
RCS	41	Back Tender (textile)	589.686-010
RCS	41	Band-Reamer-Machine Operator (nonfer. metal)	603.685-010
RCS	41	Base-Ply Hand (rubber goods)	759.684-014
RCS	41	Beveler (glass products)	673.685-018
RCS	41	Blaster Helper (any industry)	859.687-010
RCS	41	Bolter (saw. & plan.)	667.685-022
RCS	41	Bottoming-Machine Operator (paper goods)	649.685-022
RCS	41	Cable-Splicer Helper (construction; tel. & tel.; utilities)	829.667-010
RCS	41	Canoe Inspector, Final (ship-boat mfg.)	769.687-018
RCS	41	Carpet Cutter II (carpet & rug)	585.687-014
RCS	41	Circle Beveler (glass products)	673.685-034
RCS	41	Compound Finisher (chemical)	550.685-042
RCS	41	Core-Oven Tender (foundry)	518.685-010
RCS	41	Crosscutter, Rolled Glass (glass mfg.)	575.684-022
RCS	41	Cupola Charger (foundry)	512.686-010
RCS	41	Decorator, Street and Building (any industry)	899.687-010
RCS	41	Deicer-Kit Assembler (rubber goods)	759.684-030
RCS	41	Diamond-Powder Technician (nonmet. min.)	673.685-046
RCS	41	Drawing-In-Machine-Tender Helper (textile)	683.685-022
RCS	41	Dry-House Attendant (chemical)	553.585-014
RCS	41	Firer, Retort (chemical)	553.685-066
RCS	41	Former Helper, Hand (any industry)	619.684-010
RCS	41	Furnace Tender (foundry; nonfer. metal)	512.685-010

HOC	Cx	Title	DOT
RCS	41	Granulator Tender (steel & rel.)	519.665-010
RCS	41	Grinder (rubber goods; rubber reclaim.)	555.685-030
RCS	41	Heater Tender (rubber goods; rubber reclaim.; rubber tire)	553.665-038
RCS	41	Hot-Press Operator (nonmet. min.)	575.685-042
RCS	41	Hydraulic Operator (nonfer. metal)	611.685-014
RCS	41	Hydraulic-Press Operator (tobacco)	920.685-062
RCS	41	Induction-Machine Operator (heat treating)	504.685-022
RCS	41	Inspector-Grader, Agricultural Establishment (agriculture)	409.687-010
RCS	41	Laminating-Machine Tender (rubber goods)	554.665-014
RCS	41	Log Inspector (saw. & plan.)	667.687-014
RCS	41	Machine Operator, General (paper goods)	649.685-070
RCS	41	Metal-Cleaner, Immersion (any industry)	503.685-030
RCS	41	Mold-Maker Helper (smelt. & refin.)	518.687-018
RCS	41	Oxidized-Finish Plater (any industry)	599.685-062
RCS	41	Paste Mixer (chemical)	550.585-034
RCS	41	Potato-Chip Frier (food prep., n.e.c.)	526.685-046
RCS	41	Print Developer, Automatic (photofinishing)	976.685-026
RCS	41	Propellant-Charge-Zone Assembler (ordnance)	737.687-110
RCS	41	Pulper (paper & pulp; tex. prod., n.e.c.)	530.685-014
RCS	41	Rag-Cutting-Machine Tender (paper & pulp; tex. prod., n.e.c.)	530.665-014
RCS	41	Round-Corner-Cutter Operator (paper goods; print. & pub.)	640.685-074
RCS	41	Rug Cleaner, Machine (laundry & rel.)	361.682-010
RCS	41	Rug Inspector (tex. prod., n.e.c.)	585.685-090
RCS	41	Sample-Color Maker (paint & varnish)	550.584-014
RCS	41	Shell Molder (foundry)	518.685-026
RCS	41	Silica-Spray Mixer (smelt. & refin.)	570.685-090
RCS	41	Skimmer, Reverberatory (smelt. & refin.)	511.687-022
RCS	41	Sugar Grinder (sugar & conf.)	521.685-346
RCS	41	Tanker (wood prod., n.e.c.)	561.665-010
RCS	41	Thaw-Shed Heater Tender (steel & rel.)	543.685-022
RCS	41	Tire Trimmer, Hand (rubber tire)	750.684-034
RCS	41	Top-Precipitator-Operator Helper (smelt. & refin.)	511.586-010
RCS	41	Tube Balancer (rubber tire)	750.684-046
RCS	41	Tube Repairer (rubber tire)	750.684-050
RCS	41	Warper (narrow fabrics)	681.685-146
RCS	40	Ball Sorter (machinery mfg.)	609.685-010
RCS	40	Blocker, Automatic (glass mfg.; glass products)	673.685-030
RCS	40	Bucket Turner (wood. container)	669.682-018
RCS	40	Buffer (rubber goods; rubber tire)	759.684-022
RCS	40	Button Maker and Installer (tex. prod., n.e.c.)	734.685-014
RCS	40	Calender-Wind-Up Tender (rubber goods; rubber tire)	554.665-010
RCS	40	Checker (laundry & rel.)	369.687-014
RCS	40	Coffee Maker (hotel & rest.)	317.684-010
RCS	40	Collator Operator (clerical)	208.685-010
RCS	40	Condenser Setter (smelt. & refin.)	512.687-010
RCS	40	Cotton Dispatcher (furniture)	780.684-038
RCS	40	Crusher Tender (smelt. & refin.)	515.685-014
RCS	40	Driver (auto. mfg.; automotive ser.)	919.683-014

Part 2: From Holland Codes to Occupations

From Holland Codes to the Dictionary of Occupational Titles Occupations

HOC	Cx	Title	DOT
RCS	40	Driver, Starting Gate (amuse. & rec.)	919.683-030
RCS	40	Hot-Wire Glass-Tube Cutter (glass products)	772.684-014
RCS	40	Injection-Molding-Machine Offbearer (pen & pencil)	690.686-038
RCS	40	Laborer, General (leather mfg.)	589.686-026
RCS	40	Ladle Pourer (smelt. & refin.)	514.684-014
RCS	40	Lock Assembler (cutlery-hrdwr.)	706.684-074
RCS	40	Meat Clerk (retail trade)	222.684-010
RCS	40	Packer (tobacco)	920.687-130
RCS	40	Painter Helper, Automotive (automotive ser.)	845.684-014
RCS	40	Plastic-Top Assembler (furniture)	763.684-062
RCS	40	Plastics-Seasoner Operator (plastic-synth.)	553.665-042
RCS	40	Preassembler and Inspector (musical inst.)	730.684-058
RCS	40	Press Breaker (wood prod., n.e.c.)	569.686-050
RCS	40	Sander-and-Buffer (musical inst.)	730.684-066
RCS	40	Shoelace-Tipping-Machine Operator (narrow fabrics)	686.685-062
RCS	40	Spotter I (laundry & rel.)	361.684-018
RCS	40	Spray-Unit Feeder (any industry)	599.686-014
RCS	40	Tape-Folding-Machine Operator (rubber goods; tex. prod., n.e.c.)	689.685-134
RCS	40	Tone Regulator (musical inst.)	730.684-094
RCS	40	Wire Setter (glass mfg.)	579.665-018
RCS	39	Bar and Filler Assembler (furniture)	706.684-034
RCS	39	Box Repairer II (wood. container)	762.687-018
RCS	39	Cloth Spreader, Screen Printing (textile)	652.687-010
RCS	39	Comber Tender (textile)	680.685-118
RCS	39	Concrete-Pipe Maker (concrete prod.)	779.684-014
RCS	39	Curing-Press Operator (rubber tire)	553.686-018
RCS	39	Dust Collector-Treater (smelt. & refin.)	511.687-014
RCS	39	Garment Sorter (garment)	222.687-014
RCS	39	Golf-Range Attendant (amuse. & rec.)	341.683-010
RCS	39	Guider (fabrication, n.e.c.)	590.686-014
RCS	39	Ladle Liner (foundry; smelt. & refin.)	519.684-010
RCS	39	Oiler (any industry)	699.687-018
RCS	39	Putty Glazer (any industry)	749.684-042
RCS	39	Rubber (furniture; wood prod., n.e.c.)	742.684-010
RCS	39	Rug-Inspector Helper (carpet & rug)	789.687-158
RCS	39	Stainer (furniture; wood prod., n.e.c.)	742.684-014
RCS	39	Teamster (any industry)	919.664-010
RCS	39	Tinning-Equipment Tender (elec. equip.)	501.685-014
RCS	39	Tire Molder (rubber tire)	553.685-102
RCS	39	Track Laminating Machine Tender (inst. & app.)	692.685-290
RCS	39	Webbing Tacker (furniture)	780.684-130
RCS	38	Automatic-Pad-Making-Machine Operator Helper (tex. prod., n.e.c.)	689.686-010
RCS	38	Band Maker (agriculture)	619.685-010
RCS	38	Bander, Hand (tobacco)	920.687-030
RCS	38	Bark-Press Operator (paper & pulp)	563.685-010
RCS	38	Barrel Liner (wood. container)	764.687-026
RCS	38	Beamer Helper (textile)	681.686-014

Part 2: From Holland Codes to Occupations

From Holland Codes to the Dictionary of Occupational Titles Occupations

HOC	Cx	Title	DOT
RCS	38	Bottom Filler (boot & shoe)	788.684-026
RCS	38	Buffing-and-Sueding-Machine Operator (boot & shoe)	753.684-010
RCS	38	Burning-Plant Operator (ordnance)	509.685-018
RCS	38	Cloth Reeler (textile)	689.685-042
RCS	38	Cloth-Printer Helper (any industry)	652.686-010
RCS	38	Condenser-Tube Tender (smelt. & refin.)	511.685-018
RCS	38	Dipper (jewelry-silver.)	735.687-010
RCS	38	Drawer Liner (furniture)	763.684-030
RCS	38	Feather Sawyer (toy-sport equip.)	732.685-014
RCS	38	Finisher (nonmet. min.)	775.687-010
RCS	38	Fire-Hose Curer (rubber goods)	553.685-062
RCS	38	Flamer (boot & shoe)	788.684-050
RCS	38	Flasher Adjuster (light. fix.)	723.684-022
RCS	38	Foxing Cutter, Hot Knife (boot & shoe; rubber goods)	751.684-022
RCS	38	Jackhammer Operator (mine & quarry)	930.684-018
RCS	38	Log Roller (saw. & plan.)	677.687-010
RCS	38	Mold Preparer (ship-boat mfg.)	809.687-026
RCS	38	Oil-Spot Washer (tex. prod., n.e.c.; textile)	689.687-050
RCS	38	Oven Dauber (steel & rel.)	543.687-014
RCS	38	Pipe Buffer (construction)	705.684-054
RCS	38	Porter, Used-Car Lot (retail trade; wholesale tr.)	915.687-022
RCS	38	Pourer, Metal (foundry)	514.684-022
RCS	38	Rasper (boot & shoe)	788.684-094
RCS	38	Rough Opener, Jewel Hole (clock & watch)	770.684-018
RCS	38	Scraper (jewelry-silver.)	700.687-066
RCS	38	Shoe Cleaner (boot & shoe)	788.687-122
RCS	38	Snowmaker (amuse. & rec.)	969.685-010
RCS	38	Straw-Hat Brusher (hat & cap)	784.687-074
RCS	38	Stripper (glass mfg.)	673.666-014
RCS	38	Thresher, Broomcorn (agriculture)	429.685-014
RCS	38	Trimmer, Hand (any industry)	781.687-070
RCS	38	Turning-Machine-Operator Helper (wood. container)	667.686-022
RCS	38	Veneer-Stock Grader (wood. container)	769.687-050
RCS	38	Washer-Engineer Helper (paper & pulp)	533.686-014
RCS	38	Waste-Machine Offbearer (tex. prod., n.e.c.)	680.686-022
RCS	38	Wrinkle Chaser (boot & shoe)	788.684-130
RCS	37	Adhesive Primer (toy-sport equip.)	732.687-010
RCS	37	Candle Cutter (fabrication, n.e.c.)	739.687-050
RCS	37	Card Decorator (print. & pub.)	649.686-014
RCS	37	Groover (any industry)	692.686-042
RCS	37	Harvest Worker, Fruit (agriculture)	403.687-018
RCS	37	Head-Gauge-Unit Operator (ordnance)	619.685-054
RCS	37	Package Crimper (textile)	589.686-034
RCS	37	Plug Sorter (woodworking)	769.687-034
RCS	37	Rigger, Third (logging)	921.687-030
RCS	37	Tree-Trimmer Helper (utilities)	408.667-010
RCS	37	Waxer, Floor (any industry)	381.687-034
RCS	35	Smoother (hat & cap)	784.684-066

HOC to DOT

HOC	Cx	Title	DOT
RCE	67	Inspector, Electrical (government ser.)	168.167-034
RCE	64	Estimator (profess. & kin.)	169.267-038
RCE	63	Building Inspector (insurance)	168.267-010
RCE	63	Sound Controller (amuse. & rec.)	194.262-014
RCE	62	Electronic Intelligence Operations Specialist (military ser.)	193.382-010
RCE	62	Panelboard Operator (chemical)	950.562-010
RCE	62	Radio Officer (water trans.)	193.262-022
RCE	61	Camera Repairer (photo. appar.)	714.281-014
RCE	60	Developer Prover, Interior Assemblies (aircraft mfg.)	693.261-010
RCE	60	Inspector, Metal Fabricating (any industry)	619.261-010
RCE	59	Glazier Supervisor (construction)	865.131-010
RCE	59	Stonemason Supervisor (construction)	861.131-018
RCE	59	Supervisor, Inspection (sugar & conf.)	529.137-074
RCE	59	Telecine Operator (radio-tv broad.)	194.362-018
RCE	58	Chief Inspector (office machines)	706.131-018
RCE	58	Electrician, Office (tel. & tel.)	822.261-010
RCE	58	Marine-Services Technician (ship-boat mfg.)	806.261-026
RCE	58	Orthodontic Technician (protective dev.)	712.381-030
RCE	58	Pipe Fitter (construction)	862.281-022
RCE	58	Pipe-Fitter Apprentice (construction)	862.281-026
RCE	58	Radio-Intelligence Operator (government ser.)	193.362-014
RCE	57	Carpenter (construction)	860.381-022
RCE	57	Carpenter Apprentice (construction)	860.381-026
RCE	57	Engraver, Block (print. & pub.)	979.281-014
RCE	57	Gambling Monitor (amuse. & rec.)	343.367-014
RCE	57	Riveting Machine Operator, Automatic (aircraft mfg.)	806.380-010
RCE	57	Sewer-Line Repairer, Tele-Grout (sanitary ser.)	851.262-010
RCE	57	Supervisor, Waterproofing (construction)	843.137-010
RCE	56	Boat-Canvas Maker-Installer (tex. prod., n.e.c.)	789.261-010
RCE	56	Control Clerk (clock & watch)	221.387-018
RCE	56	Gauger (petrol. & gas; petrol. refin.; pipe lines)	914.384-010
RCE	56	Group Leader, Semiconductor Processing (electron. comp.)	590.362-018
RCE	56	Repairer, Art Objects (any industry)	779.381-018
RCE	56	Retort-Load Expediter (wood prod., n.e.c.)	221.167-022
RCE	56	Sample Maker II (jewelry-silver.)	735.381-018
RCE	56	Supervisor, Kennel (nonprofit org.)	410.134-018
RCE	55	Cold-Mill Operator (steel & rel.)	613.662-018
RCE	55	Fuel-Oil Clerk (clerical)	222.387-018
RCE	55	Inspector, Watch Train (clock & watch)	715.381-074
RCE	55	Motorcycle Tester (motor-bicycles)	620.384-010
RCE	55	Rolling Attendant (steel & rel.)	613.662-010
RCE	55	Supervisor, Stave Cutting (wood. container)	667.137-010
RCE	54	Assembler, Igniter (ordnance)	737.381-010
RCE	54	Contact Printer, Photoresist (inst. & app.; optical goods)	976.684-034
RCE	54	Evaporative-Cooler Installer (any industry)	637.381-010
RCE	54	Glass-Blowing-Lathe Operator (glass products)	772.482-010
RCE	54	Group Leader, Printed Circuit Board Assembly (electron. comp.)	726.361-014
RCE	54	Instructor-Trainer, Canine Service (government ser.)	379.227-010

Part 2: From Holland Codes to Occupations

From Holland Codes to the Dictionary of Occupational Titles Occupations

HOC	Cx	Title	DOT
RCE	54	Laboratory Tester (textile)	689.384-014
RCE	54	Machine Operator I (any industry)	616.380-018
RCE	54	Meter Inspector (utilities)	710.384-022
RCE	54	Painter Apprentice, Transportation Equipment (aircraft mfg.; air trans.; automotive ser.)	845.381-010
RCE	54	Painter, Transportation Equipment (aircraft mfg.; air trans.; automotive ser.)	845.381-014
RCE	54	Phosphoric-Acid Operator (chemical)	558.582-010
RCE	54	Still Operator I (beverage)	522.382-030
RCE	54	Trip Follower (air trans.)	209.367-050
RCE	53	Assistant Press Operator, Offset (print. & pub.)	651.685-026
RCE	53	Board-Machine Set-up Operator (concrete prod.)	579.380-010
RCE	53	Collating-Machine Operator (print. & pub.)	653.382-014
RCE	53	Comparator Operator (any industry)	699.384-010
RCE	53	Customer Service Representative (utilities)	959.361-010
RCE	53	Dice Maker (toy-sport equip.)	731.381-010
RCE	53	Electric Power Line Examiner (utilities)	959.367-010
RCE	53	Field Recorder (utilities)	229.367-010
RCE	53	Grinding-Mill Operator (mine & quarry; smelt. & refin.)	515.382-010
RCE	53	Process Checker (ordnance)	737.364-010
RCE	53	Refinery Operator, Assistant (grain-feed mills)	521.462-010
RCE	53	Riveting-Machine Operator I (any industry)	699.482-010
RCE	53	Station Engineer, Main Line (pipe lines)	914.362-018
RCE	53	Stock Clerk (clerical)	222.387-058
RCE	53	Tungsten Refiner (smelt. & refin.)	511.382-010
RCE	52	Batting-Machine Operator, Insulation (nonmet. min.)	677.382-010
RCE	52	Car-Retarder Operator (r.r. trans.)	910.382-010
RCE	52	Computer-Controlled-Color-Photograph-Printer Operator (photofinishing)	976.380-010
RCE	52	Deicer Inspector, Electric (rubber goods)	729.387-010
RCE	52	Engraver Apprentice, Decorative (engraving)	704.381-022
RCE	52	Engraver, Hand, Soft Metals (engraving)	704.381-030
RCE	52	Fare-Register Repairer (motor trans.)	729.384-014
RCE	52	Garment Fitter (retail trade)	785.361-014
RCE	52	Impregnator and Drier (elec. equip.; electron. comp.)	599.682-014
RCE	52	Inspector-Adjuster, Office-Machine Components (office machines)	706.384-010
RCE	52	Laser-Beam-Machine Operator (welding)	815.682-010
RCE	52	Parcel Post Clerk (clerical)	222.387-038
RCE	52	Precision Assembler, Bench (aircraft mfg.)	706.381-050
RCE	52	Sand Tester (foundry)	777.381-046
RCE	52	Shotgun-Shell-Assembly-Machine Adjuster (ordnance)	616.360-030
RCE	52	Syrup Maker (sugar & conf.)	529.482-022
RCE	52	Transportation-Equipment-Maintenance Worker (museums)	899.384-010
RCE	52	Wash Operator (chemical)	559.662-014
RCE	52	Wash-Oil-Pump Operator (steel & rel.)	549.382-018
RCE	52	Way Inspector (r.r. trans.)	910.367-030
RCE	52	Woodwork-Salvage Inspector (ordnance)	769.387-010
RCE	51	Automatic-Pad-Making-Machine Operator (tex. prod., n.e.c.)	689.382-010

Part 2: From Holland Codes to Occupations

From Holland Codes to the Dictionary of Occupational Titles Occupations

HOC	Cx	Title	DOT
RCE	51	Boring-and-Filling-Machine Operator (fabrication, n.e.c.)	692.682-018
RCE	51	Causticiser (chemical)	558.382-022
RCE	51	Checkering-Machine Adjuster (ordnance)	669.360-010
RCE	51	Chimney Repairer (business ser.)	899.364-010
RCE	51	Coil Winder, Repair (any industry)	724.381-014
RCE	51	Diamond Mounter (machine tools)	739.384-010
RCE	51	Diamond-Die Polisher (machine tools)	770.381-022
RCE	51	Fire-Equipment Inspector (any industry)	739.484-014
RCE	51	Inspector and Adjuster, Golf Club Head (toy-sport equip.)	732.384-014
RCE	51	Kitchen Clerk (hotel & rest.)	222.587-022
RCE	51	Lathe Operator (jewelry-silver.)	770.382-010
RCE	51	Machine Tester (machinery mfg.)	629.382-010
RCE	51	Music Grapher (print. & pub.)	970.581-010
RCE	51	Order Filler (retail trade; wholesale tr.)	222.487-014
RCE	51	Pleat Patternmaker (garment; tex. prod., n.e.c.)	781.484-010
RCE	51	Pole Inspector (utilities)	869.387-010
RCE	51	Pressure Sealer-and-Tester (aircraft mfg.)	806.384-038
RCE	51	Quality-Control Inspector (glass mfg.)	579.367-010
RCE	51	Record Tester (recording)	194.387-014
RCE	51	Sapphire-Stylus Grinder (comm. equip.)	770.381-038
RCE	51	Setter, Induction-Heating Equipment (welding)	813.360-014
RCE	51	Ship Runner (water trans.)	222.567-014
RCE	51	Steel-Wool-Machine Operator (nonmet. min.)	605.482-010
RCE	51	Stopboard Assembler (musical inst.)	730.684-082
RCE	51	Weatherstrip-Machine Operator (rubber goods)	690.382-014
RCE	50	Adjuster, Electrical Contacts (elec. equip.)	724.381-010
RCE	50	Assembler, Mechanical Ordnance (ordnance)	737.684-010
RCE	50	Automobile Tester (government ser.)	379.364-010
RCE	50	Batch-Records Clerk (plastic prod.)	221.387-054
RCE	50	Bullet-Grooving-Sizing-and-Lubricating-Machine Operator (ordnance)	619.382-010
RCE	50	Electrical-Discharge-Machine Operator, Production (machine shop)	609.482-010
RCE	50	Flake Miller, Wheat and Oats (grain-feed mills)	521.682-022
RCE	50	Glass Calibrator (glass products)	775.584-010
RCE	50	Grinder I (clock & watch)	603.482-030
RCE	50	Inspecting-Machine Adjuster (ordnance)	632.380-010
RCE	50	Internal-Combustion-Engine Subassembler (engine-turbine)	706.481-010
RCE	50	Laboratory Clerk (clerical)	222.587-026
RCE	50	Lumber Scaler (woodworking)	221.487-010
RCE	50	Marker I (any industry)	781.384-014
RCE	50	Maturity Checker (can. & preserv.)	529.485-022
RCE	50	Molybdenum-Steamer Operator (smelt. & refin.)	511.485-010
RCE	50	Plumber (mfd. bldgs.)	862.681-010
RCE	50	Quality Control Checker, Texturing Process (textile)	681.387-010
RCE	50	Salvage-Machine Operator (ordnance)	694.382-010
RCE	50	Skein Winder (elec. equip.)	721.484-022
RCE	50	Tile-Conduit Layer (construction)	861.381-062
RCE	50	Transfer Operator (print. & pub.)	651.382-038

Part 2: From Holland Codes to Occupations

From Holland Codes to the Dictionary of Occupational Titles Occupations

HOC	Cx	Title	DOT
RCE	50	Valve Maker II (musical inst.)	730.681-018
RCE	50	Wad-Blanking-Press Adjuster (ordnance)	690.360-010
RCE	50	Water-Treatment-Plant Operator (chemical)	551.485-010
RCE	49	Addressing-Machine Operator (clerical)	208.582-010
RCE	49	Brake-Drum-Lathe Operator (automotive ser.)	620.682-010
RCE	49	Coil Shaper (any industry)	724.684-022
RCE	49	Coiler Operator (steel & rel.)	613.382-010
RCE	49	Cook, Fast Food (hotel & rest.)	313.374-010
RCE	49	Edging-Machine Setter (glass products)	673.380-010
RCE	49	Emblem Drawer-In (tex. prod., n.e.c.)	689.380-010
RCE	49	Hogshead Inspector (tobacco)	529.367-014
RCE	49	Inspector, Assembly (ordnance)	736.387-010
RCE	49	Inspector, Finishing (tex. prod., n.e.c.)	589.387-022
RCE	49	Inspector, Mechanism (clock & watch)	715.384-014
RCE	49	Loading Inspector (r.r. trans.)	910.667-018
RCE	49	Mincemeat Maker (can. & preserv.)	520.485-018
RCE	49	Motorcycle Subassembly Repairer (motor-bicycles)	620.684-026
RCE	49	Oliving-Machine Operator (clock & watch)	770.381-034
RCE	49	Panelboard Operator (textile)	582.362-010
RCE	49	Quality-Control Inspector (bakery products)	529.367-018
RCE	49	Roller (jewelry-silver.)	613.682-018
RCE	49	Screen Maker, Photographic Process (any industry)	979.384-010
RCE	49	Tree Pruner (agriculture)	408.684-018
RCE	49	Wire Drawing Machine Operator (inst. & app.; jewelry-silver.)	614.382-018
RCE	48	Adzing-and-Boring-Machine Operator (wood prod., n.e.c.)	669.682-010
RCE	48	Armature Winder, Repair (any industry)	724.684-018
RCE	48	Barrel Filler II (beverage)	914.485-010
RCE	48	Bias-Machine Operator (rubber tire)	690.682-022
RCE	48	Boiler-Operator Helper (sugar & conf.)	950.585-014
RCE	48	Clarifier Operator (smelt. & refin.)	511.662-010
RCE	48	Colorer (brick & tile)	773.684-010
RCE	48	Cultured-Marble-Products Maker (stonework)	575.684-050
RCE	48	Doughnut-Machine Operator (bakery products)	526.682-022
RCE	48	Elevator-Constructor Helper (construction)	825.664-010
RCE	48	Fur-Machine Operator (fur goods)	783.682-010
RCE	48	Furnace Charger (nonfer. metal; smelt. & refin.; steel & rel.)	512.684-014
RCE	48	Gang Sawyer, Stone (stonework)	670.362-010
RCE	48	Glazier, Metal Furniture (furniture)	865.684-018
RCE	48	Gluing-Machine Operator, Automatic (print. & pub.)	641.682-014
RCE	48	Inspector, Open Die (cutlery-hrdwr.)	701.684-014
RCE	48	Jewel-Bearing Driller (clock & watch)	770.682-014
RCE	48	Knitting-Machine Operator, Full-Fashioned Hosiery, Automatic (knitting)	684.682-010
RCE	48	Masking-Machine Operator (plastic-synth.)	554.682-014
RCE	48	Mixer, Diamond Powder (nonmet. min.)	570.484-010
RCE	48	Mottle-Lay-Up Operator (plastic-synth.)	690.585-014
RCE	48	Nitrating-Acid Mixer (chemical)	550.585-030
RCE	48	Phonograph-Cartridge Assembler (comm. equip.)	720.684-014

HOC	Cx	Title	DOT
RCE	48	Piano Regulator-Inspector (musical inst.)	730.681-010
RCE	48	Pipe-Cleaning-and-Priming-Machine Operator (construction)	862.662-010
RCE	48	Powerhouse-Mechanic Helper (utilities)	631.684-010
RCE	48	Preparer, Making Department (jewelry-silver `)	700.684-058
RCE	48	Ram-Press Operator (pottery & porc.)	575.682-022
RCE	48	Salvage Repairer II (utilities)	729.384-018
RCE	48	Sider (construction; mfd. bldgs.; retail trade)	863.684-014
RCE	48	Sole Sewer, Hand (boot & shoe)	788.684-110
RCE	48	Starch-Treating Assistant (grain-feed mill`)	520.665-018
RCE	48	Surgical-Forceps Fabricator (inst. & app.)	712.684-054
RCE	48	Tester (musical inst.)	730.684-086
RCE	48	Testing-Machine Operator (tex. prod., n.e.c.)	586.685-038
RCE	48	Tire Classifier (rubber tire)	750.387-010
RCE	48	Tower-Loader Operator (water trans.)	921.683-074
RCE	48	Trailer Assembler I (auto. mfg.)	806.381-058
RCE	48	Transmission Tester (auto. mfg.)	806.684-134
RCE	48	Tuber-Machine Operator (rubber goods; rubber tire)	690.662-014
RCE	48	Ventilation Equipment Tender (any industry)	950.585-010
RCE	48	Water-Softener Servicer-and-Installer (business ser.)	862.684-034
RCE	48	Yeast Washer (food prep., n.e.c.)	529.685-278
RCE	47	Assorter (steel & rel.)	703.687-010
RCE	47	Balance Truer (clock & watch)	715.684-018
RCE	47	Band-Scroll-Saw Operator (woodworking)	667.682-010
RCE	47	Battery Assembler, Dry Cell (elec. equip.)	727.664-010
RCE	47	Bed Laster (boot & shoe)	690.682-018
RCE	47	Broom Stitcher (fabrication, n.e.c.)	692.682-022
RCE	47	Card Cutter, Jacquard (narrow fabrics; textile)	683.582-010
RCE	47	CD-Storage-and-Materials Make-Up Helper (chemical)	559.685-034
RCE	47	Colorer (print. & pub.)	970.681-014
RCE	47	Cupboard Builder (furniture)	703.684-014
RCE	47	Drier Tender (wood prod., n.e.c.)	563.585-010
RCE	47	Duplicating-Machine Operator I (clerical)	207.682-010
RCE	47	Extractor Operator (chemical)	552.682-018
RCE	47	Facer (clock & watch)	770.582-010
RCE	47	Foam Charger (svc. ind. mach.)	827.585-010
RCE	47	Green-Tire Inspector (rubber tire)	750.684-018
RCE	47	Hat-Finishing-Materials Preparer (hat & cap)	559.684-030
RCE	47	Hoop-Flaring-and-Coiling-Machine Operator (wood. container)	619.682-034
RCE	47	Inspector, Aligning (office machines)	706.687-022
RCE	47	Inspector, Hairspring Truing (clock & watch)	715.684-118
RCE	47	Inspector, Slide Fasteners (button & notion)	734.687-062
RCE	47	Jewel Gauger (clock & watch)	770.687-018
RCE	47	Jewel-Bearing Broacher (clock & watch)	770.682-010
RCE	47	Jewel-Bearing Facer (clock & watch)	770.682-018
RCE	47	Jewel-Bearing Grinder (clock & watch)	770.685-018
RCE	47	Jewel-Bearing Polisher (clock & watch)	770.685-022
RCE	47	Jewel-Bearing Turner (clock & watch)	770.682-022

Part 2: From Holland Codes to Occupations

From Holland Codes to the Dictionary of Occupational Titles Occupations

HOC	Cx	Title	DOT
RCE	47	Jewel-Hole Driller (clock & watch)	770.682-026
RCE	47	Kick-Press Operator I (any industry)	616.682-026
RCE	47	Leather Stamper (leather prod.)	781.381-018
RCE	47	Mailer Apprentice (print. & pub.)	222.587-032
RCE	47	Mannequin Mounter (fabrication, n.e.c.)	739.684-118
RCE	47	Microfilm-Camera Operator (business ser.)	976.682-022
RCE	47	Open-Developer Operator (textile)	582.685-098
RCE	47	Optical-Glass Etcher (optical goods)	716.681-022
RCE	47	Ornamental-Machine Operator (wood prod., n.e.c.)	690.682-054
RCE	47	Painter, Spray I (any industry)	741.684-026
RCE	47	Parachute Rigger (air trans.)	912.684-010
RCE	47	Patternmaker, Acoustical Tile (wood prod., n.e.c.)	649.685-086
RCE	47	Picture Framer (retail trade; wood prod., n.e.c.)	739.684-146
RCE	47	Piston Maker (musical inst.)	730.681-014
RCE	47	Platen Grinder (office machines)	690.385-010
RCE	47	Plater (inst. & app.)	500.684-034
RCE	47	Polisher, Sand (jewelry-silver.)	705.684-070
RCE	47	Polymerization Helper (plastic-synth.)	558.585-038
RCE	47	Power-Barker Operator (paper & pulp; saw. & plan.)	669.485-010
RCE	47	Preform-Machine Operator (button & notion)	556.380-014
RCE	47	Proof-Coin Collector (government ser.)	709.687-030
RCE	47	Reclamation Worker (wholesale tr.)	621.684-014
RCE	47	Ripening-Room Attendant (plastic-synth.)	559.682-038
RCE	47	Roller Coverer (textile)	628.682-010
RCE	47	Rug Inspector II (carpet & rug)	789.587-022
RCE	47	Sample Tester-Grinder (mine & quarry)	519.585-018
RCE	47	Scooping-Machine Tender (furniture)	665.685-026
RCE	47	Sewing-Machine Operator II (tex. prod., n.e.c.)	787.682-058
RCE	47	Stitcher (tex. prod., n.e.c.)	689.682-022
RCE	47	Tenoner Operator (wood prod., n.e.c.)	677.682-026
RCE	47	Threader (knitting)	685.680-010
RCE	47	Ticket-Chopper Assembler (furniture)	739.684-154
RCE	47	Tire Inspector (rubber tire)	750.684-030
RCE	47	Tooth Cutter, Escape Wheel (clock & watch)	605.682-026
RCE	47	Truer (metal prod., n.e.c.)	616.484-010
RCE	47	Tufting-Machine Operator (carpet & rug; textile)	687.685-018
RCE	47	Wheel Cutter (clock & watch)	605.682-030
RCE	47	Wire Repairer (carpet & rug)	628.684-038
RCE	46	Abrasive-Wheel Molder (nonmet. min.)	575.685-010
RCE	46	Assembler, Subassembly (mfd. bldgs.; vehicles, n.e.c.)	869.684-018
RCE	46	Assembler, Type-Bar-and-Segment (office machines)	706.684-026
RCE	46	Assembly Cleaner (smelt. & refin.)	519.664-010
RCE	46	Baseball Inspector and Repairer (toy-sport equip.)	732.684-030
RCE	46	Bed Operator (steel & rel.)	613.685-034
RCE	46	Blow-Molding-Machine Operator (plastic prod.)	556.682-010
RCE	46	Bright Cutter (jewelry-silver.)	700.684-018
RCE	46	Calender-Let-Off Operator (rubber goods; rubber tire)	554.682-010
RCE	46	Cap-Jewel Plate Assembler (clock & watch)	715.684-050
RCE	46	Cementer (optical goods)	711.684-014

From Holland Codes to the Dictionary of Occupational Titles Occupations

HOC	Cx	Title	DOT
RCE	46	Checker I (clerical)	222.687-010
RCE	46	Churn Tender (plastic-synth.)	550.685-034
RCE	46	Cover Inspector (furniture)	789.687-038
RCE	46	Covering-Machine Operator (print. & pub.)	653.682-014
RCE	46	Derrick-Boat Operator (water trans.)	921.683-034
RCE	46	Dust Mixer (smelt. & refin.)	510.685-010
RCE	46	Electrician Helper (any industry)	829.684-022
RCE	46	Engraver II (print. & pub.)	979.684-014
RCE	46	Engraver, Pantograph II (engraving)	704.682-014
RCE	46	Eyeglass-Lens Cutter (optical goods)	716.682-010
RCE	46	Film Laboratory Technician (motion picture; photofinishing)	976.684-014
RCE	46	Finishing-Machine Operator (nonmet. min.)	674.682-010
RCE	46	Fishing-Lure Assembler (toy-sport equip.)	732.684-058
RCE	46	Fur-Machine Operator (garment)	786.682-122
RCE	46	Gang Sawyer (saw. & plan.)	667.682-030
RCE	46	Hydrate-Control Tender (smelt. & refin.)	511.585-010
RCE	46	Ingredient Scaler (bakery products; dairy products)	529.684-014
RCE	46	Insertion Machine Tender, Electronic Components (comm. equip.; electron. comp.; office machines)	726.685-014
RCE	46	Letterer (machinery mfg.)	979.681-010
RCE	46	Manipulator Operator (forging)	612.683-010
RCE	46	Molded-Parts Inspector (elec. equip.)	727.687-074
RCE	46	Music Engraver (print. & pub.)	972.681-010
RCE	46	Needle-Control Cheniller (tex. prod., n.e.c.)	687.685-010
RCE	46	Palletizer Operator I (any industry)	921.682-014
RCE	46	Pipe-Fitter Helper (ship-boat mfg.)	862.684-018
RCE	46	Printed Circuit Board Assembly Repairer (electron. comp.)	726.684-086
RCE	46	Quality Control Inspector (furniture; millwork-plywood)	569.687-030
RCE	46	Repairer (furniture)	709.684-062
RCE	46	Ring-Rolling-Machine Operator (rubber goods)	690.682-066
RCE	46	Rip-and-Groove-Machine Operator (furniture)	667.682-062
RCE	46	Roller Maker (rubber goods)	690.685-502
RCE	46	Rubber-Goods Inspector-Tester (rubber goods)	759.684-074
RCE	46	Rubber-Mill Operator (plastic-synth.)	559.682-042
RCE	46	Salvager II (ordnance)	737.687-118
RCE	46	Sign Erector II (fabrication, n.e.c.)	869.684-054
RCE	46	Stager (print. & pub.)	971.684-014
RCE	46	Strickler Attendant (fabrication, n.e.c.)	652.665-014
RCE	46	Tamping-Machine Operator (construction)	869.683-018
RCE	46	Test Preparer (nonfer. metal; steel & rel.)	509.584-010
RCE	46	Tool-Maintenance Worker (office machines)	701.384-010
RCE	46	Tractor Operator (any industry)	929.683-014
RCE	46	Trolley-Wire Installer (mine & quarry)	821.684-022
RCE	46	Wash-Tank Tender (chemical)	559.685-182
RCE	46	Weaver (carpet & rug)	683.682-034
RCE	46	Wire-Frame Maker (button & notion)	734.481-010
RCE	45	Assembly Adjuster (comm. equip.)	720.684-010
RCE	45	Brick Setter Operator (brick & tile)	579.685-058

Part 2: From Holland Codes to Occupations

From Holland Codes to the Dictionary of Occupational Titles Occupations

HOC	Cx	Title	DOT
RCE	45	Butter Liquefier (oils & grease)	523.585-010
RCE	45	Cement Mixer (rubber goods; rubber tire)	550.685-026
RCE	45	Contact-Lens Molder (optical goods)	690.685-090
RCE	45	Crochet-Machine Operator (knitting)	685.682-010
RCE	45	De-Alcoholizer (beverage)	522.685-042
RCE	45	De-Ionizer Operator (chemical)	558.685-026
RCE	45	Diamond Blender (cutlery-hrdwr.)	590.685-018
RCE	45	Dorr Operator (sugar & conf.)	522.685-050
RCE	45	Drapery Operator (retail trade)	787.682-018
RCE	45	Drapery-Rod Assembler (retail trade)	706.484-010
RCE	45	Drawer Upfitter (furniture)	706.684-050
RCE	45	Drawer-In, Hand (textile)	683.684-014
RCE	45	Dust-Collector Operator (smelt. & refin.)	511.482-018
RCE	45	Engraver, Machine II (engraving)	704.582-010
RCE	45	Exterminator Helper (any industry)	383.684-010
RCE	45	Fitter II (any industry)	706.684-054
RCE	45	Flour Mixer (grain-feed mills)	520.485-010
RCE	45	Flux Mixer (chemical)	550.584-010
RCE	45	Freezer Tunnel Operator (can. & preserv.)	523.685-082
RCE	45	Game-Farm Helper (agriculture)	412.684-010
RCE	45	Glass Installer (automotive ser.)	865.684-010
RCE	45	Hairspring Adjuster (clock & watch)	715.684-102
RCE	45	Impregnator Operator (chemical)	559.685-106
RCE	45	Inletter (ordnance)	669.682-050
RCE	45	Ion-Exchange Operator (smelt. & refin.)	558.685-030
RCE	45	Jewel Staker (clock & watch)	715.684-134
RCE	45	Junction Maker (brick & tile)	862.684-010
RCE	45	Lacquerer (jewelry-silver.)	749.684-034
RCE	45	Log Loader (logging)	921.683-058
RCE	45	Long-Wall-Mining-Machine Tender (mine & quarry)	930.665-010
RCE	45	Marker (ordnance)	652.582-010
RCE	45	Mesh Cutter (jewelry-silver.)	700.684-050
RCE	45	Motor-Power Connector (motion picture)	962.684-018
RCE	45	Oven Tender (elec. equip.)	543.685-018
RCE	45	Pail Bailer (tinware)	703.685-010
RCE	45	Pallet Rectifier (clock & watch)	715.684-158
RCE	45	Plastic Molder (fabrication, n.e.c.)	779.684-050
RCE	45	Prepleater (tex. prod., n.e.c.)	686.685-046
RCE	45	Propellant-Charge Loader (ordnance)	737.487-010
RCE	45	Quality-Control Tester (fabrication, n.e.c.)	543.684-010
RCE	45	Recovery-Operator Helper (smelt. & refin.)	519.485-014
RCE	45	Sample Maker (boot & shoe)	690.685-506
RCE	45	Sample Selector (tex. prod., n.e.c.)	789.387-014
RCE	45	Scale-Reclamation Tender (smelt. & refin.)	515.585-010
RCE	45	Selector (fabrication, n.e.c.)	739.687-166
RCE	45	Self-Sealing-Fuel-Tank Repairer (rubber goods)	759.384-010
RCE	45	Semiconductor Processor (electron. comp.)	590.684-022
RCE	45	Sewing-Machine Operator (any industry)	787.682-046
RCE	45	Shell-Grader (button & notion)	734.687-070

Part 2: From Holland Codes to Occupations

From Holland Codes to the Dictionary of Occupational Titles Occupations

HOC	Cx	Title	DOT
RCE	45	Sizing-Machine Tender (textile)	584.665-018
RCE	45	Skip Operator (steel & rel.)	921.683-062
RCE	45	Slab Grinder (stonework)	673.682-030
RCE	45	Soda Dialyzer (plastic-synth.)	551.685-134
RCE	45	Solder-Leveler, Printed Circuit Boards (electron. comp.)	726.685-050
RCE	45	Stitcher, Standard Machine (boot & shoe)	690.682-082
RCE	45	Strap-Folding-Machine Operator (rubber goods)	554.485-014
RCE	45	Surfboard Maker (toy-sport equip.)	732.684-126
RCE	45	Synthetic-Staple Extruder (plastic-synth.)	557.665-010
RCE	45	Test-Skein Winder (glass mfg.)	575.685-082
RCE	45	Trim-Stencil Maker (any industry)	781.684-058
RCE	45	Turner, Machine (clock & watch)	770.685-034
RCE	45	Typesetting-Machine Tender (print. & pub.)	650.685-010
RCE	45	Warp-Tying-Machine Tender (narrow fabrics; textile)	683.685-034
RCE	45	Weaver (nonmet. min.; textile)	683.682-038
RCE	45	Weaver Apprentice (nonmet. min.; textile)	683.682-042
RCE	45	Weft Straightener (textile)	580.682-010
RCE	45	Wet-End Operator II (plastic-synth.)	559.685-190
RCE	45	Whiting-Machine Operator (wood prod., n.e.c.)	562.485-010
RCE	45	Winch Driver (water trans.)	921.683-082
RCE	45	Zipper-Machine Operator (button & notion)	692.685-270
RCE	44	Acetylene-Plant Operator (chemical)	549.585-010
RCE	44	Artificial-Log-Machine Operator (fabrication, n.e.c.; saw. & plan.)	569.685-010
RCE	44	Assembler, Component (mfd. bldgs.; vehicles, n.e.c.)	762.684-014
RCE	44	Barrel Repairer (ordnance)	736.684-022
RCE	44	Bench Worker (metal prod., n.e.c.)	616.485-010
RCE	44	Binder (any industry)	787.682-010
RCE	44	Blower Insulator (railroad equip.; retail trade; wholesale tr.)	863.664-010
RCE	44	Bondactor-Machine Operator (foundry)	899.684-010
RCE	44	Bowling-Ball Engraver (toy-sport equip.)	732.584-010
RCE	44	Brake Adjuster (automotive ser.)	620.684-018
RCE	44	Calender Operator (tex. prod., n.e.c.; textile)	583.685-026
RCE	44	Calibrator (cutlery-hrdwr.)	701.684-010
RCE	44	Car-Repairer Helper (railroad equip.)	622.684-014
RCE	44	Carbon-Furnace-Operator Helper (smelt. & refin.)	543.664-010
RCE	44	Card Changer, Jacquard Loom (textile)	683.685-014
RCE	44	Case Fitter (furniture)	763.684-026
RCE	44	Cigar Maker (tobacco)	790.684-014
RCE	44	Cleaner, Home Restoration Service (any industry)	389.664-010
RCE	44	Coating Operator (chemical)	550.585-022
RCE	44	Coil Winder (elec. equip.; electron. comp.)	724.684-026
RCE	44	Colleter (clock & watch)	715.684-066
RCE	44	Concrete-Building Assembler (mfd. bldgs.)	869.664-010
RCE	44	Corduroy-Cutter Operator (textile)	585.565-010
RCE	44	Crocheter, Hand (knitting)	782.684-014
RCE	44	Croze-Machine Operator (wood. container)	669.682-034
RCE	44	Deicer Repairer (rubber goods)	759.684-026
RCE	44	Deicer-Element Winder, Machine (rubber goods)	692.685-066

HOC	Cx	Title	DOT
RCE	44	Diesel-Mechanic Helper (any industry)	625.684-010
RCE	44	Driller (jewelry-silver.)	700.684-026
RCE	44	Elevator-Repairer Helper (any industry)	825.684-014
RCE	44	Embossing-Machine Operator (nonfer. metal)	617.685-018
RCE	44	End Frazer (fabrication, n.e.c.)	665.685-014
RCE	44	Etcher, Machine (cutlery-hrdwr.)	619.685-042
RCE	44	Fiberglass-Container-Winding Operator (glass products)	579.584-010
RCE	44	Gettering-Filament-Machine Operator (light. fix.)	509.685-026
RCE	44	Glue Mixer (any industry)	550.685-062
RCE	44	Grinding Machine Tender (machine shop)	603.685-062
RCE	44	Head-Bander-and-Liner Operator (print. & pub.)	653.682-018
RCE	44	Heading-Saw Operator (saw. & plan.)	667.682-038
RCE	44	Larry Operator (steel & rel.)	519.683-014
RCE	44	Laundry Worker III (any industry)	369.387-010
RCE	44	Leather Finisher (laundry & rel.)	363.682-010
RCE	44	Looper (knitting)	689.682-010
RCE	44	Matrix-Drier Tender (paper & pulp)	532.585-010
RCE	44	Mixer (food prep., n.e.c.)	520.685-138
RCE	44	Mixer Helper (concrete prod.)	530.384-010
RCE	44	Mixer, Dry-Food Products (food prep., n.e.c.)	520.685-162
RCE	44	Mixing-Machine Tender (wood prod., n.e.c.)	560.585-010
RCE	44	Mold Maker (nonmet. min.)	777.684-014
RCE	44	Mucking-Machine Operator (construction)	850.683-026
RCE	44	Napper Tender (tex. prod., n.e.c.; textile)	585.685-070
RCE	44	Netting Inspector (tex. prod., n.e.c.)	782.487-010
RCE	44	Observer Helper, Gravity Prospecting (petrol. & gas)	939.663-010
RCE	44	Oven Operator, Automatic (bakery products)	526.685-070
RCE	44	Pallet Assembler (clock & watch)	715.684-154
RCE	44	Pin Inserter, Regulator (clock & watch)	715.684-166
RCE	44	Pipe Racker (fabrication, n.e.c.)	749.687-034
RCE	44	Playground-Equipment Erector (retail trade)	801.684-018
RCE	44	Pocket Setter, Lockstitch (garment)	786.682-210
RCE	44	Precipitator I (smelt. & refin.)	511.685-038
RCE	44	Roller, Hand (tobacco)	790.684-022
RCE	44	Roof Bolter (mine & quarry)	930.683-026
RCE	44	Sampler, Wool (wholesale tr.)	222.587-042
RCE	44	Sewing-Machine-Repairer Helper (any industry)	639.684-010
RCE	44	Shot Polisher and Inspector (ordnance)	509.485-014
RCE	44	Sintering-Press Operator (nonfer. metal; steel & rel.)	617.685-038
RCE	44	Socket Puller (musical inst.)	730.682-010
RCE	44	Solderer, Torch I (welding)	813.684-026
RCE	44	Still Tender (any industry)	552.685-026
RCE	44	Straightening-Roll Operator (any industry)	613.662-022
RCE	44	Strainer Tender (rubber reclaim.)	551.365-010
RCE	44	Stretcher (jewelry-silver.)	700.684-078
RCE	44	Targeteer (ordnance)	736.684-042
RCE	44	Tenter-Frame Operator (textile)	580.685-066
RCE	44	Threading-Machine Operator (ordnance)	604.685-038
RCE	44	Ticket Scheduler (boot & shoe)	221.587-038

HOC	Cx	Title	DOT
RCE	44	Trackmobile Operator (any industry)	919.683-026
RCE	44	Transfer-Machine Operator (machine shop)	609.685-022
RCE	44	Treater Helper (petrol. refin.)	549.685-030
RCE	44	Umbrella Repairer (any industry)	369.684-018
RCE	44	Watch-Crystal Edge Grinder (glass products)	775.684-062
RCE	44	Watch-Crystal Molder (glass products)	772.684-022
RCE	44	Weaving Inspector (carpet & rug; textile)	683.684-034
RCE	43	Acid-Polymerization Operator (chemical)	558.685-010
RCE	43	Assembly Operator (woodworking)	762.684-018
RCE	43	Band-Sawing-Machine Operator (fabrication, n.e.c.)	690.485-010
RCE	43	Bench Hand (motor-bicycles)	706.684-046
RCE	43	Bisque Cleaner (pottery & porc.)	774.684-010
RCE	43	Blending-Tank Tender (beverage; can. & preserv.)	520.685-030
RCE	43	Book-Sewing-Machine Operator II (print. & pub.)	653.682-010
RCE	43	Candlemaker (fabrication, n.e.c.)	739.664-010
RCE	43	Casing-Machine Operator (tobacco)	522.685-030
RCE	43	Catalytic-Converter-Operator Helper (chemical)	558.585-010
RCE	43	Coater, Smoking Pipe (fabrication, n.e.c.)	562.685-022
RCE	43	Coating-and-Baking Operator (any industry)	554.685-014
RCE	43	Cook Helper (can. & preserv.)	529.687-050
RCE	43	Copra Processor (soap & rel.)	555.685-018
RCE	43	Crystal Cutter (clock & watch)	715.684-078
RCE	43	Die Presser (pottery & porc.)	575.685-026
RCE	43	Drier Tender (fabrication, n.e.c.)	543.685-014
RCE	43	Drill Press Tender (machine shop)	606.685-026
RCE	43	Duplicating-Machine Operator II (clerical)	207.682-014
RCE	43	Edge Bander, Machine (furniture; millwork-plywood)	762.685-010
RCE	43	Electronic-Component Processor (electron. comp.)	590.684-014
RCE	43	Expanding Machine Operator (steel & rel.)	617.685-022
RCE	43	Extractor Operator (pharmaceut.)	551.685-058
RCE	43	Food-Service Worker, Hospital (medical ser.)	319.677-014
RCE	43	Four-Slide-Machine Operator II (any industry)	619.685-050
RCE	43	Garnetter (furniture; tex. prod., n.e.c.)	680.685-054
RCE	43	Gear-Cutting-Machine Operator, Production (machine shop)	602.685-010
RCE	43	Grated-Cheese Maker (dairy products)	521.685-162
RCE	43	Grinding-Machine Operator, Portable (r.r. trans.)	910.684-010
RCE	43	Harvester Operator (chemical)	930.683-022
RCE	43	Hemmer (any industry)	787.682-026
RCE	43	Jigsawyer (jewelry-silver.)	700.684-046
RCE	43	Lapping-Machine Operator, Production (machine shop)	603.685-070
RCE	43	Lathe Tender (machine shop)	604.685-026
RCE	43	Marble-Machine Tender (glass mfg.)	575.685-058
RCE	43	Mill-Roll Rewinder (plastic-synth.)	690.585-010
RCE	43	Milling-Machine Tender (machine shop)	605.685-030
RCE	43	Mold-Filling Operator (plastic-synth.)	556.684-018
RCE	43	Mounter, Hand (light. fix.)	725.684-014
RCE	43	Oven Tender (glass mfg.)	573.585-010
RCE	43	Oven-Heater Helper (steel & rel.)	542.665-010

Part 2: From Holland Codes to Occupations

From Holland Codes to the Dictionary of Occupational Titles Occupations

HOC	Cx	Title	DOT
RCE	43	Piercing-Mill Operator (steel & rel.)	613.685-018
RCE	43	Press Tender, Pyrotechnics (chemical)	694.685-038
RCE	43	Production Machine Tender (machine shop)	609.685-018
RCE	43	Roll Builder (rubber goods)	759.484-010
RCE	43	Rotary-Driller Helper (petrol. & gas)	930.684-026
RCE	43	Rug Clipper (carpet & rug)	781.684-046
RCE	43	Salvage Winder and Inspector (paper goods)	649.685-102
RCE	43	Sandfill Operator (mine & quarry)	939.485-010
RCE	43	Screw-Machine Tender (machine shop)	604.685-034
RCE	43	Sewing-Machine Operator (furniture)	780.682-010
RCE	43	Shaper, Hand (furniture)	761.684-038
RCE	43	Signal Maintainer Helper (r.r. trans.)	822.684-018
RCE	43	Slot-Tag Inserter (clerical)	222.567-018
RCE	43	Sorter (jewelry-silver.)	735.687-030
RCE	43	Spinner, Mule (nonmet. min.; textile)	682.685-014
RCE	43	Spiral Weaver (metal prod., n.e.c.)	616.685-074
RCE	43	Stain Applicator (wood prod., n.e.c.)	561.585-010
RCE	43	Stave-Bolt Equalizer (saw. & plan.)	667.682-074
RCE	43	Stoner, Hand (clock & watch)	715.584-018
RCE	43	Tapper (beverage)	529.685-246
RCE	43	Terrazzo Finisher (construction)	861.664-014
RCE	43	Tile Finisher (construction)	861.664-018
RCE	43	Tufter (furniture)	687.684-014
RCE	43	Turret-Punch-Press Operator, Tape-Control (any industry)	615.685-042
RCE	43	Utility Worker, Molding (plastic prod.)	559.684-026
RCE	43	Vacuum-Metalizer Operator (any industry)	505.685-018
RCE	43	Vending-Machine Assembler (svc. ind. mach.)	706.684-102
RCE	43	Ware Dresser (pottery & porc.)	774.684-042
RCE	43	Welt-Trimming-Machine Operator (hat & cap)	686.685-074
RCE	43	Woven-Wood Shade Assembler (furniture)	739.684-178
RCE	42	Ager Operator (textile)	582.585-010
RCE	42	Anvil-Seating-Press Operator (ordnance)	694.685-010
RCE	42	Assembler (plastic prod.)	754.684-010
RCE	42	Assembler For Puller-Over, Machine (boot & shoe)	690.685-010
RCE	42	Assembler, Clip-On Sunglasses (optical goods)	713.684-010
RCE	42	Assembler, Metal Furniture (furniture)	709.684-014
RCE	42	Auxiliary-Equipment Tender (cement)	570.685-010
RCE	42	Band-Top Maker (furniture)	780.684-014
RCE	42	Barrel Finisher (clock & watch)	715.682-010
RCE	42	Batter Mixer (food prep., n.e.c.)	520.685-014
RCE	42	Beater-Engineer Helper (paper & pulp; tex. prod., n.e.c.)	530.665-010
RCE	42	Boat Loader II (water trans.)	921.685-010
RCE	42	Brim-Pouncing-Machine Operator (hat & cap)	585.685-010
RCE	42	Buckle Sorter (button & notion)	734.687-030
RCE	42	Bulk Filler (can. & preserv.)	529.687-022
RCE	42	Bunch Maker, Hand (tobacco)	790.684-010
RCE	42	Butcher, Chicken and Fish (hotel & rest.)	316.684-010
RCE	42	Can Patcher (can. & preserv.)	920.687-054
RCE	42	Capping-Machine Operator (elec. equip.)	692.685-042

Dictionary of Holland Occupational Codes

Part 2: From Holland Codes to Occupations

From Holland Codes to the Dictionary of Occupational Titles Occupations

HOC	Cx	Title	DOT
RCE	42	Casting-Machine Operator (dairy products)	520.685-058
RCE	42	Catcher, Filter Tip (tobacco)	529.666-010
RCE	42	Channeler, Insole (boot & shoe)	690.685-086
RCE	42	Chocolate Temperer (bakery products; grain-feed mills)	523.685-022
RCE	42	Churn Operator, Margarine (oils & grease)	520.685-070
RCE	42	Cigarette-Package Examiner (tobacco)	920.667-010
RCE	42	Clipper, Automatic (millwork-plywood)	663.585-010
RCE	42	Clock Assembler (clock & watch)	715.684-058
RCE	42	Cloth Measurer, Machine (garment; textile)	589.685-022
RCE	42	Compounder Helper (petrol. refin.)	540.686-010
RCE	42	Continuous Pillowcase Cutter (tex. prod., n.e.c.)	686.685-014
RCE	42	Core-Laying-Machine Operator (millwork-plywood)	569.685-026
RCE	42	Corn-Grinder Operator, Automatic (grain-feed mills)	521.685-086
RCE	42	Counter Cutter (boot & shoe)	690.685-094
RCE	42	Countersinker (clock & watch)	715.682-014
RCE	42	Cupola Tapper (foundry)	514.664-010
RCE	42	Curing-Press Maintainer (rubber tire)	629.684-010
RCE	42	Cushion Builder (furniture)	780.684-046
RCE	42	Cut-Lace-Machine Operator (leather prod.)	585.685-038
RCE	42	Cutter, Aluminum Sheet (ship-boat mfg.)	804.684-010
RCE	42	Cutter, Rotary Shear (tex. prod., n.e.c.)	781.684-018
RCE	42	Cutter-Machine Tender (electron. comp.)	615.685-046
RCE	42	Cutting-Machine Operator (tex. prod., n.e.c.)	686.585-010
RCE	42	Debridging-Machine Operator (nonfer. metal)	607.685-014
RCE	42	Developer, Automatic (photofinishing)	976.685-014
RCE	42	Dipper (fabrication, n.e.c.)	590.685-022
RCE	42	Drifter (steel & rel.)	503.685-018
RCE	42	Dry-Pan Operator (brick & tile)	570.665-010
RCE	42	Drying-Unit-Felting-Machine Operator (tex. prod., n.e.c.)	581.685-034
RCE	42	Edge Grinder (plastic prod.)	690.685-142
RCE	42	Edge Roller (furniture)	780.684-058
RCE	42	Electrician Helper (ship-boat mfg.)	829.684-026
RCE	42	Embosser (any industry)	583.685-030
RCE	42	Embossing-Machine Operator (ordnance)	619.685-038
RCE	42	Envelope-Machine Operator (paper goods)	649.685-042
RCE	42	Etcher, Electrolytic (cutlery-hrdwr.)	500.685-010
RCE	42	Examiner (glove & mit.)	789.687-042
RCE	42	Explosive Operator II (ordnance)	737.687-046
RCE	42	Extruder Operator (wood prod., n.e.c.)	569.685-038
RCE	42	Eyeglass-Frame Truer (optical goods)	713.684-026
RCE	42	Feed Mixer (grain-feed mills)	520.685-098
RCE	42	Filling Machine Tender (bakery products)	524.685-030
RCE	42	Filter-Press Tender (beverage; chemical)	599.685-042
RCE	42	Finisher, Machine (plastic prod.)	690.685-170
RCE	42	Flavor Extractor (grain-feed mills)	529.685-126
RCE	42	Flavoring Oil Filterer (beverage)	521.685-382
RCE	42	Focuser (light. fix.)	725.687-018
RCE	42	Folder, Machine (boot & shoe)	690.685-174
RCE	42	Folder-Seamer, Automatic (any industry)	787.685-014

Part 2: From Holland Codes to Occupations

From Holland Codes to the Dictionary of Occupational Titles Occupations

HOC	Cx	Title	DOT
RCE	42	Fountain Pen Turner (pen & pencil)	690.685-190
RCE	42	Frame Bander (textile)	628.684-014
RCE	42	Front-End Loader Operator (any industry)	921.683-042
RCE	42	Frozen Pie Maker (can. & preserv.)	529.684-010
RCE	42	Glass Polisher (glass mfg.)	775.684-038
RCE	42	Glue-Size-Machine Operator (furniture)	562.685-010
RCE	42	Gluing-Machine Operator, Electronic (woodworking)	569.685-050
RCE	42	Greenskeeper II (any industry)	406.683-010
RCE	42	Greige-Goods Marker (textile)	229.587-010
RCE	42	Grinder I (any industry)	705.684-026
RCE	42	Groundskeeper, Industrial-Commercial (any industry)	406.684-014
RCE	42	Heel Builder, Machine (boot & shoe)	690.685-206
RCE	42	Heel Pricker (boot & shoe)	690.685-218
RCE	42	Heel Sprayer, Machine (boot & shoe)	590.685-038
RCE	42	Heel-Seat Laster, Machine (boot & shoe)	690.685-230
RCE	42	Hooking-Machine Operator (textile)	580.685-034
RCE	42	Hot-Car Operator (steel & rel.)	519.663-014
RCE	42	Hydraulic Blocker (hat & cap)	580.685-038
RCE	42	Hydraulic-Press Operator (millwork-plywood)	569.685-058
RCE	42	Impregnator (pen & pencil)	562.685-014
RCE	42	Inspector, Handbag Frames (leather prod.)	222.687-042
RCE	42	Inspector, Picture Frames (wood prod., n.e.c.)	769.687-030
RCE	42	Inspector, Soldering (clock & watch)	715.687-070
RCE	42	Inspector, Timers (clock & watch)	715.687-074
RCE	42	Inspector, Type (office machines)	706.687-026
RCE	42	Instantizer Operator (dairy products)	523.685-106
RCE	42	Jewel-Cupping-Machine Operator (clock & watch)	770.685-030
RCE	42	Kerfer-Machine Operator (furniture)	667.685-042
RCE	42	Key Cutter (any industry)	709.684-050
RCE	42	Knitter, Wire Mesh (metal prod., n.e.c.)	616.685-030
RCE	42	Knitting-Machine Operator (knitting)	685.665-014
RCE	42	Lag Screwer (furniture)	763.684-046
RCE	42	Lamination Assembler, Printed Circuit Boards (electron. comp.)	726.687-026
RCE	42	Layer (glass mfg.)	673.686-026
RCE	42	Lead-Oxide-Mill Tender (elec. equip.)	558.685-042
RCE	42	Lightout Examiner (beverage)	529.687-146
RCE	42	Lumite Injector (boot & shoe)	690.685-278
RCE	42	Machine Operator II (any industry)	619.685-062
RCE	42	Marker, Machine (boot & shoe)	690.685-282
RCE	42	Mat Repairer (rubber goods)	759.684-042
RCE	42	Mat-Making Machine Tender (furniture)	692.685-122
RCE	42	Material Mixer (plastic prod.)	550.685-130
RCE	42	Matrix Worker (recording)	500.684-014
RCE	42	Meat Blender (can. & preserv.)	529.685-166
RCE	42	Metal Finisher (any industry)	705.684-034
RCE	42	Mica-Washer Gluer (mine & quarry)	729.687-022
RCE	42	Mill Operator (any industry)	599.685-058
RCE	42	Moisture-Conditioner Operator (paper & pulp)	532.685-022

Part 2: From Holland Codes to Occupations

From Holland Codes to the Dictionary of Occupational Titles Occupations

HOC	Cx	Title	DOT
RCE	42	Mold Maker, Terra Cotta (brick & tile)	575.684-038
RCE	42	Molder, Wax (petrol. refin.)	549.685-018
RCE	42	Monorail Crane Operator (any industry)	921.663-042
RCE	42	Multifocal-Lens Assembler (optical goods)	713.684-034
RCE	42	Notch Grinder (glass products)	673.685-070
RCE	42	Nozzle Tender (nonfer. metal)	512.685-014
RCE	42	Nut-Sorter Operator (can. & preserv.)	521.685-238
RCE	42	Ornament Setter (garment; tex. prod., n.e.c.)	789.685-010
RCE	42	Oven Tender (ordnance)	534.565-010
RCE	42	Pad Cutter (plastic prod.)	690.685-302
RCE	42	Paint-Line Operator (toy-sport equip.)	599.685-066
RCE	42	Painter Helper, Shipyard (ship-boat mfg.)	840.687-010
RCE	42	Pairing-Machine Operator (nonfer. metal)	691.685-022
RCE	42	Panel Laminator (struct. metal)	809.684-042
RCE	42	Paper-Reel Operator (paper goods)	640.685-046
RCE	42	Paperback-Machine Operator (metal prod., n.e.c.)	616.685-046
RCE	42	Paperhanger (concrete prod.)	574.585-010
RCE	42	Pipe-Fitter Helper (construction)	862.684-022
RCE	42	Plastics Repairer (plastic prod.)	754.684-046
RCE	42	Polisher, Dial (clock & watch)	715.684-170
RCE	42	Poultice-Machine Operator (pharmaceut.)	692.685-134
RCE	42	Press Operator (mine & quarry)	575.685-070
RCE	42	Press Operator I (chemical)	559.665-030
RCE	42	Primer-Powder Blender, Dry (ordnance)	550.565-010
RCE	42	Pusher Operator (steel & rel.)	519.663-018
RCE	42	Racker (toy-sport equip.)	749.587-010
RCE	42	Raker, Buffing Wheel (tex. prod., n.e.c.)	589.684-010
RCE	42	Relish Blender (can. & preserv.)	520.685-194
RCE	42	Remelter (elec. equip.; machinery mfg.; print. & pub.)	502.685-014
RCE	42	Resin Coater (wood prod., n.e.c.)	562.687-014
RCE	42	Rice Cleaning Machine Tender (grain-feed mills)	521.665-022
RCE	42	Rim-Fire-Priming Operator (ordnance)	694.685-050
RCE	42	Ring Stamper (jewelry-silver.)	700.684-066
RCE	42	Roll Tender (print. & pub.)	651.686-022
RCE	42	Roll-Tension Tester (plastic-synth.)	559.584-010
RCE	42	Roller, Gold Leaf (metal prod., n.e.c.)	709.685-018
RCE	42	Rotary Cutter (boot & shoe)	585.685-082
RCE	42	Rough-and-Trueing-Machine Operator (toy-sport equip.)	690.685-330
RCE	42	Rough-Rounder, Machine (boot & shoe)	690.685-334
RCE	42	Rounder (boot & shoe)	690.685-338
RCE	42	Routing Clerk (clerical)	222.687-022
RCE	42	Routing-Equipment Tender (grain-feed mills)	521.685-278
RCE	42	Sample Maker, Hand (paper goods)	794.684-030
RCE	42	Sander, Machine (woodworking)	761.682-014
RCE	42	Saw Operator, Semiconductor Wafers (electron. comp.)	726.685-046
RCE	42	Scaler-Packer (meat products)	929.687-046
RCE	42	Sealing-Machine Operator (light. fix.)	692.685-162
RCE	42	Shaker Tender (concrete prod.; mine & quarry)	934.685-018
RCE	42	Shaving-Machine Operator (leather mfg.)	585.685-094

HOC	Cx	Title	DOT
RCE	42	Shearer and Trimmer, Wire Screen and Fabric (metal prod., n.e.c.)	709.684-074
RCE	42	Shearing-Machine Feeder (leather mfg.)	585.685-098
RCE	42	Shredder Operator (plastic-synth.)	555.685-058
RCE	42	Shredder Tender, Peat (agriculture)	599.685-086
RCE	42	Side Laster, Staple (boot & shoe)	690.685-362
RCE	42	Silo Tender (cement)	579.685-050
RCE	42	Skiver (leather prod.)	690.685-374
RCE	42	Slasher (plastic-synth.)	690.665-010
RCE	42	Slubber Tender (textile)	680.685-098
RCE	42	Splicing-Machine Operator, Automatic (tex. prod., n.e.c.)	689.685-122
RCE	42	Splitting-Machine Tender (wood prod., n.e.c.)	663.685-042
RCE	42	Sport-Shoe-Spike Assembler (boot & shoe)	690.685-394
RCE	42	Spring Coiler (metal prod., n.e.c.)	616.485-014
RCE	42	Stamping-Machine Operator (boot & shoe)	690.685-398
RCE	42	Steam-Box Operator (woodworking)	562.665-014
RCE	42	Steeping-Press Tender (plastic-synth.)	551.685-138
RCE	42	Stone Trimmer (stonework)	670.685-010
RCE	42	Strap Buckler, Machine (garment)	689.665-010
RCE	42	Stretching-Machine Operator (tex. prod., n.e.c.)	580.685-058
RCE	42	Stringer-Machine Tender (protective dev.)	692.485-010
RCE	42	Stripping Cutter and Winder (boot & shoe)	585.685-118
RCE	42	Stuffing-Machine Operator (furniture)	780.685-014
RCE	42	Tankroom Tender (plastic-synth.)	559.585-018
RCE	42	Taper, Machine (boot & shoe)	690.685-414
RCE	42	Telephone-Directory-Distributor Driver (business ser.)	906.683-018
RCE	42	Tier-and-Detonator (mine & quarry)	931.664-010
RCE	42	Tipper (print. & pub.)	795.684-022
RCE	42	Tipping-Machine Operator (pen & pencil)	733.685-034
RCE	42	Tobacco-Drier Operator (tobacco)	523.685-118
RCE	42	Toe Laster, Automatic (boot & shoe)	690.685-430
RCE	42	Torque Tester (clock & watch)	715.685-066
RCE	42	Tree Driller (boot & shoe)	788.684-118
RCE	42	Truck Loader, Overhead Crane (nonfer. metal)	921.663-070
RCE	42	Tube-and-Manifold Builder (rubber goods)	759.684-062
RCE	42	Tufting-Machine Operator (furniture)	687.685-014
RCE	42	Twister Tender (glass mfg.; nonmet. min.; plastic-synth.; textile)	681.685-130
RCE	42	Type-Soldering-Machine Tender (office machines)	706.685-010
RCE	42	Upholstery Trimmer (furniture)	780.684-126
RCE	42	Vacuum Drier Operator (can. & preserv.)	523.685-122
RCE	42	Wax-Pattern Assembler (foundry)	518.684-022
RCE	42	Welt Beater (boot & shoe)	690.685-470
RCE	42	Wheel-Truing Machine Tender (motor-bicycles)	706.685-014
RCE	42	Wicker, Molded Candles (fabrication, n.e.c.)	692.685-242
RCE	42	Width Stripper (boot & shoe)	690.685-486
RCE	42	Winding-Rack Operator (tex. prod., n.e.c.)	581.685-074
RCE	42	Wine Pasteurizer (beverage)	523.685-126
RCE	42	Wrapper (metal prod., n.e.c.)	920.685-102

Part 2: From Holland Codes to Occupations

From Holland Codes to the Dictionary of Occupational Titles Occupations

HOC	Cx	Title	DOT
RCE	42	Yarn Winder (tex. prod., n.e.c.; textile)	681.685-154
RCE	41	Appliquer, Zigzag (garment)	786.682-010
RCE	41	Armhole Baster, Jumpbasting (garment)	786.682-014
RCE	41	Armhole-Sew-and-Trim Operator, Lockstitch (garment)	786.682-022
RCE	41	Armoring-Machine Operator (nonfer. metal)	691.685-010
RCE	41	Asphalt-Distributor Tender (construction)	853.665-010
RCE	41	Asphalt-Heater Tender (construction)	853.685-010
RCE	41	Assembler (cutlery-hrdwr.)	701.687-010
RCE	41	Assembler II (light. fix.)	723.684-018
RCE	41	Assembler, Filters (glass products)	739.687-018
RCE	41	Assembler, Gold Frame (optical goods)	713.384-010
RCE	41	Assembler, Production Line (struct. metal)	809.684-010
RCE	41	Assembly-Inspector Helper (agric. equip.)	801.663-010
RCE	41	Automatic Lump Making Machine Tender (tobacco)	529.685-014
RCE	41	Back Maker, Lockstitch (garment)	786.682-026
RCE	41	Ball-Warper Tender (textile)	681.685-010
RCE	41	Barrel Charrer (wood. container)	764.684-014
RCE	41	Barrel Loader and Cleaner (ordnance)	736.587-010
RCE	41	Basting-Machine Operator (garment)	786.682-030
RCE	41	Batch Mixer (soap & rel.)	550.685-010
RCE	41	Batting-Machine Operator (tex. prod., n.e.c.; textile)	680.585-010
RCE	41	Beam-Warper Tender, Automatic (knitting; narrow fabrics; nonmet. min.; textile)	681.685-018
RCE	41	Belt Repairer (any industry)	630.684-014
RCE	41	Belt-Press Operator II (rubber goods)	553.665-010
RCE	41	Bender, Machine (woodworking)	569.685-014
RCE	41	Binder, Chainstitch (garment)	786.682-034
RCE	41	Binder, Coverstitch (garment)	786.682-038
RCE	41	Binder, Lockstitch (garment)	786.682-042
RCE	41	Bit Sharpener (any industry)	603.685-026
RCE	41	Blade Groover (cutlery-hrdwr.)	705.582-010
RCE	41	Bleacher Operator (chemical; soap & rel.)	558.685-018
RCE	41	Blending-Line Attendant (tobacco)	520.685-026
RCE	41	Bobbin Presser (tex. prod., n.e.c.)	689.685-018
RCE	41	Bobbin Winder, Machine (tex. prod., n.e.c.; textile)	681.585-014
RCE	41	Bobbin Winder, Sewing Machine (textile)	681.685-026
RCE	41	Book Trimmer (print. & pub.)	640.685-010
RCE	41	Booster Assembler (ordnance)	737.687-022
RCE	41	Bottom-Turning-Lathe Tender (wood. container)	665.685-010
RCE	41	Bowling-Ball Finisher (toy-sport equip.)	690.685-038
RCE	41	Braiding-Machine Operator (narrow fabrics; nonmet. min.)	683.685-010
RCE	41	Brake Holder (any industry)	932.664-010
RCE	41	Breaker-Machine Operator (saw. & plan.; wood prod., n.e.c.)	564.685-010
RCE	41	Breaker-Machine Tender (textile)	583.685-010
RCE	41	Brim-Stretching-Machine Operator (hat & cap)	580.685-010
RCE	41	Briquetting-Machine Operator (smelt. & refin.)	519.685-010
RCE	41	Bucket Operator (concrete prod.)	575.683-010
RCE	41	Buffer (boot & shoe)	690.685-046

Part 2: From Holland Codes to Occupations

From Holland Codes to the Dictionary of Occupational Titles Occupations

HOC	Cx	Title	DOT
RCE	41	Buffer (fabrication, n.e.c.)	739.684-026
RCE	41	Buffer, Inflated-Pad (boot & shoe)	690.685-054
RCE	41	Buffing-Wheel Former, Hand (tex. prod., n.e.c.)	789.684-014
RCE	41	Button-Decorating-Machine Operator (button & notion)	690.685-062
RCE	41	Buttonhole-and-Button-Sewing-Machine Operator (garment)	786.685-042
RCE	41	Buzzsaw Operator (any industry)	667.685-026
RCE	41	Canvas Baster, Jumpbasting (garment)	786.682-050
RCE	41	Casing-Fluid Tender (tobacco)	520.685-054
RCE	41	Caster (smelt. & refin.)	514.684-010
RCE	41	Cathode Ray Tube Salvage Processor (electron. comp.)	725.684-026
RCE	41	CD-Mixer (rubber reclaim.)	550.685-022
RCE	41	Cement Loader (cement)	921.565-010
RCE	41	Cementer, Machine Joiner (boot & shoe)	690.685-074
RCE	41	Ceramic Coater, Machine (any industry)	509.685-022
RCE	41	Chalk-Extruding-Machine Operator (pen & pencil)	575.685-018
RCE	41	Chalk-Molding-Machine Operator (pen & pencil)	575.685-022
RCE	41	Chick Grader (agriculture)	411.687-010
RCE	41	Chinchilla-Machine Operator (textile)	585.685-022
RCE	41	Chip-Applying-Machine Tender (paint & varnish; print. & pub.)	641.685-030
RCE	41	Chopped-Strand Operator (textile)	680.685-022
RCE	41	Chopping-Machine Operator (meat products)	520.685-066
RCE	41	Cigarette-Making-Machine Catcher (tobacco)	529.666-014
RCE	41	Cloth Drier (knitting)	580.685-014
RCE	41	Coat Joiner, Lockstitch (garment)	786.682-058
RCE	41	Coating Operator (grain-feed mills)	524.685-018
RCE	41	Cocoa-Room Operator (sugar & conf.)	521.685-074
RCE	41	Coiler (nonfer. metal; steel & rel.)	613.685-010
RCE	41	Collar Baster, Jumpbasting (garment)	786.682-062
RCE	41	Collar Setter, Lockstitch (garment)	786.682-070
RCE	41	Collar Setter, Overlock (garment)	786.682-074
RCE	41	Collar-Turner Operator (garment)	580.685-018
RCE	41	Concaving-Machine Operator (boot & shoe)	585.685-030
RCE	41	Cone Operator (mine & quarry)	934.685-010
RCE	41	Cook, Soybean Specialties (food prep., n.e.c.)	529.685-290
RCE	41	Cooker Tender (paper & pulp)	532.685-014
RCE	41	Core-Composer-Machine Tender (millwork-plywood)	569.685-022
RCE	41	Coremaker, Machine II (foundry)	518.685-018
RCE	41	Covering-Machine Operator (textile)	681.685-038
RCE	41	Crown Attacher (clock & watch)	715.684-070
RCE	41	Cup Setter, Lockstitch (garment)	786.682-082
RCE	41	Cupola Charger, Insulation (nonmet. min.)	572.686-010
RCE	41	Cushion Maker I (furniture)	780.684-054
RCE	41	Cut-Out-and-Marking-Machine Operator (boot & shoe)	690.685-110
RCE	41	Cutter (tex. prod., n.e.c.)	686.685-022
RCE	41	Cutter I (fabrication, n.e.c.)	690.685-118
RCE	41	Cutter, V-Groove (clock & watch)	715.685-014
RCE	41	Deblocker (optical goods)	716.687-010

HOC	Cx	Title	DOT
RCE	41	Digestion Operator (smelt. & refin.)	519.565-010
RCE	41	Draw-Machine Operator (plastic-synth.)	680.665-014
RCE	41	Drum-Drier Operator (plastic-synth.)	581.685-082
RCE	41	Dry-House Attendant (woodworking)	563.685-018
RCE	41	Drying-Machine Tender (textile)	581.685-030
RCE	41	Drying-Room Attendant (tobacco)	523.587-014
RCE	41	Dye-Tub Operator (knitting)	582.685-170
RCE	41	Edge Stainer II (leather prod.)	749.684-022
RCE	41	Edge Trimmer (boot & shoe)	690.685-150
RCE	41	Edger, Touch-Up (glass products)	775.684-018
RCE	41	Elastic Attacher, Chainstitch (garment)	786.682-086
RCE	41	Elastic Attacher, Coverstitch (garment)	786.682-090
RCE	41	Elastic Attacher, Overlock (garment)	786.682-094
RCE	41	Elastic Attacher, Zigzag (garment)	786.682-098
RCE	41	Electronics Worker (electron. comp.)	726.687-010
RCE	41	Embossing-Machine-Operator Helper (plastic-synth.)	583.685-038
RCE	41	Encapsulator (elec. equip.; electron. comp.)	726.687-022
RCE	41	End Finder, Roving Department (glass mfg.)	689.687-038
RCE	41	End Finder, Twisting Department (textile)	689.687-042
RCE	41	Facing Baster, Jumpbasting (garment)	786.682-102
RCE	41	Fastener, Machine (boot & shoe)	690.685-162
RCE	41	Fastener-Sewing-Machine Operator (any industry)	787.685-010
RCE	41	Feather Shaper (button & notion)	734.684-010
RCE	41	Feather Stitcher (toy-sport equip.)	732.684-050
RCE	41	Featheredger and Reducer, Machine (boot & shoe)	690.685-166
RCE	41	Feeder (print. & pub.)	651.686-014
RCE	41	Felled-Seam Operator, Chainstitch (garment)	786.682-106
RCE	41	Felt Cutter (ordnance)	686.685-026
RCE	41	Fettler (brick & tile)	779.684-018
RCE	41	Filter Washer and Presser (beverage; chemical)	599.685-038
RCE	41	Finisher, Hand (toy-sport equip.)	731.587-010
RCE	41	Finisher, Hand (plastic prod.)	754.684-030
RCE	41	Fixing-Machine Operator (toy-sport equip.)	732.685-018
RCE	41	Flagger (construction)	372.667-022
RCE	41	Flatlock-Sewing-Machine Operator (garment)	786.682-110
RCE	41	Foam Dispenser (rubber goods)	554.684-014
RCE	41	Friction-Paint-Machine Tender (fabrication, n.e.c.)	534.685-014
RCE	41	Front Maker, Lockstitch (garment)	786.682-114
RCE	41	Front-Edge-Tape Sewer, Lockstitch (garment)	786.682-118
RCE	41	Fumigator and Sterilizer (furniture)	582.685-074
RCE	41	Fur-Blower Operator (hat & cap)	680.685-046
RCE	41	Garnett-Machine Operator (textile)	680.685-050
RCE	41	Gas-Leak Tester (svc. ind. mach.)	827.584-014
RCE	41	Glass-Cleaning-Machine Tender (glass products)	579.685-018
RCE	41	Glass-Wool-Blanket-Machine Feeder (glass products)	579.685-022
RCE	41	Glove Printer (glove & mit.)	652.685-034
RCE	41	Grader Tender (agriculture)	521.685-154
RCE	41	Grease-and-Tallow Pumper (oils & grease)	559.585-014
RCE	41	Grip Wrapper (toy-sport equip.)	732.684-082

HOC	Cx	Title	DOT
RCE	41	Groover and Turner (boot & shoe)	690.685-198
RCE	41	Grooving-Lathe Tender (plastic prod.)	690.685-202
RCE	41	Ground Layer (pottery & porc.)	574.684-010
RCE	41	Hairspring Cutter II (clock & watch)	715.687-042
RCE	41	Heat Curer (textile)	581.586-010
RCE	41	Heddle-Machine Operator (machinery mfg.)	616.685-026
RCE	41	Heel-Seat Fitter, Hand (boot & shoe)	788.684-062
RCE	41	Helmet Coverer (hat & cap)	689.685-074
RCE	41	Hose Cutter, Hand (rubber goods)	751.687-010
RCE	41	Hot-Plate-Plywood-Press Operator (millwork-plywood)	569.685-054
RCE	41	Hydraulic-Billet Maker (pen & pencil) ·	575.685-046
RCE	41	Industrial-Truck Operator (any industry)	921.683-050
RCE	41	Inker, Machine (boot & shoe)	690.685-234
RCE	41	Inseam Trimmer (boot & shoe)	690.685-238
RCE	41	Insole Reinforcer (boot & shoe)	690.685-246
RCE	41	Inspector and Hand Packager (plastic prod.)	559.687-074
RCE	41	Installer, Soft Top (automotive ser.)	807.684-026
RCE	41	Kiln-Door Builder (brick & tile)	573.684-010
RCE	41	Knife Setter, Grinder Machine (paper & pulp)	564.684-010
RCE	41	Knitter, Full-Fashioned Garment (knitting)	685.665-010
RCE	41	Laboratory Miller (grain-feed mills)	521.685-194
RCE	41	Laborer, Rags (paper & pulp)	539.587-010
RCE	41	Lacquerer (plastic prod.)	599.685-054
RCE	41	Laminator (tex. prod., n.e.c.)	584.685-034
RCE	41	Lapel Padder, Blindstitch (garment)	786.682-150
RCE	41	Last Ironer (wood prod., n.e.c.)	739.684-098
RCE	41	Lasting-Machine Operator, Hand Method (boot & shoe)	788.684-078
RCE	41	Latexer I (protective dev.)	584.685-038
RCE	41	Lehr Tender (glass mfg.)	573.685-026
RCE	41	Lens Matcher (optical goods)	713.687-030
RCE	41	Lime Mixer Tender (steel & rel.)	514.685-022
RCE	41	Liner Assembler (nonfer. metal)	613.667-010
RCE	41	Lining Baster, Jumpbasting (garment)	786.682-154
RCE	41	Lining Feller, Blindstitch (garment)	786.682-158
RCE	41	Lining Setter, Lockstitch (garment)	786.682-166
RCE	41	Lining-Machine Operator (concrete prod.)	575.565-010
RCE	41	Linter Tender (oils & grease)	521.685-198
RCE	41	Lip Cutter and Scorer (boot & shoe)	690.685-270
RCE	41	Loader Helper (any industry)	914.687-014
RCE	41	Long-Chain Beamer (textile)	681.685-058
RCE	41	Melter (jewelry-silver.)	700.687-042
RCE	41	Metal-Sponge-Making-Machine Operator (nonfer. metal)	616.685-038
RCE	41	Mingler Operator (sugar & conf.)	520.665-010
RCE	41	Mirror Specialist (glass products; wood prod., n.e.c.)	779.684-038
RCE	41	Mixing-Tank Operator (oils & grease)	520.685-170
RCE	41	Mold Dresser (any industry)	519.684-018
RCE	41	Molder (hat & cap)	580.685-042
RCE	41	Motor-Vehicle-Light Assembler (light. fix.)	729.684-034
RCE	41	Multineedle-Chainstitch-Machine Operator (garment)	786.682-178

HOC	Cx	Title	DOT
RCE	41	Nailer, Hand (any industry)	762.684-050
RCE	41	Nailing-Machine Operator, Automatic (any industry)	669.685-066
RCE	41	Necktie Operator, Pockets and Pieces (garment)	786.682-182
RCE	41	Necktie-Centralizing-Machine Operator I (garment)	786.682-186
RCE	41	Necktie-Centralizing-Machine Operator II (garment)	786.682-190
RCE	41	Needle Polisher (button & notion)	705.684-046
RCE	41	Nicker (boot & shoe)	690.685-298
RCE	41	Nozzle-and-Sleeve Worker (nonfer. metal)	514.684-018
RCE	41	Numberer and Wirer (textile)	689.587-010
RCE	41	Oriental-Rug Stretcher (any industry)	580.687-010
RCE	41	Oxidizer (jewelry-silver.)	700.684-054
RCE	41	Packager, Head (saw. & plan.)	667.682-046
RCE	41	Packing-Line Worker (rubber goods)	753.687-038
RCE	41	Paint-Roller Winder (fabrication, n.e.c.)	739.685-030
RCE	41	Pants Outseamer, Chainstitch (garment)	786.682-202
RCE	41	Parachute-Line Tier (tex. prod., n.e.c.)	789.687-118
RCE	41	Patch Worker (tobacco)	790.684-018
RCE	41	Patcher (pottery & porc.)	774.684-046
RCE	41	Patcher, Bowling Ball (toy-sport equip.)	759.684-046
RCE	41	Pattern Duplicator (textile)	683.685-026
RCE	41	Pelota Maker (toy-sport equip.)	732.684-090
RCE	41	Perforating-Machine Operator (print. & pub.)	649.685-090
RCE	41	Perforating-Machine Operator (hat & cap)	686.685-038
RCE	41	Pigment Pumper (rubber reclaim.)	914.665-010
RCE	41	Pillowcase Turner (tex. prod., n.e.c.)	583.685-078
RCE	41	Platen-Press Feeder (print. & pub.)	651.685-022
RCE	41	Plumbing-Hardware Assembler (plumbing-heat.)	706.684-086
RCE	41	Polisher and Buffer II (any industry)	705.684-062
RCE	41	Pouncing-Lathe Operator (hat & cap)	585.685-074
RCE	41	Pounder (boot & shoe)	690.685-314
RCE	41	Press Feeder (tinware)	652.685-058
RCE	41	Press Operator (textile)	583.685-086
RCE	41	Primer Assembler (ordnance)	737.687-098
RCE	41	Primer-Inserting-Machine Operator (ordnance)	694.685-042
RCE	41	Primer-Waterproofing-Machine Operator (ordnance)	694.685-046
RCE	41	Printer (pen & pencil)	652.685-062
RCE	41	Process-Machine Operator (paper goods)	640.685-050
RCE	41	Processor (plastic-synth.)	557.685-018
RCE	41	Puller Over, Machine (boot & shoe)	788.684-090
RCE	41	Punch-Press Operator (fabrication, n.e.c.)	692.665-014
RCE	41	Quiller Operator (textile)	681.685-070
RCE	41	Rag Inspector (paper & pulp)	530.687-010
RCE	41	Record-Press Tender (recording)	556.685-070
RCE	41	Reeling-Machine Operator (textile)	681.685-078
RCE	41	Reject Opener (tobacco)	790.687-026
RCE	41	Repack-Room Worker (beverage)	920.687-146
RCE	41	Reserve Operator (tobacco)	529.685-206
RCE	41	Returned-Goods Sorter (textile)	922.687-086
RCE	41	Roll-or-Tape-Edge-Machine Operator (furniture)	787.682-038

HOC	Cx	Title	DOT
RCE	41	Rope-Laying-Machine Operator (tex. prod., n.e.c.)	681.685-086
RCE	41	Route Aide (tel. & tel.)	239.687-010
RCE	41	Rubber Molder (fabrication, n.e.c.)	556.684-026
RCE	41	Rug-Cutter Helper (carpet & rug)	686.686-014
RCE	41	Sagger Maker (pottery & porc.)	774.684-030
RCE	41	Salvage Inspector (can. & preserv.)	529.687-174
RCE	41	Sandblast-or-Shotblast-Equipment Tender (any industry)	503.685-042
RCE	41	Sausage Maker (meat products)	520.685-202
RCE	41	Sausage-Meat Trimmer (meat products)	521.687-106
RCE	41	Scale Operator (chemical)	555.687-010
RCE	41	Scallop Cutter, Machine (tex. prod., n.e.c.)	686.685-058
RCE	41	Screen Maker (paper goods)	739.684-150
RCE	41	Screen Operator (chemical)	551.685-130
RCE	41	Screen-Room Operator (sugar & conf.)	521.685-282
RCE	41	Screener-Perfumer (soap & rel.)	559.685-162
RCE	41	Scroll Assembler (office machines)	710.584-010
RCE	41	Seat Joiner, Chainstitch (garment)	786.682-218
RCE	41	Sectional-Belt-Mold Assembler (rubber goods)	752.685-010
RCE	41	Separator Operator (chemical)	559.685-166
RCE	41	Shaker-Plate Operator (ordnance)	737.685-014
RCE	41	Shearing-Machine Operator (carpet & rug; textile)	585.685-102
RCE	41	Shot-Grinder Operator (ordnance)	603.685-074
RCE	41	Shoulder Joiner, Lockstitch (garment)	786.682-222
RCE	41	Side Laster, Cement (boot & shoe)	690.685-358
RCE	41	Silk Spreader (textile)	680.685-090
RCE	41	Singe Winder (textile)	681.585-018
RCE	41	Skin Former (rubber goods)	752.684-050
RCE	41	Skin Grader (meat products)	525.687-102
RCE	41	Skirt Panel Assembler (furniture)	780.687-070
RCE	41	Skiver, Blockers (boot & shoe)	585.685-110
RCE	41	Sleeve Setter, Lockstitch (garment)	786.682-230
RCE	41	Sleeve Setter, Overlock (garment)	786.682-234
RCE	41	Slinger, Sequins (plastic prod.)	692.685-178
RCE	41	Slip-Seat Coverer (furniture)	780.684-094
RCE	41	Sorter (boot & shoe)	753.587-010
RCE	41	Spinner (plastic-synth.)	557.685-026
RCE	41	Spiral Spring Winder (metal prod., n.e.c.)	616.685-070
RCE	41	Splicer Operator (millwork-plywood)	569.685-062
RCE	41	Spool Winder (nonfer. metal)	619.485-010
RCE	41	Spotter (glass mfg.)	772.687-014
RCE	41	Spray-Machine Operator (textile)	582.685-138
RCE	41	Spun-Paste-Machine Operator (elec. equip.)	692.685-190
RCE	41	Stacker Tender (millwork-plywood)	921.685-062
RCE	41	Stamp Mounter (pen & pencil)	733.684-018
RCE	41	Stamping-Mill Tender (smelt. & refin.)	515.685-018
RCE	41	Stamping-Press Operator (any industry)	652.682-030
RCE	41	Steam-Cleaning-Machine Operator (construction)	891.685-010
RCE	41	Steam-Press Tender II (rubber goods)	553.665-050
RCE	41	Stencil-Machine Operator (textile)	652.685-086

HOC	Cx	Title	DOT
RCE	41	Stop Attacher (button & notion)	692.685-206
RCE	41	Straddle-Truck Operator (any industry)	921.683-070
RCE	41	Straw-Hat-Plunger Operator (hat & cap)	583.685-114
RCE	41	Street-Light-Repairer Helper (utilities)	729.684-050
RCE	41	Strike-Off-Machine Operator (textile)	652.685-090
RCE	41	Swaging-Machine Operator (ordnance)	617.585-010
RCE	41	Take-Up Operator (plastic-synth.)	557.685-034
RCE	41	Tapper II (clock & watch)	715.685-062
RCE	41	Tensioning-Machine Operator (concrete prod.)	616.665-010
RCE	41	Toe Former, Stitchdowns (boot & shoe)	690.685-426
RCE	41	Topstitcher, Lockstitch (garment)	786.682-238
RCE	41	Topstitcher, Zigzag (garment)	786.682-242
RCE	41	Touch-Up Screener, Printed Circuit Board Assembly (electron. comp.)	726.684-110
RCE	41	Transfer-Car Operator, Drier (nonmet. min.)	921.583-010
RCE	41	Transfer-Machine Operator (knitting; tex. prod., n.e.c.)	659.685-022
RCE	41	Tray-Drier Operator (chemical)	553.665-054
RCE	41	Trim Attacher (cutlery-hrdwr.)	692.685-230
RCE	41	Trimmer, Machine (leather mfg.)	585.685-126
RCE	41	Trimmer, Machine I (boot & shoe)	690.685-434
RCE	41	Trimming Sewer, Automatic (garment; tex. prod., n.e.c.)	787.685-050
RCE	41	Tube Molder, Fiberglass (plastic prod.)	690.685-438
RCE	41	Tube Splicer (rubber tire)	690.685-442
RCE	41	Tube Winder, Hand (nonmet. min.)	692.685-234
RCE	41	Tubing-Machine Tender (clock & watch)	715.685-070
RCE	41	Tumbler (clock & watch)	599.685-106
RCE	41	Tunnel-Elastic Operator, Chainstitch (garment)	786.682-246
RCE	41	Tunnel-Elastic Operator, Lockstitch (garment)	786.682-250
RCE	41	Tunnel-Elastic Operator, Zigzag (garment)	786.682-254
RCE	41	Twister Tender, Paper (tex. prod., n.e.c.)	681.685-134
RCE	41	Uptwister Tender (textile)	681.685-138
RCE	41	V-Belt Finisher (rubber goods)	690.685-454
RCE	41	V-Belt Skiver (rubber goods)	690.685-458
RCE	41	Vacuum-Drier Operator (tex. prod., n.e.c.)	581.685-066
RCE	41	Varnishing-Machine Operator (print. & pub.)	534.685-030
RCE	41	Veneer Clipper (millwork-plywood)	663.685-050
RCE	41	Vulcanizing-Press Operator (boot & shoe)	690.685-466
RCE	41	Wad Impregnator (ordnance)	590.685-054
RCE	41	Waistline Joiner, Lockstitch (garment)	786.682-270
RCE	41	Waistline Joiner, Overlock (garment)	786.682-274
RCE	41	Wash-Oil-Pump Operator Helper (steel & rel.)	549.685-034
RCE	41	Watcher, Pantograph (tex. prod., n.e.c.)	689.685-154
RCE	41	Wax-Pot Tender (foundry)	553.685-110
RCE	41	Welt Butter, Machine (boot & shoe)	690.685-474
RCE	41	Wheel-and-Caster Repairer (any industry)	630.684-038
RCE	41	Winder (toy-sport equip.)	692.685-246
RCE	41	Winder Operator, Automatic (textile)	681.685-150
RCE	41	Wire Coiner (button & notion)	616.685-086
RCE	41	Wire Preparation Machine Tender (any industry)	728.685-010

HOC	Cx	Title	DOT
RCE	41	Wireworker (elec. equip.; electron. comp.)	728.684-022
RCE	41	Wreath and Garland Maker (fabrication, n.e.c.)	739.684-182
RCE	41	Yarn Sorter (textile)	689.687-086
RCE	41	Zipper Setter, Chainstitch (garment)	786.682-282
RCE	41	Zipper Setter, Lockstitch (garment)	786.682-286
RCE	40	Air-Bag Curer (rubber tire)	556.685-010
RCE	40	Air-Hole Driller (fabrication, n.e.c.)	692.685-018
RCE	40	Ampoule Filler (pharmaceut.)	559.685-018
RCE	40	Assembler (ordnance)	737.687-010
RCE	40	Assembler For Puller-Over, Hand (boot & shoe)	788.684-010
RCE	40	Assembler, Molded Frames (optical goods)	713.684-014
RCE	40	Assembler, Printed Products (print. & pub.)	794.687-010
RCE	40	Assembler, Production (any industry)	706.687-010
RCE	40	Assembler, Skylights (plastic prod.)	869.684-014
RCE	40	Assembly-Machine Operator (pen & pencil)	692.686-010
RCE	40	Atomizer Assembler (fabrication, n.e.c.)	706.684-030
RCE	40	Automobile Detailer (automotive ser.)	915.687-034
RCE	40	Bag Sewer (paper goods)	787.686-010
RCE	40	Bander-and-Cellophaner, Machine (tobacco)	920.685-014
RCE	40	Barrel Brander (wood. container)	764.684-010
RCE	40	Bartender Helper (hotel & rest.)	312.687-010
RCE	40	Basket Assembler I (wood. container)	669.685-014
RCE	40	Basket Assembler II (wood. container)	769.684-010
RCE	40	Basket Grader (wood. container)	769.687-010
RCE	40	Basket Patcher (wood. container)	769.684-014
RCE	40	Batch Freezer (dairy products)	523.685-010
RCE	40	Battery Charger, Conveyor Line (elec. equip.)	727.687-026
RCE	40	BB Shot Packer (ordnance)	920.685-018
RCE	40	Beading Sawyer (fabrication, n.e.c.)	667.685-018
RCE	40	Blasting-Cap Assembler (ordnance)	737.687-018
RCE	40	Bleacher, Lard (meat products; oils & grease)	521.685-026
RCE	40	Blender I (chemical)	550.685-014
RCE	40	Blender, Snuff (tobacco)	520.685-022
RCE	40	Block Feeder (fabrication, n.e.c.)	663.686-010
RCE	40	Blocker, Hand II (hat & cap)	580.684-014
RCE	40	Blocking-Machine Tender (optical goods)	716.685-010
RCE	40	Boner (garment; protective dev.)	789.687-018
RCE	40	Bottled-Beverage Inspector (beverage)	529.685-026
RCE	40	Box Maker (fabrication, n.e.c.)	762.684-026
RCE	40	Box Maker, Paperboard (any industry)	794.684-014
RCE	40	Box-Sealing Inspector (paper goods)	641.687-014
RCE	40	Braider Setter (rubber goods)	759.664-010
RCE	40	Bran Mixer (grain-feed mills)	599.685-014
RCE	40	Briar Cutter (fabrication, n.e.c.)	664.685-010
RCE	40	Brim Presser I (hat & cap)	583.685-018
RCE	40	Brush-Head Maker (fabrication, n.e.c.)	739.685-018
RCE	40	Buffer (hat & cap)	585.685-014
RCE	40	Buffer (plastic prod.)	752.684-022
RCE	40	Buffing-Machine Tender (any industry)	603.665-010
RCE	40	Buffing-Wheel Inspector (tex. prod., n.e.c.)	789.687-026

Part 2: From Holland Codes to Occupations

From Holland Codes to the Dictionary of Occupational Titles Occupations

HOC	Cx	Title	DOT
RCE	40	Bundler, Seasonal Greenery (forestry)	920.687-046
RCE	40	Button-Attaching-Machine Operator (garment; hat & cap)	699.685-010
RCE	40	Button-Sewing-Machine Operator (garment)	786.685-010
RCE	40	Buttonhole-Machine Operator (garment)	786.685-014
RCE	40	Cafeteria Attendant (hotel & rest.)	311.677-010
RCE	40	Candy Cutter, Hand (sugar & conf.)	790.687-010
RCE	40	Card Lacer, Jacquard (narrow fabrics; textile)	683.685-018
RCE	40	Carder (any industry)	920.685-034
RCE	40	Casing Grader (meat products)	529.687-026
RCE	40	Casing Sewer (meat products)	529.687-030
RCE	40	Chemical Reclamation Equipment Operator (electron. comp.)	558.685-058
RCE	40	Chin-Strap Cutter (hat & cap)	686.685-010
RCE	40	Cigar Brander (tobacco)	920.685-046
RCE	40	Cigar-Head Piercer (tobacco)	529.685-058
RCE	40	Cigarette-Packing-Machine Operator (tobacco)	920.685-050
RCE	40	Clipper (fabrication, n.e.c.)	739.685-022
RCE	40	Cloth Examiner, Hand (narrow fabrics)	689.687-022
RCE	40	Cloth Winder (textile)	689.685-046
RCE	40	Cloth-Edge Singer (textile)	585.687-018
RCE	40	Cocoa-Butter-Filter Operator (sugar & conf.)	521.685-070
RCE	40	Collar Feller, Handstitching Machine (garment)	786.682-066
RCE	40	Collector (knitting)	684.687-022
RCE	40	Collet Driller (clock & watch)	715.684-062
RCE	40	Concrete-Float Maker (concrete prod.)	869.687-022
RCE	40	Contact-Lens-Flashing Puncher (optical goods)	713.687-014
RCE	40	Continuous-Crusher Operator (textile)	586.685-014
RCE	40	Cook, Fry, Deep Fat (can. & preserv.; hotel & rest.)	526.685-014
RCE	40	Cooling-Pan Tender (can. & preserv.)	523.685-046
RCE	40	Coremaker, Machine I (foundry)	518.685-014
RCE	40	Cotton Sampler (agriculture; textile)	922.687-042
RCE	40	Cotton-Ball Bagger (protective dev.)	920.686-014
RCE	40	Counter Roller (boot & shoe)	690.685-106
RCE	40	Creeler (textile)	689.687-030
RCE	40	Cup-Trimming-Machine Operator (ordnance)	615.685-018
RCE	40	Cut-Off-Machine Operator (paper goods)	640.685-034
RCE	40	Cut-Out-Machine Operator (boot & shoe)	690.685-114
RCE	40	Cutter, Hand (rubber goods)	751.684-014
RCE	40	Cutting-Machine Tender, Decorative (glass mfg.)	775.685-010
RCE	40	Die-Casting-Machine Operator II (foundry)	514.685-018
RCE	40	Doubling-Machine Operator (textile)	681.685-046
RCE	40	Dovetail-Machine Operator (wood. container)	669.685-046
RCE	40	Drier (knitting)	581.686-014
RCE	40	Drill-Punch Operator (paper goods; print. & pub.)	649.685-034
RCE	40	Drop-Wire Builder (textile)	689.687-034
RCE	40	Duster (hat & cap)	587.685-026
RCE	40	Edge-Glue-Machine Tender (millwork-plywood)	569.685-034
RCE	40	Enrobing-Machine Operator (bakery products)	524.685-026
RCE	40	Extension Edger (paper goods)	641.685-046

Part 2: From Holland Codes to Occupations

From Holland Codes to the Dictionary of Occupational Titles Occupations

HOC	Cx	Title	DOT
RCE	40	Fertilizer Mixer (chemical)	550.665-018
RCE	40	Filler Mixer (tobacco)	520.687-030
RCE	40	Film Touch-Up Inspector (electron. comp.)	726.684-050
RCE	40	Filter Operator (any industry)	551.685-078
RCE	40	Filter-Tank-Tender Helper, Head (grain-feed mills)	521.685-134
RCE	40	Finisher-Card Tender (nonmet. min.; textile)	680.685-042
RCE	40	Fish Roe Processor (can. & preserv.)	522.687-046
RCE	40	Floor Worker (sugar & conf.)	920.687-090
RCE	40	Four-Corner-Stayer-Machine Operator (paper goods)	641.685-054
RCE	40	Frame Changer (textile)	689.686-026
RCE	40	Freezing-Room Worker (can. & preserv.)	523.687-022
RCE	40	Fruit Distributor (agriculture)	921.685-046
RCE	40	Fruit-Bar Maker (sugar & conf.)	529.685-134
RCE	40	Furnace Helper (nonfer. metal; smelt. & refin.)	512.666-010
RCE	40	Fusing-Furnace Loader (optical goods)	573.686-014
RCE	40	Glass Checker (optical goods)	716.687-014
RCE	40	Glass-Furnace Tender (paint & varnish)	572.685-010
RCE	40	Glass-Vial-Bending-Conveyor Feeder (cutlery-hrdwr.)	573.686-018
RCE	40	Glue-Machine Operator (pen & pencil)	692.685-094
RCE	40	Grout-Machine Tender (smelt. & refin.)	519.685-014
RCE	40	Handbag Framer (leather prod.)	739.684-090
RCE	40	Hander-In (narrow fabrics; textile)	683.687-018
RCE	40	Handkerchief Folder (garment)	920.687-098
RCE	40	Handle-and-Vent-Machine Operator (furniture)	686.685-034
RCE	40	Hat-Lining Blocker (hat & cap)	583.685-050
RCE	40	Heel Attacher, Wood (boot & shoe)	788.684-058
RCE	40	Hemstitching-Machine Operator (garment)	786.682-142
RCE	40	Insecticide Mixer (chemical)	550.685-070
RCE	40	Interlacer (boot & shoe)	788.684-070
RCE	40	Ironer (button & notion)	590.685-042
RCE	40	Jewel Grinder I (clock & watch)	770.685-014
RCE	40	Jewel Grinder II (clock & watch)	770.684-010
RCE	40	Joiner (glass mfg.)	673.687-010
RCE	40	Joint Cutter, Machine (boot & shoe)	690.685-250
RCE	40	Keying-Machine Operator (print. & pub.)	652.685-042
RCE	40	Kiln Cleaner (concrete prod.)	573.687-018
RCE	40	Label-Cutting-and-Folding-Machine Operator, Automatic (narrow fabrics)	689.685-086
RCE	40	Labeling-Machine Operator (recording)	920.685-066
RCE	40	Laboratory-Sample Carrier (any industry)	922.687-054
RCE	40	Laborer, General (plastic-synth.)	559.667-014
RCE	40	Laminator I (leather prod.)	690.685-258
RCE	40	Lamp-Shade Assembler (fabrication, n.e.c.)	739.684-094
RCE	40	Last Sawyer (wood prod., n.e.c.)	690.685-262
RCE	40	Laundry Worker, Domestic (domestic ser.)	302.685-010
RCE	40	Leader Tier (toy-sport equip.)	732.687-038
RCE	40	Light-Bulb Assembler (light. fix.)	692.685-118
RCE	40	Linen Grader (laundry & rel.)	361.687-022
RCE	40	Liquor Inspector (beverage)	522.667-010

Part 2: From Holland Codes to Occupations

From Holland Codes to the Dictionary of Occupational Titles Occupations

HOC	Cx	Title	DOT
RCE	40	Machine Sneller (toy-sport equip.)	732.685-026
RCE	40	Magnetic-Tape Winder (recording)	726.685-010
RCE	40	Marker II (any industry)	920.687-126
RCE	40	Marker, Semiconductor Wafers (electron. comp.)	920.587-026
RCE	40	Mat Packer (nonmet. min.)	579.686-014
RCE	40	Mattress-Spring Encaser (furniture)	780.687-030
RCE	40	Meat-Grading-Machine Operator (can. & preserv.)	521.685-218
RCE	40	Mica-Plate Layer (mine & quarry)	579.685-026
RCE	40	Mica-Plate Layer, Hand (mine & quarry)	579.684-022
RCE	40	Milker, Machine (agriculture)	410.685-010
RCE	40	Mill Attendant II (chemical)	555.685-038
RCE	40	Mill Stenciler (steel & rel.)	659.685-026
RCE	40	Mixer Operator, Snack Foods (food prep., n.e.c.)	520.685-230
RCE	40	Mixer, Foam Rubber (rubber goods)	550.685-086
RCE	40	Molded-Rubber-Goods Cutter (rubber goods)	690.685-290
RCE	40	Molder, Fiberglass Luggage (leather prod.)	575.685-066
RCE	40	Molding Cutter (woodworking)	663.685-018
RCE	40	Mounter, Automatic (photofinishing)	976.685-022
RCE	40	Mounter, Smoking Pipe (fabrication, n.e.c.)	739.684-130
RCE	40	Nail-Making-Machine Tender (steel & rel.)	617.665-010
RCE	40	Nail-Polish-Brush-Machine Feeder, Automatic (fabrication, n.e.c.)	692.686-054
RCE	40	Napper Tender (knitting)	585.665-010
RCE	40	Painter, Brush (any industry)	740.684-022
RCE	40	Parachute Inspector (tex. prod., n.e.c.)	789.687-114
RCE	40	Partition-Making-Machine Operator (paper goods)	649.685-082
RCE	40	Patch Washer (textile)	582.685-110
RCE	40	Pearler (clock & watch)	715.684-162
RCE	40	Picker-Machine Operator (furniture)	680.685-078
RCE	40	Polisher (woodworking)	761.684-026
RCE	40	Potato-Peeling-Machine Operator (food prep., n.e.c.)	521.685-250
RCE	40	Press Feeder, Broomcorn (agriculture)	429.686-010
RCE	40	Presser (soap & rel.)	559.685-142
RCE	40	Presser (rubber goods)	690.685-318
RCE	40	Profile-Stitching-Machine Operator (garment)	786.685-026
RCE	40	Red-Lead Burner (paint & varnish)	558.685-054
RCE	40	Ribbon-Lap-Machine Tender (textile)	680.685-086
RCE	40	Rigger (tex. prod., n.e.c.)	789.684-046
RCE	40	Riveter, Hand (any industry)	709.684-066
RCE	40	Rock Breaker (retail trade; stonework)	770.687-034
RCE	40	Rod-Mill Tender (cement; smelt. & refin.)	519.685-030
RCE	40	Rod-Puller and Coiler (nonfer. metal)	619.685-078
RCE	40	Roll Reclaimer (paper goods)	640.685-062
RCE	40	Roll-Forming-Machine Operator II (any industry)	617.685-034
RCE	40	Roll-Over-Press Operator (optical goods)	690.685-326
RCE	40	Roll-Slicing-Machine Tender (pen & pencil)	640.685-066
RCE	40	Rotary-Cutter Feeder (paper & pulp)	640.686-010
RCE	40	Rotary-Drier Feeder (chemical)	553.686-038
RCE	40	Saddle-and-Side Wire Stitcher (print. & pub.)	692.685-146

HOC	Cx	Title	DOT
RCE	40	Sample-Book Maker (paper goods)	659.685-014
RCE	40	Sandwich Maker (hotel & rest.)	317.664-010
RCE	40	Save-All Operator (paper & pulp)	533.685-018
RCE	40	Sawyer II (nonmet. min.)	677.685-038
RCE	40	Scorer (paper goods)	641.685-070
RCE	40	Seam Hammerer (musical inst.)	730.684-070
RCE	40	Seconds Handler (knitting)	782.687-050
RCE	40	Selvage-Machine Operator (textile)	681.685-094
RCE	40	Separator Operator (button & notion)	692.685-166
RCE	40	Shaker (knitting)	589.687-058
RCE	40	Shell-Mold-Bonding-Machine Operator (foundry)	518.685-030
RCE	40	Shoe Packer (boot & shoe)	920.687-166
RCE	40	Shot-Tube-Machine Tender (paper goods)	649.685-106
RCE	40	Silverware Assembler (jewelry-silver.)	700.684-070
RCE	40	Sinker Winder (toy-sport equip.)	732.685-030
RCE	40	Siphon Operator (medical ser.; pharmaceut.)	599.687-026
RCE	40	Ski Base Trimmer (toy-sport equip.)	732.684-110
RCE	40	Ski Topper (toy-sport equip.)	692.685-170
RCE	40	Skin-Peeling-Machine Operator (meat products)	525.685-030
RCE	40	Slicing-Machine Operator (bakery products)	521.685-302
RCE	40	Slicing-Machine Operator (dairy products; meat products)	521.685-306
RCE	40	Slicing-Machine Operator (button & notion)	692.685-174
RCE	40	Snuff Grinder and Screener (tobacco)	521.685-314
RCE	40	Soap Inspector (soap & rel.)	559.687-058
RCE	40	Sock Boarder (knitting)	589.686-042
RCE	40	Sorter (button & notion)	734.687-082
RCE	40	Sorter, Machine (button & notion)	692.685-182
RCE	40	Spike-Machine Feeder (steel & rel.)	612.666-010
RCE	40	Splitter, Machine (boot & shoe; leather prod.)	585.685-114
RCE	40	Stamper II (tex. prod., n.e.c.)	652.685-082
RCE	40	Staple Cutter (textile)	680.685-102
RCE	40	Stave-Machine Tender (wood. container)	663.685-046
RCE	40	Steamer (beverage)	529.685-226
RCE	40	Stem Mounter (light. fix.)	725.684-018
RCE	40	Stemhole Borer (fabrication, n.e.c.)	666.685-010
RCE	40	Stretch-Box Tender (textile)	680.685-110
RCE	40	Strip-Cutting-Machine Operator (textile)	686.685-066
RCE	40	Stuffer (toy-sport equip.)	731.685-014
RCE	40	Stull Installer (concrete prod.)	869.684-062
RCE	40	Swager Operator (pen & pencil)	616.685-078
RCE	40	Sweatband Separator (hat & cap)	585.685-122
RCE	40	Table Worker (boot & shoe)	788.687-142
RCE	40	Tacking-Machine Operator (garment)	786.685-034
RCE	40	Tank-Setter Helper (petrol. & gas)	801.687-018
RCE	40	Tester (pottery & porc.)	774.687-026
RCE	40	Ticket Printer and Tagger (garment)	652.685-094
RCE	40	Tinsel-Machine Operator (fabrication, n.e.c.)	692.685-226
RCE	40	Toe-Closing-Machine Tender (knitting)	787.685-046
RCE	40	Tray Filler (tobacco)	920.686-050

HOC	Cx	Title	DOT
RCE	40	Treating-Engineer Helper (wood prod., n.e.c.)	561.685-010
RCE	40	Trimmer, Machine (garment; knitting)	781.682-010
RCE	40	Trimming-Machine Operator (garment; knitting)	583.685-122
RCE	40	Tube Bender, Hand II (any industry)	709.687-050
RCE	40	Tumbler-Machine Operator (rubber goods)	559.685-178
RCE	40	Turning-Machine Operator (wood. container)	667.685-066
RCE	40	Turning-Machine Operator (tex. prod., n.e.c.)	689.685-146
RCE	40	Tying-Machine Operator, Lumber (woodworking)	929.685-018
RCE	40	Umbrella Tipper, Hand (fabrication, n.e.c.)	739.684-162
RCE	40	V-Belt Coverer (rubber goods)	690.685-450
RCE	40	Vacuum-Applicator Operator (fabrication, n.e.c.)	692.685-238
RCE	40	Valving-Machine Operator (paper goods)	641.685-094
RCE	40	Veneer Drier (millwork-plywood)	563.685-022
RCE	40	Veneer Redrier (millwork-plywood)	563.685-026
RCE	40	Wad-Printing-Machine Operator (ordnance)	652.685-102
RCE	40	Wax-Pattern Repairer (foundry)	518.684-026
RCE	40	Wedger, Machine (cutlery-hrdwr.)	701.687-034
RCE	40	Welding-Machine Tender (welding)	819.685-010
RCE	40	Wheel-Mill Operator (chemical)	555.685-066
RCE	40	Wire-Basket Maker (metal prod., n.e.c.)	709.687-062
RCE	40	Wooden-Frame Builder (furniture)	762.684-066
RCE	40	Wrapper Layer (tobacco)	529.685-266
RCE	40	Yarn Cleaner (tex. prod., n.e.c.; textile)	681.687-026
RCE	40	Yarn-Polishing-Machine Operator (textile)	583.685-126
RCE	39	Air Purifier Servicer (business ser.)	389.687-010
RCE	39	Band-Saw Operator (woodworking)	667.685-014
RCE	39	Bandoleer Straightener-Stamper (ordnance)	737.587-010
RCE	39	Barrel-Cap Setter (clock & watch)	715.687-014
RCE	39	Batch Trucker (rubber reclaim.)	550.686-010
RCE	39	Beveler (clock & watch)	715.684-030
RCE	39	Blade Balancer (agric. equip.)	701.687-014
RCE	39	Brassiere-Slide-Making-Machine Tender, Automatic (garment)	692.685-026
RCE	39	Breading Machine Tender (can. & preserv.)	524.685-010
RCE	39	Brine-Tank-Separator Operator (can. & preserv.)	521.685-038
RCE	39	Budder (agriculture)	405.684-010
RCE	39	Buffing Turner-and-Counter (tex. prod., n.e.c.)	789.687-022
RCE	39	Bulker, Cut Tobacco (tobacco)	529.685-034
RCE	39	Burnisher (boot & shoe)	690.685-058
RCE	39	Buttonhole Maker (boot & shoe)	788.684-038
RCE	39	Card Stripper (textile)	680.685-014
RCE	39	Centrifugal-Casting-Machine Operator II (foundry)	514.685-014
RCE	39	Centrifugal-Casting-Machine Tender (plastic prod.)	556.685-090
RCE	39	Checker (motor trans.)	919.687-010
RCE	39	Cigar Inspector (tobacco)	529.687-042
RCE	39	Clip-Loading-Machine Feeder (ordnance)	694.686-010
RCE	39	Clothespin-Drier Operator (woodworking)	563.685-014
RCE	39	Coffee Grinder (food prep., n.e.c.)	521.685-078
RCE	39	Confectionery-Drops-Machine Operator (sugar & conf.)	520.685-078

HOC	Cx	Title	DOT
RCE	39	Conveyor Feeder-Offbearer (any industry)	921.686-014
RCE	39	Crab Meat Processor (can. & preserv.)	525.687-126
RCE	39	Crimper (rubber goods)	690.686-026
RCE	39	Cuff Folder (knitting)	685.687-014
RCE	39	Cutlet Maker, Pork (meat products)	529.686-022
RCE	39	Cutter (food prep., n.e.c.)	529.685-082
RCE	39	Dampener Operator (paper & pulp)	534.685-010
RCE	39	Design Assembler (fabrication, n.e.c.)	692.686-034
RCE	39	Driller (optical goods)	716.685-014
RCE	39	Drop-Wire Hanger (textile)	683.687-014
RCE	39	Dry-Cans Operator (textile)	581.685-022
RCE	39	Dumping-Machine Operator (can. & preserv.; wholesale tr.)	529.685-102
RCE	39	Edging-Machine Feeder (glass mfg.)	673.686-022
RCE	39	Engraver Tender (glass products)	673.685-050
RCE	39	Filer and Sander (woodworking)	705.684-018
RCE	39	Filler Feeder (tobacco)	529.686-042
RCE	39	Folding-Machine Operator (hat & cap)	690.686-034
RCE	39	Foundation Maker (hat & cap)	784.684-030
RCE	39	Fringer (carpet & rug; tex. prod., n.e.c.)	789.687-062
RCE	39	Fuse-Cup Expander (ordnance)	694.685-022
RCE	39	Garment Folder (garment; knitting)	789.687-066
RCE	39	Getterer (light. fix.)	725.687-022
RCE	39	Glucose-and-Syrup Weigher (sugar & conf.)	520.686-026
RCE	39	Heavy-Media Operator (mine & quarry)	541.685-010
RCE	39	Heel Compressor (boot & shoe)	690.685-210
RCE	39	Hydroelectric-Plant Maintainer (utilities)	952.687-010
RCE	39	Ice Maker, Skating Rink (amuse. & rec.)	969.687-014
RCE	39	Icer, Hand (bakery products)	524.684-022
RCE	39	Inspector, Wreath (fabrication, n.e.c.)	739.687-118
RCE	39	Ironer (domestic ser.)	302.687-010
RCE	39	Jigger-Crown-Pouncing-Machine Operator (hat & cap)	585.685-058
RCE	39	Knife Changer (tobacco)	638.684-010
RCE	39	Laborer, Hoisting (any industry)	921.667-022
RCE	39	Laminated-Plastic-Tabletop-Molding Wrapper (furniture)	692.686-046
RCE	39	Laminating-Machine Offbearer (wood prod., n.e.c.)	569.686-046
RCE	39	Lamp-Shade Joiner (fabrication, n.e.c.)	692.685-110
RCE	39	Leaf-Size Picker (tobacco)	529.687-142
RCE	39	Lens Inserter (optical goods)	713.687-026
RCE	39	Machine-Pack Assembler (ordnance)	920.687-122
RCE	39	Mainspring Former, Arbor End (clock & watch)	715.687-078
RCE	39	Masker (electron. comp.)	726.687-034
RCE	39	Monitor-and-Storage-Bin Tender (grain-feed mills)	521.685-230
RCE	39	Mophead Trimmer-and-Wrapper (tex. prod., n.e.c.)	789.687-106
RCE	39	Mounter, Clock and Watch Hands (clock & watch)	715.687-094
RCE	39	Outsole Flexer (boot & shoe)	583.686-026
RCE	39	Patroller (knitting)	685.687-022
RCE	39	Pitch Worker (optical goods)	551.666-010
RCE	39	Plastic Roller (plastic prod.)	690.685-498

HOC	Cx	Title	DOT
RCE	39	Plate Stacker, Hand (elec. equip.)	729.687-026
RCE	39	Plug Wirer (elec. equip.)	726.687-014
RCE	39	Poultry Boner (meat products)	525.687-066
RCE	39	Power-Screwdriver Operator (any industry)	699.685-026
RCE	39	Pretzel Twister (bakery products)	520.587-010
RCE	39	Pulley Maintainer (mine & quarry)	630.687-010
RCE	39	Raised Printer (print. & pub.)	652.686-034
RCE	39	Raw-Juice Weigher (sugar & conf.)	529.685-194
RCE	39	Reducing-Machine Operator (optical goods)	614.685-018
RCE	39	Riveting-Machine Operator II (any industry)	699.685-030
RCE	39	Rolling-Machine Tender (knitting)	689.685-114
RCE	39	Rouge Sifter and Miller (optical goods)	579.685-046
RCE	39	Sawyer, Cork Slabs (wood prod., n.e.c.)	667.685-046
RCE	39	Sequins Stringer (plastic prod.)	754.687-014
RCE	39	Sewing-Machine Operator (toy-sport equip.)	787.682-054
RCE	39	Shellfish Shucker (can. & preserv.)	521.687-122
RCE	39	Shirt-Folding-Machine Operator (garment; laundry & rel.)	369.685-030
RCE	39	Silver Wrapper (hotel & rest.)	318.687-018
RCE	39	Skinner (meat products)	525.684-046
RCE	39	Slider Assembler (button & notion; garment)	734.687-078
RCE	39	Spiral Binder (paper goods; print. & pub.)	653.685-030
RCE	39	Spiral-Machine Operator (paper goods)	692.685-186
RCE	39	Splitting-Machine Feeder (leather mfg.)	690.686-054
RCE	39	Stapler, Machine (furniture)	692.685-198
RCE	39	Stem-Roller-or-Crusher Operator (tobacco)	521.685-330
RCE	39	Stoner and Polisher, Bevel Face (clock & watch)	603.685-082
RCE	39	Strip Presser (boot & shoe)	583.685-118
RCE	39	Strip-Cutting-Machine Operator (tobacco)	521.685-338
RCE	39	Strip-Metal-Punch-and-Straightener Operator (wood. container)	615.685-038
RCE	39	Studder, Hairspring (clock & watch)	715.684-186
RCE	39	Symbol Stamper, Semiconductor Packages (electron. comp.)	652.685-110
RCE	39	Thread Marker (garment)	782.687-058
RCE	39	Tier (meat products)	525.687-118
RCE	39	Traverse-Rod Assembler (furniture)	739.687-186
RCE	39	Trolley Operator (bakery products)	524.565-010
RCE	39	Tying-Machine Operator (paper goods; tex. prod., n.e.c.)	929.685-014
RCE	39	Unscrambler (can. & preserv.)	921.685-070
RCE	39	Warp Spooler (narrow fabrics; textile)	681.685-142
RCE	39	Waste-Machine Tender (tex. prod., n.e.c.; textile)	680.685-114
RCE	39	Wire Bender (furniture)	709.687-058
RCE	39	Wire-Turning-Machine Operator (wood. container)	692.685-258
RCE	38	Ampoule Sealer (pharmaceut.)	559.687-014
RCE	38	Ampoule-Washing-Machine Operator (pharmaceut.)	559.685-022
RCE	38	Apple-Packing Header (agriculture)	920.687-010
RCE	38	Assembler, Faucets (wood. container)	764.687-014
RCE	38	Assembly-Machine Tender (plastic prod.)	754.685-014
RCE	38	Automobile-Seat-Cover Installer (automotive ser.)	915.687-010

HOC	Cx	Title	DOT
RCE	38	Bagger (garment; laundry & rel.)	920.687-018
RCE	38	Balling-Machine Operator (textile)	681.685-014
RCE	38	Bander (pen & pencil)	733.687-018
RCE	38	Bander-and-Cellophaner Helper, Machine (tobacco)	920.686-010
RCE	38	Bandoleer Packer (ordnance)	920.687-034
RCE	38	Barrel Marker (wood. container)	764.687-030
RCE	38	Bell-Neck Hammerer (musical inst.)	730.684-014
RCE	38	Bench Worker, Hollow Handle (jewelry-silver.)	700.687-010
RCE	38	Binder Layer (tobacco)	529.685-018
RCE	38	Blind-Slat-Stapling-Machine Operator (woodworking)	669.685-018
RCE	38	Blocker (tex. prod., n.e.c.)	920.685-022
RCE	38	Bobbin Stripper (tex. prod., n.e.c.)	689.685-022
RCE	38	Boiler-Out (jewelry-silver.)	700.687-014
RCE	38	Bone-Drier Operator (chemical)	553.685-022
RCE	38	Booker (rubber goods; rubber tire)	599.687-014
RCE	38	Bow Maker (boot & shoe)	788.684-034
RCE	38	Bulb Filler (light. fix.)	692.686-022
RCE	38	Burr Grinder (optical goods)	673.686-014
RCE	38	Cadmium-Liquor Maker (paint & varnish)	553.685-026
RCE	38	Candle Wrapping-Machine Operator (fabrication, n.e.c.)	920.685-030
RCE	38	Carroter (hat & cap)	784.687-014
RCE	38	Cell Coverer (elec. equip.)	727.687-042
RCE	38	Centrifuge Operator (soap & rel.)	551.685-030
RCE	38	Centrifuge-Separator Operator (chemical)	551.685-038
RCE	38	Charger II (jewelry-silver.)	700.687-026
RCE	38	Cleaner, Signs (fabrication, n.e.c.)	739.687-062
RCE	38	Compact Assembler (jewelry-silver.)	739.687-066
RCE	38	Container Washer, Machine (any industry)	529.685-074
RCE	38	Cook-Box Filler (meat products)	523.685-030
RCE	38	Cotton-Roll Packer (protective dev.)	920.685-054
RCE	38	Covered-Buckle Assembler (button & notion)	734.687-050
RCE	38	Crusher-and-Binder Operator (tex. prod., n.e.c.)	689.685-054
RCE	38	Curing Oven Attendant (aircraft mfg.; electron. comp.)	590.685-090
RCE	38	Cutter, Woodwind Reeds (musical inst.)	730.686-010
RCE	38	Decal Applier (any industry)	749.684-010
RCE	38	Dental Floss Packer (protective dev.)	920.687-082
RCE	38	Domer (paper goods)	641.685-038
RCE	38	Drier-Take-Off Tender (elec. equip.)	921.685-034
RCE	38	Drum Straightener I (any industry)	619.685-034
RCE	38	Drum Tester (petrol. refin.)	599.687-038
RCE	38	Extractor Loader and Unloader (chemical)	551.686-014
RCE	38	Finishing Trimmer (boot & shoe)	788.687-042
RCE	38	Flower Picker (agriculture)	405.687-010
RCE	38	Folder, Hand (boot & shoe)	788.687-050
RCE	38	Foot Straightener (clock & watch)	715.687-030
RCE	38	Forming-Process-Line Worker (elec. equip.)	727.687-058
RCE	38	Fruit Cutter (sugar & conf.)	521.687-066
RCE	38	Gluer-and-Wedger (woodworking)	762.687-038
RCE	38	Golf-Shoe-Spike Assembler (boot & shoe)	788.687-054

HOC	Cx	Title	DOT
RCE	38	Hackler, Doll Wigs (toy-sport equip.)	731.687-018
RCE	38	Hardware Assembler (wood. container)	762.687-046
RCE	38	Heading-Machine Operator (pen & pencil)	669.685-062
RCE	38	Heel-Washer-Stringing-Machine Operator (rubber goods)	619.685-058
RCE	38	Hemming-and-Tacking-Machine Operator (furniture)	787.685-022
RCE	38	Hide Stretcher, Hand (leather mfg.)	580.687-014
RCE	38	Incinerator Operator I (sanitary ser.)	955.685-010
RCE	38	Incinerator Plant Laborer (sanitary ser.)	955.667-010
RCE	38	Kiss Setter, Hand (sugar & conf.)	529.687-122
RCE	38	Label Remover (beverage)	920.687-106
RCE	38	Lace Winder (tex. prod., n.e.c.)	685.687-018
RCE	38	Lacer (protective dev.)	789.687-094
RCE	38	Lacquer-Pin-Press Operator (ordnance)	737.687-078
RCE	38	Laster, Hand (boot & shoe)	788.684-074
RCE	38	Lining Cementer (hat & cap)	795.687-022
RCE	38	Log Peeler (saw. & plan.)	569.684-010
RCE	38	Log-Haul Chain Feeder (paper & pulp; saw. & plan.)	921.686-018
RCE	38	Mainspring Former, Brace End (clock & watch)	715.687-082
RCE	38	Mainspring Winder and Oiler (clock & watch)	715.685-038
RCE	38	Marking Stitcher (garment)	781.687-046
RCE	38	Mold Filler and Drainer (boot & shoe)	753.687-030
RCE	38	Oiler (clock & watch)	715.684-146
RCE	38	Opener I (hat & cap)	784.687-054
RCE	38	Package Sealer, Machine (any industry)	920.685-074
RCE	38	Packing-Machine-Pilot Can Router (tobacco)	920.685-086
RCE	38	Panel Edge Sealer (millwork-plywood)	769.685-010
RCE	38	Paper-Cone-Machine Tender (paper goods)	641.685-062
RCE	38	Paster, Hand or Machine (leather prod.)	783.687-026
RCE	38	Patcher (house. appl.)	723.687-010
RCE	38	Pick-Pulling-Machine Operator (textile)	689.685-094
RCE	38	Pin-or-Clip Fastener (jewelry-silver.)	735.687-022
RCE	38	Plasterer (furniture)	749.687-026
RCE	38	Polisher, Eyeglass Frames (optical goods)	713.684-038
RCE	38	Potato-Pancake Frier (food prep., n.e.c.)	526.685-050
RCE	38	Preparer (jewelry-silver.)	700.687-062
RCE	38	Presser, Machine (any industry)	363.682-018
RCE	38	Puller-Through (glove & mit.)	782.687-030
RCE	38	Pulverizer (jewelry-silver.)	770.687-030
RCE	38	Punchboard Assembler I (paper goods)	794.687-042
RCE	38	Puncher (woodworking)	663.685-022
RCE	38	Push-Connector Assembler (house. appl.)	706.687-030
RCE	38	Reamer, Center Hole (clock & watch)	715.687-110
RCE	38	Record-Changer Assembler (comm. equip.)	720.687-010
RCE	38	Ring-Making-Machine Operator (paper goods)	649.685-098
RCE	38	Ripper (furniture)	617.685-030
RCE	38	Ripper (garment; retail trade; tex. prod., n.e.c.)	782.687-038
RCE	38	Roller Operator (toy-sport equip.)	652.685-078
RCE	38	Roller-Skate Assembler (toy-sport equip.)	732.684-098
RCE	38	Rubber-Roller Grinder (pen & pencil)	690.686-050

HOC	Cx	Title	DOT
RCE	38	Screen Tacker (woodworking)	762.687-058
RCE	38	Screw Remover (boot & shoe)	788.684-102
RCE	38	Shuttler (tex. prod., n.e.c.)	689.687-070
RCE	38	Slasher Operator (paper & pulp; saw. & plan.)	667.685-054
RCE	38	Slat-Basket Maker, Machine (wood. container)	669.685-074
RCE	38	Slice-Plug-Cutter Operator (tobacco)	521.685-298
RCE	38	Smoking-Pipe Driller and Threader (fabrication, n.e.c.)	669.685-078
RCE	38	Smoking-Tobacco-Cutter Operator (tobacco)	521.685-310
RCE	38	Snailer (clock & watch)	603.685-078
RCE	38	Snuff-Packing-Machine Operator (tobacco)	920.685-094
RCE	38	Stamp-Pad Maker (pen & pencil)	733.687-070
RCE	38	Stamper (chemical)	556.685-078
RCE	38	Stamping-Machine Operator (pen & pencil)	692.685-194
RCE	38	Standpipe Tender (steel & rel.)	519.665-014
RCE	38	Steel-Box-Toe Inserter (boot & shoe)	788.687-138
RCE	38	Steel-Tie Adjuster, Automatic (paper goods)	649.685-110
RCE	38	Stem-Processing-Machine Operator (fabrication, n.e.c.)	739.685-042
RCE	38	Sticker (saw. & plan.)	563.686-010
RCE	38	Stretcher-Drier Operator (laundry & rel.)	363.687-022
RCE	38	Stretcher-Leveler-Operator Helper (nonfer. metal)	619.686-030
RCE	38	Stringer (jewelry-silver.)	509.687-018
RCE	38	Suture Polisher (protective dev.)	712.687-030
RCE	38	Sweep-Press Operator (clock & watch)	616.685-082
RCE	38	Tapper, Bit (fabrication, n.e.c.)	739.685-046
RCE	38	Tapper, Shank (fabrication, n.e.c.)	739.685-050
RCE	38	Tassel-Making-Machine Operator (tex. prod., n.e.c.)	689.685-142
RCE	38	Tennis-Ball Coverer, Hand (toy-sport equip.)	795.687-026
RCE	38	Thrasher Feeder (paper & pulp)	533.685-030
RCE	38	Thread Cutter (any industry)	789.684-050
RCE	38	Thread Winder, Automatic (textile)	681.685-122
RCE	38	Threshing-Machine Operator (tobacco)	521.685-362
RCE	38	Tie Binder (garment)	920.687-190
RCE	38	Tongue Presser (boot & shoe)	788.685-022
RCE	38	Top Former (boot & shoe)	788.685-026
RCE	38	Track Oiler (r.r. trans.)	910.687-026
RCE	38	Transfer-Car Operator (brick & tile)	921.683-078
RCE	38	Trimmer Helper (saw. & plan.)	667.686-018
RCE	38	Trimmer, Hand (boot & shoe)	788.687-150
RCE	38	Tube-Cleaning Operator (foundry)	514.685-026
RCE	38	Turkey-Roll Maker (meat products)	525.684-058
RCE	38	Vamp Creaser (boot & shoe)	788.687-154
RCE	38	Wafer-Line Worker (elec. equip.)	727.687-082
RCE	38	Ware Cleaner (pottery & porc.)	774.687-022
RCE	38	Winding-Machine Operator (concrete prod.)	619.665-010
RCE	38	Wing-Mailer-Machine Operator (print. & pub.)	208.685-034
RCE	38	Wiper (light. fix.)	723.687-022
RCE	38	Wiper (furniture)	742.687-010
RCE	38	Wire Threader (clock & watch)	604.686-010
RCE	38	Wrap Turner (boot & shoe)	788.685-030

HOC	Cx	Title	DOT
RCE	38	Wrapper Counter (tobacco)	929.687-050
RCE	37	Abrasive-Grader Helper (optical goods)	570.686-010
RCE	37	Advertising-Material Distributor (any industry)	230.687-010
RCE	37	Antichecking-Iron Worker (wood prod., n.e.c.)	563.687-010
RCE	37	Antisqueak Filler (boot & shoe)	788.687-010
RCE	37	Artificial-Pearl Maker (jewelry-silver.)	770.687-010
RCE	37	Assembler, Dry Cell and Battery (elec. equip.)	727.687-022
RCE	37	Assembler, Fishing Floats (toy-sport equip.)	732.687-014
RCE	37	Bag Liner (tex. prod., n.e.c.)	789.687-014
RCE	37	Ball-Machine Operator (sugar & conf.)	520.686-010
RCE	37	Band Attacher (clock & watch)	715.687-010
RCE	37	Bander (wood. container)	762.687-010
RCE	37	Battery Loader (textile)	683.686-010
RCE	37	Battery-Wrecker Operator (nonfer. metal)	515.686-010
RCE	37	Bench Hand (clock & watch)	715.684-026
RCE	37	Bin Filler (tobacco)	922.687-010
RCE	37	Binder Cutter, Hand (tobacco)	521.687-014
RCE	37	Blow-Off Worker (furniture)	763.687-010
RCE	37	Button Reclaimer (knitting)	734.687-042
RCE	37	Camouflage Assembler (ordnance)	869.687-014
RCE	37	Carbon Rod Inserter (elec. equip.)	692.686-026
RCE	37	Carding-Machine Operator (tex. prod., n.e.c.)	681.685-030
RCE	37	Casting-Plug Assembler (toy-sport equip.)	732.687-022
RCE	37	Cell Tuber, Hand (elec. equip.)	727.687-046
RCE	37	Cementer, Machine Applicator (boot & shoe)	690.686-018
RCE	37	Chilling-Hood Operator (meat products)	523.685-018
RCE	37	Circle-Cutting-Saw Operator (wood. container)	669.685-026
RCE	37	Clamp Remover (millwork-plywood)	569.687-010
RCE	37	Cleaner and Polisher (any industry)	709.687-010
RCE	37	Cleaner, Furniture (furniture)	709.687-014
RCE	37	Clipper, Machine (knitting)	684.686-010
RCE	37	Cloth-Bale Header (textile)	782.687-018
RCE	37	Coating-Machine Feeder (leather prod.)	690.686-022
RCE	37	Cob Sawyer (fabrication, n.e.c.)	667.685-030
RCE	37	Crushing-Machine Operator (beverage)	521.685-094
RCE	37	Crystal Attacher (clock & watch)	715.687-018
RCE	37	Dessert-Cup-Machine Feeder (bakery products)	520.686-014
RCE	37	Dipper (knitting; textile)	589.687-018
RCE	37	Dipper, Clock and Watch Hands (clock & watch)	715.687-026
RCE	37	Dried Fruit Washer (food prep., n.e.c.)	521.685-110
RCE	37	Drummer (hat & cap)	589.685-034
RCE	37	Dust-Mop Maker (tex. prod., n.e.c.)	739.687-078
RCE	37	Filler (fabrication, n.e.c.)	739.687-090
RCE	37	Final Assembler (optical goods)	713.687-018
RCE	37	Flare Breaker (boot & shoe)	788.685-010
RCE	37	Glass-Bulb Silverer (glass products)	779.687-018
RCE	37	Gluer (any industry)	795.687-014
RCE	37	Grinder, Hand (button & notion)	734.687-054
RCE	37	Heel Dipper (boot & shoe)	788.687-058

Part 2: From Holland Codes to Occupations

From Holland Codes to the Dictionary of Occupational Titles Occupations

HOC	Cx	Title	DOT
RCE	37	Helper, Metal Hanging (mfd. bldgs.)	806.667-010
RCE	37	Insole-and-Heel-Stiffener (boot & shoe)	788.687-062
RCE	37	Jigger (jewelry-silver.)	705.687-010
RCE	37	Kettle Tender (construction)	869.685-010
RCE	37	Kiln Worker (pottery & porc.)	573.687-022
RCE	37	Laborer, High-Density Press (agriculture)	929.687-018
RCE	37	Lacquerer (clock & watch)	715.684-138
RCE	37	Light-Fixture Servicer (any industry)	389.687-018
RCE	37	Liner Inserter (tobacco)	929.687-026
RCE	37	Log Loader Helper (logging)	921.687-022
RCE	37	Log Washer (saw. & plan.)	569.687-014
RCE	37	Lumpia Wrapper Maker (food prep., n.e.c.)	526.684-014
RCE	37	Lye-Peel Operator (can. & preserv.)	521.685-206
RCE	37	Manual-Plate Filler (ordnance)	737.687-082
RCE	37	Masker (clock & watch)	715.687-086
RCE	37	Mercury-Cracking Tester (ordnance)	737.687-086
RCE	37	Mixer Helper (build. mat., n.e.c.)	550.686-026
RCE	37	Mold-Maker Helper (jewelry-silver.)	700.687-050
RCE	37	Mounter I (light. fix.)	692.686-050
RCE	37	Necker (jewelry-silver.)	692.686-058
RCE	37	Net Washer (rubber goods)	599.687-022
RCE	37	Nut Chopper (can. & preserv.; food prep., n.e.c.; sugar & conf.)	521.686-046
RCE	37	Painter, Bottom (boot & shoe)	788.687-098
RCE	37	Painter, Clock and Watch Hands (clock & watch)	715.687-098
RCE	37	Parts Remover (clock & watch)	715.687-102
RCE	37	Paster, Screen Printing (textile)	652.687-026
RCE	37	Patch Sander (stonework)	775.684-054
RCE	37	Patch Worker (agriculture)	381.687-030
RCE	37	Patching-Machine Operator (laundry & rel.)	361.685-022
RCE	37	Pinner (garment; tex. prod., n.e.c.)	782.687-026
RCE	37	Pleater (textile)	589.685-074
RCE	37	Plug-Cutting-Machine Operator (tobacco)	529.685-182
RCE	37	Pourer (rubber goods)	556.687-026
RCE	37	Racker (jewelry-silver.)	735.687-026
RCE	37	Rag Sorter and Cutter (tex. prod., n.e.c.)	789.687-134
RCE	37	Riddler Operator (tobacco)	521.685-270
RCE	37	Roll Coverer, Burlap (textile)	929.687-042
RCE	37	Rope Cleaner (textile)	699.687-022
RCE	37	Sand-Slinger Operator (foundry)	518.683-010
RCE	37	Scrap Sorter (boot & shoe)	788.687-106
RCE	37	Seed-Potato Arranger (agriculture)	404.685-010
RCE	37	Set-Key Driver (clock & watch)	715.687-118
RCE	37	Slabber (soap & rel.)	559.686-042
RCE	37	Slice-Plug-Cutter-Operator Helper (tobacco)	521.686-054
RCE	37	Smoking-Pipe Liner (fabrication, n.e.c.)	739.687-170
RCE	37	Sorter I (wood prod., n.e.c.)	569.687-022
RCE	37	Spanner (tex. prod., n.e.c.)	689.687-074
RCE	37	Spooling-Machine Operator (tex. prod., n.e.c.)	681.685-114

HOC	Cx	Title	DOT
RCE	37	Starcher (button & notion)	739.687-178
RCE	37	Steak Tenderizer, Machine (meat products)	529.686-082
RCE	37	Steel-Barrel Reamer (wood. container)	703.687-022
RCE	37	Stem Sizer (fabrication, n.e.c.)	692.686-062
RCE	37	Stemmer, Hand (tobacco)	521.687-134
RCE	37	Stemmer, Machine (tobacco)	521.685-334
RCE	37	Sticker (hat & cap)	784.687-070
RCE	37	Sweeper-Cleaner, Industrial (any industry)	389.683-010
RCE	37	Switchbox Assembler I (comm. equip.)	722.687-010
RCE	37	Table Hand (tobacco)	521.687-138
RCE	37	Table Worker (fabrication, n.e.c.)	739.687-182
RCE	37	Tack Puller (boot & shoe)	788.687-146
RCE	37	Tack Puller, Machine (boot & shoe)	690.685-410
RCE	37	Tamale-Machine Feeder (food prep., n.e.c.)	520.686-038
RCE	37	Test Worker (foundry)	519.687-042
RCE	37	Treater (any industry)	582.687-030
RCE	37	Trimming-Machine Operator (toy-sport equip.)	732.685-038
RCE	37	Tube Cleaner (textile)	589.687-042
RCE	37	Twister, Hand (tobacco)	790.687-030
RCE	37	Umbrella Tipper, Machine (fabrication, n.e.c.)	739.685-054
RCE	37	Vamp-Strap Ironer (boot & shoe)	788.687-158
RCE	37	Varnisher (fabrication, n.e.c.)	569.685-070
RCE	37	Ware Server (glass mfg.)	652.686-046
RCE	37	Waxer (glass products)	779.687-038
RCE	37	White-Shoe Ragger (boot & shoe)	788.687-166
RCE	37	Wrapper-Layer-and-Examiner, Soft Work (tobacco)	529.685-270
RCE	36	Bagging Salvager (textile)	689.687-010
RCE	36	Bander, Hand (paper goods)	920.687-026
RCE	36	Base Filler (toy-sport equip.)	732.687-018
RCE	36	Basket Filler (can. & preserv.)	529.687-010
RCE	36	Bead Picker (rubber reclaim.)	551.686-010
RCE	36	Bone Picker (can. & preserv.)	521.687-022
RCE	36	Bone Picker (chemical)	551.687-010
RCE	36	Bung Driver (wood. container)	764.687-042
RCE	36	Burlap Spreader (tex. prod., n.e.c.)	581.687-010
RCE	36	Cane Cutter (furniture)	763.687-030
RCE	36	Cardboard Inserter (knitting)	920.687-062
RCE	36	Cartridge Loader (elec. equip.)	779.687-014
RCE	36	Casing Splitter (meat products)	525.687-014
RCE	36	Casing Tier (meat products)	529.687-034
RCE	36	Chute Loader (mine & quarry)	932.687-010
RCE	36	Core Loader (ordnance)	737.687-030
RCE	36	Drawer Waxer (furniture)	763.687-022
RCE	36	Egg Washer, Machine (agriculture; wholesale tr.)	529.686-030
RCE	36	End-Touching-Machine Operator (wood prod., n.e.c.)	662.686-010
RCE	36	Felt-Tipping-Machine Tender (pen & pencil)	686.686-010
RCE	36	Finishing-Machine Operator (paper goods)	649.686-022
RCE	36	Frame Stripper (chemical)	559.687-046
RCE	36	Garnisher (sugar & conf.)	524.687-014

Part 2: From Holland Codes to Occupations

From Holland Codes to the Dictionary of Occupational Titles Occupations

HOC	Cx	Title	DOT
RCE	36	Harvest Worker, Vegetable (agriculture)	402.687-014
RCE	36	Heat Treater (electron. comp.)	504.686-022
RCE	36	Igniter Capper (ordnance)	737.687-050
RCE	36	Last Cleaner (boot & shoe)	788.687-082
RCE	36	Leaf Tier (tobacco)	529.687-138
RCE	36	Machine Feeder (clock & watch)	715.686-014
RCE	36	Pad-Machine Offbearer (saw. & plan.)	569.686-030
RCE	36	Pairer (tex. prod., n.e.c.)	789.687-110
RCE	36	Paper-Cone-Drying-Machine Operator (paper goods)	532.686-014
RCE	36	Plastic-Design Applier (boot & shoe)	690.686-046
RCE	36	Plugger (wood. container)	764.687-098
RCE	36	Pompom Maker (knitting)	789.687-126
RCE	36	Potato-Chip Sorter (food prep., n.e.c.)	526.687-010
RCE	36	Racker (bakery products)	524.687-018
RCE	36	Remnants Cutter (textile)	789.687-150
RCE	36	Rosin-Barrel Filler (chemical)	920.687-150
RCE	36	Screw-Eye Assembler (ordnance)	737.687-122
RCE	36	Sheller I (can. & preserv.)	521.687-118
RCE	36	Stamp-Pad Finisher (pen & pencil)	733.687-066
RCE	36	Street Cleaner (government ser.)	955.687-018
RCE	36	Stuffer (tex. prod., n.e.c.)	780.687-046
RCE	36	Table Worker (leather prod.)	783.687-030
RCE	36	Third Dry-Cell-Assembling-Machine Tender (elec. equip.)	692.686-066
RCE	36	Tin-Container Straightener (tobacco)	709.687-046
RCE	36	Vine Pruner (agriculture)	403.687-022
RCE	36	Waste-Paper-Hammermill Operator (paper & pulp)	530.686-018
RCE	36	Yard Laborer (paper & pulp)	922.687-102
RCE	35	Back Tufter (furniture)	780.687-062
RCE	35	Buckler and Lacer (boot & shoe)	788.687-022
RCE	35	Bunch Trimmer, Mold (tobacco)	521.687-026
RCE	35	Dowel Inspector (woodworking)	669.687-014
RCE	35	Electrode Cleaner (elec. equip.)	729.687-014
RCE	35	Farm worker, Machine (agriculture)	409.686-010
RCE	35	Mixer II (tex. prod., n.e.c.)	789.687-098
RCE	35	Painter, Depilatory (meat products)	525.687-062
RCE	35	Pan Greaser, Machine (bakery products)	526.685-034
RCE	35	Paper Inserter (glass mfg.)	920.687-138
RCE	35	Puff Ironer (laundry & rel.)	363.687-018
RCE	35	Shank Taper (boot & shoe)	788.687-114
RCE	35	Thread Separator (tex. prod., n.e.c.)	789.687-174
RCE	35	Wire Cutter (svc. ind. mach.)	731.687-038
IRA	78	Microbiologist (profess. & kin.)	041.061-058
IRA	77	Surgeon (medical ser.)	070.101-094
IRA	71	Veterinarian, Poultry (agriculture)	073.101-014
IRS	80	Ceramic Engineer (profess. & kin.)	006.061-014
IRS	80	Crystallographer (clock & watch)	024.061-010
IRS	78	Aeronautical Engineer (aircraft mfg.)	002.061-014

From Holland Codes to the Dictionary of Occupational Titles Occupations

HOC	Cx	Title	DOT
IRS	78	Agronomist (profess. & kin.)	040.061-010
IRS	78	Animal Breeder (profess. & kin.)	041.061-014
IRS	78	Animal Scientist (profess. & kin.)	040.061-014
IRS	78	Biochemist (profess. & kin.)	041.061-026
IRS	78	Botanist (profess. & kin.)	041.061-038
IRS	78	Curator (museums)	102.017-010
IRS	78	Dairy Technologist (profess. & kin.)	040.061-022
IRS	78	Entomologist (profess. & kin.)	041.061-046
IRS	78	Forest Ecologist (profess. & kin.)	040.061-030
IRS	78	Geneticist (profess. & kin.)	041.061-050
IRS	78	Histopathologist (medical ser.)	041.061-054
IRS	78	Horticulturist (profess. & kin.)	040.061-038
IRS	78	Medical Physicist (profess. & kin.)	079.021-014
IRS	78	Mycologist (profess. & kin.)	041.061-062
IRS	78	Nematologist (profess. & kin.)	041.061-066
IRS	78	Parasitologist (profess. & kin.)	041.061-070
IRS	78	Plant Breeder (profess. & kin.)	041.061-082
IRS	78	Plant Pathologist (profess. & kin.)	041.061-086
IRS	78	Poultry Scientist (profess. & kin.)	040.061-042
IRS	78	Psychologist, Engineering (profess. & kin.)	045.061-014
IRS	78	Range Manager (profess. & kin.)	040.061-046
IRS	78	Soil Scientist (profess. & kin.)	040.061-058
IRS	77	Geophysicist (profess. & kin.)	024.061-030
IRS	77	Otolaryngologist (medical ser.)	070.101-062
IRS	77	Stratigrapher (profess. & kin.)	024.061-054
IRS	77	Urologist (medical ser.)	070.101-098
IRS	76	Fiber Technologist (profess. & kin.)	040.061-026
IRS	76	Gynecologist (medical ser.)	070.101-034
IRS	76	Internist (medical ser.)	070.101-042
IRS	76	Neurologist (medical ser.)	070.101-050
IRS	76	Obstetrician (medical ser.)	070.101-054
IRS	76	Police Surgeon (medical ser.)	070.101-082
IRS	76	Proctologist (medical ser.)	070.101-086
IRS	76	Psychologist, Developmental (profess. & kin.)	045.061-010
IRS	76	Public Health Physician (medical ser.)	070.101-046
IRS	76	Radiologist (medical ser.)	070.101-090
IRS	76	Wood Technologist (profess. & kin.)	040.061-062
IRS	75	Chemist, Food (profess. & kin.)	022.061-014
IRS	75	Orthodontist (medical ser.)	072.101-022
IRS	75	Prosthodontist (medical ser.)	072.101-034
IRS	74	Anesthesiologist (medical ser.)	070.101-010
IRS	73	Chemist, Water Purification (waterworks)	022.281-014
IRS	73	Veterinarian (medical ser.)	073.101-010
IRS	71	Chemical Design Engineer, Processes (profess. & kin.)	008.061-014
IRS	71	Chemical Research Engineer (profess. & kin.)	008.061-022
IRS	71	Data Base Design Analyst (profess. & kin.)	039.162-014
IRS	71	Electrical-Research Engineer (profess. & kin.)	003.061-026
IRS	71	Railroad Engineer (profess. & kin.)	005.061-026
IRS	71	Structural Engineer (construction)	005.061-034

HOC	Cx	Title	DOT
IRS	70	Hydraulic Engineer (profess. & kin.)	005.061-018
IRS	70	Meteorologist (profess. & kin.)	025.062-010
IRS	69	Laboratory Manager (education)	090.164-010
IRS	69	Writer, Technical Publications (profess. & kin.)	131.267-026
IRS	67	Chemical Laboratory Technician (profess. & kin.)	022.261-010
IRS	67	Radiation-Protection Specialist (government ser.)	168.261-010
IRS	66	Field Service Technician (machinery mfg.)	638.261-026
IRS	65	Air Analyst (profess. & kin.)	012.261-010
IRS	64	Restorer, Lace and Textiles (museums)	102.361-010
IRS	64	Taxidermist (profess. & kin.)	199.261-010
IRS	63	Master Control Operator (radio-tv broad.)	194.262-022
IRS	62	Photographer, Scientific (profess. & kin.)	143.062-026
IRS	61	Hydrographer (waterworks)	025.264-010
IRS	60	Technician, News Gathering (radio-tv broad.)	194.362-022
IRS	59	Network Control Operator (any industry)	031.262-014
IRS	59	Scientific Helper (profess. & kin.)	199.364-014
IRS	57	Caption Writer (motion picture; radio-tv broad.)	203.362-026
IRS	57	Cloth Tester (garment; textile)	029.381-010
IRS	54	Laboratory Assistant (textile)	029.381-014
IRS	53	Videotape Operator (radio-tv broad.)	194.382-018
IRE	80	Aerodynamicist (aircraft mfg.)	002.061-010
IRE	80	Aeronautical-Research Engineer (aircraft mfg.)	002.061-026
IRE	80	Architect, Marine (profess. & kin.)	001.061-014
IRE	80	Astronomer (profess. & kin.)	021.067-010
IRE	80	Biophysicist (profess. & kin.)	041.061-034
IRE	80	Chemical Engineer (profess. & kin.)	008.061-018
IRE	80	Chief Petroleum Engineer (petrol. & gas)	010.161-014
IRE	80	Cytologist (profess. & kin.)	041.061-042
IRE	80	Electrical-Prospecting Engineer (profess. & kin.)	003.061-022
IRE	80	Electro-Optical Engineer (profess. & kin.)	023.061-010
IRE	80	Environmental Analyst (profess. & kin.)	029.081-010
IRE	80	Geodesist (profess. & kin.)	024.061-014
IRE	80	Geologist (profess. & kin.)	024.061-018
IRE	80	Geophysical-Laboratory Chief (profess. & kin.)	024.167-010
IRE	80	Hydrologist (profess. & kin.)	024.061-034
IRE	80	Metallurgist, Extractive (profess. & kin.)	011.061-018
IRE	80	Metallurgist, Physical (profess. & kin.)	011.061-022
IRE	80	Physicist (profess. & kin.)	023.061-014
IRE	80	Physicist, Theoretical (profess. & kin.)	023.067-010
IRE	80	Planning Engineer, Central Office Facilities (tel. & tel.)	003.061-050
IRE	80	Seismologist (profess. & kin.)	024.061-050
IRE	80	Statistician, Mathematical (profess. & kin.)	020.067-022
IRE	79	Biomedical Engineer (profess. & kin.)	019.061-010
IRE	79	Central-Office Equipment Engineer (tel. & tel.)	003.187-010
IRE	79	Chemist (profess. & kin.)	022.061-010
IRE	79	Chief Engineer, Research (petrol. & gas)	010.161-010
IRE	79	Electrical Engineer, Power System (utilities)	003.167-018
IRE	79	Nuclear Engineer (profess. & kin.)	015.061-014

Part 2: From Holland Codes to Occupations

From Holland Codes to the Dictionary of Occupational Titles Occupations

HOC	Cx	Title	DOT
IRE	79	Operations-Research Analyst (profess. & kin.)	020.067-018
IRE	79	Programmer, Engineering and Scientific (profess. & kin.)	030.162-018
IRE	79	Quality Control Engineer (profess. & kin.)	012.167-054
IRE	78	Anatomist (profess. & kin.)	041.061-010
IRE	78	Apiculturist (profess. & kin.)	041.061-018
IRE	78	Aquatic Biologist (profess. & kin.)	041.061-022
IRE	78	Dairy Scientist (profess. & kin.)	040.061-018
IRE	78	Materials Scientist (profess. & kin.)	029.081-014
IRE	78	Pharmacologist (profess. & kin.)	041.061-074
IRE	78	Physiologist (profess. & kin.)	041.061-078
IRE	78	Soil Conservationist (profess. & kin.)	040.061-054
IRE	78	Zoologist (profess. & kin.)	041.061-090
IRE	77	Geographer (profess. & kin.)	029.067-010
IRE	77	Geographer, Physical (profess. & kin.)	029.067-014
IRE	77	Marine Engineer (profess. & kin.)	014.061-014
IRE	77	Pathologist (medical ser.)	070.061-010
IRE	77	Staff Toxicologist (government ser.)	041.061-094
IRE	77	Veterinary Microbiologist (profess. & kin.)	073.061-018
IRE	76	Agricultural Engineer (profess. & kin.)	013.061-010
IRE	76	Electrolysis-and-Corrosion-Control Engineer (profess. & kin.)	003.167-022
IRE	76	Environmental Epidemiologist (government ser.)	041.167-010
IRE	76	Family Practitioner (medical ser.)	070.101-026
IRE	76	Foundry Metallurgist (foundry)	011.061-010
IRE	76	Health Physicist (profess. & kin.)	015.021-010
IRE	76	Illuminating Engineer (profess. & kin.)	003.061-046
IRE	76	Metallographer (profess. & kin.)	011.061-014
IRE	76	Oral Pathologist (medical ser.)	072.061-010
IRE	76	Physiatrist (medical ser.)	070.101-070
IRE	76	Power-Distribution Engineer (utilities)	003.167-046
IRE	76	Power-Transmission Engineer (utilities)	003.167-050
IRE	76	Time-Study Engineer (profess. & kin.)	012.167-070
IRE	76	Transmission-and-Protection Engineer (tel. & tel.)	003.167-066
IRE	76	Veterinarian, Laboratory Animal Care (medical ser.)	073.061-010
IRE	76	Veterinary Pathologist (medical ser.)	073.061-030
IRE	76	Welding Engineer (profess. & kin.)	011.061-026
IRE	75	Forest Engineer (forestry; logging)	005.167-018
IRE	75	Pediatric Dentist (medical ser.)	072.101-026
IRE	75	Periodontist (medical ser.)	072.101-030
IRE	75	Public-Health Dentist (medical ser.)	072.101-038
IRE	75	Software Engineer (profess. & kin.)	030.062-010
IRE	74	Chief Engineer, Waterworks (waterworks)	005.167-010
IRE	74	Faculty Member, College or University, Life Sciences (education)	090.227-010
IRE	74	Faculty Member, College or University, Chemistry (education)	090.227-010
IRE	74	Faculty Member, College or University, Physics (education)	090.227-010
IRE	74	Faculty Member, College or University, All Other Physical Sciences (education)	090.227-010

From Holland Codes to the Dictionary of Occupational Titles Occupations

HOC	Cx	Title	DOT
IRE	74	Faculty Member, College or University, Mathematical Sciences (education)	090.227-010
IRE	74	Faculty Member, College or University, Computer Science (education)	090.227-010
IRE	74	Manufacturing Engineer (profess. & kin.)	012.167-042
IRE	74	Outside-Plant Engineer (tel. & tel.)	003.167-042
IRE	74	Silviculturist (profess. & kin.)	040.061-050
IRE	74	Statistician, Applied (profess. & kin.)	020.167-026
IRE	73	Anthropologist (profess. & kin.)	055.067-010
IRE	73	Anthropologist, Physical (profess. & kin.)	055.067-014
IRE	73	Archeologist (profess. & kin.)	055.067-018
IRE	73	Civil Engineer (profess. & kin.)	005.061-014
IRE	73	Ethnologist (profess. & kin.)	055.067-022
IRE	73	Industrial Hygienist (profess. & kin.)	079.161-010
IRE	73	Oral and Maxillofacial Surgeon (medical ser.)	072.101-018
IRE	73	Value Engineer (aircraft mfg.)	002.167-010
IRE	73	Veterinary Anatomist (profess. & kin.)	073.061-014
IRE	73	Veterinary Epidemiologist (profess. & kin.)	073.061-022
IRE	73	Veterinary Parasitologist (profess. & kin.)	073.061-026
IRE	73	Veterinary Physiologist (profess. & kin.)	073.061-038
IRE	72	Computer Systems Hardware Analyst (profess. & kin.)	033.167-010
IRE	72	Programmer-Analyst (profess. & kin.)	030.162-014
IRE	72	Supervising Airplane Pilot (government ser.)	196.163-014
IRE	72	Veterinary Meat-Inspector (government ser.)	073.264-010
IRE	72	Veterinary Pharmacologist (profess. & kin.)	073.061-034
IRE	71	Aeronautical-Design Engineer (aircraft mfg.)	002.061-022
IRE	71	Agricultural-Research Engineer (profess. & kin.)	013.061-014
IRE	71	Ceramic Design Engineer (profess. & kin.)	006.061-010
IRE	71	Ceramic Research Engineer (profess. & kin.)	006.061-018
IRE	71	Ceramics Test Engineer (profess. & kin.)	006.061-022
IRE	71	Data Base Administrator (profess. & kin.)	039.162-010
IRE	71	Design Engineer, Marine Equipment (profess. & kin.)	014.061-010
IRE	71	Design Engineer, Mining-and-Oil-Field Equipment (profess. & kin.)	010.061-010
IRE	71	Design Engineer, Nuclear Equipment (profess. & kin.)	015.061-010
IRE	71	Design-Engineer, Agricultural Equipment (profess. & kin.)	013.061-018
IRE	71	Electrical Engineer (profess. & kin.)	003.061-010
IRE	71	Geological Aide (petrol. & gas)	024.267-010
IRE	71	Research Engineer, Marine Equipment (profess. & kin.)	014.061-018
IRE	71	Research Engineer, Mining-and-Oil-Well Equipment (mine & quarry; petrol. & gas)	010.061-022
IRE	71	Research Engineer, Nuclear Equipment (profess. & kin.)	015.061-018
IRE	71	Test Engineer, Agricultural Equipment (profess. & kin.)	013.061-022
IRE	71	Test Engineer, Marine Equipment (profess. & kin.)	014.061-022
IRE	71	Test Engineer, Mining-and-Oil-Field Equipment (mine & quarry; petrol. & gas)	010.061-030
IRE	71	Test Engineer, Nuclear Equipment (profess. & kin.)	015.061-022
IRE	70	Cable Engineer, Outside Plant (tel. & tel.)	003.167-010
IRE	70	Chemical-Engineering Technician (profess. & kin.)	008.261-010

HOC	Cx	Title	DOT
IRE	70	Irrigation Engineer (profess. & kin.)	005.061-022
IRE	70	Mechanical Research Engineer (profess. & kin.)	007.161-022
IRE	70	Supervisor, Metallurgical-and-Quality-Control-Testing (profess. & kin.)	011.161-010
IRE	70	Tool Design Checker (aircraft mfg.)	007.267-014
IRE	70	Tool Planner (any industry)	012.167-074
IRE	69	Ballistics Expert, Forensic (government ser.)	199.267-010
IRE	69	Colorist (profess. & kin.)	022.161-014
IRE	69	Die-Drawing Checker (profess. & kin.)	007.167-010
IRE	69	Drafter, Patent (profess. & kin.)	007.261-018
IRE	69	Electronics Technician (profess. & kin.)	003.161-014
IRE	69	Inspector, Quality Assurance (government ser.)	168.287-014
IRE	69	Supervisor, Electronics Systems Maintenance (any industry)	828.161-010
IRE	69	Surveyor, Mine (profess. & kin.)	018.161-010
IRE	69	Technician, Semiconductor Development (profess. & kin.)	003.161-018
IRE	68	Biochemistry Technologist (medical ser.)	078.261-010
IRE	68	Industrial Engineering Technician (profess. & kin.)	012.267-010
IRE	68	Microbiology Technologist (medical ser.)	078.261-014
IRE	67	Agricultural-Engineering Technician (profess. & kin.)	013.161-010
IRE	67	Check Pilot (air trans.)	196.263-022
IRE	67	Drafter, Automotive Design (auto. mfg.)	017.261-042
IRE	67	Drafter, Mechanical (profess. & kin.)	007.281-010
IRE	67	Hazardous-Waste Management Specialist (government ser.)	168.267-086
IRE	67	Histotechnologist (medical ser.)	078.261-030
IRE	67	Laser Technician (electron. comp.; inst. & app.)	019.261-034
IRE	67	Surveyor, Geodetic (profess. & kin.)	018.167-038
IRE	67	Test Technician (profess. & kin.)	019.161-014
IRE	67	Veterinary Livestock Inspector (government ser.)	073.161-010
IRE	66	Acupuncturist (medical ser.)	079.271-010
IRE	66	Design Drafter, Electromechanisms (profess. & kin.)	017.261-014
IRE	66	Drafter Apprentice (profess. & kin.)	017.281-014
IRE	66	Drafter, Commercial (profess. & kin.)	017.261-026
IRE	66	Drafter, Electronic (profess. & kin.)	003.281-014
IRE	66	Drafter, Marine (profess. & kin.)	014.281-010
IRE	66	Inspector, Water-Pollution Control (government ser.)	168.267-090
IRE	66	Laboratory Assistant (utilities)	029.361-018
IRE	66	Mechanical-Engineering Technician (profess. & kin.)	007.161-026
IRE	66	Tool Programmer, Numerical Control (any industry)	007.167-018
IRE	64	Auto-Design Detailer (auto. mfg.)	017.281-010
IRE	64	Drafter, Civil (profess. & kin.)	005.281-010
IRE	63	Airplane Pilot (agriculture)	196.263-010
IRE	63	Laboratory Tester (plastic-synth.)	022.281-018
IRE	63	Photo-Optics Technician (profess. & kin.)	029.280-010
IRE	63	Pilot-Control Operator (chemical; plastic-synth.)	559.382-046
IRE	62	Examiner, Questioned Documents (government ser.)	199.267-022
IRE	58	Medical-Laboratory Technician (medical ser.)	078.381-014
IRE	54	Inspector, Plating (electroplating)	500.287-010

HOC	Cx	Title	DOT
IRC	80	Nuclear-Fuels Research Engineer (profess. & kin.)	015.061-030
IRC	79	Nuclear-Criticality Safety Engineer (profess. & kin.)	015.067-010
IRC	79	Research Associate (museums)	109.067-014
IRC	79	Stress Analyst (profess. & kin.)	007.061-042
IRC	77	Nuclear-Fuels Reclamation Engineer (profess. & kin.)	015.061-026
IRC	77	Nuclear-Plant Technical Advisor (utilities)	015.167-010
IRC	76	Resource-Recovery Engineer (government ser.)	019.167-018
IRC	75	Waste-Management Engineer, Radioactive Materials (profess. & kin.)	005.061-042
IRC	74	Criminalist (profess. & kin.)	029.261-026
IRC	74	Radiopharmacist (medical ser.)	074.161-014
IRC	70	Engineering Assistant, Mechanical Equipment (profess. & kin.)	007.161-018
IRC	70	Material Scheduler (aircraft mfg.)	012.167-082
IRC	70	Mathematical Technician (profess. & kin.)	020.162-010
IRC	70	Systems Programmer (profess. & kin.)	030.162-022
IRC	69	Computer Programmer (profess. & kin.)	030.162-010
IRC	69	Drafter, Tool Design (profess. & kin.)	007.261-022
IRC	68	Chemist, Instrumentation (profess. & kin.)	022.261-018
IRC	68	Chemist, Wastewater-Treatment Plant (profess. & kin.)	022.261-022
IRC	68	Cytogenetic Technologist (medical ser.)	078.261-026
IRC	68	Pheresis Specialist (medical ser.)	078.261-042
IRC	68	Toxicologist (pharmaceut.)	022.081-010
IRC	67	Controls Designer (profess. & kin.)	003.261-014
IRC	67	Drafter, Geological (petrol. & gas)	010.281-014
IRC	67	Soil-Conservation Technician (profess. & kin.)	040.261-010
IRC	66	Drafter, Aeronautical (aircraft mfg.)	002.261-010
IRC	66	Drafter, Electrical (profess. & kin.)	003.281-010
IRC	66	Drafter, Heating and Ventilating (profess. & kin.)	017.261-034
IRC	66	Drafter, Plumbing (profess. & kin.)	017.261-038
IRC	66	Drafter, Structural (profess. & kin.)	005.281-014
IRC	66	Integrated Circuit Layout Designer (profess. & kin.)	003.261-018
IRC	66	Printed Circuit Designer (profess. & kin.)	003.261-022
IRC	66	Special Procedures Technologist, CT Scan (medical ser.)	078.362-054
IRC	65	Drawings Checker, Engineering (profess. & kin.)	007.267-010
IRC	65	Flight-Test Data Acquisition Technician (aircraft mfg.)	002.262-010
IRC	64	Photogrammetrist (profess. & kin.)	018.261-026
IRC	64	Plan Checker (government ser.)	168.267-102
IRC	64	Special Procedures Technologist, Angiogram (medical ser.)	078.362-046
IRC	63	Test Technician, Semiconductor Processing Equipment (electron. comp.)	590.262-014
IRC	61	Electronics Tester (any industry)	726.261-018
IRC	60	Pulmonary-Function Technician (medical ser.)	078.262-010
IRC	60	Stenocaptioner (radio-tv broad.)	202.382-010
IRC	59	Cephalometric Analyst (medical ser.)	078.384-010
IRC	55	Herbarium Worker (profess. & kin.)	041.384-010
IRC	55	Laboratory Assistant, Culture Media (pharmaceut.)	559.384-010
IAR	80	Biologist (profess. & kin.)	041.061-030

Part 2: From Holland Codes to Occupations

From Holland Codes to the Dictionary of Occupational Titles Occupations

HOC	Cx	Title	DOT
IAS	71	Economist (profess. & kin.)	050.067-010
IAS	71	Editor, Dictionary (profess. & kin.)	132.067-018
IAS	64	Appraiser, Art (profess. & kin.)	191.287-014
●IAE	77	Psychologist, Experimental (profess. & kin.)	045.061-018
●IAE	77	Psychologist, Social (profess. & kin.)	045.067-014
ISR	78	Mineralogist (profess. & kin.)	024.061-038
ISR	77	Petrologist (profess. & kin.)	024.061-046
ISR	76	Dermatologist (medical ser.)	070.101-018
ISR	76	Dietitian, Research (profess. & kin.)	077.061-010
ISR	76	Documentation Engineer (profess. & kin.)	012.167-078
ISR	76	Ophthalmologist (medical ser.)	070.101-058
ISR	76	Osteopathic Physician (medical ser.)	071.101-010
ISR	76	Paleontologist (profess. & kin.)	024.061-042
ISR	75	Dentist (medical ser.)	072.101-010
ISR	74	Faculty Member, College or University, Health Specialties (education)	090.227-010
ISR	74	Safety Engineer (profess. & kin.)	012.061-014
ISR	72	Food Technologist (profess. & kin.)	041.081-010
ISR	71	Airport Engineer (profess. & kin.)	005.061-010
ISR	71	Sanitarian (profess. & kin.)	079.117-018
ISR	71	Transportation Engineer (profess. & kin.)	005.061-038
ISR	69	Audiologist (medical ser.)	076.101-010
ISR	69	Cardiopulmonary Technologist, Chief (medical ser.)	078.161-014
ISR	67	Chiropractor (medical ser.)	079.101-010
ISR	67	Exercise Physiologist (medical ser.)	076.121-018
ISR	66	Nurse, Private Duty (medical ser.)	075.374-018
ISR	63	Acupressurist (medical ser.)	079.271-014
ISR	62	Perfusionist (medical ser.)	078.362-034
ISR	60	Cardiopulmonary Technologist (medical ser.)	078.362-030
ISR	58	Veterinary Technician (medical ser.)	079.361-014
ISR	56	Food Tester (any industry)	029.361-014
ISR	56	Surgical Technician (medical ser.)	079.374-022
ISA	76	Psychiatrist (medical ser.)	070.107-014
ISA	68	Medical Technologist (medical ser.)	078.261-038
ISA	68	Nurse Practitioner (medical ser.)	075.264-010
ISA	66	Physician Assistant (medical ser.)	079.364-018
ISA	63	Video Operator (radio-tv broad.)	194.282-010
ISE	79	Director, Pharmacy Services (medical ser.)	074.167-010
ISE	77	Allergist-Immunologist (medical ser.)	070.101-102
ISE	77	Cardiologist (medical ser.)	070.101-014
ISE	76	General Practitioner (medical ser.)	070.101-022
ISE	76	Pediatrician (medical ser.)	070.101-066
ISE	76	Psychologist, Chief (profess. & kin.)	045.107-046
ISE	76	Zoo Veterinarian (medical ser.)	073.101-018

HOC	Cx	Title	DOT
ISE	75	Director, Speech-and-Hearing (medical ser.)	079.131-010
ISE	75	Endodontist (medical ser.)	072.101-014
ISE	74	Product-Safety Engineer (profess. & kin.)	012.061-010
ISE	72	Actuary (profess. & kin.)	020.167-010
ISE	70	Drafter, Chief, Design (utilities)	017.161-010
ISE	70	Medical Technologist, Teaching Supervisor (medical ser.)	078.121-010
ISE	69	Coroner (government ser.)	168.161-010
ISE	69	Nurse Anesthetist (medical ser.)	075.371-010
ISE	69	Nurse, Supervisor, Community-Health Nursing (medical ser.)	075.127-026
ISE	69	Optometrist (medical ser.)	079.101-018
ISE	69	Perfumer (chemical)	022.161-018
ISE	69	Photographic Engineer (profess. & kin.)	019.081-014
ISE	69	Radiologic Technologist, Chief (medical ser.)	078.162-010
ISE	68	Aerial-Photograph Interpreter (government ser.)	029.167-010
ISE	66	Customs Import Specialist (government ser.)	168.267-018
ISE	66	Nurse, Staff, Occupational Health Nursing (medical ser.)	075.374-022
ISE	66	Research Worker, Encyclopedia (profess. & kin.)	109.267-014
ISE	62	Furniture Reproducer (furniture)	149.281-010
ISC	76	Physician, Occupational (medical ser.)	070.101-078
ISC	76	Public-Health Microbiologist (government ser.)	041.261-010
ISC	72	Scientific Linguist (profess. & kin.)	059.067-014
ISC	71	Translator (profess. & kin.)	137.267-018
ISC	70	Market-Research Analyst I (profess. & kin.)	050.067-014
ISC	64	Research Assistant II (profess. & kin.)	199.267-034
ISC	57	Dialysis Technician (medical ser.)	078.362-014
IER	80	Absorption-and-Adsorption Engineer (profess. & kin.)	008.061-010
IER	80	Chief Engineer (petrol. & gas; pipe lines)	010.167-010
IER	80	Geophysical Prospector (petrol. & gas)	024.061-026
IER	78	Mathematician (profess. & kin.)	020.067-014
IER	78	Medical Coordinator, Pesticide Use (government ser.)	041.067-010
IER	77	Engineer, Soils (profess. & kin.)	024.161-010
IER	76	District Supervisor, Mud-Analysis Well Logging (petrol. & gas)	010.167-014
IER	76	Engineer of System Development (utilities)	003.167-026
IER	76	Nuclear-Test-Reactor Program Coordinator (profess. & kin.)	015.167-014
IER	76	Sanitary Engineer (profess. & kin.)	005.061-030
IER	76	Supervisor, Microwave (radio-tv broad.)	003.167-058
IER	76	Technical Director, Chemical Plant (profess. & kin.)	008.167-010
IER	75	Director, Dental Services (medical ser.)	072.117-010
IER	75	Research Worker, Social Welfare (profess. & kin.)	054.067-010
IER	74	Voice Pathologist (profess. & kin.)	076.104-010
IER	72	Information Scientist (profess. & kin.)	109.067-010
IER	71	Mechanical-Design Engineer, Products (profess. & kin.)	007.061-022
IER	70	Consultant (profess. & kin.)	189.167-010
IER	70	Engineer-In-Charge, Studio Operations (radio-tv broad.)	003.167-030

Part 2: From Holland Codes to Occupations

From Holland Codes to the Dictionary of Occupational Titles Occupations

HOC	Cx	Title	DOT
IER	70	Factory Lay-Out Engineer (profess. & kin.)	012.167-018
IER	70	Industrial Therapist (medical ser.)	076.167-010
IER	70	Project Engineer (profess. & kin.)	019.167-014
IER	69	Manager, Land Surveying (profess. & kin.)	018.167-022
IER	69	Systems Analyst (profess. & kin.)	030.167-014
IER	68	Fire-Investigation Lieutenant (government ser.)	373.267-018
IER	67	Manager, Production, Seed Corn (agriculture)	180.161-010
IER	67	Specification Writer (profess. & kin.)	019.267-010
IER	67	Surveyor Assistant, Instruments (profess. & kin.)	018.167-034
IER	67	Surveyor, Marine (profess. & kin.)	018.167-046
IER	66	Editor, Map (profess. & kin.)	018.261-018
IER	66	Geodetic Computator (profess. & kin.)	018.167-014
IER	66	Scout (petrol. & gas)	010.267-010
IER	65	Surveyor, Geophysical Prospecting (petrol. & gas)	018.167-042
IER	64	Supervisor, Laboratory (textile)	689.134-026
IER	61	Photographer, Aerial (profess. & kin.)	143.062-014
IEA	79	Chemical Laboratory Chief (profess. & kin.)	022.161-010
● IEA	74	Manager, Quality Control (profess. & kin.)	012.167-014
IEA	74	Superintendent, Water-and-Sewer Systems (waterworks)	184.161-014
IEA	73	Manager, Data Processing (profess. & kin.)	169.167-030
IEA	71	Medical Technologist, Chief (medical ser.)	078.161-010
IEA	69	School-Plant Consultant (education)	001.167-010
IEA	67	Chief of Party (profess. & kin.)	018.167-010
IEA	67	Land Surveyor (profess. & kin.)	018.167-018
IEA	57	Still Operator, Batch or Continuous (chemical)	552.362-022
IES	80	Aeronautical Project Engineer (aircraft mfg.)	002.167-018
IES	79	Engineering Manager, Electronics (profess. & kin.)	003.167-070
IES	77	Psychologist, Educational (profess. & kin.)	045.067-010
IES	76	Metrologist (profess. & kin.)	012.067-010
IES	76	Psychologist, Industrial-Organizational (profess. & kin.)	045.107-030
IES	75	Applications Engineer, Manufacturing (profess. & kin.)	007.061-038
IES	75	Clinical Therapist (profess. & kin.)	045.107-050
● IES	74	Public Health Service Officer (government ser.)	187.117-050
IES	74	Safety Manager (profess. & kin.)	012.167-058
IES	73	Electronics-Test Engineer (profess. & kin.)	003.061-042
IES	73	Occupational Analyst (profess. & kin.)	166.067-010
IES	73	Sociologist (profess. & kin.)	054.067-014
IES	72	Pharmacist (medical ser.)	074.161-010
IES	71	Electrical Test Engineer (profess. & kin.)	003.061-014
● IES	70	Appraiser (government ser.)	188.167-010
IES	70	Psychometrist (profess. & kin.)	045.067-018
IES	69	Nurse, Supervisor, Occupational Health Nursing (medical ser.)	075.137-010
IES	67	Job Analyst (profess. & kin.)	166.267-018
IEC	80	Pollution-Control Engineer (profess. & kin.)	019.081-018

Part 2: From Holland Codes to Occupations

From Holland Codes to the Dictionary of Occupational Titles Occupations

HOC	Cx	Title	DOT
IEC	79	Highway-Administrative Engineer (government ser.)	005.167-022
IEC	75	Fire-Protection Engineer (profess. & kin.)	012.167-026
IEC	73	Photogrammetric Engineer (profess. & kin.)	018.167-026
ICR	79	Reliability Engineer (profess. & kin.)	019.061-026
ICR	70	Auditor, Internal (profess. & kin.)	160.167-034
ICR	70	Management Analyst (profess. & kin.)	161.167-010
ICR	69	Chief Drafter (profess. & kin.)	007.261-010
ICR	66	Cytotechnologist (medical ser.)	078.281-010
ICR	66	Navigator (air trans.)	196.167-014
ICR	64	Mosaicist (profess. & kin.)	018.261-022
ICS	66	Immunohematologist (medical ser.)	078.261-046
ICS	63	Packaging Engineer (profess. & kin.)	019.187-010
ARI	66	Technical Illustrator (profess. & kin.)	017.281-034
ARI	64	Modeler (brick & tile)	777.081-010
ARI	63	Costumer (motion picture; radio-tv broad.)	346.261-010
ARI	61	Model Maker I (any industry)	777.261-010
ARI	60	Sketch Maker, Photoengraving (print. & pub.)	970.281-026
ARI	56	Glazier, Stained Glass (glass products)	779.381-010
ARS	62	Ornamental-Metalwork Designer (struct. metal)	142.061-034
ARS	62	Photographer, Still (profess. & kin.)	143.062-030
ARS	61	Stage Technician (amuse. & rec.)	962.261-014
ARS	51	Pewter Finisher (jewelry-silver.)	700.281-026
ARS	44	Wallcovering Texturer (paper goods)	749.684-054
ARE	65	Stone Carver (stonework)	771.281-014
ARE	61	Displayer, Merchandise (retail trade)	298.081-010
ARE	60	Miniature-Set Constructor (motion picture)	962.381-018
ARE	59	Floral Designer (retail trade)	142.081-010
ARE	58	Lay-Out Former (business ser.)	970.381-018
ARE	58	Pastry Chef (water trans.)	315.131-014
ARE	53	Engrosser (profess. & kin.)	970.661-010
ARE	53	Painter, Hand (any industry)	970.381-022
ARE	50	Cake Decorator (bakery products)	524.381-010
AIR	78	Architect (profess. & kin.)	001.061-010
AIR	75	Landscape Architect (profess. & kin.)	001.061-018
AIS	68	Restorer, Paper-and-Prints (library; museums)	109.361-010
AIS	63	Philologist (profess. & kin.)	059.067-010
AIE	74	Faculty Member, College or University, English and Foreign Languages (education)	090.227-010
AIE	73	Writer, Prose, Fiction and Nonfiction (profess. & kin.)	131.067-046
AIE	71	Cryptanalyst (government ser.)	199.267-014
AIE	67	Illustrator, Medical and Scientific (profess. & kin.)	141.061-026

Part 2: From Holland Codes to Occupations

From Holland Codes to the Dictionary of Occupational Titles Occupations

HOC	Cx	Title	DOT
AIE	66	Set Designer (motion picture; radio-tv broad.)	142.061-046
ASR	65	Fashion Designer (profess. & kin.)	142.061-018
ASR	62	Paintings Restorer (profess. & kin.)	102.261-014
ASR	60	Exhibit Builder (museums)	739.261-010
ASR	60	Optical-Effects-Camera Operator (motion picture)	143.260-010
ASR	59	Pewterer (jewelry-silver.)	700.261-010
ASR	46	Inspector, Screen Printing (print. & pub.)	979.667-010
ASI	68	Restorer, Ceramic (museums)	102.361-014
ASI	67	Copy Writer (profess. & kin.)	131.067-014
ASI	67	Reporter (print. & pub.; radio-tv broad.)	131.262-018
ASI	66	Dance Therapist (medical ser.)	076.127-018
ASI	65	Laserist (amuse. & rec.)	159.042-010
ASI	65	Painter (profess. & kin.)	144.061-010
ASI	63	Exhibit Artist (museums)	149.261-010
ASE	75	Composer (profess. & kin.)	152.067-014
ASE	74	Faculty Member, College or University, Art, Drama, and Music (education)	090.227-010
ASE	73	Editor, Technical and Scientific Publications (profess. & kin.)	132.017-018
ASE	72	Cue Selector (radio-tv broad.)	152.067-018
ASE	70	Director, Motion Picture (motion picture)	159.067-010
ASE	70	Humorist (profess. & kin.)	131.067-026
ASE	70	Playwright (profess. & kin.)	131.067-038
ASE	70	Public-Relations Representative (profess. & kin.)	165.167-014
ASE	70	Story Editor (motion picture; radio-tv broad.)	132.037-026
ASE	69	Librettist (profess. & kin.)	131.067-030
ASE	67	Exhibit Designer (museums)	142.061-058
ASE	67	Lyricist (profess. & kin.)	131.067-034
ASE	66	Stained Glass Artist (profess. & kin.)	142.061-054
ASE	66	Teacher, Art (education)	149.021-010
ASE	66	Teacher, Secondary School, English (education)	091.227-010
ASE	65	Biographer (profess. & kin.)	052.067-010
ASE	65	Dramatic Coach (profess. & kin.)	150.027-010
ASE	65	Teacher, Drama (education)	150.027-014
ASE	64	Crossword-Puzzle Maker (print. & pub.)	139.087-010
ASE	64	Supervisor, Show Operations (amuse. & rec.)	969.137-014
ASE	63	Cantor (profess. & kin.)	129.027-010
ASE	63	Instructor, Dancing (education)	151.027-014
ASE	63	Production Manager, Advertising (profess. & kin.)	141.137-010
ASE	61	Supervisor, Artist, Suspect (government ser.)	970.131-014
ASE	59	Artist, Suspect (government ser.)	970.361-018
ASE	59	Pastry Chef (hotel & rest.)	313.131-022
ASE	58	Quick Sketch Artist (amuse. & rec.)	149.041-010
ASE	56	Instructor, Modeling (education)	099.227-026
ASC	65	Musician, Instrumental (amuse. & rec.)	152.041-010

Part 2: From Holland Codes to Occupations

From Holland Codes to the Dictionary of Occupational Titles Occupations

HOC	Cx	Title	DOT
ASC	65	Police Artist (government ser.)	141.061-034
ASC	57	Type Copyist (machinery mfg.)	970.381-042
ASC	56	Optical-Effects Layout Person (motion picture)	962.361-010
ASC	48	Singing Messenger (business ser.)	230.647-010
AER	69	Safety-Clothing-and-Equipment Developer (profess. & kin.)	142.061-038
AER	66	Cloth Designer (profess. & kin.)	142.061-014
AER	66	Sculptor (profess. & kin.)	144.061-018
AER	65	Commercial Designer (profess. & kin.)	141.061-038
AER	65	Graphic Designer (profess. & kin.)	141.061-018
AER	64	Fashion Artist (retail trade)	141.061-014
AER	64	Illustrator (profess. & kin.)	141.061-022
AER	63	Bank-Note Designer (government ser.)	142.061-010
AER	63	Make-Up Artist (amuse. & rec.; motion picture; radio-tv broad.)	333.071-010
AER	62	Memorial Designer (stonework)	142.061-030
AER	61	Dancer (amuse. & rec.)	151.047-010
AER	55	Salesperson, Flowers (retail trade)	260.357-026
AER	53	Acrobat (amuse. & rec.)	159.247-010
AER	53	Equestrian (amuse. & rec.)	159.344-010
AER	52	Wire Walker (amuse. & rec.)	159.347-022
AER	49	Body-Make-Up Artist (amuse. & rec.; motion picture)	333.271-010
AER	47	Double (motion picture; radio-tv broad.)	961.364-010
AEI	77	Intelligence Research Specialist (profess. & kin.)	059.167-010
AEI	75	Arranger (profess. & kin.)	152.067-010
AEI	75	Orchestrator (profess. & kin.)	152.067-022
AEI	69	Screen Writer (motion picture; radio-tv broad.)	131.067-050
AEI	66	Newswriter (print. & pub.; radio-tv broad.)	131.262-014
AEI	65	Package Designer (profess. & kin.)	142.081-018
AEI	65	Puppeteer (amuse. & rec.)	159.041-014
AEI	59	Mime (amuse. & rec.)	159.047-022
AES	73	Editor, Book (print. & pub.)	132.067-014
AES	73	Editor, City (print. & pub.)	132.037-014
AES	73	Editor, Newspaper (print. & pub.)	132.017-014
AES	73	Editor, Publications (print. & pub.)	132.037-022
AES	72	Columnist/Commentator (print. & pub.; radio-tv broad.)	131.067-010
AES	72	Director, Music (motion picture; radio-tv broad.)	152.047-018
AES	72	Manager, Advertising (any industry)	164.117-010
AES	70	Archivist (profess. & kin.)	101.167-010
AES	70	Critic (print. & pub.; radio-tv broad.)	131.067-018
AES	70	Editorial Writer (print. & pub.)	131.067-022
AES	69	Art Director (motion picture; radio-tv broad.)	142.061-062
AES	69	Bureau Chief (print. & pub.)	132.067-010
AES	69	Choral Director (profess. & kin.)	152.047-010
AES	69	Director of Photography (motion picture; radio-tv broad.)	143.062-010
AES	69	Director, Program (radio-tv broad.)	184.167-030

Part 2: From Holland Codes to Occupations

From Holland Codes to the Dictionary of Occupational Titles Occupations

HOC	Cx	Title	DOT
AES	69	Editor, Department (print. & pub.)	132.037-018
AES	69	Editor, News (print. & pub.)	132.067-026
AES	69	Poet (profess. & kin.)	131.067-042
AES	69	Supervisor, Historic Sites (government ser.)	102.117-010
AES	69	Supervisor, Scenic Arts (motion picture; radio-tv broad.)	149.031-010
AES	67	Art Director (profess. & kin.)	141.031-010
AES	67	Audiovisual Production Specialist (profess. & kin.)	149.061-010
AES	67	Choreographer (amuse. & rec.)	151.027-010
AES	67	Conductor, Orchestra (profess. & kin.)	152.047-014
AES	67	Creative Director (profess. & kin.)	141.067-010
AES	67	Director, Stage (amuse. & rec.)	150.067-010
AES	67	Intelligence Specialist (government ser.)	059.267-010
AES	67	Sales-Service Promoter (any industry)	165.167-010
AES	66	Furniture Designer (furniture)	142.061-022
AES	66	Illustrator, Set (motion picture; radio-tv broad.)	141.061-030
AES	66	Industrial Designer (profess. & kin.)	142.061-026
AES	66	Set Designer (amuse. & rec.)	142.061-050
AES	66	Teacher, Music (education)	152.021-010
AES	65	Account Executive (business ser.)	164.167-010
AES	65	Interior Designer (profess. & kin.)	142.051-014
AES	65	Manager, Advertising Agency (business ser.)	164.117-014
AES	65	Manager, Display (retail trade)	142.031-014
AES	65	Printmaker (profess. & kin.)	144.061-014
AES	65	Set Decorator (motion picture; radio-tv broad.)	142.061-042
AES	65	Singer (amuse. & rec.; motion picture; radio-tv broad.)	152.047-022
AES	64	Color Expert (profess. & kin.)	141.051-010
AES	64	Editor, Greeting Card (print. & pub.)	132.067-022
AES	64	Reader (motion picture; radio-tv broad.)	131.087-014
AES	64	Sales Representative, Graphic Art (business ser.)	254.251-010
AES	64	Young-Adult Librarian (library)	100.167-034
AES	63	Continuity Writer (radio-tv broad.)	131.087-010
AES	63	Display Designer (profess. & kin.)	142.051-010
AES	63	Film or Videotape Editor (motion picture; radio-tv broad.)	962.262-010
AES	63	Narrator (motion picture)	150.147-010
AES	63	Program Coordinator (amuse. & rec.)	139.167-010
AES	62	Actor (amuse. & rec.)	150.047-010
AES	62	Artist and Repertoire Manager (amuse. & rec.)	159.167-010
AES	62	Camera Operator (motion picture; radio-tv broad.)	143.062-022
AES	62	Cartoonist (print. & pub.)	141.061-010
AES	62	Cartoonist, Motion Pictures (motion picture; radio-tv broad.)	141.081-010
AES	62	Photographer, Apprentice (profess. & kin.)	143.062-018
AES	61	Ventriloquist (amuse. & rec.)	159.044-010
AES	60	Impersonator (amuse. & rec.)	159.047-018
AES	60	Supervisor, Sign Shop (fabrication, n.e.c.)	970.137-010
AES	60	Wedding Consultant (retail trade)	299.357-018
AES	59	Comedian (amuse. & rec.)	159.047-014
AES	59	Copyist (garment)	142.281-010
AES	59	Sight-Effects Specialist (amuse. & rec.)	962.267-010

Part 2: From Holland Codes to Occupations

From Holland Codes to the Dictionary of Occupational Titles Occupations

HOC	Cx	Title	DOT
AES	58	Magician (amuse. & rec.)	159.041-010
AES	58	Silhouette Artist (amuse. & rec.)	149.051-010
AES	57	Contestant Coordinator (radio-tv broad.)	166.167-010
AES	57	Decorator (dairy products)	524.381-014
AES	55	Milliner (retail trade)	784.261-010
AES	52	Instructor, Painting (retail trade)	297.451-010
AES	51	Sales Representative, Dancing Instructions (education)	259.357-014
AES	49	Playroom Attendant (any industry)	359.677-026
AES	46	Amusement Park Entertainer (amuse. & rec.)	159.647-010
AES	45	Model, Photographers' (any industry)	961.367-010
AES	42	Model, Artists' (any industry)	961.667-010
AEC	59	Photojournalist (print. & pub.; radio-tv broad.)	143.062-034
AEC	50	Colorist, Photography (photofinishing)	970.381-010
AEC	49	Psychic Reader (amuse. & rec.)	159.647-018
AEC	46	Tattoo Artist (personal ser.)	339.571-010
ACS	61	Fur Designer (fur goods)	142.081-014
ACS	56	Graphologist (profess. & kin.)	199.267-038
SRI	66	Special Agent, Customs (government ser.)	188.167-090
SRI	65	Equal Opportunity Officer (any industry)	168.267-114
SRI	64	Radiologic Technologist (medical ser.)	078.362-026
SRI	57	Supervisor, Corduroy Cutting (textile)	585.130-010
SRI	55	Mental-Retardation Aide (medical ser.)	355.377-018
SRI	52	Quality Assurance Group Leader (auto. mfg.)	806.367-014
SRI	51	Phlebotomist (medical ser.)	079.364-022
SRI	51	Physical-Integration Practitioner (medical ser.)	076.264-010
SRE	69	Instructor, Pilot (air trans.)	196.223-014
SRE	68	Instructor, Flying I (education)	196.223-010
SRE	67	Apprenticeship Consultant (government ser.)	188.117-010
SRE	67	Community Dietitian (profess. & kin.)	077.127-010
SRE	67	Marine-Cargo Surveyor (business ser.)	168.267-094
SRE	67	Occupational Therapist (medical ser.)	076.121-010
SRE	66	Manual-Arts Therapist (medical ser.)	076.124-010
SRE	64	Athletic Trainer (amuse. & rec.; education)	153.224-010
SRE	63	Detective, Narcotics and Vice (government ser.)	375.267-014
SRE	61	Coach, Professional Athletes (amuse. & rec.)	153.227-010
SRE	61	Instructor, Bus, Trolley, and Taxi (motor trans.; r.r. trans.)	919.223-010
SRE	60	Coating-Mixer Supervisor (paper & pulp)	530.132-010
SRE	60	Supervisor, Paper Coating (paper & pulp; paper goods)	534.132-014
SRE	59	Animal Keeper, Head (amuse. & rec.)	412.137-010
SRE	59	Cooking, Casing, and Drying Supervisor (tobacco)	529.135-010
SRE	59	Cosmetics Supervisor (pharmaceut.)	550.131-010
SRE	59	Investigator, Narcotics (government ser.)	375.267-018
SRE	59	Supervisor, Assembly (motor-bicycles)	806.131-014
SRE	59	Supervisor, Clay Preparation (pottery & porc.)	570.130-010
SRE	59	Supervisor, Cooler Service (svc. ind. mach.)	637.131-010
SRE	59	Supervisor, Decorating (pottery & porc.)	749.131-010

HOC to DOT

HOC	Cx	Title	DOT
SRE	59	Supervisor, Film Processing (motion picture; photofinishing; radio-tv broad.)	976.131-014
SRE	59	Supervisor, Lace Tearing (tex. prod., n.e.c.)	689.134-014
SRE	59	Supervisor, Mixing (textile)	680.130-014
SRE	59	Supervisor, Mold Construction (concrete prod.)	860.131-026
SRE	59	Supervisor, Pond (chemical)	939.130-010
SRE	59	Supervisor, Silk-Screen Cutting and Printing (any industry)	979.131-018
SRE	59	Supervisor, Tufting (carpet & rug)	687.132-010
SRE	58	Supervisor, Roller Printing (textile)	652.130-018
SRE	58	Supervisor, Shipping (chemical)	550.137-018
SRE	57	Music Librarian (radio-tv broad.)	100.367-022
SRE	57	Supervisor, Char House (sugar & conf.)	523.132-010
SRE	56	Chiropractor Assistant (medical ser.)	079.364-010
SRE	56	Supervisor, Cutting Department (pen & pencil)	669.130-014
SRE	55	Cook, Larder (water trans.)	315.381-014
SRE	55	Supervisor II (chemical)	550.132-010
SRE	54	Plant Supervisor (grain-feed mills)	529.132-014
SRE	54	Recruiter (military ser.)	166.267-026
SRE	54	Survival Specialist (military ser.)	378.227-018
SRE	53	Sulky Driver (amuse. & rec.)	153.244-014
SRE	53	Supervisor, Wood-Crew (saw. & plan.)	669.137-010
SRE	52	Border Guard (government ser.)	375.363-010
SRE	52	Marksmanship Instructor (military ser.)	378.227-010
SRE	51	Animal Treatment Investigator (nonprofit org.)	379.263-010
SRE	51	Recruit Instructor (military ser.)	378.227-014
SRE	50	Kennel Manager, Dog Track (amuse. & rec.)	349.367-010
SRE	49	Checker, Dump Grounds (business ser.)	219.367-010
SRE	46	Amusement Park Worker (amuse. & rec.)	349.664-010
SRE	45	Glove-Parts Inspector (glove & mit.)	781.687-034
SRE	45	Orderly (medical ser.)	355.674-018
SRE	44	Inspector, Shipping (agric. equip.)	801.667-010
SRC	67	News Librarian (library)	100.167-038
SRC	61	Supervisor, Endless Track Vehicle (automotive ser.)	620.131-010
SRC	60	Audiometrist (profess. & kin.)	078.362-010
SRC	60	Supervisor, Phosphoric Acid (chemical)	558.132-014
SRC	58	Supervisor, Film Processing (photofinishing)	976.132-010
SRC	56	Canary Breeder (agriculture)	411.161-010
SRC	56	Job Development Specialist (profess. & kin.)	166.267-034
SRC	55	Craft Demonstrator (museums)	109.364-010
SRC	54	Certified Medication Technician (medical ser.)	355.374-014
SRC	54	Photographer, Finish (amuse. & rec.)	143.382-014
SRC	54	Professional Athlete (amuse. & rec.)	153.341-010
SRC	50	Hoof and Shoe Inspector (amuse. & rec.)	153.287-010
SRC	47	Respiratory-Therapy Aide (medical ser.)	355.674-022
SRC	45	Driver (motor trans.)	913.663-018
SRC	45	Vending-Machine Attendant (hotel & rest.)	319.464-014
SRC	43	Sales Attendant, Building Materials (retail trade)	299.677-014

HOC	Cx	Title	DOT
SIR	72	Doctor, Naturopathic (medical ser.)	079.101-014
SIR	67	Horticultural Therapist (medical ser.)	076.124-018
SIR	66	Evaluator (education)	094.267-010
SIR	65	Podiatrist (medical ser.)	079.101-022
SIR	63	Corrective Therapist (medical ser.)	076.361-010
SIR	63	Nurse, Office (medical ser.)	075.374-014
SIR	63	Nurse-Midwife (medical ser.)	075.264-014
SIR	57	Respiratory Therapist (medical ser.)	076.361-014
SIR	51	Cardiac Monitor Technician (medical ser.)	078.367-010
SIA	74	Clinical Psychologist (profess. & kin.)	045.107-022
SIA	73	Psychologist, Counseling (profess. & kin.)	045.107-026
SIA	67	Inspector, Heating and Refrigeration (government ser.)	168.167-046
SIA	66	Nurse, General Duty (medical ser.)	075.364-010
SIE	74	Faculty Member, College or University, Social Sciences (education)	090.227-010
SIE	74	Medical-Record Administrator (medical ser.)	079.167-014
SIE	73	Consultant, Educational, State Board of Nursing (government ser.)	075.117-010
SIE	71	Nurse, Instructor (medical ser.)	075.124-018
SIE	69	Chief Technologist, Nuclear Medicine (medical ser.)	078.131-010
SIE	69	Nurse, Staff, Community Health (medical ser.)	075.124-014
SIE	67	Dietitian, Clinical (profess. & kin.)	077.127-014
SIE	67	Dietitian, Teaching (profess. & kin.)	077.127-022
SIE	67	Nurse, School (medical ser.)	075.124-010
SIE	67	Nurse, Supervisor, Evening-or-Night (medical ser.)	075.127-030
SIE	67	Physical Therapist (education; medical ser.)	076.121-014
SIE	67	Veterinary Virus-Serum Inspector (government ser.)	073.261-010
SIE	66	Probation-and-Parole Officer (profess. & kin.)	195.107-046
SIE	64	Claim Examiner (insurance)	168.267-014
SIE	64	District Supervisor (motor trans.)	184.117-018
SIE	64	Investigator (government ser.)	168.267-062
SIE	56	Supervisor, Mixing (tex. prod., n.e.c.)	680.135-010
SIE	52	Comparison Shopper (retail trade; wholesale tr.)	296.367-014
SIC	63	Editor, Index (print. & pub.)	132.367-010
SIC	61	Patient-Resources-and-Reimbursement Agent (government ser.)	195.267-018
SIC	58	Telecommunicator (government ser.)	379.362-018
SAI	68	Speech Pathologist (profess. & kin.)	076.107-010
SAI	65	Librarian (library)	100.127-014
SAI	64	Acquisitions Librarian (library)	100.267-010
SAI	60	Dental Hygienist (medical ser.)	078.361-010
SAI	58	Dental Assistant (medical ser.)	079.361-018
SAE	73	Clergy Member (profess. & kin.)	120.107-010

Part 2: From Holland Codes to Occupations

From Holland Codes to the Dictionary of Occupational Titles Occupations

HOC	Cx	Title	DOT
SAE	70	Music Therapist (medical ser.)	076.127-014
SAE	69	Graduate Assistant (education)	090.227-014
SAE	68	Counselor (profess. & kin.)	045.107-010
SAE	68	Counselor, Marriage and Family (profess. & kin.)	045.107-054
SAE	67	Art Therapist (medical ser.)	076.127-010
SAE	67	Director, Instructional Material (education)	099.167-018
SAE	66	Food and Drug Inspector (government ser.)	168.267-042
SAE	66	Teacher, Elementary School (education)	092.227-010
SAE	66	Teacher, Secondary School, Home Economics (education)	091.227-010
SAE	66	Teacher, Secondary School, Speech (education)	091.227-010
SAE	66	Teacher, Secondary School, Subject Not Specified (education)	091.227-010
SAE	62	Teacher, Preschool (education)	092.227-018
SAE	49	Nursery School Attendant (any industry)	359.677-018
SAC	56	Nurse, Licensed Practical (medical ser.)	079.374-014
SER	74	Director, Unemployment Insurance (government ser.)	188.117-094
SER	73	Director, Educational, Community-Health Nursing (medical ser.)	075.117-018
SER	71	Director, Institution (any industry)	187.117-018
SER	70	Administrator, Health Care Facility (medical ser.)	187.117-010
SER	70	Director, Agricultural Services (government ser.)	188.117-038
SER	70	Director, Consumer Affairs (government ser.)	188.117-050
SER	70	Director, Licensing and Registration (government ser.)	188.117-074
SER	69	Assistant Branch Manager, Financial Institution (financial)	186.167-070
SER	69	Commissioner, Public Works (government ser.)	188.117-030
SER	69	Counselor, Nurses' Association (medical ser.)	045.107-014
SER	69	Director, Arts-and-Humanities Council (government ser.)	188.117-042
SER	69	District Customs Director (government ser.)	188.117-098
SER	69	Manager, Department Store (retail trade)	185.117-010
SER	67	Chief, Fishery Division (government ser.)	188.117-018
SER	67	Director, Athletic (education)	090.117-022
SER	67	Director, Commission For The Blind (government ser.)	094.117-010
SER	67	Director, Field Representatives (government ser.)	188.117-062
SER	67	Instructor, Correspondence School (education)	099.227-014
SER	67	Lease Buyer (mine & quarry; petrol. & gas)	191.117-030
SER	67	Research Analyst (insurance)	169.267-034
SER	67	Technical Support Specialist (profess. & kin.)	033.162-018
SER	66	Chief Librarian, Branch or Department (library)	100.127-010
SER	66	Children's Librarian (library)	100.167-018
SER	66	Counterintelligence Agent (military ser.)	378.267-010
SER	66	Data Recovery Planner (profess. & kin.)	033.162-014
SER	66	Executive Director, Sheltered Workshop (nonprofit org.)	187.117-026
SER	66	Instructor, Vocational Training (education)	097.221-010
SER	66	Manager, Recreation Establishment (amuse. & rec.)	187.117-042
SER	66	Police Chief (government ser.)	375.117-010
SER	66	Rental Manager, Public Events Facilities (business ser.)	186.117-062
SER	66	Steward, Racetrack (amuse. & rec.)	153.117-022

Part 2: From Holland Codes to Occupations

From Holland Codes to the Dictionary of Occupational Titles Occupations

HOC	Cx	Title	DOT
SER	66	Wildlife Agent, Regional (government ser.)	379.137-018
SER	65	Emergency Medical Services Coordinator (medical ser.)	079.117-010
SER	65	Executive Chef (hotel & rest.)	187.161-010
SER	65	General Claims Agent (air trans.; motor trans.; r.r. trans.; water trans.)	186.117-030
SER	65	Housing-Management Officer (government ser.)	188.117-110
SER	65	Instructor, Physical Education (education)	099.224-010
SER	65	Manager, Christmas-Tree Farm (forestry)	180.117-010
SER	65	Manager, Hotel Recreational Facilities (amuse. & rec.)	187.167-122
SER	65	Manager, Promotion (hotel & rest.)	163.117-018
SER	65	Research Assistant I (profess. & kin.)	109.267-010
SER	65	Show Host/Hostess (radio-tv broad.)	159.147-018
SER	64	Air-Traffic Coordinator (government ser.)	193.162-010
SER	64	General Manager, Road Production (amuse. & rec.)	187.117-034
SER	64	Librarian, Special Collections (library)	100.267-014
SER	64	Teacher, Learning Disabled (education)	094.227-030
SER	64	Utilization Coordinator (radio-tv broad.)	169.167-078
SER	63	Inspector, Health Care Facilities (government ser.)	168.167-042
SER	63	Manager, Internal Security (business ser.)	376.137-010
SER	63	Orientation and Mobility Therapist For The Blind (education; medical ser.; nonprofit org.)	076.224-014
SER	63	Quality Assurance Supervisor (auto. mfg.)	806.137-022
SER	63	Supervisor, Audit Clerks (clerical)	210.132-010
SER	63	Supervisor, Publications Production (print. & pub.)	979.131-010
SER	62	Air-Traffic-Control Specialist, Tower (government ser.)	193.162-018
SER	62	Customs Patrol Officer (government ser.)	168.167-010
SER	62	Supervisor, Screen Printing (textile)	652.137-014
SER	61	Manager, Casino (amuse. & rec.)	187.167-070
SER	61	Manager, Dude Ranch (amuse. & rec.)	187.167-094
SER	61	Section Supervisor (mine & quarry)	939.137-018
SER	60	Guide, Chief Airport (air trans.)	353.137-010
SER	60	Jockey Agent (amuse. & rec.)	191.117-026
SER	60	Manager, Fast Food Services (retail trade; wholesale tr.)	185.137-010
SER	60	Superintendent, Labor Utilization (any industry)	189.167-042
SER	60	Supervisor, Calendering (paper & pulp)	534.132-010
SER	60	Supervisor, Dental Laboratory (protective dev.)	712.131-010
SER	60	Supervisor, Electronic Coils (elec. equip.; electron. comp.)	724.130-010
SER	60	Supervisor, Meter-and-Regulator Shop (petrol. refin.; utilities)	710.137-014
SER	60	Teacher, Adult Education (education)	099.227-030
SER	60	Testing and Analysis Department Supervisor (can. & preserv.)	523.131-010
SER	60	Transportation Inspector (motor trans.; r.r. trans.)	168.167-082
SER	59	Attendance Officer (education)	168.367-010
SER	59	Correction Officer, Head (government ser.)	372.137-010
SER	59	Detective (government ser.)	375.267-010
SER	59	Employee Relations Specialist (profess. & kin.)	166.267-042
SER	59	Highway-Maintenance Supervisor (government ser.)	899.134-010
SER	59	Investigator, Vice (government ser.)	375.267-022

HOC	Cx	Title	DOT
SER	59	Pharmaceutical-Compounding Supervisor (pharmaceut.)	559.131-010
SER	59	Sanitary-Landfill Supervisor (sanitary ser.)	955.133-010
SER	59	Senior-Commissary Agent (air trans.)	922.137-010
SER	59	Supervisor, Artificial Breeding Ranch (agriculture)	410.131-014
SER	59	Supervisor, Assembly I (office machines)	710.137-010
SER	59	Supervisor, Automobile Body Repair (automotive ser.)	807.137-010
SER	59	Supervisor, Coin-Machine (svc. ind. mach.)	706.130-010
SER	59	Supervisor, Commissary Production (hotel & rest.)	319.137-022
SER	59	Supervisor, Finishing (furniture)	742.134-010
SER	59	Supervisor, Hospitality House (amuse. & rec.)	359.137-010
SER	59	Supervisor, Ordnance Truck Installation (ordnance)	806.137-014
SER	59	Supervisor, Ready-Mixed Food Preparation (food prep., n.e.c.)	529.137-054
SER	59	Supervisor, Sample (plastic-synth.)	754.137-010
SER	59	Supervisor, Small Appliance Assembly (house. appl.)	723.131-010
SER	59	Supervisor, Tumblers (ordnance)	599.132-010
SER	59	Taster (food prep., n.e.c.)	529.281-010
SER	59	Transfer-and-Pumphouse Operator, Chief (chemical)	559.132-138
SER	58	Assembly Supervisor (any industry)	739.137-010
SER	58	Community Worker (government ser.)	195.367-018
SER	58	Cook, Head, School Cafeteria (hotel & rest.)	313.131-018
SER	58	Supervisor, Electrical Assembly (elec. equip.)	729.130-010
SER	58	Supervisor, Hand Silvering (glass products)	574.134-010
SER	57	Animal-Ride Manager (amuse. & rec.)	349.224-010
SER	57	Follow-Up Clerk (elec. equip.)	221.367-018
SER	57	Supervisor, Blueprinting-and-Photocopy (any industry)	979.130-010
SER	57	Supervisor, Mail Carriers (government ser.)	230.137-018
SER	57	Supervisor, Mails (government ser.)	243.137-010
SER	56	Burning Supervisor (brick & tile)	573.132-010
SER	56	Cosmetologist Apprentice (personal ser.)	332.271-014
SER	56	Freight-Loading Supervisor (r.r. trans.)	910.137-026
SER	56	Hair Stylist (personal ser.)	332.271-018
SER	56	License Inspector (government ser.)	168.267-066
SER	56	Miller Supervisor (grain-feed mills)	521.130-010
SER	56	Paddock Judge (amuse. & rec.)	153.167-010
SER	56	Public-Safety Officer (government ser.)	379.263-014
SER	56	Safety Inspector (utilities)	821.367-014
SER	56	Steward/Stewardess, Third (water trans.)	350.137-026
SER	56	Supervisor, Housecleaner (hotel & rest.)	323.137-010
SER	56	Supervisor, Kosher Dietary Service (hotel & rest.)	319.137-026
SER	55	Bank Boss (mine & quarry)	932.132-010
SER	55	Police Officer I (government ser.)	375.263-014
SER	55	Police Sergeant, Precinct I (government ser.)	375.133-010
SER	55	Salesperson, Leather-and-Suede Apparel-and-Accessories (retail trade)	261.357-074
SER	55	Structural-Mill Supervisor (nonfer. metal)	619.132-022
SER	55	Supervisor, Delivery Department (tel. & tel.)	230.137-014
SER	55	Waiter/Waitress, Captain (hotel & rest.)	311.137-018
SER	54	Supervisor, Slate Splitting (stonework)	771.137-010

Part 2: From Holland Codes to Occupations

From Holland Codes to the Dictionary of Occupational Titles Occupations

HOC	Cx	Title	DOT
SER	53	Instructor (textile)	689.324-010
SER	53	Instructor, Driving (education)	099.223-010
SER	53	Route Supervisor (tel. & tel.)	239.137-018
SER	53	Sheriff, Deputy (government ser.)	377.263-010
SER	51	Furniture-Rental Consultant (retail trade)	295.357-018
SER	51	Nurse, Practical (medical ser.)	354.374-010
SER	51	Protective Officer (government ser.)	372.363-010
SER	50	Beach Lifeguard (amuse. & rec.)	379.364-014
SER	50	Deputy Sheriff, Civil Division (government ser.)	377.667-018
SER	50	Home Attendant (personal ser.)	354.377-014
SER	50	Police Officer II (government ser.)	375.367-010
SER	50	Supervisor, Parking Lot (automotive ser.)	915.133-010
SER	49	Companion (domestic ser.)	309.677-010
SER	48	Attendant, Lodging Facilities (hotel & rest.)	329.467-010
SER	48	Correction Officer (government ser.)	372.667-018
SER	46	Birth Attendant (medical ser.)	354.377-010
SER	46	Editor, School Photograph (photofinishing)	976.687-010
SER	45	Cloth-Printing Inspector (textile)	652.567-010
SER	45	Nurse Assistant (medical ser.)	355.674-014
SER	44	Veneer Matcher (millwork-plywood)	769.687-046
SER	43	Dog Catcher (government ser.)	379.673-010
SER	42	Merchant Patroller (business ser.)	372.667-038
SEI	77	Executive Director, Nurses' Association (medical ser.)	075.117-034
SEI	77	Insurance Attorney (insurance)	110.117-014
SEI	76	President, Financial Institution (financial)	186.117-054
SEI	75	Director, Correctional Agency (government ser.)	188.117-054
SEI	75	Director, Revenue (government ser.)	188.117-090
SEI	75	Psychologist, School (profess. & kin.)	045.107-034
SEI	74	Director of Guidance in Public Schools (education)	045.117-010
SEI	74	Director, Labor Standards (government ser.)	188.117-066
SEI	74	Faculty Member, College or University, All Other (education)	090.227-010
SEI	71	Community-Services-and-Health-Education Officer (government ser.)	079.167-010
SEI	71	Grant Coordinator (profess. & kin.)	169.117-014
SEI	71	Hearing Officer (government ser.)	119.107-010
SEI	70	Director, Law Enforcement (government ser.)	188.117-070
SEI	70	Political Scientist (profess. & kin.)	051.067-010
SEI	70	Research-Contracts Supervisor (government ser.)	162.117-030
SEI	70	Superintendent, Schools (education)	099.117-022
SEI	69	Coordinator of Rehabilitation Services (medical ser.)	076.117-010
SEI	69	Dietitian, Consultant (profess. & kin.)	077.127-018
SEI	69	Nurse, Head (medical ser.)	075.137-014
SEI	68	Principal (education)	099.117-018
SEI	67	Analyst, Food and Beverage (hotel & rest.)	310.267-010
SEI	67	Instructor, Ground Services (air trans.)	099.227-018
SEI	67	Nurse, Supervisor (medical ser.)	075.167-010

Part 2: From Holland Codes to Occupations

From Holland Codes to the Dictionary of Occupational Titles Occupations

HOC	Cx	Title	DOT
SEI	67	Program Specialist, Employee-Health Maintenance (profess. & kin.)	166.167-050
SEI	66	Correctional-Treatment Specialist (social ser.)	195.107-042
SEI	66	Manager, Computer Operations (profess. & kin.)	169.167-082
SEI	66	Service Representative (auto. mfg.)	191.167-022
SEI	65	Customer Services Coordinator (print. & pub.)	221.167-026
SEI	65	Dietetic Technician (profess. & kin.)	077.124-010
SEI	65	Historian (profess. & kin.)	052.067-022
SEI	65	Loan Officer (financial; insurance)	186.267-018
SEI	65	Park Naturalist (government ser.)	049.127-010
SEI	64	Teacher, Adventure Education (education)	099.224-014
SEI	63	Program Aide, Group Work (social ser.)	195.227-010
SEI	62	Supervisor, Quality Control (photofinishing)	976.131-022
SEI	61	Dianetic Counselor (profess. & kin.)	199.207-010
SEI	60	Recreation Leader (social ser.)	195.227-014
SEI	59	Fire Assistant (government ser.)	169.167-022
SEI	58	Psychiatric Technician (medical ser.)	079.374-026
SEI	53	Evaluator (nonprofit org.)	249.367-034
SEI	50	Armored-Car Guard (business ser.)	372.567-010
SEA	73	Producer (radio-tv broad.)	159.117-010
SEA	72	Appeals Reviewer, Veteran (government ser.)	119.117-010
SEA	72	Director, Special Education (education)	094.167-014
SEA	72	Program Director, Group Work (profess. & kin.)	187.117-046
SEA	71	Public Health Educator (profess. & kin.)	079.117-014
SEA	70	Director, Television (radio-tv broad.)	159.067-014
SEA	69	Academic Dean (education)	090.117-010
SEA	69	Arbitrator (profess. & kin.)	169.107-010
SEA	69	Director, Compliance (government ser.)	188.117-046
SEA	69	Instructor, Technical Training (education)	166.221-010
SEA	68	Dean of Students (education)	090.117-018
SEA	67	Caseworker, Family (social ser.)	195.107-018
SEA	67	Director, Aeronautics Commission (government ser.)	188.117-034
SEA	67	Director, Public Service (radio-tv broad.)	184.117-010
SEA	67	Fire Chief (government ser.)	373.117-010
SEA	67	Manager, Employee Welfare (profess. & kin.)	166.117-014
SEA	66	Art Conservator (museums)	102.167-010
SEA	66	Assistant Principal (education)	091.107-010
SEA	66	Caseworker, Child Welfare (social ser.)	195.107-014
SEA	66	Chief Controller (government ser.)	193.167-010
SEA	66	Christmas-Tree Contractor (any industry)	162.117-010
SEA	66	Director, Religious Education (nonprofit org.)	129.107-022
SEA	66	Director, Research (motion picture; radio-tv broad.)	052.167-010
SEA	66	District Extension Service Agent (government ser.)	096.167-010
SEA	66	Education Supervisor, Correctional Institution (education)	099.117-014
SEA	66	Field Contractor (any industry)	162.117-022
SEA	66	Home Economist (profess. & kin.)	096.121-014
SEA	66	Instructor, Extension Work (education)	090.227-018
SEA	66	Instructor, Military Science (education)	099.227-022

Part 2: From Holland Codes to Occupations

From Holland Codes to the Dictionary of Occupational Titles Occupations

HOC	Cx	Title	DOT
SEA	66	Social Group Worker (social ser.)	195.107-022
SEA	66	Social Worker, Delinquency Prevention (social ser.)	195.107-026
SEA	66	Social Worker, Psychiatric (profess. & kin.)	195.107-034
SEA	66	Substance Abuse Counselor (profess. & kin.)	045.107-058
SEA	65	Director, Community Organization (nonprofit org.)	187.167-234
SEA	65	Inservice Coordinator, Auxiliary Personnel (medical ser.)	079.127-010
SEA	63	Supervisor, Liquor Stores and Agencies (government ser.)	185.167-062
SEA	61	Supervisor, Sample Preparation (textile)	979.137-022
SEA	60	Booking Manager (amuse. & rec.)	191.117-014
SEA	60	Christian Science Practitioner (profess. & kin.)	129.107-014
SEA	60	Dyer, Supervisor (knitting; tex. prod., n.e.c.; textile)	582.131-014
SEA	60	Supervisor, Public Message Service (tel. & tel.)	239.137-026
SEA	59	Supervisor, Production (tex. prod., n.e.c.)	589.135-010
SEA	58	Supervisor, Fermenting Cellars (beverage)	529.132-058
SEA	57	Supervisor, Product Inspection (textile)	689.134-018
SEA	56	Cosmetologist (personal ser.)	332.271-010
SEA	56	Supervisor, Production (paper goods)	979.137-018
SEA	55	Supervisor II (button & notion)	734.131-010
SEA	54	Supervisor, Cigar Tobacco Processing (tobacco)	529.137-034
SEA	53	Checkroom Chief (any industry)	358.137-010
SEA	48	Caterer Helper (personal ser.)	319.677-010
SEA	47	Occupational Therapy Aide (medical ser.)	355.377-010
SEC	74	Manager, Personnel (profess. & kin.)	166.117-018
SEC	72	Library Director (library)	100.117-010
SEC	71	Claim Agent (petrol. & gas; pipe lines)	191.167-014
SEC	71	Director, School of Nursing (medical ser.)	075.117-030
SEC	71	Director, Utility Accounts (government ser.)	160.267-014
SEC	71	Manager, Schedule Planning (air trans.)	184.117-058
SEC	70	Director, Employment Research and Planning (government ser.)	050.117-010
SEC	70	Director, Translation (profess. & kin.)	137.137-010
SEC	70	Safety Manager (medical ser.)	168.167-086
SEC	69	Director, Community-Health Nursing (medical ser.)	075.117-014
SEC	69	Director, Nursing Service (medical ser.)	075.117-022
SEC	69	Librarian, Special Library (library)	100.167-026
SEC	69	Nurse, Consultant (medical ser.)	075.127-014
SEC	69	Nurse, Infection Control (medical ser.)	075.127-034
SEC	69	Residence Counselor (education)	045.107-038
SEC	69	Welfare Director (government ser.)	188.117-126
SEC	68	Financial-Aids Officer (education)	090.117-030
SEC	68	Training Representative (education)	166.227-010
SEC	68	Transplant Coordinator (medical ser.)	079.151-010
SEC	67	Continuity Director (radio-tv broad.)	132.037-010
SEC	67	Coordinator, Skill-Training Program (government ser.)	169.167-062
SEC	67	Federal Aid Coordinator (government ser.)	188.167-054
SEC	67	Import-Export Agent (any industry)	184.117-022
SEC	67	Institution Librarian (library)	100.167-022
SEC	67	Manager, City (government ser.)	188.117-114

HOC	Cx	Title	DOT
SEC	67	Supervisor, Special Education (education)	094.167-010
SEC	66	Casework Supervisor (social ser.)	195.137-010
SEC	66	Caseworker (social ser.)	195.107-010
SEC	66	Clerical-Methods Analyst (profess. & kin.)	161.267-010
SEC	66	Clinical Sociologist (profess. & kin.)	054.107-010
SEC	66	Community-Relations-and-Services Advisor, Public Housing (social ser.)	195.167-014
SEC	66	Contract Clerk (profess. & kin.)	119.267-018
SEC	66	Coordinator, Volunteer Services (social ser.)	187.167-022
SEC	66	County Home-Demonstration Agent (government ser.)	096.121-010
SEC	66	County-Agricultural Agent (government ser.)	096.127-010
SEC	66	Director, Volunteer Services (social ser.)	187.167-038
SEC	66	Extension Service Specialist (government ser.)	096.127-014
SEC	66	Paralegal (profess. & kin.)	119.267-026
SEC	66	Retirement Officer (government ser.)	166.267-030
SEC	66	Social Worker, School (profess. & kin.)	195.107-038
SEC	66	Supervisor, Education (education)	099.117-026
SEC	66	Teacher, Emotionally Impaired (education)	094.227-010
SEC	66	Teacher, Hearing Impaired (education)	094.224-010
SEC	66	Teacher, Mentally Impaired (education)	094.227-022
SEC	66	Teacher, Physically Impaired (education)	094.224-014
SEC	66	Teacher, Visually Impaired (education)	094.224-018
SEC	66	Vocational Rehabilitation Counselor (government ser.)	045.107-042
SEC	65	Claims Adjudicator (government ser.)	169.267-010
SEC	65	Director, Operations, Broadcast (radio-tv broad.)	184.167-022
SEC	65	Manager, Aquatic Facility (amuse. & rec.)	187.167-054
SEC	65	Manager, Sound Effects (radio-tv broad.)	962.167-010
SEC	65	Pastoral Assistant (nonprofit org.)	129.107-026
SEC	65	Supervisor, Network Control Operators (any industry)	031.132-010
SEC	65	Teacher, Home Therapy (social ser.)	195.227-018
SEC	65	Teacher, Vocational Training (education)	094.227-026
SEC	65	Tutor (education)	099.227-034
SEC	64	Director, Casting (motion picture; radio-tv broad.)	159.267-010
SEC	64	Disc Jockey (radio-tv broad.)	159.147-014
SEC	64	Foreign-Student Adviser (education)	090.107-010
SEC	64	Fund Raiser I (nonprofit org.)	293.157-010
SEC	64	Prisoner-Classification Interviewer (profess. & kin.)	166.267-022
SEC	64	Supervisor, Lending Activities (financial)	249.137-034
SEC	64	Work-Study Coordinator, Special Education (education)	094.107-010
SEC	63	Police Lieutenant, Community Relations (government ser.)	375.137-018
SEC	63	Recordist, Chief (motion picture)	962.134-010
SEC	63	Supervisor, Paper Testing (paper & pulp; paper goods)	539.134-010
SEC	62	Hypnotherapist (profess. & kin.)	079.157-010
SEC	62	Police Academy Program Coordinator (government ser.)	375.167-054
SEC	62	Recreational Therapist (medical ser.)	076.124-014
SEC	62	Scout, Professional Sports (amuse. & rec.)	153.117-018
SEC	62	Supervisor, Tellers (utilities)	211.137-022
SEC	62	Title Clerk (petrol. & gas; petrol. refin.; pipe lines)	162.267-010
SEC	61	Dispatcher, Traffic or System (motor trans.; r.r. trans.)	919.162-010

Part 2: From Holland Codes to Occupations

From Holland Codes to the Dictionary of Occupational Titles Occupations

HOC	Cx	Title	DOT
SEC	61	Financial-Aid Counselor (education)	169.267-018
SEC	61	Medical-Service Technician (military ser.)	079.367-018
SEC	61	Supervisor, Accounts Receivable (utilities; waterworks)	214.137-022
SEC	61	Teacher, Kindergarten (education)	092.227-014
SEC	60	Information Clerk, Automobile Club (nonprofit org.)	237.267-010
SEC	60	Manager, Touring Production (amuse. & rec.)	191.117-038
SEC	60	Supervisor, Credit and Loan Collections (clerical)	241.137-010
SEC	60	Supervisor, Rubber Stamps and Dies (pen & pencil)	733.131-010
SEC	60	Supervisor, Statement Clerks (financial)	214.137-014
SEC	60	Supervisor, Water Softener Service (business ser.)	862.134-014
SEC	59	Automobile-Club-Safety-Program Coordinator (nonprofit org.)	249.167-010
SEC	59	Counselor, Camp (amuse. & rec.)	159.124-010
SEC	59	Documentation Supervisor (water trans.)	214.137-010
SEC	59	Instructor, Apparel Manufacture (textile)	789.222-010
SEC	59	Investigator, Fraud (retail trade)	376.267-014
SEC	59	Labor Expediter (construction)	249.167-018
SEC	59	Private-Branch-Exchange Service Adviser (tel. & tel.)	235.222-010
SEC	59	Residence Supervisor (any industry)	187.167-186
SEC	59	Shipping-and-Receiving Supervisor (clerical)	222.137-030
SEC	59	Supervisor, Contact and Service Clerks (utilities)	249.137-014
SEC	59	Supervisor, Contract-Sheltered Workshop (nonprofit org.)	187.134-010
SEC	59	Supervisor, Ferry Terminal (water trans.)	911.137-026
SEC	59	Supervisor, Optical Instruments (inst. & app.)	711.137-010
SEC	59	Supervisor, Rides (amuse. & rec.)	342.137-010
SEC	59	Telephone Operator, Chief (clerical)	235.137-010
SEC	59	Travel Counselor, Automobile Club (nonprofit org.)	238.167-014
SEC	58	Astrologer (amuse. & rec.)	159.207-010
SEC	58	Christian Science Nurse (profess. & kin.)	129.107-010
SEC	58	Dispatcher (mine & quarry)	932.167-010
SEC	58	Eligibility-and-Occupancy Interviewer (government ser.)	168.267-038
SEC	58	Supervisor IV (nonmet. min.)	692.132-010
SEC	58	Supervisor, Candy (sugar & conf.)	529.130-010
SEC	58	Supervisor, Extermination (business ser.)	389.134-010
SEC	58	Supervisor, Survey Workers (clerical)	205.137-014
SEC	57	Airplane-Dispatch Clerk (air trans.)	248.367-010
SEC	57	Children's Tutor (domestic ser.)	099.227-010
SEC	57	Customer-Complaint Clerk (clerical)	241.367-014
SEC	57	Dispatcher (government ser.)	193.262-014
SEC	57	Supervisor, Animal Cruelty Investigation (nonprofit org.)	379.137-010
SEC	57	Supervisor, Finishing Department (photofinishing)	976.137-014
SEC	56	Clerk, Telegraph Service (tel. & tel.)	219.362-022
SEC	56	Customer-Service-Representative Instructor (tel. & tel.; utilities; waterworks)	239.227-010
SEC	56	Shelving Supervisor (library)	109.137-010
SEC	55	Agent-Licensing Clerk (insurance)	209.367-010
SEC	55	Case Aide (social ser.)	195.367-010
SEC	55	Central-Office-Operator Supervisor (tel. & tel.)	235.132-010
SEC	55	Customer Service Representative Supervisor (radio-tv broad.; tel. & tel.; utilities; waterworks)	239.137-014

Part 2: From Holland Codes to Occupations

From Holland Codes to the Dictionary of Occupational Titles Occupations

HOC	Cx	Title	DOT
SEC	55	Management Aide (social ser.)	195.367-014
SEC	55	Police Officer III (government ser.)	375.267-038
SEC	55	Supervisor, Inspecting (paper goods)	979.137-014
SEC	54	Homemaker (social ser.)	309.354-010
SEC	54	Instructor, Physical (amuse. & rec.; education)	153.227-014
SEC	54	Material Expediter (clerical)	221.367-042
SEC	54	Skip Tracer (clerical)	241.367-026
SEC	54	Supervisor, Circus (amuse. & rec.)	969.137-010
SEC	54	Supervisor, Marking Room (retail trade)	209.137-026
SEC	53	Deputy United States Marshal (government ser.)	377.267-010
SEC	53	Horse Trainer (agriculture; amuse. & rec.)	419.224-010
SEC	53	News Assistant (radio-tv broad.)	209.367-038
SEC	52	Bartender (hotel & rest.)	312.474-010
SEC	52	Juggler (amuse. & rec.)	159.341-010
SEC	52	Registrar (government ser.)	205.367-038
SEC	52	Wig Dresser (fabrication, n.e.c.; personal ser.)	332.361-010
SEC	51	Community Service Officer, Patrol (government ser.)	372.367-010
SEC	51	Detective I (any industry)	376.367-014
SEC	51	Psychiatric Aide (medical ser.)	355.377-014
SEC	51	Undercover Operator (retail trade)	376.367-026
SEC	51	Weight-Reduction Specialist (personal ser.)	359.367-014
SEC	50	Escort (personal ser.)	359.367-010
SEC	49	First-Aid Attendant (any industry)	354.677-010
SEC	49	Passenger Service Representative (air trans.)	359.677-022
SEC	47	Ambulance Attendant (medical ser.)	355.374-010
SEC	47	Chaperon (personal ser.)	359.667-010
SEC	46	Guard, Security (any industry)	372.667-034
SEC	45	Foster Parent (domestic ser.)	309.677-014
SEC	44	Patrol Conductor (government ser.)	372.677-010
SEC	43	Personal Attendant (domestic ser.)	309.674-014
SEC	43	School Bus Monitor (government ser.)	372.667-042
SEC	41	Child Monitor (domestic ser.)	301.677-010
SCR	69	Quality Assurance Coordinator (medical ser.)	075.167-014
SCR	62	Physical Therapist Assistant (medical ser.)	076.224-010
SCR	60	Supervisor, Sulfuric-Acid Plant (chemical)	558.132-018
SCR	59	Police Officer, Crime Prevention (government ser.)	375.264-010
SCR	56	Chief Projectionist (motion picture)	960.132-010
SCR	56	Extension Clerk (utilities)	219.362-030
SCR	56	Holter Scanning Technician (medical ser.)	078.264-010
SCR	56	Medical Assistant (medical ser.)	079.362-010
SCR	53	Police Officer, Booking (government ser.)	375.367-018
SCR	53	Storage-Facility Rental Clerk (business ser.; retail trade)	295.367-026
SCR	52	Recreation Aide (social ser.)	195.367-030
SCR	51	Food-Management Aide (government ser.)	195.367-022
SCR	50	Library Clerk, Talking Books (library)	209.387-026
SCR	48	Attendant, Arcade (amuse. & rec.)	342.667-014
SCR	44	Fast-Foods Worker (hotel & rest.)	311.472-010
SCR	40	Children's Attendant (amuse. & rec.)	349.677-018

Part 2: From Holland Codes to Occupations

From Holland Codes to the Dictionary of Occupational Titles Occupations

HOC	Cx	Title	DOT
SCI	59	Optometric Assistant (medical ser.)	079.364-014
SCI	55	Preparole-Counseling Aide (government ser.)	195.367-026
SCA	55	Sign Writer, Hand (any industry)	970.281-022
SCE	74	Consultant, Education (education)	099.167-014
SCE	69	Cost-and-Sales-Record Supervisor (utilities)	216.137-010
SCE	69	Director, Occupational Health Nursing (medical ser.)	075.117-026
SCE	68	Appeals Referee (government ser.)	119.267-014
SCE	67	Appraiser, Real Estate (real estate)	191.267-010
SCE	67	Director, State-Historical Society (profess. & kin.)	052.067-014
SCE	67	Instructor, Psychiatric Aide (education)	075.127-010
SCE	65	Contact Representative (government ser.)	169.167-018
SCE	65	Copyist (any industry)	152.267-010
SCE	65	Personnel Recruiter (profess. & kin.)	166.267-038
SCE	64	Announcer (radio-tv broad.)	159.147-010
SCE	64	Employment Interviewer (profess. & kin.)	166.267-010
SCE	63	Supervisor, Microfilm Duplicating Unit (business ser.)	976.131-018
SCE	63	Supervisor, Trust Accounts (financial)	219.132-014
SCE	62	Air-Traffic-Control Specialist, Station (government ser.)	193.162-014
SCE	62	Eligibility Worker (government ser.)	195.267-010
SCE	62	Reviewing Officer, Driver's License (government ser.)	168.167-074
SCE	62	Supervisor, Agency Appointments (insurance)	209.137-018
SCE	61	Field Cashier (construction)	219.137-010
SCE	61	Mohel (profess. & kin.)	129.271-010
SCE	60	Supervisor, Correspondence Section (insurance)	249.137-018
SCE	60	Supervisor, Securities Vault (financial)	216.132-014
SCE	59	Communication-Center Coordinator (air trans.)	235.132-014
SCE	58	Interpreter, Deaf (profess. & kin.)	137.267-014
SCE	58	Occupational Therapy Assistant (medical ser.)	076.364-010
SCE	58	Social-Services Aide (social ser.)	195.367-034
SCE	58	Teacher Aide I (education)	099.327-010
SCE	57	Agent-Contract Clerk (insurance)	241.267-010
SCE	57	Bonding Agent (business ser.)	186.267-010
SCE	57	Investigator, Cash Shortage (retail trade)	376.267-010
SCE	57	Mortgage-Closing Clerk (clerical)	219.362-038
SCE	57	Supervisor, Cutting and Splicing (motion picture; photofinishing)	976.134-010
SCE	56	Career-Guidance Technician (education)	249.367-014
SCE	55	Podiatric Assistant (medical ser.)	079.374-018
SCE	54	Stunt Performer (amuse. & rec.; motion picture; radio-tv broad.)	159.341-014
SCE	53	Police Officer, Safety Instruction (government ser.)	375.267-042
SCE	51	Scout (agriculture)	408.381-010
SCE	48	Blind Aide (personal ser.)	359.573-010
SCE	47	Taxicab Coordinator (motor trans.)	215.367-018
SCE	45	Blood-Donor-Unit Assistant (medical ser.)	245.367-014
SCE	42	Fingernail Former (personal ser.)	331.674-014
SCE	42	Jockey-Room Custodian (amuse. & rec.)	346.667-010

Dictionary of Holland Occupational Codes

HOC	Cx	Title	DOT
SCE	41	Decorator, Lighting Fixtures (light. fix.)	749.684-018
SCE	38	Print-Line Inspector (furniture)	652.687-034
ERI	75	Superintendent of Generation (utilities)	184.167-138
ERI	75	Superintendent, System Operation (utilities)	184.167-210
ERI	75	Superintendent, Transmission (utilities)	184.167-222
ERI	74	Master, Ship (water trans.)	197.167-010
ERI	70	Chemical-Equipment Sales Engineer (profess. & kin.)	008.151-010
ERI	70	Director, Research and Development (any industry)	189.117-014
ERI	70	Maintainability Engineer (profess. & kin.)	019.081-010
ERI	70	Sales Engineer, Ceramic Products (profess. & kin.)	006.151-010
ERI	70	Sales Engineer, Marine Equipment (profess. & kin.)	014.151-010
ERI	70	Sales Engineer, Mechanical Equipment (utilities)	007.151-010
ERI	70	Sales Engineer, Nuclear Equipment (profess. & kin.)	015.151-010
ERI	70	Special Agent (government ser.)	375.167-042
ERI	70	Superintendent, Maintenance (any industry)	189.167-046
ERI	69	Sales Engineer, Aeronautical Products (aircraft mfg.)	002.151-010
ERI	69	Superintendent, Drilling and Production (petrol. & gas)	181.167-014
ERI	68	Manager, Bulk Plant (petrol. refin.; retail trade)	181.117-010
ERI	68	Superintendent, Logging (logging)	183.167-038
ERI	68	Superintendent, Maintenance of Way (r.r. trans.)	182.167-030
ERI	68	Superintendent, Meters (utilities)	184.167-194
ERI	67	Revenue Agent (government ser.)	160.167-050
ERI	65	Superintendent, Greens (amuse. & rec.)	406.137-014
ERI	64	Dredge Captain (water trans.)	197.161-010
ERI	64	Manager, Branch Operation Evaluation (hotel & rest.)	187.167-062
ERI	63	Manager, Laundromat (laundry & rel.)	369.167-010
ERI	62	Manager, Marina Dry Dock (amuse. & rec.; water trans.)	187.167-226
ERI	61	Fuel-System-Maintenance Supervisor (any industry)	638.131-010
ERI	61	Sales Representative, Security Systems (business ser.)	259.257-022
ERI	60	Schedule Maker (motor trans.)	913.167-018
ERI	59	Road Supervisor (motor trans.)	913.133-010
ERI	59	Supervisor, Carbon Electrodes (steel & rel.)	549.137-010
ERI	59	Traffic-Maintenance Supervisor (government ser.)	869.137-010
ERI	58	Sanitarian (any industry)	529.137-014
ERI	58	Supervisor, Particle Board (wood prod., n.e.c.)	569.132-010
ERI	58	Supervisor, Veneer (millwork-plywood)	569.135-010
ERI	57	Disaster or Damage Control Specialist (military ser.)	378.267-014
ERI	57	Drawing-Kiln Supervisor (glass mfg.)	575.137-010
ERI	48	Drier Operator IV (chemical)	553.685-054
ERA	69	Superintendent, Measurement (petrol. & gas; pipe lines)	184.167-190
ERA	65	Park Superintendent (government ser.)	188.167-062
ERA	62	Supervisor, Reclamation (mine & quarry)	850.133-010
ERA	60	Superintendent, Maintenance (motor trans.)	184.167-170
ERA	60	Supervisor, Ovens (steel & rel.)	542.132-014
ERA	59	Supervisor, Coal Handling (steel & rel.)	549.132-018
ERA	59	Supervisor, Coke Handling (steel & rel.)	549.132-022
ERA	59	Supervisor, Marina Sales and Service (retail trade)	299.137-026

Part 2: From Holland Codes to Occupations

From Holland Codes to the Dictionary of Occupational Titles Occupations

HOC	Cx	Title	DOT
ERA	56	Converter Supervisor (smelt. & refin.)	513.132-010
ERA	55	Supervisor, Threshing Department (tobacco)	521.132-014
ERA	53	Costumer Assistant (motion picture; radio-tv broad.)	346.374-010
ERA	47	Railway-Equipment Operator (r.r. trans.)	859.683-018
ERS	70	Commissioner of Conciliation (government ser.)	188.217-010
ERS	70	Manager, Harbor Department (water trans.)	184.117-042
ERS	70	Sales Engineer, Mining-and-Oil-Well Equipment and Services (mine & quarry; petrol. & gas)	010.151-010
ERS	70	Superintendent, Oil-Well Services (petrol. & gas)	010.167-018
ERS	69	Liaison Engineer (aircraft mfg.)	012.167-038
ERS	69	Relocation Commissioner (government ser.)	188.167-070
ERS	69	Superintendent, Car Construction (railroad equip.)	183.167-034
ERS	68	Superintendent, Compressor Stations (pipe lines)	184.167-146
ERS	68	Superintendent, Distribution II (utilities)	184.167-154
ERS	68	Superintendent, Terminal (water trans.)	184.167-214
ERS	67	Inspector, Plumbing (government ser.)	168.167-050
ERS	67	Superintendent, Ammunition Storage (ordnance)	189.167-038
ERS	67	Superintendent, Construction (construction)	182.167-026
ERS	67	Wharfinger, Chief (water trans.)	184.167-274
ERS	66	Manager, Game Breeding Farm (agriculture)	180.167-034
ERS	66	Program Director, Cable Television (radio-tv broad.)	194.162-010
ERS	66	Protective-Signal Superintendent (business ser.)	822.131-022
ERS	65	Appliance-Service Supervisor (utilities)	187.167-010
ERS	65	Cloth Finisher (carpet & rug; textile)	589.130-010
ERS	65	Examiner (government ser.)	169.267-014
ERS	65	Manager, Sales (laundry & rel.)	187.167-138
ERS	65	Manager, Service Department (wholesale tr.)	187.167-142
ERS	65	Manager, Vehicle Leasing and Rental (automotive ser.)	187.167-162
ERS	65	Police Captain, Precinct (government ser.)	375.167-034
ERS	65	Superintendent, Industries, Correctional Facility (government ser.)	188.167-094
ERS	65	Unclaimed Property Officer (government ser.)	188.167-106
ERS	64	Commanding Officer, Motorized Squad (government ser.)	375.163-010
ERS	64	Inspector, Government Property (government ser.)	168.267-050
ERS	64	Intelligence Specialist (military ser.)	059.267-014
ERS	64	Manager, Traffic I (tel. & tel.)	184.167-098
ERS	64	Pilot, Highway Patrol (government ser.)	375.163-014
ERS	63	Chief Load Dispatcher (utilities)	952.137-010
ERS	63	Commander, Identification and Records (government ser.)	375.137-010
ERS	63	Customer-Facilities Supervisor (tel. & tel.)	822.131-014
ERS	63	Dispatcher, Bus and Trolley (motor trans.)	913.167-014
ERS	63	Gas Dispatcher (pipe lines; utilities)	953.167-010
ERS	63	Incinerator-Plant-General Supervisor (sanitary ser.)	184.167-046
ERS	63	Line Supervisor (tel. & tel.)	822.131-018
ERS	63	Order Department Supervisor (any industry)	169.167-038
ERS	63	Sales Representative, Foundry and Machine Shop Products (wholesale tr.)	274.257-010
ERS	63	Security Officer (any industry)	189.167-034

Dictionary of Holland Occupational Codes

HOC	Cx	Title	DOT
ERS	63	Supervisor, Air-Conditioning Installer (any industry)	827.131-018
ERS	63	Supervisor, Purification (petrol. refin.)	549.132-030
ERS	63	Transformer Assembly Supervisor (elec. equip.)	820.137-010
ERS	62	Dispatcher, Chief II (petrol. & gas; petrol. refin.; pipe lines)	914.167-010
ERS	62	Hydroelectric-Station Operator, Chief (utilities)	952.137-014
ERS	62	Manager, Poultry Hatchery (agriculture)	180.167-046
ERS	62	Signal Supervisor (r.r. trans.)	822.131-026
ERS	62	Superintendent, Laundry (laundry & rel.)	187.167-194
ERS	62	Supervisor, Aircraft Maintenance (air trans.)	621.131-014
ERS	62	Supervisor, Pulp Plant (paper & pulp)	539.132-014
ERS	62	Supervisor, Pumping (smelt. & refin.)	914.131-010
ERS	62	Supervisor, Treating and Pumping (petrol. refin.)	549.132-034
ERS	62	Supervisor, Yard (beverage)	529.137-070
ERS	61	Cable Supervisor (tel. & tel.)	184.161-010
ERS	61	Captain, Fishing Vessel (fishing & hunt.)	197.133-010
ERS	61	Harvest Contractor (agriculture)	409.117-010
ERS	61	Maintenance Supervisor (any industry)	891.137-010
ERS	61	Manager, Automobile Service Station (retail trade)	185.167-014
ERS	61	Mate, Ship (water trans.)	197.133-022
ERS	61	Pit Supervisor (mine & quarry)	939.137-014
ERS	61	Sales Representative, Radio and Television Time (radio-tv broad.)	259.357-018
ERS	61	Sales Representative, Ultrasonic Equipment (wholesale tr.)	271.352-014
ERS	61	Steel-Post-Installer Supervisor (utilities)	821.131-022
ERS	61	Supervisor (ordnance)	737.137-018
ERS	61	Supervisor, Acoustical Tile Carpenters (construction)	860.131-010
ERS	61	Supervisor, Sound Technician (business ser.)	823.131-026
ERS	61	Supervisor, Specialty Plant (petrol. refin.)	549.137-018
ERS	61	Yard Supervisor (smelt. & refin.)	929.137-026
ERS	60	Airport-Maintenance Chief (air trans.)	899.137-010
ERS	60	Dispatcher (tel. & tel.)	239.167-014
ERS	60	Estimator, Printing (print. & pub.)	221.367-014
ERS	60	Explosive-Operator Supervisor (ordnance)	694.132-010
ERS	60	Instructor, Flying II (education)	097.227-010
ERS	60	Kitchen Supervisor (hotel & rest.)	319.137-030
ERS	60	Sales Correspondent (clerical)	221.367-062
ERS	60	Sales Representative (motor trans.)	250.357-022
ERS	60	Steward/Stewardess (hotel & rest.)	310.137-018
ERS	60	Steward/Stewardess, Banquet (hotel & rest.)	310.137-022
ERS	60	Supervisor, Byproducts (steel & rel.)	542.132-010
ERS	60	Supervisor, Cab (motor trans.)	913.133-014
ERS	60	Supervisor, Garage (automotive ser.)	620.131-014
ERS	60	Supervisor, Inspection (pen & pencil)	733.137-018
ERS	60	Supervisor, Meter Repair Shop (utilities)	710.131-026
ERS	60	Supervisor, Motorcycle Repair Shop (automotive ser.)	620.131-018
ERS	60	Supervisor, Printed Circuit Board Testing (electron. comp.)	726.131-018
ERS	60	Supervisor, Repulping (paper & pulp)	539.132-018
ERS	60	Supervisor, Tower (petrol. refin.)	549.130-010

HOC	Cx	Title	DOT
ERS	60	Truck Supervisor (motor trans.)	909.137-018
ERS	60	Yard Supervisor, Building Materials or Lumber (retail trade; wholesale tr.)	929.137-030
ERS	59	Bank Boss (construction)	851.137-010
ERS	59	Bricklayer Supervisor (construction)	861.131-010
ERS	59	Cadet, Deck (water trans.)	911.133-010
ERS	59	Chest-Painting and Sealing Supervisor (ordnance)	749.137-010
ERS	59	Derrick-Boat Captain (water trans.)	911.137-014
ERS	59	Fabric-Coating Supervisor (tex. prod., n.e.c.)	589.130-014
ERS	59	Fence-Erector Supervisor (construction)	869.134-010
ERS	59	Fire Marshal (any industry)	373.167-018
ERS	59	Firearms-Assembly Supervisor (ordnance)	736.131-014
ERS	59	Gas-Pumping-Station Supervisor (utilities)	953.137-010
ERS	59	General-Handling Supervisor (smelt. & refin.)	929.137-010
ERS	59	Head Operator, Sulfide (chemical)	559.132-026
ERS	59	Inspector, Chief (foundry)	514.131-010
ERS	59	Inspector, Chief (ordnance)	737.137-010
ERS	59	Load Dispatcher (utilities)	952.167-014
ERS	59	Manager, Apartment House (real estate)	186.167-018
ERS	59	Manager, Camp (amuse. & rec.)	329.161-010
ERS	59	Melter Supervisor (steel & rel.)	512.132-010
ERS	59	Mill Supervisor (nonmet. min.)	559.132-034
ERS	59	Pressure Supervisor (utilities)	953.137-014
ERS	59	Reduction-Plant Supervisor (smelt. & refin.)	512.130-010
ERS	59	Sales Representative, Industrial Machinery (wholesale tr.)	274.357-038
ERS	59	Salvage Supervisor (paint & varnish)	559.137-010
ERS	59	Sampler, Head (smelt. & refin.)	519.130-014
ERS	59	Service Manager (retail trade)	185.164-010
ERS	59	Service Supervisor I (utilities)	953.137-018
ERS	59	Shift Supervisor, Film Processing (print. & pub.)	979.132-010
ERS	59	Stocking-and-Box-Shop Supervisor (ordnance)	769.137-010
ERS	59	Supercargo (water trans.)	248.167-010
ERS	59	Superintendent, Stevedoring (water trans.)	911.137-022
ERS	59	Supervisor (plastic prod.)	690.130-018
ERS	59	Supervisor (rubber tire)	750.130-010
ERS	59	Supervisor (leather prod.)	783.132-010
ERS	59	Supervisor (glove & mit.)	784.132-010
ERS	59	Supervisor I (rubber goods)	759.137-010
ERS	59	Supervisor II (rubber goods)	559.137-014
ERS	59	Supervisor III (fabrication, n.e.c.)	549.132-014
ERS	59	Supervisor, Alum Plant (chemical)	559.132-062
ERS	59	Supervisor, Area (agriculture)	401.137-010
ERS	59	Supervisor, Asphalt Paving (construction)	853.133-010
ERS	59	Supervisor, Assembly (woodworking)	769.137-014
ERS	59	Supervisor, Assembly-and-Packing (cutlery-hrdwr.)	701.137-010
ERS	59	Supervisor, Beet End (sugar & conf.)	529.132-018
ERS	59	Supervisor, Belt-and-Link Assembly (ordnance)	737.137-022
ERS	59	Supervisor, Bone Plant (chemical)	559.132-066
ERS	59	Supervisor, Chemical (plastic-synth.)	558.132-010

Dictionary of Holland Occupational Codes

HOC	Cx	Title	DOT
ERS	59	Supervisor, Coil Winding (elec. equip.)	724.131-010
ERS	59	Supervisor, Color-Paste Mixing (textile)	550.135-010
ERS	59	Supervisor, Compressed Yeast (food prep., n.e.c.)	520.132-014
ERS	59	Supervisor, Cook House (chemical)	559.132-074
ERS	59	Supervisor, Dials (clock & watch)	715.131-014
ERS	59	Supervisor, Dimension Warehouse (furniture)	769.134-010
ERS	59	Supervisor, Display Fabrication (fabrication, n.e.c.)	739.134-014
ERS	59	Supervisor, Dry Cleaning (laundry & rel.)	369.137-010
ERS	59	Supervisor, Egg Processing (can. & preserv.; wholesale tr.)	529.137-042
ERS	59	Supervisor, Finishing Department (pen & pencil)	733.137-014
ERS	59	Supervisor, Finishing Room (leather mfg.)	589.130-018
ERS	59	Supervisor, Gas Meter Repair (utilities)	710.131-010
ERS	59	Supervisor, Grading (construction)	859.137-010
ERS	59	Supervisor, Hairspring Fabrication (clock & watch)	715.131-018
ERS	59	Supervisor, Inspection (clock & watch)	715.131-022
ERS	59	Supervisor, Inspection and Testing (motor-bicycles)	806.131-026
ERS	59	Supervisor, Machining (woodworking)	669.130-022
ERS	59	Supervisor, Mainspring Fabrication (clock & watch)	715.131-026
ERS	59	Supervisor, Malted Milk (dairy products)	529.132-070
ERS	59	Supervisor, Painting (construction)	840.131-010
ERS	59	Supervisor, Phosphorus Processing (chemical)	559.132-118
ERS	59	Supervisor, Pigment Making (chemical)	559.132-122
ERS	59	Supervisor, Plastering (construction)	842.131-018
ERS	59	Supervisor, Powdered Sugar (sugar & conf.)	521.130-014
ERS	59	Supervisor, Pressing Department (garment)	583.132-010
ERS	59	Supervisor, Print Line (furniture)	652.132-010
ERS	59	Supervisor, Receiving and Processing (glass mfg.)	579.137-026
ERS	59	Supervisor, Shed Workers (agriculture)	404.131-014
ERS	59	Supervisor, Split and Drum Room (leather mfg.)	589.132-014
ERS	59	Supervisor, Tan Room (leather mfg.)	582.132-018
ERS	59	Supervisor, Tree-Trimming (utilities)	408.137-014
ERS	59	Supervisor, Varnish (paint & varnish)	559.132-134
ERS	59	Supervisor, Wet End (wood prod., n.e.c.)	539.131-010
ERS	59	Tracer-Bullet-Section Supervisor (ordnance)	694.131-010
ERS	59	Wood-Crew Supervisor (chemical; saw. & plan.)	564.132-010
ERS	58	Appraiser, Automobile Damage (business ser.; insurance)	241.267-014
ERS	58	Baggage-and-Mail Agent (r.r. trans.)	910.137-010
ERS	58	Blending Supervisor (grain-feed mills)	520.132-010
ERS	58	Combat Surveillance and Target Acquisition Noncommissioned Officer (military ser.)	378.161-010
ERS	58	Field Artillery Senior Sergeant (military ser.)	378.132-010
ERS	58	Flight-Information Expediter (air trans.)	912.367-010
ERS	58	Forest Nursery Supervisor (forestry)	451.137-010
ERS	58	Maintenance Supervisor, Mobile Battery Equipment (mine & quarry)	638.131-034
ERS	58	Manager, Industrial Cafeteria (hotel & rest.)	319.137-018
ERS	58	Poleyard Supervisor (utilities)	929.137-014
ERS	58	Primer Supervisor (ordnance)	737.132-010
ERS	58	Production Manager, Reproduction (print. & pub.)	652.137-010

HOC	Cx	Title	DOT
ERS	58	Salesperson, Sewing Machines (retail trade)	270.352-010
ERS	58	Sewing Supervisor (any industry)	787.132-010
ERS	58	Superintendent, Track (construction)	899.137-014
ERS	58	Supervisor, Blast Furnace (steel & rel.)	519.132-010
ERS	58	Supervisor, Broommaking (fabrication, n.e.c.)	692.130-026
ERS	58	Supervisor, Chimney Construction (construction)	801.131-010
ERS	58	Supervisor, Decorating (glass mfg.)	652.130-010
ERS	58	Supervisor, Dry Paste (chemical)	559.132-082
ERS	58	Supervisor, Drying (millwork-plywood)	563.135-010
ERS	58	Supervisor, Feed Mill (grain-feed mills)	529.132-054
ERS	58	Supervisor, Finishing (fabrication, n.e.c.)	749.134-010
ERS	58	Supervisor, Home Restoration Service (any industry)	389.137-010
ERS	58	Supervisor, Mirror Manufacturing Department (glass products)	579.131-010
ERS	58	Supervisor, Mixing Place (construction)	853.137-010
ERS	58	Supervisor, Packing and Wrapping (any industry)	920.137-026
ERS	58	Tire-Service Supervisor (automotive ser.)	915.134-010
ERS	58	Yard Manager (any industry)	910.137-046
ERS	58	Yard Supervisor, Cotton Gin (agriculture)	929.137-034
ERS	57	Car-Cleaning Supervisor (r.r. trans.)	910.137-014
ERS	57	Conductor, Pullman (r.r. trans.)	198.167-014
ERS	57	Container Coordinator (water trans.)	248.367-022
ERS	57	Salesperson, Corsets (retail trade)	261.354-010
ERS	57	Supervisor, Painting Department (pen & pencil)	692.137-010
ERS	57	Warehouse Supervisor (motor trans.)	929.137-018
ERS	56	Car Chaser (beverage)	910.167-010
ERS	56	Coin-Machine-Collector Supervisor (clerical)	292.137-010
ERS	56	Cook, Mexican Food (food prep., n.e.c.)	526.134-010
ERS	56	Heating-and-Blending Supervisor (chemical)	559.132-030
ERS	56	Manager, Pool (amuse. & rec.)	153.137-010
ERS	56	Material-Crew Supervisor (construction; mfd. bldgs.)	921.137-014
ERS	56	Supervisor (cement)	579.137-010
ERS	56	Supervisor, Cutting and Boning (meat products)	525.131-014
ERS	56	Supervisor, Ice House (food prep., n.e.c.)	523.137-010
ERS	56	Supervisor, Lamp Shades (fabrication, n.e.c.)	739.137-014
ERS	56	Supervisor, Loading and Unloading (any industry)	922.137-018
ERS	56	Supervisor, Logging (logging)	459.133-010
ERS	56	Supervisor, Shop (fabrication, n.e.c.)	692.130-042
ERS	55	Dining-Service Inspector (r.r. trans.)	168.267-030
ERS	55	Infantry Unit Leader (military ser.)	378.137-010
ERS	55	Maintenance Data Analyst (military ser.)	221.367-038
ERS	55	Property Coordinator (amuse. & rec.; radio-tv broad.)	962.167-018
ERS	55	Retread Supervisor (rubber tire)	750.132-010
ERS	55	Service Observer (tel. & tel.)	239.367-026
ERS	55	Supervisor (food prep., n.e.c.)	529.132-110
ERS	55	Supervisor, Drying and Winding (plastic-synth.)	559.134-014
ERS	55	Supervisor, Labor Gang (construction)	850.137-014
ERS	55	Supervisor, Mold-Making Plastics Sheets (plastic-synth.)	579.137-022
ERS	55	Supervisor, Putty and Caulking (paint & varnish)	559.137-042

Part 2: From Holland Codes to Occupations
From Holland Codes to the Dictionary of Occupational Titles Occupations

HOC	Cx	Title	DOT
ERS	55	Supervisor, Rag Room (paper & pulp)	539.137-010
ERS	55	Tank and Amphibian Tractor Operations Chief (military ser.)	620.137-010
ERS	55	Watch-and-Clock-Repair Clerk (retail trade)	299.367-018
ERS	55	Yard Supervisor (forestry)	922.137-030
ERS	54	Personal Property Assessor (government ser.)	191.367-010
ERS	54	Stamp Analyst (retail trade)	299.387-014
ERS	54	Supervisor (mine & quarry)	570.137-010
ERS	54	Supervisor, Christmas-Tree Farm (forestry)	451.137-014
ERS	54	Supervisor, Cigar Making, Hand (tobacco)	790.134-010
ERS	54	Supervisor, Refractory Products (brick & tile)	579.134-018
ERS	54	Supervisor, Ski Production (toy-sport equip.)	692.132-018
ERS	53	Horse-Race Starter (amuse. & rec.)	153.267-010
ERS	53	Sanitation Inspector (government ser.)	168.267-110
ERS	53	Supervisor, Epoxy Fabrication (brick & tile)	579.134-014
ERS	53	Supervisor, Tubing (textile)	689.137-014
ERS	52	Elevator Starter (any industry)	388.367-010
ERS	52	Sales Clerk, Food (retail trade)	290.477-018
ERS	52	Scalp-Treatment Operator (personal ser.)	339.371-014
ERS	51	Gate Agent (air trans.)	238.367-010
ERS	51	Ski Patroller (amuse. & rec.)	379.664-010
ERS	51	Streetcar Operator (r.r. trans.)	913.463-014
ERS	50	Identifier, Horse (amuse. & rec.)	153.387-010
ERS	49	Lunch-Truck Driver (hotel & rest.)	292.463-010
ERS	48	Pigment Processor (chemical; paint & varnish)	559.685-130
ERS	47	Inspector-Repairer (button & notion)	734.684-018
ERS	47	Steward/Stewardess, Wine (water trans.)	350.677-026
ERS	46	Print Inspector (photofinishing)	976.687-022
ERS	45	Deliverer, Merchandise (retail trade)	299.477-010
ERS	45	Deputy Sheriff, Building Guard (government ser.)	377.667-014
ERS	44	Coach Driver (business ser.)	349.677-014
ERS	44	Porter, Baggage (hotel & rest.)	324.477-010
ERS	43	Photofinishing Laboratory Worker (photofinishing)	976.687-018
ERS	42	Bellhop (hotel & rest.)	324.677-010
ERS	42	Canteen Operator (any industry)	311.674-010
ERS	41	Doorkeeper (any industry)	324.677-014
ERC	67	Supervisor, Production Department (aircraft mfg.)	806.131-042
ERC	64	Deputy Sheriff, Commander, Criminal and Patrol Division (government ser.)	377.137-014
ERC	64	Manager, Production (radio-tv broad.)	184.162-010
ERC	63	Communications Electrician Supervisor (any industry)	823.131-010
ERC	62	Industrial-Safety-and-Health Technician (any industry)	168.161-014
ERC	60	Supervisor II (protective dev.)	789.134-014
ERC	60	Supervisor, Printed Circuit Board Assembly (electron. comp.)	726.134-010
ERC	59	Lead-Burner Supervisor (welding)	819.131-010
ERC	59	Mill Supervisor (smelt. & refin.)	515.130-010
ERC	59	Production Supervisor (nonmet. min.)	539.137-014

HOC	Cx	Title	DOT
ERC	59	Supervisor (comm. equip.)	619.130-046
ERC	59	Supervisor, Burling and Joining (textile)	689.132-010
ERC	59	Supervisor, Instrument Repair (any industry)	710.131-022
ERC	59	Supervisor, Sawing and Assembly (furniture)	669.132-010
ERC	58	Supervisor, Hearing-Aid Assembly (protective dev.)	726.131-014
ERC	57	Controller, Coal or Ore (mine & quarry)	939.167-010
ERC	57	Mine Inspector (mine & quarry)	168.267-074
ERC	57	Supervisor, Dairy Farm (agriculture)	410.131-018
ERC	56	Boatswain, Otter Trawler (fishing & hunt.)	441.132-010
ERC	56	Group Leader, Semiconductor Testing (electron. comp.)	726.362-010
ERC	55	Supervisor (brick & tile)	570.132-022
ERC	54	Express Clerk (motor trans.; r.r. trans.)	222.367-022
ERC	54	Lead Hand, Inspecting and Testing (electron. comp.)	726.364-010
ERC	53	Supervisor V (tex. prod., n.e.c.)	586.130-010
ERC	51	Lead Worker, Wafer Production (electron. comp.)	590.364-010
ERC	51	Supervisor, Foam Cutting (tex. prod., n.e.c.)	690.130-022
ERC	50	Baby-Stroller and Wheelchair Rental Clerk (retail trade)	295.367-014
ERC	50	Traffic Checker (government ser.)	205.367-058
ERC	49	Bar Attendant (hotel & rest.)	312.477-010
ERC	46	Extra (amuse. & rec.; motion picture; radio-tv broad.)	159.647-014
ERC	45	Bicycle-Rental Clerk (retail trade)	295.467-010
ERC	43	Cabana Attendant (amuse. & rec.)	349.677-010
ERC	42	Service Attendant, Sleeping Car (r.r. trans.)	351.677-010
EIR	75	Industrial Engineer (profess. & kin.)	012.167-030
EIR	72	Chief Pilot (air trans.)	196.167-010
EIR	70	Program Manager (profess. & kin.)	189.167-030
EIR	70	Sales Engineer, Agricultural Equipment (profess. & kin.)	013.151-010
EIR	70	Supervisor, Sewer System (waterworks)	184.167-238
EIR	70	Supervisor, Waterworks (waterworks)	184.167-246
EIR	69	Secretary, Board-of-Education (education)	169.267-022
EIR	68	Business-Enterprise Officer (government ser.)	188.117-014
EIR	67	Port Engineer (ship-boat mfg.; water trans.)	014.167-014
EIR	67	Sales Representative, Weighing and Force-Measurement Instruments (wholesale tr.)	276.257-014
EIR	67	Superintendent, Horticulture (museums)	180.161-014
EIR	66	Maintenance Supervisor (utilities)	184.167-050
EIR	65	Wine Maker (beverage)	183.161-014
EIR	64	Division Road Supervisor (r.r. trans.)	184.167-282
EIR	64	Superintendent, Production (agriculture)	180.167-058
EIR	63	Contractor (construction)	182.167-010
EIR	58	Supervisor, Water Treatment Plant (waterworks)	954.132-010
EIR	55	Utilities Service Investigator (utilities)	821.364-010
EIA	75	District Attorney (government ser.)	110.117-010
EIA	70	Supervisor, Vendor Quality (any industry)	012.167-062
EIA	69	Assignment Editor (radio-tv broad.)	132.132-010
EIA	64	Communications Consultant (tel. & tel.)	253.157-010

Part 2: From Holland Codes to Occupations

From Holland Codes to the Dictionary of Occupational Titles Occupations

HOC	Cx	Title	DOT
EIS	76	Operations Supervisor, Nuclear Power Plant (utilities)	952.132-010
EIS	73	Controller (profess. & kin.)	160.167-058
EIS	73	Educational Specialist (education)	099.167-022
EIS	72	Auditor (profess. & kin.)	160.167-054
EIS	70	Planner, Program Services (government ser.)	188.167-110
EIS	70	Project Manager, Environmental Research (profess. & kin.)	029.167-014
EIS	69	Laboratory Supervisor (profess. & kin.)	022.137-010
EIS	69	Manager, Education and Training (education)	166.167-026
EIS	67	Buyer, Grain (grain-feed mills; wholesale tr.)	162.167-010
EIS	67	Director, Food Services (hotel & rest.)	187.167-026
EIS	67	Supervisor, Frame Sample and Pattern (furniture)	661.137-010
EIS	66	Battalion Chief (government ser.)	373.167-010
EIS	64	Manager, Dental Laboratory (protective dev.)	187.167-090
EIC	75	Industrial-Health Engineer (profess. & kin.)	012.167-034
EIC	70	Chief Bank Examiner (government ser.)	160.167-046
EIC	70	Production Engineer (profess. & kin.)	012.167-046
EIC	69	Radiation-Protection Engineer (profess. & kin.)	015.137-010
EIC	68	Foreign-Exchange Dealer (financial)	186.117-082
EIC	67	Supervisor, Drafting and Printed Circuit Design (profess. & kin.)	003.131-010
EAR	67	Traffic-Safety Administrator (government ser.)	188.167-102
EAR	63	Location Manager (motion picture; radio-tv broad.)	191.167-018
EAR	59	Supervisor, Preparation Plant (mine & quarry)	549.137-014
EAR	55	Supervisor, Sewing Room (fabrication, n.e.c.)	787.132-014
EAI	74	Director of Vital Statistics (government ser.)	188.167-022
EAI	74	Patent Agent (profess. & kin.)	119.167-014
EAI	73	Director, State-Assessed Properties (government ser.)	188.167-042
EAI	66	Manager, Records Analysis (profess. & kin.)	161.167-018
EAI	66	Sales Representative, Elevators, Escalators, and Dumbwaiters (wholesale tr.)	274.157-010
EAI	62	Supervisor, Wool-Shearing (agriculture)	410.134-014
EAI	60	Supervisor, Insect and Disease Inspection (agriculture)	408.137-010
EAS	70	Program Proposals Coordinator (radio-tv broad.)	132.067-030
EAS	70	Superintendent, Tests (utilities)	184.167-218
EAS	69	Director, Council On Aging (government ser.)	188.117-058
EAS	68	Supervising Film-or-Videotape Editor (motion picture; radio-tv broad.)	962.132-010
EAS	67	Broker-and-Market Operator, Grain (financial; wholesale tr.)	162.157-010
EAS	67	Fashion Coordinator (retail trade)	185.157-010
EAS	66	Commissioner, Conservation of Resources (government ser.)	188.117-026
EAS	66	Manager, Forms Analysis (profess. & kin.)	161.167-014
EAS	66	Manager, Housing Project (profess. & kin.)	186.167-030
EAS	66	Manager, Reports Analysis (profess. & kin.)	161.167-022

HOC	Cx	Title	DOT
EAS	65	Field Supervisor, Seed Production (agriculture)	180.167-014
EAS	65	Music Supervisor (education)	099.167-026
EAS	64	Supervisor, Properties (motion picture)	962.137-026
EAS	63	Audiovisual Librarian (library)	100.167-010
EAS	63	Commission Agent, Livestock (wholesale tr.)	162.157-026
EAS	63	Field Representative (business ser.; wholesale tr.)	163.267-010
EAS	62	Artificial-Breeding Distributor (agriculture)	180.167-010
EAS	61	Crating-and-Moving Estimator (motor trans.; r.r. trans.)	252.357-010
EAS	58	Ring Conductor (amuse. & rec.)	159.367-010
EAS	57	Sales Representative, Water-Softening Equipment (retail trade; wholesale tr.)	279.357-034
EAS	56	Sales Representative, Upholstery and Furniture Repair (retail trade)	259.357-026
EAS	56	Salesperson, Yard Goods (retail trade)	261.357-070
EAS	55	Auctioneer (retail trade; wholesale tr.)	294.257-010
EAS	55	Supervisor, Fruit Grading (wholesale tr.)	529.137-046
EAS	54	Salesperson, Men's and Boys' Clothing (retail trade)	261.357-050
EAS	54	Salesperson, Millinery (retail trade)	261.357-058
EAS	53	Salesperson, Shoes (retail trade)	261.357-062
EAS	52	Salesperson, Women's Apparel and Accessories (retail trade)	261.357-066
EAS	47	Impersonator, Character (any industry)	299.647-010
EAS	45	Model (garment; retail trade; wholesale tr.)	297.667-014
EAC	56	Clown (amuse. & rec.)	159.047-010
ESR	76	Business Manager, College or University (education)	186.117-010
ESR	74	Vice President, Financial Institution (financial)	186.117-078
ESR	72	Executive Secretary, State Board of Nursing (government ser.)	169.117-010
ESR	72	Manager, Irrigation District (waterworks)	184.117-046
ESR	72	Manager, Leasing (petrol. & gas)	186.117-046
ESR	72	President, Educational Institution (education)	090.117-034
ESR	71	Treasurer, Financial Institution (financial)	186.117-070
ESR	70	Assessor-Collector, Irrigation Tax (government ser.)	188.167-014
ESR	70	Director, Employment Services (government ser.)	188.117-078
ESR	70	Director, Museum-or-Zoo (museums)	102.117-014
ESR	70	Director, Transportation (motor trans.)	184.117-014
ESR	70	Laboratory Assistant, Liaison Inspection (steel & rel.)	169.167-026
ESR	70	Manager, Airport (air trans.)	184.117-026
ESR	70	Manager, Athlete (amuse. & rec.)	153.117-014
ESR	70	Manager, Compensation (profess. & kin.)	166.167-022
ESR	70	Manager, Regional (motor trans.)	184.117-054
ESR	70	Real-Estate Agent (profess. & kin.)	186.117-058
ESR	70	Regulatory Administrator (tel. & tel.)	168.167-070
ESR	70	Sales Representative, Data Processing Services (business ser.)	251.157-014
ESR	70	Superintendent, Pipelines (pipe lines)	184.167-198
ESR	70	Treasurer (profess. & kin.)	161.117-018

HOC	Cx	Title	DOT
ESR	69	Configuration Management Analyst (profess. & kin.)	012.167-010
ESR	69	Court Administrator (government ser.)	188.117-130
ESR	69	Customs Broker (financial)	186.117-018
ESR	69	Deputy Insurance Commissioner (government ser.)	186.117-022
ESR	69	Director, Craft Center (profess. & kin.)	187.167-202
ESR	69	Director, Medical Facilities Section (government ser.)	188.117-082
ESR	69	Director, Sports (radio-tv broad.)	184.167-034
ESR	69	Director, Summer Sessions (education)	090.167-026
ESR	69	Manager, Brokerage Office (financial)	186.117-034
ESR	69	Manager, Financial Institution (financial)	186.167-086
ESR	69	Manager, Industrial Organization (any industry)	189.117-022
ESR	69	Manager, Operations (air trans.; motor trans.; r.r. trans.; water trans.)	184.117-050
ESR	69	President (any industry)	189.117-026
ESR	69	Roads Supervisor (government ser.)	188.167-078
ESR	69	Secretary of State (government ser.)	188.167-082
ESR	69	Superintendent, Marine Oil Terminal (water trans.)	184.167-186
ESR	69	Teacher, Resource (education)	099.227-042
ESR	69	Trust Officer (financial)	186.117-074
ESR	69	Vice President (any industry)	189.117-034
ESR	69	Vocational Rehabilitation Consultant (government ser.)	094.117-018
ESR	68	Clean-Rice Broker (grain-feed mills)	162.167-018
ESR	68	Director, Service (nonprofit org.)	187.167-214
ESR	68	Gas Inspector (utilities)	168.264-018
ESR	68	General Manager, Farm (agriculture; wholesale tr.)	180.167-018
ESR	68	Manager, Automotive Services (any industry)	184.117-034
ESR	68	Manager, Bakery (bakery products)	189.117-046
ESR	68	Manager, Cargo-and-Ramp-Services (air trans.)	184.167-058
ESR	68	Manager, Flight Control (air trans.)	184.167-066
ESR	68	Manager, Utility Sales and Service (utilities)	163.167-022
ESR	68	Mine Superintendent (mine & quarry)	181.117-014
ESR	68	Permit Agent, Geophysical Prospecting (petrol. & gas)	191.117-042
ESR	68	Port Purser (water trans.)	166.167-038
ESR	68	Production Engineer, Track (r.r. trans.)	005.167-026
ESR	68	Property-Disposal Officer (any industry)	163.167-026
ESR	68	Superintendent, Commissary (water trans.)	184.117-078
ESR	68	Superintendent, Communications (tel. & tel.)	184.117-082
ESR	68	Superintendent, Marine (water trans.)	184.167-182
ESR	68	Superintendent, Power (r.r. trans.)	184.167-202
ESR	67	Director, Education (museums)	099.117-030
ESR	67	Director, Food and Beverage (amuse. & rec.)	187.167-210
ESR	67	Director, Media Marketing (radio-tv broad.)	163.117-022
ESR	67	Freight-Traffic Consultant (business ser.)	184.267-010
ESR	67	Head Coach (amuse. & rec.)	153.117-010
ESR	67	Instructor, Business Education (education)	090.222-010
ESR	67	Manager, Hotel or Motel (hotel & rest.)	187.117-038
ESR	67	Manager, Labor Relations (profess. & kin.)	166.167-034
ESR	67	Manager, Office (government ser.)	188.167-058
ESR	67	Manager, Station (radio-tv broad.)	184.117-062

HOC	Cx	Title	DOT
ESR	67	Police Commissioner I (government ser.)	188.117-118
ESR	67	Right-of-Way Agent (any industry)	191.117-046
ESR	67	Safety Inspector (insurance)	168.167-078
ESR	67	Superintendent, Transportation (any industry)	184.167-226
ESR	66	Alcohol-and-Drug-Abuse-Assistance Program Administrator (government ser.)	195.167-042
ESR	66	Director, Field Services (education)	090.167-034
ESR	66	Field-Contact Technician (dairy products)	162.117-026
ESR	66	General Superintendent, Milling (grain-feed mills)	183.167-014
ESR	66	Legislative Assistant (government ser.)	169.167-066
ESR	66	Manager, Agricultural-Labor Camp (profess. & kin.)	187.167-050
ESR	66	Manager, Auto Specialty Services (automotive ser.)	185.167-074
ESR	66	Manager, Customer Technical Services (profess. & kin.)	189.117-018
ESR	66	Manager, Field Party, Geophysical Prospecting (petrol. & gas)	181.167-010
ESR	66	Manager, Food Processing Plant (can. & preserv.)	183.167-026
ESR	66	Manager, Food Service (hotel & rest.; personal ser.)	187.167-106
ESR	66	Manager, Real-Estate Firm (real estate)	186.167-066
ESR	66	Manager, Title Search (real estate)	186.167-090
ESR	66	Manager, Traffic (any industry)	184.167-094
ESR	66	Production Superintendent (any industry)	183.117-014
ESR	66	Superintendent, Division (motor trans.; r.r. trans.)	184.167-158
ESR	66	Superintendent, Plant Protection (any industry)	189.167-050
ESR	66	Supervisor of Sales (business ser.)	185.157-014
ESR	66	Teacher (museums)	099.227-038
ESR	66	Technical Training Coordinator (education)	166.167-054
ESR	66	Transportation-Maintenance Supervisor (any industry)	184.167-266
ESR	65	Area Supervisor, Retail Chain Store (retail trade)	185.117-014
ESR	65	Child Support Officer (government ser.)	195.267-022
ESR	65	Director, Funeral (personal ser.)	187.167-030
ESR	65	Director, Photogrammetry Flight Operations (business ser.)	184.167-026
ESR	65	Director, Underwriter Solicitation (radio-tv broad.)	163.117-026
ESR	65	Dispatcher, Oil (petrol. & gas; petrol. refin.; pipe lines)	914.167-014
ESR	65	Harbor Master (government ser.)	375.167-026
ESR	65	Jailer, Chief (government ser.)	372.167-018
ESR	65	Manager, Cemetery (real estate)	187.167-074
ESR	65	Manager, Theater (amuse. & rec.)	187.167-154
ESR	65	Postmaster (government ser.)	188.167-066
ESR	65	Sales Representative, Communication Equipment (wholesale tr.)	271.257-010
ESR	65	Sectional Center Manager, Postal Service (government ser.)	188.167-086
ESR	65	Service Supervisor, Leased Machinery and Equipment (any industry)	183.167-030
ESR	65	Supervisor, Prepress (print. & pub.)	972.137-010
ESR	65	Supervisor, Welding Equipment Repairer (welding)	626.137-010
ESR	64	Claim Adjuster (business ser.; insurance)	241.217-010
ESR	64	Commanding Officer, Motor Equipment (government ser.)	375.167-018
ESR	64	Deputy Sheriff, Chief (government ser.)	377.167-010
ESR	64	Management Trainee (any industry)	189.167-018

HOC	Cx	Title	DOT
ESR	64	Manager, Front Office (hotel & rest.)	187.137-018
ESR	64	Manager, Property (real estate)	186.167-046
ESR	64	Manager, Warehouse (any industry)	184.167-114
ESR	64	Sales Representative, Computers and EDP Systems (wholesale tr.)	275.257-010
ESR	64	Supervisor, Identification and Communications (government ser.)	377.134-010
ESR	64	Supervisor, Production Control (clerical)	221.137-018
ESR	64	Supervisor, Prop-Making (motion picture)	962.137-022
ESR	64	Traffic Agent (air trans.; motor trans.; r.r. trans.; water trans.)	252.257-010
ESR	63	Bookmobile Librarian (library)	100.167-014
ESR	63	Circus Agent (amuse. & rec.)	191.117-022
ESR	63	Commission Agent, Agricultural Produce (wholesale tr.)	260.357-010
ESR	63	Deputy Sheriff, Commander, Civil Division (government ser.)	377.137-010
ESR	63	Driver Supervisor (motor trans.)	909.137-010
ESR	63	Educational Resource Coordinator (museums)	099.167-030
ESR	63	Environmental Analyst (government ser.)	199.167-022
ESR	63	Fire Warden (forestry)	452.167-010
ESR	63	Human Resource Advisor (profess. & kin.)	166.267-046
ESR	63	Instructor, Sports (amuse. & rec.; education)	153.227-018
ESR	63	Landscape Contractor (construction)	182.167-014
ESR	63	Manager, Bus Transportation (motor trans.)	184.167-054
ESR	63	Manager, Land Leases-and-Rentals (petrol. & gas)	186.167-038
ESR	63	Manager, Merchandise (retail trade; wholesale tr.)	185.167-034
ESR	63	Manager, Office (any industry)	169.167-034
ESR	63	Manager, Recreation Facility (amuse. & rec.)	187.167-230
ESR	63	Master, Riverboat (water trans.)	197.163-018
ESR	63	Pit Steward (amuse. & rec.)	153.167-014
ESR	63	Police Inspector I (government ser.)	375.267-026
ESR	63	Purchasing Agent (profess. & kin.)	162.157-038
ESR	63	Purchasing-and-Claims Supervisor (water trans.)	248.137-014
ESR	63	Sales Representative, Oil Field Supplies and Equipment (wholesale tr.)	274.357-058
ESR	63	Secretary of Police (government ser.)	375.137-022
ESR	63	Service Manager (automotive ser.)	185.167-058
ESR	63	Station Agent I (r.r. trans.)	910.137-038
ESR	63	Supervisor, Food Checkers and Cashiers (hotel & rest.)	211.137-014
ESR	63	Supervisor, Inspection (aircraft mfg.)	806.131-038
ESR	63	Supervisor, Laboratory Animal Facility (agriculture)	418.137-010
ESR	63	Supervisor, Spray, Lawn and Tree Service (agriculture)	408.131-010
ESR	63	Supervisor, Volunteer Services (profess. & kin.)	187.137-014
ESR	63	Technical Coordinator (government ser.)	209.132-014
ESR	63	Umpire (amuse. & rec.)	153.267-018
ESR	62	Boat Dispatcher (water trans.)	184.167-010
ESR	62	Buyer, Assistant (retail trade)	162.157-022
ESR	62	Commanding Officer, Homicide Squad (government ser.)	375.167-010
ESR	62	Crew Scheduler, Chief (air trans.)	215.137-010

HOC	Cx	Title	DOT
ESR	62	General Supervisor (beverage)	183.167-022
ESR	62	Manager, Customer Services (business ser.; retail trade)	187.167-082
ESR	62	Manager, Skating Rink (amuse. & rec.)	187.167-146
ESR	62	Sales Representative, Audiovisual Program Productions (motion picture)	259.157-010
ESR	62	Sales Representative, Dental and Medical Equipment and Supplies (wholesale tr.)	276.257-010
ESR	62	Sales Representative, Signs and Displays (fabrication, n.e.c.)	254.257-010
ESR	62	Sales Supervisor, Malt Liquors (wholesale tr.)	299.137-014
ESR	62	Sample-Room Supervisor (textile)	299.137-018
ESR	62	Senior Reservations Agent (air trans.)	238.137-014
ESR	62	Stock-Control Supervisor (clerical)	222.137-038
ESR	62	Supervisor, Communications-and-Signals (r.r. trans.)	184.167-290
ESR	62	Supervisor, Gate Services (air trans.)	238.137-018
ESR	62	Supervisor, Motion-Picture Equipment (motion picture; photo. appar.)	714.131-010
ESR	62	Supervisor, Train Operations (r.r. trans.)	184.167-294
ESR	61	Advance Agent (amuse. & rec.)	191.167-010
ESR	61	Commanding Officer, Investigation Division (government ser.)	375.167-014
ESR	61	Commissary Manager (any industry)	185.167-010
ESR	61	Electrical-Appliance-Servicer Supervisor (any industry)	827.131-010
ESR	61	Electrician, Chief (motion picture)	824.137-010
ESR	61	Energy-Control Officer (education)	199.167-018
ESR	61	Investigator, Utility-Bill Complaints (utilities)	241.267-034
ESR	61	Manager, Cardroom (amuse. & rec.)	343.137-010
ESR	61	Manager, Dairy Farm (agriculture)	180.167-026
ESR	61	Manager, Tobacco Warehouse (wholesale tr.)	185.167-054
ESR	61	Manager, Travel Agency (business ser.; retail trade)	187.167-158
ESR	61	Sales Representative, Advertising (print. & pub.)	254.357-014
ESR	61	Sales Representative, Aircraft Equipment and Parts (wholesale tr.)	273.357-010
ESR	61	Sales Representative, Construction Machinery (wholesale tr.)	274.357-022
ESR	61	Sales Representative, Education Courses (education)	259.257-010
ESR	61	Sales Representative, Electronics Parts (wholesale tr.)	271.357-010
ESR	61	Sales Representative, Metals (wholesale tr.)	274.357-054
ESR	61	Sales Representative, Motor Vehicles and Supplies (wholesale tr.)	273.357-022
ESR	61	Sales Representative, Musical Instruments and Accessories (wholesale tr.)	277.357-014
ESR	61	Sales Representative, Poultry Equipment and Supplies (retail trade; wholesale tr.)	272.357-018
ESR	61	Sales Representative, Precision Instruments (wholesale tr.)	276.357-014
ESR	61	Sales Representative, Public Utilities (tel. & tel.; utilities)	253.357-010
ESR	61	Sales Representative, Railroad Equipment and Supplies (wholesale tr.)	273.357-026
ESR	61	Sales Representative, Textile Machinery (wholesale tr.)	274.357-070

Part 2: From Holland Codes to Occupations

From Holland Codes to the Dictionary of Occupational Titles Occupations

HOC	Cx	Title	DOT
ESR	61	Supervisor, Beater Room (paper & pulp)	530.132-014
ESR	61	Supervisor, Electronics Processing (electron. comp.)	590.130-010
ESR	61	Supervisor, Phosphatic Fertilizer (chemical)	558.130-010
ESR	61	Tariff Publishing Agent (business ser.)	184.167-250
ESR	61	Traffic Inspector (motor trans.; r.r. trans.)	184.163-010
ESR	61	Traffic Lieutenant (government ser.)	375.167-046
ESR	60	Agricultural-Chemicals Inspector (government ser.)	168.267-082
ESR	60	Booking Supervisor (water trans.)	248.137-010
ESR	60	Dredge Mate (water trans.)	197.137-010
ESR	60	Examination Proctor (government ser.)	199.267-018
ESR	60	Grip Boss (motion picture)	962.137-010
ESR	60	Manager, Health Club (personal ser.)	339.137-010
ESR	60	Manager, Liquor Establishment (hotel & rest.)	187.167-126
ESR	60	Manager, Lodging Facilities (hotel & rest.)	320.137-014
ESR	60	Manager, Machinery-or-Equipment, Rental and Leasing (any industry)	185.167-026
ESR	60	Park Ranger (government ser.)	169.167-042
ESR	60	Pesticide-Control Inspector (government ser.)	168.267-098
ESR	60	Police Lieutenant, Patrol (government ser.)	375.167-038
ESR	60	Police-Academy Instructor (government ser.)	375.227-010
ESR	60	Public Health Registrar (government ser.)	169.167-046
ESR	60	Sales Representative, Architectural and Engineering Supplies (wholesale tr.)	276.357-010
ESR	60	Sales Representative, Dairy Supplies (wholesale tr.)	274.357-030
ESR	60	Sales Representative, Industrial Rubber Goods (wholesale tr.)	274.357-042
ESR	60	Sales Representative, Mortician Supplies (wholesale tr.)	275.357-030
ESR	60	Sales Representative, Veterinarian Supplies (wholesale tr.)	276.357-018
ESR	60	Salesperson, Orthopedic Shoes (retail trade)	276.257-018
ESR	60	Salesperson, Pianos and Organs (retail trade)	277.354-010
ESR	60	Supervisor V (nonmet. min.)	692.132-014
ESR	60	Supervisor, Cardroom (amuse. & rec.)	343.137-014
ESR	60	Supervisor, Malt House (beverage)	522.132-010
ESR	60	Supervisor, Payroll (clerical)	215.137-014
ESR	60	Supervisor, Rose-Grading (agriculture)	405.137-010
ESR	60	Yard Supervisor (construction)	229.137-014
ESR	59	Acid Supervisor (chemical)	559.132-010
ESR	59	Announcer (amuse. & rec.)	159.347-010
ESR	59	Barn Boss (any industry)	410.131-010
ESR	59	Calender Supervisor (plastic-synth.)	559.132-014
ESR	59	Catalyst Operator, Chief (chemical)	559.132-018
ESR	59	Chef (hotel & rest.)	313.131-014
ESR	59	Control Clerk, Head (clock & watch)	221.137-010
ESR	59	Credit Analyst (clerical)	241.267-022
ESR	59	Dispatcher, Chief, Service or Work (utilities)	959.137-010
ESR	59	Dispatcher, Service or Work (utilities)	952.167-010
ESR	59	Dispatcher, Service, Chief (utilities)	959.137-014
ESR	59	Electric Motor Repairing Supervisor (any industry)	721.131-010
ESR	59	Film-Vault Supervisor (motion picture)	222.137-010

HOC	Cx	Title	DOT
ESR	59	Fire Marshal (government ser.)	373.267-014
ESR	59	Host/Hostess, Restaurant (hotel & rest.)	310.137-010
ESR	59	Instructor, Wastewater-Treatment Plant (sanitary ser.)	955.222-010
ESR	59	Mailroom Supervisor (clerical)	209.137-010
ESR	59	Manager, Department (retail trade)	299.137-010
ESR	59	Manager, Solid-Waste-Disposal (government ser.)	184.167-078
ESR	59	Manager, Truck Terminal (motor trans.)	184.167-110
ESR	59	Material Coordinator (clerical)	221.167-014
ESR	59	Office-Machine-Service Supervisor (any industry)	633.131-010
ESR	59	Porcelain-Enameling Supervisor (any industry)	590.131-010
ESR	59	Prize Coordinator (radio-tv broad.)	162.167-026
ESR	59	Production Coordinator (clerical)	221.167-018
ESR	59	Production Supervisor, Anhydrous Ammonia (chemical)	559.132-046
ESR	59	Sales Representative, Bottles and Bottling Equipment (wholesale tr.)	274.357-014
ESR	59	Sales Representative, Containers (wholesale tr.)	274.357-026
ESR	59	Sales Representative, Material-Handling Equipment (wholesale tr.)	274.357-050
ESR	59	Sales Representative, Office Machines (retail trade; wholesale tr.)	275.357-034
ESR	59	Sales Representative, School Equipment and Supplies (wholesale tr.)	275.357-042
ESR	59	Salesperson, Sheet Music (retail trade)	277.357-054
ESR	59	Service Observer, Chief (tel. & tel.)	239.137-022
ESR	59	Shift Superintendent, Caustic Cresylate (chemical)	552.132-010
ESR	59	Steward/Stewardess, Chief, Cargo Vessel (water trans.)	350.137-014
ESR	59	Steward/Stewardess, Chief, Passenger Ship (water trans.)	350.137-018
ESR	59	Steward/Stewardess, Railroad Dining Car (r.r. trans.)	310.137-026
ESR	59	Street-Light-Servicer Supervisor (utilities)	824.137-014
ESR	59	Superintendent, Cold Storage (any industry)	184.167-142
ESR	59	Superintendent, Local (utilities)	952.137-018
ESR	59	Supervisor III (tex. prod., n.e.c.)	789.132-018
ESR	59	Supervisor, Candle Making (fabrication, n.e.c.)	590.132-010
ESR	59	Supervisor, Cap-and-Hat Production (hat & cap)	784.130-010
ESR	59	Supervisor, Core Drilling (construction)	850.137-010
ESR	59	Supervisor, Dog License Officer (nonprofit org.)	379.137-014
ESR	59	Supervisor, Dry-Cell Assembly (elec. equip.)	727.137-010
ESR	59	Supervisor, Facepiece Line (protective dev.)	712.137-010
ESR	59	Supervisor, Fiberglass Boat Assembly (ship-boat mfg.)	806.134-014
ESR	59	Supervisor, Final Assembly and Packing (protective dev.)	712.137-014
ESR	59	Supervisor, Game Farm (agriculture)	412.131-010
ESR	59	Supervisor, Gelatin Plant (chemical)	559.137-030
ESR	59	Supervisor, Glue Specialty (chemical)	559.137-034
ESR	59	Supervisor, Grain and Yeast Plants (beverage)	529.132-062
ESR	59	Supervisor, Inspection (plastic-synth.)	559.137-038
ESR	59	Supervisor, Inspection (agric. equip.)	801.137-014
ESR	59	Supervisor, Metal Furniture Assembly (furniture)	709.134-010
ESR	59	Supervisor, Paint (paint & varnish)	559.132-114
ESR	59	Supervisor, Picking (tobacco)	521.137-010

HOC	Cx	Title	DOT
ESR	59	Supervisor, Powdered Metal (nonfer. metal; steel & rel.)	509.130-010
ESR	59	Supervisor, Route Sales-Delivery Drivers (retail trade; wholesale tr.)	292.137-014
ESR	59	Supervisor, Shipping Track (railroad equip.)	806.137-018
ESR	59	Supervisor, Ticket Sales (air trans.)	238.137-022
ESR	59	Supervisor, Upholstery Department (any industry)	780.131-014
ESR	59	Transformer Shop Supervisor (any industry)	724.131-014
ESR	59	Warehouse Supervisor (any industry)	929.137-022
ESR	58	Boxing-and-Pressing Supervisor (knitting)	789.137-010
ESR	58	Concrete-Batching and Mixing-Plant Supervisor (construction)	570.132-010
ESR	58	Dispatcher (construction)	849.137-010
ESR	58	Food-Service Supervisor (hotel & rest.)	319.137-010
ESR	58	Hearing Aid Specialist (retail trade)	276.354-010
ESR	58	Laboratory Chief (photofinishing)	976.131-010
ESR	58	Land-Leasing Examiner (government ser.)	237.367-026
ESR	58	Linen-Room Supervisor (laundry & rel.)	222.137-014
ESR	58	Mailroom Supervisor (print. & pub.)	222.137-022
ESR	58	Manager, Bowling Alley (amuse. & rec.)	187.167-222
ESR	58	Manager, Camp (construction; logging)	187.167-066
ESR	58	Milling Supervisor (brick & tile)	570.132-014
ESR	58	Packing-House Supervisor (agriculture; wholesale tr.)	920.137-010
ESR	58	Potato-Chip-Processing Supervisor (food prep., n.e.c.)	526.137-010
ESR	58	Preparation Supervisor (can. & preserv.)	529.137-010
ESR	58	Row Boss, Hoeing (agriculture)	409.137-014
ESR	58	Sales Agent, Pest Control Service (business ser.)	251.357-018
ESR	58	Sales Representative, Abrasives (wholesale tr.)	274.357-010
ESR	58	Sales Representative, Animal-Feed Products (wholesale tr.)	272.357-010
ESR	58	Sales Representative, Building Equipment and Supplies (wholesale tr.)	274.357-018
ESR	58	Sales Representative, Canvas Products (wholesale tr.)	261.357-014
ESR	58	Sales Representative, Men's and Boys' Apparel (wholesale tr.)	261.357-022
ESR	58	Sales Representative, Petroleum Products (wholesale tr.)	269.357-014
ESR	58	Sales Representative, Water-Treatment Chemicals (wholesale tr.)	262.357-022
ESR	58	Sales Representative, Welding Equipment (wholesale tr.)	274.357-074
ESR	58	Sales Representative, Wire Rope (wholesale tr.)	274.357-078
ESR	58	Salesperson, Automobiles (retail trade)	273.353-010
ESR	58	Steward/Stewardess, Second (water trans.)	350.137-022
ESR	58	Stock Supervisor (clerical)	222.137-034
ESR	58	Supervisor (tobacco)	529.137-026
ESR	58	Supervisor I (fabrication, n.e.c.)	739.131-010
ESR	58	Supervisor I (tex. prod., n.e.c.)	789.132-014
ESR	58	Supervisor, Advertising-Material Distributors (business ser.)	230.137-010
ESR	58	Supervisor, Asbestos Textile (nonmet. min.)	579.137-014
ESR	58	Supervisor, Assembly (agric. equip.)	801.137-010
ESR	58	Supervisor, Boat Outfitting (ship-boat mfg.)	806.131-018
ESR	58	Supervisor, Coffee (food prep., n.e.c.)	529.130-018

Part 2: From Holland Codes to Occupations

From Holland Codes to the Dictionary of Occupational Titles Occupations

HOC	Cx	Title	DOT
ESR	58	Supervisor, Composing-Room (print. & pub.)	973.137-010
ESR	58	Supervisor, Ice Storage, Sale, and Delivery (food prep., n.e.c.)	299.137-022
ESR	58	Supervisor, Inspection (glass mfg.)	579.134-010
ESR	58	Supervisor, Lime (concrete prod.)	579.132-014
ESR	58	Supervisor, Safety Deposit (financial)	295.137-010
ESR	58	Supervisor, Sewing Department (carpet & rug)	689.137-010
ESR	58	Supervisor, Sugar House (grain-feed mills)	529.132-090
ESR	58	Tool-Crib Supervisor (clerical)	222.137-046
ESR	57	Bus Dispatcher, Interstate (motor trans.)	913.167-010
ESR	57	Chief Clerk, Print Shop (clerical)	207.137-010
ESR	57	Dealer-Compliance Representative (retail trade; wholesale tr.)	168.267-026
ESR	57	Header (water trans.)	911.137-018
ESR	57	Housekeeper, Home (domestic ser.)	301.137-010
ESR	57	Manager, Boarding House (hotel & rest.)	320.137-010
ESR	57	Manager, Food Concession (hotel & rest.)	185.167-022
ESR	57	Manager, Storage Garage (automotive ser.)	187.167-150
ESR	57	Mixing Supervisor (plastic prod.)	550.135-014
ESR	57	Sack-Department Supervisor (grain-feed mills)	229.137-010
ESR	57	Sales Representative, Automotive-Leasing (business ser.)	273.357-014
ESR	57	Sales Representative, Church Furniture and Religious Supplies (wholesale tr.)	275.357-014
ESR	57	Sales Representative, Farm and Garden Equipment and Supplies (wholesale tr.)	272.357-014
ESR	57	Sales Representative, Franchise (business ser.)	251.357-022
ESR	57	Sales Representative, Hobbies and Crafts (retail trade; wholesale tr.)	277.357-010
ESR	57	Supervisor, Advertising-Dispatch Clerks (print. & pub.)	247.137-010
ESR	57	Supervisor, Asbestos Removal (construction)	869.134-026
ESR	57	Supervisor, Beehive Kiln (chemical)	563.137-010
ESR	57	Supervisor, Telephone Clerks (tel. & tel.)	239.132-010
ESR	57	Top Screw (agriculture)	410.137-014
ESR	56	Assistant Construction Superintendent (construction)	869.367-010
ESR	56	Conductor, Yard (r.r. trans.)	910.137-022
ESR	56	Counter Supervisor (hotel & rest.)	311.137-010
ESR	56	Headwaiter/Headwaitress (water trans.)	350.137-010
ESR	56	Inspector, Motor Vehicles (government ser.)	168.267-058
ESR	56	Manager, Reservations (hotel & rest.)	238.137-010
ESR	56	Personal Shopper (retail trade)	296.357-010
ESR	56	Police Inspector II (government ser.)	375.267-030
ESR	56	Program Assistant (radio-tv broad.)	962.167-014
ESR	56	Superintendent, Seed Mill (agriculture)	599.137-010
ESR	56	Superintendent, Service (hotel & rest.)	329.137-010
ESR	56	Supervisor, Cured-Meat Packing (meat products)	529.135-014
ESR	56	Supervisor, Finishing Room (print. & pub.)	979.137-010
ESR	56	Supervisor, Silvering Department (glass products)	574.132-014
ESR	56	Supervisor, Syrup Shed (sugar & conf.)	529.137-058
ESR	56	Supervisor, Wall Mirror Department (glass products)	739.137-022

Part 2: From Holland Codes to Occupations

From Holland Codes to the Dictionary of Occupational Titles Occupations

HOC	Cx	Title	DOT
ESR	56	Supervisor, Wet Pour (concrete prod.)	575.137-014
ESR	55	Airplane-Flight Attendant (air trans.)	352.367-010
ESR	55	Baggage Porter, Head (hotel & rest.)	324.137-010
ESR	55	Claims Clerk (auto. mfg.)	241.387-010
ESR	55	Magazine Supervisor (chemical; ordnance)	222.137-018
ESR	55	Migrant Leader (agriculture)	180.167-050
ESR	55	Sales Representative, Shipping Services (motor trans.)	252.357-014
ESR	55	Subscription Crew Leader (retail trade)	291.157-010
ESR	55	Supervisor, Contingents (retail trade)	205.367-050
ESR	55	Supervisor, Hide House (leather mfg.)	922.137-014
ESR	55	Supervisor, Janitorial Services (any industry)	381.137-010
ESR	55	Supervisor, Poultry Hatchery (agriculture)	411.137-010
ESR	55	Transportation Agent (air trans.)	912.367-014
ESR	54	Deputy, Court (government ser.)	377.137-018
ESR	54	Exhibit-Display Representative (any industry)	297.367-010
ESR	54	Group Leader (agriculture)	180.167-022
ESR	54	Guard, Chief (any industry)	372.167-014
ESR	54	Housekeeper (hotel & rest.; medical ser.; real estate)	321.137-010
ESR	54	Rater, Travel Accommodations (profess. & kin.)	168.367-014
ESR	54	Salesperson, Phonograph Records and Tape Recordings (retail trade)	277.357-046
ESR	54	Supervisor, Detasseling Crew (agriculture)	401.137-014
ESR	54	Tool-and-Equipment-Rental Clerk (business ser.; retail trade)	295.357-014
ESR	54	Trailer-Rental Clerk (automotive ser.)	295.467-022
ESR	53	Barber (personal ser.)	330.371-010
ESR	53	Barber Apprentice (personal ser.)	330.371-014
ESR	53	Bell Captain (hotel & rest.)	324.137-014
ESR	53	Caddie Supervisor (amuse. & rec.)	341.137-010
ESR	53	Dog Licenser (nonprofit org.)	249.367-030
ESR	53	Investigator (utilities)	376.367-022
ESR	53	Passenger Representative (r.r. trans.)	910.367-026
ESR	53	Personnel Quality Assurance Auditor (electron. comp.)	168.367-022
ESR	52	Driver, Sales Route (retail trade; wholesale tr.)	292.353-010
ESR	52	Game Attendant (amuse. & rec.)	342.657-014
ESR	52	Salesperson, Art Objects (retail trade)	277.457-010
ESR	52	Warehouse Traffic Supervisor (wholesale tr.)	922.137-026
ESR	51	Fire Ranger (forestry)	452.367-014
ESR	51	Host/Hostess, Ground (air trans.)	352.377-010
ESR	51	Sales Clerk (retail trade)	290.477-014
ESR	50	Guard, Immigration (government ser.)	372.567-014
ESR	50	Jailer (government ser.)	372.367-014
ESR	49	Attendant, Children's Institution (any industry)	359.677-010
ESR	49	Host/Hostess (any industry)	352.667-010
ESR	49	Thrill Performer (amuse. & rec.)	159.347-018
ESR	49	Waiter/Waitress, Bar (hotel & rest.)	311.477-018
ESR	48	Repossessor (clerical)	241.367-022
ESR	47	Lifeguard (amuse. & rec.)	379.667-014
ESR	47	Waiter/Waitress, Room Service (hotel & rest.)	311.477-034

HOC	Cx	Title	DOT
ESR	46	Parlor Chaperone (hotel & rest.)	352.667-014
ESR	45	Bailiff (government ser.)	377.667-010
ESR	45	Bouncer (amuse. & rec.)	376.667-010
ESR	44	Car Hop (hotel & rest.)	311.477-010
ESR	44	Sales Attendant (retail trade)	299.677-010
ESR	44	Waiter/Waitress, Take Out (hotel & rest.)	311.477-038
ESR	43	Escort (any industry)	353.667-010
ESR	43	Jockey Valet (amuse. & rec.)	346.677-010
ESR	43	Self-Service-Laundry-and-Dry-Cleaning Attendant (laundry & rel.)	369.677-010
ESR	42	Funeral Attendant (personal ser.)	359.677-014
ESR	40	Flagger (amuse. & rec.)	372.667-026
ESI	77	Lawyer (profess. & kin.)	110.107-010
ESI	77	Magistrate (government ser.)	111.107-014
ESI	76	Director, Quality Assurance (profess. & kin.)	189.117-042
ESI	75	Tax Attorney (profess. & kin.)	110.117-038
ESI	74	Manager, Land Development (real estate)	186.117-042
ESI	73	Bar Examiner (profess. & kin.)	110.167-010
ESI	73	Department Head, College or University (education)	090.167-010
ESI	73	Library Consultant (library)	100.117-014
ESI	73	Title Attorney (profess. & kin.)	110.117-042
ESI	72	Budget Officer (profess. & kin.)	161.117-010
ESI	72	Certification and Selection Specialist (education)	099.167-010
ESI	72	Estate Planner (insurance)	186.167-010
ESI	71	Credit Counselor (profess. & kin.)	160.207-010
ESI	71	Executive Director, Red Cross (nonprofit org.)	187.117-066
ESI	71	Urban Planner (profess. & kin.)	199.167-014
ESI	70	District Customs Director, Deputy (government ser.)	188.167-046
ESI	70	Factor (financial)	186.167-082
ESI	70	Manager, Flight Operations (air trans.)	184.117-038
ESI	70	Project Director (profess. & kin.)	189.117-030
ESI	70	Sales-Engineer, Electrical Products (profess. & kin.)	003.151-010
ESI	70	Sales-Engineer, Electronics Products and Systems (profess. & kin.)	003.151-014
ESI	70	Supervisor, Estimator and Drafter (utilities)	019.161-010
ESI	69	Chief, Computer Programmer (profess. & kin.)	030.167-010
ESI	69	Dietitian, Chief (profess. & kin.)	077.117-010
ESI	69	Director, Industrial Relations (profess. & kin.)	166.117-010
ESI	69	Manager, Exchange Floor (financial)	186.117-086
ESI	69	Manager, Traffic II (tel. & tel.)	184.167-106
ESI	68	Dispatcher (air trans.)	912.167-010
ESI	67	Group Worker (social ser.)	195.164-010
ESI	67	Producer (amuse. & rec.)	187.167-178
ESI	67	Revenue Officer (government ser.)	188.167-074
ESI	67	Superintendent, Sanitation (government ser.)	188.167-098
ESI	67	Supervisor, Bridges and Buildings (r.r. trans.)	182.167-034
ESI	67	Supervisor, Computer Operations (clerical)	213.132-010
ESI	67	Supervisor, Special Services (education)	169.267-026

Part 2: From Holland Codes to Occupations

From Holland Codes to the Dictionary of Occupational Titles Occupations

HOC	Cx	Title	DOT
ESI	66	Newscaster (radio-tv broad.)	131.262-010
ESI	66	Service Representative, Elevators, Escalators, and Dumbwaiters (wholesale tr.)	259.257-018
ESI	66	Vending-Stand Supervisor (government ser.)	185.167-066
ESI	65	Director, Merit System (government ser.)	188.117-086
ESI	65	Health Officer, Field (government ser.)	168.167-018
ESI	65	Supervisor (government ser.)	188.137-010
ESI	65	Supervisor, Operations (utilities)	952.137-026
ESI	64	Floor Broker (financial)	162.167-034
ESI	63	Ferryboat Captain (water trans.)	197.163-010
ESI	60	Molding Supervisor (plastic prod.)	556.130-018
ESI	60	Safety Coordinator (motor trans.)	909.127-010
ESI	59	Quality-Control Supervisor (plastic prod.)	559.134-010
ESI	58	Investigator, Private (business ser.)	376.267-018
ESI	58	Library Technical Assistant (library)	100.367-018
ESI	58	Operations Manager (motor trans.)	184.167-118
ESI	57	Blending Supervisor (tobacco)	520.136-010
ESI	57	Cheese Blender (dairy products)	520.487-010
ESI	56	Handicapper, Harness Racing (amuse. & rec.)	219.267-010
ESA	77	Judge (government ser.)	111.107-010
ESA	77	Lawyer, Admiralty (profess. & kin.)	110.117-018
ESA	77	Lawyer, Corporation (profess. & kin.)	110.117-022
ESA	77	Lawyer, Criminal (profess. & kin.)	110.107-014
ESA	77	Lawyer, Patent (profess. & kin.)	110.117-026
ESA	77	Lawyer, Probate (profess. & kin.)	110.117-030
ESA	77	Lawyer, Real Estate (profess. & kin.)	110.117-034
ESA	75	Director of Placement (education)	166.167-014
ESA	74	Director of Counseling (profess. & kin.)	045.107-018
ESA	74	Producer (motion picture)	187.167-174
ESA	74	Revenue-Settlements Administrator (tel. & tel.)	184.117-074
ESA	73	Director, Extension Work (education)	090.117-026
ESA	73	Editor, Managing, Newspaper (print. & pub.)	132.017-010
ESA	73	Right-of-Way Supervisor (any industry)	191.117-050
ESA	72	Superintendent, Recreation (government ser.)	187.117-054
ESA	70	Executive Vice President, Chamber of Commerce (nonprofit org.)	187.117-030
ESA	70	Manager, Export (any industry)	163.117-014
ESA	70	Manager, Traffic (air trans.; motor trans.; water trans.)	184.117-066
ESA	70	Operations Manager (tel. & tel.)	184.117-070
ESA	70	Producer, Assistant (motion picture)	187.167-182
ESA	69	Association Executive (profess. & kin.)	189.117-010
ESA	69	Conciliator (profess. & kin.)	169.207-010
ESA	69	Director, Camp (social ser.)	195.167-018
ESA	69	Director, Safety Council (government ser.)	188.167-034
ESA	69	Director, Securities and Real Estate (government ser.)	188.167-038
ESA	69	Economic Development Coordinator (government ser.)	188.117-102
ESA	69	Foreign-Service Officer (government ser.)	188.117-106
ESA	69	Manager, Customer Service (tel. & tel.)	168.167-058

Part 2: From Holland Codes to Occupations

From Holland Codes to the Dictionary of Occupational Titles Occupations

HOC	Cx	Title	DOT
ESA	69	Port-Traffic Manager (water trans.)	184.167-122
ESA	69	Recreation Supervisor (profess. & kin.)	187.167-238
ESA	69	Superintendent, Sales (construction)	250.157-010
ESA	69	Wholesaler I (wholesale tr.)	185.167-070
ESA	68	Brewing Director (beverage)	183.167-010
ESA	68	Director, Fundraising (nonprofit org.)	165.117-010
ESA	68	Lobbyist (profess. & kin.)	165.017-010
ESA	68	Manager, Advertising (print. & pub.)	163.167-010
ESA	68	Manager, Branch (any industry)	183.117-010
ESA	68	Manager, Sales (any industry)	163.167-018
ESA	68	Risk and Insurance Manager (any industry)	186.117-066
ESA	68	Sales Representative, Financial Services (financial)	250.257-022
ESA	68	Superintendent, Maintenance (air trans.)	184.167-174
ESA	67	Artist's Manager (amuse. & rec.)	191.117-010
ESA	67	Civil Preparedness Officer (government ser.)	188.117-022
ESA	67	Commercial Loan Collection Officer (financial)	186.167-078
ESA	67	Director, Classification and Treatment (government ser.)	188.167-026
ESA	67	Director, Field (social ser.)	195.167-022
ESA	67	District Adviser (nonprofit org.)	187.117-022
ESA	67	Division Manager, Chamber of Commerce (nonprofit org.)	187.167-042
ESA	67	Field Representative (profess. & kin.)	189.267-010
ESA	67	Literary Agent (business ser.)	191.117-034
ESA	67	Manager, Area Development (utilities)	184.117-030
ESA	67	Manager, Nursery (agriculture; retail trade; wholesale tr.)	180.167-042
ESA	67	Manager, World Trade and Maritime Division (nonprofit org.)	187.167-170
ESA	67	Rehabilitation Center Manager (government ser.)	195.167-038
ESA	67	Veterans Contact Representative (nonprofit org.)	187.167-198
ESA	67	Wholesaler II (wholesale tr.)	185.157-018
ESA	66	Administrator, Social Welfare (profess. & kin.)	195.117-010
ESA	66	Alumni Secretary (education)	090.117-014
ESA	66	Business-Opportunity-and-Property-Investment Broker (business ser.; real estate)	189.157-010
ESA	66	Captain, Fire-Prevention Bureau (government ser.)	373.167-014
ESA	66	Community Organization Worker (social ser.)	195.167-010
ESA	66	Contract Administrator (any industry)	162.117-014
ESA	66	Contract Specialist (profess. & kin.)	162.117-018
ESA	66	Director of Admissions (education)	090.167-014
ESA	66	Director of Religious Activities (education)	129.107-018
ESA	66	Director, News (radio-tv broad.)	184.167-014
ESA	66	Director, Recreation Center (social ser.)	195.167-026
ESA	66	Director, Vocational Training (education)	097.167-010
ESA	66	Four-H Club Agent (education)	096.127-022
ESA	66	Home-Service Director (profess. & kin.)	096.161-010
ESA	66	Legal Investigator (profess. & kin.)	119.267-022
ESA	66	Manager, Convention (hotel & rest.)	187.167-078
ESA	66	Manager, Department (any industry)	189.167-022
ESA	66	Manager, Game Preserve (agriculture)	180.167-038
ESA	66	Manager, Professional Equipment Sales-and-Service (business ser.)	185.167-042

HOC	Cx	Title	DOT
ESA	66	Manager, Station (air trans.)	184.167-082
ESA	66	Media Specialist, School Library (library)	100.167-030
ESA	66	Membership Director (profess. & kin.)	189.167-026
ESA	66	Outside Property Agent (motion picture)	162.157-030
ESA	66	Pharmaceutical Detailer (wholesale tr.)	262.157-010
ESA	66	Property-Utilization Officer (government ser.)	188.117-122
ESA	66	Sales Agent, Psychological Tests and Industrial Relations (business ser.; print. & pub.)	251.257-014
ESA	66	Social Worker, Medical (profess. & kin.)	195.107-030
ESA	66	Specialist-In-Charge, Extension Service (government ser.)	096.167-014
ESA	66	Superintendent (agriculture; can. & preserv.)	180.167-054
ESA	66	Water Control Supervisor (waterworks)	184.167-270
ESA	65	Business Representative, Labor Union (profess. & kin.)	187.167-018
ESA	65	Chief Warden (government ser.)	188.167-018
ESA	65	Election Assistant (government ser.)	188.167-050
ESA	65	Equal-Opportunity Representative (government ser.)	168.167-014
ESA	65	Manager, Fish Hatchery (fishing & hunt.)	180.167-030
ESA	65	Sales Representative, Electroplating (wholesale tr.)	259.257-014
ESA	64	Conductor, Passenger Car (r.r. trans.)	198.167-010
ESA	64	Demonstrator, Electric-Gas Appliances (utilities)	297.357-010
ESA	64	Director, Technical (radio-tv broad.)	962.162-010
ESA	64	Representative, Personal Service (tel. & tel.)	236.252-010
ESA	63	Civil Preparedness Training Officer (government ser.)	169.127-010
ESA	63	Interpreter (profess. & kin.)	137.267-010
ESA	63	Manufacturer's Representative (wholesale tr.)	279.157-010
ESA	63	Reports Analyst (profess. & kin.)	161.267-026
ESA	63	Sales Representative, Telephone Services (tel. & tel.)	253.257-010
ESA	63	Salesperson, Surgical Appliances (retail trade)	276.257-022
ESA	63	Supervisor, Airplane-Flight Attendant (air trans.)	352.137-010
ESA	63	Supervisor, Travel-Information Center (government ser.)	237.137-014
ESA	63	Testing-and-Regulating Chief (tel. & tel.)	184.167-258
ESA	62	Buyer, Tobacco, Head (wholesale tr.)	162.167-014
ESA	62	Manager, Parts (retail trade; wholesale tr.)	185.167-038
ESA	62	Manager, Telegraph Office (tel. & tel.)	184.167-086
ESA	62	Manager, Textile Conversion (business ser.; wholesale tr.)	185.167-050
ESA	62	Supervisor, Tar Distillation (chemical)	542.130-014
ESA	61	Building Consultant (wholesale tr.)	250.357-010
ESA	61	Manager, Armored Transport Service (business ser.)	372.167-022
ESA	61	Sales Agent, Financial-Report Service (business ser.)	250.357-026
ESA	61	Sales Representative, Livestock (wholesale tr.)	260.257-010
ESA	61	Sales Representative, Radiographic-Inspection Equipment and Services (wholesale tr.)	271.352-010
ESA	61	Sales Representative, Textiles (wholesale tr.)	261.357-030
ESA	61	Special Agent (r.r. trans.)	372.267-010
ESA	61	Supervisor, Customer Services (motor trans.)	248.137-018
ESA	61	Supervisor, Terminal Operations (motor trans.)	184.167-242
ESA	60	Dispatcher, Security Guard (business ser.)	372.167-010
ESA	60	Leasing Agent, Residence (real estate)	250.357-014
ESA	60	Patrol Judge (amuse. & rec.)	153.267-014

HOC	Cx	Title	DOT
ESA	60	Sales Representative, Hotel and Restaurant Equipment and Supplies (wholesale tr.)	275.357-026
ESA	60	Salesperson, Musical Instruments and Accessories (retail trade)	277.357-038
ESA	60	Sous Chef (water trans.)	315.137-014
ESA	60	Supervisor, Costuming (motion picture; radio-tv broad.)	962.137-018
ESA	60	Supervisor, Dock (petrol. refin.; pipe lines)	914.137-018
ESA	60	Supervisor, Paint Department (any industry)	749.131-014
ESA	59	CD-Storage-and-Materials-Make-Up Operator, Head (chemical)	559.167-010
ESA	59	Chef, Passenger Vessel (water trans.)	315.137-010
ESA	59	Sales Representative, Printing Supplies (wholesale tr.)	274.357-062
ESA	59	Sales Representative, Textile Designs (wholesale tr.)	274.357-066
ESA	59	Salesperson, Burial Needs (retail trade)	279.357-042
ESA	59	Song Plugger (recording)	165.157-010
ESA	59	Supervisor (knitting)	684.137-010
ESA	59	Supervisor, Channel Process (chemical)	559.137-022
ESA	59	Supervisor, Maintenance (petrol. refin.)	899.137-018
ESA	59	Supervisor, Painting, Shipyard (ship-boat mfg.)	840.131-014
ESA	59	Waiter/Waitress, Head (hotel & rest.)	311.137-022
ESA	58	Manager, Meat Sales and Storage (retail trade; wholesale tr.)	185.167-030
ESA	58	Sales Representative, Commercial Equipment and Supplies (wholesale tr.)	275.357-018
ESA	58	Sales Representative, Footwear (wholesale tr.)	261.357-018
ESA	58	Sales Representative, Jewelry (wholesale tr.)	279.357-018
ESA	58	Sales Representative, Leather Goods (wholesale tr.)	279.357-022
ESA	58	Sales Representative, Signs (fabrication, n.e.c.)	254.357-022
ESA	58	Sales Representative, Uniforms (retail trade; wholesale tr.)	261.357-034
ESA	58	Salesperson, Flying Squad (retail trade)	279.357-046
ESA	58	Supervisor, Maple Products (food prep., n.e.c.)	529.137-050
ESA	58	Supervisor, Packing Room (leather mfg.)	589.137-010
ESA	58	Supervisor, Reclamation (wholesale tr.)	621.137-010
ESA	58	Ticket Broker (amuse. & rec.)	259.357-034
ESA	58	Waiter/Waitress, Banquet, Head (hotel & rest.)	311.137-014
ESA	57	Circulation-Sales Representative (print. & pub.)	299.167-010
ESA	57	Collection Clerk (clerical)	241.357-010
ESA	57	Flight Attendant, Ramp (air trans.)	352.367-014
ESA	57	Manager, Dance Studio (education)	187.167-086
ESA	57	Sales Agent, Business Services (business ser.)	251.357-010
ESA	57	Sales Representative, Apparel Trimmings (wholesale tr.)	261.357-010
ESA	57	Sales Representative, Barber and Beauty Equipment and Supplies (wholesale tr.)	275.357-010
ESA	57	Sales Representative, Boats and Marine Supplies (retail trade; wholesale tr.)	273.357-018
ESA	57	Sales Representative, Chemicals and Drugs (wholesale tr.)	262.357-010
ESA	57	Sales Representative, Cordage (wholesale tr.)	275.357-022
ESA	57	Sales Representative, Food Products (wholesale tr.)	260.357-014
ESA	57	Sales Representative, Fuels (retail trade; wholesale tr.)	269.357-010

HOC	Cx	Title	DOT
ESA	57	Sales Representative, General Merchandise (wholesale tr.)	279.357-014
ESA	57	Sales Representative, Hardware Supplies (wholesale tr.)	274.357-034
ESA	57	Sales Representative, Herbicide Service (business ser.)	251.357-026
ESA	57	Sales Representative, Home Furnishings (wholesale tr.)	270.357-010
ESA	57	Sales Representative, Household Appliances (wholesale tr.)	270.357-014
ESA	57	Sales Representative, Novelties (wholesale tr.)	277.357-018
ESA	57	Sales Representative, Paper and Paper Products (wholesale tr.)	279.357-026
ESA	57	Sales Representative, Pressure-Sensitive Tape (wholesale tr.)	275.357-038
ESA	57	Sales Representative, Printing (wholesale tr.)	254.357-018
ESA	57	Sales Representative, Publications (wholesale tr.)	277.357-022
ESA	57	Sales Representative, Recreation and Sporting Goods (wholesale tr.)	277.357-026
ESA	57	Sales Representative, Safety Apparel and Equipment (wholesale tr.)	261.357-026
ESA	57	Sales Representative, Shoe Leather and Findings (wholesale tr.)	275.357-046
ESA	57	Sales Representative, Toilet Preparations (wholesale tr.)	262.357-014
ESA	57	Sales Representative, Vending and Coin Machines (wholesale tr.)	275.357-050
ESA	57	Sales Representative, Weather-Forecasting Service (business ser.)	259.357-030
ESA	57	Sales Representative, Women's and Girls' Apparel (wholesale tr.)	261.357-038
ESA	57	Salesperson, Automobile Accessories (retail trade; wholesale tr.)	273.357-030
ESA	57	Salesperson, China and Silverware (retail trade; wholesale tr.)	270.357-018
ESA	57	Salesperson, Curtains and Draperies (retail trade)	270.357-022
ESA	57	Salesperson, Floor Coverings (retail trade; wholesale tr.)	270.357-026
ESA	57	Salesperson, Florist Supplies (wholesale tr.)	275.357-054
ESA	57	Salesperson, Furs (retail trade)	261.357-042
ESA	57	Salesperson, Horticultural and Nursery Products (retail trade; wholesale tr.)	272.357-022
ESA	57	Salesperson, Household Appliances (retail trade)	270.357-034
ESA	57	Salesperson, Jewelry (retail trade)	279.357-058
ESA	57	Salesperson, Men's Furnishings (retail trade)	261.357-054
ESA	57	Salesperson, Pets and Pet Supplies (retail trade)	277.357-042
ESA	57	Salesperson, Photographic Supplies and Equipment (retail trade; wholesale tr.)	277.357-050
ESA	57	Salesperson, Sporting Goods (retail trade)	277.357-058
ESA	57	Salesperson, Stamps or Coins (retail trade; wholesale tr.)	277.357-062
ESA	57	Salesperson, Stereo Equipment (retail trade)	270.357-038
ESA	57	Salesperson, Trailers and Motor Homes (retail trade)	273.357-034
ESA	57	Salesperson-Demonstrator, Party Plan (retail trade)	279.357-038
ESA	56	Circus-Train Supervisor (amuse. & rec.)	910.137-018
ESA	56	Garbage-Collection Supervisor (motor trans.)	909.137-014
ESA	56	Linen Controller (laundry & rel.)	299.357-010

HOC	Cx	Title	DOT
ESA	56	Sales Representative, Television Cable Service (radio-tv broad.)	259.357-022
ESA	56	Sales Representative, Tobacco Products and Smoking Supplies (retail trade; wholesale tr.)	260.357-022
ESA	56	Sales Representative, Writing and Marking Pens (wholesale tr.)	277.357-030
ESA	56	Salesperson, Infants' and Children's Wear (retail trade)	261.357-046
ESA	56	Supervisor, Rug Cleaning (laundry & rel.)	369.137-014
ESA	56	Wine Steward/Stewardess (hotel & rest.)	310.357-010
ESA	55	Blood-Donor Recruiter (medical ser.)	293.357-010
ESA	55	Launch Commander, Harbor Police (government ser.)	375.167-030
ESA	55	Sales Representative, Malt Liquors (wholesale tr.)	260.357-018
ESA	55	Supervisor, Tank Cleaning (paint & varnish)	559.137-050
ESA	54	Salesperson, Cosmetics and Toiletries (retail trade)	262.357-018
ESA	54	Salesperson, Furniture (retail trade)	270.357-030
ESA	53	Salesperson, Wigs (personal ser.; retail trade)	261.351-010
ESA	52	Fire Lookout (forestry)	452.367-010
ESA	52	Fund Raiser II (nonprofit org.)	293.357-014
ESA	52	Photographer (amuse. & rec.)	143.457-010
ESA	52	Sales Exhibitor (nonprofit org.)	279.357-010
ESA	52	Sales Representative, Door-To-Door (retail trade)	291.357-010
ESA	52	Sales-Promotion Representative (wholesale tr.)	269.357-018
ESA	52	Salesperson, General Hardware (retail trade; wholesale tr.)	279.357-050
ESA	52	Track Supervisor (grain-feed mills)	921.132-010
ESA	51	Salesperson, General Merchandise (retail trade; wholesale tr.)	279.357-054
ESA	51	Show-Horse Driver (amuse. & rec.)	159.344-018
ESA	51	Tobacco-Warehouse Agent (business ser.)	259.357-038
ESA	50	Alarm Investigator (business ser.)	376.367-010
ESA	50	Guide, Establishment (any industry)	353.367-014
ESA	49	Detective II (any industry)	376.667-014
ESA	49	House Officer (hotel & rest.)	376.367-018
ESA	48	Barker (amuse. & rec.)	342.657-010
ESA	48	Weight Guesser (amuse. & rec.)	342.357-010
ESA	44	Cigarette Vendor (hotel & rest.)	291.457-010
ESC	74	Director, Outpatient Services (medical ser.)	187.117-058
ESC	73	Director of Institutional Research (education)	090.167-018
ESC	73	Manager, Insurance Office (insurance)	186.167-034
ESC	72	Manager, Regulated Program (government ser.)	168.167-090
ESC	72	User Representative, International Accounting (profess. & kin.)	189.117-038
ESC	71	Manager, Contracts (petrol. & gas; petrol. refin.; pipe lines)	163.117-010
ESC	70	Dietary Manager (hotel & rest.)	187.167-206
ESC	70	Logistics Engineer (profess. & kin.)	019.167-010
ESC	70	Radiology Administrator (medical ser.)	187.117-062
ESC	70	Registrar, College or University (education)	090.167-030
ESC	70	Reserve Officer (financial; insurance)	186.167-054
ESC	69	Adjudicator (government ser.)	119.167-010

Part 2: From Holland Codes to Occupations

From Holland Codes to the Dictionary of Occupational Titles Occupations

HOC	Cx	Title	DOT
ESC	69	Manager, Traffic I (motor trans.)	184.167-102
ESC	69	Media Director (profess. & kin.)	164.117-018
ESC	68	Director of Student Affairs (education)	090.167-022
ESC	68	Director, Educational Program (education)	099.117-010
ESC	68	Dispatcher, Chief I (petrol. & gas; petrol. refin.; pipe lines)	184.167-038
ESC	68	Manager, Flight-Reservations (air trans.)	184.167-070
ESC	68	Superintendent, Stations (motor trans.; r.r. trans.)	184.167-206
ESC	67	Administrative Secretary (any industry)	169.167-014
ESC	67	Business Manager (amuse. & rec.)	191.117-018
ESC	67	Director of Pupil Personnel Program (education)	099.167-034
ESC	67	Director, Educational Programming (radio-tv broad.)	169.167-070
ESC	67	Director, Operations (radio-tv broad.)	184.167-018
ESC	67	Director, Regulatory Agency (government ser.)	188.117-134
ESC	67	Field Supervisor, Broadcast (radio-tv broad.)	193.167-014
ESC	67	Letter-of-Credit Document Examiner (financial)	169.267-042
ESC	67	Manager, Car Inspection and Repair (r.r. trans.)	184.117-086
ESC	67	Manager, Circulation (print. & pub.)	163.167-014
ESC	67	Manager, Employment (profess. & kin.)	166.167-030
ESC	67	Operations Officer (financial)	186.137-014
ESC	67	Regional Superintendent, Railroad Car Inspection and Repair (r.r. trans.)	184.117-090
ESC	67	Stations-Relations-Contact Representative (radio-tv broad.)	184.167-134
ESC	67	Superintendent, Radio Communications (government ser.)	193.167-018
ESC	67	Supervisor of Way (r.r. trans.)	184.167-234
ESC	66	Administrative Assistant (any industry)	169.167-010
ESC	66	Director, Nurses' Registry (medical ser.)	187.167-034
ESC	66	Director, Service (retail trade)	189.167-014
ESC	66	General Agent, Operations (air trans.; motor trans.; r.r. trans.)	184.167-042
ESC	66	Historic-Site Administrator (museums)	102.167-014
ESC	66	Instructor, Bridge (education)	159.227-010
ESC	66	Manager, Benefits (profess. & kin.)	166.167-018
ESC	66	Manager, Communications Station (tel. & tel.)	184.167-062
ESC	66	Manager, Traffic (radio-tv broad.)	184.167-090
ESC	66	Special Agent (insurance)	166.167-046
ESC	66	Special Agent, Group Insurance (insurance)	169.167-050
ESC	66	Superintendent, Concrete-Mixing Plant (construction)	182.167-022
ESC	66	Teller, Head (financial)	211.132-010
ESC	66	Terminal Superintendent (r.r. trans.)	184.167-254
ESC	66	User Support Analyst Supervisor (profess. & kin.)	032.132-010
ESC	65	Chief Dispatcher (petrol. & gas)	939.137-010
ESC	65	Financial Planner (profess. & kin.)	250.257-014
ESC	65	Genealogist (profess. & kin.)	052.067-018
ESC	65	Historian, Dramatic Arts (profess. & kin.)	052.067-026
ESC	65	Manager, Animal Shelter (nonprofit org.)	187.167-218
ESC	65	Manager, Credit and Collection (any industry)	169.167-086
ESC	65	Manager, Retail Store (retail trade)	185.167-046
ESC	65	Racing Secretary and Handicapper (amuse. & rec.)	153.167-018
ESC	65	Supervisor of Communications (any industry)	184.167-230

From Holland Codes to the Dictionary of Occupational Titles Occupations

HOC	Cx	Title	DOT
ESC	64	Buyer (profess. & kin.)	162.157-018
ESC	64	Commander, Internal Affairs (government ser.)	375.167-050
ESC	64	Commanding Officer, Police (government ser.)	375.137-034
ESC	64	Commercial-Instructor Supervisor (tel. & tel.; utilities; waterworks)	239.137-010
ESC	64	Director, Financial Responsibility Division (government ser.)	188.167-030
ESC	64	Executive Producer, Promos (radio-tv broad.)	159.167-022
ESC	64	Manager, Distribution Warehouse (wholesale tr.)	185.167-018
ESC	64	Manager, Fish-and-Game Club (amuse. & rec.)	187.167-102
ESC	64	Manager, Winter Sports (amuse. & rec.)	187.167-166
ESC	64	Purser (water trans.)	197.167-014
ESC	64	Registered Representative (financial)	250.257-018
ESC	64	Registration Specialist, Agricultural Chemicals (government ser.)	168.267-106
ESC	64	Sales Agent, Insurance (insurance)	250.257-010
ESC	64	Security Consultant (business ser.; personal ser.)	189.167-054
ESC	63	Claim Examiner (business ser.; insurance)	241.267-018
ESC	63	Condominium Manager (real estate)	186.167-062
ESC	63	Director, Day Care Center (education)	092.167-010
ESC	63	Director, Radio (radio-tv broad.)	159.167-014
ESC	63	Forms Analyst (profess. & kin.)	161.267-018
ESC	63	Guide, Travel (personal ser.)	353.167-010
ESC	63	Manager, Employment Agency (profess. & kin.)	187.167-098
ESC	63	Manager, Stage (amuse. & rec.; radio-tv broad.)	159.167-018
ESC	63	Office Supervisor, Animal Hospital (nonprofit org.)	249.137-010
ESC	63	Records-Management Analyst (profess. & kin.)	161.267-022
ESC	63	Sales Representative, Hotel Services (hotel & rest.)	259.157-014
ESC	63	Special Agent-In-Charge (r.r. trans.)	376.167-010
ESC	63	Supervisor, Claims (insurance)	241.137-018
ESC	63	Supervisor, Customer Records Division (utilities)	249.137-022
ESC	63	Supervisor, Force Adjustment (tel. & tel.)	215.137-018
ESC	63	Travel Clerk (government ser.)	238.167-010
ESC	62	Admissions Evaluator (education)	205.367-010
ESC	62	Deposit Clerk (utilities)	241.267-026
ESC	62	Feed and Farm Management Adviser (agriculture; retail trade)	096.127-018
ESC	62	Hospital-Insurance Representative (insurance)	166.267-014
ESC	62	Manager, Market (retail trade; wholesale tr.)	186.167-042
ESC	62	Station Manager (r.r. trans.)	184.167-130
ESC	62	Transfer Clerk, Head (financial)	216.137-014
ESC	61	Commander, Police Reserves (government ser.)	375.137-030
ESC	61	Communications Coordinator (medical ser.)	239.167-010
ESC	61	Director, Social (hotel & rest.; water trans.)	352.167-010
ESC	61	Manager, Barber or Beauty Shop (personal ser.)	187.167-058
ESC	61	Sales Agent, Real Estate (real estate)	250.357-018
ESC	61	Supervisor, Blood-Donor Recruiters (medical ser.)	293.137-010
ESC	61	Supervisor, Cashiers (hotel & rest.; retail trade)	211.137-010
ESC	61	Supervisor, Classified Advertising (print. & pub.)	247.137-014

HOC to DOT

From Holland Codes to the Dictionary of Occupational Titles Occupations

HOC	Cx	Title	DOT
ESC	61	Supervisor, Customer-Complaint Service (clerical)	241.137-014
ESC	61	Supervisor, Home-Energy Consultant (utilities)	959.137-022
ESC	61	Yard Manager (r.r. trans.)	184.167-278
ESC	60	Complaint Evaluation Supervisor (government ser.)	375.137-038
ESC	60	Employer Relations Representative (profess. & kin.)	166.257-010
ESC	60	Investigator (clerical)	241.267-030
ESC	60	Loading-Rack Supervisor (petrol. refin.)	914.137-014
ESC	60	Supervisor, Surgical Garment Assembly (protective dev.)	712.132-010
ESC	60	Tester, Food Products (any industry)	199.251-010
ESC	59	Alarm Operator (government ser.)	379.162-010
ESC	59	Detective Chief (government ser.)	375.167-022
ESC	59	Manager, Flight Kitchen (hotel & rest.)	319.137-014
ESC	59	Petroleum-Inspector Supervisor (business ser.)	222.137-026
ESC	59	Sales Representative, Lubricating Equipment (wholesale tr.)	274.357-046
ESC	59	Superintendent, Grain Elevator (beverage; grain-feed mills)	529.137-022
ESC	59	Supervisor (oils & grease)	529.137-030
ESC	59	Supervisor, Aircraft Cleaning (air trans.)	891.137-014
ESC	59	Supervisor, Coating (plastic-synth.)	554.137-014
ESC	59	Supervisor, Compounding-and-Finishing (chemical)	550.137-010
ESC	59	Supervisor, Flame Cutting (steel & rel.)	819.132-010
ESC	59	Supervisor, Order Takers (clerical)	249.137-026
ESC	59	Supervisor, Toilet-and-Laundry Soap (soap & rel.)	559.132-130
ESC	58	Bookmaker (amuse. & rec.)	187.167-014
ESC	58	Car Clerk, Pullman (r.r. trans.)	215.167-010
ESC	58	Demonstrator, Knitting (retail trade)	297.354-014
ESC	58	Desk Officer (government ser.)	375.137-014
ESC	58	Instrument-Shop Supervisor (tel. & tel.)	722.131-010
ESC	58	Rate Supervisor (clerical)	214.137-018
ESC	58	Salesperson, Books (retail trade)	277.357-034
ESC	58	Senior Enlisted Advisor (military ser.)	166.167-042
ESC	58	Supervisor, Bonding (textile)	589.137-014
ESC	58	Supervisor, Car Installations (railroad equip.)	806.137-010
ESC	58	Supervisor, Cutting Department (any industry)	781.134-010
ESC	58	Supervisor, Taping (construction)	842.134-010
ESC	57	Butler (domestic ser.)	309.137-010
ESC	57	Dispatcher, Tugboat (water trans.)	911.167-010
ESC	57	Film-Rental Clerk (business ser.; retail trade)	295.367-018
ESC	57	Fruit Coordinator (can. & preserv.)	529.167-010
ESC	57	Loan Interviewer, Mortgage (financial)	241.367-018
ESC	57	Meter Reader, Chief (utilities; waterworks)	209.137-014
ESC	57	Order Dispatcher, Chief (utilities)	959.137-018
ESC	57	Sales Representative, Plastic Products (wholesale tr.)	279.357-030
ESC	57	Supervisor, Files (clerical)	206.137-010
ESC	57	Vault Cashier (business ser.)	222.137-050
ESC	56	Airplane-Charter Clerk (air trans.)	295.367-010
ESC	56	Mail-Distribution-Scheme Examiner (government ser.)	239.367-018
ESC	56	Sales Representative, Videotape (wholesale tr.)	271.357-014
ESC	56	Salesperson, Parts (retail trade; wholesale tr.)	279.357-062
ESC	56	Salesperson, Toy Trains and Accessories (retail trade)	277.357-066

HOC	Cx	Title	DOT
ESC	55	Car Distributor (r.r. trans.)	910.367-014
ESC	55	Decorating-and-Assembly Supervisor (plastic prod.)	754.130-010
ESC	55	Employment-and-Claims Aide (government ser.)	169.367-010
ESC	55	Membership Solicitor (any industry)	293.357-022
ESC	55	Supervisor, Filling-and-Packing (paint & varnish)	920.137-022
ESC	55	Typing Section Chief (clerical)	203.137-014
ESC	54	Apparel-Rental Clerk (retail trade)	295.357-010
ESC	54	Automobile Rental Clerk (automotive ser.)	295.467-026
ESC	54	Claims Clerk II (insurance)	205.367-018
ESC	54	Collector (clerical)	241.367-010
ESC	54	Customer-Service Clerk (retail trade)	299.367-010
ESC	54	Demonstrator (retail trade; wholesale tr.)	297.354-010
ESC	54	Desk Clerk, Bowling Floor (amuse. & rec.)	340.367-010
ESC	54	Driver's License Examiner (government ser.)	168.267-034
ESC	54	Group-Sales Representative (amuse. & rec.)	259.357-010
ESC	54	Pay-Station Attendant (tel. & tel.)	237.367-034
ESC	54	Recreation-Facility Attendant (amuse. & rec.)	341.367-010
ESC	54	Scorer (amuse. & rec.)	153.387-014
ESC	54	Shopping Investigator (business ser.)	376.267-022
ESC	54	Teacher Aide II (education)	249.367-074
ESC	54	Telephone Solicitor (any industry)	299.357-014
ESC	54	Travel Clerk (hotel & rest.)	238.367-030
ESC	53	Animal-Hospital Clerk (medical ser.)	245.367-010
ESC	53	Dispatcher, Motor Vehicle (clerical)	249.167-014
ESC	53	Leasing Agent, Outdoor Advertising (business ser.)	254.357-010
ESC	53	Receiver-Dispatcher (nonprofit org.)	239.367-022
ESC	53	Usher, Head (amuse. & rec.)	344.137-010
ESC	51	Cardroom Attendant I (amuse. & rec.)	343.467-010
ESC	51	Dude Wrangler (amuse. & rec.)	353.364-010
ESC	51	Guide, Plant (any industry)	353.367-018
ESC	51	Guide, Sightseeing (amuse. & rec.; personal ser.)	353.363-010
ESC	51	Physical Therapy Aide (medical ser.)	355.354-010
ESC	51	Process Server (business ser.)	249.367-062
ESC	51	Receiving-Barn Custodian (amuse. & rec.)	349.367-014
ESC	50	Communication-Center Operator (air trans.)	235.662-014
ESC	50	Goodwill Ambassador (business ser.)	293.357-018
ESC	50	Lost-and-Found Clerk (clerical)	222.367-034
ESC	49	Clocker (amuse. & rec.)	153.367-010
ESC	49	Golf-Course Ranger (amuse. & rec.)	379.667-010
ESC	49	Waiter/Waitress, Informal (hotel & rest.)	311.477-030
ESC	48	Guide (personal ser.)	353.367-010
ESC	48	Host/Hostess, Head (amuse. & rec.)	349.667-014
ESC	45	Bodyguard (personal ser.)	372.667-014
ESC	45	Guard, School-Crossing (government ser.)	371.567-010
ESC	45	Newspaper Carrier (retail trade)	292.457-010
ESC	45	Patroller (r.r. trans.)	376.667-018
ESC	45	Steward/Stewardess (water trans.)	350.677-022
ESC	44	Lei Seller (retail trade)	291.454-010
ESC	43	Dresser (amuse. & rec.)	346.674-010

Dictionary of Holland Occupational Codes

HOC	Cx	Title	DOT
ESC	43	Peddler (retail trade)	291.457-018
ESC	42	Grader (can. & preserv.)	529.687-098
ESC	42	Manicurist (personal ser.)	331.674-010
ESC	41	Waiter/Waitress, Club (hotel & rest.)	352.677-018
ECR	66	Executive Housekeeper (any industry)	187.167-046
ECR	66	Supervisor, Mapping (petrol. & gas; pipe lines)	018.167-030
ECR	65	Central-Office-Repairer Supervisor (tel. & tel.)	822.131-010
ECR	61	Rigger Supervisor (radio-tv broad.; tel. & tel.)	823.131-014
ECR	61	Test-Desk Supervisor (tel. & tel.)	822.131-030
ECR	60	Supervisor I (protective dev.)	692.137-014
ECR	60	Supervisor, Yarn Preparation (textile)	689.130-034
ECR	59	Supervisor, Fiber-Locking (textile)	689.132-014
ECR	59	Supervisor, Instant Potato Processing (food prep., n.e.c.)	529.137-078
ECR	59	Supervisor, Locomotive (r.r. trans.)	625.137-010
ECR	58	Rate Reviewer (utilities)	214.387-014
ECR	58	Supervisor, Animal Maintenance (pharmaceut.)	410.137-018
ECR	58	Supervisor, Furniture Assembly (furniture)	763.134-014
ECR	55	Dispatcher, Relay (pipe lines)	221.362-014
ECR	55	Supervisor, Incinerator Plant (sanitary ser.)	955.131-010
ECR	54	Supervisor, Brake Repair (r.r. trans.)	622.137-010
ECR	53	Job Tracer (clerical)	221.387-034
ECR	53	Supervisor, Car and Yard (r.r. trans.)	622.137-014
ECR	52	Circulation Clerk (print. & pub.)	209.362-010
ECR	51	Head Doffer (textile)	689.366-010
ECR	47	Grain Receiver (grain-feed mills)	921.365-010
ECR	45	Office Helper (clerical)	239.567-010
ECR	45	Trapper, Bird (fishing & hunt.)	461.684-018
ECR	44	Laborer, Poultry Hatchery (agriculture)	411.687-022
ECR	41	Lard Refiner (meat products; oils & grease)	529.685-158
ECR	40	Coal Sampler (utilities)	922.687-038
ECR	40	Sorting-Machine Operator (paper goods)	649.665-010
ECI	76	Superintendent, Electric Power (utilities)	184.167-162
ECI	75	Superintendent, Distribution I (utilities)	184.167-150
ECI	70	Procurement Engineer (aircraft mfg.)	162.157-034
ECI	69	Auditor, County or City (government ser.)	160.167-030
ECI	63	Town Clerk (government ser.)	243.367-018
ECS	70	Accountant, Tax (profess. & kin.)	160.162-010
ECS	69	Director, Funds Development (profess. & kin.)	165.117-014
ECS	69	Purchase-Price Analyst (profess. & kin.)	162.167-030
ECS	69	Securities Trader (financial)	162.167-038
ECS	68	Utilization-Review Coordinator (medical ser.)	079.267-010
ECS	67	Director, Records Management (profess. & kin.)	161.117-014
ECS	67	Occupational-Safety-and-Health Inspector (government ser.)	168.167-062
ECS	66	Manager, Golf Club (amuse. & rec.)	187.167-114
ECS	66	Manager, Procurement Services (profess. & kin.)	162.167-022

Part 2: From Holland Codes to Occupations

From Holland Codes to the Dictionary of Occupational Titles Occupations

HOC	Cx	Title	DOT
ECS	65	Supervisor, Real-Estate Office (real estate)	249.137-030
ECS	64	Superintendent, Maintenance of Equipment (motor trans.; r.r. trans.)	184.167-178
ECS	62	Escrow Officer (profess. & kin.)	119.367-010
ECS	62	Train Dispatcher (r.r. trans.)	184.167-262
ECS	61	Distribution Supervisor (pipe lines; wholesale tr.)	914.137-010
ECS	61	Supervisor, Keymodule Assembly (office machines)	692.130-038
ECS	60	Pawnbroker (retail trade)	191.157-010
ECS	60	Supervisor, Telecommunicator (government ser.)	379.132-010
ECS	60	Supervisor, Type Photography (machinery mfg.)	976.131-026
ECS	60	Supervisor, Type-Disk Quality Control (machinery mfg.)	979.137-026
ECS	60	Travel Agent (business ser.; motor trans.; retail trade)	252.152-010
ECS	59	Building-Insulation Supervisor (construction)	863.134-010
ECS	59	Dispatcher, Service (utilities)	959.167-010
ECS	59	Production Supervisor, Defluorinated Phosphate (chemical)	559.132-050
ECS	59	Supervisor, Dehydrogenation (chemical; petrol. refin.)	559.132-078
ECS	59	Supervisor, Processing (sugar & conf.)	529.137-082
ECS	59	Supervisor, Smoke Control (steel & rel.)	861.134-010
ECS	58	Admitting Officer (medical ser.)	205.162-010
ECS	58	Conductor, Road Freight (r.r. trans.)	198.167-018
ECS	58	Supervisor, Dry-Starch (grain-feed mills)	529.132-046
ECS	58	Train Dispatcher, Assistant Chief (r.r. trans.)	910.167-014
ECS	57	Dispatcher, Concrete Products (concrete prod.; construction)	579.137-030
ECS	57	General Car Supervisor, Yard (r.r. trans.)	184.167-286
ECS	56	Sugar-Reprocess Operator, Head (sugar & conf.)	529.137-018
ECS	56	Supervisor, Artificial Breast Fabrication (protective dev.)	712.134-010
ECS	54	Cashier, Courtesy Booth (retail trade)	211.467-010
ECS	54	Complaint Evaluation Officer (government ser.)	375.367-014
ECS	54	Hotel Clerk (hotel & rest.)	238.367-038
ECS	54	Reproduction Order Processor (clerical)	221.367-058
ECS	54	Safe-Deposit-Box Rental Clerk (financial)	295.367-022
ECS	54	Unit Clerk (medical ser.)	245.362-014
ECS	53	Hospital-Admitting Clerk (medical ser.)	205.362-018
ECS	53	Information Clerk (clerical)	237.367-022
ECS	53	Scheduler, Maintenance (clerical)	221.367-066
ECS	52	Charter (amuse. & rec.)	249.367-018
ECS	51	Alterations Workroom Clerk (retail trade)	221.367-010
ECS	51	Automobile Locator (retail trade)	296.367-010
ECS	51	Demonstrator, Sewing Techniques (retail trade)	297.454-010
ECS	51	Food Order Expediter (hotel & rest.)	319.467-010
ECS	51	Manager, Branch Store (laundry & rel.)	369.467-010
ECS	51	Order-Control Clerk, Blood Bank (medical ser.; nonprofit organ.)	245.367-026
ECS	51	Service-Establishment Attendant (laundry & rel.; personal ser.)	369.477-014
ECS	50	Card Player (amuse. & rec.)	343.367-010
ECS	50	Service Clerk (clerical)	221.367-070
ECS	50	Waiter/Waitress, Formal (hotel & rest.)	311.477-026

HOC	Cx	Title	DOT
ECS	49	Passenger Service Representative I (r.r. trans.)	352.677-010
ECS	49	Waiter/Waitress, Dining Car (r.r. trans.)	311.477-022
ECS	45	Lounge-Car Attendant (r.r. trans.)	291.457-014
ECS	43	Room-Service Clerk (hotel & rest.)	324.577-010
ECS	42	Field Inspector, Disease and Insect Control (agriculture)	408.687-010
ECS	42	Host/Hostess, Dance Hall (amuse. & rec.)	349.667-010
ECS	42	Sampler (petrol. refin.)	549.587-014
ECS	41	Press-Box Custodian (amuse. & rec.)	344.677-010
CRI	70	Accountant, Budget (profess. & kin.)	160.162-022
CRI	66	Fire-Protection Engineering Technician (profess. & kin.)	019.261-026
CRI	59	Infantry Operations Specialist (military ser.)	378.367-022
CRI	58	Fixed-Capital Clerk (utilities)	210.382-042
CRI	58	Polysomnographic Technician (medical ser.)	078.362-042
CRI	57	Canceling and Cutting Control Clerk (financial)	219.367-042
CRI	57	Nesting Operator, Numerical Control (aircraft mfg.)	007.362-010
CRI	56	Clearing-House Clerk (financial)	216.382-026
CRI	56	Photo Mask Technician, Electron-Beam (electron. comp.)	972.382-022
CRI	56	Receipt-and-Report Clerk (water trans.)	216.382-054
CRI	56	Stock Control Clerk (clerical)	219.387-030
CRI	55	Teller, Vault (financial)	211.382-010
CRI	51	Notereader (clerical)	203.582-078
CRI	47	Instrument Inspector (inst. & app.)	710.684-050
CRI	42	Liquid-Fertilizer Servicer (agriculture)	906.683-014
CRA	58	Computer Typesetter-Keyliner (print. & pub.)	979.382-026
CRA	44	Photo Checker and Assembler (photofinishing)	976.687-014
CRS	69	Credit Analyst (financial)	160.267-022
CRS	69	Underwriter, Mortgage Loan (financial)	186.267-026
CRS	59	General-Ledger Bookkeeper (clerical)	210.382-046
CRS	59	Night Auditor (hotel & rest.)	210.382-054
CRS	59	Paste-Up Artist (print. & pub.)	972.381-030
CRS	59	Paste-Up Artist Apprentice (print. & pub.)	972.381-038
CRS	57	Police Clerk (government ser.)	375.362-010
CRS	56	Interline Clerk (motor trans.; r.r. trans.)	214.382-022
CRS	56	Margin Clerk I (financial)	216.362-042
CRS	56	Media Clerk (business ser.)	247.382-010
CRS	56	Progress Clerk (construction)	221.362-022
CRS	56	Sound Cutter (motion picture)	962.382-014
CRS	56	Tonnage-Compilation Clerk (water trans.)	248.387-014
CRS	55	Billing Clerk (clerical)	214.362-042
CRS	55	Clerk, Television Production (radio-tv broad.)	221.367-086
CRS	55	Crew Scheduler (air trans.)	215.362-010
CRS	55	Mortgage Clerk (financial)	249.362-014
CRS	55	Mortgage Loan Processor (financial)	249.362-022
CRS	55	Mortgage-Accounting Clerk (clerical)	216.362-026
CRS	55	Radiotelegraph Operator (tel. & tel.)	193.262-030
CRS	54	Aircraft-Log Clerk (air trans.)	221.362-010

HOC	Cx	Title	DOT
CRS	54	Billing-Machine Operator (clerical)	214.482-010
CRS	54	Cost Clerk (clerical)	216.382-034
CRS	54	Disbursement Clerk (financial)	219.367-046
CRS	54	Film-or-Tape Librarian (clerical)	222.367-026
CRS	54	Lumber Estimator (wood. container)	221.482-014
CRS	54	Returned-Item Clerk (financial)	216.382-058
CRS	54	Statistical Clerk (clerical)	216.382-062
CRS	53	Digitizer Operator (business ser.; petrol. & gas)	213.582-010
CRS	53	Dividend Clerk (financial)	216.482-034
CRS	53	Fabric-and-Accessories Estimator (garment)	221.482-010
CRS	53	Parts-Order-and-Stock Clerk (clerical)	249.367-058
CRS	53	Policy-Value Calculator (insurance)	216.382-050
CRS	53	Sample Clerk (furniture)	221.382-026
CRS	53	Statement Clerk (financial)	214.362-046
CRS	53	Tape Librarian (clerical)	206.367-018
CRS	53	Title Searcher (real estate)	209.367-046
CRS	52	Expediter, Service Order (furniture)	222.367-070
CRS	52	Money Counter (amuse. & rec.)	211.467-014
CRS	52	Property Clerk (government ser.)	222.367-054
CRS	52	Terminal-Makeup Operator (print. & pub.)	208.382-010
CRS	52	Weather Clerk (air trans.)	248.362-014
CRS	52	Word Processing Machine Operator (clerical)	203.382-030
CRS	51	Audit-Machine Operator (clerical)	216.482-018
CRS	51	Booking Prizer (tobacco)	216.462-010
CRS	51	Char-Filter Operator (sugar & conf.)	521.365-010
CRS	51	Clerk, General (clerical)	209.562-010
CRS	51	Jacket Preparer (print. & pub.)	221.387-030
CRS	51	Mail Carrier (government ser.)	230.367-010
CRS	51	Naphtha-Washing-System Operator (plastic-synth.)	559.382-038
CRS	51	Pricer, Message and Delivery Service (business ser.)	214.467-014
CRS	51	Statistical Clerk, Advertising (retail trade)	216.382-066
CRS	50	Checker II (clerical)	209.687-010
CRS	50	Contact Worker, Lithography (print. & pub.)	976.684-038
CRS	50	Functional Tester, Typewriters (office machines)	706.382-010
CRS	50	Music Copyist (print. & pub.)	209.582-010
CRS	50	Tester, Sound (machinery mfg.)	706.382-014
CRS	50	Traffic Clerk (radio-tv broad.)	209.382-022
CRS	50	Traffic Clerk (clerical)	214.587-014
CRS	50	Winding Inspector and Tester (elec. equip.)	724.364-010
CRS	49	Armature Tester I (elec. equip.)	724.384-010
CRS	49	Braille Operator (print. & pub.)	203.582-010
CRS	49	Cut-File Clerk (print. & pub.)	222.367-014
CRS	49	Gas Usage Meter Clerk (petrol. refin.; pipe lines; utilities)	216.685-010
CRS	49	Inspector (toy-sport equip.)	732.684-130
CRS	49	Insulator Tester (utilities)	729.387-026
CRS	49	Metal-Finish Inspector (any industry)	703.687-014
CRS	49	Pantry Worker (sugar & conf.)	520.487-018
CRS	49	Plate Inspector (print. & pub.)	972.687-010
CRS	49	Rug Dyer II (laundry & rel.)	364.684-010

HOC	Cx	Title	DOT
CRS	49	Sterilizer (medical ser.; pharmaceut.; protective dev.)	599.585-010
CRS	49	Weaver, Hand (personal ser.)	782.381-022
CRS	48	Assembly-Line Inspector (furniture)	709.684-018
CRS	48	Body Wirer (vehicles, n.e.c.)	829.684-014
CRS	48	Candle-Extrusion-Machine Operator (fabrication, n.e.c.)	692.682-026
CRS	48	Chart Changer (clerical)	221.584-010
CRS	48	Control Inspector (paper & pulp; wood prod., n.e.c.)	539.667-010
CRS	48	Conveyor-System Operator (any industry)	921.662-018
CRS	48	Die Cutter (any industry)	699.682-022
CRS	48	Electronics Tester (comm. equip.; electron. comp.; inst. & app.; office machines)	726.684-026
CRS	48	Icicle-Machine Operator (dairy products)	920.482-010
CRS	48	Inspector (nonmet. min.)	776.667-010
CRS	48	Jewel Inspector (clock & watch)	770.687-022
CRS	48	Line Walker (petrol. & gas; petrol. refin.; pipe lines)	869.564-010
CRS	48	Mold Operator (elec. equip.)	729.684-030
CRS	48	Pilot-Control-Operator Helper (chemical; plastic-synth.)	559.664-014
CRS	48	Reduction-Furnace Operator (chemical)	553.682-022
CRS	48	Street-Light-Servicer Helper (utilities)	824.664-010
CRS	48	Subassembler (office machines)	706.684-094
CRS	48	Tip Printer (hat & cap)	651.682-022
CRS	47	Battery Assembler (elec. equip.)	727.684-010
CRS	47	Canopy Stringer (tex. prod., n.e.c.)	789.684-018
CRS	47	Carpenter I (mfd. bldgs.)	860.664-010
CRS	47	Drawbridge Operator (r.r. trans.)	371.362-010
CRS	47	Embossograph Operator (any industry)	652.682-014
CRS	47	File Cutter (cutlery-hrdwr.)	605.685-014
CRS	47	Fur Plucker (leather mfg.)	585.681-014
CRS	47	Furniture Assembler (furniture)	763.684-038
CRS	47	Glass-Cutting-Machine Operator, Automatic (glass mfg.)	677.562-010
CRS	47	Inspector (jewelry-silver.)	700.687-034
CRS	47	Inspector, Wheel and Pinion (clock & watch)	715.684-126
CRS	47	Loader I (any industry)	914.667-010
CRS	47	Mother Repairer (recording)	705.684-042
CRS	47	Needle Straightener (knitting)	628.684-018
CRS	47	Outside Cutter, Hand (boot & shoe)	788.684-082
CRS	47	Protective-Signal-Installer Helper (business ser.)	822.664-010
CRS	47	Pump Tester (plastic-synth.)	557.564-014
CRS	47	Safety-Lamp Keeper (mine & quarry)	729.684-042
CRS	47	Sail Cutter (tex. prod., n.e.c.)	781.384-018
CRS	47	Screwmaker, Automatic (clock & watch)	609.682-030
CRS	47	Sports-Equipment Repairer (any industry)	732.684-122
CRS	47	Strap-Machine Operator (paper goods)	534.682-034
CRS	47	Thickener Operator (smelt. & refin.)	511.485-014
CRS	47	Upholstery Sewer (any industry)	780.682-018
CRS	46	Assembler, Musical Instruments (musical inst.)	730.684-010
CRS	46	Assembly Inspector (furniture)	763.684-010
CRS	46	Ball-Mill Operator (chemical)	558.685-014
CRS	46	Bow Rehairer (any industry)	730.684-022

Part 2: From Holland Codes to Occupations

From Holland Codes to the Dictionary of Occupational Titles Occupations

HOC	Cx	Title	DOT
CRS	46	Cannon-Pinion Adjuster (clock & watch)	715.684-046
CRS	46	Carbonation Equipment Tender (beverage)	522.685-026
CRS	46	Carpet Inspector, Finished (carpet & rug)	689.564-010
CRS	46	Chain Maker, Machine (jewelry-silver.)	700.684-022
CRS	46	Coiled-Coil Inspector (light. fix.)	725.684-010
CRS	46	Coloring-Machine Operator (hat & cap)	582.685-034
CRS	46	Crown-Wheel Assembler (clock & watch)	715.684-074
CRS	46	Earring Maker (jewelry-silver.)	700.684-030
CRS	46	Electronics Inspector (electron. comp.)	726.684-022
CRS	46	Element Winding Machine Tender (elec. equip.; inst. & app.)	724.685-010
CRS	46	Embossing-Machine Operator I (clerical)	208.582-014
CRS	46	Fiberglass-Dowel-Drawing-Machine Operator (plastic prod.)	575.682-010
CRS	46	Formula-Room Worker (dairy products)	520.487-014
CRS	46	Fuse Assembler (ordnance)	737.684-022
CRS	46	Iron-Launder Operator (smelt. & refin.)	511.565-018
CRS	46	Motor-and-Generator-Brush Maker (elec. equip.)	724.684-038
CRS	46	Put-In-Beat Adjuster (clock & watch)	715.684-174
CRS	46	Receiving Checker (clerical)	222.687-018
CRS	46	Screen Printer (textile)	979.684-030
CRS	46	Sewing Machine Operator I (tex. prod., n.e.c.)	787.682-066
CRS	46	Ticket-Dispenser Changer (amuse. & rec.)	349.680-010
CRS	46	Wirer, Subassemblies (office machines)	729.684-062
CRS	45	Antenna Installer (any industry)	823.684-010
CRS	45	Artist, Mannequin Coloring (fabrication, n.e.c.)	741.684-010
CRS	45	Assembler, Carbon Brushes (elec. equip.)	721.684-014
CRS	45	Bone-Cooking Operator (chemical)	551.685-018
CRS	45	Box Printer (any industry)	652.682-010
CRS	45	Carton Inspector (tobacco)	920.687-070
CRS	45	Classifier Tender (smelt. & refin.)	511.685-014
CRS	45	Diver Helper (any industry)	899.664-010
CRS	45	Document Preparer, Microfilming (business ser.)	249.587-018
CRS	45	Embossing-Machine Operator II (clerical)	208.682-010
CRS	45	Fat-Purification Worker (oils & grease)	551.685-070
CRS	45	Glove Sewer (glove & mit.)	784.682-010
CRS	45	Hands Assembler (clock & watch)	715.684-110
CRS	45	Heel-Seat Fitter, Machine (boot & shoe)	690.682-046
CRS	45	Inspector (woodworking)	769.687-026
CRS	45	Jewel Inserter (clock & watch)	715.684-130
CRS	45	Job Putter-Up and Ticket Preparer (boot & shoe)	788.587-010
CRS	45	Leather Etcher (garment)	583.685-066
CRS	45	Liner (pottery & porc.)	740.681-010
CRS	45	Office Copy Selector (print. & pub.)	249.687-010
CRS	45	Overedge Sewer (any industry)	787.682-034
CRS	45	Pole Inspector (wood prod., n.e.c.)	561.587-010
CRS	45	Printer Operator, Black-and-White (photofinishing)	976.682-014
CRS	45	Saw-Edge Fuser, Circular (cutlery-hrdwr.)	701.684-026
CRS	45	Shuttle Fixer (textile)	628.684-026

HOC	Cx	Title	DOT
CRS	45	Sizer (knitting)	684.684-014
CRS	45	Smash Hand (narrow fabrics; textile)	683.684-026
CRS	45	Trimmer, Machine II (boot & shoe)	690.682-086
CRS	44	Annealer (glass products)	573.685-010
CRS	44	Boat-Hoist Operator (retail trade)	921.683-010
CRS	44	Caner I (furniture)	763.684-018
CRS	44	Coater Operator (plastic-synth.)	554.585-014
CRS	44	Creaser (leather prod.)	783.685-014
CRS	44	Cupola Hoist Operator (foundry)	921.683-030
CRS	44	Cupola Patcher (foundry)	861.684-010
CRS	44	Curb Attendant (laundry & rel.)	369.477-010
CRS	44	Curing-Oven Tender (chemical)	553.685-038
CRS	44	Cutting-Machine Tender (any industry)	690.685-122
CRS	44	Deicer Finisher (rubber goods)	739.684-054
CRS	44	Finger Cobbler (boot & shoe)	788.684-046
CRS	44	Flower-Machine Operator (tex. prod., n.e.c.)	687.682-010
CRS	44	Hobbing-Press Operator (any industry)	617.682-018
CRS	44	Inlayer (print. & pub.)	977.684-014
CRS	44	Inspector, Rubber-Stamp Die (pen & pencil)	733.687-054
CRS	44	Inspector-Repairer (leather prod.)	783.684-018
CRS	44	Integrated Circuit Fabricator (electron. comp.)	590.684-042
CRS	44	Mattress Finisher (furniture)	780.684-070
CRS	44	Mechanism Assembler (clock & watch)	715.684-142
CRS	44	Meter-Repairer Helper (any industry)	710.684-034
CRS	44	Mixer Operator, Carbon Paste (elec. equip.; smelt. & refin.)	540.585-010
CRS	44	Needle-Punch-Machine Operator (textile)	689.682-014
CRS	44	Nib Finisher (pen & pencil)	705.684-050
CRS	44	Olive Brine Tester (can. & preserv.)	522.584-010
CRS	44	Overcoiler (clock & watch)	715.684-150
CRS	44	Padded-Products Finisher (rubber goods)	752.684-034
CRS	44	Priming-Powder-Premix Blender (chemical)	550.684-022
CRS	44	Reagent Tender (smelt. & refin.)	511.685-046
CRS	44	Sewer and Inspector (knitting)	684.682-014
CRS	44	Slip-Cover Sewer (tex. prod., n.e.c.)	780.682-014
CRS	44	Steam-Press Tender (textile)	583.685-106
CRS	44	Temperature Inspector (meat products)	529.687-202
CRS	44	Tester, Electrical Continuity (elec. equip.; house. appl.; light. fix.)	729.684-058
CRS	44	Tuft-Machine Operator (carpet & rug; tex. prod., n.e.c.)	687.682-014
CRS	44	Wooden-Shade Hardware Installer (furniture)	739.684-174
CRS	44	Wrong-Address Clerk (retail trade)	209.587-050
CRS	43	Band Builder (rubber tire)	750.684-010
CRS	43	Banding-Machine Operator (pottery & porc.)	679.682-010
CRS	43	Bevel Polisher (clock & watch)	603.685-022
CRS	43	Feltmaker and Weigher (tex. prod., n.e.c.)	586.685-022
CRS	43	Filter Tender, Jelly (can. & preserv.)	529.685-114
CRS	43	Fire-Equipment-Inspector Helper (any industry)	739.687-094
CRS	43	Frame Repairer (glass products)	739.684-074

Part 2: From Holland Codes to Occupations

From Holland Codes to the Dictionary of Occupational Titles Occupations

HOC	Cx	Title	DOT
CRS	43	Fur Cleaner, Hand (laundry & rel.)	362.684-018
CRS	43	Guide Winder (toy-sport equip.)	732.684-086
CRS	43	Inspector, Balance Wheel Motion (clock & watch)	715.687-054
CRS	43	Inspector, Ball Points (nonfer. metal)	733.687-046
CRS	43	Oil-Seal Assembler (leather prod.)	739.684-138
CRS	43	Press-Pipe Inspector (brick & tile)	575.687-030
CRS	43	Serging-Machine Operator, Automatic (any industry)	787.685-030
CRS	43	Shirring-Machine Operator (any industry)	787.682-078
CRS	43	Solderer, Ultrasonic, Hand (welding)	813.684-030
CRS	43	Spoilage Worker (tinware)	709.587-014
CRS	43	Swatch Clerk (garment)	222.587-050
CRS	43	Tester (rubber goods)	899.487-010
CRS	43	Toy Assembler (retail trade)	731.684-018
CRS	43	Tube Builder, Airplane (rubber tire)	750.384-014
CRS	43	Waste Salvager (garment)	781.684-062
CRS	42	Acetylene-Cylinder-Packing Mixer (chemical)	549.665-010
CRS	42	Ampoule Examiner (pharmaceut.)	559.687-010
CRS	42	Assembler (laundry & rel.)	369.687-010
CRS	42	Bead Builder (rubber tire)	750.684-014
CRS	42	Boxing Inspector (garment)	789.587-010
CRS	42	Chain-Testing-Machine Operator (forging)	616.685-010
CRS	42	Coin-Machine Assembler (svc. ind. mach.)	731.684-010
CRS	42	Crayon Grader (mine & quarry)	579.684-014
CRS	42	Cripple Worker (boot & shoe)	788.684-042
CRS	42	Curtain-Roller Assembler (furniture)	739.684-042
CRS	42	Decay-Control Operator (wholesale tr.)	529.685-086
CRS	42	Dialer (clock & watch)	715.684-086
CRS	42	Drier (garment)	581.685-014
CRS	42	Edge Stripper (paper goods; wood. container)	795.684-014
CRS	42	Electronic-Scale Subassembler (office machines)	726.684-014
CRS	42	Electronics Assembler (comm. equip.; electron. comp.; inst. & app.)	726.684-018
CRS	42	Felt-Washing-Machine Tender (tex. prod., n.e.c.)	582.685-070
CRS	42	Fiberglass-Bonding-Machine Tender (glass mfg.)	574.665-010
CRS	42	Fly Tier (toy-sport equip.)	732.684-074
CRS	42	Formula Weigher (rubber goods)	550.663-010
CRS	42	Hand Filer, Balance Wheel (clock & watch)	715.684-106
CRS	42	Inspector (pen & pencil)	733.687-042
CRS	42	Inspector, Barrel (ordnance)	736.687-014
CRS	42	Level-Vial Setter (cutlery-hrdwr.)	701.684-018
CRS	42	Machine-Made-Shoe Unit Worker (boot & shoe)	753.584-010
CRS	42	Nylon-Hot-Wire Cutter (tex. prod., n.e.c.)	781.684-038
CRS	42	Outsole Scheduler (boot & shoe)	221.587-022
CRS	42	Parachute Mender (tex. prod., n.e.c.)	789.684-038
CRS	42	Primer Inspector (ordnance)	737.687-106
CRS	42	Protective-Clothing Issuer (chemical)	222.687-046
CRS	42	Quill-Buncher-and-Sorter (tex. prod., n.e.c.)	734.687-066
CRS	42	Quilling-Machine Operator, Automatic (textile)	681.685-074
CRS	42	Roller-Skate Repairer (any industry)	732.684-102

HOC	Cx	Title	DOT
CRS	42	Rug Inspector I (carpet & rug)	689.667-010
CRS	42	Solderer, Production Line (welding)	813.684-022
CRS	42	Solderer-Dipper (welding)	813.684-018
CRS	42	Sorter, Upholstery Parts (furniture)	780.587-010
CRS	42	Spring Clipper (furniture)	780.684-102
CRS	42	Thermostat-Assembly-Machine-Tender, Automatic (inst. & app.)	692.685-218
CRS	42	Thread-Cutter Tender (tex. prod., n.e.c.)	689.665-014
CRS	42	Tire-Bladder Maker (rubber tire)	750.684-042
CRS	42	Washer Engineer (paper & pulp)	533.685-034
CRS	42	Weave-Defect-Charting Clerk (textile)	221.587-042
CRS	42	Weigher, Production (any industry)	929.687-062
CRS	42	Welt Cutter (boot & shoe)	690.685-478
CRS	41	Aerial-Tram Operator (mine & quarry)	932.685-010
CRS	41	Airline Security Representative (air trans.)	372.667-010
CRS	41	Assembler, Marking Devices (pen & pencil)	733.687-010
CRS	41	Assembler, Movement (clock & watch)	715.684-014
CRS	41	Bench Worker, Binding (print. & pub.)	977.684-026
CRS	41	Binder and Box Builder (textile)	628.684-010
CRS	41	Bit Bender (fabrication, n.e.c.)	752.684-018
CRS	41	Blender Helper (plastic prod.; plastic-synth.)	550.586-010
CRS	41	Bonder, Semiconductor (electron. comp.)	726.685-066
CRS	41	Brim Ironer, Hand (hat & cap)	784.684-014
CRS	41	Brush Polisher (clock & watch)	603.685-038
CRS	41	Bullet-Lubricant Mixer (ordnance)	543.685-010
CRS	41	Caner II (furniture)	763.684-022
CRS	41	Carton-Packaging-Machine Operator (tobacco)	920.665-010
CRS	41	Cell Inspector (plastic-synth.)	556.684-010
CRS	41	Churner (oils & grease)	520.565-010
CRS	41	Coiler (light. fix.)	725.687-014
CRS	41	Cutter-Inspector (nonmet. min.)	751.684-010
CRS	41	Decorator (leather prod.)	739.684-046
CRS	41	Deli Cutter-Slicer (retail trade)	316.684-014
CRS	41	Dielectric-Press Operator (auto. mfg.)	692.685-074
CRS	41	Disassembler (clock & watch)	715.684-090
CRS	41	Doweling-Machine Operator (woodworking)	669.685-050
CRS	41	Drier Operator, Drum (food prep., n.e.c.)	529.685-098
CRS	41	Fan-Blade Aligner (elec. equip.)	706.687-018
CRS	41	Filer (jewelry-silver.)	700.684-034
CRS	41	Fish-Stringer Assembler (toy-sport equip.)	732.684-054
CRS	41	Gasser (textile)	585.685-050
CRS	41	Glass Driller (glass mfg.)	775.687-014
CRS	41	Glass Grinder (glass mfg.)	775.684-034
CRS	41	Glass-Worker, Pressed or Blown (glass mfg.)	772.687-010
CRS	41	Gold-Nib Grinder (pen & pencil)	705.682-010
CRS	41	Golf-Club Assembler (toy-sport equip.)	732.684-078
CRS	41	Hardware Assembler (furniture)	763.684-042
CRS	41	Hat-Forming-Machine Feeder (hat & cap)	586.686-018
CRS	41	Hot Box Operator (metal prod., n.e.c.)	709.685-014

HOC	Cx	Title	DOT
CRS	41	Inspector (sugar & conf.)	529.687-114
CRS	41	Jewel Stripper (clock & watch)	605.685-022
CRS	41	Label Coder (any industry)	920.587-014
CRS	41	Machine Operator, Ceramics (pottery & porc.)	679.685-010
CRS	41	Mold Worker (steel & rel.)	514.567-010
CRS	41	Naphthalene Operator (steel & rel.)	551.665-010
CRS	41	Order Caller (clerical)	209.667-014
CRS	41	Paper Cutter (beverage)	640.565-010
CRS	41	Parking-Lot Attendant (automotive ser.)	915.473-010
CRS	41	Pinner (tex. prod., n.e.c.)	782.684-054
CRS	41	Presser (print. & pub.)	977.684-018
CRS	41	Repairer (boot & shoe)	753.684-026
CRS	41	Rubber-Tubing Splicer (rubber goods)	752.684-042
CRS	41	Rug-Backing Stenciler (carpet & rug)	781.687-054
CRS	41	Sample Clerk (textile)	789.587-026
CRS	41	Sample Maker, Veneer (millwork-plywood)	769.684-042
CRS	41	Sealer, Dry Cell (elec. equip.)	692.685-158
CRS	41	Seamless-Hosiery Knitter (knitting)	684.685-010
CRS	41	Sewing-Machine Operator (knitting)	787.682-074
CRS	41	Shade-Cloth Finisher (furniture)	585.687-026
CRS	41	Spring Tester II (metal prod., n.e.c.)	709.687-042
CRS	41	Stoner (jewelry-silver.)	735.684-014
CRS	41	Strike-Out-Machine Operator (textile)	587.685-030
CRS	41	Tip Finisher (boot & shoe)	690.685-418
CRS	41	Turret-Lathe Operator, Tumble Tailstock (clock & watch)	604.685-042
CRS	41	Warp-Yarn Sorter (textile)	681.687-022
CRS	40	Binding Printer (textile)	652.685-014
CRS	40	Bit-Sharpener Operator (mine & quarry)	603.685-030
CRS	40	Blemish Remover (boot & shoe)	788.684-022
CRS	40	Bobbin Sorter (glass mfg.; plastic-synth.; textile)	922.687-018
CRS	40	Can Reconditioner (can. & preserv.)	920.687-058
CRS	40	Candy Dipper, Hand (sugar & conf.)	524.684-010
CRS	40	Chicle-Grinder Feeder (sugar & conf.)	521.686-018
CRS	40	Cut-Off-Machine Operator (ordnance)	615.685-022
CRS	40	Cutter, Hand II (any industry)	781.687-026
CRS	40	Cutter, Hot Knife (boot & shoe; rubber goods)	751.684-018
CRS	40	Decorator (furniture; toy-sport equip.)	749.684-014
CRS	40	Detonator Assembler (ordnance)	737.687-038
CRS	40	Dining Room Attendant (hotel & rest.)	311.677-018
CRS	40	Dipper and Baker (any industry)	599.685-030
CRS	40	Driller, Machine (glass products)	676.685-014
CRS	40	Enrobing-Machine Feeder (sugar & conf.)	524.686-010
CRS	40	Golf-Club Weighter (toy-sport equip.)	732.687-026
CRS	40	Groover (nonmet. min.)	673.685-062
CRS	40	Insole Beveler (boot & shoe)	690.685-242
CRS	40	Inspector, Bullet Slugs (ordnance)	737.687-058
CRS	40	Lap Cutter-Truer Operator (optical goods)	604.685-022
CRS	40	Leak Hunter (beverage)	764.687-090
CRS	40	Level-Vial Sealer (cutlery-hrdwr.)	779.684-034

HOC	Cx	Title	DOT
CRS	40	Lime-Sludge Kiln Operator (paper & pulp)	553.685-074
CRS	40	Lump Inspector (tobacco)	790.687-018
CRS	40	Mender, Knit Goods (garment; knitting)	782.684-046
CRS	40	Molder, Shoulder Pad (garment)	789.684-026
CRS	40	Monogram-and-Letter Paster (tex. prod., n.e.c.)	789.687-102
CRS	40	Name-Plate Stamper (any industry)	652.685-054
CRS	40	Paper-Pattern Inspector (paper goods)	649.687-018
CRS	40	Passementerie Worker (tex. prod., n.e.c.)	782.684-050
CRS	40	Production Helper (can. & preserv.; food prep., n.e.c.)	529.686-070
CRS	40	Reagent Tender Helper (smelt. & refin.)	511.686-010
CRS	40	Rounder, Hand (hat & cap)	784.684-050
CRS	40	Sanding-Machine Tender (wood prod., n.e.c.)	662.685-026
CRS	40	Sealer (elec. equip.)	727.684-030
CRS	40	Shank Threader (fabrication, n.e.c.)	739.685-034
CRS	40	Slitter (knitting)	781.684-054
CRS	40	Stencil Inspector (pen & pencil)	733.687-074
CRS	40	Stocklayer (boot & shoe)	753.687-042
CRS	40	Surgical-Dressing Maker (protective dev.)	689.685-130
CRS	40	Thermal-Surfacing-Machine Operator (stonework)	679.685-018
CRS	40	Thermometer Production Worker (inst. & app.)	710.685-014
CRS	40	Tire Balancer (rubber tire)	750.687-014
CRS	39	Bakery Worker, Conveyor Line (bakery products)	524.687-022
CRS	39	Bow Maker (garment; hat & cap)	784.684-010
CRS	39	Bow-String Maker (toy-sport equip.)	732.684-042
CRS	39	Box Inspector (wood. container)	762.687-014
CRS	39	Candy Molder, Hand (sugar & conf.)	520.687-018
CRS	39	Forwarder (print. & pub.)	794.687-026
CRS	39	Inspector, Live Ammunition (ordnance)	736.687-018
CRS	39	Landscape Specialist (government ser.)	406.687-010
CRS	39	Lens-Block Gauger (optical goods)	716.687-030
CRS	39	Ornament Maker, Hand (fabrication, n.e.c.)	739.687-130
CRS	39	Pasting-Machine Offbearer (elec. equip.)	509.686-014
CRS	39	Pinion Polisher (clock & watch)	715.685-042
CRS	39	Rotor Assembler (clock & watch)	715.687-114
CRS	39	Starchmaker (sugar & conf.)	526.687-014
CRS	39	Warm-In Worker (glass mfg.)	772.684-018
CRS	38	Arborer (jewelry-silver.)	700.684-010
CRS	38	Assembler, Small Products I (any industry)	706.684-022
CRS	38	Balcony Worker (glass mfg.)	575.687-010
CRS	38	Billposter (business ser.)	841.684-010
CRS	38	Bottom Polisher (elec. equip.)	603.685-034
CRS	38	Brim Stitcher I (hat & cap)	784.685-014
CRS	38	Caponizer (agriculture)	411.684-010
CRS	38	Color-Card Maker (paint & varnish)	794.687-014
CRS	38	Compression-Molding-Machine Tender (plastic prod.)	556.685-022
CRS	38	Cut-and-Cover Line Worker (boot & shoe)	753.684-014
CRS	38	Dowel Pointer (woodworking)	667.685-038
CRS	38	Drying-Rack Changer (boot & shoe)	581.686-026
CRS	38	Edge Bander, Hand (furniture)	762.684-038

HOC	Cx	Title	DOT
CRS	38	Frame Trimmer I (wood prod., n.e.c.)	749.684-030
CRS	38	Fruit-Grader Operator (agriculture; wholesale tr.)	529.665-010
CRS	38	Fur Blower (retail trade)	369.685-010
CRS	38	Grinder Operator, Automatic (cutlery-hrdwr.)	603.685-058
CRS	38	Inker (boot & shoe)	788.684-066
CRS	38	Lead Pony Rider (amuse. & rec.)	153.674-014
CRS	38	Middle-Card Tender (nonmet. min.; textile)	680.665-018
CRS	38	Planisher (jewelry-silver.)	700.687-054
CRS	38	Poultry Vaccinator (agriculture)	411.684-014
CRS	38	Reed-Press Feeder (wood prod., n.e.c.)	669.686-022
CRS	38	Roller-Stitcher (boot & shoe)	753.684-030
CRS	38	Spring Layer (clock & watch)	715.687-122
CRS	38	Sticker-On (nonmet. min.)	774.684-034
CRS	38	Varnishing-Unit Operator (ordnance)	737.687-138
CRS	38	X-Ray Inspector (can. & preserv.; tobacco)	529.685-274
CRS	37	Pulverizer (meat products)	521.685-266
CRS	37	Returned-Case Inspector (beverage)	929.687-038
CRE	64	Airline-Radio Operator (air trans.; business ser.)	193.262-010
CRE	64	Preventive Maintenance Coordinator (any industry)	169.167-074
CRE	60	Audit Clerk (clerical)	210.382-010
CRE	59	Foreign-Exchange-Position Clerk (financial)	210.367-014
CRE	59	Photoradio Operator (print. & pub.; tel. & tel.)	193.362-010
CRE	59	Supervisor, Protective-Signal Operations (business ser.)	379.137-022
CRE	58	Central-Office Repairer (tel. & tel.)	822.281-014
CRE	58	Quality-Control Technician (glass mfg.)	579.367-014
CRE	57	Material Lister (construction)	229.387-010
CRE	57	Property-Assessment Monitor (government ser.)	241.367-042
CRE	56	Distribution-Accounting Clerk (utilities)	210.362-010
CRE	56	Quartermaster (water trans.)	911.363-014
CRE	56	Services Clerk (water trans.)	214.387-018
CRE	55	Demurrage Clerk (r.r. trans.)	214.362-010
CRE	55	Payroll Clerk (clerical)	215.382-014
CRE	54	Assignment Clerk (tel. & tel.)	219.387-010
CRE	54	Melter Clerk (foundry)	221.387-042
CRE	54	Mill Recorder, Computerized Mill (steel & rel.)	221.367-046
CRE	54	Proof-Machine Operator (financial)	217.382-010
CRE	54	Revising Clerk (motor trans.; r.r. trans.)	214.382-026
CRE	54	Settlement Clerk (smelt. & refin.)	214.382-030
CRE	54	Special-Certificate Dictator (insurance)	209.382-014
CRE	53	Chronograph Operator (ordnance)	739.484-010
CRE	53	Cloth Tester, Quality (textile)	689.384-010
CRE	53	Revival Clerk (insurance)	219.362-050
CRE	52	Clerk, Route (tel. & tel.)	235.562-010
CRE	52	Electrologist (personal ser.)	339.371-010
CRE	52	Knitter, Hand (tex. prod., n.e.c.)	782.684-034
CRE	52	Laundry Pricing Clerk (laundry & rel.)	216.482-030
CRE	52	Machine-Stoppage-Frequency Checker (textile)	221.367-034
CRE	52	Photocomposition-Keyboard Operator (print. & pub.)	203.582-046

Part 2: From Holland Codes to Occupations

From Holland Codes to the Dictionary of Occupational Titles Occupations

HOC	Cx	Title	DOT
CRE	52	Quality-Control Tester (knitting)	684.384-010
CRE	52	Varitype Operator (clerical)	203.382-026
CRE	52	Waterway Traffic Checker (water trans.)	248.367-030
CRE	51	Command and Control Specialist (military ser.)	235.662-010
CRE	51	Drop Tester (ordnance)	737.387-010
CRE	51	Food-and-Beverage Checker (hotel & rest.)	211.482-018
CRE	51	Injector Assembler (engine-turbine)	706.684-062
CRE	51	Space-and-Storage Clerk (ordnance)	219.387-026
CRE	51	Tile Shader (brick & tile)	574.367-010
CRE	51	Water-Service Dispatcher (waterworks)	954.367-010
CRE	50	Direct-Mail Clerk (clerical)	209.587-018
CRE	50	Electrotype Servicer (print. & pub.)	659.462-010
CRE	50	Food Checker (hotel & rest.)	211.482-014
CRE	50	Machine Tester (office machines)	706.387-014
CRE	50	Protective-Signal-Repairer Helper (business ser.)	822.684-014
CRE	50	Quality-Control Checker (garment)	789.387-010
CRE	50	Steep Tender (grain-feed mills)	522.465-010
CRE	49	Chip Tester (paper & pulp)	539.387-010
CRE	49	Coke Inspector (steel & rel.)	542.567-010
CRE	49	Currency Counter (financial)	217.485-010
CRE	49	Etched-Circuit Processor (electron. comp.)	590.684-018
CRE	49	Inspector (house. appl.)	729.387-022
CRE	49	Insulation Cutter and Former (elec. equip.)	721.484-018
CRE	49	Lot Attendant (retail trade)	915.583-010
CRE	49	Perishable-Freight Inspector (r.r. trans.)	910.667-022
CRE	49	Rectification Printer (any industry)	976.682-018
CRE	49	Typesetter-Perforator Operator (print. & pub.)	203.582-062
CRE	48	Assembler, Billiard-Table (toy-sport equip.)	732.384-010
CRE	48	Assembler, Electrical Accessories II (elec. equip.)	729.384-010
CRE	48	Balance Assembler (clock & watch)	715.384-010
CRE	48	Bottle Gauger (beverage)	529.587-010
CRE	48	Electrical-Control Assembler (comm. equip.; elec. equip.)	729.684-026
CRE	48	Hat Trimmer (laundry & rel.)	782.381-010
CRE	48	Moisture-Meter Operator (tobacco)	529.687-162
CRE	48	Sample Clerk, Paper (paper & pulp; paper goods)	209.587-046
CRE	48	Spice Mixer (can. & preserv.)	520.687-062
CRE	48	Switchboard Operator, Police District (government ser.)	235.562-014
CRE	48	Venetian-Blind Installer (furniture; retail trade)	869.484-018
CRE	47	Acid Adjuster (elec. equip.)	727.484-010
CRE	47	Black-Mill Operator (chemical)	553.665-014
CRE	47	Cantilever-Crane Operator (water trans.)	921.683-018
CRE	47	Deicer Inspector, Pneumatic (rubber goods)	759.687-010
CRE	47	Driller and Broacher (clock & watch)	715.685-022
CRE	47	Fire-Extinguisher-Sprinkler Inspector (any industry)	379.687-010
CRE	47	Gauger (clock & watch)	715.687-034
CRE	47	Preparer, Samples and Repairs (jewelry-silver.)	700.684-062
CRE	47	Racket Stringer (toy-sport equip.)	732.684-094
CRE	47	Sample Checker (carpet & rug; textile)	229.687-010
CRE	47	Shipping-and-Receiving Weigher (clerical)	222.387-074

Part 2: From Holland Codes to Occupations

From Holland Codes to the Dictionary of Occupational Titles Occupations

HOC	Cx	Title	DOT
CRE	47	Spray-Machine Tender (tinware)	599.685-090
CRE	46	Assembler I (light. fix.)	723.684-014
CRE	46	Assembler, Leather Goods I (leather prod.)	783.684-010
CRE	46	Battery-Charger Tester (elec. equip.)	729.684-010
CRE	46	Bowling-Ball Weigher and Packer (toy-sport equip.)	732.487-010
CRE	46	Dial Marker (elec. equip.)	729.684-018
CRE	46	Inspector, Publications (print. & pub.)	653.667-010
CRE	46	Mail Clerk (clerical)	209.687-026
CRE	46	Manual Winder (musical inst.)	730.684-046
CRE	46	Overhead Cleaner Maintainer (textile)	628.684-022
CRE	46	Plate Assembler, Small Battery (elec. equip.)	727.684-026
CRE	46	Racker, Octave Board (musical inst.)	730.684-062
CRE	46	Raw Sampler (smelt. & refin.)	519.484-014
CRE	46	Retort-Condenser Attendant (chemical)	552.685-022
CRE	46	Towel-Cabinet Repairer (business ser.)	709.364-014
CRE	45	Assembler (toy-sport equip.)	732.684-014
CRE	45	Automat-Car Attendant (r.r. trans.)	319.464-010
CRE	45	Burler (carpet & rug; textile)	689.684-010
CRE	45	Cell Repairer (elec. equip.)	727.684-018
CRE	45	Clip-and-Hanger Attacher (glass products)	739.684-038
CRE	45	Colorer, Citrus Fruit (wholesale tr.)	529.685-070
CRE	45	Crystallizer Operator I (chemical)	559.685-042
CRE	45	Dustless Operator (chemical)	550.685-058
CRE	45	Explosive Operator I (ordnance)	737.687-042
CRE	45	Finer (clock & watch)	715.684-098
CRE	45	Fountain Server (hotel & rest.)	319.474-010
CRE	45	Ginner (agriculture)	429.685-010
CRE	45	Gold Cutter (metal prod., n.e.c.)	700.684-038
CRE	45	Heddles Tier, Jacquard Loom (narrow fabrics; textile)	683.680-014
CRE	45	Inspector, Casing (clock & watch)	715.687-062
CRE	45	Inspector, Fabric (any industry)	789.587-014
CRE	45	Mender (any industry)	787.682-030
CRE	45	Page (library)	249.687-014
CRE	45	Photolettering-Machine Operator (print. & pub.)	652.585-010
CRE	45	Roll Inspector (plastic-synth.)	554.587-010
CRE	45	Roller-Bearing Inspector (machinery mfg.; motor-bicycles)	706.687-034
CRE	45	Rounding-and-Backing-Machine Operator (print. & pub.)	653.685-026
CRE	45	Shotgun-Shell-Loading-Machine Operator (ordnance)	694.665-010
CRE	45	Silk-Screen-Frame Assembler (any industry)	709.484-010
CRE	45	Staker (clock & watch)	715.684-182
CRE	45	Wirer, Street Light (utilities)	821.684-018
CRE	44	Abrasive Grinder (nonmet. min.)	673.685-010
CRE	44	Adhesive-Bandage-Machine Operator (protective dev.)	692.685-014
CRE	44	Battery Assembler, Plastic (elec. equip.)	727.684-014
CRE	44	Bead Stringer (jewelry-silver.)	735.684-010
CRE	44	Book-Jacket-Cover-Machine Operator (paper goods)	640.685-014
CRE	44	Calciner-Operator Helper (mine & quarry; smelt. & refin.)	513.667-010
CRE	44	Caser (clock & watch)	715.684-054
CRE	44	Centrifuge-Separator Tender (nonfer. metal)	541.585-010

HOC	Cx	Title	DOT
CRE	44	Cigar Packer (tobacco)	790.687-014
CRE	44	Counter Clerk (photofinishing)	249.366-010
CRE	44	Cutting Inspector (tex. prod., n.e.c.)	781.684-022
CRE	44	Decorating-Machine Operator (glass products)	652.685-026
CRE	44	End Polisher (clock & watch)	715.685-026
CRE	44	Engraver, Machine I (engraving)	704.682-010
CRE	44	Flat Surfacer, Jewel (clock & watch)	770.685-010
CRE	44	Flotation Tender (smelt. & refin.)	511.685-026
CRE	44	Fur Cleaner, Machine (fur goods; laundry & rel.; retail trade; wholesale tr.)	369.685-014
CRE	44	Fur Ironer (laundry & rel.)	369.685-018
CRE	44	Hat Finisher (hat & cap)	589.685-062
CRE	44	Inspector (cutlery-hrdwr.)	709.587-010
CRE	44	Inspector, Balance-Bridge (clock & watch)	715.687-058
CRE	44	Laminator (rubber goods)	899.684-018
CRE	44	Lens-Fabricating-Machine Tender (optical goods)	716.685-022
CRE	44	Nitroglycerin-Separator Operator (chemical)	551.685-102
CRE	44	Pleater (tex. prod., n.e.c.)	787.685-026
CRE	44	Pleater, Hand (tex. prod., n.e.c.)	583.684-010
CRE	44	Rabble-Furnace Tender (chemical)	553.685-090
CRE	44	Rooter Operator (fabrication, n.e.c.)	731.685-010
CRE	44	Rug Hooker (carpet & rug)	687.684-010
CRE	44	Shade Matcher (textile)	582.687-022
CRE	44	Spark Tester (elec. equip.; nonfer. metal)	728.684-018
CRE	44	Tape-Making-Machine Operator (tex. prod., n.e.c.)	689.685-138
CRE	44	Template Cutter (cutlery-hrdwr.)	703.684-018
CRE	44	Transferrer (clock & watch)	715.684-190
CRE	44	Tube Assembler, Electron (electron. comp.)	725.384-010
CRE	44	Tube Sizer-and-Cutter Operator (ordnance)	640.685-086
CRE	44	Waiter/Waitress, Buffet (hotel & rest.)	311.674-018
CRE	44	Weaver (wood. container)	769.684-054
CRE	44	Weaver, Hand (narrow fabrics; textile)	782.684-062
CRE	43	Aircraft Skin Burnisher (aircraft mfg.)	807.684-018
CRE	43	Aluminum-Container Tester (elec. equip.)	727.687-018
CRE	43	Armature Connector II (elec. equip.)	724.684-014
CRE	43	Assembler (house. appl.)	723.684-010
CRE	43	Ball Assembler (toy-sport equip.)	732.684-026
CRE	43	Bead Inspector (light. fix.)	725.687-010
CRE	43	Bearing-Ring Assembler (machinery mfg.)	706.684-038
CRE	43	Bench Assembler (agric. equip.)	706.684-042
CRE	43	Case Finisher (leather prod.)	739.684-034
CRE	43	Casting Inspector (foundry)	514.687-010
CRE	43	Centrifuge Operator (grain-feed mills)	521.685-046
CRE	43	Ceramic Capacitor Processor (electron. comp.)	590.684-010
CRE	43	Chainstitch Sewing Machine Operator (garment)	786.682-054
CRE	43	Change Person (amuse. & rec.)	211.467-034
CRE	43	Coffee Roaster, Continuous Process (food prep., n.e.c.)	523.685-026
CRE	43	Coin-Machine Collector (business ser.; tel. & tel.)	292.687-010
CRE	43	Cold-Roll Inspector (plastic-synth.)	751.584-010

Part 2: From Holland Codes to Occupations

From Holland Codes to the Dictionary of Occupational Titles Occupations

HOC	Cx	Title	DOT
CRE	43	Counter Molder (boot & shoe)	690.685-102
CRE	43	Electric-Container Tester (elec. equip.)	727.687-050
CRE	43	Elevator Operator (any industry)	388.663-010
CRE	43	Finisher (toy-sport equip.)	732.584-014
CRE	43	Flatwork Tier (laundry & rel.)	361.587-010
CRE	43	Food Assembler, Kitchen (hotel & rest.)	319.484-010
CRE	43	Frame Carver, Spindle (optical goods)	713.684-030
CRE	43	Framer (glass products; wood prod., n.e.c.)	739.684-078
CRE	43	Gas-Transfer Operator (chemical)	914.585-010
CRE	43	Harness Rigger (tex. prod., n.e.c.)	789.687-082
CRE	43	Heading Matcher and Assembler (wood. container)	764.687-062
CRE	43	Inspector, Final Assembly (pen & pencil)	733.687-050
CRE	43	Linen-Supply Load-Builder (laundry & rel.)	920.687-118
CRE	43	Lockstitch-Machine Operator (garment)	786.682-170
CRE	43	Malt-House Operator (beverage)	522.685-074
CRE	43	Patcher (leather mfg.)	585.687-022
CRE	43	Pattern Assembler (knitting)	685.685-014
CRE	43	Pick-Up Operator (textile)	689.685-098
CRE	43	Repair Operator (garment)	786.682-214
CRE	43	Ribbon Winder (pen & pencil)	733.685-022
CRE	43	Saturator Tender (build. mat., n.e.c.)	582.685-118
CRE	43	Seasoning Mixer (chemical)	550.685-106
CRE	43	Stab Setter and Driller (cutlery-hrdwr.)	709.684-082
CRE	43	Strap-Cutting-Machine Operator (rubber goods)	690.685-402
CRE	43	Tester, Waste Disposal Leakage (house. appl.)	723.687-018
CRE	43	Thread Laster (boot & shoe)	788.684-114
CRE	43	Tile Setter (mfd. bldgs.)	861.684-018
CRE	43	Tooth Cutter (clock & watch)	605.685-050
CRE	43	Tucking-Machine Operator (any industry)	787.682-082
CRE	43	Weaver (fabrication, n.e.c.)	739.684-170
CRE	43	Zipper Setter (any industry)	787.682-086
CRE	42	Acetone-Recovery Worker (plastic-synth.)	552.685-010
CRE	42	Asbestos-Shingle Inspector (nonmet. min.)	679.687-010
CRE	42	Assembler (jewelry-silver.)	700.684-014
CRE	42	Assembler, Filters (auto. mfg.)	739.687-026
CRE	42	Barrel Inspector, Tight (wood. container)	764.687-022
CRE	42	Barrel Rifler (ordnance)	605.685-010
CRE	42	Battery Charger (elec. equip.)	727.587-010
CRE	42	Bellows Assembler (inst. & app.)	710.684-042
CRE	42	Boarding-Machine Operator (knitting)	589.685-010
CRE	42	Bonder, Automobile Brakes (automotive ser.)	620.685-010
CRE	42	Bow Maker (any industry)	789.684-010
CRE	42	Brine Maker II (can. & preserv.)	522.685-022
CRE	42	Burrer (clock & watch)	715.684-042
CRE	42	Caddie (amuse. & rec.)	341.677-010
CRE	42	Can Inspector (beverage; can. & preserv.)	920.687-050
CRE	42	Cap Maker (hat & cap)	784.684-018
CRE	42	Chair Inspector and Leveler (furniture)	763.687-014
CRE	42	Chiller Operator (chemical)	551.685-042

Part 2: From Holland Codes to Occupations

From Holland Codes to the Dictionary of Occupational Titles Occupations

HOC	Cx	Title	DOT
CRE	42	Cigarette-Filter-Making-Machine Operator (tobacco)	529.685-062
CRE	42	Cigarette-Lighter Repairer (any industry)	709.684-034
CRE	42	Clarifier (beverage)	521.685-058
CRE	42	Cracker Sprayer (bakery products)	524.685-022
CRE	42	Culler (wood. container)	764.687-054
CRE	42	Decorator (hat & cap)	784.684-022
CRE	42	Design Inserter (plastic prod.)	692.685-070
CRE	42	Dyer (fabrication, n.e.c.)	599.685-034
CRE	42	Electric-Motor Assembler (elec. equip.)	721.684-022
CRE	42	Embosser (optical goods)	713.684-022
CRE	42	Extractor Operator (beverage)	521.685-118
CRE	42	Extractor Operator, Solvent Process (chemical)	551.685-062
CRE	42	Fiber-Machine Tender (glass mfg.)	575.685-030
CRE	42	Finisher (fabrication, n.e.c.)	731.687-014
CRE	42	Firer (jewelry-silver.)	590.685-034
CRE	42	Fishing-Rod Marker (toy-sport equip.)	732.684-070
CRE	42	Flanger (inst. & app.)	712.684-018
CRE	42	Flanger (hat & cap)	784.684-026
CRE	42	Flyer Repairer (textile)	628.687-010
CRE	42	Fur Trimmer (fur goods)	783.687-014
CRE	42	Garment Inspector (any industry)	789.687-070
CRE	42	Gauge-and-Weigh-Machine Operator (ordnance)	737.685-010
CRE	42	Grain Picker (grain-feed mills)	529.687-110
CRE	42	Grinder Operator (grain-feed mills)	521.685-166
CRE	42	Grinder, Hand (optical goods)	716.685-018
CRE	42	Hair Worker (fabrication, n.e.c.)	739.684-086
CRE	42	Hat-and-Cap Sewer (hat & cap)	784.682-014
CRE	42	Heel Gouger (boot & shoe)	690.685-214
CRE	42	Hemmer, Automatic (tex. prod., n.e.c.)	787.685-018
CRE	42	Inspector, Container Finishing (elec. equip.)	727.687-066
CRE	42	Inspector, Hairspring II (clock & watch)	715.684-122
CRE	42	Inspector, Wire Products (metal prod., n.e.c.)	709.687-026
CRE	42	Jacquard-Twine-Polisher Operator (tex. prod., n.e.c.)	583.685-062
CRE	42	Kick-Press Operator (protective dev.)	692.685-102
CRE	42	Knitting-Machine Operator (tex. prod., n.e.c.)	685.685-010
CRE	42	Lamination Assembler (elec. equip.; electron. comp.)	729.684-066
CRE	42	Leather-Belt Maker (leather prod.)	690.685-266
CRE	42	Level-Vial Curvature Gauger (cutlery-hrdwr.)	701.687-022
CRE	42	Level-Vial Marker (cutlery-hrdwr.)	775.684-046
CRE	42	Linker (jewelry-silver.)	735.687-014
CRE	42	Looper (musical inst.)	730.685-010
CRE	42	Magnet-Valve Assembler (elec. equip.)	724.684-034
CRE	42	Matcher, Leather Parts (leather prod.)	783.687-022
CRE	42	Molding-Machine Tender (paper & pulp)	539.685-018
CRE	42	Needle Grinder (button & notion)	734.584-010
CRE	42	Needle Leader (button & notion)	502.684-022
CRE	42	Needle-Board Repairer (tex. prod., n.e.c.)	739.684-134
CRE	42	Net Maker (tex. prod., n.e.c.)	789.684-030
CRE	42	Padder, Cushion (furniture)	780.684-078

HOC	Cx	Title	DOT
CRE	42	Painting-Machine Operator (any industry)	599.685-074
CRE	42	Pellet-Mill Operator (grain-feed mills)	520.685-178
CRE	42	Pinking-Machine Operator (boot & shoe; garment)	686.685-042
CRE	42	Plate Slitter-and-Inspector (elec. equip.)	727.685-010
CRE	42	Ribbon-Hanking-Machine Operator (paper goods)	640.385-010
CRE	42	Router (clerical)	222.587-038
CRE	42	Sampler (beverage)	529.687-178
CRE	42	Scribing-Machine Operator (cutlery-hrdwr.)	605.685-042
CRE	42	Selector (glass mfg.)	579.687-030
CRE	42	Sheet-Metal-Pattern Cutter (musical inst.)	730.684-074
CRE	42	Skiver, Machine (boot & shoe; rubber goods)	690.685-378
CRE	42	Slide-Fastener Repairer (button & notion)	734.684-022
CRE	42	Spark Tester (elec. equip.)	727.687-078
CRE	42	Spinner, Frame (nonmet. min.; textile)	682.685-010
CRE	42	Spinning-Bath Patroller (plastic-synth.)	557.685-030
CRE	42	Spot Cleaner (garment; knitting)	582.684-014
CRE	42	Spring Inspector II (metal prod., n.e.c.)	709.687-038
CRE	42	Stringing-Machine Tender (tex. prod., n.e.c.)	689.585-018
CRE	42	Sublimer (chemical)	542.685-014
CRE	42	Ticketer (textile)	229.587-018
CRE	42	Ticketer (any industry)	652.685-098
CRE	42	Tobacco-Packing-Machine Operator (tobacco)	920.685-098
CRE	42	Top-Hat-Body Maker (hat & cap)	784.684-074
CRE	42	Turning-and-Beading-Machine Operator (button & notion)	679.685-026
CRE	42	Upper-and-Bottom Lacer, Hand (boot & shoe)	788.684-122
CRE	42	Wallpaper Inspector and Shipper (paper goods)	652.687-046
CRE	42	Watch-Band Assembler (jewelry-silver.)	700.684-082
CRE	42	Watcher, Automat (tex. prod., n.e.c.)	689.685-150
CRE	42	Water Leak Repairer (auto. mfg.)	807.684-034
CRE	42	Wax-Machine Operator (textile)	584.685-050
CRE	42	Wet-End Helper (wood prod., n.e.c.)	534.685-034
CRE	42	Wheel-Press Clerk (railroad equip.)	221.587-046
CRE	42	Wool Puller (leather mfg.; meat products)	589.687-050
CRE	42	Yarn Examiner, Skeins (textile)	689.687-082
CRE	42	Yarn-Texturing-Machine Operator (plastic-synth.)	589.685-102
CRE	42	Zipper Trimmer, Hand (button & notion)	734.687-094
CRE	41	Abrasive Sawyer (nonmet. min.)	677.685-010
CRE	41	Acid Purifier (chemical)	559.685-010
CRE	41	Adjuster, Alarm Mechanism (clock & watch)	715.684-010
CRE	41	Artificial-Flower Maker (button & notion)	739.684-014
CRE	41	Assembler II (ordnance)	736.684-014
CRE	41	Assembler, Electrical Accessories I (elec. equip.; light. fix.)	729.687-010
CRE	41	Assembly Loader (inst. & app.)	711.684-010
CRE	41	Assembly-Press Operator (any industry)	690.685-014
CRE	41	Balance Recesser (clock & watch)	604.685-010
CRE	41	Barrel Polisher, Inside (ordnance)	603.685-014
CRE	41	Basket Mender (wood. container)	762.684-022
CRE	41	Beater Operator (chemical)	555.685-010
CRE	41	Belt Maker (nonmet. min.)	776.684-010

HOC	Cx	Title	DOT
CRE	41	Bird-Cage Assembler (metal prod., n.e.c.)	709.684-026
CRE	41	Bow-Maker-Machine Tender, Automatic (tex. prod., n.e.c.)	689.685-030
CRE	41	Broommaker (fabrication, n.e.c.)	739.684-018
CRE	41	Buckle-Strap-Drum Operator (rubber goods)	554.485-010
CRE	41	Burnisher, Balance Wheel Arm (clock & watch)	715.684-038
CRE	41	Casing-Material Weigher (tobacco)	520.687-026
CRE	41	Catheter Builder (rubber goods)	752.684-026
CRE	41	Chip Unloader (paper & pulp)	921.663-018
CRE	41	Choke Reamer (ordnance)	606.685-022
CRE	41	Coater Operator, Insulation Board (wood prod., n.e.c.)	539.685-010
CRE	41	Coater, Brake Linings (nonmet. min.)	574.685-010
CRE	41	Color Matcher (boot & shoe)	788.687-034
CRE	41	Composition-Weatherboard Applier (construction)	863.684-010
CRE	41	Counter Former (boot & shoe)	690.685-098
CRE	41	Cutter, Machine II (any industry)	699.685-014
CRE	41	Dater Assembler (pen & pencil)	733.687-030
CRE	41	Deicer-Element Winder, Hand (rubber goods)	739.684-058
CRE	41	Deskidding-Machine Operator (boot & shoe)	690.685-126
CRE	41	Dial-Screw Assembler (clock & watch)	715.684-082
CRE	41	Doll Repairer (any industry)	731.684-014
CRE	41	Drilling-Machine Operator, Automatic (clock & watch)	606.685-030
CRE	41	Drum-Drier Operator (chemical)	553.665-030
CRE	41	Dust-Collector Operator (soap & rel.)	551.685-050
CRE	41	Dyed-Yarn Operator (textile)	582.685-058
CRE	41	Edge Stainer I (leather prod.)	589.685-046
CRE	41	Electric-Sealing-Machine Operator (any industry)	690.685-154
CRE	41	End Finder, Forming Department (textile)	681.687-010
CRE	41	Etcher, Hand (cutlery-hrdwr.)	704.687-014
CRE	41	Evaporator Operator (paper & pulp)	532.685-018
CRE	41	Extruder Tender (rubber goods)	557.685-014
CRE	41	Facing-Machine Operator (clock & watch)	604.685-014
CRE	41	Feather-Duster Winder (tex. prod., n.e.c.)	734.684-014
CRE	41	Final Inspector (elec. equip.)	727.687-054
CRE	41	Fishing-Rod Assembler (toy-sport equip.)	732.684-066
CRE	41	Flat Polisher (clock & watch)	603.685-054
CRE	41	Folder (narrow fabrics)	686.685-030
CRE	41	Foot-Miter Operator (wood prod., n.e.c.)	739.684-066
CRE	41	Form Coverer (fabrication, n.e.c.)	739.684-070
CRE	41	Fur-Cutting-Machine Operator (hat & cap)	585.685-046
CRE	41	Fur-Glazing-and-Polishing-Machine Operator (laundry & rel.)	369.685-022
CRE	41	Gas-Meter Mechanic II (utilities)	710.684-026
CRE	41	Gauger (protective dev.)	712.687-018
CRE	41	Gig Tender (textile)	585.685-054
CRE	41	Glue Spreader, Veneer (millwork-plywood; wood prod., n.e.c.)	569.685-042
CRE	41	Golf-Ball Trimmer (toy-sport equip.)	732.587-010
CRE	41	Grinder II (clock & watch)	715.685-030
CRE	41	Grinder, Lap (clock & watch)	603.685-066

HOC	Cx	Title	DOT
CRE	41	Hat Braider (hat & cap)	784.684-038
CRE	41	Heading Repairer (wood. container)	764.687-066
CRE	41	Heel Scorer (boot & shoe)	690.685-222
CRE	41	Heel-Nailing-Machine Operator (boot & shoe)	690.685-226
CRE	41	Holiday-Detector Operator (construction)	862.687-014
CRE	41	Hooking-Machine Operator (clock & watch)	605.685-018
CRE	41	Hydraulic-Press Operator (tex. prod., n.e.c.)	583.685-058
CRE	41	Inspector, Salvage (ordnance)	737.684-026
CRE	41	Inspector, Surgical Instruments (inst. & app.)	712.684-050
CRE	41	Jewelry Coater (jewelry-silver.)	590.685-046
CRE	41	Lacer II (boot & shoe)	690.685-254
CRE	41	Leacher (paper & pulp)	551.685-090
CRE	41	Lens Hardener (optical goods)	573.685-030
CRE	41	Level-Vial Inside Grinder (cutlery-hrdwr.)	673.685-066
CRE	41	Lever Miller (clock & watch)	605.685-026
CRE	41	Loading-Machine Operator (ordnance)	694.685-026
CRE	41	Loading-Unit Operator (ordnance)	694.685-030
CRE	41	Lubricator-Granulator (nonfer. metal; steel & rel.)	509.685-042
CRE	41	Mangle Tender (textile)	584.685-042
CRE	41	Marking-Machine Operator (textile)	652.685-046
CRE	41	Match-Up Worker (garment)	782.684-038
CRE	41	Metallic-Yarn-Slitting-Machine Operator (nonfer. metal)	619.685-070
CRE	41	Mix-House Tender (smelt. & refin.)	510.685-014
CRE	41	Mixer (glass mfg.)	570.685-054
CRE	41	Moisture Tester (woodworking)	563.687-014
CRE	41	Overlock Sewing Machine Operator (garment)	786.682-194
CRE	41	Panel Maker (furniture)	780.684-086
CRE	41	Paper Coater (paper & pulp; paper goods)	534.685-022
CRE	41	Pasteurizer (beverage; can. & preserv.)	523.685-110
CRE	41	Patcher (fabrication, n.e.c.)	739.687-146
CRE	41	Pattern Hand (woodworking)	652.687-030
CRE	41	Pegger, Dobby Looms (narrow fabrics; textile)	689.687-054
CRE	41	Perforator (tex. prod., n.e.c.)	781.684-042
CRE	41	Pinking-Machine Operator (button & notion)	692.685-130
CRE	41	Planing-Machine Operator (clock & watch)	605.685-034
CRE	41	Plug Cutter (pen & pencil)	690.685-306
CRE	41	Pocket-Machine Operator (furniture)	616.685-050
CRE	41	Pocketed-Spring Assembler (furniture)	780.684-090
CRE	41	Polisher, Balance Screwhead (clock & watch)	715.685-046
CRE	41	Production-Machine Tender, Glass Cutting-or-Grinding (electron. comp.; glass mfg.)	679.685-014
CRE	41	Pulp-Press Tender (sugar & conf.)	521.685-258
CRE	41	Quilt Stuffer, Machine (tex. prod., n.e.c.)	689.685-102
CRE	41	Repairer, Auto Clocks (clock & watch)	715.584-014
CRE	41	Ribbon Inker (pen & pencil)	692.685-142
CRE	41	Rim-Turning Finisher (clock & watch)	604.685-030
CRE	41	Roller Checker (textile)	682.684-010
CRE	41	Rubber-Mold Maker (jewelry-silver.)	559.684-018
CRE	41	Sanitary-Napkin-Machine Tender (protective dev.)	692.685-150

From Holland Codes to the Dictionary of Occupational Titles Occupations

HOC	Cx	Title	DOT
CRE	41	Seam Presser (hat & cap)	583.685-098
CRE	41	Seasoning Mixer (meat products)	520.687-054
CRE	41	Sewer, Hand (any industry)	782.684-058
CRE	41	Sewing-Machine Operator (knitting; protective dev.)	787.682-050
CRE	41	Sewing-Machine Operator, Semiautomatic (garment)	786.685-030
CRE	41	Sewing-Machine Operator, Special Equipment (furniture)	689.685-118
CRE	41	Shadowgraph-Scale Operator (ordnance)	737.687-126
CRE	41	Sheetrock Applicator (mfd. bldgs.)	869.684-050
CRE	41	Shotgun-Shell-Reprinting-Unit Operator (ordnance)	659.685-018
CRE	41	Silk-Screen Etcher (engraving)	704.684-014
CRE	41	Sizing-Machine Operator (nonmet. min.)	554.685-026
CRE	41	Slicker (hat & cap)	784.684-062
CRE	41	Sole Leveler, Machine (boot & shoe)	690.685-382
CRE	41	Splicer (rubber tire)	759.684-058
CRE	41	Spreading-Machine Operator (chemical)	559.685-170
CRE	41	Stitcher, Hand (print. & pub.)	977.684-022
CRE	41	Subassembler (elec. equip.)	729.684-054
CRE	41	Tacking-Machine Operator (any industry)	787.685-042
CRE	41	Tobacco-Sample Puller (tobacco)	529.587-022
CRE	41	Transplanter, Orchid (agriculture)	405.687-018
CRE	41	Tuber-Machine Cutter (rubber goods; rubber tire)	690.685-446
CRE	41	Twister (tex. prod., n.e.c.)	681.685-126
CRE	41	Type-Copy Examiner (machinery mfg.)	979.687-026
CRE	41	Ultrasonic-Seaming-Machine Operator (garment)	786.682-258
CRE	41	Veneer Taper (millwork-plywood)	569.685-074
CRE	41	Wad Lubricator (ordnance)	590.685-058
CRE	41	Wader-Boot-Top Assembler (rubber goods)	795.684-026
CRE	41	Washer (optical goods)	713.684-042
CRE	41	Wax Molder (foundry; jewelry-silver.)	549.685-038
CRE	41	Weigher (toy-sport equip.)	732.687-086
CRE	41	Window-Shade Cutter and Mounter (furniture)	692.685-250
CRE	41	Wood Inspector (paper & pulp)	663.687-010
CRE	41	Yarn-Texturing-Machine Operator I (textile)	681.685-158
CRE	41	Yarn-Texturing-Machine Operator II (textile)	689.685-158
CRE	40	Acid Filler (elec. equip.)	727.687-014
CRE	40	Airplane-Gas-Tank-Liner Assembler (rubber goods)	759.684-010
CRE	40	Almond-Blancher Operator (can. & preserv.)	521.685-014
CRE	40	Annealer (jewelry-silver.)	504.687-010
CRE	40	Armhole Feller, Handstitching Machine (garment)	786.682-018
CRE	40	Back Padder (furniture)	780.684-010
CRE	40	Back Tender, Insulation Board (wood prod., n.e.c.)	532.685-010
CRE	40	Bag Repairer (paper goods)	794.684-010
CRE	40	Band-and-Cuff Cutter (glove & mit.)	784.685-010
CRE	40	Bit Shaver (fabrication, n.e.c.)	754.684-018
CRE	40	Blindstitch-Machine Operator (garment)	786.682-046
CRE	40	Blueprint Trimmer (any industry)	920.687-038
CRE	40	Bobbin Inspector (woodworking)	769.687-014
CRE	40	Brim-and-Crown Presser (hat & cap)	583.685-022
CRE	40	Brine-Mixer Operator, Automatic (can. & preserv.)	520.685-034

Part 2: From Holland Codes to Occupations

From Holland Codes to the Dictionary of Occupational Titles Occupations

HOC	Cx	Title	DOT
CRE	40	Bunch Maker, Machine (tobacco)	529.685-038
CRE	40	Burrer, Machine (clock & watch)	603.685-046
CRE	40	Butt Maker (tobacco)	529.685-042
CRE	40	Cell Tuber, Machine (elec. equip.)	692.685-046
CRE	40	Clip Coater (optical goods)	713.687-010
CRE	40	Coverstitch-Machine Operator (garment)	786.682-078
CRE	40	Crusher (fabrication, n.e.c.)	780.684-042
CRE	40	Cutter (photofinishing)	976.685-010
CRE	40	Deburrer (button & notion)	603.685-050
CRE	40	Deflector Operator (beverage)	529.687-058
CRE	40	Disk-and-Tape-Machine Tender (leather prod.)	783.685-018
CRE	40	Drawstring Knotter (tex. prod., n.e.c.)	689.685-058
CRE	40	Drier Operator II (plastic-synth.)	553.685-046
CRE	40	Driller, Brake Lining (nonmet. min.)	676.685-010
CRE	40	Driller, Hand (button & notion)	754.684-026
CRE	40	Dry Cleaner (knitting)	589.685-038
CRE	40	Embroidery-Machine Operator (garment)	786.685-018
CRE	40	Endband Cutter, Hand (hat & cap)	784.687-026
CRE	40	Engraver, Automatic (clock & watch)	609.685-014
CRE	40	Extractor-and-Wringer Operator (chemical)	551.685-066
CRE	40	Eye-Dropper Assembler (glass products)	739.687-086
CRE	40	Eyelet-Machine Operator (any industry)	699.685-018
CRE	40	Eyelet-Punch Operator (furniture)	699.685-022
CRE	40	Fabricator, Foam Rubber (any industry)	780.684-062
CRE	40	Firer Helper (paper & pulp)	553.665-034
CRE	40	Fishing-Reel Assembler (toy-sport equip.)	732.684-062
CRE	40	Floorworker-Distributor (hat & cap)	784.687-030
CRE	40	Folding-Machine Operator (leather prod.)	690.685-178
CRE	40	Front-Sight Attacher (ordnance)	736.684-030
CRE	40	Glazier (inst. & app.)	712.684-026
CRE	40	Glazing-Machine Operator (glass mfg.)	573.685-018
CRE	40	Gluer, Wet Suit (plastic prod.)	795.687-018
CRE	40	Grooving-Machine Operator (pen & pencil)	733.685-018
CRE	40	Guide-Base Winder, Machine (toy-sport equip.)	732.685-022
CRE	40	Hairspring Cutter I (clock & watch)	715.687-038
CRE	40	Hemmer, Blindstitch (garment)	786.682-126
CRE	40	Hemmer, Chainstitch (garment)	786.682-130
CRE	40	Hemmer, Lockstitch (garment)	786.682-134
CRE	40	Hemmer, Overlock (garment)	786.682-138
CRE	40	Hogshead Mat Inspector (wood. container)	764.687-086
CRE	40	Hollow-Handle-Knife Assembler (jewelry-silver.)	700.684-042
CRE	40	Hop Strainer (beverage)	521.685-178
CRE	40	Jet Wiper (plastic-synth.)	557.684-014
CRE	40	Jumpbasting-Machine Operator (garment)	786.682-146
CRE	40	Label Pinker (narrow fabrics)	585.685-062
CRE	40	Last Chalker (boot & shoe)	788.687-078
CRE	40	Last Marker (wood prod., n.e.c.)	739.684-102
CRE	40	Last-Repairer Helper (boot & shoe)	739.684-114
CRE	40	Layboy Tender (paper & pulp; paper goods; print. & pub.)	649.685-066

HOC	Cx	Title	DOT
CRE	40	Lead Former (elec. equip.)	691.685-018
CRE	40	Lead-Caster Helper (elec. equip.)	502.687-018
CRE	40	Level-Glass-Forming-Machine Operator (cutlery-hrdwr.)	679.665-010
CRE	40	Liner (glove & mit.)	784.687-046
CRE	40	Lining Maker, Lockstitch (garment)	786.682-162
CRE	40	Lip-of-Shank Cutter (boot & shoe)	690.685-274
CRE	40	Making-Line Worker (boot & shoe)	753.687-026
CRE	40	Marking-Machine Tender (boot & shoe; leather prod.)	783.685-026
CRE	40	Mat Cutter (wood prod., n.e.c.)	739.684-126
CRE	40	Moisture-Machine Tender (tobacco)	529.685-170
CRE	40	Molder, Labels (boot & shoe)	690.685-294
CRE	40	Needle-Bar Molder (carpet & rug)	556.684-022
CRE	40	Packer Operator, Automatic (tobacco)	920.685-082
CRE	40	Paint-Roller Assembler (fabrication, n.e.c.)	739.687-134
CRE	40	Painter and Grader, Cork (toy-sport equip.)	732.687-062
CRE	40	Panel Coverer, Metal Furniture (furniture)	780.684-082
CRE	40	Panel Installer (mfd. bldgs.)	869.684-038
CRE	40	Paper-Core-Machine Operator (paper goods)	640.685-042
CRE	40	Paper-Novelty Maker (paper goods)	794.684-022
CRE	40	Paradichlorobenzene Tender (chemical)	556.685-054
CRE	40	Picked-Edge Sewing-Machine Operator (garment)	786.682-206
CRE	40	Piped-Pocket-Machine Operator (garment)	786.685-022
CRE	40	Pleat Taper (tex. prod., n.e.c.)	789.487-010
CRE	40	Polisher, Implant (optical goods)	713.687-034
CRE	40	Poly-Packer and Heat-Sealer (protective dev.)	920.686-038
CRE	40	Precise Winder (textile)	681.685-066
CRE	40	Pretzel-Twisting-Machine Operator (bakery products)	520.685-190
CRE	40	Printing-Machine Operator, Folding Rules (cutlery-hrdwr.)	652.685-074
CRE	40	Profiling-Machine Operator (clock & watch)	605.685-038
CRE	40	Puller and Laster, Machine (boot & shoe)	788.684-086
CRE	40	Puzzle Assembler (toy-sport equip.)	731.687-030
CRE	40	Rebrander (rubber goods)	559.685-150
CRE	40	Remnant Sorter (textile)	789.687-146
CRE	40	Rivet-Hole Puncher (garment)	686.685-054
CRE	40	Riveter, Hand (garment)	789.687-154
CRE	40	Rounding-Machine Operator (hat & cap; tex. prod., n.e.c.)	585.685-086
CRE	40	Rubber-Thread Spooler (toy-sport equip.)	681.685-090
CRE	40	Sack Repairer (any industry)	782.687-046
CRE	40	Sander (toy-sport equip.)	690.685-346
CRE	40	Sanding-Machine Buffer (wood prod., n.e.c.)	662.685-022
CRE	40	Seal-Extrusion Operator (elec. equip.)	692.685-154
CRE	40	Seam-Rubbing-Machine Operator (boot & shoe)	690.685-350
CRE	40	Shank Inspector (boot & shoe)	788.687-110
CRE	40	Shaper and Presser (garment)	583.685-102
CRE	40	Sifter (pharmaceut.)	551.687-030
CRE	40	Slate Mixer (build. mat., n.e.c.)	570.685-094
CRE	40	Sleeve Maker, Lockstitch (garment)	786.682-226
CRE	40	Slide-Fastener-Chain Assembler (button & notion)	734.687-074
CRE	40	Smoother (pen & pencil)	733.685-026

Part 2: From Holland Codes to Occupations

From Holland Codes to the Dictionary of Occupational Titles Occupations

HOC	Cx	Title	DOT
CRE	40	Soap-Drier Operator (soap & rel.)	553.685-098
CRE	40	Splicer (photofinishing)	976.684-026
CRE	40	Sponge Clipper (fishing & hunt.; wholesale tr.)	447.687-026
CRE	40	Squaring-Machine Operator (clock & watch)	605.685-046
CRE	40	Steaming-Cabinet Tender (garment)	582.685-150
CRE	40	Straw Hat Presser, Machine (hat & cap)	583.685-110
CRE	40	Stripping-Machine Operator (paper goods)	641.685-090
CRE	40	Tape-Fastener-Machine Operator (paper goods)	649.685-122
CRE	40	Ticket Puller (tobacco)	221.687-014
CRE	40	Trimmer (hat & cap)	784.684-078
CRE	40	Vacuum Plastic-Forming-Machine Operator (plastic prod.)	556.685-082
CRE	40	Waistband Setter, Lockstitch (garment)	786.682-266
CRE	40	Wax Pourer (chemical)	737.685-018
CRE	40	Wet Mixer (chemical)	550.685-126
CRE	40	Whizzer (hat & cap)	581.685-070
CRE	40	Winterizer (oils & grease)	521.685-374
CRE	40	Wire Inserter (hat & cap)	784.687-082
CRE	40	Wool-Washing-Machine Operator (textile)	582.685-166
CRE	40	Yarn-Mercerizer Operator I (textile)	584.685-054
CRE	40	Yeast-Cutting-and-Wrapping-Machine Operator (food prep., n.e.c.)	529.665-022
CRE	40	Zigzag-Machine Operator (garment)	786.682-278
CRE	40	Zipper Trimmer, Machine (button & notion)	692.685-266
CRE	39	Assembler, Corncob Pipes (fabrication, n.e.c.)	739.687-014
CRE	39	Assembler, Sandal Parts (boot & shoe)	788.684-014
CRE	39	Baseball Sewer, Hand (toy-sport equip.)	732.684-034
CRE	39	Cementer, Machine (boot & shoe)	692.685-050
CRE	39	Center-Punch Operator (recording)	690.685-078
CRE	39	Check Weigher (ordnance)	737.687-026
CRE	39	Cheese Sprayer (sugar & conf.)	524.685-014
CRE	39	Cleaner, Hospital (medical ser.)	323.687-010
CRE	39	Cleaner, Housekeeping (any industry)	323.687-014
CRE	39	Crayon Sawyer (mine & quarry)	677.685-022
CRE	39	Crown Pouncer, Hand (hat & cap)	784.687-018
CRE	39	Drop-Wire Aligner (textile)	689.685-062
CRE	39	Ending-Machine Operator (paper goods)	641.685-042
CRE	39	Gluing-Machine Operator (rubber goods)	692.685-098
CRE	39	Laborer, General (rubber goods; rubber reclaim.; rubber tire)	559.686-026
CRE	39	Level-Glass-Vial Filler (cutlery-hrdwr.)	692.685-114
CRE	39	Measuring-Machine Operator (leather mfg.)	589.685-070
CRE	39	Mender (hat & cap)	784.684-046
CRE	39	Metal Sander and Finisher (furniture)	705.687-018
CRE	39	Nut Grinder (can. & preserv.)	521.685-234
CRE	39	Press Operator (protective dev.)	686.685-050
CRE	39	Protector-Plate Attacher (cutlery-hrdwr.)	692.685-138
CRE	39	Puller, Machine (leather mfg.)	589.685-078
CRE	39	Reel-Blade-Bender Furnace Tender (agric. equip.)	504.685-030
CRE	39	Sample Sawyer (brick & tile)	677.685-034

HOC	Cx	Title	DOT
CRE	39	Sausage Inspector (meat products)	529.587-014
CRE	39	Scrap Separator (food prep., n.e.c.)	529.587-018
CRE	39	Sorter II (wood prod., n.e.c.)	769.687-042
CRE	39	Sprayer, Hand (leather mfg.)	584.687-014
CRE	39	Stone Setter (jewelry-silver.)	735.687-034
CRE	39	Tester and Inspector, Lamps (light. fix.)	723.687-014
CRE	39	Tumbler Tender (food prep., n.e.c.)	520.685-222
CRE	39	Ultrasonic-Seaming-Machine Operator, Semiautomatic (garment)	786.685-038
CRE	39	Undercoater (automotive ser.)	843.684-014
CRE	39	Wood-Heel Finisher (boot & shoe)	788.684-126
CRE	38	Auto Roller (tobacco)	529.685-010
CRE	38	Bone-Char Kiln Tender (chemical)	553.685-018
CRE	38	Bottling-Line Attendant (beverage)	920.687-042
CRE	38	Burnisher (clock & watch)	603.685-042
CRE	38	Celluloid Trimmer (toy-sport equip.)	732.684-046
CRE	38	Convex-Grinder Operator (button & notion)	673.685-042
CRE	38	Core Extruder (elec. equip.)	557.685-010
CRE	38	Covering-Machine Tender (leather prod.)	783.685-010
CRE	38	Egg Processor (pharmaceut.)	559.687-034
CRE	38	Gasket Inspector (nonmet. min.)	739.687-102
CRE	38	Hand Sewer, Shoes (boot & shoe)	788.684-054
CRE	38	Jewel Stringer (clock & watch)	770.687-026
CRE	38	Lacer (nonmet. min.)	774.687-014
CRE	38	Laminator II (leather prod.)	783.685-022
CRE	38	Mica Patcher (mine & quarry)	579.687-026
CRE	38	Paper-Cone Grader (paper goods)	649.687-014
CRE	38	Paper-Pattern Folder (paper goods)	794.687-034
CRE	38	Rubber-Goods Assembler (rubber goods)	752.684-038
CRE	38	Sander, Portable Machine (woodworking)	761.684-034
CRE	38	Set-Staff Fitter (clock & watch)	715.684-178
CRE	38	Skein-Winding Operator (any industry)	559.687-054
CRE	38	Slip Laster (boot & shoe)	788.684-106
CRE	38	Solderer (clock & watch)	715.685-058
CRE	38	Staker, Machine (leather mfg.)	580.685-050
CRE	38	String-Top Sealer (paper goods)	641.685-086
CRE	38	Striper, Spray Gun (any industry)	741.687-022
CRE	38	Synthetic-Gem-Press Operator (jewelry-silver.)	575.685-078
CRE	38	Tape Stringer (garment; knitting)	782.687-054
CRE	38	Tire Setter (toy-sport equip.)	731.685-018
CRE	38	Toy Assembler (toy-sport equip.)	731.687-034
CRE	38	Trimmer, Hand (paper goods)	794.687-062
CRE	38	Vacuum-Bottle Assembler (glass products)	739.687-194
CRE	38	Veneer Repairer, Machine (millwork-plywood)	669.685-098
CRE	37	Acetone-Button Paster (button & notion)	734.687-010
CRE	37	Assembler (button & notion)	734.687-018
CRE	37	Button Spindler (button & notion)	740.687-010
CRE	37	Dial Brusher (clock & watch)	715.687-022
CRE	37	Fitter-Placer (rubber goods)	753.687-022

HOC	Cx	Title	DOT
CRE	37	Hot-Stone Setter (button & notion)	734.687-058
CRE	37	Nailer (tinware)	739.687-126
CRE	37	Nut Sorter (can. & preserv.)	521.687-086
CRE	37	Pattern Ruler (tex. prod., n.e.c.)	794.687-038
CRE	37	Shoe Shiner (personal ser.)	366.677-010
CRE	37	Vacuum Tester, Cans (can. & preserv.)	920.687-194
CRE	37	Veneer-Jointer Helper (millwork-plywood)	665.686-018
CRE	36	Buckle-Wire Inserter (button & notion)	734.687-034
CRE	36	Buttoner (garment; knitting)	782.687-014
CRE	36	Felt-Hat Steamer (hat & cap)	582.687-018
CRE	36	Fusing-Machine Feeder (garment)	583.686-014
CRE	36	Punchboard Assembler II (paper goods)	794.687-046
CRE	36	Raveler (knitting)	782.687-034
CRE	36	Sticker (button & notion)	734.687-090
CRE	36	Stringer (paper goods)	794.687-054
CRE	36	Tabber (paper goods)	794.687-058
CIR	69	Medical Radiation Dosimetrist (medical ser.)	078.261-034
CIR	61	Medical Record Technician (medical ser.)	079.362-014
CIR	58	Echocardiograph Technician (medical ser.)	078.364-014
CIR	58	Electromyographic Technician (medical ser.)	078.362-038
CIR	58	Electronic Prepress System Operator (print. & pub.)	979.282-010
CIR	57	Flash Ranging Crewmember (military ser.)	378.367-018
CIA	65	Editorial Assistant (print. & pub.)	132.267-014
CIS	69	Auditor, Data Processing (profess. & kin.)	160.162-030
CIS	64	Polygraph Examiner (profess. & kin.)	199.267-026
CIS	63	Computer Security Coordinator (profess. & kin.)	033.162-010
CIS	59	Ophthalmic Photographer (medical ser.)	143.362-014
CIS	59	Ophthalmic Technician (medical ser.)	078.361-038
CIS	57	Computer Security Specialist (profess. & kin.)	033.362-010
CIS	57	Foreign Clerk (clerical)	214.467-010
CIS	57	Stress Test Technician (medical ser.)	078.362-062
CIE	70	Accountant, Cost (profess. & kin.)	160.162-026
CIE	70	Investment Analyst (financial; insurance)	160.267-026
CIE	65	Inspector, Building (government ser.)	168.167-030
CIE	64	Editor, Telegraph (print. & pub.; radio-tv broad.)	132.267-010
CSR	69	Loan Review Analyst (financial)	186.267-022
CSR	64	Bibliographer (profess. & kin.)	100.367-010
CSR	61	Flight-Crew-Time Clerk (air trans.)	215.362-018
CSR	60	Classifier (library)	100.367-014
CSR	59	Budget Clerk (clerical)	216.382-022
CSR	58	Classification-Control Clerk (clerical)	210.382-030
CSR	58	Collection Clerk (financial)	216.362-014
CSR	58	Music Librarian, International Broadcast (radio-tv broad.)	100.367-026
CSR	58	Real-Estate Clerk (real estate)	219.362-046

Part 2: From Holland Codes to Occupations

From Holland Codes to the Dictionary of Occupational Titles Occupations

HOC	Cx	Title	DOT
CSR	57	Computer Processing Scheduler (clerical)	221.362-030
CSR	57	Policy-Change Clerk (insurance)	219.362-042
CSR	57	Voucher Clerk (r.r. trans.)	219.362-066
CSR	56	Computer Operator (clerical)	213.362-010
CSR	55	Accounting Clerk (clerical)	216.482-010
CSR	55	Brokerage Clerk I (financial)	219.482-010
CSR	55	Food-and-Beverage Controller (hotel & rest.)	216.362-022
CSR	55	Invoice-Control Clerk (clerical)	214.362-026
CSR	55	Reinsurance Clerk (insurance)	219.482-018
CSR	54	Brokerage Clerk II (financial)	219.362-018
CSR	54	Chart Clerk (clerical)	221.382-010
CSR	54	Documentation-Billing Clerk (air trans.; motor trans.; r.r. trans.; water trans.)	214.362-014
CSR	54	Insurance Checker (insurance)	219.482-014
CSR	54	Keno Writer (amuse. & rec.)	343.467-022
CSR	54	Production Assistant (chemical)	221.387-050
CSR	54	Production Clerk (clerical)	221.382-018
CSR	54	Protective-Signal Operator (any industry)	379.362-014
CSR	54	Railroad-Maintenance Clerk (r.r. trans.)	221.362-026
CSR	54	Rater (insurance)	214.482-022
CSR	54	Ticketing Clerk (air trans.)	248.382-010
CSR	53	Accounts-Adjustable Clerk (r.r. trans.)	214.462-010
CSR	53	Custodian, Athletic Equipment (amuse. & rec.)	969.367-010
CSR	53	Mail Censor (government ser.)	243.367-010
CSR	53	Order Detailer (clerical)	221.387-046
CSR	53	Wire-Transfer Clerk (financial)	203.562-010
CSR	52	Deposit-Refund Clerk (utilities)	214.482-014
CSR	52	Dispatcher Clerk (r.r. trans.)	215.362-014
CSR	52	Medical-Voucher Clerk (insurance)	214.482-018
CSR	52	Work-Order-Sorting Clerk (utilities)	221.367-082
CSR	51	Braille Typist (education; nonprofit organ.; print. & pub.)	203.582-014
CSR	51	C.O.D. Clerk (clerical)	214.382-018
CSR	51	Cashier, Tube Room (retail trade)	211.482-010
CSR	51	Computer Peripheral Equipment Operator (clerical)	213.382-010
CSR	51	Credit-Card Clerk (hotel & rest.)	210.382-038
CSR	51	Dividend-Deposit-Voucher Clerk (insurance)	216.482-026
CSR	51	File Clerk II (clerical)	206.367-014
CSR	51	Laundry Clerk (clerical)	221.387-038
CSR	51	Train Clerk (r.r. trans.)	219.462-014
CSR	50	Assignment Clerk (motor trans.)	215.367-010
CSR	50	Record Clerk (textile)	206.387-022
CSR	50	Tip-Length Checker (tobacco)	529.467-010
CSR	49	Quality-Control Clerk (pharmaceut.)	229.587-014
CSR	49	Surveillance-System Monitor (government ser.)	379.367-010
CSR	48	File Clerk I (clerical)	206.387-034
CSR	48	Film-Replacement Orderer (motion picture)	976.567-010
CSR	48	Scoreboard Operator (amuse. & rec.)	349.665-010
CSR	47	Cabinet Assembler (furniture)	763.684-014
CSR	47	Complaint Clerk (boot & shoe)	221.387-014

Part 2: From Holland Codes to Occupations

From Holland Codes to the Dictionary of Occupational Titles Occupations

HOC	Cx	Title	DOT
CSR	47	Heel Sorter (boot & shoe)	788.584-010
CSR	47	Route-Delivery Clerk (clerical)	222.587-034
CSR	47	String-Winding-Machine Operator (musical inst.)	692.682-062
CSR	47	Tire Inspector (automotive ser.)	750.687-018
CSR	46	Nib Inspector (pen & pencil)	733.687-058
CSR	45	Bisque Grader (pottery & porc.)	774.687-010
CSR	45	Checker, Film Tests (photo. appar.)	714.687-010
CSR	45	Painter, Plate (print. & pub.)	970.681-030
CSR	45	Salvager I (ordnance)	737.687-114
CSR	45	Sample Worker (any industry)	920.687-154
CSR	44	Garment-Alteration Examiner (retail trade)	789.687-078
CSR	44	Striping-Machine Operator (nonfer. metal)	652.682-026
CSR	43	Booking Clerk (wholesale tr.)	216.587-010
CSR	43	Embroiderer, Hand (tex. prod., n.e.c.)	782.684-018
CSR	43	Marker, Company (tobacco)	529.567-014
CSR	43	Reinspector (knitting)	684.687-014
CSR	42	Assembler (garment; glove & mit.)	781.687-010
CSR	42	Checkroom Attendant (any industry)	358.677-010
CSR	42	Defect Repairer, Glassware (glass mfg.)	772.684-010
CSR	42	Hat-Body Sorter (hat & cap)	784.587-010
CSR	42	Pairer (knitting)	684.687-010
CSR	42	Plastic-Card Grader, Cardroom (amuse. & rec.)	343.687-010
CSR	42	Sprayer, Leather (laundry & rel.)	364.684-018
CSR	42	Wire Harness Assembler (elec. equip.; electron. comp.; office machines)	728.684-010
CSR	41	Collator (print. & pub.)	653.687-010
CSR	41	Decorating Inspector (glass mfg.)	579.687-014
CSR	41	Decorator (bakery products; sugar & conf.)	524.684-014
CSR	41	Inspector-Packer (hat & cap)	784.687-042
CSR	41	Marker (retail trade; wholesale tr.)	209.587-034
CSR	40	Assembler, Small Products II (any industry)	739.687-030
CSR	40	Buckle Inspector (button & notion)	734.687-026
CSR	40	Inspector (laundry & rel.)	369.687-022
CSR	40	Inspector, Bicycle (motor-bicycles)	806.687-030
CSR	40	Mexican-Food-Machine Tender (food prep., n.e.c.)	524.685-038
CSR	40	Microfilm Mounter (clerical)	208.685-022
CSR	40	Painter, Ski Edge (toy-sport equip.)	749.687-022
CSR	40	Part Maker (jewelry-silver.)	739.687-138
CSR	40	Pressroom Worker, Fat (oils & grease)	559.685-146
CSR	40	Swage Tender (ordnance)	617.685-042
CSR	40	Thread Inspector (plastic-synth.)	681.687-018
CSR	40	Tile Grinder (brick & tile)	679.685-022
CSR	39	Produce Weigher (retail trade)	299.587-010
CSR	39	Spout Tender II (chemical)	921.685-058
CSR	38	Parking Lot Signaler (automotive ser.)	915.667-014
CSR	38	Riding-Silks Custodian (amuse. & rec.)	346.677-014
CSR	38	Stamper I (tex. prod., n.e.c.)	781.687-062
CSR	38	Stenciler (garment; tex. prod., n.e.c.)	781.687-066
CSR	38	Touch-Up Painter, Hand (any industry)	740.684-026

HOC	Cx	Title	DOT
CSI	70	Accountant (profess. & kin.)	160.162-018
CSI	64	Abstractor (profess. & kin.)	119.267-010
CSI	63	User Support Analyst (profess. & kin.)	032.262-010
CSI	60	Bookkeeper (clerical)	210.382-014
CSI	57	Proofreader (print. & pub.)	209.387-030
CSI	55	Medical-Record Clerk (medical ser.)	245.362-010
CSE	70	Accountant, Systems (profess. & kin.)	160.167-026
CSE	70	Supervisor, Cartography (profess. & kin.)	018.131-010
CSE	70	Underwriter (insurance)	169.267-046
CSE	68	Title Supervisor (profess. & kin.)	119.167-018
CSE	66	Chief Clerk, Measurement Department (petrol. & gas; pipe lines)	221.132-010
CSE	65	Closer (real estate)	186.167-074
CSE	65	Supervisor, Accounting Clerks (clerical)	216.132-010
CSE	65	Title Examiner (profess. & kin.)	119.287-010
CSE	63	Caseworker (government ser.)	169.262-010
CSE	63	Investigator, Internal Affairs (government ser.)	375.267-034
CSE	63	Proof-Machine-Operator Supervisor (financial)	217.132-010
CSE	63	Supervisor, Underwriting Clerks (insurance)	219.132-022
CSE	62	Supervisor, Personnel Clerks (clerical)	209.132-010
CSE	62	Supervisor, Policy-Change Clerks (insurance)	219.132-010
CSE	61	Paymaster of Purses (amuse. & rec.)	211.367-010
CSE	61	Policyholder-Information Clerk (insurance)	249.262-010
CSE	61	Rate Analyst, Freight (air trans.; motor trans.; r.r. trans.; water trans.)	214.267-010
CSE	60	Electronic Funds Transfer Coordinator (financial)	216.362-038
CSE	60	Legal Secretary (clerical)	201.362-010
CSE	60	Prompter (amuse. & rec.)	152.367-010
CSE	60	Secretary (clerical)	201.362-030
CSE	60	Securities Clerk (clerical)	210.382-062
CSE	60	Tourist-Information Assistant (government ser.)	237.367-050
CSE	59	City Planning Aide (profess. & kin.)	199.364-010
CSE	59	Securities Clerk (financial)	219.362-054
CSE	59	Supervisor, Money-Room (amuse. & rec.)	211.137-018
CSE	58	Attendance Clerk (education)	219.362-014
CSE	58	Customer Service Representative (financial)	205.362-026
CSE	58	Inspector, Chief (elec. equip.)	729.131-010
CSE	58	Script Supervisor (motion picture; radio-tv broad.)	201.362-026
CSE	58	Tariff Inspector (r.r. trans.)	214.362-034
CSE	57	Account-Information Clerk (utilities)	210.367-010
CSE	57	Braille Proofreader (nonprofit org.; print. & pub.)	209.367-014
CSE	57	Coupon Clerk (financial)	219.462-010
CSE	57	Court Clerk (government ser.)	243.362-010
CSE	57	Credit Clerk (clerical)	205.367-022
CSE	57	Gas-Distribution-and-Emergency Clerk (utilities)	249.367-042
CSE	57	Industrial-Order Clerk (clerical)	221.367-022
CSE	57	Insurance Clerk (medical ser.)	214.362-022
CSE	57	Mortgage Loan Closer (financial)	249.362-018

HOC	Cx	Title	DOT
CSE	57	Supervisor, Telegraphic-Typewriter Operators (clerical)	203.132-010
CSE	57	Television-Schedule Coordinator (radio-tv broad.)	199.382-010
CSE	57	Trust-Vault Clerk (financial)	216.367-014
CSE	56	Cashier I (clerical)	211.362-010
CSE	56	Catalog Librarian (library)	100.387-010
CSE	56	Contract Clerk, Automobile (retail trade)	219.362-026
CSE	56	Counter Clerk (tel. & tel.)	249.362-010
CSE	56	Engineering-Document-Control Clerk (aircraft mfg.; electron. comp.)	206.367-010
CSE	56	Expediter (clerical)	222.367-018
CSE	56	Margin Clerk II (financial)	216.382-046
CSE	56	Reserves Clerk (financial)	216.362-034
CSE	56	School Secretary (education)	201.362-022
CSE	56	Shorthand Reporter (clerical)	202.362-010
CSE	56	Supervisor, Transcribing Operators (clerical)	203.132-014
CSE	56	Teller (financial)	211.362-018
CSE	56	Ticket Agent (any industry)	238.367-026
CSE	56	Traffic-Rate Clerk (clerical)	214.362-038
CSE	55	Administrative Clerk (clerical)	219.362-010
CSE	55	Advertising-Space Clerk (print. & pub.)	247.387-018
CSE	55	Billing-Control Clerk (utilities)	214.387-010
CSE	55	Cancellation Clerk (insurance)	203.382-014
CSE	55	Claims Clerk I (insurance)	241.362-010
CSE	55	Code and Test Clerk (financial)	209.667-018
CSE	55	Insurance Clerk (clerical)	219.387-014
CSE	55	Membership Secretary (nonprofit org.)	201.362-018
CSE	55	Paper-Control Clerk (water trans.)	219.367-022
CSE	55	Personnel Clerk (clerical)	209.362-026
CSE	55	Personnel Scheduler (clerical)	215.367-014
CSE	55	Rate Clerk, Passenger (motor trans.)	214.362-030
CSE	55	Supervisor, Billposting (business ser.)	841.137-010
CSE	54	Billing Typist (clerical)	214.382-014
CSE	54	Bulk-Plant Operator (sugar & conf.)	520.362-010
CSE	54	Classified-Ad Clerk II (print. & pub.)	247.387-022
CSE	54	Clerk-Typist (clerical)	203.362-010
CSE	54	Control Clerk, Auditing (insurance)	209.362-014
CSE	54	Grading Clerk (education)	219.467-010
CSE	54	Laboratory Assistant, Blood and Plasma (medical ser.; pharmaceut.)	078.687-010
CSE	54	Mortgage-Loan-Computation Clerk (insurance)	210.382-050
CSE	54	Post-Office Clerk (government ser.)	243.367-014
CSE	54	Reconsignment Clerk (clerical)	209.367-042
CSE	54	Repair-Order Clerk (clerical)	221.382-022
CSE	54	Space Scheduler (clerical)	238.367-022
CSE	54	Stenographer (clerical)	202.362-014
CSE	54	Stenographer, Print Shop (print. & pub.)	202.362-018
CSE	54	Stenotype Operator (clerical)	202.362-022
CSE	54	Throw-Out Clerk (retail trade)	241.367-030
CSE	54	Underwriting Clerk (insurance)	219.367-038

Part 2: From Holland Codes to Occupations

From Holland Codes to the Dictionary of Occupational Titles Occupations

HOC	Cx	Title	DOT
CSE	53	Cashier, Gambling (amuse. & rec.)	211.462-022
CSE	53	Gambling Dealer (amuse. & rec.)	343.464-010
CSE	53	Information Clerk-Cashier (amuse. & rec.)	249.467-010
CSE	53	Manager, Traffic II (motor trans.)	237.367-030
CSE	53	Test Technician (clerical)	249.367-078
CSE	53	Traffic Clerk (business ser.)	221.367-078
CSE	53	Wire-Photo Operator, News (print. & pub.)	239.382-010
CSE	52	Advertising Clerk (business ser.)	247.387-010
CSE	52	Calculating-Machine Operator (clerical)	216.482-022
CSE	52	Check Cashier (business ser.)	211.462-026
CSE	52	Copy Holder (print. & pub.)	209.667-010
CSE	52	Library Assistant (library)	249.367-046
CSE	52	Referral-and-Information Aide (government ser.)	237.367-042
CSE	52	Rural Mail Carrier (government ser.)	230.363-010
CSE	52	Telegrapher Agent (r.r. trans.)	236.562-014
CSE	52	Telephone Clerk, Telegraph Office (tel. & tel.)	239.362-010
CSE	51	Advertising-Dispatch Clerk (print. & pub.)	247.387-014
CSE	51	Appointment Clerk (clerical)	237.367-010
CSE	51	Back-Shoe Worker (boot & shoe)	221.387-010
CSE	51	Cashier-Wrapper (retail trade)	211.462-018
CSE	51	Check Writer (retail trade)	219.382-010
CSE	51	Civil-Service Clerk (government ser.)	205.362-010
CSE	51	Compiler (clerical)	209.387-014
CSE	51	Contact Clerk (utilities)	209.387-018
CSE	51	Continuity Clerk (motion picture)	209.382-010
CSE	51	Correspondence-Review Clerk (clerical)	209.367-018
CSE	51	Credit Clerk, Blood Bank (medical ser.)	245.367-022
CSE	51	Credit Reporting Clerk (business ser.)	203.362-014
CSE	51	Data-Examination Clerk (clerical)	209.387-022
CSE	51	Dispatcher, Radio (government ser.)	379.362-010
CSE	51	Gin Clerk (agriculture)	221.467-010
CSE	51	Layaway Clerk (retail trade)	299.467-010
CSE	51	License Clerk (government ser.)	205.367-034
CSE	51	Outpatient-Admitting Clerk (medical ser.)	205.362-030
CSE	51	Pedigree Tracer (clerical)	249.387-018
CSE	51	Petroleum Inspector (business ser.)	222.367-046
CSE	51	Police Aide (government ser.)	243.362-014
CSE	51	Receptionist (clerical)	237.367-038
CSE	51	Registration Clerk (government ser.)	205.367-042
CSE	51	Registration Clerk (library)	249.365-010
CSE	51	Teller (utilities)	211.462-034
CSE	51	Timekeeper (clerical)	215.362-022
CSE	51	Weight Tester (paper & pulp)	539.485-010
CSE	51	Weight-Yardage Checker (textile)	589.487-010
CSE	50	Call-Out Operator (business ser.; retail trade)	237.367-014
CSE	50	Car Checker (r.r. trans.)	222.387-014
CSE	50	Cashier II (clerical)	211.462-010
CSE	50	Charge-Account Clerk (clerical)	205.367-014
CSE	50	Checker (chemical)	559.165-010

From Holland Codes to the Dictionary of Occupational Titles Occupations

HOC	Cx	Title	DOT
CSE	50	Credit Card Control Clerk (financial)	249.367-026
CSE	50	Data Entry Clerk (clerical)	203.582-054
CSE	50	Drivers'-Cash Clerk (motor trans.)	211.462-030
CSE	50	Floor-Space Allocator (tobacco; wholesale tr.)	222.367-030
CSE	50	Identification Clerk (clerical)	205.362-022
CSE	50	Line-Up Worker (auto. mfg.)	221.367-026
CSE	50	Meter Reader (utilities; waterworks)	209.567-010
CSE	50	Milk Sampler (agriculture)	410.357-010
CSE	50	Parimutuel-Ticket Cashier (amuse. & rec.)	211.467-018
CSE	50	Parimutuel-Ticket Seller (amuse. & rec.)	211.467-022
CSE	50	Reader (business ser.)	249.387-022
CSE	50	Rehabilitation Clerk (nonprofit org.)	205.367-046
CSE	50	Suggestion Clerk (clerical)	209.387-034
CSE	50	Telegraphic-Typewriter Operator (clerical)	203.582-050
CSE	50	Transcribing-Machine Operator (clerical)	203.582-058
CSE	50	Yard Clerk (r.r. trans.)	209.367-054
CSE	49	Braille Transcriber, Hand (education; nonprofit organ.; print. & pub.)	209.584-010
CSE	49	CD-Reactor Operator (chemical)	558.385-010
CSE	49	Central-Office Operator (tel. & tel.)	235.462-010
CSE	49	Election Clerk (government ser.)	205.367-030
CSE	49	Perforator Typist (clerical)	203.582-038
CSE	49	Production Proofreader (print. & pub.; retail trade)	247.667-010
CSE	49	Telephone Operator (clerical)	235.662-022
CSE	49	Telephone-Answering-Service Operator (business ser.)	235.662-026
CSE	49	Ticket Marker (wholesale tr.)	216.567-010
CSE	49	Typist (clerical)	203.582-066
CSE	48	Creel Clerk (government ser.)	205.367-026
CSE	48	Return-To-Factory Clerk (clerical)	209.587-042
CSE	48	Reviewer (insurance)	209.687-018
CSE	48	Spotter, Photographic (photofinishing)	970.381-034
CSE	48	Survey Worker (clerical)	205.367-054
CSE	47	Enameler (jewelry-silver.)	740.684-018
CSE	47	Map Clerk (insurance)	209.587-030
CSE	47	Order Clerk, Food and Beverage (hotel & rest.)	209.567-014
CSE	47	Receptionist, Airline Lounge (air trans.)	352.677-014
CSE	47	Sample Display Preparer (knitting)	222.687-026
CSE	47	Tallier (clerical)	221.587-030
CSE	47	Tooth Clerk (protective dev.)	222.687-038
CSE	46	Board Attendant (amuse. & rec.)	249.587-010
CSE	46	Braille-and-Talking Books Clerk (library)	222.587-014
CSE	46	Brand Recorder (government ser.)	206.587-010
CSE	46	Caller (r.r. trans.)	215.563-010
CSE	46	Carbonation Tester (beverage)	522.587-010
CSE	46	Tower-Crane Operator (construction)	921.663-054
CSE	45	Bouffant-Curtain-Machine Tender (tex. prod., n.e.c.)	689.685-026
CSE	45	Decorator (pottery & porc.)	740.684-014
CSE	45	Telegraph-Service Rater (tel. & tel.)	214.587-010
CSE	44	Charger I (jewelry-silver.)	740.684-010

HOC	Cx	Title	DOT
CSE	44	Hosiery Mender (knitting)	782.684-030
CSE	44	Sorter (office machines)	706.587-014
CSE	44	Take-Down Sorter (photofinishing)	976.665-010
CSE	43	Kosher Inspector (dairy products)	529.687-126
CSE	43	Material Assembler (hat & cap)	784.687-050
CSE	43	Recorder (knitting)	221.587-026
CSE	43	Ride Operator (amuse. & rec.)	342.663-010
CSE	42	Checker (textile)	221.587-010
CSE	42	Shoe Dyer (personal ser.)	364.684-014
CSE	42	Tufting-Machine Operator, Single-Needle (carpet & rug)	687.685-022
CSE	41	Cooling-Room Attendant (personal ser.)	335.677-010
CSE	41	Printer, Machine (hat & cap)	652.685-070
CSE	41	Threading-Machine Tender (carpet & rug)	683.685-030
CSE	40	Finisher (tex. prod., n.e.c.)	789.687-050
CSE	40	Marker (garment; retail trade; tex. prod., n.e.c.)	781.687-042
CSE	40	Rug Braider, Hand (carpet & rug)	782.687-042
CSE	38	Assembler, Plastic Hospital Products (inst. & app.)	712.687-010
CSE	38	Second (amuse. & rec.)	346.677-018
CSE	38	Show Girl (amuse. & rec.)	159.647-022
CSE	38	Tooth Inspector (protective dev.)	712.687-038
CER	70	Accountant, Property (profess. & kin.)	160.167-022
CER	68	Registrar, Museum (museums)	102.167-018
CER	66	Budget Analyst (government ser.)	161.267-030
CER	63	Supervisor (optical goods)	716.130-010
CER	61	Relay-Shop Supervisor (utilities)	729.131-014
CER	56	Flight Operations Specialist (military ser.)	248.387-010
CER	56	Utility Clerk (utilities)	239.367-034
CER	55	Investigator, Dealer Accounts (financial)	241.367-038
CER	54	Cryptographic-Machine Operator (clerical)	203.582-018
CER	54	Parts Lister (electron. comp.)	229.367-014
CER	54	Stamp Classifier (retail trade)	299.387-018
CER	54	Telegrapher (r.r. trans.)	236.562-010
CER	53	Radio-Message Router (tel. & tel.)	235.387-010
CER	53	Transfer Clerk (financial)	216.362-046
CER	52	Locomotive Lubricating-Systems Clerk (r.r. trans.)	221.367-030
CER	51	Automobile-Self-Serve-Service-Station Attendant (automotive ser.)	915.477-010
CER	51	Broadcast Checker (radio-tv broad.)	249.387-010
CER	51	Classifier (rubber goods)	753.467-010
CER	51	Detailer, School Photographs (photofinishing)	976.564-010
CER	51	Rough-Rice Grader (grain-feed mills)	529.367-026
CER	50	Purification-Operator Helper (chemical)	551.465-010
CER	50	Sheet Writer (amuse. & rec.)	211.467-026
CER	50	Ticket Worker (tobacco)	221.482-018
CER	49	Directory-Assistance Operator (tel. & tel.)	235.662-018
CER	49	Ski-Tow Operator (amuse. & rec.)	341.665-010
CER	48	Central-Supply Worker (medical ser.)	381.687-010
CER	48	Centrifuge Operator, Plasma Processing (medical ser.; pharmaceut.)	599.685-018

HOC	Cx	Title	DOT
CER	48	Credit-Card Clerk (retail trade)	209.587-014
CER	48	Quality-Control Inspector (light. fix.)	725.687-026
CER	47	Cellophane-Bath Mixer (plastic-synth.)	550.585-014
CER	46	Inspector, Balance Truing (clock & watch)	715.687-050
CER	45	Crossing Tender (any industry)	371.667-010
CER	45	Tube Operator (clerical)	239.687-014
CER	44	Acid-Plant Helper (chemical)	558.565-010
CER	44	Barrel Filler (grain-feed mills)	529.485-010
CER	44	Nodulizer (cement)	579.685-034
CER	44	Painter, Animated Cartoons (motion picture; radio-tv broad.)	970.681-026
CER	44	Second Operator, Mill Tender (chemical)	555.685-054
CER	44	Stock Patcher (ordnance)	761.684-042
CER	44	Twitchell Operator (chemical)	558.585-042
CER	43	Brush Filler, Hand (fabrication, n.e.c.)	739.687-046
CER	43	Grain Mixer (grain-feed mills)	520.485-014
CER	43	Paper Sorter and Counter (paper & pulp)	649.687-010
CER	43	Passenger Service Representative II (r.r. trans.)	910.677-010
CER	43	Tablet Tester (pharmaceut.)	559.667-010
CER	42	Assembler, Leather Goods II (leather prod.)	783.687-010
CER	42	Broomcorn Grader (fabrication, n.e.c.)	739.687-042
CER	42	Counter Attendant, Cafeteria (hotel & rest.)	311.677-014
CER	42	Glass Inspector (any industry)	579.687-022
CER	42	Grader, Dressed Poultry (meat products)	529.687-102
CER	42	Leaf Sorter (tobacco)	529.687-134
CER	42	Mixer Operator (beverage)	520.685-146
CER	42	Pull-Out Operator (fabrication, n.e.c.)	739.687-162
CER	42	Sample Clerk, Handkerchief (garment)	920.587-022
CER	41	Batch-Tank Controller (grain-feed mills)	521.685-022
CER	41	Cooler Tender (grain-feed mills)	523.685-038
CER	41	Cutter-and-Paster, Press Clippings (business ser.)	249.587-014
CER	41	Escort-Vehicle Driver (motor trans.)	919.663-022
CER	41	Line-Out Worker I (tobacco)	920.687-110
CER	41	Painter (jewelry-silver.)	735.687-018
CER	41	Raw Shellfish Preparer (hotel & rest.)	311.674-014
CER	41	Roll Examiner (paper & pulp)	640.687-010
CER	41	Sample Collector (chemical)	550.587-014
CER	41	Steward/Stewardess, Bath (water trans.)	350.677-018
CER	41	Stocking Inspector (knitting)	684.684-010
CER	41	Transporter, Patients (medical ser.)	355.677-014
CER	41	Wheat Cleaner (grain-feed mills)	529.685-262
CER	41	Wrapper Selector (tobacco)	529.687-218
CER	40	Abrasive-Band Winder (nonmet. min.)	692.685-010
CER	40	Collet Gluer (clock & watch)	715.685-010
CER	40	Egg Candler (any industry)	529.687-074
CER	40	Folder-Tier (nonmet. min.)	759.684-034
CER	40	Ion Exchange Operator (beverage)	521.685-190
CER	40	Mounter, Hand (photofinishing)	976.684-018
CER	40	Pegger (boot & shoe)	788.687-102

HOC	Cx	Title	DOT
CER	40	Pencil Inspector (pen & pencil)	733.687-062
CER	40	Rest Room Attendant (any industry)	358.677-018
CER	40	Tab-Machine Operator (nonmet. min.)	754.685-010
CER	39	Laborer, General (tex. prod., n.e.c.)	589.687-026
CER	39	Mill Operator (grain-feed mills)	521.685-226
CER	38	Processor, Grain (grain-feed mills)	521.685-254
CER	38	Sandwich-Board Carrier (any industry)	299.687-014
CER	37	Racker (paper goods)	659.687-010
CEI	70	Bursar (education)	160.167-042
CEI	65	Customs Inspector (government ser.)	168.267-022
CEI	53	Fingerprint Clerk II (government ser.)	206.387-014
CES	72	Auditor, Tax (profess. & kin.)	160.167-038
CES	70	Fire-Prevention Research Engineer (profess. & kin.)	012.167-022
CES	66	Quality-Control Coordinator (pharmaceut.)	168.167-066
CES	66	Supervisor, Production Clerks (clerical)	221.137-014
CES	65	Airline-Radio Operator, Chief (air trans.; business ser.)	193.162-022
CES	65	Manager, Mutuel Department (amuse. & rec.)	187.167-134
CES	64	Tumor Registrar (medical ser.)	079.362-018
CES	63	Manager, Gun Club (amuse. & rec.)	187.167-118
CES	63	Supervisor, Word Processing (clerical)	203.137-010
CES	62	Foreign Banknote Teller-Trader (financial)	211.362-014
CES	62	Social Secretary (clerical)	201.162-010
CES	61	Medical Secretary (medical ser.)	201.362-014
CES	60	Copyright Expert (radio-tv broad.)	249.267-010
CES	60	Employment Clerk (clerical)	205.362-014
CES	60	Passport-Application Examiner (government ser.)	169.267-030
CES	60	Placer (insurance)	239.267-010
CES	60	Production Scheduler, Paperboard Products (paper goods)	221.162-010
CES	60	Supervisor, Central Supply (medical ser.)	381.137-014
CES	59	Copy Cutter (print. & pub.)	221.167-010
CES	58	Chart Calculator (utilities)	214.487-010
CES	58	Trust Operations Assistant (financial)	219.362-074
CES	57	Congressional-District Aide (government ser.)	209.362-030
CES	57	Fire Inspector (government ser.)	373.267-010
CES	57	Operations and Intelligence Assistant (military ser.)	378.367-026
CES	57	Script Reader (radio-tv broad.)	131.267-022
CES	57	Tax Preparer (business ser.)	219.362-070
CES	56	Intelligence Clerk (military ser.)	249.387-014
CES	56	Letter-of-Credit Clerk (financial)	219.367-050
CES	56	Supervisor, Steno Pool (clerical)	202.132-010
CES	55	Information Clerk (motor trans.; r.r. trans.; water trans.)	237.367-018
CES	55	Photocomposing-Perforator-Machine Operator (print. & pub.)	203.582-042
CES	55	Procurement Clerk (clerical)	249.367-066
CES	55	Quality-Control Technician (photofinishing)	976.267-010
CES	55	Relay-Record Clerk (utilities)	221.367-054
CES	55	Reservation Clerk (clerical)	238.362-014

HOC	Cx	Title	DOT
CES	55	Reservations Agent (air trans.)	238.367-018
CES	54	Classified-Ad Clerk I (print. & pub.)	247.367-010
CES	54	Dispatcher, Ship Pilot (water trans.)	248.367-026
CES	54	Insurance Clerk (financial; insurance)	219.367-014
CES	54	Magnetic-Tape-Composer Operator (print. & pub.)	203.382-018
CES	54	Museum Attendant (museums)	109.367-010
CES	54	Order Clerk (clerical)	249.362-026
CES	54	Park Aide (government ser.)	249.367-082
CES	54	Scheduler (museums)	238.367-034
CES	53	Benefits Clerk II (clerical)	205.567-010
CES	53	Booking Clerk (water trans.)	248.367-014
CES	53	Dispatcher, Oil Well Services (petrol. & gas)	939.362-010
CES	53	Shipping-Order Clerk (clerical)	219.367-030
CES	52	Classification Clerk (clerical)	206.387-010
CES	52	Correspondence Clerk (clerical)	209.362-034
CES	52	Customer Service Representative (radio-tv broad.; tel. & tel.; utilities; waterworks)	239.362-014
CES	52	Diet Clerk (medical ser.)	245.587-010
CES	52	Dispatcher, Maintenance Service (clerical)	239.367-014
CES	52	History-Card Clerk (utilities)	209.587-022
CES	52	Referral Clerk, Temporary Help Agency (clerical)	205.367-062
CES	51	Animal-Shelter Clerk (nonprofit org.)	249.367-010
CES	51	Assignment Clerk (clerical)	249.367-090
CES	51	Braker, Passenger Train (r.r. trans.)	910.364-010
CES	51	Calendar-Control Clerk, Blood Bank (medical ser.)	245.367-018
CES	51	Cashier-Checker (retail trade)	211.462-014
CES	51	Credit Reference Clerk (financial; retail trade)	209.362-018
CES	51	Grain Elevator Clerk (beverage; grain-feed mills)	222.567-010
CES	51	Lost-Charge-Card Clerk (clerical)	209.367-034
CES	51	Reservation Clerk (r.r. trans.)	238.367-014
CES	51	Routing Clerk (nonprofit org.)	249.367-070
CES	51	Satellite-Instruction Facilitator (education)	249.367-086
CES	51	Tax Clerk (clerical)	219.487-010
CES	51	Taxicab Starter (motor trans.)	913.367-010
CES	50	Coupon-Redemption Clerk (retail trade)	290.477-010
CES	50	Credit Authorizer (clerical)	249.367-022
CES	50	Page (radio-tv broad.)	353.367-022
CES	50	Parimutuel-Ticket Checker (amuse. & rec.)	219.587-010
CES	50	Planimeter Operator (government ser.)	219.387-022
CES	50	Telephone Quotation Clerk (financial)	237.367-046
CES	50	Ticket Seller (clerical)	211.467-030
CES	50	Toll Collector (government ser.)	211.462-038
CES	49	Bus Attendant (motor trans.)	352.577-010
CES	49	Fingerprint Clerk I (government ser.)	209.367-026
CES	49	Skate-Shop Attendant (amuse. & rec.)	341.464-010
CES	48	Color Mixer (furniture)	589.464-010
CES	48	Dispatcher, Street Department (government ser.)	239.367-030
CES	48	Fermenter, Wine (beverage)	522.685-062
CES	48	Gate Guard (any industry)	372.667-030

Part 2: From Holland Codes to Occupations

From Holland Codes to the Dictionary of Occupational Titles Occupations

HOC	Cx	Title	DOT
CES	48	Hair-Sample Matcher (fabrication, n.e.c.)	739.387-014
CES	48	Outboard-Motor Inspector (engine-turbine)	806.687-042
CES	48	Temperature-Control Inspector (plastic-synth.)	559.467-010
CES	47	Auction Clerk (retail trade; wholesale tr.)	294.567-010
CES	47	Counter Attendant, Lunchroom or Coffee Shop (hotel & rest.)	311.477-014
CES	47	Waiter/Waitress (water trans.)	350.677-030
CES	45	Color Tester (smelt. & refin.)	511.667-014
CES	45	Hospital-Television-Rental Clerk (business ser.)	295.467-018
CES	45	Plant Operator, Channel Process (chemical)	542.685-010
CES	45	Unit Operator (chemical)	542.685-018
CES	44	Redye Hand (knitting)	789.687-142
CES	44	Regenerator Operator (sugar & conf.)	573.685-034
CES	43	Drive-In Theater Attendant (amuse. & rec.)	349.673-010
CES	43	Racker (amuse. & rec.)	340.477-010
CES	42	Addresser (clerical)	209.587-010
CES	42	Cardroom Attendant II (amuse. & rec.)	343.577-010
CES	42	Impregnation Operator (paper goods)	539.685-014
CES	42	Mica Sizer (mine & quarry)	779.687-030
CES	42	Parking Enforcement Officer (government ser.)	375.587-010
CES	42	Sorter (clerical)	209.687-022
CES	41	Auction Assistant (retail trade; wholesale tr.)	294.667-010
CES	41	Collator, Hand (print. & pub.)	977.687-010
CES	41	Deliverer, Outside (clerical)	230.663-010
CES	41	Floor Attendant (amuse. & rec.)	343.467-014
CES	41	Messenger, Copy (print. & pub.)	239.677-010
CES	41	Paint-Spray Inspector (any industry)	741.687-010
CES	41	Passenger Attendant (water trans.)	350.677-014
CES	41	Ride Attendant (amuse. & rec.)	342.677-010
CES	41	Ticket Taker (amuse. & rec.)	344.667-010
CES	40	Sizing-Machine Tender (clock & watch)	690.685-366
CES	40	Usher (amuse. & rec.)	344.677-014
CES	40	Window-Shade-Ring Sewer (furniture)	692.685-254
CES	38	Belt-Maker Helper (nonmet. min.)	776.687-010
CES	38	Drier Helper (chemical)	553.687-010
CES	38	Suture Winder, Hand (protective dev.)	712.687-034

Note. n.e.c. = not elsewhere classified.

Part 2: From Holland Codes to Occupations

From Holland Codes to the Occupational Employment Statistics
and Occupational Outlook Handbook Occupations

HOC	Cx	Title	OES
RIA	58	Photographers	34023
RIS	69	Occupational Therapists	32305
RIS	62	Broadcast Technicians	34028
RIS	62	Data Processing Equipment Repairers	85705
RIS	61	Embalmers	39014
RIS	60	Radiation Therapists	32913
RIS	59	Cabinetmakers and Bench Carpenters	89311
RIS	59	Elevator Installers and Repairers	85932
RIS	59	Emergency Medical Technicians	32508
RIS	59	Maintenance Repairers, General Utility	85132
RIS	59	Pattern Markers, Wood	89305
RIS	59	Signal or Track Switch Maintainers	85511
RIS	58	Opticians, Dispensing and Measuring	32514
RIS	58	Telephone and Cable Television Line Installers and Repairers	85702
RIS	57	Biological, Agricultural, and Food Technicians and Technologists, Except Health	24502
RIS	57	Food Batchmakers	89808
RIS	57	Petroleum Pump System Operators	95011
RIS	56	Electrical Installers and Repairers, Transportation Equipment	85728
RIS	54	Screen Printing Machine Setters and Set-up Operators	92524
RIS	51	Forging Machine Setters and Set-up Operators, Metal and Plastic	91317
RIS	47	Furnace Operators and Tenders	91935
RIS	47	Loading Machine Operators, Underground Mining	97932
RIS	47	Longshore Equipment Operators	97902
RIS	47	Operating Engineers	97956
RIS	47	Sprayers/Applicators	79036
RIS	46	Brattice Builders	87121
RIE	74	Engineering Teachers, Postsecondary	31222
RIE	72	Mining Engineers, Including Mine Safety	22108
RIE	71	Mechanical Engineers	22135
RIE	68	Industrial Engineering Technicians and Technologists	22508
RIE	67	Aircraft Pilots and Flight Engineers	97702
RIE	67	Mechanical Engineering Technicians and Technologists	22511
RIE	65	Electrical and Electronic Engineering Technicians and Technologists	22505
RIE	65	Petroleum Technicians and Technologists	24511
RIE	63	Construction and Building Inspectors	21908
RIE	61	All Other Engineering and Related Technicians and Technologists	22599
RIE	60	Aircraft Engine Specialists	85326
RIE	60	Machinists	89108
RIE	59	All Other Electrical and Electronic Equipment Mechanics, Installers, and Repairers	85799
RIE	59	Job Printers	89705

HOC to OES and OOH

Part 2: From Holland Codes to Occupations

From Holland Codes to the Occupational Employment Statistics
and Occupational Outlook Handbook Occupations

HOC	Cx	Title	OES
RIE	59	Medical and Clinical Laboratory Technicians	32905
RIE	59	Pattern and Model Makers, Metal	89114
RIE	59	Precision Instrument Makers	89105
RIE	59	Precision Instrument Repairers	85905
RIE	59	Tool and Die Makers	89102
RIE	58	Aircraft Structure, Surfaces, Rigging, and Systems Assemblers, Precision	93102
RIE	58	Gas Appliance Repairers	85944
RIE	58	Precision Lay-Out Workers, Metal	89117
RIE	58	Precision Patternmakers, Model Makers, Lay-Out Workers, and Cutters	89908
RIE	58	Sheet Metal Workers	89132
RIE	57	All Other Precision Woodworkers	89399
RIE	57	Combination Machine Tool Setters and Set-up Operators, Metal and Plastic	91505
RIE	57	Electrolytic Plating and Coating Machine Setters and Set-up Operators, Metal and Plastic	91917
RIE	57	Electromechanical Equipment Assemblers, Precision	93111
RIE	57	Lathe and Turning Machine Tool Setters and Set-up Operators, Metal and Plastic	91105
RIE	57	Photoengravers	89712
RIE	57	Shipfitters	89121
RIE	57	Underground Mine Machinery Mechanics	85117
RIE	56	Letterpress Setters and Set-up Operators	92515
RIE	55	All Other Precision Printing Workers	89799
RIE	55	Camera Operators	89713
RIE	55	Drilling and Boring Machine Tool Setters and Set-up Operators, Metal and Plastic	91108
RIE	55	Precision Molders, Shapers, Casters, and Carvers, Except Jewelry and Foundry	89905
RIE	54	Locomotive Firers	97311
RIE	54	Milling and Planing Machine Setters and Set-up Operators, Metal and Plastic	91111
RIE	54	Wood Machinists	89308
RIE	53	Soldering and Brazing Machine Setters and Set-up Operators	91708
RIE	52	Grinding, Lapping, and Buffing Machine Tool Setters and Set-up Operators, Metal and Plastic	91114
RIE	52	Motorcycle Repairers	85308
RIE	51	Welders and Cutters	93914
RIE	50	Extruding and Drawing Machine Setters and Set-up Operators, Metal and Plastic	91311
RIE	50	Metal Molding, Coremaking, and Casting Machine Setters and Set-up Operators	91908
RIE	49	Paper Goods Machine Setters and Set-up Operators	92914
RIE	49	Pile-Driver Operators	87705
RIE	48	Carpet Cutters, Diagrammers, and Seamers	93932
RIE	48	Head Sawyers	92305
RIE	48	Mine Cutting and Channeling Machine Operators	87943

HOC	Cx	Title	OES
RIE	48	Motorboat Operators	97511
RIE	48	Rail Yard Engineers, Dinkey Operators, and Hostlers	97308
RIE	48	Septic Tank Servicers and Sewer Pipe Cleaners	87511
RIE	48	Woodworking Machine Setters and Set-up Operators, Except Sawing	92311
RIE	47	Heat Treating, Annealing, and Tempering Machine Operators and Tenders, Metal and Plastic	91932
RIE	47	Shuttle Car Operators	97935
RIC	68	Civil Engineering Technicians and Technologists	22502
RIC	60	Electronics Repairers, Commercial and Industrial Equipment	85717
RIC	60	Programmers, Numerical Tool and Process Control	25111
RIC	59	Metal Fabricators, Structural Metal Products	91714
RIC	59	Station Installers and Repairers, Telephone	85726
RIC	55	Precision Foundry Mold and Coremakers	89902
RIC	54	Motion Picture Projectionists	92905
RIC	54	Tank Car and Truck Loaders	97905
RIC	51	Punching Machine Setters and Set-up Operators, Metal and Plastic	91302
RAI	61	Merchandise Displayers and Window Trimmers	34044
RAS	53	All Other Precision Food and Tobacco Workers	89899
RAC	52	Precision Detail Design Decorators and Painters	89911
RSI	61	All Other Health Professionals, Paraprofessionals, and Technicians	32999
RSI	56	Medical Appliance Makers	89923
RSI	56	Power Distributors and Dispatchers	95028
RSI	53	Heating Equipment Setters and Set-up Operators, Metal and Plastic	91928
RSI	51	Shear and Slitter Machine Setters and Set-up Operators, Metal and Plastic	91308
RSA	54	Bakers, Bread and Pastry	65021
RSE	58	Telegraph and Teletype Installers and Maintainers	85508
RSE	57	Gas Compressor Operators	97921
RSE	57	Petroleum Refinery and Control Panel Operators	95014
RSE	57	Radio Mechanics	85514
RSE	56	Central Office and PBX Installers and Repairers	85502
RSE	56	Electronic Home Entertainment Equipment Repairers	85708
RSE	56	Power-Generating Plant Operators, Except Auxiliary Equipment Operators	95021
RSE	55	Electrical Power-Line Installers and Repairers	85723
RSE	53	Bakers, Manufacturing	89805
RSE	53	Cooks, Restaurant	65026

HOC	Cx	Title	OES
RSE	53	Precision Dyers	89521
RSE	51	Glaziers	87811
RSE	51	Press and Press-Brake Machine Setters and Set-up Operators, Metal and Plastic	91305
RSE	51	Riggers	85935
RSE	50	Coin and Vending Machine Servicers and Repairers	85947
RSE	50	Cooks, Short order	65035
RSE	49	Bus Drivers	97108
RSE	49	Butchers and Meat Cutters	65023
RSE	49	Cooks, Specialty Fast Food	65032
RSE	49	Painters and Paperhangers, Construction and Maintenance	87402
RSE	47	Continuous Mining Machine Operators	87941
RSE	47	Fence Erectors	87817
RSE	47	Stock Clerks, Sales Floor	49021
RSE	45	Portable Machine Cutters	93928
RSC	57	Hand Compositors and Typesetters	89702
RSC	52	Furniture Finishers	89314
RSC	51	Musical Instrument Repairers and Tuners	85921
RSC	48	All Other Inspectors, Testers, and Related Workers	83099
RSC	48	Bicycle Repairers	85951
RSC	43	Helpers, Carpenters and Related Workers	98312
RSC	43	Rock Splitters, Quarry	87908
REI	68	Pilots, Ship	97508
REI	68	Traffic Technicians	39005
REI	67	Criminal Investigators, Public Service	63028
REI	61	Electromedical and Biomedical Equipment Repairers	85908
REI	59	Machinery Maintenance Mechanics, Water or Power Generation Plant	85118
REI	59	Pattern and Model Makers, Wood	89302
REI	58	All Other Lithography and Photoengraving Workers	89719
REI	58	Bus and Truck Mechanics and Diesel Engine Specialists	85311
REI	57	All Other Communications Equipment Mechanics, Installers, and Repairers	85599
REI	57	Custom Tailors and Sewers	89505
REI	57	Fitters, Structural Metal, Precision	93108
REI	57	Mobile Heavy Equipment Mechanics, Except Engines	85314
REI	57	Precision Inspectors, Testers, and Graders	83002
REI	57	Small Engine Specialists	85328
REI	56	Electric Meter Installers and Repairers	85911
REI	56	Stationary Engineers	95032
REI	56	Strippers	89717
REI	55	All Other Machinery Maintenance Mechanics	85119
REI	55	Fabric and Apparel Patternmakers and Lay-Out Workers	89502
REI	55	Numerical Control Machine Tool Operators and Tenders, Metal and Plastic	91502
REI	55	Platemakers	89718
REI	55	Plumbers, Pipefitters, and Steamfitters	87502

HOC to OES and OOH

HOC	Cx	Title	OES
REI	55	Precision Etchers and Engravers, Hand or Machine	89128
REI	55	Precision Optical Goods Workers	89917
REI	55	Tool Grinders, Filers, Sharpeners, and Other Precision Grinders	89111
REI	54	Aircraft Mechanics	85323
REI	54	All Other Precision Metal Workers	89199
REI	54	Carpet Installers	87602
REI	54	Electrical and Electronic Equipment Assemblers, Precision	93114
REI	54	Mechanical Control and Valve Installers and Repairers	85928
REI	54	Plasterers and Stucco Masons	87317
REI	54	Rotary Drill Operators, Oil and Gas Extraction	87911
REI	54	Structural Metal Workers	87814
REI	54	Water and Liquid Waste Treatment Plant and System Operators	95002
REI	54	Welding Machine Setters and Set-up Operators	91702
REI	53	All Other Metal and Plastic (cutting, forming, fabricating, or processing) Machine Setters and Set-up Operators	92197
REI	53	All Other Plant and System Operators	95099
REI	53	All Other Precision Workers	89999
REI	53	Electric Motor, Transformer, and Related Repairers	85714
REI	53	Nonelectrolytic Plating and Coating Machine Setters and Set-up Operators, Metal and Plastic	91923
REI	52	Dairy Processing Equipment Operators, Including Setters	92932
REI	51	All Other Printing Press Setters and Set-up Operators	92519
REI	51	Chemical Equipment Controllers and Operators	92935
REI	51	Concrete and Terrazzo Finishers	87311
REI	51	Rolling Machine Setters and Set-up Operators, Metal and Plastic	91314
REI	50	All Other Agricultural, Forestry, Fishing, and Related Workers	79999
REI	50	All Other Machine Setters and Set-up Operators	92997
REI	50	All Other Printing Related Machine Setters and Set-up Operators	92529
REI	50	Automotive Body and Related Repairers	85305
REI	50	Log Graders and Scalers	79008
REI	50	Plastic Molding and Casting Machine Setters and Set-up Operators	91902
REI	49	Subway and Streetcar Operators	97314
REI	49	Welding Machine Operators and Tenders	91705
REI	48	Earth Drillers, Except Oil and Gas	87902
REI	47	Rail-Track Laying and Maintenance Equipment Operators	87714
REI	46	Ordinary Seamen and Marine Oilers	97517
REI	46	Truck Drivers, Heavy or Tractor-Trailer	97102
REI	45	Grader, Bulldozer, and Scraper Operators	97938
REI	44	Logging Tractor Operators	73011
REI	39	Forest and Conservation Workers	79002
RES	63	Fish and Game Wardens	63041

HOC	Cx	Title	OES
RES	62	Millwrights	85123
RES	61	Power Reactor Operators	95026
RES	60	Powerhouse, Substation, and Relay Electricians	85721
RES	59	First-Line Supervisors and Managers/Supervisors - Construction Trades and Extractive Workers	81005
RES	59	First-Line Supervisors and Managers/Supervisors - Production and Operating Workers	81008
RES	59	Service Unit Operators	87917
RES	59	Ship Engineers	97521
RES	58	Animal Breeders	79015
RES	58	Machinery Maintenance Mechanics, Marine Equipment	85116
RES	58	Scanner Operators	89715
RES	57	Boilermakers	89135
RES	57	Electricians	87202
RES	57	Machinery Maintenance Mechanics, Sewing Machines	85113
RES	57	Office Machine and Cash Register Servicers	85926
RES	56	Ceiling Tile Installers and Acoustical Carpenters	87105
RES	56	Heating, Air Conditioning, and Refrigeration Mechanics and Installers	85902
RES	56	Machine Builders and Other Precision Machine Assemblers	93105
RES	56	Oil Pumpers, Except Wellhead	97908
RES	56	Wellhead Pumpers	97911
RES	55	Locomotive Engineers	97305
RES	55	Rail Car Repairers	85317
RES	54	All Other Precision Assemblers	93197
RES	54	Electric Home Appliance and Power Tool Repairers	85711
RES	54	Floor Layers, Except Carpet, Wood, and Hard Tiles	87605
RES	54	Gas Plant Operators	95005
RES	54	Jewelers and Silversmiths	89123
RES	54	Precision Hand Workers, Jewelry and Related Products	89126
RES	53	All Other Precision Textile, Apparel, and Furnishings Workers	89599
RES	53	Carpenters	87102
RES	53	Farm Equipment Mechanics	85321
RES	53	Stonemasons	87305
RES	53	Textile Machine Setters and Set-up Operators	92702
RES	52	Automotive Mechanics	85302
RES	52	Blasters and Explosives Workers	87905
RES	52	Bookbinders	89721
RES	52	Shoe and Leather Workers and Repairers, Precision	89511
RES	52	Watch, Clock, and Chronometer Assemblers, Adjusters, Calibrators, Precision	93117
RES	51	Cooks, Institution or Cafeteria	65028
RES	51	Slaughterers and Butchers	89802
RES	50	Auxiliary Equipment Operators, Power	95023
RES	50	Bus Drivers, School	97111
RES	50	Fire Fighters	63008
RES	49	Spotters, Dry-Cleaning	89514
RES	48	Driver/Sales Workers	97117

HOC	Cx	Title	OES
RES	48	Photoengraving and Lithographing Machine Operators and Tenders	92545
RES	47	Dragline Operators	97926
RES	47	Tapers	87111
RES	46	Animal Caretakers, Except Farm	79017
RES	46	Heaters, Metal and Plastic	91938
RES	46	Reinforcing Metal Workers	87314
RES	45	All Other Extractive Workers, Except Helpers	87989
RES	45	Boiler Operators and Tenders, Low Pressure	92926
RES	44	Baggage Porters and Bellhops	68023
RES	44	Refractory Materials Repairers, Except Brickmasons	85126
RES	44	Roasting, Baking, and Drying Machine Operators and Tenders, Food and Tobacco	92921
RES	42	Fallers and Buckers	73002
RES	41	All Other Cleaning and Building Service Workers	67099
RES	40	All Other Construction and Extractive Workers, Except Helpers	87999
RES	40	All Other Freight, Stock, and Material Movers, Hand	98799
RES	38	Stevedores, Except Equipment Operators	98702
RES	37	Choke Setters	73005
RES	36	Refuse and Recyclable Material Collectors	98705
REC	57	Locksmiths and Safe Repairers	85923
REC	56	Precision Dental Laboratory Technicians	89921
REC	54	Gas Pumping Station Operators	97917
REC	54	Pharmacy Technicians	32518
REC	53	Able Seamen	97514
REC	53	Derrick Operators, Oil and Gas Extraction	87914
REC	53	Installers and Repairers, Manufactured Buildings, Mobile Homes, and Travel Trailers	85938
REC	53	Upholsterers	89508
REC	53	Watchmakers	85917
REC	52	Gem and Diamond Workers	89926
REC	51	Frame Wirers, Central Office	85505
REC	51	Shipping, Receiving, and Traffic Clerks	58028
REC	50	Roofers	87808
REC	49	Bindery Machine Setters and Set-up Operators	92525
REC	49	Brickmasons	87302
REC	49	Dredge Operators	97928
REC	49	Extruding, Forming, Pressing, and Compacting Machine Setters and Set-up Operators	92968
REC	48	All Other Mining Machine Operators	87949
REC	47	All Other Rail Vehicle Operators and Controllers	97399
REC	47	Electrolytic Plating and Coating Machine Operators and Tenders, Metal and Plastic	91921
REC	47	Glaziers, Manufacturing	93911
REC	47	Graders and Sorters, Agricultural Products	79011
REC	47	Railroad Brake, Signal, and Switch Operators	97317
REC	46	Chemical Equipment Tenders	92938

From Holland Codes to the Occupational Employment Statistics
and Occupational Outlook Handbook Occupations

HOC	Cx	Title	OES
REC	46	Pest Controllers and Assistants	67008
REC	45	Combination Machine Tool Operators and Tenders, Metal and Plastic	91508
REC	45	Cooking Machine Operators and Tenders, Food and Tobacco	92917
REC	45	Metal Molding, Coremaking, and Casting Machine Operators and Tenders	91911
REC	45	Pressers, Delicate Fabrics	89517
REC	45	Service Station Attendants	97805
REC	45	Taxi Drivers and Chauffeurs	97114
REC	44	Coating, Painting, and Spraying Machine Operators and Tenders	92953
REC	44	Crushing, Grinding, Mixing, and Blending Machine Operators and Tenders	92965
REC	44	Duplicating Machine Operators	56005
REC	44	Farm Equipment Operators	79021
REC	44	Helpers, Mechanics and Repairers	98102
REC	44	Hoist and Winch Operators	97941
REC	44	Mail Machine Operators, Preparation and Handling	56008
REC	44	Paving, Surfacing, and Tamping Equipment Operators	87708
REC	44	Separating, Filtering, Clarifying, Precipitating, and Still Machine Operators and Tenders	92962
REC	44	Textile Bleaching and Dyeing Machine Operators and Tenders	92714
REC	43	All Other Material-Moving Equipment Operators	97989
REC	43	Cooling and Freezing Equipment Operators and Tenders	92928
REC	43	Extruding, Forming, Pressing, and Compacting Machine Operators and Tenders	92971
REC	43	Farmworkers, Farm and Ranch Animals	79858
REC	43	Molders and Casters, Hand	93944
REC	42	All Other Timber Cutting and Related Logging Workers	73099
REC	42	Cannery Workers	93935
REC	42	Cleaning, Washing, and Pickling Equipment Operators and Tenders	92958
REC	42	Elevator Operators	67011
REC	42	Helpers, All Other Construction Trades Workers	98319
REC	42	Helpers, Extractive Workers	98323
REC	42	Laundry and Dry-Cleaning Machine Operators and Tenders, Except Pressing	92726
REC	42	Woodworking Machine Operators and Tenders, Except Sawing	92314
REC	41	Helpers, Brick and Stonemasons and Hard Tile Setters	98311
REC	41	Tire Repairers and Changers	85953
REC	40	Janitors and Cleaners, Except Maids and Housekeeping Cleaners	67005
REC	39	All Other Helpers, Laborers, and Material Movers, Hand	98999
REC	39	Hand Packers and Packagers	98902
REC	39	Machine Feeders and Offbearers	98502
REC	39	Meat, Poultry, and Fish Cutters and Trimmers, Hand	93938

From Holland Codes to the Occupational Employment Statistics
and Occupational Outlook Handbook Occupations

HOC	Cx	Title	OES
REC	39	Pressers, Hand	93921
REC	39	Vehicle Washers and Equipment Cleaners	98905
REC	38	Farmworkers, Food and Fiber Crops	79856
RCI	59	Nuclear Technicians and Technologists	24508
RCI	57	Offset Lithographic Press Setters and Set-up Operators	92512
RCI	54	Electrocardiograph Technicians	32926
RCI	49	Sawing Machine Tool Setters and Set-up Operators, Metal and Plastic	91102
RCI	49	Typesetting and Composing Machine Operators and Tenders	92541
RCI	48	Electronic Semiconductor Processors	92902
RCI	46	Tire Building Machine Operators	92911
RCI	45	Solderers and Brazers	93917
RCI	45	Soldering and Brazing Machine Operators and Tenders	91711
RCA	59	Paste-Up Workers	89706
RCS	61	Camera and Photographic Equipment Repairers	85914
RCS	59	Electroneurodiagnostic Technologists	32923
RCS	52	Lathers	87114
RCS	51	Bridge, Lock, and Lighthouse Tenders	97802
RCS	50	Hard Tile Setters	87308
RCS	50	Machinery Maintenance Mechanics, Textile Machines	85112
RCS	49	Specialty Materials Printing Machine Setters and Set-up Operators	92522
RCS	48	Coating, Painting, and Spraying Machine Setters and Set-up Operators	92951
RCS	47	Coil Winders, Tapers, and Finishers	93908
RCS	47	Drywall Installers	87108
RCS	47	Highway Maintenance Workers	87711
RCS	46	Roustabouts	87921
RCS	44	Excavating and Loading Machine Operators	97923
RCS	44	Log-Handling Equipment Operators	73008
RCS	44	Roof Bolters	87923
RCS	42	Metal Pourers and Casters, Basic Shapes	93941
RCS	38	Air Hammer Operators	87702
RCE	64	Cost Estimators	21902
RCE	61	Radio Operators	39008
RCE	56	Gaugers	95017
RCE	54	Chemical Plant and System Operators	95008
RCE	53	Main-Line Station Engineers	97914
RCE	53	Precision Photographic Process Workers	89914
RCE	52	Painters, Transportation Equipment	92947
RCE	51	Order Fillers, Wholesale and Retail Sales	58026
RCE	51	Transportation Inspectors	83008
RCE	50	Stock Clerks - Stockroom, Warehouse or Storage Yard	58023
RCE	49	All Other Mechanics, Installers, and Repairers	85999
RCE	49	Insulation Workers	87802

Part 2: From Holland Codes to Occupations

From Holland Codes to the Occupational Employment Statistics and Occupational Outlook Handbook Occupations

HOC	Cx	Title	OES
RCE	49	Mail Clerks, Except Mail Machine Operators and Postal Service	57302
RCE	49	Pruners	79033
RCE	48	All Other Construction Trades Workers	87899
RCE	48	Cutting and Slicing Machine Setters and Set-up Operators	92941
RCE	47	Photographic Processing Machine Operators and Tenders	92908
RCE	47	Sawing Machine Setters and Set-up Operators	92302
RCE	46	All Other Transportation and Related Workers	97899
RCE	46	Electrical and Electronic Assemblers	93905
RCE	46	Engraving and Printing Workers, Hand	93951
RCE	46	Machine Assemblers	93902
RCE	46	Pump Operators	97953
RCE	45	Crane and Tower Operators	97944
RCE	45	Helpers, Electricians and Power-Line Transmission Installers	98313
RCE	45	Laborers, Landscaping and Groundskeeping	79041
RCE	45	Production Inspectors, Testers, Graders, Sorters, Samplers, and Weighers	83005
RCE	44	All Other Printing, Binding, and Related Machine Operators and Tenders	92549
RCE	44	Bindery Machine Operators and Tenders	92546
RCE	44	Furnace, Kiln, Oven, Drier, or Kettle Operators and Tenders	92923
RCE	44	Helpers, Plumbers, Pipefitters, and Steamfitters	98315
RCE	44	Machine Forming Operators and Tenders, Metal and Plastic	91321
RCE	44	Nonelectrolytic Plating and Coating Machine Operators and Tenders, Metal and Plastic	91926
RCE	44	Sawing Machine Operators and Tenders	92308
RCE	43	All Other Metal and Plastic (cutting, forming, fabricating, or processing) Machine Operators and Tenders	92198
RCE	43	Machine Tool Cutting Operators and Tenders, Metal and Plastic	91117
RCE	43	Machinery Maintenance Workers	85128
RCE	43	Printing Press Machine Operators and Tenders	92543
RCE	43	Sewing Machine Operators, Nongarment	92721
RCE	43	Shoe Sewing Machine Operators and Tenders	92723
RCE	43	Truck Drivers, Light, Include Delivery and Route Workers	97105
RCE	42	All Other Machine Operators and Tenders	92998
RCE	42	Assemblers and Fabricators, Except Machine, Electrical, Electronic, and Precision	93956
RCE	42	Conveyor Operators and Tenders	97951
RCE	42	Extruding and Forming Machine Operators and Tenders, Synthetic or Glass Fibers	92708
RCE	42	Food Preparation Workers	65038
RCE	42	Grinding and Polishing Workers, Hand	93953
RCE	42	Helpers, Painters, Paperhangers, Plasterers, and Stucco Masons	98314

From Holland Codes to the Occupational Employment Statistics
and Occupational Outlook Handbook Occupations

HOC	Cx	Title	OES
RCE	42	Industrial Truck and Tractor Operators	97947
RCE	42	Plastic Molding and Casting Machine Operators and Tenders	91905
RCE	42	Sewers, Hand	93923
RCE	42	Textile Machine Operators and Tenders, Winding, Twisting, Knitting, Weaving, and Cutting	92705
RCE	41	All Other Hand Workers	93999
RCE	41	All Other Motor Vehicle Operators	97199
RCE	41	Cementing and Gluing Machine Operators and Tenders	92956
RCE	41	Cutters and Trimmers, Hand	93926
RCE	41	Cutting and Slicing Machine Operators and Tenders	92944
RCE	41	Packaging and Filling Machine Operators and Tenders	92974
RCE	41	Painting, Coating, and Decorating Workers, Hand	93947
RCE	41	Pressing Machine Operators and Tenders, Textile, Garment, and Related Materials	92728
RCE	41	Sewing Machine Operators, Garment	92717
RCE	41	Textile Draw-Out Machine Operators and Tenders	92711
RCE	40	Dining Room and Cafeteria Attendants and Bartender Helpers	65014
RCE	39	Foundry Mold Assembly and Shake-Out Workers	91914
RCE	39	Maids and Housekeeping Cleaners	67002
IRA	73	All Other Mathematical Scientists	25319
IRS	78	Biological Scientists	24308
IRS	78	Geologists, Geophysicists, and Oceanographers	24111
IRS	78	Medical Scientists	24311
IRS	77	Agricultural and Food Scientists	24305
IRS	76	Physicians and Surgeons	32102
IRS	73	Foresters and Conservation Scientists	24302
IRS	72	Civil Engineers, Including Traffic	22121
IRS	71	Data Base Administrators	25103
IRS	70	Atmospheric and Space Scientists	24108
IRS	69	Technical Writers	34005
IRS	68	Nuclear Medicine Technologists	32914
IRS	66	Radiologic Technologists	32919
IRS	65	Chemical Technicians and Technologists, Except Health	24505
IRE	80	Marine Architects	22305
IRE	79	Operations and Systems Researchers and Analysts, Except Computer	25302
IRE	79	Physicists and Astronomers	24102
IRE	78	All Other Physical Scientists	24199
IRE	77	Statisticians	25312
IRE	76	Aeronautical and Astronautical Engineers	22102
IRE	75	Chemical Engineers	22114
IRE	75	Dentists	32105
IRE	75	Metallurgists and Metallurgical, Ceramic, and Materials Engineers	22105

Part 2: From Holland Codes to Occupations

From Holland Codes to the Occupational Employment Statistics
and Occupational Outlook Handbook Occupations

HOC	Cx	Title	OES
IRE	75	Nuclear Engineers	22117
IRE	75	Petroleum Engineers	22111
IRE	74	All Other Physical Sciences Teachers, Postsecondary	31209
IRE	74	Chemistry Teachers, Postsecondary	31204
IRE	74	Computer Engineers	22127
IRE	74	Computer Science Teachers, Postsecondary	31226
IRE	74	Electrical and Electronic Engineers	22126
IRE	74	Life Sciences Teachers, Postsecondary	31202
IRE	74	Mathematical Sciences Teachers, Postsecondary	31224
IRE	74	Physics Teachers, Postsecondary	31206
IRE	73	All Other Engineers	22199
IRE	73	Veterinarians and Veterinary Inspectors	32114
IRE	72	Agricultural Engineers	22123
IRE	71	Marine Engineers	22138
IRE	69	Systems Analysts, Electronic Data Processing	25102
IRE	68	Computer Programmers	25105
IRE	68	Medical and Clinical Laboratory Technologists	32902
IRE	68	Surveyors and Mapping Scientists	22311
IRE	66	Drafters	22514
IRE	62	All Other Physical and Life Science Technicians and Technologists	24599
IRC	70	Mathematical Technicians	25323
IRC	69	Computer Programmer Aides	25108
IAE	74	Architects, Except Landscape and Marine	22302
ISR	74	Health Specialties Teachers, Postsecondary	31212
ISR	70	Speech-Language Pathologists and Audiologists	32314
ISR	67	Chiropractors	32113
ISR	66	All Other Health Diagnosing and Treating Practitioners	32199
ISR	58	Veterinary Assistants	79806
ISR	58	Veterinary Technicians and Technologists	32951
ISR	56	Surgical Technologists and Technicians	32928
ISA	71	Economists, Including Market Research Analysts	27102
ISA	66	Physician's Assistants	32511
ISE	75	Pharmacists	32517
ISE	75	Psychologists	27108
ISE	72	Actuaries	25313
ISE	69	Optometrists	32108
IER	73	Engineering, Mathematical, and Natural Sciences Managers	13017
IER	72	Chemists, Except Biochemists	24105
IER	72	Industrial Engineers, Except Safety	22128
IER	65	Surveying and Mapping Technicians	22521
IES	74	Safety Engineers, Except Mining	22132

Part 2: From Holland Codes to Occupations

From Holland Codes to the Occupational Employment Statistics
and Occupational Outlook Handbook Occupations

HOC	Cx	Title	OES
ICR	62	Cardiology Technologists	32925
ARS	62	Camera Operators, Television and Motion Picture	34026
AIR	75	Landscape Architects	22308
AIE	74	English and Foreign Languages Teachers, Postsecondary	31216
ASI	67	Reporters and Correspondents	34011
ASE	74	Art, Drama, and Music Teachers, Postsecondary	31218
ASC	65	Musicians, Instrumental	34051
AER	64	Dancers and Choreographers	34053
AES	70	Music Directors, Singers, Composers, and Related Workers	34047
AES	68	Public Relations Specialists and Publicity Writers	34008
AES	68	Writers and Editors	34002
AES	67	Audio-Visual Specialists	31508
AES	65	Designers, Except Interior Designers	34038
AES	65	Interior Designers	34041
AES	63	Artists and Related Workers	34035
AES	62	Film Editors	34032
SRI	64	All Other Computer Scientists	25199
SRI	60	Corrective and Manual Arts Therapists	32311
SRE	54	Medical Assistants	66005
SRE	53	Psychiatric Aides	66014
SRE	47	Ambulance Drivers and Attendants, Except Emergency Medical Technicians	66023
SRC	54	Pharmacy Aides	66026
SIR	65	Podiatrists	32111
SIR	57	Respiratory Therapists	32302
SIE	74	Social Sciences Teachers, Postsecondary	31210
SIE	71	Nursing Instructors, Postsecondary	31114
SIE	69	Dietitians and Nutritionists	32521
SIE	68	All Other Therapists	32399
SIE	67	Physical Therapists	32308
SIE	67	Registered Nurses	32502
SIE	64	Claims Examiners, Property and Casualty Insurance	21921
SIE	58	Psychiatric Technicians	32931
SAI	60	Dental Hygienists	32908
SAI	58	Dental Assistants	66002

Part 2: From Holland Codes to Occupations

From Holland Codes to the Occupational Employment Statistics
and Occupational Outlook Handbook Occupations

HOC	Cx	Title	OES
SAE	73	Clergy	27502
SAE	69	Graduate Assistants, Teaching	31117
SAE	66	Recreational Therapists	32317
SAE	62	Teachers, Preschool	31303
SAC	56	Licensed Practical Nurses	32505
SER	66	Curators, Archivists, Museum Technicians, and Restorers	31511
SER	66	Teachers, Secondary School	31308
SER	65	Personnel, Training, and Labor Relations Specialists	21511
SER	64	Airplane Dispatchers and Air Traffic Controllers	39002
SER	62	Teachers and Instructors, Vocational Education and Training	31314
SER	61	Instructors and Coaches, Sports and Physical Training	31321
SER	59	Police Detectives	63011
SER	56	Animal Trainers	79016
SER	55	Police Patrol Officers	63014
SER	50	All Other Protective Service Workers	63099
SER	50	Home Health Aides	66011
SER	50	Sheriffs and Deputy Sheriffs	63032
SER	48	Correction Officers and Jailers	63017
SER	47	Nursing Aides, Orderlies, and Attendants	66008
SEI	74	All Other Postsecondary Teachers	31299
SEI	68	Instructional Coordinators	31517
SEI	65	Dietetic Technicians	32523
SEA	69	Vocational and Educational Counselors	31514
SEA	66	Directors, Religious Activities and Education	27505
SEA	66	Social Workers, Medical and Psychiatric	27302
SEA	66	Teachers, Elementary School	31305
SEA	65	Librarians, Professional	31502
SEA	64	All Other Teachers and Instructors	31399
SEA	62	Instructors, Nonvocational Education	31317
SEA	61	All Other Religious Workers	27599
SEA	56	Shampooers	68011
SEC	71	Medicine and Health Services Managers	15008
SEC	69	Adjudicators, Hearings Officers, and Judicial Reviewers	28105
SEC	67	Public Administration Chief Executives, Legislators, and General Administrators	19002
SEC	66	Law Clerks	28302
SEC	66	Paralegal Personnel	28305
SEC	66	Teachers, Special Education	31311
SEC	65	Farm and Home Management Advisors	31323
SEC	64	Announcers, Radio and Television	34017
SEC	64	Social Workers, Except Medical and Psychiatric	27305
SEC	61	Teachers, Kindergarten	31304
SEC	59	Residential Counselors	27307
SEC	57	Dispatchers, Police, Fire, and Ambulance	58002

HOC	Cx	Title	OES
SEC	57	Physical and Corrective Therapy Assistants and Aides	66017
SEC	55	Insurance Claims Clerks	53311
SEC	54	All Other Communications Equipment Operators	57199
SEC	53	Occupational Therapy Assistants and Aides	66021
SEC	53	United States Marshals	63026
SEC	52	License Clerks	53708
SEC	51	Personal and Home Care Aides	68035
SEC	46	Guards and Watch Guards	63047
SEC	42	Manicurists	68008
SCR	63	Computer Support Specialists	25104
SCR	59	Technical Assistants, Library	31505
SCR	44	Combined Food Preparation and Service Workers	65041
SCE	68	Loan Officers and Counselors	21108
SCE	67	Appraisers, Real Estate	43011
SCE	64	Employment Interviewers, Private or Public Employment Service	21508
SCE	58	Teacher Aides, Paraprofessional	31521
SCE	57	Welfare Eligibility Workers and Interviewers	53502
SCE	55	Human Services Workers	27308
SCE	52	Postal Service Clerks	57308
ERI	70	Estimators and Drafters, Utilities	22517
ERI	70	Sales Engineers	49002
ERI	67	Tax Examiners, Collectors, and Revenue Agents	21914
ERS	67	Mining, Quarrying, and Oil and Gas Well Drilling Managers	15021
ERS	65	Construction Managers	15017
ERS	62	Fire Fighting and Prevention Supervisors	61002
ERS	61	First-Line Supervisors and Managers/Supervisors - Mechanics, Installers, and Repairers	81002
ERS	60	All Other Professional, Paraprofessional, and Technical Workers	39999
ERS	60	Captains, Water Vessel	97502
ERS	59	First-Line Supervisors and Managers/Supervisors - Transportation and Material-Moving Machine and Vehicle Operators	81011
ERS	59	Mates, Ship, Boat, and Barge	97505
ERS	58	First-Line Supervisors and Managers/Supervisors - Agricultural, Forestry, Fishing, and Related Workers	72002
ERS	58	Insurance Appraisers, Auto Damage	53305
ERS	57	First-Line Supervisors and Managers/Supervisors - Helpers, Laborers, and Material Movers, Hand	81017
ERS	55	Transportation Agents	58011
ERS	54	All Other Sales and Related Workers	49999
ERS	47	Bartenders	65005
ERS	45	Food Servers, Outside	65011

From Holland Codes to the Occupational Employment Statistics
and Occupational Outlook Handbook Occupations

HOC	Cx	Title	OES
ERC	57	Fire Inspectors	63002
ERC	46	Wardrobe, and Locker and Dressing Room Attendants	68032
EIR	62	Assessors	21917
EIS	71	Urban and Regional Planners	27105
EIS	69	All Other Social Scientists	27199
EAS	69	Broadcast News Analysts	34014
EAS	59	Producers, Directors, Actors, and Other Entertainers	34056
ESR	70	Financial Managers	13002
ESR	69	General Managers and Top Executives	19005
ESR	68	Personnel, Training, and Labor Relations Managers	13005
ESR	67	Communications, Transportation, and Utilities Operations Managers	15023
ESR	67	Industrial Production Managers	15014
ESR	66	Administrative Services Managers	13014
ESR	66	Property and Real Estate Managers and Administrators	15011
ESR	66	Purchasing Managers	13008
ESR	65	All Other Management Support Workers	21999
ESR	65	All Other Managers and Administrators	19999
ESR	65	Funeral Directors and Morticians	39011
ESR	65	Postmasters and Mail Superintendents	15002
ESR	64	Food Service and Lodging Managers	15026
ESR	63	Compliance Officers and Enforcement Inspectors, Except Construction	21911
ESR	63	Lawn Service Managers	15032
ESR	63	Wholesale and Retail Buyers, Except Farm Products	21302
ESR	62	First-Line Supervisors and Managers/Supervisors - Sales and Related Workers	41002
ESR	62	Recreation Workers	27311
ESR	61	Police and Detective Supervisors	61005
ESR	61	Sales Representatives, Scientific and Related Products and Services, Except Retail	49005
ESR	59	All Other First-Line Supervisors and Managers/ Supervisors - Production, Construction, Maintenance, and Related Workers	81099
ESR	59	Announcers, Except Radio and Television	34021
ESR	59	Hosts and Hostesses, Restaurant, Lounge, or Coffee Shop	65002
ESR	58	Adjustment Clerks	53123
ESR	58	All Other Supervisors and Managers/Supervisors - Service Workers	61099
ESR	56	Forest Fire Inspectors and Prevention Specialists	63005
ESR	55	Athletes, Coaches, Umpires, and Related Workers	34058
ESR	55	Flight Attendants	68026
ESR	54	Hairdressers, Hairstylists, and Cosmetologists	68005
ESR	54	Housekeeping Supervisors	61008
ESR	53	Barbers	68002

HOC to OES and OOH

Part 2: From Holland Codes to Occupations

From Holland Codes to the Occupational Employment Statistics
and Occupational Outlook Handbook Occupations

HOC	Cx	Title	OES
ESR	53	Bill and Account Collectors	53508
ESR	53	Guides	68017
ESR	51	Counter and Rental Clerks	49017
ESR	46	All Other Service Workers	69999
ESR	45	Bailiffs	63023
ESR	42	Funeral Attendants	68041
ESI	77	Judges and Magistrates	28102
ESI	76	Lawyers	28108
ESI	67	All Other Financial Specialists	21199
ESA	68	Education Administrators	15005
ESA	67	Marketing, Advertising, and Public Relations Managers	13011
ESA	67	Nursery and Greenhouse Managers	15031
ESA	66	Purchasing Agents and Buyers, Farm Products	21305
ESA	63	Sales Agents, Real Estate	43008
ESA	61	Sales Agents, Selected Business Services	43017
ESA	59	Sales Agents, Advertising	43023
ESA	58	Sales Representatives, Except Retail and Scientific and Related Products and Services	49008
ESA	57	All Other Sales Representatives and Salespersons, Services	43099
ESA	56	Salespersons, Retail	49011
ESA	50	Demonstrators, Promoters, and Models	49032
ESA	47	Child Care Workers	68038
ESC	67	Purchasing Agents, Except Wholesale, Retail, and Farm Products	21308
ESC	66	All Other Legal Assistants and Technicians, Except Clerical	28399
ESC	66	Management Analysts	21905
ESC	66	Special Agents, Insurance	21505
ESC	65	Credit Analysts	21105
ESC	65	Insurance Adjusters, Examiners, and Investigators	53302
ESC	65	Sales Agents, Securities, Commodities, and Financial Services	43014
ESC	63	Sales Agents and Placers, Insurance	43002
ESC	61	Brokers, Real Estate	43005
ESC	60	First-Line Supervisors and Managers/Supervisors - Clerical and Administrative Support Workers	51002
ESC	60	Railroad Conductors and Yardmasters	97302
ESC	58	Travel Clerks	53802
ESC	57	Loan Interviewers	53111
ESC	56	Railroad and Transit Police and Special Agents	63038
ESC	56	Salespersons, Parts	49014
ESC	55	Claims Takers, Unemployment Benefits	21502
ESC	55	Detectives and Investigators, Except Public	63035
ESC	48	Telemarketers, Door-To-Door Sales Workers, News and Street Venders, and Other Related Workers	49026

Dictionary of Holland Occupational Codes

Part 2: From Holland Codes to Occupations

From Holland Codes to the Occupational Employment Statistics
and Occupational Outlook Handbook Occupations

HOC	Cx	Title	OES
ECR	44	Counter Attendants - Lunchroom, Coffee Shop, or Cafeteria	65017
ECR	44	Crossing Guards	63044
ECI	63	Municipal Clerks	53705
ECS	69	Budget Analysts	21117
ECS	60	Travel Agents	43021
ECS	58	Investigators, Clerical	53505
ECS	55	Dispatchers, Except Police, Fire, and Ambulance	58005
ECS	54	Correspondence Clerks	55317
ECS	54	Hotel Desk Clerks	53808
ECS	48	All Other Food Service Workers	65099
ECS	47	Amusement and Recreation Attendants	68014
ECS	47	Waiters and Waitresses	65008
ECS	46	Transportation Attendants, Except Flight Attendants and Baggage Porters	68028
CRS	53	Statement Clerks	53126
CRS	53	Title Searchers	28308
CRS	52	Billing, Posting, and Calculating Machine Operators	56002
CRS	52	Peripheral EDP Equipment Operators	56014
CRS	49	All Other Health Service Workers	66099
CRS	49	All Other Material Recording, Scheduling, and Distributing Workers	58099
CRS	45	All Other Office Machine Operators	56099
CRS	43	Parking Lot Attendants	97808
CRE	54	Production, Planning, and Expediting Clerks	58008
CRE	54	Transit Clerks	53108
CRE	52	Data Keyers, Composing	56021
CRE	47	Weighers, Measurers, Checkers, and Samplers, Recordkeeping	58017
CRE	41	Menders, Garments, Linens, and Related	85956
CIR	58	Electronic Pagination System Operators	89707
CIE	70	Financial Analysts, Statistical	25315
CIE	63	Medical Records Technicians	32911
CSR	58	Real Estate Clerks	53914
CSR	56	Bookkeeping, Accounting, and Auditing Clerks	55338
CSR	56	Computer Operators, Except Peripheral Equipment	56011
CSR	56	Loan and Credit Clerks	53121
CSR	56	Payroll and Timekeeping Clerks	55341
CSR	55	Billing, Cost, and Rate Clerks	55344
CSR	55	Brokerage Clerks	53128
CSR	54	Insurance Policy Processing Clerks	53314
CSR	53	Statistical Clerks	55328

Part 2: From Holland Codes to Occupations

From Holland Codes to the Occupational Employment Statistics
and Occupational Outlook Handbook Occupations

HOC	Cx	Title	OES
CSR	52	Postal Mail Carriers	57305
CSR	51	Data Entry Keyers, Except Composing	56017
CSR	51	File Clerks	55321
CSR	51	Typists, Including Word Processing	55307
CSR	49	Library Assistants and Bookmobile Drivers	53902
CSR	45	Marking Clerks	58021
CSE	70	Underwriters	21102
CSE	66	Title Examiners and Abstractors	28311
CSE	60	Legal Secretaries	55102
CSE	58	New Accounts Clerks	53105
CSE	58	Secretaries, Except Legal and Medical	55108
CSE	58	Tellers	53102
CSE	57	Court Clerks	53702
CSE	55	Stenographers and/or Court Reporters	55302
CSE	54	Advertising Clerks	53908
CSE	54	General Office Clerks	55347
CSE	54	Personnel Clerks, Except Payroll and Timekeeping	55314
CSE	54	Receptionists and Information Clerks	55305
CSE	53	Proofreaders and Copy Markers	53911
CSE	52	Credit Checkers	53117
CSE	52	Procurement Clerks	55326
CSE	52	Telegraph and Teletype Operators	57111
CSE	51	Cashiers	49023
CSE	50	Interviewing Clerks, Except Personnel and Social Welfare	55332
CSE	50	Meter Readers, Utilities	58014
CSE	50	Switchboard Operators	57102
CSE	49	Central Office Operators	57108
CER	54	Customer Service Representatives, Utilities	55335
CER	49	Directory Assistance Operators	57105
CER	45	Messengers	57311
CEI	70	Accountants and Auditors	21114
CES	61	Medical Secretaries	55105
CES	57	Tax Preparers	21111
CES	54	Insurance Examining Clerks	53308
CES	53	Order Clerks, Materials, Merchandise, and Service	55323
CES	53	Reservation and Transportation Ticket Agents	53805
CES	53	Teacher Aides and Educational Assistants, Clerical	53905
CES	51	All Other Clerical and Administrative Support Workers	59999
CES	50	Credit Authorizers	53114
CES	42	Parking Enforcement Officers	63021
CES	41	Ushers, Lobby Attendants, and Ticket Takers	68021

HOC	Cx	Title	SOC
RIS	69	Occupational Therapists	3032
RIS	63	General Farmers	5512
RIS	62	Electrical and Electronic Repairers, Commercial and Industrial Equipment	6153
RIS	60	Health Technologists and Technicians, n.e.c.	3690
RIS	59	Elevator Installers and Repairers	6176
RIS	58	Batchmakers (candymakers, cheesemakers, etc.)	6873
RIS	58	Biological Technologists and Technicians, Except Health	3820
RIS	57	Cabinet Makers and Bench Carpenters	6832
RIS	51	Forging Machine Setup Operators	7319
RIS	51	Punching and Shearing Machine Setup Operators	7314
RIS	49	Shaping and Joining Machine Setup Operators	7435
RIS	47	Longshore Equipment Operators	8313
RIS	47	Operating Engineers	8312
RIE	74	Engineering Teachers*	2226
RIE	71	Mechanical Engineers	1635
RIE	67	Airplane Pilots and Navigators	8250
RIE	65	Petroleum Technologists and Technicians	3833
RIE	64	Electrical and Electronic Engineering Technologists and Technicians	3711
RIE	63	Construction Inspectors	1472
RIE	62	Engineering Technologists and Technicians, n.e.c.	3719
RIE	61	Cartographers	1644
RIE	61	Science Technologists and Technicians, n.e.c.	3890
RIE	60	Machinists	6813
RIE	59	Horticultural Specialty Farmers	5515
RIE	59	Patternmakers and Model Makers (metal)	6817
RIE	59	Technicians, n.e.c.	3990
RIE	59	Tool and Die Makers	6811
RIE	58	Camera, Watch, and Other Precision Instrument Repairers	6171
RIE	58	Precision Patternmakers, Lay-Out Workers and Cutters	6862
RIE	58	Still, Clarifying, and Precipitating Machine Setup Operators	7476
RIE	57	Lathe and Turning Machine Setup Operators	7312
RIE	57	Lay-Out Workers	6821
RIE	57	Miscellaneous Precision Woodworkers	6839
RIE	57	Precision Lithographers and Photoengravers	6842
RIE	56	Aircraft Mechanics (except Engine Specialists)	6116
RIE	56	Miscellaneous Electrical and Electronic Equipment Repairers	6159
RIE	55	Drilling and Boring Machine Setup Operators	7318
RIE	55	Miscellaneous Precision Printing Occupations	6849
RIE	55	Plating and Coating Machine Setup Operators	7343
RIE	54	Milling and Planing Machine Setup Operators	7313
RIE	54	Miscellaneous Metalworking and Plastic Working Machine Setup Operators	7329
RIE	54	Printing Press Setup Operators	7443
RIE	53	Lapping and Honing Machine Setup Operators	7324
RIE	53	Soldering and Brazing Machine Setup Operators	7333
RIE	50	Extruding and Drawing Machine Setup Operators	7315

HOC	Cx	Title	SOC
RIE	50	Locomotive Operating Occupations	8232
RIE	50	Molding and Casting Machine Setup Operators	7342
RIE	50	Welders and Cutters	7714
RIE	49	Pile Driving Operators	6476
RIE	48	Heating Equipment Operators and Tenders	7544
RIE	48	Lathe and Turning Machine Setup Operators	7431
RIE	48	Router and Planner Machine Setup Operators	7432
RIE	48	Truck Drivers, Tractor-Trailer	8212
RIE	46	Rail and Track Laying Equipment Operators	6467
RIC	65	Cartographic Technicians	3734
RIC	60	Mechanics and Repairers	6100
RIC	60	Programmers, Numerical, Tool and Process Control	3974
RIC	59	Telephone Installers and Repairers	6158
RIC	52	Photoengraving and Lithographing Machine Setup Operators	7444
RAS	53	Miscellaneous Precision Food Workers	6879
RSI	58	Precision Typesetters	6841
RSI	53	Heating Equipment Setup Operators	7344
RSE	59	Supervisors—Electricians and Power Transmission Installers	6314
RSE	57	Petroleum Plant Operators	6950
RSE	56	Electronic Repairers, Home-Entertainment Equipment	6155
RSE	54	Chemical Plant Operators	6940
RSE	54	Furniture Finishers	6835
RSE	54	Household Appliance and Power Tool Repairers	6156
RSE	53	Bakers	6872
RSE	52	Cooks, Except Short Order	5214
RSE	52	Cooks, Private Household	5040
RSE	52	Riggers	6177
RSE	51	Glaciers	6464
RSE	51	Press and Brake Machine Setup Operators	7317
RSE	50	Short-Order Cooks	5215
RSE	48	Bus Drivers	8215
RSE	43	Private Household Cleaners and Servants	5070
RSC	57	Telephone Line Installers and Repairers	6157
RSC	51	Musical Instrument Repairers and Tuners	6172
RSC	47	Paperhangers	6443
RSC	45	Helpers—Surveyor's	8646
RSC	43	Helpers—Carpenters and Related Workers	8642
RSC	41	Air Hammer Operators	6475
REI	68	Trade and Industrial Teachers*	2246
REI	61	Crop, Vegetable, Fruit and Tree Nut Farmers	5513
REI	59	Patternmakers and Model Makers, Wood	6831
REI	59	Sheet Metal Workers	6824
REI	58	Livestock, Dairy, Poultry and Fish Farmers	5514

HOC to SOC

Part 2: From Holland Codes to Occupations

From Holland Codes to the Standard Occupational Classification

HOC	Cx	Title	SOC
REI	57	Communications Equipment Repairers	6151
REI	57	Precision Inspectors, Testers and Graders	6881
REI	57	Stationary Engineers	6931
REI	57	Tailers and Dressmakers, Hand	6852
REI	56	Apparel and Fabric Patternmakers	6856
REI	56	Data Processing Equipment Repairers	6154
REI	56	Heavy Equipment Mechanics	6117
REI	56	Precision Hand Molders and Shapers (except jewelers)	6861
REI	56	Small Engine Repairers	6114
REI	55	Engravers	6823
REI	55	Industrial Machinery Repairers	6130
REI	55	Miscellaneous Precision Workers, n.e.c.	6869
REI	55	Numerical Control Machine Setup Operators	7326
REI	55	Optical Goods Workers	6864
REI	55	Plumbers, Pipefitters and Steamfitters	6450
REI	55	Precision Assemblers (metal)	6812
REI	55	Precision Electrical and Electronic Equipment Assemblers	6867
REI	55	Precision Grinders, Filers, and Tool Sharpeners	6816
REI	55	Water and Sewage Treatment Plant Operators	6910
REI	54	Miscellaneous Fabricating Machine Setup Operators	7339
REI	54	Plasterers	6444
REI	54	Welding Machine Setup Operators	7332
REI	53	Drillers, Oil Well	6520
REI	53	Electric Motor, Transformer, and Related Repairers	6152
REI	53	Miscellaneous Precision Metal Workers	6829
REI	52	Miscellaneous Plant or System Operators	6960
REI	51	Concrete and Terrazzo Finishers	6463
REI	51	Grinding, Abrading, Buffing, and Polishing Machine Setup Operators	7322
REI	51	Miscellaneous Printing Machine Setup Operators	7449
REI	51	Precision Adjusters and Calibrators	6882
REI	51	Rolling Machine Setup Operators	7316
REI	50	Automotive Body and Related Repairers	6115
REI	50	Brickmasons	6412
REI	50	Miscellaneous Machine Setup Operators	7479
REI	49	Miscellaneous Woodworking Machine Setup Operators	7439
REI	48	Drillers, Earth	6474
REI	48	Folding Machine Setup Operators	7474
REI	48	Sailors and Deckhands	8243
REI	47	Crushing, Grinding, and Polishing Machine Setup Operators	7477
REI	47	Mining Machine Operators	6540
REI	47	Rail Vehicle Operators, n.e.c.	8239
REI	46	Sanding Machine Setup Operators	7434
REI	45	Grader, Dozer, and Scraper Operators	8317
REI	45	Truck Drivers, Heavy	8213
REI	44	Farm Machinery Operators	5616
REI	44	Logging Occupations, n.e.c.	5790
REI	39	Forestry Workers, Except Logging	5720

HOC	Cx	Title	SOC
RES	62	Millwrights	6178
RES	61	Supervisors—Mechanics and Repairers	6000
RES	60	Supervisors—Carpenters and Related Workers	6313
RES	60	Supervisors—Precision Production Occupations	6700
RES	59	Marine Engineers	8244
RES	59	Supervisors—Brickmasons, Stonemasons, and Hard Tile Setters	6312
RES	59	Supervisors—other Construction Trades	6318
RES	59	Supervisors—Plumbers and Pipefitters and Steamfitters	6316
RES	59	Supervisors—Related Agricultural Workers	5621
RES	58	Bus and Truck Engine, and Diesel Engine Mechanics	6112
RES	58	Sheetmetal Duct Installers*	6472
RES	58	Supervisors—Extractive Occupations	6320
RES	58	Supervisors—Overall Construction	6311
RES	57	Boilermakers	6814
RES	56	Boat and Barge Operators	8242
RES	56	Electricians	6432
RES	56	Office Machine Repairers	6174
RES	56	Power Plant and Systems Operators, Except Stationary Engineers	6932
RES	56	Roasting and Baking Machine Setup Operators	7472
RES	55	Electrical Power Installers and Repairers	6433
RES	55	Winding and Twisting Machine Setup Operators	7451
RES	54	Carpet and Soft Tile Installers	6462
RES	54	Gas Plant Operators	6920
RES	54	Miscellaneous Precision Apparel and Fabric Workers	6859
RES	54	Precision Hand Molders and Shapers (jewelers)	6822
RES	54	Textile Machine Setup Operators, n.e.c.	7459
RES	53	Explosive Workers	6530
RES	53	Farm Equipment Mechanics	6118
RES	53	Stonemasons	6413
RES	53	Upholsterers	6853
RES	52	Automobile Mechanics	6111
RES	52	Bookbinders	6844
RES	52	Knitting and Weaving Machine Setup Operators	7452
RES	52	Sales Occupations —other, n.e.c.	4490
RES	52	Shoemakers and Leather Workers and Repairers	6854
RES	52	Structural Metal Workers	6473
RES	51	Military Occupations	9100
RES	51	Precision Laundering, Cleaning, and Dyeing Occupations	6855
RES	50	Butchers and Meat Cutters	6871
RES	50	Firefighting Occupations	5123
RES	50	Painters (construction and maintenance)	6442
RES	48	Compressing and Compacting Machine Setup Operators	7467
RES	48	Driver-Sales Workers	8218
RES	48	Hunters and Trappers	5840
RES	46	Animal Caretakers, Except Farm	5624
RES	46	Extractive Occupations, n.e.c.	6560
RES	45	Boiler Operators and Tenders (low pressure)	7668

HOC to SOC

Part 2: From Holland Codes to Occupations

From Holland Codes to the Standard Occupational Classification

HOC	Cx	Title	SOC
RES	45	Excavating and Loading Machine Operators	8316
RES	44	Baggage Porters and Bellhops	5262
RES	44	Roasting and Baking Machine Operators and Tenders	7672
RES	43	General Farm Workers	5612
RES	42	Marine Life Cultivation Workers	5618
RES	41	Construction Laborers	8710
RES	41	Helpers—other Construction Trades	8648
RES	41	Helpers—Printing Machine Operators and Tenders	8616
RES	41	Timber Cutting and Related Occupations	5730
RES	40	Day Workers	5020
RES	40	Freight, Stock and Material Movers, n.e.c.	8726
RES	40	Helpers—Brickmasons, Stonemasons, and Hard Tile Setters	8641
RES	40	Helpers—Metal and Plastic Processing Machine Operators and Tenders	8614
RES	40	Helpers—Metalworking and Plastic Working Machine Operators and Tenders	8611
RES	39	Helpers—Textile, Apparel and Furnishings Machine Operators and Tenders	8617
RES	39	Helpers—Woodworking Machine Operators and Tenders	8615
RES	39	Stock Handlers and Baggers	8724
RES	38	Stevedores	8723
RES	36	Garbage Collectors	8722
REC	57	Dental Laboratory Technicians	6865
REC	57	Locksmiths and Safe Repairers	6173
REC	55	Heating, Air-Conditioning, and Refrigeration Mechanics	6160
REC	53	Carpenters	6422
REC	53	Mechanical Controls and Valve Repairers	6175
REC	52	Gem and Diamond Working Occupations	6866
REC	50	Extruding and Forming Machine Setup Operators	7463
REC	50	Roofers	6468
REC	49	Inspectors—Agricultural Products	5627
REC	49	Production Expediters	7870
REC	49	Welding Machine Operators and Tenders	7532
REC	48	Graders and Sorters—Agricultural Products	5625
REC	48	Miscellaneous Metal and Plastic Processing Machine Setup Operators	7349
REC	48	Slicing and Cutting Machine Setup Operators	7478
REC	47	Photoengraving and Lithographing Machine Operators and Tenders	7644
REC	47	Railroad brake, Signal, and Switch Operators	8233
REC	47	Rolling Machine Operators and Tenders	7516
REC	47	Still, Clarifier and Precipitator Operators and Tenders	7676
REC	46	Garage and Service Station Related Occupations	8730
REC	46	Groundskeepers and Gardeners, Except Farm	5622
REC	46	Pest Control Occupations	5246
REC	45	Extruding and Drawing Machine Operators and Tenders	7515
REC	45	Miscellaneous Material Moving Equipment Operators	8319
REC	45	Miscellaneous Metal and Plastic Processing Machine Operators and Tenders	7549

HOC	Cx	Title	SOC
REC	45	Mixing and Blending Machine Operators and Tenders	7664
REC	45	Taxicab Drivers and Chauffeurs	8216
REC	44	Duplicating Machine Operators	4722
REC	44	Forging Machine Operators and Tenders	7519
REC	44	Helpers—Vehicle and Mobile Equipment Mechanics and Repairers	8632
REC	44	Hoist and Winch Operators	8314
REC	44	Mail Preparing and Handling Machine Operators	4723
REC	44	Paving, Surfacing, and Tamping Equipment Operators	6466
REC	43	Cooling and Freezing Equipment Operators and Tenders	7665
REC	43	Extruding and Forming Machine Operators and Tenders	7663
REC	43	Hand Molding and Casting Occupations	7754
REC	43	Helpers—Miscellaneous Mechanics and Repairers	8637
REC	43	Helpers—Precision Production Occupations and Setup Operators	8619
REC	43	Nursery Workers	5619
REC	43	Other Motor Transportation Occupations, n.e.c.	8219
REC	43	Separating and Filtering Machine Operators and Tenders	7666
REC	42	Elevator Operators	5245
REC	42	Fishers	5830
REC	42	Helpers—Extractive Occupations	8650
REC	42	Laundering and Dry Cleaning Machine Operators and Tenders	7658
REC	42	Livestock Workers	5617
REC	42	Miscellaneous Food and Beverage Preparation Occupations	5219
REC	42	Washing, Cleaning and Pickling Equipment Operators and Tenders	7673
REC	41	Cleaning and Building Service Occupations, n.e.c.	5249
REC	41	Compressing and Compacting Machine Operators and Tenders	7667
REC	41	Folding Machine Operators and Tenders	7674
REC	41	Helpers—Fabricators and Inspectors	8620
REC	41	Irrigation Workers	5615
REC	41	Lathe and Turning Machine Operators and Tenders	7631
REC	41	Sanding Machine Operators and Tenders	7634
REC	41	Shaping and Joining Machine Operators and Tenders	7635
REC	40	Helpers—Machine Operators and Tenders, Assorted Materials	8618
REC	40	Janitors and Cleaners	5244
REC	39	Hand Packers and Packagers	8761
REC	39	Machine Feeders and Offbearers	8725
REC	39	Manual Occupations, n.e.c.	8769
REC	39	Vehicle Washers and Equipment Cleaners	8750
REC	38	Field Crop and Vegetable Farm Workers (hand)	5613
RCI	66	Engineering Technologists and Technicians	3710
RCI	59	Nuclear Technologists and Technicians	3832
RCI	51	Handlers, Equipment Cleaners and Laborers	8700
RCI	49	Typesetting and Composing Machine Operators and Tenders	7642
RCI	45	Soldering and Brazing Machine Operators and Tenders	7533

HOC to SOC

HOC	Cx	Title	SOC
RCA	52	Detail Design Painters and Decorators	6863
RCS	61	Radio and Related Operators	3930
RCS	51	Bridge, Lock, and Lighthouse Tenders	8245
RCS	50	Packaging and Filling Machine Setup Operators	7462
RCS	50	Tile Setters, Hard	6414
RCS	49	Drywall Installers	6424
RCS	46	Helpers—Electricians and Power Transmission Installers	8643
RCS	45	Knitting and Weaving Machine Operators and Tenders	7652
RCS	44	Kitchen Workers, Food Preparation	5217
RCE	55	Photographic Process Workers	6868
RCE	51	Traffic, Shipping, and Receiving Clerks	4753
RCE	51	Transportation Inspectors	8280
RCE	50	Stock and Inventory Clerks	4754
RCE	49	Insulation Workers	6465
RCE	49	Mail Clerks, Except Post Office	4744
RCE	48	Mechanics and Repairers, n.e.c.	6179
RCE	48	Production Testers	7830
RCE	48	Weighers, Measurers, and Checkers	4756
RCE	47	Construction Trades, n.e.c.	6479
RCE	47	Photographic Processing Machine Operators	7671
RCE	47	Sawing Machine Setup Operators	7433
RCE	46	Hand Engraving and Printing Occupations	7757
RCE	46	Production Inspectors, Checkers and Examiners	7820
RCE	46	Router and Planner Machine Operators and Tenders	7632
RCE	45	Crane and Tower Operators	8315
RCE	45	Furnace, Kiln, and Oven Operators and Tenders	7675
RCE	45	Helpers—Industrial Machinery Repairers	8633
RCE	44	Coating, Painting, and Spraying Machine Operators and Tenders	7669
RCE	44	Lathe and Turning Machine Operators and Tenders	7512
RCE	44	Miscellaneous Metalworking and Plastic Working Machine Operators and Tenders	7529
RCE	44	Molding and Casting Machine Operators and Tenders	7542
RCE	44	Plating and Coating Machine Operators and Tenders	7543
RCE	44	Printing Machine Operators and Tenders, n.e.c.	7649
RCE	44	Production Samplers and Weighers	7840
RCE	44	Punching and Shearing Machine Operators and Tenders	7514
RCE	44	Sawing Machine Operators and Tenders	7633
RCE	44	Shoe Machine Operators and Tenders	7656
RCE	44	Solderers and Brazers	7717
RCE	44	Truck Drivers, Light (including delivery and route drivers)	8214
RCE	43	Assemblers	7720
RCE	43	Crushing, Grinding and Polishing Machine Operators and Tenders	7677
RCE	43	Drilling and Boring Machine Operators and Tenders	7518
RCE	43	Graders and Sorters, Except Agricultural	7850
RCE	43	Grinding, Abrading, Buffing and Polishing Machine Operators and Tenders	7522

HOC	Cx	Title	SOC
RCE	43	Hand Forming and Shaping Occupations	7755
RCE	43	Helpers—Electrical and Electronic Equipment Repairers	8635
RCE	43	Helpers—Plumbers, Pipefitters and Steamfitters	8645
RCE	43	Industrial Truck and Tractor Equipment Operators	8318
RCE	43	Machinery Maintenance Occupations	6140
RCE	43	Miscellaneous Machine Operators and Tenders, n.e.c.	7679
RCE	43	Miscellaneous Woodworking Machine Operators and Tenders	7639
RCE	43	Press and Brake Machine Operators and Tenders	7517
RCE	43	Printing Machine Operators and Tenders	7643
RCE	43	Textile Cutting Machine Operators and Tenders	7654
RCE	42	Hand Cutting and Trimming Occupations	7753
RCE	42	Hand Grinding and Polishing Occupations	7758
RCE	42	Hand Painting, Coating and Decorating Occupations	7756
RCE	42	Hand Sewing Occupations	7752
RCE	42	Helpers—Painters, Paperhangers, and Plasterers	8644
RCE	42	Milling and Planning Machine Operators and Tenders	7513
RCE	42	Miscellaneous Fabricating Machine Operators and Tenders	7539
RCE	42	Miscellaneous Hand Working Occupations	7759
RCE	42	Miscellaneous Textile Machine Operators and Tenders	7659
RCE	42	Orchard and Vineyard and Related Workers (hand)	5614
RCE	42	Slicing and Cutting Machine Operators and Tenders	7678
RCE	42	Textile Sewing Machine Operators and Tenders	7655
RCE	41	Cementing and Gluing Machine Operators and Tenders	7661
RCE	41	Packaging and Filling Machine Operators and Tenders	7662
RCE	41	Pressing Machine Operators	7657
RCE	41	Winding and Twisting Machine Operators and Tenders	7651
RCE	40	Launderers and Ironers	5030
RCE	40	Waiters'/Waitresses' Assistants	5218
RCE	39	Fabricators, n.e.c.	7740
RCE	39	Maids and Housemen	5242
RCE	39	Nailing and Tacking Machine Operators and Tenders	7636
IRA	73	Mathematical Scientists, n.e.c.	1739
IRS	78	Agriculture Teachers*	2234
IRS	78	Geologists	1847
IRS	78	Medical Scientists	1855
IRS	77	Agricultural and Food Scientists	1853
IRS	76	Physicians	2610
IRS	72	Civil Engineers	1628
IRS	72	Forestry and Conservation Scientists	1852
IRS	70	Atmospheric and Space Scientists	1846
IRS	69	Technical Writers	3980
IRS	68	Computer Scientists, n.e.c.	1719
IRS	66	Radiologic Technologists and Technicians	3650
IRS	65	Chemical Technologists and Technicians	3831
IRS	64	Appraisers and Related Occupations	4440

Part 2: From Holland Codes to Occupations

From Holland Codes to the Standard Occupational Classification

HOC	Cx	Title	SOC
IRE	80	Astronomers	1842
IRE	79	Operations Researchers and Analysts	1721
IRE	79	Physicists	1843
IRE	79	Programmers, Scientific	3972
IRE	78	Biological Scientists	1854
IRE	78	Petroleum Engineers	1625
IRE	78	Physical Scientists, n.e.c.	1849
IRE	77	Statisticians	1733
IRE	76	Aerospace Engineers	1622
IRE	75	Chemical Engineers	1626
IRE	75	Dentists	2620
IRE	75	Metallurgical and Materials Engineers	1623
IRE	75	Nuclear Engineers	1627
IRE	74	Atmospheric, Earth, Marine, and Space Sciences Teachers*	2212
IRE	74	Biological Sciences Teachers*	2213
IRE	74	Chemistry Teachers*	2214
IRE	74	Computer Engineers	1636
IRE	74	Computer Science Teachers*	2228
IRE	74	Electrical and Electronic Engineers	1633
IRE	74	Mathematical Science Teachers*	2227
IRE	74	Natural Sciences Teachers, n.e.c.*	2216
IRE	74	Physics Teachers*	2215
IRE	73	Veterinarians	2700
IRE	72	Agricultural Engineers	1632
IRE	72	Marine Engineers and Naval Architects	1637
IRE	71	Mining Engineers	1624
IRE	70	Computer Systems Analysts	1712
IRE	69	Mechanical Engineering Technologists and Technicians	3713
IRE	69	Programmers, Business	3971
IRE	69	Social Scientists, n.e.c.	1919
IRE	68	Clinical Laboratory Technologists and Technicians	3620
IRE	68	Industrial Engineering Technologists and Technicians	3712
IRE	66	Drafting Occupations	3720
IRE	65	Surveying and Mapping Technicians, n.e.c.	3739
IRC	70	Mathematical Technicians	3840
IAR	74	Architects	1610
ISR	74	Medical Science Teachers*	2231
ISR	70	Speech Pathologists and Audiologists	3034
ISR	66	Health Diagnosing and Treating Practitioners, n.e.c.	2890
ISA	71	Economics Teachers*	2218
ISA	71	Economists	1912
ISA	66	Physicians Assistants	3040
ISE	75	Pharmacists	3010
ISE	75	Psychologists	1915

HOC	Cx	Title	SOC
ISE	75	Psychology Teachers*	2217
ISE	72	Actuaries	1732
ISE	69	Optometrists	2810
IER	73	Chemists, Except Biochemists	1845
IER	73	Engineers, n.e.c.	1639
IER	72	Industrial Engineers	1634
IER	69	Surveyors and Mapping Scientists, n.e.c.	1649
IER	67	Surveying Technicians	3733
IEA	67	Land Surveyors	1643
IES	71	Sociologists	1916
IES	71	Sociology Teachers*	2224
ARS	60	Photographers	3260
AIE	74	English Teachers*	2238
AIE	74	Foreign Language Teachers*	2242
ASE	74	Art, Drama, and Music Teachers*	2235
AER	64	Dancers	3270
AES	69	Musicians and Composers	3230
AES	69	Reporters	3313
AES	68	Authors	3210
AES	68	Editors	3312
AES	64	Designers	3220
AES	63	Painters, Sculptors, Craft-Artists, and Artist Printmakers	3250
SRI	62	Physical Therapists	3033
SRE	67	Secondary School Teachers	2330
SRE	46	Private Household Occupations, n.e.c.	5090
SRC	52	Health Aides, Except Nursing	5233
SIR	65	Podiatrists	2830
SIR	57	Respiratory Therapists	3031
SIE	74	Social Science Teachers, n.e.c.*	2225
SIE	71	Health Specialties Teachers, n.e.c.	2232
SIE	69	Dietitians	3020
SIE	67	Registered Nurses	2900
SIE	67	Therapists, n.e.c.	3039
SAI	60	Dental Hygienists	3630
SAI	58	Dental Assistants	5232

HOC to SOC

Part 2: From Holland Codes to Occupations

From Holland Codes to the Standard Occupational Classification

HOC	Cx	Title	SOC
SAE	73	Clergy	2042
SAE	73	Theology Teachers*	2245
SAE	66	Elementary School Teachers	2320
SAE	64	Writers, Artists, and Related Workers, n.e.c.	3290
SER	70	Human Resources Program Administrators	1132
SER	66	Archivists and Curators	2520
SER	65	Physical Education Teachers*	2236
SER	64	Air Traffic Controllers	3920
SER	62	Adult Education and Other Teachers, n.e.c.	2390
SER	58	Police and Detectives, Public Service	5132
SER	58	Supervisors—Mail and Message Distribution Clerks	4524
SER	53	Housekeepers and Butlers	5050
SER	52	Hairdressers and Cosmetologists	5253
SER	51	Protective Service Occupations, n.e.c.	5149
SER	50	Correctional Institution Officers	5133
SER	49	Sales Clerk	4362
SER	48	Nursing Aides, Orderlies, and Attendants	5236
SEI	70	Political Science Teachers*	2223
SEI	70	Political Scientists	1914
SEI	67	Administrators—Elementary and Secondary Education	1282
SEI	67	Education Teachers*	2237
SEI	62	Recreation Workers	2033
SEA	69	Instructional Coordinators	2360
SEA	69	Vocational and Educational Counselors	2400
SEA	66	Historians	1913
SEA	66	History Teachers*	2222
SEA	66	Home Economics Teachers*	2247
SEA	64	Teachers—Postsecondary, n.e.c.	2249
SEA	63	Religious Workers, n.e.c.	2049
SEA	62	Prekindergarten and Kindergarten Teachers	2310
SEA	55	Licensed Practical Nurses	3660
SEC	71	Judges	2120
SEC	70	Managers—Medicine and Health	1310
SEC	67	Chief Executives and General Administrators	1120
SEC	65	Loan Officers	1415
SEC	65	Personnel, Training, and Labor Relations Specialists	1430
SEC	65	Teachers—Special Education	2350
SEC	64	Librarians	2510
SEC	63	Radio, Television, and Other Announcers	3330
SEC	63	Social Work Teachers*	2244
SEC	63	Social Workers	2032
SEC	63	Supervisors—Financial Record Processing Occupations	4521
SEC	60	Clerks, Social Welfare	4784
SEC	60	Supervisors—Correspondence Clerks and Order Clerks	4516
SEC	58	Chief Communications Operators	4523

Part 2: From Holland Codes to Occupations

From Holland Codes to the Standard Occupational Classification

HOC	Cx	Title	SOC
SEC	52	License Clerks	4787
SEC	51	Welfare Service Aides	5263
SEC	43	Child Care Workers, Private Household	5060
SCE	65	Legal Technicians	3960
SCE	60	Supervisors—Record Clerks	4519
SCE	52	Postal Clerks, Except Mail Carriers	4742
ERI	70	Sales Engineers	4210
ERI	66	Managers—Crop, Vegetable, Fruit and Tree Nut Farm	5523
ERS	70	Electricity, Gas, Water Supply, and Sanitary Services Managers	1343
ERS	67	Managers—Mining, Quarrying, Well Drilling, and Similar Operations	1360
ERS	65	Construction Managers	1330
ERS	64	Ship Captains and Mates	8241
ERS	62	Supervisors—Firefighting and Fire Prevention Occupations	5111
ERS	62	Technical Sales Workers, Aircraft	4232
ERS	59	Supervisors—Production Occupations	7100
ERS	58	Supervisors—Farm Workers	5611
ERS	57	Fire Inspection and Fire Prevention Occupations	5122
ERS	57	Supervisors—Material Moving Equipment Operators	8120
ERS	56	Supervisors—Forestry and Logging Workers	5710
ERS	56	Supervisors—Handlers, Equipment Cleaners, Helpers, and Laborers	8500
ERS	47	Bartenders	5212
ERS	45	Personal Service Occupations, n.e.c.	5269
EIR	71	Managers—Engineering, Mathematics, and Natural Sciences	1260
EIS	71	Urban and Regional Planners	1920
EIS	63	Miscellaneous Occupations	9900
EAS	66	Public Relations Specialists and Publicity Writers	3320
EAS	55	Auctioneers	4470
EAS	55	Performers, n.e.c.	3280
ESR	70	Financial Managers	1220
ESR	70	General Managers and Other Top Executives	1210
ESR	70	Public Finance, Taxation, and Other Monetary Program Administrators	1135
ESR	70	Rural, Urban, and Community Development Program Administrators	1134
ESR	69	Teachers, Except Postsecondary Institutions	2300
ESR	68	Administrators—Education and Related Fields, n.e.c.	1283
ESR	68	Managers—General Farm	5522
ESR	67	Business, Commerce, and Marketing Teachers	2233

Part 2: From Holland Codes to Occupations

From Holland Codes to the Standard Occupational Classification

HOC	Cx	Title	SOC
ESR	67	Judicial, Public Safety, and Correctional Administrators	1131
ESR	67	Managers—Property and Leasing	1353
ESR	67	Officials and Administrators, Public Administration, n.e.c.	1139
ESR	67	Production Managers, Industrial	1320
ESR	67	Purchasing Agents and Buyers, n.e.c.	1449
ESR	66	Communications Operations Managers	1341
ESR	66	Managers—Administrative Services	1370
ESR	66	Managers—Horticultural Specialty Farm	5525
ESR	66	Natural Resources Program Administrators	1133
ESR	66	Purchasing Managers	1240
ESR	66	Transportation Facilities and Operations Managers	1342
ESR	65	Postmasters and Mail Superintendents	1344
ESR	65	Supervisors—Sales Occupations, Insurance, Real Estate, and Business Services	4010
ESR	64	Managers—Food Serving and Lodging Establishments	1351
ESR	64	Managers—Livestock, Dairy, Poultry and Fish Farm	5524
ESR	64	Managers—Service Organizations, n.e.c.	1359
ESR	63	Buyers, Wholesale and Retail Trade, Except Farm Products	1442
ESR	63	Inspectors and Compliance Officers, Except Construction	1473
ESR	63	Managers—Entertainment and Recreation Facilities	1352
ESR	63	Technical Sales Workers, Electronic Equipment	4234
ESR	63	Technical Sales Workers, Medical and Dental Equipment and Supplies	4236
ESR	63	Technical Sales Workers, n.e.c.	4239
ESR	61	Sales Representatives, Motor Vehicles and Supplies	4244
ESR	61	Supervisors—Information Clerks	4514
ESR	61	Supervisors—Police and Detectives	5112
ESR	60	Supervisors—Motor Vehicle Operators	8111
ESR	60	Supervisors—Sales Occupations, Retail	4030
ESR	60	Technical Sales Workers, Industrial Machinery, Equipment, and Supplies	4235
ESR	59	Railroad Conductors and Yardmasters	8113
ESR	59	Sales Representatives, Commercial and Industrial Equipment and Supplies	4242
ESR	59	Salespersons—Musical Instruments and Supplies	4343
ESR	59	Supervisors—Material Recording, Scheduling, and Distribution Clerks	4525
ESR	59	Technical Sales Workers, Agricultural Equipment and Supplies	4233
ESR	58	Supervisors—Duplicating, Mail and Other Office Machine Operators	4522
ESR	58	Supervisors—Food and Beverage Preparation and Service Occupations	5211
ESR	58	Supervisors—Guards	5113
ESR	58	Supervisors—Painters, Paperhangers, and Plasterers	6315
ESR	58	Supervisors—Personal Service Occupations	5251
ESR	58	Technical Sales Workers—Chemicals and Chemical Products	4237
ESR	56	Supervisors—Cleaning and Building Service Workers	5241

Part 2: From Holland Codes to Occupations

From Holland Codes to the Standard Occupational Classification

HOC	Cx	Title	SOC
ESR	55	Athletes and Related Workers	3400
ESR	54	Sheriffs, Bailiffs, and Other Law Enforcement Officers	5134
ESR	53	Barbers	5252
ESR	53	Bill and Account Collectors	4786
ESR	53	Guides	5255
ESR	51	Counter Clerks	4363
ESR	45	Wardrobe and Dressing Room Attendants	5258
ESI	76	Law Teachers*	2243
ESI	76	Lawyers	2110
ESI	76	Legislators*	1110
ESI	69	Personnel and Labor Relations Managers	1230
ESI	67	Supervisors—Computer and Peripheral Equipment Operators	4512
ESI	53	Shoppers	4460
ESA	69	Administrators—Colleges and Universities	1281
ESA	69	Managers—Membership Organizations	1354
ESA	67	Managers—Marketing, Advertising, and Public Relations	1250
ESA	67	Managers—Social Sciences and Related Fields	1270
ESA	66	Purchasing Agents and Buyers, Farm Products	1443
ESA	64	Actors and Directors	3240
ESA	63	Business and Promotion Agents	1450
ESA	63	Supervisors—Sales Occupations, Commodities Except Retail	4020
ESA	62	Sales Representatives—Farm Products and Livestock	4246
ESA	61	Business Service, Except Advertising, Sales Occupations	4152
ESA	59	Advertising and Related Sales Occupations	4153
ESA	58	Sales Representatives, Garments and Related Textile Products	4243
ESA	58	Salespersons—Books, Stamps, Coins, and Stationery	4347
ESA	58	Salespersons—Jewelry and Related Products	4356
ESA	57	Sales Occupations—Services, n.e.c.	4369
ESA	57	Sales Representatives—Pulp, Paper and Paper Products	4245
ESA	57	Sales Representatives—n.e.c.	4249
ESA	57	Salespersons—Boats, and Marine Equipment and Supplies	4344
ESA	57	Salespersons—Motor Vehicles, Motor Homes and Supplies	4342
ESA	57	Salespersons—Radio, Television, High Fidelity, and Household Appliances	4352
ESA	57	Salespersons—Shoes	4351
ESA	57	Salespersons—Sporting Goods	4345
ESA	56	Salespersons—Furniture and Home Furnishings	4348
ESA	55	Salespersons—Cosmetics, Toiletries, and Allied Products	4354
ESA	55	Salespersons—Garments and Textile Products	4346
ESA	55	Salespersons—Hardware	4353
ESA	55	Salespersons—n.e.c.	4359
ESA	51	Demonstrators, Promoters, and Models	4450
ESA	47	Child Care Workers, Except Private Household	5264

Part 2: From Holland Codes to Occupations

From Holland Codes to the Standard Occupational Classification

HOC	Cx	Title	SOC
ESC	67	Officials and Administrators—Other, n.e.c.	1390
ESC	67	Other Financial Officers	1419
ESC	65	Insurance, Securities, Real Estate, and Business Service Sales Occupations	4100
ESC	65	Management Analysts	1420
ESC	65	Management Related Occupations, n.e.c.	1490
ESC	65	Securities and Financial Services Sales Occupations	4124
ESC	64	Real Estate Sales Occupations	4123
ESC	64	Supervisors—General Office Occupations	4511
ESC	62	Supervisors—Miscellaneous Administrative Support Occupations	4529
ESC	61	Supervisors—Adjusters, Investigators, and Collectors	4528
ESC	60	Insurance Adjusters, Examiners, and Investigators	4782
ESC	56	Investigators and Adjusters, Except Insurance	4783
ESC	56	Salespersons—Parts	4367
ESC	51	Guards and Police, Except Public Service	5144
ESC	49	Street Vendors, Door-to-Door Sales Workers, and Related Occupations	4366
ESC	45	News Vendors	4365
ECR	44	Crossing Guards	5142
ECR	44	Food Counter, Fountain and Related Occupations	5216
ECS	62	Insurance Sales Occupations	4122
ECS	56	Dispatchers	4751
ECS	55	Reservation Agents and Transportation Clerks	4644
ECS	54	Correspondence Clerks	4663
ECS	54	Hotel Clerks	4643
ECS	48	Public Transportation Attendants	5257
ECS	47	Attendants, Amusement and Recreation Facilities	5254
ECS	47	Waiters and Waitresses	5213
CRS	53	Billing, Posting, and Calculating Machine Operators	4718
CRS	52	Peripheral Equipment Operators	4613
CRS	49	Samplers	4757
CRS	48	Material Recording, Scheduling, and Distributing Clerks, n.e.c.	4759
CRS	45	Office Machine Operators, n.e.c.	4729
CRS	43	Parking Lot Attendants	8740
CRE	54	Production and Planning Clerks	4752
CRE	52	Data Entry Keyers	4793
CIE	63	Health Record Technologists and Technicians	3640
CSR	56	Bookkeepers and Accounting and Auditing Clerks	4712
CSR	56	Computer Operators	4612
CSR	56	Payroll and Timekeeping Clerks	4713
CSR	55	Cost and Rate Clerks	4716

Part 2: From Holland Codes to Occupations

From Holland Codes to the Standard Occupational Classification

HOC	Cx	Title	SOC
CSR	54	Billing Clerks	4715
CSR	53	Statistical Clerks	4794
CSR	52	Mail Carriers, Post Office	4743
CSR	51	File Clerks	4696
CSR	51	Typists	4624
CSR	49	Library Clerks	4694
CSE	70	Underwriters	1414
CSE	59	Secretaries	4622
CSE	58	Bank Tellers	4791
CSE	55	Information Clerks, n.e.c.	4649
CSE	55	Stenographers	4623
CSE	54	Classified-Ad Clerks	4662
CSE	54	Personnel Clerks, Except Payroll and Timekeeping	4692
CSE	53	Communications Equipment Operators, n.e.c.	4739
CSE	53	Expediters	4758
CSE	53	General Office Occupations	4630
CSE	53	Proof Readers	4792
CSE	52	Interviewing Clerks	4642
CSE	52	Receptionists	4645
CSE	52	Record Clerks, n.e.c.	4699
CSE	52	Telegraphers	4733
CSE	51	Cashiers	4364
CSE	50	Meter Readers	4755
CER	45	Messengers	4745
CEI	70	Accountants and Auditors	1412
CES	58	Supervisors—Secretaries, Stenographers and Typists	4513
CES	53	Administrative Support Occupations, Including Clerical, n.e.c.	4799
CES	53	Teacher Aides	4795
CES	52	Order Clerks	4664
CES	50	Telephone Operators	4732
CES	41	Ushers	5256

Note. n.e.c. = not elsewhere classified.

*No occupation in the *Dictionary of Occupational Titles* or its *Supplements* was assigned to this category. The Holland code shown is not an aggregation of the empirically derived codes; in most cases, it is a code for a closely related SOC category.

Part 2: From Holland Codes to Occupations

From Holland Codes to the Census Occupational Classification

HOC	Cx	Title	COC
RIS	69	Occupational Therapists	099
RIS	60	Health Technologists and Technicians, n.e.c.	208
RIS	59	Elevator Installers and Repairer	543
RIS	58	Biological Technicians	223
RIS	57	Cabinet Makers and Bench Carpenters	657
RIS	56	Brickmason and Stonemason Apprentices	564
RIS	47	Longshore Equipment Operators	845
RIS	47	Operating Engineers	844
RIE	71	Mechanical Engineers	057
RIE	67	Airplane pilots and Navigators	226
RIE	64	Electrical and Electronic Technicians	213
RIE	63	Construction Inspectors	035
RIE	63	Science Technicians, n.e.c.	225
RIE	62	Engineering Technicians, n.e.c.	216
RIE	60	Machinists	637
RIE	60	Machinist Apprentices	639
RIE	60	Patternmakers and Model Makers, Metal	645
RIE	59	Horticultural Specialty Farmers	474
RIE	59	Tool and Die Makers	634
RIE	58	Electronic Repairers, Communications and Industrial Equipment	523
RIE	58	Patternmakers, Lay-Out Workers, and Cutters	676
RIE	58	Technicians, n.e.c.	235
RIE	58	Tool and Die Maker Apprentices	635
RIE	57	Lathe and Turning Machine Set-up Operators	703
RIE	57	Lay-Out Workers	646
RIE	57	Tailors	667
RIE	56	Aircraft Mechanics, Except Engine	515
RIE	56	Miscellaneous Precision Woodworkers	659
RIE	54	Motion Picture Projectionists	773
RIE	50	Locomotive Operating Occupations	824
RIE	48	Heat Treating Equipment Operators	724
RIC	67	Mechanical Engineering Technicians	215
RIC	61	Tool Programmers, Numerical Control	233
RIC	59	Telephone Installers and Repairers	529
RSE	59	Supervisors, Electricians and Power Transmission Installers	555
RSE	56	Automobile Mechanic Apprentices	506
RSE	55	Food Batchmakers	688
RSE	54	Furniture and Wood Finishers	658
RSE	53	Bakers	687
RSE	52	Cooks	436
RSE	52	Cooks, Private Household	404
RSE	51	Glaziers	589
RSE	44	Private Household Cleaners and Servants	407
RSC	57	Telephone Line Installers and Repairers	527

HOC	Cx	Title	COC
RSC	47	Paperhangers	583
RSC	45	Helpers, Surveyor	867
REI	61	Captains and Other Officers, Fishing Vessels	497
REI	60	Farmers, Except Horticultural	473
REI	59	Patternmakers and Model Makers, Wood	656
REI	59	Sheet Metal Workers	653
REI	59	Sheet Metal Worker Apprentices	654
REI	56	Data Processing Equipment Repairers	525
REI	56	Heavy Equipment Mechanics	516
REI	56	Inspectors, Testers, and Graders	689
REI	56	Small Engine Repairers	509
REI	55	Electrical and Electronic Equipment Assemblers	683
REI	55	Engravers, Metal	649
REI	55	Hand Molders and Shapers, Except Jewelers	675
REI	55	Industrial Machinery Repairers	518
REI	55	Miscellaneous Precision Workers, n.e.c.	684
REI	55	Numerical Control Machine Operators	714
REI	55	Precision Assemblers, Metal	636
REI	55	Precision Grinders, Fitters, and Tool Sharpeners	644
REI	54	Carpet Installers	566
REI	54	Miscellaneous Electrical and Electronic Equipment Repairers	533
REI	54	Miscellaneous Precision Metal Workers	655
REI	54	Plasterers	584
REI	54	Plumbers, Pipefitters, and Steamfitters	585
REI	54	Water and Sewage Treatment Plant Operators	694
REI	53	Drillers, Oil Well	614
REI	53	Photoengravers and Lithographers	735
REI	52	Automobile Mechanics	505
REI	52	Optical Goods Workers	677
REI	51	Adjusters and Calibrators	693
REI	51	Concrete and Terrazzo Finishers	588
REI	51	Welders and Cutters	783
REI	50	Miscellaneous Printing Machine Operators	737
REI	50	Non-Commissioned Officers and Other Enlisted Personnel	904
REI	49	Forging Machine Operators	713
REI	48	Drillers, Earth	598
REI	48	Sailors and Deckhands	829
REI	47	Mining Machine Operators	616
REI	47	Rail Vehicle Operators, n.e.c.	826
REI	45	Grader, Dozer, and Scraper Operators	855
REI	45	Truck Drivers	804
REI	39	Forestry Workers, Except Logging	495
RES	62	Millwrights	544
RES	61	Electrician Apprentices	576
RES	60	Supervisors, Carpenters and Related Workers	554
RES	59	Marine Engineers	833

HOC	Cx	Title	COC
RES	59	Supervisors, Related Agricultural Occupations	485
RES	59	Supervisors; Brickmasons, Stonemasons, and Tile Setters	553
RES	59	Supervisors; Plumbers, Pipefitters and Steamfitters	557
RES	59	Supervisors, n.e.c.	558
RES	58	Bus, Truck, and Stationary Engine Mechanics	507
RES	58	Plumber, Pipefitter, and Steamfitter Apprentices	587
RES	58	Supervisors, Extractive Occupations	613
RES	57	Boilermakers	643
RES	57	Carpenter Apprentices	569
RES	56	Electricians	575
RES	56	Office Machine Repairers	538
RES	56	Power Plant Operators	695
RES	55	Electrical Power Installers and Repairers	577
RES	54	Household Appliance and Power Tool Repairers	526
RES	53	Explosives Workers	615
RES	53	Farm Equipment Mechanics	517
RES	53	Miscellaneous Plant and System Operators	699
RES	52	Bookbinders	679
RES	52	Shoe Repairers	669
RES	52	Structural Metal Workers	597
RES	52	Tile setters, Hard and Soft	565
RES	51	Brickmasons and Stonemasons	563
RES	51	Stationary Engineers	696
RES	50	Automobile Body and Related Repairers	514
RES	50	Butchers and Meat Cutters	686
RES	50	Firefighting Occupations	417
RES	50	Painters, Construction and Maintenance	579
RES	49	Bus Drivers	808
RES	49	Rolling Machine Operators	707
RES	48	Driver-Sales Workers	806
RES	48	Hunters and Trappers	499
RES	46	Animal Caretakers, Except Farm	487
RES	46	Mining Occupations, n.e.c.	617
RES	45	Excavating and Loading Machine Operators	853
RES	44	Baggage Porters and Bellhops	464
RES	44	Roasting and Baking Machine Operators, Food	763
RES	42	Marine Life Cultivation Workers	483
RES	42	Timber Cutting and Logging Occupations	496
RES	41	Construction Laborers	869
RES	40	Freight, Stock, and Material Handlers, n.e.c.	883
RES	39	Stock Handlers and Baggers	877
RES	38	Stevedores	876
RES	36	Garbage Collectors	875
REC	57	Dental Laboratory and Medical Appliance Technicians	678
REC	57	Locksmiths and Safe Repairers	536
REC	55	Camera, Watch, and Musical Instrument Repairers	535
REC	55	Heating, Air Conditioning, and Refrigeration Mechanics	534
REC	54	Dressmakers	666

HOC to COC

Part 2: From Holland Codes to Occupations
From Holland Codes to the Census Occupational Classification

HOC	Cx	Title	COC
REC	53	Mechanical Controls and Valve Repairers	539
REC	53	Precious Stones and Metals Workers (jewelers)	647
REC	53	Upholsterers	668
REC	52	Carpenters	567
REC	50	Miscellaneous Precision Apparel and Fabric Workers	674
REC	50	Roofers	595
REC	49	Inspectors, Agricultural Products	489
REC	47	Graders and Sorters, Agricultural Products	488
REC	47	Railroad Brake, Signal, and Switch Operators	825
REC	46	Fabricating Machine Operators, n.e.c.	717
REC	46	Garage and Service Station Related Occupations	885
REC	46	Groundskeepers and Gardeners, Except Farm	486
REC	46	Pest Control Occupations	455
REC	45	Miscellaneous Metal and Plastic Processing Machine Operators	725
REC	45	Miscellaneous Material Moving Equipment Operators	859
REC	45	Mixing and Blending Machine Operators	756
REC	45	Molding and Casting Machine Operators	719
REC	45	Separating, Filtering, and Clarifying Machine Operators	757
REC	45	Taxicab Drivers and Chauffeurs	809
REC	45	Wood Lathe, Routing, and Planing Machine Operators	726
REC	44	Duplicating Machine Operators	345
REC	44	Extruding and Forming Machine Operators	755
REC	44	Helpers, Mechanics and Repairers	865
REC	44	Hoist and Winch Operators	848
REC	44	Laundering and Dry Cleaning Machine Operators	748
REC	44	Mail Preparing and Paper Handling Machine Operators	346
REC	44	Paving, Surfacing, and Tamping Equipment Operators	594
REC	43	Crushing and Grinding Machine Operators	768
REC	43	Folding Machine Operators	765
REC	43	Nursery Workers	484
REC	42	Elevator Operators	454
REC	42	Farm Workers	479
REC	42	Fishers	498
REC	42	Helpers, Construction Trades	866
REC	42	Helpers, Extractive Occupations	868
REC	42	Miscellaneous Food Preparation Occupations	444
REC	42	Shaping and Joining Machine Operators	728
REC	42	Washing, Cleaning, and Pickling Machine Operators	764
REC	41	Compressing and Compacting Machine Operators	758
REC	40	Janitors and Cleaners	453
REC	40	Production Helpers	874
REC	39	Hand Packers and Packagers	888
REC	39	Laborers, Except Construction	889
REC	39	Machine Feeders and Offbearers	878
REC	39	Vehicle Washers and Equipment Cleaners	887
RCI	61	Broadcast Equipment Operators	228
RCI	53	Typesetters and Compositors	736

Part 2: From Holland Codes to Occupations

From Holland Codes to the Census Occupational Classification

HOC	Cx	Title	COC
RCI	46	Solderers and Brazers	784
RCS	51	Bridge, Lock, and Lighthouse Tenders	834
RCS	49	Drywall Installers	573
RCS	44	Kitchen Workers, Food Preparation	439
RCE	51	Photographic Process Machine Operators	774
RCE	51	Traffic, Shipping, and Receiving Clerks	364
RCE	50	Stock and Inventory Clerks	365
RCE	49	Insulation Workers	593
RCE	49	Mail Clerks, exc. Postal Service	356
RCE	49	Milling and Planing Machine Operators	705
RCE	49	Specified Mechanics and Repairers, n.e.c.	547
RCE	48	Production Testers	797
RCE	47	Construction Trades, n.e.c.	599
RCE	47	Drilling and Boring Machine Operators	708
RCE	47	Knitting, Looping, Taping, and Weaving Machine Operators	739
RCE	47	Miscellaneous Metal, Plastic, Stone and Glass Working Machine Operators	715
RCE	46	Grinding, Abrading, Buffing, and Polishing Machine Operators	709
RCE	46	Hand Engraving and Printing Occupations	793
RCE	46	Metal Plating Machine Operators	723
RCE	46	Printing Press Operators	734
RCE	46	Production Inspectors, Checkers, and Examiners	796
RCE	46	Punching and Stamping Press Machine Operators	706
RCE	45	Crane and Tower Operators	849
RCE	45	Furnace, Kiln, and Oven Operators, Except Food	766
RCE	44	Lathe and Turning Machine Operators	704
RCE	44	Miscellaneous Woodworking Machine Operators	733
RCE	44	Miscellaneous Machine Operators, n.e.c.	777
RCE	44	Painting and Paint Spraying Machine Operators	759
RCE	44	Production Samplers and Weighers	798
RCE	44	Sawing Machine Operators	727
RCE	44	Shoe Machine Operators	745
RCE	43	Graders and Sorters, Except Agricultural	799
RCE	43	Hand Molding, Casting, and Forming Occupations	787
RCE	43	Industrial Truck and Tractor Equipment Operators	856
RCE	43	Machinery Maintenance Occupations	519
RCE	43	Slicing and Cutting Machine Operators	769
RCE	42	Assemblers	785
RCE	42	Hand Cutting and Trimming Occupations	786
RCE	42	Hand Painting, Coating, and Decorating Occupations	789
RCE	42	Miscellaneous Textile Machine Operators	749
RCE	42	Miscellaneous Hand Working Occupations	795
RCE	42	Packaging and Filling Machine Operators	754
RCE	42	Textile Cutting Machine Operators	743
RCE	42	Textile Sewing Machine Operators	744
RCE	41	Cementing and Gluing Machine Operators	753

HOC	Cx	Title	COC
RCE	41	Motor Transportation Occupations, n.e.c.	814
RCE	41	Pressing Machine Operators	747
RCE	41	Winding and Twisting Machine Operators	738
RCE	40	Launderers and Ironers	403
RCE	40	Maids and Housemen	449
RCE	40	Waiters'/Waitresses' Assistants	443
RCE	39	Nailing and Tacking Machine Operators	729
IRA	73	Mathematical Scientists, n.e.c.	068
IRS	78	Geologists and Geodesists	075
IRS	78	Medical Scientists	083
IRS	77	Agricultural and Food Scientists	077
IRS	76	Physicians	084
IRS	74	Postsecondary Teachers, Subject not Specified	154
IRS	72	Civil Engineers	053
IRS	72	Forestry and Conservation Scientists	079
IRS	70	Atmospheric and Space Scientists	074
IRS	69	Technical Writers	184
IRS	67	Computer Systems Analysts and Scientists	064
IRS	66	Radiologic Technicians	206
IRS	65	Chemical Technicians	224
IRE	79	Operations and Systems Researchers and Analysts	065
IRE	79	Physicists and Astronomers	069
IRE	78	Biological and Life Scientists	078
IRE	78	Petroleum Engineers	047
IRE	78	Physical Scientists, n.e.c.	076
IRE	76	Aerospace Engineers	044
IRE	75	Chemical Engineers	048
IRE	75	Dentists	085
IRE	75	Nuclear Engineers	049
IRE	75	Statisticians	067
IRE	74	Electrical and Electronic Engineers	055
IRE	74	Metallurgical and Materials Engineers	045
IRE	73	Veterinarians	086
IRE	72	Agricultural Engineers	054
IRE	72	Marine and Naval Architects	058
IRE	71	Mining Engineers	046
IRE	68	Industrial Engineering Technicians	214
IRE	66	Clinical Laboratory Technologists and Technicians	203
IRE	66	Drafting Occupations	217
IRE	66	Surveying and Mapping Technicians	218
IRC	68	Computer Programmers	229
IAR	74	Architects	043
ISR	70	Speech Therapists	104

Part 2: From Holland Codes to Occupations

From Holland Codes to the Census Occupational Classification

HOC	Cx	Title	COC
ISR	66	Health Diagnosing Practitioners, n.e.c.	089
ISA	71	Economists	166
ISA	66	Physicians' Assistants	106
ISE	75	Pharmacists	096
ISE	75	Psychologists	167
ISE	72	Actuaries	066
ISE	69	Optometrists	087
IER	73	Chemists, Except Biochemists	073
IER	73	Engineers, n.e.c.	059
IER	72	Industrial Engineers	056
IER	68	Surveyors and Mapping Scientists	063
IES	71	Sociologists	168
ARS	60	Photographers	189
AER	64	Dancers	193
AES	69	Musicians and Composers	186
AES	68	Editors and Reporters	195
AES	67	Authors	183
AES	64	Designers	185
AES	63	Painters, Sculptors, Craft-Artists, and Artist Printmakers	188
SRI	62	Physical Therapists	103
SRE	67	Teachers, Secondary School	157
SRC	52	Health Aides, Except Nursing	446
SIR	65	Podiatrists	088
SIR	57	Respiratory Therapists	098
SIE	71	Health Specialties Teachers	134
SIE	69	Dietitians	097
SIE	67	Registered Nurses	095
SIE	67	Therapists, n.e.c.	105
SAI	60	Dental Hygienists	204
SAI	58	Dental Assistants	445
SAE	73	Clergy	176
SAE	66	Teachers, Elementary School	156
SER	66	Archivists and Curators	165
SER	64	Air Traffic Controllers	227

HOC to COC

HOC	Cx	Title	COC
SER	63	Teachers, n.e.c.	159
SER	58	Police and Detectives, Public Service	418
SER	53	Housekeepers and Butlers	405
SER	52	Hairdressers and Cosmetologists	458
SER	51	Protective Service Occupations, n.e.c.	427
SER	50	Correctional Institution Officers	424
SER	48	Nursing Aides, Orderlies, and Attendants	447
SEA	69	Counselors, Educational and Vocational	163
SEA	64	Teachers, Postsecondary, n.e.c.	153
SEA	63	Religious Workers, n.e.c.	177
SEA	62	Teachers, Prekindergarten and Kindergarten	155
SEA	55	Licensed Practical Nurses	207
SEC	71	Judges	179
SEC	70	Managers, Medicine and Health	015
SEC	67	Chief Executives and General Administrators, Public Administrators	004
SEC	66	Teachers, Special Education	158
SEC	65	Personnel, Training, and Labor Relations Specialists	027
SEC	64	Librarians	164
SEC	63	Announcers	198
SEC	63	Social Workers	174
SEC	63	Supervisors, Financial Records Processing	305
SEC	60	Eligibility Clerks, Social Welfare	377
SEC	58	Chief Communications Operators	306
SEC	51	Welfare Service Aides	465
SEC	43	Child Care Workers, Private Household	406
SCE	65	Legal Assistants	234
SCE	52	Postal Clerks, Except Mail Carriers	354
ERI	70	Sales Engineers	258
ERS	65	Managers, Farms, Except Horticultural	475
ERS	62	Supervisors, Firefighting and Fire Prevention Occupations	413
ERS	61	Supervisors, Mechanics and Repairers	503
ERS	59	Ship Captains and Mates, Except Fishing Boats	828
ERS	59	Supervisors, Production Occupations	628
ERS	58	Supervisors, Farm Workers	477
ERS	57	Fire Inspection and Fire Prevention Occupations	416
ERS	57	Supervisors, Material Moving Equipment Operators	843
ERS	56	Supervisors, Forestry and Logging Workers	494
ERS	56	Supervisors, Handlers, Equipment Cleaners, and Laborers, n.e.c.	864
ERS	54	Sales Support Occupations, n.e.c.	285
ERS	47	Bartenders	434
ERS	45	Personal Service Occupations, n.e.c.	469

Part 2: From Holland Codes to Occupations

From Holland Codes to the Census Occupational Classification

HOC	Cx	Title	COC
EIS	71	Urban Planners	173
EAS	66	Public Relations Specialists	197
EAS	57	Artists, Performers, and Related Workers, n.e.c.	194
EAS	55	Auctioneers	284
ESR	70	Financial Managers	007
ESR	68	Administrators and Officials, Public Administration	005
ESR	67	Administrators, Protective Services	006
ESR	67	Managers and Administrators, n.e.c.	022
ESR	67	Purchasing Agents and Buyers, n.e.c.	033
ESR	66	Managers, Properties and Real Estate	018
ESR	66	Managers, Horticultural Specialty Farms	476
ESR	66	Purchasing Managers	009
ESR	65	Funeral Directors	019
ESR	65	Managers, Service Organizations, n.e.c.	021
ESR	65	Postmasters and Mail Superintendents	016
ESR	64	Managers, Food Serving and Lodging Establishments	017
ESR	63	Buyers, Wholesale and Retail Trade Except Farm Products	029
ESR	63	Inspectors and Compliance Officers, Except Construction	036
ESR	62	Recreation Workers	175
ESR	62	Supervisors and Proprietors, Sales Occupations	243
ESR	61	Supervisors, Police and Detectives	414
ESR	60	Railroad Conductors and Yardmasters	823
ESR	60	Supervisors, Motor Vehicle Operators	803
ESR	59	Sales Representatives, Mining, Manufacturing, and Wholesale	259
ESR	59	Supervisors, Distribution, Scheduling and Adjusting Clerks	307
ESR	58	Sales Workers, Radio, TV, Hi-Fi, and Appliances	267
ESR	58	Supervisors, Guards	415
ESR	58	Supervisors, Food Preparation and Service Occupations	433
ESR	58	Supervisors, Personal Service Occupations	456
ESR	58	Supervisors; Painters, Paperhangers and Plasterers	556
ESR	56	Supervisors, Cleaning and Building Service Workers	448
ESR	55	Athletes	199
ESR	54	Sheriffs, Bailiffs, and Other Law Enforcement Officers	423
ESR	53	Barbers	457
ESR	53	Bill and Account Collectors	378
ESR	53	Guides	461
ESR	51	Sales Counter Clerks	275
ESI	76	Lawyers	178
ESI	69	Personnel and Labor Relations Managers	008
ESI	67	Social Scientists, n.e.c.	169
ESI	67	Supervisors, Computer Equipment Operators	304
ESA	68	Administrators, Education and Related Fields	014
ESA	67	Managers, Marketing, Advertising, and Public Relations	013
ESA	66	Purchasing Agents and Buyers, Farm Products	028

Part 2: From Holland Codes to Occupations

From Holland Codes to the Census Occupational Classification

HOC	Cx	Title	COC
ESA	64	Actors and Directors	187
ESA	63	Business and Promotion Agents	034
ESA	61	Sales Occupations, Other Business Services	257
ESA	59	Advertising and Related Sales Occupations	256
ESA	57	Sales Workers, Motor Vehicles and Boats	263
ESA	57	Sales Workers, Shoes	265
ESA	56	Sales Workers, Furniture and Home Furnishings	266
ESA	55	Sales Workers, Apparel	264
ESA	55	Sales Workers, Hardware and Building Supplies	268
ESA	55	Sales Workers, Other Commodities	274
ESA	51	Demonstrators, Promoters and Models, Sales	283
ESA	47	Child Care Workers, n.e.c.	468
ESC	67	Other Financial Officers	025
ESC	65	Management Analysts	026
ESC	65	Management Related Occupations, n.e.c.	037
ESC	65	Securities and Financial Services Sales Occupations	255
ESC	63	Real Estate Sales Occupations	254
ESC	61	Supervisors, General Office	303
ESC	60	Insurance Adjusters, Examiners, and Investigators	375
ESC	56	Investigators and Adjusters, Except Insurance	376
ESC	56	Sales Workers, Parts	269
ESC	51	Guards and Police, Except Public Service	426
ESC	48	Street and Door-to-Door Sales Workers	277
ESC	45	News Vendors	278
ECR	44	Crossing Guards	425
ECR	44	Food Counter, Fountain and Related Occupations	438
ECS	62	Insurance Sales Occupations	253
ECS	56	Dispatchers	359
ECS	55	Transportation Ticket and Reservation Agents	318
ECS	54	Correspondence Clerks	326
ECS	54	Hotel Clerks	317
ECS	48	Public Transportation Attendants	463
ECS	47	Attendants, Amusement and Recreation Facilities	459
ECS	47	Waiters and Waitresses	435
CRS	53	Billing, Posting, and Calculating Machine Operators	344
CRS	52	Peripheral Equipment Operators	309
CRS	48	Material Recording, Scheduling, and Distributing Clerks, n.e.c.	374
CRS	45	Office Machine Operators, n.e.c.	347
CRS	43	Parking Lot Attendants	813
CRE	54	Production Coordinators	363
CRE	52	Data-Entry Keyers	385
CRE	48	Weighers, Measurers, Checkers and Samplers	368

Dictionary of Holland Occupational Codes

HOC	Cx	Title	COC
CIE	63	Health Record Technologists and Technicians	205
CSR	56	Bookkeepers, Accounting and Auditing Clerks	337
CSR	56	Computer Operators	308
CSR	56	Payroll and Timekeeping Clerks	338
CSR	55	Cost and Rate Clerks	343
CSR	54	Billing Clerks	339
CSR	53	Statistical Clerks	386
CSR	52	Mail Carriers, Postal Service	355
CSR	51	File Clerks	335
CSR	51	Typists	315
CSR	49	Library Clerks	329
CSE	70	Underwriters	024
CSE	59	Secretaries	313
CSE	58	Bank tellers	383
CSE	55	Information Clerks, n.e.c.	323
CSE	55	Stenographers	314
CSE	54	Classified-Ad Clerks	325
CSE	54	General Office Clerks	379
CSE	54	Personnel Clerks, Except Payroll and Timekeeping	328
CSE	54	Proofreaders	384
CSE	53	Communications Equipment Operators, n.e.c.	353
CSE	53	Expediters	373
CSE	52	Interviewers	316
CSE	52	Receptionists	319
CSE	52	Records Clerks	336
CSE	51	Cashiers	276
CSE	50	Meter readers	366
CER	45	Messengers	357
CEI	70	Accountants and Auditors	023
CES	53	Administrative Support Occupations, n.e.c.	389
CES	53	Order Clerks	327
CES	53	Teachers' Aides	387
CES	50	Telephone Operators	348
CES	41	Ushers	462

Note. n.e.c. = not elsewhere classified.

HOC to COC

HOC	Title	CIP
RIA	Commercial Photography	50.0406
RIS	Biological Technology/Technician	41.0101
RIS	Computer Engineering	14.0901
RIS	Computer Installer and Repairer	47.0104
RIS	Electrocardiograph Technology/Technician	51.0902
RIS	Environmental and Pollution Control Technology/Technician	15.0507
RIS	Environmental Control Technology/Technicians, Other	15.0599
RIS	Forestry, General	03.0501
RIS	Health Physics/Radiologic Health	51.2205
RIS	Industrial Radiologic Technology/Technician	41.0204
RIS	Mechanics and Repairers, Other	47.9999
RIS	Mining Technology/Technician	15.0901
RIS	Poultry Science	02.0209
RIS	Surgical/Operating Room Technician	51.0909
RIE	Aeronautical and Aerospace Engineering Technology/Technician	15.0801
RIE	Agricultural Animal Nutrition	02.0204
RIE	Aircraft Pilot and Navigator (Professional)	49.0102
RIE	Animal Sciences, General	02.0201
RIE	Architectural Engineering Technology/Technician	15.0101
RIE	Automotive Engineering Technology/Technician	15.0803
RIE	Aviation and Airway Science	49.0101
RIE	Aviation Systems and Avionics Main. Technologist/Technician	47.0609
RIE	Chemical Technology/Technician	41.0301
RIE	Civil/Structural Drafting	48.0103
RIE	Computer Main. Technology/Technician	15.0402
RIE	Design and Visual Communications	50.0401
RIE	Electrical, Electronic and Communications Engin. Technology/Technician	15.0303
RIE	Electromechanical Technology/Technician	15.0403
RIE	Engineering Design	14.2901
RIE	Engineering/Industrial Management	14.3001
RIE	Forest Products Technology/Technician	03.0404
RIE	Geological Engineering	14.1501
RIE	Geophysical Engineering	14.1601
RIE	Industrial/Manufacturing Technology/Technician	15.0603
RIE	Instrumentation Technology/Technician	15.0404
RIE	Laser and Optical Technology/Technician	15.0304
RIE	Lithographer and Platemaker	48.0206
RIE	Machinist/Machine Technologist	48.0501
RIE	Material Engineering	14.1801
RIE	Materials Science	14.3101
RIE	Mechanical Engineering	14.1901
RIE	Mining and Mineral Engineering	14.2101
RIE	Ocean Engineering	14.2401
RIE	Opticianry/Dispensing Optician	51.1801
RIE	Petroleum Technology/Technician	15.0903
RIE	Physical Science Technology/Technicians, Other	41.0399

HOC	Title	CIP
RIE	Tool and Die Maker/Technologist	48.0507
RIE	Water Quality and Wastewater Treatment Technology/Technician	15.0506
RIE	Wood Science and Pulp/Paper Technology	03.0509
RIC	Civil Engineering/Civil Technology/Technician	15.0201
RIC	Diagnostic Medical Sonography	51.0910
RIC	Heating, Air Conditioning and Refrigeration Technology/Technician	15.0501
RIC	Quality Control Technology/Technician	15.0702
RIC	Sheet Metal Worker	48.0506
RIC	Solar Technology/Technician	15.0505
RAE	Graphic Design, Commercial Art and Illustration	50.0402
RAE	Interior Architecture	04.0501
RSI	Emergency Medical Technology/Technician	51.0904
RSI	Orthoptics	51.1804
RSE	Animal Trainer	01.0505
RSE	Baker/Pastry Chef	12.0501
RSE	Bicycle Mechanic and Repairer	47.0610
RSE	Funeral Services and Mortuary Science	12.0301
RSE	Kitchen Personnel/Cook and Assistant Training	12.0505
RSE	Leatherworkers and Upholsterers, Other	48.0399
RSE	Lineworker	46.0303
RSE	Major Appliance Installer and Repairer	47.0106
RSE	Medical Assistant	51.0801
RSE	Orthotics/Prosthetics	51.2307
RSE	Painter and Wall Coverer	46.0408
RSE	Pharmacy Technician/Assistant	51.0805
RSC	Nuclear/Nuclear Power Technology/Technician	41.0205
REI	Agricultural Mechanization, General	01.0201
REI	Aircraft Mechanic/Technician, Airframe	47.0607
REI	Aircraft Mechanic/Technician, Powerplant	47.0608
REI	Auto/Automotive Mechanic/Technician	47.0604
REI	Biomedical Engineering-Related Technology/Technician	15.0401
REI	Cabinet Maker and Millworker	48.0703
REI	Construction Equipment Operator	49.0202
REI	Construction/Building Inspector	46.0403
REI	Construction/Building Technology/Technician	15.1001
REI	Diesel Engine Mechanic and Repairer	47.0605
REI	Diver	49.0304
REI	Graphic and Printing Equipment Operator, General	48.0201
REI	Greenhouse Operations and Management	01.0604
REI	Horticulture Science	02.0403
REI	Industrial Equipment Main. and Repairers, Other	47.0399
REI	Industrial Machinery Main. and Repairer	47.0303
REI	Instrument Calibration and Repairer	47.0401

HOC	Title	CIP
REI	Landscaping Operations and Management	01.0605
REI	Machine Shop Assistant	48.0503
REI	Mechanical Typesetter and Composer	48.0205
REI	Metallurgical Technology/Technician	15.0611
REI	Motorcycle Mechanic and Repairer	47.0611
REI	Nursery Operations and Management	01.0606
REI	Optical Technician/Assistant	51.1802
REI	Optometric/Ophthalmic Laboratory Technician	51.1006
REI	Plant Sciences, General	02.0401
REI	Plumber and Pipefitter	46.0501
REI	Precision Metal Workers, Other	48.0599
REI	Precision Production Trades, Other	48.9999
REI	Printing Press Operator	48.0208
REI	Small Engine Mechanic and Repairer	47.0606
REI	Turf Management	01.0607
REI	Welder/Welding Technologist	48.0508
REI	Woodworkers, General	48.0701
RES	Agricultural and Food Products Processing Operations and Management	01.0401
RES	Agricultural Animal Husbandry and Production Management	01.0302
RES	Agricultural Power Machinery Operator	01.0204
RES	Agricultural Production Workers and Managers, General	01.0301
RES	Aquaculture Operations and Production Management	01.0303
RES	Art, General	50.0701
RES	Building/Property Main. and Manager	46.0401
RES	Carpenter	46.0201
RES	Construction and Building Finishers and Managers, Other	46.0499
RES	Crop Production Operations and Management	01.0304
RES	Custodian/Caretaker	20.0604
RES	Custom Tailor	20.0305
RES	Drycleaner and Launderer (Commercial)	20.0309
RES	Electrical and Electronics Equipment Installer and Repairer, Other	47.0199
RES	Electrical and Power Transmission Installer, General	46.0301
RES	Electrician	46.0302
RES	Energy Management and Systems Technology/Technician	15.0503
RES	Equestrian/Equine Studies, Horse Management and Training	01.0507
RES	Fire Science/Firefighting	43.0203
RES	Fishing and Fisheries Sciences and Management	03.0301
RES	Fishing Technology/Commercial Fishing	49.0303
RES	Heating, Air Conditioning and Refrigeration Mechanic and Repairer	47.0201
RES	Horticulture Services Operations and Management, General	01.0601
RES	Horticulture Services Operations and Management, Other	01.0699
RES	Industrial Production Technology/Technicians, Other	15.0699
RES	Logging/Timber Harvesting	03.0405
RES	Marine Main. and Ship Repairer	49.0306
RES	Marine Science/Merchant Marine Officer	49.0309
RES	Mason and Tile Setter	46.0101

Dictionary of Holland Occupational Codes

HOC	Title	CIP
RES	Massage	12.0405
RES	Meatcutter	12.0506
RES	Metal and Jewelry Arts	50.0713
RES	Occupational Safety and Health Technology/Technician	15.0701
RES	Operations Management and Supervision	52.0205
RES	Ornamental Horticulture Operations and Management	01.0603
RES	Radio and Television Broadcasting Technology/Technician	10.0104
RES	Stationary Energy Sources Installer and Operator	47.0501
RES	Truck, Bus and Other Commercial Vehicle Operator	49.0205
RES	Water Transportation Workers, Other	49.0399
RES	Wildlife and Wildlands Management	03.0601
RES	Woodworkers, Other	48.0799
REC	Auto/Automotive Body Repairer	47.0603
REC	Business Machine Repairer	47.0102
REC	Ceramics Arts and Ceramics	50.0711
REC	Clothing, Apparel and Textile Workers and Managers, General	20.0301
REC	Communication Systems Installer and Repairer	47.0103
REC	Construction Trades, Other	46.9999
REC	Dental Laboratory Technician	51.0603
REC	Graphic and Printing Equipment Operators, Other	48.0299
REC	Gunsmith	47.0402
REC	Heavy Equipment Main. and Repairer	47.0302
REC	Locksmith and Safe Repairer	47.0403
REC	Musical Instrument Repairer	47.0404
REC	Plastics Technology/Technician	15.0607
REC	Vehicle and Equipment Operators, Other	49.0299
REC	Watch, Clock and Jewelry Repairer	47.0408
RCI	Air Transportation Workers, Other	49.0199
RCI	Industrial Electronics Installer and Repairer	47.0105
RCI	Nuclear and Industrial Radiologic Technology/Technicians, Other	41.0299
RCA	Educational/Instructional Media Technology/Technician	10.0101
RCS	Crafts, Folk Art and Artisanry	50.0201
RCS	Electroencephalograph Technology/Technician	51.0903
RCS	Furniture Designer and Maker	48.0702
RCE	Administrative and Secretarial Services, Other	52.0499
RCE	Commercial Garment and Apparel Worker	20.0303
RCE	Electrical and Electronics Equipment Installer and Repairer, General	47.0101
RCE	Miscellaneous Mechanics and Repairers, Other	47.0499
RCE	Photographic Technology/Technician	10.0103
RCE	Shoe, Boot and Leather Repairer	48.0304
RCE	Upholsterer	48.0303
RCE	Window Treatment Maker and Installer	20.0502

HOC	Title	CIP
IRA	Biopsychology	30.1001
IRA	Cell Biology	26.0401
IRA	Critical Care Surgery Residency	51.2912
IRA	General Surgery Residency	51.2921
IRA	Hand Surgery Residency	51.2923
IRA	Medical Microbiology	51.1308
IRA	Orthopedics/Orthopedic Surgery Residency	51.2942
IRA	Pediatric Orthopedics Residency	51.2949
IRA	Pediatric Surgery Residency	51.2950
IRA	Plastic Surgery Residency	51.2953
IRA	Thoracic Surgery Residency	51.2962
IRA	Vascular Surgery Residency	51.2964
IRA	Virology	26.0619
IRS	Acupuncture and Oriental Medicine	51.2701
IRS	Aerospace Medicine Residency	51.2901
IRS	Agricultural Animal Breeding and Genetics	02.0202
IRS	Agricultural Animal Health	02.0203
IRS	Agricultural Plant Pathology	02.0406
IRS	Agriculture/Agricultural Sciences, General	02.0101
IRS	Agronomy and Crop Science	02.0402
IRS	Anesthesiology Residency	51.2903
IRS	Architectural Engineering	14.0401
IRS	Atmospheric Sciences and Meteorology	40.0401
IRS	Basic Medical Sciences, Other	51.1399
IRS	Biochemistry	26.0202
IRS	Biological Immunology	26.0618
IRS	Biophysics	26.0203
IRS	Biotechnology Research	26.0616
IRS	Botany, General	26.0301
IRS	Botany, Other	26.0399
IRS	Colon and Rectal Surgery Residency	51.2909
IRS	Computer and Information Sciences, General	11.0101
IRS	Critical Care Anesthesiology Residency	51.2910
IRS	Critical Care Medicine Residency	51.2911
IRS	Dairy Science	02.0206
IRS	Dental Clinical Sciences/Graduate Dentistry (M.S., Ph.D.)	51.0501
IRS	Dentistry (D.D.S., D.M.D.)	51.0401
IRS	Developmental and Child Psychology	42.0701
IRS	Diagnostic Radiology Residency	51.2915
IRS	Ecology	26.0603
IRS	Entomology	26.0702
IRS	Epidemiology	51.2203
IRS	Evolutionary Biology	26.0617
IRS	Family Medicine Residency	51.2918
IRS	Forensic Pathology Residency	51.2919
IRS	Forest Management	03.0506
IRS	Forestry Sciences	03.0502
IRS	Gastroenterology Residency	51.2920

HOC	Title	CIP
IRS	Genetics, Plant and Animal	26.0613
IRS	Geochemistry	40.0602
IRS	Geology	40.0601
IRS	Infectious Disease Residency	51.2927
IRS	Internal Medicine Residency	51.2928
IRS	Mathematics and Computer Science	30.0801
IRS	Medical Biochemistry	51.1302
IRS	Medical Clinical Sciences (M.S., Ph.D.)	51.1401
IRS	Medical Genetics	51.1306
IRS	Medical Molecular Biology	51.1309
IRS	Medical Neurobiology	51.1310
IRS	Medical Pathology	51.1312
IRS	Medical Physics/Biophysics	51.1304
IRS	Medical Radiologic Technology/Technician	51.0907
IRS	Medical Residency Programs, Other	51.2999
IRS	Medicine (M.D.)	51.1201
IRS	Microbiology/Bacteriology	26.0501
IRS	Molecular Biology	26.0402
IRS	Neurological Surgery/Neurosurgery Residency	51.2933
IRS	Neurology Residency	51.2934
IRS	Nuclear Medical Technology/Technician	51.0905
IRS	Nuclear Medicine Residency	51.2936
IRS	Nuclear Radiology Residency	51.2937
IRS	Obstetrics and Gynecology Residency	51.2938
IRS	Oceanography	40.0702
IRS	Oncology Residency	51.2940
IRS	Orthodontics Specialty	51.2805
IRS	Otolaryngology Residency	51.2943
IRS	Paleontology	40.0604
IRS	Parasitology	26.0610
IRS	Pharmacology, Human and Animal	26.0705
IRS	Plant Breeding and Genetics	02.0405
IRS	Plant Pathology	26.0305
IRS	Plant Physiology	26.0307
IRS	Polymer/Plastics Engineering	14.3201
IRS	Preventive Medicine Residency	51.2954
IRS	Prosthodontics Specialty	51.2808
IRS	Public Health Medicine Residency	51.2956
IRS	Pulmonary Disease Residency	51.2957
IRS	Radiation Oncology Residency	51.2958
IRS	Radioisotopic Pathology Residency	51.2959
IRS	Soil Sciences	02.0501
IRS	Structural Engineering	14.0803
IRS	Theriogenology	51.3015
IRS	Urology Residency	51.2963
IRS	Veterinary Anesthesiology	51.3001
IRS	Veterinary Dentistry	51.3002
IRS	Veterinary Dermatology	51.3003
IRS	Veterinary Emergency and Critical Care Medicine	51.3004

HOC to CIP

HOC	Title	CIP
IRS	Veterinary Internal Medicine	51.3005
IRS	Veterinary Nutrition	51.3008
IRS	Veterinary Ophthalmology	51.3009
IRS	Veterinary Practice	51.3011
IRS	Veterinary Radiology	51.3013
IRS	Veterinary Surgery	51.3014
IRS	Veterinary Toxicology	51.3016
IRE	Acoustics	40.0809
IRE	Aerospace, Aeronautical and Astronautical Engineering	14.0201
IRE	Agricultural Animal Physiology	02.0205
IRE	Agricultural Engineering	14.0301
IRE	Agricultural Plant Physiology	02.0407
IRE	Analytical Chemistry	40.0502
IRE	Anatomy	26.0601
IRE	Anthropology	45.0201
IRE	Applied Mathematics, General	27.0301
IRE	Archeology	45.0301
IRE	Astronomy	40.0201
IRE	Astrophysics	40.0301
IRE	Bioengineering and Biomedical Engineering	14.0501
IRE	Biological and Physical Sciences	30.0101
IRE	Biometrics	26.0614
IRE	Biostatistics	26.0615
IRE	Blood Banking Residency	51.2904
IRE	Business Statistics	52.1302
IRE	Cartography	45.0702
IRE	Ceramic Sciences and Engineering	14.0601
IRE	Chemical and Atomic/Molecular Physics	40.0802
IRE	Chemical Engineering	14.0701
IRE	Chemical Pathology Residency	51.2906
IRE	Chemistry, General	40.0501
IRE	Civil Engineering, General	14.0801
IRE	Computer Engineering Technology/Technician	15.0301
IRE	Computer Programming	11.0201
IRE	Computer Systems Analysis	11.0501
IRE	Dental Public Health Specialty	51.2802
IRE	Dental/Oral Surgery Specialty	51.2801
IRE	Drafting, General	48.0101
IRE	Earth and Planetary Sciences	40.0703
IRE	Electrical, Electronics and Communication Engineering	14.1001
IRE	Elementary Particle Physics	40.0804
IRE	Endocrinology and Metabolism Residency	51.2917
IRE	Engineering Mechanics	14.1101
IRE	Engineering Physics	14.1201
IRE	Engineering Science	14.1301
IRE	Engineering, General	14.0101
IRE	Engineering-Related Technology/Technician, General	15.1101
IRE	Environmental Health	51.2202

HOC	Title	CIP
IRE	Geography	45.0701
IRE	Geophysics and Seismology	40.0603
IRE	Geotechnical Engineering	14.0802
IRE	Geriatric Medicine Residency	51.2922
IRE	Gerontology	30.1101
IRE	Health and Medical Biostatistics	51.2204
IRE	Hematological Pathology Residency	51.2925
IRE	Hematology Residency	51.2924
IRE	Information Sciences and Systems	11.0401
IRE	Laboratory Animal Medicine	51.3006
IRE	Laboratory Medicine Residency	51.2929
IRE	Management Science	52.1301
IRE	Marine/Aquatic Biology	26.0607
IRE	Mathematical Statistics	27.0501
IRE	Mathematics	27.0101
IRE	Mechanical Drafting	48.0105
IRE	Mechanical Engineering/Mechanical Technology/Technician	15.0805
IRE	Medical Anatomy	51.1301
IRE	Medical Biomathematics and Biometrics	51.1303
IRE	Medical Cell Biology	51.1305
IRE	Medical Laboratory Technician	51.1004
IRE	Medical Pharmacology and Pharmaceutical Sciences	51.2003
IRE	Medical Physiology	51.1313
IRE	Medical Toxicology	51.1314
IRE	Medicinal/Pharmaceutical Chemistry	40.0505
IRE	Metallurgical Engineering	14.2001
IRE	Metallurgy	40.0701
IRE	Musculoskeletal Oncology Residency	51.2930
IRE	Natural Resources Conservation, General	03.0101
IRE	Naval Architecture and Marine Engineering	14.2201
IRE	Nephrology Residency	51.2932
IRE	Neuropathology Residency	51.2935
IRE	Neuroscience	26.0608
IRE	Nuclear Engineering	14.2301
IRE	Nuclear Physics	40.0806
IRE	Operations Research	27.0302
IRE	Optics	40.0807
IRE	Oral Pathology Specialty	51.2804
IRE	Organic Chemistry	40.0504
IRE	Pathology Residency	51.2944
IRE	Pathology, Human and Animal	26.0704
IRE	Pedodontics Specialty	51.2806
IRE	Periodontics Specialty	51.2807
IRE	Petroleum Engineering	14.2501
IRE	Physical and Rehabilitation Medicine Residency	51.2952
IRE	Physical and Theoretical Chemistry	40.0506
IRE	Physical Sciences, General	40.0101
IRE	Physics, General	40.0801
IRE	Physiology, Human and Animal	26.0706

HOC to CIP

HOC	Title	CIP
IRE	Plasma and High-Temperature Physics	40.0805
IRE	Polymer Chemistry	40.0507
IRE	Rheumatology Residency	51.2960
IRE	Robotics Technology/Technician	15.0405
IRE	Solid State and Low-Temperature Physics	40.0808
IRE	Sports Medicine Residency	51.2961
IRE	Textile Sciences and Engineering	14.2801
IRE	Theoretical and Mathematical Physics	40.0810
IRE	Toxicology	26.0612
IRE	Veterinary Clinical Sciences (M.S., Ph.D.)	51.2501
IRE	Veterinary Medicine (D.V.M.)	51.2401
IRE	Veterinary Microbiology	51.3007
IRE	Veterinary Pathology	51.3010
IRE	Veterinary Preventive Medicine	51.3012
IRE	Water Resources Engineering	14.0805
IRE	Zoology, General	26.0701
IRC	Architectural Drafting	48.0102
IRC	Business Computer Programming/Programmer	52.1202
IRC	Cytotechnologist	51.1002
IRC	Electrical/Electronics Drafting	48.0104
IRC	Forensic Technology/Technician	43.0106
IRC	Health and Medical Laboratory Technology/Technicians, Other	51.1099
IAR	Biology, General	26.0101
IAS	Agricultural Economics	01.0103
IAS	Business/Managerial Economics	52.0601
IAS	Development Economics and International Development	45.0604
IAS	Economics, Other	45.0699
IAS	International Economics	45.0605
IAS	Linguistics	16.0102
IAE	Architecture	04.0201
IAE	Experimental Psychology	42.0801
IAE	Peace and Conflict Studies	30.0501
IAE	Physiological Psychology/Psychobiology	42.1101
IAE	Socio-Psychological Sports Studies	31.0506
ISR	Audiology/Hearing Sciences	51.0202
ISR	Business Systems Analysis and Design	52.1203
ISR	Cardiovascular Technology/Technician	51.0901
ISR	Child/Pediatric Neurology Residency	51.2907
ISR	Chiropractic (D.C., D.C.M.)	51.0101
ISR	Dermatology Residency	51.2913
ISR	Dermatopathology Residency	51.2914
ISR	Econometrics and Quantitative Economics	45.0603
ISR	Management Information Systems and Business Data Processing, General	52.1201

HOC	Title	CIP
ISR	Medical Nutrition	51.1311
ISR	Neonatal-Perinatal Medicine Residency	51.2931
ISR	Ophthalmology Residency	51.2941
ISR	Osteopathic Medicine (D.O.)	51.1901
ISR	Perfusion Technology/Technician	51.0906
ISR	Radiation Biology/Radiobiology	26.0611
ISR	Speech-Language Pathology and Audiology	51.0204
ISR	Transportation and Highway Engineering	14.0804
ISA	Applied and Resource Economics	45.0602
ISA	Child Psychiatry Residency	51.2908
ISA	Nursing, Family Practice (Post-R.N.)	51.1605
ISA	Physician Assistant	51.0807
ISA	Psychiatry Residency	51.2955
ISA	Speech-Language Pathology	51.0203
ISE	Actuarial Science	52.0802
ISE	Allergies and Immunology Residency	51.2902
ISE	Cardiology Residency	51.2905
ISE	Communication Disorders Sciences and Services, Other	51.0299
ISE	Criminology	45.0401
ISE	Economics, General	45.0601
ISE	Endodontics Specialty	51.2803
ISE	Foreign Languages and Literatures, General	16.0101
ISE	Immunopathology Residency	51.2926
ISE	Medical Immunology	51.1307
ISE	Medical Technology	51.1005
ISE	Nursing Anesthetist (Post-R.N.)	51.1604
ISE	Nutritional Sciences	26.0609
ISE	Optometry (O.D.)	51.1701
ISE	Pediatric Cardiology Residency	51.2945
ISE	Pediatric Endocrinology Residency	51.2946
ISE	Pediatric Hemato-Oncology Residency	51.2947
ISE	Pediatric Nephrology Residency	51.2948
ISE	Pediatrics Residency	51.2951
ISE	Psychology, General	42.0101
ISE	School Psychology	42.1701
ISE	Zoological Medicine	51.3017
ISC	Occupational Medicine Residency	51.2939
IER	Cognitive Psychology and Psycholinguistics	42.0301
IER	Demography/Population Studies	45.0501
IER	Dental Residency Programs, Other	51.2899
IER	Environmental Science/Studies	03.0102
IER	Industrial/Manufacturing Engineering	14.1701
IER	Inorganic Chemistry	40.0503
IER	Marketing Research	52.1402
IER	Plant Protection (Pest Management)	02.0408

HOC to CIP

From Holland Codes to the Classification of Instructional Programs

HOC	Title	CIP
IER	Sociology	45.1101
IER	Surveying	15.1102
IEA	Social Psychology	42.1601
IES	Criminal Justice Studies	43.0104
IES	Educational Psychology	13.0802
IES	Environmental/Environmental Health Engineering	14.1401
IES	Industrial and Organizational Psychology	42.0901
IES	International Relations and Affairs	45.0901
IES	Pharmacy Administration and Pharmaceutics	51.2002
IES	Urban Affairs/Studies	45.1201
IEC	Pharmacy (B. Pharm., Pharm. D.)	51.2001
ICS	Computer Science	11.0701
AIR	Architectural Environmental Design	04.0401
AIR	Landscape Architecture	04.0601
AIS	English Technical and Business Writing	23.1101
AIE	Arabic Language and Literature	16.1101
AIE	Biblical and Other Theological Languages and Literatures	39.0101
AIE	Chinese Language and Literature	16.0301
AIE	Classical and Ancient Near Eastern Languages and Literatures	16.1299
AIE	Classics and Classical Languages and Literatures	16.1201
AIE	East and Southeast Asian Languages and Literatures, Other	16.0399
AIE	East European Languages and Literatures, Other	16.0499
AIE	French Language and Literature	16.0901
AIE	German Language and Literature	16.0501
AIE	Germanic Languages and Literatures, Other	16.0599
AIE	Greek Language and Literature (Ancient and Medieval)	16.1202
AIE	Greek Language and Literature (Modern)	16.0601
AIE	Hebrew Language and Literature	16.1102
AIE	Italian Language and Literature	16.0902
AIE	Japanese Language and Literature	16.0302
AIE	Latin Language and Literature (Ancient and Medieval)	16.1203
AIE	Medical Illustrating	51.2703
AIE	Middle Eastern Languages and Literatures, Other	16.1199
AIE	Musicology and Ethnomusicology (IAE)	50.0905
AIE	Philosophy	38.0101
AIE	Portuguese Language and Literature	16.0904
AIE	Romance Languages and Literatures, Other	16.0999
AIE	Russian Language and Literature	16.0402
AIE	Scandinavian Languages and Literatures	16.0502
AIE	Slavic Languages and Literatures (other than Russian)	16.0403
AIE	South Asian Languages and Literatures	16.0703
AIE	Spanish Language and Literature	16.0905

HOC	Title	CIP
ASI	Dance Therapy	51.2302
ASE	American Literature (United States)	23.0701
ASE	Comparative Literature	23.0301
ASE	Drawing	50.0705
ASE	English Composition	23.0401
ASE	English Creative Writing	23.0501
ASE	English Language and Literature, General	23.0101
ASE	English Literature (British and Commonwealth)	23.0801
ASE	Music Theory and Composition	50.0904
ASE	Painting	50.0708
ASE	Playwriting and Screenwriting	50.0504
ASE	Religious/Sacred Music	39.0501
ASE	Speech and Rhetorical Studies	23.1001
ASC	Music - Piano and Organ Performance	50.0907
AER	Dance	50.0301
AER	Fashion Design and Illustration	50.0407
AER	Industrial Design	50.0404
AER	Intermedia	50.0706
AER	Make-Up Artist	12.0406
AER	Printmaking	50.0710
AER	Sculpture	50.0709
AER	Technical Theater/Theater Design and Stagecraft	50.0502
AEI	Dramatic/Theater Arts and Stagecraft, Other	50.0599
AES	Drama/Theater Arts, General	50.0501
AES	Fashion Modeling	08.0103
AES	Film/Cinema Studies	50.0601
AES	Fine/Studio Arts	50.0702
AES	Historic Preservation, Conservation and Architectural History	30.1201
AES	Housing Studies, General	19.0601
AES	Interior Design	50.0408
AES	Interior Environments	19.0603
AES	Journalism	09.0401
AES	Music - General Performance	50.0903
AES	Music - Voice and Choral/Opera Performance	50.0908
AES	Music Conducting	50.0906
AES	Music History and Literature	50.0902
AES	Music, General	50.0901
AES	Personal Services Marketing Operations	08.0205
AES	Photography	50.0605
SRI	Athletic Training and Sports Medicine	31.0503
SRI	Emergency Medicine Residency	51.2916
SRI	Physical Therapy	51.2308
SRI	Respiratory Therapy Technician	51.0908

HOC	Title	CIP
SRE	Occupational Therapy	51.2306
SRE	Physical Therapy Assistant	51.0806
SRC	Business Information and Data Processing Services, Other	52.1299
SRC	Data Processing Technology/Technician	11.0301
SIR	Adapted Physical Education/Therapeutic Recreation	31.0502
SIR	Chemistry Teacher Education	13.1323
SIR	Exercise Sciences/Physiology and Movement Studies	31.0505
SIR	Naturopathic Medicine	51.2704
SIR	Nursing Midwifery (Post-R.N.)	51.1607
SIR	Physics Teacher Education	13.1329
SIR	Podiatry (D.P.M., D.P., Pod.D.)	51.2101
SIA	Art Therapy	51.2301
SIA	Biology Teacher Education	13.1322
SIA	Nursing, Adult Health (Post-R.N.)	51.1603
SIA	Nursing, Pediatric (Post-R.N.)	51.1609
SIA	Nursing, Psychiatric/Mental Health (Post-R.N.)	51.1610
SIA	Nursing, Surgical (Post-R.N.)	51.1612
SIA	Psychoanalysis	51.2705
SIE	Communication Disorders, General	51.0201
SIE	Counseling Psychology	42.0601
SIE	Food Sciences and Technology	02.0301
SIE	Foods and Nutrition Science	19.0502
SIE	Foreign Language Interpretation and Translation	16.0103
SIE	Medical Dietician	51.2702
SIE	Medical Records Administration	51.0706
SIE	Medieval and Renaissance Studies	30.1301
SIE	Movement Therapy	51.2304
SIE	Nursing (R.N. Training)	51.1601
SIE	Nursing Science (Post-R.N.)	51.1608
SIE	Nursing, Maternal/Child Health (Post-R.N.)	51.1606
SIE	Nursing, Public Health (Post-R.N.)	51.1611
SIE	Rehabilitation/Therapeutic Services, Other	51.2399
SIE	Science, Technology and Society	30.1501
SIE	Social and Philosophical Foundations of Education	13.0901
SIE	Social Sciences, General	45.0101
SIE	Veterinarian Assistant/Animal Health Technician	51.0808
SAI	Dental Assistant	51.0601
SAI	Dental Hygienist	51.0602
SAE	Art Teacher Education	13.1302
SAE	Computer Teacher Education	13.1321
SAE	Divinity/Ministry (B.D., M.Div.)	39.0602
SAE	Drama and Dance Teacher Education	13.1324
SAE	English Teacher Education	13.1305

HOC	Title	CIP
SAE	Family and Marriage Counseling	19.0703
SAE	Foreign Languages Teacher Education	13.1306
SAE	French Language Teacher Education	13.1325
SAE	German Language Teacher Education	13.1326
SAE	Health Teacher Education	13.1307
SAE	History Teacher Education	13.1328
SAE	Junior High/Intermediate/Middle School Teacher Education	13.1203
SAE	Marketing Operations Teacher Education/Marketing and Distributive Teacher Education	13.1310
SAE	Mathematics Teacher Education	13.1311
SAE	Music Teacher Education	13.1312
SAE	Music Therapy	51.2305
SAE	Philosophy and Religion	38.9999
SAE	Pre-Theological/Pre-Ministerial Studies	39.0605
SAE	Rabbinical and Talmudic Studies (M.H.L./Rav.)	39.0604
SAE	Reading Teacher Education	13.1315
SAE	Religion/Religious Studies	38.0201
SAE	Science Teacher Education, General	13.1316
SAE	Social Science Teacher Education	13.1317
SAE	Social Studies Teacher Education	13.1318
SAE	Spanish Language Teacher Education	13.1330
SAE	Speech Teacher Education	13.1331
SAE	Technology Teacher Education/Industrial Arts Teacher Education	13.1309
SAE	Theology/Theological Studies	39.0601
SAC	Practical Nurse (L.P.N. Training)	51.1613
SER	Air Traffic Controller	49.0105
SER	Business Systems Networking and Telecommunications	52.1204
SER	Criminal Justice and Corrections, Other	43.0199
SER	Custodial, Housekeeping and Home Services Workers and Managers, General	20.0601
SER	Education Administration and Supervision, General	13.0401
SER	Education, General	13.0101
SER	Health Aide	51.2601
SER	Health and Physical Education, General	31.0501
SER	Home Health Aide	51.1615
SER	Homemaker's Aide	20.0606
SER	Hospital/Health Facilities Administration	51.0702
SER	Law Enforcement/Police Science	43.0107
SER	Nurse Assistant/Aide	51.1614
SER	Protective Services, Other	43.9999
SER	Range Science and Management	02.0409
SER	Teaching English as a Second Language/Foreign Language	13.1401
SER	Vocational Rehabilitation Counseling	51.2310
SEI	African Studies	05.0101
SEI	Afro-American (Black) Studies	05.0201
SEI	Alcohol/Drug Abuse Counseling	51.1501

HOC	Title	CIP
SEI	American (United States) History	45.0802
SEI	American Government and Politics	45.1002
SEI	American Indian/Native American Studies	05.0202
SEI	American Studies/Civilization	05.0102
SEI	Asian Studies	05.0103
SEI	Asian-American Studies	05.0206
SEI	Business Home Economics	19.0201
SEI	Canadian Studies	05.0115
SEI	Clinical Psychology	42.0201
SEI	Community Health Liaison	51.0301
SEI	Community Psychology (IAE)	42.0401
SEI	Consumer Economics and Science	19.0402
SEI	Counselor Education Counseling and Guidance Services	13.1101
SEI	Dietetics/Human Nutritional Services	19.0503
SEI	East Asian Studies	05.0104
SEI	Eastern European Area Studies	05.0105
SEI	Education of the Gifted and Talented	13.1004
SEI	Educational Assessment, Testing and Measurement	13.0604
SEI	European History	45.0803
SEI	European Studies	05.0106
SEI	Family and Community Studies	19.0301
SEI	Foods and Nutrition Studies, General	19.0501
SEI	Hispanic-American Studies	05.0203
SEI	History and Philosophy of Science and Technology	45.0804
SEI	Home Economics Communications	19.0202
SEI	Home Economics, General	19.0101
SEI	International and Comparative Education	13.0701
SEI	Islamic Studies	05.0204
SEI	Jewish/Judaic Studies	05.0205
SEI	Latin American Studies	05.0107
SEI	Middle Eastern Studies	05.0108
SEI	Nursing Administration (Post-R.N.)	51.1602
SEI	Pacific Area Studies	05.0109
SEI	Political Science and Government, Other	45.1099
SEI	Psychiatric/Mental Health Services Technician	51.1502
SEI	Russian and Slavic Area Studies	05.0110
SEI	Scandinavian Area Studies	05.0111
SEI	South Asian Studies	05.0112
SEI	Southeast Asian Studies	05.0113
SEI	Western European Studies	05.0114
SEI	Women's Studies	05.0207
SEA	Adult and Continuing Teacher Education	13.1201
SEA	Agricultural Teacher Education (Vocational)	13.1301
SEA	Bible/Biblical Studies	39.0201
SEA	Bilingual/Bicultural Education	13.0201
SEA	Business Teacher Education (Vocational)	13.1303
SEA	Child Care Services Manager	20.0203
SEA	Clinical and Medical Social Work	51.1503

Part 2: From Holland Codes to Occupations

From Holland Codes to the Classification of Instructional Programs

HOC	Title	CIP
SEA	College/Postsecondary Student Counseling and Personnel Services	13.1102
SEA	Driver and Safety Teacher Education	13.1304
SEA	Educational Supervision	13.0404
SEA	Elementary Teacher Education	13.1202
SEA	General Teacher Education, Other	13.1299
SEA	Gerontological Services	19.0705
SEA	Health Occupations Teacher Education (Vocational)	13.1327
SEA	Home Economics Teacher Education (Vocational)	13.1308
SEA	Individual and Family Development Studies, General	19.0701
SEA	Library Science/Librarianship	25.0101
SEA	Marketing Operations/Marketing and Distribution, Other	08.9999
SEA	Missions/Missionary Studies and Evangelism	39.0301
SEA	Pastoral Counseling and Specialized Ministries	39.0701
SEA	Physical Education Teaching and Coaching	13.1314
SEA	Pre-Elementary/Early Childhood/Kindergarten Teacher Education	13.1204
SEA	Public Health Education and Promotion	51.2207
SEA	Religious Education	39.0401
SEA	Secondary Teacher Education	13.1205
SEA	Teacher Education, Multiple Levels	13.1206
SEA	Teacher Education, Specific Academic and Vocational Programs	13.1399
SEA	Technical Teacher Education (Vocational)	13.1319
SEA	Trade and Industrial Teacher Education (Vocational)	13.1320
SEC	Administration of Special Education	13.0402
SEC	Agricultural Extension	02.0102
SEC	Arts Management	50.0704
SEC	Bartender/Mixologist	12.0502
SEC	Child Care and Guidance Workers and Managers, General	20.0201
SEC	Child Care Provider/Assistant	20.0202
SEC	Child Growth, Care and Development Studies	19.0706
SEC	Community Organization, Resources and Services	44.0201
SEC	Dietician Assistant	20.0404
SEC	Education of the Autistic	13.1013
SEC	Education of the Blind and Visually Handicapped	13.1009
SEC	Education of the Deaf and Hearing Impaired	13.1003
SEC	Education of the Emotionally Handicapped	13.1005
SEC	Education of the Mentally Handicapped	13.1006
SEC	Education of the Multiple Handicapped	13.1007
SEC	Education of the Physically Handicapped	13.1008
SEC	Education of the Specific Learning Disabled	13.1011
SEC	Education of the Speech Impaired	13.1012
SEC	Elder Care Provider/Companion	20.0602
SEC	Human Resources Management	52.1001
SEC	Hypnotherapy	51.2303
SEC	Mental Health Services, Other	51.1599
SEC	Paralegal/Legal Assistant	22.0103
SEC	Recreational Therapy	51.2309
SEC	Social Work	44.0701
SEC	Special Education, General	13.1001

Part 2: From Holland Codes to Occupations

From Holland Codes to the Classification of Instructional Programs

HOC	Title	CIP
SEC	Teacher Assistant/Aide	13.1501
SCR	Blood Bank Technology/Technician	51.1001
SCR	Health and Medical Assistants, Other	51.0899
SCR	Nursing, Other	51.1699
SCE	Business Computer Facilities Operator	52.1205
SCE	Food Sales Operations	08.0906
SCE	Library Assistant	25.0301
SCE	Occupational Therapy Assistant	51.0803
SCE	Sign Language Interpreter	51.0205
ERI	Systems Engineering	14.2701
ERS	Agricultural Mechanization, Other	01.0299
ERS	Agricultural Supplies Retailing and Wholesaling	01.0501
ERS	Art History, Criticism and Conservation	50.0703
ERS	Business Administration and Management, General	52.0201
ERS	Business, General	52.0101
ERS	Culinary Arts/Chef Training	12.0503
ERS	Forest Harvesting and Production Technology/Technician	03.0401
ERS	Home Furnishings and Equipment Installers and Consultants	20.0501
ERS	Natural Resources Law Enforcement and Protective Services	03.0203
ERS	Sport and Fitness Administration/Management	31.0504
ERC	Petroleum Products Retailing Operations	08.1209
EIR	Natural Resources Management and Policy	03.0201
EIS	Architectural Urban Design and Planning	04.0701
EIS	City/Urban, Community and Regional Planning	04.0301
EIS	Public Health, General	51.2201
EIS	Public Policy Analysis	44.0501
EAR	Floristry Marketing Operations	08.0503
EAS	Acting and Directing	50.0503
EAS	Auctioneering	08.0701
EAS	Broadcast Journalism	09.0402
ESR	Adult and Continuing Education Administration	13.0403
ESR	Agricultural Business and Management, General	01.0101
ESR	Agricultural Business/Agribusiness Operations	01.0102
ESR	Aviation Management	49.0104
ESR	Barber/Hairstylist	12.0402
ESR	Business and Personal Services Marketing Operations, Other	08.0299
ESR	Business Marketing and Marketing Management	52.1401
ESR	Business Services Marketing Operations	08.0204
ESR	Communications, General	09.0101

Part 2: From Holland Codes to Occupations

From Holland Codes to the Classification of Instructional Programs

HOC	Title	CIP
ESR	Corrections/Correctional Administration	43.0102
ESR	Cosmetologist	12.0403
ESR	Criminal Justice/Law Enforcement Administration	43.0103
ESR	Enterprise Management and Operation, General	52.0701
ESR	Entrepreneurship	08.0301
ESR	Executive Housekeeper	20.0605
ESR	Farm and Ranch Management	01.0104
ESR	Fire Protection and Safety Technology/Technician	43.0201
ESR	Fire Services Administration	43.0202
ESR	Flight Attendant	49.0106
ESR	Food and Beverage/Restaurant Operations Manager	12.0504
ESR	Food Caterer	20.0405
ESR	Food Products Retailing and Wholesaling Operations	08.0601
ESR	Food Systems Administration	19.0505
ESR	Franchise Operation	52.0702
ESR	General Distribution Operations	08.0709
ESR	General Marketing Operations	08.0708
ESR	Health Products and Services Marketing Operations	08.1301
ESR	Higher Education Administration	13.0406
ESR	History, General	45.0801
ESR	Hospitality/Administration Management	52.0901
ESR	Hotel/Motel and Restaurant Management	52.0902
ESR	Institutional Food Services Administrator	20.0409
ESR	Institutional Food Workers and Administrators, General	20.0401
ESR	Labor/Personnel Relations and Studies	52.1002
ESR	Logistics and Materials Management	52.0203
ESR	Museology/Museum Studies	30.1401
ESR	Organizational Behavior Studies	52.1003
ESR	Parks, Recreation and Leisure Facilities Management	31.0301
ESR	Public Administration	44.0401
ESR	Public/Applied History and Archival Administration	45.0805
ESR	Purchasing, Procurement and Contracts Management	52.0202
ESR	Real Estate	52.1501
ESR	Recreation Products/Services Marketing Operations	08.0903
ESR	Umpires and Other Sports Officials	12.0204
ESR	Vehicle and Petroleum Products Marketing Operations, Other	08.1299
ESR	Vehicle Marketing Operations	08.1208
ESR	Vehicle Parts and Accessories Marketing Operations	08.1203
ESR	Waiter/Waitress and Dining Room Manager	12.0507
ESI	Educational Evaluation and Research	13.0601
ESI	Educational Statistics and Research Methods	13.0603
ESI	Elementary, Middle and Secondary Education Administration	13.0405
ESI	International Business	52.1101
ESI	International Finance	52.0806
ESI	Law (LL.B., J.D.)	22.0101
ESI	Non-Profit and Public Management	52.0206
ESI	Political Science, General	45.1001
ESI	Public Finance	52.0808

From Holland Codes to the Classification of Instructional Programs

HOC	Title	CIP
ESA	Advertising	09.0201
ESA	Apparel and Accessories Marketing Operations, General	08.0101
ESA	Apparel and Accessories Marketing Operations, Other	08.0199
ESA	Clothing/Apparel and Textile Studies	19.0901
ESA	Community and Junior College Administration	13.0407
ESA	Curriculum and Instruction	13.0301
ESA	Drama/Theater Literature, History and Criticism	50.0505
ESA	Educational/Instructional Media Design	13.0501
ESA	Fashion and Fabric Consultant	20.0306
ESA	Fashion Merchandising	08.0102
ESA	Film-Video Making/Cinematography and Production	50.0602
ESA	General Buying Operations	08.0704
ESA	General Retailing Operations	08.0705
ESA	General Selling Skills and Sales Operations	08.0706
ESA	Home Products Marketing Operations	08.0809
ESA	Juridical Science/Legal Specialization (LL.M., M.C.L., J.S.D./S.J.D.)	22.0104
ESA	Mass Communications	09.0403
ESA	Music Business Management and Merchandising	50.0909
ESA	Office Products Marketing Operations	08.0810
ESA	Public Relations and Organizational Communications	09.0501
ESA	Travel-Tourism Management	52.0903
ESC	Card Dealer	12.0203
ESC	Executive Assistant/Secretary	52.0402
ESC	Finance, General	52.0801
ESC	Financial Planning	52.0804
ESC	Financial Services Marketing Operations	08.0401
ESC	Health and Medical Administrative Services, Other	51.0799
ESC	Health System/Health Services Administration	51.0701
ESC	Hospitality and Recreation Marketing Operations, General	08.0901
ESC	Hotel/Motel Services Marketing Operations	08.0902
ESC	Insurance and Risk Management	52.0805
ESC	Insurance Marketing Operations	08.1001
ESC	International Business Marketing	52.1403
ESC	Investments and Securities	52.0807
ESC	Occupational Health and Industrial Hygiene	51.2206
ESC	Office Supervision and Management	52.0204
ESC	Parks, Recreation and Leisure Studies	31.0101
ESC	Radio and Television Broadcasting	09.0701
ESC	Security and Loss Prevention Services	43.0109
ESC	Taxation	52.1601
ESC	Tourism Promotion Operations	08.1104
ESC	Travel Services Marketing Operations	08.1105
ECS	Health Unit Coordinator/Ward Clerk	51.0703
ECS	Health Unit Manager/Ward Supervisor	51.0704
CRI	Medical Laboratory Assistant	51.0802

Part 2: From Holland Codes to Occupations

From Holland Codes to the Classification of Instructional Programs

HOC	Title	CIP
CRA	Desktop Publishing Equipment Operator	48.0212
CRE	Computer Typography and Composition Equipment Operator	48.0211
CRE	Electrolysis Technician	12.0404
CIR	Health and Medical Diagnostic and Treatment Services, Other	51.0999
CIS	Medical Records Technology/Technician	51.0707
CIS	Ophthalmic Medical Assistant	51.0804
CIS	Ophthalmic Medical Technologist	51.1803
CSR	Accounting Technician	52.0302
CSR	Court Reporter	52.0405
CSI	Business Communications	52.0501
CSE	Banking and Financial Support Services	52.0803
CSE	Fiber, Textile and Weaving Arts	50.0712
CSE	General Office/Clerical and Typing Services	52.0408
CSE	Hematology Technology/Technician	51.1003
CSE	Information Processing/Data Entry Technician	52.0407
CSE	Legal Administrative Assistant/Secretary	52.0403
CSE	Medical Office Management	51.0705
CSE	Medical Transcription	51.0708
CEI	Accounting	52.0301
CES	Administrative Assistant/Secretarial Science, General	52.0401
CES	Medical Administrative Assistant/Secretary	52.0404
CES	Receptionist	52.0406
—-	General Studies	24.0102
—-	Humanities/Humanistic Studies	24.0103
—-	Liberal Arts and Sciences/Liberal Studies	24.0101
—-	Military Technologies	29.0101

HOC	Cx	Title	GOE
RIS	67	Forestry and Logging	03.01.04
RIE	67	Air	05.04.01
RIE	65	Industrial and Safety	05.03.06
RIE	64	Drafting	05.03.02
RIE	64	Petroleum	05.03.04
RIE	62	Physical Sciences	02.04.01
RIE	60	Packaging and Storing	05.03.09
RIE	59	Machining	05.05.07
RIE	58	Electrical-Electronic	05.03.05
RIE	57	Machine Set-up and Operation	06.01.03
RIE	56	Printing	05.05.13
RIE	56	Woodworking	05.05.08
RIC	65	Mechanical	05.03.07
RSE	60	Environmental Control	05.03.08
RSE	59	Electrical	05.07.03
RSE	58	Mechanical	05.07.02
RSE	54	Performing	12.01.03
RSE	51	Food Preparation	05.10.08
RSE	49	Group Transportation	09.03.01
RSE	48	Animal Service	03.03.02
REI	61	Specialty Cropping	03.01.03
REI	61	Water	05.04.02
REI	59	Electrical-Electronic Equipment Repair	05.05.10
REI	59	Scientific, Medical, and Technical Equipment Fabrication and Repair	05.05.11
REI	58	Construction and Maintenance	05.05.02
REI	58	Mechanical Work	05.05.09
REI	56	Inspection	06.01.05
REI	56	Metal Fabrication and Repair	05.05.06
REI	55	Dyeing	05.05.16
REI	55	Graphic Arts and Related Crafts	01.06.01
REI	54	Precision Hand Work	06.01.04
REI	53	Machine Set-up	06.01.02
REI	52	Drilling and Oil Exploration	05.11.03
REI	52	Rail Vehicle Operation	05.08.02
REI	51	Equipment Operation, Chemical Processing	06.02.11
REI	51	Equipment Operation, Welding, Brazing, and Soldering	06.02.19
REI	50	Coating and Plating	06.02.21
REI	50	Environmental	05.07.04
REI	50	Equipment Operation, Rubber, Plastics, and Glass Processing	06.02.13
REI	50	Equipment Operation, Clay and Coke Processing	06.02.17
REI	50	Equipment Operation, Assorted materials Processing	06.02.18
REI	50	Logging and Lumber	05.07.06
REI	49	Equipment Operation, Paper and Paper Products Processing	06.02.14

Part 2: From Holland Codes to Occupations

From Holland Codes to the Guide for Occupational Exploration

HOC	Cx	Title	GOE
REI	49	Machine Work, Stone, Glass, and Clay	06.02.08
REI	49	Mining and Quarrying	05.11.02
REI	48	Construction	05.11.01
REI	48	Truck Driving	05.08.01
REI	47	Boat Operation	05.08.04
REI	47	Braking, Switching, and Coupling	05.12.05
REI	47	Individual Transportation	09.03.02
REI	47	Machine Work, Wood	06.02.03
REA	57	Arts and Crafts	01.06.02
RES	62	Farming	03.01.01
RES	60	Nursery and Groundskeeping	03.02.03
RES	59	Electrical-Electronic Systems Installation and Repair	05.05.05
RES	59	Specialty Breeding	03.01.02
RES	59	Supervision and Instruction	06.01.01
RES	58	Supervision	06.02.01
RES	57	Electricity Generation and Transmission	05.06.01
RES	57	Farming	03.02.01
RES	57	Forestry and Logging	03.02.02
RES	57	Oil, Gas, and Water Distribution	05.06.03
RES	57	Plumbing and Pipefitting	05.05.03
RES	56	Painting, Plastering, and Paperhanging	05.05.04
RES	55	Gem Cutting and Finishing	05.05.14
RES	55	Musical Instrument Fabrication and Repair	05.05.12
RES	54	Custom Sewing, Tailoring, and Upholstering	05.05.15
RES	54	Masonry, Stone, and Brick Work	05.05.01
RES	53	Animal Training	03.03.01
RES	53	Blasting	05.10.06
RES	53	Emergency Responding	04.02.04
RES	53	Mechanical	05.10.02
RES	53	Stationary Engineering	05.06.02
RES	52	Equipment Operation, Petroleum and Gas Processing	06.02.12
RES	52	Manual Work, Food Processing	06.02.28
RES	52	Structural-Mechanical-Electrical-Electronic	05.10.04
RES	51	Environmental	05.10.09
RES	51	Structural	05.10.01
RES	50	Equipment Operation, Metal Processing	06.02.10
RES	50	Equipment Operation, Food Processing	06.02.15
RES	49	Equipment Operation, Textile, Fabric, and Leather Processing	06.02.16
RES	49	Machine Work, Paper	06.02.04
RES	47	Services	03.04.05
RES	42	Forestry and Logging	03.04.02
RES	42	Hoisting, Conveying	05.12.04
RES	40	Loading, Moving	05.12.03
RES	40	Packaging-Wrapping	09.05.10
RES	40	Welding	05.12.11

HOC	Cx	Title	GOE
REC	58	Processing	05.06.04
REC	54	Structural	05.07.01
REC	53	Electrical-Electronic	05.10.03
REC	53	Estimating, Scheduling, and Record Keeping	05.09.02
REC	53	Painting, Dyeing, and Coating	05.10.07
REC	51	Inspecting, Testing, and Repairing	06.03.01
REC	51	Shipping, Receiving, and Stock Checking	05.09.01
REC	50	Machine Work, Metal and Plastics	06.02.02
REC	50	Manual Work, Laying Out and Marking	06.02.31
REC	48	Elevator Services	09.05.09
REC	48	Machine Work, Rubber	06.02.07
REC	46	Manual Work, Stone, Glass, and Clay	06.02.30
REC	46	Materials Handling	05.11.04
REC	45	Nursery and Groundskeeping	03.04.04
REC	45	Services Requiring Driving	05.08.03
REC	44	General Wardrobe Services	09.05.07
REC	44	Mechanical Work	05.12.15
REC	43	Equipment Operation, Chemical Processing	06.04.11
REC	43	Hunting and Fishing	03.04.03
REC	43	Mining, Quarrying, Drilling	05.12.02
REC	43	Pumping	05.12.06
REC	43	Structural Work	05.12.12
REC	42	Crushing, Mixing, Separating, and Chipping	05.12.07
REC	42	Farming	03.04.01
REC	42	Reproduction Services	05.12.19
REC	41	Cleaning and Maintenance	05.12.18
REC	41	Equipment Operation, Food Processing	06.04.15
REC	41	Equipment Operation, Textile, Fabric and Leather Processing	06.04.16
REC	41	Equipment Operation, Clay Processing	06.04.17
REC	41	Equipment Operation, Wood Processing	06.04.18
REC	41	Heating and Melting	05.12.10
REC	41	Lubricating	05.12.08
REC	41	Manual Work, Assembly Large Parts	06.04.22
REC	40	Laundering, Dry Cleaning	06.04.35
REC	40	Loading, Moving, Hoisting, and Conveying	06.04.40
REC	40	Machine Work, Paper	06.04.04
REC	40	Manual Work, Wood	06.04.25
REC	40	Masonry	05.12.09
REC	39	Cleaning	06.04.39
REC	39	Manual Work, Food Processing	06.04.28
RCS	48	Machine Assembling	06.02.20
RCS	46	Machine Work, Textiles	06.02.06
RCE	52	Reproduction	05.10.05
RCE	51	Hand Lettering, Painting, and Decorating	01.06.03
RCE	49	Manual Work, Assembly Large Parts	06.02.22
RCE	48	Machine Work, Assorted Materials	06.02.09

HOC	Cx	Title	GOE
RCE	48	Manual Work, Assembly Small Parts	06.02.23
RCE	47	Manual Work, Assorted Materials	06.02.32
RCE	47	Manual Work, Wood	06.02.25
RCE	47	Verifying, Recording, and Marking	05.09.03
RCE	46	Manual Work, Metal and Plastics	06.02.24
RCE	46	Manual Work, Textile, Fabric and Leather	06.02.27
RCE	45	Cutting and Finishing	05.12.13
RCE	45	Manual Work, Rubber	06.02.29
RCE	44	Electrical Work	05.12.16
RCE	44	Equipment Operation, Petroleum, Gas, and Coal Processing	06.04.12
RCE	44	Manual Work, Paper	06.02.26
RCE	43	Equipment Operation, Metal Processing	06.04.10
RCE	43	Inspecting, Grading, Sorting, Weighing, and Recording	06.03.02
RCE	43	Machine Work, Leather and Fabrics	06.02.05
RCE	43	Painting, Caulking, and Coating	05.12.14
RCE	43	Signalling	05.12.20
RCE	42	Equipment Operation, Assorted Materials Processing	06.04.19
RCE	42	Manual Work, Welding and Flame Cutting	06.04.31
RCE	41	Equipment Operation, Rubber, Plastics, and Glass Processing	06.04.13
RCE	41	Equipment Operation, Paper Making	06.04.14
RCE	41	Food Preparation	05.12.17
RCE	41	Machine Work, Assorted Materials	06.04.09
RCE	41	Machine Work, Brushing, Spraying, and Coating	06.04.21
RCE	41	Machine Work, Fabric and Leather	06.04.05
RCE	41	Machine Work, Metal and Plastics	06.04.02
RCE	41	Machine Work, Stone, Glass, and Clay	06.04.08
RCE	41	Manual Work, Casting and Molding	06.04.32
RCE	41	Manual Work, Metal and Plastics	06.04.24
RCE	41	Manual Work, Stamping, Marking, Labeling, and Ticketing	06.04.37
RCE	41	Manual Work, Stone, Glass, and Clay	06.04.30
RCE	40	Filling	06.04.36
RCE	40	Machine Assembling	06.04.20
RCE	40	Machine Work, Rubber	06.04.07
RCE	40	Machine Work, Textiles	06.04.06
RCE	40	Machine Work, Wood	06.04.03
RCE	40	Manual Work, Assembly Small Parts	06.04.23
RCE	40	Manual Work, Assorted Materials	06.04.34
RCE	40	Manual Work, Brushing, Spraying, and Coating	06.04.33
RCE	40	Manual Work, Paper	06.04.26
RCE	40	Manual Work, Rubber	06.04.29
RCE	40	Wrapping and Packing	06.04.38
RCE	39	Manual Work, Textile, Fabric and Leather	06.04.27
IRS	76	Medicine and Surgery	02.03.01
IRS	76	Plant Specialization	02.02.02
IRS	75	Food Research	02.02.04
IRS	68	Veterinary Medicine	02.03.03
IRS	61	Life Sciences	02.04.02

Part 2: From Holland Codes to Occupations
From Holland Codes to the Guide for Occupational Exploration

HOC	Cx	Title	GOE
IRE	79	Plant and Animal Specialization	02.02.03
IRE	77	Theoretical Research	02.01.01
IRE	76	Animal Specialization	02.02.01
IRE	75	Dentistry	02.03.02
IRE	75	Systems Design	05.01.03
IRE	74	General Engineering	05.01.08
IRE	73	Design	05.01.07
IRE	72	Testing and Quality Control	05.01.04
IRE	71	Research	05.01.01
IRE	70	Data Processing Design	11.01.01
IRE	70	Work Planning and Utilization	05.01.06
IAS	71	Economic	11.03.05
ISR	69	Health Specialties	02.03.04
ISA	66	Writing	11.08.02
IER	76	Technology	02.01.02
IER	75	Environmental Protection	05.01.02
IER	72	Data Analysis	11.01.02
IER	66	Surveying	05.03.01
IES	76	Psychological	11.03.01
AIS	65	Instructing and Appraising	01.02.01
ASE	70	Composing and Arranging	01.04.02
ASE	68	Creative Writing	01.01.02
ASE	62	Studio Art	01.02.02
ASC	65	Instrumental Performing	01.04.04
AER	61	Performing	01.05.02
AES	70	Critiquing	01.01.03
AES	69	Editing	11.08.01
AES	68	Editing	01.01.01
AES	67	Instructing and Directing	01.04.01
AES	65	Vocal Performing	01.04.03
AES	64	Commercial Art	01.02.03
AES	62	Instructing and Choreography	01.05.01
AES	60	Performing	01.03.02
AES	45	Personal Appearance	01.08.01
AEC	49	Psychic Science	01.07.01
SRE	53	Patient Care	10.03.02

Part 2: From Holland Codes to Occupations

From Holland Codes to the Guide for Occupational Exploration

HOC	Cx	Title	GOE
SIR	64	Therapy and Rehabilitation	10.02.02
SIE	67	Nursing	10.02.01
SER	67	Teaching and Instructing, General	11.02.01
SER	67	Teaching, Vocational and Industrial	11.02.02
SER	66	Individual Rights	11.10.02
SER	63	Coaching and Instructing	12.01.01
SER	60	Food Preparation	05.05.17
SER	59	Investigating	04.01.02
SER	55	Cosmetology	09.02.01
SER	49	Detention	04.02.01
SEI	73	Justice Administration	11.04.01
SEI	66	Counseling and Social Work	10.01.02
SEI	66	Immigration and Customs	11.10.04
SEI	66	Translating and Interpreting	11.08.04
SEI	64	Occupational	11.03.04
SEA	65	Religious	10.01.01
SEA	64	Instructing and Directing	01.03.01
SEA	64	Narrating and Announcing	01.03.03
SEC	70	Health and Safety Services	11.07.02
SEC	65	Specialized Teaching	10.02.03
SEC	65	Teaching, Home Economics, Agriculture, and Related	11.02.03
SEC	63	Certifying	07.01.05
SEC	62	Expediting and Coordinating	05.03.03
SEC	62	Interviewing	07.01.01
SEC	61	Library Services	11.02.04
SEC	47	Care of Others	10.03.03
SCE	52	Switchboard Services	07.04.06
ERI	70	Sales Engineering	05.01.05
ERA	52	Performing	12.02.01
ERS	68	Systems	05.02.01
ERS	67	Processing and Manufacturing	05.02.03
ERS	65	Materials Handling	05.02.07
ERS	63	Maintenance and Construction	05.02.02
ERS	62	Investigating	07.01.06
ERS	62	Mining, Logging, and Petroleum Production	05.02.05
ERS	62	Services	05.02.06
ERS	58	Instruction and Supervision	09.03.03
ERS	58	Supervision	06.04.01
ERS	57	Supervision	05.12.01
ERS	52	Driving-Selling	08.02.07

Part 2: From Holland Codes to Occupations

From Holland Codes to the Guide for Occupational Exploration

HOC	Cx	Title	GOE
ERS	49	Property and People	04.02.02
ERS	45	Individualized Services	09.05.06
ERS	45	Portering and Baggage Services	09.05.03
ERC	55	Petroleum	05.07.05
ERC	54	Services	03.02.04
ERC	46	Food Services	09.05.02
EIS	69	Sociological	11.03.02
EAS	70	Writing and Broadcasting	11.08.03
EAS	66	Records Systems Analysis	11.06.02
ESR	71	Management Services: Non-Government	11.05.01
ESR	71	Recreation Services	11.07.04
ESR	70	Budget and Financial Control	11.06.05
ESR	69	Conciliation	11.04.03
ESR	68	Administrative Specialization	11.05.02
ESR	68	Management Services: Government	11.05.03
ESR	67	Sales and Purchasing Management	11.05.04
ESR	66	Claims Settlement	11.12.01
ESR	66	Communications	05.02.04
ESR	66	Rental and Leasing	11.12.02
ESR	64	Booking	11.12.03
ESR	64	Services	11.11.04
ESR	64	Transportation	11.11.03
ESR	63	Health and Safety	11.10.03
ESR	63	Lodging	11.11.01
ESR	63	Recreation and Amusement	11.11.02
ESR	62	Intangible Sales	08.01.02
ESR	62	Managing	04.01.01
ESR	62	Technical Sales	08.01.01
ESR	62	Wholesale-Retail	11.11.05
ESR	59	Company Policy	11.10.05
ESR	55	Social and Recreational Services	09.01.01
ESR	53	Barbering	09.02.02
ESR	52	Officiating	12.01.02
ESR	49	Law and Order	04.02.03
ESR	45	Entertaining	01.07.03
ESR	44	Physical Conditioning	09.05.01
ESI	69	Historical	11.03.03
ESI	66	Procurement Negotiations	11.12.04
ESA	74	Legal Practice	11.04.02
ESA	68	Educational Services	11.07.03
ESA	67	Social Services	11.07.01
ESA	66	Public Relations	11.09.03
ESA	65	Sales	11.09.01

Dictionary of Holland Occupational Codes

HOC	Cx	Title	GOE
ESA	64	Fund and Membership Solicitation	11.09.02
ESA	63	Brokering	11.06.04
ESA	63	Purchasing Sales	08.01.03
ESA	62	Real Estate	08.02.04
ESA	58	Services	08.02.06
ESA	58	Wholesale	08.02.01
ESA	57	Retail	08.02.02
ESA	57	Wholesale and Retail	08.02.03
ESA	56	Demonstration and Sales	08.02.05
ESA	54	Soliciting-Selling	08.02.08
ESA	53	Announcing	01.07.02
ESC	67	Abstracting, Document Preparation	11.04.04
ESC	66	Risk and Profit Analysis	11.06.03
ESC	64	Finance	11.10.01
ESC	61	Administration	07.01.02
ESC	56	Food Services	09.01.03
ESC	56	Order, Complaint, and Claims handling	07.04.02
ESC	56	Test Administration	07.01.07
ESC	52	Guide Services	09.01.02
ESC	52	Safety and Comfort Services	09.01.04
ESC	49	Food Services	09.04.01
ESC	49	Sales Services	09.04.02
ESC	48	Doorkeeping Services	09.05.04
ESC	45	Peddling and Hawking	08.03.01
ECS	56	Coordinating and Scheduling	07.05.01
ECS	56	Information Transmitting and Receiving	07.04.05
ECS	53	Registration	07.04.03
CRS	53	Keyboard Machine Operations	07.06.02
CRE	46	Sorting and Distribution	07.07.02
CIR	58	Data Collection	10.03.01
CSR	59	Bookkeeping and Auditing	07.02.01
CSR	59	Statistical Reporting and Analysis	07.02.03
CSR	56	Accounting	07.02.02
CSR	56	Payroll and Timekeeping	07.02.05
CSR	55	Computer Operation	07.06.01
CSR	54	Billing and Rate Computation	07.02.04
CSR	49	Filing	07.07.01
CSE	60	Secretarial Work	07.01.03
CSE	59	Financial Work	07.01.04
CSE	54	Record Preparation and Maintenance	07.05.03
CSE	54	Record Verification and Proofing	07.05.02
CSE	53	Interviewing	07.04.01

Part 2: From Holland Codes to Occupations

From Holland Codes to the Guide for Occupational Exploration

HOC	Cx	Title	GOE
CSE	52	Routing and Distribution	07.05.04
CER	38	Promoting	08.03.02
CEI	70	Accounting and Auditing	11.06.01
CES	56	Reception and Information Giving	07.04.04
CES	54	Paying and Receiving	07.03.01
CES	47	General Clerical Work	07.07.03
CES	44	Card and Game Room Services	09.05.05
CES	44	Ticket Taking, Ushering	09.05.08

From the Dictionary of Occupational Titles Occupations to Holland Codes

Title	HOC	Cx	DOT
Able Seaman (water trans.)	RES	49	911.364-010
Abrasive Grader (optical goods)	RIE	47	570.682-010
Abrasive Grinder (nonmet. min.)	CRE	44	673.685-010
Abrasive Mixer (nonmet. min.)	RES	47	570.485-010
Abrasive Sawyer (nonmet. min.)	CRE	41	677.685-010
Abrasive-Band Winder (nonmet. min.)	CER	40	692.685-010
Abrasive-Coating-Machine Operator (nonmet. min.)	RES	49	574.462-010
Abrasive-Grader Helper (optical goods)	RCE	37	570.686-010
Abrasive-Mixer Helper (nonmet. min.)	REC	40	570.686-014
Abrasive-Wheel Molder (nonmet. min.)	RCE	46	575.685-010
Absorption Operator (chemical)	REI	53	551.382-010
Absorption-and-Adsorption Engineer (profess. & kin.)	IER	80	008.061-010
Abstractor (profess. & kin.)	CSI	64	119.267-010
Academic Dean (education)	SEA	69	090.117-010
Accelerator Operator (profess. & kin.)	RCI	64	015.362-010
Access Coordinator, Cable Television (radio-tv broad.)	REI	63	194.122-010
Accident-Prevention-Squad Police Officer (government ser.)	RES	60	375.263-010
Accordion Maker (musical inst.)	RES	59	730.281-010
Accordion Repairer (any industry)	RSE	56	730.281-014
Accordion Tuner (any industry)	RCS	50	730.381-010
Account Executive (business ser.)	AES	65	164.167-010
Account-Information Clerk (utilities)	CSE	57	210.367-010
Accountant (profess. & kin.)	CSI	70	160.162-018
Accountant, Budget (profess. & kin.)	CRI	70	160.162-022
Accountant, Cost (profess. & kin.)	CIE	70	160.162-026
Accountant, Property (profess. & kin.)	CER	70	160.167-022
Accountant, Systems (profess. & kin.)	CSE	70	160.167-026
Accountant, Tax (profess. & kin.)	ECS	70	160.162-010
Accounting Clerk (clerical)	CSR	55	216.482-010
Accounts-Adjustable Clerk (r.r. trans.)	CSR	53	214.462-010
Acetone-Button Paster (button & notion)	CRE	37	734.687-010
Acetone-Recovery Worker (plastic-synth.)	CRE	42	552.685-010
Acetylene-Cylinder-Packing Mixer (chemical)	CRS	42	549.665-010
Acetylene-Plant Operator (chemical)	RCE	44	549.585-010
Acid Adjuster (elec. equip.)	CRE	47	727.484-010
Acid Dumper (elec. equip.)	RES	38	727.687-010
Acid Extractor (steel & rel.)	REI	52	558.382-010
Acid Filler (elec. equip.)	CRE	40	727.687-014
Acid Maker (paper & pulp)	RES	47	559.662-010
Acid Purifier (chemical)	CRE	41	559.685-010
Acid Supervisor (chemical)	ESR	59	559.132-010
Acid-Plant Helper (chemical)	CER	44	558.565-010
Acid-Polymerization Operator (chemical)	RCE	43	558.685-010
Acid-Tank Liner (construction)	RIE	57	861.381-010
Acoustical Carpenter (construction)	RES	56	860.381-010
Acquisitions Librarian (library)	SAI	64	100.267-010
Acrobat (amuse. & rec.)	AER	53	159.247-010
Acrobatic Rigger (amuse. & rec.)	RSC	46	962.684-010

Title	HOC	Cx	DOT
Actor (amuse. & rec.)	AES	62	150.047-010
Actuary (profess. & kin.)	ISE	72	020.167-010
Acupressurist (medical ser.)	ISR	63	079.271-014
Acupuncturist (medical ser.)	IRE	66	079.271-010
Addresser (clerical)	CES	42	209.587-010
Addressing-Machine Operator (clerical)	RCE	49	208.582-010
Adhesive Primer (toy-sport equip.)	RCS	37	732.687-010
Adhesive-Bandage-Machine Operator (protective dev.)	CRE	44	692.685-014
Adjudicator (government ser.)	ESC	69	119.167-010
Adjuster (furniture)	REC	46	709.684-010
Adjuster, Alarm Mechanism (clock & watch)	CRE	41	715.684-010
Adjuster, Electrical Contacts (elec. equip.)	RCE	50	724.381-010
Admeasurer (government ser.)	RIE	68	169.284-010
Administrative Assistant (any industry)	ESC	66	169.167-010
Administrative Clerk (clerical)	CSE	55	219.362-010
Administrative Secretary (any industry)	ESC	67	169.167-014
Administrator, Health Care Facility (medical ser.)	SER	70	187.117-010
Administrator, Social Welfare (profess. & kin.)	ESA	66	195.117-010
Admissions Evaluator (education)	ESC	62	205.367-010
Admitting Officer (medical ser.)	ECS	58	205.162-010
Advance Agent (amuse. & rec.)	ESR	61	191.167-010
Advertising Clerk (business ser.)	CSE	52	247.387-010
Advertising-Dispatch Clerk (print. & pub.)	CSE	51	247.387-014
Advertising-Material Distributor (any industry)	RCE	37	230.687-010
Advertising-Space Clerk (print. & pub.)	CSE	55	247.387-018
Adzing-and-Boring-Machine Operator (wood prod., n.e.c.)	RCE	48	669.682-010
Aerial-Photograph Interpreter (government ser.)	ISE	68	029.167-010
Aerial-Tram Operator (mine & quarry)	CRS	41	932.685-010
Aerialist (amuse. & rec.)	REA	55	159.247-014
Aerodynamicist (aircraft mfg.)	IRE	80	002.061-010
Aeronautical Engineer (aircraft mfg.)	IRS	78	002.061-014
Aeronautical Project Engineer (aircraft mfg.)	IES	80	002.167-018
Aeronautical Test Engineer (aircraft mfg.)	RIE	71	002.061-018
Aeronautical-Design Engineer (aircraft mfg.)	IRE	71	002.061-022
Aeronautical-Research Engineer (aircraft mfg.)	IRE	80	002.061-026
Aerospace Physiological Technician (military ser.)	RSE	51	199.682-010
Agate Setter (office machines)	RCS	45	710.684-010
Agent-Contract Clerk (insurance)	SCE	57	241.267-010
Agent-Licensing Clerk (insurance)	SEC	55	209.367-010
Ager Operator (plastic-synth.)	RES	50	553.482-010
Ager Operator (textile)	RCE	42	582.585-010
Aging-Department Supervisor (textile)	RSE	56	582.132-010
Agricultural Engineer (profess. & kin.)	IRE	76	013.061-010
Agricultural-Chemicals Inspector (government ser.)	ESR	60	168.267-082
Agricultural-Engineering Technician (profess. & kin.)	IRE	67	013.161-010
Agricultural-Research Engineer (profess. & kin.)	IRE	71	013.061-014
Agronomist (profess. & kin.)	IRS	78	040.061-010
Air Analyst (profess. & kin.)	IRS	65	012.261-010
Air and Hydronic Balancing Technician (any industry)	RCI	58	637.261-034

Title	HOC	Cx	DOT
Air Purifier Servicer (business ser.)	RCE	39	389.687-010
Air-and-Water Filler (wood. container)	RES	40	764.687-010
Air-Bag Curer (rubber tire)	RCE	40	556.685-010
Air-Compressor Mechanic (railroad equip.)	RCS	50	622.684-010
Air-Compressor Operator (any industry)	RES	47	950.685-010
Air-Conditioning Installer-Servicer Helper, Window Unit (construction)	REC	42	637.687-010
Air-Conditioning Installer-Servicer, Window Unit (construction)	RES	59	637.261-010
Air-Conditioning Mechanic (automotive ser.)	RES	55	620.281-010
Air-Conditioning-Coil Assembler (svc. ind. mach.)	REC	46	706.684-010
Air-Conditioning-Unit Tester (svc. ind. mach.)	RES	52	827.361-010
Air-Drier-Machine Operator (paper & pulp)	RES	47	534.682-010
Air-Hole Driller (fabrication, n.e.c.)	RCE	40	692.685-018
Air-Table Operator (mine & quarry)	REC	40	549.685-010
Air-Traffic Coordinator (government ser.)	SER	64	193.162-010
Air-Traffic-Control Specialist, Station (government ser.)	SCE	62	193.162-014
Air-Traffic-Control Specialist, Tower (government ser.)	SER	62	193.162-018
Air-Valve Repairer (railroad equip.)	RCS	50	622.381-010
Airborne Sensor Specialist (military ser.)	RIE	57	378.382-010
Airbrush Artist (profess. & kin.)	RCA	57	970.281-010
Aircraft Body Repairer (air trans.)	RIE	58	807.261-010
Aircraft Launch and Recovery Technician (military ser.)	RIE	52	912.682-010
Aircraft Mechanic, Armament (aircraft mfg.)	REI	57	806.361-030
Aircraft Mechanic, Electrical and Radio (aircraft mfg.)	RIE	59	825.381-010
Aircraft Mechanic, Environmental Control System (aircraft mfg.)	REI	57	806.381-014
Aircraft Mechanic, Plumbing and Hydraulics (aircraft mfg.)	RCI	56	806.381-066
Aircraft Mechanic, Rigging and Controls (aircraft mfg.)	REI	58	806.381-018
Aircraft Skin Burnisher (aircraft mfg.)	CRE	43	807.684-018
Aircraft-Armament Mechanic (government ser.)	RIE	61	632.261-010
Aircraft-Log Clerk (air trans.)	CRS	54	221.362-010
Aircraft-Photographic-Equipment Mechanic (photo. appar.)	RCS	63	714.281-010
Aircraft-Shipping Checker (aircraft mfg.)	REC	55	222.387-010
Airframe-and-Power-Plant Mechanic (aircraft mfg.; air trans.)	RIE	60	621.281-014
Airframe-and-Power-Plant-Mechanic Apprentice (air trans.)	RIE	60	621.281-018
Airframe-and-Power-Plant-Mechanic Helper (aircraft mfg.; air trans.)	RES	47	621.684-010
Airline Security Representative (air trans.)	CRS	41	372.667-010
Airline-Radio Operator (air trans.; business ser.)	CRE	64	193.262-010
Airline-Radio Operator, Chief (air trans.; business ser.)	CES	65	193.162-022
Airplane Coverer (aircraft mfg.; air trans.)	RES	52	849.381-010
Airplane Inspector (air trans.)	RES	63	621.261-010
Airplane Pilot (agriculture)	IRE	63	196.263-010
Airplane Pilot, Commercial (air trans.)	RIE	67	196.263-014
Airplane Pilot, Photogrammetry (business ser.)	RIE	65	196.263-018

Title	HOC	Cx	DOT
Airplane-Charter Clerk (air trans.)	ESC	56	295.367-010
Airplane-Dispatch Clerk (air trans.)	SEC	57	248.367-010
Airplane-Flight Attendant (air trans.)	ESR	55	352.367-010
Airplane-Gas-Tank-Liner Assembler (rubber goods)	CRE	40	759.684-010
Airplane-Pilot Helper (agriculture)	REA	43	409.667-010
Airport Attendant (air trans.)	RES	52	912.364-010
Airport Electrician (air trans.)	RSE	61	824.281-010
Airport Engineer (profess. & kin.)	ISR	71	005.061-010
Airport Utility Worker (air trans.)	RCI	51	912.663-010
Airport-Maintenance Chief (air trans.)	ERS	60	899.137-010
Alarm Investigator (business ser.)	ESA	50	376.367-010
Alarm Operator (government ser.)	ESC	59	379.162-010
Alcohol-and-Drug-Abuse-Assistance Program Administrator (government ser.)	ESR	66	195.167-042
Aligner, Barrel and Receiver (ordnance)	RIE	45	736.684-010
Aligner, Typewriter (office machines)	RCS	49	706.381-010
Allergist-Immunologist (medical ser.)	ISE	77	070.101-102
Almond Blancher, Hand (can. & preserv.)	REC	36	521.687-010
Almond Huller (can. & preserv.)	REC	42	521.685-010
Almond-Blancher Operator (can. & preserv.)	CRE	40	521.685-014
Almond-Cutting-Machine Tender (can. & preserv.)	RES	39	521.685-018
Almond-Paste Mixer (sugar & conf.)	RIE	57	529.361-010
Almond-Paste Molder (sugar & conf.)	RCS	43	520.684-010
Alodize-Machine Helper (nonfer. metal)	REC	41	509.685-010
Alodize-Machine Operator (nonfer. metal)	RES	50	509.462-010
Alteration Tailor (garment; personal ser.; retail trade)	RIE	58	785.261-010
Alterations Workroom Clerk (retail trade)	ECS	51	221.367-010
Alum-Plant Operator (chemical)	REI	49	559.362-010
Alumina-Plant Supervisor (smelt. & refin.)	RES	59	511.130-010
Aluminum-Container Tester (elec. equip.)	CRE	43	727.687-018
Aluminum-Hydroxide-Process Operator (chemical; pharmaceut.)	RES	47	559.685-014
Aluminum-Pool Installer (construction)	RES	46	809.664-010
Alumni Secretary (education)	ESA	66	090.117-014
Amalgamator (smelt. & refin.)	REI	44	511.685-010
Ambulance Attendant (medical ser.)	SEC	47	355.374-010
Ambulance Driver (medical ser.)	RSI	47	913.683-010
Ammonia-Still Operator (steel & rel.)	REA	54	559.382-010
Ammonium-Nitrate Crystallizer (chemical)	RCS	47	553.685-010
Amphibian Crewmember (military ser.)	RES	41	378.683-010
Ampoule Examiner (pharmaceut.)	CRS	42	559.687-010
Ampoule Filler (pharmaceut.)	RCE	40	559.685-018
Ampoule Sealer (pharmaceut.)	RCE	38	559.687-014
Ampoule-Washing-Machine Operator (pharmaceut.)	RCE	38	559.685-022
Amusement Park Entertainer (amuse. & rec.)	AES	46	159.647-010
Amusement Park Worker (amuse. & rec.)	SRE	46	349.664-010
Analyst, Food and Beverage (hotel & rest.)	SEI	67	310.267-010
Anatomist (profess. & kin.)	IRE	78	041.061-010
Anesthesiologist (medical ser.)	IRS	74	070.101-010

Part 3: From Occupational Titles to Holland Codes

From the Dictionary of Occupational Titles Occupations to Holland Codes

Title	HOC	Cx	DOT
Angle Shear Operator (any industry)	RIE	47	615.482-010
Animal Breeder (agriculture)	RES	58	410.161-010
Animal Breeder (profess. & kin.)	IRS	78	041.061-014
Animal Caretaker (any industry)	RCS	43	410.674-010
Animal Eviscerator (meat products)	RES	40	525.687-010
Animal Keeper (amuse. & rec.)	RSE	47	412.674-010
Animal Keeper, Head (amuse. & rec.)	SRE	59	412.137-010
Animal Scientist (profess. & kin.)	IRS	78	040.061-014
Animal Trainer (amuse. & rec.)	RES	58	159.224-010
Animal Treatment Investigator (nonprofit org.)	SRE	51	379.263-010
Animal-Hospital Clerk (medical ser.)	ESC	53	245.367-010
Animal-Nursery Worker (amuse. & rec.; museums)	RCI	49	412.674-014
Animal-Ride Attendant (amuse. & rec.)	RCS	44	349.674-010
Animal-Ride Manager (amuse. & rec.)	SER	57	349.224-010
Animal-Shelter Clerk (nonprofit org.)	CES	51	249.367-010
Ankle-Patch Molder (boot & shoe)	REC	46	692.682-010
Annealer (glass products)	CRS	44	573.685-010
Annealer (heat treating)	RCS	44	504.682-010
Annealer (jewelry-silver.)	CRE	40	504.687-010
Announcer (amuse. & rec.)	ESR	59	159.347-010
Announcer (radio-tv broad.)	SCE	64	159.147-010
Anode Builder (chemical)	REI	47	826.684-010
Anode Rebuilder (smelt. & refin.)	RSE	45	630.684-010
Anode-Crew Supervisor (smelt. & refin.)	RES	57	630.134-010
Anodizer (any industry)	REI	48	500.682-010
Antenna Installer (any industry)	CRS	45	823.684-010
Antenna Installer, Satellite Communications (any industry)	RCI	56	823.261-022
Anthropologist (profess. & kin.)	IRE	73	055.067-010
Anthropologist, Physical (profess. & kin.)	IRE	73	055.067-014
Antichecking-Iron Worker (wood prod., n.e.c.)	RCE	37	563.687-010
Antisqueak Filler (boot & shoe)	RCE	37	788.687-010
Antitank Assault Gunner (military ser.)	REI	44	378.464-010
Anvil-Seating-Press Operator (ordnance)	RCE	42	694.685-010
Apiculturist (profess. & kin.)	IRE	78	041.061-018
Apparel-Rental Clerk (retail trade)	ESC	54	295.357-010
Appeals Referee (government ser.)	SCE	68	119.267-014
Appeals Reviewer, Veteran (government ser.)	SEA	72	119.117-010
Apple-Packing Header (agriculture)	RCE	38	920.687-010
Appliance Assembler, Line (house. appl.; svc. ind. mach.)	REC	44	827.684-010
Appliance Repairer (house. appl.)	RIE	47	723.584-010
Appliance-Service Supervisor (utilities)	ERS	65	187.167-010
Applications Engineer, Manufacturing (profess. & kin.)	IES	75	007.061-038
Appliquer, Zigzag (garment)	RCE	41	786.682-010
Appointment Clerk (clerical)	CSE	51	237.367-010
Appraiser (any industry)	RIS	67	191.287-010
Appraiser (government ser.)	IES	70	188.167-010
Appraiser, Art (profess. & kin.)	IAS	64	191.287-014
Appraiser, Automobile Damage (business ser.; insurance)	ERS	58	241.267-014
Appraiser, Real Estate (real estate)	SCE	67	191.267-010

Part 3: From Occupational Titles to Holland Codes

From the Dictionary of Occupational Titles Occupations to Holland Codes

Title	HOC	Cx	DOT
Apprenticeship Consultant (government ser.)	SRE	67	188.117-010
Apron Cleaner (nonmet. min.)	RES	37	680.687-010
Aquarist (amuse. & rec.)	REI	48	449.674-010
Aquatic Biologist (profess. & kin.)	IRE	78	041.061-022
Aquatic Performer (amuse. & rec.)	REI	53	159.347-014
Arbitrator (profess. & kin.)	SEA	69	169.107-010
Arbor-Press Operator I (any industry)	REI	44	616.682-010
Arborer (jewelry-silver.)	CRS	38	700.684-010
Arc Cutter (welding)	REI	50	816.364-010
Arch-Cushion-Press Operator (rubber goods)	RES	52	556.362-010
Arch-Cushion-Skiving-Machine Operator (rubber goods)	RIE	48	690.682-010
Arch-Support Technician (protective dev.)	RSE	49	712.381-010
Archeologist (profess. & kin.)	IRE	73	055.067-018
Architect (profess. & kin.)	AIR	78	001.061-010
Architect, Marine (profess. & kin.)	IRE	80	001.061-014
Archivist (profess. & kin.)	AES	70	101.167-010
Area Supervisor, Retail Chain Store (retail trade)	ESR	65	185.117-014
Armature Bander (any industry)	RCS	47	724.684-010
Armature Connector II (elec. equip.)	CRE	43	724.684-014
Armature Tester I (elec. equip.)	CRS	49	724.384-010
Armature Winder, Repair (any industry)	RCE	48	724.684-018
Armature-Winder Helper, Repair (any industry)	REC	41	721.684-010
Armhole Baster, Jumpbasting (garment)	RCE	41	786.682-014
Armhole Feller, Handstitching Machine (garment)	CRE	40	786.682-018
Armhole-Sew-and-Trim Operator, Lockstitch (garment)	RCE	41	786.682-022
Armor Reconnaissance Specialist (military ser.)	REI	55	378.363-010
Armored-Car Guard (business ser.)	SEI	50	372.567-010
Armored-Car Guard and Driver (business ser.)	RSC	48	372.563-010
Armorer Technician (museums)	RSI	61	109.281-010
Armoring-Machine Operator (nonfer. metal)	RCE	41	691.685-010
Arranger (profess. & kin.)	AEI	75	152.067-010
Arrowsmith (toy-sport equip.)	REC	42	732.684-010
Art Conservator (museums)	SEA	66	102.167-010
Art Director (motion picture; radio-tv broad.)	AES	69	142.061-062
Art Director (profess. & kin.)	AES	67	141.031-010
Art Therapist (medical ser.)	SAE	67	076.127-010
Artificial Inseminator (agriculture)	REI	51	418.384-010
Artificial-Breeding Distributor (agriculture)	EAS	62	180.167-010
Artificial-Breeding Technician (agriculture)	RCS	54	418.384-014
Artificial-Candy Maker (fabrication, n.e.c.)	RCS	47	739.684-010
Artificial-Flower Maker (button & notion)	CRE	41	739.684-014
Artificial-Foliage Arranger (retail trade)	RCI	53	899.364-014
Artificial-Glass-Eye Maker (optical goods)	RES	59	713.261-010
Artificial-Log-Machine Operator (fabrication, n.e.c.; saw. & plan.)	RCE	44	569.685-010
Artificial-Pearl Maker (jewelry-silver.)	RCE	37	770.687-010
Artificial-Plastic-Eye Maker (optical goods)	RES	60	713.261-014
Artillery or Naval Gunfire Observer (military ser.)	REC	53	378.367-010
Artillery-Maintenance Supervisor (ordnance)	RES	61	632.131-010

Part 3: From Occupational Titles to Holland Codes

From the Dictionary of Occupational Titles Occupations to Holland Codes

Title	HOC	Cx	DOT
Artist and Repertoire Manager (amuse. & rec.)	AES	62	159.167-010
Artist's Manager (amuse. & rec.)	ESA	67	191.117-010
Artist, Mannequin Coloring (fabrication, n.e.c.)	CRS	45	741.684-010
Artist, Suspect (government ser.)	ASE	59	970.361-018
Asbestos Removal Worker (construction)	RES	47	869.684-082
Asbestos-Shingle Inspector (nonmet. min.)	CRE	42	679.687-010
Asbestos-Shingle Shearing-Machine Operator (nonmet. min.)	REC	37	679.686-010
Asbestos-Wire Finisher (nonfer. metal)	RES	48	691.682-010
Asphalt-Distributor Tender (construction)	RCE	41	853.665-010
Asphalt-Heater Tender (construction)	RCE	41	853.685-010
Asphalt-Paving-Machine Operator (construction)	RES	43	853.663-010
Assayer (profess. & kin.)	RIS	66	022.281-010
Assembler (button & notion)	CRE	37	734.687-018
Assembler (clock & watch)	RSE	53	715.381-010
Assembler (cutlery-hrdwr.)	RCE	41	701.687-010
Assembler (garment; glove & mit.)	CSR	42	781.687-010
Assembler (glove & mit.)	RCS	41	781.667-010
Assembler (house. appl.)	CRE	43	723.684-010
Assembler (jewelry-silver.)	CRE	42	700.684-014
Assembler (laundry & rel.)	CRS	42	369.687-010
Assembler (machinery mfg.)	RCS	52	706.361-010
Assembler (mfd. bldgs.; vehicles, n.e.c.)	RES	47	869.684-010
Assembler (ordnance)	RCE	40	737.687-010
Assembler (pen & pencil)	RES	41	733.685-010
Assembler (plastic prod.)	RCE	42	754.684-010
Assembler (svc. ind. mach.)	REC	37	731.687-010
Assembler (tel. & tel.)	RCI	57	722.381-010
Assembler (tex. prod., n.e.c.)	REC	38	734.687-014
Assembler (toy-sport equip.)	CRE	45	732.684-014
Assembler (wood. container)	REI	44	762.684-010
Assembler and Tester, Electronics (office machines)	RIC	57	710.281-010
Assembler and Wirer, Industrial Equipment (elec. equip.; machinery mfg.)	RES	55	826.361-010
Assembler for Puller-Over, Hand (boot & shoe)	RCE	40	788.684-010
Assembler for Puller-Over, Machine (boot & shoe)	RCE	42	690.685-010
Assembler Helper, Internal Combustion Engine (engine-turbine)	RES	40	801.687-010
Assembler I (light. fix.)	CRE	46	723.684-014
Assembler I (office machines)	RIC	50	706.684-014
Assembler I (ordnance)	RSE	50	736.381-010
Assembler II (light. fix.)	RCE	41	723.684-018
Assembler II (office machines)	RES	51	710.381-010
Assembler II (ordnance)	CRE	41	736.684-014
Assembler, Aircraft Power Plant (aircraft mfg.)	REI	54	806.381-022
Assembler, Aircraft, Structures and Surfaces (aircraft mfg.)	RIE	57	806.381-026
Assembler, Aluminum Boats (ship-boat mfg.)	REI	52	806.481-010
Assembler, Bicycle I (motor-bicycles)	RES	41	806.684-014
Assembler, Bicycle II (motor-bicycles)	REC	39	806.687-010

DOT to HOC

Title	HOC	Cx	DOT
Assembler, Billiard-Table (toy-sport equip.)	CRE	48	732.384-010
Assembler, Camper (vehicles, n.e.c.)	REI	46	806.684-018
Assembler, Carbon Brushes (elec. equip.)	CRS	45	721.684-014
Assembler, Clip-On Sunglasses (optical goods)	RCE	42	713.684-010
Assembler, Component (mfd. bldgs.; vehicles, n.e.c.)	RCE	44	762.684-014
Assembler, Corncob Pipes (fabrication, n.e.c.)	CRE	39	739.687-014
Assembler, Deck and Hull (ship-boat mfg.)	RES	44	806.684-022
Assembler, Dry Cell and Battery (elec. equip.)	RCE	37	727.687-022
Assembler, Electrical Accessories I (elec. equip.; light. fix.)	CRE	41	729.687-010
Assembler, Electrical Accessories II (elec. equip.)	CRE	48	729.384-010
Assembler, Electromechanical (aircraft mfg.; electron. comp.; inst. & app.)	RCI	57	828.381-018
Assembler, Faucets (wood. container)	RCE	38	764.687-014
Assembler, Filters (auto. mfg.)	CRE	42	739.687-026
Assembler, Filters (glass products)	RCE	41	739.687-018
Assembler, Finger Buffs (tex. prod., n.e.c.)	REI	40	739.685-010
Assembler, Fishing Floats (toy-sport equip.)	RCE	37	732.687-014
Assembler, Garment Form (fabrication, n.e.c.)	RES	41	739.687-022
Assembler, Gold Frame (optical goods)	RCE	41	713.384-010
Assembler, Ground Support Equipment (aircraft mfg.)	REI	58	809.261-010
Assembler, Igniter (ordnance)	RCE	54	737.381-010
Assembler, Insulation and Flooring (ship-boat mfg.)	REC	41	806.684-026
Assembler, Internal Combustion Engine (engine-turbine)	RIE	56	806.481-014
Assembler, Lay-Ups (toy-sport equip.)	RSE	40	677.685-014
Assembler, Leather Goods I (leather prod.)	CRE	46	783.684-010
Assembler, Leather Goods II (leather prod.)	CER	42	783.687-010
Assembler, Liquid Center (toy-sport equip.)	REC	40	732.684-018
Assembler, Marking Devices (pen & pencil)	CRS	41	733.687-010
Assembler, Mechanical Ordnance (ordnance)	RCE	50	737.684-010
Assembler, Mechanical Pencils and Ballpoint Pens (pen & pencil)	REC	42	733.687-014
Assembler, Metal Bonding (aircraft mfg.)	RES	52	806.384-030
Assembler, Metal Building (construction)	RES	53	801.381-010
Assembler, Metal Furniture (furniture)	RCE	42	709.684-014
Assembler, Mining Machinery (machinery mfg.)	RSC	59	801.261-010
Assembler, Molded Frames (optical goods)	RCE	40	713.684-014
Assembler, Motor Vehicle (auto. mfg.)	REC	41	806.684-010
Assembler, Movement (clock & watch)	CRS	41	715.684-014
Assembler, Musical Instruments (musical inst.)	CRS	46	730.684-010
Assembler, Photographic Equipment (photo. appar.)	RIE	57	714.381-010
Assembler, Piano (musical inst.)	RCS	47	730.384-010
Assembler, Ping-Pong Table (toy-sport equip.)	REC	40	732.684-022
Assembler, Plastic Hospital Products (inst. & app.)	CSE	38	712.687-010
Assembler, Printed Products (print. & pub.)	RCE	40	794.687-010
Assembler, Product (machine shop)	RCI	46	706.684-018
Assembler, Production (any industry)	RCE	40	706.687-010
Assembler, Production Line (photo. appar.)	RES	47	714.684-010
Assembler, Production Line (struct. metal)	RCE	41	809.684-010
Assembler, Sandal Parts (boot & shoe)	CRE	39	788.684-014

Part 3: From Occupational Titles to Holland Codes

From the Dictionary of Occupational Titles Occupations to Holland Codes

Title	HOC	Cx	DOT
Assembler, Semiconductor (electron. comp.)	RCI	48	726.684-034
Assembler, Skylights (plastic prod.)	RCE	40	869.684-014
Assembler, Small Products I (any industry)	CRS	38	706.684-022
Assembler, Small Products II (any industry)	CSR	40	739.687-030
Assembler, Steam-and-Gas Turbine (engine-turbine)	REI	59	600.261-010
Assembler, Subassembly (aircraft mfg.)	RCI	52	806.384-034
Assembler, Subassembly (mfd. bldgs.; vehicles, n.e.c.)	RCE	46	869.684-018
Assembler, Surgical Garment (protective dev.)	REC	45	712.684-010
Assembler, Tubing (aircraft mfg.)	RIE	56	806.381-034
Assembler, Type-Bar-and-Segment (office machines)	RCE	46	706.684-026
Assembler, Unit (struct. metal)	RSI	47	809.681-010
Assembler, Watch Train (clock & watch)	RIE	54	715.381-014
Assembler, Wet Wash (laundry & rel.)	RES	40	361.687-010
Assembler, Wire-Mesh Gate (metal prod., n.e.c.)	REI	46	801.384-010
Assembler-and-Gluer, Laminated Plastics (plastic prod.)	RCS	44	754.684-014
Assembler-Arranger (fabrication, n.e.c.)	REC	40	739.687-010
Assembler-Installer, General (aircraft mfg.)	RIE	57	806.361-014
Assembly Adjuster (comm. equip.)	RCE	45	720.684-010
Assembly Cleaner (smelt. & refin.)	RCE	46	519.664-010
Assembly Inspector (agric. equip.)	RES	48	706.361-014
Assembly Inspector (furniture)	CRS	46	763.684-010
Assembly Loader (inst. & app.)	CRE	41	711.684-010
Assembly Operator (woodworking)	RCE	43	762.684-018
Assembly Repairer (agric. equip.)	RES	51	624.381-010
Assembly Supervisor (any industry)	SER	58	739.137-010
Assembly Technician (office machines)	RIE	59	633.261-010
Assembly-Inspector Helper (agric. equip.)	RCE	41	801.663-010
Assembly-Line Inspector (furniture)	CRS	48	709.684-018
Assembly-Machine Operator (pen & pencil)	RCE	40	692.686-010
Assembly-Machine Tender (plastic prod.)	RCE	38	754.685-014
Assembly-Machine-Set-up Mechanic (elec. equip.)	RSE	55	692.360-010
Assembly-Press Operator (any industry)	CRE	41	690.685-014
Assessor-Collector, Irrigation Tax (government ser.)	ESR	70	188.167-014
Assignment Clerk (clerical)	CES	51	249.367-090
Assignment Clerk (motor trans.)	CSR	50	215.367-010
Assignment Clerk (tel. & tel.)	CRE	54	219.387-010
Assignment Editor (radio-tv broad.)	EIA	69	132.132-010
Assistant Branch Manager, Financial Institution (financial)	SER	69	186.167-070
Assistant Construction Superintendent (construction)	ESR	56	869.367-010
Assistant Designer (garment)	RCI	53	781.361-010
Assistant Press Operator, Offset (print. & pub.)	RCE	53	651.685-026
Assistant Principal (education)	SEA	66	091.107-010
Assistant-Press Operator (print. & pub.)	RES	50	651.585-010
Association Executive (profess. & kin.)	ESA	69	189.117-010
Assorter (steel & rel.)	RCE	47	703.687-010
Astrologer (amuse. & rec.)	SEC	58	159.207-010
Astronomer (profess. & kin.)	IRE	80	021.067-010
Athletic Trainer (amuse. & rec.; education)	SRE	64	153.224-010
Atomic-Fuel Assembler (chemical)	RCS	50	709.381-010

Part 3: From Occupational Titles to Holland Codes

From the Dictionary of Occupational Titles Occupations to Holland Codes

Title	HOC	Cx	DOT
Atomizer Assembler (fabrication, n.e.c.)	RCE	40	706.684-030
Attendance Clerk (education)	CSE	58	219.362-014
Attendance Officer (education)	SER	59	168.367-010
Attendant, Arcade (amuse. & rec.)	SCR	48	342.667-014
Attendant, Campground (amuse. & rec.)	RES	40	329.683-010
Attendant, Children's Institution (any industry)	ESR	49	359.677-010
Attendant, Lodging Facilities (hotel & rest.)	SER	48	329.467-010
Auction Assistant (retail trade; wholesale tr.)	CES	41	294.667-010
Auction Clerk (retail trade; wholesale tr.)	CES	47	294.567-010
Auctioneer (retail trade; wholesale tr.)	EAS	55	294.257-010
Audio Operator (radio-tv broad.)	RES	59	194.262-010
Audio-Video Repairer (any industry)	RSE	54	729.281-010
Audiologist (medical ser.)	ISR	69	076.101-010
Audiometrist (profess. & kin.)	SRC	60	078.362-010
Audiovisual Librarian (library)	EAS	63	100.167-010
Audiovisual Production Specialist (profess. & kin.)	AES	67	149.061-010
Audiovisual Technician (any industry)	RCI	53	960.382-010
Audit Clerk (clerical)	CRE	60	210.382-010
Audit-Machine Operator (clerical)	CRS	51	216.482-018
Auditor (profess. & kin.)	EIS	72	160.167-054
Auditor, County or City (government ser.)	ECI	69	160.167-030
Auditor, Data Processing (profess. & kin.)	CIS	69	160.162-030
Auditor, Internal (profess. & kin.)	ICR	70	160.167-034
Auditor, Tax (profess. & kin.)	CES	72	160.167-038
Auger Press Operator, Manual Control (brick & tile)	RES	51	575.462-010
Auto Roller (tobacco)	CRE	38	529.685-010
Auto-Body Repairer, Fiberglass (automotive ser.)	RCI	54	807.381-030
Auto-Design Checker (auto. mfg.)	RIE	67	017.261-010
Auto-Design Detailer (auto. mfg.)	IRE	64	017.281-010
Autoclave Operator (aircraft mfg.)	RCI	57	553.362-014
Autoclave Operator (knitting)	REC	42	587.585-010
Autoclave Operator (textile)	RSC	47	587.682-010
Autoclave Operator I (chemical)	RIE	53	553.382-010
Autoclave Operator II (chemical)	RCS	49	709.682-010
Automat-Car Attendant (r.r. trans.)	CRE	45	319.464-010
Automated Cutting Machine Operator (aircraft mfg.)	RES	51	699.362-010
Automated Equipment Engineer-Technician (machinery mfg.)	RES	64	638.261-010
Automatic Bandsaw Tender (furniture)	RCI	45	667.685-070
Automatic Casting-Forging Machine Operator (forging)	RCI	51	611.682-014
Automatic Lump Making Machine Tender (tobacco)	RCE	41	529.685-014
Automatic Pattern Edger (glass products)	REI	44	673.682-010
Automatic Stacker (tinware)	RES	35	619.686-010
Automatic-Door Mechanic (construction)	REI	56	829.281-010
Automatic-Equipment Technician (tel. & tel.)	RES	59	822.281-010
Automatic-Machine Attendant (paper goods)	REI	40	649.685-010
Automatic-Nailing-Machine Feeder (woodworking)	REC	35	669.686-010
Automatic-Pad-Making-Machine Operator (tex. prod., n.e.c.)	RCE	51	689.382-010

Title	HOC	Cx	DOT
Automatic-Pad-Making-Machine Operator Helper (tex. prod., n.e.c.)	RCS	38	689.686-010
Automatic-Wheel-Line Operator (machine shop)	RSE	50	609.682-010
Automatic-Window-Seat-and-Top-Lift Repairer (automotive ser.)	REA	51	825.381-014
Automobile Detailer (automotive ser.)	RCE	40	915.687-034
Automobile Locator (retail trade)	ECS	51	296.367-010
Automobile Mechanic (automotive ser.)	RCI	56	620.261-010
Automobile Racer (amuse. & rec.)	RES	56	153.243-010
Automobile Rental Clerk (automotive ser.)	ESC	54	295.467-026
Automobile Tester (automotive ser.)	RSE	56	620.261-014
Automobile Tester (government ser.)	RCE	50	379.364-010
Automobile Upholsterer (automotive ser.)	RES	54	780.381-010
Automobile Wrecker (wholesale tr.)	RES	45	620.684-010
Automobile-Accessories Installer (automotive ser.)	RES	44	806.684-038
Automobile-Body Customizer (automotive ser.)	RES	53	807.361-010
Automobile-Body Repairer (automotive ser.)	RIE	53	807.381-010
Automobile-Body-Repairer Helper (automotive ser.)	RES	38	807.687-010
Automobile-Bumper Straightener (automotive ser.)	RES	42	807.684-010
Automobile-Club-Safety-Program Coordinator (nonprofit org.)	SEC	59	249.167-010
Automobile-Mechanic Apprentice (automotive ser.)	RSE	56	620.261-012
Automobile-Mechanic Helper (automotive ser.)	REI	42	620.684-014
Automobile-Radiator Mechanic (automotive ser.)	RSE	49	620.381-010
Automobile-Repair-Service Estimator (automotive ser.)	RSE	58	620.261-018
Automobile-Seat-Cover Installer (automotive ser.)	RCE	38	915.687-010
Automobile-Seat-Cover-and-Convertible-Top Installer (automotive ser.)	RES	52	780.384-010
Automobile-Self-Serve-Service-Station Attendant (automotive ser.)	CER	51	915.477-010
Automobile-Service-Station Attendant (automotive ser.)	RES	51	915.467-010
Automobile-Service-Station Mechanic (automotive ser.)	RIC	54	620.261-030
Automobile-Upholsterer Apprentice (automotive ser.)	RES	54	780.381-014
Automotive Engineer (auto. mfg.)	RIE	71	007.061-010
Automotive Technician, Exhaust Emissions (government ser.)	RIE	55	620.281-014
Automotive-Cooling-System Diagnostic Technician (automotive ser.)	RCI	60	620.261-034
Automotive-Generator-and-Starter Repairer (automotive ser.)	RSE	55	721.281-010
Automotive-Maintenance-Equipment Servicer (any industry)	RIE	58	620.281-018
Automotive-Tire Tester (ordnance)	RES	58	736.367-010
Automotive-Tire-Testing Supervisor (ordnance)	RES	59	736.131-010
Auxiliary-Equipment Operator (utilities)	RES	52	952.362-010
Auxiliary-Equipment Tender (cement)	RCE	42	570.685-010
Auxiliary-Equipment Tender (construction)	RCS	48	869.665-010
Aviation Support Equipment Repairer (military ser.)	RIE	56	639.281-010
Avionics Technician (aircraft mfg.; air trans.)	RIS	62	823.261-026

Part 3: From Occupational Titles to Holland Codes
From the Dictionary of Occupational Titles Occupations to Holland Codes

Title	HOC	Cx	DOT
Awning Hanger (construction; retail trade; tex. prod., n.e.c.)	REI	48	869.484-010
Awning Maker-and-Installer (furniture; retail trade)	REI	51	869.481-010
Awning-Frame Maker (tex. prod., n.e.c.)	RES	49	809.484-010
Awning-Hanger Helper (construction; retail trade; tex. prod., n.e.c.)	RES	41	869.687-010
Babbitter (machine shop)	REI	47	709.684-022
Baby-Stroller and Wheelchair Rental Clerk (retail trade)	ERC	50	295.367-014
Back Feeder, Plywood Layup Line (millwork-plywood)	RES	37	569.686-010
Back Maker, Lockstitch (garment)	RCE	41	786.682-026
Back Padder (furniture)	CRE	40	780.684-010
Back Tender (textile)	RCS	41	589.686-010
Back Tender, Cloth Printing (textile)	REC	40	652.685-010
Back Tender, Insulation Board (wood prod., n.e.c.)	CRE	40	532.685-010
Back Tender, Paper Machine (paper & pulp)	RES	50	534.662-010
Back Tufter (furniture)	RCE	35	780.687-062
Back Washer (textile)	RES	41	582.685-010
Back-Shoe Worker (boot & shoe)	CSE	51	221.387-010
Back-Strip-Machine Operator (boot & shoe)	REC	39	690.685-018
Backing-in-Machine Tender (fabrication, n.e.c.)	RES	38	590.685-010
Bag Cutter (tex. prod., n.e.c.)	REC	38	789.687-010
Bag Liner (tex. prod., n.e.c.)	RCE	37	789.687-014
Bag Loader (ordnance)	REC	36	737.687-014
Bag Printer (print. & pub.)	RCS	44	651.685-010
Bag Repairer (paper goods)	CRE	40	794.684-010
Bag Sewer (paper goods)	RCE	40	787.686-010
Bag-Machine Operator (paper goods)	REI	41	649.685-014
Bag-Machine-Operator Helper (paper goods)	REC	40	649.686-010
Baggage Checker (air trans.; motor trans.)	RES	48	357.477-010
Baggage Handler (r.r. trans.)	REC	40	910.687-010
Baggage Porter, Head (hotel & rest.)	ESR	55	324.137-010
Baggage-and-Mail Agent (r.r. trans.)	ERS	58	910.137-010
Bagger (garment; laundry & rel.)	RCE	38	920.687-018
Bagger (knitting)	REC	39	582.687-010
Bagger (plastic prod.)	REC	41	553.685-014
Bagger (retail trade)	RES	40	920.687-014
Bagging Salvager (textile)	RCE	36	689.687-010
Bailiff (government ser.)	ESR	45	377.667-010
Baker (bakery products)	RSE	54	526.381-010
Baker (hotel & rest.)	RSE	50	313.381-010
Baker Apprentice (bakery products)	RSE	54	526.381-014
Baker Helper (bakery products)	REC	40	526.686-010
Baker Helper (hotel & rest.)	RES	41	313.684-010
Baker, Head (hotel & rest.)	RES	57	313.131-010
Baker, Pizza (hotel & rest.)	RSE	48	313.381-014
Baker, Second (hotel & rest.)	RSI	57	313.361-010
Baker, Test (grain-feed mills)	RSE	52	526.381-018
Bakery Supervisor (bakery products)	RES	59	526.131-010
Bakery Worker, Conveyor Line (bakery products)	CRS	39	524.687-022
Bakery-Machine Mechanic (bakery products)	RIE	58	629.281-010

Dictionary of Holland Occupational Codes

DOT to HOC

Part 3: From Occupational Titles to Holland Codes

From the Dictionary of Occupational Titles Occupations to Holland Codes

Title	HOC	Cx	DOT
Bakery-Machine-Mechanic Supervisor (bakery products)	RES	60	629.131-010
Balance Assembler (clock & watch)	CRE	48	715.384-010
Balance Recesser (clock & watch)	CRE	41	604.685-010
Balance Truer (clock & watch)	RCE	47	715.684-018
Balance-Bridge Assembler (clock & watch)	RCI	46	715.684-022
Balancer, Scale (office machines)	RIS	54	710.381-014
Balancing-Machine Operator (any industry)	RSE	51	609.462-010
Balancing-Machine Set-up Worker (any industry)	RIE	57	809.382-010
Balcony Worker (glass mfg.)	CRS	38	575.687-010
Bale Sewer (agriculture)	REC	37	920.687-022
Bale-Tie-Machine Operator (metal prod., n.e.c.)	RES	41	616.682-014
Baler (plastic-synth.)	REC	40	690.685-022
Baling-Machine Tender (any industry)	RES	38	920.685-010
Ball Assembler (toy-sport equip.)	CRE	43	732.684-026
Ball Sorter (machinery mfg.)	RCS	40	609.685-010
Ball-Fringe-Machine Operator (tex. prod., n.e.c.)	RES	39	689.685-010
Ball-Machine Operator (sugar & conf.)	RCE	37	520.686-010
Ball-Mill Operator (chemical)	CRS	46	558.685-014
Ball-Truing-Machine Operator (toy-sport equip.)	REI	49	690.682-014
Ball-Warper Tender (textile)	RCE	41	681.685-010
Balling-Machine Operator (textile)	RCE	38	681.685-014
Ballistics Expert, Forensic (government ser.)	IRE	69	199.267-010
Balloon Dipper (rubber goods)	RES	40	599.687-010
Balloon Maker (rubber goods)	REC	48	752.684-010
Ballpoint Pen Cartridge Tester (pen & pencil)	REI	53	733.281-010
Ballpoint-Pen-Assembly-Machine Operator (pen & pencil)	RSI	53	692.382-010
Band Attacher (clock & watch)	RCE	37	715.687-010
Band Builder (rubber tire)	CRS	43	750.684-010
Band Cutter (rubber goods)	REC	41	690.685-026
Band Maker (agriculture)	RCS	38	619.685-010
Band Salvager (agriculture)	REC	36	929.686-014
Band Tumbler (rubber goods)	REC	39	551.685-010
Band-and-Cuff Cutter (glove & mit.)	CRE	40	784.685-010
Band-Machine Operator (rubber goods)	REC	44	690.685-030
Band-Reamer-Machine Operator (nonfer. metal)	RCS	41	603.685-010
Band-Saw Operator (meat products)	REI	40	525.685-010
Band-Saw Operator (paper goods)	RCI	44	640.685-090
Band-Saw Operator (tex. prod., n.e.c.)	RCS	44	686.682-010
Band-Saw Operator (wood. container)	REI	40	667.685-010
Band-Saw Operator (woodworking)	RCE	39	667.685-014
Band-Sawing-Machine Operator (fabrication, n.e.c.)	RCE	43	690.485-010
Band-Scroll-Saw Operator (woodworking)	RCE	47	667.682-010
Band-Top Maker (furniture)	RCE	42	780.684-014
Bander (pen & pencil)	RCE	38	733.687-018
Bander (wood. container)	RCE	37	762.687-010
Bander, Hand (any industry)	RCI	42	929.687-058
Bander, Hand (paper goods)	RCE	36	920.687-026
Bander, Hand (tobacco)	RCS	38	920.687-030
Bander-and-Cellophaner Helper, Machine (tobacco)	RCE	38	920.686-010

Title	HOC	Cx	DOT
Bander-and-Cellophaner, Machine (tobacco)	RCE	40	920.685-014
Banding-Machine Operator (furniture)	REC	40	619.685-014
Banding-Machine Operator (ordnance)	RES	41	619.685-018
Banding-Machine Operator (pottery & porc.)	CRS	43	679.682-010
Bandoleer Packer (ordnance)	RCE	38	920.687-034
Bandoleer Straightener-Stamper (ordnance)	RCE	39	737.587-010
Bank Boss (construction)	ERS	59	851.137-010
Bank Boss (mine & quarry)	SER	55	932.132-010
Bank-Note Designer (government ser.)	AER	63	142.061-010
Banking Pin Adjuster (clock & watch)	REC	49	715.381-018
Bar and Filler Assembler (furniture)	RCS	39	706.684-034
Bar Attendant (hotel & rest.)	ERC	49	312.477-010
Bar Examiner (profess. & kin.)	ESI	73	110.167-010
Barbed-Wire-Machine Operator (metal prod., n.e.c.)	RCS	47	616.382-010
Barber (personal ser.)	ESR	53	330.371-010
Barber Apprentice (personal ser.)	ESR	53	330.371-014
Barge Captain (water trans.)	REI	56	911.137-010
Bark-Press Operator (paper & pulp)	RCS	38	563.685-010
Barker (amuse. & rec.)	ESA	48	342.657-010
Barker Operator (millwork-plywood)	RES	41	663.682-010
Barley Steeper (beverage)	RCS	42	522.685-114
Barn Boss (any industry)	ESR	59	410.131-010
Barrel Assembler (clock & watch)	RCS	50	715.381-022
Barrel Assembler (wood. container)	RCS	47	669.682-014
Barrel Brander (wood. container)	RCE	40	764.684-010
Barrel Charrer (wood. container)	RCE	41	764.684-014
Barrel Drainer (wood. container)	RES	36	764.687-018
Barrel Filler (grain-feed mills)	CER	44	529.485-010
Barrel Filler I (beverage)	RES	35	522.687-010
Barrel Filler II (beverage)	RCE	48	914.485-010
Barrel Finisher (clock & watch)	RCE	42	715.682-010
Barrel Finisher (ordnance)	RCS	44	736.684-018
Barrel Inspector, Tight (wood. container)	CRE	42	764.687-022
Barrel Liner (wood. container)	RCS	38	764.687-026
Barrel Loader and Cleaner (ordnance)	RCE	41	736.587-010
Barrel Marker (wood. container)	RCE	38	764.687-030
Barrel Polisher, Inside (ordnance)	CRE	41	603.685-014
Barrel Raiser (wood. container)	REC	41	764.684-018
Barrel Repairer (ordnance)	RCE	44	736.684-022
Barrel Rifler (ordnance)	CRE	42	605.685-010
Barrel Straightener I (ordnance)	RES	45	736.684-026
Barrel-Assembler Helper (wood. container)	RES	39	669.685-010
Barrel-Bridge Assembler (clock & watch)	REC	49	715.381-026
Barrel-Cap Setter (clock & watch)	RCE	39	715.687-014
Barrel-Charrer Helper (wood. container)	RES	38	764.687-034
Barrel-Dedenting-Machine Operator (beverage)	REC	43	617.682-010
Barrel-Endshake Adjuster (clock & watch)	RSE	50	715.381-030
Barrel-Lathe Operator, Inside (wood. container)	RES	44	664.682-010
Barrel-Lathe Operator, Outside (wood. container)	RES	41	664.682-014

DOT to HOC

Part 3: From Occupational Titles to Holland Codes

From the Dictionary of Occupational Titles Occupations to Holland Codes

Title	HOC	Cx	DOT
Barrel-Raiser Helper (wood. container)	RES	38	764.687-038
Barrel-Rib Matting-Machine Operator (ordnance)	REI	45	605.682-010
Bartender (hotel & rest.)	SEC	52	312.474-010
Bartender Helper (hotel & rest.)	RCE	40	312.687-010
Base Filler (toy-sport equip.)	RCE	36	732.687-018
Base Remover (light. fix.)	REC	37	692.686-014
Base-Draw Operator (ordnance)	RES	44	504.685-010
Base-Filler Operator (toy-sport equip.)	REC	40	732.685-010
Base-Ply Hand (rubber goods)	RCS	41	759.684-014
Baseball Inspector and Repairer (toy-sport equip.)	RCE	46	732.684-030
Baseball Sewer, Hand (toy-sport equip.)	CRE	39	732.684-034
Basin Operator (waterworks)	REC	47	954.385-010
Basket Assembler I (wood. container)	RCE	40	669.685-014
Basket Assembler II (wood. container)	RCE	40	769.684-010
Basket Filler (can. & preserv.)	RCE	36	529.687-010
Basket Grader (wood. container)	RCE	40	769.687-010
Basket Mender (wood. container)	CRE	41	762.684-022
Basket Patcher (wood. container)	RCE	40	769.684-014
Basting Puller (garment)	REC	39	782.687-010
Basting-Machine Operator (garment)	RCE	41	786.682-030
Batch Freezer (dairy products)	RCE	40	523.685-010
Batch Maker (nonfer. metal; steel & rel.)	REC	40	515.685-010
Batch Mixer (brick & tile)	REC	40	570.687-010
Batch Mixer (soap & rel.)	RCE	41	550.685-010
Batch Trucker (rubber reclaim.)	RCE	39	550.686-010
Batch-and-Furnace Operator (glass mfg.)	RIS	57	572.382-010
Batch-Records Clerk (plastic prod.)	RCE	50	221.387-054
Batch-Still Operator I (chemical)	RES	47	552.685-014
Batch-Tank Controller (grain-feed mills)	CER	41	521.685-022
Bath-Mix Operator (plastic-synth.)	REI	38	552.685-018
Battalion Chief (government ser.)	EIS	66	373.167-010
Batter Mixer (bakery products)	RCS	47	520.685-010
Batter Mixer (food prep., n.e.c.)	RCE	42	520.685-014
Batter Scaler (bakery products)	RES	47	526.682-010
Batter-Out (pottery & porc.)	REI	42	575.684-010
Battery Assembler (elec. equip.)	CRS	47	727.684-010
Battery Assembler, Dry Cell (elec. equip.)	RCE	47	727.664-010
Battery Assembler, Plastic (elec. equip.)	CRE	44	727.684-014
Battery Charger (any industry)	RCI	42	825.684-018
Battery Charger (elec. equip.)	CRE	42	727.587-010
Battery Charger, Conveyor Line (elec. equip.)	RCE	40	727.687-026
Battery Inspector (railroad equip.; r.r. trans.)	RES	51	829.684-010
Battery Loader (textile)	RCE	37	683.686-010
Battery Maintainer, Large Emergency Storage (utilities)	RSE	52	820.381-010
Battery Recharger (elec. equip.)	RES	49	727.381-010
Battery Repairer (any industry)	REI	50	727.381-014
Battery Stacker (elec. equip.)	REC	37	727.687-030
Battery Tester (elec. equip.)	REI	51	727.384-010
Battery-Charger Tester (elec. equip.)	CRE	46	729.684-010

Title	HOC	Cx	DOT
Battery-Container-Finishing Hand (elec. equip.)	REC	39	727.687-034
Battery-Parts Assembler (elec. equip.)	REC	42	727.687-038
Battery-Wrecker Operator (nonfer. metal)	RCE	37	515.686-010
Batting-Machine Operator (tex. prod., n.e.c.; textile)	RCE	41	680.585-010
Batting-Machine Operator, Insulation (nonmet. min.)	RCE	52	677.382-010
BB Shot Packer (ordnance)	RCE	40	920.685-018
Beach Lifeguard (amuse. & rec.)	SER	50	379.364-014
Bead Builder (rubber tire)	CRS	42	750.684-014
Bead Inspector (light. fix.)	CRE	43	725.687-010
Bead Maker (jewelry-silver.)	REC	54	770.381-010
Bead Picker (rubber reclaim.)	RCE	36	551.686-010
Bead Preparer (rubber goods)	REC	41	692.685-022
Bead Stringer (jewelry-silver.)	CRE	44	735.684-010
Bead-Forming-Machine Operator (rubber tire)	RCS	47	692.682-014
Bead-Machine Operator (hat & cap)	REC	41	583.686-010
Beader (furniture)	REC	39	739.687-034
Beading Sawyer (fabrication, n.e.c.)	RCE	40	667.685-018
Beadworker (fabrication, n.e.c.)	REI	50	789.381-010
Beam Racker (textile)	RSE	38	681.686-010
Beam-Dyer Operator (textile)	REC	46	582.685-014
Beam-Warper Tender, Automatic (knitting; narrow fabrics; nonmet. min.; textile)	RCE	41	681.685-018
Beamer (textile)	REC	41	681.585-010
Beamer Helper (textile)	RCS	38	681.686-014
Beaming Inspector (leather mfg.)	REC	42	585.687-010
Bearing-Ring Assembler (machinery mfg.)	CRE	43	706.684-038
Beater Engineer (paper & pulp; tex. prod., n.e.c.)	RES	50	530.662-010
Beater Operator (chemical)	CRE	41	555.685-010
Beater-and-Pulper Feeder (paper & pulp; tex. prod., n.e.c.)	RES	40	530.686-010
Beater-Engineer Helper (paper & pulp; tex. prod., n.e.c.)	RCE	42	530.665-010
Bed Laster (boot & shoe)	RCE	47	690.682-018
Bed Operator (steel & rel.)	RCE	46	613.685-034
Bed Rubber (stonework)	REI	46	673.685-014
Bed Setter (stonework)	RSC	41	679.664-010
Bedder (pottery & porc.)	REC	41	573.687-010
Bee Worker (agriculture)	RCI	40	413.687-018
Beekeeper (agriculture)	RES	58	413.161-010
Bell Captain (hotel & rest.)	ESR	53	324.137-014
Bell Maker (musical inst.)	RES	53	730.381-014
Bell Spinner (musical inst.)	RSE	50	619.682-010
Bell-Neck Hammerer (musical inst.)	RCE	38	730.684-014
Bellhop (hotel & rest.)	ERS	42	324.677-010
Bellows Assembler (inst. & app.)	CRE	42	710.684-042
Bellows Filler (inst. & app.)	RIE	47	710.684-014
Bellows Maker (photo. appar.)	REC	47	714.684-014
Bellows Tester (inst. & app.)	REI	48	710.687-014
Belly Builder (musical inst.)	RIE	48	730.684-018
Belt Builder (rubber goods)	RCS	42	752.684-014
Belt Maker (nonmet. min.)	CRE	41	776.684-010

Title	HOC	Cx	DOT
Belt Picker (mine & quarry)	REC	36	939.687-010
Belt Repairer (any industry)	RCE	41	630.684-014
Belt Sander, Stone (stonework)	RIE	40	673.666-010
Belt-Builder Helper (rubber goods)	REI	41	759.684-018
Belt-Maker Helper (nonmet. min.)	CES	38	776.687-010
Belt-Press Operator I (rubber goods)	RIE	53	553.362-010
Belt-Press Operator II (rubber goods)	RCE	41	553.665-010
Belting-and-Webbing Inspector (narrow fabrics)	REC	41	683.487-010
Ben-Day Artist (print. & pub.)	REA	47	970.681-010
Bench Assembler (agric. equip.)	CRE	43	706.684-042
Bench Carpenter (woodworking)	RSC	43	760.684-010
Bench Grinder (any industry)	REI	41	705.684-010
Bench Hand (bakery products)	RES	52	520.384-010
Bench Hand (clock & watch)	RCE	37	715.684-026
Bench Hand (furniture)	REI	54	706.381-014
Bench Hand (jewelry-silver.)	RSC	49	735.381-010
Bench Hand (motor-bicycles)	RCE	43	706.684-046
Bench Worker (metal prod., n.e.c.)	RCE	44	616.485-010
Bench Worker (optical goods)	REC	41	713.684-018
Bench Worker, Binding (print. & pub.)	CRS	41	977.684-026
Bench Worker, Hollow Handle (jewelry-silver.)	RCE	38	700.687-010
Bench-Molder Apprentice (jewelry-silver.)	RSE	56	518.381-010
Bench-Shear Operator (furniture)	RCS	48	703.684-010
Bender, Hand (woodworking)	REC	38	769.684-018
Bender, Machine (paper goods)	REC	42	641.685-010
Bender, Machine (woodworking)	RCE	41	569.685-014
Bending-Machine Operator I (any industry)	RCS	49	617.482-010
Bending-Machine Operator II (any industry)	REC	41	617.685-010
Benefits Clerk II (clerical)	CES	53	205.567-010
Benzene-Washer Operator (chemical; steel & rel.)	RIE	50	551.682-010
Bevel Polisher (clock & watch)	CRS	43	603.685-022
Beveler (clock & watch)	RCE	39	715.684-030
Beveler (glass mfg.; glass products)	REI	47	775.684-010
Beveler (glass products)	RCS	41	673.685-018
Beveler (nonmet. min.)	RIE	40	673.685-022
Beveler (stonework)	RES	50	771.484-010
Beveler, Printed Circuit Boards (electron. comp.)	RCI	41	699.682-034
Beveling-and-Edging-Machine Operator (glass mfg.; glass products)	RIE	48	673.682-014
Beveling-and-Edging-Machine-Operator Helper (glass mfg.; glass products)	RES	40	673.686-010
Beveling-Machine Operator (hat & cap)	REC	39	690.686-010
Bias-Cutting-Machine Operator (tex. prod., n.e.c.)	REC	44	686.682-014
Bias-Machine Operator (rubber tire)	RCE	48	690.682-022
Bias-Machine-Operator Helper (rubber tire)	REC	39	690.686-014
Bibliographer (profess. & kin.)	CSR	64	100.367-010
Bicycle Repairer (any industry)	RSC	48	639.681-010
Bicycle-Rental Clerk (retail trade)	ERC	45	295.467-010
Billet Assembler (chemical)	RCS	47	614.684-010

From the Dictionary of Occupational Titles Occupations to Holland Codes

Title	HOC	Cx	DOT
Billing Clerk (clerical)	CRS	55	214.362-042
Billing Typist (clerical)	CSE	54	214.382-014
Billing-Control Clerk (utilities)	CSE	55	214.387-010
Billing-Machine Operator (clerical)	CRS	54	214.482-010
Billposter (any industry)	REC	41	299.667-010
Billposter (business ser.)	CRS	38	841.684-010
Bin Cleaner (beverage; grain-feed mills)	REC	39	529.687-014
Bin Filler (tobacco)	RCE	37	922.687-010
Bin Tripper Operator (steel & rel.)	RCI	41	922.665-014
Binder (any industry)	RCE	44	787.682-010
Binder and Box Builder (textile)	CRS	41	628.684-010
Binder Cutter, Hand (tobacco)	RCE	37	521.687-014
Binder Layer (tobacco)	RCE	38	529.685-018
Binder Selector (tobacco)	REI	40	521.687-018
Binder Technician (glass mfg.)	REI	45	550.585-010
Binder, Chainstitch (garment)	RCE	41	786.682-034
Binder, Coverstitch (garment)	RCE	41	786.682-038
Binder, Lockstitch (garment)	RCE	41	786.682-042
Binder-and-Wrapper Packer (tobacco)	RES	38	922.687-014
Bindery Worker (paper goods)	RES	41	649.685-018
Bindery Worker (print. & pub.)	REC	44	653.685-010
Bindery-Machine Feeder-Offbearer (print. & pub.)	REC	39	653.686-026
Bindery-Machine Setter (print. & pub.)	RES	55	653.360-018
Binding Cutter, Synthetic Cloth (tex. prod., n.e.c.)	RSE	47	699.682-010
Binding Folder, Machine (boot & shoe)	RCS	44	788.684-018
Binding Printer (textile)	CRS	40	652.685-014
Biochemist (profess. & kin.)	IRS	78	041.061-026
Biochemistry Technologist (medical ser.)	IRE	68	078.261-010
Biographer (profess. & kin.)	ASE	65	052.067-010
Biological Aide (agriculture)	RSI	54	049.364-018
Biological Photographer (profess. & kin.)	RIS	60	143.362-010
Biologist (profess. & kin.)	IAR	80	041.061-030
Biology Specimen Technician (profess. & kin.)	RCS	56	041.381-010
Biomedical Engineer (profess. & kin.)	IRE	79	019.061-010
Biomedical Equipment Technician (profess. & kin.)	RIE	60	019.261-010
Biophysicist (profess. & kin.)	IRE	80	041.061-034
Bird-Cage Assembler (metal prod., n.e.c.)	CRE	41	709.684-026
Birth Attendant (medical ser.)	SER	46	354.377-010
Bisque Cleaner (pottery & porc.)	RCE	43	774.684-010
Bisque Grader (pottery & porc.)	CSR	45	774.687-010
Bit Bender (fabrication, n.e.c.)	CRS	41	752.684-018
Bit Sharpener (any industry)	RCE	41	603.685-026
Bit Shaver (fabrication, n.e.c.)	CRE	40	754.684-018
Bit-Sharpener Operator (mine & quarry)	CRS	40	603.685-030
Bite-Block Maker (protective dev.)	RES	44	712.684-014
Black Oxide Coating Equipment Tender (electron. comp.)	RCI	42	501.685-018
Black-Ash-Burner Operator (paper & pulp)	RES	47	553.682-010
Black-Mill Operator (chemical)	CRE	47	553.665-014
Blacksmith (forging)	RIE	56	610.381-010

Title	HOC	Cx	DOT
Blacksmith Apprentice (forging)	RIE	56	610.381-014
Blacksmith Helper (forging)	RES	41	610.684-010
Blade Balancer (agric. equip.)	RCE	39	701.687-014
Blade Groover (cutlery-hrdwr.)	RCE	41	705.582-010
Blanching-Machine Operator (can. & preserv.)	RES	43	523.685-014
Blanket Washer (smelt. & refin.)	RES	40	511.687-010
Blanket-Cutting-Machine Operator (tex. prod., n.e.c.)	REC	42	689.585-010
Blanket-Winder Helper (paper goods)	RES	40	641.686-010
Blanket-Winder Operator (paper goods)	RSE	47	641.682-010
Blankmaker (glass mfg.)	RCI	56	579.382-022
Blast-Furnace Keeper (steel & rel.)	RSE	48	502.664-010
Blast-Furnace-Keeper Helper (steel & rel.)	RES	43	502.687-010
Blaster (any industry)	RIE	60	859.261-010
Blaster (mine & quarry)	RSE	54	931.261-010
Blaster Helper (any industry)	RCS	41	859.687-010
Blasting-Cap Assembler (ordnance)	RCE	40	737.687-018
Bleach Packer (chemical)	REC	38	558.687-010
Bleach-Boiler Filler (paper & pulp)	REC	41	533.685-010
Bleach-Liquor Maker (paper & pulp)	RES	47	550.662-010
Bleach-Range Operator (textile)	REC	42	582.685-018
Bleacher Operator (chemical; soap & rel.)	RCE	41	558.685-018
Bleacher, Lard (meat products; oils & grease)	RCE	40	521.685-026
Bleacher, Pulp (paper & pulp)	RSE	51	533.362-010
Blemish Remover (boot & shoe)	CRS	40	788.684-022
Blender (bakery products)	REC	39	520.585-010
Blender (petrol. refin.)	RES	54	540.462-010
Blender (tobacco)	RCS	49	520.387-010
Blender Helper (plastic prod.; plastic-synth.)	CRS	41	550.586-010
Blender I (chemical)	RCE	40	550.685-014
Blender II (chemical)	RSC	47	550.665-010
Blender Laborer (tobacco)	RES	36	520.687-010
Blender, Snuff (tobacco)	RCE	40	520.685-022
Blender-Conveyor Operator (dairy products)	REC	41	529.685-022
Blender-Machine Operator (oils & grease)	REC	40	520.685-018
Blending Supervisor (grain-feed mills)	ERS	58	520.132-010
Blending Supervisor (tobacco)	ESI	57	520.136-010
Blending-Line Attendant (tobacco)	RCE	41	520.685-026
Blending-Machine Operator (dairy products)	RES	46	522.685-010
Blending-Machine Operator (textile)	RCS	42	680.685-010
Blending-Plant Operator (oils & grease)	REI	50	520.682-010
Blending-Tank Tender (beverage; can. & preserv.)	RCE	43	520.685-030
Blending-Tank Tender Helper (can. & preserv.)	RCI	40	520.687-066
Blind Aide (personal ser.)	SCE	48	359.573-010
Blind-Slat-Stapling-Machine Operator (woodworking)	RCE	38	669.685-018
Blindstitch-Machine Operator (garment)	CRE	40	786.682-046
Blintze Roller (food prep., n.e.c.)	REC	37	520.687-014
Block Feeder (fabrication, n.e.c.)	RCE	40	663.686-010
Block Inspector (fabrication, n.e.c.)	REC	37	739.687-038
Block Maker (protective dev.)	RCI	54	719.381-018

DOT to HOC

Title	HOC	Cx	DOT
Block-Breaker Operator (chemical)	RES	40	555.686-010
Block-Making-Machine Operator (concrete prod.)	RES	42	575.685-014
Block-Press Operator (chemical)	REC	40	556.685-014
Block-Splitter Operator (paper & pulp)	RES	39	663.685-010
Blocker (clock & watch)	REC	43	715.684-034
Blocker (glass mfg.; glass products)	REC	42	673.685-026
Blocker (laundry & rel.)	REC	45	363.684-010
Blocker (narrow fabrics; nonmet. min.)	REC	41	689.685-014
Blocker (tex. prod., n.e.c.)	RCE	38	920.685-022
Blocker and Cutter, Contact Lens (optical goods)	REI	50	716.681-010
Blocker and Polisher, Gold Wheel (clock & watch)	RES	49	715.381-034
Blocker I (print. & pub.)	RES	52	979.682-010
Blocker II (print. & pub.)	REI	48	971.684-010
Blocker, Automatic (glass mfg.; glass products)	RCS	40	673.685-030
Blocker, Hand (optical goods)	RES	44	716.684-010
Blocker, Hand I (hat & cap)	REC	42	580.684-010
Blocker, Hand II (hat & cap)	RCE	40	580.684-014
Blocker, Metal Base (print. & pub.)	RIE	53	974.682-010
Blocking-Machine Tender (optical goods)	RCE	40	716.685-010
Blood Tester, Fowl (agriculture)	RIE	49	411.364-010
Blood-Donor Recruiter (medical ser.)	ESA	55	293.357-010
Blood-Donor-Unit Assistant (medical ser.)	SCE	45	245.367-014
Blow-Molding-Machine Operator (plastic prod.)	RCE	46	556.682-010
Blow-Molding-Machine Tender (toy-sport equip.)	RCI	38	556.685-086
Blow-Off Worker (furniture)	RCE	37	763.687-010
Blow-Pit Helper (paper & pulp)	RES	38	533.686-010
Blow-Pit Operator (paper & pulp)	RES	41	533.665-010
Blow-Up Operator (sugar & conf.)	REI	52	529.485-014
Blower and Compressor Assembler (machinery mfg.)	RIS	57	801.361-010
Blower Feeder, Dyed Raw Stock (textile)	RES	37	581.686-010
Blower Insulator (railroad equip.; retail trade; wholesale tr.)	RCE	44	863.664-010
Blueprint Trimmer (any industry)	CRE	40	920.687-038
Blueprinting-Machine Operator (any industry)	RCS	47	979.682-014
Board Attendant (amuse. & rec.)	CSE	46	249.587-010
Board-Liner Operator (wood. container)	RES	41	641.685-014
Board-Machine Set-up Operator (concrete prod.)	RCE	53	579.380-010
Boarding-Machine Operator (knitting)	CRE	42	589.685-010
Boat Buffer, Plastic (ship-boat mfg.)	REC	38	849.684-010
Boat Dispatcher (water trans.)	ESR	62	184.167-010
Boat Loader I (water trans.)	REC	47	911.364-014
Boat Loader II (water trans.)	RCE	42	921.685-010
Boat Outfitter (ship-boat mfg.)	REI	48	806.684-146
Boat Patcher, Plastic (ship-boat mfg.)	REA	44	807.684-014
Boat Repairer (ship-boat mfg.)	RES	57	807.361-014
Boat Rigger (retail trade; ship-boat mfg.)	RSE	47	806.464-010
Boat-Canvas Maker-Installer (tex. prod., n.e.c.)	RCE	56	789.261-010
Boat-Hoist Operator (retail trade)	CRS	44	921.683-010
Boat-Hoist-Operator Helper (retail trade)	RES	39	921.667-010

Part 3: From Occupational Titles to Holland Codes

From the Dictionary of Occupational Titles Occupations to Holland Codes

Title	HOC	Cx	DOT
Boat-Loader Helper (water trans.)	RES	40	911.687-010
Boat-Oar Maker (woodworking)	RIS	53	761.381-010
Boat-Rental Clerk (amuse. & rec.)	RES	51	295.467-014
Boatbuilder Apprentice, Wood (ship-boat mfg.)	REI	53	860.361-014
Boatbuilder, Wood (ship-boat mfg.)	REI	53	860.361-010
Boatswain (water trans.)	RES	56	911.131-010
Boatswain, Otter Trawler (fishing & hunt.)	ERC	56	441.132-010
Bobbin Cleaner, Hand (textile)	RES	37	689.687-014
Bobbin Disker (glass mfg.)	REC	40	734.687-022
Bobbin Inspector (woodworking)	CRE	40	769.687-014
Bobbin Presser (tex. prod., n.e.c.)	RCE	41	689.685-018
Bobbin Sorter (glass mfg.; plastic-synth.; textile)	CRS	40	922.687-018
Bobbin Stripper (tex. prod., n.e.c.)	RCE	38	689.685-022
Bobbin Winder, Machine (boot & shoe)	REC	37	681.685-022
Bobbin Winder, Machine (tex. prod., n.e.c.; textile)	RCE	41	681.585-014
Bobbin Winder, Sewing Machine (textile)	RCE	41	681.685-026
Bobbin-Cleaning-Machine Operator (textile)	REC	39	689.686-014
Bobbin-Winder Tender (glass mfg.)	RES	39	619.685-022
Body Wirer (vehicles, n.e.c.)	CRS	48	829.684-014
Body-Make-Up Artist (amuse. & rec.; motion picture)	AER	49	333.271-010
Body-Maker-Machine Setter (tinware)	REI	52	616.360-010
Bodyguard (personal ser.)	ESC	45	372.667-014
Boil-Off-Machine Operator, Cloth (textile)	REI	43	582.685-022
Boiler (soap & rel.)	REI	57	553.382-014
Boiler House Inspector (any industry)	RSE	46	805.667-010
Boiler Operator (any industry)	RSE	57	950.382-010
Boiler Reliner, Plastic Block (foundry)	RES	47	849.484-010
Boiler-Operator Helper (sugar & conf.)	RCE	48	950.585-014
Boiler-Out (jewelry-silver.)	RCE	38	700.687-014
Boiler-Room Helper (any industry)	RES	44	950.685-014
Boilerhouse Mechanic (any industry)	RES	57	805.361-010
Boilermaker Apprentice (struct. metal)	RSE	59	805.261-010
Boilermaker Fitter (struct. metal)	RIE	56	805.361-014
Boilermaker Helper I (struct. metal)	RES	40	805.687-010
Boilermaker Helper II (struct. metal)	RES	46	805.664-010
Boilermaker I (struct. metal)	RSE	59	805.261-014
Boilermaker II (struct. metal)	RES	54	805.381-010
Boiling-Tub Operator (chemical)	REC	40	551.685-014
Bolt Loader (saw. & plan.)	RES	35	922.687-022
Bolter (grain-feed mills)	REC	41	521.685-030
Bolter (saw. & plan.)	RCS	41	667.685-022
Bolter Helper (grain-feed mills)	REC	40	521.686-010
Bomb Loader (ordnance)	RES	46	737.684-014
Bondactor-Machine Operator (foundry)	RCE	44	899.684-010
Bonded Structures Repairer (aircraft mfg.)	REC	54	807.381-014
Bonder, Automobile Brakes (automotive ser.)	CRE	42	620.685-010
Bonder, Semiconductor (electron. comp.)	CRS	41	726.685-066
Bonding Agent (business ser.)	SCE	57	186.267-010
Bonding-Machine Setter (textile)	REI	54	589.360-010

Title	HOC	Cx	DOT
Bonding-Machine Tender (textile)	RES	45	589.665-010
Bone Crusher (chemical)	REC	38	555.685-014
Bone Picker (can. & preserv.)	RCE	36	521.687-022
Bone Picker (chemical)	RCE	36	551.687-010
Bone-Char Kiln Operator (grain-feed mills)	RES	48	523.662-010
Bone-Char Kiln Tender (chemical)	CRE	38	553.685-018
Bone-Char Operator (chemical)	REC	38	553.686-010
Bone-Cooking Operator (chemical)	CRS	45	551.685-018
Bone-Drier Operator (chemical)	RCE	38	553.685-022
Bone-Process Operator (chemical)	RCS	44	559.665-010
Boner (garment; protective dev.)	RCE	40	789.687-018
Boner, Meat (meat products)	REC	41	525.684-010
Bonsai Culturist (agriculture)	RAE	59	405.161-010
Book Repairer (any industry)	REC	42	977.684-010
Book Trimmer (print. & pub.)	RCE	41	640.685-010
Book-Jacket-Cover-Machine Operator (paper goods)	CRE	44	640.685-014
Book-Sewing-Machine Operator I (print. & pub.)	REC	41	653.685-014
Book-Sewing-Machine Operator II (print. & pub.)	RCE	43	653.682-010
Bookbinder (print. & pub.)	RES	52	977.381-010
Bookbinder Apprentice (print. & pub.)	RES	52	977.381-014
Booker (rubber goods; rubber tire)	RCE	38	599.687-014
Booking Clerk (water trans.)	CES	53	248.367-014
Booking Clerk (wholesale tr.)	CSR	43	216.587-010
Booking Manager (amuse. & rec.)	SEA	60	191.117-014
Booking Prizer (tobacco)	CRS	51	216.462-010
Booking Supervisor (water trans.)	ESR	60	248.137-010
Bookkeeper (clerical)	CSI	60	210.382-014
Bookmaker (amuse. & rec.)	ESC	58	187.167-014
Bookmobile Driver (library)	RCS	51	249.363-010
Bookmobile Librarian (library)	ESR	63	100.167-014
Boom-Conveyor Operator (any industry)	REI	42	921.683-014
Booster Assembler (ordnance)	RCE	41	737.687-022
Bootmaker, Hand (rubber goods)	REC	50	753.381-010
Border Guard (government ser.)	SRE	52	375.363-010
Border Measurer and Cutter (furniture)	REC	38	780.687-010
Boring-and-Filling-Machine Operator (fabrication, n.e.c.)	RCE	51	692.682-018
Boring-Machine Operator (furniture)	RCI	44	666.685-014
Boring-Machine Operator (machine shop)	RCI	56	606.382-022
Boring-Machine Operator (woodworking)	REI	50	666.382-010
Boring-Machine Operator, Production (machine shop)	REI	43	606.685-010
Boring-Machine Set-up Operator, Jig (machine shop)	RIE	59	606.280-010
Boring-Mill Set-up Operator, Horizontal (machine shop)	RIE	59	606.280-014
Botanist (profess. & kin.)	IRS	78	041.061-038
Bottle Gauger (beverage)	CRE	48	529.587-010
Bottle Packer (beverage)	REC	40	920.685-026
Bottle-House Quality-Control Technician (beverage)	RIE	59	029.361-010
Bottled-Beverage Inspector (beverage)	RCE	40	529.685-026
Bottling-Line Attendant (beverage)	CRE	38	920.687-042
Bottom Bleacher (boot & shoe)	REC	37	788.687-014

Title	HOC	Cx	DOT
Bottom Filler (boot & shoe)	RCS	38	788.684-026
Bottom Maker (steel & rel.)	RES	41	509.687-010
Bottom Polisher (elec. equip.)	CRS	38	603.685-034
Bottom Presser (boot & shoe)	REC	39	690.685-034
Bottom Wheeler (boot & shoe)	REC	41	788.684-030
Bottom-Hole-Pressure-Recording-Operator Helper (petrol. & gas)	RES	40	930.687-010
Bottom-Hoop Driver (wood. container)	RES	39	669.685-022
Bottom-Precipitator Operator (smelt. & refin.)	RSC	44	511.664-010
Bottom-Saw Operator (saw. & plan.)	RCS	44	667.682-014
Bottom-Turning-Lathe Tender (wood. container)	RCE	41	665.685-010
Bottomer I (mine & quarry)	RES	41	932.667-010
Bottoming-Machine Operator (paper goods)	RCS	41	649.685-022
Bouffant-Curtain-Machine Tender (tex. prod., n.e.c.)	CSE	45	689.685-026
Bouncer (amuse. & rec.)	ESR	45	376.667-010
Bow Maker (any industry)	CRE	42	789.684-010
Bow Maker (boot & shoe)	RCE	38	788.684-034
Bow Maker (garment; hat & cap)	CRS	39	784.684-010
Bow Maker (musical inst.)	RCI	55	730.281-058
Bow Maker, Custom (toy-sport equip.)	RIE	53	732.381-010
Bow Maker, Production (toy-sport equip.)	REI	50	732.684-038
Bow Rehairer (any industry)	CRS	46	730.684-022
Bow-Maker-Machine Tender, Automatic (tex. prod., n.e.c.)	CRE	41	689.685-030
Bow-String Maker (toy-sport equip.)	CRS	39	732.684-042
Bowl Turner (fabrication, n.e.c.)	REI	40	664.684-010
Bowling-Ball Engraver (toy-sport equip.)	RCE	44	732.584-010
Bowling-Ball Finisher (toy-sport equip.)	RCE	41	690.685-038
Bowling-Ball Grader and Marker (toy-sport equip.)	REI	53	732.381-014
Bowling-Ball Molder (toy-sport equip.)	RES	41	556.685-018
Bowling-Ball Weigher and Packer (toy-sport equip.)	CRE	46	732.487-010
Bowling-Ball-Mold Assembler (toy-sport equip.)	RES	38	556.687-010
Box Bender (paper goods)	RES	36	641.687-010
Box Inspector (wood. container)	CRS	39	762.687-014
Box Maker (fabrication, n.e.c.)	RCE	40	762.684-026
Box Maker, Paperboard (any industry)	RCE	40	794.684-014
Box Maker, Wood (wood. container)	RCS	46	760.684-014
Box Printer (any industry)	CRS	45	652.682-010
Box Repairer II (wood. container)	RCS	39	762.687-018
Box Tender (plastic-synth.)	RES	57	689.280-010
Box-Blank-Machine Operator (wood. container)	REC	48	669.662-010
Box-Blank-Machine-Operator Helper (wood. container)	RES	40	669.686-014
Box-Folding-Machine Operator (paper goods)	RIE	47	649.682-010
Box-Lining-Machine Feeder (paper goods)	REC	40	641.685-018
Box-Sealing Inspector (paper goods)	RCE	40	641.687-014
Box-Sealing-Machine Operator (paper goods)	RSE	45	641.662-010
Box-Spring Maker I (furniture)	REC	41	780.684-018
Box-Spring Maker II (furniture)	RES	39	780.684-022
Box-Truck Washer (meat products)	REC	38	529.687-018
Boxing Inspector (garment)	CRS	42	789.587-010

DOT to HOC

Title	HOC	Cx	DOT
Boxing-and-Pressing Supervisor (knitting)	ESR	58	789.137-010
Bracelet and Brooch Maker (jewelry-silver.)	RCS	49	735.681-010
Braid-Pattern Setter (narrow fabrics)	RES	59	683.260-010
Braider Operator (nonfer. metal)	REC	47	691.682-014
Braider Setter (rubber goods)	RCE	40	759.664-010
Braiding-Machine Operator (narrow fabrics; nonmet. min.)	RCE	41	683.685-010
Braiding-Machine Tender (rubber goods)	REC	42	692.665-010
Braille Operator (print. & pub.)	CRS	49	203.582-010
Braille Proofreader (nonprofit org.; print. & pub.)	CSE	57	209.367-014
Braille Transcriber, Hand (education; nonprofit organ.; print. & pub.)	CSE	49	209.584-010
Braille Typist (education; nonprofit organ.; print. & pub.)	CSR	51	203.582-014
Braille-and-Talking Books Clerk (library)	CSE	46	222.587-014
Braille-Duplicating-Machine Operator (print. & pub.)	REC	41	207.685-010
Brake Adjuster (automotive ser.)	RCE	44	620.684-018
Brake Coupler, Road Freight (r.r. trans.)	RIE	51	910.367-010
Brake Holder (any industry)	RCE	41	932.664-010
Brake Operator I (any industry)	RSI	54	617.360-010
Brake Operator II (any industry)	RES	47	619.685-026
Brake Repairer (automotive ser.)	RES	56	620.281-026
Brake Repairer, Railroad (r.r. trans.)	RCI	50	622.261-010
Brake-Drum-Lathe Operator (automotive ser.)	RCE	49	620.682-010
Brake-Lining Curer (nonmet. min.)	REC	39	573.686-010
Brake-Lining Finisher, Asbestos (nonmet. min.)	RSC	44	579.665-010
Brake-Lining-Finisher Helper, Asbestos (nonmet. min.)	RES	40	579.687-010
Braker, Passenger Train (r.r. trans.)	CES	51	910.364-010
Bran Mixer (grain-feed mills)	RCE	40	599.685-014
Brand Recorder (government ser.)	CSE	46	206.587-010
Branding-Machine Tender (rubber goods)	RES	41	690.685-042
Branner-Machine Tender (galvanizing)	RSC	45	509.685-014
Brass-Wind-Instrument Maker (musical inst.)	RIE	60	730.381-018
Brassiere-Slide-Making-Machine Tender, Automatic (garment)	RCE	39	692.685-026
Brazer, Assembler (welding)	RSI	51	813.684-010
Brazer, Controlled Atmospheric Furnace (welding)	RSC	48	813.685-010
Brazer, Furnace (welding)	RIE	51	813.482-010
Brazer, Induction (welding)	RIE	50	813.382-010
Brazer, Resistance (welding)	RIE	47	813.682-010
Brazing-Machine Operator (welding)	RIE	52	813.382-014
Brazing-Machine Setter (welding)	RIE	60	813.360-010
Breading Machine Tender (can. & preserv.)	RCE	39	524.685-010
Break-and-Load Operator (electron. comp.)	RCI	41	726.685-018
Break-Off Worker (millwork-plywood)	RES	38	663.686-014
Breaker (glass products)	RSE	38	779.687-010
Breaker Tender (steel & rel.)	REC	39	544.685-010
Breaker-Machine Operator (saw. & plan.; wood prod., n.e.c.)	RCE	41	564.685-010
Breaker-Machine Tender (textile)	RCE	41	583.685-010
Breaker-Up-Machine Operator (hat & cap)	REC	37	589.685-014

Title	HOC	Cx	DOT
Breaking-Machine Operator (sugar & conf.)	RES	38	521.685-034
Brewery Cellar Worker (beverage)	REC	40	522.685-014
Brewing Director (beverage)	ESA	68	183.167-010
Briar Cutter (fabrication, n.e.c.)	RCE	40	664.685-010
Briar-Wood Sorter (fabrication, n.e.c.)	RCI	40	769.687-058
Brick Setter Operator (brick & tile)	RCE	45	579.685-058
Brick Tester (brick & tile)	REI	50	579.384-010
Brick Unloader Tender (brick & tile)	RCI	43	579.685-062
Brick-and-Tile-Making-Machine Operator (brick & tile)	RSE	49	575.382-010
Bricklayer (brick & tile)	REI	55	861.381-014
Bricklayer (construction)	RSE	58	861.381-018
Bricklayer Apprentice (construction)	RIE	58	861.381-022
Bricklayer Helper, Firebrick and Refractory Tile (construction)	RES	41	861.687-010
Bricklayer Supervisor (construction)	ERS	59	861.131-010
Bricklayer, Firebrick and Refractory Tile (construction)	REI	54	861.381-026
Bridge Inspector (r.r. trans.)	RSI	61	869.287-010
Bridge Operator, Slip (r.r. trans.)	RCS	47	919.682-010
Bright Cutter (jewelry-silver.)	RCE	46	700.684-018
Brilliandeer-Lopper (jewelry-silver.)	REI	52	770.261-010
Brim Curler (hat & cap)	REC	40	583.685-014
Brim Ironer, Hand (hat & cap)	CRS	41	784.684-014
Brim Presser I (hat & cap)	RCE	40	583.685-018
Brim Raiser (hat & cap)	REC	38	784.687-010
Brim Stitcher I (hat & cap)	CRS	38	784.685-014
Brim-and-Crown Presser (hat & cap)	CRE	40	583.685-022
Brim-Pouncing-Machine Operator (hat & cap)	RCE	42	585.685-010
Brim-Stretching-Machine Operator (hat & cap)	RCE	41	580.685-010
Brimer (metal prod., n.e.c.)	REC	39	700.687-018
Brine Maker I (can. & preserv.)	REC	46	522.685-018
Brine Maker I (chemical)	RIE	46	550.685-018
Brine Maker II (can. & preserv.)	CRE	42	522.685-022
Brine Maker II (chemical)	REC	41	551.687-014
Brine-Mixer Operator, Automatic (can. & preserv.)	CRE	40	520.685-034
Brine-Tank Tender (dairy products)	REI	40	529.685-030
Brine-Tank-Separator Operator (can. & preserv.)	RCE	39	521.685-038
Brine-Well Operator (chemical)	RSE	45	559.685-026
Briner (can. & preserv.)	REI	39	522.687-014
Briquette Operator (brick & tile)	RCI	43	579.685-066
Briquette-Machine Operator (fabrication, n.e.c.)	REC	47	549.662-010
Briquette-Machine-Operator Helper (fabrication, n.e.c.)	RES	38	549.686-010
Briquetter Operator (chemical)	RES	44	559.685-030
Briquetting-Machine Operator (smelt. & refin.)	RCE	41	519.685-010
Broaching-Machine Operator, Production (machine shop)	RIE	45	605.682-014
Broaching-Machine Set-up Operator (machine shop)	RIE	51	605.382-010
Broadcast Checker (radio-tv broad.)	CER	51	249.387-010
Broker-and-Market Operator, Grain (financial; wholesale tr.)	EAS	67	162.157-010
Brokerage Clerk I (financial)	CSR	55	219.482-010

Title	HOC	Cx	DOT
Brokerage Clerk II (financial)	CSR	54	219.362-018
Broom Bundler (fabrication, n.e.c.)	REC	41	692.685-030
Broom Stitcher (fabrication, n.e.c.)	RCE	47	692.682-022
Broomcorn Grader (fabrication, n.e.c.)	CER	42	739.687-042
Broomcorn Seeder (fabrication, n.e.c.)	REC	37	692.686-018
Broommaker (fabrication, n.e.c.)	CRE	41	739.684-018
Broth Mixer (bakery products)	REI	47	520.585-014
Brown-Stock Washer (paper & pulp)	REC	39	533.685-014
Browning Processor (ordnance)	REC	43	505.685-010
Brush Filler, Hand (fabrication, n.e.c.)	CER	43	739.687-046
Brush Loader and Handle Attacher (fabrication, n.e.c.)	RCI	40	739.687-206
Brush Maker, Machine (fabrication, n.e.c.)	RES	38	739.685-014
Brush Material Preparer (fabrication, n.e.c.)	RCS	42	739.684-022
Brush Operator (textile)	REC	40	587.685-010
Brush Polisher (clock & watch)	CRS	41	603.685-038
Brush-Fabrication Supervisor (fabrication, n.e.c.)	RES	59	692.130-010
Brush-Head Maker (fabrication, n.e.c.)	RCE	40	739.685-018
Brush-Machine Setter (fabrication, n.e.c.)	RES	52	692.360-014
Brusher (boot & shoe)	REC	37	788.687-018
Brusher, Machine (hat & cap)	REC	40	587.685-014
Bucker (logging)	REC	39	454.684-010
Bucket Chucker (wood. container)	REC	41	664.685-014
Bucket Operator (concrete prod.)	RCE	41	575.683-010
Bucket Turner (wood. container)	RCS	40	669.682-018
Buckle Inspector (button & notion)	CSR	40	734.687-026
Buckle Sorter (button & notion)	RCE	42	734.687-030
Buckle-Frame Shaper (button & notion)	REC	42	692.685-034
Buckle-Strap-Drum Operator (rubber goods)	CRE	41	554.485-010
Buckle-Wire Inserter (button & notion)	CRE	36	734.687-034
Buckler and Lacer (boot & shoe)	RCE	35	788.687-022
Buckshot-Swage Operator (ordnance)	RIE	50	612.682-010
Budder (agriculture)	RCE	39	405.684-010
Budget Analyst (government ser.)	CER	66	161.267-030
Budget Clerk (clerical)	CSR	59	216.382-022
Budget Officer (profess. & kin.)	ESI	72	161.117-010
Buffer (boot & shoe)	RCE	41	690.685-046
Buffer (fabrication, n.e.c.)	RCE	41	739.684-026
Buffer (hat & cap)	RCE	40	585.685-014
Buffer (plastic prod.)	RCE	40	752.684-022
Buffer (rubber goods; rubber tire)	RCS	40	759.684-022
Buffer I (any industry)	RCS	44	705.684-014
Buffer, Automatic (boot & shoe)	REC	39	690.685-050
Buffer, Inflated-Pad (boot & shoe)	RCE	41	690.685-054
Buffer, Machine (leather mfg.)	REC	41	585.685-018
Buffing Turner-and-Counter (tex. prod., n.e.c.)	RCE	39	789.687-022
Buffing-and-Polishing-Wheel Repairer (any industry)	REC	42	739.684-030
Buffing-and-Sueding-Machine Operator (boot & shoe)	RCS	38	753.684-010
Buffing-Line Set-up Worker (any industry)	REI	53	603.360-010
Buffing-Machine Operator (any industry)	RIE	52	603.382-010

Title	HOC	Cx	DOT
Buffing-Machine Operator, Silverware (jewelry-silver.)	RIE	48	603.682-010
Buffing-Machine Tender (any industry)	RCE	40	603.665-010
Buffing-Wheel Former, Automatic (tex. prod., n.e.c.)	REC	41	689.685-034
Buffing-Wheel Former, Hand (tex. prod., n.e.c.)	RCE	41	789.684-014
Buffing-Wheel Inspector (tex. prod., n.e.c.)	RCE	40	789.687-026
Builder, Beam (mfd. bldgs.)	RCS	46	860.684-010
Building Cleaner (any industry)	RCS	47	891.684-022
Building Consultant (wholesale tr.)	ESA	61	250.357-010
Building Inspector (insurance)	RCE	63	168.267-010
Building-Equipment Inspector (utilities)	REI	54	956.387-010
Building-Insulation Supervisor (construction)	ECS	59	863.134-010
Bulb Filler (light. fix.)	RCE	38	692.686-022
Bulk Filler (can. & preserv.)	RCE	42	529.687-022
Bulk-Plant Operator (sugar & conf.)	CSE	54	520.362-010
Bulk-Sealer Operator (plastic-synth.)	REC	40	554.685-010
Bulk-Station Operator (petrol. & gas)	RIE	53	570.362-010
Bulker (tobacco)	REC	39	522.687-018
Bulker, Cut Tobacco (tobacco)	RCE	39	529.685-034
Bull-Chain Operator (saw. & plan.)	REC	40	921.685-014
Bull-Gang Worker (tobacco)	RES	37	922.687-026
Bulldozer Operator I (any industry)	REC	47	850.683-010
Bullet-Assembly-Press Operator (ordnance)	REC	42	694.685-014
Bullet-Assembly-Press Setter-Operator (ordnance)	REC	48	694.682-010
Bullet-Casting Operator (ordnance)	RSC	47	502.682-010
Bullet-Grooving-Sizing-and-Lubricating-Machine Operator (ordnance)	RCE	50	619.382-010
Bullet-Lubricant Mixer (ordnance)	CRS	41	543.685-010
Bullet-Lubricating-Machine Operator (ordnance)	REC	39	694.685-018
Bullet-Slug-Casting-Machine Operator (ordnance)	RIS	49	502.382-010
Bunch Maker, Hand (tobacco)	RCE	42	790.684-010
Bunch Maker, Machine (tobacco)	CRE	40	529.685-038
Bunch Trimmer, Mold (tobacco)	RCE	35	521.687-026
Bundle Breaker (tex. prod., n.e.c.)	REC	37	689.687-018
Bundle Tier and Labeler (saw. & plan.)	REC	40	920.685-110
Bundler, Seasonal Greenery (forestry)	RCE	40	920.687-046
Bundles Hanger (tobacco)	REC	36	529.686-010
Bung Driver (wood. container)	RCE	36	764.687-042
Bureau Chief (print. & pub.)	AES	69	132.067-010
Burlap Spreader (tex. prod., n.e.c.)	RCE	36	581.687-010
Burler (carpet & rug; textile)	CRE	45	689.684-010
Burn-Out Tender, Lace (tex. prod., n.e.c.)	RES	42	589.685-018
Burner (brick & tile)	RCI	40	573.685-038
Burner Operator (chemical)	REI	55	558.382-014
Burner Tender (mine & quarry)	REC	40	571.685-010
Burning Supervisor (brick & tile)	SER	56	573.132-010
Burning-Plant Operator (ordnance)	RCS	38	509.685-018
Burnisher (boot & shoe)	RCE	39	690.685-058
Burnisher (clock & watch)	CRE	38	603.685-042
Burnisher, Balance Wheel Arm (clock & watch)	CRE	41	715.684-038

Title	HOC	Cx	DOT
Burr Grinder (optical goods)	RCE	38	673.686-014
Burrer (clock & watch)	CRE	42	715.684-042
Burrer, Machine (clock & watch)	CRE	40	603.685-046
Burring-Machine Operator (nut & bolt)	REC	41	615.685-010
Bursar (education)	CEI	70	160.167-042
Bus Attendant (motor trans.)	CES	49	352.577-010
Bus Dispatcher, Interstate (motor trans.)	ESR	57	913.167-010
Bus Driver (motor trans.)	RES	50	913.463-010
Bus Driver, Day-Haul or Farm Charter (agriculture)	RIE	51	913.363-010
Bus Inspector (automotive ser.)	REI	60	620.281-030
Busher (nonmet. min.)	RES	38	502.687-014
Business Manager (amuse. & rec.)	ESC	67	191.117-018
Business Manager, College or University (education)	ESR	76	186.117-010
Business Representative, Labor Union (profess. & kin.)	ESA	65	187.167-018
Business-Enterprise Officer (government ser.)	EIR	68	188.117-014
Business-Opportunity-and-Property-Investment Broker (business ser.; real estate)	ESA	66	189.157-010
Butcher Apprentice (meat products)	RES	52	525.381-010
Butcher, All-Round (meat products)	RES	52	525.381-014
Butcher, Chicken and Fish (hotel & rest.)	RCE	42	316.684-010
Butcher, Fish (can. & preserv.)	REI	37	525.684-014
Butcher, Meat (hotel & rest.)	RSE	48	316.681-010
Butler (domestic ser.)	ESC	57	309.137-010
Butler, Second (domestic ser.)	RSC	45	309.674-010
Butt Maker (tobacco)	CRE	40	529.685-042
Butter Liquefier (oils & grease)	RCE	45	523.585-010
Buttermaker (dairy products)	REI	54	529.362-010
Buttermaker, Continuous Churn (dairy products)	REI	52	529.382-010
Button Grader (button & notion)	RES	42	734.687-038
Button Maker and Installer (tex. prod., n.e.c.)	RCS	40	734.685-014
Button Reclaimer (knitting)	RCE	37	734.687-042
Button Spindler (button & notion)	CRE	37	740.687-010
Button-and-Buckle Maker (any industry)	REC	41	734.687-046
Button-Attaching-Machine Operator (garment; hat & cap)	RCE	40	699.685-010
Button-Cutting-Machine Operator (button & notion)	REC	43	734.384-010
Button-Decorating-Machine Operator (button & notion)	RCE	41	690.685-062
Button-Facing-Machine Operator (button & notion)	REC	41	690.685-066
Button-Sewing-Machine Operator (garment)	RCE	40	786.685-010
Buttoner (garment; knitting)	CRE	36	782.687-014
Buttonhole Maker (boot & shoe)	RCE	39	788.684-038
Buttonhole-and-Button-Sewing-Machine Operator (garment)	RCE	41	786.685-042
Buttonhole-Machine Operator (garment)	RCE	40	786.685-014
Buyer (profess. & kin.)	ESC	64	162.157-018
Buyer, Assistant (retail trade)	ESR	62	162.157-022
Buyer, Grain (grain-feed mills; wholesale tr.)	EIS	67	162.167-010
Buyer, Tobacco, Head (wholesale tr.)	ESA	62	162.167-014
Buzzsaw Operator (any industry)	RCE	41	667.685-026
Buzzsaw-Operator Helper (any industry)	RES	36	667.687-010

Part 3: From Occupational Titles to Holland Codes

From the Dictionary of Occupational Titles Occupations to Holland Codes

Title	HOC	Cx	DOT
C.O.D. Clerk (clerical)	CSR	51	214.382-018
Cabana Attendant (amuse. & rec.)	ERC	43	349.677-010
Cabin-Equipment Supervisor (air trans.)	RES	59	869.131-010
Cabinet Assembler (furniture)	CSR	47	763.684-014
Cabinetmaker (woodworking)	RIS	59	660.280-010
Cabinetmaker Apprentice (woodworking)	RIS	59	660.280-014
Cabinetmaker, Supervisor (woodworking)	RES	62	660.130-010
Cable Assembler and Swager (aircraft mfg.)	RSC	56	806.381-042
Cable Engineer, Outside Plant (tel. & tel.)	IRE	70	003.167-010
Cable Installer-Repairer (utilities)	RSE	59	821.361-010
Cable Maintainer (utilities)	REC	54	952.464-010
Cable Puller (construction; utilities)	REC	40	829.684-018
Cable Splicer (construction; tel. & tel.; utilities)	RCS	57	829.361-010
Cable Supervisor (construction; tel. & tel.; utilities)	RES	59	829.131-010
Cable Supervisor (tel. & tel.)	ERS	61	184.161-010
Cable Television Installer (radio-tv broad.)	RIE	58	821.281-010
Cable Television Line Technician (radio-tv broad.)	REC	56	821.261-010
Cable Tester (tel. & tel.)	RSE	57	822.361-010
Cable-Splicer Apprentice (construction; tel. & tel.; utilities)	RCS	57	829.361-014
Cable-Splicer Helper (construction; tel. & tel.; utilities)	RCS	41	829.667-010
Caddie (amuse. & rec.)	CRE	42	341.677-010
Caddie Supervisor (amuse. & rec.)	ESR	53	341.137-010
Cadet, Deck (water trans.)	ERS	59	911.133-010
Cadmium Burner (chemical)	RCI	41	553.685-114
Cadmium-Liquor Maker (paint & varnish)	RCE	38	553.685-026
Cafeteria Attendant (hotel & rest.)	RCE	40	311.677-010
Cage Maker (concrete prod.)	RSC	46	709.684-030
Cage Maker, Machine (concrete prod.)	RES	46	616.682-018
Cager (mine & quarry)	RES	44	939.667-010
Cager Operator (can. & preserv.)	RES	40	921.685-018
Cake Decorator (bakery products)	ARE	50	524.381-010
Cake Former (oils & grease)	REC	38	520.685-038
Cake Puller (oils & grease)	RES	37	521.686-014
Cake Stripper (oils & grease)	REC	38	520.685-042
Cake Tester (grain-feed mills)	RSE	53	526.381-022
Cake Wrapper (plastic-synth.)	REC	37	589.687-010
Cake-Press Operator (plastic-synth.)	RSC	46	556.665-010
Cake-Press-Operator Helper (plastic-synth.)	RSE	38	556.686-010
Calcine Furnace Loader (paint & varnish)	RES	38	553.486-010
Calcine-Furnace Tender (paint & varnish)	REI	42	553.685-030
Calciner Operator (mine & quarry; smelt. & refin.)	REC	52	513.362-010
Calciner, Gypsum (concrete prod.)	RES	49	579.382-010
Calciner-Operator Helper (mine & quarry; smelt. & refin.)	CRE	44	513.667-010
Calculating-Machine Operator (clerical)	CSE	52	216.482-022
Calendar-Control Clerk, Blood Bank (medical ser.)	CES	51	245.367-018
Calender Feeder (rubber goods)	RES	37	554.686-010
Calender Operator (fabrication, n.e.c.)	RIE	49	590.682-010
Calender Operator (rubber goods; rubber tire)	RIE	49	554.362-010

Part 3: From Occupational Titles to Holland Codes

From the Dictionary of Occupational Titles Occupations to Holland Codes

Title	HOC	Cx	DOT
Calender Operator (tex. prod., n.e.c.; textile)	RCE	44	583.685-026
Calender Operator, Artificial Leather (tex. prod., n.e.c.)	RCS	43	584.685-010
Calender Operator, Four-Roll (plastic prod.; rubber goods; rubber tire)	RSE	49	554.662-010
Calender Operator, Insulation Board (wood prod., n.e.c.)	REI	50	539.482-010
Calender Supervisor (plastic-synth.)	ESR	59	559.132-014
Calender-Let-Off Helper (rubber goods; rubber tire)	REI	40	554.686-014
Calender-Let-Off Operator (rubber goods; rubber tire)	RCE	46	554.682-010
Calender-Machine Operator (nonmet. min.)	REI	47	583.585-010
Calender-Operator Helper (rubber goods; rubber tire)	RES	40	554.686-018
Calender-Roll Press Operator (machinery mfg.)	RCS	51	692.462-010
Calender-Wind-Up Helper (rubber goods; rubber tire)	RES	37	554.686-022
Calender-Wind-Up Tender (rubber goods; rubber tire)	RCS	40	554.665-010
Calendering-Machine Operator (knitting)	REI	47	580.485-010
Calibration Laboratory Technician (aircraft mfg.; electron. comp.)	RCI	66	019.281-010
Calibrator (cutlery-hrdwr.)	RCE	44	701.684-010
Calibrator (inst. & app.)	RIE	57	710.381-034
Calibrator, Barometers (inst. & app.)	RIE	57	710.381-042
Call-Out Operator (business ser.; retail trade)	CSE	50	237.367-014
Caller (r.r. trans.)	CSE	46	215.563-010
Camera Operator (motion picture; radio-tv broad.)	AES	62	143.062-022
Camera Operator, Animation (motion picture)	RIC	57	143.382-010
Camera Operator, Title (motion picture)	RCS	54	976.382-010
Camera Repairer (photo. appar.)	RCE	61	714.281-014
Camouflage Assembler (ordnance)	RCE	37	869.687-014
Camouflage Specialist (military ser.)	RES	44	378.684-010
Camp Tender (agriculture)	RES	54	410.137-010
Can Doffer (textile)	RES	37	680.686-010
Can Filler (tobacco)	RES	35	922.687-030
Can Inspector (beverage; can. & preserv.)	CRE	42	920.687-050
Can Patcher (can. & preserv.)	RCE	42	920.687-054
Can Reconditioner (can. & preserv.)	CRS	40	920.687-058
Can-Conveyor Feeder (food prep., n.e.c.)	REC	38	529.685-046
Can-Filling-and-Closing-Machine Tender (can. & preserv.)	RCI	40	529.685-282
Canal-Equipment Mechanic (waterworks)	REI	56	899.281-010
Canary Breeder (agriculture)	SRC	56	411.161-010
Canceling and Cutting Control Clerk (financial)	CRI	57	219.367-042
Cancellation Clerk (insurance)	CSE	55	203.382-014
Candle Cutter (fabrication, n.e.c.)	RCS	37	739.687-050
Candle Molder, Hand (fabrication, n.e.c.)	REC	39	739.687-054
Candle Molder, Machine (fabrication, n.e.c.)	RES	42	692.685-038
Candle Wrapping-Machine Operator (fabrication, n.e.c.)	RCE	38	920.685-030
Candle-Extrusion-Machine Operator (fabrication, n.e.c.)	CRS	48	692.682-026
Candlemaker (fabrication, n.e.c.)	RCE	43	739.664-010
Candy Cutter, Hand (sugar & conf.)	RCE	40	790.687-010
Candy Dipper, Hand (sugar & conf.)	CRS	40	524.684-010
Candy Maker (sugar & conf.)	RSE	58	529.361-014

Part 3: From Occupational Titles to Holland Codes

From the Dictionary of Occupational Titles Occupations to Holland Codes

Title	HOC	Cx	DOT
Candy Molder, Hand (sugar & conf.)	CRS	39	520.687-018
Candy Puller (sugar & conf.)	RSE	44	520.685-046
Candy Spreader (sugar & conf.)	REC	39	520.687-022
Candy-Maker Helper (sugar & conf.)	RCS	47	520.685-050
Cane Cutter (furniture)	RCE	36	763.687-030
Caner I (furniture)	CRS	44	763.684-018
Caner II (furniture)	CRS	41	763.684-022
Cannery Worker (can. & preserv.)	REC	42	529.686-014
Cannon-Pinion Adjuster (clock & watch)	CRS	46	715.684-046
Canoe Inspector, Final (ship-boat mfg.)	RCS	41	769.687-018
Canopy Stringer (tex. prod., n.e.c.)	CRS	47	789.684-018
Canteen Operator (any industry)	ERS	42	311.674-010
Cantilever-Crane Operator (water trans.)	CRE	47	921.683-018
Cantor (profess. & kin.)	ASE	63	129.027-010
Canvas Baster, Jumpbasting (garment)	RCE	41	786.682-050
Canvas Repairer (any industry)	REC	41	782.684-010
Canvas Shrinker (textile)	RES	39	587.687-010
Canvas Worker (ship-boat mfg.; tex. prod., n.e.c.)	RSE	55	739.381-010
Canvas-Worker Apprentice (ship-boat mfg.; tex. prod., n.e.c.)	RSE	55	739.381-014
Cap Maker (hat & cap)	CRE	42	784.684-018
Cap-Jewel Plate Assembler (clock & watch)	RCE	46	715.684-050
Capacitor Assembler (elec. equip.)	RCS	47	729.684-014
Capacitor-Pack-Press Operator (elec. equip.)	RES	41	726.684-010
Caponizer (agriculture)	CRS	38	411.684-010
Capping-Machine Operator (elec. equip.)	RCE	42	692.685-042
Capsule-Filling-Machine Operator (pharmaceut.)	RIE	48	559.682-010
Captain, Fire-Prevention Bureau (government ser.)	ESA	66	373.167-014
Captain, Fishing Vessel (fishing & hunt.)	ERS	61	197.133-010
Caption Writer (motion picture; radio-tv broad.)	IRS	57	203.362-026
Car Blocker (any industry)	RCI	45	860.684-018
Car Chaser (beverage)	ERS	56	910.167-010
Car Checker (r.r. trans.)	CSE	50	222.387-014
Car Clerk, Pullman (r.r. trans.)	ESC	58	215.167-010
Car Cooper (any industry)	REC	40	910.687-014
Car Distributor (r.r. trans.)	ESC	55	910.367-014
Car Dropper (mine & quarry)	REC	41	932.683-010
Car Hop (hotel & rest.)	ESR	44	311.477-010
Car Icer (food prep., n.e.c.; meat products)	RES	40	910.687-018
Car Inspector (railroad equip.)	RCS	46	910.667-010
Car Pincher (steel & rel.)	RES	36	922.687-034
Car Repairer (railroad equip.)	RES	57	622.381-014
Car Repairer, Pullman (r.r. trans.)	REI	57	622.381-018
Car Scrubber (railroad equip.)	REC	41	845.684-010
Car Trimmer (railroad equip.)	RES	45	806.684-046
Car-Cleaning Supervisor (r.r. trans.)	ERS	57	910.137-014
Car-Dumper Operator (beverage)	RSE	44	921.662-010
Car-Dumper-Operator Helper (beverage)	REC	40	921.687-010
Car-Repairer Apprentice (railroad equip.)	RES	57	622.381-022

Part 3: From Occupational Titles to Holland Codes

From the Dictionary of Occupational Titles Occupations to Holland Codes

Title	HOC	Cx	DOT
Car-Repairer Helper (railroad equip.)	RCE	44	622.684-014
Car-Retarder Operator (r.r. trans.)	RCE	52	910.382-010
Car-Wash Attendant, Automatic (automotive ser.)	REC	41	915.667-010
Car-Wash Supervisor (automotive ser.)	RES	52	915.137-010
Carbide Operator (machine shop)	RIE	58	601.380-010
Carbide-Powder Processor (machine shop)	RSE	49	510.465-010
Carbon Cutter (elec. equip.)	REC	47	677.685-018
Carbon Printer (print. & pub.)	REI	47	979.684-010
Carbon Rod Inserter (elec. equip.)	RCE	37	692.686-026
Carbon Setter (smelt. & refin.)	RES	40	519.667-010
Carbon-and-Graphite-Brush-Machine Operator (elec. equip.)	RSE	50	692.482-010
Carbon-Coater-Machine Operator (pen & pencil)	RIE	48	534.682-014
Carbon-Furnace Operator (smelt. & refin.)	REA	51	543.562-010
Carbon-Furnace-Operator Helper (smelt. & refin.)	RCE	44	543.664-010
Carbon-Paper Interleafer (pen & pencil)	RES	41	640.685-018
Carbon-Paper-Coating-Machine Setter (pen & pencil)	RCS	53	534.380-010
Carbonation Equipment Operator (sugar & conf.)	RSI	54	529.582-010
Carbonation Equipment Tender (beverage)	CRS	46	522.685-026
Carbonation Tester (beverage)	CSE	46	522.587-010
Carbonizer (textile)	REC	44	581.585-010
Carburetor Mechanic (automotive ser.)	RSE	52	620.281-034
Carcass Splitter (meat products)	REC	40	525.684-018
Card Changer, Jacquard Loom (textile)	RCE	44	683.685-014
Card Clothier (textile)	RES	56	628.381-010
Card Cutter, Jacquard (narrow fabrics; textile)	RCE	47	683.582-010
Card Decorator (print. & pub.)	RCS	37	649.686-014
Card Grinder (nonmet. min.; textile)	RSE	56	680.380-010
Card Grinder Helper (textile)	RCI	45	680.684-010
Card Lacer, Jacquard (narrow fabrics; textile)	RCE	40	683.685-018
Card Player (amuse. & rec.)	ECS	50	343.367-010
Card Stripper (textile)	RCE	39	680.685-014
Card Tender (nonmet. min.; textile)	RSC	40	680.685-018
Cardboard Inserter (knitting)	RCE	36	920.687-062
Carder (any industry)	RCE	40	920.685-034
Cardiac Monitor Technician (medical ser.)	SIR	51	078.367-010
Carding-Machine Operator (tex. prod., n.e.c.)	RCE	37	681.685-030
Cardiologist (medical ser.)	ISE	77	070.101-014
Cardiopulmonary Technologist (medical ser.)	ISR	60	078.362-030
Cardiopulmonary Technologist, Chief (medical ser.)	ISR	69	078.161-014
Cardroom Attendant I (amuse. & rec.)	ESC	51	343.467-010
Cardroom Attendant II (amuse. & rec.)	CES	42	343.577-010
Career-Guidance Technician (education)	SCE	56	249.367-014
Caretaker (domestic ser.)	RES	41	301.687-010
Cargo Agent (air trans.)	RES	55	248.367-018
Cargo Checker (water trans.)	RSE	53	222.367-010
Cargo Inspector (petrol. refin.; pipe lines)	REC	54	549.387-010
Carnallite-Plant Operator (smelt. & refin.)	RCS	44	519.484-010
Carpenter (construction)	RCE	57	860.381-022

Part 3: From Occupational Titles to Holland Codes

From the Dictionary of Occupational Titles Occupations to Holland Codes

Title	HOC	Cx	DOT
Carpenter Apprentice (construction)	RCE	57	860.381-026
Carpenter I (mfd. bldgs.)	CRS	47	860.664-010
Carpenter II (mfd. bldgs.)	REI	47	860.681-010
Carpenter Inspector (any industry)	RSC	57	860.261-010
Carpenter, Bridge (r.r. trans.)	RES	55	860.381-030
Carpenter, Maintenance (any industry)	REI	59	860.281-010
Carpenter, Mold (brick & tile; concrete prod.)	RIE	57	860.381-034
Carpenter, Prototype (ship-boat mfg.)	RIC	60	806.281-058
Carpenter, Railcar (railroad equip.)	RES	56	860.381-038
Carpenter, Rough (construction)	RIS	56	860.381-042
Carpenter, Ship (ship-boat mfg.)	REI	58	860.281-014
Carpenter-Labor Supervisor (construction)	RES	59	860.137-010
Carpet Cutter (retail trade)	RIE	51	929.381-010
Carpet Cutter I (carpet & rug)	REC	45	781.684-010
Carpet Cutter II (carpet & rug)	RCS	41	585.687-014
Carpet Inspector, Finished (carpet & rug)	CRS	46	689.564-010
Carpet Layer (retail trade)	REI	54	864.381-010
Carpet Sewer (carpet & rug; retail trade)	RCI	46	787.682-014
Carpet Weaver (carpet & rug)	RCS	45	683.682-010
Carpet Weaver, Jacquard Loom (carpet & rug)	RCS	45	683.682-014
Carpet-Layer Helper (retail trade)	RES	42	864.687-010
Carpet-Loom Fixer (carpet & rug)	RSI	55	683.260-014
Carrier Packer (protective dev.)	RES	38	920.687-066
Carroter (hat & cap)	RCE	38	784.687-014
Carroting-Machine Offbearer (hat & cap)	REC	36	586.686-010
Carroting-Machine Operator (hat & cap)	REC	40	586.685-010
Carton Inspector (tobacco)	CRS	45	920.687-070
Carton Marker, Machine (boot & shoe; garment)	REI	40	652.685-018
Carton-Counter Feeder (tobacco)	RES	37	921.686-010
Carton-Forming-Machine Helper (any industry)	RES	40	641.686-014
Carton-Forming-Machine Operator (any industry)	REC	40	641.685-022
Carton-Forming-Machine Tender (paper goods)	REI	40	641.685-026
Carton-Packaging-Machine Operator (tobacco)	CRS	41	920.665-010
Cartoon Designer (tex. prod., n.e.c.)	RAE	57	781.381-010
Cartoonist (print. & pub.)	AES	62	141.061-010
Cartoonist, Motion Pictures (motion picture; radio-tv broad.)	AES	62	141.081-010
Cartridge Loader (elec. equip.)	RCE	36	779.687-014
Carver (hotel & rest.)	RCS	47	316.661-010
Carver, Hand (woodworking)	RIE	62	761.281-010
Case Aide (social ser.)	SEC	55	195.367-010
Case Finisher (leather prod.)	CRE	43	739.684-034
Case Fitter (furniture)	RCE	44	763.684-026
Case Hardener (heat treating)	RCI	48	504.682-014
Case Packer and Sealer (tobacco)	REC	42	920.685-038
Case Preparer-and-Liner (ordnance)	RCS	49	509.384-010
Case-Finishing-Machine Adjuster (ordnance)	RES	51	626.381-010
Case-Loader Operator (beverage)	REI	38	920.685-042
Case-Making-Machine Operator (print. & pub.)	RES	41	653.685-018

Part 3: From Occupational Titles to Holland Codes

From the Dictionary of Occupational Titles Occupations to Holland Codes

Title	HOC	Cx	DOT
Caser (clock & watch)	CRE	44	715.684-054
Caser (petrol. & gas)	RES	39	930.664-010
Caser, Shoe Parts (boot & shoe)	RIE	46	788.687-026
Casework Supervisor (social ser.)	SEC	66	195.137-010
Caseworker (government ser.)	CSE	63	169.262-010
Caseworker (social ser.)	SEC	66	195.107-010
Caseworker, Child Welfare (social ser.)	SEA	66	195.107-014
Caseworker, Family (social ser.)	SEA	67	195.107-018
Cash-Register Servicer (any industry)	RES	58	633.281-010
Cashier I (clerical)	CSE	56	211.362-010
Cashier II (clerical)	CSE	50	211.462-010
Cashier, Courtesy Booth (retail trade)	ECS	54	211.467-010
Cashier, Gambling (amuse. & rec.)	CSE	53	211.462-022
Cashier, Tube Room (retail trade)	CSR	51	211.482-010
Cashier-Checker (retail trade)	CES	51	211.462-014
Cashier-Wrapper (retail trade)	CSE	51	211.462-018
Casing Cleaner (meat products)	REC	38	525.686-010
Casing Grader (meat products)	RCE	40	529.687-026
Casing Sewer (meat products)	RCE	40	529.687-030
Casing Splitter (meat products)	RCE	36	525.687-014
Casing Tier (meat products)	RCE	36	529.687-034
Casing-Fluid Tender (tobacco)	RCE	41	520.685-054
Casing-in-Line Feeder (print. & pub.)	REC	37	653.686-010
Casing-in-Line Setter (print. & pub.)	REI	56	653.360-010
Casing-Machine Operator (tobacco)	RCE	43	522.685-030
Casing-Material Weigher (tobacco)	CRE	41	520.687-026
Casing-Running-Machine Tender (meat products)	REC	37	525.685-014
Casket Assembler (fabrication, n.e.c.)	RCI	48	739.684-190
Casket Assembler, Metal (fabrication, n.e.c.)	REI	44	809.684-014
Casket Coverer (fabrication, n.e.c.)	REC	42	780.684-026
Casket Inspector (fabrication, n.e.c.)	REC	47	739.387-010
Casket Liner (fabrication, n.e.c.)	RES	44	780.684-030
Caster (brick & tile)	RCI	42	579.684-026
Caster (jewelry-silver.)	REC	50	502.381-010
Caster (nonfer. metal)	RES	46	502.482-010
Caster (nonmet. min.)	RES	43	575.684-018
Caster (plastic prod.)	REC	42	754.684-022
Caster (pottery & porc.)	REI	38	575.684-014
Caster (smelt. & refin.)	RCE	41	514.684-010
Caster Helper (jewelry-silver.)	RES	39	700.687-022
Casting Inspector (foundry)	CRE	43	514.687-010
Casting Operator (nonfer. metal)	RCS	47	514.662-010
Casting Repairer (any industry)	RES	56	619.281-010
Casting-and-Curing Operator (chemical)	RCS	47	559.682-014
Casting-House Worker (nonfer. metal)	RES	38	514.687-014
Casting-Machine Operator (dairy products)	RCE	42	520.685-058
Casting-Machine Operator (machinery mfg.; print. & pub.)	REI	52	654.382-010
Casting-Machine Operator (nonfer. metal)	RCS	47	502.682-014
Casting-Machine Operator (sugar & conf.)	REC	40	520.685-062

DOT to HOC

Title	HOC	Cx	DOT
Casting-Machine Operator, Automatic (elec. equip.)	RIE	48	502.482-014
Casting-Machine-Operator Helper (elec. equip.)	RES	40	502.686-010
Casting-Machine-Service Operator (plastic-synth.)	RES	41	559.687-018
Casting-Operator Helper (nonfer. metal)	RCS	42	514.687-018
Casting-Plug Assembler (toy-sport equip.)	RCE	37	732.687-022
Casting-Room Operator (plastic-synth.)	RES	47	556.585-010
Casting-Wheel Operator (smelt. & refin.)	RIE	47	514.682-010
Casting-Wheel-Operator Helper (smelt. & refin.)	RSE	38	514.667-010
Catalog Librarian (library)	CSE	56	100.387-010
Catalyst Operator, Chief (chemical)	ESR	59	559.132-018
Catalyst Operator, Gasoline (chemical)	REI	52	559.382-014
Catalyst-Recovery Operator (chemical)	RIE	46	551.685-022
Catalytic-Converter Operator (chemical)	RSE	50	558.362-010
Catalytic-Converter-Operator Helper (chemical)	RCE	43	558.585-010
Catcher (steel & rel.)	RES	41	613.686-010
Catcher, Filter Tip (tobacco)	RCE	42	529.666-010
Caterer Helper (personal ser.)	SEA	48	319.677-010
Catheter Builder (rubber goods)	CRE	41	752.684-026
Cathode Maker (chemical)	REI	49	554.585-010
Cathode Ray Tube Salvage Processor (electron. comp.)	RCE	41	725.684-026
Caustic Operator (paper & pulp)	REI	53	558.485-010
Caustic Operator (plastic-synth.)	REC	41	554.684-010
Causticiser (chemical)	RCE	51	558.382-022
Causticiser (paper & pulp)	REC	47	558.382-018
CD-Mixer (rubber reclaim.)	RCE	41	550.685-022
CD-Mixer Helper (rubber reclaim.)	RES	37	553.686-014
CD-Reactor Operator (chemical)	CSE	49	558.385-010
CD-Reactor Operator, Head (chemical)	RES	56	558.362-014
CD-Storage-and-Materials Make-Up Helper (chemical)	RCE	47	559.685-034
CD-Storage-and-Materials-Make-Up Operator, Head (chemical)	ESA	59	559.167-010
Cell Changer (chemical)	REI	47	826.684-014
Cell Cleaner (chemical)	RES	38	559.687-022
Cell Coverer (elec. equip.)	RCE	38	727.687-042
Cell Inspector (plastic-synth.)	CRS	41	556.684-010
Cell Installer (chemical)	RCS	48	826.684-018
Cell Maker (chemical)	RSE	47	844.681-010
Cell Plasterer (smelt. & refin.)	RES	37	519.687-010
Cell Preparer (plastic-synth.)	RES	40	556.687-014
Cell Repairer (chemical)	RIE	49	826.384-010
Cell Repairer (elec. equip.)	CRE	45	727.684-018
Cell Stripper (plastic-synth.)	RES	38	556.686-014
Cell Tender (chemical)	REI	54	558.382-026
Cell Tester (chemical)	RIE	47	558.584-010
Cell Tuber, Hand (elec. equip.)	RCE	37	727.687-046
Cell Tuber, Machine (elec. equip.)	CRE	40	692.685-046
Cell-Feed-Department Supervisor (smelt. & refin.)	REC	59	519.130-010
Cell-Tender Helper (chemical)	REC	44	558.685-022
Cellar Supervisor (beverage)	REA	58	529.131-010

From the Dictionary of Occupational Titles Occupations to Holland Codes

Title	HOC	Cx	DOT
Cellophane-Bath Mixer (plastic-synth.)	CER	47	550.585-014
Cellophane-Casting-Machine Repairer (plastic prod.)	RIE	57	629.281-014
Celluloid Trimmer (toy-sport equip.)	CRE	38	732.684-046
Cement Fittings Maker (concrete prod.)	REC	44	779.684-010
Cement Loader (cement)	RCE	41	921.565-010
Cement Mason (construction)	RES	52	844.364-010
Cement Mixer (rubber goods; rubber tire)	RCE	45	550.685-026
Cement Sprayer Helper, Nozzle (concrete prod.; construction)	REC	37	844.687-010
Cement-Boat-and-Barge Loader (cement)	REI	40	921.665-010
Cement-Mason Apprentice (construction)	RES	52	844.364-014
Cementer (optical goods)	RCE	46	711.684-014
Cementer and Folder, Machine (boot & shoe)	REC	42	690.685-070
Cementer, Hand (boot & shoe)	RES	37	788.687-030
Cementer, Machine (boot & shoe)	CRE	39	692.685-050
Cementer, Machine Applicator (boot & shoe)	RCE	37	690.686-018
Cementer, Machine Joiner (boot & shoe)	RCE	41	690.685-074
Cemetery Worker (real estate)	RSE	46	406.684-010
Center-Machine Operator (sugar & conf.)	RIE	51	520.682-014
Center-Punch Operator (recording)	CRE	39	690.685-078
Central-Office Equipment Engineer (tel. & tel.)	IRE	79	003.187-010
Central-Office Installer (tel. & tel.)	RSE	56	822.361-014
Central-Office Operator (tel. & tel.)	CSE	49	235.462-010
Central-Office Repairer (tel. & tel.)	CRE	58	822.281-014
Central-Office-Operator Supervisor (tel. & tel.)	SEC	55	235.132-010
Central-Office-Repairer Supervisor (tel. & tel.)	ECR	65	822.131-010
Central-Supply Worker (medical ser.)	CER	48	381.687-010
Centrifugal Operator (grain-feed mills; sugar & conf.)	REI	48	521.682-010
Centrifugal Spinner (concrete prod.)	REC	40	575.664-010
Centrifugal-Casting-Machine Operator (jewelry-silver.)	RCS	47	502.682-018
Centrifugal-Casting-Machine Operator I (foundry)	RES	42	514.685-010
Centrifugal-Casting-Machine Operator II (foundry)	RCE	39	514.685-014
Centrifugal-Casting-Machine Operator III (foundry)	RSE	49	514.562-010
Centrifugal-Casting-Machine Tender (button & notion)	RCS	48	556.385-010
Centrifugal-Casting-Machine Tender (plastic prod.)	RCE	39	556.685-090
Centrifugal-Drier Operator (chemical)	RES	44	551.685-026
Centrifugal-Station Operator, Automatic (sugar & conf.)	RES	46	521.585-010
Centrifuge Operator (dairy products)	REI	42	521.685-042
Centrifuge Operator (grain-feed mills)	CRE	43	521.685-046
Centrifuge Operator (oils & grease)	REI	42	521.685-050
Centrifuge Operator (paint & varnish)	RES	38	551.685-034
Centrifuge Operator (soap & rel.)	RCE	38	551.685-030
Centrifuge Operator (sugar & conf.)	RES	47	529.682-010
Centrifuge Operator, Plasma Processing (medical ser.; pharmaceut.)	CER	48	599.685-018
Centrifuge-Separator Operator (chemical)	RCE	38	551.685-038
Centrifuge-Separator Tender (nonfer. metal)	CRE	44	541.585-010
Cephalometric Analyst (medical ser.)	IRC	59	078.384-010
Ceramic Capacitor Processor (electron. comp.)	CRE	43	590.684-010

Title	HOC	Cx	DOT
Ceramic Coater, Machine (any industry)	RCE	41	509.685-022
Ceramic Design Engineer (profess. & kin.)	IRE	71	006.061-010
Ceramic Engineer (profess. & kin.)	IRS	80	006.061-014
Ceramic Research Engineer (profess. & kin.)	IRE	71	006.061-018
Ceramics Test Engineer (profess. & kin.)	IRE	71	006.061-022
Certification and Selection Specialist (education)	ESI	72	099.167-010
Certified Medication Technician (medical ser.)	SRC	54	355.374-014
Chain Builder, Loom Control (textile)	RCS	48	683.381-010
Chain Maker, Hand (jewelry-silver.)	RES	56	700.381-010
Chain Maker, Machine (jewelry-silver.)	CRS	46	700.684-022
Chain Offbearer (saw. & plan.)	RSE	38	669.686-018
Chain Repairer (carpet & rug)	REA	46	683.684-010
Chain Saw Operator (chemical; logging; millwork-plywood)	RES	40	454.687-010
Chain-Testing-Machine Operator (forging)	CRS	42	616.685-010
Chainstitch Sewing Machine Operator (garment)	CRE	43	786.682-054
Chair Inspector and Leveler (furniture)	CRE	42	763.687-014
Chair Upholsterer (furniture)	RSC	47	780.684-034
Chalk Cutter (pen & pencil)	REC	39	733.687-022
Chalk-Extruding-Machine Operator (pen & pencil)	RCE	41	575.685-018
Chalk-Molding-Machine Operator (pen & pencil)	RCE	41	575.685-022
Chamfering-Machine Operator I (ordnance)	REI	48	606.685-014
Chamfering-Machine Operator II (ordnance)	REC	42	606.685-018
Change Person (amuse. & rec.)	CRE	43	211.467-034
Change-House Attendant (any industry)	REI	41	358.687-010
Channel Installer (wood. container)	RES	38	764.687-046
Channel Opener, Outsoles (boot & shoe)	REC	39	690.685-082
Channeler, Insole (boot & shoe)	RCE	42	690.685-086
Channeling-Machine Runner (mine & quarry)	RIE	47	930.383-010
Chaperon (personal ser.)	SEC	47	359.667-010
Char Puller (grain-feed mills; sugar & conf.)	REI	38	521.687-030
Char-Conveyor Tender (sugar & conf.)	REC	40	529.685-050
Char-Dust Cleaner and Salvager (sugar & conf.)	RES	40	529.687-038
Char-Filter Operator (sugar & conf.)	CRS	51	521.365-010
Char-Filter-Operator Helper (sugar & conf.)	RES	41	521.687-034
Char-Filter-Tank Tender, Head (grain-feed mills)	RES	45	521.665-010
Charcoal Burner, Beehive Kiln (chemical)	RSE	45	563.682-010
Charge Preparation Technician (electron. comp.)	RCI	47	590.384-010
Charge-Account Clerk (clerical)	CSE	50	205.367-014
Charge-Machine Operator (chemical)	RCS	50	921.662-014
Charger I (jewelry-silver.)	CSE	44	740.684-010
Charger II (jewelry-silver.)	RCE	38	700.687-026
Charger Operator (steel & rel.)	RCS	47	504.665-014
Charger-Operator Helper (steel & rel.)	REC	39	504.686-010
Charging-Machine Operator (steel & rel.)	RCS	45	512.683-010
Chart Calculator (utilities)	CES	58	214.487-010
Chart Changer (clerical)	CRS	48	221.584-010
Chart Clerk (clerical)	CSR	54	221.382-010
Charter (amuse. & rec.)	ECS	52	249.367-018

Title	HOC	Cx	DOT
Chaser (jewelry-silver.)	RIE	56	704.381-010
Chaser (logging)	RES	39	921.667-014
Chaser, Tar (steel & rel.)	REC	37	549.687-010
Chauffeur (any industry)	REC	46	913.663-010
Chauffeur (domestic ser.)	RES	44	359.673-010
Chauffeur, Funeral Car (personal ser.)	RES	44	359.673-014
Check Cashier (business ser.)	CSE	52	211.462-026
Check Pilot (air trans.)	IRE	67	196.263-022
Check Weigher (ordnance)	CRE	39	737.687-026
Check Writer (retail trade)	CSE	51	219.382-010
Checker (chemical)	CSE	50	559.165-010
Checker (laundry & rel.)	RCS	40	369.687-014
Checker (motor trans.)	RCE	39	919.687-010
Checker (textile)	CSE	42	221.587-010
Checker I (clerical)	RCE	46	222.687-010
Checker II (clerical)	CRS	50	209.687-010
Checker, Bakery Products (bakery products)	REC	44	222.487-010
Checker, Dump Grounds (business ser.)	SRE	49	219.367-010
Checker, Film Tests (photo. appar.)	CSR	45	714.687-010
Checker-In (boot & shoe)	RCS	42	221.587-014
Checkering-Machine Adjuster (ordnance)	RCE	51	669.360-010
Checkroom Attendant (any industry)	CSR	42	358.677-010
Checkroom Chief (any industry)	SEA	53	358.137-010
Cheese Blender (dairy products)	ESI	57	520.487-010
Cheese Cutter (dairy products)	REI	41	529.585-010
Cheese Grader (dairy products)	RES	49	529.387-010
Cheese Sprayer (sugar & conf.)	CRE	39	524.685-014
Cheesemaker (dairy products)	RES	58	529.361-018
Cheesemaker Helper (dairy products)	REI	50	529.682-014
Chef (hotel & rest.)	ESR	59	313.131-014
Chef De Froid (hotel & rest.)	RAE	58	313.281-010
Chef, Passenger Vessel (water trans.)	ESA	59	315.137-010
Chemical Compounder (chemical)	RIE	48	559.682-018
Chemical Design Engineer, Processes (profess. & kin.)	IRS	71	008.061-014
Chemical Engineer (profess. & kin.)	IRE	80	008.061-018
Chemical Laboratory Chief (profess. & kin.)	IEA	79	022.161-010
Chemical Laboratory Technician (profess. & kin.)	IRS	67	022.261-010
Chemical Mixer (photofinishing)	RES	51	550.485-010
Chemical Mixer (textile)	RES	47	550.585-018
Chemical Operator II (chemical)	RIC	48	558.685-062
Chemical Operator III (chemical)	REI	55	559.382-018
Chemical Preparer (chemical; electron. comp.)	RIE	52	550.685-030
Chemical Reclamation Equipment Operator (electron. comp.)	RCE	40	558.685-058
Chemical Research Engineer (profess. & kin.)	IRS	71	008.061-022
Chemical-Compounder Helper (chemical)	RSE	38	550.687-010
Chemical-Engineering Technician (profess. & kin.)	IRE	70	008.261-010
Chemical-Equipment Sales Engineer (profess. & kin.)	ERI	70	008.151-010
Chemical-Etching Processor (aircraft mfg.)	RIE	54	704.381-014

Title	HOC	Cx	DOT
Chemical-Processing Supervisor (pharmaceut.)	RES	59	559.130-010
Chemical-Radiation Technician (government ser.)	RCS	57	015.261-010
Chemical-Strength Tester (textile)	REC	46	582.587-010
Chemical-Test Engineer (profess. & kin.)	RIE	71	008.061-026
Chemist (profess. & kin.)	IRE	79	022.061-010
Chemist, Food (profess. & kin.)	IRS	75	022.061-014
Chemist, Instrumentation (profess. & kin.)	IRC	68	022.261-018
Chemist, Wastewater-Treatment Plant (profess. & kin.)	IRC	68	022.261-022
Chemist, Water Purification (waterworks)	IRS	73	022.281-014
Cherry Cutter (can. & preserv.)	REC	35	524.687-010
Cherry-Picker Operator (construction)	RES	41	921.663-014
Chest-Painting and Sealing Supervisor (ordnance)	ERS	59	749.137-010
Chick Grader (agriculture)	RCE	41	411.687-010
Chick Sexer (agriculture)	REC	42	411.687-014
Chicle-Grinder Feeder (sugar & conf.)	CRS	40	521.686-018
Chief Bank Examiner (government ser.)	EIC	70	160.167-046
Chief Clerk, Measurement Department (petrol. & gas; pipe lines)	CSE	66	221.132-010
Chief Clerk, Print Shop (clerical)	ESR	57	207.137-010
Chief Controller (government ser.)	SEA	66	193.167-010
Chief Dispatcher (petrol. & gas)	ESC	65	939.137-010
Chief Drafter (profess. & kin.)	ICR	69	007.261-010
Chief Engineer (petrol. & gas; pipe lines)	IER	80	010.167-010
Chief Engineer, Research (petrol. & gas)	IRE	79	010.161-010
Chief Engineer, Waterworks (waterworks)	IRE	74	005.167-010
Chief Inspector (office machines)	RCE	58	706.131-018
Chief Librarian, Branch or Department (library)	SER	66	100.127-010
Chief Load Dispatcher (utilities)	ERS	63	952.137-010
Chief of Party (profess. & kin.)	IEA	67	018.167-010
Chief Operator (chemical)	RSE	59	558.260-010
Chief Petroleum Engineer (petrol. & gas)	IRE	80	010.161-014
Chief Pilot (air trans.)	EIR	72	196.167-010
Chief Projectionist (motion picture)	SCR	56	960.132-010
Chief Technologist, Nuclear Medicine (medical ser.)	SIE	69	078.131-010
Chief Warden (government ser.)	ESA	65	188.167-018
Chief, Computer Programmer (profess. & kin.)	ESI	69	030.167-010
Chief, Fishery Division (government ser.)	SER	67	188.117-018
Child Monitor (domestic ser.)	SEC	41	301.677-010
Child Support Officer (government ser.)	ESR	65	195.267-022
Child-Care Attendant, School (personal ser.)	RES	42	355.674-010
Children's Attendant (amuse. & rec.)	SCR	40	349.677-018
Children's Librarian (library)	SER	66	100.167-018
Children's Tutor (domestic ser.)	SEC	57	099.227-010
Chiller Operator (chemical)	CRE	42	551.685-042
Chiller Tender (meat products)	REC	45	523.585-014
Chilling-Hood Operator (meat products)	RCE	37	523.685-018
Chimney Repairer (business ser.)	RCE	51	899.364-010
Chimney Supervisor, Brick (construction)	RES	59	861.131-014
Chimney Sweep (any industry)	REC	42	891.687-010

DOT to HOC

Title	HOC	Cx	DOT
Chin-Strap Cutter (hat & cap)	RCE	40	686.685-010
Chinchilla-Machine Operator (textile)	RCE	41	585.685-022
Chip Tester (paper & pulp)	CRE	49	539.387-010
Chip Tuner (musical inst.)	RSC	45	730.684-026
Chip Unloader (paper & pulp)	CRE	41	921.663-018
Chip Washer (beverage)	RES	39	522.686-010
Chip-Applying-Machine Tender (paint & varnish; print. & pub.)	RCE	41	641.685-030
Chip-Bin Conveyor Tender (chemical; paper & pulp)	REC	39	921.685-022
Chip-Mixing-Machine Operator (wood prod., n.e.c.)	RCS	48	560.465-010
Chipper (chemical; paper & pulp; saw. & plan.)	REC	40	564.685-014
Chipping-Machine Operator (wood prod., n.e.c.)	RES	45	564.682-010
Chiropractor (medical ser.)	ISR	67	079.101-010
Chiropractor Assistant (medical ser.)	SRE	56	079.364-010
Chlorinator Operator (chemical)	RES	49	558.382-030
Chocolate Molder, Machine (sugar & conf.)	RES	47	529.685-054
Chocolate Temperer (bakery products; grain-feed mills)	RCE	42	523.685-022
Chocolate Temperer (sugar & conf.)	RSC	47	523.682-010
Chocolate-Production-Machine Operator (sugar & conf.)	RES	57	529.382-014
Choke Reamer (ordnance)	CRE	41	606.685-022
Choke Setter (logging)	RES	37	921.687-014
Chopped-Strand Operator (textile)	RCE	41	680.685-022
Chopper (chemical)	RES	36	564.687-010
Chopping-Machine Operator (meat products)	RCE	41	520.685-066
Choral Director (profess. & kin.)	AES	69	152.047-010
Choreographer (amuse. & rec.)	AES	67	151.027-010
Christian Science Nurse (profess. & kin.)	SEC	58	129.107-010
Christian Science Practitioner (profess. & kin.)	SEA	60	129.107-014
Christmas-Tree Contractor (any industry)	SEA	66	162.117-010
Christmas-Tree Farm Worker (forestry)	REI	35	451.687-010
Christmas-Tree Grader (forestry)	REI	41	451.687-014
Chronograph Operator (ordnance)	CRE	53	739.484-010
Chronometer Assembler and Adjuster (clock & watch)	RIE	57	715.381-038
Chronometer-Balance-and-Hairspring Assembler (clock & watch)	REC	53	715.381-042
Chucking-and-Boring-Machine Operator (furniture)	RCS	47	669.682-022
Chucking-and-Sawing-Machine Operator (woodworking)	REC	46	669.682-026
Chucking-Machine Operator (woodworking)	REI	46	665.382-010
Chucking-Machine Set-up Operator (machine shop)	RIE	59	604.380-010
Chucking-Machine Set-up Operator, Multiple Spindle, Vertical (machine shop)	RIE	59	604.380-014
Churn Operator, Margarine (oils & grease)	RCE	42	520.685-070
Churn Tender (plastic-synth.)	RCE	46	550.685-034
Churner (oils & grease)	CRS	41	520.565-010
Chute Loader (mine & quarry)	RCE	36	932.687-010
Cigar Brander (tobacco)	RCE	40	920.685-046
Cigar Inspector (tobacco)	RCE	39	529.687-042
Cigar Maker (tobacco)	RCE	44	790.684-014
Cigar Packer (tobacco)	CRE	44	790.687-014

Part 3: From Occupational Titles to Holland Codes

From the Dictionary of Occupational Titles Occupations to Holland Codes

Title	HOC	Cx	DOT
Cigar-Head Piercer (tobacco)	RCE	40	529.685-058
Cigar-Wrapper Tender, Automatic (tobacco)	RCI	41	529.685-286
Cigarette Inspector (tobacco)	RCS	44	529.567-010
Cigarette Tester (tobacco)	REC	55	529.387-014
Cigarette Vendor (hotel & rest.)	ESA	44	291.457-010
Cigarette-and-Filter Chief Inspector (tobacco)	RSE	51	529.367-010
Cigarette-Filter-Making-Machine Operator (tobacco)	CRE	42	529.685-062
Cigarette-Lighter Repairer (any industry)	CRE	42	709.684-034
Cigarette-Making-Machine Catcher (tobacco)	RCE	41	529.666-014
Cigarette-Making-Machine Operator (tobacco)	REC	42	529.685-066
Cigarette-Making-Machine-Hopper Feeder (tobacco)	RES	39	529.686-018
Cigarette-Package Examiner (tobacco)	RCE	42	920.667-010
Cigarette-Packing-Machine Operator (tobacco)	RCE	40	920.685-050
Circle Beveler (glass products)	RCS	41	673.685-034
Circle Edger (glass products)	REC	38	673.685-038
Circle-Cutting-Saw Operator (wood. container)	RCE	37	669.685-026
Circular Saw Operator (construction)	RCS	46	869.682-010
Circular Sawyer, Stone (stonework)	REI	47	677.462-010
Circular-Sawyer Helper (stonework)	REI	42	677.486-010
Circulating Process Inspector (elec. equip.)	RES	54	829.361-018
Circulation Clerk (print. & pub.)	ECR	52	209.362-010
Circulation-Sales Representative (print. & pub.)	ESA	57	299.167-010
Circus Agent (amuse. & rec.)	ESR	63	191.117-022
Circus Laborer (amuse. & rec.)	RES	40	969.687-010
Circus-Train Supervisor (amuse. & rec.)	ESA	56	910.137-018
Cistern-Room Operator (beverage)	REC	53	520.382-010
City Planning Aide (profess. & kin.)	CSE	59	199.364-010
Civil Engineer (profess. & kin.)	IRE	73	005.061-014
Civil Engineering Technician (profess. & kin.)	RIC	66	005.261-014
Civil Preparedness Officer (government ser.)	ESA	67	188.117-022
Civil Preparedness Training Officer (government ser.)	ESA	63	169.127-010
Civil-Service Clerk (government ser.)	CSE	51	205.362-010
Claim Adjuster (business ser.; insurance)	ESR	64	241.217-010
Claim Agent (petrol. & gas; pipe lines)	SEC	71	191.167-014
Claim Examiner (business ser.; insurance)	ESC	63	241.267-018
Claim Examiner (insurance)	SIE	64	168.267-014
Claims Adjudicator (government ser.)	SEC	65	169.267-010
Claims Clerk (auto. mfg.)	ESR	55	241.387-010
Claims Clerk I (insurance)	CSE	55	241.362-010
Claims Clerk II (insurance)	ESC	54	205.367-018
Clam Sorter (fishing & hunt.)	REC	41	446.687-010
Clamp Remover (millwork-plywood)	RCE	37	569.687-010
Clamp-Jig Assembler (woodworking)	RES	42	762.687-022
Clamper (pen & pencil)	REC	37	733.687-026
Clamper (print. & pub.)	RES	52	979.382-010
Clamper (woodworking)	RSC	39	669.685-030
Clarifier (beverage)	CRE	42	521.685-058
Clarifier (grain-feed mills; oils & grease)	REC	40	521.685-054
Clarifier Operator (smelt. & refin.)	RCE	48	511.662-010

Title	HOC	Cx	DOT
Clarifier-Operator Helper (smelt. & refin.)	REC	41	511.667-010
Clarifying-Plant Operator (textile)	REI	52	955.382-010
Classification Clerk (clerical)	CES	52	206.387-010
Classification-Control Clerk (clerical)	CSR	58	210.382-030
Classified-Ad Clerk I (print. & pub.)	CES	54	247.367-010
Classified-Ad Clerk II (print. & pub.)	CSE	54	247.387-022
Classifier (laundry & rel.)	REC	39	361.687-014
Classifier (library)	CSR	60	100.367-014
Classifier (rubber goods)	CER	51	753.467-010
Classifier Operator (smelt. & refin.)	RSC	48	511.562-010
Classifier Tender (smelt. & refin.)	CRS	45	511.685-014
Clay Maker (brick & tile; pottery & porc.)	REI	49	570.482-010
Clay Mixer (brick & tile)	REC	40	570.685-014
Clay Modeler (any industry)	RAE	61	779.281-010
Clay Roaster (petrol. refin.)	RES	45	573.685-014
Clay-Stain Mixer (brick & tile)	RIE	49	773.487-010
Clay-Structure Builder and Servicer (glass mfg.)	RSE	48	579.664-010
Clean-Out Driller (petrol. & gas)	RIE	51	930.363-010
Clean-Out-Driller Helper (petrol. & gas)	REI	42	930.664-014
Clean-Rice Broker (grain-feed mills)	ESR	68	162.167-018
Clean-Rice Grader and Reel Tender (grain-feed mills)	REC	41	521.685-062
Cleaner (engraving)	REC	39	704.687-010
Cleaner (fabrication, n.e.c.)	REC	38	739.687-058
Cleaner (mfd. bldgs.)	RES	40	869.687-018
Cleaner (ordnance)	REC	41	503.684-010
Cleaner and Polisher (any industry)	RCE	37	709.687-010
Cleaner and Preparer (elec. equip.)	REC	39	721.687-010
Cleaner II (any industry)	REI	39	919.687-014
Cleaner III (any industry)	REC	40	911.687-014
Cleaner, Commercial or Institutional (any industry)	REC	37	381.687-014
Cleaner, Furniture (furniture)	RCE	37	709.687-014
Cleaner, Home Restoration Service (any industry)	RCE	44	389.664-010
Cleaner, Hospital (medical ser.)	CRE	39	323.687-010
Cleaner, Housekeeping (any industry)	CRE	39	323.687-014
Cleaner, Industrial (any industry)	RSE	39	381.687-018
Cleaner, Laboratory Equipment (any industry)	RES	41	381.687-022
Cleaner, Signs (fabrication, n.e.c.)	RCE	38	739.687-062
Cleaner, Wall (any industry)	REC	37	381.687-026
Cleaner, Window (any industry)	RES	39	389.687-014
Cleaner-Touch-Up Worker (office machines)	REC	42	706.587-010
Cleaning Machine Tender, Semiconductor Wafers (electron. comp.)	RCI	42	590.685-062
Clearance Cutter (clock & watch)	REC	38	615.685-014
Clearing Supervisor (construction)	RES	59	869.133-010
Clearing-House Clerk (financial)	CRI	56	216.382-026
Cleat Feeder (wood. container)	REC	39	669.687-010
Clergy Member (profess. & kin.)	SAE	73	120.107-010
Clerical-Methods Analyst (profess. & kin.)	SEC	66	161.267-010
Clerk, General (clerical)	CRS	51	209.562-010

Part 3: From Occupational Titles to Holland Codes

From the Dictionary of Occupational Titles Occupations to Holland Codes

Title	HOC	Cx	DOT
Clerk, Route (tel. & tel.)	CRE	52	235.562-010
Clerk, Telegraph Service (tel. & tel.)	SEC	56	219.362-022
Clerk, Television Production (radio-tv broad.)	CRS	55	221.367-086
Clerk-of-Scales (amuse. & rec.)	REI	51	153.467-010
Clerk-Typist (clerical)	CSE	54	203.362-010
Clicking-Machine Operator (boot & shoe; glove & mit.; leather prod.)	RCS	49	789.382-010
Clinching-Machine Operator (elec. equip.)	REC	40	616.685-014
Clinical Psychologist (profess. & kin.)	SIA	74	045.107-022
Clinical Sociologist (profess. & kin.)	SEC	66	054.107-010
Clinical Therapist (profess. & kin.)	IES	75	045.107-050
Clip Coater (optical goods)	CRE	40	713.687-010
Clip-and-Hanger Attacher (glass products)	CRE	45	739.684-038
Clip-Bolter and Wrapper (metal prod., n.e.c.)	REC	42	709.684-038
Clip-Loading-Machine Adjuster (ordnance)	RSC	50	694.362-010
Clip-Loading-Machine Feeder (ordnance)	RCE	39	694.686-010
Clipper (any industry)	REC	39	789.687-030
Clipper (boot & shoe)	RES	38	753.687-010
Clipper (fabrication, n.e.c.)	RCE	40	739.685-022
Clipper and Turner (furniture)	RES	37	780.687-014
Clipper, Automatic (millwork-plywood)	RCE	42	663.585-010
Clipper, Machine (knitting)	RCE	37	684.686-010
Clock Assembler (clock & watch)	RCE	42	715.684-058
Clocker (amuse. & rec.)	ESC	49	153.367-010
Closer (real estate)	CSE	65	186.167-074
Cloth Designer (profess. & kin.)	AER	66	142.061-014
Cloth Doffer (textile)	RES	41	689.686-058
Cloth Drier (knitting)	RCE	41	580.685-014
Cloth Examiner, Hand (narrow fabrics)	RCE	40	689.687-022
Cloth Examiner, Hand (textile)	RES	42	781.687-014
Cloth Examiner, Machine (textile)	REI	46	689.685-038
Cloth Feeder (textile)	RES	39	589.686-014
Cloth Finisher (carpet & rug; textile)	ERS	65	589.130-010
Cloth Folder, Hand (tex. prod., n.e.c.; textile)	REC	41	589.687-014
Cloth Framer (textile)	RSE	38	689.687-026
Cloth Grader (textile)	RES	48	689.387-010
Cloth Inspector (knitting)	REC	44	685.687-010
Cloth Measurer, Machine (garment; textile)	RCE	42	589.685-022
Cloth Printer (any industry)	RIS	52	652.382-010
Cloth Reeler (textile)	RCS	38	689.685-042
Cloth Sander (textile)	REC	37	581.685-010
Cloth Shader (garment; textile)	RES	42	582.685-026
Cloth Spreader, Screen Printing (textile)	RCS	39	652.687-010
Cloth Tearer (garment)	RES	40	781.687-018
Cloth Tester (garment; textile)	IRS	57	029.381-010
Cloth Tester, Quality (textile)	CRE	53	689.384-010
Cloth Trimmer, Machine (textile)	RCS	42	585.685-026
Cloth Winder (textile)	RCE	40	689.685-046
Cloth-Bale Header (textile)	RCE	37	782.687-018

Title	HOC	Cx	DOT
Cloth-Bolt Bander (textile)	RES	41	920.587-010
Cloth-Doubling-and-Winding-Machine Operator (textile)	REC	41	689.685-050
Cloth-Edge Singer (textile)	RCE	40	585.687-018
Cloth-Finishing-Range Operator (textile)	REC	42	589.665-014
Cloth-Finishing-Range Operator, Chief (textile)	REI	51	589.562-010
Cloth-Finishing-Range Tender (textile)	REI	45	589.685-026
Cloth-Grader Supervisor (textile)	RES	59	689.134-010
Cloth-Mercerizer Operator (textile)	RCS	46	584.685-014
Cloth-Printer Helper (any industry)	RCS	38	652.686-010
Cloth-Printing Inspector (textile)	SER	45	652.567-010
Cloth-Shrinking Tester (textile)	RIE	51	587.384-010
Cloth-Shrinking-Machine Operator (textile)	REC	42	587.685-018
Cloth-Shrinking-Machine-Operator Helper (textile)	REC	39	587.686-010
Cloth-Stock Sorter (tex. prod., n.e.c.; textile)	REC	41	789.687-034
Cloth-Washer Operator (textile)	REC	41	582.685-030
Clothespin-Drier Operator (woodworking)	RCE	39	563.685-014
Clothespin-Machine Operator (woodworking)	REC	37	667.686-010
Clothing-Pattern Preparer (garment)	RES	57	781.287-010
Clown (amuse. & rec.)	EAC	56	159.047-010
Clutch Rebuilder (automotive ser.)	RCS	48	620.684-022
Coach Driver (business ser.)	ERS	44	349.677-014
Coach, Professional Athletes (amuse. & rec.)	SRE	61	153.227-010
Coagulating-Bath Mixer (plastic-synth.)	REI	48	550.684-010
Coagulation Operator (plastic-synth.)	REC	51	559.582-010
Coal Pipeline Operator (pipe lines)	RES	53	914.362-010
Coal Sampler (utilities)	ECR	40	922.687-038
Coal Trimmer (water trans.)	RES	39	911.687-018
Coal Washer (mine & quarry)	RES	51	541.382-010
Coal-Equipment Operator (utilities)	RIE	49	921.683-022
Coal-Yard Supervisor (any industry)	RES	59	921.137-010
Coat Joiner, Lockstitch (garment)	RCE	41	786.682-058
Coat-Hanger-Shaper-Machine Operator (woodworking)	REC	39	669.685-034
Coater (business ser.)	RCS	45	503.685-010
Coater (pharmaceut.)	REI	51	554.382-010
Coater (textile)	RSE	47	584.682-010
Coater Helper (textile)	RSC	42	584.665-010
Coater Operator (any industry)	RIE	53	509.382-010
Coater Operator (plastic-synth.)	CRS	44	554.585-014
Coater Operator, Insulation Board (wood prod., n.e.c.)	CRE	41	539.685-010
Coater, Brake Linings (nonmet. min.)	CRE	41	574.685-010
Coater, Smoking Pipe (fabrication, n.e.c.)	RCE	43	562.685-022
Coating Equipment Operator, Printed Circuit Boards (electron. comp.)	RCI	45	590.685-066
Coating Operator (chemical)	RCE	44	550.585-022
Coating Operator (grain-feed mills)	RCE	41	524.685-018
Coating-and-Baking Operator (any industry)	RCE	43	554.685-014
Coating-and-Embossing-Unit Operator (tex. prod., n.e.c.; textile)	RES	50	583.682-010
Coating-Machine Feeder (leather prod.)	RCE	37	690.686-022

Title	HOC	Cx	DOT
Coating-Machine Operator (carpet & rug; tex. prod., n.e.c.)	RCS	50	584.562-010
Coating-Machine Operator (fabrication, n.e.c.)	REC	49	590.685-014
Coating-Machine Operator (galvanizing)	RES	54	501.362-010
Coating-Machine Operator (paper & pulp; paper goods)	REI	47	534.682-018
Coating-Machine Operator (pen & pencil)	RES	41	692.685-054
Coating-Machine Operator (sugar & conf.)	RSE	50	524.382-010
Coating-Machine Operator I (tex. prod., n.e.c.)	RIE	51	584.382-010
Coating-Machine Operator II (tex. prod., n.e.c.)	REC	41	584.685-018
Coating-Machine Operator, Hardboard (paper goods; wood prod., n.e.c.)	REI	47	534.682-022
Coating-Machine-Operator Helper (fabrication, n.e.c.)	REI	40	590.686-010
Coating-Mixer Supervisor (paper & pulp)	SRE	60	530.132-010
Coating-Mixer Tender (paper & pulp)	RES	42	530.685-010
Cob Sawyer (fabrication, n.e.c.)	RCE	37	667.685-030
Cobbler (boot & shoe)	RES	46	788.381-010
Cocoa-Bean Cleaner (sugar & conf.)	REI	40	521.685-066
Cocoa-Bean Roaster I (sugar & conf.)	RSE	48	523.362-010
Cocoa-Bean Roaster II (sugar & conf.)	RES	56	523.380-010
Cocoa-Bean-Roaster Helper (sugar & conf.)	RES	41	523.666-010
Cocoa-Butter-Filter Operator (sugar & conf.)	RCE	40	521.685-070
Cocoa-Powder-Mixer Operator (sugar & conf.)	RSC	47	520.685-074
Cocoa-Press Operator (sugar & conf.)	RES	47	521.682-014
Cocoa-Room Operator (sugar & conf.)	RCE	41	521.685-074
Code and Test Clerk (financial)	CSE	55	209.667-018
Code Inspector (government ser.)	RCI	52	168.367-018
Coffee Grinder (food prep., n.e.c.)	RCE	39	521.685-078
Coffee Maker (hotel & rest.)	RCS	40	317.684-010
Coffee Roaster (food prep., n.e.c.)	RSE	49	523.682-014
Coffee Roaster, Continuous Process (food prep., n.e.c.)	CRE	43	523.685-026
Coffee Weigher (food prep., n.e.c.)	RES	38	529.687-046
Coffee-Roaster Helper (food prep., n.e.c.)	REC	37	523.687-010
Coil Assembler, Machine (furniture)	RES	41	616.685-018
Coil Binder (nonfer. metal)	RES	38	619.687-010
Coil Connector (elec. equip.)	RES	49	721.684-018
Coil Shaper (any industry)	RCE	49	724.684-022
Coil Winder (elec. equip.; electron. comp.)	RCE	44	724.684-026
Coil Winder, Repair (any industry)	RCE	51	724.381-014
Coil-Rewind-Machine Operator (nonfer. metal)	REC	40	619.685-030
Coiled-Coil Inspector (light. fix.)	CRS	46	725.684-010
Coiler (light. fix.)	CRS	41	725.687-014
Coiler (nonfer. metal; steel & rel.)	RCE	41	613.685-010
Coiler (protective dev.)	REC	40	712.687-014
Coiler (tex. prod., n.e.c.)	REI	40	681.685-034
Coiler Operator (steel & rel.)	RCE	49	613.382-010
Coin Collector (business ser.)	REC	48	292.483-010
Coin-Counter-and-Wrapper (clerical)	RES	48	217.585-010
Coin-Machine Assembler (svc. ind. mach.)	CRS	42	731.684-010
Coin-Machine Collector (business ser.; tel. & tel.)	CRE	43	292.687-010
Coin-Machine-Collector Supervisor (clerical)	ERS	56	292.137-010

Title	HOC	Cx	DOT
Coin-Machine-Service Repairer (svc. ind. mach.)	RSE	54	639.281-014
Coke Burner (steel & rel.)	RES	48	543.682-010
Coke Drawer, Hand (steel & rel.)	REC	37	543.687-010
Coke Inspector (steel & rel.)	CRE	49	542.567-010
Coke Loader (steel & rel.)	RES	50	921.563-010
Coke-Crusher Operator (steel & rel.)	RIS	47	544.662-010
Cold-Mill Operator (steel & rel.)	RCE	55	613.662-018
Cold-Press Loader (cutlery-hrdwr.)	RES	40	701.687-018
Cold-Roll Inspector (plastic-synth.)	CRE	43	751.584-010
Collar Baster, Jumpbasting (garment)	RCE	41	786.682-062
Collar Feller, Handstitching Machine (garment)	RCE	40	786.682-066
Collar Setter, Lockstitch (garment)	RCE	41	786.682-070
Collar Setter, Overlock (garment)	RCE	41	786.682-074
Collar-Turner Operator (garment)	RCE	41	580.685-018
Collating-Machine Operator (print. & pub.)	RCE	53	653.382-014
Collator (print. & pub.)	CSR	41	653.687-010
Collator Operator (clerical)	RCS	40	208.685-010
Collator, Hand (print. & pub.)	CES	41	977.687-010
Collection Clerk (clerical)	ESA	57	241.357-010
Collection Clerk (financial)	CSR	58	216.362-014
Collector (clerical)	ESC	54	241.367-010
Collector (knitting)	RCE	40	684.687-022
Collet Driller (clock & watch)	RCE	40	715.684-062
Collet Gluer (clock & watch)	CER	40	715.685-010
Collet Maker (clock & watch)	REC	49	609.682-014
Colleter (clock & watch)	RCE	44	715.684-066
Color Checker, Roving or Yarn (textile)	REI	51	582.387-010
Color Developer (paper & pulp)	RIS	64	530.261-010
Color Dipper (textile)	RSE	38	652.687-014
Color Expert (profess. & kin.)	AES	64	141.051-010
Color Maker (chemical)	RES	53	550.382-010
Color Maker (tex. prod., n.e.c.)	RIE	50	550.382-014
Color Matcher (boot & shoe)	CRE	41	788.687-034
Color Matcher (knitting)	RSC	53	582.261-010
Color Matcher (leather mfg.; plastic-synth.; tex. prod., n.e.c.)	RIE	54	550.381-010
Color Mixer (furniture)	CES	48	589.464-010
Color Strainer (textile)	RES	37	550.687-014
Color Tester (smelt. & refin.)	CES	45	511.667-014
Color Weigher (fabrication, n.e.c.)	REI	51	590.487-010
Color-Card Maker (paint & varnish)	CRS	38	794.687-014
Color-Paste Mixer (textile)	RCS	46	550.685-038
Color-Printer Operator (photofinishing)	RIE	51	976.382-014
Colorer (brick & tile)	RCE	48	773.684-010
Colorer (print. & pub.)	RCE	47	970.681-014
Colorer, Citrus Fruit (wholesale tr.)	CRE	45	529.685-070
Colorer, Hides and Skins (leather mfg.)	REI	50	582.482-010
Coloring Checker (jewelry-silver.)	RIE	48	735.587-010
Coloring-Machine Operator (hat & cap)	CRS	46	582.685-034

Title	HOC	Cx	DOT
Colorist (profess. & kin.)	IRE	69	022.161-014
Colorist, Photography (photofinishing)	AEC	50	970.381-010
Column Precaster (mfd. bldgs.)	RES	38	869.667-010
Columnist/Commentator (print. & pub.; radio-tv broad.)	AES	72	131.067-010
Comb-Machine Operator (fabrication, n.e.c.)	REC	41	640.685-022
Combat Rifle Crewmember (military ser.)	REC	41	378.684-014
Combat Surveillance and Target Acquisition Crewmember (military ser.)	RES	42	378.687-010
Combat Surveillance and Target Acquisition Noncommissioned Officer (military ser.)	ERS	58	378.161-010
Comber Tender (textile)	RCS	39	680.685-118
Combiner Operator (paper & pulp; paper goods)	RIE	47	534.682-026
Combining-Machine Operator (plastic-synth.)	RCS	44	554.685-018
Comedian (amuse. & rec.)	AES	59	159.047-014
Command and Control Specialist (military ser.)	CRE	51	235.662-010
Commander, Identification and Records (government ser.)	ERS	63	375.137-010
Commander, Internal Affairs (government ser.)	ESC	64	375.167-050
Commander, Police Reserves (government ser.)	ESC	61	375.137-030
Commanding Officer, Homicide Squad (government ser.)	ESR	62	375.167-010
Commanding Officer, Investigation Division (government ser.)	ESR	61	375.167-014
Commanding Officer, Motor Equipment (government ser.)	ESR	64	375.167-018
Commanding Officer, Motorized Squad (government ser.)	ERS	64	375.163-010
Commanding Officer, Police (government ser.)	ESC	64	375.137-034
Commercial Designer (profess. & kin.)	AER	65	141.061-038
Commercial Engineer (radio-tv broad.)	RIE	71	003.187-014
Commercial Loan Collection Officer (financial)	ESA	67	186.167-078
Commercial-Instructor Supervisor (tel. & tel.; utilities; waterworks)	ESC	64	239.137-010
Commissary Assistant (amuse. & rec.; museums)	RCI	41	412.687-010
Commissary Manager (any industry)	ESR	61	185.167-010
Commission Agent, Agricultural Produce (wholesale tr.)	ESR	63	260.357-010
Commission Agent, Livestock (wholesale tr.)	EAS	63	162.157-026
Commissioner of Conciliation (government ser.)	ERS	70	188.217-010
Commissioner, Conservation of Resources (government ser.)	EAS	66	188.117-026
Commissioner, Public Works (government ser.)	SER	69	188.117-030
Communication-Center Coordinator (air trans.)	SCE	59	235.132-014
Communication-Center Operator (air trans.)	ESC	50	235.662-014
Communications Consultant (tel. & tel.)	EIA	64	253.157-010
Communications Coordinator (medical ser.)	ESC	61	239.167-010
Communications Electrician Supervisor (any industry)	ERC	63	823.131-010
Communications Technician (education)	RSE	56	962.362-010
Community Dietitian (profess. & kin.)	SRE	67	077.127-010
Community Organization Worker (social ser.)	ESA	66	195.167-010
Community Service Officer, Patrol (government ser.)	SEC	51	372.367-010
Community Worker (government ser.)	SER	58	195.367-018
Community-Relations-and-Services Advisor, Public Housing (social ser.)	SEC	66	195.167-014

Title	HOC	Cx	DOT
Community-Services-and-Health-Education Officer (government ser.)	SEI	71	079.167-010
Commutator Assembler (elec. equip.)	RES	49	724.684-030
Compact Assembler (jewelry-silver.)	RCE	38	739.687-066
Companion (domestic ser.)	SER	49	309.677-010
Company Laborer (mine & quarry)	RES	40	939.687-014
Comparator Operator (any industry)	RCE	53	699.384-010
Comparison Shopper (retail trade; wholesale tr.)	SIE	52	296.367-014
Compensator (paper goods)	REC	35	640.685-026
Compiler (clerical)	CSE	51	209.387-014
Complaint Clerk (boot & shoe)	CSR	47	221.387-014
Complaint Evaluation Officer (government ser.)	ECS	54	375.367-014
Complaint Evaluation Supervisor (government ser.)	ESC	60	375.137-038
Complaint Inspector (utilities)	RSI	58	829.261-010
Compo Caster (wood prod., n.e.c.)	RES	50	769.381-010
Composer (profess. & kin.)	ASE	75	152.067-014
Composing-Room Machinist (print. & pub.)	RES	59	627.261-010
Composition Mixer (fabrication, n.e.c.)	REI	45	550.665-014
Composition-Roll Maker and Cutter (rubber goods)	RES	48	559.482-010
Composition-Stone Applicator (construction)	REC	50	861.361-010
Composition-Weatherboard Applier (construction)	CRE	41	863.684-010
Compositor (print. & pub.)	RCS	59	973.381-010
Compositor Apprentice (print. & pub.)	RSC	59	973.381-014
Compound Filler (chemical)	REI	37	550.686-014
Compound Finisher (chemical)	RCS	41	550.685-042
Compound Mixer (tinware)	REC	50	509.485-010
Compound Worker (recording)	REC	39	559.686-010
Compound-Coating-Machine Offbearer (tinware)	RES	37	509.666-010
Compounder (chemical)	RSE	41	550.685-050
Compounder (petrol. refin.)	RES	56	540.382-010
Compounder (pharmaceut.; soap & rel.)	REI	47	550.685-046
Compounder Helper (petrol. refin.)	RCE	42	540.686-010
Compounder, Cork (wood prod., n.e.c.)	REC	43	560.587-010
Compounder, Flavorings (beverage)	RIS	56	529.381-010
Compressed-Gas-Plant Worker (chemical)	REC	43	549.587-010
Compression-Molding-Machine Operator (elec. equip.; plastic prod.)	RSE	47	556.682-014
Compression-Molding-Machine Tender (plastic prod.)	CRS	38	556.685-022
Compressor (elec. equip.; pharmaceut.)	RCS	47	556.682-022
Compressor Operator II (chemical)	RES	40	559.685-038
Compressor-Station Engineer, Chief (pipe lines)	RES	62	914.132-010
Computer Operator (clerical)	CSR	56	213.362-010
Computer Peripheral Equipment Operator (clerical)	CSR	51	213.382-010
Computer Processing Scheduler (clerical)	CSR	57	221.362-030
Computer Programmer (profess. & kin.)	IRC	69	030.162-010
Computer Security Coordinator (profess. & kin.)	CIS	63	033.162-010
Computer Security Specialist (profess. & kin.)	CIS	57	033.362-010
Computer Systems Hardware Analyst (profess. & kin.)	IRE	72	033.167-010
Computer Typesetter-Keyliner (print. & pub.)	CRA	58	979.382-026

Title	HOC	Cx	DOT
Computer-Controlled-Color-Photograph-Printer Operator (photofinishing)	RCE	52	976.380-010
Computerized Environmental Control Installer (electron. comp.)	RCI	64	828.281-026
Concaving-Machine Operator (boot & shoe)	RCE	41	585.685-030
Concentrator Operator (smelt. & refin.)	RES	55	511.462-010
Conche Operator (sugar & conf.)	RSE	49	526.382-010
Conciliator (profess. & kin.)	ESA	69	169.207-010
Concrete Rubber (concrete prod.)	RES	45	844.684-010
Concrete Sculptor (concrete prod.)	RAI	58	777.281-010
Concrete-Batching and Mixing-Plant Supervisor (construction)	ESR	58	570.132-010
Concrete-Building Assembler (mfd. bldgs.)	RCE	44	869.664-010
Concrete-Fence Builder (construction)	REI	48	869.681-010
Concrete-Float Maker (concrete prod.)	RCE	40	869.687-022
Concrete-Mixing-Truck Driver (construction)	REI	44	900.683-010
Concrete-Paving-Machine Operator (construction)	REI	44	853.663-014
Concrete-Pipe Maker (concrete prod.)	RCS	39	779.684-014
Concrete-Pipe-Making-Machine Operator (concrete prod.)	REC	40	575.665-010
Concrete-Stone Fabricator (concrete prod.)	REI	52	575.461-010
Concrete-Stone Finisher (concrete prod.)	REI	53	844.461-010
Concrete-Vault Maker (concrete prod.)	REC	38	579.684-010
Concreting Supervisor (construction)	RES	59	869.131-014
Condenser Setter (smelt. & refin.)	RCS	40	512.687-010
Condenser-Tube Tender (smelt. & refin.)	RCS	38	511.685-018
Conditioner Tender (textile)	RES	41	587.685-022
Conditioner-Tumbler Operator (laundry & rel.)	RES	39	361.685-010
Condominium Manager (real estate)	ESC	63	186.167-062
Conductor (r.r. trans.)	RSC	49	910.667-014
Conductor, Orchestra (profess. & kin.)	AES	67	152.047-014
Conductor, Passenger Car (r.r. trans.)	ESA	64	198.167-010
Conductor, Pullman (r.r. trans.)	ERS	57	198.167-014
Conductor, Road Freight (r.r. trans.)	ECS	58	198.167-018
Conductor, Yard (r.r. trans.)	ESR	56	910.137-022
Conduit Mechanic (construction; utilities)	REI	56	869.361-010
Cone Operator (mine & quarry)	RCE	41	934.685-010
Cone Treater (paper goods)	RES	38	534.687-010
Confectionery Cooker (sugar & conf.)	RIE	56	526.382-014
Confectionery-Drops-Machine Operator (sugar & conf.)	RCE	39	520.685-078
Configuration Management Analyst (profess. & kin.)	ESR	69	012.167-010
Congressional-District Aide (government ser.)	CES	57	209.362-030
Conservation Technician (museums)	RIE	63	102.261-010
Conservator, Artifacts (profess. & kin.)	RIS	59	055.381-010
Console Assembler (musical inst.)	RIE	47	730.684-030
Construction Checker (utilities)	RCI	58	821.367-010
Construction Inspector (construction)	REC	62	182.267-010
Construction Worker I (construction)	RIE	49	869.664-014
Construction Worker II (construction)	RES	40	869.687-026
Construction-and-Maintenance Inspector (petrol. refin.)	RCS	53	914.362-014

Title	HOC	Cx	DOT
Construction-Equipment Mechanic (construction)	REI	56	620.261-022
Construction-Equipment-Mechanic Helper (construction)	RES	44	620.664-010
Consultant (profess. & kin.)	IER	70	189.167-010
Consultant, Education (education)	SCE	74	099.167-014
Consultant, Educational, State Board of Nursing (government ser.)	SIE	73	075.117-010
Contact Clerk (utilities)	CSE	51	209.387-018
Contact Printer, Photoresist (inst. & app.; optical goods)	RCE	54	976.684-034
Contact Printer, Printed Circuit Boards (electron. comp.)	RCI	43	976.684-030
Contact Representative (government ser.)	SCE	65	169.167-018
Contact Worker, Lithography (print. & pub.)	CRS	50	976.684-038
Contact-Acid-Plant Operator (chemical)	REI	50	558.585-018
Contact-Acid-Plant-Operator Helper (chemical)	RES	40	559.687-026
Contact-Lens Molder (optical goods)	RCE	45	690.685-090
Contact-Lens-Flashing Puncher (optical goods)	RCE	40	713.687-014
Container Coordinator (water trans.)	ERS	57	248.367-022
Container Washer, Machine (any industry)	RCE	38	529.685-074
Contestant Coordinator (radio-tv broad.)	AES	57	166.167-010
Continuity Clerk (motion picture)	CSE	51	209.382-010
Continuity Director (radio-tv broad.)	SEC	67	132.037-010
Continuity Writer (radio-tv broad.)	AES	63	131.087-010
Continuous Pillowcase Cutter (tex. prod., n.e.c.)	RCE	42	686.685-014
Continuous-Absorption-Process Operator (sugar & conf.)	RSE	49	521.362-010
Continuous-Crusher Operator (textile)	RCE	40	586.685-014
Continuous-Linter-Drier Operator (chemical)	REI	40	553.685-034
Continuous-Mining-Machine Operator (mine & quarry)	RSE	47	930.683-010
Continuous-Towel Roller (laundry & rel.)	REC	38	361.685-014
Contour Grinder (stonework)	REI	48	675.682-010
Contour Wire Specialist, Denture (protective dev.)	REI	57	712.381-014
Contour-Band-Saw Operator, Vertical (machine shop)	RIE	51	607.382-010
Contract Administrator (any industry)	ESA	66	162.117-014
Contract Clerk (profess. & kin.)	SEC	66	119.267-018
Contract Clerk, Automobile (retail trade)	CSE	56	219.362-026
Contract Specialist (profess. & kin.)	ESA	66	162.117-018
Contractor (construction)	EIR	63	182.167-010
Control Clerk (clock & watch)	RCE	56	221.387-018
Control Clerk, Auditing (insurance)	CSE	54	209.362-014
Control Clerk, Head (clock & watch)	ESR	59	221.137-010
Control Inspector (paper & pulp; wood prod., n.e.c.)	CRS	48	539.667-010
Control Operator (smelt. & refin.)	RSI	53	511.482-010
Control-Panel Operator (petrol. refin.)	RSC	53	546.382-010
Control-Panel Tester (elec. equip.)	RES	60	827.381-010
Controller (profess. & kin.)	EIS	73	160.167-058
Controller Repairer-and-Tester (railroad equip.)	RES	57	825.381-018
Controller, Coal or Ore (mine & quarry)	ERC	57	939.167-010
Controller, Remotely-Piloted Vehicle (aircraft mfg.)	RIE	69	196.263-026
Controls Designer (profess. & kin.)	IRC	67	003.261-014
Controls Operator, Molded Goods (fabrication, n.e.c.)	RES	50	590.662-010
Converter Operator (grain-feed mills)	REC	49	526.382-018

Part 3: From Occupational Titles to Holland Codes
From the Dictionary of Occupational Titles Occupations to Holland Codes

Title	HOC	Cx	DOT
Converter Supervisor (smelt. & refin.)	ERA	56	513.132-010
Convex-Grinder Operator (button & notion)	CRE	38	673.685-042
Conveyor Feeder-Offbearer (any industry)	RCE	39	921.686-014
Conveyor Loader I (meat products)	RES	39	525.687-018
Conveyor Loader II (meat products)	REC	40	525.686-014
Conveyor Operator, Pneumatic System (food prep., n.e.c.)	REC	52	921.382-010
Conveyor Tender (any industry)	REC	40	921.685-026
Conveyor-Maintenance Mechanic (any industry)	RES	52	630.381-010
Conveyor-System Operator (any industry)	CRS	48	921.662-018
Convolute-Tube Winder (paper goods)	REI	47	640.682-010
Cook (any industry)	RES	52	315.361-010
Cook (chemical)	REC	48	553.665-018
Cook (domestic ser.)	RSE	52	305.281-010
Cook (fishing & hunt.)	RES	49	315.381-010
Cook (hotel & rest.)	RSE	56	313.361-014
Cook (meat products)	REI	44	526.685-010
Cook Apprentice (hotel & rest.)	RSE	56	313.361-018
Cook Apprentice, Pastry (hotel & rest.)	RAS	56	313.381-018
Cook Helper (can. & preserv.)	RCE	43	529.687-050
Cook Helper (hotel & rest.)	RES	40	317.687-010
Cook Helper, Pastry (hotel & rest.)	RES	41	313.687-010
Cook, Barbecue (hotel & rest.)	RSE	49	313.381-022
Cook, Chief (water trans.)	REA	58	315.131-010
Cook, Dog-and-Cat Food (meat products)	RES	48	526.682-014
Cook, Fast Food (hotel & rest.)	RCE	49	313.374-010
Cook, Fry, Deep Fat (can. & preserv.; hotel & rest.)	RCE	40	526.685-014
Cook, Head, School Cafeteria (hotel & rest.)	SER	58	313.131-018
Cook, Kettle (beverage; can. & preserv.; grain-feed mills)	RSE	52	526.381-026
Cook, Larder (water trans.)	SRE	55	315.381-014
Cook, Mess (water trans.)	RES	50	315.371-010
Cook, Mexican Food (food prep., n.e.c.)	ERS	56	526.134-010
Cook, Pastry (hotel & rest.)	RAS	56	313.381-026
Cook, Railroad (r.r. trans.)	RES	53	315.381-018
Cook, School Cafeteria (hotel & rest.)	RSE	50	313.381-030
Cook, Short Order (hotel & rest.)	RSE	50	313.374-014
Cook, Soybean Specialties (food prep., n.e.c.)	RCE	41	529.685-290
Cook, Specialty (hotel & rest.)	RSE	49	313.361-026
Cook, Specialty, Foreign Food (hotel & rest.)	RSE	55	313.361-030
Cook, Station (water trans.)	RSE	52	315.361-022
Cook, Syrup Maker (beverage)	REI	50	526.682-018
Cook, Third (water trans.)	RES	50	315.381-022
Cook, Vacuum Kettle (can. & preserv.)	REC	40	526.685-018
Cook-Box Filler (meat products)	RCE	38	523.685-030
Cooker (grain-feed mills)	RES	42	526.685-022
Cooker Cleaner (can. & preserv.)	REC	39	529.687-054
Cooker Loader (oils & grease)	REC	37	921.685-030
Cooker Tender (oils & grease)	REI	38	553.665-022
Cooker Tender (paper & pulp)	RCE	41	532.685-014
Cooker, Casing (tobacco)	REC	41	520.685-082

Title	HOC	Cx	DOT
Cooker, Meal (oils & grease)	REC	42	523.685-034
Cooker, Process Cheese (dairy products)	RES	46	526.665-010
Cooking, Casing, and Drying Supervisor (tobacco)	SRE	59	529.135-010
Cooler Room Worker (meat products)	REI	41	525.687-022
Cooler Tender (grain-feed mills)	CER	41	523.685-038
Cooler Tender (sugar & conf.)	RES	42	520.585-018
Cooling-Machine Operator (beverage)	REC	40	523.685-042
Cooling-Pan Tender (can. & preserv.)	RCE	40	523.685-046
Cooling-Pipe Inspector (construction)	REI	46	862.687-010
Cooling-Room Attendant (personal ser.)	CSE	41	335.677-010
Cooper (wood. container)	RSC	45	764.684-022
Cooper Helper (wood. container)	RES	42	764.687-050
Coordinate Measuring Equipment Operator (electron. comp.)	RCI	51	726.682-018
Coordinator of Rehabilitation Services (medical ser.)	SEI	69	076.117-010
Coordinator, Skill-Training Program (government ser.)	SEC	67	169.167-062
Coordinator, Volunteer Services (social ser.)	SEC	66	187.167-022
Coper, Hand (stonework)	REI	47	771.384-010
Coppersmith (ship-boat mfg.)	RSE	58	862.281-010
Coppersmith Apprentice (ship-boat mfg.)	RSE	58	862.281-014
Copra Processor (soap & rel.)	RCE	43	555.685-018
Copy Cutter (print. & pub.)	CES	59	221.167-010
Copy Holder (print. & pub.)	CSE	52	209.667-010
Copy Writer (profess. & kin.)	ASI	67	131.067-014
Copy-Lathe Tender (woodworking)	REC	41	664.685-018
Copyist (any industry)	SCE	65	152.267-010
Copyist (garment)	AES	59	142.281-010
Copyright Expert (radio-tv broad.)	CES	60	249.267-010
Corduroy-Brusher Operator (textile)	REI	41	585.685-034
Corduroy-Cutter Operator (textile)	RCE	44	585.565-010
Core Checker (foundry)	REC	45	518.687-010
Core Extruder (elec. equip.)	CRE	38	557.685-010
Core Feeder, Plywood Layup Line (millwork-plywood)	REC	41	569.685-018
Core Layer, Plywood Layup Line (millwork-plywood)	REC	40	569.686-014
Core Loader (ordnance)	RCE	36	737.687-030
Core Setter (foundry)	REC	40	518.684-010
Core Shaper (toy-sport equip.)	REC	41	692.685-058
Core Winding Operator (paper & pulp)	RSE	50	640.682-014
Core-Composer Feeder (millwork-plywood)	REC	41	669.685-038
Core-Composer-Machine Tender (millwork-plywood)	RCE	41	569.685-022
Core-Cutter and Reamer (paper goods)	RSE	45	649.685-026
Core-Drill Operator (any industry)	RSE	48	930.682-010
Core-Drill Operator (construction)	RCS	46	869.682-014
Core-Drill-Operator Helper (any industry)	RES	44	930.687-014
Core-Laying-Machine Operator (millwork-plywood)	RCE	42	569.685-026
Core-Oven Tender (foundry)	RCS	41	518.685-010
Coremaker (foundry)	RCI	51	518.381-014
Coremaker Apprentice (foundry)	RCI	51	518.381-018
Coremaker, Machine I (foundry)	RCE	40	518.685-014

From the Dictionary of Occupational Titles Occupations to Holland Codes

Title	HOC	Cx	DOT
Coremaker, Machine II (foundry)	RCE	41	518.685-018
Coremaker, Machine III (foundry)	REC	41	518.685-022
Coremaker, Pipe (foundry)	REC	41	518.684-014
Coremaking-Machine Operator (elec. equip.)	RCS	47	692.682-030
Cork Grinder (toy-sport equip.)	REC	40	662.685-010
Cork Insulator, Refrigeration Plant (construction)	RCS	50	863.381-010
Cork Molder (wood prod., n.e.c.)	RCS	42	569.685-030
Cork-Pressing-Machine Operator (wood prod., n.e.c.)	REC	37	569.686-018
Corn Cooker (food prep., n.e.c.)	REC	42	522.685-034
Corn Grinder (food prep., n.e.c.)	REC	39	521.685-082
Corn Popper (sugar & conf.)	REC	39	526.685-026
Corn-Grinder Operator, Automatic (grain-feed mills)	RCE	42	521.685-086
Corn-Press Operator (food prep., n.e.c.)	RES	41	529.685-078
Corner Cutter (paper goods)	REC	40	640.685-030
Corner Former (wood. container)	RES	39	617.685-014
Corner-Brace-Block-Machine Operator (furniture)	RCS	47	669.682-030
Corner-Trimmer Operator (wood. container)	RES	45	667.682-018
Coroner (government ser.)	ISE	69	168.161-010
Correction Officer (government ser.)	SER	48	372.667-018
Correction Officer, Head (government ser.)	SER	59	372.137-010
Correctional-Treatment Specialist (social ser.)	SEI	66	195.107-042
Corrective Therapist (medical ser.)	SIR	63	076.361-010
Correspondence Clerk (clerical)	CES	52	209.362-034
Correspondence-Review Clerk (clerical)	CSE	51	209.367-018
Corrosion-Control Fitter (pipe lines; utilities)	REI	57	820.361-010
Corrugated-Fastener Driver (woodworking)	REC	38	669.685-042
Corrugator Operator (paper goods)	RSE	48	641.562-010
Corrugator Operator (plastic-synth.)	RSE	47	556.665-014
Corrugator-Operator Helper (paper goods)	RES	41	641.686-018
Corset Fitter (retail trade)	RES	53	782.361-010
Cosmetics Presser (pharmaceut.)	REC	41	556.685-026
Cosmetics Supervisor (pharmaceut.)	SRE	59	550.131-010
Cosmetologist (personal ser.)	SEA	56	332.271-010
Cosmetologist Apprentice (personal ser.)	SER	56	332.271-014
Cost Clerk (clerical)	CRS	54	216.382-034
Cost-and-Sales-Record Supervisor (utilities)	SCE	69	216.137-010
Costumer (motion picture; radio-tv broad.)	ARI	63	346.261-010
Costumer Assistant (motion picture; radio-tv broad.)	ERA	53	346.374-010
Cottage-Cheese Maker (dairy products)	RES	51	522.382-010
Cotton Baler (agriculture)	REC	45	920.685-114
Cotton Classer (agriculture; textile)	RSE	57	429.387-010
Cotton Classer Aide (agriculture)	RCI	42	429.587-010
Cotton Dispatcher (furniture)	RCS	40	780.684-038
Cotton Puller (oils & grease)	REC	36	521.686-022
Cotton Sampler (agriculture; textile)	RCE	40	922.687-042
Cotton Tier (agriculture)	REC	37	920.687-074
Cotton Washer (plastic-synth.)	RES	36	559.687-030
Cotton-Ball Bagger (protective dev.)	RCE	40	920.686-014
Cotton-Ball-Machine Tender (protective dev.)	RCS	47	580.685-022

Title	HOC	Cx	DOT
Cotton-Roll Packer (protective dev.)	RCE	38	920.685-054
Counselor (profess. & kin.)	SAE	68	045.107-010
Counselor, Camp (amuse. & rec.)	SEC	59	159.124-010
Counselor, Marriage and Family (profess. & kin.)	SAE	68	045.107-054
Counselor, Nurses' Association (medical ser.)	SER	69	045.107-014
Counter Attendant, Cafeteria (hotel & rest.)	CER	42	311.677-014
Counter Attendant, Lunchroom or Coffee Shop (hotel & rest.)	CES	47	311.477-014
Counter Clerk (photofinishing)	CRE	44	249.366-010
Counter Clerk (tel. & tel.)	CSE	56	249.362-010
Counter Cutter (boot & shoe)	RCE	42	690.685-094
Counter Former (boot & shoe)	CRE	41	690.685-098
Counter Molder (boot & shoe)	CRE	43	690.685-102
Counter Roller (boot & shoe)	RCE	40	690.685-106
Counter Supervisor (hotel & rest.)	ESR	56	311.137-010
Counter, Hand (paper goods)	REC	43	794.687-018
Counter-Supply Worker (hotel & rest.)	RES	40	319.687-010
Counterintelligence Agent (military ser.)	SER	66	378.267-010
Countersinker (clock & watch)	RCE	42	715.682-014
Counting-Machine Operator (paper goods)	RSC	41	649.685-030
County Home-Demonstration Agent (government ser.)	SEC	66	096.121-010
County-Agricultural Agent (government ser.)	SEC	66	096.127-010
Coupling-Machine Operator (steel & rel.)	RCS	47	619.682-014
Coupon Clerk (financial)	CSE	57	219.462-010
Coupon-Redemption Clerk (retail trade)	CES	50	290.477-010
Court Administrator (government ser.)	ESR	69	188.117-130
Court Clerk (government ser.)	CSE	57	243.362-010
Cover Inspector (furniture)	RCE	46	789.687-038
Cover Stripper (paper goods)	REI	40	641.685-034
Covered-Buckle Assembler (button & notion)	RCE	38	734.687-050
Coverer, Looseleaf Binder (print. & pub.)	REC	42	795.687-010
Covering-Machine Operator (print. & pub.)	RCE	46	653.682-014
Covering-Machine Operator (textile)	RCE	41	681.685-038
Covering-Machine Tender (leather prod.)	CRE	38	783.685-010
Covering-Machine-Operator Helper (textile)	RES	42	681.685-042
Coverstitch-Machine Operator (garment)	CRE	40	786.682-078
Cowpuncher (agriculture)	RES	45	410.674-014
Crab Butcher (can. & preserv.)	REI	37	525.684-022
Crab Meat Processor (can. & preserv.)	RCE	39	525.687-126
Crabber (textile)	REC	42	582.685-038
Cracker Sprayer (bakery products)	CRE	42	524.685-022
Cracker-and-Cookie-Machine Operator (bakery products)	RES	47	520.682-034
Cracking-and-Fanning-Machine Operator (sugar & conf.)	REC	43	521.385-010
Cracking-Unit Operator (plastic-synth.)	RCS	47	558.682-010
Craft Demonstrator (museums)	SRC	55	109.364-010
Crane-Crew Supervisor (any industry)	RES	58	921.133-010
Crate Liner (furniture)	RES	38	920.687-078
Crate Opener (furniture)	RES	38	929.685-010
Crater (any industry)	REC	46	920.684-010

Title	HOC	Cx	DOT
Crating-and-Moving Estimator (motor trans.; r.r. trans.)	EAS	61	252.357-010
Crayon Grader (mine & quarry)	CRS	42	579.684-014
Crayon Sawyer (mine & quarry)	CRE	39	677.685-022
Crayon-Sorting-Machine Feeder (pen & pencil)	REC	40	929.686-018
Creaser (leather prod.)	CRS	44	783.685-014
Creative Director (profess. & kin.)	AES	67	141.067-010
Credit Analyst (clerical)	ESR	59	241.267-022
Credit Analyst (financial)	CRS	69	160.267-022
Credit Authorizer (clerical)	CES	50	249.367-022
Credit Card Control Clerk (financial)	CSE	50	249.367-026
Credit Clerk (clerical)	CSE	57	205.367-022
Credit Clerk, Blood Bank (medical ser.)	CSE	51	245.367-022
Credit Counselor (profess. & kin.)	ESI	71	160.207-010
Credit Reference Clerk (financial; retail trade)	CES	51	209.362-018
Credit Reporting Clerk (business ser.)	CSE	51	203.362-014
Credit-Card Clerk (hotel & rest.)	CSR	51	210.382-038
Credit-Card Clerk (retail trade)	CER	48	209.587-014
Creel Clerk (government ser.)	CSE	48	205.367-026
Creeler (textile)	RCE	40	689.687-030
Cremator (personal ser.)	RES	46	359.685-010
Creping-Machine Operator (paper goods)	RCS	46	534.682-030
Creping-Machine-Operator Helper (paper goods)	REI	41	534.687-014
Crew Leader, Gluing (millwork-plywood)	REC	50	569.565-010
Crew Scheduler (air trans.)	CRS	55	215.362-010
Crew Scheduler, Chief (air trans.)	ESR	62	215.137-010
Criminalist (profess. & kin.)	IRC	74	029.261-026
Crimp Setter (textile)	RES	41	680.685-026
Crimper (rubber goods)	RCE	39	690.686-026
Crimping-Machine Operator (any industry)	RES	47	616.682-022
Crimping-Machine Operator (textile)	REC	41	680.685-030
Cripple Worker (boot & shoe)	CRS	42	788.684-042
Critic (print. & pub.; radio-tv broad.)	AES	70	131.067-018
Crochet-Machine Operator (knitting)	RCE	45	685.682-010
Crocheter, Hand (knitting)	RCE	44	782.684-014
Crook Operator (musical inst.)	RES	48	609.682-018
Crossband Layer (millwork-plywood)	REI	40	762.687-026
Crosscutter, Rolled Glass (glass mfg.)	RCS	41	575.684-022
Crossing Tender (any industry)	CER	45	371.667-010
Crossword-Puzzle Maker (print. & pub.)	ASE	64	139.087-010
Crown Attacher (clock & watch)	RCE	41	715.684-070
Crown Pouncer, Hand (hat & cap)	CRE	39	784.687-018
Crown-Assembly-Machine Operator (any industry)	REC	40	692.685-062
Crown-Wheel Assembler (clock & watch)	CRS	46	715.684-074
Croze-Machine Operator (wood. container)	RCE	44	669.682-034
Crude-Oil Treater (petrol. & gas)	REI	55	541.382-014
Cruiser (forestry; logging)	RIE	57	459.387-010
Crusher (fabrication, n.e.c.)	CRE	40	780.684-042
Crusher Operator (concrete prod.)	RIE	41	570.685-018
Crusher Operator (sugar & conf.)	RES	39	521.685-090

Title	HOC	Cx	DOT
Crusher Setter (mine & quarry)	RES	44	933.664-010
Crusher Supervisor (smelt. & refin.)	RES	59	515.132-010
Crusher Tender (any industry)	REI	42	570.685-022
Crusher Tender (fabrication, n.e.c.)	REI	40	555.685-022
Crusher Tender (smelt. & refin.)	RCS	40	515.685-014
Crusher-and-Binder Operator (tex. prod., n.e.c.)	RCE	38	689.685-054
Crusher-and-Blender Operator (steel & rel.)	RCS	49	544.582-010
Crushing-Machine Operator (beverage)	RCE	37	521.685-094
Crutcher (soap & rel.)	RES	47	550.685-054
Crutcher Helper (soap & rel.)	RES	38	550.686-018
Cryolite-Recovery Operator (smelt. & refin.)	REC	50	511.482-014
Cryptanalyst (government ser.)	AIE	71	199.267-014
Cryptographic-Machine Operator (clerical)	CER	54	203.582-018
Crystal Attacher (clock & watch)	RCE	37	715.687-018
Crystal Cutter (clock & watch)	RCE	43	715.684-078
Crystal Grinder (electron. comp.)	RCI	49	673.382-026
Crystal Grower (comm. equip.; electron. comp.)	RIC	54	590.382-014
Crystal Growing Technician (electron. comp.)	RIC	61	590.262-010
Crystal Machining Coordinator (electron. comp.)	RIS	56	679.362-010
Crystal Mounter (electron. comp.)	RCI	41	677.687-014
Crystal Slicer (electron. comp.)	RCI	49	677.382-018
Crystallizer Operator (grain-feed mills)	REC	43	523.685-050
Crystallizer Operator (sugar & conf.)	REC	44	523.585-018
Crystallizer Operator I (chemical)	CRE	45	559.685-042
Crystallographer (clock & watch)	IRS	80	024.061-010
Cubing-Machine Tender (concrete prod.)	RCI	40	920.685-106
Cue Selector (radio-tv broad.)	ASE	72	152.067-018
Cuff Cutter (glove & mit.)	RCS	42	686.685-018
Cuff Folder (knitting)	RCE	39	685.687-014
Culler (wood. container)	CRE	42	764.687-054
Cullet Crusher-and-Washer (glass mfg.)	REI	41	570.685-026
Cultured-Marble-Products Maker (stonework)	RCE	48	575.684-050
Cup Setter, Lockstitch (garment)	RCE	41	786.682-082
Cup-Trimming-Machine Operator (ordnance)	RCE	40	615.685-018
Cupboard Builder (furniture)	RCE	47	703.684-014
Cupola Charger (foundry)	RCS	41	512.686-010
Cupola Charger, Insulation (nonmet. min.)	RCE	41	572.686-010
Cupola Hoist Operator (foundry)	CRS	44	921.683-030
Cupola Operator, Insulation (nonmet. min.)	RSE	50	579.382-014
Cupola Patcher (foundry)	CRS	44	861.684-010
Cupola Tapper (foundry)	RCE	42	514.664-010
Cupola Tender (foundry)	RIS	47	512.662-010
Cuprous-Chloride Helper (chemical)	REC	42	558.585-022
Cuprous-Chloride Operator (chemical)	RIE	50	558.382-034
Curator (museums)	IRS	78	102.017-010
Curb Attendant (laundry & rel.)	CRS	44	369.477-010
Curb-Machine Operator (construction)	RIE	46	853.683-010
Curer, Foam Rubber (rubber goods)	REI	48	553.682-014
Curing Oven Attendant (aircraft mfg.; electron. comp.)	RCE	38	590.685-090

Title	HOC	Cx	DOT
Curing-Bin Operator (grain-feed mills)	RES	43	522.685-038
Curing-Oven Tender (chemical)	CRS	44	553.685-038
Curing-Press Maintainer (rubber tire)	RCE	42	629.684-010
Curing-Press Operator (rubber tire)	RCS	39	553.686-018
Currency Counter (financial)	CRE	49	217.485-010
Curtain-Roller Assembler (furniture)	CRS	42	739.684-042
Curtain-Stretcher Assembler (woodworking)	REC	41	762.684-030
Cushion Builder (furniture)	RCE	42	780.684-046
Cushion Maker I (furniture)	RCE	41	780.684-054
Custodian, Athletic Equipment (amuse. & rec.)	CSR	53	969.367-010
Custom Ski Maker (toy-sport equip.)	RIS	62	732.281-010
Custom Tailor (garment; personal ser.; retail trade)	RES	62	785.261-014
Custom Van Converter (auto. mfg.; automotive ser.)	RCI	56	806.381-070
Custom-Feed-Mill Operator (grain-feed mills)	RSE	56	529.132-010
Custom-Feed-Mill-Operator Helper (grain-feed mills)	REC	39	521.686-026
Custom-Leather-Products Maker (leather prod.)	RCI	53	783.361-010
Customer Service Representative (financial)	CSE	58	205.362-026
Customer Service Representative (radio-tv broad.; tel. & tel.; utilities; waterworks)	CES	52	239.362-014
Customer Service Representative (utilities)	RCE	53	959.361-010
Customer Service Representative Supervisor (radio-tv broad.; tel. & tel.; utilities; waterworks)	SEC	55	239.137-014
Customer Services Coordinator (print. & pub.)	SEI	65	221.167-026
Customer-Complaint Clerk (clerical)	SEC	57	241.367-014
Customer-Equipment Engineer (tel. & tel.)	RIE	70	003.187-018
Customer-Facilities Supervisor (tel. & tel.)	ERS	63	822.131-014
Customer-Service Clerk (retail trade)	ESC	54	299.367-010
Customer-Service-Representative Instructor (tel. & tel.; utilities; waterworks)	SEC	56	239.227-010
Customs Broker (financial)	ESR	69	186.117-018
Customs Import Specialist (government ser.)	ISE	66	168.267-018
Customs Inspector (government ser.)	CEI	65	168.267-022
Customs Patrol Officer (government ser.)	SER	62	168.167-010
Cut-and-Cover Line Worker (boot & shoe)	CRS	38	753.684-014
Cut-and-Print-Machine Operator (ordnance)	RIE	47	659.682-010
Cut-File Clerk (print. & pub.)	CRS	49	222.367-014
Cut-In Worker (grain-feed mills)	RES	36	521.686-030
Cut-Lace-Machine Operator (leather prod.)	RCE	42	585.685-038
Cut-Off Saw Tender, Metal (machine shop)	RIE	42	607.685-010
Cut-Off Sawyer, Log (paper & pulp; saw. & plan.)	REI	40	667.685-034
Cut-Off-Machine Operator (ordnance)	CRS	40	615.685-022
Cut-Off-Machine Operator (paper goods)	RCE	40	640.685-034
Cut-Off-Machine Operator (steel & rel.)	RCI	43	619.685-094
Cut-Off-Saw Operator I (woodworking)	RSC	47	667.682-022
Cut-Off-Saw Operator II (woodworking)	RCI	40	667.685-074
Cut-Off-Saw Operator, Metal (machine shop)	RIE	47	607.682-010
Cut-Off-Saw Operator, Pipe Blanks (nonmet. min.)	REC	41	677.685-026
Cut-Out-and-Marking-Machine Operator (boot & shoe)	RCE	41	690.685-110
Cut-Out-Machine Operator (boot & shoe)	RCE	40	690.685-114

DOT to HOC

Part 3: From Occupational Titles to Holland Codes

From the Dictionary of Occupational Titles Occupations to Holland Codes

Title	HOC	Cx	DOT
Cutch Cleaner (metal prod., n.e.c.)	REC	40	700.687-030
Cutlet Maker, Pork (meat products)	RCE	39	529.686-022
Cutter (brick & tile)	RCI	40	579.684-030
Cutter (food prep., n.e.c.)	RCE	39	529.685-082
Cutter (glove & mit.; tex. prod., n.e.c.)	RSE	47	699.682-014
Cutter (photofinishing)	CRE	40	976.685-010
Cutter (tex. prod., n.e.c.)	RCE	41	686.685-022
Cutter Apprentice, Hand (any industry)	RCS	44	781.684-078
Cutter Helper (any industry)	REC	40	781.687-022
Cutter I (fabrication, n.e.c.)	RCE	41	690.685-118
Cutter II (fabrication, n.e.c.)	REC	39	692.686-030
Cutter Operator (any industry)	RSC	47	699.682-018
Cutter Operator (mine & quarry)	RCS	48	930.683-014
Cutter Operator (plastic-synth.)	RCS	44	555.585-010
Cutter, Aluminum Sheet (ship-boat mfg.)	RCE	42	804.684-010
Cutter, Banana Room (wholesale tr.)	RES	40	929.687-010
Cutter, Barrel Drum (tex. prod., n.e.c.)	RCS	45	690.682-026
Cutter, Frozen Meat (can. & preserv.)	REC	40	521.685-098
Cutter, Hand (rubber goods)	RCE	40	751.684-014
Cutter, Hand I (any industry)	RCS	44	781.684-074
Cutter, Hand II (any industry)	CRS	40	781.687-026
Cutter, Hand III (any industry)	REC	37	781.687-030
Cutter, Hot Knife (boot & shoe; rubber goods)	CRS	40	751.684-018
Cutter, Machine I (any industry)	RES	47	781.684-014
Cutter, Machine II (any industry)	CRE	41	699.685-014
Cutter, Rotary Shear (tex. prod., n.e.c.)	RCE	42	781.684-018
Cutter, V-Groove (clock & watch)	RCE	41	715.685-014
Cutter, Wet Machine (paper & pulp)	RSC	38	539.686-010
Cutter, Woodwind Reeds (musical inst.)	RCE	38	730.686-010
Cutter-and-Paster, Press Clippings (business ser.)	CER	41	249.587-014
Cutter-Inspector (nonmet. min.)	CRS	41	751.684-010
Cutter-Machine Tender (electron. comp.)	RCE	42	615.685-046
Cutter-Operator Helper (mine & quarry)	RES	38	930.687-018
Cutting Inspector (tex. prod., n.e.c.)	CRE	44	781.684-022
Cutting Supervisor (glass products)	RSE	59	775.134-010
Cutting-and-Printing-Machine Operator (tex. prod., n.e.c.)	RCS	43	652.685-022
Cutting-Machine Fixer (textile)	RIE	57	585.380-010
Cutting-Machine Offbearer (tex. prod., n.e.c.)	REC	40	689.686-018
Cutting-Machine Operator (print. & pub.)	RIE	47	640.682-018
Cutting-Machine Operator (sugar & conf.)	REC	44	521.685-102
Cutting-Machine Operator (tex. prod., n.e.c.)	RCE	42	686.585-010
Cutting-Machine Tender (any industry)	CRS	44	690.685-122
Cutting-Machine Tender, Decorative (glass mfg.)	RCE	40	775.685-010
Cutting-Machine-Tender Helper (any industry)	RES	40	690.686-030
Cylinder Batcher (textile)	REC	40	582.665-010
Cylinder Filler (chemical)	RSE	45	559.565-010
Cylinder Grinder (print. & pub.)	RCS	54	500.381-010
Cylinder Inspector-and-Tester (chemical)	REC	51	953.387-010
Cylinder-Die-Machine Helper (paper goods)	RES	40	649.686-018

Title	HOC	Cx	DOT
Cylinder-Die-Machine Operator (paper goods)	REI	47	649.682-014
Cylinder-Machine Operator (paper & pulp; wood prod., n.e.c.)	REI	53	539.362-010
Cylinder-Press Feeder (print. & pub.)	REI	41	651.686-010
Cylinder-Press Operator (print. & pub.)	RIE	57	651.362-010
Cylinder-Press-Operator Apprentice (print. & pub.)	RIE	57	651.362-014
Cylinder-Sander Operator (woodworking)	REI	40	662.685-014
Cytogenetic Technologist (medical ser.)	IRC	68	078.261-026
Cytologist (profess. & kin.)	IRE	80	041.061-042
Cytotechnologist (medical ser.)	ICR	66	078.281-010
Dado Operator (woodworking)	RIE	48	669.382-010
Dairy Helper (dairy products)	REC	40	529.686-026
Dairy Scientist (profess. & kin.)	IRE	78	040.061-018
Dairy Technologist (profess. & kin.)	IRS	78	040.061-022
Dairy-Equipment Repairer (dairy products)	REI	58	629.281-018
Dairy-Processing-Equipment Operator (dairy products)	REI	53	529.382-018
Dampener Operator (paper & pulp)	RCE	39	534.685-010
Dance Therapist (medical ser.)	ASI	66	076.127-018
Dancer (amuse. & rec.)	AER	61	151.047-010
Data Base Administrator (profess. & kin.)	IRE	71	039.162-010
Data Base Design Analyst (profess. & kin.)	IRS	71	039.162-014
Data Communications Analyst (profess. & kin.)	RSI	65	031.262-010
Data Communications Technician (any industry)	RIS	61	823.261-030
Data Entry Clerk (clerical)	CSE	50	203.582-054
Data Recovery Planner (profess. & kin.)	SER	66	033.162-014
Data-Examination Clerk (clerical)	CSE	51	209.387-022
Dater Assembler (pen & pencil)	CRE	41	733.687-030
Day Worker (domestic ser.)	RES	40	301.687-014
De-Alcoholizer (beverage)	RCE	45	522.685-042
De-Ionizer Operator (chemical)	RCE	45	558.685-026
Dealer-Compliance Representative (retail trade; wholesale tr.)	ESR	57	168.267-026
Dean of Students (education)	SEA	68	090.117-018
Deblocker (optical goods)	RCE	41	716.687-010
Deboner, Pet Food (can. & preserv.)	RCI	39	521.685-378
Debrander (boot & shoe)	REC	37	753.687-014
Debridging-Machine Operator (nonfer. metal)	RCE	42	607.685-014
Debubblizer (plastic-synth.)	REC	41	553.585-010
Deburrer (button & notion)	CRE	40	603.685-050
Deburrer, Machine (clock & watch)	REC	42	715.685-018
Deburrer, Printed Circuit Board Panels (electron. comp.)	RCI	39	603.686-014
Deburrer, Strip (clock & watch)	REI	53	603.482-010
Deburring-and-Tooling-Machine Operator (office machines)	RCI	60	690.280-010
Decal Applier (any industry)	RCE	38	749.684-010
Decating-Machine Operator (textile)	REC	43	582.685-042
Decay-Control Operator (wholesale tr.)	CRS	42	529.685-086
Deck Engineer (water trans.)	RSE	56	623.281-010
Decker Operator (paper & pulp)	REC	47	533.682-010

Title	HOC	Cx	DOT
Deckhand (chemical)	RES	37	553.686-022
Deckhand (water trans.)	REI	45	911.687-022
Deckhand, Fishing Vessel (fishing & hunt.)	REI	41	449.667-010
Decontaminator (any industry)	REI	54	199.384-010
Decorating Inspector (glass mfg.)	CSR	41	579.687-014
Decorating-and-Assembly Supervisor (plastic prod.)	ESC	55	754.130-010
Decorating-Equipment Setter (glass mfg.; glass products)	REI	49	652.380-010
Decorating-Machine Operator (glass products)	CRE	44	652.685-026
Decorator (any industry)	RIE	60	298.381-010
Decorator (bakery products; sugar & conf.)	CSR	41	524.684-014
Decorator (dairy products)	AES	57	524.381-014
Decorator (furniture; toy-sport equip.)	CRS	40	749.684-014
Decorator (glass mfg.; glass products)	RIA	54	740.381-010
Decorator (hat & cap)	CRE	42	784.684-022
Decorator (leather prod.)	CRS	41	739.684-046
Decorator (pottery & porc.)	CSE	45	740.684-014
Decorator, Lighting Fixtures (light. fix.)	SCE	41	749.684-018
Decorator, Mannequin (fabrication, n.e.c.)	RAE	52	970.381-014
Decorator, Street and Building (any industry)	RCS	41	899.687-010
Deep Submergence Vehicle Crewmember (military ser.)	RIE	57	623.281-014
Deep Submergence Vehicle Operator (military ser.)	RES	51	911.263-010
Defect Repairer, Glassware (glass mfg.)	CSR	42	772.684-010
Defective-Cigarette Slitter (tobacco)	REC	38	529.685-090
Defensive Fire Control Systems Operator (military ser.)	REI	55	378.382-014
Definer (button & notion)	REI	40	599.685-022
Deflash and Wash Operator (electron. comp.)	RCI	39	726.685-022
Deflector Operator (beverage)	CRE	40	529.687-058
Dehairing-Machine Tender (meat products)	REC	40	525.685-018
Dehydrating-Press Operator (chemical; plastic-synth.)	REC	41	551.685-046
Dehydrator Tender (can. & preserv.)	RES	43	523.685-054
Deicer Assembler, Electric (rubber goods)	RCS	51	739.684-050
Deicer Finisher (rubber goods)	CRS	44	739.684-054
Deicer Inspector, Electric (rubber goods)	RCE	52	729.387-010
Deicer Inspector, Pneumatic (rubber goods)	CRE	47	759.687-010
Deicer Repairer (rubber goods)	RCE	44	759.684-026
Deicer Tester (rubber goods)	REC	52	729.387-014
Deicer-Element Winder, Hand (rubber goods)	CRE	41	739.684-058
Deicer-Element Winder, Machine (rubber goods)	RCE	44	692.685-066
Deicer-Kit Assembler (rubber goods)	RCS	41	759.684-030
Deli Cutter-Slicer (retail trade)	CRS	41	316.684-014
Delineator (profess. & kin.)	REI	62	970.281-014
Deliverer, Car Rental (automotive ser.; retail trade)	REC	43	919.663-010
Deliverer, Merchandise (retail trade)	ERS	45	299.477-010
Deliverer, Outside (clerical)	CES	41	230.663-010
Demolition Specialist (ordnance)	RES	40	737.687-034
Demonstrator (retail trade; wholesale tr.)	ESC	54	297.354-010
Demonstrator, Electric-Gas Appliances (utilities)	ESA	64	297.357-010
Demonstrator, Knitting (retail trade)	ESC	58	297.354-014
Demonstrator, Sewing Techniques (retail trade)	ECS	51	297.454-010

Title	HOC	Cx	DOT
Demurrage Clerk (r.r. trans.)	CRE	55	214.362-010
Density Control Puncher (motion picture)	RES	44	976.684-010
Dental Assistant (medical ser.)	SAI	58	079.361-018
Dental Ceramist (protective dev.)	REC	58	712.381-042
Dental Ceramist Assistant (protective dev.)	REA	51	712.664-010
Dental Floss Packer (protective dev.)	RCE	38	920.687-082
Dental Hygienist (medical ser.)	SAI	60	078.361-010
Dental-Amalgam Processor (nonfer. metal)	REI	49	509.382-014
Dental-Equipment Installer and Servicer (wholesale tr.)	RSE	59	829.261-014
Dental-Laboratory Technician (protective dev.)	REI	58	712.381-018
Dental-Laboratory-Technician Apprentice (protective dev.)	REI	58	712.381-022
Dentist (medical ser.)	ISR	75	072.101-010
Denture Waxer (protective dev.)	RCI	56	712.381-046
Denture-Model Maker (protective dev.)	RES	50	712.684-046
Deodorizer (chemical)	RES	43	522.685-046
Deoiling-Machine and Pasteurizing-Machine Operator (beverage)	REC	41	529.685-094
Department Head, College or University (education)	ESI	73	090.167-010
Deposit Clerk (utilities)	ESC	62	241.267-026
Deposit-Refund Clerk (utilities)	CSR	52	214.482-014
Depositing-Machine Operator (bakery products)	RSC	44	524.682-010
Depositing-Machine Operator (sugar & conf.)	RES	49	529.682-018
Deputy Insurance Commissioner (government ser.)	ESR	69	186.117-022
Deputy Sheriff, Building Guard (government ser.)	ERS	45	377.667-014
Deputy Sheriff, Chief (government ser.)	ESR	64	377.167-010
Deputy Sheriff, Civil Division (government ser.)	SER	50	377.667-018
Deputy Sheriff, Commander, Civil Division (government ser.)	ESR	63	377.137-010
Deputy Sheriff, Commander, Criminal and Patrol Division (government ser.)	ERC	64	377.137-014
Deputy Sheriff, Grand Jury (government ser.)	RSE	50	377.363-010
Deputy United States Marshal (government ser.)	SEC	53	377.267-010
Deputy, Court (government ser.)	ESR	54	377.137-018
Dermatologist (medical ser.)	ISR	76	070.101-018
Derrick Operator (any industry)	RES	44	921.663-022
Derrick Worker, Well Service (petrol. & gas)	RES	41	930.683-018
Derrick-Boat Captain (water trans.)	ERS	59	911.137-014
Derrick-Boat Operator (water trans.)	RCE	46	921.683-034
Design Assembler (fabrication, n.e.c.)	RCE	39	692.686-034
Design Drafter, Electromechanisms (profess. & kin.)	IRE	66	017.261-014
Design Engineer, Marine Equipment (profess. & kin.)	IRE	71	014.061-010
Design Engineer, Mining-and-Oil-Field Equipment (profess. & kin.)	IRE	71	010.061-010
Design Engineer, Nuclear Equipment (profess. & kin.)	IRE	71	015.061-010
Design Inserter (plastic prod.)	CRE	42	692.685-070
Design Printer, Balloon (rubber goods)	REC	40	651.685-014
Design Technician, Computer-Aided (electron. comp.)	RCI	57	003.362-010
Design-Engineer, Agricultural Equipment (profess. & kin.)	IRE	71	013.061-018
Designer (protective dev.)	RSI	58	712.281-014

Title	HOC	Cx	DOT
Designer and Patternmaker (boot & shoe)	RIE	63	788.281-010
Desizing-Machine Operator, Head-End (textile)	REI	44	582.685-046
Desk Clerk, Bowling Floor (amuse. & rec.)	ESC	54	340.367-010
Desk Officer (government ser.)	ESC	58	375.137-014
Desk-Pen-Set Assembler (pen & pencil)	REC	40	733.687-034
Deskidding-Machine Operator (boot & shoe)	CRE	41	690.685-126
Dessert-Cup-Machine Feeder (bakery products)	RCE	37	520.686-014
Destaticizer Feeder (clock & watch)	REC	40	715.686-010
Desulfurizer Operator (steel & rel.)	RIE	52	541.362-010
Detacker (knitting; textile)	REC	37	589.685-030
Detailer (profess. & kin.)	RIE	66	017.261-018
Detailer, Furniture (profess. & kin.)	RIE	66	017.261-022
Detailer, School Photographs (photofinishing)	CER	51	976.564-010
Detective (government ser.)	SER	59	375.267-010
Detective Chief (government ser.)	ESC	59	375.167-022
Detective I (any industry)	SEC	51	376.367-014
Detective II (any industry)	ESA	49	376.667-014
Detective, Narcotics and Vice (government ser.)	SRE	63	375.267-014
Dethistler Operator (can. & preserv.)	REC	43	521.685-106
Detonator Assembler (ordnance)	CRS	40	737.687-038
Developer (photofinishing)	REI	48	976.681-010
Developer Prover, Interior Assemblies (aircraft mfg.)	RCE	60	693.261-010
Developer, Automatic (photofinishing)	RCE	42	976.685-014
Developer, Printed Circuit Board Panels (electron. comp.)	RCI	42	976.685-034
Development Mechanic (aircraft mfg.)	RIS	64	693.261-014
Devulcanizer Charger (rubber reclaim.)	RES	40	558.666-010
Devulcanizer Tender (rubber reclaim.)	REC	44	558.585-026
Dewaterer Operator (smelt. & refin.)	RES	47	511.565-010
Dextrine Mixer (grain-feed mills)	RSE	45	523.682-018
Diagrammer and Seamer (carpet & rug)	RIE	55	789.484-010
Dial Brusher (clock & watch)	CRE	37	715.687-022
Dial Maker (clock & watch)	RES	53	715.381-046
Dial Maker (office machines)	REC	47	710.684-018
Dial Marker (elec. equip.)	CRE	46	729.684-018
Dial Refinisher (clock & watch)	RCS	44	715.584-010
Dial-Screw Assembler (clock & watch)	CRE	41	715.684-082
Dialer (clock & watch)	CRS	42	715.684-086
Dialysis Technician (medical ser.)	ISC	57	078.362-014
Diamond Blender (cutlery-hrdwr.)	RCE	45	590.685-018
Diamond Cleaver (jewelry-silver.)	REC	50	770.381-014
Diamond Driller (machine tools)	RCI	49	770.381-018
Diamond Expert (jewelry-silver.)	RSE	61	770.267-010
Diamond Mounter (machine tools)	RCE	51	739.384-010
Diamond Selector (jewelry-silver.)	REI	58	770.281-010
Diamond Sizer and Sorter (clock & watch; jewelry-silver.)	REC	48	770.687-014
Diamond-Die Polisher (machine tools)	RCE	51	770.381-022
Diamond-Powder Technician (nonmet. min.)	RCS	41	673.685-046
Dianetic Counselor (profess. & kin.)	SEI	61	199.207-010
Diaper Machine Tender (protective dev.)	RCI	48	692.685-278

Title	HOC	Cx	DOT
Dice Maker (toy-sport equip.)	RCE	53	731.381-010
Dicer Operator (plastic-synth.)	REC	40	690.685-130
Dictating-Transcribing-Machine Servicer (any industry)	RES	58	633.281-014
Die Attacher (electron. comp.)	RCI	41	726.684-042
Die Attaching Machine Tender (electron. comp.)	RCI	39	726.685-026
Die Barber (machine shop)	REI	51	705.381-010
Die Cleaner (food prep., n.e.c.)	REI	42	529.687-062
Die Cutter (any industry)	CRS	48	699.682-022
Die Designer (machine shop)	RIE	66	007.161-010
Die Finisher (machine shop)	RIS	56	601.381-010
Die Maker (jewelry-silver.)	RIE	57	601.381-014
Die Maker (paper goods)	RIE	58	739.381-018
Die Maker (print. & pub.)	RIE	60	979.281-010
Die Maker, Bench, Stamping (machine shop)	RIE	62	601.281-010
Die Maker, Electronic (machine shop)	RCI	55	601.381-042
Die Maker, Stamping (machine shop)	RIE	61	601.280-010
Die Maker, Trim (machine shop)	RIE	59	601.280-014
Die Maker, Wire Drawing (machine shop)	RIE	59	601.280-018
Die Mounter (paper goods)	RES	47	659.684-010
Die Polisher (nonfer. metal)	RES	53	601.381-018
Die Presser (pottery & porc.)	RCE	43	575.685-026
Die Set-up Operator, Printed Circuit Boards (electron. comp.)	RCI	48	699.380-010
Die Setter (forging)	RIE	57	612.360-010
Die Sinker (machine shop)	RIE	58	601.280-022
Die Tester (electron. comp.)	RCI	43	726.685-030
Die Tripper (brick & tile)	RES	41	575.665-014
Die-Casting-Machine Operator I (foundry)	RIE	49	514.382-010
Die-Casting-Machine Operator II (foundry)	RCE	40	514.685-018
Die-Casting-Machine Setter (foundry)	RIE	57	514.360-010
Die-Cutting-Machine Operator, Automatic (tex. prod., n.e.c.; textile)	RSE	45	686.462-010
Die-Designer Apprentice (machine shop)	RIE	66	007.161-014
Die-Drawing Checker (profess. & kin.)	IRE	69	007.167-010
Die-Maker Apprentice (jewelry-silver.)	RIE	57	601.381-022
Die-Maker Apprentice (paper goods)	RIE	58	739.381-022
Die-Try-Out Worker, Stamping (machine shop)	RIE	58	601.281-014
Dielectric-Press Operator (auto. mfg.)	CRS	41	692.685-074
Diesel Mechanic (any industry)	REI	58	625.281-010
Diesel-Engine Erector (engine-turbine)	REI	57	625.361-010
Diesel-Engine Tester (engine-turbine)	RSI	58	625.261-010
Diesel-Mechanic Apprentice (any industry)	REI	58	625.281-014
Diesel-Mechanic Helper (any industry)	RCE	44	625.684-010
Diesel-Plant Operator (utilities)	RCS	57	952.382-010
Diet Clerk (medical ser.)	CES	52	245.587-010
Dietary Manager (hotel & rest.)	ESC	70	187.167-206
Dietetic Technician (profess. & kin.)	SEI	65	077.124-010
Dietitian, Chief (profess. & kin.)	ESI	69	077.117-010
Dietitian, Clinical (profess. & kin.)	SIE	67	077.127-014

Part 3: From Occupational Titles to Holland Codes

From the Dictionary of Occupational Titles Occupations to Holland Codes

Title	HOC	Cx	DOT
Dietitian, Consultant (profess. & kin.)	SEI	69	077.127-018
Dietitian, Research (profess. & kin.)	ISR	76	077.061-010
Dietitian, Teaching (profess. & kin.)	SIE	67	077.127-022
Diffuser Operator (sugar & conf.)	RSE	50	523.562-010
Diffusion Furnace Operator, Semiconductor Wafers (electron. comp.)	RCI	44	590.685-070
Digester Operator (paper & pulp; paper goods)	RES	54	532.362-010
Digester-Operator Helper (paper & pulp; paper goods)	REC	41	532.686-010
Digestion Operator (smelt. & refin.)	RCE	41	519.565-010
Digger (fabrication, n.e.c.)	RES	44	739.687-070
Digitizer Operator (business ser.; petrol. & gas)	CRS	53	213.582-010
Dining Room Attendant (hotel & rest.)	CRS	40	311.677-018
Dining-Service Inspector (r.r. trans.)	ERS	55	168.267-030
Dinkey Operator (any industry)	RIS	47	919.663-014
Dip-Lube Operator (ordnance)	REI	40	503.685-014
Dipper (any industry)	REC	40	599.685-026
Dipper (fabrication, n.e.c.)	RCE	42	590.685-022
Dipper (jewelry-silver.)	RCS	38	735.687-010
Dipper (knitting; textile)	RCE	37	589.687-018
Dipper (pen & pencil)	REC	37	733.687-038
Dipper (pottery & porc.)	RCS	45	774.684-014
Dipper (rubber goods)	REC	40	556.685-030
Dipper and Baker (any industry)	CRS	40	599.685-030
Dipper and Drier (woodworking)	REC	37	749.687-010
Dipper, Clock and Watch Hands (clock & watch)	RCE	37	715.687-026
Dipping-Machine Operator (rubber goods)	REC	42	556.685-034
Direct-Mail Clerk (clerical)	CRE	50	209.587-018
Director of Admissions (education)	ESA	66	090.167-014
Director of Counseling (profess. & kin.)	ESA	74	045.107-018
Director of Guidance in Public Schools (education)	SEI	74	045.117-010
Director of Institutional Research (education)	ESC	73	090.167-018
Director of Photography (motion picture; radio-tv broad.)	AES	69	143.062-010
Director of Placement (education)	ESA	75	166.167-014
Director of Pupil Personnel Program (education)	ESC	67	099.167-034
Director of Religious Activities (education)	ESA	66	129.107-018
Director of Student Affairs (education)	ESC	68	090.167-022
Director of Vital Statistics (government ser.)	EAI	74	188.167-022
Director, Aeronautics Commission (government ser.)	SEA	67	188.117-034
Director, Agricultural Services (government ser.)	SER	70	188.117-038
Director, Arts-and-Humanities Council (government ser.)	SER	69	188.117-042
Director, Athletic (education)	SER	67	090.117-022
Director, Camp (social ser.)	ESA	69	195.167-018
Director, Casting (motion picture; radio-tv broad.)	SEC	64	159.267-010
Director, Classification and Treatment (government ser.)	ESA	67	188.167-026
Director, Commission for the Blind (government ser.)	SER	67	094.117-010
Director, Community Organization (nonprofit org.)	SEA	65	187.167-234
Director, Community-Health Nursing (medical ser.)	SEC	69	075.117-014
Director, Compliance (government ser.)	SEA	69	188.117-046
Director, Consumer Affairs (government ser.)	SER	70	188.117-050

DOT to HOC

Part 3: From Occupational Titles to Holland Codes

From the Dictionary of Occupational Titles Occupations to Holland Codes

Title	HOC	Cx	DOT
Director, Correctional Agency (government ser.)	SEI	75	188.117-054
Director, Council on Aging (government ser.)	EAS	69	188.117-058
Director, Craft Center (profess. & kin.)	ESR	69	187.167-202
Director, Day Care Center (education)	ESC	63	092.167-010
Director, Dental Services (medical ser.)	IER	75	072.117-010
Director, Education (museums)	ESR	67	099.117-030
Director, Educational Program (education)	ESC	68	099.117-010
Director, Educational Programming (radio-tv broad.)	ESC	67	169.167-070
Director, Educational, Community-Health Nursing (medical ser.)	SER	73	075.117-018
Director, Employment Research and Planning (government ser.)	SEC	70	050.117-010
Director, Employment Services (government ser.)	ESR	70	188.117-078
Director, Extension Work (education)	ESA	73	090.117-026
Director, Field (social ser.)	ESA	67	195.167-022
Director, Field Representatives (government ser.)	SER	67	188.117-062
Director, Field Services (education)	ESR	66	090.167-034
Director, Financial Responsibility Division (government ser.)	ESC	64	188.167-030
Director, Food and Beverage (amuse. & rec.)	ESR	67	187.167-210
Director, Food Services (hotel & rest.)	EIS	67	187.167-026
Director, Fundraising (nonprofit org.)	ESA	68	165.117-010
Director, Funds Development (profess. & kin.)	ECS	69	165.117-014
Director, Funeral (personal ser.)	ESR	65	187.167-030
Director, Industrial Relations (profess. & kin.)	ESI	69	166.117-010
Director, Institution (any industry)	SER	71	187.117-018
Director, Instructional Material (education)	SAE	67	099.167-018
Director, Labor Standards (government ser.)	SEI	74	188.117-066
Director, Law Enforcement (government ser.)	SEI	70	188.117-070
Director, Licensing and Registration (government ser.)	SER	70	188.117-074
Director, Media Marketing (radio-tv broad.)	ESR	67	163.117-022
Director, Medical Facilities Section (government ser.)	ESR	69	188.117-082
Director, Merit System (government ser.)	ESI	65	188.117-086
Director, Motion Picture (motion picture)	ASE	70	159.067-010
Director, Museum-or-Zoo (museums)	ESR	70	102.117-014
Director, Music (motion picture; radio-tv broad.)	AES	72	152.047-018
Director, News (radio-tv broad.)	ESA	66	184.167-014
Director, Nurses' Registry (medical ser.)	ESC	66	187.167-034
Director, Nursing Service (medical ser.)	SEC	69	075.117-022
Director, Occupational Health Nursing (medical ser.)	SCE	69	075.117-026
Director, Operations (radio-tv broad.)	ESC	67	184.167-018
Director, Operations, Broadcast (radio-tv broad.)	SEC	65	184.167-022
Director, Outpatient Services (medical ser.)	ESC	74	187.117-058
Director, Pharmacy Services (medical ser.)	ISE	79	074.167-010
Director, Photogrammetry Flight Operations (business ser.)	ESR	65	184.167-026
Director, Program (radio-tv broad.)	AES	69	184.167-030
Director, Public Service (radio-tv broad.)	SEA	67	184.117-010
Director, Quality Assurance (profess. & kin.)	ESI	76	189.117-042
Director, Radio (radio-tv broad.)	ESC	63	159.167-014

Title	HOC	Cx	DOT
Director, Records Management (profess. & kin.)	ECS	67	161.117-014
Director, Recreation Center (social ser.)	ESA	66	195.167-026
Director, Regulatory Agency (government ser.)	ESC	67	188.117-134
Director, Religious Education (nonprofit org.)	SEA	66	129.107-022
Director, Research (motion picture; radio-tv broad.)	SEA	66	052.167-010
Director, Research and Development (any industry)	ERI	70	189.117-014
Director, Revenue (government ser.)	SEI	75	188.117-090
Director, Safety Council (government ser.)	ESA	69	188.167-034
Director, School of Nursing (medical ser.)	SEC	71	075.117-030
Director, Securities and Real Estate (government ser.)	ESA	69	188.167-038
Director, Service (nonprofit org.)	ESR	68	187.167-214
Director, Service (retail trade)	ESC	66	189.167-014
Director, Social (hotel & rest.; water trans.)	ESC	61	352.167-010
Director, Special Education (education)	SEA	72	094.167-014
Director, Speech-and-Hearing (medical ser.)	ISE	75	079.131-010
Director, Sports (radio-tv broad.)	ESR	69	184.167-034
Director, Stage (amuse. & rec.)	AES	67	150.067-010
Director, State-Assessed Properties (government ser.)	EAI	73	188.167-042
Director, State-Historical Society (profess. & kin.)	SCE	67	052.067-014
Director, Summer Sessions (education)	ESR	69	090.167-026
Director, Technical (radio-tv broad.)	ESA	64	962.162-010
Director, Television (radio-tv broad.)	SEA	70	159.067-014
Director, Translation (profess. & kin.)	SEC	70	137.137-010
Director, Transportation (motor trans.)	ESR	70	184.117-014
Director, Underwriter Solicitation (radio-tv broad.)	ESR	65	163.117-026
Director, Unemployment Insurance (government ser.)	SER	74	188.117-094
Director, Utility Accounts (government ser.)	SEC	71	160.267-014
Director, Vocational Training (education)	ESA	66	097.167-010
Director, Volunteer Services (social ser.)	SEC	66	187.167-038
Directory-Assistance Operator (tel. & tel.)	CER	49	235.662-018
Disassembler (clock & watch)	CRS	41	715.684-090
Disaster or Damage Control Specialist (military ser.)	ERI	57	378.267-014
Disbursement Clerk (financial)	CRS	54	219.367-046
Disc Jockey (radio-tv broad.)	SEC	64	159.147-014
Disc-Pad Grinder (nonmet. min.)	RCI	41	673.685-086
Disc-Pad Grinding Machine Feeder (nonmet. min.)	RCI	37	673.686-030
Disc-Pad Knockout Worker (nonmet. min.)	RCI	39	579.687-034
Disc-Pad-Plate Filler (nonmet. min.)	RCI	39	579.687-038
Disk-and-Tape-Machine Tender (leather prod.)	CRE	40	783.685-018
Dispatcher (air trans.)	ESI	68	912.167-010
Dispatcher (construction)	ESR	58	849.137-010
Dispatcher (government ser.)	SEC	57	193.262-014
Dispatcher (mine & quarry)	SEC	58	932.167-010
Dispatcher (tel. & tel.)	ERS	60	239.167-014
Dispatcher Clerk (r.r. trans.)	CSR	52	215.362-014
Dispatcher, Bus and Trolley (motor trans.)	ERS	63	913.167-014
Dispatcher, Chief I (petrol. & gas; petrol. refin.; pipe lines)	ESC	68	184.167-038
Dispatcher, Chief II (petrol. & gas; petrol. refin.; pipe lines)	ERS	62	914.167-010
Dispatcher, Chief, Service or Work (utilities)	ESR	59	959.137-010

DOT to HOC

Title	HOC	Cx	DOT
Dispatcher, Concrete Products (concrete prod.; construction)	ECS	57	579.137-030
Dispatcher, Maintenance Service (clerical)	CES	52	239.367-014
Dispatcher, Motor Vehicle (clerical)	ESC	53	249.167-014
Dispatcher, Oil (petrol. & gas; petrol. refin.; pipe lines)	ESR	65	914.167-014
Dispatcher, Oil Well Services (petrol. & gas)	CES	53	939.362-010
Dispatcher, Radio (government ser.)	CSE	51	379.362-010
Dispatcher, Radioactive-Waste-Disposal (chemical)	RES	65	955.167-010
Dispatcher, Relay (pipe lines)	ECR	55	221.362-014
Dispatcher, Security Guard (business ser.)	ESA	60	372.167-010
Dispatcher, Service (utilities)	ECS	59	959.167-010
Dispatcher, Service or Work (utilities)	ESR	59	952.167-010
Dispatcher, Service, Chief (utilities)	ESR	59	959.137-014
Dispatcher, Ship Pilot (water trans.)	CES	54	248.367-026
Dispatcher, Street Department (government ser.)	CES	48	239.367-030
Dispatcher, Traffic or System (motor trans.; r.r. trans.)	SEC	61	919.162-010
Dispatcher, Tugboat (water trans.)	ESC	57	911.167-010
Display Designer (profess. & kin.)	AES	63	142.051-010
Display Fabricator (fabrication, n.e.c.)	RCI	43	860.684-022
Display Maker (fabrication, n.e.c.)	RSI	57	739.361-010
Display-Screen Fabricator (electron. comp.)	REC	42	725.685-010
Displayer, Merchandise (retail trade)	ARE	61	298.081-010
Dissolver Operator (chemical)	RES	48	558.682-014
Distillation Operator (chemical)	RIE	56	552.462-010
Distillation-Operator Helper (chemical)	RES	40	552.687-010
Distiller I (chemical)	REC	47	552.682-010
Distiller II (chemical)	RES	47	552.682-014
Distillery Worker, General (beverage)	REI	40	529.687-066
Distilling-Department Supervisor (beverage)	RES	63	522.131-010
Distresser (furniture)	RES	39	763.687-018
Distributing Clerk (clerical)	RES	49	222.587-018
Distribution Supervisor (pipe lines; wholesale tr.)	ECS	61	914.137-010
Distribution-Accounting Clerk (utilities)	CRE	56	210.362-010
Distribution-Field Engineer (utilities)	RIE	70	003.167-014
Distributor-Cleaner (tobacco)	REC	38	529.687-070
District Adviser (nonprofit org.)	ESA	67	187.117-022
District Attorney (government ser.)	EIA	75	110.117-010
District Customs Director (government ser.)	SER	69	188.117-098
District Customs Director, Deputy (government ser.)	ESI	70	188.167-046
District Extension Service Agent (government ser.)	SEA	66	096.167-010
District Supervisor (motor trans.)	SIE	64	184.117-018
District Supervisor, Mud-Analysis Well Logging (petrol. & gas)	IER	76	010.167-014
Ditch Rider (waterworks)	REI	55	954.362-010
Ditcher Operator (r.r. trans.)	RES	44	850.683-014
Diver (amuse. & rec.)	RES	52	349.247-010
Diver (any industry)	RES	58	899.261-010
Diver Helper (any industry)	CRS	45	899.664-010
Diver Pumper (construction; fishing & hunt.)	RCS	46	899.682-010

Title	HOC	Cx	DOT
Dividend Clerk (financial)	CRS	53	216.482-034
Dividend-Deposit-Voucher Clerk (insurance)	CSR	51	216.482-026
Dividing-Machine Operator (bakery products)	RES	44	520.685-086
Division Manager, Chamber of Commerce (nonprofit org.)	ESA	67	187.167-042
Division Road Supervisor (r.r. trans.)	EIR	64	184.167-282
Dock Hand (air trans.)	REI	47	919.683-010
Dock Hand (ship-boat mfg.)	REI	42	891.684-010
Dock Supervisor (ship-boat mfg.)	RES	59	891.131-010
Doctor, Naturopathic (medical ser.)	SIR	72	079.101-014
Document Preparer, Microfilming (business ser.)	CRS	45	249.587-018
Document Restorer (profess. & kin.)	RIE	57	979.361-010
Documentation Engineer (profess. & kin.)	ISR	76	012.167-078
Documentation Supervisor (water trans.)	SEC	59	214.137-010
Documentation-Billing Clerk (air trans.; motor trans.; r.r. trans.; water trans.)	CSR	54	214.362-014
Doffer (textile)	REC	41	689.686-022
Dog Bather (personal ser.)	REC	45	418.677-010
Dog Catcher (government ser.)	SER	43	379.673-010
Dog Groomer (personal ser.)	RSE	48	418.674-010
Dog Licenser (nonprofit org.)	ESR	53	249.367-030
Doll Repairer (any industry)	CRE	41	731.684-014
Dolly Pusher (radio-tv broad.)	RES	38	962.687-010
Domer (paper goods)	RCE	38	641.685-038
Door Assembler (mfd. bldgs.; vehicles, n.e.c.)	RIE	45	806.684-050
Door Assembler I (woodworking)	REC	41	762.684-034
Door Core Assembler (woodworking)	RES	38	762.687-030
Door-Closer Mechanic (any industry)	RES	56	630.381-014
Door-Machine Operator (steel & rel.)	RIE	46	519.663-010
Doorkeeper (any industry)	ERS	41	324.677-014
Dope-Dry-House Operator (chemical)	REC	40	559.685-046
Dorr Operator (sugar & conf.)	RCE	45	522.685-050
Dot Etcher (print. & pub.)	REA	58	972.281-010
Dot Etcher Apprentice (print. & pub.)	REA	58	972.281-018
Double (motion picture; radio-tv broad.)	AER	47	961.364-010
Double-End-Trimmer-and-Boring-Machine Operator (furniture)	REI	48	669.682-038
Doubling-Machine Operator (textile)	RCE	40	681.685-046
Dough Mixer (bakery products)	RCS	51	520.685-234
Dough-Brake-Machine Operator (bakery products)	REC	42	520.685-090
Dough-Mixer Operator (bakery products)	REI	50	520.462-010
Doughnut Maker (bakery products)	RES	44	526.684-010
Doughnut-Machine Operator (bakery products)	RCE	48	526.682-022
Dovetail-Machine Operator (wood. container)	RCE	40	669.685-046
Dowel Inspector (woodworking)	RCE	35	669.687-014
Dowel Pointer (woodworking)	CRS	38	667.685-038
Dowel-Inserting-Machine Operator (woodworking)	REC	43	669.682-042
Dowel-Machine Operator (woodworking)	REI	48	665.682-010
Doweling-Machine Operator (woodworking)	CRS	41	669.685-050
Drafter Apprentice (profess. & kin.)	IRE	66	017.281-014

Title	HOC	Cx	DOT
Drafter, Aeronautical (aircraft mfg.)	IRC	66	002.261-010
Drafter, Architectural (profess. & kin.)	RCI	64	001.261-010
Drafter, Assistant (profess. & kin.)	RCS	58	017.281-018
Drafter, Automotive Design (auto. mfg.)	IRE	67	017.261-042
Drafter, Automotive Design Layout (auto. mfg.)	RIE	65	017.281-026
Drafter, Cartographic (profess. & kin.)	RIE	63	018.261-010
Drafter, Castings (profess. & kin.)	RIE	66	007.261-014
Drafter, Chief, Design (utilities)	ISE	70	017.161-010
Drafter, Civil (profess. & kin.)	IRE	64	005.281-010
Drafter, Commercial (profess. & kin.)	IRE	66	017.261-026
Drafter, Detail (profess. & kin.)	RIE	64	017.261-030
Drafter, Directional Survey (petrol. & gas)	RIE	67	010.281-010
Drafter, Electrical (profess. & kin.)	IRC	66	003.281-010
Drafter, Electronic (profess. & kin.)	IRE	66	003.281-014
Drafter, Geological (petrol. & gas)	IRC	67	010.281-014
Drafter, Geophysical (petrol. & gas)	RIE	67	010.281-018
Drafter, Heating and Ventilating (profess. & kin.)	IRC	66	017.261-034
Drafter, Landscape (profess. & kin.)	RIE	63	001.261-014
Drafter, Marine (profess. & kin.)	IRE	66	014.281-010
Drafter, Mechanical (profess. & kin.)	IRE	67	007.281-010
Drafter, Oil and Gas (petrol. & gas; petrol. refin.)	RIE	63	017.281-030
Drafter, Patent (profess. & kin.)	IRE	69	007.261-018
Drafter, Plumbing (profess. & kin.)	IRC	66	017.261-038
Drafter, Structural (profess. & kin.)	IRC	66	005.281-014
Drafter, Tool Design (profess. & kin.)	IRC	69	007.261-022
Dragline Operator (any industry)	RES	47	850.683-018
Drainage-Design Coordinator (waterworks)	RIE	69	005.167-014
Dramatic Coach (profess. & kin.)	ASE	65	150.027-010
Draper (garment; knitting)	REC	48	781.684-026
Draper (motion picture; radio-tv broad.)	REI	54	962.381-010
Drapery and Upholstery Estimator (retail trade)	REC	54	299.387-010
Drapery and Upholstery Measurer (retail trade)	RES	54	299.364-010
Drapery Hanger (retail trade)	RES	50	869.484-014
Drapery Operator (retail trade)	RCE	45	787.682-018
Drapery-Head Former (retail trade)	REC	40	781.684-030
Drapery-Rod Assembler (retail trade)	RCE	45	706.484-010
Draw-Bench Operator (any industry)	RIE	52	614.682-010
Draw-Bench Operator (nonfer. metal; steel & rel.)	RIE	47	614.482-010
Draw-Bench-Operator Helper (nonfer. metal; steel & rel.)	RES	38	614.686-010
Draw-Frame Tender (tex. prod., n.e.c.)	REC	42	680.685-034
Draw-Machine Operator (plastic-synth.)	RCE	41	680.665-014
Drawbridge Operator (r.r. trans.)	CRS	47	371.362-010
Drawer Liner (furniture)	RCS	38	763.684-030
Drawer Upfitter (furniture)	RCE	45	706.684-050
Drawer Waxer (furniture)	RCE	36	763.687-022
Drawer-In Helper, Hand (textile)	REC	40	683.687-010
Drawer-In, Hand (textile)	RCE	45	683.684-014
Drawer-In, Stitch-Bonding Machine (textile)	REC	40	689.684-014
Drawing-Frame Tender (textile)	REC	40	680.685-038

Title	HOC	Cx	DOT
Drawing-in-Machine Tender (textile)	RSC	46	683.682-018
Drawing-in-Machine-Tender Helper (textile)	RCS	41	683.685-022
Drawing-Kiln Operator (glass mfg.)	RCS	48	575.362-010
Drawing-Kiln Supervisor (glass mfg.)	ERI	57	575.137-010
Drawings Checker, Engineering (profess. & kin.)	IRC	65	007.267-010
Drawstring Knotter (tex. prod., n.e.c.)	CRE	40	689.685-058
Dredge Captain (water trans.)	ERI	64	197.161-010
Dredge Mate (water trans.)	ESR	60	197.137-010
Dredge Operator (construction; mine & quarry)	REC	49	850.663-010
Dredge Operator Supervisor (mine & quarry)	RES	57	939.132-010
Dresser (amuse. & rec.)	ESC	43	346.674-010
Dresser (boot & shoe)	RES	38	788.687-038
Dresser Tender (textile)	RCS	45	681.682-010
Dressmaker (any industry)	RSE	54	785.361-010
Dried Fruit Washer (food prep., n.e.c.)	RCE	37	521.685-110
Drier (garment)	CRS	42	581.685-014
Drier (knitting)	RCE	40	581.686-014
Drier Attendant (can. & preserv.; grain-feed mills)	REC	42	523.685-058
Drier Attendant (garment)	REC	38	581.686-018
Drier Feeder (rubber reclaim.)	RES	37	559.686-014
Drier Helper (chemical)	CES	38	553.687-010
Drier Operator (can. & preserv.)	REC	37	523.685-062
Drier Operator (can. & preserv.; dairy products)	RCS	48	523.682-022
Drier Operator (chemical; pharmaceut.)	REI	46	553.685-042
Drier Operator (food prep., n.e.c.)	RES	56	523.362-014
Drier Operator (mine & quarry)	RIE	47	543.682-014
Drier Operator (sugar & conf.)	RSE	50	529.682-022
Drier Operator (utilities)	REC	49	543.382-010
Drier Operator I (chemical)	RSE	41	553.665-026
Drier Operator I (plastic-synth.)	RSE	51	559.562-010
Drier Operator II (chemical)	RES	47	553.582-010
Drier Operator II (plastic-synth.)	CRE	40	553.685-046
Drier Operator III (chemical)	RCS	47	553.685-050
Drier Operator III (plastic-synth.)	REC	41	581.685-018
Drier Operator IV (chemical)	ERI	48	553.685-054
Drier Operator V (chemical)	RES	40	553.686-026
Drier Operator VI (chemical)	RCS	43	553.685-118
Drier Operator, Drum (food prep., n.e.c.)	CRS	41	529.685-098
Drier Tender (can. & preserv.)	RES	42	523.685-066
Drier Tender (fabrication, n.e.c.)	RCE	43	543.685-014
Drier Tender (grain-feed mills)	RCS	45	523.685-070
Drier Tender (smelt. & refin.)	RSE	47	511.565-014
Drier Tender (wood prod., n.e.c.)	RCE	47	563.585-010
Drier Tender I (oils & grease)	REC	39	523.685-074
Drier, Belt Conveyor (food prep., n.e.c.)	REI	44	529.485-018
Drier, Long Goods (food prep., n.e.c.)	REC	43	523.585-022
Drier, Short Goods (food prep., n.e.c.)	REC	44	523.587-010
Drier-and-Grinder Tender (mine & quarry)	RCS	43	579.685-010
Drier-and-Pulverizer Tender (chemical)	REC	40	559.685-050

Title	HOC	Cx	DOT
Drier-Operator Helper (chemical)	REC	37	553.685-058
Drier-Operator Helper (rubber reclaim.)	RES	37	553.686-030
Drier-Take-Off Tender (elec. equip.)	RCE	38	921.685-034
Drifter (steel & rel.)	RCE	42	503.685-018
Drill Operator, Automatic (glass products)	REI	46	676.682-010
Drill Press Tender (machine shop)	RCE	43	606.685-026
Drill-Bit Sharpener (electron. comp.)	RCS	42	603.682-030
Drill-Press Operator (machine shop)	RCS	44	606.682-014
Drill-Press Operator, Acoustical Tile (wood prod., n.e.c.)	REC	47	649.682-018
Drill-Press Operator, Numerical Control (machine shop)	REI	56	606.362-010
Drill-Press Operator, Printed Circuit Boards (electron. comp.)	RCS	50	676.382-010
Drill-Press Set-up Operator, Multiple Spindle (machine shop)	RIE	58	606.380-010
Drill-Press Set-up Operator, Radial (machine shop)	RIE	58	606.380-014
Drill-Press Set-up Operator, Radial, Tool (machine shop)	RIE	58	606.380-018
Drill-Press Set-up Operator, Single Spindle (machine shop)	RIE	46	606.682-018
Drill-Punch Operator (paper goods; print. & pub.)	RCE	40	649.685-034
Driller (jewelry-silver.)	RCE	44	700.684-026
Driller (optical goods)	RCE	39	716.685-014
Driller and Broacher (clock & watch)	CRE	47	715.685-022
Driller and Deburrer, Reflector (light. fix.)	RCI	38	676.686-014
Driller Helper (construction; mine & quarry)	REI	41	930.666-010
Driller, Brake Lining (nonmet. min.)	CRE	40	676.685-010
Driller, Hand (any industry)	REI	40	809.684-018
Driller, Hand (button & notion)	CRE	40	754.684-026
Driller, Machine (construction; mine & quarry)	RIE	49	930.382-010
Driller, Machine (glass products)	CRS	40	676.685-014
Driller-and-Reamer, Automatic (musical inst.)	RES	50	606.382-010
Drilling-Machine Operator (mine & quarry)	RIE	50	930.482-010
Drilling-Machine Operator, Automatic (clock & watch)	CRE	41	606.685-030
Drip Pumper (pipe lines; utilities)	REC	47	953.583-010
Drip-Box Tender (grain-feed mills)	REC	36	521.687-038
Drive-In Theater Attendant (amuse. & rec.)	CES	43	349.673-010
Driver (auto. mfg.; automotive ser.)	RCS	40	919.683-014
Driver (motor trans.)	SRC	45	913.663-018
Driver Helper, Sales Route (retail trade; wholesale tr.)	REC	44	292.667-010
Driver Supervisor (motor trans.)	ESR	63	909.137-010
Driver's License Examiner (government ser.)	ESC	54	168.267-034
Driver, Sales Route (retail trade; wholesale tr.)	ESR	52	292.353-010
Driver, Starting Gate (amuse. & rec.)	RCS	40	919.683-030
Driver-Utility Worker (auto. mfg.; automotive ser.)	RES	44	919.663-018
Drivers'-Cash Clerk (motor trans.)	CSE	50	211.462-030
Drop Tester (ordnance)	CRE	51	737.387-010
Drop-Wire Aligner (textile)	CRE	39	689.685-062
Drop-Wire Builder (textile)	RCE	40	689.687-034
Drop-Wire Hanger (textile)	RCE	39	683.687-014
Drophammer Operator (aircraft mfg.; forging)	RSE	52	610.362-010

Title	HOC	Cx	DOT
Dropper, Fermenting Cellar (beverage)	RES	41	522.685-054
Dross Skimmer (smelt. & refin.)	RSC	40	519.683-010
Drum Attendant (leather mfg.; tex. prod., n.e.c.)	REC	37	582.685-050
Drum Cleaner (petrol. refin.)	RCI	38	599.687-034
Drum Drier (grain-feed mills)	RSE	47	523.682-026
Drum Loader and Unloader (beverage)	RES	38	522.685-058
Drum Straightener I (any industry)	RCE	38	619.685-034
Drum Tester (petrol. refin.)	RCE	38	599.687-038
Drum-Drier Operator (chemical)	CRE	41	553.665-030
Drum-Drier Operator (plastic-synth.)	RCE	41	581.685-082
Drummer (hat & cap)	RCE	37	589.685-034
Dry Cleaner (knitting)	CRE	40	589.685-038
Dry Cleaner (laundry & rel.)	RES	49	362.382-014
Dry Cleaner, Hand (laundry & rel.)	REI	41	362.684-010
Dry Curer (meat products)	RES	40	525.687-026
Dry-Cans Operator (textile)	RCE	39	581.685-022
Dry-Cell Tester (elec. equip.)	RIE	57	727.381-018
Dry-Cell-Assembly-Machine Tender (elec. equip.)	RCI	46	692.665-018
Dry-Charge-Process Attendant (elec. equip.)	RIE	47	590.685-026
Dry-Cleaner Apprentice (laundry & rel.)	RES	49	362.382-010
Dry-Cleaner Helper (laundry & rel.)	RES	38	362.686-010
Dry-End Operator (plastic-synth.)	RCS	46	559.665-014
Dry-House Attendant (chemical)	RCS	41	553.585-014
Dry-House Attendant (woodworking)	RCE	41	563.685-018
Dry-House Tender (ordnance)	REC	43	559.585-010
Dry-Kiln Operator (brick & tile)	REI	50	573.362-010
Dry-Kiln Operator Helper (brick & tile)	RES	39	573.687-014
Dry-Pan Charger (brick & tile)	REI	49	570.683-010
Dry-Pan Operator (brick & tile)	RCE	42	570.665-010
Dry-Placer-Machine Operator (mine & quarry)	RES	49	939.382-010
Dry-Press Operator (brick & tile)	RIE	49	575.662-010
Dry-Press-Operator Helper (brick & tile)	REC	39	575.686-010
Dry-Starch Operator (grain-feed mills)	RES	55	520.362-014
Dry-Starch Operator, Automatic (grain-feed mills)	RES	54	529.362-014
Dry-Wall Applicator (construction)	RCS	54	842.361-030
Dry-Wall Applicator (construction; mfd. bldgs.)	RCS	47	842.684-014
Dry-Wall Sprayer (mfd. bldgs.)	RES	46	842.684-010
Drying-Machine Operator, Package Yarns (textile)	REC	40	581.685-026
Drying-Machine Tender (textile)	RCE	41	581.685-030
Drying-Oven Attendant (hat & cap)	REI	36	581.686-022
Drying-Rack Changer (boot & shoe)	CRS	38	581.686-026
Drying-Room Attendant (hat & cap)	REC	38	581.687-014
Drying-Room Attendant (soap & rel.)	REC	39	553.585-018
Drying-Room Attendant (tobacco)	RCE	41	523.587-014
Drying-Unit-Felting-Machine Operator (tex. prod., n.e.c.)	RCE	42	581.685-034
Drying-Unit-Felting-Machine-Operator Helper (tex. prod., n.e.c.)	RES	37	581.687-018
Dual-Hose Cementer (rubber goods)	REC	41	690.685-134
Dubbing-Machine Operator (motion picture; radio-tv broad.)	RSC	44	962.665-010

Title	HOC	Cx	DOT
Duct Maker (construction; mfd. bldgs.)	REC	41	809.687-010
Dude Wrangler (amuse. & rec.)	ESC	51	353.364-010
Dulser (fishing & hunt.)	REC	37	447.687-010
Dump Operator (any industry)	REC	41	921.685-038
Dump-Truck Driver (any industry)	RIE	43	902.683-010
Dumper (any industry)	REI	40	921.667-018
Dumper (chemical)	REC	36	922.686-010
Dumper-Bailer Operator (petrol. & gas)	REC	50	931.684-010
Dumping-Machine Operator (can. & preserv.; wholesale tr.)	RCE	39	529.685-102
Duplicating-Machine Operator I (clerical)	RCE	47	207.682-010
Duplicating-Machine Operator II (clerical)	RCE	43	207.682-014
Duplicator-Punch Operator (any industry)	RIE	54	615.482-014
Dust Box Worker (build. mat., n.e.c.)	REA	40	574.667-010
Dust Collector, Ore Crushing (smelt. & refin.)	REC	45	511.682-010
Dust Collector-Treater (smelt. & refin.)	RCS	39	511.687-014
Dust Mixer (smelt. & refin.)	RCE	46	510.685-010
Dust Puller (smelt. & refin.)	RES	37	519.687-014
Dust Sampler (mine & quarry)	REC	44	939.585-010
Dust-Brush Assembler (house. appl.)	REC	37	739.687-074
Dust-Collector Attendant (mine & quarry)	REI	44	511.685-022
Dust-Collector Operator (smelt. & refin.)	RCE	45	511.482-018
Dust-Collector Operator (soap & rel.)	CRE	41	551.685-050
Dust-Mill Operator (tex. prod., n.e.c.)	REI	38	581.686-030
Dust-Mop Maker (tex. prod., n.e.c.)	RCE	37	739.687-078
Duster (hat & cap)	RCE	40	587.685-026
Dusting-and-Brushing-Machine Operator (rubber goods)	REC	38	559.685-054
Dustless Operator (chemical)	CRE	45	550.685-058
Dye Automation Operator (textile)	RCI	55	582.362-014
Dye Weigher (any industry)	RES	46	550.684-014
Dye-House Supervisor (leather mfg.)	REA	59	582.131-010
Dye-House Worker (leather mfg.)	RES	35	582.686-010
Dye-Lab Technician (knitting)	RIC	52	582.384-010
Dye-Range Operator, Cloth (textile)	REI	47	582.582-010
Dye-Reel Operator (textile)	REC	44	582.665-014
Dye-Reel-Operator Helper (textile)	REI	41	582.686-014
Dye-Stand Loader (textile)	REC	39	589.687-062
Dye-Tank Tender (tex. prod., n.e.c.)	REC	45	582.685-054
Dye-Tub Operator (knitting)	RCE	41	582.685-170
Dye-Weigher Helper (any industry)	REC	40	550.687-018
Dyed-Yarn Operator (textile)	CRE	41	582.685-058
Dyer (button & notion)	REC	37	582.687-014
Dyer (chemical)	REI	50	554.384-010
Dyer (fabrication, n.e.c.)	CRE	42	599.685-034
Dyer (laundry & rel.)	REI	55	364.361-010
Dyer (woodworking)	RES	40	562.687-010
Dyer Helper (hat & cap)	REC	42	589.685-042
Dyer Helper (laundry & rel.)	RES	39	364.687-010
Dyer, Supervisor (knitting; tex. prod., n.e.c.; textile)	SEA	60	582.131-014
Dynamite Reclaimer (chemical)	RSE	38	551.687-018

Part 3: From Occupational Titles to Holland Codes

From the Dictionary of Occupational Titles Occupations to Holland Codes

Title	HOC	Cx	DOT
Dynamite-Cartridge Crimper (chemical)	REI	47	692.685-078
Dynamite-Packing-Machine Feeder (chemical)	RES	40	692.686-038
Dynamite-Packing-Machine Operator (chemical)	RSE	48	692.662-010
Dynamometer Tester, Engine (auto. mfg.)	REI	57	806.281-010
Ear-Mold Laboratory Technician (plastic prod.)	RIE	56	777.361-010
Ear-Muff Assembler (hat & cap)	REC	40	784.687-022
Earring Maker (jewelry-silver.)	CRS	46	700.684-030
Earth-Boring-Machine Operator (construction; utilities)	RES	44	859.682-010
Echocardiograph Technician (medical ser.)	CIR	58	078.364-014
Economic Development Coordinator (government ser.)	ESA	69	188.117-102
Economist (profess. & kin.)	IAS	71	050.067-010
Eddy-Current Inspector (steel & rel.)	RCI	51	619.381-014
Edge Bander, Hand (furniture)	CRS	38	762.684-038
Edge Bander, Machine (furniture; millwork-plywood)	RCE	43	762.685-010
Edge Burnisher, Uppers (boot & shoe)	REC	41	690.685-138
Edge Grinder (plastic prod.)	RCE	42	690.685-142
Edge Roller (furniture)	RCE	42	780.684-058
Edge Setter (boot & shoe)	RES	42	690.685-146
Edge Stainer I (leather prod.)	CRE	41	589.685-046
Edge Stainer II (leather prod.)	RCE	41	749.684-022
Edge Stripper (paper goods; wood. container)	CRS	42	795.684-014
Edge Trimmer (boot & shoe)	RCE	41	690.685-150
Edge-Banding-Machine Offbearer (furniture; millwork-plywood)	RES	37	762.686-010
Edge-Glue-Machine Tender (millwork-plywood)	RCE	40	569.685-034
Edger, Automatic (saw. & plan.)	RES	48	667.682-026
Edger, Hand (glass mfg.; glass products)	REC	42	775.684-014
Edger, Touch-Up (glass products)	RCE	41	775.684-018
Edger-Machine Helper (stonework)	RES	40	673.686-018
Edger-Machine Operator (stonework)	REI	41	673.682-018
Edging-Machine Feeder (glass mfg.)	RCE	39	673.686-022
Edging-Machine Setter (glass products)	RCE	49	673.380-010
Editor, Book (print. & pub.)	AES	73	132.067-014
Editor, City (print. & pub.)	AES	73	132.037-014
Editor, Department (print. & pub.)	AES	69	132.037-018
Editor, Dictionary (profess. & kin.)	IAS	71	132.067-018
Editor, Greeting Card (print. & pub.)	AES	64	132.067-022
Editor, Index (print. & pub.)	SIC	63	132.367-010
Editor, Managing, Newspaper (print. & pub.)	ESA	73	132.017-010
Editor, Map (profess. & kin.)	IER	66	018.261-018
Editor, News (print. & pub.)	AES	69	132.067-026
Editor, Newspaper (print. & pub.)	AES	73	132.017-014
Editor, Publications (print. & pub.)	AES	73	132.037-022
Editor, School Photograph (photofinishing)	SER	46	976.687-010
Editor, Technical and Scientific Publications (profess. & kin.)	ASE	73	132.017-018
Editor, Telegraph (print. & pub.; radio-tv broad.)	CIE	64	132.267-010
Editorial Assistant (print. & pub.)	CIA	65	132.267-014
Editorial Writer (print. & pub.)	AES	70	131.067-022

Part 3: From Occupational Titles to Holland Codes

From the Dictionary of Occupational Titles Occupations to Holland Codes

Title	HOC	Cx	DOT
Education Supervisor, Correctional Institution (education)	SEA	66	099.117-014
Educational Resource Coordinator (museums)	ESR	63	099.167-030
Educational Specialist (education)	EIS	73	099.167-022
Effervescent-Salts Compounder (pharmaceut.)	RES	48	559.685-058
Egg Breaker (any industry)	REC	37	521.687-042
Egg Candler (any industry)	CER	40	529.687-074
Egg Pasteurizer (agriculture)	RCI	51	529.682-038
Egg Processor (pharmaceut.)	CRE	38	559.687-034
Egg Washer, Machine (agriculture; wholesale tr.)	RCE	36	529.686-030
Egg-Breaking-Machine Operator (can. & preserv.)	REC	39	521.685-114
Elastic Attacher, Chainstitch (garment)	RCE	41	786.682-086
Elastic Attacher, Coverstitch (garment)	RCE	41	786.682-090
Elastic Attacher, Overlock (garment)	RCE	41	786.682-094
Elastic Attacher, Zigzag (garment)	RCE	41	786.682-098
Elastic-Tape Inserter (garment)	RES	40	782.687-022
Election Assistant (government ser.)	ESA	65	188.167-050
Election Clerk (government ser.)	CSE	49	205.367-030
Electric Blanket Wirer (tex. prod., n.e.c.)	RCI	39	789.684-054
Electric Motor Repairing Supervisor (any industry)	ESR	59	721.131-010
Electric Power Line Examiner (utilities)	RCE	53	959.367-010
Electric-Cell Tender (chemical)	RES	49	558.565-014
Electric-Container Tester (elec. equip.)	CRE	43	727.687-050
Electric-Distribution Checker (construction; utilities)	RES	59	824.281-014
Electric-Fork Operator (agriculture)	RES	35	921.685-042
Electric-Golf-Cart Repairer (amuse. & rec.; automotive ser.)	REI	54	620.261-026
Electric-Meter Installer I (utilities)	RES	59	821.361-014
Electric-Meter Installer II (utilities)	REC	48	821.684-010
Electric-Meter Repairer (utilities)	RIE	57	729.281-014
Electric-Meter Tester (utilities)	RIE	59	821.381-010
Electric-Meter-Repairer Apprentice (utilities)	RIE	57	729.281-018
Electric-Motor Analyst (any industry)	RSE	57	721.261-010
Electric-Motor Assembler (elec. equip.)	CRE	42	721.684-022
Electric-Motor Assembler and Tester (any industry)	REI	57	721.281-014
Electric-Motor Fitter (railroad equip.)	RES	56	721.381-010
Electric-Motor Repairer (any industry)	RIE	58	721.281-018
Electric-Motor Winder (elec. equip.)	RES	51	721.484-010
Electric-Motor-and-Generator Assembler (elec. equip.)	RSE	59	820.361-014
Electric-Motor-Control Assembler (elec. equip.)	RIE	54	721.381-014
Electric-Organ Assembler and Checker (musical inst.)	RES	50	730.381-022
Electric-Organ Inspector and Repairer (musical inst.)	RSC	57	730.281-018
Electric-Sealing-Machine Operator (any industry)	CRE	41	690.685-154
Electric-Sign Assembler (fabrication, n.e.c.)	RCS	46	729.684-022
Electric-Tool Repairer (any industry)	REI	57	729.281-022
Electric-Track-Switch Maintainer (r.r. trans.)	RSE	59	825.261-010
Electrical and Radio Mock-Up Mechanic (aircraft mfg.)	RIE	57	693.381-026
Electrical Assembler (aircraft mfg.)	RCI	51	729.384-026
Electrical Engineer (profess. & kin.)	IRE	71	003.061-010
Electrical Engineer, Power System (utilities)	IRE	79	003.167-018
Electrical Inspector (aircraft mfg.; air trans.)	RES	57	825.381-026

Part 3: From Occupational Titles to Holland Codes

From the Dictionary of Occupational Titles Occupations to Holland Codes

Title	HOC	Cx	DOT
Electrical Supervisor (petrol. & gas)	RSE	61	826.131-010
Electrical Technician (profess. & kin.)	RIE	66	003.161-010
Electrical Test Engineer (profess. & kin.)	IES	71	003.061-014
Electrical-Appliance Preparer (any industry)	RCS	45	827.584-010
Electrical-Appliance Repairer (any industry)	RSE	52	723.381-010
Electrical-Appliance Servicer (any industry)	RSE	58	827.261-010
Electrical-Appliance-Servicer Apprentice (any industry)	RSE	58	827.261-014
Electrical-Appliance-Servicer Supervisor (any industry)	ESR	61	827.131-010
Electrical-Control Assembler (comm. equip.; elec. equip.)	CRE	48	729.684-026
Electrical-Design Engineer (profess. & kin.)	RIS	71	003.061-018
Electrical-Discharge-Machine Operator, Production (machine shop)	RCE	50	609.482-010
Electrical-Discharge-Machine Set-up Operator (machine shop)	RIE	61	609.380-010
Electrical-Equipment Tester (aircraft mfg.)	RES	56	729.381-010
Electrical-Installation Supervisor (utilities)	RES	62	821.131-010
Electrical-Instrument Repairer (any industry)	RIE	61	729.281-026
Electrical-Line Splicer (petrol. & gas)	RCS	47	728.684-014
Electrical-Prospecting Engineer (profess. & kin.)	IRE	80	003.061-022
Electrical-Research Engineer (profess. & kin.)	IRS	71	003.061-026
Electrician (construction)	RIE	63	824.261-010
Electrician (mfd. bldgs.)	REI	49	824.681-010
Electrician (ship-boat mfg.)	RIE	58	825.381-030
Electrician (water trans.)	RES	58	825.281-014
Electrician Apprentice (construction)	REI	63	824.261-014
Electrician Apprentice (ship-boat mfg.)	RSE	58	825.381-034
Electrician Apprentice, Powerhouse (utilities)	RES	62	820.261-010
Electrician Helper (any industry)	RCE	46	829.684-022
Electrician Helper (ship-boat mfg.)	RCE	42	829.684-026
Electrician Helper, Automotive (automotive ser.)	REC	42	825.684-010
Electrician Supervisor (any industry)	RES	59	829.131-014
Electrician Supervisor (ship-boat mfg.)	RSC	59	825.131-010
Electrician Supervisor, Substation (utilities)	RES	63	820.131-010
Electrician, Aircraft (aircraft mfg.; air trans.)	RIS	60	825.261-018
Electrician, Automotive (automotive ser.)	RIE	58	825.281-022
Electrician, Chief (motion picture)	ESR	61	824.137-010
Electrician, Locomotive (railroad equip.)	RIE	62	825.281-026
Electrician, Maintenance (any industry)	RCI	65	829.261-018
Electrician, Office (tel. & tel.)	RCE	58	822.261-010
Electrician, Powerhouse (utilities)	RES	62	820.261-014
Electrician, Radio (any industry)	RSC	59	823.281-014
Electrician, Research (aircraft mfg.)	RIE	63	726.261-014
Electrician, Substation (utilities)	RSE	60	820.261-018
Electrifier Operator (textile)	REC	42	585.685-042
Electro-Optical Engineer (profess. & kin.)	IRE	80	023.061-010
Electrocardiograph Technician (medical ser.)	RCI	54	078.362-018
Electrode Cleaner (elec. equip.)	RCE	35	729.687-014
Electrode Turner-and-Finisher (elec. equip.)	RIE	50	692.682-034
Electrode-Cleaning-Machine Operator (elec. equip.)	REI	40	559.685-062

Dictionary of Holland Occupational Codes

Title	HOC	Cx	DOT
Electroencephalographic Technologist (medical ser.)	RCS	59	078.362-022
Electroformer (electroplating)	RES	43	500.684-010
Electrogalvanizing-Machine Operator (electroplating)	RIE	57	500.362-010
Electroless Plater (any industry)	REC	43	505.684-010
Electroless Plater, Printed Circuit Board Panels (electron. comp.)	RCI	42	501.685-022
Electrologist (personal ser.)	CRE	52	339.371-010
Electrolysis-and-Corrosion-Control Engineer (profess. & kin.)	IRE	76	003.167-022
Electromechanical Technician (inst. & app.)	RIE	64	710.281-018
Electromedical-Equipment Repairer (any industry)	RIE	57	729.281-030
Electromyographic Technician (medical ser.)	CIR	58	078.362-038
Electronic Equipment Repairer (comm. equip.; electron. comp.)	RSE	56	726.381-014
Electronic Equipment Set-up Operator (electron. comp.)	RCI	60	726.380-010
Electronic Funds Transfer Coordinator (financial)	CSE	60	216.362-038
Electronic Intelligence Operations Specialist (military ser.)	RCE	62	193.382-010
Electronic Masking System Operator (print. & pub.)	RIE	59	972.282-018
Electronic Prepress System Operator (print. & pub.)	CIR	58	979.282-010
Electronic-Component Processor (electron. comp.)	RCE	43	590.684-014
Electronic-Organ Technician (any industry)	RSE	59	828.261-010
Electronic-Production-Line-Maintenance Mechanic (electron. comp.)	RIS	62	629.261-022
Electronic-Sales-and-Service Technician (profess. & kin.)	RIE	63	828.251-010
Electronic-Scale Subassembler (office machines)	CRS	42	726.684-014
Electronics Assembler (comm. equip.; electron. comp.; inst. & app.)	CRS	42	726.684-018
Electronics Assembler, Developmental (any industry)	RES	62	726.261-010
Electronics Engineer (profess. & kin.)	RIE	71	003.061-030
Electronics Inspector (comm. equip.; electron. comp.; inst. & app.)	RIE	59	726.381-010
Electronics Inspector (electron. comp.)	CRS	46	726.684-022
Electronics Mechanic (any industry)	RIS	62	828.261-022
Electronics Technician (profess. & kin.)	IRE	69	003.161-014
Electronics Tester (any industry)	IRC	61	726.261-018
Electronics Tester (comm. equip.; electron. comp.; inst. & app.; office machines)	CRS	48	726.684-026
Electronics Utility Worker (comm. equip.; electron. comp.)	RES	54	726.364-018
Electronics Worker (electron. comp.)	RCE	41	726.687-010
Electronics-Design Engineer (profess. & kin.)	RIS	76	003.061-034
Electronics-Mechanic Apprentice (any industry)	RIS	62	828.261-026
Electronics-Research Engineer (profess. & kin.)	RIS	71	003.061-038
Electronics-Test Engineer (profess. & kin.)	IES	73	003.061-042
Electrotype Servicer (print. & pub.)	CRE	50	659.462-010
Electrotyper (print. & pub.)	RIE	58	974.381-010
Electrotyper Apprentice (print. & pub.)	RIE	58	974.381-014
Element Winding Machine Tender (elec. equip.; inst. & app.)	CRS	46	724.685-010
Elevating-Grader Operator (construction)	RIE	46	850.663-014
Elevator Constructor (construction)	RIE	57	825.361-010

DOT to HOC

Title	HOC	Cx	DOT
Elevator Examiner-and-Adjuster (any industry)	RES	61	825.261-014
Elevator Operator (any industry)	CRE	43	388.663-010
Elevator Operator, Freight (any industry)	RES	40	921.683-038
Elevator Repairer (any industry)	RIS	58	825.281-030
Elevator Starter (any industry)	ERS	52	388.367-010
Elevator-Constructor Helper (construction)	RCE	48	825.664-010
Elevator-Constructor Supervisor (construction)	RES	59	825.131-014
Elevator-Repairer Apprentice (any industry)	RIS	58	825.281-034
Elevator-Repairer Helper (any industry)	RCE	44	825.684-014
Eligibility Worker (government ser.)	SCE	62	195.267-010
Eligibility-and-Occupancy Interviewer (government ser.)	SEC	58	168.267-038
Embalmer (personal ser.)	RIS	61	338.371-014
Embalmer Apprentice (personal ser.)	RIS	61	338.371-010
Emblem Drawer-In (tex. prod., n.e.c.)	RCE	49	689.380-010
Embosser (any industry)	RCE	42	583.685-030
Embosser (boot & shoe)	REC	41	690.685-158
Embosser (leather mfg.; leather prod.)	RIC	46	690.682-030
Embosser (optical goods)	CRE	42	713.684-022
Embosser (print. & pub.)	RIE	51	659.382-010
Embosser Operator (paper goods)	REI	47	649.682-022
Embossing Toolsetter (ordnance)	RES	55	616.260-010
Embossing-Machine Operator (nonfer. metal)	RCE	44	617.685-018
Embossing-Machine Operator (ordnance)	RCE	42	619.685-038
Embossing-Machine Operator (tex. prod., n.e.c.)	RCS	47	583.685-034
Embossing-Machine Operator (wood prod., n.e.c.)	RCS	47	669.682-046
Embossing-Machine Operator I (clerical)	CRS	46	208.582-014
Embossing-Machine Operator II (clerical)	CRS	45	208.682-010
Embossing-Machine Tender (paper goods)	RES	40	649.685-038
Embossing-Machine-Operator Helper (plastic-synth.)	RCE	41	583.685-038
Embossing-Press Operator (print. & pub.)	RES	49	659.682-014
Embossing-Press Operator, Molded Goods (fabrication, n.e.c.)	REI	49	690.682-034
Embossing-Press-Operator Apprentice (print. & pub.)	RES	49	659.682-018
Embossograph Operator (any industry)	CRS	47	652.682-014
Embroiderer, Hand (tex. prod., n.e.c.)	CSR	43	782.684-018
Embroidery Patternmaker (retail trade; wholesale tr.)	RIE	59	782.361-014
Embroidery Supervisor (tex. prod., n.e.c.)	RES	60	689.130-010
Embroidery-Machine Operator (any industry)	REI	47	787.682-022
Embroidery-Machine Operator (garment)	CRE	40	786.685-018
Emergency Medical Services Coordinator (medical ser.)	SER	65	079.117-010
Emergency Medical Technician (medical ser.)	RSI	57	079.374-010
Employee Relations Specialist (profess. & kin.)	SER	59	166.267-042
Employer Relations Representative (profess. & kin.)	ESC	60	166.257-010
Employment Clerk (clerical)	CES	60	205.362-014
Employment Interviewer (profess. & kin.)	SCE	64	166.267-010
Employment-and-Claims Aide (government ser.)	ESC	55	169.367-010
Enameler (jewelry-silver.)	CSE	47	740.684-018
Enameler (plumbing-heat.)	RES	45	509.684-010
Encapsulator (aircraft mfg.)	RCS	47	556.684-014

Dictionary of Holland Occupational Codes

Part 3: From Occupational Titles to Holland Codes

From the Dictionary of Occupational Titles Occupations to Holland Codes

Title	HOC	Cx	DOT
Encapsulator (elec. equip.; electron. comp.)	RCE	41	726.687-022
End Finder, Forming Department (textile)	CRE	41	681.687-010
End Finder, Roving Department (glass mfg.)	RCE	41	689.687-038
End Finder, Twisting Department (textile)	RCE	41	689.687-042
End Frazer (fabrication, n.e.c.)	RCE	44	665.685-014
End Polisher (clock & watch)	CRE	44	715.685-026
End Stapler (wood. container)	REI	41	669.685-054
End-Touching-Machine Operator (wood prod., n.e.c.)	RCE	36	662.686-010
Endband Cutter, Hand (hat & cap)	CRE	40	784.687-026
Ending-Machine Operator (paper goods)	CRE	39	641.685-042
Endodontist (medical ser.)	ISE	75	072.101-014
Energy-Conservation Representative (utilities)	RES	54	959.367-018
Energy-Control Officer (education)	ESR	61	199.167-018
Engine Dispatcher (r.r. trans.)	REC	51	910.367-018
Engine Repairer, Production (engine-turbine)	RIE	57	625.381-010
Engine Repairer, Service (engine-turbine)	RIE	58	625.281-018
Engine Tester (aircraft mfg.; air trans.)	RIS	62	621.261-014
Engine Turner (jewelry-silver.)	REC	50	704.381-018
Engine-Lathe Set-up Operator (machine shop)	RIE	58	604.380-018
Engine-Lathe Set-up Operator, Tool (machine shop)	RIE	60	604.280-010
Engine-Testing Supervisor (engine-turbine)	RES	62	625.131-010
Engineer (water trans.)	RES	59	197.130-010
Engineer of System Development (utilities)	IER	76	003.167-026
Engineer, Exhauster (steel & rel.)	REC	56	950.362-010
Engineer, Soils (profess. & kin.)	IER	77	024.161-010
Engineer-in-Charge, Studio Operations (radio-tv broad.)	IER	70	003.167-030
Engineer-in-Charge, Transmitter (radio-tv broad.)	RIE	70	003.167-034
Engineering Assistant, Mechanical Equipment (profess. & kin.)	IRC	70	007.161-018
Engineering Manager, Electronics (profess. & kin.)	IES	79	003.167-070
Engineering Model Maker (inst. & app.; office machines)	RIE	65	693.260-018
Engineering-Document-Control Clerk (aircraft mfg.; electron. comp.)	CSE	56	206.367-010
Engraver (glass products)	REA	50	775.381-010
Engraver Apprentice, Decorative (engraving)	RCE	52	704.381-022
Engraver I (print. & pub.)	RES	50	979.381-010
Engraver II (print. & pub.)	RCE	46	979.684-014
Engraver Tender (glass products)	RCE	39	673.685-050
Engraver, Automatic (clock & watch)	CRE	40	609.685-014
Engraver, Block (print. & pub.)	RCE	57	979.281-014
Engraver, Hand, Hard Metals (engraving)	RIE	58	704.381-026
Engraver, Hand, Soft Metals (engraving)	RCE	52	704.381-030
Engraver, Machine (print. & pub.)	RIE	56	979.382-014
Engraver, Machine I (engraving)	CRE	44	704.682-010
Engraver, Machine II (engraving)	RCE	45	704.582-010
Engraver, Pantograph I (engraving)	REI	53	704.382-010
Engraver, Pantograph II (engraving)	RCE	46	704.682-014
Engraver, Picture (print. & pub.)	RIE	59	979.281-018
Engraver, Rubber (pen & pencil)	RSC	55	733.381-010

Part 3: From Occupational Titles to Holland Codes

From the Dictionary of Occupational Titles Occupations to Holland Codes

Title	HOC	Cx	DOT
Engraver, Rubber (print. & pub.)	RSC	46	979.581-010
Engraver, Seals (pen & pencil)	REI	56	704.381-034
Engraver, Tire Mold (machine shop)	REI	52	605.382-014
Engraving Supervisor (engraving)	RES	59	704.131-010
Engraving-Press Operator (print. & pub.)	RCS	55	651.382-010
Engrosser (profess. & kin.)	ARE	53	970.661-010
Enrobing-Machine Corder (sugar & conf.)	REC	40	524.684-018
Enrobing-Machine Feeder (sugar & conf.)	CRS	40	524.686-010
Enrobing-Machine Operator (bakery products)	RCE	40	524.685-026
Enrobing-Machine Operator (bakery products; sugar & conf.)	RES	49	524.382-014
Entomologist (profess. & kin.)	IRS	78	041.061-046
Envelope-Folding-Machine Adjuster (paper goods)	RIS	52	641.380-010
Envelope-Machine Operator (paper goods)	RCE	42	649.685-042
Environmental Analyst (government ser.)	ESR	63	199.167-022
Environmental Analyst (profess. & kin.)	IRE	80	029.081-010
Environmental Epidemiologist (government ser.)	IRE	76	041.167-010
Epitaxial Reactor Operator (electron. comp.)	RCI	54	590.382-018
Epitaxial Reactor Technician (electron. comp.)	RCI	62	590.282-010
Equal Opportunity Officer (any industry)	SRI	65	168.267-114
Equal-Opportunity Representative (government ser.)	ESA	65	168.167-014
Equestrian (amuse. & rec.)	AER	53	159.344-010
Equipment Cleaner (any industry)	REI	41	599.684-010
Equipment Cleaner-and-Tester (smelt. & refin.)	REC	47	630.584-010
Equipment Inspector (tel. & tel.)	RES	62	822.261-014
Equipment Installer (any industry)	RSE	57	828.381-010
Equipment Installer (tel. & tel.)	RSE	57	822.381-010
Equipment Monitor, Phototypesetting (print. & pub.)	RCS	45	650.682-010
Escort (any industry)	ESR	43	353.667-010
Escort (personal ser.)	SEC	50	359.367-010
Escort-Vehicle Driver (motor trans.)	CER	41	919.663-022
Escrow Officer (profess. & kin.)	ECS	62	119.367-010
Estate Planner (insurance)	ESI	72	186.167-010
Estimator (profess. & kin.)	RCE	64	169.267-038
Estimator and Drafter (utilities)	RIE	69	019.261-014
Estimator, Jewelry (jewelry-silver.)	REC	59	221.387-022
Estimator, Paperboard Boxes (paper goods)	RCI	64	221.362-018
Estimator, Printing (print. & pub.)	ERS	60	221.367-014
Etch Operator, Semiconductor Wafers (electron. comp.)	RCI	41	590.685-074
Etched-Circuit Processor (electron. comp.)	CRE	49	590.684-018
Etcher (electron. comp.)	RCI	42	590.685-078
Etcher (engraving)	REI	48	704.684-010
Etcher Apprentice, Photoengraving (print. & pub.)	RIE	58	971.381-010
Etcher Helper, Hand (print. & pub.)	RES	38	971.687-010
Etcher, Electrolytic (cutlery-hrdwr.)	RCE	42	500.685-010
Etcher, Hand (cutlery-hrdwr.)	CRE	41	704.687-014
Etcher, Hand (print. & pub.)	RSI	55	971.261-010
Etcher, Machine (cutlery-hrdwr.)	RCE	44	619.685-042
Etcher, Photoengraving (print. & pub.)	RIE	58	971.381-014

Dictionary of Holland Occupational Codes

Part 3: From Occupational Titles to Holland Codes

From the Dictionary of Occupational Titles Occupations to Holland Codes

Title	HOC	Cx	DOT
Etcher-Stripper, Semiconductor Wafers (electron. comp.)	RCI	39	590.684-026
Ethnologist (profess. & kin.)	IRE	73	055.067-022
Evaluator (education)	SIR	66	094.267-010
Evaluator (nonprofit org.)	SEI	53	249.367-034
Evaporative-Cooler Installer (any industry)	RCE	54	637.381-010
Evaporator Operator (can. & preserv.; dairy products; sugar & conf.)	REC	51	521.382-010
Evaporator Operator (paper & pulp)	CRE	41	532.685-018
Evaporator Operator I (chemical)	RIC	57	553.382-018
Evaporator Operator II (chemical)	RCS	45	553.682-018
Examination Proctor (government ser.)	ESR	60	199.267-018
Examiner (fabrication, n.e.c.)	REC	40	739.687-082
Examiner (glove & mit.)	RCE	42	789.687-042
Examiner (government ser.)	ERS	65	169.267-014
Examiner (print. & pub.)	RES	42	979.687-010
Examiner, Questioned Documents (government ser.)	IRE	62	199.267-022
Excavator (any industry)	RSC	42	850.684-010
Excelsior-Machine Tender (saw. & plan.)	REI	40	663.685-014
Executive Chef (hotel & rest.)	SER	65	187.161-010
Executive Director, Nurses' Association (medical ser.)	SEI	77	075.117-034
Executive Director, Red Cross (nonprofit org.)	ESI	71	187.117-066
Executive Director, Sheltered Workshop (nonprofit org.)	SER	66	187.117-026
Executive Housekeeper (any industry)	ECR	66	187.167-046
Executive Pilot (any industry)	RIE	66	196.263-030
Executive Producer, Promos (radio-tv broad.)	ESC	64	159.167-022
Executive Secretary, State Board of Nursing (government ser.)	ESR	72	169.117-010
Executive Vice President, Chamber of Commerce (nonprofit org.)	ESA	70	187.117-030
Exercise Physiologist (medical ser.)	ISR	67	076.121-018
Exerciser, Horse (amuse. & rec.)	REA	41	153.674-010
Exhaust Equipment Operator (electron. comp.)	RIS	59	599.382-014
Exhibit Artist (museums)	ASI	63	149.261-010
Exhibit Builder (museums)	ASR	60	739.261-010
Exhibit Designer (museums)	ASE	67	142.061-058
Exhibit-Display Representative (any industry)	ESR	54	297.367-010
Expanding Machine Operator (steel & rel.)	RCE	43	617.685-022
Expansion Envelope Maker, Hand (paper goods)	RES	40	794.684-018
Expansion-Joint Builder (rubber goods)	RIE	48	759.664-014
Expediter (clerical)	CSE	56	222.367-018
Expediter Clerk (optical goods)	RCS	51	221.387-026
Expediter, Service Order (furniture)	CRS	52	222.367-070
Expedition Supervisor (fishing & hunt.)	REI	55	461.134-010
Expeller Operator (grain-feed mills; oils & grease)	REC	41	529.685-106
Experimental Aircraft Mechanic (aircraft mfg.)	RIE	61	621.261-022
Experimental Assembler (any industry)	RIE	59	739.381-026
Experimental Mechanic (motor-bicycles)	RIS	60	600.260-014
Experimental Mechanic, Electrical (motor-bicycles)	REI	59	806.281-014
Experimental Mechanic, Outboard Motors (engine-turbine)	RES	60	623.261-010

Part 3: From Occupational Titles to Holland Codes
From the Dictionary of Occupational Titles Occupations to Holland Codes

Title	HOC	Cx	DOT
Experimental-Box Tester (wood. container)	RIE	63	761.281-014
Experimental-Rocket-Sled Mechanic (aircraft mfg.)	REI	60	825.281-038
Explosive Operator I (ordnance)	CRE	45	737.687-042
Explosive Operator II (ordnance)	RCE	42	737.687-046
Explosive-Operator Supervisor (ordnance)	ERS	60	694.132-010
Explosives-Truck Driver (ordnance)	RSE	45	903.683-010
Express Clerk (motor trans.; r.r. trans.)	ERC	54	222.367-022
Extension Clerk (utilities)	SCR	56	219.362-030
Extension Edger (paper goods)	RCE	40	641.685-046
Extension Service Specialist (government ser.)	SEC	66	096.127-014
Exterminator (business ser.)	RES	45	389.684-010
Exterminator Helper (any industry)	RCE	45	383.684-010
Exterminator Helper, Termite (business ser.)	RES	37	383.687-010
Exterminator, Termite (business ser.)	REI	52	383.364-010
Extra (amuse. & rec.; motion picture; radio-tv broad.)	ERC	46	159.647-014
Extractor Loader and Unloader (chemical)	RCE	38	551.686-014
Extractor Operator (any industry)	REC	38	581.685-038
Extractor Operator (beverage)	CRE	42	521.685-118
Extractor Operator (chemical)	RCE	47	552.682-018
Extractor Operator (chemical; oils & grease)	RES	40	551.685-054
Extractor Operator (pharmaceut.)	RCE	43	551.685-058
Extractor Operator (tex. prod., n.e.c.)	RES	42	582.685-062
Extractor Operator (textile)	REC	41	581.685-042
Extractor Operator, Solvent Process (chemical)	CRE	42	551.685-062
Extractor-and-Wringer Operator (chemical)	CRE	40	551.685-066
Extractor-Machine Operator (can. & preserv.)	REC	39	521.665-014
Extractor-Operator Helper (chemical)	RES	38	552.686-010
Extractor-Plant Operator (chemical; oils & grease)	RES	47	559.665-018
Extruder Operator (forging)	RIE	50	614.482-014
Extruder Operator (grain-feed mills)	RES	47	520.682-018
Extruder Operator (plastic prod.; plastic-synth.)	REI	49	557.382-010
Extruder Operator (wood prod., n.e.c.)	RCE	42	569.685-038
Extruder Tender (rubber goods)	CRE	41	557.685-014
Extruder-Operator Helper (plastic prod.; plastic-synth.)	REC	42	557.564-010
Extruding-Machine Operator (nonfer. metal)	RCI	49	691.382-010
Extruding-Machine Operator (tex. prod., n.e.c.)	RES	41	557.565-010
Extruding-Press Operator (ordnance)	RES	44	614.685-010
Extrusion Bender (ship-boat mfg.)	RES	47	804.684-014
Extrusion-Die Repairer (nonfer. metal)	RCI	56	705.381-014
Extrusion-Press Adjuster (elec. equip.)	RIE	54	614.380-010
Extrusion-Press Operator I (elec. equip.)	REI	51	614.482-018
Extrusion-Press Operator II (elec. equip.)	REI	44	614.685-014
Eye-Dropper Assembler (glass products)	CRE	40	739.687-086
Eyeglass-Frame Truer (optical goods)	RCE	42	713.684-026
Eyeglass-Lens Cutter (optical goods)	RCE	46	716.682-010
Eyelet-Machine Operator (any industry)	CRE	40	699.685-018
Eyelet-Punch Operator (furniture)	CRE	40	699.685-022
Fabric Normalizer (rubber goods)	RES	39	559.685-066
Fabric Stretcher (furniture)	REC	41	709.667-010

DOT to HOC

Title	HOC	Cx	DOT
Fabric-and-Accessories Estimator (garment)	CRS	53	221.482-010
Fabric-Coating Supervisor (tex. prod., n.e.c.)	ERS	59	589.130-014
Fabric-Lay-Out Worker (textile)	REC	41	589.687-022
Fabric-Machine Operator I (furniture)	REI	56	616.362-010
Fabric-Machine Operator II (furniture)	REC	41	616.685-022
Fabricator, Artificial Breast (protective dev.)	RCI	40	712.684-042
Fabricator, Foam Rubber (any industry)	CRE	40	780.684-062
Fabricator, Industrial Furnace (machinery mfg.)	RSE	52	826.381-010
Fabricator, Shower Doors and Panels (struct. metal)	RES	50	739.381-030
Fabricator-Assembler, Metal Products (any industry)	RIE	53	809.381-010
Facer (clock & watch)	RCE	47	770.582-010
Facilities Planner (any industry)	RIE	69	019.261-018
Facilities-Flight-Check Pilot (government ser.)	RIE	69	196.263-034
Facility Examiner (tel. & tel.)	REC	53	959.367-014
Facing Baster, Jumpbasting (garment)	RCE	41	786.682-102
Facing-Machine Operator (clock & watch)	CRE	41	604.685-014
Factor (financial)	ESI	70	186.167-082
Factory Helper (sugar & conf.)	REC	39	529.686-034
Factory Lay-Out Engineer (profess. & kin.)	IER	70	012.167-018
Faculty Member, College or University, All Other (education)	SEI	74	090.227-010
Faculty Member, College or University, All Other Physical Sciences (education)	IRE	74	090.227-010
Faculty Member, College or University, Art, Drama, and Music (education)	ASE	74	090.227-010
Faculty Member, College or University, Chemistry (education)	IRE	74	090.227-010
Faculty Member, College or University, Computer Science (education)	IRE	74	090.227-010
Faculty Member, College or University, Engineering (education)	RIE	74	090.227-010
Faculty Member, College or University, English and Foreign Languages (education)	AIE	74	090.227-010
Faculty Member, College or University, Health Specialties (education)	ISR	74	090.227-010
Faculty Member, College or University, Life Sciences (education)	IRE	74	090.227-010
Faculty Member, College or University, Mathematical Sciences (education)	IRE	74	090.227-010
Faculty Member, College or University, Physics (education)	IRE	74	090.227-010
Faculty Member, College or University, Social Sciences (education)	SIE	74	090.227-010
Faller I (logging)	RES	49	454.384-010
Faller II (logging)	RES	39	454.684-014
Family Practitioner (medical ser.)	IRE	76	070.101-026
Fan-Blade Aligner (elec. equip.)	CRS	41	706.687-018
Fancy-Wire Drawer (jewelry-silver.)	REI	57	700.381-014
Fare-Register Repairer (motor trans.)	RCE	52	729.384-014

Title	HOC	Cx	DOT
Farm-Equipment Mechanic I (agric. equip.)	RES	58	624.281-010
Farm-Equipment Mechanic II (agric. equip.)	RSC	49	624.381-014
Farm-Equipment-Mechanic Apprentice (agric. equip.)	RES	58	624.281-014
Farm-Machine Operator (agriculture)	RIE	48	409.683-010
Farm-Machine Tender (agriculture)	REI	39	409.685-010
Farm-Machinery Set-up Mechanic (agric. equip.)	RSE	54	624.381-018
Farmer, Cash Grain (agriculture)	RIE	59	401.161-010
Farmer, Diversified Crops (agriculture)	RSI	63	407.161-010
Farmer, Field Crop (agriculture)	REI	63	404.161-010
Farmer, Fruit Crops, Bush and Vine (agriculture)	RIE	61	403.161-014
Farmer, General (agriculture)	RIS	63	421.161-010
Farmer, Tree-Fruit-and-Nut Crops (agriculture)	REI	61	403.161-010
Farmer, Vegetable (agriculture)	REI	63	402.161-010
Farmworker, Bulbs (agriculture)	RES	47	405.683-010
Farmworker, Dairy (agriculture)	RES	41	410.684-010
Farmworker, Diversified Crops I (agriculture)	RES	48	407.663-010
Farmworker, Diversified Crops II (agriculture)	REC	39	407.687-010
Farmworker, Field Crop I (agriculture)	RSE	48	404.663-010
Farmworker, Field Crop II (agriculture)	REC	39	404.687-010
Farmworker, Fruit I (agriculture)	REI	48	403.683-010
Farmworker, Fruit II (agriculture)	REC	39	403.687-010
Farmworker, General I (agriculture)	RES	48	421.683-010
Farmworker, General II (agriculture)	REC	38	421.687-010
Farmworker, Grain I (agriculture)	REI	45	401.683-010
Farmworker, Grain II (agriculture)	RES	37	401.687-010
Farmworker, Livestock (agriculture)	RSE	47	410.664-010
Farmworker, Machine (agriculture)	RCE	35	409.686-010
Farmworker, Poultry (agriculture)	RCS	45	411.584-010
Farmworker, Rice (agriculture)	REI	47	401.683-014
Farmworker, Vegetable I (agriculture)	REC	49	402.663-010
Farmworker, Vegetable II (agriculture)	REC	39	402.687-010
Fashion Artist (retail trade)	AER	64	141.061-014
Fashion Coordinator (retail trade)	EAS	67	185.157-010
Fashion Designer (profess. & kin.)	ASR	65	142.061-018
Fast-Foods Worker (hotel & rest.)	SCR	44	311.472-010
Fastener Technologist (nut & bolt)	RIC	63	612.260-010
Fastener, Machine (boot & shoe)	RCE	41	690.685-162
Fastener-Sewing-Machine Operator (any industry)	RCE	41	787.685-010
Fat-Purification Worker (oils & grease)	CRS	45	551.685-070
Feather Mixer (tex. prod., n.e.c.)	REI	40	589.685-050
Feather Renovator (laundry & rel.)	REC	37	362.685-010
Feather Sawyer (toy-sport equip.)	RCS	38	732.685-014
Feather Separator (tex. prod., n.e.c.)	REI	41	589.685-054
Feather Shaper (button & notion)	RCE	41	734.684-010
Feather Stitcher (toy-sport equip.)	RCE	41	732.684-050
Feather Washer (tex. prod., n.e.c.)	REC	40	582.685-066
Feather-Curling-Machine Operator (tex. prod., n.e.c.)	RES	38	589.686-018
Feather-Cutting-Machine Feeder (tex. prod., n.e.c.)	REC	36	585.686-010
Feather-Drying-Machine Operator (tex. prod., n.e.c.)	RES	39	581.686-034

Part 3: From Occupational Titles to Holland Codes
From the Dictionary of Occupational Titles Occupations to Holland Codes

Title	HOC	Cx	DOT
Feather-Duster Winder (tex. prod., n.e.c.)	CRE	41	734.684-014
Featheredger and Reducer, Machine (boot & shoe)	RCE	41	690.685-166
Federal Aid Coordinator (government ser.)	SEC	67	188.167-054
Feed and Farm Management Adviser (agriculture; retail trade)	ESC	62	096.127-018
Feed Blender (grain-feed mills)	REI	40	520.685-094
Feed Grinder (grain-feed mills)	REI	40	521.685-122
Feed Mixer (grain-feed mills)	RCE	42	520.685-098
Feed Weigher (grain-feed mills)	REI	38	920.685-058
Feed-In Worker (grain-feed mills)	RES	37	929.686-022
Feed-Mixer Helper (grain-feed mills)	RES	37	520.686-018
Feed-Research Aide (agriculture)	RES	52	049.364-010
Feeder (print. & pub.)	RCE	41	651.686-014
Feeder-Catcher, Tobacco (tobacco)	RES	37	529.686-038
Feeder-Switchboard Operator (utilities)	RSC	52	952.362-014
Felled-Seam Operator, Chainstitch (garment)	RCE	41	786.682-106
Felt Carbonizer (tex. prod., n.e.c.)	REI	42	586.687-010
Felt Cutter (ordnance)	RCE	41	686.685-026
Felt Hanger (build. mat., n.e.c.)	RES	42	549.686-014
Felt-Cutting-Machine Operator (tex. prod., n.e.c.)	REC	48	686.682-018
Felt-Goods Supervisor, Needle Process (tex. prod., n.e.c.)	REC	59	689.130-014
Felt-Hat Steamer (hat & cap)	CRE	36	582.687-018
Felt-Strip Finisher (tex. prod., n.e.c.)	REC	42	586.685-018
Felt-Tipping-Machine Tender (pen & pencil)	RCE	36	686.686-010
Felt-Washing-Machine Tender (tex. prod., n.e.c.)	CRS	42	582.685-070
Felting-Machine Operator (tex. prod., n.e.c.)	RSC	48	586.662-010
Felting-Machine-Operator Helper (tex. prod., n.e.c.)	REC	39	586.686-014
Feltmaker and Weigher (tex. prod., n.e.c.)	CRS	43	586.685-022
Fence Erector (construction)	RSE	47	869.684-022
Fence-Erector Supervisor (construction)	ERS	59	869.134-010
Fence-Making Machine Operator (metal prod., n.e.c.)	RIE	46	616.582-010
Fermentation Operator (beverage)	RIE	55	522.382-014
Fermentation Operator (chemical)	RES	49	558.682-018
Fermenter Operator (pharmaceut.)	REC	47	559.685-070
Fermenter, Wine (beverage)	CES	48	522.685-062
Ferryboat Captain (water trans.)	ESI	63	197.163-010
Ferryboat Operator (water trans.)	RES	50	911.363-010
Ferryboat Operator, Cable (water trans.)	RES	45	911.664-010
Ferryboat-Operator Helper (water trans.)	REI	42	911.667-010
Fertilizer Mixer (chemical)	RCE	40	550.665-018
Fettler (brick & tile)	RCE	41	779.684-018
Fiber Technologist (profess. & kin.)	IRS	76	040.061-026
Fiber-Machine Tender (glass mfg.)	CRE	42	575.685-030
Fiberglass Laminator (ship-boat mfg.; vehicles, n.e.c.)	RES	46	806.684-054
Fiberglass-Bonding-Machine Tender (glass mfg.)	CRS	42	574.665-010
Fiberglass-Container-Winding Operator (glass products)	RCE	44	579.584-010
Fiberglass-Dowel-Drawing-Machine Operator (plastic prod.)	CRS	46	575.682-010

Part 3: From Occupational Titles to Holland Codes

From the Dictionary of Occupational Titles Occupations to Holland Codes

Title	HOC	Cx	DOT
Fiberglass-Machine Operator (glass products)	RCS	44	574.682-010
Field Artillery Crewmember (military ser.)	RES	41	378.684-018
Field Artillery Operations Specialist (military ser.)	RIE	59	378.367-014
Field Artillery Senior Sergeant (military ser.)	ERS	58	378.132-010
Field Cashier (construction)	SCE	61	219.137-010
Field Contractor (any industry)	SEA	66	162.117-022
Field Engineer (radio-tv broad.)	RIS	66	193.262-018
Field Engineer, Specialist (petrol. & gas)	RIE	64	010.261-010
Field Hauler (agriculture)	RSE	41	409.683-014
Field Inspector, Disease and Insect Control (agriculture)	ECS	42	408.687-010
Field Recorder (utilities)	RCE	53	229.367-010
Field Representative (business ser.; wholesale tr.)	EAS	63	163.267-010
Field Representative (profess. & kin.)	ESA	67	189.267-010
Field Service Engineer (profess. & kin.)	RIE	66	828.261-014
Field Service Technician (machinery mfg.)	IRS	66	638.261-026
Field Service Technician, Poultry (agriculture)	RES	58	411.267-010
Field Supervisor, Broadcast (radio-tv broad.)	ESC	67	193.167-014
Field Supervisor, Oil-Well Services (petrol. & gas)	RES	59	930.131-010
Field Supervisor, Seed Production (agriculture)	EAS	65	180.167-014
Field-Assembly Supervisor (mfd. bldgs.)	RES	59	869.131-018
Field-Contact Technician (dairy products)	ESR	66	162.117-026
Field-Map Editor (profess. & kin.)	RIE	61	018.262-010
Field-Mechanical-Meter Tester (petrol. refin.; pipe lines; utilities)	RSE	65	953.281-010
Field-Ring Assembler (elec. equip.)	RES	51	721.484-014
Field-Service Engineer (aircraft mfg.)	RIE	76	002.167-014
Field-Service Engineer (photo. appar.)	RSE	63	826.261-010
Field-Service Representative (aircraft mfg.)	RES	65	621.221-010
Fig Caprifier (agriculture)	RES	41	403.687-014
Figure Refinisher and Repairer (retail trade)	RSE	54	739.381-034
File Clerk I (clerical)	CSR	48	206.387-034
File Clerk II (clerical)	CSR	51	206.367-014
File Cutter (cutlery-hrdwr.)	CRS	47	605.685-014
Filer (jewelry-silver.)	CRS	41	700.684-034
Filer and Sander (woodworking)	RCE	39	705.684-018
Filer, Finish (ordnance)	REI	50	705.481-010
Filer, Hand, Tool (machine shop)	REI	49	705.484-010
Filing-and-Polishing Supervisor (ordnance)	REI	61	603.137-010
Filler (fabrication, n.e.c.)	RCE	37	739.687-090
Filler (tex. prod., n.e.c.)	REC	40	780.684-066
Filler Feeder (tobacco)	RCE	39	529.686-042
Filler Mixer (tobacco)	RCE	40	520.687-030
Filler Room Attendant (tobacco)	RES	39	522.687-022
Filler Shredder, Machine (tobacco)	REC	41	529.685-110
Filler Spreader (tobacco)	RES	35	521.687-046
Filler-Block Inserter-Remover (furniture)	RES	36	652.687-018
Filler-Shredder Helper (tobacco)	REC	37	529.687-078
Filling Machine Tender (bakery products)	RCE	42	524.685-030
Filling-and-Stapling-Machine Operator (fabrication, n.e.c.)	RCS	45	692.682-038

Title	HOC	Cx	DOT
Filling-Machine Operator (nonfer. metal)	RCI	42	699.685-038
Filling-Machine Operator (pen & pencil)	RCS	42	733.685-014
Filling-Machine Set-up Mechanic (food prep., n.e.c.)	RIE	45	920.680-010
Film Developer (motion picture; photofinishing)	RES	48	976.382-018
Film Flat Inspector (print. & pub.)	RIC	58	972.284-010
Film Inspector (photofinishing)	RIE	54	976.362-010
Film Laboratory Technician (motion picture; photofinishing)	RCE	46	976.684-014
Film Laboratory Technician I (motion picture)	RIE	63	976.381-010
Film Laboratory Technician II (motion picture)	RES	47	976.685-018
Film Loader (motion picture)	RES	40	962.687-014
Film or Videotape Editor (motion picture; radio-tv broad.)	AES	63	962.262-010
Film Printer (motion picture)	RES	45	976.682-010
Film Spooler (photo. appar.)	REC	40	692.685-082
Film Touch-Up Inspector (electron. comp.)	RCE	40	726.684-050
Film-Casting Operator (plastic-synth.)	REI	46	559.682-022
Film-or-Tape Librarian (clerical)	CRS	54	222.367-026
Film-Rental Clerk (business ser.; retail trade)	ESC	57	295.367-018
Film-Replacement Orderer (motion picture)	CSR	48	976.567-010
Film-Vault Supervisor (motion picture)	ESR	59	222.137-010
Filter Changer (beverage)	REC	39	521.687-050
Filter Cleaner (plastic-synth.)	REC	38	559.687-038
Filter Helper (chemical)	REC	40	551.685-074
Filter Operator (any industry)	RCE	40	551.685-078
Filter Operator (beverage; sugar & conf.)	RES	41	521.685-126
Filter Operator (grain-feed mills)	REC	47	521.682-018
Filter Tender (grain-feed mills)	REC	47	522.665-010
Filter Tender, Jelly (can. & preserv.)	CRS	43	529.685-114
Filter Washer (chemical)	RES	40	559.687-042
Filter Washer and Presser (beverage; chemical)	RCE	41	599.685-038
Filter-Plant Supervisor (smelt. & refin.)	REI	58	511.135-010
Filter-Press Operator (any industry)	REC	41	551.685-082
Filter-Press Tender (beverage)	REC	40	521.685-130
Filter-Press Tender (beverage; chemical)	RCE	42	599.685-042
Filter-Press Tender, Head (grain-feed mills)	REI	41	521.665-018
Filter-Screen Cleaner (beverage)	REI	40	521.687-054
Filter-Tank Operator (chemical)	REC	41	551.585-010
Filter-Tank-Tender Helper, Head (grain-feed mills)	RCE	40	521.685-134
Filtering-Machine Tender (grain-feed mills)	REC	42	521.685-138
Filtration Operator, Polyethylene Catalyst (chemical)	REC	48	551.562-010
Final Assembler (garment)	REC	40	789.687-046
Final Assembler (office machines)	REI	54	706.381-018
Final Assembler (optical goods)	RCE	37	713.687-018
Final Finisher, Forging Dies (machine shop)	REI	51	705.484-014
Final Inspector (auto. mfg.)	REI	49	806.687-018
Final Inspector (boot & shoe)	RIE	48	753.687-018
Final Inspector (clock & watch)	REC	57	715.381-050
Final Inspector (elec. equip.)	CRE	41	727.687-054
Final Inspector (glass products)	REI	51	779.387-010

DOT to HOC

Part 3: From Occupational Titles to Holland Codes

From the Dictionary of Occupational Titles Occupations to Holland Codes

Title	HOC	Cx	DOT
Final Inspector (musical inst.)	RES	50	730.367-010
Final Inspector, Motorcycles (motor-bicycles)	RIE	56	806.281-018
Final Inspector, Movement Assembly (clock & watch)	REC	47	715.684-094
Final Inspector, Paper (paper & pulp)	RSC	53	539.367-010
Final Inspector, Shuttle (woodworking)	RES	47	769.684-022
Final Inspector, Truck Trailer (auto. mfg.)	RSE	59	806.361-018
Final Tester (elec. equip.)	RSI	58	721.261-014
Final-Dressing Cutter (meat products)	REC	44	525.684-026
Financial Planner (profess. & kin.)	ESC	65	250.257-014
Financial-Aid Counselor (education)	SEC	61	169.267-018
Financial-Aids Officer (education)	SEC	68	090.117-030
Fine Arts Packer (museums)	REI	61	102.367-010
Finer (clock & watch)	CRE	45	715.684-098
Finger Cobbler (boot & shoe)	CRS	44	788.684-046
Finger-Grip-Machine Operator (glass products)	REC	45	673.685-054
Fingernail Former (personal ser.)	SCE	42	331.674-014
Fingerprint Classifier (government ser.)	RCI	52	375.387-010
Fingerprint Clerk I (government ser.)	CES	49	209.367-026
Fingerprint Clerk II (government ser.)	CEI	53	206.387-014
Finish Opener, Jewel Hole (clock & watch)	REC	48	673.682-022
Finish Patcher (furniture)	RCS	45	763.684-034
Finish-Machine Tender (pottery & porc.)	RSE	45	673.685-058
Finished-Stock Inspector (furniture)	RCS	47	763.687-026
Finisher (fabrication, n.e.c.)	CRE	42	731.687-014
Finisher (nonmet. min.)	RCS	38	775.687-010
Finisher (plastic-synth.)	RES	41	554.586-010
Finisher (pottery & porc.)	REC	43	774.684-018
Finisher (steel & rel.)	RES	52	613.382-014
Finisher (tex. prod., n.e.c.)	CSE	40	789.687-050
Finisher (toy-sport equip.)	CRE	43	732.584-014
Finisher (wood. container)	RES	43	749.684-026
Finisher Operator (can. & preserv.)	REI	38	521.685-142
Finisher, Brush (fabrication, n.e.c.)	REC	42	739.684-062
Finisher, Denture (protective dev.)	RCI	54	712.381-050
Finisher, Fiberglass Boat Parts (ship-boat mfg.)	REC	43	809.684-022
Finisher, Hand (plastic prod.)	RCE	41	754.684-030
Finisher, Hand (tex. prod., n.e.c.)	RCS	47	789.484-014
Finisher, Hand (toy-sport equip.)	RCE	41	731.587-010
Finisher, Machine (plastic prod.)	RCE	42	690.685-170
Finisher-Card Tender (nonmet. min.; textile)	RCE	40	680.685-042
Finishing Inspector (elec. equip.)	REI	54	729.387-018
Finishing Supervisor (elec. equip.)	RES	59	692.130-014
Finishing Supervisor, Plastic Sheets (plastic-synth.)	RES	55	554.137-010
Finishing Trimmer (boot & shoe)	RCE	38	788.687-042
Finishing-Area Operator (plastic-synth.)	RSE	50	559.362-014
Finishing-Area Supervisor (plastic-synth.)	RES	59	559.132-022
Finishing-Machine Operator (narrow fabrics)	RSC	47	582.682-010
Finishing-Machine Operator (nonmet. min.)	RCE	46	674.682-010
Finishing-Machine Operator (paper goods)	RCE	36	649.686-022

Dictionary of Holland Occupational Codes

Title	HOC	Cx	DOT
Fire Assistant (government ser.)	SEI	59	169.167-022
Fire Captain (government ser.)	RES	62	373.134-010
Fire Chief (government ser.)	SEA	67	373.117-010
Fire Chief's Aide (government ser.)	REI	55	373.363-010
Fire Fighter (any industry)	RES	54	373.364-010
Fire Fighter, Crash, Fire, and Rescue (air trans.)	RES	50	373.663-010
Fire Inspector (any industry)	REI	55	373.367-010
Fire Inspector (government ser.)	CES	57	373.267-010
Fire Lookout (forestry)	ESA	52	452.367-010
Fire Marshal (any industry)	ERS	59	373.167-018
Fire Marshal (government ser.)	ESR	59	373.267-014
Fire Ranger (forestry)	ESR	51	452.367-014
Fire Warden (forestry)	ESR	63	452.167-010
Fire-Control Mechanic (government ser.)	RIE	61	632.261-014
Fire-Equipment Inspector (any industry)	RCE	51	739.484-014
Fire-Equipment-Inspector Helper (any industry)	CRS	43	739.687-094
Fire-Extinguisher Repairer (any industry)	RSE	50	709.384-010
Fire-Extinguisher-Sprinkler Inspector (any industry)	CRE	47	379.687-010
Fire-Fighting-Equipment Specialist (government ser.)	RIS	59	638.281-010
Fire-Hose Curer (rubber goods)	RCS	38	553.685-062
Fire-Investigation Lieutenant (government ser.)	IER	68	373.267-018
Fire-Prevention Research Engineer (profess. & kin.)	CES	70	012.167-022
Fire-Protection Engineer (profess. & kin.)	IEC	75	012.167-026
Fire-Protection Engineering Technician (profess. & kin.)	CRI	66	019.261-026
Firearms-Assembly Supervisor (ordnance)	ERS	59	736.131-014
Firer (jewelry-silver.)	CRE	42	590.685-034
Firer Helper (paper & pulp)	CRE	40	553.665-034
Firer, High Pressure (any industry)	RES	47	951.685-010
Firer, Kiln (pottery & porc.)	RIS	53	573.662-010
Firer, Kiln (sugar & conf.)	RES	44	523.685-078
Firer, Locomotive (r.r. trans.)	RIE	54	910.363-010
Firer, Low Pressure (any industry)	RES	44	951.685-014
Firer, Marine (water trans.)	RES	48	951.685-018
Firer, Retort (chemical)	RCS	41	553.685-066
Firesetter (elec. equip.; electron. comp.; inst. & app.)	RIE	57	692.360-018
Fireworks Assembler (chemical)	REC	41	737.587-014
Fireworks Display Specialist (chemical)	REI	52	969.664-010
Fireworks Maker (chemical)	RES	47	737.684-018
First Helper (steel & rel.)	RSE	52	512.362-010
First-Aid Attendant (any industry)	SEC	49	354.677-010
First-Breaker Feeder (tex. prod., n.e.c.)	REC	37	680.686-014
Fish and Game Warden (government ser.)	RES	63	379.167-010
Fish Bailer (fishing & hunt.)	REC	37	914.685-010
Fish Chopper, Gang Knife (can. & preserv.)	RES	37	521.687-058
Fish Cleaner (can. & preserv.; fishing & hunt.)	REC	39	525.684-030
Fish Cleaner Machine Tender (can. & preserv.)	REC	40	529.685-118
Fish Drier (can. & preserv.)	RES	35	523.687-014
Fish Farmer (fishing & hunt.)	REI	53	446.161-010
Fish Hatchery Worker (fishing & hunt.)	RES	46	446.684-010

DOT to HOC

Title	HOC	Cx	DOT
Fish Packer (can. & preserv.)	REC	40	920.687-086
Fish Roe Processor (can. & preserv.)	RCE	40	522.687-046
Fish Roe Technician (can. & preserv.)	RCS	52	522.384-010
Fish Smoker (can. & preserv.)	REC	42	522.685-066
Fish-Bin Tender (can. & preserv.)	REC	40	529.687-082
Fish-Cake Maker (food prep., n.e.c.)	REI	43	529.685-122
Fish-Egg Packer (can. & preserv.)	REI	39	529.687-086
Fish-Liver Sorter (can. & preserv.; fishing & hunt.)	REI	40	521.687-062
Fish-Machine Feeder (can. & preserv.)	REI	40	521.686-034
Fish-Net Stringer (tex. prod., n.e.c.)	REC	42	782.684-026
Fish-Stringer Assembler (toy-sport equip.)	CRS	41	732.684-054
Fisher, Diving (fishing & hunt.)	RES	47	443.664-010
Fisher, Line (fishing & hunt.)	REC	41	442.684-010
Fisher, Net (fishing & hunt.)	RES	43	441.684-010
Fisher, Pot (fishing & hunt.)	REI	40	441.684-014
Fisher, Spear (fishing & hunt.)	REI	41	443.684-010
Fisher, Terrapin (fishing & hunt.)	REI	38	441.684-018
Fisher, Weir (fishing & hunt.)	RES	43	441.684-022
Fishing Accessories Maker (toy-sport equip.)	RCS	47	619.682-018
Fishing-Line-Winding-Machine Operator (tex. prod., n.e.c.)	REC	40	689.685-066
Fishing-Lure Assembler (toy-sport equip.)	RCE	46	732.684-058
Fishing-Reel Assembler (toy-sport equip.)	CRE	40	732.684-062
Fishing-Rod Assembler (toy-sport equip.)	CRE	41	732.684-066
Fishing-Rod Marker (toy-sport equip.)	CRE	42	732.684-070
Fishing-Tool Technician, Oil Well (petrol. & gas)	RES	63	930.261-010
Fitter (machine shop)	RES	55	801.381-014
Fitter Helper (any industry)	RES	41	801.687-014
Fitter I (any industry)	RIE	58	801.261-014
Fitter II (any industry)	RCE	45	706.684-054
Fitter, Ventilated Rib (ordnance)	RIE	49	736.381-014
Fitter-Placer (rubber goods)	CRE	37	753.687-022
Fittings Finisher (plumbing-heat.)	RCS	49	619.382-014
Fixed-Capital Clerk (utilities)	CRI	58	210.382-042
Fixer, Boarding Room (knitting)	RSI	53	580.380-010
Fixing-Machine Operator (toy-sport equip.)	RCE	41	732.685-018
Fixture Maker (light. fix.)	RES	57	600.380-010
Fixture Repairer-Fabricator (any industry)	RIE	51	630.384-010
Flagger (amuse. & rec.)	ESR	40	372.667-026
Flagger (construction)	RCE	41	372.667-022
Flake Miller, Wheat and Oats (grain-feed mills)	RCE	50	521.682-022
Flake-Cutter Operator (wood prod., n.e.c.)	RCS	47	564.682-014
Flaker Operator (chemical; smelt. & refin.)	REC	43	559.685-074
Flaking-Roll Operator (grain-feed mills)	RES	44	520.685-102
Flame Channeler (construction; mine & quarry)	REI	43	930.684-010
Flame Degreaser (automotive ser.)	REC	37	503.685-022
Flame-Annealing-Machine Setter (heat treating)	RSC	53	504.360-010
Flame-Hardening-Machine Operator (heat treating)	RES	41	504.685-014
Flame-Hardening-Machine Setter (heat treating)	RIS	54	504.380-010

Dictionary of Holland Occupational Codes

Title	HOC	Cx	DOT
Flamer (boot & shoe)	RCS	38	788.684-050
Flanger (hat & cap)	CRE	42	784.684-026
Flanger (inst. & app.)	CRE	42	712.684-018
Flanging-Roll Operator (any industry)	RSE	50	619.362-010
Flare Breaker (boot & shoe)	RCE	37	788.685-010
Flash Ranging Crewmember (military ser.)	CIR	57	378.367-018
Flash-Drier Operator (chemical)	RIE	50	553.462-010
Flash-Drier Operator (grain-feed mills)	RCS	51	529.582-014
Flasher Adjuster (light. fix.)	RCS	38	723.684-022
Flat Clothier (textile)	RSC	50	628.382-010
Flat Drier (tex. prod., n.e.c.)	RCI	45	581.685-078
Flat Polisher (clock & watch)	CRE	41	603.685-054
Flat Surfacer, Jewel (clock & watch)	CRE	44	770.685-010
Flatcar Whacker (saw. & plan.)	RES	41	807.667-010
Flatlock-Sewing-Machine Operator (garment)	RCE	41	786.682-110
Flatware Maker (jewelry-silver.)	RES	50	700.682-010
Flatwork Finisher (laundry & rel.)	REC	38	363.686-010
Flatwork Tier (laundry & rel.)	CRE	43	361.587-010
Flavor Extractor (grain-feed mills)	RCE	42	529.685-126
Flavor Room Worker (dairy products)	REI	49	529.685-130
Flavoring Oil Filterer (beverage)	RCE	42	521.685-382
Fleece Tier (agriculture)	RES	38	410.687-010
Flesher (leather mfg.)	RCS	47	585.681-010
Flexographic-Press Operator (paper goods; print. & pub.)	RIE	48	651.682-010
Flight Attendant, Ramp (air trans.)	ESA	57	352.367-014
Flight Engineer (air trans.)	RIE	66	621.261-018
Flight Operations Specialist (military ser.)	CER	56	248.387-010
Flight-Crew-Time Clerk (air trans.)	CSR	61	215.362-018
Flight-Information Expediter (air trans.)	ERS	58	912.367-010
Flight-Operations Inspector (government ser.)	RIE	71	196.163-010
Flight-Test Data Acquisition Technician (aircraft mfg.)	IRC	65	002.262-010
Flocker (tex. prod., n.e.c.)	REC	40	789.687-054
Floor and Wall Applier, Liquid (construction)	RCS	45	864.684-010
Floor Attendant (amuse. & rec.)	CES	41	343.467-014
Floor Attendant (glass mfg.)	RES	40	579.687-018
Floor Broker (financial)	ESI	64	162.167-034
Floor Layer (construction; retail trade)	RES	53	864.481-010
Floor Service Worker, Spring (automotive ser.)	RSE	40	807.684-022
Floor Supervisor, Endless-Belt-Weaving Department (narrow fabrics)	RES	61	683.130-010
Floor Winder (textile)	RES	45	681.685-050
Floor Worker (sugar & conf.)	RCE	40	920.687-090
Floor Worker (wood prod., n.e.c.)	REC	36	739.687-098
Floor Worker, Well Service (petrol. & gas)	RES	41	930.684-014
Floor-Covering Layer (railroad equip.)	RIS	57	622.381-026
Floor-Layer Apprentice (construction; retail trade)	RES	53	864.481-014
Floor-Space Allocator (tobacco; wholesale tr.)	CSE	50	222.367-030
Floorworker, Lasting (boot & shoe)	REC	41	788.687-046
Floorworker-Distributor (hat & cap)	CRE	40	784.687-030

Title	HOC	Cx	DOT
Floral Designer (retail trade)	ARE	59	142.081-010
Flotation Tender (smelt. & refin.)	CRE	44	511.685-026
Flotation-Tender Helper (smelt. & refin.)	REC	38	511.687-018
Flour Blender (grain-feed mills)	REI	41	520.685-106
Flour Mixer (grain-feed mills)	RCE	45	520.485-010
Flour-Blender Helper (grain-feed mills)	REC	39	520.686-022
Flower Picker (agriculture)	RCE	38	405.687-010
Flower-Machine Operator (tex. prod., n.e.c.)	CRS	44	687.682-010
Flower-Pot-Press Operator (pottery & porc.)	REC	40	575.685-034
Fluid Jet Cutter Operator (aircraft mfg.)	RCS	52	699.382-010
Fluid-Power Mechanic (any industry)	RIE	63	600.281-010
Flumer (grain-feed mills)	REC	36	521.686-038
Flumer I (sugar & conf.)	REC	39	922.665-010
Flumer II (sugar & conf.)	REC	36	521.686-042
Fluoroscope Operator (nonfer. metal)	RCS	53	502.382-014
Flusher (chemical)	RES	47	559.682-026
Flux Mixer (chemical)	RCE	45	550.584-010
Flux-Tube Attendant (nonfer. metal; smelt. & refin.)	RCS	43	519.687-018
Fly Tier (toy-sport equip.)	CRS	42	732.684-074
Flyer (amuse. & rec.; radio-tv broad.)	RSE	41	962.687-018
Flyer Repairer (textile)	CRE	42	628.687-010
Flying-Shear Operator (steel & rel.)	RCS	48	615.682-010
Foam Charger (svc. ind. mach.)	RCE	47	827.585-010
Foam Dispenser (rubber goods)	RCE	41	554.684-014
Foam-Gun Operator (plastic prod.)	REC	46	741.684-014
Foam-Machine Operator (plastic prod.; plastic-synth.)	REI	40	559.685-078
Focuser (light. fix.)	RCE	42	725.687-018
Foiling-Machine Adjuster (ordnance)	REC	50	629.381-010
Foiling-Machine Operator (ordnance)	REC	39	692.685-086
Folder (laundry & rel.)	RES	38	369.687-018
Folder (narrow fabrics)	CRE	41	686.685-030
Folder (tex. prod., n.e.c.)	REC	39	789.687-058
Folder, Hand (boot & shoe)	RCE	38	788.687-050
Folder, Hand (paper goods)	REC	41	794.687-022
Folder, Machine (boot & shoe)	RCE	42	690.685-174
Folder-Seamer, Automatic (any industry)	RCE	42	787.685-014
Folder-Tier (nonmet. min.)	CER	40	759.684-034
Folding-Machine Feeder (paper goods)	REC	40	641.685-050
Folding-Machine Feeder (tex. prod., n.e.c.)	REC	37	920.686-018
Folding-Machine Operator (clerical)	REC	40	208.685-014
Folding-Machine Operator (garment)	REC	40	583.685-042
Folding-Machine Operator (hat & cap)	RCE	39	690.686-034
Folding-Machine Operator (knitting; textile)	REC	41	589.685-058
Folding-Machine Operator (laundry & rel.)	REC	40	369.686-010
Folding-Machine Operator (leather prod.)	CRE	40	690.685-178
Folding-Machine Operator (paper goods)	REI	44	649.685-046
Folding-Machine Operator (print. & pub.)	RES	49	653.382-010
Folding-Machine Operator (textile)	REC	41	689.585-014
Folding-Machine Tender (boot & shoe)	REC	38	788.685-014

Title	HOC	Cx	DOT
Follow-Up Clerk (elec. equip.)	SER	57	221.367-018
Food and Drug Inspector (government ser.)	SAE	66	168.267-042
Food Assembler, Kitchen (hotel & rest.)	CRE	43	319.484-010
Food Checker (hotel & rest.)	CRE	50	211.482-014
Food Mixer (grain-feed mills)	REC	42	520.687-034
Food Order Expediter (hotel & rest.)	ECS	51	319.467-010
Food Technologist (profess. & kin.)	ISR	72	041.081-010
Food Tester (any industry)	ISR	56	029.361-014
Food-and-Beverage Checker (hotel & rest.)	CRE	51	211.482-018
Food-and-Beverage Controller (hotel & rest.)	CSR	55	216.362-022
Food-Management Aide (government ser.)	SCR	51	195.367-022
Food-Service Driver (hotel & rest.)	REI	41	906.683-010
Food-Service Supervisor (hotel & rest.)	ESR	58	319.137-010
Food-Service Worker, Hospital (medical ser.)	RCE	43	319.677-014
Foot Straightener (clock & watch)	RCE	38	715.687-030
Foot Worker (chemical)	REC	38	934.687-010
Foot-Miter Operator (wood prod., n.e.c.)	CRE	41	739.684-066
Force-Variation Equipment Tender (rubber tire)	RES	41	690.685-182
Foreign Banknote Teller-Trader (financial)	CES	62	211.362-014
Foreign Clerk (clerical)	CIS	57	214.467-010
Foreign-Exchange Dealer (financial)	EIC	68	186.117-082
Foreign-Exchange-Position Clerk (financial)	CRE	59	210.367-014
Foreign-Service Officer (government ser.)	ESA	69	188.117-106
Foreign-Student Adviser (education)	SEC	64	090.107-010
Forepart Laster (boot & shoe)	REC	41	690.685-186
Forest Ecologist (profess. & kin.)	IRS	78	040.061-030
Forest Engineer (forestry; logging)	IRE	75	005.167-018
Forest Nursery Supervisor (forestry)	ERS	58	451.137-010
Forest Worker (forestry)	RES	40	452.687-010
Forest-Fire Fighter (forestry)	RES	38	452.687-014
Forest-Products Gatherer (agriculture; forestry)	RES	38	453.687-010
Forester (profess. & kin.)	RIS	70	040.167-010
Forester Aide (forestry)	REI	57	452.364-010
Forge Helper (forging)	RSE	38	619.686-034
Forge-Shop Supervisor (forging)	RES	59	612.131-010
Forge-Shop-Machine Repairer (forging)	RES	58	626.261-010
Forging-Press Operator I (forging)	RIE	50	611.482-010
Forging-Press Operator II (forging)	REI	44	611.685-010
Forging-Roll Operator (forging)	RSC	47	612.682-014
Form Builder (construction)	RIE	56	860.381-046
Form Coverer (fabrication, n.e.c.)	CRE	41	739.684-070
Form Designer (print. & pub.)	RCS	56	970.361-010
Form Maker, Plaster (plastic prod.)	REI	45	777.684-010
Form-Grader Operator (construction)	RIE	46	850.683-022
Form-Tamper Operator (construction)	RSC	40	869.683-010
Formation-Testing Operator (petrol. & gas)	REC	57	930.261-014
Former Helper, Hand (any industry)	RCS	41	619.684-010
Former, Hand (any industry)	RES	56	619.361-010
Forming-Machine Adjuster (glass mfg.)	RIE	55	629.281-026

From the Dictionary of Occupational Titles Occupations to Holland Codes

Title	HOC	Cx	DOT
Forming-Machine Operator (button & notion)	RSE	47	559.665-022
Forming-Machine Operator (glass mfg.)	REI	53	575.382-014
Forming-Machine Tender (glass mfg.)	RES	45	575.685-038
Forming-Machine Upkeep Mechanic (glass mfg.)	RES	57	575.380-010
Forming-Machine Upkeep-Mechanic Helper (glass mfg.)	RES	44	575.687-014
Forming-Process Worker (elec. equip.)	RES	51	590.362-010
Forming-Process-Line Worker (elec. equip.)	RCE	38	727.687-058
Forming-Roll Operator I (any industry)	RIE	48	617.482-014
Forming-Roll Operator II (any industry)	RES	39	619.685-046
Forms Analyst (profess. & kin.)	ESC	63	161.267-018
Formula Clerk (textile)	RCI	54	221.367-090
Formula Weigher (pen & pencil)	REC	47	559.685-082
Formula Weigher (rubber goods)	CRS	42	550.663-010
Formula-Room Worker (dairy products)	CRS	46	520.487-014
Forwarder (print. & pub.)	CRS	39	794.687-026
Foster Parent (domestic ser.)	SEC	45	309.677-014
Foundation Maker (fabrication, n.e.c.)	RES	50	739.384-014
Foundation Maker (hat & cap)	RCE	39	784.684-030
Foundation-Drill Operator (construction)	RIE	47	859.682-014
Foundry Laborer, Coreroom (foundry)	REC	38	518.687-014
Foundry Metallurgist (foundry)	IRE	76	011.061-010
Foundry Supervisor (foundry)	RES	59	519.131-010
Foundry Worker, General (foundry)	RES	40	519.687-022
Fountain Pen Turner (pen & pencil)	RCE	42	690.685-190
Fountain Server (hotel & rest.)	CRE	45	319.474-010
Four-Corner-Stayer-Machine Operator (paper goods)	RCE	40	641.685-054
Four-H Club Agent (education)	ESA	66	096.127-022
Four-Slide-Machine Operator I (any industry)	RIE	56	619.382-018
Four-Slide-Machine Operator II (any industry)	RCE	43	619.685-050
Four-Slide-Machine Setter (any industry)	RIE	56	616.380-010
Fourdrinier-Machine Operator (paper & pulp; paper goods)	REI	53	539.362-014
Foxing Cutter, Hot Knife (boot & shoe; rubber goods)	RCS	38	751.684-022
Foxing Painter (rubber goods)	REC	42	584.685-022
Foxing-Cutting-Machine Operator, Automatic (boot & shoe)	REC	45	690.682-038
Frame Bander (textile)	RCE	42	628.684-014
Frame Carver, Spindle (optical goods)	CRE	43	713.684-030
Frame Changer (textile)	RCE	40	689.686-026
Frame Feeder (chemical)	REC	37	553.686-034
Frame Hand (tex. prod., n.e.c.)	RES	37	689.687-046
Frame Repairer (furniture)	RCI	49	763.681-010
Frame Repairer (glass products)	CRS	43	739.684-074
Frame Repairer (motor-bicycles)	RES	49	807.381-018
Frame Straightener (motor-bicycles)	RIE	49	807.484-010
Frame Stripper (chemical)	RCE	36	559.687-046
Frame Stripper (soap & rel.)	REC	40	559.685-086
Frame Trimmer I (wood prod., n.e.c.)	CRS	38	749.684-030
Frame Trimmer II (wood prod., n.e.c.)	REC	38	769.687-022
Frame Wirer (tel. & tel.)	REC	51	822.684-010

Part 3: From Occupational Titles to Holland Codes
From the Dictionary of Occupational Titles Occupations to Holland Codes

Title	HOC	Cx	DOT
Frame-Table Operator (wood prod., n.e.c.)	RES	47	669.662-014
Frame-Table-Operator Helper (wood prod., n.e.c.)	RES	41	669.685-058
Framer (glass products; wood prod., n.e.c.)	CRE	43	739.684-078
Framer (wood prod., n.e.c.)	REI	42	666.684-010
Frazer (fabrication, n.e.c.)	RES	41	664.685-022
Freezer Operator (dairy products)	RES	49	529.482-010
Freezer Tunnel Operator (can. & preserv.)	RCE	45	523.685-082
Freezing-Machine Operator (pharmaceut.)	REC	46	559.685-090
Freezing-Room Worker (can. & preserv.)	RCE	40	523.687-022
Freight-Car Cleaner, Delta System (r.r. trans.)	REI	40	910.687-022
Freight-Loading Supervisor (r.r. trans.)	SER	56	910.137-026
Freight-Traffic Consultant (business ser.)	ESR	67	184.267-010
Fresh-Work Inspector (tobacco)	REC	43	529.687-090
Fretted-Instrument Inspector (musical inst.)	REI	47	730.684-034
Fretted-Instrument Maker, Hand (musical inst.)	RES	60	730.281-022
Fretted-Instrument Repairer (any industry)	REI	59	730.281-026
Friction-Paint-Machine Tender (fabrication, n.e.c.)	RCE	41	534.685-014
Fringer (carpet & rug; tex. prod., n.e.c.)	RCE	39	789.687-062
Fringing-Machine Operator (knitting)	REC	40	685.686-010
Frit-Mixer-and-Burner (brick & tile; pottery & porc.)	RES	42	579.685-014
Front Maker, Lockstitch (garment)	RCE	41	786.682-114
Front-Edge-Tape Sewer, Lockstitch (garment)	RCE	41	786.682-118
Front-End Loader Operator (any industry)	RCE	42	921.683-042
Front-End Mechanic (automotive ser.)	RCS	54	620.281-038
Front-Sight Attacher (ordnance)	CRE	40	736.684-030
Frothing-Machine Operator (rubber goods)	RCS	51	550.362-010
Frozen Pie Maker (can. & preserv.)	RCE	42	529.684-010
Fruit Coordinator (can. & preserv.)	ESC	57	529.167-010
Fruit Cutter (sugar & conf.)	RCE	38	521.687-066
Fruit Distributor (agriculture)	RCE	40	921.685-046
Fruit-Bar Maker (sugar & conf.)	RCE	40	529.685-134
Fruit-Buying Grader (can. & preserv.; wholesale tr.)	RIE	53	529.387-018
Fruit-Grader Operator (agriculture; wholesale tr.)	CRS	38	529.665-010
Fruit-Press Operator (beverage; can. & preserv.)	REI	37	521.685-146
Fuel Attendant (any industry)	RSE	49	953.362-010
Fuel-House Attendant (saw. & plan.)	REI	40	951.686-010
Fuel-Injection Servicer (any industry)	RIE	56	625.281-022
Fuel-Oil Clerk (clerical)	RCE	55	222.387-018
Fuel-System-Maintenance Supervisor (any industry)	ERI	61	638.131-010
Fuel-System-Maintenance Worker (any industry)	RIE	54	638.381-010
Fuller (textile)	RCS	48	586.682-010
Fulling-Machine Operator (tex. prod., n.e.c.)	REI	50	586.382-010
Fumigator (business ser.)	REI	56	383.361-010
Fumigator and Sterilizer (furniture)	RCE	41	582.685-074
Fun-House Operator (amuse. & rec.)	RES	43	342.665-010
Functional Tester, Typewriters (office machines)	CRS	50	706.382-010
Fund Raiser I (nonprofit org.)	SEC	64	293.157-010
Fund Raiser II (nonprofit org.)	ESA	52	293.357-014
Funeral Attendant (personal ser.)	ESR	42	359.677-014

DOT to HOC

Part 3: From Occupational Titles to Holland Codes

From the Dictionary of Occupational Titles Occupations to Holland Codes

Title	HOC	Cx	DOT
Fur Blender (leather mfg.)	RES	47	783.681-010
Fur Blower (retail trade)	CRS	38	369.685-010
Fur Cleaner (laundry & rel.)	RES	47	362.684-014
Fur Cleaner, Hand (laundry & rel.)	CRS	43	362.684-018
Fur Cleaner, Machine (fur goods; laundry & rel.; retail trade; wholesale tr.)	CRE	44	369.685-014
Fur Cutter (fur goods)	RES	52	783.381-010
Fur Designer (fur goods)	ACS	61	142.081-014
Fur Dresser (leather mfg.)	RES	55	589.361-010
Fur Farmer (agriculture)	REI	58	410.161-014
Fur Finisher (fur goods)	RES	50	783.381-014
Fur Glazer (fur goods)	RES	39	369.684-010
Fur Ironer (laundry & rel.)	CRE	44	369.685-018
Fur Nailer (fur goods)	RSE	48	783.684-014
Fur Plucker (leather mfg.)	CRS	47	585.681-014
Fur Sorter (fur goods)	REI	55	783.384-010
Fur Trimmer (fur goods)	CRE	42	783.687-014
Fur-Blower Operator (hat & cap)	RCE	41	680.685-046
Fur-Cutting-Machine Operator (hat & cap)	CRE	41	585.685-046
Fur-Floor Worker (leather mfg.)	REC	39	589.686-022
Fur-Glazing-and-Polishing-Machine Operator (laundry & rel.)	CRE	41	369.685-022
Fur-Machine Operator (fur goods)	RCE	48	783.682-010
Fur-Machine Operator (garment)	RCE	46	786.682-122
Fur-Repair Inspector (retail trade)	RES	51	783.387-010
Fur-Storage Clerk (retail trade)	RSE	57	369.367-010
Furnace Charger (nonfer. metal; smelt. & refin.; steel & rel.)	RCE	48	512.684-014
Furnace Cleaner (any industry)	REI	40	891.687-014
Furnace Helper (chemical)	RES	39	558.686-010
Furnace Helper (chemical)	REC	40	553.687-014
Furnace Helper (heat treating)	REI	41	504.686-014
Furnace Helper (nonfer. metal; smelt. & refin.)	RCE	40	512.666-010
Furnace Installer (utilities)	RES	56	862.361-010
Furnace Installer-and-Repairer, Hot Air (any industry)	REI	58	869.281-010
Furnace Operator (chemical)	RES	51	558.482-010
Furnace Operator (elec. equip.)	REI	46	543.682-018
Furnace Operator (foundry; steel & rel.)	RSE	50	512.362-018
Furnace Operator (nonfer. metal)	RSE	51	613.462-014
Furnace Operator (nonfer. metal; smelt. & refin.)	RIS	50	512.362-014
Furnace Operator (petrol. refin.)	RES	50	542.562-010
Furnace Operator (smelt. & refin.)	RIE	48	513.462-010
Furnace Tender (foundry; nonfer. metal)	RCS	41	512.685-010
Furnace Worker (elec. equip.)	RCS	42	543.666-010
Furnace-and-Wash-Equipment Operator (ordnance)	RIE	42	503.685-026
Furnace-Combustion Analyst (glass mfg.)	RSI	57	572.360-010
Furnace-Installer-and-Repairer Helper, Hot Air (any industry)	RES	40	869.687-030
Furnace-Stock Inspector (elec. equip.)	REC	51	559.364-010
Furniture Assembler (furniture)	CRS	47	763.684-038
Furniture Assembler-and-Installer (retail trade)	REI	46	739.684-082

Dictionary of Holland Occupational Codes

Title	HOC	Cx	DOT
Furniture Cleaner (laundry & rel.)	RES	42	362.684-022
Furniture Designer (furniture)	AES	66	142.061-022
Furniture Finisher (woodworking)	RSE	52	763.381-010
Furniture Reproducer (furniture)	ISE	62	149.281-010
Furniture Restorer (museums)	RCI	58	763.380-010
Furniture Upholsterer (any industry)	RCS	57	780.381-018
Furniture-Finisher Apprentice (woodworking)	RSE	52	763.381-014
Furniture-Rental Consultant (retail trade)	SER	51	295.357-018
Furniture-Upholsterer Apprentice (any industry)	RIE	57	780.381-022
Furrier (fur goods)	REI	62	783.261-010
Fuse Assembler (ordnance)	CRS	46	737.684-022
Fuse Maker (chemical)	RES	42	559.685-094
Fuse-Cup Expander (ordnance)	RCE	39	694.685-022
Fusing-Furnace Loader (optical goods)	RCE	40	573.686-014
Fusing-Machine Feeder (garment)	CRE	36	583.686-014
Fusing-Machine Tender (garment; knitting)	REC	39	583.685-046
Galley Stripper (print. & pub.)	REC	51	973.681-010
Gambling Dealer (amuse. & rec.)	CSE	53	343.464-010
Gambling Monitor (amuse. & rec.)	RCE	57	343.367-014
Gambreler (meat products)	RES	37	525.687-030
Gambreler Helper (meat products)	RES	37	525.687-034
Game Attendant (amuse. & rec.)	ESR	52	342.657-014
Game-Bird Farmer (agriculture)	REI	58	412.161-010
Game-Farm Helper (agriculture)	RCE	45	412.684-010
Gamekeeper (agriculture)	RSE	55	169.171-010
Gamma-Facilities Operator (profess. & kin.)	RSE	60	015.362-014
Gang Sawyer (saw. & plan.)	RCE	46	667.682-030
Gang Sawyer, Stone (stonework)	RCE	48	670.362-010
Garage Servicer, Industrial (any industry)	REC	42	915.687-014
Garbage Collector (motor trans.)	RES	36	955.687-022
Garbage Collector Driver (motor trans.)	RIE	44	905.663-010
Garbage-Collection Supervisor (motor trans.)	ESA	56	909.137-014
Garde Manger (hotel & rest.)	RSE	50	313.361-034
Garden Worker (agriculture; museums)	RCI	48	406.684-018
Gardener, Special Effects and Instruction Models (motion picture; museums)	RIS	54	406.381-010
Garland-Machine Operator (fabrication, n.e.c.)	REC	40	692.685-090
Garment Fitter (retail trade)	RCE	52	785.361-014
Garment Folder (garment; knitting)	RCE	39	789.687-066
Garment Inspector (any industry)	CRE	42	789.687-070
Garment Sorter (garment)	RCS	39	222.687-014
Garment Steamer (knitting)	REC	40	582.685-078
Garment Turner (garment; knitting)	REC	37	789.687-074
Garment-Alteration Examiner (retail trade)	CSR	44	789.687-078
Garnett-Machine Operator (textile)	RCE	41	680.685-050
Garnetter (furniture; tex. prod., n.e.c.)	RCE	43	680.685-054
Garnisher (sugar & conf.)	RCE	36	524.687-014
Gas Charger (svc. ind. mach.)	REC	47	827.485-010
Gas Dispatcher (pipe lines; utilities)	ERS	63	953.167-010

DOT to HOC

Title	HOC	Cx	DOT
Gas Inspector (utilities)	ESR	68	168.264-018
Gas Treater (any industry)	REC	50	546.385-010
Gas Usage Meter Clerk (petrol. refin.; pipe lines; utilities)	CRS	49	216.685-010
Gas-and-Oil Servicer (motor trans.)	REC	41	915.587-010
Gas-Appliance Servicer (any industry)	RIE	58	637.261-018
Gas-Appliance-Servicer Helper (any industry)	REI	45	637.684-010
Gas-Check-Pad Maker (ordnance)	RCS	47	736.684-034
Gas-Compressor Operator (any industry)	RSE	57	950.382-014
Gas-Distribution-and-Emergency Clerk (utilities)	CSE	57	249.367-042
Gas-Engine Operator (any industry)	REI	53	950.382-018
Gas-Engine Repairer (any industry)	REI	56	625.281-026
Gas-Leak Inspector (pipe lines; utilities)	RES	51	953.367-010
Gas-Leak Inspector Helper (pipe lines; utilities)	RES	47	953.667-010
Gas-Leak Tester (svc. ind. mach.)	RCE	41	827.584-014
Gas-Main Fitter (utilities)	RIE	56	862.361-014
Gas-Mask Assembler (protective dev.)	REC	43	712.684-022
Gas-Mask Inspector (protective dev.)	RES	47	712.687-022
Gas-Meter Checker (utilities)	RSE	49	953.367-014
Gas-Meter Installer (utilities)	RES	53	953.364-010
Gas-Meter Mechanic I (utilities)	REC	55	710.381-022
Gas-Meter Mechanic II (utilities)	CRE	41	710.684-026
Gas-Meter Prover (utilities)	RES	57	710.281-022
Gas-Meter-Installer Helper (utilities)	REC	41	953.687-010
Gas-Pumping-Station Helper (utilities)	RES	42	953.684-010
Gas-Pumping-Station Operator (utilities)	REC	54	953.382-010
Gas-Pumping-Station Supervisor (utilities)	ERS	59	953.137-010
Gas-Regulator Repairer (petrol. refin.; pipe lines; utilities)	RIE	57	710.381-026
Gas-Regulator-Repairer Helper (petrol. refin.; pipe lines; utilities)	REC	49	710.384-010
Gas-Transfer Operator (chemical)	CRE	43	914.585-010
Gas-Welding-Equipment Mechanic (any industry)	RES	56	626.381-014
Gasket Inspector (nonmet. min.)	CRE	38	739.687-102
Gasket Supervisor (wood prod., n.e.c.)	RES	58	569.130-010
Gasser (textile)	CRS	41	585.685-050
Gate Agent (air trans.)	ERS	51	238.367-010
Gate Guard (any industry)	CES	48	372.667-030
Gatherer (glass mfg.)	RSC	43	575.684-026
Gauge Operator (fabrication, n.e.c.)	RCS	44	692.682-042
Gauge-and-Weigh-Machine Adjuster (ordnance)	RCS	50	632.360-010
Gauge-and-Weigh-Machine Operator (ordnance)	CRE	42	737.685-010
Gauger (beverage)	REC	53	529.387-022
Gauger (clock & watch)	CRE	47	715.687-034
Gauger (petrol. & gas; petrol. refin.; pipe lines)	RCE	56	914.384-010
Gauger (protective dev.)	CRE	41	712.687-018
Gauger, Chief (petrol. & gas; petrol. refin.; pipe lines)	RES	62	914.134-010
Gear Hobber Set-up Operator (machine shop)	RIE	55	602.382-010
Gear Inspector (machine shop)	RIE	57	602.362-010
Gear Repairer (water trans.)	RIE	54	623.381-010
Gear-Cutting-Machine Operator, Production (machine shop)	RCE	43	602.685-010

DOT to HOC

Title	HOC	Cx	DOT
Gear-Cutting-Machine Set-up Operator (machine shop)	RIE	57	602.380-010
Gear-Cutting-Machine Set-up Operator, Tool (machine shop)	RIE	59	602.280-010
Gear-Generator Set-up Operator, Spiral Bevel (machine shop)	RIE	55	602.382-014
Gear-Generator Set-up Operator, Straight Bevel (machine shop)	RIE	55	602.382-018
Gear-Lapping-Machine Operator (machine shop)	RIE	54	602.482-010
Gear-Milling-Machine Set-up Operator (machine shop)	RIE	55	602.382-022
Gear-Shaper Set-up Operator (machine shop)	RIE	55	602.382-026
Gear-Shaver Set-up Operator (machine shop)	RIE	56	602.382-030
Gear-Sorting-and-Inspecting Machine Operator (machine shop)	REC	50	602.362-014
Gelatin Maker, Utility (chemical)	RES	50	529.382-022
Gelatin-Dynamite-Packing Operator (chemical)	RSE	48	692.662-014
Gem Cutter (jewelry-silver.)	RES	56	770.281-014
Gemologist (jewelry-silver.)	REI	63	199.281-010
Genealogist (profess. & kin.)	ESC	65	052.067-018
General Agent, Operations (air trans.; motor trans.; r.r. trans.)	ESC	66	184.167-042
General Car Supervisor, Yard (r.r. trans.)	ECS	57	184.167-286
General Claims Agent (air trans.; motor trans.; r.r. trans.; water trans.)	SER	65	186.117-030
General Helper (food prep., n.e.c.)	REC	39	522.686-014
General Helper (oils & grease)	REC	37	529.687-094
General Helper (sugar & conf.)	REC	39	529.686-046
General Manager, Farm (agriculture; wholesale tr.)	ESR	68	180.167-018
General Manager, Road Production (amuse. & rec.)	SER	64	187.117-034
General Practitioner (medical ser.)	ISE	76	070.101-022
General Superintendent, Milling (grain-feed mills)	ESR	66	183.167-014
General Supervisor (any industry)	REI	66	183.167-018
General Supervisor (beverage)	ESR	62	183.167-022
General Worker, Lithographic (print. & pub.)	RSE	42	979.687-034
General-Handling Supervisor (smelt. & refin.)	ERS	59	929.137-010
General-Ledger Bookkeeper (clerical)	CRS	59	210.382-046
Geneticist (profess. & kin.)	IRS	78	041.061-050
Geodesist (profess. & kin.)	IRE	80	024.061-014
Geodetic Computator (profess. & kin.)	IER	66	018.167-014
Geographer (profess. & kin.)	IRE	77	029.067-010
Geographer, Physical (profess. & kin.)	IRE	77	029.067-014
Geological Aide (petrol. & gas)	IRE	71	024.267-010
Geologist (profess. & kin.)	IRE	80	024.061-018
Geologist, Petroleum (petrol. & gas)	RIE	77	024.061-022
Geophysical Prospector (petrol. & gas)	IER	80	024.061-026
Geophysical-Laboratory Chief (profess. & kin.)	IRE	80	024.167-010
Geophysicist (profess. & kin.)	IRS	77	024.061-030
Germination Worker (beverage)	REC	48	522.585-014
Getterer (light. fix.)	RCE	39	725.687-022
Gettering-Filament-Machine Operator (light. fix.)	RCE	44	509.685-026
Gift Wrapper (retail trade)	RCS	45	299.364-014

DOT to HOC

Title	HOC	Cx	DOT
Gig Tender (textile)	CRE	41	585.685-054
Gilder (any industry)	RSE	48	749.381-010
Gill-Box Tender (textile)	RES	41	680.685-058
Gin Clerk (agriculture)	CSE	51	221.467-010
Ginner (agriculture)	CRE	45	429.685-010
Girdler (jewelry-silver.)	RCS	52	770.261-014
Glass Bender (fabrication, n.e.c.)	REI	56	772.381-010
Glass Blower (glass mfg.)	RCS	50	772.381-022
Glass Blower, Laboratory Apparatus (glass products; inst. & app.)	RCA	58	772.281-010
Glass Calibrator (glass products)	RCE	50	775.584-010
Glass Checker (optical goods)	RCE	40	716.687-014
Glass Cut-Off Tender (glass mfg.)	RCS	42	677.685-030
Glass Cutter (any industry)	RCS	44	775.684-022
Glass Cutter, Hand (optical goods)	REI	48	716.681-014
Glass Cutter, Oval or Circular (glass mfg.)	RCS	42	779.684-022
Glass Decorator (glass mfg.; glass products)	RAE	55	775.381-014
Glass Driller (glass mfg.)	CRS	41	775.687-014
Glass Finisher (glass products)	RSC	47	775.684-026
Glass Grinder (glass mfg.)	CRS	41	775.684-034
Glass Grinder (glass products)	RSC	48	775.684-030
Glass Grinder, Laboratory Apparatus (glass products; inst. & app.)	REI	50	775.382-010
Glass Inspector (any industry)	CER	42	579.687-022
Glass Installer (automotive ser.)	RCE	45	865.684-010
Glass Installer (woodworking)	RCS	44	865.684-014
Glass Polisher (glass mfg.)	RCE	42	775.684-038
Glass Sander, Belt (glass products)	REC	40	775.684-042
Glass Tinter (glass products)	REC	45	840.684-010
Glass-Blowing-Lathe Operator (glass products)	RCE	54	772.482-010
Glass-Bulb Silverer (glass products)	RCE	37	779.687-018
Glass-Bulb-Machine Adjuster (glass mfg.)	RSI	53	575.360-010
Glass-Bulb-Machine Former, Tubular Stock (glass mfg.)	RSE	50	575.382-018
Glass-Cleaning-Machine Tender (glass products)	RCE	41	579.685-018
Glass-Cut-Off Supervisor (glass mfg.)	RSE	61	677.131-010
Glass-Cutter Helper (any industry)	RSC	42	775.687-018
Glass-Cutting-Machine Feeder (glass products)	RCI	37	677.686-014
Glass-Cutting-Machine Operator, Automatic (glass mfg.)	CRS	47	677.562-010
Glass-Furnace Tender (paint & varnish)	RCE	40	572.685-010
Glass-Lathe Operator (electron. comp.)	RCS	50	674.382-010
Glass-Lined Tank Repairer (beverage)	REC	45	779.684-026
Glass-Ribbon-Machine Operator (glass mfg.)	RSE	56	575.362-014
Glass-Ribbon-Machine-Operator Assistant (glass mfg.)	RES	51	575.365-010
Glass-Rolling-Machine Operator (glass mfg.)	REI	53	575.382-022
Glass-Unloading-Equipment Tender (glass mfg.)	REC	40	677.665-010
Glass-Vial-Bending-Conveyor Feeder (cutlery-hrdwr.)	RCE	40	573.686-018
Glass-Wool-Blanket-Machine Feeder (glass products)	RCE	41	579.685-022
Glass-Worker, Pressed or Blown (glass mfg.)	CRS	41	772.687-010
Glaze Handler (brick & tile)	RES	41	571.685-014

From the Dictionary of Occupational Titles Occupations to Holland Codes

Title	HOC	Cx	DOT
Glaze Maker (brick & tile; pottery & porc.)	RSE	45	570.685-098
Glaze Supervisor (brick & tile)	REI	56	574.130-010
Glaze Supervisor (pottery & porc.)	RES	58	574.132-010
Glazier (construction)	RSE	50	865.381-010
Glazier (inst. & app.)	CRE	40	712.684-026
Glazier Apprentice (construction)	RSE	50	865.381-014
Glazier Supervisor (construction)	RCE	59	865.131-010
Glazier, Metal Furniture (furniture)	RCE	48	865.684-018
Glazier, Stained Glass (glass products)	ARI	56	779.381-010
Glazing Operator, Black Powder (chemical)	RSE	44	550.686-022
Glazing-Machine Operator (glass mfg.)	CRE	40	573.685-018
Globe Mounter (print. & pub.)	RSE	41	795.684-018
Glove Cleaner, Hand (laundry & rel.)	REC	41	362.687-010
Glove Former (glove & mit.; laundry & rel.)	REC	39	363.687-010
Glove Pairer (glove & mit.)	REC	40	784.687-034
Glove Printer (glove & mit.)	RCE	41	652.685-034
Glove Sewer (glove & mit.)	CRS	45	784.682-010
Glove Turner (glove & mit.)	REC	41	784.687-038
Glove Turner and Former, Automatic (glove & mit.)	REC	39	583.686-018
Glove-Parts Inspector (glove & mit.)	SRE	45	781.687-034
Glucose-and-Syrup Weigher (sugar & conf.)	RCE	39	520.686-026
Glue Maker, Bone (chemical)	REI	49	559.382-022
Glue Mixer (any industry)	RCE	44	550.685-062
Glue Spreader, Veneer (millwork-plywood; wood prod., n.e.c.)	CRE	41	569.685-042
Glue-Machine Operator (pen & pencil)	RCE	40	692.685-094
Glue-Mill Operator (chemical)	RES	42	559.685-098
Glue-Size-Machine Operator (furniture)	RCE	42	562.685-010
Glue-Spreading-Machine Operator (leather prod.)	REC	40	584.665-014
Glued Wood Tester (woodworking)	RES	58	762.384-010
Gluer (any industry)	RCE	37	795.687-014
Gluer (woodworking)	RES	43	762.687-034
Gluer and Slicer, Hand (paper goods)	RES	40	794.687-030
Gluer, Wet Suit (plastic prod.)	CRE	40	795.687-018
Gluer-and-Wedger (woodworking)	RCE	38	762.687-038
Gluing-Machine Feeder (woodworking)	RCI	38	569.686-038
Gluing-Machine Offbearer (woodworking)	RES	38	569.686-022
Gluing-Machine Operator (rubber goods)	CRE	39	692.685-098
Gluing-Machine Operator (woodworking)	REC	43	569.685-046
Gluing-Machine Operator, Automatic (print. & pub.)	RCE	48	641.682-014
Gluing-Machine Operator, Electronic (woodworking)	RCE	42	569.685-050
Gluten-Settling Tender (grain-feed mills)	REC	37	521.685-150
Goat Herder (agriculture)	REC	39	410.687-014
Gold Burnisher (pottery & porc.)	REC	40	775.687-022
Gold Cutter (metal prod., n.e.c.)	CRE	45	700.684-038
Gold Reclaimer (metal prod., n.e.c.)	RCS	42	709.685-010
Gold-Nib Grinder (pen & pencil)	CRS	41	705.682-010
Goldbeater (metal prod., n.e.c.)	RSE	50	700.381-018
Golf-Ball Trimmer (toy-sport equip.)	CRE	41	732.587-010

Title	HOC	Cx	DOT
Golf-Ball-Cover Treater (toy-sport equip.)	RCS	42	559.685-102
Golf-Club Assembler (toy-sport equip.)	CRS	41	732.684-078
Golf-Club Facer (toy-sport equip.)	RES	46	761.684-010
Golf-Club Head Former (toy-sport equip.)	RES	52	732.381-018
Golf-Club Repairer (toy-sport equip.)	RES	52	732.381-022
Golf-Club Weigher (toy-sport equip.)	RCS	42	732.587-014
Golf-Club Weighter (toy-sport equip.)	CRS	40	732.687-026
Golf-Course Ranger (amuse. & rec.)	ESC	49	379.667-010
Golf-Range Attendant (amuse. & rec.)	RCS	39	341.683-010
Golf-Shoe-Spike Assembler (boot & shoe)	RCE	38	788.687-054
Goods Layer (textile)	RES	40	781.687-038
Goodwill Ambassador (business ser.)	ESC	50	293.357-018
Governor Assembler, Hydraulic (elec. equip.)	RIE	56	721.381-018
Grade Checker (construction)	REA	50	850.467-010
Grader (can. & preserv.)	ESC	42	529.687-098
Grader (woodworking)	RCI	48	669.687-030
Grader Marker (garment)	RCI	53	781.381-034
Grader Tender (agriculture)	RCE	41	521.685-154
Grader, Dressed Poultry (meat products)	CER	42	529.687-102
Grader, Green Meat (meat products)	REC	44	529.687-106
Grader, Meat (meat products)	RES	48	525.387-010
Grading Clerk (education)	CSE	54	219.467-010
Graduate Assistant (education)	SAE	69	090.227-014
Grain Drier (beverage)	RES	42	523.685-086
Grain Elevator Clerk (beverage; grain-feed mills)	CES	51	222.567-010
Grain Mixer (grain-feed mills)	CER	43	520.485-014
Grain Picker (grain-feed mills)	CRE	42	529.687-110
Grain Receiver (grain-feed mills)	ECR	47	921.365-010
Grain-Drier Operator (grain-feed mills)	REC	43	523.685-090
Grain-Wafer-Machine Operator (bakery products)	RES	42	523.685-094
Grainer, Machine (any industry)	REC	42	652.686-014
Graining-Press Operator (chemical)	RES	41	557.682-010
Grant Coordinator (profess. & kin.)	SEI	71	169.117-014
Granulating-Machine Operator (tobacco)	REC	40	521.685-158
Granulator Operator (sugar & conf.)	REC	41	523.685-098
Granulator Tender (steel & rel.)	RCS	41	519.665-010
Granulator-Machine Operator (pharmaceut.)	RIE	51	559.382-026
Graphic Designer (profess. & kin.)	AER	65	141.061-018
Graphite Pan-Drier Tender (nonmet. min.)	REC	44	549.685-014
Graphologist (profess. & kin.)	ACS	56	199.267-038
Grated-Cheese Maker (dairy products)	RCE	43	521.685-162
Gravel Inspector (construction)	RCI	57	859.281-010
Graves Registration Specialist (military ser.)	RES	43	355.687-014
Gray-Cloth Tender, Printing (textile)	REC	40	652.686-018
Grease Buffer (jewelry-silver.)	RCS	45	705.684-022
Grease Maker (petrol. refin.)	REI	52	549.682-010
Grease Maker, Head (petrol. refin.)	RES	62	549.132-010
Grease-and-Tallow Pumper (oils & grease)	RCE	41	559.585-014
Grease-Refiner Operator (oils & grease)	REC	39	551.685-086

Part 3: From Occupational Titles to Holland Codes

From the Dictionary of Occupational Titles Occupations to Holland Codes

Title	HOC	Cx	DOT
Greaser (agric. equip.)	RCS	42	624.684-010
Greaser (ordnance)	REC	37	736.687-010
Greaser Operator (hat & cap)	REC	41	582.685-082
Green Inspector (elec. equip.)	REC	52	726.367-010
Green-Chain Offbearer (millwork-plywood)	REI	40	663.686-018
Green-Coffee Blender (food prep., n.e.c.)	REC	41	520.685-110
Green-Tire Inspector (rubber tire)	RCE	47	750.684-018
Greens Tier (wholesale tr.)	REC	38	920.687-094
Greenskeeper I (any industry)	RES	58	406.137-010
Greenskeeper II (any industry)	RCE	42	406.683-010
Greige-Goods Marker (textile)	RCE	42	229.587-010
Grinder (plastic prod.; plastic-synth.)	REI	38	555.685-026
Grinder (rubber goods; rubber reclaim.)	RCS	41	555.685-030
Grinder I (any industry)	RCE	42	705.684-026
Grinder I (clock & watch)	RCE	50	603.482-030
Grinder II (clock & watch)	CRE	41	715.685-030
Grinder Machine Setter (machine shop)	RIE	57	603.380-010
Grinder Operator (chemical)	REC	42	555.685-034
Grinder Operator (grain-feed mills)	RSE	49	521.682-026
Grinder Operator (grain-feed mills)	CRE	42	521.685-166
Grinder Operator, Automatic (cutlery-hrdwr.)	CRS	38	603.685-058
Grinder Operator, External, Tool (machine shop)	RIE	58	603.280-010
Grinder Operator, Surface, Tool (machine shop)	RIE	58	603.280-014
Grinder Operator, Tool (machine shop)	RIE	59	603.280-018
Grinder Set-up Operator (machine shop)	RIE	56	603.382-034
Grinder Set-up Operator, Centerless (machine shop)	RES	51	603.382-014
Grinder Set-up Operator, Gear, Tool (machine shop)	RIE	57	602.360-010
Grinder Set-up Operator, Internal (machine shop)	RIE	58	603.280-022
Grinder Set-up Operator, Jig (machine shop)	RIE	59	603.280-026
Grinder Set-up Operator, Thread Tooi (machine shop)	RIC	59	603.260-010
Grinder Set-up Operator, Universal (machine shop)	RIE	59	603.280-030
Grinder, Carbon Plant (smelt. & refin.)	RCS	46	544.565-010
Grinder, Gear (machine shop)	REI	53	602.382-034
Grinder, Hand (button & notion)	RCE	37	734.687-054
Grinder, Hand (optical goods)	CRE	42	716.685-018
Grinder, Hardboard (wood prod., n.e.c.)	REI	53	569.682-010
Grinder, Lap (clock & watch)	CRE	41	603.685-066
Grinder-Chipper I (any industry)	REI	47	705.684-030
Grinder-Chipper II (any industry)	RES	42	809.684-026
Grinder-Mill Operator (smelt. & refin.)	REC	46	519.485-010
Grinding Machine Tender (machine shop)	RCE	44	603.685-062
Grinding-Machine Operator, Automatic (button & notion)	REC	41	690.685-194
Grinding-Machine Operator, Portable (r.r. trans.)	RCE	43	910.684-010
Grinding-Mill Operator (mine & quarry; smelt. & refin.)	RCE	53	515.382-010
Grinding-Wheel Inspector (nonmet. min.)	REI	48	776.487-010
Grip (amuse. & rec.; radio-tv broad.)	RES	47	962.684-014
Grip (motion picture; radio-tv broad.)	RES	47	962.687-022
Grip Assembler (woodworking)	RCS	47	762.684-042
Grip Boss (motion picture)	ESR	60	962.137-010

Title	HOC	Cx	DOT
Grip Wrapper (toy-sport equip.)	RCE	41	732.684-082
Grizzly Worker (mine & quarry; smelt. & refin.)	RES	37	933.687-010
Groover (any industry)	RCS	37	692.686-042
Groover (nonmet. min.)	CRS	40	673.685-062
Groover and Turner (boot & shoe)	RCE	41	690.685-198
Groover-and-Striper Operator (wood prod., n.e.c.)	RCI	42	669.685-102
Grooving-Lathe Tender (plastic prod.)	RCE	41	690.685-202
Grooving-Machine Operator (pen & pencil)	CRE	40	733.685-018
Ground Layer (pottery & porc.)	RCE	41	574.684-010
Ground Mixer (chemical)	RES	40	550.685-066
Groundskeeper, Industrial-Commercial (any industry)	RCE	42	406.684-014
Group Leader (agriculture)	ESR	54	180.167-022
Group Leader, Printed Circuit Board Assembly (electron. comp.)	RCE	54	726.361-014
Group Leader, Printed Circuit Board Quality Control (electron. comp.)	RSE	56	726.361-018
Group Leader, Semiconductor Processing (electron. comp.)	RCE	56	590.362-018
Group Leader, Semiconductor Testing (electron. comp.)	ERC	56	726.362-010
Group Worker (social ser.)	ESI	67	195.164-010
Group-Sales Representative (amuse. & rec.)	ESC	54	259.357-010
Grout-Machine Tender (smelt. & refin.)	RCE	40	519.685-014
Growth-Media Mixer, Mushroom (agriculture)	RIE	46	405.683-014
Guard, Chief (any industry)	ESR	54	372.167-014
Guard, Immigration (government ser.)	ESR	50	372.567-014
Guard, School-Crossing (government ser.)	ESC	45	371.567-010
Guard, Security (any industry)	SEC	46	372.667-034
Guide (personal ser.)	ESC	48	353.367-010
Guide Setter (steel & rel.)	RSI	52	613.361-010
Guide Winder (toy-sport equip.)	CRS	43	732.684-086
Guide, Alpine (personal ser.)	REI	62	353.164-010
Guide, Chief Airport (air trans.)	SER	60	353.137-010
Guide, Establishment (any industry)	ESA	50	353.367-014
Guide, Hunting and Fishing (amuse. & rec.)	RES	59	353.161-010
Guide, Plant (any industry)	ESC	51	353.367-018
Guide, Sightseeing (amuse. & rec.; personal ser.)	ESC	51	353.363-010
Guide, Travel (personal ser.)	ESC	63	353.167-010
Guide-Base Winder, Machine (toy-sport equip.)	CRE	40	732.685-022
Guider (fabrication, n.e.c.)	RCS	39	590.686-014
Gum Puller (sugar & conf.)	RES	40	520.687-038
Gum-Scoring-Machine Operator (sugar & conf.)	RIE	44	520.682-022
Gun Examiner (ordnance)	RIS	56	736.281-010
Gun Synchronizer (ordnance)	RCS	50	632.381-010
Gun-Perforator Loader (petrol. & gas)	RSE	49	931.384-010
Gun-Repair Clerk (ordnance)	RES	51	222.387-022
Gunner (grain-feed mills)	REC	46	523.382-010
Gunsmith (any industry)	RIE	61	632.281-010
Gunsmith, Ballistics Laboratory (ordnance)	RIS	61	609.260-010
Gynecologist (medical ser.)	IRS	76	070.101-034
Hacker (brick & tile)	REC	39	573.686-022

Title	HOC	Cx	DOT
Hackler, Doll Wigs (toy-sport equip.)	RCE	38	731.687-018
Hair Clipper, Power (leather mfg.)	REI	38	789.684-022
Hair Preparer (fabrication, n.e.c.)	RES	48	739.384-018
Hair Stylist (personal ser.)	SER	56	332.271-018
Hair Worker (fabrication, n.e.c.)	CRE	42	739.684-086
Hair-Boiler Operator (leather mfg.)	RES	41	582.685-086
Hair-Sample Matcher (fabrication, n.e.c.)	CES	48	739.387-014
Hair-Spinning-Machine Operator (leather mfg.)	REI	38	689.686-030
Hairspring Adjuster (clock & watch)	RCE	45	715.684-102
Hairspring Assembler (clock & watch)	RES	48	715.381-054
Hairspring Cutter I (clock & watch)	CRE	40	715.687-038
Hairspring Cutter II (clock & watch)	RCE	41	715.687-042
Hairspring Truer (clock & watch)	RES	50	715.381-058
Hairspring Vibrator (clock & watch)	RES	50	715.381-062
Ham-Rolling-Machine Operator (meat products)	REC	35	529.685-138
Hammer Adjuster (clock & watch)	REC	36	715.687-046
Hammer Operator (aircraft mfg.)	RCS	49	617.382-014
Hammer-Mill Operator (nonmet. min.)	REC	41	570.685-030
Hammer-Mill Operator (smelt. & refin.)	REC	41	515.687-010
Hammersmith (jewelry-silver.)	RES	50	700.381-022
Hand Filer, Balance Wheel (clock & watch)	CRS	42	715.684-106
Hand Sewer, Shoes (boot & shoe)	CRE	38	788.684-054
Hand Stamper (any industry)	RCS	44	709.684-042
Handbag Framer (leather prod.)	RCE	40	739.684-090
Hander-In (narrow fabrics; textile)	RCE	40	683.687-018
Handicapper, Harness Racing (amuse. & rec.)	ESI	56	219.267-010
Handkerchief Folder (garment)	RCE	40	920.687-098
Handle Assembler (woodworking)	RES	38	762.687-042
Handle Maker (pottery & porc.)	REI	41	575.684-030
Handle-and-Vent-Machine Operator (furniture)	RCE	40	686.685-034
Handle-Machine Operator (paper goods)	RES	41	649.685-050
Handler (pottery & porc.)	REC	45	774.684-022
Hands Assembler (clock & watch)	CRS	45	715.684-110
Harbor Master (government ser.)	ESR	65	375.167-026
Hardener (clock & watch)	RIE	57	504.382-010
Hardener (hat & cap)	REC	44	784.684-034
Hardener Helper (clock & watch)	RES	37	504.686-018
Hardening-Machine Operator (hat & cap)	REC	42	586.685-026
Hardness Inspector (heat treating)	REI	51	504.387-010
Hardness Tester (mine & quarry)	REC	48	519.585-010
Hardware Assembler (furniture)	CRS	41	763.684-042
Hardware Assembler (wood. container)	RCE	38	762.687-046
Hardware Assembler (woodworking)	RES	38	762.684-046
Harness Builder (textile)	RSI	50	683.380-010
Harness Cleaner (textile)	REC	37	699.687-010
Harness Maker (leather prod.; retail trade)	RES	53	783.381-018
Harness Placer (textile)	RCS	45	683.680-010
Harness Puller (textile)	REI	47	683.684-018
Harness Rigger (tex. prod., n.e.c.)	CRE	43	789.687-082

DOT to HOC

DOT to HOC

Title	HOC	Cx	DOT
Harness-and-Bag Inspector (tex. prod., n.e.c.)	RES	41	789.687-086
Harp Maker (musical inst.)	RSE	60	730.281-030
Harp Regulator (musical inst.)	RSE	49	730.381-026
Harp-Action Assembler (musical inst.)	RIE	54	730.381-030
Harpsichord Maker (musical inst.)	RIE	59	730.281-034
Harvest Contractor (agriculture)	ERS	61	409.117-010
Harvest Worker, Field Crop (agriculture)	REC	36	404.687-014
Harvest Worker, Fruit (agriculture)	RCS	37	403.687-018
Harvest Worker, Vegetable (agriculture)	RCE	36	402.687-014
Harvester Operator (chemical)	RCE	43	930.683-022
Hasher Operator (meat products)	REI	38	521.685-170
Hassock Maker (tex. prod., n.e.c.)	RES	37	780.687-018
Hat Blocker (laundry & rel.)	REC	44	363.684-014
Hat Braider (hat & cap)	CRE	41	784.684-038
Hat Conditioner (hat & cap)	RCI	37	784.687-086
Hat Finisher (hat & cap)	CRE	44	589.685-062
Hat Maker (hat & cap)	RSE	46	784.684-042
Hat Trimmer (laundry & rel.)	CRE	48	782.381-010
Hat-and-Cap Sewer (hat & cap)	CRE	42	784.682-014
Hat-Block Maker (woodworking)	REI	53	661.381-010
Hat-Blocking-Machine Operator I (hat & cap)	REC	41	580.685-026
Hat-Blocking-Machine Operator II (hat & cap)	REC	39	580.685-030
Hat-Body Sorter (hat & cap)	CSR	42	784.587-010
Hat-Finishing-Materials Preparer (hat & cap)	RCE	47	559.684-030
Hat-Forming-Machine Feeder (hat & cap)	CRS	41	586.686-018
Hat-Forming-Machine Operator (hat & cap)	REI	44	586.685-030
Hat-Lining Blocker (hat & cap)	RCE	40	583.685-050
Hat-Stock-Laminating-Machine Operator (hat & cap)	RES	42	584.685-026
Hatch Tender (water trans.)	RES	40	911.667-014
Hatter (laundry & rel.)	RES	47	369.384-010
Hay Sorter (toy-sport equip.)	REC	36	732.686-010
Hazardous-Waste Management Specialist (government ser.)	IRE	67	168.267-086
Head Coach (amuse. & rec.)	ESR	67	153.117-010
Head Doffer (textile)	ECR	51	689.366-010
Head Inspector (wood. container)	REI	53	764.387-010
Head Operator, Sulfide (chemical)	ERS	59	559.132-026
Head Sawyer (saw. & plan.)	RIE	47	667.662-010
Head Sawyer, Automatic (paper & pulp; saw. & plan.)	REI	49	667.682-034
Head Trimmer (meat products)	REI	41	525.684-034
Head-Bander-and-Liner Operator (print. & pub.)	RCE	44	653.682-018
Head-Gauge-Unit Operator (ordnance)	RCS	37	619.685-054
Head-Machine Feeder (meat products)	RES	38	525.686-018
Head-Saw Operator, Insulation Board (wood prod., n.e.c.)	REC	49	677.682-010
Header (water trans.)	ESR	57	911.137-018
Header (wood prod., n.e.c.)	RIE	49	665.682-014
Header (wood. container)	RES	40	764.687-058
Heading Matcher and Assembler (wood. container)	CRE	43	764.687-062
Heading Repairer (wood. container)	CRE	41	764.687-066
Heading-Machine Operator (pen & pencil)	RCE	38	669.685-062

Title	HOC	Cx	DOT
Heading-Saw Operator (saw. & plan.)	RCE	44	667.682-038
Headwaiter/Headwaitress (water trans.)	ESR	56	350.137-010
Health Officer, Field (government ser.)	ESI	65	168.167-018
Health Physicist (profess. & kin.)	IRE	76	015.021-010
Health-Equipment Servicer (medical ser.)	RCI	52	359.363-010
Hearing Aid Specialist (retail trade)	ESR	58	276.354-010
Hearing Officer (government ser.)	SEI	71	119.107-010
Hearing-Aid Repairer (inst. & app.)	RES	58	719.381-014
Heat Curer (textile)	RCE	41	581.586-010
Heat Reader (forging)	RES	43	612.687-010
Heat Treater (electron. comp.)	RCE	36	504.686-022
Heat Treater I (heat treating)	RIE	57	504.382-014
Heat Treater II (heat treating)	RIS	48	504.682-018
Heat Welder, Plastics (plastic prod.)	RIE	42	553.684-010
Heat-Transfer Technician (profess. & kin.)	RIC	70	007.181-010
Heat-Treat Inspector (heat treating)	RSI	58	504.281-010
Heat-Treat Supervisor (heat treating)	RES	59	504.131-010
Heat-Treater Apprentice (heat treating)	RIE	57	504.382-018
Heat-Treater Helper (heat treating)	REC	42	504.685-018
Heat-Treating Bluer (heat treating)	REI	49	504.682-022
Heater (forging)	RIE	47	619.682-022
Heater Helper (steel & rel.)	RES	45	613.685-014
Heater I (steel & rel.)	RES	52	613.362-010
Heater II (steel & rel.)	RIE	53	542.362-010
Heater Tender (rubber goods; rubber reclaim.; rubber tire)	RCS	41	553.665-038
Heater-Planer Operator (construction)	RIE	44	853.683-014
Heating-and-Air-Conditioning Installer-Servicer (construction)	RES	58	637.261-014
Heating-and-Air-Conditioning Installer-Servicer Helper (construction)	RSE	48	637.664-010
Heating-and-Blending Supervisor (chemical)	ERS	56	559.132-030
Heating-Element Winder (elec. equip.; house. appl.)	REC	41	723.685-010
Heating-Plant Superintendent (any industry)	RSE	59	959.131-010
Heavy Forger (forging)	REI	59	612.361-010
Heavy-Forger Helper (forging)	REI	41	612.687-014
Heavy-Media Operator (mine & quarry)	RCE	39	541.685-010
Heddle Cleaner, Machine (textile)	RSE	40	689.685-070
Heddle-Machine Operator (machinery mfg.)	RCE	41	616.685-026
Heddles Tier, Jacquard Loom (narrow fabrics; textile)	CRE	45	683.680-014
Heel Attacher, Wood (boot & shoe)	RCE	40	788.684-058
Heel Breaster, Leather (boot & shoe)	RCS	45	690.682-042
Heel Builder, Machine (boot & shoe)	RCE	42	690.685-206
Heel Compressor (boot & shoe)	RCE	39	690.685-210
Heel Dipper (boot & shoe)	RCE	37	788.687-058
Heel Gouger (boot & shoe)	CRE	42	690.685-214
Heel Pricker (boot & shoe)	RCE	42	690.685-218
Heel Scorer (boot & shoe)	CRE	41	690.685-222
Heel Sorter (boot & shoe)	CSR	47	788.584-010
Heel Sprayer, Machine (boot & shoe)	RCE	42	590.685-038

Part 3: From Occupational Titles to Holland Codes

From the Dictionary of Occupational Titles Occupations to Holland Codes

Title	HOC	Cx	DOT
Heel-Nailing-Machine Operator (boot & shoe)	CRE	41	690.685-226
Heel-Seat Fitter, Hand (boot & shoe)	RCE	41	788.684-062
Heel-Seat Fitter, Machine (boot & shoe)	CRS	45	690.682-046
Heel-Seat Laster, Machine (boot & shoe)	RCE	42	690.685-230
Heel-Washer-Stringing-Machine Operator (rubber goods)	RCE	38	619.685-058
Helicopter Pilot (any industry)	RIS	62	196.263-038
Helmet Coverer (hat & cap)	RCE	41	689.685-074
Helper, Electrical (utilities)	RSE	41	821.667-010
Helper, Liquefaction-and-Regasification (utilities)	RCS	49	953.584-010
Helper, Manufacturing (aircraft mfg.)	REC	40	809.687-014
Helper, Metal Bonding (aircraft mfg.)	RES	43	806.687-022
Helper, Metal Hanging (mfd. bldgs.)	RCE	37	806.667-010
Helper, Shear Operator (steel & rel.)	RCI	41	615.687-010
Hemmer (any industry)	RCE	43	787.682-026
Hemmer, Automatic (tex. prod., n.e.c.)	CRE	42	787.685-018
Hemmer, Blindstitch (garment)	CRE	40	786.682-126
Hemmer, Chainstitch (garment)	CRE	40	786.682-130
Hemmer, Lockstitch (garment)	CRE	40	786.682-134
Hemmer, Overlock (garment)	CRE	40	786.682-138
Hemming-and-Tacking-Machine Operator (furniture)	RCE	38	787.685-022
Hemstitching-Machine Operator (garment)	RCE	40	786.682-142
Herbarium Worker (profess. & kin.)	IRC	55	041.384-010
Hide Handler (meat products; oils & grease)	REI	38	525.687-038
Hide Inspector (leather mfg.)	RSE	45	783.687-018
Hide Inspector (meat products)	REC	42	525.687-042
Hide Puller (meat products)	REI	40	525.685-022
Hide Splitter (leather mfg.)	REI	47	690.580-010
Hide Stretcher, Hand (leather mfg.)	RCE	38	580.687-014
Hide Trimmer (meat products; oils & grease)	RES	37	525.687-046
High Rigger (amuse. & rec.; radio-tv broad.)	RES	48	962.664-010
High-Density Finishing Operator (wood prod., n.e.c.)	RIE	47	539.562-010
High-Energy-Forming Equipment Operator (aircraft mfg.)	RIE	57	619.380-010
Highway-Administrative Engineer (government ser.)	IEC	79	005.167-022
Highway-Maintenance Supervisor (government ser.)	SER	59	899.134-010
Highway-Maintenance Worker (government ser.)	RCS	45	899.684-014
Histopathologist (medical ser.)	IRS	78	041.061-054
Historian (profess. & kin.)	SEI	65	052.067-022
Historian, Dramatic Arts (profess. & kin.)	ESC	65	052.067-026
Historic-Site Administrator (museums)	ESC	66	102.167-014
History-Card Clerk (utilities)	CES	52	209.587-022
Histotechnologist (medical ser.)	IRE	67	078.261-030
Hobbing-Press Operator (any industry)	CRS	44	617.682-018
Hog Tender (woodworking)	REC	38	564.685-018
Hog-Confinement-System Manager (agriculture)	RIC	66	410.161-022
Hogshead Cooper I (wood. container)	RES	38	764.684-026
Hogshead Cooper II (wood. container)	RES	38	764.687-070
Hogshead Cooper III (wood. container)	RES	38	764.687-074
Hogshead Hooper (wood. container)	REC	37	764.687-078
Hogshead Inspector (tobacco)	RCE	49	529.367-014

Part 3: From Occupational Titles to Holland Codes
From the Dictionary of Occupational Titles Occupations to Holland Codes

Title	HOC	Cx	DOT
Hogshead Mat Assembler (wood. container)	REC	38	764.687-082
Hogshead Mat Inspector (wood. container)	CRE	40	764.687-086
Hogshead Opener (tobacco)	RES	41	920.687-102
Hoist Operator (mine & quarry)	RCS	45	921.663-026
Hoist Operator (petrol. & gas)	RCS	49	932.363-010
Hoisting Engineer (any industry)	RCS	44	921.663-030
Holiday-Detector Operator (construction)	CRE	41	862.687-014
Hollow-Handle-Knife Assembler (jewelry-silver.)	CRE	40	700.684-042
Holter Scanning Technician (medical ser.)	SCR	56	078.264-010
Home Attendant (personal ser.)	SER	50	354.377-014
Home Economist (profess. & kin.)	SEA	66	096.121-014
Home-Service Director (profess. & kin.)	ESA	66	096.161-010
Homemaker (social ser.)	SEC	54	309.354-010
Honey Extractor (food prep., n.e.c.)	REC	39	521.685-174
Honey Grader-and-Blender (food prep., n.e.c.)	RIS	57	520.361-010
Honey Processor (food prep., n.e.c.)	REC	42	522.685-070
Honeycomb Decapper (food prep., n.e.c.)	RES	41	521.687-070
Honing-Machine Operator, Production (machine shop)	RIE	48	603.482-034
Honing-Machine Set-up Operator (machine shop)	REI	51	603.382-018
Honing-Machine Set-up Operator, Tool (machine shop)	RIE	57	603.382-022
Hood Maker (tex. prod., n.e.c.)	RIS	55	804.481-010
Hoof and Shoe Inspector (amuse. & rec.)	SRC	50	153.287-010
Hook Puller (narrow fabrics)	REC	38	683.687-022
Hook Tender (logging)	RES	55	921.131-010
Hooker Inspector (textile)	RIE	45	689.685-078
Hooker-Laster (boot & shoe)	REC	40	753.684-018
Hooking-Machine Operator (clock & watch)	CRE	41	605.685-018
Hooking-Machine Operator (textile)	RCE	42	580.685-034
Hoop Bender, Tank (wood. container)	RCS	46	619.682-026
Hoop Coiler (wood. container)	REC	37	617.686-010
Hoop Maker, Machine (wood. container)	RIS	47	619.682-030
Hoop-Flaring-and-Coiling-Machine Operator (wood. container)	RCE	47	619.682-034
Hoop-Maker Helper, Machine (wood. container)	RES	40	619.686-014
Hop Strainer (beverage)	CRE	40	521.685-178
Hop Weigher (beverage)	REC	42	520.687-042
Hopper Attendant (sugar & conf.)	REC	40	521.685-182
Hopper Feeder (oils & grease)	REC	37	551.686-018
Hopper Feeder (ordnance)	RES	37	619.686-018
Horizontal-Earth-Boring-Machine Operator (construction)	REI	47	850.662-010
Horizontal-Earth-Boring-Machine-Operator Helper (construction)	REC	40	850.684-014
Horse Trainer (agriculture; amuse. & rec.)	SEC	53	419.224-010
Horse-Race Starter (amuse. & rec.)	ERS	53	153.267-010
Horse-Race Timer (amuse. & rec.)	RES	50	153.367-014
Horseradish Maker (can. & preserv.)	REC	38	529.685-142
Horseshoer (agriculture)	RSE	50	418.381-010
Horticultural Therapist (medical ser.)	SIR	67	076.124-018
Horticultural Worker I (agriculture)	RIE	47	405.684-014

Title	HOC	Cx	DOT
Horticultural Worker II (agriculture)	RES	38	405.687-014
Horticultural-Specialty Grower, Field (agriculture)	RIE	59	405.161-014
Horticultural-Specialty Grower, Inside (agriculture)	REI	62	405.161-018
Horticulturist (profess. & kin.)	IRS	78	040.061-038
Hose Cutter, Hand (rubber goods)	RCE	41	751.687-010
Hose Cutter, Machine (rubber goods)	RES	38	751.686-010
Hose Inspector and Patcher (rubber goods)	REI	49	759.364-010
Hose Maker (rubber goods)	RIE	48	752.684-030
Hose Wrapper (rubber goods)	RES	41	759.684-038
Hose-Coupling Joiner (rubber goods)	RES	41	759.687-014
Hose-Tubing Backer (rubber goods)	RES	38	559.686-018
Hosiery Mender (knitting)	CSE	44	782.684-030
Hospital-Admitting Clerk (medical ser.)	ECS	53	205.362-018
Hospital-Insurance Representative (insurance)	ESC	62	166.267-014
Hospital-Television-Rental Clerk (business ser.)	CES	45	295.467-018
Host/Hostess (any industry)	ESR	49	352.667-010
Host/Hostess, Dance Hall (amuse. & rec.)	ECS	42	349.667-010
Host/Hostess, Ground (air trans.)	ESR	51	352.377-010
Host/Hostess, Head (amuse. & rec.)	ESC	48	349.667-014
Host/Hostess, Restaurant (hotel & rest.)	ESR	59	310.137-010
Hostler (motor trans.)	RIE	47	909.663-010
Hostler (r.r. trans.)	RIE	47	910.683-010
Hot Box Operator (metal prod., n.e.c.)	CRS	41	709.685-014
Hot-Car Operator (steel & rel.)	RCE	42	519.663-014
Hot-Cell Technician (profess. & kin.)	RIC	58	015.362-018
Hot-Die-Press Operator (boot & shoe)	RCS	45	690.682-050
Hot-Plate-Plywood-Press Operator (millwork-plywood)	RCE	41	569.685-054
Hot-Press Operator (nonmet. min.)	RCS	41	575.685-042
Hot-Room Attendant (personal ser.)	REC	41	335.677-014
Hot-Stone Setter (button & notion)	CRE	37	734.687-058
Hot-Top Liner (steel & rel.)	REI	41	709.684-046
Hot-Top-Liner Helper (steel & rel.)	REI	39	709.687-018
Hot-Wire Glass-Tube Cutter (glass products)	RCS	40	772.684-014
Hot-Wort Settler (beverage)	REC	39	521.685-186
Hotel Clerk (hotel & rest.)	ECS	54	238.367-038
Hothouse Worker (chemical)	REC	41	549.687-014
House Builder (construction)	RES	57	869.281-014
House Mover (construction)	RSE	56	869.261-010
House Officer (hotel & rest.)	ESA	49	376.367-018
House Repairer (construction)	REI	57	869.381-010
House Sitter (domestic ser.)	RCS	47	309.367-010
House Worker, General (domestic ser.)	RSE	45	301.474-010
House-Mover Helper (construction)	RES	37	869.687-034
House-Mover Supervisor (construction)	RSE	59	869.131-022
House-Piping Inspector (utilities)	REC	52	953.367-018
Housecleaner (hotel & rest.)	REC	40	323.687-018
Household-Appliance Installer (any industry)	RSE	50	827.661-010
Housekeeper (hotel & rest.; medical ser.; real estate)	ESR	54	321.137-010
Housekeeper, Home (domestic ser.)	ESR	57	301.137-010

From the Dictionary of Occupational Titles Occupations to Holland Codes

Title	HOC	Cx	DOT
Housing-Management Officer (government ser.)	SER	65	188.117-110
Hull and Deck Remover (ship-boat mfg.)	RSE	39	809.667-010
Hull Inspector (ship-boat mfg.)	RCS	56	806.264-010
Huller Operator (grain-feed mills)	REA	45	521.682-030
Human Resource Advisor (profess. & kin.)	ESR	63	166.267-046
Humidifier Attendant (textile; tobacco)	RES	47	950.485-010
Humidifier Operator (wood prod., n.e.c.)	REI	48	562.682-010
Humorist (profess. & kin.)	ASE	70	131.067-026
Hydrate-Control Tender (smelt. & refin.)	RCE	46	511.585-010
Hydraulic Blocker (hat & cap)	RCE	42	580.685-038
Hydraulic Engineer (profess. & kin.)	IRS	70	005.061-018
Hydraulic Operator (nonfer. metal)	RCS	41	611.685-014
Hydraulic Press Operator (construction)	RSE	44	616.662-010
Hydraulic Repairer (any industry)	RCI	57	638.281-034
Hydraulic-Billet Maker (pen & pencil)	RCE	41	575.685-046
Hydraulic-Boom Operator (smelt. & refin.)	REI	41	921.683-046
Hydraulic-Chair Assembler (furniture)	RCS	47	706.684-058
Hydraulic-Jack Adjuster (construction)	RCS	52	869.361-014
Hydraulic-Press Operator (knitting)	REC	40	583.685-054
Hydraulic-Press Operator (millwork-plywood)	RCE	42	569.685-058
Hydraulic-Press Operator (tex. prod., n.e.c.)	CRE	41	583.685-058
Hydraulic-Press Operator (tobacco)	RCS	41	920.685-062
Hydraulic-Press Servicer (ordnance)	REI	53	626.381-018
Hydraulic-Pressure-Auto-Frettage-Machine Operator (ordnance)	RES	47	694.682-014
Hydraulic-Pressure-Auto-Frettage-Machine-Operator Supervisor (ordnance)	RSE	60	619.130-010
Hydraulic-Rubbish-Compactor Mechanic (sanitary ser.)	RCI	59	638.281-030
Hydraulic-Strainer Operator (plastic-synth.)	RCS	47	551.582-010
Hydro-Pneumatic Tester (any industry)	RES	47	862.687-018
Hydro-Sprayer Operator (agriculture)	RIS	47	408.662-010
Hydroelectric-Machinery Mechanic (utilities)	RIE	58	631.261-010
Hydroelectric-Machinery-Mechanic Helper (utilities)	RIE	52	631.364-010
Hydroelectric-Plant Maintainer (utilities)	RCE	39	952.687-010
Hydroelectric-Station Operator (utilities)	RCS	57	952.362-018
Hydroelectric-Station Operator, Chief (utilities)	ERS	62	952.137-014
Hydrogenation Operator (oils & grease)	REI	50	529.382-026
Hydrographer (waterworks)	IRS	61	025.264-010
Hydrologist (profess. & kin.)	IRE	80	024.061-034
Hydrometer Calibrator (inst. & app.)	RES	52	710.381-030
Hypnotherapist (profess. & kin.)	SEC	62	079.157-010
Ice Cream Freezer Assistant (dairy products)	REC	40	529.685-146
Ice Cutter (food prep., n.e.c.)	REI	39	529.685-150
Ice Maker (food prep., n.e.c.)	REC	42	523.685-102
Ice Maker, Skating Rink (amuse. & rec.)	RCE	39	969.687-014
Ice-Cream Chef (hotel & rest.)	RAS	49	313.381-034
Icer (wholesale tr.)	RES	36	922.687-046
Icer, Hand (bakery products)	RCE	39	524.684-022
Icer, Machine (bakery products)	RES	39	524.685-034

DOT to HOC

Title	HOC	Cx	DOT
Icicle-Machine Operator (dairy products)	CRS	48	920.482-010
Icing Mixer (bakery products)	RSE	45	520.685-114
Identification Clerk (clerical)	CSE	50	205.362-022
Identification Clerk (government ser.)	REI	51	209.362-022
Identification Officer (government ser.)	RIE	63	377.264-010
Identifier, Horse (amuse. & rec.)	ERS	50	153.387-010
Igniter Capper (ordnance)	RCE	36	737.687-050
Illuminating Engineer (profess. & kin.)	IRE	76	003.061-046
Illustrator (profess. & kin.)	AER	64	141.061-022
Illustrator, Medical and Scientific (profess. & kin.)	AIE	67	141.061-026
Illustrator, Set (motion picture; radio-tv broad.)	AES	66	141.061-030
Immigration Inspector (government ser.)	RSE	59	168.167-022
Immunohematologist (medical ser.)	ICS	66	078.261-046
Impersonator (amuse. & rec.)	AES	60	159.047-018
Impersonator, Character (any industry)	EAS	47	299.647-010
Import-Export Agent (any industry)	SEC	67	184.117-022
Impregnating-Machine Operator (metal prod., n.e.c.)	REI	50	590.362-014
Impregnating-Tank Operator (any industry)	RIE	48	599.685-046
Impregnation Operator (paper goods)	CES	42	539.685-014
Impregnator (nonfer. metal; steel & rel.)	RCS	42	509.685-030
Impregnator (pen & pencil)	RCE	42	562.685-014
Impregnator and Drier (elec. equip.; electron. comp.)	RCE	52	599.682-014
Impregnator Operator (chemical)	RCE	45	559.685-106
Impregnator-and-Drier Helper (elec. equip.; light. fix.)	RCS	42	599.685-050
In-Flight Refueling Operator (military ser.)	RES	55	912.662-010
In-Flight Refueling System Repairer (military ser.)	REI	57	829.281-018
Incinerator Operator I (sanitary ser.)	RCE	38	955.685-010
Incinerator Operator II (sanitary ser.)	RCI	53	955.362-014
Incinerator Plant Laborer (sanitary ser.)	RCE	38	955.667-010
Incinerator-Plant-General Supervisor (sanitary ser.)	ERS	63	184.167-046
Incising-Machine Operator (wood prod., n.e.c.)	RCS	47	569.662-010
Incoming-Freight Clerk (water trans.)	RES	55	248.362-010
Induction-Coordination Power Engineer (utilities)	RIE	76	003.167-038
Induction-Machine Operator (heat treating)	RCS	41	504.685-022
Induction-Machine Setter (heat treating)	RSE	53	504.380-014
Industrial Designer (profess. & kin.)	AES	66	142.061-026
Industrial Engineer (profess. & kin.)	EIR	75	012.167-030
Industrial Engineering Technician (profess. & kin.)	IRE	68	012.267-010
Industrial Hygienist (profess. & kin.)	IRE	73	079.161-010
Industrial Therapist (medical ser.)	IER	70	076.167-010
Industrial-Gas Fitter (utilities)	RIE	54	862.381-014
Industrial-Gas Servicer (utilities)	RIS	58	637.261-022
Industrial-Gas-Servicer Helper (utilities)	RES	49	637.384-010
Industrial-Health Engineer (profess. & kin.)	EIC	75	012.167-034
Industrial-Order Clerk (clerical)	CSE	57	221.367-022
Industrial-Safety-and-Health Technician (any industry)	ERC	62	168.161-014
Industrial-Truck Operator (any industry)	RCE	41	921.683-050
Infantry Indirect Fire Crewmember (military ser.)	RES	42	378.684-022
Infantry Operations Specialist (military ser.)	CRI	59	378.367-022

Part 3: From Occupational Titles to Holland Codes

From the Dictionary of Occupational Titles Occupations to Holland Codes

Title	HOC	Cx	DOT
Infantry Unit Leader (military ser.)	ERS	55	378.137-010
Infantry Weapons Crewmember (military ser.)	RES	41	378.684-026
Information Clerk (clerical)	ECS	53	237.367-022
Information Clerk (motor trans.; r.r. trans.; water trans.)	CES	55	237.367-018
Information Clerk, Automobile Club (nonprofit org.)	SEC	60	237.267-010
Information Clerk-Cashier (amuse. & rec.)	CSE	53	249.467-010
Information Scientist (profess. & kin.)	IER	72	109.067-010
Ingot Header (nonfer. metal; smelt. & refin.)	RCS	45	514.584-010
Ingredient Scaler (bakery products; dairy products)	RCE	46	529.684-014
Injection-Molding-Machine Offbearer (musical inst.)	RES	39	690.686-042
Injection-Molding-Machine Offbearer (pen & pencil)	RCS	40	690.686-038
Injection-Molding-Machine Operator (plastic prod.)	REI	49	556.382-014
Injection-Molding-Machine Tender (plastic prod.; recording; rubber goods)	REC	40	556.685-038
Injector Assembler (engine-turbine)	CRE	51	706.684-062
Ink Printer (jewelry-silver.; leather prod.; plastic prod.)	REC	39	652.685-038
Inker (boot & shoe)	CRS	38	788.684-066
Inker (print. & pub.)	RES	48	659.667-010
Inker and Opaquer (motion picture)	RCA	46	970.681-018
Inker, Machine (boot & shoe)	RCE	41	690.685-234
Inlayer (print. & pub.)	CRS	44	977.684-014
Inletter (ordnance)	RCE	45	669.682-050
Inner-Tube Inserter (rubber tire)	RES	35	750.687-010
Inseam Trimmer (boot & shoe)	RCE	41	690.685-238
Insecticide Mixer (chemical)	RCE	40	550.685-070
Inserting-Machine Operator (clerical)	REC	41	208.685-018
Insertion Machine Tender, Electronic Components (comm. equip.; electron. comp.)	RCE	46	726.685-014
Inservice Coordinator, Auxiliary Personnel (medical ser.)	SEA	65	079.127-010
Inset Cutter (fabrication, n.e.c.)	RIS	57	739.381-038
Inside-Meter Tester (utilities)	RIE	58	729.281-034
Insole Beveler (boot & shoe)	CRS	40	690.685-242
Insole Reinforcer (boot & shoe)	RCE	41	690.685-246
Insole-and-Heel-Stiffener (boot & shoe)	RCE	37	788.687-062
Inspecting-Machine Adjuster (ordnance)	RCE	50	632.380-010
Inspection Clerk (fabrication, n.e.c.)	RSE	50	739.587-010
Inspection Supervisor (chemical; nonfer. metal)	RES	63	709.137-010
Inspection Supervisor (machine shop)	RES	62	609.131-010
Inspection Supervisor I (ordnance)	RES	59	736.131-018
Inspection Supervisor II (ordnance)	RES	58	737.134-010
Inspector (boot & shoe)	RIE	49	788.384-010
Inspector (build. mat., n.e.c.)	RCS	49	549.367-010
Inspector (chemical)	RES	47	709.687-022
Inspector (cutlery-hrdwr.)	CRE	44	709.587-010
Inspector (elec. equip.)	REC	40	727.687-062
Inspector (forging)	RIS	57	612.261-010
Inspector (hat & cap)	REC	43	784.387-010
Inspector (hotel & rest.)	RES	56	321.137-014
Inspector (house. appl.)	CRE	49	729.387-022

Title	HOC	Cx	DOT
Inspector (jewelry-silver.)	CRS	47	700.687-034
Inspector (laundry & rel.)	CSR	40	369.687-022
Inspector (mfd. bldgs.)	RES	49	869.687-038
Inspector (nonmet. min.)	CRS	48	776.667-010
Inspector (office machines)	RSE	57	710.384-014
Inspector (paper & pulp)	REI	45	649.487-010
Inspector (pen & pencil)	CRS	42	733.687-042
Inspector (pharmaceut.)	RCI	51	559.387-014
Inspector (plastic prod.; plastic-synth.)	RIE	55	559.381-010
Inspector (steel & rel.)	REI	54	619.381-010
Inspector (sugar & conf.)	CRS	41	529.687-114
Inspector (toy-sport equip.)	CRS	49	732.684-130
Inspector (woodworking)	CRS	45	769.687-026
Inspector and Adjuster, Golf Club Head (toy-sport equip.)	RCE	51	732.384-014
Inspector and Hand Packager (plastic prod.)	RCE	41	559.687-074
Inspector and Sorter (leather mfg.)	RES	50	589.387-010
Inspector and Tester (agric. equip.)	RSE	53	624.361-010
Inspector and Tester (struct. metal)	REC	42	809.687-018
Inspector I (concrete prod.)	REC	52	779.387-014
Inspector I (fabrication, n.e.c.)	REI	42	739.687-106
Inspector I (furniture)	RCI	48	780.687-066
Inspector I (nonfer. metal)	RES	56	619.364-010
Inspector I (ordnance)	RES	49	737.387-014
Inspector I (pottery & porc.)	RCI	40	575.687-034
Inspector II (concrete prod.)	RES	49	579.664-014
Inspector II (fabrication, n.e.c.)	REI	51	590.367-010
Inspector II (furniture)	REC	42	780.687-022
Inspector II (ordnance)	RCS	48	737.687-054
Inspector II (pottery & porc.)	REI	49	774.384-010
Inspector III (furniture)	RSC	39	739.687-110
Inspector III (ordnance)	REI	57	737.367-010
Inspector IV (ordnance)	RES	53	559.387-010
Inspector of Dredging (water trans.)	RIE	57	850.387-010
Inspector, Agricultural Commodities (government ser.)	REI	61	168.287-010
Inspector, Air-Carrier (government ser.)	RIE	66	168.264-010
Inspector, Aircraft Launching and Arresting Systems (government ser.)	RIE	63	806.264-014
Inspector, Aligning (office machines)	RCE	47	706.687-022
Inspector, Aluminum Boat (ship-boat mfg.)	RES	42	806.687-026
Inspector, Assemblies and Installations (aircraft mfg.)	RIC	62	806.261-030
Inspector, Assembly (furniture)	RCI	53	669.364-010
Inspector, Assembly (ordnance)	RCE	49	736.387-010
Inspector, Automatic Typewriter (office machines)	REC	50	706.387-010
Inspector, Balance Truing (clock & watch)	CER	46	715.687-050
Inspector, Balance Wheel Motion (clock & watch)	CRS	43	715.687-054
Inspector, Balance-Bridge (clock & watch)	CRE	44	715.687-058
Inspector, Ball Points (nonfer. metal)	CRS	43	733.687-046
Inspector, Barrel (ordnance)	CRS	42	736.687-014
Inspector, Barrel Assembly (clock & watch)	RCS	48	715.684-114

Part 3: From Occupational Titles to Holland Codes

From the Dictionary of Occupational Titles Occupations to Holland Codes

Title	HOC	Cx	DOT
Inspector, Bicycle (motor-bicycles)	CSR	40	806.687-030
Inspector, Boiler (profess. & kin.)	RSI	67	168.167-026
Inspector, Building (government ser.)	CIE	65	168.167-030
Inspector, Bullet Slugs (ordnance)	CRS	40	737.687-058
Inspector, Canned Food Reconditioning (can. & preserv.)	REC	42	529.687-118
Inspector, Casing (clock & watch)	CRE	45	715.687-062
Inspector, Chief (elec. equip.)	CSE	58	729.131-010
Inspector, Chief (foundry)	ERS	59	514.131-010
Inspector, Chief (ordnance)	ERS	59	737.137-010
Inspector, Chief (utilities)	RIE	59	956.267-010
Inspector, Circuitry Negative (electron. comp.)	RCI	53	726.384-014
Inspector, Clip-On Sunglasses (optical goods)	REC	42	713.667-010
Inspector, Cold Working (ordnance)	RIE	54	612.384-010
Inspector, Container Finishing (elec. equip.)	CRE	42	727.687-066
Inspector, Crystal (electron. comp.)	RCI	48	726.684-054
Inspector, Dials (clock & watch)	RES	48	715.687-066
Inspector, Electrical (government ser.)	RCE	67	168.167-034
Inspector, Electromechanical (inst. & app.)	RIC	58	729.361-010
Inspector, Elevators (government ser.)	RIS	69	168.167-038
Inspector, Exhaust Emissions (auto. mfg.)	REI	55	806.364-010
Inspector, Eyeglass (optical goods)	REI	54	713.384-014
Inspector, Eyeglass Frames (optical goods)	REC	42	713.687-022
Inspector, Fabric (any industry)	CRE	45	789.587-014
Inspector, Fabrication (aircraft mfg.)	REC	60	806.361-022
Inspector, Fibrous Wallboard (wood prod., n.e.c.)	REC	53	539.487-010
Inspector, Filter Tip (tobacco)	RES	43	529.667-010
Inspector, Final Assembly (pen & pencil)	CRE	43	733.687-050
Inspector, Finishing (tex. prod., n.e.c.)	RCE	49	589.387-022
Inspector, Firearms (ordnance)	RCI	57	632.381-014
Inspector, Fireworks (chemical)	RCS	42	737.687-062
Inspector, Floor (machine shop)	REI	56	609.361-010
Inspector, Furniture and Bedding (government ser.)	RSE	59	168.267-046
Inspector, Furniture Decals (furniture)	RCI	40	979.687-030
Inspector, Gauge and Instrument (machine shop)	RIE	61	601.281-018
Inspector, General (any industry)	RCS	45	609.684-010
Inspector, Glass or Mirror (glass products)	REI	47	779.687-022
Inspector, Golf Ball (toy-sport equip.)	RES	47	732.567-010
Inspector, Government Property (government ser.)	ERS	64	168.267-050
Inspector, Grain Mill Products (grain-feed mills)	REI	51	529.387-026
Inspector, Hairspring I (clock & watch)	REC	50	715.381-066
Inspector, Hairspring II (clock & watch)	CRE	42	715.684-122
Inspector, Hairspring Truing (clock & watch)	RCE	47	715.684-118
Inspector, Handbag Frames (leather prod.)	RCE	42	222.687-042
Inspector, Health Care Facilities (government ser.)	SER	63	168.167-042
Inspector, Heating and Refrigeration (government ser.)	SIA	67	168.167-046
Inspector, Industrial Waste (government ser.)	RIE	66	168.267-054
Inspector, Insulation (nonfer. metal)	REC	55	691.387-010
Inspector, Integrated Circuits (electron. comp.)	RCI	43	726.684-058
Inspector, Live Ammunition (ordnance)	CRS	39	736.687-018

From the Dictionary of Occupational Titles Occupations to Holland Codes

Title	HOC	Cx	DOT
Inspector, Magnetic Particle and Penetrant (any industry)	REI	53	709.364-010
Inspector, Material Disposition (aircraft mfg.)	RIE	64	806.261-034
Inspector, Mechanism (clock & watch)	RCE	49	715.384-014
Inspector, Metal Can (tinware)	RIE	56	709.367-010
Inspector, Metal Fabricating (any industry)	RCE	60	619.261-010
Inspector, Missile (aircraft mfg.)	RIE	66	806.261-038
Inspector, Motor Vehicles (government ser.)	ESR	56	168.267-058
Inspector, Motors and Generators (elec. equip.)	RES	57	721.361-010
Inspector, Multifocal Lens (optical goods)	REC	46	716.687-018
Inspector, Open Die (cutlery-hrdwr.)	RCE	48	701.684-014
Inspector, Optical Instrument (optical goods)	REI	64	711.281-010
Inspector, Outside Production (aircraft mfg.)	RIE	62	806.261-042
Inspector, Packaging Materials (pharmaceut.)	REC	53	920.387-010
Inspector, Paper Products (paper goods)	REI	49	649.367-010
Inspector, Photographic Equipment (photo. appar.)	RIE	57	714.381-014
Inspector, Picture Frames (wood prod., n.e.c.)	RCE	42	769.687-030
Inspector, Plastics and Composites (aircraft mfg.)	RIE	62	806.261-046
Inspector, Plating (electroplating)	IRE	54	500.287-010
Inspector, Plumbing (government ser.)	ERS	67	168.167-050
Inspector, Poising (clock & watch)	REI	49	715.384-018
Inspector, Precision (optical goods)	RIE	58	716.381-010
Inspector, Precision Assembly (aircraft mfg.)	RIE	59	806.281-026
Inspector, Printed Circuit Boards (electron. comp.)	RCI	48	726.684-062
Inspector, Processing (aircraft mfg.)	RIC	55	806.381-074
Inspector, Processing (sugar & conf.)	RCI	50	529.687-226
Inspector, Publications (print. & pub.)	CRE	46	653.667-010
Inspector, Quality Assurance (government ser.)	IRE	69	168.287-014
Inspector, Railroad (government ser.)	RIE	59	168.287-018
Inspector, Receiving (aircraft mfg.; elec. equip.; electron. comp.)	RCI	54	222.384-010
Inspector, Returned Materials (auto. mfg.)	REI	54	806.384-014
Inspector, Rubber-Stamp Die (pen & pencil)	CRS	44	733.687-054
Inspector, Salvage (ordnance)	CRE	41	737.684-026
Inspector, Screen Printing (print. & pub.)	ASR	46	979.667-010
Inspector, Semiconductor Wafer (electron. comp.)	RCI	46	726.684-066
Inspector, Semiconductor Wafer Processing (electron. comp.)	RCI	49	726.384-018
Inspector, Set-up and Lay-Out (machine shop)	REI	65	601.261-010
Inspector, Shells (ordnance)	REI	43	737.687-066
Inspector, Shipping (agric. equip.)	SRE	44	801.667-010
Inspector, Slide Fasteners (button & notion)	RCE	47	734.687-062
Inspector, Soldering (clock & watch)	RCE	42	715.687-070
Inspector, Surgical Garment (protective dev.)	REI	50	712.487-010
Inspector, Surgical Instruments (inst. & app.)	CRE	41	712.684-050
Inspector, Timers (clock & watch)	RCE	42	715.687-074
Inspector, Timing (clock & watch)	REC	47	715.685-034
Inspector, Tool (machine shop)	RIE	65	601.281-022
Inspector, Toys (toy-sport equip.)	RES	47	731.687-022
Inspector, Type (office machines)	RCE	42	706.687-026

From the Dictionary of Occupational Titles Occupations to Holland Codes

Title	HOC	Cx	DOT
Inspector, Typewriter Assembly and Parts (office machines)	RIE	56	706.381-022
Inspector, Watch Assembly (clock & watch)	REC	52	715.381-070
Inspector, Watch Parts (clock & watch)	REC	54	715.384-022
Inspector, Watch Train (clock & watch)	RCE	55	715.381-074
Inspector, Water-Pollution Control (government ser.)	IRE	66	168.267-090
Inspector, Wheel and Pinion (clock & watch)	CRS	47	715.684-126
Inspector, Wire (metal prod., n.e.c.; nonfer. metal)	RES	55	691.367-010
Inspector, Wire Products (metal prod., n.e.c.)	CRE	42	709.687-026
Inspector, Woodwind Instruments (musical inst.)	REC	47	730.684-038
Inspector, Wreath (fabrication, n.e.c.)	RCE	39	739.687-118
Inspector-Adjuster, Office-Machine Components (office machines)	RCE	52	706.384-010
Inspector-Grader, Agricultural Establishment (agriculture)	RCS	41	409.687-010
Inspector-Packer (hat & cap)	CSR	41	784.687-042
Inspector-Repairer (button & notion)	ERS	47	734.684-018
Inspector-Repairer (leather prod.)	CRS	44	783.684-018
Inspector-Repairer, Sandstone (stonework)	RSI	46	779.684-030
Installation Superintendent, Pin-Setting Machine (construction)	RES	59	829.131-018
Installer (mfd. bldgs.; vehicles, n.e.c.)	RES	50	869.684-026
Installer (museums)	RES	38	922.687-050
Installer, Door Furring (railroad equip.)	RES	40	806.687-034
Installer, Electrical, Plumbing, Mechanical (ship-boat mfg.)	RCI	56	806.381-062
Installer, Interior Assemblies (aircraft mfg.)	RCS	53	806.381-078
Installer, Metal Flooring (railroad equip.)	RES	41	806.684-070
Installer, Movable Bulkhead (railroad equip.)	RES	44	806.684-074
Installer, Soft Top (automotive ser.)	RCE	41	807.684-026
Installer-Inspector, Final (vehicles, n.e.c.)	REI	47	806.684-066
Instant Print Operator (print. & pub.)	RCS	54	979.362-010
Instantizer Operator (dairy products)	RCE	42	523.685-106
Institution Librarian (library)	SEC	67	100.167-022
Instructor (boot & shoe)	RES	62	788.222-010
Instructor (textile)	SER	53	689.324-010
Instructor, Apparel Manufacture (textile)	SEC	59	789.222-010
Instructor, Bridge (education)	ESC	66	159.227-010
Instructor, Bus, Trolley, and Taxi (motor trans.; r.r. trans.)	SRE	61	919.223-010
Instructor, Business Education (education)	ESR	67	090.222-010
Instructor, Correspondence School (education)	SER	67	099.227-014
Instructor, Dancing (education)	ASE	63	151.027-014
Instructor, Decorating (pottery & porc.)	RSE	60	740.221-010
Instructor, Driving (education)	SER	53	099.223-010
Instructor, Extension Work (education)	SEA	66	090.227-018
Instructor, Flying I (education)	SRE	68	196.223-010
Instructor, Flying II (education)	ERS	60	097.227-010
Instructor, Ground Services (air trans.)	SEI	67	099.227-018
Instructor, Military Science (education)	SEA	66	099.227-022
Instructor, Modeling (education)	ASE	56	099.227-026
Instructor, Painting (retail trade)	AES	52	297.451-010

Title	HOC	Cx	DOT
Instructor, Physical (amuse. & rec.; education)	SEC	54	153.227-014
Instructor, Physical Education (education)	SER	65	099.224-010
Instructor, Pilot (air trans.)	SRE	69	196.223-014
Instructor, Psychiatric Aide (education)	SCE	67	075.127-010
Instructor, Sports (amuse. & rec.; education)	ESR	63	153.227-018
Instructor, Technical Training (education)	SEA	69	166.221-010
Instructor, Vocational Training (education)	SER	66	097.221-010
Instructor, Wastewater-Treatment Plant (sanitary ser.)	ESR	59	955.222-010
Instructor, Watch Assembly (clock & watch)	RES	63	715.221-010
Instructor, Weaving (textile)	RES	54	683.222-010
Instructor-Trainer, Canine Service (government ser.)	RCE	54	379.227-010
Instrument Assembler (inst. & app.)	RCI	47	710.684-046
Instrument Inspector (aircraft mfg.; air trans.)	RIE	60	722.381-014
Instrument Inspector (inst. & app.)	CRI	47	710.684-050
Instrument Maker (any industry)	RIE	59	600.280-010
Instrument Mechanic (any industry)	RCS	59	710.281-026
Instrument Mechanic, Weapons System (inst. & app.)	RIE	59	711.281-014
Instrument Repairer (any industry)	RCS	60	710.261-010
Instrument Repairer (tel. & tel.)	RIE	58	722.281-010
Instrument Technician (utilities)	REI	59	710.281-030
Instrument-Maker and Repairer (petrol. & gas)	RIE	58	600.280-014
Instrument-Maker Apprentice (any industry)	RIE	59	600.280-018
Instrument-Repairer Helper (any industry)	REI	53	710.384-018
Instrument-Shop Supervisor (tel. & tel.)	ESC	58	722.131-010
Instrument-Technician Apprentice (utilities)	REI	59	710.281-042
Instrument-Technician Helper (utilities)	REI	50	710.684-030
Instrumentation Technician (profess. & kin.)	RIC	68	003.261-010
Insulating-Machine Operator (nonfer. metal)	RCI	45	691.682-018
Insulation Cutter and Former (elec. equip.)	CRE	49	721.484-018
Insulation Worker (construction)	RCI	51	863.364-014
Insulation-Power-Unit Tender (construction; retail trade; wholesale tr.)	REC	41	863.685-010
Insulation-Worker Apprentice (construction)	REC	51	863.364-010
Insulator Tester (utilities)	CRS	49	729.387-026
Insurance Attorney (insurance)	SEI	77	110.117-014
Insurance Checker (insurance)	CSR	54	219.482-014
Insurance Clerk (clerical)	CSE	55	219.387-014
Insurance Clerk (financial; insurance)	CES	54	219.367-014
Insurance Clerk (medical ser.)	CSE	57	214.362-022
Integrated Circuit Fabricator (electron. comp.)	CRS	44	590.684-042
Integrated Circuit Layout Designer (profess. & kin.)	IRC	66	003.261-018
Intelligence Clerk (military ser.)	CES	56	249.387-014
Intelligence Research Specialist (profess. & kin.)	AEI	77	059.167-010
Intelligence Specialist (government ser.)	AES	67	059.267-010
Intelligence Specialist (military ser.)	ERS	64	059.267-014
Interior Designer (profess. & kin.)	AES	65	142.051-014
Interlacer (boot & shoe)	RCE	40	788.684-070
Interline Clerk (motor trans.; r.r. trans.)	CRS	56	214.382-022
Internal Carver (plastic prod.)	RIA	57	754.381-010

From the Dictionary of Occupational Titles Occupations to Holland Codes

Title	HOC	Cx	DOT
Internal-Combustion-Engine Inspector (engine-turbine)	RIE	59	806.261-010
Internal-Combustion-Engine Subassembler (engine-turbine)	RCE	50	706.481-010
Internist (medical ser.)	IRS	76	070.101-042
Interpreter (profess. & kin.)	ESA	63	137.267-010
Interpreter, Deaf (profess. & kin.)	SCE	58	137.267-014
Inventory Clerk (clerical)	RCI	54	222.387-026
Investigator (clerical)	ESC	60	241.267-030
Investigator (government ser.)	SIE	64	168.267-062
Investigator (utilities)	ESR	53	376.367-022
Investigator, Cash Shortage (retail trade)	SCE	57	376.267-010
Investigator, Dealer Accounts (financial)	CER	55	241.367-038
Investigator, Fraud (retail trade)	SEC	59	376.267-014
Investigator, Internal Affairs (government ser.)	CSE	63	375.267-034
Investigator, Narcotics (government ser.)	SRE	59	375.267-018
Investigator, Private (business ser.)	ESI	58	376.267-018
Investigator, Utility-Bill Complaints (utilities)	ESR	61	241.267-034
Investigator, Vice (government ser.)	SER	59	375.267-022
Investment Analyst (financial; insurance)	CIE	70	160.267-026
Invoice-Control Clerk (clerical)	CSR	55	214.362-026
Ion Exchange Operator (beverage)	CER	40	521.685-190
Ion Implant Machine Operator (electron. comp.)	RCI	54	590.382-022
Ion-Exchange Operator (chemical)	RES	48	558.685-034
Ion-Exchange Operator (pharmaceut.)	RSC	47	558.685-038
Ion-Exchange Operator (smelt. & refin.)	RCE	45	558.685-030
Irish-Moss Bleacher (fishing & hunt.)	REC	40	447.687-014
Irish-Moss Gatherer (fishing & hunt.)	REC	39	447.687-018
Irish-Moss Operator (chemical)	RSE	48	529.382-030
Iron-Launder Operator (smelt. & refin.)	CRS	46	511.565-018
Iron-Plastic Bullet Maker (ordnance)	RIE	51	590.365-010
Ironer (button & notion)	RCE	40	590.685-042
Ironer (domestic ser.)	RCE	39	302.687-010
Ironer, Sock (laundry & rel.)	REC	35	363.687-014
Ironworker-Machine Operator (any industry)	RSC	48	615.482-018
Irradiated-Fuel Handler (chemical)	RSC	45	921.663-034
Irrigation Engineer (profess. & kin.)	IRE	70	005.061-022
Irrigation System Installer (construction)	REI	51	851.383-010
Irrigator, Gravity Flow (agriculture)	REI	40	409.687-014
Irrigator, Head (agriculture)	RES	55	409.137-010
Irrigator, Sprinkling System (agriculture)	REC	41	409.685-014
Irrigator, Valve Pipe (agriculture)	REC	42	409.684-010
Jack Setter (mine & quarry)	RCS	44	939.684-010
Jacket Preparer (print. & pub.)	CRS	51	221.387-030
Jackhammer Operator (mine & quarry)	RCS	38	930.684-018
Jacquard-Loom Weaver (narrow fabrics)	RCS	46	683.682-022
Jacquard-Loom Weaver (textile)	REC	45	683.662-010
Jacquard-Plate Maker (knitting)	RES	49	685.381-010
Jacquard-Twine-Polisher Operator (tex. prod., n.e.c.)	CRE	42	583.685-062
Jailer (government ser.)	ESR	50	372.367-014

Title	HOC	Cx	DOT
Jailer, Chief (government ser.)	ESR	65	372.167-018
Jammer Operator (logging)	REC	41	921.683-054
Janitor (any industry)	RES	49	382.664-010
Jet Handler (plastic-synth.)	REI	41	557.684-010
Jet Wiper (plastic-synth.)	CRE	40	557.684-014
Jet-Dyeing-Machine Tender (textile)	RES	42	582.685-090
Jewel Blocker and Sawyer (clock & watch)	RCS	50	770.381-026
Jewel Gauger (clock & watch)	RCE	47	770.687-018
Jewel Grinder I (clock & watch)	RCE	40	770.685-014
Jewel Grinder II (clock & watch)	RCE	40	770.684-010
Jewel Inserter (clock & watch)	CRS	45	715.684-130
Jewel Inspector (clock & watch)	CRS	48	770.687-022
Jewel Staker (clock & watch)	RCE	45	715.684-134
Jewel Stringer (clock & watch)	CRE	38	770.687-026
Jewel Stripper (clock & watch)	CRS	41	605.685-022
Jewel Supervisor (clock & watch)	REC	60	770.131-010
Jewel-Bearing Broacher (clock & watch)	RCE	47	770.682-010
Jewel-Bearing Driller (clock & watch)	RCE	48	770.682-014
Jewel-Bearing Facer (clock & watch)	RCE	47	770.682-018
Jewel-Bearing Grinder (clock & watch)	RCE	47	770.685-018
Jewel-Bearing Maker (clock & watch)	REI	57	770.381-030
Jewel-Bearing Polisher (clock & watch)	RCE	47	770.685-022
Jewel-Bearing Turner (clock & watch)	RCE	47	770.682-022
Jewel-Corner-Brushing-Machine Operator (clock & watch)	REC	41	770.685-026
Jewel-Cupping-Machine Operator (clock & watch)	RCE	42	770.685-030
Jewel-Hole Cornerer (clock & watch)	RES	39	770.684-014
Jewel-Hole Driller (clock & watch)	RCE	47	770.682-026
Jeweler (jewelry-silver.)	REC	58	700.281-010
Jeweler Apprentice (jewelry-silver.)	REC	58	700.281-014
Jewelry Coater (jewelry-silver.)	CRE	41	590.685-046
Jig Builder (metal prod., n.e.c.)	REC	42	761.684-014
Jig Builder (wood. container)	RSE	50	761.381-014
Jig Fitter (machinery mfg.)	REI	50	801.684-010
Jig-Boring Machine Operator, Numerical Control (machine shop)	RIE	59	606.382-014
Jigger (jewelry-silver.)	RCE	37	705.687-010
Jigger (textile)	REC	44	582.665-018
Jigger-Crown-Pouncing-Machine Operator (hat & cap)	RCE	39	585.685-058
Jigsaw Operator (woodworking)	RCS	44	667.682-042
Jigsawyer (jewelry-silver.)	RCE	43	700.684-046
Jinrikisha Driver (amuse. & rec.)	RSE	43	349.477-010
Job Analyst (profess. & kin.)	IES	67	166.267-018
Job Development Specialist (profess. & kin.)	SRC	56	166.267-034
Job Printer (print. & pub.)	RIE	59	973.381-018
Job Putter-Up and Ticket Preparer (boot & shoe)	CRS	45	788.587-010
Job Setter (electron. comp.)	REC	55	616.380-014
Job Setter, Honing (machine shop)	RIE	57	603.280-034
Job Setter, Spline-Rolling Machine (machine shop)	REI	51	617.480-010
Job Tracer (clerical)	ECR	53	221.387-034

DOT to HOC

Title	HOC	Cx	DOT
Job-Printer Apprentice (print. & pub.)	RIE	59	973.381-022
Jockey (amuse. & rec.)	RES	55	153.244-010
Jockey Agent (amuse. & rec.)	SER	60	191.117-026
Jockey Valet (amuse. & rec.)	ESR	43	346.677-010
Jockey-Room Custodian (amuse. & rec.)	SCE	42	346.667-010
Jogger (print. & pub.)	RSE	40	651.686-018
Joiner (glass mfg.)	RCE	40	673.687-010
Joiner (ship-boat mfg.)	RES	55	860.381-050
Joiner Apprentice (ship-boat mfg.)	RES	55	860.381-054
Joiner Helper (ship-boat mfg.)	RCS	46	860.664-014
Joint Cutter, Machine (boot & shoe)	RCE	40	690.685-250
Joint-Cleaning-and-Grooving-Machine Operator (construction)	RIE	44	853.683-018
Jointer Operator (woodworking)	RIS	48	665.682-042
Judge (government ser.)	ESA	77	111.107-010
Juggler (amuse. & rec.)	SEC	52	159.341-010
Jumpbasting-Machine Operator (garment)	CRE	40	786.682-146
Junction Maker (brick & tile)	RCE	45	862.684-010
Kapok-and-Cotton-Machine Operator (tex. prod., n.e.c.)	REI	41	689.685-082
Keg Varnisher (wood. container)	REC	37	749.687-014
Kelp Cutter (fishing & hunt.)	REI	40	447.687-022
Kennel Manager, Dog Track (amuse. & rec.)	SRE	50	349.367-010
Keno Writer (amuse. & rec.)	CSR	54	343.467-022
Kerfer-Machine Operator (furniture)	RCE	42	667.685-042
Kettle Operator (beverage)	RES	46	522.682-010
Kettle Operator (plastic-synth.)	REI	53	558.382-042
Kettle Operator (smelt. & refin.)	REC	48	519.685-018
Kettle Operator I (chemical)	REI	49	558.382-038
Kettle Tender (beverage)	REI	40	526.665-014
Kettle Tender (construction)	RCE	37	869.685-010
Kettle Tender (sugar & conf.)	REI	40	520.685-118
Kettle Tender I (smelt. & refin.)	RSC	45	519.685-022
Kettle Tender II (smelt. & refin.)	REC	45	511.685-030
Kettle Tender, Platinum and Palladium (smelt. & refin.)	RES	45	511.685-034
Kettle Worker (soap & rel.)	REI	47	553.685-070
Key Cutter (any industry)	RCE	42	709.684-050
Keyboard-Action Assembler (musical inst.)	RES	48	730.684-042
Keying-Machine Operator (print. & pub.)	RCE	40	652.685-042
Keymodule-Assembly-Machine Tender (office machines)	RCI	42	692.685-274
Keyseating-Machine Set-up Operator (machine shop)	REI	51	605.382-018
Kick Press Setter (button & notion)	RCS	50	617.380-010
Kick-Press Operator (protective dev.)	CRE	42	692.685-102
Kick-Press Operator I (any industry)	RCE	47	616.682-026
Kiln Burner (brick & tile)	RSC	49	573.682-010
Kiln Cleaner (concrete prod.)	RCE	40	573.687-018
Kiln Drawer (brick & tile)	REI	40	929.687-014
Kiln Drawer (pottery & porc.)	REC	40	573.667-010
Kiln Loader (beverage)	REC	39	523.687-018
Kiln Operator (smelt. & refin.)	RCS	46	513.565-010

DOT to HOC

Part 3: From Occupational Titles to Holland Codes

From the Dictionary of Occupational Titles Occupations to Holland Codes

DOT to HOC

Title	HOC	Cx	DOT
Kiln Operator (steel & rel.)	RCS	44	509.565-010
Kiln Operator (woodworking)	REC	53	563.382-010
Kiln Operator, Malt House (beverage)	RSE	45	523.682-030
Kiln Placer (pottery & porc.)	REC	40	573.686-026
Kiln Worker (pottery & porc.)	RCE	37	573.687-022
Kiln-Burner Helper (brick & tile)	RES	41	573.687-026
Kiln-Door Builder (brick & tile)	RCE	41	573.684-010
Kiln-Furniture Caster (pottery & porc.)	REC	43	579.684-018
Kiln-Operator Helper (concrete prod.)	REC	38	573.685-022
Kiln-Operator Helper (smelt. & refin.)	RCS	43	513.587-010
Kiln-Transfer Operator (woodworking)	REI	41	569.683-010
Kiss Setter, Hand (sugar & conf.)	RCE	38	529.687-122
Kitchen Clerk (hotel & rest.)	RCE	51	222.587-022
Kitchen Helper (hotel & rest.)	RES	38	318.687-010
Kitchen Steward/Stewardess (hotel & rest.)	RES	59	318.137-010
Kitchen Supervisor (hotel & rest.)	ERS	60	319.137-030
Knife Changer (tobacco)	RCE	39	638.684-010
Knife Grinder (machine shop)	RCI	50	603.382-038
Knife Operator (concrete prod.)	REC	51	579.382-018
Knife Setter (saw. & plan.)	RCS	47	663.380-010
Knife Setter (sugar & conf.)	REC	48	638.684-014
Knife Setter, Grinder Machine (paper & pulp)	RCE	41	564.684-010
Knife-Machine Operator (textile)	REC	42	584.685-030
Knit-Goods Washer (knitting)	RSC	45	582.685-094
Knitter Mechanic (knitting)	RIE	57	685.360-010
Knitter, Full-Fashioned Garment (knitting)	RCE	41	685.665-010
Knitter, Hand (tex. prod., n.e.c.)	CRE	52	782.684-034
Knitter, Wire Mesh (metal prod., n.e.c.)	RCE	42	616.685-030
Knitting-Machine Fixer (knitting)	REI	56	689.260-026
Knitting-Machine Fixer, Head (knitting)	RSE	60	689.130-018
Knitting-Machine Operator (knitting)	RCE	42	685.665-014
Knitting-Machine Operator (tex. prod., n.e.c.)	CRE	42	685.685-010
Knitting-Machine Operator Helper (knitting)	REC	41	685.686-014
Knitting-Machine Operator, Full-Fashioned Hosiery, Automatic (knitting)	RCE	48	684.682-010
Knock-Out Hand (plastic prod.)	REC	39	754.684-034
Knock-Up Assembler (woodworking)	RES	38	762.687-050
Knotting-Machine Operator (paper goods)	REC	40	649.685-054
Knurling-Machine Operator (ordnance)	RCS	43	604.685-018
Kosher Inspector (dairy products)	CSE	43	529.687-126
Label Coder (any industry)	CRS	41	920.587-014
Label Drier (recording)	REC	40	532.687-010
Label Pinker (narrow fabrics)	CRE	40	585.685-062
Label Remover (beverage)	RCE	38	920.687-106
Label-Cutting-and-Folding-Machine Operator, Automatic (narrow fabrics)	RCE	40	689.685-086
Labeling-Machine Operator (recording)	RCE	40	920.685-066
Labor Expediter (construction)	SEC	59	249.167-018
Labor-Crew Supervisor (construction; utilities)	RES	59	899.131-010

Title	HOC	Cx	DOT
Laboratory Assistant (petrol. & gas)	RIE	63	024.381-010
Laboratory Assistant (textile)	IRS	54	029.381-014
Laboratory Assistant (utilities)	IRE	66	029.361-018
Laboratory Assistant, Blood and Plasma (medical ser.; pharmaceut.)	CSE	54	078.687-010
Laboratory Assistant, Culture Media (pharmaceut.)	IRC	55	559.384-010
Laboratory Assistant, Liaison Inspection (steel & rel.)	ESR	70	169.167-026
Laboratory Assistant, Metallurgical (steel & rel.)	RCI	60	011.261-022
Laboratory Chief (photofinishing)	ESR	58	976.131-010
Laboratory Clerk (clerical)	RCE	50	222.587-026
Laboratory Helper (utilities)	RCS	42	821.564-010
Laboratory Manager (education)	IRS	69	090.164-010
Laboratory Miller (grain-feed mills)	RCE	41	521.685-194
Laboratory Supervisor (machine shop)	RES	59	706.131-010
Laboratory Supervisor (profess. & kin.)	EIS	69	022.137-010
Laboratory Technician (auto. mfg.)	RIE	59	019.261-030
Laboratory Technician, Artificial Breeding (agriculture)	RCS	58	040.361-010
Laboratory Technician, Pharmaceutical (pharmaceut.)	RIC	60	559.361-010
Laboratory Tester (any industry)	RIC	60	029.261-010
Laboratory Tester (plastic-synth.)	IRE	63	022.281-018
Laboratory Tester (textile)	RCE	54	689.384-014
Laboratory-Equipment Installer (construction)	REI	56	869.381-014
Laboratory-Sample Carrier (any industry)	RCE	40	922.687-054
Laborer (fabrication, n.e.c.)	RSE	40	590.687-010
Laborer (meat products)	REI	40	529.687-130
Laborer (petrol. & gas)	REI	38	939.687-018
Laborer (pharmaceut.)	RES	41	559.686-022
Laborer (toy-sport equip.)	RES	39	732.687-030
Laborer, Airport Maintenance (air trans.)	RES	40	899.687-014
Laborer, Ammunition Assembly I (ordnance)	RES	41	737.687-070
Laborer, Ammunition Assembly II (ordnance)	RES	40	737.687-074
Laborer, Aquatic Life (fishing & hunt.)	RES	40	446.687-014
Laborer, Boot and Shoe (boot & shoe)	RES	38	788.687-066
Laborer, Brush Clearing (any industry)	RES	37	459.687-010
Laborer, Canvas Shop (tex. prod., n.e.c.)	RES	40	789.687-090
Laborer, Car Barn (r.r. trans.)	RIE	47	910.583-010
Laborer, Cheesemaking (dairy products)	REC	40	529.686-050
Laborer, Chemical Processing (chemical)	REI	41	559.687-050
Laborer, Concrete Plant (concrete prod.)	REC	40	579.687-042
Laborer, Concrete-Mixing Plant (construction)	REC	38	579.665-014
Laborer, Construction or Leak Gang (utilities)	RES	41	862.684-014
Laborer, Cook House (chemical)	REC	37	551.687-022
Laborer, Electroplating (electroplating)	REC	42	500.686-010
Laborer, General (brick & tile)	RES	38	579.667-010
Laborer, General (leather mfg.)	RCS	40	589.686-026
Laborer, General (machine shop)	RES	40	609.684-014
Laborer, General (motor trans.)	REC	37	909.687-014
Laborer, General (nonfer. metal)	RES	40	519.686-010
Laborer, General (paint & varnish)	RIE	40	559.685-110

Title	HOC	Cx	DOT
Laborer, General (plastic prod.)	RES	38	754.687-010
Laborer, General (plastic-synth.)	RCE	40	559.667-014
Laborer, General (rubber goods; rubber reclaim.; rubber tire)	CRE	39	559.686-026
Laborer, General (smelt. & refin.)	REI	40	519.687-026
Laborer, General (steel & rel.)	REI	41	509.687-026
Laborer, General (tex. prod., n.e.c.)	CER	39	589.687-026
Laborer, Gold Leaf (metal prod., n.e.c.)	RES	38	700.687-038
Laborer, Grinding and Polishing (any industry)	REC	42	705.687-014
Laborer, High-Density Press (agriculture)	RCE	37	929.687-018
Laborer, Hoisting (any industry)	RCE	39	921.667-022
Laborer, Hot-Plate Plywood Press (millwork-plywood)	RSE	40	569.686-026
Laborer, Landscape (agriculture)	RES	42	408.687-014
Laborer, Petroleum Refinery (petrol. refin.)	RES	41	549.687-018
Laborer, Pie Bakery (bakery products)	RES	38	529.686-054
Laborer, Pipelines (pipe lines)	RES	40	914.687-010
Laborer, Poultry Farm (agriculture)	RIE	41	411.687-018
Laborer, Poultry Hatchery (agriculture)	ECR	44	411.687-022
Laborer, Powerhouse (utilities)	RES	41	952.665-010
Laborer, Prestressed Concrete (concrete prod.)	RES	39	575.687-018
Laborer, Rags (paper & pulp)	RCE	41	539.587-010
Laborer, Salvage (any industry)	RSE	40	929.687-022
Laborer, Shellfish Processing (can. & preserv.)	REC	40	529.687-230
Laborer, Shipyard (ship-boat mfg.)	RSE	38	809.687-022
Laborer, Solder Making (nonfer. metal)	RSE	41	519.667-014
Laborer, Starch Factory (grain-feed mills)	RES	41	529.685-154
Laborer, Stores (any industry)	RES	40	922.687-058
Laborer, Syrup Machine (grain-feed mills)	RES	36	521.687-074
Laborer, Tanbark (logging)	REC	41	454.687-014
Laborer, Tin Can (tinware)	RSE	38	709.686-010
Laborer, Tree Tapping (agriculture; forestry)	REC	37	453.687-014
Laborer, Vat House (chemical)	REC	37	559.686-030
Laborer, Wharf (can. & preserv.)	REI	39	922.687-062
Laborer, Wood-Preserving Plant (wood prod., n.e.c.)	RES	40	561.686-010
Lace Winder (tex. prod., n.e.c.)	RCE	38	685.687-018
Lace-Paper-Machine Operator (paper goods)	RES	41	649.685-058
Lace-Roller Operator (leather prod.)	REC	38	920.685-070
Lacer (nonmet. min.)	CRE	38	774.687-014
Lacer (protective dev.)	RCE	38	789.687-094
Lacer (toy-sport equip.)	REC	41	732.687-034
Lacer and Tier (elec. equip.)	REC	39	724.687-010
Lacer I (boot & shoe)	REC	37	788.687-070
Lacer II (boot & shoe)	CRE	41	690.685-254
Lacing-String Cutter (boot & shoe)	REC	35	788.687-074
Lacquer Maker (paint & varnish)	RSC	45	559.682-030
Lacquer-Dipping-Machine Operator (button & notion)	REC	41	509.685-034
Lacquer-Pin-Press Operator (ordnance)	RCE	38	737.687-078
Lacquerer (clock & watch)	RCE	37	715.684-138
Lacquerer (jewelry-silver.)	RCE	45	749.684-034

DOT to HOC

Title	HOC	Cx	DOT
Lacquerer (plastic prod.)	RCE	41	599.685-054
Ladle Liner (foundry; smelt. & refin.)	RCS	39	519.684-010
Ladle Pourer (smelt. & refin.)	RCS	40	514.684-014
Lag Screwer (furniture)	RCE	42	763.684-046
Lagging-Machine Operator (nonfer. metal)	REC	40	691.685-014
Lamber (agriculture)	RIS	47	410.364-010
Laminated-Plastic-Tabletop-Molding Wrapper (furniture)	RCE	39	692.686-046
Laminating-Machine Feeder (wood prod., n.e.c.)	RCI	36	569.686-042
Laminating-Machine Offbearer (wood prod., n.e.c.)	RCE	39	569.686-046
Laminating-Machine Operator (furniture)	RCS	45	692.685-106
Laminating-Machine Operator (knitting; textile)	REC	48	584.682-014
Laminating-Machine Tender (rubber goods)	RCS	41	554.665-014
Lamination Assembler (elec. equip.; electron. comp.)	CRE	42	729.684-066
Lamination Assembler, Printed Circuit Boards (electron. comp.)	RCE	42	726.687-026
Lamination Spinner (elec. equip.)	REC	38	729.687-018
Laminator (rubber goods)	CRE	44	899.684-018
Laminator (tex. prod., n.e.c.)	RCE	41	584.685-034
Laminator (wood prod., n.e.c.)	RCI	43	554.685-030
Laminator I (leather prod.)	RCE	40	690.685-258
Laminator II (leather prod.)	CRE	38	783.685-022
Laminator, Hand (furniture)	RES	42	763.684-050
Laminator, Preforms (plastic prod.)	RES	42	754.684-050
Laminator, Printed Circuit Boards (electron. comp.)	RCI	40	692.685-282
Lamp-Shade Assembler (fabrication, n.e.c.)	RCE	40	739.684-094
Lamp-Shade Joiner (fabrication, n.e.c.)	RCE	39	692.685-110
Lamp-Shade Sewer (fabrication, n.e.c.)	RSE	50	787.381-010
Land Surveyor (profess. & kin.)	IEA	67	018.167-018
Land-Leasing Examiner (government ser.)	ESR	58	237.367-026
Landscape Architect (profess. & kin.)	AIR	75	001.061-018
Landscape Contractor (construction)	ESR	63	182.167-014
Landscape Gardener (agriculture)	RIS	61	408.161-010
Landscape Specialist (government ser.)	CRS	39	406.687-010
Lane-Marker Installer (construction)	REC	42	859.684-010
Lap Cutter-Truer Operator (optical goods)	CRS	40	604.685-022
Lapel Padder, Blindstitch (garment)	RCE	41	786.682-150
Lapper (textile)	RCI	40	689.687-090
Lapper, Hand, Tool (machine shop)	RES	51	705.481-014
Lapping-Machine Operator, Production (machine shop)	RCE	43	603.685-070
Lapping-Machine Set-up Operator (machine shop)	REI	52	603.382-026
Lard Refiner (meat products; oils & grease)	ECR	41	529.685-158
Larry Operator (steel & rel.)	RCE	44	519.683-014
Laser Technician (electron. comp.; inst. & app.)	IRE	67	019.261-034
Laser-Beam-Machine Operator (welding)	RCE	52	815.682-010
Laser-Beam-Trim Operator (electron. comp.)	RCI	51	726.682-010
Laserist (amuse. & rec.)	ASI	65	159.042-010
Last Chalker (boot & shoe)	CRE	40	788.687-078
Last Cleaner (boot & shoe)	RCE	36	788.687-082
Last Ironer (wood prod., n.e.c.)	RCE	41	739.684-098

Part 3: From Occupational Titles to Holland Codes

From the Dictionary of Occupational Titles Occupations to Holland Codes

Title	HOC	Cx	DOT
Last Marker (wood prod., n.e.c.)	CRE	40	739.684-102
Last Puller (boot & shoe)	REC	38	788.687-086
Last Putter-Away (boot & shoe; rubber goods)	RES	39	922.687-066
Last Remodeler-Repairer (boot & shoe; wood prod., n.e.c.)	REI	47	739.684-106
Last Repairer (boot & shoe; wood prod., n.e.c.)	REC	41	739.684-110
Last Sawyer (wood prod., n.e.c.)	RCE	40	690.685-262
Last Scourer (wood prod., n.e.c.)	REC	41	662.685-018
Last Trimmer (wood prod., n.e.c.)	REI	46	669.682-054
Last-Model Maker (wood prod., n.e.c.)	RIE	57	761.381-018
Last-Pattern Grader (wood prod., n.e.c.)	RIE	56	693.382-010
Last-Repairer Helper (boot & shoe)	CRE	40	739.684-114
Laster (boot & shoe)	REC	40	753.684-022
Laster, Hand (boot & shoe)	RCE	38	788.684-074
Lasting-Machine Operator, Hand Method (boot & shoe)	RCE	41	788.684-078
Latex Spooler (rubber goods)	REC	41	559.685-114
Latex-Ribbon-Machine Operator (rubber goods)	REI	50	559.682-034
Latexer (carpet & rug)	RES	42	584.684-010
Latexer I (protective dev.)	RCE	41	584.685-038
Lathe Hand (jewelry-silver.)	REC	47	700.682-014
Lathe Operator (jewelry-silver.)	RCE	51	770.382-010
Lathe Operator, Contact Lens (optical goods)	REI	55	716.382-010
Lathe Operator, Numerical Control (machine shop)	RIE	57	604.362-010
Lathe Sander (woodworking)	REC	42	761.682-010
Lathe Spotter (millwork-plywood)	RES	41	663.686-022
Lathe Tender (machine shop)	RCE	43	604.685-026
Lathe Winder (metal prod., n.e.c.)	REC	51	619.482-010
Lather (construction)	RCS	52	842.361-010
Lather Apprentice (construction)	RCS	52	842.361-014
Latrine Cleaner (mine & quarry)	REC	37	939.687-022
Launch Commander, Harbor Police (government ser.)	ESA	55	375.167-030
Launderer, Hand (laundry & rel.)	RES	41	361.684-010
Laundry Clerk (clerical)	CSR	51	221.387-038
Laundry Laborer (laundry & rel.)	REC	39	361.687-018
Laundry Operator (laundry & rel.)	REI	42	369.684-014
Laundry Pricing Clerk (laundry & rel.)	CRE	52	216.482-030
Laundry Worker I (any industry)	REI	40	361.684-014
Laundry Worker II (any industry)	REC	40	361.685-018
Laundry Worker III (any industry)	RCE	44	369.387-010
Laundry Worker, Domestic (domestic ser.)	RCE	40	302.685-010
Laundry-Bag-Punch Operator (paper goods)	REC	37	649.685-062
Laundry-Machine Mechanic (laundry & rel.)	RES	52	629.261-010
Laundry-Machine Tender (tex. prod., n.e.c.)	REC	41	589.685-066
Laundry-Tub Maker (concrete prod.)	RSE	43	575.684-034
Lawn-Service Worker (agriculture)	REI	47	408.684-010
Lawn-Sprinkler Installer (construction)	REI	47	869.684-030
Lawyer (profess. & kin.)	ESI	77	110.107-010
Lawyer, Admiralty (profess. & kin.)	ESA	77	110.117-018
Lawyer, Corporation (profess. & kin.)	ESA	77	110.117-022
Lawyer, Criminal (profess. & kin.)	ESA	77	110.107-014

Part 3: From Occupational Titles to Holland Codes

From the Dictionary of Occupational Titles Occupations to Holland Codes

Title	HOC	Cx	DOT
Lawyer, Patent (profess. & kin.)	ESA	77	110.117-026
Lawyer, Probate (profess. & kin.)	ESA	77	110.117-030
Lawyer, Real Estate (profess. & kin.)	ESA	77	110.117-034
Lay-Out Former (business ser.)	ARE	58	970.381-018
Lay-Out Inspector (machine shop)	RIE	60	600.281-014
Lay-Out Technician (optical goods)	REI	56	716.381-014
Lay-Out Worker (jewelry-silver.)	RIE	56	700.381-026
Lay-Out Worker (machine shop)	RIE	61	600.281-018
Lay-Out Worker (mfd. bldgs.)	RES	48	869.684-034
Lay-Out Worker I (any industry)	RIE	62	809.281-010
Lay-Out Worker II (any industry)	REI	52	809.381-014
Lay-Out-Machine Operator (tex. prod., n.e.c.)	RES	44	781.684-034
Layaway Clerk (retail trade)	CSE	51	299.467-010
Layboy Tender (paper & pulp; paper goods; print. & pub.)	CRE	40	649.685-066
Layer (glass mfg.)	RCE	42	673.686-026
Leacher (paper & pulp)	CRE	41	551.685-090
Leacher (smelt. & refin.)	RES	48	511.582-010
Lead Burner (elec. equip.)	RCS	44	727.684-022
Lead Burner (welding)	RIE	58	819.281-010
Lead Burner, Machine (elec. equip.)	RES	47	727.662-010
Lead Caster (elec. equip.)	REI	45	502.684-010
Lead Former (elec. equip.)	CRE	40	691.685-018
Lead Former (pen & pencil)	REC	39	575.685-050
Lead Hand, Inspecting and Testing (electron. comp.)	ERC	54	726.364-010
Lead Handler (ordnance)	RES	41	599.687-018
Lead Operator (smelt. & refin.)	REI	55	630.381-018
Lead Operator, Automatic Vulcanizing (rubber goods)	RES	53	690.362-010
Lead Pony Rider (amuse. & rec.)	CRS	38	153.674-014
Lead Recoverer, Continuous-Naphtha-Treating Plant (petrol. refin.)	RCS	47	541.685-014
Lead Worker, Wafer Polishing (electron. comp.)	REC	56	673.364-010
Lead Worker, Wafer Production (electron. comp.)	ERC	51	590.364-010
Lead-Burner Apprentice (welding)	RIE	58	819.281-014
Lead-Burner Helper (elec. equip.)	RSE	41	727.687-070
Lead-Burner Supervisor (welding)	ERC	59	819.131-010
Lead-Caster Helper (elec. equip.)	CRE	40	502.687-018
Lead-Nitrate Processor (chemical)	REI	42	558.585-030
Lead-Oxide-Mill Tender (elec. equip.)	RCE	42	558.685-042
Lead-Press Operator (nonfer. metal)	RSC	47	691.382-014
Lead-Section Supervisor (ordnance)	REI	59	619.132-010
Leader Tier (toy-sport equip.)	RCE	40	732.687-038
Leaf Conditioner (tobacco)	REC	39	522.687-026
Leaf Coverer (smelt. & refin.)	REC	41	519.684-014
Leaf Sorter (tobacco)	CER	42	529.687-134
Leaf Tier (tobacco)	RCE	36	529.687-138
Leaf-Conditioner Helper (tobacco)	REC	39	522.687-030
Leaf-Size Picker (tobacco)	RCE	39	529.687-142
Leak Hunter (beverage)	CRS	40	764.687-090
Leak Tester, Semiconductor Packages (electron. comp.)	RCI	39	726.685-034

DOT to HOC

Title	HOC	Cx	DOT
Lease Buyer (mine & quarry; petrol. & gas)	SER	67	191.117-030
Lease Picker (textile)	RCI	45	689.684-018
Lease-Out Worker (textile)	REC	40	683.684-022
Leasing Agent, Outdoor Advertising (business ser.)	ESC	53	254.357-010
Leasing Agent, Residence (real estate)	ESA	60	250.357-014
Leasing-Machine Tender (textile)	RES	40	681.685-054
Leather Cleaner (laundry & rel.)	REC	46	362.684-026
Leather Coater (leather mfg.)	REC	36	584.687-010
Leather Cutter (leather prod.)	RES	47	783.684-022
Leather Etcher (garment)	CRS	45	583.685-066
Leather Finisher (laundry & rel.)	RCE	44	363.682-010
Leather Grader (glove & mit.)	RIE	51	784.387-014
Leather Softener (boot & shoe)	REI	40	788.687-090
Leather Stamper (leather prod.)	RCE	47	781.381-018
Leather Tooler (furniture)	RCS	47	763.684-054
Leather Worker (leather prod.)	RSE	45	783.684-026
Leather-Belt Maker (leather prod.)	CRE	42	690.685-266
Legal Investigator (profess. & kin.)	ESA	66	119.267-022
Legal Secretary (clerical)	CSE	60	201.362-010
Legend Maker (fabrication, n.e.c.)	REC	42	979.684-018
Legislative Assistant (government ser.)	ESR	66	169.167-066
Lehr Tender (glass mfg.)	RCE	41	573.685-026
Lei Seller (retail trade)	ESC	44	291.454-010
Lens Examiner (optical goods)	RES	42	716.687-022
Lens Hardener (optical goods)	CRE	41	573.685-030
Lens Inserter (optical goods)	RCE	39	713.687-026
Lens Matcher (optical goods)	RCE	41	713.687-030
Lens Mounter II (optical goods)	RES	49	713.681-010
Lens Polisher, Hand (optical goods)	REI	51	716.681-018
Lens-Blank Gauger (optical goods)	REC	46	716.687-026
Lens-Block Gauger (optical goods)	CRS	39	716.687-030
Lens-Fabricating-Machine Tender (optical goods)	CRE	44	716.685-022
Lens-Mold Setter (optical goods)	REI	54	713.381-010
Lens-Molding-Equipment Operator (glass mfg.)	RES	41	575.685-054
Letter-of-Credit Clerk (financial)	CES	56	219.367-050
Letter-of-Credit Document Examiner (financial)	ESC	67	169.267-042
Letterer (machinery mfg.)	RCE	46	979.681-010
Letterer (profess. & kin.)	REA	51	970.661-014
Level-Glass-Forming-Machine Operator (cutlery-hrdwr.)	CRE	40	679.665-010
Level-Glass-Vial Filler (cutlery-hrdwr.)	CRE	39	692.685-114
Level-Vial Curvature Gauger (cutlery-hrdwr.)	CRE	42	701.687-022
Level-Vial Inside Grinder (cutlery-hrdwr.)	CRE	41	673.685-066
Level-Vial Inspector-and-Tester (cutlery-hrdwr.)	REC	42	701.687-026
Level-Vial Marker (cutlery-hrdwr.)	CRE	42	775.684-046
Level-Vial Sealer (cutlery-hrdwr.)	CRS	40	779.684-034
Level-Vial Setter (cutlery-hrdwr.)	CRS	42	701.684-018
Leveler I (wood. container)	REC	37	764.687-094
Lever Miller (clock & watch)	CRE	41	605.685-026
Lever Tender (forging)	REC	41	612.685-010

Title	HOC	Cx	DOT
Levers-Lace Machine Operator (tex. prod., n.e.c.)	RCS	47	683.682-026
Liaison Engineer (aircraft mfg.)	ERS	69	012.167-038
Librarian (library)	SAI	65	100.127-014
Librarian, Special Collections (library)	SER	64	100.267-014
Librarian, Special Library (library)	SEC	69	100.167-026
Library Assistant (library)	CSE	52	249.367-046
Library Clerk, Talking Books (library)	SCR	50	209.387-026
Library Consultant (library)	ESI	73	100.117-014
Library Director (library)	SEC	72	100.117-010
Library Technical Assistant (library)	ESI	58	100.367-018
Librettist (profess. & kin.)	ASE	69	131.067-030
License Clerk (government ser.)	CSE	51	205.367-034
License Inspector (government ser.)	SER	56	168.267-066
Lifeguard (amuse. & rec.)	ESR	47	379.667-014
Lift-Slab Operator (construction)	RES	54	869.662-010
Light Air Defense Artillery Crewmember (military ser.)	REC	41	378.684-030
Light Technician (motion picture; radio-tv broad.)	REI	56	962.362-014
Light-Bulb Assembler (light. fix.)	RCE	40	692.685-118
Light-Fixture Servicer (any industry)	RCE	37	389.687-018
Lighting-Equipment Operator (amuse. & rec.)	RIA	54	962.381-014
Lightout Examiner (beverage)	RCE	42	529.687-146
Lime Mixer Tender (steel & rel.)	RCE	41	514.685-022
Lime Slaker (concrete prod.)	REC	42	570.685-034
Lime-Kiln Operator (concrete prod.)	REI	49	573.462-010
Lime-Kiln Operator (paper & pulp)	RES	47	559.685-118
Lime-Sludge Kiln Operator (paper & pulp)	CRS	40	553.685-074
Lime-Sludge Mixer (paper & pulp)	REC	43	550.585-026
Line Erector (construction; utilities)	RES	56	821.361-018
Line Inspector (tel. & tel.)	RSC	60	822.267-010
Line Installer, Street Railway (r.r. trans.)	RIE	59	821.361-022
Line Installer-Repairer (tel. & tel.)	RSE	57	822.381-014
Line Maintainer (any industry)	RSI	58	821.261-014
Line Mover (railroad equip.)	RES	42	921.664-010
Line Repairer (utilities)	RES	58	821.361-026
Line Supervisor (tel. & tel.)	ERS	63	822.131-018
Line Supervisor (utilities)	RES	63	821.131-014
Line Tender, Flakeboard (wood prod., n.e.c.)	RIE	51	569.382-010
Line Walker (petrol. & gas; petrol. refin.; pipe lines)	CRS	48	869.564-010
Line-Erector Apprentice (construction; utilities)	RES	56	821.361-030
Line-Out Worker I (tobacco)	CER	41	920.687-110
Line-Out Worker II (tobacco)	REC	40	920.687-114
Line-Service Attendant (air trans.)	RIE	45	912.687-010
Line-Up Examiner (print. & pub.)	RES	55	979.381-014
Line-Up Worker (auto. mfg.)	CSE	50	221.367-026
Linen Controller (laundry & rel.)	ESA	56	299.357-010
Linen Grader (laundry & rel.)	RCE	40	361.687-022
Linen-Room Attendant (hotel & rest.; medical ser.)	REI	45	222.387-030
Linen-Room Supervisor (laundry & rel.)	ESR	58	222.137-014
Linen-Supply Load-Builder (laundry & rel.)	CRE	43	920.687-118

Part 3: From Occupational Titles to Holland Codes
From the Dictionary of Occupational Titles Occupations to Holland Codes

Title	HOC	Cx	DOT
Liner (glove & mit.)	CRE	40	784.687-046
Liner (pottery & porc.)	CRS	45	740.681-010
Liner Assembler (nonfer. metal)	RCE	41	613.667-010
Liner Inserter (tobacco)	RCE	37	929.687-026
Liner Replacer (mine & quarry; smelt. & refin.)	RES	41	801.664-010
Liner Reroll Tender (rubber goods; rubber tire)	REI	40	554.685-022
Liner-Machine Operator (paper goods)	RES	41	641.685-058
Liner-Machine-Operator Helper (paper goods)	RES	40	641.686-022
Lines Tender (water trans.)	RES	38	911.687-026
Lingo Cleaner (textile)	REC	40	683.687-026
Lining Baster, Jumpbasting (garment)	RCE	41	786.682-154
Lining Cementer (hat & cap)	RCE	38	795.687-022
Lining Feller, Blindstitch (garment)	RCE	41	786.682-158
Lining Inserter (toy-sport equip.)	RES	38	732.687-042
Lining Maker, Lockstitch (garment)	CRE	40	786.682-162
Lining Scrubber (laundry & rel.)	REC	37	362.687-014
Lining Setter, Lockstitch (garment)	RCE	41	786.682-166
Lining-Machine Operator (concrete prod.)	RCE	41	575.565-010
Link-and-Link-Knitting-Machine Operator (knitting)	REI	54	685.380-010
Linker (jewelry-silver.)	CRE	42	735.687-014
Linker (meat products)	RES	41	529.687-150
Linking-Machine Operator (meat products)	REC	38	529.685-162
Linotype Operator (print. & pub.)	RIE	55	650.582-010
Linseed-Oil Refiner (oils & grease)	RSE	49	559.382-030
Linseed-Oil-Press Tender (oils & grease)	RES	42	559.685-122
Linter Tender (oils & grease)	RCE	41	521.685-198
Linter-Saw Sharpener (oils & grease)	REI	49	603.682-018
Lip Cutter and Scorer (boot & shoe)	RCE	41	690.685-270
Lip-of-Shank Cutter (boot & shoe)	CRE	40	690.685-274
Liquefaction-and-Regasification-Plant Operator (utilities)	RSC	57	953.362-014
Liquefaction-Plant Operator (chemical)	REC	53	559.362-018
Liquid-Fertilizer Servicer (agriculture)	CRI	42	906.683-014
Liquid-Sugar Fortifier (sugar & conf.)	REC	46	520.585-022
Liquid-Sugar Melter (sugar & conf.)	REI	50	520.382-014
Liquor Blender (beverage)	REI	57	522.382-018
Liquor Inspector (beverage)	RCE	40	522.667-010
Liquor-Bridge Operator (sugar & conf.)	REI	47	521.565-010
Liquor-Bridge-Operator Helper (sugar & conf.)	RSE	41	521.687-078
Liquor-Grinding-Mill Operator (sugar & conf.)	REC	41	521.685-202
Literary Agent (business ser.)	ESA	67	191.117-034
Lithograph-Press Operator, Tinware (tinware)	REI	54	651.382-014
Lithographed-Plate Inspector (tinware)	RES	39	651.687-010
Lithographic Platemaker (print. & pub.)	REI	57	972.381-010
Lithographic-Plate-Maker Apprentice (print. & pub.)	REI	57	972.381-014
Lithographic-Proofer Apprentice (print. & pub.)	REI	50	651.582-014
Livestock Rancher (agriculture)	RSI	59	410.161-018
Livestock-Yard Attendant (any industry)	REI	47	410.674-018
Load Checker (utilities)	REI	56	952.367-010
Load Dispatcher (utilities)	ERS	59	952.167-014

Title	HOC	Cx	DOT
Load Tester (metal prod., n.e.c.)	RCS	45	616.685-034
Load-Out Supervisor (mine & quarry)	REI	54	921.133-014
Load-Test Mechanic (aircraft mfg.)	RES	51	929.382-010
Loader (mfd. bldgs.)	RES	42	921.687-018
Loader Helper (any industry)	RCE	41	914.687-014
Loader I (any industry)	CRS	47	914.667-010
Loader, Magazine Grinder (paper & pulp)	RES	40	530.686-014
Loader, Malt House (beverage)	REI	42	921.682-010
Loader, Semiconductor Dies (electron. comp.)	RCI	39	726.687-030
Loader-Demolder (furniture)	RCI	42	556.684-030
Loader-Unloader, Screen-Printing Machine (textile)	RES	38	652.686-022
Loading Inspector (r.r. trans.)	RCE	49	910.667-018
Loading-Machine Adjuster (ordnance)	RCS	48	632.360-014
Loading-Machine Operator (mine & quarry)	RIE	47	932.683-014
Loading-Machine Operator (ordnance)	CRE	41	694.685-026
Loading-Machine Tool-Setter (ordnance)	RCS	56	694.260-010
Loading-Machine-Operator Helper (mine & quarry)	REC	39	939.686-010
Loading-Rack Supervisor (petrol. refin.)	ESC	60	914.137-014
Loading-Shovel Oiler (mine & quarry)	RES	39	932.667-014
Loading-Unit Operator (ordnance)	CRE	41	694.685-030
Loading-Unit Tool-Setter (ordnance)	REC	52	632.380-014
Loan Interviewer, Mortgage (financial)	ESC	57	241.367-018
Loan Officer (financial; insurance)	SEI	65	186.267-018
Loan Review Analyst (financial)	CSR	69	186.267-022
Lobbyist (profess. & kin.)	ESA	68	165.017-010
Location Manager (motion picture; radio-tv broad.)	EAR	63	191.167-018
Location-and-Measurement Technician (clock & watch)	RIE	57	715.381-078
Lock Assembler (cutlery-hrdwr.)	RCS	40	706.684-074
Lock Assembler (furniture)	RES	51	706.684-070
Lock Installer (furniture)	REC	44	706.684-078
Lock Maintenance Supervisor (construction)	RES	61	899.131-014
Lock Operator (water trans.)	RSC	51	911.362-010
Lock Tender II (construction)	REI	44	850.663-018
Lock Tender, Chief Operator (water trans.)	RES	59	911.131-014
Lock-Corner-Machine Operator (woodworking)	RIE	49	665.382-014
Locker-Plant Attendant (retail trade; wholesale tr.)	RSE	45	922.684-010
Locker-Room Attendant (personal ser.)	RES	42	358.677-014
Locket Maker (jewelry-silver.)	RES	50	700.381-030
Locksmith (any industry)	REC	57	709.281-010
Locksmith Apprentice (any industry)	REC	57	709.281-014
Lockstitch-Machine Operator (garment)	CRE	43	786.682-170
Lockstitch-Sewing-Machine Operator, Complete Garment (garment)	REC	45	786.682-174
Locomotive Engineer (r.r. trans.)	RES	55	910.363-014
Locomotive Inspector (railroad equip.)	RES	58	622.281-010
Locomotive Lubricating-Systems Clerk (r.r. trans.)	CER	52	221.367-030
Locomotive Operator Helper (r.r. trans.)	REA	48	910.367-022
Locomotive-Crane Operator (any industry)	RSI	46	921.663-038
Loft Worker (ship-boat mfg.)	RES	59	661.281-010

Title	HOC	Cx	DOT
Loft Worker Apprentice (ship-boat mfg.)	RES	59	661.281-014
Loft Worker, Head (ship-boat mfg.)	RES	61	661.131-010
Log Cooker (wood. container)	REC	40	562.665-010
Log Grader (logging; saw. & plan.)	REI	54	455.367-010
Log Inspector (saw. & plan.)	RCS	41	667.687-014
Log Loader (logging)	RCE	45	921.683-058
Log Loader Helper (logging)	RCE	37	921.687-022
Log Marker (logging)	REI	40	455.687-010
Log Marker (logging; millwork-plywood)	RIE	45	454.687-018
Log Peeler (saw. & plan.)	RCE	38	569.684-010
Log Roller (saw. & plan.)	RCS	38	677.687-010
Log Scaler (logging; millwork-plywood; paper & pulp; saw. & plan.)	REI	51	455.487-010
Log Sorter (logging)	REI	44	455.684-010
Log Washer (saw. & plan.)	RCE	37	569.687-014
Log-Chipper Operator (logging)	RCS	45	564.662-010
Log-Cut-Off Sawyer, Automatic (saw. & plan.)	REC	49	667.682-090
Log-Haul Chain Feeder (paper & pulp; saw. & plan.)	RCE	38	921.686-018
Log-Truck Driver (logging)	RIS	45	904.683-010
Logger, All-Round (logging)	RES	42	454.684-018
Logging-Equipment Mechanic (logging)	REI	58	620.281-042
Logging-Operations Inspector (forestry; logging)	RES	64	168.267-070
Logging-Tractor Operator (forestry; logging; saw. & plan.)	RES	44	929.663-010
Logistics Engineer (profess. & kin.)	ESC	70	019.167-010
Long-Chain Beamer (textile)	RCE	41	681.685-058
Long-Goods Helper, Machine (food prep., n.e.c.)	RES	38	529.686-062
Long-Wall Shear Operator (mine & quarry)	RCS	47	930.662-010
Long-Wall-Mining-Machine Tender (mine & quarry)	RCE	45	930.665-010
Loom Changeover Operator (carpet & rug)	RES	41	683.687-030
Loom Changer (textile)	REI	54	683.360-010
Loom Fixer (narrow fabrics; nonmet. min.; textile)	RSE	55	683.260-018
Loom Setter, Wire Weaving (metal prod., n.e.c.)	RES	56	616.360-014
Loom Starter (textile)	RSE	53	683.360-014
Loom-Fixer Supervisor (narrow fabrics)	RES	60	683.130-014
Loom-Winder Tender (textile)	RES	40	681.685-062
Looper (knitting)	RCE	44	689.682-010
Looper (musical inst.)	CRE	42	730.685-010
Loose-End Finder, Bobbin (knitting)	REC	39	681.687-014
Lost-and-Found Clerk (clerical)	ESC	50	222.367-034
Lost-Charge-Card Clerk (clerical)	CES	51	209.367-034
Lot Attendant (retail trade)	CRE	49	915.583-010
Lounge-Car Attendant (r.r. trans.)	ECS	45	291.457-014
Lowerator Operator (fabrication, n.e.c.)	REC	39	922.686-014
Lozenge Maker (sugar & conf.)	RIE	48	529.682-026
Lozenge-Dough Mixer (sugar & conf.)	RES	44	520.685-122
Lubricating-Machine Tender (ordnance)	REC	41	509.685-038
Lubrication Servicer (automotive ser.)	RES	43	915.687-018
Lubrication-Equipment Servicer (any industry)	RES	50	630.381-022
Lubricator-Granulator (nonfer. metal; steel & rel.)	CRE	41	509.685-042

Part 3: From Occupational Titles to Holland Codes

From the Dictionary of Occupational Titles Occupations to Holland Codes

Title	HOC	Cx	DOT
Luggage Maker (leather prod.)	REC	52	783.381-022
Luggage Repairer (any industry)	RSE	50	365.361-010
Lumber Estimator (wood. container)	CRS	54	221.482-014
Lumber Handler (woodworking)	RSE	40	922.687-070
Lumber Scaler (woodworking)	RCE	50	221.487-010
Lumber Sorter (woodworking)	RES	39	922.687-074
Lumber Straightener (saw. & plan.)	RES	40	669.687-018
Lumite Injector (boot & shoe)	RCE	42	690.685-278
Lump Inspector (tobacco)	CRS	40	790.687-018
Lumpia Wrapper Maker (food prep., n.e.c.)	RCE	37	526.684-014
Lunch-Truck Driver (hotel & rest.)	ERS	49	292.463-010
Luster Applicator (glass mfg.; glass products)	RSE	50	740.381-014
Lye Treater (chemical; soap & rel.)	RIE	46	551.685-094
Lye-Peel Operator (can. & preserv.)	RCE	37	521.685-206
Lyricist (profess. & kin.)	ASE	67	131.067-034
Machine Assembler (machinery mfg.)	RES	56	638.361-010
Machine Builder (machinery mfg.; machine tools)	RIE	59	600.281-022
Machine Cleaner (any industry)	REC	38	699.687-014
Machine Feeder (any industry)	REC	37	699.686-010
Machine Feeder (clock & watch)	RCE	36	715.686-014
Machine Feeder (welding)	REC	40	819.686-010
Machine Feeder, Raw Stock (tex. prod., n.e.c.; textile)	RES	39	680.686-018
Machine Fixer (carpet & rug)	REI	59	628.281-010
Machine Fixer (textile)	RES	55	689.260-010
Machine Helper (any industry)	RSE	41	619.687-014
Machine Helper (tex. prod., n.e.c.)	RES	40	586.686-022
Machine Helper (welding)	RES	41	819.666-010
Machine Molder (foundry)	RIE	47	518.682-010
Machine Operator I (any industry)	RCE	54	616.380-018
Machine Operator II (any industry)	RCE	42	619.685-062
Machine Operator, Centrifugal-Control Switches (elec. equip.)	REI	50	609.682-022
Machine Operator, Ceramics (pottery & porc.)	CRS	41	679.685-010
Machine Operator, General (paper goods)	RCS	41	649.685-070
Machine Repairer, Maintenance (any industry)	RIC	64	638.261-030
Machine Set-up Operator (machine shop)	RIE	58	600.380-018
Machine Set-up Operator, Paper Goods (paper goods)	RIE	52	649.380-010
Machine Setter (any industry)	RIE	57	616.360-022
Machine Setter (button & notion)	RIE	54	690.380-010
Machine Setter (clock & watch)	RIE	59	600.380-022
Machine Setter (machine shop)	RIE	59	600.360-014
Machine Setter (nonmet. min.)	RCS	56	692.260-010
Machine Setter (woodworking)	RIE	57	669.280-010
Machine Setter-and-Repairer (plastic prod.)	RCS	49	690.380-014
Machine Sneller (toy-sport equip.)	RCE	40	732.685-026
Machine Tester (machinery mfg.)	RCE	51	629.382-010
Machine Tester (office machines)	CRE	50	706.387-014
Machine Try-Out Setter (machine tools)	RIS	59	600.360-010
Machine-Adjuster Leader (ordnance)	REA	59	619.137-010

From the Dictionary of Occupational Titles Occupations to Holland Codes

Title	HOC	Cx	DOT
Machine-Assembler Supervisor (machinery mfg.)	RES	65	638.131-014
Machine-Castings Plasterer (foundry)	REC	40	519.687-030
Machine-Clothing Replacer (paper & pulp)	RSE	54	629.361-010
Machine-Made-Shoe Unit Worker (boot & shoe)	CRS	42	753.584-010
Machine-Pack Assembler (ordnance)	RCE	39	920.687-122
Machine-Shop Supervisor, Production (machine shop)	RES	61	609.130-010
Machine-Shop Supervisor, Tool (machine shop)	RES	63	600.130-010
Machine-Stoppage-Frequency Checker (textile)	CRE	52	221.367-034
Machine-Tank Operator (wood. container)	RSE	47	667.662-014
Machinery Erector (engine-turbine; machinery mfg.)	REI	61	638.261-014
Machining-and-Assembly Supervisor (elec. equip.)	REI	56	619.131-010
Machinist (machine shop)	RIE	62	600.280-022
Machinist Apprentice (machine shop)	RIE	62	600.280-026
Machinist Apprentice, Automotive (automotive ser.)	RIE	58	600.280-030
Machinist Apprentice, Composing Room (print. & pub.)	RES	59	627.261-014
Machinist Apprentice, Linotype (print. & pub.)	REI	58	627.261-018
Machinist Apprentice, Marine Engine (ship-boat mfg.)	RSE	58	623.281-018
Machinist Apprentice, Outside (ship-boat mfg.)	RIE	58	623.281-022
Machinist Apprentice, Wood (woodworking)	RIE	54	669.380-010
Machinist Helper, Outside (ship-boat mfg.)	RCS	42	623.687-010
Machinist Supervisor, Outside (ship-boat mfg.)	RSE	59	623.131-010
Machinist, Automotive (automotive ser.)	RIE	58	600.280-034
Machinist, Experimental (machine shop)	RIS	62	600.260-022
Machinist, Linotype (print. & pub.)	REI	58	627.261-022
Machinist, Marine Engine (ship-boat mfg.)	RSE	58	623.281-026
Machinist, Motion-Picture Equipment (motion picture; photo. appar.)	RIE	61	714.281-018
Machinist, Outside (ship-boat mfg.)	RIE	58	623.281-030
Machinist, Wood (woodworking)	RIE	54	669.380-014
Magazine Keeper (clerical)	RSE	51	222.367-038
Magazine Repairer (print. & pub.)	RCS	42	653.685-022
Magazine Supervisor (chemical; ordnance)	ESR	55	222.137-018
Magician (amuse. & rec.)	AES	58	159.041-010
Magistrate (government ser.)	ESI	77	111.107-014
Magnesium-Mill Operator (nonfer. metal)	RES	40	607.686-010
Magnet-Valve Assembler (elec. equip.)	CRE	42	724.684-034
Magnetic-Tape Winder (recording)	RCE	40	726.685-010
Magnetic-Tape-Composer Operator (print. & pub.)	CES	54	203.382-018
Magneto Repairer (any industry)	REI	55	721.281-022
Mail Carrier (government ser.)	CRS	51	230.367-010
Mail Censor (government ser.)	CSR	53	243.367-010
Mail Clerk (clerical)	CRE	46	209.687-026
Mail Handler (government ser.)	RSC	47	209.687-014
Mail-Distribution-Scheme Examiner (government ser.)	ESC	56	239.367-018
Mail-Processing-Equipment Mechanic (government ser.)	RIE	57	633.261-014
Mailer (print. & pub.)	REC	47	222.587-030
Mailer Apprentice (print. & pub.)	RCE	47	222.587-032
Mailing-Machine Operator (print. & pub.)	RIE	53	208.462-010
Mailroom Supervisor (clerical)	ESR	59	209.137-010

Part 3: From Occupational Titles to Holland Codes
From the Dictionary of Occupational Titles Occupations to Holland Codes

Title	HOC	Cx	DOT
Mailroom Supervisor (print. & pub.)	ESR	58	222.137-022
Mains-and-Service Supervisor (utilities)	RES	59	862.137-010
Mainspring Former, Arbor End (clock & watch)	RCE	39	715.687-078
Mainspring Former, Brace End (clock & watch)	RCE	38	715.687-082
Mainspring Winder and Oiler (clock & watch)	RCE	38	715.685-038
Maintainability Engineer (profess. & kin.)	ERI	70	019.081-010
Maintenance Data Analyst (military ser.)	ERS	55	221.367-038
Maintenance Inspector (tel. & tel.)	RES	59	822.261-018
Maintenance Machinist (machine shop)	RIE	59	600.280-042
Maintenance Mechanic (any industry)	REI	59	638.281-014
Maintenance Mechanic (construction; petrol. & gas; pipe lines)	RIE	58	620.281-046
Maintenance Mechanic (grain-feed mills)	RES	54	629.281-030
Maintenance Mechanic (leather mfg.)	RIS	57	629.280-010
Maintenance Mechanic Helper (construction; petrol. & gas; pipe lines)	RSC	47	620.664-014
Maintenance Mechanic, Compressed-Gas Plant (chemical)	RIE	58	630.261-010
Maintenance Mechanic, Engine (water trans.)	REI	57	623.281-034
Maintenance Mechanic, Telephone (any industry)	RIE	59	822.281-018
Maintenance Repairer, Building (any industry)	RES	57	899.381-010
Maintenance Repairer, Industrial (any industry)	RIC	60	899.261-014
Maintenance Supervisor (any industry)	ERS	61	891.137-010
Maintenance Supervisor (utilities)	EIR	66	184.167-050
Maintenance Supervisor, Fire-Fighting-Equipment (government ser.)	REI	60	638.131-018
Maintenance Supervisor, Mobile Battery Equipment (mine & quarry)	ERS	58	638.131-034
Maintenance Worker, Municipal (government ser.)	RCS	48	899.684-046
Maintenance-Mechanic Helper (any industry)	REC	42	638.684-018
Maintenance-Mechanic Supervisor (any industry)	RES	67	638.131-022
Maintenance-Repairer Helper, Industrial (any industry)	RES	46	899.684-022
Major-Assembly Inspector (agric. equip.)	RIE	53	801.381-018
Make-Up Arranger (print. & pub.)	RSI	55	973.381-026
Make-Up Artist (amuse. & rec.; motion picture; radio-tv broad.)	AER	63	333.071-010
Make-Up Operator (chemical)	REI	51	559.382-034
Make-Up Operator Helper (chemical)	RCS	42	550.587-010
Making-Line Worker (boot & shoe)	CRE	40	753.687-026
Malt Roaster (beverage)	RES	47	526.682-026
Malt-House Operator (beverage)	CRE	43	522.685-074
Malt-Specifications-Control Assistant (beverage)	RIS	65	022.261-014
Management Aide (social ser.)	SEC	55	195.367-014
Management Analyst (profess. & kin.)	ICR	70	161.167-010
Management Trainee (any industry)	ESR	64	189.167-018
Manager, Advertising (any industry)	AES	72	164.117-010
Manager, Advertising (print. & pub.)	ESA	68	163.167-010
Manager, Advertising Agency (business ser.)	AES	65	164.117-014
Manager, Aerial Planting and Cultivation (agriculture)	REC	61	180.167-062
Manager, Agricultural-Labor Camp (profess. & kin.)	ESR	66	187.167-050

Part 3: From Occupational Titles to Holland Codes
From the Dictionary of Occupational Titles Occupations to Holland Codes

Title	HOC	Cx	DOT
Manager, Airport (air trans.)	ESR	70	184.117-026
Manager, Animal Shelter (nonprofit org.)	ESC	65	187.167-218
Manager, Apartment House (real estate)	ERS	59	186.167-018
Manager, Aquatic Facility (amuse. & rec.)	SEC	65	187.167-054
Manager, Area Development (utilities)	ESA	67	184.117-030
Manager, Armored Transport Service (business ser.)	ESA	61	372.167-022
Manager, Athlete (amuse. & rec.)	ESR	70	153.117-014
Manager, Auto Specialty Services (automotive ser.)	ESR	66	185.167-074
Manager, Automobile Service Station (retail trade)	ERS	61	185.167-014
Manager, Automotive Services (any industry)	ESR	68	184.117-034
Manager, Bakery (bakery products)	ESR	68	189.117-046
Manager, Barber or Beauty Shop (personal ser.)	ESC	61	187.167-058
Manager, Benefits (profess. & kin.)	ESC	66	166.167-018
Manager, Boarding House (hotel & rest.)	ESR	57	320.137-010
Manager, Bowling Alley (amuse. & rec.)	ESR	58	187.167-222
Manager, Branch (any industry)	ESA	68	183.117-010
Manager, Branch Operation Evaluation (hotel & rest.)	ERI	64	187.167-062
Manager, Branch Store (laundry & rel.)	ECS	51	369.467-010
Manager, Brokerage Office (financial)	ESR	69	186.117-034
Manager, Bulk Plant (petrol. refin.; retail trade)	ERI	68	181.117-010
Manager, Bus Transportation (motor trans.)	ESR	63	184.167-054
Manager, Camp (amuse. & rec.)	ERS	59	329.161-010
Manager, Camp (construction; logging)	ESR	58	187.167-066
Manager, Car Inspection and Repair (r.r. trans.)	ESC	67	184.117-086
Manager, Cardroom (amuse. & rec.)	ESR	61	343.137-010
Manager, Cargo-and-Ramp-Services (air trans.)	ESR	68	184.167-058
Manager, Casino (amuse. & rec.)	SER	61	187.167-070
Manager, Cemetery (real estate)	ESR	65	187.167-074
Manager, Christmas-Tree Farm (forestry)	SER	65	180.117-010
Manager, Circulation (print. & pub.)	ESC	67	163.167-014
Manager, City (government ser.)	SEC	67	188.117-114
Manager, Communications Station (tel. & tel.)	ESC	66	184.167-062
Manager, Compensation (profess. & kin.)	ESR	70	166.167-022
Manager, Computer Operations (profess. & kin.)	SEI	66	169.167-082
Manager, Contracts (petrol. & gas; petrol. refin.; pipe lines)	ESC	71	163.117-010
Manager, Convention (hotel & rest.)	ESA	66	187.167-078
Manager, Credit and Collection (any industry)	ESC	65	169.167-086
Manager, Customer Service (tel. & tel.)	ESA	69	168.167-058
Manager, Customer Services (business ser.; retail trade)	ESR	62	187.167-082
Manager, Customer Technical Services (profess. & kin.)	ESR	66	189.117-018
Manager, Dairy Farm (agriculture)	ESR	61	180.167-026
Manager, Dance Studio (education)	ESA	57	187.167-086
Manager, Data Processing (profess. & kin.)	IEA	73	169.167-030
Manager, Dental Laboratory (protective dev.)	EIS	64	187.167-090
Manager, Department (any industry)	ESA	66	189.167-022
Manager, Department (retail trade)	ESR	59	299.137-010
Manager, Department Store (retail trade)	SER	69	185.117-010
Manager, Display (retail trade)	AES	65	142.031-014

Part 3: From Occupational Titles to Holland Codes
From the Dictionary of Occupational Titles Occupations to Holland Codes

Title	HOC	Cx	DOT
Manager, Distribution Warehouse (wholesale tr.)	ESC	64	185.167-018
Manager, Dude Ranch (amuse. & rec.)	SER	61	187.167-094
Manager, Education and Training (education)	EIS	69	166.167-026
Manager, Employee Welfare (profess. & kin.)	SEA	67	166.117-014
Manager, Employment (profess. & kin.)	ESC	67	166.167-030
Manager, Employment Agency (profess. & kin.)	ESC	63	187.167-098
Manager, Exchange Floor (financial)	ESI	69	186.117-086
Manager, Export (any industry)	ESA	70	163.117-014
Manager, Fast Food Services (retail trade; wholesale tr.)	SER	60	185.137-010
Manager, Field Party, Geophysical Prospecting (petrol. & gas)	ESR	66	181.167-010
Manager, Financial Institution (financial)	ESR	69	186.167-086
Manager, Fish Hatchery (fishing & hunt.)	ESA	65	180.167-030
Manager, Fish-and-Game Club (amuse. & rec.)	ESC	64	187.167-102
Manager, Flight Control (air trans.)	ESR	68	184.167-066
Manager, Flight Kitchen (hotel & rest.)	ESC	59	319.137-014
Manager, Flight Operations (air trans.)	ESI	70	184.117-038
Manager, Flight-Reservations (air trans.)	ESC	68	184.167-070
Manager, Food Concession (hotel & rest.)	ESR	57	185.167-022
Manager, Food Processing Plant (can. & preserv.)	ESR	66	183.167-026
Manager, Food Service (hotel & rest.; personal ser.)	ESR	66	187.167-106
Manager, Forms Analysis (profess. & kin.)	EAS	66	161.167-014
Manager, Front Office (hotel & rest.)	ESR	64	187.137-018
Manager, Game Breeding Farm (agriculture)	ERS	66	180.167-034
Manager, Game Preserve (agriculture)	ESA	66	180.167-038
Manager, Golf Club (amuse. & rec.)	ECS	66	187.167-114
Manager, Gun Club (amuse. & rec.)	CES	63	187.167-118
Manager, Handicraft-or-Hobby Shop (amuse. & rec.)	RES	65	187.161-014
Manager, Harbor Department (water trans.)	ERS	70	184.117-042
Manager, Health Club (personal ser.)	ESR	60	339.137-010
Manager, Hotel or Motel (hotel & rest.)	ESR	67	187.117-038
Manager, Hotel Recreational Facilities (amuse. & rec.)	SER	65	187.167-122
Manager, Housing Project (profess. & kin.)	EAS	66	186.167-030
Manager, Industrial Cafeteria (hotel & rest.)	ERS	58	319.137-018
Manager, Industrial Organization (any industry)	ESR	69	189.117-022
Manager, Insurance Office (insurance)	ESC	73	186.167-034
Manager, Internal Security (business ser.)	SER	63	376.137-010
Manager, Irrigation District (waterworks)	ESR	72	184.117-046
Manager, Labor Relations (profess. & kin.)	ESR	67	166.167-034
Manager, Land Development (real estate)	ESI	74	186.117-042
Manager, Land Leases-and-Rentals (petrol. & gas)	ESR	63	186.167-038
Manager, Land Surveying (profess. & kin.)	IER	69	018.167-022
Manager, Laundromat (laundry & rel.)	ERI	63	369.167-010
Manager, Leasing (petrol. & gas)	ESR	72	186.117-046
Manager, Liquor Establishment (hotel & rest.)	ESR	60	187.167-126
Manager, Lodging Facilities (hotel & rest.)	ESR	60	320.137-014
Manager, Machinery-or-Equipment, Rental and Leasing (any industry)	ESR	60	185.167-026
Manager, Marina Dry Dock (amuse. & rec.; water trans.)	ERI	62	187.167-226

From the Dictionary of Occupational Titles Occupations to Holland Codes

Title	HOC	Cx	DOT
Manager, Marine Service (ship-boat mfg.)	REA	61	187.167-130
Manager, Market (retail trade; wholesale tr.)	ESC	62	186.167-042
Manager, Meat Sales and Storage (retail trade; wholesale tr.)	ESA	58	185.167-030
Manager, Merchandise (retail trade; wholesale tr.)	ESR	63	185.167-034
Manager, Mutuel Department (amuse. & rec.)	CES	65	187.167-134
Manager, Nursery (agriculture; retail trade; wholesale tr.)	ESA	67	180.167-042
Manager, Office (any industry)	ESR	63	169.167-034
Manager, Office (government ser.)	ESR	67	188.167-058
Manager, Operations (air trans.; motor trans.; r.r. trans.; water trans.)	ESR	69	184.117-050
Manager, Orchard (agriculture)	REC	66	180.167-066
Manager, Parts (retail trade; wholesale tr.)	ESA	62	185.167-038
Manager, Personnel (profess. & kin.)	SEC	74	166.117-018
Manager, Pool (amuse. & rec.)	ERS	56	153.137-010
Manager, Poultry Hatchery (agriculture)	ERS	62	180.167-046
Manager, Procurement Services (profess. & kin.)	ECS	66	162.167-022
Manager, Production (radio-tv broad.)	ERC	64	184.162-010
Manager, Production, Seed Corn (agriculture)	IER	67	180.161-010
Manager, Professional Equipment Sales-and-Service (business ser.)	ESA	66	185.167-042
Manager, Promotion (hotel & rest.)	SER	65	163.117-018
Manager, Property (real estate)	ESR	64	186.167-046
Manager, Quality Control (profess. & kin.)	IEA	74	012.167-014
Manager, Real-Estate Firm (real estate)	ESR	66	186.167-066
Manager, Records Analysis (profess. & kin.)	EAI	66	161.167-018
Manager, Recreation Establishment (amuse. & rec.)	SER	66	187.117-042
Manager, Recreation Facility (amuse. & rec.)	ESR	63	187.167-230
Manager, Regional (motor trans.)	ESR	70	184.117-054
Manager, Regulated Program (government ser.)	ESC	72	168.167-090
Manager, Reports Analysis (profess. & kin.)	EAS	66	161.167-022
Manager, Reservations (hotel & rest.)	ESR	56	238.137-010
Manager, Retail Store (retail trade)	ESC	65	185.167-046
Manager, Sales (any industry)	ESA	68	163.167-018
Manager, Sales (laundry & rel.)	ERS	65	187.167-138
Manager, Schedule Planning (air trans.)	SEC	71	184.117-058
Manager, Service Department (wholesale tr.)	ERS	65	187.167-142
Manager, Skating Rink (amuse. & rec.)	ESR	62	187.167-146
Manager, Solid-Waste-Disposal (government ser.)	ESR	59	184.167-078
Manager, Sound Effects (radio-tv broad.)	SEC	65	962.167-010
Manager, Stage (amuse. & rec.; radio-tv broad.)	ESC	63	159.167-018
Manager, Station (air trans.)	ESA	66	184.167-082
Manager, Station (radio-tv broad.)	ESR	67	184.117-062
Manager, Storage Garage (automotive ser.)	ESR	57	187.167-150
Manager, Telegraph Office (tel. & tel.)	ESA	62	184.167-086
Manager, Textile Conversion (business ser.; wholesale tr.)	ESA	62	185.167-050
Manager, Theater (amuse. & rec.)	ESR	65	187.167-154
Manager, Title Search (real estate)	ESR	66	186.167-090
Manager, Tobacco Warehouse (wholesale tr.)	ESR	61	185.167-054

Title	HOC	Cx	DOT
Manager, Touring Production (amuse. & rec.)	SEC	60	191.117-038
Manager, Traffic (air trans.; motor trans.; water trans.)	ESA	70	184.117-066
Manager, Traffic (any industry)	ESR	66	184.167-094
Manager, Traffic (radio-tv broad.)	ESC	66	184.167-090
Manager, Traffic I (motor trans.)	ESC	69	184.167-102
Manager, Traffic I (tel. & tel.)	ERS	64	184.167-098
Manager, Traffic II (motor trans.)	CSE	53	237.367-030
Manager, Traffic II (tel. & tel.)	ESI	69	184.167-106
Manager, Travel Agency (business ser.; retail trade)	ESR	61	187.167-158
Manager, Truck Terminal (motor trans.)	ESR	59	184.167-110
Manager, Utility Sales and Service (utilities)	ESR	68	163.167-022
Manager, Vehicle Leasing and Rental (automotive ser.)	ERS	65	187.167-162
Manager, Warehouse (any industry)	ESR	64	184.167-114
Manager, Winter Sports (amuse. & rec.)	ESC	64	187.167-166
Manager, World Trade and Maritime Division (nonprofit org.)	ESA	67	187.167-170
Mangle Tender (textile)	CRE	41	584.685-042
Mangle-Press Catcher (textile)	REC	39	583.686-022
Mangler (knitting)	REC	41	583.685-070
Manicurist (personal ser.)	ESC	42	331.674-010
Manipulator (steel & rel.)	RSE	47	613.682-010
Manipulator Operator (forging)	RCE	46	612.683-010
Mannequin Mounter (fabrication, n.e.c.)	RCE	47	739.684-118
Mannequin Sander and Finisher (fabrication, n.e.c.)	REC	44	739.684-122
Mannequin Wig Maker (fabrication, n.e.c.)	RSE	50	739.381-042
Mannequin-Mold Maker (fabrication, n.e.c.)	RSE	52	739.381-046
Manometer Technician (smelt. & refin.)	REC	50	519.387-010
Manual Winder (musical inst.)	CRE	46	730.684-046
Manual-Arts Therapist (medical ser.)	SRE	66	076.124-010
Manual-Plate Filler (ordnance)	RCE	37	737.687-082
Manufacturer's Representative (wholesale tr.)	ESA	63	279.157-010
Manufacturer's Service Representative (machinery mfg.; machine tools)	RES	59	638.261-018
Manufacturing Engineer (profess. & kin.)	IRE	74	012.167-042
Manugrapher (fabrication, n.e.c.)	RCA	47	970.681-022
Map Clerk (insurance)	CSE	47	209.587-030
Map-and-Chart Mounter (print. & pub.)	REC	47	979.684-022
Maple-Syrup Maker (food prep., n.e.c.)	RES	51	523.382-014
Marble Finisher (construction)	RCS	42	861.664-010
Marble Setter (construction)	RIE	54	861.381-030
Marble-Machine Tender (glass mfg.)	RCE	43	575.685-058
Margin Clerk I (financial)	CRS	56	216.362-042
Margin Clerk II (financial)	CSE	56	216.382-046
Marine Engineer (profess. & kin.)	IRE	77	014.061-014
Marine Oiler (water trans.)	REI	45	911.584-010
Marine Railway Operator (ship-boat mfg.)	RSE	47	921.662-022
Marine Surveyor (profess. & kin.)	REC	68	014.167-010
Marine-Cargo Surveyor (business ser.)	SRE	67	168.267-094
Marine-Services Technician (ship-boat mfg.)	RCE	58	806.261-026

Part 3: From Occupational Titles to Holland Codes

From the Dictionary of Occupational Titles Occupations to Holland Codes

Title	HOC	Cx	DOT
Mark-Up Designer (glass mfg.)	RCS	47	775.684-050
Marker (garment; retail trade; tex. prod., n.e.c.)	CSE	40	781.687-042
Marker (laundry & rel.)	REC	40	369.687-026
Marker (ordnance)	RCE	45	652.582-010
Marker (retail trade; wholesale tr.)	CSR	41	209.587-034
Marker I (any industry)	RCE	50	781.384-014
Marker II (any industry)	RCE	40	920.687-126
Marker Machine Attendant (glass mfg.)	RCI	39	579.685-070
Marker, Company (tobacco)	CSR	43	529.567-014
Marker, Hand (boot & shoe)	REC	41	788.584-014
Marker, Machine (boot & shoe)	RCE	42	690.685-282
Marker, Semiconductor Wafers (electron. comp.)	RCE	40	920.587-026
Market-Research Analyst I (profess. & kin.)	ISC	70	050.067-014
Marking Stitcher (garment)	RCE	38	781.687-046
Marking-Machine Operator (knitting; tex. prod., n.e.c.)	REC	40	652.685-050
Marking-Machine Operator (textile)	CRE	41	652.685-046
Marking-Machine Tender (boot & shoe; leather prod.)	CRE	40	783.685-026
Marksmanship Instructor (military ser.)	SRE	52	378.227-010
Marquetry Worker (furniture)	RCI	63	761.281-018
Marshal (amuse. & rec.)	RES	46	153.384-010
Mash Grinder (dairy products)	REC	42	520.685-130
Mash-Filter Operator (beverage)	REC	39	521.565-014
Mash-Filter-Cloth Changer (beverage)	RES	39	529.667-014
Mash-Tub-Cooker Operator (beverage)	RCS	55	522.382-022
Masher (beverage)	REC	51	522.482-010
Masker (any industry)	REC	41	749.687-018
Masker (clock & watch)	RCE	37	715.687-086
Masker (electron. comp.)	RCE	39	726.687-034
Masking-Machine Feeder (plastic-synth.)	REC	41	920.586-010
Masking-Machine Operator (plastic-synth.)	RCE	48	554.682-014
Masseur/Masseuse (personal ser.)	RES	51	334.374-010
Master Control Operator (radio-tv broad.)	IRS	63	194.262-022
Master, Passenger Barge (water trans.)	REI	63	197.163-014
Master, Riverboat (water trans.)	ESR	63	197.163-018
Master, Ship (water trans.)	ERI	74	197.167-010
Master, Yacht (water trans.)	REI	63	197.133-014
Mat Cutter (wood prod., n.e.c.)	CRE	40	739.684-126
Mat Inspector (concrete prod.)	REI	46	575.687-022
Mat Packer (nonmet. min.)	RCE	40	579.686-014
Mat Puncher (rubber goods)	REC	41	690.685-286
Mat Repairer (rubber goods)	RCE	42	759.684-042
Mat Sewer (oils & grease)	REC	38	529.687-154
Mat Tester (nonmet. min.)	REI	50	579.387-010
Mat-Machine Operator (nonmet. min.)	RES	46	579.662-010
Mat-Making Machine Tender (furniture)	RCE	42	692.685-122
Match-Up Worker (garment)	CRE	41	782.684-038
Matchbook Assembler (fabrication, n.e.c.)	RES	41	649.685-074
Matcher, Leather Parts (leather prod.)	CRE	42	783.687-022
Mate, Fishing Vessel (fishing & hunt.)	REI	61	197.133-018

DOT to HOC

Title	HOC	Cx	DOT
Mate, Ship (water trans.)	ERS	61	197.133-022
Material Assembler (furniture)	RCI	45	781.684-066
Material Assembler (hat & cap)	CSE	43	784.687-050
Material Clerk (clerical)	REC	55	222.387-034
Material Coordinator (clerical)	ESR	59	221.167-014
Material Expediter (clerical)	SEC	54	221.367-042
Material Handler (any industry)	REI	41	929.687-030
Material Inspector (wood. container)	RES	54	764.387-014
Material Lister (construction)	CRE	57	229.387-010
Material Mixer (plastic prod.)	RCE	42	550.685-130
Material Preparation Worker (electron. comp.)	RCI	45	590.684-030
Material Scheduler (aircraft mfg.)	IRC	70	012.167-082
Material-Crew Supervisor (construction; mfd. bldgs.)	ERS	56	921.137-014
Material-Handling Supervisor (any industry)	RES	58	921.133-018
Materials Engineer (profess. & kin.)	REI	71	019.061-014
Materials Scientist (profess. & kin.)	IRE	78	029.081-014
Mathematical Technician (profess. & kin.)	IRC	70	020.162-010
Mathematician (profess. & kin.)	IER	78	020.067-014
Matrix Inspector (machinery mfg.)	REI	42	654.687-010
Matrix Plater (recording)	REC	50	500.384-010
Matrix Worker (recording)	RCE	42	500.684-014
Matrix-Bath Attendant (recording)	REI	53	500.384-014
Matrix-Drier Tender (paper & pulp)	RCE	44	532.585-010
Matting-Press Tender (rubber goods)	REC	38	556.685-042
Mattress Finisher (furniture)	CRS	44	780.684-070
Mattress Maker (furniture)	RCS	45	780.684-074
Mattress Stripper (furniture)	RES	38	780.687-026
Mattress-Filling-Machine Tender (furniture)	REC	38	780.685-010
Mattress-Spring Encaser (furniture)	RCE	40	780.687-030
Maturity Checker (can. & preserv.)	RCE	50	529.485-022
Meal-Grinder Tender (grain-feed mills)	REC	37	521.685-210
Measurer (retail trade)	RIS	50	869.367-014
Measurer (struct. metal)	RCS	48	869.487-010
Measuring-Machine Operator (leather mfg.)	CRE	39	589.685-070
Meat Blender (can. & preserv.)	RCE	42	529.685-166
Meat Clerk (retail trade)	RCS	40	222.684-010
Meat Cutter (retail trade; wholesale tr.)	RSE	49	316.684-018
Meat Dresser (agriculture)	RES	50	525.664-010
Meat Grinder (meat products)	RES	37	521.685-214
Meat-Cutter Apprentice (retail trade; wholesale tr.)	RSE	49	316.684-022
Meat-Grading-Machine Operator (can. & preserv.)	RCE	40	521.685-218
Mechanic, Endless Track Vehicle (automotive ser.)	RES	56	620.381-014
Mechanic, Industrial Truck (any industry)	RES	58	620.281-050
Mechanical Engineer (profess. & kin.)	RIS	73	007.061-014
Mechanical Inspector (petrol. refin.)	RSC	58	549.261-010
Mechanical Oxidizer (fabrication, n.e.c.)	RSE	51	590.662-014
Mechanical Research Engineer (profess. & kin.)	IRE	70	007.161-022
Mechanical Technician, Laboratory (clock & watch)	RSE	59	715.261-010
Mechanical-Design Engineer, Facilities (profess. & kin.)	RIE	75	007.061-018

Part 3: From Occupational Titles to Holland Codes

From the Dictionary of Occupational Titles Occupations to Holland Codes

DOT to HOC

Title	HOC	Cx	DOT
Mechanical-Design Engineer, Products (profess. & kin.)	IER	71	007.061-022
Mechanical-Engineering Technician (profess. & kin.)	IRE	66	007.161-026
Mechanical-Maintenance Supervisor (any industry)	RES	59	638.131-026
Mechanical-Shovel Operator (mine & quarry)	RSE	46	932.683-018
Mechanical-Test Technician (inst. & app.)	RES	58	869.261-014
Mechanical-Unit Repairer (automotive ser.; railroad equip.)	RES	57	620.381-018
Mechanism Assembler (clock & watch)	CRS	44	715.684-142
Media Clerk (business ser.)	CRS	56	247.382-010
Media Director (profess. & kin.)	ESC	69	164.117-018
Media Specialist, School Library (library)	ESA	66	100.167-030
Medical Assistant (medical ser.)	SCR	56	079.362-010
Medical Coordinator, Pesticide Use (government ser.)	IER	78	041.067-010
Medical Physicist (profess. & kin.)	IRS	78	079.021-014
Medical Radiation Dosimetrist (medical ser.)	CIR	69	078.261-034
Medical Record Technician (medical ser.)	CIR	61	079.362-014
Medical Secretary (medical ser.)	CES	61	201.362-014
Medical Technologist (medical ser.)	ISA	68	078.261-038
Medical Technologist, Chief (medical ser.)	IEA	71	078.161-010
Medical Technologist, Teaching Supervisor (medical ser.)	ISE	70	078.121-010
Medical-Equipment Repairer (protective dev.; retail trade)	RCI	51	639.281-022
Medical-Laboratory Technician (medical ser.)	IRE	58	078.381-014
Medical-Record Administrator (medical ser.)	SIE	74	079.167-014
Medical-Record Clerk (medical ser.)	CSI	55	245.362-010
Medical-Service Technician (military ser.)	SEC	61	079.367-018
Medical-Voucher Clerk (insurance)	CSR	52	214.482-018
Mellowing-Machine Operator (hat & cap)	REC	40	585.685-066
Melt-House Drag Operator (sugar & conf.)	RES	41	529.687-158
Melter (jewelry-silver.)	RCE	41	700.687-042
Melter Clerk (foundry)	CRE	54	221.387-042
Melter Operator (sugar & conf.)	REI	52	523.382-018
Melter Supervisor (steel & rel.)	ERS	59	512.132-010
Membership Director (profess. & kin.)	ESA	66	189.167-026
Membership Secretary (nonprofit org.)	CSE	55	201.362-018
Membership Solicitor (any industry)	ESC	55	293.357-022
Memorial Designer (stonework)	AER	62	142.061-030
Mender (any industry)	CRE	45	787.682-030
Mender (carpet & rug; textile)	RES	45	782.684-042
Mender (hat & cap)	CRE	39	784.684-046
Mender, Knit Goods (garment; knitting)	CRS	40	782.684-046
Mental-Retardation Aide (medical ser.)	SRI	55	355.377-018
Merchandise Distributor (retail trade)	RCS	51	219.367-018
Merchant Patroller (business ser.)	SER	42	372.667-038
Mercury Purifier (chemical)	REC	43	551.585-014
Mercury Washer (chemical)	RES	41	551.685-098
Mercury-Cracking Tester (ordnance)	RCE	37	737.687-086
Mesh Cutter (jewelry-silver.)	RCE	45	700.684-050
Mess Attendant (water trans.)	REC	42	350.677-010
Messenger, Copy (print. & pub.)	CES	41	239.677-010
Metal Control Worker (foundry)	RIE	49	512.487-010

Part 3: From Occupational Titles to Holland Codes

From the Dictionary of Occupational Titles Occupations to Holland Codes

Title	HOC	Cx	DOT
Metal Fabricator (any industry)	RIC	59	619.361-014
Metal Fabricator Helper (any industry)	RES	43	619.685-066
Metal Finisher (any industry)	RCE	42	705.684-034
Metal Hanger (mfd. bldgs.; vehicles, n.e.c.)	REI	48	809.684-030
Metal Sander and Finisher (furniture)	CRE	39	705.687-018
Metal Sprayer, Corrosion Prevention (any industry)	RIE	50	843.482-010
Metal Sprayer, Machined Parts (any industry)	RIE	57	505.380-010
Metal Sprayer, Production (any industry)	REC	43	505.684-014
Metal-Bed Assembler (furniture)	RES	45	706.684-082
Metal-Bonding Crib Attendant (chemical)	RES	49	550.564-010
Metal-Bonding Press Operator (aircraft mfg.)	RES	49	553.382-026
Metal-Cleaner, Immersion (any industry)	RCS	41	503.685-030
Metal-Control Coordinator (nonfer. metal)	RES	58	222.167-010
Metal-Fabricating-Shop Helper (any industry)	RSE	40	619.686-022
Metal-Fabricator Apprentice (any industry)	RIC	59	619.361-018
Metal-Finish Inspector (any industry)	CRS	49	703.687-014
Metal-Finish Inspector (furniture)	REI	47	703.687-018
Metal-Reed Tuner (any industry)	RCS	50	730.381-034
Metal-Sponge-Making-Machine Operator (nonfer. metal)	RCE	41	616.685-038
Metal-Spraying-Machine Operator, Automatic I (any industry)	RIE	55	505.382-010
Metal-Spraying-Machine Operator, Automatic II (any industry)	RES	42	505.685-014
Metal-Washing-Machine Operator (svc. ind. mach.)	REC	42	503.685-034
Metallic-Yarn-Slitting-Machine Operator (nonfer. metal)	CRE	41	619.685-070
Metallization Equipment Tender, Semiconductors (comm. equip.; electron. comp.)	RCI	46	590.685-086
Metallographer (profess. & kin.)	IRE	76	011.061-014
Metallurgical Technician (profess. & kin.)	RIS	60	011.261-010
Metallurgist, Extractive (profess. & kin.)	IRE	80	011.061-018
Metallurgist, Physical (profess. & kin.)	IRE	80	011.061-022
Meteorological-Equipment Repairer (any industry)	RIE	60	823.281-018
Meteorologist (profess. & kin.)	IRS	70	025.062-010
Meter Inspector (utilities)	RCE	54	710.384-022
Meter Reader (utilities; waterworks)	CSE	50	209.567-010
Meter Reader, Chief (utilities; waterworks)	ESC	57	209.137-014
Meter Repairer (any industry)	RIE	56	710.281-034
Meter-Repairer Helper (any industry)	CRS	44	710.684-034
Metrologist (profess. & kin.)	IES	76	012.067-010
Mexican Food Maker, Hand (food prep., n.e.c.)	REC	38	520.687-046
Mexican-Food-Machine Tender (food prep., n.e.c.)	CSR	40	524.685-038
Mica Inspector (mine & quarry)	RCS	47	779.687-026
Mica Patcher (mine & quarry)	CRE	38	579.687-026
Mica Sizer (mine & quarry)	CES	42	779.687-030
Mica Splitter (mine & quarry)	REC	49	779.681-010
Mica-Laminating-Machine Feeder (mine & quarry)	REC	40	579.686-018
Mica-Plate Layer (mine & quarry)	RCE	40	579.685-026
Mica-Plate Layer, Hand (mine & quarry)	RCE	40	579.684-022
Mica-Washer Gluer (mine & quarry)	RCE	42	729.687-022

DOT to HOC

Part 3: From Occupational Titles to Holland Codes

From the Dictionary of Occupational Titles Occupations to Holland Codes

Title	HOC	Cx	DOT
Microbiologist (profess. & kin.)	IRA	78	041.061-058
Microbiology Technologist (medical ser.)	IRE	68	078.261-014
Microcomputer Support Specialist (profess. & kin.)	RSI	61	039.264-010
Microelectronics Technician (electron. comp.)	RCI	58	590.362-022
Microfiche Duplicator (business ser.)	RIE	54	976.381-014
Microfilm Mounter (clerical)	CSR	40	208.685-022
Microfilm Processor (business ser.)	RCI	47	976.385-010
Microfilm-Camera Operator (business ser.)	RCE	47	976.682-022
Microphone-Boom Operator (motion picture; radio-tv broad.)	RES	50	962.384-010
Middle-Card Tender (nonmet. min.; textile)	CRS	38	680.665-018
Migrant Leader (agriculture)	ESR	55	180.167-050
Milk Driver (dairy products)	RIE	49	905.483-010
Milk Receiver (dairy products)	REC	45	222.585-010
Milk Sampler (agriculture)	CSE	50	410.357-010
Milk-Powder Grinder (dairy products)	RES	39	521.685-222
Milk-Receiver, Tank Truck (dairy products)	REC	47	222.485-010
Milker, Machine (agriculture)	RCE	40	410.685-010
Milking-System Installer (agric. equip.; retail trade)	RIE	57	809.381-018
Mill Attendant I (chemical)	RIE	44	555.565-010
Mill Attendant II (chemical)	RCE	40	555.685-038
Mill Feeder (grain-feed mills)	REC	39	520.685-134
Mill Hand, Plate Mill (steel & rel.)	RES	41	613.667-014
Mill Helper (nonfer. metal)	RIE	43	502.684-014
Mill Operator (any industry)	RCE	42	599.685-058
Mill Operator (brick & tile; pottery & porc.)	REI	50	570.382-010
Mill Operator (grain-feed mills)	CER	39	521.685-226
Mill Operator, Rolls (any industry)	RCS	49	613.682-030
Mill Platform Supervisor (sugar & conf.)	REI	58	521.132-010
Mill Recorder, Computerized Mill (steel & rel.)	CRE	54	221.367-046
Mill Stenciler (steel & rel.)	RCE	40	659.685-026
Mill Supervisor (nonmet. min.)	ERS	59	559.132-034
Mill Supervisor (smelt. & refin.)	ERC	59	515.130-010
Mill-and-Coal-Transport Operator (utilities)	REC	43	544.665-010
Mill-Labor Supervisor (smelt. & refin.)	RES	59	519.131-014
Mill-Operator Helper (any industry)	REC	39	599.686-010
Mill-Roll Rewinder (plastic-synth.)	RCE	43	690.585-010
Milled-Rubber Tender (rubber goods; rubber tire)	REI	40	553.685-078
Miller (beverage)	REC	39	521.585-014
Miller (cement)	REI	39	570.685-046
Miller (mine & quarry)	RES	40	570.685-038
Miller Helper, Distillery (beverage)	REI	41	521.687-082
Miller I (chemical)	REC	38	570.685-042
Miller II (chemical)	REI	46	555.682-010
Miller Supervisor (grain-feed mills)	SER	56	521.130-010
Miller, Distillery (beverage)	REI	53	521.362-014
Miller, Head, Assistant, Wet Process (grain-feed mills)	REC	45	629.684-014
Miller, Head, Wet Process (grain-feed mills)	REI	55	629.261-014
Miller, Wet Process (grain-feed mills)	RSE	51	521.662-010

DOT to HOC

Title	HOC	Cx	DOT
Miller, Wood Flour (woodworking)	REI	48	564.682-018
Milliner (retail trade)	AES	55	784.261-010
Milling Supervisor (brick & tile)	ESR	58	570.132-014
Milling-Machine Set-up Operator I (machine shop)	RIE	61	605.280-010
Milling-Machine Set-up Operator II (machine shop)	RIE	59	605.282-010
Milling-Machine Set-up Operator, Numerical Control (machine shop)	RES	56	605.380-010
Milling-Machine Tender (machine shop)	RCE	43	605.685-030
Millwright (any industry)	RES	60	638.281-018
Millwright Apprentice (any industry)	RES	60	638.281-022
Millwright Helper (any industry)	REC	46	638.484-010
Millwright Supervisor (any industry)	REC	65	638.131-030
Mime (amuse. & rec.)	AEI	59	159.047-022
Mincemeat Maker (can. & preserv.)	RCE	49	520.485-018
Mine Inspector (mine & quarry)	ERC	57	168.267-074
Mine Superintendent (mine & quarry)	ESR	68	181.117-014
Mine-Car Repairer (mine & quarry)	RIE	57	622.381-030
Miner (construction)	RIE	56	850.381-010
Miner I (mine & quarry)	RIE	55	939.281-010
Miner, Placer (mine & quarry)	REC	41	939.684-014
Mineralogist (profess. & kin.)	ISR	78	024.061-038
Mingler Operator (sugar & conf.)	RCE	41	520.665-010
Miniature-Set Constructor (motion picture)	ARE	60	962.381-018
Mining Engineer (mine & quarry)	RIE	74	010.061-014
Mirror Installer (construction)	RCI	53	865.361-010
Mirror Specialist (glass products; wood prod., n.e.c.)	RCE	41	779.684-038
Mirror-Finishing-Machine Operator (jewelry-silver.)	RES	47	603.682-022
Mirror-Machine Feeder (glass products)	RES	37	579.686-022
Missile Facilities Repairer (military ser.)	RIE	55	828.281-018
Miter Grinder Operator (glass mfg.; glass products)	RIE	48	673.682-026
Mix-Crusher Operator (elec. equip.)	REC	39	544.585-010
Mix-House Tender (smelt. & refin.)	CRE	41	510.685-014
Mixer (brick & tile)	RCI	40	579.685-074
Mixer (food prep., n.e.c.)	RCE	44	520.685-138
Mixer (glass mfg.)	CRE	41	570.685-054
Mixer (hat & cap)	REC	41	680.685-062
Mixer (nonfer. metal; steel & rel.)	RCS	43	510.685-018
Mixer (nonmet. min.)	REC	40	570.685-050
Mixer (paint & varnish)	RIE	43	550.685-078
Mixer Helper (build. mat., n.e.c.)	RCE	37	550.686-026
Mixer Helper (concrete prod.)	RCE	44	530.384-010
Mixer I (chemical)	RES	44	559.665-026
Mixer I (tex. prod., n.e.c.)	RIE	45	550.685-074
Mixer II (chemical)	RIE	42	737.687-090
Mixer II (tex. prod., n.e.c.)	RCE	35	789.687-098
Mixer Operator (beverage)	CER	42	520.685-146
Mixer Operator (chemical; electron. comp.)	RES	43	550.685-082
Mixer Operator (concrete prod.)	REC	39	570.685-058
Mixer Operator (sugar & conf.)	REI	47	520.685-150

DOT to HOC

Title	HOC	Cx	DOT
Mixer Operator Helper, Hot Metal (steel & rel.)	REC	43	509.566-010
Mixer Operator I (chemical)	RIS	49	550.382-018
Mixer Operator II (chemical)	REC	40	520.685-142
Mixer Operator, Carbon Paste (elec. equip.; smelt. & refin.)	CRS	44	540.585-010
Mixer Operator, Hot Metal (steel & rel.)	RES	49	509.362-010
Mixer Operator, Snack Foods (food prep., n.e.c.)	RCE	40	520.685-230
Mixer Tender, Board (concrete prod.)	RES	46	570.685-062
Mixer, Chili Powder (food prep., n.e.c.)	RES	42	520.685-158
Mixer, Diamond Powder (nonmet. min.)	RCE	48	570.484-010
Mixer, Dry-Food Products (food prep., n.e.c.)	RCE	44	520.685-162
Mixer, Foam Rubber (rubber goods)	RCE	40	550.685-086
Mixer, Wet Pour (concrete prod.)	REI	44	579.682-010
Mixer, Whipped Topping (food prep., n.e.c.)	RES	48	520.385-010
Mixer-and-Blender (food prep., n.e.c.)	RES	48	520.685-154
Mixing Supervisor (plastic prod.)	ESR	57	550.135-014
Mixing-Machine Feeder (chemical)	RES	39	550.686-030
Mixing-Machine Operator (any industry)	RIE	50	550.382-022
Mixing-Machine Operator (can. & preserv.)	RES	39	520.685-166
Mixing-Machine Operator (fabrication, n.e.c.)	REI	40	680.685-066
Mixing-Machine Operator (food prep., n.e.c.)	RES	42	520.665-014
Mixing-Machine Operator (plastic prod.; plastic-synth.)	RES	47	550.685-134
Mixing-Machine Tender (chemical; pharmaceut.)	RIE	47	550.685-090
Mixing-Machine Tender (wood prod., n.e.c.)	RCE	44	560.585-010
Mixing-Roll Operator (fabrication, n.e.c.)	RSC	49	590.662-018
Mixing-Tank Operator (oils & grease)	RCE	41	520.685-170
Mobile-Home-Lot Utility Worker (retail trade)	RSE	48	899.484-010
Mobile-Lounge Driver (motor trans.)	RSC	46	913.663-014
Mock-Up Builder (aircraft mfg.)	RIE	60	693.361-014
Mock-Up Builder (vehicles, n.e.c.)	RIE	58	693.381-018
Model (garment; retail trade; wholesale tr.)	EAS	45	297.667-014
Model Builder (furniture)	REI	55	709.381-014
Model Maker (aircraft mfg.)	RIS	64	693.261-018
Model Maker (auto. mfg.)	REA	56	693.380-014
Model Maker (clock & watch)	RIE	58	693.380-010
Model Maker (pottery & porc.)	RAE	59	777.281-014
Model Maker (toy-sport equip.)	RSA	59	731.280-010
Model Maker I (any industry)	ARI	61	777.261-010
Model Maker I (jewelry-silver.)	RIS	60	700.281-018
Model Maker II (jewelry-silver.)	REI	57	709.381-018
Model Maker, Fiberglass (concrete prod.)	RIS	56	777.381-010
Model Maker, Firearms (ordnance)	RES	60	600.260-018
Model Maker, Fluorescent Lighting (light. fix.)	RIS	57	723.361-010
Model Maker, Scale (office machines)	RIE	57	710.361-010
Model Maker, Wood (any industry)	REI	59	661.380-010
Model, Artists' (any industry)	AES	42	961.667-010
Model, Photographers' (any industry)	AES	45	961.367-010
Model-and-Mold Maker (brick & tile)	RIE	54	777.381-014
Model-and-Mold Maker, Plaster (concrete prod.)	REA	56	777.381-018
Model-Maker Apprentice (jewelry-silver.)	REI	57	709.381-022

Title	HOC	Cx	DOT
Modeler (brick & tile)	ARI	64	777.081-010
Mohel (profess. & kin.)	SCE	61	129.271-010
Moisture Tester (woodworking)	CRE	41	563.687-014
Moisture-Conditioner Operator (paper & pulp)	RCE	42	532.685-022
Moisture-Machine Tender (tobacco)	CRE	40	529.685-170
Moisture-Meter Operator (tobacco)	CRE	48	529.687-162
Molasses and Caramel Operator (grain-feed mills)	REI	51	526.382-022
Molasses Preparer (food prep., n.e.c.)	REI	48	522.685-078
Mold Cleaner (rubber goods)	RES	40	556.687-018
Mold Cleaner (toy-sport equip.)	REC	37	732.687-046
Mold Closer (foundry)	RES	41	518.684-018
Mold Dresser (any industry)	RCE	41	519.684-018
Mold Filler (toy-sport equip.)	RCI	36	556.687-030
Mold Filler and Drainer (boot & shoe)	RCE	38	753.687-030
Mold Filler, Plastic Dolls (toy-sport equip.)	RES	41	731.687-026
Mold Finisher (machine shop)	RES	47	705.684-038
Mold Laminator (concrete prod.; ship-boat mfg.)	REI	44	806.684-086
Mold Maker (nonmet. min.)	RCE	44	777.684-014
Mold Maker (pottery & porc.)	RES	47	777.684-018
Mold Maker (smelt. & refin.)	RCS	42	518.664-010
Mold Maker I (jewelry-silver.)	RES	58	700.381-034
Mold Maker II (jewelry-silver.)	RES	49	777.381-022
Mold Maker, Die-Casting and Plastic Molding (machine shop)	RIE	60	601.280-030
Mold Maker, Terra Cotta (brick & tile)	RCE	42	575.684-038
Mold Operator (elec. equip.)	CRS	48	729.684-030
Mold Parter (plastic-synth.)	RES	41	556.587-010
Mold Polisher (glass mfg.)	RCS	43	579.685-030
Mold Preparer (ship-boat mfg.)	RCS	38	809.687-026
Mold Presser (tobacco)	RES	38	790.687-022
Mold Setter (elec. equip.)	REI	48	502.684-018
Mold Setter (inst. & app.; office machines; plastic prod.; recording)	RIE	54	556.380-010
Mold Sheet Cleaner (metal prod., n.e.c.)	REC	37	700.687-046
Mold Stamper (machine shop)	RES	50	709.684-054
Mold Stamper and Repairer (rubber tire)	RSE	53	709.381-026
Mold Stripper (toy-sport equip.)	REC	37	732.687-050
Mold Worker (steel & rel.)	CRS	41	514.567-010
Mold-Filling Operator (plastic-synth.)	RCE	43	556.684-018
Mold-Insert Changer (boot & shoe)	RES	41	753.687-034
Mold-Maker Apprentice (jewelry-silver.)	RES	58	700.381-038
Mold-Maker Helper (jewelry-silver.)	RCE	37	700.687-050
Mold-Maker Helper (smelt. & refin.)	RCS	41	518.687-018
Molded-Parts Inspector (elec. equip.)	RCE	46	727.687-074
Molded-Rubber-Goods Cutter (rubber goods)	RCE	40	690.685-290
Molder (aircraft mfg.; concrete prod.; foundry)	RIE	57	518.361-010
Molder (hat & cap)	RCE	41	580.685-042
Molder (optical goods)	RSE	50	575.381-010
Molder Apprentice (aircraft mfg.; concrete prod.; foundry)	RIE	57	518.361-014

Part 3: From Occupational Titles to Holland Codes

From the Dictionary of Occupational Titles Occupations to Holland Codes

Title	HOC	Cx	DOT
Molder Helper (optical goods)	REC	39	575.686-014
Molder Operator (woodworking)	RCS	50	665.682-018
Molder, Automobile Carpets (tex. prod., n.e.c.)	RCI	39	692.685-286
Molder, Bench (jewelry-silver.)	RSE	56	518.381-022
Molder, Fiberglass Luggage (leather prod.)	RCE	40	575.685-066
Molder, Foam Rubber (rubber goods)	RES	39	556.685-046
Molder, Hand (brick & tile; elec. equip.)	REI	44	575.684-042
Molder, Inflated Ball (toy-sport equip.)	RES	40	732.687-054
Molder, Labels (boot & shoe)	CRE	40	690.685-294
Molder, Lead Ingot (ordnance)	REC	42	502.685-010
Molder, Machine (pharmaceut.)	REC	47	556.685-050
Molder, Meat (meat products)	RES	38	520.685-174
Molder, Pattern (foundry)	REI	56	693.381-022
Molder, Pipe Covering (plastic prod.)	RES	41	556.665-018
Molder, Punch (aircraft mfg.)	RSC	57	502.381-014
Molder, Shoe Parts (boot & shoe)	REC	38	788.687-094
Molder, Shoulder Pad (garment)	CRS	40	789.684-026
Molder, Sweep (foundry)	RIE	57	518.361-018
Molder, Toilet Products (pharmaceut.)	REC	41	556.687-022
Molder, Wax (petrol. refin.)	RCE	42	549.685-018
Molder, Wax Ball (toy-sport equip.)	RES	40	732.687-058
Molder-Machine Tender (nonmet. min.)	REI	40	575.685-062
Molding Cutter (woodworking)	RCE	40	663.685-018
Molding Sander (woodworking)	RES	44	662.682-010
Molding Supervisor (plastic prod.)	ESI	60	556.130-018
Molding-Machine Operator (sugar & conf.)	REC	52	520.682-026
Molding-Machine Operator (toy-sport equip.)	RSE	44	575.682-014
Molding-Machine Tender (paper & pulp)	CRE	42	539.685-018
Molding-Machine Tender (pen & pencil)	RES	38	570.685-066
Molding-Machine-Operator Helper (sugar & conf.)	REC	37	520.686-030
Molybdenum-Steamer Operator (smelt. & refin.)	RCE	50	511.485-010
Money Counter (amuse. & rec.)	CRS	52	211.467-014
Monitor Car Operator (mine & quarry)	RCS	47	939.682-010
Monitor-and-Storage-Bin Tender (grain-feed mills)	RCE	39	521.685-230
Monogram-and-Letter Paster (tex. prod., n.e.c.)	CRS	40	789.687-102
Monomer-Purification Operator (chemical)	RES	51	552.362-010
Monorail Crane Operator (any industry)	RCE	42	921.663-042
Monotype-Keyboard Operator (machinery mfg.; print. & pub.)	RCI	54	650.582-014
Monument Setter (construction)	RSE	55	861.361-014
Mop Maker (tex. prod., n.e.c.)	REC	42	739.685-026
Mop-Handle Assembler (tex. prod., n.e.c.)	REC	40	739.687-122
Mophead Trimmer-and-Wrapper (tex. prod., n.e.c.)	RCE	39	789.687-106
Morgue Attendant (medical ser.)	REI	47	355.667-010
Mortgage Clerk (financial)	CRS	55	249.362-014
Mortgage Loan Closer (financial)	CSE	57	249.362-018
Mortgage Loan Processor (financial)	CRS	55	249.362-022
Mortgage-Accounting Clerk (clerical)	CRS	55	216.362-026
Mortgage-Closing Clerk (clerical)	SCE	57	219.362-038

Title	HOC	Cx	DOT
Mortgage-Loan-Computation Clerk (insurance)	CSE	54	210.382-050
Mortician Investigator (government ser.)	RES	59	168.267-078
Mortising-Machine Operator (woodworking)	RIE	51	665.482-014
Mortuary Beautician (personal ser.)	RSE	52	339.361-010
Mosaic Worker (glass products; nonmet. min.)	RCS	49	779.381-014
Mosaicist (profess. & kin.)	ICR	64	018.261-022
Mosquito Sprayer (government ser.)	REC	39	379.687-014
Mother Repairer (recording)	CRS	47	705.684-042
Motion-Picture Projectionist (amuse. & rec.; motion picture)	RIE	54	960.362-010
Motor Operator (r.r. trans.)	RIE	47	910.683-014
Motor Polarizer (clock & watch)	REC	39	715.687-090
Motor-and-Generator-Brush Maker (elec. equip.)	CRS	46	724.684-038
Motor-Grader Operator (construction)	REA	45	850.663-022
Motor-Power Connector (motion picture)	RCE	45	962.684-018
Motor-Room Controller (utilities)	RES	57	820.662-010
Motor-Vehicle-Light Assembler (light. fix.)	RCE	41	729.684-034
Motorboat Mechanic (engine-turbine; ship-boat mfg.)	RES	58	623.281-038
Motorboat Operator (any industry)	RIE	48	911.663-010
Motorboat-Mechanic Helper (engine-turbine; ship-boat mfg.)	REC	42	623.684-010
Motorcycle Assembler (motor-bicycles)	RES	45	806.684-090
Motorcycle Racer (amuse. & rec.)	RES	53	153.243-014
Motorcycle Repairer (automotive ser.)	RIE	54	620.281-054
Motorcycle Subassembler (motor-bicycles)	RES	48	806.684-094
Motorcycle Subassembly Repairer (motor-bicycles)	RCE	49	620.684-026
Motorcycle Tester (motor-bicycles)	RCE	55	620.384-010
Mottle-Lay-Up Operator (plastic-synth.)	RCE	48	690.585-014
Mottler Operator (fabrication, n.e.c.)	RES	41	550.665-022
Mottler-Machine Feeder (fabrication, n.e.c.)	REI	40	550.686-034
Mounter I (light. fix.)	RCE	37	692.686-050
Mounter II (light. fix.)	REC	39	692.685-126
Mounter, Automatic (photofinishing)	RCE	40	976.685-022
Mounter, Clock and Watch Hands (clock & watch)	RCE	39	715.687-094
Mounter, Hand (light. fix.)	RCE	43	725.684-014
Mounter, Hand (photofinishing)	CER	40	976.684-018
Mounter, Smoking Pipe (fabrication, n.e.c.)	RCE	40	739.684-130
Mouthpiece Maker (musical inst.)	RES	44	730.685-014
Mucking-Machine Operator (construction)	RCE	44	850.683-026
Mud Boss (smelt. & refin.)	REI	47	519.585-014
Mud-Mill Tender (smelt. & refin.)	REC	40	519.685-026
Mud-Mixer Helper (steel & rel.)	REC	37	549.687-022
Mud-Mixer Operator (smelt. & refin.; steel & rel.)	REC	40	570.685-070
Mud-Plant Operator (petrol. & gas)	RES	48	930.685-010
Muffler Installer (automotive ser.)	RES	47	807.664-010
Multi-Operation-Forming-Machine Operator I (any industry)	RIS	55	616.360-026
Multi-Operation-Forming-Machine Operator II (any industry)	REC	40	616.685-042

Title	HOC	Cx	DOT
Multi-Operation-Forming-Machine Setter (any industry)	RIS	58	616.260-014
Multi-Operation-Machine Operator (any industry)	RSE	50	612.462-010
Multi-Purpose Machine Operator (furniture)	RCI	52	669.382-022
Multifocal-Lens Assembler (optical goods)	RCE	42	713.684-034
Multineedle-Chainstitch-Machine Operator (garment)	RCE	41	786.682-178
Multiple-Drum Sander (woodworking)	RIE	47	662.682-014
Multiple-Drum-Sander Helper (woodworking)	RES	39	662.686-014
Munitions Handler (ordnance)	REC	40	929.687-034
Museum Attendant (museums)	CES	54	109.367-010
Museum Technician (museums)	REI	57	102.381-010
Music Copyist (print. & pub.)	CRS	50	209.582-010
Music Engraver (print. & pub.)	RCE	46	972.681-010
Music Grapher (print. & pub.)	RCE	51	970.581-010
Music Librarian (radio-tv broad.)	SRE	57	100.367-022
Music Librarian, International Broadcast (radio-tv broad.)	CSR	58	100.367-026
Music Supervisor (education)	EAS	65	099.167-026
Music Therapist (medical ser.)	SAE	70	076.127-014
Musical-String Maker (musical inst.)	REC	44	730.684-050
Musician, Instrumental (amuse. & rec.)	ASC	65	152.041-010
MVA-Reactor Operator (chemical)	REI	45	558.685-046
MVA-Reactor Operator, Head (chemical)	RES	56	559.362-022
Mycologist (profess. & kin.)	IRS	78	041.061-062
Nail-Assembly-Machine Operator (steel & rel.)	RCS	47	616.682-030
Nail-Making-Machine Setter (steel & rel.)	RES	54	616.460-010
Nail-Making-Machine Tender (steel & rel.)	RCE	40	617.665-010
Nail-Polish-Brush-Machine Feeder, Automatic (fabrication, n.e.c.)	RCE	40	692.686-054
Nailer (tinware)	CRE	37	739.687-126
Nailer, Hand (any industry)	RCE	41	762.684-050
Nailing-Machine Operator (any industry)	REC	41	669.682-058
Nailing-Machine Operator, Automatic (any industry)	RCE	41	669.685-066
Name-Plate Stamper (any industry)	CRS	40	652.685-054
Naphtha-Washing-System Operator (plastic-synth.)	CRS	51	559.382-038
Naphthalene Operator (steel & rel.)	CRS	41	551.665-010
Naphthalene-Operator Helper (steel & rel.)	REI	37	551.687-026
Napper Tender (knitting)	RCE	40	585.665-010
Napper Tender (tex. prod., n.e.c.; textile)	RCE	44	585.685-070
Narrator (motion picture)	AES	63	150.147-010
Narrow-Fabric Calenderer (narrow fabrics)	REC	40	583.685-074
Natural-Gas-Treating-Unit Operator (petrol. & gas)	REI	54	549.382-010
Navigator (air trans.)	ICR	66	196.167-014
Neck Skewer (meat products)	REC	39	525.687-050
Necker (jewelry-silver.)	RCE	37	692.686-058
Necktie Operator, Pockets and Pieces (garment)	RCE	41	786.682-182
Necktie-Centralizing-Machine Operator I (garment)	RCE	41	786.682-186
Necktie-Centralizing-Machine Operator II (garment)	RCE	41	786.682-190
Needle Grinder (button & notion)	CRE	42	734.584-010
Needle Leader (button & notion)	CRE	42	502.684-022
Needle Polisher (button & notion)	RCE	41	705.684-046

Title	HOC	Cx	DOT
Needle Straightener (knitting)	CRS	47	628.684-018
Needle-Bar Molder (carpet & rug)	CRE	40	556.684-022
Needle-Board Repairer (tex. prod., n.e.c.)	CRE	42	739.684-134
Needle-Control Cheniller (tex. prod., n.e.c.)	RCE	46	687.685-010
Needle-Felt-Making-Machine Operator (tex. prod., n.e.c.)	RCS	52	689.362-010
Needle-Loom Operator (tex. prod., n.e.c.)	RSC	48	689.662-010
Needle-Loom Setter (tex. prod., n.e.c.)	RSE	53	689.360-010
Needle-Loom Tender (tex. prod., n.e.c.)	RCS	43	689.685-090
Needle-Punch-Machine Operator (textile)	CRS	44	689.682-014
Needle-Punch-Machine-Operator Helper (textile)	REC	39	689.686-034
Needlemaker (button & notion)	RIE	59	619.280-010
Nematologist (profess. & kin.)	IRS	78	041.061-066
Neon-Sign Servicer (fabrication, n.e.c.)	RSE	54	824.281-018
Neon-Tube Pumper (fabrication, n.e.c.)	RSE	47	824.684-010
Nesting Operator, Numerical Control (aircraft mfg.)	CRI	57	007.362-010
Net Maker (tex. prod., n.e.c.)	CRE	42	789.684-030
Net Repairer (fishing & hunt.)	RES	47	449.664-010
Net Washer (rubber goods)	RCE	37	599.687-022
Netting Inspector (tex. prod., n.e.c.)	RCE	44	782.487-010
Network Control Operator (any industry)	IRS	59	031.262-014
Neurologist (medical ser.)	IRS	76	070.101-050
Neutralizer (grain-feed mills)	REI	48	522.685-082
Neutralizer (soap & rel.)	REC	44	558.585-034
New-Car Get-Ready Mechanic (automotive ser.; retail trade)	RIS	52	806.361-026
New-Car Inspector (motor trans.)	RIE	50	919.363-010
News Assistant (radio-tv broad.)	SEC	53	209.367-038
News Librarian (library)	SRC	67	100.167-038
Newscaster (radio-tv broad.)	ESI	66	131.262-010
Newspaper Carrier (retail trade)	ESC	45	292.457-010
Newspaper-Delivery Driver (wholesale tr.)	RSE	49	292.363-010
Newswriter (print. & pub.; radio-tv broad.)	AEI	66	131.262-014
Nib Finisher (pen & pencil)	CRS	44	705.684-050
Nib Inspector (pen & pencil)	CSR	46	733.687-058
Nibbler Operator (any industry)	RCS	45	615.685-026
Nickel-Plant Operator (smelt. & refin.)	RES	52	519.362-010
Nicker (boot & shoe)	RCE	41	690.685-298
Nicking-Machine Operator (cutlery-hrdwr.)	RES	47	609.682-026
Night Auditor (hotel & rest.)	CRS	59	210.382-054
Night-Patrol Inspector (fabrication, n.e.c.)	RCI	41	824.683-010
Nitrating-Acid Mixer (chemical)	RCE	48	550.585-030
Nitrator Operator (chemical)	RSE	50	558.382-046
Nitrocellulose Operator (chemical)	RES	44	553.684-014
Nitroglycerin Distributor (chemical)	RES	40	559.664-010
Nitroglycerin Neutralizer (chemical)	RSC	46	558.685-050
Nitroglycerin Supervisor (chemical)	RES	59	559.132-038
Nitroglycerin-Separator Operator (chemical)	CRE	44	551.685-102
Nodulizer (cement)	CER	44	579.685-034
Nondestructive Tester (profess. & kin.)	RCI	57	011.261-018

DOT to HOC

Title	HOC	Cx	DOT
Noodle Maker (food prep., n.e.c.)	RES	44	529.385-010
Noodle-Catalyst Maker (chemical)	REC	40	559.685-126
Noodle-Press Operator (food prep., n.e.c.)	REI	49	520.662-010
Notch Grinder (glass products)	RCE	42	673.685-070
Notereader (clerical)	CRI	51	203.582-078
Novelty Maker I (dairy products)	REI	51	529.482-014
Novelty Maker II (dairy products)	REI	52	529.482-018
Novelty Worker (dairy products)	REC	40	524.686-014
Nozzle Tender (nonfer. metal)	RCE	42	512.685-014
Nozzle-and-Sleeve Worker (nonfer. metal)	RCE	41	514.684-018
Nuclear Engineer (profess. & kin.)	IRE	79	015.061-014
Nuclear Medicine Technologist (medical ser.)	RIS	67	078.361-018
Nuclear-Criticality Safety Engineer (profess. & kin.)	IRC	79	015.067-010
Nuclear-Fuels Reclamation Engineer (profess. & kin.)	IRC	77	015.061-026
Nuclear-Fuels Research Engineer (profess. & kin.)	IRC	80	015.061-030
Nuclear-Plant Technical Advisor (utilities)	IRC	77	015.167-010
Nuclear-Test-Reactor Program Coordinator (profess. & kin.)	IER	76	015.167-014
Numberer and Wirer (textile)	RCE	41	689.587-010
Numerical Control Machine Operator (machine shop)	REI	55	609.362-010
Numerical Control Machine Set-up Operator (machine shop)	RSE	58	609.360-010
Numerical-Control Drill Operator, Printed Circuit Boards (electron. comp.)	RCI	54	606.382-018
Numerical-Control Router Operator (aircraft mfg.; electron. comp.)	RCI	50	605.382-046
Nurse Anesthetist (medical ser.)	ISE	69	075.371-010
Nurse Assistant (medical ser.)	SER	45	355.674-014
Nurse Practitioner (medical ser.)	ISA	68	075.264-010
Nurse, Consultant (medical ser.)	SEC	69	075.127-014
Nurse, General Duty (medical ser.)	SIA	66	075.364-010
Nurse, Head (medical ser.)	SEI	69	075.137-014
Nurse, Infection Control (medical ser.)	SEC	69	075.127-034
Nurse, Instructor (medical ser.)	SIE	71	075.124-018
Nurse, Licensed Practical (medical ser.)	SAC	56	079.374-014
Nurse, Office (medical ser.)	SIR	63	075.374-014
Nurse, Practical (medical ser.)	SER	51	354.374-010
Nurse, Private Duty (medical ser.)	ISR	66	075.374-018
Nurse, School (medical ser.)	SIE	67	075.124-010
Nurse, Staff, Community Health (medical ser.)	SIE	69	075.124-014
Nurse, Staff, Occupational Health Nursing (medical ser.)	ISE	66	075.374-022
Nurse, Supervisor (medical ser.)	SEI	67	075.167-010
Nurse, Supervisor, Community-Health Nursing (medical ser.)	ISE	69	075.127-026
Nurse, Supervisor, Evening-or-Night (medical ser.)	SIE	67	075.127-030
Nurse, Supervisor, Occupational Health Nursing (medical ser.)	IES	69	075.137-010
Nurse-Midwife (medical ser.)	SIR	63	075.264-014
Nursery School Attendant (any industry)	SAE	49	359.677-018

Dictionary of Holland Occupational Codes

Title	HOC	Cx	DOT
Nut Chopper (can. & preserv.; food prep., n.e.c.; sugar & conf.)	RCE	37	521.686-046
Nut Former (nut & bolt)	RES	50	612.462-014
Nut Grinder (can. & preserv.)	CRE	39	521.685-234
Nut Roaster (can. & preserv.)	RES	45	529.685-174
Nut Sorter (can. & preserv.)	CRE	37	521.687-086
Nut Steamer (can. & preserv.)	REC	40	521.687-090
Nut-and-Bolt Assembler (nut & bolt)	REC	39	929.587-010
Nut-Process Helper (can. & preserv.)	RES	40	529.486-010
Nut-Sorter Operator (can. & preserv.)	RCE	42	521.685-238
Nylon-Hot-Wire Cutter (tex. prod., n.e.c.)	CRS	42	781.684-038
Observer Helper, Gravity Prospecting (petrol. & gas)	RCE	44	939.663-010
Observer Helper, Seismic Prospecting (petrol. & gas)	RCS	48	939.364-010
Observer, Electrical Prospecting (petrol. & gas)	RIE	63	010.261-014
Observer, Gravity Prospecting (petrol. & gas)	RIE	65	010.261-018
Observer, Seismic Prospecting (petrol. & gas)	RIE	66	010.161-018
Obstetrician (medical ser.)	IRS	76	070.101-054
Occupational Analyst (profess. & kin.)	IES	73	166.067-010
Occupational Therapist (medical ser.)	SRE	67	076.121-010
Occupational Therapy Aide (medical ser.)	SEA	47	355.377-010
Occupational Therapy Assistant (medical ser.)	SCE	58	076.364-010
Occupational-Safety-and-Health Inspector (government ser.)	ECS	67	168.167-062
Oceanographer, Assistant (military ser.)	RIE	68	025.267-010
Odd Bundle Worker (tobacco)	REC	37	529.687-166
Odd-Piece Checker (knitting)	REC	42	221.587-018
Odd-Shoe Examiner (boot & shoe)	RES	44	788.667-010
Offal Icer, Poultry (meat products)	RSE	35	525.687-054
Offal Separator (meat products)	REC	40	525.684-038
Offbearer, Pipe Smoking Machine (fabrication, n.e.c.)	RCI	39	563.686-018
Offbearer, Sewer Pipe (brick & tile)	RES	39	579.686-026
Office Copy Selector (print. & pub.)	CRS	45	249.687-010
Office Helper (clerical)	ECR	45	239.567-010
Office Supervisor, Animal Hospital (nonprofit org.)	ESC	63	249.137-010
Office-Machine Servicer (any industry)	RES	58	633.281-018
Office-Machine-Service Supervisor (any industry)	ESR	59	633.131-010
Office-Machine-Servicer Apprentice (any industry)	RES	58	633.281-022
Offset-Duplicating-Machine Operator (clerical)	RES	48	207.682-018
Offset-Duplicating-Machine Operator (print. & pub.)	RES	45	651.682-014
Offset-Press Operator I (print. & pub.)	RCI	57	651.382-042
Offset-Press Operator II (print. & pub.)	REC	41	651.685-018
Offset-Press-Operator Apprentice (print. & pub.)	RCI	57	651.382-046
Oil Boiler (tex. prod., n.e.c.)	RIE	54	543.362-010
Oil Dipper (woodworking)	REC	41	769.684-026
Oil Pumper (petrol. & gas)	RES	56	914.382-010
Oil-Burner-Servicer-and-Installer (any industry)	RES	52	862.281-018
Oil-Burner-Servicer-and-Installer Helper (any industry)	RSE	37	862.687-022
Oil-Field Equipment Mechanic (petrol. & gas)	RIE	57	629.381-014
Oil-Field Equipment Mechanic Supervisor (petrol. & gas)	RES	59	629.131-014

Part 3: From Occupational Titles to Holland Codes
From the Dictionary of Occupational Titles Occupations to Holland Codes

Title	HOC	Cx	DOT
Oil-Pipe Inspector (petrol. & gas)	REC	59	930.267-010
Oil-Pipe-Inspector Helper (petrol. & gas)	RSC	48	930.364-010
Oil-Recovery-Unit Operator (petrol. refin.)	RIE	53	549.382-014
Oil-Seal Assembler (leather prod.)	CRS	43	739.684-138
Oil-Spot Washer (tex. prod., n.e.c.; textile)	RCS	38	689.687-050
Oil-Well-Service Operator (petrol. & gas)	RIS	56	939.462-010
Oil-Well-Service-Operator Helper (petrol. & gas)	RCS	47	939.684-018
Oil-Well-Services Supervisor (petrol. & gas)	RSE	61	939.132-014
Oiler (any industry)	RCS	39	699.687-018
Oiler (clock & watch)	RCE	38	715.684-146
Oiling-Machine Operator (paper & pulp; paper goods)	REI	40	534.685-018
Oilseed-Meat Presser (oils & grease)	RES	37	521.685-242
Olive Brine Tester (can. & preserv.)	CRS	44	522.584-010
Oliving-Machine Operator (clock & watch)	RCE	49	770.381-034
Opaquer (protective dev.)	RES	47	712.684-030
Open-Developer Operator (textile)	RCE	47	582.685-098
Opener (rubber goods)	REC	37	559.686-034
Opener I (hat & cap)	RCE	38	784.687-054
Opener II (hat & cap)	REC	37	589.686-030
Opener Tender (textile)	RES	40	680.685-070
Opener-Verifier-Packer, Customs (government ser.)	RIE	53	168.387-010
Operating Engineer (construction; mine & quarry)	RIS	47	859.683-010
Operating-Engineer Apprentice (construction; mine & quarry)	RIS	47	859.683-014
Operating-Table Assembler (furniture)	RIE	57	706.381-026
Operational Test Mechanic (aircraft mfg.)	RIC	59	806.261-050
Operations and Intelligence Assistant (military ser.)	CES	57	378.367-026
Operations Manager (motor trans.)	ESI	58	184.167-118
Operations Manager (tel. & tel.)	ESA	70	184.117-070
Operations Officer (financial)	ESC	67	186.137-014
Operations Supervisor, Nuclear Power Plant (utilities)	EIS	76	952.132-010
Operations-Research Analyst (profess. & kin.)	IRE	79	020.067-018
Operator, Automated Process (electron. comp.)	REI	54	590.382-010
Operator, Catalyst Concentration (plastic-synth.)	RIE	51	550.382-026
Operator, Cavity Pump (elec. equip.)	RCS	49	729.682-010
Operator, Prefinish (millwork-plywood)	RSC	47	562.685-018
Ophthalmic Photographer (medical ser.)	CIS	59	143.362-014
Ophthalmic Technician (medical ser.)	CIS	59	078.361-038
Ophthalmologist (medical ser.)	ISR	76	070.101-058
Optical Engineer (profess. & kin.)	RIC	72	019.061-018
Optical-Effects Layout Person (motion picture)	ASC	56	962.361-010
Optical-Effects-Camera Operator (motion picture)	ASR	60	143.260-010
Optical-Element Coater (optical goods)	RES	51	716.382-014
Optical-Glass Etcher (optical goods)	RCE	47	716.681-022
Optical-Glass Silverer (optical goods)	RES	47	574.484-010
Optical-Instrument Assembler (optical goods)	RIE	60	711.381-010
Optician (optical goods)	RIE	61	716.280-018
Optician (optical goods; retail trade)	REI	61	716.280-014
Optician Apprentice (optical goods; retail trade)	REI	61	716.280-010

Title	HOC	Cx	DOT
Optician Apprentice, Dispensing (optical goods; retail trade)	RIS	58	299.361-014
Optician, Dispensing (optical goods; retail trade)	RIS	58	299.361-010
Optomechanical Technician (optical goods; photo. appar.)	RIC	68	007.161-030
Optometric Assistant (medical ser.)	SCI	59	079.364-014
Optometrist (medical ser.)	ISE	69	079.101-018
Oral and Maxillofacial Surgeon (medical ser.)	IRE	73	072.101-018
Oral Pathologist (medical ser.)	IRE	76	072.061-010
Orchestrator (profess. & kin.)	AEI	75	152.067-022
Order Caller (clerical)	CRS	41	209.667-014
Order Clerk (clerical)	CES	54	249.362-026
Order Clerk, Food and Beverage (hotel & rest.)	CSE	47	209.567-014
Order Department Supervisor (any industry)	ERS	63	169.167-038
Order Detailer (clerical)	CSR	53	221.387-046
Order Dispatcher, Chief (utilities)	ESC	57	959.137-018
Order Filler (retail trade; wholesale tr.)	RCE	51	222.487-014
Order Filler, Linseed Oil (oils & grease)	REC	40	920.686-022
Order Runner (meat products)	REC	39	525.687-058
Order-Control Clerk, Blood Bank (medical ser.; nonprofit organ.)	ECS	51	245.367-026
Ordering-Machine Operator (tobacco)	RCS	47	522.682-014
Orderly (medical ser.)	SRE	45	355.674-018
Ordinary Seaman (water trans.)	REI	44	911.687-030
Ordnance Artificer (government ser.)	REI	63	632.261-018
Ordnance Engineer (chemical; ordnance)	RIE	77	019.061-022
Ordnance Truck Installation Mechanic (ordnance)	RIE	45	806.684-098
Ordnance-Artificer Helper (government ser.)	RSE	44	632.684-010
Organ-Pipe Maker, Metal (musical inst.)	RSE	52	709.381-030
Organ-Pipe Voicer (musical inst.)	RES	55	730.381-038
Oriental-Rug Repairer (any industry)	RSE	53	782.381-014
Oriental-Rug Stretcher (any industry)	RCE	41	580.687-010
Orientation and Mobility Therapist for the Blind (education; medical ser.; nonprofit org.)	SER	63	076.224-014
Ornament Maker, Hand (fabrication, n.e.c.)	CRS	39	739.687-130
Ornament Setter (garment; tex. prod., n.e.c.)	RCE	42	789.685-010
Ornamental-Iron Worker (construction)	RIS	57	809.381-022
Ornamental-Iron-Worker Apprentice (construction)	RIS	57	809.381-026
Ornamental-Machine Operator (wood prod., n.e.c.)	RCE	47	690.682-054
Ornamental-Metal Worker (metal prod., n.e.c.)	RIC	59	619.260-014
Ornamental-Metal-Worker Apprentice (metal prod., n.e.c.)	RSE	59	619.260-010
Ornamental-Metal-Worker Helper (metal prod., n.e.c.)	RES	43	619.484-010
Ornamental-Metalwork Designer (struct. metal)	ARS	62	142.061-034
Orthodontic Band Maker (protective dev.)	RES	58	712.381-026
Orthodontic Technician (protective dev.)	RCE	58	712.381-030
Orthodontist (medical ser.)	IRS	75	072.101-022
Orthopedic Assistant (medical ser.)	RSE	49	078.664-010
Orthopedic-Boot-and-Shoe Designer and Maker (boot & shoe; protective dev.)	RCS	63	788.261-010
Orthoptist (medical ser.)	RSI	61	079.371-014

DOT to HOC

Part 3: From Occupational Titles to Holland Codes

From the Dictionary of Occupational Titles Occupations to Holland Codes

Title	HOC	Cx	DOT
Orthotics Assistant (medical ser.)	RSE	61	078.361-022
Orthotics Technician (protective dev.)	RSC	58	712.381-034
Orthotist (medical ser.)	RSE	64	078.261-018
Osteopathic Physician (medical ser.)	ISR	76	071.101-010
Otolaryngologist (medical ser.)	IRS	77	070.101-062
Outboard-Motor Inspector (engine-turbine)	CES	48	806.687-042
Outboard-Motor Mechanic (engine-turbine; ship-boat mfg.)	RIE	58	623.281-042
Outboard-Motor Tester (engine-turbine)	REI	57	623.261-014
Outfitter, Cabin (ship-boat mfg.)	REC	47	806.684-102
Outpatient-Admitting Clerk (medical ser.)	CSE	51	205.362-030
Outside Cutter, Hand (boot & shoe)	CRS	47	788.684-082
Outside Property Agent (motion picture)	ESA	66	162.157-030
Outside-Plant Engineer (tel. & tel.)	IRE	74	003.167-042
Outsole Cutter, Automatic (rubber goods)	RCS	51	690.462-010
Outsole Flexer (boot & shoe)	RCE	39	583.686-026
Outsole Scheduler (boot & shoe)	CRS	42	221.587-022
Oven Dauber (steel & rel.)	RCS	38	543.687-014
Oven Operator (fabrication, n.e.c.)	REC	42	590.665-010
Oven Operator (grain-feed mills)	RES	43	526.585-010
Oven Operator, Automatic (bakery products)	RCE	44	526.685-070
Oven Tender (bakery products)	RES	44	526.685-030
Oven Tender (elec. equip.)	RCE	45	543.685-018
Oven Tender (glass mfg.)	RCE	43	573.585-010
Oven Tender (ordnance)	RCE	42	534.565-010
Oven Tender (paint & varnish)	RES	44	553.685-082
Oven-Equipment Repairer (steel & rel.)	RES	54	630.261-014
Oven-Heater Helper (steel & rel.)	RCE	43	542.665-010
Oven-Press Tender I (nonmet. min.)	RCI	41	573.685-042
Oven-Press Tender II (nonmet. min.)	RCI	41	573.685-046
Overcoiler (clock & watch)	CRS	44	715.684-150
Overedge Sewer (any industry)	CRS	45	787.682-034
Overhauler (textile)	RIE	59	628.261-010
Overhauler Helper (textile)	RCS	42	628.664-010
Overhead Cleaner Maintainer (textile)	CRE	46	628.684-022
Overhead Crane Operator (any industry)	RCS	47	921.663-010
Overlay Plastician (ship-boat mfg.)	RES	43	806.684-106
Overlock Sewing Machine Operator (garment)	CRE	41	786.682-194
Overlock-Machine Operator, Complete Garment (garment)	REC	44	786.682-198
Oxidized-Finish Plater (any industry)	RCS	41	599.685-062
Oxidizer (jewelry-silver.)	RCE	41	700.684-054
Oxygen-Furnace Operator (steel & rel.)	RIE	51	512.382-010
Oxygen-Plant Operator (chemical)	REI	54	552.362-014
Oyster Floater (fishing & hunt.)	REC	38	449.687-010
Pack-Room Operator (plastic-synth.)	RIE	47	559.684-010
Package Crimper (textile)	RCS	37	589.686-034
Package Designer (profess. & kin.)	AEI	65	142.081-018
Package Sealer, Machine (any industry)	RCE	38	920.685-074
Package-Dyeing-Machine Operator (textile)	REI	47	582.685-102

Dictionary of Holland Occupational Codes

Title	HOC	Cx	DOT
Packager, Hand (any industry)	RES	41	920.587-018
Packager, Head (saw. & plan.)	RCE	41	667.682-046
Packager, Machine (any industry)	REC	40	920.685-078
Packaging Engineer (profess. & kin.)	ICS	63	019.187-010
Packaging Supervisor (any industry)	REI	57	920.132-010
Packaging Technician (paper goods)	RES	56	739.281-010
Packer (ordnance)	RCS	44	929.684-010
Packer (tobacco)	RCS	40	920.687-130
Packer Operator, Automatic (tobacco)	CRE	40	920.685-082
Packer, Agricultural Produce (agriculture)	RES	40	920.687-134
Packer, Denture (protective dev.)	RES	48	712.684-034
Packer, Insulation (nonmet. min.)	RES	38	579.685-038
Packer-Fuser (chemical)	REC	38	737.687-094
Packing-Floor Worker (tobacco)	RES	40	920.686-026
Packing-House Supervisor (agriculture; wholesale tr.)	ESR	58	920.137-010
Packing-Line Worker (rubber goods)	RCE	41	753.687-038
Packing-Machine Can Feeder (tobacco)	REC	40	920.686-030
Packing-Machine-Pilot Can Router (tobacco)	RCE	38	920.685-086
Pad Cutter (plastic prod.)	RCE	42	690.685-302
Pad Hand (leather prod.)	RCS	50	780.381-030
Pad Maker (textile)	RES	42	589.687-030
Pad-Extractor Tender (knitting)	REC	43	589.485-010
Pad-Machine Feeder (saw. & plan.)	REC	37	920.686-034
Pad-Machine Offbearer (saw. & plan.)	RCE	36	569.686-030
Padded-Products Finisher (rubber goods)	CRS	44	752.684-034
Padder, Cushion (furniture)	CRE	42	780.684-078
Padding Gluer (furniture)	RES	38	780.687-034
Padding-Machine Operator (textile)	REC	40	582.685-106
Paddock Judge (amuse. & rec.)	SER	56	153.167-010
Page (library)	CRE	45	249.687-014
Page (radio-tv broad.)	CES	50	353.367-022
Pager (machinery mfg.)	REC	40	654.687-014
Pail Bailer (tinware)	RCE	45	703.685-010
Paint Mixer, Hand (any industry)	REI	41	550.684-018
Paint Mixer, Machine (any industry)	RES	44	550.485-018
Paint Pourer (fabrication, n.e.c.)	RES	38	652.687-022
Paint Sprayer, Sandblaster (concrete prod.)	RCS	47	845.381-018
Paint Stripper (petrol. refin.)	RCI	45	599.685-130
Paint Trimmer, Pipe Bowls (fabrication, n.e.c.)	RCI	40	749.684-050
Paint-Brush Maker (fabrication, n.e.c.)	RCS	44	733.684-010
Paint-Line Operator (toy-sport equip.)	RCE	42	599.685-066
Paint-Roller Assembler (fabrication, n.e.c.)	CRE	40	739.687-134
Paint-Roller Covermaker (fabrication, n.e.c.)	REC	40	739.684-142
Paint-Roller Winder (fabrication, n.e.c.)	RCE	41	739.685-030
Paint-Roller-Cover-Machine Setter (fabrication, n.e.c.)	REI	52	692.682-046
Paint-Spray Inspector (any industry)	CES	41	741.687-010
Paint-Spray Tender (glass products)	RCS	44	574.685-014
Paint-Sprayer Operator, Automatic (any industry)	RIE	52	599.382-010
Painter (button & notion)	RAC	49	740.381-018

Part 3: From Occupational Titles to Holland Codes

From the Dictionary of Occupational Titles Occupations to Holland Codes

Title	HOC	Cx	DOT
Painter (construction)	RSE	50	840.381-010
Painter (jewelry-silver.)	CER	41	735.687-018
Painter (profess. & kin.)	ASI	65	144.061-010
Painter and Grader, Cork (toy-sport equip.)	CRE	40	732.687-062
Painter Apprentice, Shipyard (ship-boat mfg.)	RES	54	840.381-014
Painter Apprentice, Transportation Equipment (aircraft mfg.; air trans.; automotive ser.)	RCE	54	845.381-010
Painter Helper, Automotive (automotive ser.)	RCS	40	845.684-014
Painter Helper, Shipyard (ship-boat mfg.)	RCE	42	840.687-010
Painter Helper, Sign (any industry)	RES	48	970.664-010
Painter Helper, Spray (any industry)	RES	41	741.687-014
Painter, Airbrush (any industry)	RES	45	741.684-018
Painter, Animated Cartoons (motion picture; radio-tv broad.)	CER	44	970.681-026
Painter, Bottom (boot & shoe)	RCE	37	788.687-098
Painter, Brush (any industry)	RCE	40	740.684-022
Painter, Clock and Watch Hands (clock & watch)	RCE	37	715.687-098
Painter, Depilatory (meat products)	RCE	35	525.687-062
Painter, Electrostatic (any industry)	RIC	51	599.682-010
Painter, Embossed or Impressed Lettering (any industry)	RES	38	740.687-018
Painter, Hand (any industry)	ARE	53	970.381-022
Painter, Mirror (glass products)	REC	47	741.684-022
Painter, Panel Edge (furniture)	REC	37	740.687-022
Painter, Plate (print. & pub.)	CSR	45	970.681-030
Painter, Rug Touch-Up (laundry & rel.)	RSE	47	364.381-010
Painter, Shipyard (ship-boat mfg.)	RES	54	840.381-018
Painter, Sign (any industry)	RAE	57	970.381-026
Painter, Ski Edge (toy-sport equip.)	CSR	40	749.687-022
Painter, Spray I (any industry)	RCE	47	741.684-026
Painter, Spray II (any industry)	REI	40	741.687-018
Painter, Stage Settings (motion picture)	RCS	47	840.681-010
Painter, Touch-Up (any industry)	RIE	44	749.684-038
Painter, Transportation Equipment (aircraft mfg.; air trans.; automotive ser.)	RCE	54	845.381-014
Painter, Tumbling Barrel (any industry)	RIE	44	599.685-070
Painting-Machine Operator (any industry)	CRE	42	599.685-074
Paintings Restorer (profess. & kin.)	ASR	62	102.261-014
Pairer (knitting)	CSR	42	684.687-010
Pairer (tex. prod., n.e.c.)	RCE	36	789.687-110
Pairing-Machine Operator (nonfer. metal)	RCE	42	691.685-022
Paleontological Helper (profess. & kin.)	REI	53	024.364-010
Paleontologist (profess. & kin.)	ISR	76	024.061-042
Pallbearer (personal ser.)	REC	36	359.687-010
Pallet Assembler (clock & watch)	RCE	44	715.684-154
Pallet Rectifier (clock & watch)	RCE	45	715.684-158
Pallet-Stone Inserter (clock & watch)	REC	52	715.381-082
Pallet-Stone Positioner (clock & watch)	REC	52	715.381-086
Palletizer (nonfer. metal)	RCI	42	929.687-054
Palletizer Operator I (any industry)	RCE	46	921.682-014

Dictionary of Holland Occupational Codes

Title	HOC	Cx	DOT
Pan Greaser, Machine (bakery products)	RCE	35	526.685-034
Pan Helper (chemical)	RES	46	551.585-018
Panel Coverer, Metal Furniture (furniture)	CRE	40	780.684-082
Panel Cutter (furniture)	RCI	42	761.684-050
Panel Edge Sealer (millwork-plywood)	RCE	38	769.685-010
Panel Installer (mfd. bldgs.)	CRE	40	869.684-038
Panel Laminator (struct. metal)	RCE	42	809.684-042
Panel Maker (furniture)	CRE	41	780.684-086
Panel-Lay-Up Worker (woodworking)	RES	45	761.684-018
Panel-Machine Operator (paper goods)	REC	40	640.685-038
Panel-Machine Setter (paper goods)	RES	53	640.360-010
Panelboard Operator (chemical)	RCE	62	950.562-010
Panelboard Operator (mine & quarry; smelt. & refin.)	RIE	56	939.362-014
Panelboard Operator (textile)	RCE	49	582.362-010
Pantograph Setter (print. & pub.)	RSI	51	979.380-010
Pantograph-Machine Set-up Operator (machine shop)	REI	54	605.382-022
Pantographer (print. & pub.)	RES	46	979.382-022
Pantry Goods Maker (hotel & rest.)	RCS	47	317.684-014
Pantry Worker (sugar & conf.)	CRS	49	520.487-018
Pants Outseamer, Chainstitch (garment)	RCE	41	786.682-202
Paper Coater (paper & pulp; paper goods)	CRE	41	534.685-022
Paper Cutter (beverage)	CRS	41	640.565-010
Paper Inserter (glass mfg.)	RCE	35	920.687-138
Paper Sorter and Counter (paper & pulp)	CER	43	649.687-010
Paper Stripper (paper goods; print. & pub.)	RES	37	922.687-078
Paper-Bag-Press Operator (paper goods)	REC	39	641.686-026
Paper-Coating-Machine Operator (photo. appar.)	REI	51	534.582-010
Paper-Cone Grader (paper goods)	CRE	38	649.687-014
Paper-Cone-Drying-Machine Operator (paper goods)	RCE	36	532.686-014
Paper-Cone-Machine Tender (paper goods)	RCE	38	641.685-062
Paper-Control Clerk (water trans.)	CSE	55	219.367-022
Paper-Core-Machine Operator (paper goods)	CRE	40	640.685-042
Paper-Cup-Machine Operator (paper goods)	RES	41	649.685-078
Paper-Novelty Maker (paper goods)	CRE	40	794.684-022
Paper-Pattern Folder (paper goods)	CRE	38	794.687-034
Paper-Pattern Inspector (paper goods)	CRS	40	649.687-018
Paper-Processing-Machine Helper (paper & pulp; paper goods)	RES	38	534.686-010
Paper-Reel Operator (paper goods)	RCE	42	640.685-046
Paperback-Machine Operator (metal prod., n.e.c.)	RCE	42	616.685-046
Paperhanger (concrete prod.)	RCE	42	574.585-010
Paperhanger (construction)	RSE	55	841.381-010
Papier Mache Molder (fabrication, n.e.c.)	REC	47	794.684-026
Parachute Folder (tex. prod., n.e.c.)	RES	41	789.684-034
Parachute Inspector (tex. prod., n.e.c.)	RCE	40	789.687-114
Parachute Marker (tex. prod., n.e.c.)	REC	41	789.587-018
Parachute Mender (tex. prod., n.e.c.)	CRS	42	789.684-038
Parachute Rigger (air trans.)	RCE	47	912.684-010
Parachute-Line Tier (tex. prod., n.e.c.)	RCE	41	789.687-118

Part 3: From Occupational Titles to Holland Codes

From the Dictionary of Occupational Titles Occupations to Holland Codes

Title	HOC	Cx	DOT
Paradichlorobenzene Tender (chemical)	CRE	40	556.685-054
Paraffin-Machine Operator (paper goods)	REC	38	534.685-026
Paraffin-Plant Operator (petrol. refin.)	RSE	47	541.682-010
Paraffin-Plant-Sweater Operator (petrol. refin.)	RES	47	543.682-022
Paralegal (profess. & kin.)	SEC	66	119.267-026
Paramedic (medical ser.)	RIS	60	079.364-026
Parasitologist (profess. & kin.)	IRS	78	041.061-070
Parcel Post Clerk (clerical)	RCE	52	222.387-038
Parimutuel-Ticket Cashier (amuse. & rec.)	CSE	50	211.467-018
Parimutuel-Ticket Checker (amuse. & rec.)	CES	50	219.587-010
Parimutuel-Ticket Seller (amuse. & rec.)	CSE	50	211.467-022
Park Aide (government ser.)	CES	54	249.367-082
Park Naturalist (government ser.)	SEI	65	049.127-010
Park Ranger (government ser.)	ESR	60	169.167-042
Park Superintendent (government ser.)	ERA	65	188.167-062
Parking Analyst (government ser.)	RIC	68	199.261-014
Parking Enforcement Officer (government ser.)	CES	42	375.587-010
Parking Lot Signaler (automotive ser.)	CSR	38	915.667-014
Parking-Lot Attendant (automotive ser.)	CRS	41	915.473-010
Parking-Meter Servicer (government ser.)	RES	49	710.384-026
Parlor Chaperone (hotel & rest.)	ESR	46	352.667-014
Part Maker (jewelry-silver.)	CSR	40	739.687-138
Partition Assembler (wood. container)	REC	38	762.687-054
Partition-Assembly-Machine Operator (any industry)	RSE	48	649.582-010
Partition-Making-Machine Operator (paper goods)	RCE	40	649.685-082
Parts Cataloger (any industry)	REI	62	229.267-010
Parts Clerk (clerical)	RCS	54	222.367-042
Parts Lister (electron. comp.)	CER	54	229.367-014
Parts Remover (clock & watch)	RCE	37	715.687-102
Parts Salvager (any industry)	RIE	58	638.281-026
Parts-Order-and-Stock Clerk (clerical)	CRS	53	249.367-058
Passementerie Worker (tex. prod., n.e.c.)	CRS	40	782.684-050
Passenger Attendant (water trans.)	CES	41	350.677-014
Passenger Representative (r.r. trans.)	ESR	53	910.367-026
Passenger Service Representative (air trans.)	SEC	49	359.677-022
Passenger Service Representative I (r.r. trans.)	ECS	49	352.677-010
Passenger Service Representative II (r.r. trans.)	CER	43	910.677-010
Passport-Application Examiner (government ser.)	CES	60	169.267-030
Paste Mixer (chemical)	RCS	41	550.585-034
Paste-Up Artist (print. & pub.)	CRS	59	972.381-030
Paste-Up Artist Apprentice (print. & pub.)	CRS	59	972.381-038
Paster (brick & tile)	REC	42	773.684-014
Paster Supervisor (brick & tile)	RES	56	773.131-010
Paster, Hand or Machine (leather prod.)	RCE	38	783.687-026
Paster, Hat Lining (hat & cap)	RCI	39	692.686-070
Paster, Screen Printing (textile)	RCE	37	652.687-026
Pasteurizer (beverage; can. & preserv.)	CRE	41	523.685-110
Pasteurizer (oils & grease)	RES	44	523.585-026
Pasting Inspector (brick & tile)	RES	41	773.687-010

Dictionary of Holland Occupational Codes

From the Dictionary of Occupational Titles Occupations to Holland Codes

Title	HOC	Cx	DOT
Pasting-Machine Offbearer (elec. equip.)	CRS	39	509.686-014
Pasting-Machine Operator (elec. equip.)	REI	50	505.482-010
Pastoral Assistant (nonprofit org.)	SEC	65	129.107-026
Pastry Chef (hotel & rest.)	ASE	59	313.131-022
Pastry Chef (water trans.)	ARE	58	315.131-014
Patch Driller (fabrication, n.e.c.)	REI	41	739.687-142
Patch Finisher (textile)	RES	41	582.684-010
Patch Sander (stonework)	RCE	37	775.684-054
Patch Washer (textile)	RCE	40	582.685-110
Patch Worker (agriculture)	RCE	37	381.687-030
Patch Worker (tobacco)	RCE	41	790.684-018
Patch-Machine Operator (paper goods)	REC	40	641.685-066
Patcher (fabrication, n.e.c.)	CRE	41	739.687-146
Patcher (house. appl.)	RCE	38	723.687-010
Patcher (leather mfg.)	CRE	43	585.687-022
Patcher (pottery & porc.)	RCE	41	774.684-046
Patcher (steel & rel.)	REC	41	861.684-014
Patcher (woodworking)	REC	42	769.684-030
Patcher Helper (steel & rel.)	RES	39	861.687-014
Patcher, Bowling Ball (toy-sport equip.)	RCE	41	759.684-046
Patching-Machine Operator (laundry & rel.)	RCE	37	361.685-022
Patent Agent (profess. & kin.)	EAI	74	119.167-014
Pathologist (medical ser.)	IRE	77	070.061-010
Patient-Resources-and-Reimbursement Agent (government ser.)	SIC	61	195.267-018
Patrol Conductor (government ser.)	SEC	44	372.677-010
Patrol Judge (amuse. & rec.)	ESA	60	153.267-014
Patroller (knitting)	RCE	39	685.687-022
Patroller (r.r. trans.)	ESC	45	376.667-018
Pattern Assembler (knitting)	CRE	43	685.685-014
Pattern Chart-Writer (paper goods)	REC	53	789.381-014
Pattern Duplicator (textile)	RCE	41	683.685-026
Pattern Gater (foundry)	REC	41	801.684-014
Pattern Grader-Cutter (garment)	REI	54	781.381-022
Pattern Hand (woodworking)	CRE	41	652.687-030
Pattern Marker I (woodworking)	RIS	59	761.381-022
Pattern Marker II (woodworking)	REC	42	761.684-022
Pattern Ruler (tex. prod., n.e.c.)	CRE	37	794.687-038
Pattern Wheel Maker (knitting)	RCS	45	685.684-010
Pattern-Chain Maker Supervisor (textile)	RES	61	683.132-010
Pattern-Grader Supervisor (wood prod., n.e.c.)	RSE	59	693.132-010
Pattern-Lease Inspector (textile)	REA	46	683.384-010
Pattern-Shop Supervisor (foundry)	RES	59	693.131-010
Patternmaker (engraving)	RIE	57	751.381-010
Patternmaker (fabrication, n.e.c.)	RIE	59	772.381-014
Patternmaker (furniture)	RIE	61	709.381-034
Patternmaker (furniture)	RCI	62	661.280-010
Patternmaker (furniture; garment; tex. prod., n.e.c.)	RIC	57	781.361-014
Patternmaker (glass products)	RCS	49	779.584-010

DOT to HOC

Title	HOC	Cx	DOT
Patternmaker (hat & cap)	RSE	54	784.361-010
Patternmaker (metal prod., n.e.c.)	RES	58	693.281-014
Patternmaker (stonework)	RIE	57	703.381-010
Patternmaker Apprentice, Metal (foundry)	RIE	60	600.280-046
Patternmaker Apprentice, Wood (foundry)	RIE	62	661.281-018
Patternmaker, Acoustical Tile (wood prod., n.e.c.)	RCE	47	649.685-086
Patternmaker, All-Around (foundry; plastic prod.)	RCI	62	693.280-014
Patternmaker, Envelope (paper goods)	RIE	62	649.361-010
Patternmaker, Metal (foundry)	RIE	60	600.280-050
Patternmaker, Metal, Bench (foundry)	RIE	60	693.281-018
Patternmaker, Plaster (aircraft mfg.)	RIE	64	777.281-018
Patternmaker, Plastics (plastic prod.)	RIS	57	754.381-014
Patternmaker, Sample (cutlery-hrdwr.)	REI	60	693.281-022
Patternmaker, Wood (foundry)	RIE	62	661.281-022
Pawnbroker (retail trade)	ECS	60	191.157-010
Pay-Station Attendant (tel. & tel.)	ESC	54	237.367-034
Paymaster of Purses (amuse. & rec.)	CSE	61	211.367-010
Payroll Clerk (clerical)	CRE	55	215.382-014
Peanut Blancher (can. & preserv.)	REC	39	521.685-246
Peanut-Butter Maker (can. & preserv.; food prep., n.e.c.)	RES	41	529.685-178
Pearl Restorer (jewelry-silver.)	RES	50	735.381-014
Pearl-Glue Operator (chemical)	REC	41	550.685-094
Pearler (clock & watch)	RCE	40	715.684-162
Peddler (retail trade)	ESC	43	291.457-018
Pediatric Dentist (medical ser.)	IRE	75	072.101-026
Pediatrician (medical ser.)	ISE	76	070.101-066
Pedigree Tracer (clerical)	CSE	51	249.387-018
Peeled-Potato Inspector (food prep., n.e.c.)	REC	37	521.687-094
Pegger (boot & shoe)	CER	40	788.687-102
Pegger, Dobby Looms (narrow fabrics; textile)	CRE	41	689.687-054
Pellet-Mill Operator (grain-feed mills)	CRE	42	520.685-178
Pellet-Press Operator (chemical)	REI	45	555.685-042
Pellet-Press Operator (ordnance)	RCS	42	694.685-034
Pelota Maker (toy-sport equip.)	RCE	41	732.684-090
Pelter (agriculture)	REI	41	410.687-018
Pen-and-Pencil Repairer (any industry)	RCS	47	733.684-014
Pencil Inspector (pen & pencil)	CER	40	733.687-062
Percolator Operator (grain-feed mills)	RES	48	523.682-034
Percussion-Instrument Repairer (any industry)	REI	50	730.381-042
Perforating-Machine Operator (hat & cap)	RCE	41	686.685-038
Perforating-Machine Operator (print. & pub.)	RCE	41	649.685-090
Perforator (tex. prod., n.e.c.)	CRE	41	781.684-042
Perforator Operator, Oil Well (petrol. & gas)	RES	53	931.382-010
Perforator Typist (clerical)	CSE	49	203.582-038
Perfumer (chemical)	ISE	69	022.161-018
Perfusionist (medical ser.)	ISR	62	078.362-034
Periodontist (medical ser.)	IRE	75	072.101-030
Perishable-Freight Inspector (r.r. trans.)	CRE	49	910.667-022
Perishable-Fruit Inspector (wholesale tr.)	REI	52	910.387-010

Part 3: From Occupational Titles to Holland Codes

From the Dictionary of Occupational Titles Occupations to Holland Codes

Title	HOC	Cx	DOT
Permanent-Mold Supervisor (foundry; nonfer. metal)	RSE	61	514.130-010
Permit Agent, Geophysical Prospecting (petrol. & gas)	ESR	68	191.117-042
Personal Attendant (domestic ser.)	SEC	43	309.674-014
Personal Property Assessor (government ser.)	ERS	54	191.367-010
Personal Shopper (retail trade)	ESR	56	296.357-010
Personnel Clerk (clerical)	CSE	55	209.362-026
Personnel Quality Assurance Auditor (electron. comp.)	ESR	53	168.367-022
Personnel Recruiter (profess. & kin.)	SCE	65	166.267-038
Personnel Scheduler (clerical)	CSE	55	215.367-014
Pesticide-Control Inspector (government ser.)	ESR	60	168.267-098
Petroleum Engineer (petrol. & gas)	RIE	76	010.061-018
Petroleum Inspector (business ser.)	CSE	51	222.367-046
Petroleum-Inspector Supervisor (business ser.)	ESC	59	222.137-026
Petrologist (profess. & kin.)	ISR	77	024.061-046
Pewter Caster (jewelry-silver.)	RCI	50	502.384-010
Pewter Finisher (jewelry-silver.)	ARS	51	700.281-026
Pewterer (jewelry-silver.)	ASR	59	700.261-010
Pharmaceutical Detailer (wholesale tr.)	ESA	66	262.157-010
Pharmaceutical Operator (pharmaceut.)	RIE	53	559.382-042
Pharmaceutical-Compounding Supervisor (pharmaceut.)	SER	59	559.131-010
Pharmacist (medical ser.)	IES	72	074.161-010
Pharmacist Assistant (military ser.)	RIE	61	074.381-010
Pharmacologist (profess. & kin.)	IRE	78	041.061-074
Pharmacy Technician (medical ser.)	REC	54	074.382-010
Pheresis Specialist (medical ser.)	IRC	68	078.261-042
Philologist (profess. & kin.)	AIS	63	059.067-010
Phlebotomist (medical ser.)	SRI	51	079.364-022
Phonograph-Cartridge Assembler (comm. equip.)	RCE	48	720.684-014
Phonograph-Needle-Tip Maker (comm. equip.)	REC	51	770.382-014
Phosphoric-Acid Operator (chemical)	RCE	54	558.582-010
Photo Checker and Assembler (photofinishing)	CRA	44	976.687-014
Photo Mask Cleaner (electron. comp.)	RCI	39	590.684-034
Photo Mask Inspector (electron. comp.)	RCI	58	726.384-022
Photo Mask Maker, Electron-Beam (electron. comp.)	RCI	54	972.382-018
Photo Mask Pattern Generator (electron. comp.)	RCI	55	976.382-038
Photo Mask Processor (electron. comp.)	RCI	51	976.384-014
Photo Mask Technician, Electron-Beam (electron. comp.)	CRI	56	972.382-022
Photo Technician (electron. comp.)	RCI	51	976.384-010
Photo-Optics Technician (profess. & kin.)	IRE	63	029.280-010
Photocomposing-Machine Operator (print. & pub.)	RCS	48	650.582-018
Photocomposing-Perforator-Machine Operator (print. & pub.)	CES	55	203.582-042
Photocomposition-Keyboard Operator (print. & pub.)	CRE	52	203.582-046
Photocopying-Machine Operator (clerical)	REC	40	207.685-014
Photoengraver (print. & pub.)	RIE	58	971.381-022
Photoengraver Apprentice (print. & pub.)	RIE	58	971.381-026
Photoengraving Finisher (print. & pub.)	RIE	56	971.381-030
Photoengraving Printer (print. & pub.)	RIE	56	971.381-034
Photoengraving Proofer (print. & pub.)	RIS	56	971.381-038

DOT to HOC

Title	HOC	Cx	DOT
Photoengraving-Proofer Apprentice (print. & pub.)	RIS	56	971.381-040
Photofinishing Laboratory Worker (photofinishing)	ERS	43	976.687-018
Photogrammetric Engineer (profess. & kin.)	IEC	73	018.167-026
Photogrammetrist (profess. & kin.)	IRC	64	018.261-026
Photograph Finisher (photofinishing)	REC	43	976.487-010
Photograph Retoucher (photofinishing)	RCA	55	970.281-018
Photographer (amuse. & rec.)	ESA	52	143.457-010
Photographer Apprentice, Lithographic (print. & pub.)	RIE	56	972.382-010
Photographer Helper (any industry)	REI	47	976.667-010
Photographer, Aerial (profess. & kin.)	IER	61	143.062-014
Photographer, Apprentice (profess. & kin.)	AES	62	143.062-018
Photographer, Finish (amuse. & rec.)	SRC	54	143.382-014
Photographer, Lithographic (print. & pub.)	RIE	56	972.382-014
Photographer, Photoengraving (electron. comp.; print. & pub.)	RIE	58	971.382-014
Photographer, Scientific (profess. & kin.)	IRS	62	143.062-026
Photographer, Still (profess. & kin.)	ARS	62	143.062-030
Photographic Aligner, Semiconductor Wafers (electron. comp.)	RCI	49	976.382-030
Photographic Engineer (profess. & kin.)	ISE	69	019.081-014
Photographic Equipment Technician (photo. appar.)	RIE	61	714.281-022
Photographic Processor, Semiconductor Wafers (electron. comp.)	RCI	41	976.685-038
Photographic-Equipment-Maintenance Technician (photo. appar.)	RSE	59	714.281-026
Photographic-Machine Operator (clerical)	RES	43	207.685-018
Photographic-Plate Maker (electron. comp.)	RIE	57	714.381-018
Photojournalist (print. & pub.; radio-tv broad.)	AEC	59	143.062-034
Photolettering-Machine Operator (print. & pub.)	CRE	45	652.585-010
Photoradio Operator (print. & pub.; tel. & tel.)	CRE	59	193.362-010
Photoresist Laminator, Printed Circuit Board (electron. comp.)	RCI	41	554.685-034
Photostat Operator (any industry)	REI	53	976.382-022
Photostat-Operator Helper (any industry)	REC	40	979.687-014
Phototypesetter Operator (print. & pub.)	RCI	54	650.582-022
Physiatrist (medical ser.)	IRE	76	070.101-070
Physical Therapist (education; medical ser.)	SIE	67	076.121-014
Physical Therapist Assistant (medical ser.)	SCR	62	076.224-010
Physical Therapy Aide (medical ser.)	ESC	51	355.354-010
Physical-Integration Practitioner (medical ser.)	SRI	51	076.264-010
Physician Assistant (medical ser.)	ISA	66	079.364-018
Physician, Occupational (medical ser.)	ISC	76	070.101-078
Physicist (profess. & kin.)	IRE	80	023.061-014
Physicist, Theoretical (profess. & kin.)	IRE	80	023.067-010
Physiologist (profess. & kin.)	IRE	78	041.061-078
Piano Case and Bench Assembler (musical inst.)	RCS	42	763.684-058
Piano Regulator-Inspector (musical inst.)	RCE	48	730.681-010
Piano Stringer (musical inst.)	RCS	42	730.684-054
Piano Technician (any industry)	RAE	56	730.281-038

Part 3: From Occupational Titles to Holland Codes

From the Dictionary of Occupational Titles Occupations to Holland Codes

Title	HOC	Cx	DOT
Piano Tuner (any industry)	RCS	52	730.361-010
Pick Remover (textile)	REC	37	689.687-058
Pick-Pulling-Machine Operator (textile)	RCE	38	689.685-094
Pick-Up Operator (textile)	CRE	43	689.685-098
Picked-Edge Sewing-Machine Operator (garment)	CRE	40	786.682-206
Picker (saw. & plan.)	REI	41	669.687-022
Picker (tobacco)	REC	37	521.687-098
Picker Tender (textile)	RIC	42	680.685-074
Picker-Machine Operator (furniture)	RCE	40	680.685-078
Picking-Machine Operator (any industry)	REC	38	680.685-082
Picking-Table Worker (sugar & conf.)	REC	36	521.687-102
Pickle Pumper (meat products)	RES	43	522.685-086
Pickler (can. & preserv.)	REC	43	522.684-010
Pickler (meat products)	REC	38	522.687-034
Pickler Helper, Continuous Pickling Line (any industry)	REC	43	503.686-010
Pickler, Continuous Pickling Line (any industry)	RSI	53	503.362-010
Pickling Solution Maker (meat products)	RES	44	522.485-010
Picture Framer (retail trade; wood prod., n.e.c.)	RCE	47	739.684-146
Pie Maker (hotel & rest.)	RSE	50	313.361-038
Pie Maker, Machine (bakery products)	RES	44	526.685-038
Piercing-Machine Operator (nonfer. metal)	RES	49	613.482-014
Piercing-Mill Operator (steel & rel.)	RCE	43	613.685-018
Pig-Machine Operator (steel & rel.)	RSE	49	514.362-010
Pig-Machine-Operator Helper (steel & rel.)	REI	41	514.667-014
Pigment Furnace Tender (chemical)	RIE	46	553.685-086
Pigment Processor (chemical; paint & varnish)	ERS	48	559.685-130
Pigment Pumper (rubber reclaim.)	RCE	41	914.665-010
Pile-Driver Operator (construction)	RIE	49	859.682-018
Pilling-Machine Operator (plastic prod.; plastic-synth.)	REC	41	556.685-058
Pillow Cleaner (tex. prod., n.e.c.)	REC	36	789.687-122
Pillowcase Turner (tex. prod., n.e.c.)	RCE	41	583.685-078
Pilot, Highway Patrol (government ser.)	ERS	64	375.163-014
Pilot, Ship (water trans.)	REI	68	197.133-026
Pilot, Submersible (any industry)	RIE	62	029.383-010
Pilot-Control Operator (chemical; plastic-synth.)	IRE	63	559.382-046
Pilot-Control-Operator Helper (chemical; plastic-synth.)	CRS	48	559.664-014
Pin Inserter, Regulator (clock & watch)	RCE	44	715.684-166
Pin Maker (pottery & porc.)	REC	40	575.686-018
Pin-Game-Machine Inspector (svc. ind. mach.)	REC	55	729.381-014
Pin-or-Clip Fastener (jewelry-silver.)	RCE	38	735.687-022
Pinion Polisher (clock & watch)	CRS	39	715.685-042
Pinking-Machine Operator (boot & shoe; garment)	CRE	42	686.685-042
Pinking-Machine Operator (button & notion)	CRE	41	692.685-130
Pinner (garment; tex. prod., n.e.c.)	RCE	37	782.687-026
Pinner (tex. prod., n.e.c.)	CRS	41	782.684-054
Pinner, Printed Circuit Boards (electron. comp.)	RCI	41	699.685-046
Pinsetter Adjuster, Automatic (toy-sport equip.)	RSI	57	829.381-010
Pinsetter Mechanic, Automatic (any industry)	REC	51	638.261-022
Pinsetter-Mechanic Helper (any industry)	REC	42	829.667-014

Part 3: From Occupational Titles to Holland Codes
From the Dictionary of Occupational Titles Occupations to Holland Codes

Title	HOC	Cx	DOT
Pipe Buffer (construction)	RCS	38	705.684-054
Pipe Changer (mine & quarry)	RES	42	891.564-010
Pipe Coverer and Insulator (ship-boat mfg.)	REI	55	863.381-014
Pipe Cutter (mfd. bldgs.)	RIS	49	862.682-010
Pipe Finisher (brick & tile)	RCS	42	779.684-042
Pipe Fitter (construction)	RCE	58	862.281-022
Pipe Fitter (ship-boat mfg.)	RIE	59	862.261-010
Pipe Fitter, Diesel Engine I (engine-turbine)	RSE	57	862.361-018
Pipe Fitter, Diesel Engine II (engine-turbine)	RES	56	862.381-022
Pipe Installer (construction; utilities)	RES	53	869.381-018
Pipe Racker (fabrication, n.e.c.)	RCE	44	749.687-034
Pipe Stem Aligner (fabrication, n.e.c.)	RCI	39	739.687-210
Pipe Stem Repairer (fabrication, n.e.c.)	RCI	43	739.684-186
Pipe Stripper (concrete prod.)	RES	37	575.687-026
Pipe Tester (petrol. & gas)	RIE	54	930.382-014
Pipe-and-Tank Fabricator (wood. container)	RES	50	669.380-018
Pipe-Cleaning-and-Priming-Machine Operator (construction)	RCE	48	862.662-010
Pipe-Fitter Apprentice (construction)	RCE	58	862.281-026
Pipe-Fitter Helper (construction)	RCE	42	862.684-022
Pipe-Fitter Helper (ship-boat mfg.)	RCE	46	862.684-018
Pipe-Fitter Supervisor (construction)	RES	59	862.131-010
Pipe-Fitter Supervisor (ship-boat mfg.)	RSE	59	862.131-014
Pipe-Organ Builder (musical inst.)	RES	59	730.281-042
Pipe-Organ Installer (musical inst.)	RES	57	730.381-046
Pipe-Organ Tuner and Repairer (any industry)	RSC	55	730.361-014
Pipe-Smoker-Machine Operator (fabrication, n.e.c.)	RES	42	739.687-150
Pipe-Wrapping-Machine Operator (construction; pipe lines)	RIE	46	862.682-014
Piped-Pocket-Machine Operator (garment)	CRE	40	786.685-022
Pipeline Construction Inspector (construction)	RES	58	869.367-018
Pipeliner (pipe lines)	RES	46	899.684-026
Piston Maker (musical inst.)	RCE	47	730.681-014
Pit Steward (amuse. & rec.)	ESR	63	153.167-014
Pit Supervisor (mine & quarry)	ERS	61	939.137-014
Pitch Filler (any industry)	RES	40	619.687-018
Pitch Worker (optical goods)	RCE	39	551.666-010
Placer (insurance)	CES	60	239.267-010
Plan Checker (government ser.)	IRC	64	168.267-102
Planer Operator (elec. equip.)	REI	47	675.682-014
Planer Operator (woodworking)	RIE	47	665.682-022
Planer Set-up Operator, Tool (machine shop)	RIE	58	605.282-014
Planer, Stone (stonework)	RIE	49	675.682-018
Planer-Type-Milling-Machine Set-up Operator (machine shop)	RIE	58	605.282-018
Planetarium Technician (museums)	RCI	64	962.261-010
Planimeter Operator (government ser.)	CES	50	219.387-022
Planing-Machine Operator (clock & watch)	CRE	41	605.685-034
Planisher (jewelry-silver.)	CRS	38	700.687-054

Dictionary of Holland Occupational Codes

Part 3: From Occupational Titles to Holland Codes

From the Dictionary of Occupational Titles Occupations to Holland Codes

Title	HOC	Cx	DOT
Planishing-Press Operator (plastic-synth.)	RSC	47	690.682-058
Planner, Program Services (government ser.)	EIS	70	188.167-110
Planning Engineer, Central Office Facilities (tel. & tel.)	IRE	80	003.061-050
Plant Breeder (profess. & kin.)	IRS	78	041.061-082
Plant Engineer (profess. & kin.)	RIE	70	007.167-014
Plant Operator (concrete prod.; construction)	RIE	47	570.682-014
Plant Operator, Channel Process (chemical)	CES	45	542.685-010
Plant Operator, Furnace Process (chemical)	RES	54	559.362-026
Plant Pathologist (profess. & kin.)	IRS	78	041.061-086
Plant Propagator (agriculture)	RIS	57	405.361-010
Plant Supervisor (grain-feed mills)	SRE	54	529.132-014
Plant-Care Worker (agriculture)	RCI	51	408.364-010
Plasma Etcher, Printed Circuit Boards (electron. comp.)	RCI	47	590.685-094
Plaster Maker (nonmet. min.)	RES	46	779.684-046
Plaster Mixer, Machine (concrete prod.)	REI	50	570.382-014
Plaster Molder I (foundry)	RIE	57	777.381-034
Plaster Molder II (foundry)	REC	47	518.484-010
Plaster-Die Maker (pottery & porc.)	RES	45	774.684-026
Plaster-Machine Tender (construction)	REC	40	842.665-010
Plaster-Pattern Caster (machine tools)	RIE	57	777.381-038
Plasterer (construction)	RES	52	842.361-018
Plasterer (furniture)	RCE	38	749.687-026
Plasterer Apprentice (construction)	RES	52	842.361-022
Plasterer, Molding (concrete prod.; construction)	RIE	56	842.361-026
Plastic Duplicator (machine tools)	REI	47	754.684-038
Plastic Molder (fabrication, n.e.c.)	RCE	45	779.684-050
Plastic Roller (plastic prod.)	RCE	39	690.685-498
Plastic Tool Maker (machine shop)	RIE	57	601.381-026
Plastic-Card Grader, Cardroom (amuse. & rec.)	CSR	42	343.687-010
Plastic-Design Applier (boot & shoe)	RCE	36	690.686-046
Plastic-Fixture Builder (machine shop)	RIE	59	601.381-030
Plastic-Joint Maker (brick & tile)	RES	41	590.687-014
Plastic-Top Assembler (furniture)	RCS	40	763.684-062
Plastics Fabricator (aircraft mfg.; plastic prod.)	RIE	60	754.381-018
Plastics Repairer (plastic prod.)	RCE	42	754.684-046
Plastics Worker (aircraft mfg.)	REC	47	754.684-042
Plastics-Seasoner Operator (plastic-synth.)	RCS	40	553.665-042
Plastics-Spreading-Machine Operator (plastic-synth.)	RIE	50	554.382-014
Plate Assembler, Small Battery (elec. equip.)	CRE	46	727.684-026
Plate Conditioner (steel & rel.)	RCI	44	819.664-010
Plate Finisher (print. & pub.)	RIE	56	659.360-010
Plate Former (elec. equip.)	RCS	47	500.684-018
Plate Gauger (print. & pub.)	REC	42	979.687-018
Plate Grainer (print. & pub.)	RES	50	972.682-010
Plate Inspector (print. & pub.)	CRS	49	972.687-010
Plate Molder (pen & pencil; print. & pub.)	RES	47	556.582-010
Plate Setter, Flexographic Press (print. & pub.)	RIE	54	659.381-010
Plate Slitter-and-Inspector (elec. equip.)	CRE	42	727.685-010
Plate Stacker, Hand (elec. equip.)	RCE	39	729.687-026

Title	HOC	Cx	DOT
Plate Stacker, Machine (elec. equip.)	RCS	49	692.382-014
Plate Worker (paper & pulp)	REC	41	535.685-010
Plate-Grainer Apprentice (print. & pub.)	RES	50	972.682-014
Plate-Take-Out Worker (elec. equip.)	RES	40	500.687-010
Platemaker, Semiconductor Packages (electron. comp.)	RCI	51	972.384-014
Platen Builder-Up (print. & pub.)	REC	46	651.384-010
Platen Grinder (office machines)	RCE	47	690.385-010
Platen-Press Feeder (print. & pub.)	RCE	41	651.685-022
Platen-Press Operator (paper goods)	RES	47	649.682-026
Platen-Press Operator (print. & pub.)	RIE	55	651.362-018
Platen-Press-Operator Apprentice (print. & pub.)	RIE	55	651.362-022
Plater (electroplating)	RIE	57	500.380-010
Plater (inst. & app.)	RCE	47	500.684-034
Plater Apprentice (electroplating)	RIE	57	500.380-014
Plater, Barrel (electroplating)	REI	51	500.362-014
Plater, Hot Dip (galvanizing)	REI	41	501.685-010
Plater, Printed Circuit Board Panels (electron. comp.)	RCI	42	500.684-026
Plater, Semiconductor Wafers and Components (electron. comp.)	RCS	46	500.684-030
Platform Attendant (food prep., n.e.c.)	REI	50	299.377-010
Plating Equipment Tender (electroplating)	RCI	45	500.685-014
Plating-Machine Operator (paper & pulp)	REC	40	649.686-026
Player-Piano Technician (musical inst.)	RIE	53	730.381-050
Playground-Equipment Erector (retail trade)	RCE	44	801.684-018
Playroom Attendant (any industry)	AES	49	359.677-026
Playwright (profess. & kin.)	ASE	70	131.067-038
Pleat Patternmaker (garment; tex. prod., n.e.c.)	RCE	51	781.484-010
Pleat Taper (tex. prod., n.e.c.)	CRE	40	789.487-010
Pleater (tex. prod., n.e.c.)	CRE	44	787.685-026
Pleater (textile)	RCE	37	589.685-074
Pleater, Hand (tex. prod., n.e.c.)	CRE	44	583.684-010
Pleating-Machine Operator (any industry)	REC	46	583.685-082
Plodder Operator (soap & rel.)	RES	45	556.682-018
Plow-and-Boring-Machine Tender (woodworking)	RES	40	665.685-018
Plug Cutter (pen & pencil)	CRE	41	690.685-306
Plug Shaper, Hand (tobacco)	REC	39	520.687-050
Plug Shaper, Machine (tobacco)	RES	37	520.686-034
Plug Sorter (woodworking)	RCS	37	769.687-034
Plug Wirer (elec. equip.)	RCE	39	726.687-014
Plug-Cutting-Machine Operator (tobacco)	RCE	37	529.685-182
Plug-Overwrap-Machine Tender (tobacco)	REC	40	529.685-186
Plugger (steel & rel.)	RES	42	613.687-010
Plugger (wood. container)	RCE	36	764.687-098
Plugging-Machine Operator (woodworking)	RES	44	669.682-062
Plumber (construction)	REI	57	862.381-030
Plumber (mfd. bldgs.)	RCE	50	862.681-010
Plumber Apprentice (construction)	REI	57	862.381-034
Plumber Supervisor (construction)	RES	59	862.131-018
Plumbing Assembler-Installer (mfd. bldgs.)	RCS	45	862.684-026

Part 3: From Occupational Titles to Holland Codes

From the Dictionary of Occupational Titles Occupations to Holland Codes

Title	HOC	Cx	DOT
Plumbing-Hardware Assembler (plumbing-heat.)	RCE	41	706.684-086
Plush Weaver (textile)	RCS	45	683.682-030
Plywood-Scarfer Tender (millwork-plywood)	REC	41	665.685-022
Pneumatic Jacketer (nonfer. metal)	RES	37	691.667-010
Pneumatic-Hoist Operator (construction; mfd. bldgs.)	RSE	41	921.663-046
Pneumatic-Jack Operator (petrol. & gas)	REI	47	939.682-014
Pneumatic-Tool Operator (ship-boat mfg.)	RES	52	809.381-030
Pneumatic-Tool Repairer (any industry)	RIE	58	630.281-010
Pneumatic-Tube Repairer (any industry)	RES	56	630.281-014
Poacher Operator (chemical)	REC	45	551.685-106
Pocket Cutter (woodworking)	RIS	48	667.482-014
Pocket Setter, Lockstitch (garment)	RCE	44	786.682-210
Pocket-Machine Operator (furniture)	CRE	41	616.685-050
Pocketed-Spring Assembler (furniture)	CRE	41	780.684-090
Podiatric Assistant (medical ser.)	SCE	55	079.374-018
Podiatrist (medical ser.)	SIR	65	079.101-022
Poet (profess. & kin.)	AES	69	131.067-042
Pointing-Machine Operator (plastic prod.; rubber goods)	REC	39	690.685-310
Pole Framer (utilities; wood prod., n.e.c.)	REI	42	959.684-010
Pole Inspector (utilities)	RCE	51	869.387-010
Pole Inspector (wood prod., n.e.c.)	CRS	45	561.587-010
Pole-Peeling-Machine Operator (saw. & plan.; wood prod., n.e.c.)	REA	44	663.682-014
Pole-Peeling-Machine-Operator Helper (wood prod., n.e.c.)	RES	37	665.686-010
Poleyard Supervisor (utilities)	ERS	58	929.137-014
Police Academy Program Coordinator (government ser.)	SEC	62	375.167-054
Police Aide (government ser.)	CSE	51	243.362-014
Police Artist (government ser.)	ASC	65	141.061-034
Police Captain, Precinct (government ser.)	ERS	65	375.167-034
Police Chief (government ser.)	SER	66	375.117-010
Police Clerk (government ser.)	CRS	57	375.362-010
Police Commissioner I (government ser.)	ESR	67	188.117-118
Police Inspector I (government ser.)	ESR	63	375.267-026
Police Inspector II (government ser.)	ESR	56	375.267-030
Police Lieutenant, Community Relations (government ser.)	SEC	63	375.137-018
Police Lieutenant, Patrol (government ser.)	ESR	60	375.167-038
Police Officer I (government ser.)	SER	55	375.263-014
Police Officer II (government ser.)	SER	50	375.367-010
Police Officer III (government ser.)	SEC	55	375.267-038
Police Officer, Booking (government ser.)	SCR	53	375.367-018
Police Officer, Crime Prevention (government ser.)	SCR	59	375.264-010
Police Officer, Identification and Records (government ser.)	REI	57	375.384-010
Police Officer, Safety Instruction (government ser.)	SCE	53	375.267-042
Police Sergeant, Precinct I (government ser.)	SER	55	375.133-010
Police Surgeon (medical ser.)	IRS	76	070.101-082
Police-Academy Instructor (government ser.)	ESR	60	375.227-010
Policy-Change Clerk (insurance)	CSR	57	219.362-042
Policy-Value Calculator (insurance)	CRS	53	216.382-050

DOT to HOC

Title	HOC	Cx	DOT
Policyholder-Information Clerk (insurance)	CSE	61	249.262-010
Polisher (any industry)	RES	48	705.684-058
Polisher (button & notion)	REI	41	599.685-078
Polisher (clock & watch)	RCS	47	715.682-018
Polisher (glass mfg.; glass products)	RSE	41	775.684-058
Polisher (jewelry-silver.)	REI	42	700.687-058
Polisher (woodworking)	RCE	40	761.684-026
Polisher and Buffer II (any industry)	RCE	41	705.684-062
Polisher Apprentice (any industry)	RES	48	705.684-066
Polisher, Balance Screwhead (clock & watch)	CRE	41	715.685-046
Polisher, Dial (clock & watch)	RCE	42	715.684-170
Polisher, Eyeglass Frames (optical goods)	RCE	38	713.684-038
Polisher, Implant (optical goods)	CRE	40	713.687-034
Polisher, Sand (jewelry-silver.)	RCE	47	705.684-070
Polishing Machine Tender (electron. comp.)	RCI	46	673.685-094
Polishing-Machine Operator (any industry)	REI	47	603.682-026
Polishing-Machine-Operator Helper (any industry)	REI	40	603.686-010
Polishing-Pad Mounter (optical goods)	REC	40	739.687-154
Polishing-Wheel Setter (any industry)	RSC	40	776.684-014
Political Scientist (profess. & kin.)	SEI	70	051.067-010
Pollution-Control Engineer (profess. & kin.)	IEC	80	019.081-018
Pollution-Control Technician (profess. & kin.)	RSI	60	029.261-014
Poly-Packer and Heat-Sealer (protective dev.)	CRE	40	920.686-038
Polygraph Examiner (profess. & kin.)	CIS	64	199.267-026
Polymerization Helper (plastic-synth.)	RCE	47	558.585-038
Polymerization-Kettle Operator (plastic-synth.)	RIE	57	558.382-050
Polymerization-Oven Operator (plastic-synth.)	REC	41	556.585-014
Polysilicon Preparation Worker (electron. comp.)	RCS	42	590.684-038
Polysomnographic Technician (medical ser.)	CRI	58	078.362-042
Polystyrene-Bead Molder (plastic prod.)	REI	50	556.382-018
Polystyrene-Molding-Machine Tender (plastic prod.)	REC	38	556.685-062
Pompom Maker (knitting)	RCE	36	789.687-126
Pond Tender (chemical)	REI	44	939.685-010
Pond Worker (millwork-plywood; paper & pulp; saw. & plan.)	REI	37	921.686-022
Pony Edger (saw. & plan.)	RES	47	667.682-050
Popcorn-Candy Maker (sugar & conf.)	RES	42	526.685-042
Porcelain-Enamel Laborer (any industry)	RES	39	509.687-014
Porcelain-Enamel Repairer (any industry)	RIE	41	741.684-030
Porcelain-Enameling Supervisor (any industry)	ESR	59	590.131-010
Port Engineer (ship-boat mfg.; water trans.)	EIR	67	014.167-014
Port Purser (water trans.)	ESR	68	166.167-038
Port-Traffic Manager (water trans.)	ESA	69	184.167-122
Portable Sawyer (railroad equip.)	RSE	45	899.684-030
Porter (air trans.; motor trans.; r.r. trans.)	REC	41	357.677-010
Porter, Baggage (hotel & rest.)	ERS	44	324.477-010
Porter, Marina (water trans.)	RES	43	329.677-010
Porter, Sample Case (wholesale tr.)	RES	40	299.687-010
Porter, Used-Car Lot (retail trade; wholesale tr.)	RCS	38	915.687-022

Title	HOC	Cx	DOT
Post-Office Clerk (government ser.)	CSE	54	243.367-014
Postmaster (government ser.)	ESR	65	188.167-066
Pot Builder (chemical)	RIE	47	826.684-022
Pot Firer (chemical)	RES	48	553.582-014
Pot Liner (smelt. & refin.)	RES	45	519.664-014
Pot Tender (smelt. & refin.)	RCS	42	512.685-018
Pot-Lining Supervisor (smelt. & refin.)	RES	59	519.134-010
Pot-Room Supervisor (smelt. & refin.)	RES	59	512.135-010
Potato-Chip Frier (food prep., n.e.c.)	RCS	41	526.685-046
Potato-Chip Sorter (food prep., n.e.c.)	RCE	36	526.687-010
Potato-Chip-Processing Supervisor (food prep., n.e.c.)	ESR	58	526.137-010
Potato-Pancake Frier (food prep., n.e.c.)	RCE	38	526.685-050
Potato-Peeling-Machine Operator (food prep., n.e.c.)	RCE	40	521.685-250
Potline Monitor (smelt. & refin.)	REC	48	512.467-010
Pottery-Machine Operator (pottery & porc.)	RIE	49	774.382-010
Poultice-Machine Operator (pharmaceut.)	RCE	42	692.685-134
Poultry Boner (meat products)	RCE	39	525.687-066
Poultry Breeder (agriculture)	RIE	62	411.161-014
Poultry Debeaker (agriculture)	REC	41	411.687-026
Poultry Dresser (agriculture; meat products)	REC	37	525.687-070
Poultry Eviscerator (meat products)	REC	37	525.687-074
Poultry Farmer (agriculture)	RSE	57	411.161-018
Poultry Hanger (meat products)	REC	36	525.687-078
Poultry Inseminator (agriculture)	RIE	50	411.384-010
Poultry Killer (meat products)	REC	37	525.684-042
Poultry Scientist (profess. & kin.)	IRS	78	040.061-042
Poultry Tender (agriculture)	RES	51	411.364-014
Poultry Vaccinator (agriculture)	CRS	38	411.684-014
Poultry-Dressing Worker (meat products)	RES	39	525.687-082
Poultry-Picking Machine Tender (meat products)	REI	40	525.685-026
Pouncing-Lathe Operator (hat & cap)	RCE	41	585.685-074
Pounder (boot & shoe)	RCE	41	690.685-314
Poured-Concrete-Wall Technician (construction)	RCI	58	869.261-018
Pourer (fabrication, n.e.c.)	REC	39	739.687-158
Pourer (rubber goods)	RCE	37	556.687-026
Pourer, Metal (foundry)	RCS	38	514.684-022
Powder Blender and Pourer (chemical)	RIE	48	550.485-022
Powder Loader (mine & quarry)	RSE	42	931.667-010
Powder Worker, TNT (ordnance)	RES	47	737.684-030
Powder-and-Primer-Canning Leader (ordnance)	RES	59	737.137-014
Powder-Cutting Operator (chemical)	REC	40	559.685-134
Powder-Line Repairer (chemical)	RSE	56	629.261-018
Powder-Mill Operator (sugar & conf.)	RES	44	521.585-018
Powder-Truck Driver (ordnance)	RSE	47	903.683-014
Powderer (hat & cap)	REC	38	784.687-058
Power Operator (tel. & tel.)	RES	53	952.382-014
Power-Barker Operator (paper & pulp; saw. & plan.)	RCE	47	669.485-010
Power-Chisel Operator (cutlery-hrdwr.)	RES	38	701.687-030
Power-Distribution Engineer (utilities)	IRE	76	003.167-046

Part 3: From Occupational Titles to Holland Codes

From the Dictionary of Occupational Titles Occupations to Holland Codes

Title	HOC	Cx	DOT
Power-Driven-Brush Maker (fabrication, n.e.c.)	RSC	51	692.682-050
Power-Plant Operator (utilities)	RES	60	952.382-018
Power-Press Tender (any industry)	REC	42	617.685-026
Power-Reactor Operator (utilities)	RES	61	952.362-022
Power-Saw Mechanic (any industry)	REI	56	625.281-030
Power-Screwdriver Operator (any industry)	RCE	39	699.685-026
Power-Shovel Operator (any industry)	RES	43	850.683-030
Power-Transformer Repairer (utilities)	RIE	56	821.361-034
Power-Transmission Engineer (utilities)	IRE	76	003.167-050
Powered Bridge Specialist (military ser.)	REC	48	378.683-014
Powerhouse Helper (chemical)	REI	41	550.685-098
Powerhouse Mechanic (utilities)	REI	61	631.261-014
Powerhouse-Mechanic Apprentice (utilities)	REI	61	631.261-018
Powerhouse-Mechanic Helper (utilities)	RCE	48	631.684-010
Powerhouse-Mechanic Supervisor (utilities)	RES	63	631.131-010
Preassembler and Inspector (musical inst.)	RCS	40	730.684-058
Preassembler, Printed Circuit Board (electron. comp.)	RCI	41	726.687-038
Precast Molder (concrete prod.)	REC	42	579.685-042
Precipitate Washer (chemical)	REI	42	551.685-110
Precipitator I (smelt. & refin.)	RCE	44	511.685-038
Precipitator II (smelt. & refin.)	RCS	45	511.685-042
Precipitator Supervisor (smelt. & refin.; steel & rel.)	REI	54	511.132-010
Precise Winder (textile)	CRE	40	681.685-066
Precision Assembler (aircraft mfg.)	RIE	60	806.381-082
Precision Assembler, Bench (aircraft mfg.)	RCE	52	706.381-050
Precision-Lens Centerer and Edger (optical goods)	REI	54	716.462-010
Precision-Lens Generator (optical goods)	REI	54	716.682-014
Precision-Lens Grinder (optical goods)	RIE	58	716.382-018
Precision-Lens Polisher (optical goods)	REI	52	716.682-018
Precision-Lens-Grinder Apprentice (optical goods)	RIE	58	716.382-022
Predatory-Animal Hunter (fishing & hunt.)	RES	45	461.661-010
Prefitter, Doors (woodworking)	RIE	47	666.582-010
Preform Plate Maker (ship-boat mfg.)	RCS	47	751.684-026
Preform-Machine Operator (button & notion)	RCE	47	556.380-014
Preparation Supervisor (can. & preserv.)	ESR	58	529.137-010
Preparation-Room Worker (nonmet. min.)	REC	39	570.686-018
Preparer (jewelry-silver.)	RCE	38	700.687-062
Preparer, Making Department (jewelry-silver.)	RCE	48	700.684-058
Preparer, Samples and Repairs (jewelry-silver.)	CRE	47	700.684-062
Preparole-Counseling Aide (government ser.)	SCI	55	195.367-026
Prepleater (tex. prod., n.e.c.)	RCE	45	686.685-046
Prescription Clerk, Lens-and-Frames (optical goods)	RES	53	222.367-050
Preservation Inspector, Marine Equipment (government ser.)	RIE	55	929.367-010
Preservative Filler, Machine (can. & preserv.)	REC	42	529.685-190
President (any industry)	ESR	69	189.117-026
President, Educational Institution (education)	ESR	72	090.117-034
President, Financial Institution (financial)	SEI	76	186.117-054
Press Breaker (wood prod., n.e.c.)	RCS	40	569.686-050

Part 3: From Occupational Titles to Holland Codes

From the Dictionary of Occupational Titles Occupations to Holland Codes

Title	HOC	Cx	DOT
Press Bucker (any industry)	RES	36	920.686-042
Press Feeder (knitting; textile)	REC	39	583.686-030
Press Feeder (tinware)	RCE	41	652.685-058
Press Feeder, Broomcorn (agriculture)	RCE	40	429.686-010
Press Hand (knitting)	REC	39	583.687-010
Press Helper (plastic prod.)	RES	41	651.586-010
Press Machine Feeder (tobacco)	REC	39	529.686-066
Press Offbearer (brick & tile)	RCI	38	579.686-030
Press Operator (brick & tile)	RSE	41	575.682-018
Press Operator (laundry & rel.)	REC	38	363.685-010
Press Operator (mine & quarry)	RCE	42	575.685-070
Press Operator (oils & grease)	RES	38	551.685-114
Press Operator (plastic prod.)	RSC	45	690.682-062
Press Operator (protective dev.)	CRE	39	686.685-050
Press Operator (rubber reclaim.)	REC	39	559.685-138
Press Operator (textile)	RCE	41	583.685-086
Press Operator I (chemical)	RCE	42	559.665-030
Press Operator II (chemical)	REC	40	551.685-118
Press Operator, Carbon Blocks (smelt. & refin.)	RCS	44	514.682-014
Press Operator, Hardboard (wood prod., n.e.c.)	RIE	47	569.682-014
Press Operator, Heavy Duty (any industry)	RSE	53	617.260-010
Press Operator, Meat (meat products)	REC	37	520.685-182
Press Operator, Pierce and Shave (clock & watch)	REC	40	715.685-050
Press Puller (grain-feed mills)	RES	37	529.687-170
Press Setter (nonfer. metal; steel & rel.)	RIE	52	617.480-014
Press Supervisor (brick & tile)	RES	58	575.130-010
Press Tender (food prep., n.e.c.)	REA	44	520.685-186
Press Tender (rubber goods; rubber tire; toy-sport equip.)	REC	40	556.685-066
Press Tender, Pyrotechnics (chemical)	RCE	43	694.685-038
Press-Box Custodian (amuse. & rec.)	ECS	41	344.677-010
Press-Hand Supervisor (jewelry-silver.)	RES	59	615.130-010
Press-Machine Operator (fabrication, n.e.c.)	RES	44	590.665-014
Press-Pipe Inspector (brick & tile)	CRS	43	575.687-030
Presser (glass mfg.)	RES	41	575.685-074
Presser (print. & pub.)	CRS	41	977.684-018
Presser (rubber goods)	RCE	40	690.685-318
Presser (soap & rel.)	RCE	40	559.685-142
Presser, All-Around (laundry & rel.)	REI	42	363.682-014
Presser, Automatic (laundry & rel.)	REC	39	363.685-014
Presser, Buffing Wheel (tex. prod., n.e.c.)	REC	40	583.685-090
Presser, Form (any industry)	REC	41	363.685-018
Presser, Hand (any industry)	REC	38	363.684-018
Presser, Handkerchief (laundry & rel.)	REC	37	363.685-022
Presser, Machine (any industry)	RCE	38	363.682-018
Pressroom Worker, Fat (oils & grease)	CSR	40	559.685-146
Pressure Controller (utilities)	REI	56	953.362-018
Pressure Sealer-and-Tester (aircraft mfg.)	RCE	51	806.384-038
Pressure Supervisor (utilities)	ERS	59	953.137-014
Pressure-Tank Operator (chemical)	REC	44	523.385-010

DOT to HOC

Title	HOC	Cx	DOT
Pressure-Test Operator (ordnance)	REI	51	737.387-018
Pretzel Cooker (bakery products)	RES	42	526.685-054
Pretzel Twister (bakery products)	RCE	39	520.587-010
Pretzel-Twisting-Machine Operator (bakery products)	CRE	40	520.685-190
Preventive Maintenance Coordinator (any industry)	CRE	64	169.167-074
Pricer, Message and Delivery Service (business ser.)	CRS	51	214.467-014
Primer Assembler (ordnance)	RCE	41	737.687-098
Primer Boxer (ordnance)	RCS	42	737.587-018
Primer Charger (ordnance)	RSC	39	737.687-102
Primer Expeditor and Drier (chemical)	RCS	44	553.385-014
Primer Inspector (ordnance)	CRS	42	737.687-106
Primer Supervisor (ordnance)	ERS	58	737.132-010
Primer-Charging Tool Setter (ordnance)	RSI	55	694.360-010
Primer-Inserting-Machine Adjuster (ordnance)	RSE	50	632.360-018
Primer-Inserting-Machine Operator (ordnance)	RCE	41	694.685-042
Primer-Powder Blender, Dry (ordnance)	RCE	42	550.565-010
Primer-Powder Blender, Wet (chemical)	RCS	47	550.582-010
Primer-Waterproofing-Machine Adjuster (ordnance)	RCS	50	632.380-018
Primer-Waterproofing-Machine Operator (ordnance)	RCE	41	694.685-046
Priming-Mixture Carrier (ordnance)	RCS	42	922.587-010
Priming-Powder-Premix Blender (chemical)	CRS	44	550.684-022
Principal (education)	SEI	68	099.117-018
Print Controller (photofinishing)	RSE	56	976.360-010
Print Developer, Automatic (photofinishing)	RCS	41	976.685-026
Print Inspector (photofinishing)	ERS	46	976.687-022
Print Inspector (pottery & porc.)	REI	46	774.687-018
Print Washer (photofinishing)	REC	39	976.684-022
Print-Line Feeder (furniture)	RES	36	652.686-026
Print-Line Inspector (furniture)	SCE	38	652.687-034
Print-Line Operator (furniture; wood prod., n.e.c.)	RES	49	652.662-018
Print-Line Tailer (furniture)	REC	36	652.686-030
Print-Shop Helper (print. & pub.)	REC	41	979.684-026
Printed Circuit Board Assembler, Hand (comm. equip.; electron. comp.; inst. & app.; office machines)	RCI	44	726.684-070
Printed Circuit Board Assembly Repairer (electron. comp.)	RCE	46	726.684-086
Printed Circuit Board Component Tester, Chemical (electron. comp.)	RCI	51	726.684-074
Printed Circuit Board Component Tester, Pre-Assembly (electron. comp.)	RCI	51	726.684-078
Printed Circuit Board Inspector, Pre-Assembly (electron. comp.)	RCI	51	726.684-082
Printed Circuit Designer (profess. & kin.)	IRC	66	003.261-022
Printer (glass products)	RSE	46	979.681-014
Printer (pen & pencil)	RCE	41	652.685-062
Printer (print. & pub.)	RIE	53	979.382-018
Printer Operator, Black-and-White (photofinishing)	CRS	45	976.682-014
Printer, Floor Covering (fabrication, n.e.c.)	REC	42	652.685-066
Printer, Floor Covering, Assistant (fabrication, n.e.c.)	REC	40	652.687-038
Printer, Machine (hat & cap)	CSE	41	652.685-070

Title	HOC	Cx	DOT
Printer, Plastic (plastic prod.; tex. prod., n.e.c.)	RIE	50	651.382-026
Printer-Slotter Helper (paper goods)	RES	40	659.686-014
Printer-Slotter Operator (paper goods)	RSI	49	659.662-010
Printing Screen Assembler (electron. comp.)	RCI	38	979.684-042
Printing-Machine Operator, Folding Rules (cutlery-hrdwr.)	CRE	40	652.685-074
Printing-Machine Operator, Tape Rules (cutlery-hrdwr.)	RCS	48	652.662-010
Printing-Roller Handler (textile)	RES	42	652.385-010
Printing-Roller Polisher (machine shop)	REI	50	603.382-030
Printmaker (profess. & kin.)	AES	65	144.061-014
Prisoner-Classification Interviewer (profess. & kin.)	SEC	64	166.267-022
Private-Branch-Exchange Installer (tel. & tel.)	RIS	56	822.381-018
Private-Branch-Exchange Repairer (tel. & tel.)	REI	55	822.281-022
Private-Branch-Exchange Service Adviser (tel. & tel.)	SEC	59	235.222-010
Prize Coordinator (radio-tv broad.)	ESR	59	162.167-026
Prizer (tobacco)	RES	38	920.687-142
Probation-and-Parole Officer (profess. & kin.)	SIE	66	195.107-046
Probe Test Equipment Technician, Semiconductor Wafers (electron. comp.)	RCI	52	729.360-010
Process Checker (ordnance)	RCE	53	737.364-010
Process Controller (textile)	RCI	54	689.364-014
Process Inspector (ordnance)	RCS	51	736.381-018
Process Server (business ser.)	ESC	51	249.367-062
Process-Area Supervisor (plastic-synth.)	RES	59	559.132-042
Process-Machine Operator (paper goods)	RCE	41	640.685-050
Processor (plastic-synth.)	RCE	41	557.685-018
Processor Helper (grain-feed mills)	RES	37	521.686-050
Processor, Grain (grain-feed mills)	CER	38	521.685-254
Processor, Instant Potato (food prep., n.e.c.)	RCI	51	523.382-022
Processor, Solid Propellant (chemical)	RIE	57	590.464-010
Proctologist (medical ser.)	IRS	76	070.101-086
Procurement Clerk (clerical)	CES	55	249.367-066
Procurement Engineer (aircraft mfg.)	ECI	70	162.157-034
Produce Weigher (retail trade)	CSR	39	299.587-010
Producer (amuse. & rec.)	ESI	67	187.167-178
Producer (motion picture)	ESA	74	187.167-174
Producer (radio-tv broad.)	SEA	73	159.117-010
Producer, Assistant (motion picture)	ESA	70	187.167-182
Product Tester, Fiberglass (textile)	REI	54	589.384-010
Product-Safety Engineer (profess. & kin.)	ISE	74	012.061-010
Production Assembler (ordnance)	RCS	45	737.684-034
Production Assistant (chemical)	CSR	54	221.387-050
Production Clerk (clerical)	CSR	54	221.382-018
Production Coordinator (clerical)	ESR	59	221.167-018
Production Engineer (profess. & kin.)	EIC	70	012.167-046
Production Engineer, Track (r.r. trans.)	ESR	68	005.167-026
Production Hardener (heat treating)	REI	43	504.685-026
Production Helper (can. & preserv.; food prep., n.e.c.)	CRS	40	529.686-070
Production Helper (nonfer. metal)	REC	38	691.687-010
Production Machine Tender (machine shop)	RCE	43	609.685-018

Title	HOC	Cx	DOT
Production Manager, Advertising (profess. & kin.)	ASE	63	141.137-010
Production Manager, Reproduction (print. & pub.)	ERS	58	652.137-010
Production Planner (profess. & kin.)	REI	67	012.167-050
Production Proofreader (print. & pub.; retail trade)	CSE	49	247.667-010
Production Scheduler, Paperboard Products (paper goods)	CES	60	221.162-010
Production Superintendent (any industry)	ESR	66	183.117-014
Production Supervisor (any industry)	RES	60	699.130-010
Production Supervisor (nonmet. min.)	ERC	59	539.137-014
Production Supervisor, Anhydrous Ammonia (chemical)	ESR	59	559.132-046
Production Supervisor, Defluorinated Phosphate (chemical)	ECS	59	559.132-050
Production Technician, Semiconductor Processing Equipment (electron. comp.)	RCI	53	590.384-014
Production-Machine Tender (auto. mfg.)	RCI	44	699.685-050
Production-Machine Tender (nut & bolt)	RCS	44	619.365-010
Production-Machine Tender, Glass Cutting-or-Grinding (electron. comp.; glass)	CRE	41	679.685-014
Production-Supply-Equipment Tender (food prep., n.e.c.)	RCS	45	921.685-050
Professional Athlete (amuse. & rec.)	SRC	54	153.341-010
Profile Trimmer (jewelry-silver.)	RCS	47	607.682-014
Profile-Grinder Technician (clock & watch)	REI	53	601.482-010
Profile-Saw Operator (jewelry-silver.)	RCS	48	700.682-018
Profile-Shaper Operator, Automatic (woodworking)	RIE	46	665.682-026
Profile-Stitching-Machine Operator (garment)	RCE	40	786.685-026
Profiler, Hand (clock & watch)	REC	47	715.685-054
Profiling-Machine Operator (clock & watch)	CRE	40	605.685-038
Profiling-Machine Set-up Operator I (machine shop)	RIE	58	605.280-014
Profiling-Machine Set-up Operator II (machine shop)	RIE	53	605.382-026
Profiling-Machine Set-up Operator, Tool (machine shop)	RIE	59	605.280-018
Program Aide, Group Work (social ser.)	SEI	63	195.227-010
Program Assistant (radio-tv broad.)	ESR	56	962.167-014
Program Coordinator (amuse. & rec.)	AES	63	139.167-010
Program Director, Cable Television (radio-tv broad.)	ERS	66	194.162-010
Program Director, Group Work (profess. & kin.)	SEA	72	187.117-046
Program Manager (profess. & kin.)	EIR	70	189.167-030
Program Proposals Coordinator (radio-tv broad.)	EAS	70	132.067-030
Program Specialist, Employee-Health Maintenance (profess. & kin.)	SEI	67	166.167-050
Programmer, Engineering and Scientific (profess. & kin.)	IRE	79	030.162-018
Programmer-Analyst (profess. & kin.)	IRE	72	030.162-014
Programming Equipment Operator (electron. comp.)	RCI	49	726.685-062
Progress Clerk (construction)	CRS	56	221.362-022
Progressive Assembler and Fitter (agric. equip.)	REC	41	801.684-022
Project Director (profess. & kin.)	ESI	70	189.117-030
Project Engineer (profess. & kin.)	IER	70	019.167-014
Project Manager, Environmental Research (profess. & kin.)	EIS	70	029.167-014
Project-Crew Worker (any industry)	REC	41	891.687-018
Projection Printer (photofinishing)	RSE	54	976.381-018
Prompter (amuse. & rec.)	CSE	60	152.367-010
Proof Inspector (ordnance)	RCS	48	736.384-010

Title	HOC	Cx	DOT
Proof Technician (ordnance)	RIE	64	199.171-010
Proof-Coin Collector (government ser.)	RCE	47	709.687-030
Proof-Machine Operator (financial)	CRE	54	217.382-010
Proof-Machine-Operator Supervisor (financial)	CSE	63	217.132-010
Proof-Press Operator (print. & pub.)	REI	50	651.582-010
Proof-Technician Helper (ordnance)	RIE	50	736.387-014
Proofer, Prepress (print. & pub.)	RCI	54	972.381-034
Proofreader (print. & pub.)	CSI	57	209.387-030
Proofsheet Corrector (print. & pub.)	RSE	55	973.381-030
Prop Attendant (amuse. & rec.)	RCS	46	962.684-022
Prop Maker (amuse. & rec.; motion picture)	REI	60	962.281-010
Propellant-Charge Loader (ordnance)	RCE	45	737.487-010
Propellant-Charge-Zone Assembler (ordnance)	RCS	41	737.687-110
Property Clerk (government ser.)	CRS	52	222.367-054
Property Coordinator (amuse. & rec.; radio-tv broad.)	ERS	55	962.167-018
Property Custodian (motion picture)	REI	54	222.387-042
Property-Assessment Monitor (government ser.)	CRE	57	241.367-042
Property-Disposal Officer (any industry)	ESR	68	163.167-026
Property-Utilization Officer (government ser.)	ESA	66	188.117-122
Propulsion-Motor-and-Generator Repairer (automotive ser.)	RIE	55	721.281-026
Prospecting Driller (petrol. & gas)	REI	54	930.382-018
Prospector (any industry)	RIS	60	024.284-010
Prosthetics Assistant (medical ser.)	RSE	61	078.361-026
Prosthetics Technician (protective dev.)	RIE	61	712.381-038
Prosthetist (medical ser.)	RSE	64	078.261-022
Prosthodontist (medical ser.)	IRS	75	072.101-034
Protection Engineer (utilities)	RIE	76	003.167-054
Protective Officer (government ser.)	SER	51	372.363-010
Protective-Clothing Issuer (chemical)	CRS	42	222.687-046
Protective-Signal Installer (business ser.)	RCS	56	822.361-018
Protective-Signal Operator (any industry)	CSR	54	379.362-014
Protective-Signal Repairer (business ser.)	RES	57	822.361-022
Protective-Signal Superintendent (business ser.)	ERS	66	822.131-022
Protective-Signal-Installer Helper (business ser.)	CRS	47	822.664-010
Protective-Signal-Repairer Helper (business ser.)	CRE	50	822.684-014
Protector-Plate Attacher (cutlery-hrdwr.)	CRE	39	692.685-138
Prototype-Deicer Assembler (rubber goods)	RIE	57	759.261-010
Psychiatric Aide (medical ser.)	SEC	51	355.377-014
Psychiatric Technician (medical ser.)	SEI	58	079.374-026
Psychiatrist (medical ser.)	ISA	76	070.107-014
Psychic Reader (amuse. & rec.)	AEC	49	159.647-018
Psychologist, Chief (profess. & kin.)	ISE	76	045.107-046
Psychologist, Counseling (profess. & kin.)	SIA	73	045.107-026
Psychologist, Developmental (profess. & kin.)	IRS	76	045.061-010
Psychologist, Educational (profess. & kin.)	IES	77	045.067-010
Psychologist, Engineering (profess. & kin.)	IRS	78	045.061-014
Psychologist, Experimental (profess. & kin.)	IAE	77	045.061-018
Psychologist, Industrial-Organizational (profess. & kin.)	IES	76	045.107-030
Psychologist, School (profess. & kin.)	SEI	75	045.107-034

DOT to HOC

DOT to HOC

Title	HOC	Cx	DOT
Psychologist, Social (profess. & kin.)	IAE	77	045.067-014
Psychometrist (profess. & kin.)	IES	70	045.067-018
Public Health Educator (profess. & kin.)	SEA	71	079.117-014
Public Health Physician (medical ser.)	IRS	76	070.101-046
Public Health Registrar (government ser.)	ESR	60	169.167-046
Public Health Service Officer (government ser.)	IES	74	187.117-050
Public-Address Servicer (any industry)	RES	57	823.261-010
Public-Health Dentist (medical ser.)	IRE	75	072.101-038
Public-Health Microbiologist (government ser.)	ISC	76	041.261-010
Public-Relations Representative (profess. & kin.)	ASE	70	165.167-014
Public-Safety Officer (government ser.)	SER	56	379.263-014
Puff Ironer (laundry & rel.)	RCE	35	363.687-018
Pug-Mill Operator (smelt. & refin.)	RES	45	510.685-022
Pug-Mill-Operator Helper (brick & tile; pottery & porc.)	REI	40	570.685-074
Pull-Out Operator (fabrication, n.e.c.)	CER	42	739.687-162
Puller and Laster, Machine (boot & shoe)	CRE	40	788.684-086
Puller Over, Machine (boot & shoe)	RCE	41	788.684-090
Puller, Machine (leather mfg.)	CRE	39	589.685-078
Puller-Through (glove & mit.)	RCE	38	782.687-030
Pulley Maintainer (mine & quarry)	RCE	39	630.687-010
Pulley-Mortiser Operator (woodworking)	RES	48	666.482-010
Pulmonary-Function Technician (medical ser.)	IRC	60	078.262-010
Pulp Grinder and Blender (paper & pulp; wood prod., n.e.c.)	REI	51	530.682-010
Pulp Piler (logging)	RES	37	922.687-082
Pulp-and-Paper Tester (paper & pulp)	RIE	55	539.364-010
Pulp-Drier Firer (sugar & conf.)	REC	45	523.585-030
Pulp-Press Tender (paper & pulp)	RES	40	532.685-026
Pulp-Press Tender (sugar & conf.)	CRE	41	521.685-258
Pulp-Refiner Operator (paper & pulp)	REI	50	530.382-010
Pulper (paper & pulp; tex. prod., n.e.c.)	RCS	41	530.685-014
Pulper Tender (can. & preserv.)	REC	37	521.685-262
Pulper, Synthetic Soil Blocks (paper & pulp)	REI	50	530.582-010
Pulverizer (chemical)	RES	40	555.685-046
Pulverizer (jewelry-silver.)	RCE	38	770.687-030
Pulverizer (meat products)	CRS	37	521.685-266
Pulverizer-Mill Operator (rubber goods; rubber reclaim.)	RIC	50	555.382-010
Pulverizing-and-Sifting Operator (chemical)	RCS	48	550.485-026
Pump Erector (construction)	RIS	57	637.281-010
Pump Installer (any industry)	RES	52	630.684-018
Pump Mechanic (paper & pulp)	RSE	54	629.281-034
Pump Operator, Byproducts (steel & rel.)	REC	51	541.362-014
Pump Servicer (any industry)	REI	57	630.281-018
Pump Tender, Cement Based Materials (concrete prod.; construction)	REC	41	849.665-010
Pump Tester (plastic-synth.)	CRS	47	557.564-014
Pump-Press Operator (paper & pulp)	RCS	43	539.685-022
Pump-Servicer Helper (any industry)	RCS	45	630.684-022
Pump-Servicer Supervisor (any industry)	RES	59	630.131-010

From the Dictionary of Occupational Titles Occupations to Holland Codes

Title	HOC	Cx	DOT
Pump-Station Operator, Waterworks (waterworks)	REC	50	954.382-010
Pumper (any industry)	REI	52	914.682-010
Pumper (petrol. refin.)	RIS	57	549.360-010
Pumper Helper (any industry)	RES	38	914.687-018
Pumper Helper (petrol. refin.)	RCS	43	549.684-010
Pumper, Brewery (beverage)	REI	46	914.665-014
Pumper, Head (petrol. & gas)	RES	56	914.382-022
Pumper-Gauger (chemical; petrol. refin.; pipe lines)	RIE	57	914.382-014
Pumper-Gauger Apprentice (chemical; petrol. refin.; pipe lines)	RIE	57	914.382-018
Punch Press Operator (wood prod., n.e.c.)	RCI	42	669.685-106
Punch-Press Operator (fabrication, n.e.c.)	RCE	41	692.665-014
Punch-Press Operator I (any industry)	RCS	51	615.382-010
Punch-Press Operator II (any industry)	REI	42	615.685-030
Punch-Press Operator III (any industry)	RIS	47	615.682-014
Punch-Press Operator, Automatic (any industry)	RIS	50	615.482-026
Punch-Press Setter (any industry)	RIE	53	619.380-014
Punchboard Assembler I (paper goods)	RCE	38	794.687-042
Punchboard Assembler II (paper goods)	CRE	36	794.687-046
Punchboard-Filling-Machine Operator (paper goods)	REC	38	649.685-094
Puncher (tex. prod., n.e.c.)	RCS	44	689.582-010
Puncher (woodworking)	RCE	38	663.685-022
Puppeteer (amuse. & rec.)	AEI	65	159.041-014
Purchase-Price Analyst (profess. & kin.)	ECS	69	162.167-030
Purchasing Agent (profess. & kin.)	ESR	63	162.157-038
Purchasing-and-Claims Supervisor (water trans.)	ESR	63	248.137-014
Purification Operator I (chemical)	REC	47	551.685-122
Purification Operator II (chemical)	RSE	53	551.362-010
Purification-Operator Helper (chemical)	CER	50	551.465-010
Purser (water trans.)	ESC	64	197.167-014
Push-Connector Assembler (house. appl.)	RCE	38	706.687-030
Pusher Operator (steel & rel.)	RCE	42	519.663-018
Put-in-Beat Adjuster (clock & watch)	CRS	46	715.684-174
Putty Glazer (any industry)	RCS	39	749.684-042
Putty Mixer and Applier (wood. container)	REC	38	769.687-038
Putty Tinter-Maker (paint & varnish)	RSE	49	559.482-014
Puzzle Assembler (toy-sport equip.)	CRE	40	731.687-030
Pyridine Operator (steel & rel.)	REI	56	552.382-010
Quality Assurance Analyst (profess. & kin.)	RIC	63	033.262-010
Quality Assurance Coordinator (medical ser.)	SCR	69	075.167-014
Quality Assurance Group Leader (auto. mfg.)	SRI	52	806.367-014
Quality Assurance Monitor (auto. mfg.)	RIE	50	806.367-018
Quality Assurance Supervisor (auto. mfg.)	SER	63	806.137-022
Quality Control Checker, Texturing Process (textile)	RCE	50	681.387-010
Quality Control Engineer (profess. & kin.)	IRE	79	012.167-054
Quality Control Inspector (furniture; millwork-plywood)	RCE	46	569.687-030
Quality Control Inspector (sugar & conf.)	RIC	54	529.367-034
Quality Control Technician (concrete prod.)	RCI	56	579.364-010
Quality Control Technician (profess. & kin.)	RIE	68	012.261-014

Title	HOC	Cx	DOT
Quality Technician, Fiberglass (glass mfg.)	RIE	54	579.384-014
Quality-Control Checker (garment)	CRE	50	789.387-010
Quality-Control Clerk (pharmaceut.)	CSR	49	229.587-014
Quality-Control Coordinator (pharmaceut.)	CES	66	168.167-066
Quality-Control Inspector (bakery products)	RCE	49	529.367-018
Quality-Control Inspector (cutlery-hrdwr.)	RSC	57	701.261-010
Quality-Control Inspector (glass mfg.)	RCE	51	579.367-010
Quality-Control Inspector (light. fix.)	CER	48	725.687-026
Quality-Control Inspector (recording)	REI	50	194.387-010
Quality-Control Inspector (rubber tire)	REI	53	750.367-010
Quality-Control Supervisor (plastic prod.)	ESI	59	559.134-010
Quality-Control Supervisor (plastic-synth.)	RES	59	559.131-014
Quality-Control Technician (beverage)	REC	54	529.367-022
Quality-Control Technician (can. & preserv.; food prep., n.e.c.)	REI	51	529.387-030
Quality-Control Technician (glass mfg.)	CRE	58	579.367-014
Quality-Control Technician (photofinishing)	CES	55	976.267-010
Quality-Control Technician (svc. ind. mach.)	REI	50	637.684-014
Quality-Control Technician, Inked Ribbons (pen & pencil)	RCI	55	733.364-010
Quality-Control Tester (fabrication, n.e.c.)	RCE	45	543.684-010
Quality-Control Tester (knitting)	CRE	52	684.384-010
Quality-Control Tester (paper goods; plastic-synth.)	RIE	53	559.367-010
Quality-Control Tester (wood prod., n.e.c.)	RCI	57	569.384-010
Quarry Plug-and-Feather Driller (mine & quarry)	RSC	43	930.684-022
Quarry Supervisor, Dimension Stone (mine & quarry)	RIE	58	930.134-010
Quarry Supervisor, Open Pit (mine & quarry)	REC	57	939.131-010
Quarry Worker (mine & quarry)	RES	38	939.667-014
Quartermaster (water trans.)	CRE	56	911.363-014
Quick Sketch Artist (amuse. & rec.)	ASE	58	149.041-010
Quill-Buncher-and-Sorter (tex. prod., n.e.c.)	CRS	42	734.687-066
Quiller Operator (textile)	RCE	41	681.685-070
Quilling-Machine Operator, Automatic (textile)	CRS	42	681.685-074
Quilt Stuffer (tex. prod., n.e.c.)	REC	38	789.687-130
Quilt Stuffer, Machine (tex. prod., n.e.c.)	CRE	41	689.685-102
Quilter Fixer (tex. prod., n.e.c.)	RSE	56	689.260-014
Quilting-Machine Operator (glove & mit.; tex. prod., n.e.c.)	RCS	44	689.685-106
Quilting-Machine Operator (tex. prod., n.e.c.)	RCI	49	584.382-014
Rabble-Furnace Tender (chemical)	CRE	44	553.685-090
Racing Secretary and Handicapper (amuse. & rec.)	ESC	65	153.167-018
Rack Loader (fabrication, n.e.c.)	REC	38	590.687-018
Rack Loader I (tobacco)	RES	37	529.686-074
Rack-Room Worker (beverage)	REI	40	920.665-014
Racker (amuse. & rec.)	CES	43	340.477-010
Racker (bakery products)	RCE	36	524.687-018
Racker (clock & watch)	REC	39	715.687-106
Racker (jewelry-silver.)	RCE	37	735.687-026
Racker (paper goods)	CER	37	659.687-010
Racker (toy-sport equip.)	RCE	42	749.587-010
Racker, Octave Board (musical inst.)	CRE	46	730.684-062

Title	HOC	Cx	DOT
Racker, Silk-Screen Printing (any industry)	REC	39	659.687-014
Racket Stringer (toy-sport equip.)	CRE	47	732.684-094
Radial-Arm-Saw Operator (woodworking)	RSC	44	667.682-054
Radiation Monitor (profess. & kin.)	RCS	60	199.167-010
Radiation-Protection Engineer (profess. & kin.)	EIC	69	015.137-010
Radiation-Protection Specialist (government ser.)	IRS	67	168.261-010
Radiation-Therapy Technologist (medical ser.)	RIS	60	078.361-034
Radio Interference Investigator (electron. comp.)	RSC	58	823.261-014
Radio Mechanic (any industry)	REI	57	823.261-018
Radio Officer (water trans.)	RCE	62	193.262-022
Radio Repairer (any industry)	REI	55	720.281-010
Radio Station Operator (aircraft mfg.)	RIC	64	193.262-026
Radio-Intelligence Operator (government ser.)	RCE	58	193.362-014
Radio-Message Router (tel. & tel.)	CER	53	235.387-010
Radioactivity-Instrument Maintenance Technician (petrol. & gas)	RIE	64	828.281-022
Radiographer (any industry)	RIS	58	199.361-010
Radioisotope-Production Operator (profess. & kin.)	RIS	58	015.362-022
Radiologic Technologist (medical ser.)	SRI	64	078.362-026
Radiologic Technologist, Chief (medical ser.)	ISE	69	078.162-010
Radiological-Equipment Specialist (inst. & app.)	RES	69	719.261-014
Radiologist (medical ser.)	IRS	76	070.101-090
Radiology Administrator (medical ser.)	ESC	70	187.117-062
Radiopharmacist (medical ser.)	IRC	74	074.161-014
Radiotelegraph Operator (tel. & tel.)	CRS	55	193.262-030
Radiotelephone Operator (any industry)	RSC	59	193.262-034
Radius Corner Machine Operator (glass products)	RCI	40	673.685-098
Rafter (logging)	REI	42	455.664-010
Rafter-Cutting-Machine Operator (mfd. bldgs.)	RIE	51	669.382-014
Rag Inspector (paper & pulp)	RCE	41	530.687-010
Rag Sorter and Cutter (tex. prod., n.e.c.)	RCE	37	789.687-134
Rag-Cutting-Machine Feeder (paper & pulp; tex. prod., n.e.c.)	REC	40	530.666-010
Rag-Cutting-Machine Tender (paper & pulp; tex. prod., n.e.c.)	RCS	41	530.665-014
Rail-Flaw-Detector Operator (r.r. trans.)	REI	61	910.263-010
Rail-Tractor Operator (steel & rel.)	REI	47	919.683-018
Railroad Engineer (profess. & kin.)	IRS	71	005.061-026
Railroad Wheels and Axle Inspector (railroad equip.)	RES	57	622.381-034
Railroad-Car Inspector (r.r. trans.)	RES	52	910.387-014
Railroad-Car Letterer (r.r. trans.)	REI	52	845.681-010
Railroad-Car-Truck Builder (railroad equip.)	RSE	44	806.684-114
Railroad-Construction Director (r.r. trans.)	RES	63	182.167-018
Railroad-Maintenance Clerk (r.r. trans.)	CSR	54	221.362-026
Railway-Equipment Operator (r.r. trans.)	ERA	47	859.683-018
Raised Printer (print. & pub.)	RCE	39	652.686-034
Raker (carpet & rug)	REC	37	789.687-138
Raker, Buffing Wheel (tex. prod., n.e.c.)	RCE	42	589.684-010
Ram-Press Operator (pottery & porc.)	RCE	48	575.682-022

DOT to HOC

Title	HOC	Cx	DOT
Range Manager (profess. & kin.)	IRS	78	040.061-046
Rasper (boot & shoe)	RCS	38	788.684-094
Rate Analyst, Freight (air trans.; motor trans.; r.r. trans.; water trans.)	CSE	61	214.267-010
Rate Clerk, Passenger (motor trans.)	CSE	55	214.362-030
Rate Reviewer (utilities)	ECR	58	214.387-014
Rate Supervisor (clerical)	ESC	58	214.137-018
Rater (insurance)	CSR	54	214.482-022
Rater, Travel Accommodations (profess. & kin.)	ESR	54	168.367-014
Raveler (knitting)	CRE	36	782.687-034
Raw Sampler (smelt. & refin.)	CRE	46	519.484-014
Raw Shellfish Preparer (hotel & rest.)	CER	41	311.674-014
Raw-Cheese Worker (dairy products)	REI	40	529.686-078
Raw-Juice Weigher (sugar & conf.)	RCE	39	529.685-194
Raw-Silk Grader (textile)	RES	48	689.687-062
Raw-Stock-Drier Tender (textile)	REC	38	581.685-046
Raw-Stock-Machine Loader (textile)	REC	39	582.686-018
Rawhide-Bone Roller (leather prod.)	REC	40	789.684-042
Reactor Operator, Test-and-Research (profess. & kin.)	RCS	60	015.362-026
Reader (business ser.)	CSE	50	249.387-022
Reader (motion picture; radio-tv broad.)	AES	64	131.087-014
Reagent Tender (smelt. & refin.)	CRS	44	511.685-046
Reagent Tender Helper (smelt. & refin.)	CRS	40	511.686-010
Real-Estate Agent (profess. & kin.)	ESR	70	186.117-058
Real-Estate Clerk (real estate)	CSR	58	219.362-046
Reamer, Center Hole (clock & watch)	RCE	38	715.687-110
Reamer, Hand (machine shop)	RCS	46	709.684-058
Reaming-Machine Tender (nonfer. metal)	REC	40	606.685-034
Rebrander (rubber goods)	CRE	40	559.685-150
Receipt-and-Report Clerk (water trans.)	CRI	56	216.382-054
Receiver, Fermenting Cellars (beverage)	REI	47	522.662-010
Receiver-Dispatcher (nonprofit org.)	ESC	53	239.367-022
Receiving Checker (clerical)	CRS	46	222.687-018
Receiving-Barn Custodian (amuse. & rec.)	ESC	51	349.367-014
Receptionist (clerical)	CSE	51	237.367-038
Receptionist, Airline Lounge (air trans.)	CSE	47	352.677-014
Reclamation Kettle Tender, Metal (smelt. & refin.)	REC	41	512.685-022
Reclamation Supervisor (nonfer. metal)	RES	58	512.132-014
Reclamation Worker (wholesale tr.)	RCE	47	621.684-014
Reconnaissance Crewmember (military ser.)	REC	54	378.367-030
Reconsignment Clerk (clerical)	CSE	54	209.367-042
Record Clerk (textile)	CSR	50	206.387-022
Record Tester (recording)	RCE	51	194.387-014
Record-Changer Assembler (comm. equip.)	RCE	38	720.687-010
Record-Changer Tester (comm. equip.)	REC	38	720.687-014
Record-Press Tender (recording)	RCE	41	556.685-070
Recorder (knitting)	CSE	43	221.587-026
Recorder (steel & rel.)	RES	52	221.367-050
Recording Engineer (radio-tv broad.; recording)	RES	56	194.362-010

Dictionary of Holland Occupational Codes

Part 3: From Occupational Titles to Holland Codes

From the Dictionary of Occupational Titles Occupations to Holland Codes

Title	HOC	Cx	DOT
Recording Studio Set-up Worker (recording)	RCS	44	962.664-014
Recordist (motion picture)	REC	53	962.382-010
Recordist, Chief (motion picture)	SEC	63	962.134-010
Records-Management Analyst (profess. & kin.)	ESC	63	161.267-022
Recovery Operator (chemical)	RCS	45	558.682-022
Recovery Operator (paper & pulp)	RIE	56	552.362-018
Recovery Operator (smelt. & refin.)	REC	48	519.582-010
Recovery-Operator Helper (smelt. & refin.)	RCE	45	519.485-014
Recreation Aide (social ser.)	SCR	52	195.367-030
Recreation Leader (social ser.)	SEI	60	195.227-014
Recreation Supervisor (profess. & kin.)	ESA	69	187.167-238
Recreation-Facility Attendant (amuse. & rec.)	ESC	54	341.367-010
Recreational Therapist (medical ser.)	SEC	62	076.124-014
Recruit Instructor (military ser.)	SRE	51	378.227-014
Recruiter (military ser.)	SRE	54	166.267-026
Rectification Printer (any industry)	CRE	49	976.682-018
Red-Lead Burner (paint & varnish)	RCE	40	558.685-054
Redeye Gunner (military ser.)	RIE	48	378.682-010
Redrying-Machine Operator (tobacco)	RSE	47	522.662-014
Reducing-Machine Operator (optical goods)	RCE	39	614.685-018
Reducing-Salon Attendant (personal ser.)	RES	43	359.567-010
Reduction-Furnace Operator (chemical)	CRS	48	553.682-022
Reduction-Furnace-Operator Helper (chemical; oils & grease)	RES	40	559.686-038
Reduction-Plant Supervisor (smelt. & refin.)	ERS	59	512.130-010
Redye Hand (knitting)	CES	44	789.687-142
Reed Maker (machinery mfg.)	RES	52	709.381-038
Reed Repairer (textile)	RCS	50	628.484-010
Reed-Press Feeder (wood prod., n.e.c.)	CRS	38	669.686-022
Reel Assembler (woodworking)	RCS	46	762.484-010
Reel-Blade-Bender Furnace Tender (agric. equip.)	CRE	39	504.685-030
Reeler (build. mat., n.e.c.)	RES	40	549.685-022
Reeler (paper goods)	RES	38	640.685-054
Reeler (woodworking)	RES	40	769.684-034
Reeling-Machine Operator (steel & rel.)	RSE	46	613.682-014
Reeling-Machine Operator (textile)	RCE	41	681.685-078
Referral Clerk, Temporary Help Agency (clerical)	CES	52	205.367-062
Referral-and-Information Aide (government ser.)	CSE	52	237.367-042
Refined-Syrup Operator (sugar & conf.)	REI	54	520.485-022
Refiner (protective dev.)	RES	47	712.684-038
Refinery Operator (grain-feed mills)	RES	57	521.362-018
Refinery Operator (petrol. refin.)	RES	61	549.260-010
Refinery Operator Helper (petrol. refin.)	REC	52	542.362-014
Refinery Operator, Assistant (grain-feed mills)	RCE	53	521.462-010
Refining-Machine Operator (oils & grease)	RSC	46	529.685-198
Refining-Machine Operator (sugar & conf.)	RES	48	521.682-034
Reflow Operator (electron. comp.)	RCI	42	726.685-038
Refractory Mixer (steel & rel.)	REC	41	570.685-078
Refractory-Grinder Operator (brick & tile)	REC	45	677.682-014

Title	HOC	Cx	DOT
Refrigerating Engineer (any industry)	REI	57	950.362-014
Refrigerating Engineer, Head (any industry)	RES	60	950.131-010
Refrigeration Mechanic (any industry)	RES	59	637.261-026
Refrigeration Mechanic (svc. ind. mach.)	RES	57	827.361-014
Refrigeration Unit Repairer (svc. ind. mach.)	RSE	51	637.381-014
Refrigeration-Mechanic Helper (any industry)	RES	41	637.687-014
Refrigerator Glazier (svc. ind. mach.)	REC	45	865.684-022
Refrigerator Tester (svc. ind. mach.)	RSE	52	827.384-010
Regenerator Operator (sugar & conf.)	CES	44	573.685-034
Regional Superintendent, Railroad Car Inspection and Repair (r.r. trans.)	ESC	67	184.117-090
Register Repairer (r.r. trans.)	RES	50	710.681-018
Registered Representative (financial)	ESC	64	250.257-018
Registrar (government ser.)	SEC	52	205.367-038
Registrar, College or University (education)	ESC	70	090.167-030
Registrar, Museum (museums)	CER	68	102.167-018
Registration Clerk (government ser.)	CSE	51	205.367-042
Registration Clerk (library)	CSE	51	249.365-010
Registration Specialist, Agricultural Chemicals (government ser.)	ESC	64	168.267-106
Regulator Inspector (utilities)	RES	59	820.361-018
Regulatory Administrator (tel. & tel.)	ESR	70	168.167-070
Rehabilitation Center Manager (government ser.)	ESA	67	195.167-038
Rehabilitation Clerk (nonprofit org.)	CSE	50	205.367-046
Reinforcing-Metal Worker (construction)	RES	46	801.684-026
Reinforcing-Steel-Machine Operator (construction)	RCS	44	859.683-022
Reinspector (knitting)	CSR	43	684.687-014
Reinsurance Clerk (insurance)	CSR	55	219.482-018
Reject Opener (tobacco)	RCE	41	790.687-026
Relay Technician (utilities)	RIE	63	821.261-018
Relay Tester (utilities)	RIE	59	729.281-038
Relay-Record Clerk (utilities)	CES	55	221.367-054
Relay-Shop Supervisor (utilities)	CER	61	729.131-014
Reliability Engineer (profess. & kin.)	ICR	79	019.061-026
Relief-Map Modeler (any industry)	RIA	55	777.381-042
Relish Blender (can. & preserv.)	RCE	42	520.685-194
Relocation Commissioner (government ser.)	ERS	69	188.167-070
Remelt-Furnace Expediter (nonfer. metal)	RES	58	512.132-018
Remelter (elec. equip.; machinery mfg.; print. & pub.)	RCE	42	502.685-014
Remnant Sorter (textile)	CRE	40	789.687-146
Remnants Cutter (textile)	RCE	36	789.687-150
Rendering-Equipment Tender (meat products)	REA	44	529.685-202
Renovator-Machine Operator (tex. prod., n.e.c.)	RES	37	589.685-082
Rental Manager, Public Events Facilities (business ser.)	SER	66	186.117-062
Repack-Room Worker (beverage)	RCE	41	920.687-146
Repair Operator (garment)	CRE	43	786.682-214
Repair-Order Clerk (clerical)	CSE	54	221.382-022
Repairer (boot & shoe)	CRS	41	753.684-026
Repairer (furniture)	RCE	46	709.684-062

Title	HOC	Cx	DOT
Repairer (mine & quarry)	RES	57	630.281-022
Repairer (smelt. & refin.)	REI	58	630.281-026
Repairer Helper (smelt. & refin.)	RES	45	630.664-010
Repairer I (chemical)	RES	55	630.261-018
Repairer II (chemical)	RES	47	630.684-026
Repairer, Art Objects (any industry)	RCE	56	779.381-018
Repairer, Assembled Wood Products (woodworking)	RSE	44	769.684-038
Repairer, Auto Clocks (clock & watch)	CRE	41	715.584-014
Repairer, Finished Metal (any industry)	RSE	45	809.684-034
Repairer, General (auto. mfg.)	RES	47	806.684-118
Repairer, Gyroscope (inst. & app.)	RCI	56	710.381-054
Repairer, Handtools (cutlery-hrdwr.)	RES	51	701.381-010
Repairer, Heavy (auto. mfg.)	RIE	51	620.381-022
Repairer, Kiln Car (brick & tile)	RCI	42	861.684-022
Repairer, Manufactured Buildings (mfd. bldgs.; vehicles, n.e.c.)	RES	49	869.384-010
Repairer, Pens and Pencils (pen & pencil)	REI	45	733.384-010
Repairer, Probe Test Card, Semiconductor Wafers (electron. comp.)	RCI	52	726.361-022
Repairer, Recreational Vehicle (vehicles, n.e.c.)	RCI	57	869.261-022
Repairer, Shoe Sticks (rubber goods)	RES	39	619.685-074
Repairer, Switchgear (comm. equip.; elec. equip.)	RES	47	729.684-038
Repairer, Typewriter (office machines)	REI	54	706.381-030
Repairer, Veneer Sheet (furniture)	RCI	40	769.684-058
Repairer, Welding Equipment (welding)	REI	49	626.384-010
Repairer, Welding Systems and Equipment (welding)	RCI	64	626.261-014
Repairer, Welding, Brazing, and Burning Machines (welding)	RIS	56	626.361-010
Repeat Chief (print. & pub.)	REI	57	970.361-014
Repeat-Photocomposing-Machine Operator (print. & pub.)	REI	57	971.382-018
Reporter (print. & pub.; radio-tv broad.)	ASI	67	131.262-018
Reports Analyst (profess. & kin.)	ESA	63	161.267-026
Repossessor (clerical)	ESR	48	241.367-022
Representative, Personal Service (tel. & tel.)	ESA	64	236.252-010
Reproduction Order Processor (clerical)	ECS	54	221.367-058
Reproduction Technician (any industry)	RIE	54	976.361-010
Reptile Farmer (agriculture)	RIE	63	413.161-014
Rerecording Mixer (motion picture; radio-tv broad.)	RSE	60	194.362-014
Resaw Operator (woodworking)	RIS	47	667.682-058
Research Analyst (insurance)	SER	67	169.267-034
Research Assistant I (profess. & kin.)	SER	65	109.267-010
Research Assistant II (profess. & kin.)	ISC	64	199.267-034
Research Associate (museums)	IRC	79	109.067-014
Research Engineer, Marine Equipment (profess. & kin.)	IRE	71	014.061-018
Research Engineer, Mining-and-Oil-Well Equipment (mine & quarry; petrol. & gas)	IRE	71	010.061-022
Research Engineer, Nuclear Equipment (profess. & kin.)	IRE	71	015.061-018
Research Mechanic (aircraft mfg.)	RIE	64	002.261-014
Research Subject (any industry)	RCS	47	359.677-030

Title	HOC	Cx	DOT
Research Worker, Encyclopedia (profess. & kin.)	ISE	66	109.267-014
Research Worker, Social Welfare (profess. & kin.)	IER	75	054.067-010
Research-Contracts Supervisor (government ser.)	SEI	70	162.117-030
Reservation Clerk (clerical)	CES	55	238.362-014
Reservation Clerk (r.r. trans.)	CES	51	238.367-014
Reservations Agent (air trans.)	CES	55	238.367-018
Reserve Officer (financial; insurance)	ESC	70	186.167-054
Reserve Operator (tobacco)	RCE	41	529.685-206
Reserves Clerk (financial)	CSE	56	216.362-034
Residence Counselor (education)	SEC	69	045.107-038
Residence Supervisor (any industry)	SEC	59	187.167-186
Resin Coater (wood prod., n.e.c.)	RCE	42	562.687-014
Resource-Recovery Engineer (government ser.)	IRC	76	019.167-018
Respiratory Therapist (medical ser.)	SIR	57	076.361-014
Respiratory-Therapy Aide (medical ser.)	SRC	47	355.674-022
Rest Room Attendant (any industry)	CER	40	358.677-018
Restorer, Ceramic (museums)	ASI	68	102.361-014
Restorer, Lace and Textiles (museums)	IRS	64	102.361-010
Restorer, Paper-and-Prints (library; museums)	AIS	68	109.361-010
Restrictive-Preparation Operator (ordnance)	REI	42	559.685-154
Retirement Officer (government ser.)	SEC	66	166.267-030
Retort Operator (can. & preserv.)	RES	45	526.682-034
Retort Unloader (chemical)	RES	37	569.686-034
Retort-Condenser Attendant (chemical)	CRE	46	552.685-022
Retort-Load Expediter (wood prod., n.e.c.)	RCE	56	221.167-022
Retort-or-Condenser Press Operator (brick & tile)	RES	46	575.382-026
Retoucher, Photoengraving (print. & pub.)	RES	56	970.381-030
Retread Supervisor (rubber tire)	ERS	55	750.132-010
Return-to-Factory Clerk (clerical)	CSE	48	209.587-042
Returned-Case Inspector (beverage)	CRS	37	929.687-038
Returned-Goods Sorter (textile)	RCE	41	922.687-086
Returned-Item Clerk (financial)	CRS	54	216.382-058
Returned-Telephone-Equipment Appraiser (comm. equip.)	REC	54	222.387-046
Revenue Agent (government ser.)	ERI	67	160.167-050
Revenue Officer (government ser.)	ESI	67	188.167-074
Revenue-Settlements Administrator (tel. & tel.)	ESA	74	184.117-074
Reverser (toy-sport equip.)	RES	38	732.687-066
Reviewer (insurance)	CSE	48	209.687-018
Reviewing Officer, Driver's License (government ser.)	SCE	62	168.167-074
Revising Clerk (motor trans.; r.r. trans.)	CRE	54	214.382-026
Revival Clerk (insurance)	CRE	53	219.362-050
Rewinder Operator (paper goods)	REI	45	640.685-058
Reworker, Printed Circuit Board (electron. comp.)	RCI	45	726.684-090
Ribbon Cutter (narrow fabrics)	RES	40	781.687-050
Ribbon Inker (pen & pencil)	CRE	41	692.685-142
Ribbon Winder (pen & pencil)	CRE	43	733.685-022
Ribbon-Hanking-Machine Operator (paper goods)	CRE	42	640.385-010
Ribbon-Lap-Machine Tender (textile)	RCE	40	680.685-086
Rice Cleaning Machine Tender (grain-feed mills)	RCE	42	521.665-022

Title	HOC	Cx	DOT
Riddler Operator (tobacco)	RCE	37	521.685-270
Ride Attendant (amuse. & rec.)	CES	41	342.677-010
Ride Operator (amuse. & rec.)	CSE	43	342.663-010
Riding-Silks Custodian (amuse. & rec.)	CSR	38	346.677-014
Rigger (any industry)	RSC	53	921.260-010
Rigger (construction)	RES	45	869.683-014
Rigger (logging)	RSC	47	921.664-014
Rigger (radio-tv broad.)	RSI	56	823.281-022
Rigger (ship-boat mfg.)	RES	56	806.261-014
Rigger (tex. prod., n.e.c.)	RCE	40	789.684-046
Rigger Apprentice (ship-boat mfg.)	RES	56	806.261-018
Rigger Helper (any industry)	RSE	39	921.687-026
Rigger Helper (ship-boat mfg.)	RES	45	806.684-122
Rigger Supervisor (radio-tv broad.; tel. & tel.)	ECR	61	823.131-014
Rigger, Third (logging)	RCS	37	921.687-030
Rigging Slinger (logging)	RES	50	921.364-010
Rigging Supervisor (construction)	RES	59	921.130-010
Right-of-Way Agent (any industry)	ESR	67	191.117-046
Right-of-Way Supervisor (any industry)	ESA	73	191.117-050
Rim-Fire-Priming Operator (ordnance)	RCE	42	694.685-050
Rim-Fire-Priming Tool Setter (ordnance)	RIC	54	632.380-022
Rim-Turning Finisher (clock & watch)	CRE	41	604.685-030
Ring Conductor (amuse. & rec.)	EAS	58	159.367-010
Ring Maker (jewelry-silver.)	RES	52	700.381-042
Ring Stamper (jewelry-silver.)	RCE	42	700.684-066
Ring-Making-Machine Operator (paper goods)	RCE	38	649.685-098
Ring-Rolling-Machine Operator (rubber goods)	RCE	46	690.682-066
Rip-and-Groove-Machine Operator (furniture)	RCE	46	667.682-062
Ripening-Room Attendant (plastic-synth.)	RCE	47	559.682-038
Ripper (furniture)	RCE	38	617.685-030
Ripper (garment; retail trade; tex. prod., n.e.c.)	RCE	38	782.687-038
Ripsaw Operator (woodworking)	RCS	47	667.682-066
Risk and Insurance Manager (any industry)	ESA	68	186.117-066
River (logging)	REC	40	454.684-022
Rivet Heater (heat treating)	RCS	48	504.485-010
Rivet-Hole Puncher (garment)	CRE	40	686.685-054
Riveter (light. fix.)	REC	40	616.685-054
Riveter (railroad equip.)	RSE	44	800.684-010
Riveter Helper (any industry)	RES	39	800.687-010
Riveter, Hand (any industry)	RCE	40	709.684-066
Riveter, Hand (garment)	CRE	40	789.687-154
Riveter, Hydraulic (any industry)	REC	45	800.662-010
Riveter, Pneumatic (any industry)	RES	44	800.684-014
Riveter, Portable Pinch (any industry)	REC	44	800.682-010
Riveting Machine Operator, Automatic (aircraft mfg.)	RCE	57	806.380-010
Riveting-Machine Operator (furniture)	REI	40	616.685-058
Riveting-Machine Operator I (any industry)	RCE	53	699.482-010
Riveting-Machine Operator II (any industry)	RCE	39	699.685-030
Road Supervisor (motor trans.)	ERI	59	913.133-010

DOT to HOC

Title	HOC	Cx	DOT
Road Supervisor of Engines (r.r. trans.)	REI	63	910.137-034
Road-Mixer Operator (construction)	RIE	45	859.683-026
Road-Oiling-Truck Driver (construction)	REI	45	853.663-018
Road-Roller Operator (construction)	REC	41	859.683-030
Roadability-Machine Operator (auto. mfg.)	REC	51	806.383-010
Roads Supervisor (government ser.)	ESR	69	188.167-078
Roaster, Grain (grain-feed mills)	RSE	47	523.585-034
Robotic Machine Operator (aircraft mfg.)	RSE	52	606.382-026
Rock Breaker (retail trade; stonework)	RCE	40	770.687-034
Rock Splitter (stonework)	REI	46	771.684-010
Rock-Drill Operator I (construction)	RCS	47	850.683-034
Rock-Drill Operator II (construction)	RIE	48	850.662-014
Rock-Dust Sprayer (mine & quarry)	REC	40	939.687-026
Rocket-Engine-Component Mechanic (aircraft mfg.)	RIE	60	621.281-030
Rocket-Motor Mechanic (aircraft mfg.)	RIE	62	693.261-022
Rocket-Test-Fire Worker (ordnance)	RSE	47	806.384-022
Rod Tape Operator (electron. comp.)	RCI	41	726.685-042
Rod-and-Tube Straightener (plastic-synth.)	REC	41	559.587-010
Rod-Mill Tender (cement; smelt. & refin.)	RCE	40	519.685-030
Rod-Puller and Coiler (nonfer. metal)	RCE	40	619.685-078
Rodding Machine Tender (furniture)	RCI	38	665.685-038
Rodding-Anode Worker (smelt. & refin.)	RES	41	519.687-034
Rodeo Performer (amuse. & rec.)	RES	52	159.344-014
Roll Builder (rubber goods)	RCE	43	759.484-010
Roll Builder (steel & rel.)	RES	48	801.664-018
Roll Coverer, Burlap (textile)	RCE	37	929.687-042
Roll Cutter (rubber goods)	REC	39	690.685-322
Roll Examiner (paper & pulp)	CER	41	640.687-010
Roll Finisher (paper & pulp)	RES	38	920.685-090
Roll Grinder (rubber reclaim.)	RIE	48	629.682-010
Roll Inspector (plastic-synth.)	CRE	45	554.587-010
Roll Operator (plastic-synth.)	RIE	45	554.682-018
Roll Operator I (any industry)	RSE	56	619.362-014
Roll Reclaimer (paper goods)	RCE	40	640.685-062
Roll Tender (chemical)	REI	51	559.362-030
Roll Tender (print. & pub.)	RCE	42	651.686-022
Roll Turner (knitting)	REC	39	689.685-110
Roll-Forming-Machine Operator I (any industry)	RIE	53	617.482-018
Roll-Forming-Machine Operator II (any industry)	RCE	40	617.685-034
Roll-Forming-Machine Set-up Mechanic (any industry)	RIE	54	613.360-010
Roll-or-Tape-Edge-Machine Operator (furniture)	RCE	41	787.682-038
Roll-Over-Press Operator (optical goods)	RCE	40	690.685-326
Roll-Sheeting Cutter (tex. prod., n.e.c.)	RIC	48	699.682-026
Roll-Slicing-Machine Tender (pen & pencil)	RCE	40	640.685-066
Roll-Tension Tester (plastic-synth.)	RCE	42	559.584-010
Roll-Threader Operator (nut & bolt)	REI	50	619.462-010
Roll-Tube Setter (steel & rel.)	RES	50	613.360-014
Roll-Up-Guider Operator (fabrication, n.e.c.)	RCS	43	590.685-050
Roller (jewelry-silver.)	RCE	49	613.682-018

Part 3: From Occupational Titles to Holland Codes

From the Dictionary of Occupational Titles Occupations to Holland Codes

Title	HOC	Cx	DOT
Roller (ship-boat mfg.)	RES	41	806.687-046
Roller Checker (textile)	CRE	41	682.684-010
Roller Cleaner (textile)	REC	39	680.687-014
Roller Coverer (textile)	RCE	47	628.682-010
Roller Engraver, Hand (print. & pub.)	RES	50	979.681-018
Roller I (sugar & conf.)	REI	44	520.684-014
Roller Maker (print. & pub.)	RSI	44	759.664-018
Roller Maker (rubber goods)	RCE	46	690.685-502
Roller Operator (hat & cap)	REC	41	580.685-046
Roller Operator (toy-sport equip.)	RCE	38	652.685-078
Roller Repairer (textile)	RIE	53	979.381-026
Roller Varnisher (print. & pub.)	RES	46	979.682-022
Roller, Gold Leaf (metal prod., n.e.c.)	RCE	42	709.685-018
Roller, Hand (tobacco)	RCE	44	790.684-022
Roller, Primary Mill (steel & rel.)	RIE	58	613.362-014
Roller-Bearing Inspector (machinery mfg.; motor-bicycles)	CRE	45	706.687-034
Roller-Leveler Operator (steel & rel.)	REC	40	613.685-022
Roller-Machine Operator (leather mfg.)	REI	41	583.685-094
Roller-Machine Operator (metal prod., n.e.c.)	RIE	47	611.482-014
Roller-Mill Operator (paint & varnish)	RCS	47	555.682-014
Roller-Print Tender (print. & pub.)	RIE	45	971.685-010
Roller-Skate Assembler (toy-sport equip.)	RCE	38	732.684-098
Roller-Skate Repairer (any industry)	CRS	42	732.684-102
Roller-Stitcher (boot & shoe)	CRS	38	753.684-030
Rolling Attendant (steel & rel.)	RCE	55	613.662-010
Rolling-Down-Machine Operator (knitting; textile)	REC	41	589.685-086
Rolling-Machine Operator (paper goods)	REC	40	640.685-070
Rolling-Machine Operator (sugar & conf.)	RES	41	520.685-198
Rolling-Machine Operator (textile)	REC	40	585.685-078
Rolling-Machine Tender (knitting)	RCE	39	689.685-114
Rolling-Mill Operator (nonfer. metal)	RSE	48	613.462-018
Rolling-Mill-Operator Helper (nonfer. metal)	REC	41	613.685-026
Roof Assembler I (mfd. bldgs.)	RSC	45	869.684-042
Roof Bolter (mine & quarry)	RCE	44	930.683-026
Roof Fitter (railroad equip.)	REI	46	806.684-126
Roof-Cement-and-Paint Maker (build. mat., n.e.c.; nonmet. min.)	RIE	49	550.382-030
Roof-Cement-and-Paint-Maker Helper (build. mat., n.e.c.; nonmet. min.)	RES	39	550.686-038
Roof-Truss-Machine Tender (mfd. bldgs.)	REC	38	669.685-070
Roofer (construction)	REC	52	866.381-010
Roofer Applicator (construction)	RCS	47	866.684-010
Roofer Apprentice (construction)	REC	52	866.381-014
Roofing Supervisor (construction)	RES	58	866.131-010
Roofing-Machine Operator (build. mat., n.e.c.)	REI	45	554.682-022
Roofing-Machine Tender (nonmet. min.)	RCI	42	590.685-098
Room-Service Clerk (hotel & rest.)	ECS	43	324.577-010
Rooter Operator (fabrication, n.e.c.)	CRE	44	731.685-010
Rope Cleaner (textile)	RCE	37	699.687-022

Title	HOC	Cx	DOT
Rope Maker, Machine (nonmet. min.)	REC	41	681.685-082
Rope-Laying-Machine Operator (tex. prod., n.e.c.)	RCE	41	681.685-086
Rope-Machine Setter (tex. prod., n.e.c.)	RES	53	681.380-010
Rope-Maker, Ropewalk (tex. prod., n.e.c.)	REI	45	681.682-014
Rope-Silica-Machine Operator (textile)	RCS	44	582.685-114
Rosin-Barrel Filler (chemical)	RCE	36	920.687-150
Rotary Cutter (boot & shoe)	RCE	42	585.685-082
Rotary Derrick Operator (petrol. & gas)	REC	53	930.382-022
Rotary Driller (petrol. & gas)	REI	53	930.382-026
Rotary-Cutter Feeder (paper & pulp)	RCE	40	640.686-010
Rotary-Cutter Operator (rubber goods)	REI	39	551.585-022
Rotary-Drier Feeder (chemical)	RCE	40	553.686-038
Rotary-Driller Helper (petrol. & gas)	RCE	43	930.684-026
Rotary-Engine Assembler (engine-turbine)	RCI	60	801.261-018
Rotary-Furnace Tender (chemical)	REC	41	553.685-094
Rotary-Head-Milling-Machine Set-up Operator (machine shop)	RIE	57	605.382-030
Rotary-Kiln Operator (cement; chemical; mine & quarry)	REI	50	573.382-010
Rotary-Kiln Operator (smelt. & refin.)	RCS	47	513.682-010
Rotary-Rig Engine Operator (petrol. & gas)	RES	57	950.382-022
Rotary-Screen-Printing-Machine Operator (textile)	RIE	45	652.582-014
Rotary-Shear Operator (any industry)	RIS	48	615.482-030
Rotogravure-Press Operator (print. & pub.)	REI	54	651.362-026
Rotor Assembler (clock & watch)	CRS	39	715.687-114
Rotor Casting-Machine Operator (elec. equip.)	RSE	49	502.482-018
Rouge Mixer (optical goods)	REC	39	570.685-082
Rouge Sifter and Miller (optical goods)	RCE	39	579.685-046
Rough Opener, Jewel Hole (clock & watch)	RCS	38	770.684-018
Rough Planer Tender (woodworking)	RCI	45	665.665-010
Rough-and-Trueing-Machine Operator (toy-sport equip.)	RCE	42	690.685-330
Rough-Rice Grader (grain-feed mills)	CER	51	529.367-026
Rough-Rice Tender (grain-feed mills)	REC	41	521.685-274
Rough-Rounder, Machine (boot & shoe)	RCE	42	690.685-334
Rougher (steel & rel.)	RES	56	613.362-018
Rougher Operator (steel & rel.)	RCS	47	613.662-014
Round-Corner-Cutter Operator (paper goods; print. & pub.)	RCS	41	640.685-074
Round-Up-Ring Hand (concrete prod.)	RES	42	579.587-010
Rounder (boot & shoe)	RCE	42	690.685-338
Rounder, Hand (hat & cap)	CRS	40	784.684-050
Rounding-and-Backing-Machine Operator (print. & pub.)	CRE	45	653.685-026
Rounding-Machine Operator (hat & cap; tex. prod., n.e.c.)	CRE	40	585.685-086
Rounding-Machine Tender (pen & pencil)	RES	40	663.685-026
Roustabout (petrol. & gas)	RCS	46	869.684-046
Route Aide (tel. & tel.)	RCE	41	239.687-010
Route Supervisor (tel. & tel.)	SER	53	239.137-018
Route-Delivery Clerk (clerical)	CSR	47	222.587-034
Router (clerical)	CRE	42	222.587-038
Router (print. & pub.)	REC	45	979.682-026
Router Machine Operator (plastic prod.)	RCI	40	605.685-054

Part 3: From Occupational Titles to Holland Codes

From the Dictionary of Occupational Titles Occupations to Holland Codes

Title	HOC	Cx	DOT
Router Operator (any industry)	RIE	56	605.382-034
Router Operator (stonework)	RIE	51	676.462-010
Router Operator (woodworking)	RIE	47	665.682-030
Router Operator, Hand (aircraft mfg.; railroad equip.)	RSC	45	806.684-150
Router Set-up Operator, Numerical Control (machine shop)	RIE	57	605.360-010
Router Tender (furniture)	RCI	40	665.685-042
Router, Printed Circuit Boards (electron. comp.)	RCI	45	605.682-034
Routing Clerk (clerical)	RCE	42	222.687-022
Routing Clerk (nonprofit org.)	CES	51	249.367-070
Routing-Equipment Tender (grain-feed mills)	RCE	42	521.685-278
Roving Sizer (textile)	RSE	51	680.367-010
Roving Winder, Fiberglass (textile)	RCS	43	681.485-010
Roving-Weight Gauger (textile)	REC	42	680.687-018
Row Boss, Hoeing (agriculture)	ESR	58	409.137-014
Rubber (furniture; wood prod., n.e.c.)	RCS	39	742.684-010
Rubber (personal ser.)	RES	41	334.677-010
Rubber and Plastics Worker (military ser.)	RIE	49	891.684-014
Rubber Cutter (rubber goods; rubber tire)	RES	37	559.685-158
Rubber Liner (machinery mfg.)	REI	45	759.684-050
Rubber Molder (fabrication, n.e.c.)	RCE	41	556.684-026
Rubber Tester (rubber goods; rubber tire)	RES	53	559.381-014
Rubber-Cutting-Machine Tender (rubber goods)	RES	40	690.685-342
Rubber-Goods Assembler (rubber goods)	CRE	38	752.684-038
Rubber-Goods Cutter-Finisher (rubber goods)	RCI	49	690.680-010
Rubber-Goods Inspector-Tester (rubber goods)	RCE	46	759.684-074
Rubber-Goods Repairer (any industry)	RCS	44	759.684-054
Rubber-Goods Tester (elec. equip.; utilities)	RCS	53	759.381-010
Rubber-Mill Operator (plastic-synth.)	RCE	46	559.682-042
Rubber-Mill Tender (plastic-synth.; rubber goods; rubber reclaim.; rubber tire)	REI	43	550.685-102
Rubber-Mold Maker (jewelry-silver.)	CRE	41	559.684-018
Rubber-Printing-Machine Operator (rubber goods)	RCI	50	652.462-010
Rubber-Roller Grinder (pen & pencil)	RCE	38	690.686-050
Rubber-Stamp Maker (pen & pencil)	RSC	55	733.381-014
Rubber-Thread Spooler (toy-sport equip.)	CRE	40	681.685-090
Rubber-Tubing Splicer (rubber goods)	CRS	41	752.684-042
Rubberizing Mechanic (any industry)	RIE	58	630.281-030
Rug Braider, Hand (carpet & rug)	CSE	40	782.687-042
Rug Cleaner (carpet & rug)	REI	40	689.687-066
Rug Cleaner, Hand (laundry & rel.)	RCS	46	369.384-014
Rug Cleaner, Machine (laundry & rel.)	RCS	41	361.682-010
Rug Clipper (carpet & rug)	RCE	43	781.684-046
Rug Cutter (carpet & rug)	RSC	45	686.662-010
Rug Cutter (fabrication, n.e.c.)	REC	38	590.687-022
Rug Dyer I (laundry & rel.)	RES	55	364.361-014
Rug Dyer II (laundry & rel.)	CRS	49	364.684-010
Rug Hooker (carpet & rug)	CRE	44	687.684-010
Rug Inspector (laundry & rel.)	RSE	42	369.687-030
Rug Inspector (tex. prod., n.e.c.)	RCS	41	585.685-090

From the Dictionary of Occupational Titles Occupations to Holland Codes

Title	HOC	Cx	DOT
Rug Inspector I (carpet & rug)	CRS	42	689.667-010
Rug Inspector II (carpet & rug)	RCE	47	789.587-022
Rug Measurer (laundry & rel.; retail trade)	RES	50	369.367-014
Rug Repairer (laundry & rel.)	RES	53	782.381-018
Rug Setter, Axminster (carpet & rug)	REI	46	681.682-018
Rug-Backing Stenciler (carpet & rug)	CRS	41	781.687-054
Rug-Cleaner Helper (laundry & rel.)	RES	39	362.686-014
Rug-Cutter Helper (carpet & rug)	RCE	41	686.686-014
Rug-Dry-Room Attendant (laundry & rel.)	REC	38	369.685-026
Rug-Drying-Machine Operator (carpet & rug)	REC	42	581.685-050
Rug-Dyer Helper (laundry & rel.)	RES	39	364.687-014
Rug-Frame Mounter (carpet & rug)	RES	43	687.464-010
Rug-Inspector Helper (carpet & rug)	RCS	39	789.687-158
Rug-Inspector Helper (tex. prod., n.e.c.)	REC	39	589.686-038
Rug-Sample Beveler (carpet & rug)	REC	37	781.684-050
Ruling-Machine Set-up Operator (paper goods; print. & pub.)	REI	48	659.682-022
Running Rigger (ship-boat mfg.)	RCI	48	806.684-142
Rural Mail Carrier (government ser.)	CSE	52	230.363-010
Sack Repairer (any industry)	CRE	40	782.687-046
Sack-Department Supervisor (grain-feed mills)	ESR	57	229.137-010
Saddle Maker (leather prod.)	RSE	53	783.381-026
Saddle-and-Side Wire Stitcher (print. & pub.)	RCE	40	692.685-146
Safe-and-Vault Service Mechanic (business ser.; wholesale tr.)	REI	56	869.381-022
Safe-Deposit-Box Rental Clerk (financial)	ECS	54	295.367-022
Safety Coordinator (motor trans.)	ESI	60	909.127-010
Safety Engineer (profess. & kin.)	ISR	74	012.061-014
Safety Engineer, Mines (mine & quarry)	REI	71	010.061-026
Safety Inspector (any industry)	RCS	59	168.264-014
Safety Inspector (insurance)	ESR	67	168.167-078
Safety Inspector (utilities)	SER	56	821.367-014
Safety Inspector, Truck (automotive ser.; motor trans.)	REC	47	919.687-018
Safety Manager (medical ser.)	SEC	70	168.167-086
Safety Manager (profess. & kin.)	IES	74	012.167-058
Safety-Clothing-and-Equipment Developer (profess. & kin.)	AER	69	142.061-038
Safety-Lamp Keeper (mine & quarry)	CRS	47	729.684-042
Safety-Pin-Assembling-Machine Operator (button & notion)	RIE	52	616.482-010
Sagger Maker (pottery & porc.)	RCE	41	774.684-030
Sagger Preparer (pottery & porc.)	REC	41	570.685-086
Sail Cutter (tex. prod., n.e.c.)	CRS	47	781.384-018
Sail-Lay-Out Worker (tex. prod., n.e.c.)	RES	57	781.381-030
Sailor, Pleasure Craft (water trans.)	RIE	51	911.664-014
Salad Maker (water trans.)	RSC	50	317.384-010
Sales Agent, Business Services (business ser.)	ESA	57	251.357-010
Sales Agent, Financial-Report Service (business ser.)	ESA	61	250.357-026
Sales Agent, Insurance (insurance)	ESC	64	250.257-010
Sales Agent, Pest Control Service (business ser.)	ESR	58	251.357-018

Title	HOC	Cx	DOT
Sales Agent, Psychological Tests and Industrial Relations (business ser.; print. & pub.)	ESA	66	251.257-014
Sales Agent, Real Estate (real estate)	ESC	61	250.357-018
Sales Attendant (retail trade)	ESR	44	299.677-010
Sales Attendant, Building Materials (retail trade)	SRC	43	299.677-014
Sales Clerk (retail trade)	ESR	51	290.477-014
Sales Clerk, Food (retail trade)	ERS	52	290.477-018
Sales Correspondent (clerical)	ERS	60	221.367-062
Sales Engineer, Aeronautical Products (aircraft mfg.)	ERI	69	002.151-010
Sales Engineer, Agricultural Equipment (profess. & kin.)	EIR	70	013.151-010
Sales Engineer, Ceramic Products (profess. & kin.)	ERI	70	006.151-010
Sales Engineer, Marine Equipment (profess. & kin.)	ERI	70	014.151-010
Sales Engineer, Mechanical Equipment (utilities)	ERI	70	007.151-010
Sales Engineer, Mining-and-Oil-Well Equipment and Services (mine & quarry; petrol. & gas)	ERS	70	010.151-010
Sales Engineer, Nuclear Equipment (profess. & kin.)	ERI	70	015.151-010
Sales Exhibitor (nonprofit org.)	ESA	52	279.357-010
Sales Representative (motor trans.)	ERS	60	250.357-022
Sales Representative, Abrasives (wholesale tr.)	ESR	58	274.357-010
Sales Representative, Advertising (print. & pub.)	ESR	61	254.357-014
Sales Representative, Aircraft (retail trade; wholesale tr.)	REI	63	273.253-010
Sales Representative, Aircraft Equipment and Parts (wholesale tr.)	ESR	61	273.357-010
Sales Representative, Animal-Feed Products (wholesale tr.)	ESR	58	272.357-010
Sales Representative, Apparel Trimmings (wholesale tr.)	ESA	57	261.357-010
Sales Representative, Architectural and Engineering Supplies (wholesale tr.)	ESR	60	276.357-010
Sales Representative, Audiovisual Program Productions (motion picture)	ESR	62	259.157-010
Sales Representative, Automotive-Leasing (business ser.)	ESR	57	273.357-014
Sales Representative, Barber and Beauty Equipment and Supplies (wholesale tr.)	ESA	57	275.357-010
Sales Representative, Boats and Marine Supplies (retail trade; wholesale tr.)	ESA	57	273.357-018
Sales Representative, Bottles and Bottling Equipment (wholesale tr.)	ESR	59	274.357-014
Sales Representative, Building Equipment and Supplies (wholesale tr.)	ESR	58	274.357-018
Sales Representative, Canvas Products (wholesale tr.)	ESR	58	261.357-014
Sales Representative, Chemicals and Drugs (wholesale tr.)	ESA	57	262.357-010
Sales Representative, Church Furniture and Religious Supplies (wholesale tr.)	ESR	57	275.357-014
Sales Representative, Commercial Equipment and Supplies (wholesale tr.)	ESA	58	275.357-018
Sales Representative, Communication Equipment (wholesale tr.)	ESR	65	271.257-010
Sales Representative, Computers and EDP Systems (wholesale tr.)	ESR	64	275.257-010
Sales Representative, Construction Machinery (wholesale tr.)	ESR	61	274.357-022

DOT to HOC

Title	HOC	Cx	DOT
Sales Representative, Containers (wholesale tr.)	ESR	59	274.357-026
Sales Representative, Cordage (wholesale tr.)	ESA	57	275.357-022
Sales Representative, Dairy Supplies (wholesale tr.)	ESR	60	274.357-030
Sales Representative, Dancing Instructions (education)	AES	51	259.357-014
Sales Representative, Data Processing Services (business ser.)	ESR	70	251.157-014
Sales Representative, Dental and Medical Equipment and Supplies (wholesale tr.)	ESR	62	276.257-010
Sales Representative, Door-To-Door (retail trade)	ESA	52	291.357-010
Sales Representative, Education Courses (education)	ESR	61	259.257-010
Sales Representative, Electronics Parts (wholesale tr.)	ESR	61	271.357-010
Sales Representative, Electroplating (wholesale tr.)	ESA	65	259.257-014
Sales Representative, Elevators, Escalators, and Dumbwaiters (wholesale tr.)	EAI	66	274.157-010
Sales Representative, Farm and Garden Equipment and Supplies (wholesale tr.)	ESR	57	272.357-014
Sales Representative, Financial Services (financial)	ESA	68	250.257-022
Sales Representative, Food Products (wholesale tr.)	ESA	57	260.357-014
Sales Representative, Footwear (wholesale tr.)	ESA	58	261.357-018
Sales Representative, Foundry and Machine Shop Products (wholesale tr.)	ERS	63	274.257-010
Sales Representative, Franchise (business ser.)	ESR	57	251.357-022
Sales Representative, Fuels (retail trade; wholesale tr.)	ESA	57	269.357-010
Sales Representative, General Merchandise (wholesale tr.)	ESA	57	279.357-014
Sales Representative, Graphic Art (business ser.)	AES	64	254.251-010
Sales Representative, Hardware Supplies (wholesale tr.)	ESA	57	274.357-034
Sales Representative, Herbicide Service (business ser.)	ESA	57	251.357-026
Sales Representative, Hobbies and Crafts (retail trade; wholesale tr.)	ESR	57	277.357-010
Sales Representative, Home Furnishings (wholesale tr.)	ESA	57	270.357-010
Sales Representative, Hotel and Restaurant Equipment and Supplies (wholesale tr.)	ESA	60	275.357-026
Sales Representative, Hotel Services (hotel & rest.)	ESC	63	259.157-014
Sales Representative, Household Appliances (wholesale tr.)	ESA	57	270.357-014
Sales Representative, Industrial Machinery (wholesale tr.)	ERS	59	274.357-038
Sales Representative, Industrial Rubber Goods (wholesale tr.)	ESR	60	274.357-042
Sales Representative, Jewelry (wholesale tr.)	ESA	58	279.357-018
Sales Representative, Leather Goods (wholesale tr.)	ESA	58	279.357-022
Sales Representative, Livestock (wholesale tr.)	ESA	61	260.257-010
Sales Representative, Lubricating Equipment (wholesale tr.)	ESC	59	274.357-046
Sales Representative, Malt Liquors (wholesale tr.)	ESA	55	260.357-018
Sales Representative, Material-Handling Equipment (wholesale tr.)	ESR	59	274.357-050
Sales Representative, Men's and Boys' Apparel (wholesale tr.)	ESR	58	261.357-022
Sales Representative, Metals (wholesale tr.)	ESR	61	274.357-054
Sales Representative, Mortician Supplies (wholesale tr.)	ESR	60	275.357-030
Sales Representative, Motor Vehicles and Supplies (wholesale tr.)	ESR	61	273.357-022

Part 3: From Occupational Titles to Holland Codes

From the Dictionary of Occupational Titles Occupations to Holland Codes

Title	HOC	Cx	DOT
Sales Representative, Musical Instruments and Accessories (wholesale tr.)	ESR	61	277.357-014
Sales Representative, Novelties (wholesale tr.)	ESA	57	277.357-018
Sales Representative, Office Machines (retail trade; wholesale tr.)	ESR	59	275.357-034
Sales Representative, Oil Field Supplies and Equipment (wholesale tr.)	ESR	63	274.357-058
Sales Representative, Paper and Paper Products (wholesale tr.)	ESA	57	279.357-026
Sales Representative, Petroleum Products (wholesale tr.)	ESR	58	269.357-014
Sales Representative, Plastic Products (wholesale tr.)	ESC	57	279.357-030
Sales Representative, Poultry Equipment and Supplies (retail trade; wholesale tr.)	ESR	61	272.357-018
Sales Representative, Precision Instruments (wholesale tr.)	ESR	61	276.357-014
Sales Representative, Pressure-Sensitive Tape (wholesale tr.)	ESA	57	275.357-038
Sales Representative, Printing (wholesale tr.)	ESA	57	254.357-018
Sales Representative, Printing Supplies (wholesale tr.)	ESA	59	274.357-062
Sales Representative, Public Utilities (tel. & tel.; utilities)	ESR	61	253.357-010
Sales Representative, Publications (wholesale tr.)	ESA	57	277.357-022
Sales Representative, Radio and Television Time (radio-tv broad.)	ERS	61	259.357-018
Sales Representative, Radiographic-Inspection Equipment and Services (wholesale tr.)	ESA	61	271.352-010
Sales Representative, Railroad Equipment and Supplies (wholesale tr.)	ESR	61	273.357-026
Sales Representative, Recreation and Sporting Goods (wholesale tr.)	ESA	57	277.357-026
Sales Representative, Safety Apparel and Equipment (wholesale tr.)	ESA	57	261.357-026
Sales Representative, School Equipment and Supplies (wholesale tr.)	ESR	59	275.357-042
Sales Representative, Security Systems (business ser.)	ERI	61	259.257-022
Sales Representative, Shipping Services (motor trans.)	ESR	55	252.357-014
Sales Representative, Shoe Leather and Findings (wholesale tr.)	ESA	57	275.357-046
Sales Representative, Signs (fabrication, n.e.c.)	ESA	58	254.357-022
Sales Representative, Signs and Displays (fabrication, n.e.c.)	ESR	62	254.257-010
Sales Representative, Telephone Services (tel. & tel.)	ESA	63	253.257-010
Sales Representative, Television Cable Service (radio-tv broad.)	ESA	56	259.357-022
Sales Representative, Textile Designs (wholesale tr.)	ESA	59	274.357-066
Sales Representative, Textile Machinery (wholesale tr.)	ESR	61	274.357-070
Sales Representative, Textiles (wholesale tr.)	ESA	61	261.357-030
Sales Representative, Tobacco Products and Smoking Supplies (retail trade; wholesale tr.)	ESA	56	260.357-022
Sales Representative, Toilet Preparations (wholesale tr.)	ESA	57	262.357-014
Sales Representative, Ultrasonic Equipment (wholesale tr.)	ERS	61	271.352-014
Sales Representative, Uniforms (retail trade; wholesale tr.)	ESA	58	261.357-034
Sales Representative, Upholstery and Furniture Repair (retail trade)	EAS	56	259.357-026

DOT to HOC

Title	HOC	Cx	DOT
Sales Representative, Vending and Coin Machines (wholesale tr.)	ESA	57	275.357-050
Sales Representative, Veterinarian Supplies (wholesale tr.)	ESR	60	276.357-018
Sales Representative, Videotape (wholesale tr.)	ESC	56	271.357-014
Sales Representative, Water-Softening Equipment (retail trade; wholesale tr.)	EAS	57	279.357-034
Sales Representative, Water-Treatment Chemicals (wholesale tr.)	ESR	58	262.357-022
Sales Representative, Weather-Forecasting Service (business ser.)	ESA	57	259.357-030
Sales Representative, Weighing and Force-Measurement Instruments (wholesale tr.)	EIR	67	276.257-014
Sales Representative, Welding Equipment (wholesale tr.)	ESR	58	274.357-074
Sales Representative, Wire Rope (wholesale tr.)	ESR	58	274.357-078
Sales Representative, Women's and Girls' Apparel (wholesale tr.)	ESA	57	261.357-038
Sales Representative, Writing and Marking Pens (wholesale tr.)	ESA	56	277.357-030
Sales Supervisor, Malt Liquors (wholesale tr.)	ESR	62	299.137-014
Sales-Engineer, Electrical Products (profess. & kin.)	ESI	70	003.151-010
Sales-Engineer, Electronics Products and Systems (profess. & kin.)	ESI	70	003.151-014
Sales-Promotion Representative (wholesale tr.)	ESA	52	269.357-018
Sales-Service Promoter (any industry)	AES	67	165.167-010
Sales-Service Representative, Milking Machines (retail trade)	REI	60	299.251-010
Salesperson, Art Objects (retail trade)	ESR	52	277.457-010
Salesperson, Automobile Accessories (retail trade; wholesale tr.)	ESA	57	273.357-030
Salesperson, Automobiles (retail trade)	ESR	58	273.353-010
Salesperson, Books (retail trade)	ESC	58	277.357-034
Salesperson, Burial Needs (retail trade)	ESA	59	279.357-042
Salesperson, China and Silverware (retail trade; wholesale tr.)	ESA	57	270.357-018
Salesperson, Corsets (retail trade)	ERS	57	261.354-010
Salesperson, Cosmetics and Toiletries (retail trade)	ESA	54	262.357-018
Salesperson, Curtains and Draperies (retail trade)	ESA	57	270.357-022
Salesperson, Electric Motors (retail trade; wholesale tr.)	RES	58	271.354-010
Salesperson, Floor Coverings (retail trade; wholesale tr.)	ESA	57	270.357-026
Salesperson, Florist Supplies (wholesale tr.)	ESA	57	275.357-054
Salesperson, Flowers (retail trade)	AER	55	260.357-026
Salesperson, Flying Squad (retail trade)	ESA	58	279.357-046
Salesperson, Furniture (retail trade)	ESA	54	270.357-030
Salesperson, Furs (retail trade)	ESA	57	261.357-042
Salesperson, General Hardware (retail trade; wholesale tr.)	ESA	52	279.357-050
Salesperson, General Merchandise (retail trade; wholesale tr.)	ESA	51	279.357-054
Salesperson, Horticultural and Nursery Products (retail trade; wholesale tr.)	ESA	57	272.357-022

Title	HOC	Cx	DOT
Salesperson, Household Appliances (retail trade)	ESA	57	270.357-034
Salesperson, Infants' and Children's Wear (retail trade)	ESA	56	261.357-046
Salesperson, Jewelry (retail trade)	ESA	57	279.357-058
Salesperson, Leather-and-Suede Apparel-and-Accessories (retail trade)	SER	55	261.357-074
Salesperson, Men's and Boys' Clothing (retail trade)	EAS	54	261.357-050
Salesperson, Men's Furnishings (retail trade)	ESA	57	261.357-054
Salesperson, Millinery (retail trade)	EAS	54	261.357-058
Salesperson, Musical Instruments and Accessories (retail trade)	ESA	60	277.357-038
Salesperson, Orthopedic Shoes (retail trade)	ESR	60	276.257-018
Salesperson, Parts (retail trade; wholesale tr.)	ESC	56	279.357-062
Salesperson, Pets and Pet Supplies (retail trade)	ESA	57	277.357-042
Salesperson, Phonograph Records and Tape Recordings (retail trade)	ESR	54	277.357-046
Salesperson, Photographic Supplies and Equipment (retail trade; wholesale tr.)	ESA	57	277.357-050
Salesperson, Pianos and Organs (retail trade)	ESR	60	277.354-010
Salesperson, Sewing Machines (retail trade)	ERS	58	270.352-010
Salesperson, Sheet Music (retail trade)	ESR	59	277.357-054
Salesperson, Shoes (retail trade)	EAS	53	261.357-062
Salesperson, Sporting Goods (retail trade)	ESA	57	277.357-058
Salesperson, Stamps or Coins (retail trade; wholesale tr.)	ESA	57	277.357-062
Salesperson, Stereo Equipment (retail trade)	ESA	57	270.357-038
Salesperson, Surgical Appliances (retail trade)	ESA	63	276.257-022
Salesperson, Toy Trains and Accessories (retail trade)	ESC	56	277.357-066
Salesperson, Trailers and Motor Homes (retail trade)	ESA	57	273.357-034
Salesperson, Wigs (personal ser.; retail trade)	ESA	53	261.351-010
Salesperson, Women's Apparel and Accessories (retail trade)	EAS	52	261.357-066
Salesperson, Yard Goods (retail trade)	EAS	56	261.357-070
Salesperson-Demonstrator, Party Plan (retail trade)	ESA	57	279.357-038
Salt Washer (chemical)	REC	45	551.685-126
Salvage Engineer (machinery mfg.)	REI	60	600.131-014
Salvage Inspector (can. & preserv.)	RCE	41	529.687-174
Salvage Inspector (railroad equip.)	RIS	57	622.381-038
Salvage Repairer II (utilities)	RCE	48	729.384-018
Salvage Supervisor (paint & varnish)	ERS	59	559.137-010
Salvage Winder and Inspector (paper goods)	RCE	43	649.685-102
Salvage Worker (nonfer. metal)	RCS	49	619.387-010
Salvage-Machine Operator (ordnance)	RCE	50	694.382-010
Salvager (optical goods)	REC	40	713.687-038
Salvager (petrol. refin.)	RCS	47	709.684-070
Salvager (utilities)	RES	39	729.687-030
Salvager Helper (petrol. refin.)	RES	41	709.687-034
Salvager I (ordnance)	CSR	45	737.687-114
Salvager II (ordnance)	RCE	46	737.687-118
Sample Checker (carpet & rug; textile)	CRE	47	229.687-010
Sample Clerk (furniture)	CRS	53	221.382-026

DOT to HOC

From the Dictionary of Occupational Titles Occupations to Holland Codes

Title	HOC	Cx	DOT
Sample Clerk (plastic prod.)	RCI	51	222.387-066
Sample Clerk (textile)	CRS	41	789.587-026
Sample Clerk, Handkerchief (garment)	CER	42	920.587-022
Sample Clerk, Paper (paper & pulp; paper goods)	CRE	48	209.587-046
Sample Collector (chemical)	CER	41	550.587-014
Sample Cutter (furniture)	RCS	42	781.684-070
Sample Display Preparer (knitting)	CSE	47	222.687-026
Sample Maker (boot & shoe)	RCE	45	690.685-506
Sample Maker I (jewelry-silver.)	REC	52	700.381-046
Sample Maker II (jewelry-silver.)	RCE	56	735.381-018
Sample Maker, Appliances (house. appl.; light. fix.)	RIS	59	600.280-054
Sample Maker, Hand (paper goods)	RCE	42	794.684-030
Sample Maker, Veneer (millwork-plywood)	CRS	41	769.684-042
Sample Sawyer (brick & tile)	CRE	39	677.685-034
Sample Selector (tex. prod., n.e.c.)	RCE	45	789.387-014
Sample Shoe Inspector and Reworker (boot & shoe)	RCS	44	788.684-098
Sample Stitcher (garment)	RIE	57	785.361-018
Sample Tester (chemical)	RCS	52	553.364-010
Sample Tester-Grinder (mine & quarry)	RCE	47	519.585-018
Sample Washer (petrol. & gas)	REC	37	939.687-030
Sample Worker (any industry)	CSR	45	920.687-154
Sample-Book Maker (paper goods)	RCE	40	659.685-014
Sample-Color Maker (paint & varnish)	RCS	41	550.584-014
Sample-Room Supervisor (textile)	ESR	62	299.137-018
Sample-Taker Operator (petrol. & gas)	RCS	52	931.361-010
Sampler (beverage)	CRE	42	529.687-178
Sampler (elec. equip.)	REC	42	549.587-018
Sampler (mine & quarry)	RIC	49	579.484-010
Sampler (oils & grease)	REI	52	529.387-034
Sampler (petrol. refin.)	ECS	42	549.587-014
Sampler (steel & rel.)	RCS	46	599.684-014
Sampler, First (smelt. & refin.)	RES	51	619.682-038
Sampler, Head (smelt. & refin.)	ERS	59	519.130-014
Sampler, Wool (wholesale tr.)	RCE	44	222.587-042
Sampler-Tester (nonmet. min.)	REC	45	579.585-010
Sand Filler (mine & quarry)	RES	40	939.687-034
Sand Mixer, Machine (foundry)	RES	44	570.682-018
Sand Plant Attendant (concrete prod.; mine & quarry)	REC	41	934.685-014
Sand Tester (foundry)	RCE	52	777.381-046
Sand-Cutter Operator (foundry)	REI	41	570.683-014
Sand-Mill Grinder (paint & varnish)	REI	45	555.682-018
Sand-Slinger Operator (foundry)	RCE	37	518.683-010
Sandblast Operator (ordnance)	REC	42	503.685-038
Sandblast-or-Shotblast-Equipment Tender (any industry)	RCE	41	503.685-042
Sandblaster (any industry)	REI	41	503.687-010
Sandblaster, Stone (stonework)	RIE	48	673.382-010
Sandblaster, Stone Apprentice (stonework)	RIE	48	673.382-014
Sander (fabrication, n.e.c.)	RCS	42	761.684-030
Sander (toy-sport equip.)	CRE	40	690.685-346

Part 3: From Occupational Titles to Holland Codes

From the Dictionary of Occupational Titles Occupations to Holland Codes

Title	HOC	Cx	DOT
Sander, Hand (woodworking)	REC	38	761.687-010
Sander, Machine (woodworking)	RCE	42	761.682-014
Sander, Portable Machine (woodworking)	CRE	38	761.684-034
Sander-and-Buffer (musical inst.)	RCS	40	730.684-066
Sandfill Operator (mine & quarry)	RCE	43	939.485-010
Sanding-Machine Buffer (wood prod., n.e.c.)	CRE	40	662.685-022
Sanding-Machine Operator (sugar & conf.)	RES	39	524.665-010
Sanding-Machine Tender (wood prod., n.e.c.)	CRS	40	662.685-026
Sandwich Maker (hotel & rest.)	RCE	40	317.664-010
Sandwich-Board Carrier (any industry)	CER	38	299.687-014
Sandwich-Machine Operator (dairy products)	REC	41	529.685-210
Sanitarian (any industry)	ERI	58	529.137-014
Sanitarian (profess. & kin.)	ISR	71	079.117-018
Sanitary Engineer (profess. & kin.)	IER	76	005.061-030
Sanitary Landfill Operator (sanitary ser.)	RSC	45	955.463-010
Sanitary-Landfill Supervisor (sanitary ser.)	SER	59	955.133-010
Sanitary-Napkin-Machine Tender (protective dev.)	CRE	41	692.685-150
Sanitation Inspector (government ser.)	ERS	53	168.267-110
Sapphire-Stylus Grinder (comm. equip.)	RCE	51	770.381-038
Satellite-Instruction Facilitator (education)	CES	51	249.367-086
Saturation-Equipment Operator (fabrication, n.e.c.)	RIE	50	582.665-022
Saturator Operator (chemical; steel & rel.)	RIE	51	558.362-018
Saturator Tender (build. mat., n.e.c.)	CRE	43	582.685-118
Sausage Inspector (meat products)	CRE	39	529.587-014
Sausage Maker (meat products)	RCE	41	520.685-202
Sausage Mixer (meat products)	REC	42	520.685-206
Sausage-Meat Trimmer (meat products)	RCE	41	521.687-106
Save-All Operator (paper & pulp)	RCE	40	533.685-018
Saw Filer (any industry)	RIE	56	701.381-014
Saw Maker (cutlery-hrdwr.)	RIS	56	601.381-034
Saw Operator (aircraft mfg.)	RCI	49	607.382-014
Saw Operator (brick & tile)	RCI	40	677.685-054
Saw Operator (electron. comp.)	RCI	44	726.682-026
Saw Operator, Semiconductor Wafers (electron. comp.)	RCE	42	726.685-046
Saw Setter (stonework)	REI	46	701.684-022
Saw-Edge Fuser, Circular (cutlery-hrdwr.)	CRS	45	701.684-026
Sawmill Worker (saw. & plan.)	RCS	44	667.687-018
Sawyer (plastic prod.; plastic-synth.)	RCS	47	690.482-010
Sawyer I (nonmet. min.)	REC	40	677.686-010
Sawyer II (nonmet. min.)	RCE	40	677.685-038
Sawyer, Cork Slabs (wood prod., n.e.c.)	RCE	39	667.685-046
Sawyer, Optical Glass (optical goods)	RES	50	677.382-014
Scagliola Mechanic (nonmet. min.)	RSE	46	556.484-010
Scale Assembly Set-up Worker (office machines)	RES	59	710.360-010
Scale Mechanic (any industry)	RES	58	633.281-026
Scale Operator (chemical)	RCE	41	555.687-010
Scale-Reclamation Tender (smelt. & refin.)	RCE	45	515.585-010
Scaler-Packer (meat products)	RCE	42	929.687-046
Scaling Machine Operator (can. & preserv.)	RCI	37	521.685-386

DOT to HOC

Title	HOC	Cx	DOT
Scallop Cutter, Machine (tex. prod., n.e.c.)	RCE	41	686.685-058
Scalp-Treatment Operator (personal ser.)	ERS	52	339.371-014
Scalper Operator (nonfer. metal)	RIE	47	605.682-022
Scanner (profess. & kin.)	RIC	58	015.384-010
Scanner Operator (print. & pub.)	RES	58	972.282-010
Scarf Gluer (millwork-plywood)	RES	41	762.684-054
Scarfing Machine Operator (steel & rel.)	RCS	47	816.682-010
Schedule Maker (motor trans.)	ERI	60	913.167-018
Scheduler (museums)	CES	54	238.367-034
Scheduler, Maintenance (clerical)	ECS	53	221.367-066
School Bus Monitor (government ser.)	SEC	43	372.667-042
School Secretary (education)	CSE	56	201.362-022
School-Plant Consultant (education)	IEA	69	001.167-010
Scientific Glass Blower (glass products)	RIE	66	006.261-010
Scientific Helper (profess. & kin.)	IRS	59	199.364-014
Scientific Linguist (profess. & kin.)	ISC	72	059.067-014
Scooping-Machine Tender (furniture)	RCE	47	665.685-026
Scoreboard Operator (amuse. & rec.)	CSR	48	349.665-010
Scorer (amuse. & rec.)	ESC	54	153.387-014
Scorer (paper goods)	RCE	40	641.685-070
Scorer Helper (paper goods)	RES	40	641.686-030
Scouring-Train Operator (carpet & rug; textile)	REI	49	589.662-010
Scout (agriculture)	SCE	51	408.381-010
Scout (petrol. & gas)	IER	66	010.267-010
Scout, Professional Sports (amuse. & rec.)	SEC	62	153.117-018
Scrap Baller (nonfer. metal; steel & rel.)	RES	41	509.685-046
Scrap Handler (any industry)	REI	46	509.685-050
Scrap Separator (food prep., n.e.c.)	CRE	39	529.587-018
Scrap Sorter (boot & shoe)	RCE	37	788.687-106
Scrap Sorter (nonfer. metal)	RES	40	509.686-018
Scraper (jewelry-silver.)	RCS	38	700.687-066
Scraper Operator (construction)	RIE	46	850.683-038
Scraper, Hand (machine shop)	RES	49	705.384-010
Scraper-Loader Operator (mine & quarry)	RES	45	921.663-050
Scrapper (paper goods)	RSE	40	794.687-050
Scratcher Tender (fabrication, n.e.c.)	REI	41	555.685-050
Screen Cleaner (wood prod., n.e.c.)	REC	37	569.687-018
Screen Handler (paper & pulp)	REC	38	539.685-026
Screen Maker (paper goods)	RCE	41	739.684-150
Screen Maker, Photographic Process (any industry)	RCE	49	979.384-010
Screen Maker, Textile (textile)	RIE	55	971.381-046
Screen Operator (chemical)	RCE	41	551.685-130
Screen Operator (smelt. & refin.)	REC	45	511.685-050
Screen Printer (any industry)	REC	42	979.684-034
Screen Printer (textile)	CRS	46	979.684-030
Screen Printer Helper (any industry)	RSC	38	979.687-022
Screen Repairer, Crusher (mine & quarry)	RSE	47	630.684-030
Screen Tacker (woodworking)	RCE	38	762.687-058
Screen Tender (paper & pulp)	REC	44	533.685-022

Title	HOC	Cx	DOT
Screen Tender (paper & pulp; wood prod., n.e.c.)	REC	42	534.665-010
Screen Tender, Chips (paper & pulp)	RES	41	533.685-026
Screen Writer (motion picture; radio-tv broad.)	AEI	69	131.067-050
Screen-and-Cyclone Repairer (mine & quarry)	RES	47	630.664-014
Screen-Machine Operator (tex. prod., n.e.c.)	RCI	46	559.682-070
Screen-Printing-Equipment Setter (paper goods)	RSE	56	979.360-010
Screen-Printing-Machine Operator (textile)	REI	44	652.682-018
Screen-Printing-Machine-Operator Helper (textile)	RES	40	652.686-038
Screen-Room Operator (sugar & conf.)	RCE	41	521.685-282
Screen-Tender Helper (paper & pulp)	REC	38	533.687-010
Screener Operator (any industry)	REI	41	599.685-082
Screener-and-Blender Operator (steel & rel.)	REI	42	549.685-026
Screener-Perfumer (soap & rel.)	RCE	41	559.685-162
Screw Remover (boot & shoe)	RCE	38	788.684-102
Screw Supervisor (clock & watch)	RES	59	609.130-014
Screw-Eye Assembler (ordnance)	RCE	36	737.687-122
Screw-Machine Operator, Multiple Spindle (machine shop)	REI	52	604.382-010
Screw-Machine Operator, Single Spindle (machine shop)	REI	51	604.382-014
Screw-Machine Operator, Swiss-Type (clock & watch)	REI	53	604.682-010
Screw-Machine Set-up Operator (machine shop)	RIE	56	604.380-022
Screw-Machine Set-up Operator, Multiple Spindle (machine shop)	RIE	59	604.280-014
Screw-Machine Set-up Operator, Single Spindle (machine shop)	RIE	58	604.280-018
Screw-Machine Set-up Operator, Swiss-Type (clock & watch)	RIE	58	604.260-010
Screw-Machine Tender (machine shop)	RCE	43	604.685-034
Screwdown Operator (steel & rel.)	RIS	49	613.382-018
Screwhead Polisher (clock & watch)	REC	51	715.381-090
Screwmaker, Automatic (clock & watch)	CRS	47	609.682-030
Scribing-Machine Operator (cutlery-hrdwr.)	CRE	42	605.685-042
Script Reader (radio-tv broad.)	CES	57	131.267-022
Script Supervisor (motion picture; radio-tv broad.)	CSE	58	201.362-026
Scroll Assembler (office machines)	RCE	41	710.584-010
Scroll-Machine Operator (struct. metal)	REC	40	616.685-062
Scrubber Machine Tender (electron. comp.)	RCI	39	599.685-134
Scrubbing-Machine Operator (tex. prod., n.e.c.)	REC	42	582.685-122
Scuba Diver (any industry)	REI	49	379.384-010
Scullion (water trans.)	REC	40	318.687-014
Sculptor (profess. & kin.)	AER	66	144.061-018
Scutcher Tender (textile)	REI	40	589.685-090
Seal Mixer (elec. equip.)	RCS	42	540.687-010
Seal-Extrusion Operator (elec. equip.)	CRE	40	692.685-154
Sealer (elec. equip.)	CRS	40	727.684-030
Sealer (fishing & hunt.)	REC	39	461.684-010
Sealer (office machines)	RSE	47	710.684-038
Sealer, Dry Cell (elec. equip.)	CRS	41	692.685-158
Sealer, Semiconductor Packages (electron. comp.)	RCI	40	726.687-042
Sealing-and-Canceling-Machine Operator (clerical)	REC	42	208.685-026

Title	HOC	Cx	DOT
Sealing-Machine Operator (light. fix.)	RCE	42	692.685-162
Sealing-Machine Operator (paper goods)	REC	40	641.685-074
Seam Hammerer (musical inst.)	RCE	40	730.684-070
Seam Presser (hat & cap)	CRE	41	583.685-098
Seam Steamer (garment)	REC	38	789.687-166
Seam-Rubbing-Machine Operator (boot & shoe)	CRE	40	690.685-350
Seamless-Hosiery Knitter (knitting)	CRS	41	684.685-010
Seamless-Tube Roller (steel & rel.)	RSC	47	619.682-042
Seasoning Mixer (chemical)	CRE	43	550.685-106
Seasoning Mixer (meat products)	CRE	41	520.687-054
Seat Joiner, Chainstitch (garment)	RCE	41	786.682-218
Second (amuse. & rec.)	CSE	38	346.677-018
Second Cook and Baker (water trans.)	RES	52	315.381-026
Second Cutter (glass mfg.)	RCS	43	779.684-054
Second Helper (steel & rel.)	REI	41	512.684-010
Second Operator, Mill Tender (chemical)	CER	44	555.685-054
Second-Floor Operator (plastic-synth.)	REI	41	557.685-022
Seconds Handler (knitting)	RCE	40	782.687-050
Secretary (clerical)	CSE	60	201.362-030
Secretary of Police (government ser.)	ESR	63	375.137-022
Secretary of State (government ser.)	ESR	69	188.167-082
Secretary, Board-of-Education (education)	EIR	69	169.267-022
Section Leader and Machine Setter (textile)	REI	57	689.260-018
Section Leader and Machine Setter, Polishing (textile)	RES	56	689.260-022
Section Leader, Screen Printing (textile)	RIS	57	652.260-010
Section Supervisor (mine & quarry)	SER	61	939.137-018
Section-Plotter Operator (petrol. & gas)	REI	55	194.382-010
Sectional Center Manager, Postal Service (government ser.)	ESR	65	188.167-086
Sectional-Belt-Mold Assembler (rubber goods)	RCE	41	752.685-010
Securities Clerk (clerical)	CSE	60	210.382-062
Securities Clerk (financial)	CSE	59	219.362-054
Securities Trader (financial)	ECS	69	162.167-038
Security Consultant (business ser.; personal ser.)	ESC	64	189.167-054
Security Officer (any industry)	ERS	63	189.167-034
Seed Analyst (profess. & kin.)	RIS	60	040.361-014
Seed Core Operator (electron. comp.)	RCI	50	679.384-010
Seed Cutter (agriculture)	RES	35	404.686-010
Seed Pelleter (agriculture)	RCI	41	599.685-126
Seed-Cleaner Operator (agriculture; oils & grease)	REC	40	599.665-010
Seed-Potato Arranger (agriculture)	RCE	37	404.685-010
Seed-Yeast Operator (food prep., n.e.c.)	REI	46	522.685-090
Seedling Puller (forestry)	RES	35	451.687-018
Seedling Sorter (forestry)	REC	37	451.687-022
Seismologist (profess. & kin.)	IRE	80	024.061-050
Selector (fabrication, n.e.c.)	RCE	45	739.687-166
Selector (glass mfg.)	CRE	42	579.687-030
Self-Sealing-Fuel-Tank Builder (rubber goods)	RCS	47	752.684-046
Self-Sealing-Fuel-Tank Repairer (rubber goods)	RCE	45	759.384-010
Self-Service-Laundry-and-Dry-Cleaning Attendant (laundry & rel.)	ESR	43	369.677-010

Part 3: From Occupational Titles to Holland Codes

From the Dictionary of Occupational Titles Occupations to Holland Codes

Title	HOC	Cx	DOT
Selvage-Machine Operator (textile)	RCE	40	681.685-094
Semiconductor Processor (electron. comp.)	RCE	45	590.684-022
Senior Enlisted Advisor (military ser.)	ESC	58	166.167-042
Senior Reservations Agent (air trans.)	ESR	62	238.137-014
Senior Technician, Controls (pipe lines)	RES	62	828.261-018
Senior-Commissary Agent (air trans.)	SER	59	922.137-010
Sensitized-Paper Tester (photo. appar.)	RES	41	714.667-010
Separator Operator (button & notion)	RCE	40	692.685-166
Separator Operator (chemical)	RCE	41	559.685-166
Separator Operator (grain-feed mills)	REC	51	521.382-014
Separator Operator, Shellfish Meats (can. & preserv.)	REC	40	521.685-286
Separator Tender II (grain-feed mills)	REI	41	521.685-290
Septic-Tank Installer (construction)	RSE	47	851.663-010
Sequencing-Machine Operator (electron. comp.)	RCI	48	726.382-010
Sequins Stringer (plastic prod.)	RCE	39	754.687-014
Serging-Machine Operator, Automatic (any industry)	CRS	43	787.685-030
Service Attendant, Sleeping Car (r.r. trans.)	ERC	42	351.677-010
Service Clerk (clerical)	ECS	50	221.367-070
Service Manager (automotive ser.)	ESR	63	185.167-058
Service Manager (retail trade)	ERS	59	185.164-010
Service Mechanic (auto. mfg.)	RES	53	807.381-022
Service Mechanic, Compressed-Gas Equipment (chemical)	REI	58	630.281-034
Service Observer (tel. & tel.)	ERS	55	239.367-026
Service Observer, Chief (tel. & tel.)	ESR	59	239.137-022
Service Representative (auto. mfg.)	SEI	66	191.167-022
Service Representative (utilities; waterworks)	REI	47	959.574-010
Service Representative, Elevators, Escalators, and Dumbwaiters (wholesale tr.)	ESI	66	259.257-018
Service Restorer, Emergency (r.r. trans.)	RSE	55	821.261-022
Service Supervisor I (utilities)	ERS	59	953.137-018
Service Supervisor II (utilities)	RES	62	821.131-018
Service Supervisor III (utilities)	RES	63	184.167-126
Service Supervisor, Leased Machinery and Equipment (any industry)	ESR	65	183.167-030
Service Technician, Computerized-Photofinishing Equipment (photofinishing)	RCI	59	714.281-030
Service-Establishment Attendant (laundry & rel.; personal ser.)	ECS	51	369.477-014
Service-Mechanic Helper, Compressed-Gas Equipment (chemical)	RES	42	630.664-018
Service-Unit Operator, Oil Well (petrol. & gas)	RES	54	930.361-010
Services Clerk (water trans.)	CRE	56	214.387-018
Set Decorator (motion picture; radio-tv broad.)	AES	65	142.061-042
Set Designer (amuse. & rec.)	AES	66	142.061-050
Set Designer (motion picture; radio-tv broad.)	AIE	66	142.061-046
Set-Key Driver (clock & watch)	RCE	37	715.687-118
Set-Staff Fitter (clock & watch)	CRE	38	715.684-178
Set-up Mechanic (pen & pencil)	RSE	53	692.380-010
Set-up Mechanic, Automatic Line (pen & pencil)	REI	57	692.380-014

Part 3: From Occupational Titles to Holland Codes

From the Dictionary of Occupational Titles Occupations to Holland Codes

Title	HOC	Cx	DOT
Set-up Mechanic, Coil-Winding Machines (elec. equip.)	RSE	58	724.360-010
Set-up Mechanic, Crown Assembly Machine (any industry)	RES	53	692.362-010
Set-up Worker (clock & watch)	REC	48	715.660-010
Setter (brick & tile)	RCS	44	573.684-014
Setter Helper (brick & tile)	RES	39	573.687-030
Setter, Automatic-Spinning Lathe (any industry)	RIE	57	604.360-010
Setter, Cold-Rolling Machine (machine shop)	RIE	54	617.682-022
Setter, Induction-Heating Equipment (welding)	RCE	51	813.360-014
Setter, Juice Packaging Machines (can. & preserv.)	RCI	53	920.380-010
Setter, Molding-and-Coremaking Machines (foundry)	RIE	50	518.380-010
Settlement Clerk (smelt. & refin.)	CRE	54	214.382-030
Sewage-Disposal Worker (sanitary ser.)	REI	40	955.687-010
Sewer and Inspector (knitting)	CRS	44	684.682-014
Sewer, Hand (any industry)	CRE	41	782.684-058
Sewer-Line Photo-Inspector (sanitary ser.)	RCI	51	851.362-010
Sewer-Line Repairer (sanitary ser.)	RIC	51	869.664-018
Sewer-Line Repairer, Tele-Grout (sanitary ser.)	RCE	57	851.262-010
Sewer-Pipe Cleaner (business ser.)	REI	45	899.664-014
Sewing Machine Operator (leather prod.)	REC	44	783.682-014
Sewing Machine Operator I (tex. prod., n.e.c.)	CRS	46	787.682-066
Sewing Supervisor (any industry)	ERS	58	787.132-010
Sewing-Machine Assembler (machinery mfg.)	RES	52	706.381-034
Sewing-Machine Operator (any industry)	RCE	45	787.682-046
Sewing-Machine Operator (furniture)	RCE	43	780.682-010
Sewing-Machine Operator (knitting)	CRS	41	787.682-074
Sewing-Machine Operator (knitting; protective dev.)	CRE	41	787.682-050
Sewing-Machine Operator (toy-sport equip.)	RCE	39	787.682-054
Sewing-Machine Operator II (tex. prod., n.e.c.)	RCE	47	787.682-058
Sewing-Machine Operator, Paper Bags (paper goods)	RCI	41	787.685-054
Sewing-Machine Operator, Semiautomatic (garment)	CRE	41	786.685-030
Sewing-Machine Operator, Special Equipment (furniture)	CRE	41	689.685-118
Sewing-Machine Operator, Zipper (button & notion)	REC	40	787.685-034
Sewing-Machine Repairer (any industry)	RES	57	639.281-018
Sewing-Machine Tester (machinery mfg.)	RCI	51	709.382-010
Sewing-Machine-Repairer Helper (any industry)	RCE	44	639.684-010
Sexton (nonprofit org.)	RES	41	389.667-010
Shackler (meat products)	REC	37	525.687-086
Shactor Helper (meat products)	RES	37	525.687-090
Shade Matcher (textile)	CRE	44	582.687-022
Shade-Cloth Finisher (furniture)	CRS	41	585.687-026
Shadowgraph-Scale Operator (ordnance)	CRE	41	737.687-126
Shaft Mechanic (mine & quarry)	RES	46	899.684-034
Shake Backboard Notcher (saw. & plan.)	REC	40	663.685-030
Shake Sawyer (saw. & plan.)	RES	46	667.682-070
Shaker (hat & cap)	REC	39	589.685-094
Shaker (knitting)	RCE	40	589.687-058
Shaker (tobacco)	REC	35	521.687-110
Shaker Repairer (grain-feed mills)	REC	40	769.664-010

Part 3: From Occupational Titles to Holland Codes

From the Dictionary of Occupational Titles Occupations to Holland Codes

Title	HOC	Cx	DOT
Shaker Tender (concrete prod.; mine & quarry)	RCE	42	934.685-018
Shaker Tender (steel & rel.)	REC	42	541.665-010
Shaker Washer (grain-feed mills)	REI	38	521.687-114
Shaker, Wearing Apparel (laundry & rel.)	REC	37	361.687-026
Shaker-Plate Operator (ordnance)	RCE	41	737.685-014
Shale Planer Operator (mine & quarry)	REI	49	930.663-010
Shale Planer Operator Helper (mine & quarry)	REC	38	930.667-010
Shank Inspector (boot & shoe)	CRE	40	788.687-110
Shank Taper (boot & shoe)	RCE	35	788.687-114
Shank Threader (fabrication, n.e.c.)	CRS	40	739.685-034
Shank-Piece Tacker (boot & shoe)	REC	37	788.687-118
Shaper and Presser (garment)	CRE	40	583.685-102
Shaper Operator (woodworking)	RIE	47	665.682-034
Shaper Set-up Operator, Tool (machine shop)	RIE	57	605.382-038
Shaper, Baseball Glove (toy-sport equip.)	RES	38	732.684-106
Shaper, Hand (furniture)	RCE	43	761.684-038
Shaping Machine Tender (furniture)	RCI	43	665.685-046
Shaping-Machine Operator (plastic prod.)	REC	39	690.685-354
Shaver (laundry & rel.)	RES	35	362.687-018
Shaver (meat products)	REC	37	525.687-094
Shaving-Machine Operator (leather mfg.)	RCE	42	585.685-094
Shear Operator I (any industry)	RCS	47	615.682-018
Shear Operator II (any industry)	REC	45	615.685-034
Shear Setter (any industry)	RIE	56	615.380-010
Shear-Grinder Operator (textile)	REI	53	628.382-014
Shear-Grinder-Operator Helper (textile)	RES	40	628.687-014
Shearer and Trimmer, Wire Screen and Fabric (metal prod., n.e.c.)	RCE	42	709.684-074
Shearing-Machine Feeder (leather mfg.)	RCE	42	585.685-098
Shearing-Machine Operator (carpet & rug; textile)	RCE	41	585.685-102
Sheep Herder (agriculture)	RES	39	410.687-022
Sheep Shearer (agriculture)	RSE	39	410.684-014
Sheepskin Pickler (meat products)	REC	41	582.685-126
Sheet Turner (millwork-plywood)	REC	37	762.687-062
Sheet Writer (amuse. & rec.)	CER	50	211.467-026
Sheet-Metal Worker (any industry)	REI	59	804.281-010
Sheet-Metal-Pattern Cutter (musical inst.)	CRE	42	730.684-074
Sheet-Metal-Worker Apprentice (any industry)	REI	59	804.281-014
Sheet-Mill Supervisor (nonfer. metal)	RES	55	619.132-014
Sheeter Operator (plastic-synth.)	RCS	50	690.382-010
Sheetrock Applicator (mfd. bldgs.)	CRE	41	869.684-050
Shell Assembler (ordnance)	REC	45	737.684-038
Shell Molder (foundry)	RCS	41	518.685-026
Shell-Grader (button & notion)	RCE	45	734.687-070
Shell-Machine Operator (chemical)	RIE	47	649.682-030
Shell-Mold-Bonding-Machine Operator (foundry)	RCE	40	518.685-030
Shell-Shop Supervisor (ordnance)	RES	58	619.132-018
Shell-Sieve Operator (ordnance)	RES	39	694.585-010
Shellacker (ordnance)	REC	39	737.687-130

Title	HOC	Cx	DOT
Sheller I (can. & preserv.)	RCE	36	521.687-118
Sheller II (can. & preserv.)	REI	39	521.685-294
Shellfish Dredge Operator (fishing & hunt.)	REI	47	446.663-010
Shellfish Grower (fishing & hunt.)	REI	53	446.161-014
Shellfish Shucker (can. & preserv.)	RCE	39	521.687-122
Shellfish-Bed Worker (fishing & hunt.)	REI	41	446.684-014
Shellfish-Processing-Machine Tender (can. & preserv.)	REC	40	529.685-214
Shelving Supervisor (library)	SEC	56	109.137-010
Sheriff, Deputy (government ser.)	SER	53	377.263-010
Shield Runner (construction)	RES	45	850.682-010
Shift Superintendent, Caustic Cresylate (chemical)	ESR	59	552.132-010
Shift Supervisor, Film Processing (print. & pub.)	ERS	59	979.132-010
Shingle Packer (saw. & plan.)	RES	38	920.687-158
Shingle Sawyer (saw. & plan.)	RCS	44	667.485-010
Shingle Trimmer (saw. & plan.)	REC	44	667.685-050
Ship Runner (water trans.)	RCE	51	222.567-014
Shipfitter (ship-boat mfg.)	RIE	57	806.381-046
Shipfitter Apprentice (ship-boat mfg.)	RIE	57	806.381-050
Shipfitter Helper (ship-boat mfg.)	REC	40	806.687-050
Shipping and Receiving Clerk (clerical)	REI	54	222.387-050
Shipping Checker (clerical)	REI	51	222.687-030
Shipping-and-Receiving Supervisor (clerical)	SEC	59	222.137-030
Shipping-and-Receiving Weigher (clerical)	CRE	47	222.387-074
Shipping-Order Clerk (clerical)	CES	53	219.367-030
Shipwright (ship-boat mfg.)	RES	59	860.381-058
Shipwright Apprentice (ship-boat mfg.)	RES	59	860.381-062
Shipwright Helper (ship-boat mfg.)	RSC	41	860.664-018
Shirring-Machine Operator (any industry)	CRS	43	787.682-078
Shirring-Machine Operator, Automatic (tex. prod., n.e.c.)	REC	41	787.685-038
Shirt Presser (laundry & rel.)	REC	38	363.685-026
Shirt-Folding-Machine Operator (garment; laundry & rel.)	RCE	39	369.685-030
Shoe Cleaner (boot & shoe)	RCS	38	788.687-122
Shoe Coverer (boot & shoe)	REC	39	788.687-126
Shoe Dyer (personal ser.)	CSE	42	364.684-014
Shoe Packer (boot & shoe)	RCE	40	920.687-166
Shoe Repairer (personal ser.)	RSE	50	365.361-014
Shoe Shiner (personal ser.)	CRE	37	366.677-010
Shoe Turner (boot & shoe)	REC	38	788.687-130
Shoe-Lay-Out Planner (boot & shoe)	RIE	64	012.187-014
Shoe-Repair Supervisor (personal ser.)	RES	51	365.131-010
Shoe-Repairer Helper (personal ser.)	RES	42	365.674-010
Shoelace-Tipping-Machine Operator (narrow fabrics)	RCS	40	686.685-062
Shoemaker, Custom (boot & shoe)	RIE	57	788.381-014
Shooter (petrol. & gas)	RES	52	931.361-014
Shooter, Seismograph (petrol. & gas)	RSE	53	931.361-018
Shop Estimator (automotive ser.)	RES	57	807.267-010
Shop Supervisor (struct. metal)	RES	59	619.131-014
Shop Tailor (garment; retail trade)	RIE	57	785.361-022
Shop Tailor Apprentice (garment; retail trade)	RIE	57	785.361-026

Dictionary of Holland Occupational Codes

Part 3: From Occupational Titles to Holland Codes

From the Dictionary of Occupational Titles Occupations to Holland Codes

Title	HOC	Cx	DOT
Shopping Investigator (business ser.)	ESC	54	376.267-022
Shore Hand, Dredge or Barge (construction; mine & quarry)	RES	40	939.667-018
Shorthand Reporter (clerical)	CSE	56	202.362-010
Shot Bagger (ordnance)	REC	40	920.687-170
Shot Dropper (ordnance)	REI	54	502.362-010
Shot Polisher and Inspector (ordnance)	RCE	44	509.485-014
Shot-Coat Tender (concrete prod.)	REC	38	575.665-018
Shot-Grinder Operator (ordnance)	RCE	41	603.685-074
Shot-Peening Operator (aircraft mfg.)	RIE	59	617.280-010
Shot-Tube-Machine Tender (paper goods)	RCE	40	649.685-106
Shotblast-Equipment Operator (foundry)	RCI	52	503.362-014
Shotgun-Shell-Assembly-Machine Adjuster (ordnance)	RCE	52	616.360-030
Shotgun-Shell-Assembly-Machine Operator (ordnance)	RCS	44	694.385-010
Shotgun-Shell-Loading-Machine Operator (ordnance)	CRE	45	694.665-010
Shotgun-Shell-Reprinting-Unit Operator (ordnance)	CRE	41	659.685-018
Shoulder Joiner, Lockstitch (garment)	RCE	41	786.682-222
Show Girl (amuse. & rec.)	CSE	38	159.647-022
Show Host/Hostess (radio-tv broad.)	SER	65	159.147-018
Show-Horse Driver (amuse. & rec.)	ESA	51	159.344-018
Shredded-Filler Hopper-Feeder (tobacco)	RES	37	529.687-182
Shredder Operator (plastic-synth.)	RCE	42	555.685-058
Shredder Tender (chemical)	REI	38	555.665-010
Shredder Tender, Peat (agriculture)	RCE	42	599.685-086
Shredding-Floor-Equipment Operator (plastic-synth.)	RES	49	559.382-050
Shrimp-Peeling-Machine Operator (can. & preserv.)	REC	46	521.682-038
Shrink-Pit Operator (ordnance)	RSE	47	619.662-010
Shrink-Pit Supervisor (ordnance)	RES	60	619.131-018
Shrinking-Machine Operator (hat & cap)	REC	42	586.685-034
Shrouder (meat products)	REC	39	525.587-010
Shuttle Fixer (textile)	CRS	45	628.684-026
Shuttle Hand (textile)	REC	38	689.686-038
Shuttle Inspector (woodworking)	REC	47	769.684-046
Shuttle Spotter (woodworking)	RES	38	664.685-026
Shuttle-Car Operator (mine & quarry)	RIE	47	932.683-022
Shuttler (tex. prod., n.e.c.)	RCE	38	689.687-070
Side Laster, Cement (boot & shoe)	RCE	41	690.685-358
Side Laster, Staple (boot & shoe)	RCE	42	690.685-362
Sider (construction; mfd. bldgs.; retail trade)	RCE	48	863.684-014
Sider (mfd. bldgs.)	RSC	45	860.684-014
Siderographer (print. & pub.)	RIS	56	979.381-030
Siding Stapler (millwork-plywood)	RCS	42	762.684-058
Sieve Maker (grain-feed mills)	REC	40	529.684-018
Sieve-Grader Tender (can. & preserv.)	REC	38	521.665-026
Sifter (pharmaceut.)	CRE	40	551.687-030
Sight Mounter (ordnance)	REC	51	736.481-010
Sight-Effects Specialist (amuse. & rec.)	AES	59	962.267-010
Sign Erector I (fabrication, n.e.c.)	RIE	54	869.381-026
Sign Erector II (fabrication, n.e.c.)	RCE	46	869.684-054

Part 3: From Occupational Titles to Holland Codes

From the Dictionary of Occupational Titles Occupations to Holland Codes

Title	HOC	Cx	DOT
Sign Erector-and-Repairer (fabrication, n.e.c.)	RSE	50	869.361-018
Sign Writer, Hand (any industry)	SCA	55	970.281-022
Sign Writer, Machine (any industry)	RIC	47	659.682-026
Signal Maintainer (r.r. trans.)	RIE	58	822.281-026
Signal Maintainer Helper (r.r. trans.)	RCE	43	822.684-018
Signal Supervisor (r.r. trans.)	ERS	62	822.131-026
Signaler (construction)	RES	41	869.667-014
Silhouette Artist (amuse. & rec.)	AES	58	149.051-010
Silica-Filter Operator (beverage)	RES	43	521.582-010
Silica-Spray Mixer (smelt. & refin.)	RCS	41	570.685-090
Silk Finisher (laundry & rel.)	REC	45	363.681-010
Silk Spreader (textile)	RCE	41	680.685-090
Silk-Screen Cutter (any industry)	REC	48	979.681-022
Silk-Screen Etcher (engraving)	CRE	41	704.684-014
Silk-Screen Printer, Machine (any industry)	RCS	42	979.685-010
Silk-Screen Repairer (any industry)	RSE	45	979.684-038
Silk-Screen-Frame Assembler (any industry)	CRE	45	709.484-010
Silo Operator (tobacco)	REI	48	529.682-030
Silo Tender (cement)	RCE	42	579.685-050
Silver Spray Worker (recording)	REI	45	500.684-022
Silver Stripper, Machine (glass products)	REC	41	579.685-054
Silver Wrapper (hotel & rest.)	RCE	39	318.687-018
Silver-Solution Mixer (chemical)	REI	48	550.684-026
Silverer (glass products)	RSC	44	574.684-014
Silvering Applicator (glass products)	RIE	48	574.582-010
Silversmith II (jewelry-silver.)	RSC	53	700.281-022
Silverware Assembler (jewelry-silver.)	RCE	40	700.684-070
Silviculturist (profess. & kin.)	IRE	74	040.061-050
Singe Winder (textile)	RCE	41	681.585-018
Singer (amuse. & rec.; motion picture; radio-tv broad.)	AES	65	152.047-022
Singer (hat & cap)	REC	38	784.687-062
Singer (meat products)	REC	40	525.687-098
Singer (narrow fabrics)	REC	39	585.687-030
Singer (textile)	RIE	42	585.685-106
Singing Messenger (business ser.)	ASC	48	230.647-010
Sink Cutter (stonework)	REI	44	677.682-018
Sinker Winder (toy-sport equip.)	RCE	40	732.685-030
Sinter Feeder (steel & rel.)	REC	47	513.685-010
Sinter-Machine Operator (smelt. & refin.; steel & rel.)	RCS	45	510.685-026
Sintering-Press Operator (nonfer. metal; steel & rel.)	RCE	44	617.685-038
Siphon Operator (medical ser.; pharmaceut.)	RCE	40	599.687-026
Size Maker (paper & pulp)	REI	47	550.682-010
Sizer (knitting)	CRS	45	684.684-014
Sizer (textile)	RES	41	582.687-026
Sizer, Hand (hat & cap)	REC	41	784.684-054
Sizer, Machine (hat & cap)	REC	40	784.684-058
Sizer, Machine (optical goods)	RES	54	716.360-010
Sizing-Machine Operator (nonmet. min.)	CRE	41	554.685-026
Sizing-Machine Operator (ordnance)	REI	45	649.582-014

Part 3: From Occupational Titles to Holland Codes
From the Dictionary of Occupational Titles Occupations to Holland Codes

Title	HOC	Cx	DOT
Sizing-Machine Tender (clock & watch)	CES	40	690.685-366
Sizing-Machine Tender (pen & pencil)	RES	38	662.685-030
Sizing-Machine Tender (textile)	RCE	45	584.665-018
Sizing-Machine-and-Drier Operator (tex. prod., n.e.c.)	RSC	44	582.665-026
Skate-Shop Attendant (amuse. & rec.)	CES	49	341.464-010
Skein Winder (elec. equip.)	RCE	50	721.484-022
Skein Winder (textile)	REC	39	681.685-098
Skein-Winding Operator (any industry)	CRE	38	559.687-054
Skein-Yarn Drier (textile)	REC	39	581.685-054
Skein-Yarn Dyer (textile)	REC	42	582.685-130
Skein-Yarn-Dyer Helper (textile)	RES	40	582.686-022
Skeiner (narrow fabrics)	REC	40	681.685-102
Skelp Processor (steel & rel.)	RCI	50	619.662-014
Sketch Maker I (print. & pub.)	REC	46	979.381-034
Sketch Maker II (print. & pub.)	REI	55	972.381-018
Sketch Maker, Photoengraving (print. & pub.)	ARI	60	970.281-026
Ski Base Trimmer (toy-sport equip.)	RCE	40	732.684-110
Ski Maker, Wood (toy-sport equip.)	RES	50	761.381-026
Ski Molder (toy-sport equip.)	RES	43	732.684-114
Ski Patroller (amuse. & rec.)	ERS	51	379.664-010
Ski Repairer, Production (toy-sport equip.)	RSE	42	732.684-118
Ski Topper (toy-sport equip.)	RCE	40	692.685-170
Ski-Binding Fitter-and-Repairer (toy-sport equip.)	RCI	56	732.364-014
Ski-Top Trimmer (plastic prod.)	RIE	40	690.685-370
Ski-Tow Operator (amuse. & rec.)	CER	49	341.665-010
Skiff Operator (fishing & hunt.)	REI	45	441.683-010
Skimmer, Reverberatory (smelt. & refin.)	RCS	41	511.687-022
Skin Former (rubber goods)	RCE	41	752.684-050
Skin Grader (meat products)	RCE	41	525.687-102
Skin Lifter, Bacon (meat products)	REC	38	521.687-126
Skin-Lap Bonder (aircraft mfg.)	REC	49	806.684-130
Skin-Peeling-Machine Operator (meat products)	RCE	40	525.685-030
Skinner (meat products)	RCE	39	525.684-046
Skinning-Machine Feeder (meat products)	RES	38	525.686-022
Skip Operator (steel & rel.)	RCE	45	921.683-062
Skip Tracer (clerical)	SEC	54	241.367-026
Skirt Panel Assembler (furniture)	RCE	41	780.687-070
Skiver (leather prod.)	RCE	42	690.685-374
Skiver, Blockers (boot & shoe)	RCE	41	585.685-110
Skiver, Machine (boot & shoe; rubber goods)	CRE	42	690.685-378
Skiving-Machine Operator (ordnance)	REI	41	664.682-018
Skull Grinder (meat products)	REC	39	521.687-130
Slab Grinder (stonework)	RCE	45	673.682-030
Slab-Conditioner Supervisor (nonfer. metal)	RES	56	609.132-010
Slab-Depiler Operator (steel & rel.)	RIE	47	504.665-010
Slabber (soap & rel.)	RCE	37	559.686-042
Slasher (plastic-synth.)	RCE	42	690.665-010
Slasher Operator (paper & pulp; saw. & plan.)	RCE	38	667.685-054
Slasher Tender (textile)	RES	50	582.562-010

Title	HOC	Cx	DOT
Slasher-Tender Helper (textile)	RES	41	582.686-026
Slat Twister (furniture)	REC	37	616.685-066
Slat-Basket Maker Helper, Machine (wood. container)	REC	37	669.686-026
Slat-Basket Maker, Machine (wood. container)	RCE	38	669.685-074
Slate Mixer (build. mat., n.e.c.)	CRE	40	570.685-094
Slaughterer, Religious Ritual (meat products)	RES	49	525.361-010
Sleeve Maker, Lockstitch (garment)	CRE	40	786.682-226
Sleeve Setter, Lockstitch (garment)	RCE	41	786.682-230
Sleeve Setter, Overlock (garment)	RCE	41	786.682-234
Sleever (paper goods)	REC	35	641.686-034
Slice-Plug-Cutter Operator (tobacco)	RCE	38	521.685-298
Slice-Plug-Cutter-Operator Helper (tobacco)	RCE	37	521.686-054
Slicing-Machine Operator (bakery products)	RCE	40	521.685-302
Slicing-Machine Operator (button & notion)	RCE	40	692.685-174
Slicing-Machine Operator (dairy products; meat products)	RCE	40	521.685-306
Slicing-Machine Tender (furniture)	REC	41	663.685-034
Slicing-Machine Tender (wood prod., n.e.c.)	REC	38	663.686-026
Slicker (hat & cap)	CRE	41	784.684-062
Slide-Fastener Repairer (button & notion)	CRE	42	734.684-022
Slide-Fastener-Chain Assembler (button & notion)	CRE	40	734.687-074
Slide-Machine Tender (fabrication, n.e.c.)	REC	40	641.685-078
Slider Assembler (button & notion; garment)	RCE	39	734.687-078
Sliding-Joint Maker (musical inst.)	REC	46	730.684-078
Slime-Plant Operator I (smelt. & refin.)	RES	47	510.685-030
Slime-Plant Operator II (smelt. & refin.)	REC	45	511.685-054
Slime-Plant-Operator Helper (smelt. & refin.)	REC	42	511.685-058
Slinger, Sequins (plastic prod.)	RCE	41	692.685-178
Slip Laster (boot & shoe)	CRE	38	788.684-106
Slip-Cover Sewer (tex. prod., n.e.c.)	CRS	44	780.682-014
Slip-Seat Coverer (furniture)	RCE	41	780.684-094
Slipcover Cutter (retail trade; tex. prod., n.e.c.)	RES	54	780.381-034
Slitter (knitting)	CRS	40	781.684-054
Slitter Service and Setter (tinware)	RSI	56	615.280-010
Slitter-Creaser-Slotter Helper (paper goods)	RES	38	649.686-030
Slitter-Creaser-Slotter Operator (paper goods)	RES	45	649.682-034
Slitter-Scorer-Cut-Off Operator (paper goods)	RIS	47	649.682-038
Slitting-Machine Operator I (any industry)	RSI	48	699.682-030
Slitting-Machine Operator II (any industry)	RSE	51	615.662-010
Slitting-Machine-Operator Helper I (any industry)	RSC	41	699.587-010
Sliver-Lap-Machine Tender (textile)	RES	40	680.685-094
Slot Router (furniture)	RSE	42	763.684-066
Slot-Tag Inserter (clerical)	RCE	43	222.567-018
Slotter Operator (paper goods)	RCS	42	640.685-078
Slotter-Operator Helper (paper goods)	REC	37	640.686-014
Slubber Tender (textile)	RCE	42	680.685-098
Slug-Press Operator (elec. equip.)	REC	40	556.685-074
Slunk-Skin Curer (meat products)	RES	38	525.687-106
Slurry Mixer (ordnance)	REI	50	539.362-018
Slurry-Control Tender (smelt. & refin.)	REI	50	510.465-014

DOT to HOC

Part 3: From Occupational Titles to Holland Codes

From the Dictionary of Occupational Titles Occupations to Holland Codes

Title	HOC	Cx	DOT
Small-Engine Mechanic (any industry)	REC	54	625.281-034
Smash Hand (narrow fabrics; textile)	CRS	45	683.684-026
Smoke and Flame Specialist (military ser.)	RES	47	378.682-014
Smoke Jumper (forestry)	REI	52	452.364-014
Smoke Jumper Supervisor (forestry)	RES	55	452.134-010
Smoke Tester (smelt. & refin.)	RIC	58	012.281-010
Smoke-Room Operator (hat & cap)	RES	37	784.687-066
Smoked Meat Preparer (meat products)	RES	38	525.587-014
Smoker (meat products)	RES	46	525.682-010
Smoking-Pipe Driller and Threader (fabrication, n.e.c.)	RCE	38	669.685-078
Smoking-Pipe Liner (fabrication, n.e.c.)	RCE	37	739.687-170
Smoking-Pipe Maker (fabrication, n.e.c.)	RIE	55	761.381-030
Smoking-Pipe Repairer (any industry)	REC	52	739.484-018
Smoking-Tobacco-Cutter Operator (tobacco)	RCE	38	521.685-310
Smoother (hat & cap)	RCS	35	784.684-066
Smoother (pen & pencil)	CRE	40	733.685-026
Snag Grinder (foundry)	REI	42	705.684-074
Snailer (clock & watch)	RCE	38	603.685-078
Snow Shoveler (government ser.)	REC	36	955.687-014
Snow-Removing Supervisor (government ser.)	REI	58	955.137-010
Snowmaker (amuse. & rec.)	RCS	38	969.685-010
Snuff Grinder and Screener (tobacco)	RCE	40	521.685-314
Snuff-Box Finisher (tobacco)	REC	40	920.687-174
Snuff-Container Inspector (tobacco)	RCS	44	920.667-014
Snuff-Packing-Machine Operator (tobacco)	RCE	38	920.685-094
Soaker, Hides (meat products)	REI	41	582.685-134
Soap Chipper (soap & rel.)	RES	37	555.686-014
Soap Grinder (soap & rel.)	RES	38	555.685-062
Soap Inspector (soap & rel.)	RCE	40	559.687-058
Soap Maker (soap & rel.)	REI	53	559.382-054
Soap-Drier Operator (soap & rel.)	CRE	40	553.685-098
Soaping-Department Supervisor (textile)	RES	56	582.132-014
Social Group Worker (social ser.)	SEA	66	195.107-022
Social Secretary (clerical)	CES	62	201.162-010
Social Worker, Delinquency Prevention (social ser.)	SEA	66	195.107-026
Social Worker, Medical (profess. & kin.)	ESA	66	195.107-030
Social Worker, Psychiatric (profess. & kin.)	SEA	66	195.107-034
Social Worker, School (profess. & kin.)	SEC	66	195.107-038
Social-Services Aide (social ser.)	SCE	58	195.367-034
Sociologist (profess. & kin.)	IES	73	054.067-014
Sock Boarder (knitting)	RCE	40	589.686-042
Socket Puller (musical inst.)	RCE	44	730.682-010
Soda Dialyzer (plastic-synth.)	RCE	45	551.685-134
Soda-Column Operator (chemical)	RIE	50	558.382-054
Soda-Room Operator (beverage)	REI	45	559.682-046
Soda-Room Operator (plastic-synth.)	REC	37	551.687-034
Soft Crab Shedder (fishing & hunt.)	REC	41	446.684-018
Soft-Sugar Operator, Head (sugar & conf.)	RES	50	521.565-018
Soft-Tile Setter (construction; retail trade)	RES	53	861.381-034

From the Dictionary of Occupational Titles Occupations to Holland Codes

Title	HOC	Cx	DOT
Softball Core Molder (toy-sport equip.)	RES	40	732.687-070
Software Engineer (profess. & kin.)	IRE	75	030.062-010
Soil Conservationist (profess. & kin.)	IRE	78	040.061-054
Soil Scientist (profess. & kin.)	IRS	78	040.061-058
Soil-Conservation Technician (profess. & kin.)	IRC	67	040.261-010
Solar-Energy-System Installer (any industry)	RCI	59	637.261-030
Solar-Energy-System-Installer Helper (any industry)	RCI	45	637.687-018
Solar-Energy-Systems Designer (profess. & kin.)	RIC	66	007.161-038
Solar-Fabrication Technician (machine shop)	RCI	51	809.381-034
Solder Deposit Operator (electron. comp.)	RCI	42	726.684-094
Solder-Leveler, Printed Circuit Boards (electron. comp.)	RCE	45	726.685-050
Solderer (clock & watch)	CRE	38	715.685-058
Solderer (jewelry-silver.)	RSE	50	700.381-050
Solderer, Barrel Ribs (ordnance)	REC	41	736.684-038
Solderer, Production Line (welding)	CRS	42	813.684-022
Solderer, Torch I (welding)	RCE	44	813.684-026
Solderer, Ultrasonic, Hand (welding)	CRS	43	813.684-030
Solderer-Assembler (welding)	RIE	49	813.684-014
Solderer-Dipper (welding)	CRS	42	813.684-018
Sole Leveler, Machine (boot & shoe)	CRE	41	690.685-382
Sole Scraper (boot & shoe)	RES	35	788.687-134
Sole Sewer, Hand (boot & shoe)	RCE	48	788.684-110
Sole-Conforming-Machine Operator (boot & shoe)	RCS	45	690.682-070
Solutions Operator (plastic-synth.)	REI	53	550.382-034
Song Plugger (recording)	ESA	59	165.157-010
Sorter (boot & shoe)	RCE	41	753.587-010
Sorter (brick & tile)	RES	42	573.687-034
Sorter (button & notion)	RCE	40	734.687-082
Sorter (clerical)	CES	42	209.687-022
Sorter (jewelry-silver.)	RCE	43	735.687-030
Sorter (office machines)	CSE	44	706.587-014
Sorter I (wood prod., n.e.c.)	RCE	37	569.687-022
Sorter II (wood prod., n.e.c.)	CRE	39	769.687-042
Sorter Operator (saw. & plan.)	RES	43	921.685-054
Sorter, Agricultural Produce (agriculture; can. & preserv.; wholesale tr.)	REC	39	529.687-186
Sorter, Machine (button & notion)	RCE	40	692.685-182
Sorter, Upholstery Parts (furniture)	CRS	42	780.587-010
Sorter-Pricer (nonprofit org.)	RES	53	222.387-054
Sorting Supervisor (brick & tile)	RES	55	920.137-014
Sorting-Grapple Operator (logging)	RES	48	921.683-066
Sorting-Machine Operator (can. & preserv.)	RES	40	521.685-318
Sorting-Machine Operator (paper goods)	ECR	40	649.665-010
Sound Controller (amuse. & rec.)	RCE	63	194.262-014
Sound Cutter (motion picture)	CRS	56	962.382-014
Sound Mixer (motion picture; radio-tv broad.; recording)	RCS	63	194.262-018
Sound Ranging Crewmember (military ser.)	REC	55	378.362-010
Sound Technician (any industry)	RIE	54	829.281-022
Sound-Effects Technician (radio-tv broad.)	RAE	57	962.281-014

Title	HOC	Cx	DOT
Sounder (any industry)	RSC	45	911.667-018
Sous Chef (hotel & rest.)	RSE	59	313.131-026
Sous Chef (water trans.)	ESA	60	315.137-014
Souvenir and Novelty Maker (metal prod., n.e.c.)	RES	53	739.381-050
Space Scheduler (clerical)	CSE	54	238.367-022
Space-and-Storage Clerk (ordnance)	CRE	51	219.387-026
Spaghetti-Machine Operator (plastic prod.)	RCS	48	690.682-074
Spanner (tex. prod., n.e.c.)	RCE	37	689.687-074
Spar-Machine Operator (wood prod., n.e.c.)	RES	47	664.682-022
Spar-Machine-Operator Helper (wood prod., n.e.c.)	RES	43	664.685-030
Spark Tester (elec. equip.)	CRE	42	727.687-078
Spark Tester (elec. equip.; nonfer. metal)	CRE	44	728.684-018
Spark-Plug Assembler (elec. equip.)	REC	40	729.684-046
Special Agent (government ser.)	ERI	70	375.167-042
Special Agent (insurance)	ESC	66	166.167-046
Special Agent (r.r. trans.)	ESA	61	372.267-010
Special Agent, Customs (government ser.)	SRI	66	188.167-090
Special Agent, Group Insurance (insurance)	ESC	66	169.167-050
Special Agent-in-Charge (r.r. trans.)	ESC	63	376.167-010
Special Effects Specialist (amuse. & rec.; motion picture; radio-tv broad.)	RIE	57	962.281-018
Special Procedures Technologist, Angiogram (medical ser.)	IRC	64	078.362-046
Special Procedures Technologist, Cardiac Catheterization (medical ser.)	RIC	66	078.362-050
Special Procedures Technologist, CT Scan (medical ser.)	IRC	66	078.362-054
Special Procedures Technologist, Magnetic Resonance Imaging (MRI) (medical ser.)	RIC	66	078.362-058
Special Tester (tobacco)	REC	53	529.487-010
Special-Certificate Dictator (insurance)	CRE	54	209.382-014
Specialist-in-Charge, Extension Service (government ser.)	ESA	66	096.167-014
Specialties Operator (chemical)	REI	53	559.582-014
Specification Writer (profess. & kin.)	IER	67	019.267-010
Spectroscopist (profess. & kin.)	RIE	64	011.281-014
Speech Pathologist (profess. & kin.)	SAI	68	076.107-010
Speed Operator (steel & rel.)	RSE	53	613.362-022
Speed-Belt-Sander Tender (woodworking)	REC	40	662.685-034
Speeder Tender (textile)	REC	40	681.685-106
Spice Cleaner (food prep., n.e.c.)	REI	40	521.685-322
Spice Fumigator (food prep., n.e.c.)	RCS	45	529.685-218
Spice Miller (food prep., n.e.c.)	REC	41	521.685-326
Spice Mixer (can. & preserv.)	CRE	48	520.687-062
Spice Mixer (food prep., n.e.c.)	RSE	41	520.585-026
Spider Assembler (elec. equip.)	RSI	51	721.684-026
Spike-Machine Feeder (steel & rel.)	RCE	40	612.666-010
Spike-Machine Heater (steel & rel.)	RES	37	619.686-026
Spike-Machine Operator (steel & rel.)	RSC	49	612.662-010
Spikemaking Supervisor (steel & rel.)	RSE	54	612.130-010
Spin-Table Operator (toy-sport equip.)	RES	39	732.687-074
Spindle Carver (woodworking)	RES	47	761.682-018

DOT to HOC

Part 3: From Occupational Titles to Holland Codes

From the Dictionary of Occupational Titles Occupations to Holland Codes

Title	HOC	Cx	DOT
Spindle Plumber (textile)	RCS	47	628.684-030
Spindle Repairer (textile)	RCI	38	628.684-042
Spinner (jewelry-silver.)	REC	47	700.684-074
Spinner (plastic-synth.)	RCE	41	557.685-026
Spinner (sugar & conf.)	RSC	48	520.682-030
Spinner, Frame (nonmet. min.; textile)	CRE	42	682.685-010
Spinner, Hand (any industry)	RIE	57	619.362-018
Spinner, Hydraulic (any industry)	RIE	57	619.362-022
Spinner, Mule (nonmet. min.; textile)	RCE	43	682.685-014
Spinning-Bath Patroller (plastic-synth.)	CRE	42	557.685-030
Spinning-Lathe Operator, Automatic (any industry)	REC	40	619.685-082
Spinning-Machine Tender (tex. prod., n.e.c.)	REI	38	681.685-110
Spiral Binder (paper goods; print. & pub.)	RCE	39	653.685-030
Spiral Runner (mine & quarry)	REC	43	934.685-022
Spiral Spring Winder (metal prod., n.e.c.)	RCE	41	616.685-070
Spiral Weaver (metal prod., n.e.c.)	RCE	43	616.685-074
Spiral-Machine Operator (paper goods)	RCE	39	692.685-186
Spiral-Tube Winder (paper goods)	REI	47	640.682-022
Spiral-Tube-Winder Helper (paper goods)	REC	38	640.687-014
Splash-Line Operator (fabrication, n.e.c.)	RES	44	559.665-034
Splicer (fabrication, n.e.c.)	REC	37	692.687-010
Splicer (photofinishing)	CRE	40	976.684-026
Splicer (protective dev.)	RCI	40	759.684-070
Splicer (rubber tire)	CRE	41	759.684-058
Splicer Operator (millwork-plywood)	RCE	41	569.685-062
Splicing-Machine Operator (tex. prod., n.e.c.)	REC	41	689.682-018
Splicing-Machine Operator, Automatic (tex. prod., n.e.c.)	RCE	42	689.685-122
Splitter Operator (stonework)	REI	40	677.685-042
Splitter Tender (saw. & plan.)	RIE	40	663.685-038
Splitter, Hand (button & notion)	REC	37	734.687-086
Splitter, Machine (boot & shoe; leather prod.)	RCE	40	585.685-114
Splitting-Machine Feeder (leather mfg.)	RCE	39	690.686-054
Splitting-Machine Operator (rubber goods; rubber reclaim.)	REC	41	690.685-386
Splitting-Machine Operator (stonework)	RCI	45	677.685-046
Splitting-Machine Tender (wood prod., n.e.c.)	RCE	42	663.685-042
Splitting-Machine-Operator Helper (stonework)	RES	37	677.666-010
Spoilage Worker (tinware)	CRS	43	709.587-014
Sponge Buffer (plastic prod.)	REI	41	690.685-390
Sponge Clipper (fishing & hunt.; wholesale tr.)	CRE	40	447.687-026
Sponge Hooker (fishing & hunt.)	REC	40	447.684-010
Sponge-Press Operator (rubber goods)	RES	47	559.682-050
Spool Maker (paper goods)	REC	35	641.685-082
Spool Winder (nonfer. metal)	RCE	41	619.485-010
Spooler Operator, Automatic (textile)	REC	40	681.686-018
Spooler, Sequins (plastic prod.)	REC	40	920.686-046
Spooling-Machine Operator (metal prod., n.e.c.; nonfer. metal)	REC	42	691.685-026
Spooling-Machine Operator (tex. prod., n.e.c.)	RCE	37	681.685-114
Sport-Shoe-Spike Assembler (boot & shoe)	RCE	42	690.685-394

Dictionary of Holland Occupational Codes

Part 3: From Occupational Titles to Holland Codes
From the Dictionary of Occupational Titles Occupations to Holland Codes

Title	HOC	Cx	DOT
Sports-Equipment Repairer (any industry)	CRS	47	732.684-122
Spot Cleaner (garment; knitting)	CRE	42	582.684-014
Spot Picker, Molded Goods (fabrication, n.e.c.)	RES	41	739.667-010
Spotter (glass mfg.)	RCE	41	772.687-014
Spotter (machine tools)	RES	53	770.381-042
Spotter I (laundry & rel.)	RCS	40	361.684-018
Spotter II (laundry & rel.)	RES	49	362.381-010
Spotter, Photographic (photofinishing)	CSE	48	970.381-034
Spout Tender I (chemical)	RES	41	932.664-014
Spout Tender II (chemical)	CSR	39	921.685-058
Spout Worker (smelt. & refin.)	REI	40	514.667-018
Spray-Drier Operator (brick & tile)	RES	47	573.382-014
Spray-Gun Repairer (any industry)	RES	54	630.381-026
Spray-Gun-Repairer Helper (any industry)	REC	42	630.684-034
Spray-Machine Loader (brick & tile; pottery & porc.)	RES	40	574.686-010
Spray-Machine Operator (brick & tile; pottery & porc.)	REI	43	574.682-014
Spray-Machine Operator (textile)	RCE	41	582.685-138
Spray-Machine Tender (tinware)	CRE	47	599.685-090
Spray-Painting-Machine Operator (any industry)	REI	40	741.685-010
Spray-Unit Feeder (any industry)	RCS	40	599.686-014
Sprayer Operator (smelt. & refin.)	RIC	46	505.682-010
Sprayer, Hand (agriculture)	RIE	47	408.684-014
Sprayer, Hand (leather mfg.)	CRE	39	584.687-014
Sprayer, Leather (laundry & rel.)	CSR	42	364.684-018
Sprayer, Machine (leather mfg.)	REC	41	599.685-094
Spreader (hat & cap)	REI	38	581.687-022
Spreader (plastic-synth.)	RES	37	554.687-010
Spreader I (any industry)	RES	38	781.687-058
Spreader Operator, Automatic (tobacco)	REC	37	529.685-222
Spreader, Machine (any industry)	REC	46	781.685-010
Spreading-Machine Operator (chemical)	CRE	41	559.685-170
Spring Assembler (furniture)	REC	40	780.684-098
Spring Assembler (metal prod., n.e.c.)	RES	41	706.684-090
Spring Clipper (furniture)	CRS	42	780.684-102
Spring Coiler (metal prod., n.e.c.)	RCE	42	616.485-014
Spring Coiling Machine Setter (metal prod., n.e.c.)	RIE	59	616.260-018
Spring Coverer (furniture)	RES	40	780.687-038
Spring Fitter (metal prod., n.e.c.)	REI	47	709.684-078
Spring Former, Hand (metal prod., n.e.c.)	RES	50	709.381-042
Spring Former, Machine (metal prod., n.e.c.)	REI	47	617.482-022
Spring Inspector I (metal prod., n.e.c.)	RSE	57	616.361-010
Spring Inspector II (metal prod., n.e.c.)	CRE	42	709.687-038
Spring Layer (clock & watch)	CRS	38	715.687-122
Spring Maker (metal prod., n.e.c.)	RIE	58	616.280-010
Spring Repairer, Hand (automotive ser.)	RES	57	619.380-018
Spring Salvage Worker (metal prod., n.e.c.)	RES	41	610.684-014
Spring Tester I (metal prod., n.e.c.)	RCS	45	612.685-014
Spring Tester II (metal prod., n.e.c.)	CRS	41	709.687-042
Spring-Manufacturing Set-up Technician (clock & watch)	RIE	60	619.280-018

Part 3: From Occupational Titles to Holland Codes

From the Dictionary of Occupational Titles Occupations to Holland Codes

Title	HOC	Cx	DOT
Spring-Repairer Helper, Hand (automotive ser.)	RES	43	620.584-010
Springer (furniture)	RCS	45	780.684-106
Sprinkler-Irrigation-Equipment Mechanic (agric. equip.)	REI	54	624.361-014
Spun-Paste-Machine Operator (elec. equip.)	RCE	41	692.685-190
Squaring-Machine Operator (clock & watch)	CRE	40	605.685-046
Squeak, Rattle, and Leak Repairer (automotive ser.)	RES	47	620.364-010
Squeegee Tender (rubber tire)	RES	41	750.685-010
Squeezer Operator (wood. container)	REI	41	669.685-082
Stab Setter and Driller (cutlery-hrdwr.)	CRE	43	709.684-082
Stable Attendant (any industry)	RIE	40	410.674-022
Stacker (leather prod.)	REC	42	222.587-046
Stacker Tender (millwork-plywood)	RCE	41	921.685-062
Stacker, Machine (woodworking)	REC	40	569.685-066
Stacker-and-Sorter Operator (saw. & plan.)	REC	41	921.682-018
Stacking-Machine Operator I (any industry)	RCS	48	692.682-054
Stacking-Machine Operator II (any industry)	RES	40	739.685-038
Staff Toxicologist (government ser.)	IRE	77	041.061-094
Stage Technician (amuse. & rec.)	ARS	61	962.261-014
Stager (print. & pub.)	RCE	46	971.684-014
Stain Applicator (wood prod., n.e.c.)	RCE	43	561.585-010
Stained Glass Artist (profess. & kin.)	ASE	66	142.061-054
Stainer (fabrication, n.e.c.)	RES	40	739.687-174
Stainer (furniture; wood prod., n.e.c.)	RCS	39	742.684-014
Stainer (leather prod.)	REC	40	589.687-034
Staining-Machine Operator (tex. prod., n.e.c.)	REC	42	582.685-142
Staker (clock & watch)	CRE	45	715.684-182
Staker, Machine (leather mfg.)	CRE	38	580.685-050
Stamp Analyst (retail trade)	ERS	54	299.387-014
Stamp Classifier (retail trade)	CER	54	299.387-018
Stamp Mounter (pen & pencil)	RCE	41	733.684-018
Stamp-Pad Finisher (pen & pencil)	RCE	36	733.687-066
Stamp-Pad Maker (pen & pencil)	RCE	38	733.687-070
Stamper (button & notion)	REC	38	734.685-010
Stamper (chemical)	RCE	38	556.685-078
Stamper I (tex. prod., n.e.c.)	CSR	38	781.687-062
Stamper II (tex. prod., n.e.c.)	RCE	40	652.685-082
Stamper, Machine (pottery & porc.)	RIE	44	652.682-022
Stamping-Machine Operator (boot & shoe)	RCE	42	690.685-398
Stamping-Machine Operator (pen & pencil)	RCE	38	692.685-194
Stamping-Mill Tender (smelt. & refin.)	RCE	41	515.685-018
Stamping-Press Operator (any industry)	RCE	41	652.682-030
Stand-In (motion picture; radio-tv broad.)	RSC	38	961.667-014
Standards Engineer (profess. & kin.)	RIE	76	012.061-018
Standpipe Tender (steel & rel.)	RCE	38	519.665-014
Staple Cutter (textile)	RCE	40	680.685-102
Staple-Processing-Machine Operator (textile)	RCS	42	680.585-014
Stapler, Hand (furniture)	RES	38	780.687-042
Stapler, Machine (furniture)	RCE	39	692.685-198
Stapling-Machine Operator (any industry)	REC	41	692.685-202

Title	HOC	Cx	DOT
Starch-Treating Assistant (grain-feed mills)	RCE	48	520.665-018
Starcher (button & notion)	RCE	37	739.687-178
Starchmaker (grain-feed mills)	REI	50	520.485-030
Starchmaker (sugar & conf.)	CRS	39	526.687-014
Starter (amuse. & rec.)	RSE	47	153.667-010
State-Highway Police Officer (government ser.)	RSE	55	375.263-018
Statement Clerk (financial)	CRS	53	214.362-046
Static Balancer (any industry)	REI	46	724.384-014
Station Agent I (r.r. trans.)	ESR	63	910.137-038
Station Engineer, Chief (pipe lines)	RES	62	914.132-014
Station Engineer, Main Line (pipe lines)	RCE	53	914.362-018
Station Installer-and-Repairer (tel. & tel.)	RCS	59	822.261-022
Station Manager (r.r. trans.)	ESC	62	184.167-130
Stationary Engineer (any industry)	REI	59	950.382-026
Stationary-Engineer Apprentice (any industry)	REI	59	950.382-030
Stationary-Engineer Supervisor (any industry)	RES	59	950.131-014
Stations-Relations-Contact Representative (radio-tv broad.)	ESC	67	184.167-134
Statistical Clerk (clerical)	CRS	54	216.382-062
Statistical Clerk, Advertising (retail trade)	CRS	51	216.382-066
Statistical-Machine Servicer (any industry)	RES	58	633.281-030
Statistician, Applied (profess. & kin.)	IRE	74	020.167-026
Statistician, Mathematical (profess. & kin.)	IRE	80	020.067-022
Stave Jointer (wood. container)	RES	41	665.685-030
Stave-Bolt Equalizer (saw. & plan.)	RCE	43	667.682-074
Stave-Log-Cut-Off Saw Operator (saw. & plan.)	RSC	46	667.682-078
Stave-Log-Ripsaw Operator (saw. & plan.)	REI	41	667.685-058
Stave-Machine Tender (wood. container)	RCE	40	663.685-046
Stave-Planer Tender (saw. & plan.)	REC	38	665.686-014
Stave-Saw Operator (wood. container)	REC	44	667.685-062
Steak Sauce Maker (can. & preserv.)	RES	47	529.484-010
Steak Tenderizer, Machine (meat products)	RCE	37	529.686-082
Steam Cleaner (automotive ser.)	RES	40	915.687-026
Steam Service Inspector (utilities)	REI	57	862.361-022
Steam-Box Operator (woodworking)	RCE	42	562.665-014
Steam-Cleaning-Machine Operator (construction)	RCE	41	891.685-010
Steam-Conditioner Operator (tobacco)	RSE	40	522.685-094
Steam-Distribution Supervisor (utilities)	RES	61	862.137-014
Steam-Drier Tender (carpet & rug)	RSC	48	581.685-058
Steam-Oven Operator (can. & preserv.)	REC	44	526.382-026
Steam-Press Tender (textile)	CRS	44	583.685-106
Steam-Press Tender I (rubber goods)	RES	41	553.665-046
Steam-Press Tender II (rubber goods)	RCE	41	553.665-050
Steam-Tank Operator (nonmet. min.)	RSE	44	573.683-010
Steam-Tunnel Feeder (saw. & plan.)	REC	36	562.686-010
Steamer (beverage)	RCE	40	529.685-226
Steamer (meat products)	REC	38	525.687-110
Steamer (tex. prod., n.e.c.)	RES	37	789.687-170
Steamer Tender (textile)	REC	41	582.685-146
Steamer-Blocker (hat & cap; knitting)	RES	38	784.684-070

Title	HOC	Cx	DOT
Steaming-Cabinet Tender (garment)	CRE	40	582.685-150
Steel Pourer (steel & rel.)	RSE	48	502.664-014
Steel-Barrel Reamer (wood. container)	RCE	37	703.687-022
Steel-Box-Toe Inserter (boot & shoe)	RCE	38	788.687-138
Steel-Die Printer (print. & pub.)	RSE	50	651.382-030
Steel-Pan-Form-Placing Supervisor (construction)	REC	59	869.131-026
Steel-Plate Caulker (any industry)	RES	40	843.684-010
Steel-Post Installer (utilities)	RES	41	821.687-010
Steel-Post-Installer Supervisor (utilities)	ERS	61	821.131-022
Steel-Pourer Helper (steel & rel.)	RES	46	502.664-018
Steel-Shot-Header Operator (ordnance)	REI	45	611.682-010
Steel-Tie Adjuster, Automatic (paper goods)	RCE	38	649.685-110
Steel-Wool-Machine Operator (nonmet. min.)	RCE	51	605.482-010
Steep Tender (grain-feed mills)	CRE	50	522.465-010
Steeping-Press Tender (plastic-synth.)	RCE	42	551.685-138
Steeple Jack (construction)	RSE	53	869.381-030
Stem Mounter (light. fix.)	RCE	40	725.684-018
Stem Sizer (fabrication, n.e.c.)	RCE	37	692.686-062
Stem-Dryer Maintainer (tobacco)	REC	37	529.685-230
Stem-Processing-Machine Operator (fabrication, n.e.c.)	RCE	38	739.685-042
Stem-Roller-or-Crusher Operator (tobacco)	RCE	39	521.685-330
Stemhole Borer (fabrication, n.e.c.)	RCE	40	666.685-010
Stemmer, Hand (tobacco)	RCE	37	521.687-134
Stemmer, Machine (tobacco)	RCE	37	521.685-334
Stencil Cutter (railroad equip.)	RIE	57	970.381-038
Stencil Cutter (stonework)	RIE	53	771.281-010
Stencil Inspector (pen & pencil)	CRS	40	733.687-074
Stencil Maker (carpet & rug)	RES	53	979.381-038
Stencil-Machine Operator (textile)	RCE	41	652.685-086
Stenciler (any industry)	REC	39	920.687-178
Stenciler (garment; tex. prod., n.e.c.)	CSR	38	781.687-066
Stenocaptioner (radio-tv broad.)	IRC	60	202.382-010
Stenographer (clerical)	CSE	54	202.362-014
Stenographer, Print Shop (print. & pub.)	CSE	54	202.362-018
Stenotype Operator (clerical)	CSE	54	202.362-022
Step-and-Repeat Reduction Camera Operator (electron. comp.)	RCI	53	976.382-034
Stereo-Plotter Operator (profess. & kin.)	RCI	62	018.281-010
Stereotyper (print. & pub.)	RIE	56	974.382-014
Stereotyper Apprentice (print. & pub.)	RIE	56	974.382-010
Sterile-Products Processor (pharmaceut.)	RES	51	559.682-054
Sterilizer (beverage)	RES	38	920.687-182
Sterilizer (medical ser.; pharmaceut.; protective dev.)	CRS	49	599.585-010
Sterilizer Operator (dairy products)	RES	43	523.685-114
Stevedore I (water trans.)	RIS	47	911.663-014
Stevedore II (water trans.)	RES	38	922.687-090
Steward, Racetrack (amuse. & rec.)	SER	66	153.117-022
Steward/Stewardess (hotel & rest.)	ERS	60	310.137-018
Steward/Stewardess (water trans.)	ESC	45	350.677-022

From the Dictionary of Occupational Titles Occupations to Holland Codes

Title	HOC	Cx	DOT
Steward/Stewardess, Banquet (hotel & rest.)	ERS	60	310.137-022
Steward/Stewardess, Bath (water trans.)	CER	41	350.677-018
Steward/Stewardess, Chief, Cargo Vessel (water trans.)	ESR	59	350.137-014
Steward/Stewardess, Chief, Passenger Ship (water trans.)	ESR	59	350.137-018
Steward/Stewardess, Railroad Dining Car (r.r. trans.)	ESR	59	310.137-026
Steward/Stewardess, Second (water trans.)	ESR	58	350.137-022
Steward/Stewardess, Third (water trans.)	SER	56	350.137-026
Steward/Stewardess, Wine (water trans.)	ERS	47	350.677-026
Sticker (button & notion)	CRE	36	734.687-090
Sticker (hat & cap)	RCE	37	784.687-070
Sticker (saw. & plan.)	RCE	38	563.686-010
Sticker, Animal (meat products)	REC	40	525.684-050
Sticker-On (nonmet. min.)	CRS	38	774.684-034
Stiffener (hat & cap)	REI	41	589.687-038
Still Operator (agriculture; can. & preserv.)	RES	47	522.685-098
Still Operator (build. mat., n.e.c.)	REC	47	543.682-026
Still Operator I (beverage)	RCE	54	522.382-030
Still Operator II (beverage)	REI	58	522.382-026
Still Operator, Batch or Continuous (chemical)	IEA	57	552.362-022
Still Tender (any industry)	RCE	44	552.685-026
Still-Operator Helper (chemical)	RES	46	552.685-030
Still-Pump Operator (petrol. refin.)	RCS	49	549.362-010
Stitch-Bonding-Machine Tender (textile)	RES	41	689.685-126
Stitch-Bonding-Machine-Tender Helper (textile)	RES	39	689.686-042
Stitcher (tex. prod., n.e.c.)	RCE	47	689.682-022
Stitcher Operator (paper goods)	RES	41	649.685-114
Stitcher, Hand (print. & pub.)	CRE	41	977.684-022
Stitcher, Special Machine (boot & shoe)	RCS	45	690.682-078
Stitcher, Standard Machine (boot & shoe)	RCE	45	690.682-082
Stitcher, Tape-Controlled Machine (boot & shoe)	RCI	40	690.685-494
Stitching-Machine Operator (print. & pub.)	RCS	48	653.662-010
Stitching-Machine Operator (wood. container)	RES	38	669.685-086
Stock Checker, Apparel (retail trade)	RSE	40	299.667-014
Stock Checker I (ordnance)	RSE	50	761.381-034
Stock Checker II (ordnance)	REC	40	665.685-034
Stock Clerk (clerical)	RCE	53	222.387-058
Stock Clerk (retail trade)	RSE	50	299.367-014
Stock Control Clerk (clerical)	CRI	56	219.387-030
Stock Cutter (saw. & plan.)	RIE	50	667.482-018
Stock Fitter (boot & shoe)	RES	47	788.685-018
Stock Grader (woodworking)	RIE	49	667.382-010
Stock Maker, Custom (ordnance)	RSI	57	761.381-038
Stock Patcher (ordnance)	CER	44	761.684-042
Stock Preparer (plastic prod.)	RCS	43	751.387-010
Stock Shaper (ordnance)	REC	41	761.684-046
Stock Sheets Cleaner-Inspector (glass products)	RES	47	779.687-034
Stock Supervisor (clerical)	ESR	58	222.137-034
Stock-Control Supervisor (clerical)	ESR	62	222.137-038
Stock-Parts Fabricator (ship-boat mfg.)	RCS	44	769.684-050

DOT to HOC

Title	HOC	Cx	DOT
Stock-Parts Inspector (furniture)	REI	47	763.684-070
Stock-Patch Sawyer (woodworking)	RIE	46	667.682-082
Stocking Inspector (knitting)	CER	41	684.684-010
Stocking-and-Box-Shop Supervisor (ordnance)	ERS	59	769.137-010
Stocklayer (boot & shoe)	CRS	40	753.687-042
Stoker Erector-and-Servicer (any industry)	RIS	56	637.281-014
Stone Carver (stonework)	ARE	65	771.281-014
Stone Cleaner (beverage)	REC	38	529.687-190
Stone Driller (stonework)	REI	48	676.682-014
Stone Grader (mine & quarry)	RES	48	679.567-010
Stone Grader (stonework)	RIE	50	670.384-010
Stone Layout Marker (stonework)	RIE	47	670.587-010
Stone Polisher, Hand (stonework)	REI	43	775.664-010
Stone Polisher, Machine (stonework)	REI	48	673.382-018
Stone Polisher, Machine Apprentice (stonework)	REI	48	673.382-022
Stone Repairer (stonework)	RES	48	779.684-058
Stone Rougher (optical goods)	REI	41	673.685-074
Stone Setter (jewelry-silver.)	CRE	39	735.687-034
Stone Setter (jewelry-silver.; optical goods)	REI	54	700.381-054
Stone Splitter (concrete prod.)	REC	41	677.685-050
Stone Trimmer (stonework)	RCE	42	670.685-010
Stone-Driller Helper (stonework)	REI	39	676.686-010
Stone-Lathe Operator (stonework)	RIE	51	674.662-010
Stone-Mill Operator (paint & varnish)	RSC	43	555.682-022
Stone-Setter Apprentice (jewelry-silver.; optical goods)	REI	54	700.381-058
Stone-Spreader Operator (construction)	RCS	45	853.663-022
Stonecutter Apprentice, Hand (stonework)	RIE	54	771.381-010
Stonecutter, Hand (stonework)	RIS	54	771.381-014
Stonecutter, Machine (stonework)	RIE	49	677.682-022
Stonemason (construction)	RSE	54	861.381-038
Stonemason Apprentice (construction)	RSE	54	861.381-042
Stonemason Supervisor (construction)	RCE	59	861.131-018
Stoner (jewelry-silver.)	CRS	41	735.684-014
Stoner and Polisher, Bevel Face (clock & watch)	RCE	39	603.685-082
Stoner, Hand (clock & watch)	RCE	43	715.584-018
Stop Attacher (button & notion)	RCE	41	692.685-206
Stopboard Assembler (musical inst.)	RCE	51	730.684-082
Stopper Maker (steel & rel.)	RES	41	519.684-022
Stopper-Maker Helper (steel & rel.)	RES	40	519.687-038
Stopping Builder (mine & quarry)	RIS	46	869.684-058
Storage Battery Inspector and Tester (elec. equip.)	RIE	57	727.381-022
Storage-Facility Rental Clerk (business ser.; retail trade)	SCR	53	295.367-026
Storekeeper (water trans.)	RES	54	222.387-062
Story Editor (motion picture; radio-tv broad.)	ASE	70	132.037-026
Stove Refinisher (any industry)	RSE	41	749.684-046
Stove Tender (steel & rel.)	RES	48	512.382-014
Stove-Bottom Worker (fabrication, n.e.c.)	REC	41	590.667-010
Stove-Carriage Operator (fabrication, n.e.c.)	RIS	48	590.662-022
Straddle-Truck Operator (any industry)	RCE	41	921.683-070

DOT to HOC

Title	HOC	Cx	DOT
Straight-Line Edger (glass mfg.; glass products)	RES	43	673.685-078
Straight-Line-Press Setter (ordnance)	RES	49	616.360-034
Straight-Pin-Making-Machine Operator (button & notion)	RIE	54	609.482-014
Straightener, Hand (any industry)	REI	52	709.484-014
Straightening-Press Operator II (any industry)	REI	47	617.482-026
Straightening-Roll Operator (any industry)	RCE	44	613.662-022
Strainer Tender (rubber reclaim.)	RCE	44	551.365-010
Strand-and-Binder Controller (nonmet. min.)	REI	40	680.685-106
Strand-Forming-Machine Operator (tex. prod., n.e.c.)	REC	41	681.685-118
Stranding-Machine Operator (elec. equip.; light. fix.; metal prod., n.e.c.; nonfer. metal)	RIE	47	616.682-034
Stranding-Machine-Operator Helper (nonfer. metal)	RES	40	616.687-010
Strap Buckler, Machine (garment)	RCE	42	689.665-010
Strap-Cutting-Machine Operator (rubber goods)	CRE	43	690.685-402
Strap-Folding-Machine Operator (rubber goods)	RCE	45	554.485-014
Strap-Machine Operator (paper goods)	CRS	47	534.682-034
Strapping-Machine Operator (wood. container)	RSE	45	692.682-058
Stratigrapher (profess. & kin.)	IRS	77	024.061-054
Straw Hat Presser, Machine (hat & cap)	CRE	40	583.685-110
Straw-Hat Brusher (hat & cap)	RCS	38	784.687-074
Straw-Hat-Plunger Operator (hat & cap)	RCE	41	583.685-114
Straw-Hat-Washer Operator (hat & cap)	REC	36	784.687-078
Street Cleaner (government ser.)	RCE	36	955.687-018
Street-Light Cleaner (utilities)	REC	40	952.667-010
Street-Light Repairer (utilities)	RIE	56	729.381-018
Street-Light Servicer (utilities)	RES	56	824.381-010
Street-Light-Repairer Helper (utilities)	RCE	41	729.684-050
Street-Light-Servicer Helper (utilities)	CRS	48	824.664-010
Street-Light-Servicer Supervisor (utilities)	ESR	59	824.137-014
Street-Openings Inspector (utilities)	REI	59	859.267-010
Street-Sweeper Operator (government ser.)	REC	41	919.683-022
Streetcar Operator (r.r. trans.)	ERS	51	913.463-014
Streetcar Repairer (railroad equip.)	RIS	53	807.381-026
Streetcar-Repairer Helper (railroad equip.)	RES	41	807.687-014
Stress Analyst (aircraft mfg.)	RIE	76	002.061-030
Stress Analyst (profess. & kin.)	IRC	79	007.061-042
Stress Test Technician (medical ser.)	CIS	57	078.362-062
Stretch-Box Tender (textile)	RCE	40	680.685-110
Stretch-Machine Operator (plastic prod.)	RES	47	559.682-058
Stretcher (hat & cap)	REC	40	580.685-054
Stretcher (jewelry-silver.)	RCE	44	700.684-078
Stretcher-Drier Operator (laundry & rel.)	RCE	38	363.687-022
Stretcher-Leveler Operator (nonfer. metal)	REI	50	619.582-010
Stretcher-Leveler-Operator Helper (nonfer. metal)	RCE	38	619.686-030
Stretching-Machine Operator (tex. prod., n.e.c.)	RCE	42	580.685-058
Strickler Attendant (fabrication, n.e.c.)	RCE	46	652.665-014
Strike-Off-Machine Operator (textile)	RCE	41	652.685-090
Strike-Out-Machine Operator (textile)	CRS	41	587.685-030
String Laster (boot & shoe)	RIE	41	690.685-406

Title	HOC	Cx	DOT
String-Top Sealer (paper goods)	CRE	38	641.685-086
String-Winding-Machine Operator (musical inst.)	CSR	47	692.682-062
Stringer (jewelry-silver.)	RCE	38	509.687-018
Stringer (paper goods)	CRE	36	794.687-054
Stringer-Machine Tender (protective dev.)	RCE	42	692.485-010
Stringing-Machine Tender (tex. prod., n.e.c.)	CRE	42	689.585-018
Strip Polisher (stonework)	REC	40	673.685-082
Strip Presser (boot & shoe)	RCE	39	583.685-118
Strip Roller (metal prod., n.e.c.)	REI	49	613.682-022
Strip-Cutting-Machine Operator (textile)	RCE	40	686.685-066
Strip-Cutting-Machine Operator (tobacco)	RCE	39	521.685-338
Strip-Metal-Punch-and-Straightener Operator (wood. container)	RCE	39	615.685-038
Strip-Tank Tender (ordnance)	REC	42	503.685-046
Stripe Matcher (knitting)	RSC	46	689.662-014
Striper (paper goods)	RCS	45	651.682-018
Striper, Hand (any industry)	RSC	49	740.484-010
Striper, Machine (motor-bicycles)	RES	40	749.686-010
Striper, Spray Gun (any industry)	CRE	38	741.687-022
Striping-Machine Operator (nonfer. metal)	CSR	44	652.682-026
Stripper (furniture)	RES	38	749.687-030
Stripper (glass mfg.)	RCS	38	673.666-014
Stripper (plastic prod.; rubber goods)	REC	37	556.686-018
Stripper (print. & pub.)	REI	57	971.381-050
Stripper and Taper (rubber goods)	RCS	42	899.684-038
Stripper Apprentice (print. & pub.)	REI	57	971.381-054
Stripper, Lithographic I (print. & pub.)	RIC	59	972.281-022
Stripper, Lithographic II (print. & pub.)	RIE	57	972.381-022
Stripper-Cutter, Machine (food prep., n.e.c.)	REC	40	521.685-342
Stripper-Etcher, Printed Circuit Boards (electron. comp.)	RCI	43	590.685-082
Stripping Cutter and Winder (boot & shoe)	RCE	42	585.685-118
Stripping-Machine Operator (paper goods)	CRE	40	641.685-090
Stripping-Shovel Oiler (mine & quarry)	RES	46	850.684-018
Stripping-Shovel Operator (mine & quarry)	RSC	43	850.663-026
Stroboscope Operator (textile)	RES	50	689.364-010
Stroke-Belt-Sander Operator (woodworking)	RIE	47	662.682-018
Strong-Nitric Operator (chemical)	RES	48	559.682-062
Structural Engineer (construction)	IRS	71	005.061-034
Structural-Mill Supervisor (nonfer. metal)	SER	55	619.132-022
Structural-Steel Worker (construction)	REI	55	801.361-014
Structural-Steel-Worker Apprentice (construction)	REI	55	801.361-018
Stubber (retail trade)	RES	42	222.687-034
Stucco Mason (construction)	REI	57	842.381-014
Studder, Hairspring (clock & watch)	RCE	39	715.684-186
Stuffer (meat products)	REC	38	520.685-210
Stuffer (tex. prod., n.e.c.)	RCE	36	780.687-046
Stuffer (toy-sport equip.)	RCE	40	731.685-014
Stuffing-Machine Operator (furniture)	RCE	42	780.685-014
Stuffing-Machine Operator (toy-sport equip.)	REC	40	732.685-034

Part 3: From Occupational Titles to Holland Codes

From the Dictionary of Occupational Titles Occupations to Holland Codes

Title	HOC	Cx	DOT
Stull Installer (concrete prod.)	RCE	40	869.684-062
Stunner, Animal (meat products)	RES	37	525.687-114
Stunt Performer (amuse. & rec.; motion picture; radio-tv broad.)	SCE	54	159.341-014
Subassembler (elec. equip.)	CRE	41	729.684-054
Subassembler (machinery mfg.)	REI	53	706.381-038
Subassembler (office machines)	CRS	48	706.684-094
Sublimer (chemical)	CRE	42	542.685-014
Subscription Crew Leader (retail trade)	ESR	55	291.157-010
Substance Abuse Counselor (profess. & kin.)	SEA	66	045.107-058
Substation Inspector (utilities)	RSE	58	952.261-010
Substation Operator (utilities)	RIS	57	952.362-026
Substation Operator Apprentice (utilities)	RIS	57	952.362-030
Substation Operator, Chief (utilities)	RES	59	952.131-010
Substation-Operator Helper (utilities)	REC	42	952.687-014
Sucker-Machine Operator (sugar & conf.)	RES	39	529.685-234
Suction-Dredge-Pipeline-Placing Supervisor (construction)	REI	59	862.134-010
Suction-Plate-Carrier Cleaner (tobacco)	REC	37	529.687-194
Sugar Boiler (sugar & conf.)	RES	53	522.382-034
Sugar Controller (sugar & conf.)	REC	49	529.565-010
Sugar Drier (grain-feed mills)	RES	41	523.665-010
Sugar Grinder (sugar & conf.)	RCS	41	521.685-346
Sugar Presser (grain-feed mills)	REC	37	521.685-350
Sugar-Chipper-Machine Operator (grain-feed mills)	RES	37	521.685-354
Sugar-Reprocess Operator, Head (sugar & conf.)	ECS	56	529.137-018
Suggestion Clerk (clerical)	CSE	50	209.387-034
Sulfate Drier-Machine Operator (steel & rel.)	REC	41	551.685-142
Sulky Driver (amuse. & rec.)	SRE	53	153.244-014
Sumatra Opener (tobacco)	REC	39	529.687-198
Sunglass-Clip Attacher (optical goods)	REC	40	713.687-042
Supercalender Operator (paper & pulp)	REA	47	534.682-038
Supercargo (water trans.)	ERS	59	248.167-010
Supercharger-Repair Supervisor (air trans.)	RES	61	621.131-010
Superintendent (agriculture; can. & preserv.)	ESA	66	180.167-054
Superintendent of Generation (utilities)	ERI	75	184.167-138
Superintendent, Ammunition Storage (ordnance)	ERS	67	189.167-038
Superintendent, Building (any industry)	RES	65	187.167-190
Superintendent, Car Construction (railroad equip.)	ERS	69	183.167-034
Superintendent, Cold Storage (any industry)	ESR	59	184.167-142
Superintendent, Commissary (water trans.)	ESR	68	184.117-078
Superintendent, Communications (tel. & tel.)	ESR	68	184.117-082
Superintendent, Compressor Stations (pipe lines)	ERS	68	184.167-146
Superintendent, Concrete-Mixing Plant (construction)	ESC	66	182.167-022
Superintendent, Construction (construction)	ERS	67	182.167-026
Superintendent, Distribution I (utilities)	ECI	75	184.167-150
Superintendent, Distribution II (utilities)	ERS	68	184.167-154
Superintendent, Division (motor trans.; r.r. trans.)	ESR	66	184.167-158
Superintendent, Drilling and Production (petrol. & gas)	ERI	69	181.167-014
Superintendent, Electric Power (utilities)	ECI	76	184.167-162

Title	HOC	Cx	DOT
Superintendent, Generating Plant (utilities)	REI	70	184.167-166
Superintendent, Grain Elevator (beverage; grain-feed mills)	ESC	59	529.137-022
Superintendent, Greens (amuse. & rec.)	ERI	65	406.137-014
Superintendent, Horticulture (museums)	EIR	67	180.161-014
Superintendent, Industries, Correctional Facility (government ser.)	ERS	65	188.167-094
Superintendent, Labor Utilization (any industry)	SER	60	189.167-042
Superintendent, Laundry (laundry & rel.)	ERS	62	187.167-194
Superintendent, Local (utilities)	ESR	59	952.137-018
Superintendent, Logging (logging)	ERI	68	183.167-038
Superintendent, Maintenance (air trans.)	ESA	68	184.167-174
Superintendent, Maintenance (any industry)	ERI	70	189.167-046
Superintendent, Maintenance (motor trans.)	ERA	60	184.167-170
Superintendent, Maintenance of Equipment (motor trans.; r.r. trans.)	ECS	64	184.167-178
Superintendent, Maintenance of Way (r.r. trans.)	ERI	68	182.167-030
Superintendent, Marine (water trans.)	ESR	68	184.167-182
Superintendent, Marine Oil Terminal (water trans.)	ESR	69	184.167-186
Superintendent, Measurement (petrol. & gas; pipe lines)	ERA	69	184.167-190
Superintendent, Meters (utilities)	ERI	68	184.167-194
Superintendent, Oil-Well Services (petrol. & gas)	ERS	70	010.167-018
Superintendent, Pipelines (pipe lines)	ESR	70	184.167-198
Superintendent, Plant Protection (any industry)	ESR	66	189.167-050
Superintendent, Power (r.r. trans.)	ESR	68	184.167-202
Superintendent, Production (agriculture)	EIR	64	180.167-058
Superintendent, Radio Communications (government ser.)	ESC	67	193.167-018
Superintendent, Recreation (government ser.)	ESA	72	187.117-054
Superintendent, Sales (construction)	ESA	69	250.157-010
Superintendent, Sanitation (government ser.)	ESI	67	188.167-098
Superintendent, Schools (education)	SEI	70	099.117-022
Superintendent, Seed Mill (agriculture)	ESR	56	599.137-010
Superintendent, Service (hotel & rest.)	ESR	56	329.137-010
Superintendent, Stations (motor trans.; r.r. trans.)	ESC	68	184.167-206
Superintendent, Stevedoring (water trans.)	ERS	59	911.137-022
Superintendent, System Operation (utilities)	ERI	75	184.167-210
Superintendent, Terminal (water trans.)	ERS	68	184.167-214
Superintendent, Tests (utilities)	EAS	70	184.167-218
Superintendent, Track (construction)	ERS	58	899.137-014
Superintendent, Transmission (utilities)	ERI	75	184.167-222
Superintendent, Transportation (any industry)	ESR	67	184.167-226
Superintendent, Water-and-Sewer Systems (waterworks)	IEA	74	184.161-014
Supervising Airplane Pilot (government ser.)	IRE	72	196.163-014
Supervising Film-or-Videotape Editor (motion picture; radio-tv broad.)	EAS	68	962.132-010
Supervisor (boot & shoe)	RES	60	788.131-010
Supervisor (brick & tile)	ERC	55	570.132-022
Supervisor (cement)	ERS	56	579.137-010
Supervisor (clock & watch)	RES	59	715.131-010
Supervisor (comm. equip.)	ERC	59	619.130-046

Part 3: From Occupational Titles to Holland Codes
From the Dictionary of Occupational Titles Occupations to Holland Codes

Title	HOC	Cx	DOT
Supervisor (cutlery-hrdwr.)	RES	59	615.130-014
Supervisor (electroplating)	RES	60	500.131-010
Supervisor (food prep., n.e.c.)	ERS	55	529.132-110
Supervisor (glove & mit.)	ERS	59	784.132-010
Supervisor (government ser.)	ESI	65	188.137-010
Supervisor (jewelry-silver.)	RES	59	700.130-010
Supervisor (jewelry-silver.; plastic prod.)	RES	59	700.131-010
Supervisor (knitting)	ESA	59	684.137-010
Supervisor (leather prod.)	ERS	59	783.132-010
Supervisor (metal prod., n.e.c.)	RES	59	700.131-014
Supervisor (mine & quarry)	ERS	54	570.137-010
Supervisor (musical inst.)	RES	59	730.131-010
Supervisor (nonfer. metal)	RES	59	691.130-010
Supervisor (nut & bolt)	RES	59	616.130-010
Supervisor (office machines)	RCS	60	706.131-014
Supervisor (oils & grease)	ESC	59	529.137-030
Supervisor (optical goods)	CER	63	716.130-010
Supervisor (ordnance)	ERS	61	737.137-018
Supervisor (plastic prod.)	ERS	59	690.130-018
Supervisor (plumbing-heat.)	RES	61	609.130-018
Supervisor (rubber reclaim.)	RES	58	559.132-058
Supervisor (rubber tire)	ERS	59	750.130-010
Supervisor (stonework)	RSE	60	679.130-010
Supervisor (struct. metal)	RES	61	617.130-010
Supervisor (sugar & conf.)	RES	56	920.137-018
Supervisor (tobacco)	ESR	58	529.137-026
Supervisor (toy-sport equip.)	RES	58	732.130-010
Supervisor I (button & notion)	RES	59	692.130-018
Supervisor I (chemical)	RES	61	559.132-054
Supervisor I (fabrication, n.e.c.)	ESR	58	739.131-010
Supervisor I (nonmet. min.)	RSE	59	779.131-010
Supervisor I (protective dev.)	ECR	60	692.137-014
Supervisor I (rubber goods)	ERS	59	759.137-010
Supervisor I (tex. prod., n.e.c.)	ESR	58	789.132-014
Supervisor II (button & notion)	SEA	55	734.131-010
Supervisor II (chemical)	SRE	55	550.132-010
Supervisor II (fabrication, n.e.c.)	RES	58	739.131-014
Supervisor II (nonmet. min.)	RES	59	579.132-010
Supervisor II (protective dev.)	ERC	60	789.134-014
Supervisor II (rubber goods)	ERS	59	559.137-014
Supervisor II (tex. prod., n.e.c.)	RES	58	789.134-010
Supervisor III (button & notion)	RES	56	690.130-010
Supervisor III (fabrication, n.e.c.)	ERS	59	549.132-014
Supervisor III (nonmet. min.)	RES	54	575.130-014
Supervisor III (tex. prod., n.e.c.)	ESR	59	789.132-018
Supervisor IV (nonmet. min.)	SEC	58	692.132-010
Supervisor IV (tex. prod., n.e.c.)	RES	56	789.132-010
Supervisor of Communications (any industry)	ESC	65	184.167-230
Supervisor of Sales (business ser.)	ESR	66	185.157-014

Title	HOC	Cx	DOT
Supervisor of Way (r.r. trans.)	ESC	67	184.167-234
Supervisor V (nonmet. min.)	ESR	60	692.132-014
Supervisor V (tex. prod., n.e.c.)	ERC	53	586.130-010
Supervisor VI (nonmet. min.)	RES	58	692.130-022
Supervisor VI (tex. prod., n.e.c.)	RES	59	589.132-010
Supervisor, Abattoir (meat products)	RES	56	525.131-010
Supervisor, Accounting Clerks (clerical)	CSE	65	216.132-010
Supervisor, Accounts Receivable (utilities; waterworks)	SEC	61	214.137-022
Supervisor, Acoustical Tile Carpenters (construction)	ERS	61	860.131-010
Supervisor, Adjustable-Steel-Joist-Setting (construction)	RES	59	869.134-014
Supervisor, Advertising-Dispatch Clerks (print. & pub.)	ESR	57	247.137-010
Supervisor, Advertising-Material Distributors (business ser.)	ESR	58	230.137-010
Supervisor, Agency Appointments (insurance)	SCE	62	209.137-018
Supervisor, Air-Conditioning Installer (any industry)	ERS	63	827.131-018
Supervisor, Aircraft Cleaning (air trans.)	ESC	59	891.137-014
Supervisor, Aircraft Maintenance (air trans.)	ERS	62	621.131-014
Supervisor, Airplane-Flight Attendant (air trans.)	ESA	63	352.137-010
Supervisor, Alteration Workroom (retail trade)	RES	57	785.131-010
Supervisor, Alum Plant (chemical)	ERS	59	559.132-062
Supervisor, Aluminum Boat Assembly (ship-boat mfg.)	RSE	59	806.131-010
Supervisor, Aluminum Fabrication (ship-boat mfg.)	RES	59	619.130-014
Supervisor, Animal Cruelty Investigation (nonprofit org.)	SEC	57	379.137-010
Supervisor, Animal Maintenance (pharmaceut.)	ECR	58	410.137-018
Supervisor, Area (agriculture)	ERS	59	401.137-010
Supervisor, Artificial Breast Fabrication (protective dev.)	ECS	56	712.134-010
Supervisor, Artificial Breeding Ranch (agriculture)	SER	59	410.131-014
Supervisor, Artist, Suspect (government ser.)	ASE	61	970.131-014
Supervisor, Asbestos Pipe (nonmet. min.)	RSE	58	679.130-014
Supervisor, Asbestos Removal (construction)	ESR	57	869.134-026
Supervisor, Asbestos Textile (nonmet. min.)	ESR	58	579.137-014
Supervisor, Asbestos-Cement Sheet (nonmet. min.)	RIE	59	679.130-018
Supervisor, Asphalt Paving (construction)	ERS	59	853.133-010
Supervisor, Assembly (agric. equip.)	ESR	58	801.137-010
Supervisor, Assembly (motor-bicycles)	SRE	59	806.131-014
Supervisor, Assembly (pen & pencil)	RES	60	733.137-010
Supervisor, Assembly (woodworking)	ERS	59	769.137-014
Supervisor, Assembly Department (struct. metal)	RES	59	809.130-010
Supervisor, Assembly I (office machines)	SER	59	710.137-010
Supervisor, Assembly Room (fabrication, n.e.c.)	RES	59	739.134-010
Supervisor, Assembly Room (furniture)	RES	59	669.130-010
Supervisor, Assembly Stock (clerical)	RES	57	222.137-042
Supervisor, Assembly-and-Packing (cutlery-hrdwr.)	ERS	59	701.137-010
Supervisor, Audit Clerks (clerical)	SER	63	210.132-010
Supervisor, Automatic Machines (clock & watch)	RSE	57	609.130-022
Supervisor, Automobile Body Repair (automotive ser.)	SER	59	807.137-010
Supervisor, Avionics Shop (air trans.)	RSE	63	823.131-018
Supervisor, Beam Department (leather mfg.)	REI	59	589.134-010
Supervisor, Beater Room (paper & pulp)	ESR	61	530.132-014
Supervisor, Beehive Kiln (chemical)	ESR	57	563.137-010

Part 3: From Occupational Titles to Holland Codes

From the Dictionary of Occupational Titles Occupations to Holland Codes

Title	HOC	Cx	DOT
Supervisor, Beet End (sugar & conf.)	ERS	59	529.132-018
Supervisor, Belt-and-Link Assembly (ordnance)	ERS	59	737.137-022
Supervisor, Billposting (business ser.)	CSE	55	841.137-010
Supervisor, Bindery (print. & pub.)	RES	59	653.131-010
Supervisor, Bit and Shank Department (fabrication, n.e.c.)	RES	59	739.130-010
Supervisor, Blast Furnace (smelt. & refin.)	RES	59	512.132-022
Supervisor, Blast Furnace (steel & rel.)	ERS	58	519.132-010
Supervisor, Blast-Furnace-Auxiliaries (steel & rel.)	RES	58	519.132-014
Supervisor, Bleach (chemical)	RES	59	559.137-018
Supervisor, Blood-Donor Recruiters (medical ser.)	ESC	61	293.137-010
Supervisor, Blooming Mill (steel & rel.)	RSE	60	613.130-010
Supervisor, Blueprinting-and-Photocopy (any industry)	SER	57	979.130-010
Supervisor, Board Mill (concrete prod.)	RES	59	579.130-010
Supervisor, Boat Outfitting (ship-boat mfg.)	ESR	58	806.131-018
Supervisor, Boatbuilders, Wood (ship-boat mfg.)	RES	59	860.131-014
Supervisor, Boiler Repair (any industry)	RES	59	805.137-010
Supervisor, Boilermaking (struct. metal)	RSE	61	805.131-010
Supervisor, Bonding (textile)	ESC	58	589.137-014
Supervisor, Bone Plant (chemical)	ERS	59	559.132-066
Supervisor, Bottle-House Cleaners (beverage)	REI	59	529.132-022
Supervisor, Brake Repair (r.r. trans.)	ECR	54	622.137-010
Supervisor, Brew House (beverage)	RES	58	529.132-026
Supervisor, Briar Shop (fabrication, n.e.c.)	RSE	59	761.130-010
Supervisor, Bridges and Buildings (r.r. trans.)	ESI	67	182.167-034
Supervisor, Brine (chemical)	REI	59	558.134-010
Supervisor, Brineyard (can. & preserv.)	RES	59	522.134-010
Supervisor, Broommaking (fabrication, n.e.c.)	ERS	58	692.130-026
Supervisor, Burling and Joining (textile)	ERC	59	689.132-010
Supervisor, Burning, Forming, and Assembly (elec. equip.)	RSE	59	727.130-010
Supervisor, Byproducts (steel & rel.)	ERS	60	542.132-010
Supervisor, Cab (motor trans.)	ERS	60	913.133-014
Supervisor, Calendering (paper & pulp)	SER	60	534.132-010
Supervisor, Canal-Equipment Maintenance (waterworks)	RES	59	899.130-010
Supervisor, Candle Making (fabrication, n.e.c.)	ESR	59	590.132-010
Supervisor, Candy (sugar & conf.)	SEC	58	529.130-010
Supervisor, Cap-and-Hat Production (hat & cap)	ESR	59	784.130-010
Supervisor, Car and Yard (r.r. trans.)	ECR	53	622.137-014
Supervisor, Car Installations (railroad equip.)	ESC	58	806.137-010
Supervisor, Carbon Electrodes (steel & rel.)	ERI	59	549.137-010
Supervisor, Carbon-Paper-Coating (pen & pencil)	RES	60	534.137-010
Supervisor, Carding (textile)	RSE	60	680.130-010
Supervisor, Cardroom (amuse. & rec.)	ESR	60	343.137-014
Supervisor, Carpenters (construction)	RES	61	860.131-018
Supervisor, Cartography (profess. & kin.)	CSE	70	018.131-010
Supervisor, Carton and Can Supply (beverage)	RES	59	920.132-014
Supervisor, Cashiers (hotel & rest.; retail trade)	ESC	61	211.137-010
Supervisor, Casting-and-Pasting (elec. equip.)	RES	59	502.130-010
Supervisor, CD-Area (chemical)	REI	60	559.132-070
Supervisor, Cell Operation (smelt. & refin.)	RES	59	519.132-018

Part 3: From Occupational Titles to Holland Codes

From the Dictionary of Occupational Titles Occupations to Holland Codes

Title	HOC	Cx	DOT
Supervisor, Cell Room (chemical)	REI	59	558.134-014
Supervisor, Cell-Efficiency (chemical)	REI	60	558.134-018
Supervisor, Cellars (beverage)	RES	56	914.132-018
Supervisor, Cemetery Workers (real estate)	RES	56	406.134-010
Supervisor, Central Supply (medical ser.)	CES	60	381.137-014
Supervisor, Cereal (grain-feed mills)	RES	59	529.132-030
Supervisor, Channel Process (chemical)	ESA	59	559.137-022
Supervisor, Char House (sugar & conf.)	SRE	57	523.132-010
Supervisor, Chemical (plastic-synth.)	ERS	59	558.132-010
Supervisor, Chimney Construction (construction)	ERS	58	801.131-010
Supervisor, Chocolate-and-Cocoa Processing (sugar & conf.)	RES	63	529.130-014
Supervisor, Christmas-Tree Farm (forestry)	ERS	54	451.137-014
Supervisor, Cigar Making, Hand (tobacco)	ERS	54	790.134-010
Supervisor, Cigar Tobacco Processing (tobacco)	SEA	54	529.137-034
Supervisor, Cigar-Making Machine (tobacco)	RSE	56	529.132-034
Supervisor, Circus (amuse. & rec.)	SEC	54	969.137-010
Supervisor, Claims (insurance)	ESC	63	241.137-018
Supervisor, Classified Advertising (print. & pub.)	ESC	61	247.137-014
Supervisor, Clay Preparation (pottery & porc.)	SRE	59	570.130-010
Supervisor, Clay Shop (pottery & porc.)	RES	59	774.130-010
Supervisor, Cleaning (beverage; can. & preserv.; dairy products; food prep., n.e.c.)	RES	58	699.137-010
Supervisor, Cloth Winding (tex. prod., n.e.c.)	RSE	56	689.130-022
Supervisor, Coal Handling (steel & rel.)	ERA	59	549.132-018
Supervisor, Coating (photo. appar.)	RES	59	534.130-010
Supervisor, Coating (plastic-synth.)	ESC	59	554.137-014
Supervisor, Coffee (food prep., n.e.c.)	ESR	58	529.130-018
Supervisor, Coil Winding (elec. equip.)	ERS	59	724.131-010
Supervisor, Coin-Machine (svc. ind. mach.)	SER	59	706.130-010
Supervisor, Coke Handling (steel & rel.)	ERA	59	549.132-022
Supervisor, Cold Rolling (steel & rel.)	REI	58	619.130-018
Supervisor, Color-Paste Mixing (textile)	ERS	59	550.135-010
Supervisor, Commissary Production (hotel & rest.)	SER	59	319.137-022
Supervisor, Communications-and-Signals (r.r. trans.)	ESR	62	184.167-290
Supervisor, Component Assembler (mfd. bldgs.)	RSE	59	762.134-010
Supervisor, Composing-Room (print. & pub.)	ESR	58	973.137-010
Supervisor, Compounding-and-Finishing (chemical)	ESC	59	550.137-010
Supervisor, Compressed Yeast (food prep., n.e.c.)	ERS	59	520.132-014
Supervisor, Computer Operations (clerical)	ESI	67	213.132-010
Supervisor, Concrete Block Plant (concrete prod.)	RES	59	579.130-014
Supervisor, Concrete Pipe Plant (concrete prod.)	RES	59	579.130-018
Supervisor, Concrete-Stone Fabricating (concrete prod.)	RES	58	575.131-010
Supervisor, Concrete-Stone Finishing (concrete prod.)	RES	59	775.131-010
Supervisor, Conditioning Yard (steel & rel.)	RES	56	619.134-010
Supervisor, Contact and Service Clerks (utilities)	SEC	59	249.137-014
Supervisor, Contingents (retail trade)	ESR	55	205.367-050
Supervisor, Continuous-Weld-Pipe Mill (steel & rel.)	RES	59	619.130-022
Supervisor, Contract-Sheltered Workshop (nonprofit org.)	SEC	59	187.134-010

Title	HOC	Cx	DOT
Supervisor, Cook House (chemical)	ERS	59	559.132-074
Supervisor, Cook Room (can. & preserv.)	RES	58	529.132-038
Supervisor, Cooler Service (svc. ind. mach.)	SRE	59	637.131-010
Supervisor, Cooperage Shop (wood. container)	RES	58	764.134-010
Supervisor, Corduroy Cutting (textile)	SRI	57	585.130-010
Supervisor, Core Drilling (construction)	ESR	59	850.137-010
Supervisor, Coremaker (paper & pulp)	REI	59	640.132-010
Supervisor, Corncob Pipe Manufacturing (fabrication, n.e.c.)	RES	54	739.132-010
Supervisor, Correspondence Section (insurance)	SCE	60	249.137-018
Supervisor, Costuming (motion picture; radio-tv broad.)	ESA	60	962.137-018
Supervisor, Covering and Lining (fabrication, n.e.c.)	REI	55	780.134-010
Supervisor, Credit and Loan Collections (clerical)	SEC	60	241.137-010
Supervisor, Cured Meats (meat products)	RES	56	525.132-010
Supervisor, Cured-Meat Packing (meat products)	ESR	56	529.135-014
Supervisor, Curing Room (tobacco)	RES	59	529.137-038
Supervisor, Customer Records Division (utilities)	ESC	63	249.137-022
Supervisor, Customer Services (motor trans.)	ESA	61	248.137-018
Supervisor, Customer-Complaint Service (clerical)	ESC	61	241.137-014
Supervisor, Cutting and Boning (meat products)	ERS	56	525.131-014
Supervisor, Cutting and Splicing (motion picture; photofinishing)	SCE	57	976.134-010
Supervisor, Cutting Department (any industry)	ESC	58	781.134-010
Supervisor, Cutting Department (pen & pencil)	SRE	56	669.130-014
Supervisor, Cutting-and-Sewing Department (furniture)	RES	59	780.131-010
Supervisor, Dairy Farm (agriculture)	ERC	57	410.131-018
Supervisor, Dairy Processing (dairy products)	RES	59	529.131-014
Supervisor, Decorating (glass mfg.)	ERS	58	652.130-010
Supervisor, Decorating (pottery & porc.)	SRE	59	749.131-010
Supervisor, Dehydrogenation (chemical; petrol. refin.)	ECS	59	559.132-078
Supervisor, Delivery Department (tel. & tel.)	SER	55	230.137-014
Supervisor, Dental Laboratory (protective dev.)	SER	60	712.131-010
Supervisor, Detasseling Crew (agriculture)	ESR	54	401.137-014
Supervisor, Dials (clock & watch)	ERS	59	715.131-014
Supervisor, Diamond Finishing (jewelry-silver.)	REA	61	770.131-014
Supervisor, Die Casting (foundry; smelt. & refin.)	RES	59	514.130-014
Supervisor, Dimension Warehouse (furniture)	ERS	59	769.134-010
Supervisor, Display Fabrication (fabrication, n.e.c.)	ERS	59	739.134-014
Supervisor, Diversified Crops (agriculture)	RES	60	407.131-010
Supervisor, Dock (petrol. refin.; pipe lines)	ESA	60	914.137-018
Supervisor, Dog License Officer (nonprofit org.)	ESR	59	379.137-014
Supervisor, Doping (construction)	REC	56	843.134-010
Supervisor, Drafting and Printed Circuit Design (profess. & kin.)	EIC	67	003.131-010
Supervisor, Drawing (nonfer. metal; steel & rel.)	RES	59	614.132-010
Supervisor, Dried Yeast (food prep., n.e.c.)	RES	60	529.132-042
Supervisor, Dry Cleaning (laundry & rel.)	ERS	59	369.137-010
Supervisor, Dry Paste (chemical)	ERS	58	559.132-082
Supervisor, Dry-Cell Assembly (elec. equip.)	ESR	59	727.137-010

Title	HOC	Cx	DOT
Supervisor, Dry-Starch (grain-feed mills)	ECS	58	529.132-046
Supervisor, Dry-Wall Application (construction)	RES	59	842.131-010
Supervisor, Drying (millwork-plywood)	ERS	58	563.135-010
Supervisor, Drying and Winding (plastic-synth.)	ERS	55	559.134-014
Supervisor, Edging (glass products)	RES	53	673.130-010
Supervisor, Education (education)	SEC	66	099.117-026
Supervisor, Egg Processing (can. & preserv.; wholesale tr.)	ERS	59	529.137-042
Supervisor, Electrical Assemblies (elec. equip.; machinery mfg.)	RSE	61	826.131-014
Supervisor, Electrical Assembly (elec. equip.)	SER	58	729.130-010
Supervisor, Electrical Repair and Telephone Line Maintenance (utilities)	RES	61	829.131-022
Supervisor, Electronic Coils (elec. equip.; electron. comp.)	SER	60	724.130-010
Supervisor, Electronic Controls Repairer (engine-turbine)	RIS	62	828.131-010
Supervisor, Electronics Processing (electron. comp.)	ESR	61	590.130-010
Supervisor, Electronics Production (comm. equip.; electron. comp.; office machines)	RSE	59	726.130-010
Supervisor, Electronics Systems Maintenance (any industry)	IRE	69	828.161-010
Supervisor, Electrotyping and Stereotyping (print. & pub.)	RSE	59	974.131-010
Supervisor, Endless Track Vehicle (automotive ser.)	SRC	61	620.131-010
Supervisor, Engine Assembly (engine-turbine)	RSE	58	806.130-010
Supervisor, Engine-Repair (engine-turbine)	RES	62	625.131-014
Supervisor, Engraving (pen & pencil)	RES	59	704.131-014
Supervisor, Epoxy Fabrication (brick & tile)	ERS	53	579.134-014
Supervisor, Erection Shop (railroad equip.)	RES	59	806.131-022
Supervisor, Esters-and-Emulsifiers (chemical)	RES	59	559.132-086
Supervisor, Estimator and Drafter (utilities)	ESI	70	019.161-010
Supervisor, Eváporator (chemical)	RES	60	559.137-026
Supervisor, Extermination (business ser.)	SEC	58	389.134-010
Supervisor, Extruding Department (plastic prod.)	RES	59	557.130-010
Supervisor, Extrusion (forging)	RES	59	614.132-014
Supervisor, Fabrication (wood prod., n.e.c.)	RES	58	769.130-010
Supervisor, Fabrication and Assembly (toy-sport equip.)	RES	59	809.131-010
Supervisor, Fabrication Department (light. fix.)	RES	59	723.132-010
Supervisor, Facepiece Line (protective dev.)	ESR	59	712.137-010
Supervisor, Farm-Equipment Maintenance (agric. equip.)	RSE	60	624.131-010
Supervisor, Feed House (grain-feed mills)	RES	58	529.132-050
Supervisor, Feed Mill (grain-feed mills)	ERS	58	529.132-054
Supervisor, Felling-Bucking (logging)	RES	58	454.134-010
Supervisor, Fence Manufacture (metal prod., n.e.c.)	REI	54	617.130-014
Supervisor, Fermenting Cellars (beverage)	SEA	58	529.132-058
Supervisor, Ferry Terminal (water trans.)	SEC	59	911.137-026
Supervisor, Fertilizer (chemical)	RES	58	559.132-090
Supervisor, Fertilizer Processing (chemical)	RES	59	559.130-014
Supervisor, Fiber-Locking (textile)	ECR	59	689.132-014
Supervisor, Fiberglass Boat Assembly (ship-boat mfg.)	ESR	59	806.134-014
Supervisor, Field Pipelines (pipe lines)	RES	62	914.132-022
Supervisor, Field-Crop Farming (agriculture)	RES	57	404.131-010

Part 3: From Occupational Titles to Holland Codes

From the Dictionary of Occupational Titles Occupations to Holland Codes

Title	HOC	Cx	DOT
Supervisor, Files (clerical)	ESC	57	206.137-010
Supervisor, Filling-and-Packing (paint & varnish)	ESC	55	920.137-022
Supervisor, Film Processing (motion picture; photofinishing; radio-tv broad.)	SRE	59	976.131-014
Supervisor, Film Processing (photofinishing)	SRC	58	976.132-010
Supervisor, Filtration (sugar & conf.)	RES	58	529.130-022
Supervisor, Final Assembly and Packing (protective dev.)	ESR	59	712.137-014
Supervisor, Finishing (fabrication, n.e.c.)	ERS	58	749.134-010
Supervisor, Finishing (furniture)	SER	59	742.134-010
Supervisor, Finishing (glass mfg.)	RSE	58	775.130-010
Supervisor, Finishing Department (nonmet. min.)	RIE	53	679.137-010
Supervisor, Finishing Department (pen & pencil)	ERS	59	733.137-014
Supervisor, Finishing Department (photofinishing)	SEC	57	976.137-014
Supervisor, Finishing Room (leather mfg.)	ERS	59	589.130-018
Supervisor, Finishing Room (print. & pub.)	ESR	56	979.137-010
Supervisor, Finishing-and-Shipping (steel & rel.)	REI	58	619.132-026
Supervisor, Fireworks Assembly (chemical)	RSE	58	737.131-010
Supervisor, Fish Bait Processing (toy-sport equip.)	RSE	56	550.132-014
Supervisor, Fish Hatchery (fishing & hunt.)	RES	58	446.134-010
Supervisor, Fish Processing (can. & preserv.)	RES	55	525.134-010
Supervisor, Fitting (any industry)	REA	62	801.131-014
Supervisor, Flame Cutting (steel & rel.)	ESC	59	819.132-010
Supervisor, Foam Cutting (tex. prod., n.e.c.)	ERC	51	690.130-022
Supervisor, Food Checkers and Cashiers (hotel & rest.)	ESR	63	211.137-014
Supervisor, Force Adjustment (tel. & tel.)	ESC	63	215.137-018
Supervisor, Forming Department I (glass mfg.)	RES	59	575.130-018
Supervisor, Forming Department II (glass mfg.)	RSE	56	579.130-022
Supervisor, Frame Sample and Pattern (furniture)	EIS	67	661.137-010
Supervisor, Framing Mill (wood prod., n.e.c.)	RSC	57	669.130-018
Supervisor, Fruit Grading (wholesale tr.)	EAS	55	529.137-046
Supervisor, Fur Dressing (leather mfg.)	RES	59	589.130-022
Supervisor, Furnace Process (chemical)	RES	59	559.132-094
Supervisor, Furniture Assembly (furniture)	ECR	58	763.134-014
Supervisor, Furrier Shop (fur goods)	RES	62	783.131-010
Supervisor, Game Farm (agriculture)	ESR	59	412.131-010
Supervisor, Garage (automotive ser.)	ERS	60	620.131-014
Supervisor, Garment Manufacturing (garment)	REI	55	786.132-010
Supervisor, Gas Meter Repair (utilities)	ERS	59	710.131-010
Supervisor, Gate Services (air trans.)	ESR	62	238.137-018
Supervisor, Gear Repair (water trans.)	RES	59	623.131-014
Supervisor, Gelatin Plant (chemical)	ESR	59	559.137-030
Supervisor, Glazing Department (textile)	RES	59	582.130-010
Supervisor, Glue Specialty (chemical)	ESR	59	559.137-034
Supervisor, Glycerin (soap & rel.)	RSE	60	559.132-098
Supervisor, Grading (construction)	ERS	59	859.137-010
Supervisor, Grain and Yeast Plants (beverage)	ESR	59	529.132-062
Supervisor, Grease Refining (oils & grease)	REC	59	553.132-010
Supervisor, Green End Department (millwork-plywood)	RES	59	663.132-010
Supervisor, Grinding (any industry)	REI	59	603.130-010

Title	HOC	Cx	DOT
Supervisor, Grinding and Spraying (struct. metal)	RSE	57	809.134-010
Supervisor, Hairspring Fabrication (clock & watch)	ERS	59	715.131-018
Supervisor, Hand Silvering (glass products)	SER	58	574.134-010
Supervisor, Hardboard (wood prod., n.e.c.)	RES	60	539.130-010
Supervisor, Harvesting (chemical)	RES	56	939.137-022
Supervisor, Hearing-Aid Assembly (protective dev.)	ERC	58	726.131-014
Supervisor, Hide House (leather mfg.)	ESR	55	922.137-014
Supervisor, Historic Sites (government ser.)	AES	69	102.117-010
Supervisor, Home Restoration Service (any industry)	ERS	58	389.137-010
Supervisor, Home-Energy Consultant (utilities)	ESC	61	959.137-022
Supervisor, Horticultural-Specialty Farming (agriculture)	RES	60	405.131-010
Supervisor, Hospitality House (amuse. & rec.)	SER	59	359.137-010
Supervisor, Hot-Dip Plating (galvanizing)	REI	60	501.137-010
Supervisor, Hot-Dip-Tinning (steel & rel.)	REI	60	501.130-010
Supervisor, Hot-Strip Mill (steel & rel.)	RES	59	613.132-010
Supervisor, Hot-Wound Spring Production (metal prod., n.e.c.)	RES	61	619.130-026
Supervisor, Housecleaner (hotel & rest.)	SER	56	323.137-010
Supervisor, Hydrochloric Area (chemical)	REI	59	558.134-022
Supervisor, Ice House (food prep., n.e.c.)	ERS	56	523.137-010
Supervisor, Ice Storage, Sale, and Delivery (food prep., n.e.c.)	ESR	58	299.137-022
Supervisor, Identification and Communications (government ser.)	ESR	64	377.134-010
Supervisor, Incinerator Plant (sanitary ser.)	ECR	55	955.131-010
Supervisor, Insect and Disease Inspection (agriculture)	EAI	60	408.137-010
Supervisor, Insecticide (chemical)	RES	59	559.132-102
Supervisor, Inspecting (paper goods)	SEC	55	979.137-014
Supervisor, Inspection (agric. equip.)	ESR	59	801.137-014
Supervisor, Inspection (aircraft mfg.)	ESR	63	806.131-038
Supervisor, Inspection (clock & watch)	ERS	59	715.131-022
Supervisor, Inspection (glass mfg.)	ESR	58	579.134-010
Supervisor, Inspection (pen & pencil)	ERS	60	733.137-018
Supervisor, Inspection (plastic-synth.)	ESR	59	559.137-038
Supervisor, Inspection (sugar & conf.)	RCE	59	529.137-074
Supervisor, Inspection and Testing (elec. equip.)	REI	61	721.131-014
Supervisor, Inspection and Testing (motor-bicycles)	ERS	59	806.131-026
Supervisor, Instant Potato Processing (food prep., n.e.c.)	ECR	59	529.137-078
Supervisor, Instrument Assembly (electron. comp.; inst. & app.)	RES	59	710.131-038
Supervisor, Instrument Maintenance (any industry)	RES	63	710.131-014
Supervisor, Instrument Mechanics (utilities)	RES	63	710.131-018
Supervisor, Instrument Repair (any industry)	ERC	59	710.131-022
Supervisor, Insulation (construction)	RES	59	863.134-014
Supervisor, Insulation (nonmet. min.)	RES	60	590.130-014
Supervisor, Janitorial Services (any industry)	ESR	55	381.137-010
Supervisor, Jewelry Department (jewelry-silver.)	RES	60	700.131-018
Supervisor, Joiners (ship-boat mfg.)	RES	61	860.131-022
Supervisor, Kennel (nonprofit org.)	RCE	56	410.134-018

Part 3: From Occupational Titles to Holland Codes

From the Dictionary of Occupational Titles Occupations to Holland Codes

Title	HOC	Cx	DOT
Supervisor, Keymodule Assembly (office machines)	ECS	61	692.130-038
Supervisor, Knitting II (knitting)	RIS	59	685.130-010
Supervisor, Kosher Dietary Service (hotel & rest.)	SER	56	319.137-026
Supervisor, Labor Gang (any industry)	RES	59	899.133-010
Supervisor, Labor Gang (construction)	ERS	55	850.137-014
Supervisor, Laboratory (textile)	IER	64	689.134-026
Supervisor, Laboratory Animal Facility (agriculture)	ESR	63	418.137-010
Supervisor, Lace Tearing (tex. prod., n.e.c.)	SRE	59	689.134-014
Supervisor, Lamp Shades (fabrication, n.e.c.)	ERS	56	739.137-014
Supervisor, Landscape (museums; waterworks)	RES	59	406.134-014
Supervisor, Last-Model Department (wood prod., n.e.c.)	RES	59	761.131-010
Supervisor, Lathing (construction)	RES	59	842.131-014
Supervisor, Laundry (laundry & rel.)	RES	55	361.137-010
Supervisor, Lead Refinery (smelt. & refin.)	RSE	59	519.130-018
Supervisor, Lending Activities (financial)	SEC	64	249.137-034
Supervisor, Lime (concrete prod.)	ESR	58	579.132-014
Supervisor, Line (any industry)	RES	58	619.130-030
Supervisor, Line Department (r.r. trans.)	RES	59	825.137-010
Supervisor, Liquefaction (chemical)	RES	59	559.132-106
Supervisor, Liquefaction-and-Regasification (utilities)	RES	64	953.132-010
Supervisor, Liquid Yeast (food prep., n.e.c.)	RES	59	529.132-066
Supervisor, Liquor Stores and Agencies (government ser.)	SEA	63	185.167-062
Supervisor, Litharge (paint & varnish)	RES	59	559.132-110
Supervisor, Livestock-Yard (any industry)	REA	55	410.134-010
Supervisor, Loading and Unloading (any industry)	ERS	56	922.137-018
Supervisor, Locomotive (r.r. trans.)	ECR	59	625.137-010
Supervisor, Log Sorting (logging; millwork-plywood)	RES	56	455.134-010
Supervisor, Logging (logging)	ERS	56	459.133-010
Supervisor, Lubrication (any industry)	REC	59	699.131-010
Supervisor, Lump Room (tobacco)	RES	58	520.137-010
Supervisor, Machine Setter (any industry)	RES	60	619.130-034
Supervisor, Machining (woodworking)	ERS	59	669.130-022
Supervisor, Mail Carriers (government ser.)	SER	57	230.137-018
Supervisor, Mails (government ser.)	SER	57	243.137-010
Supervisor, Mainspring Fabrication (clock & watch)	ERS	59	715.131-026
Supervisor, Maintenance (chemical)	RES	56	382.137-010
Supervisor, Maintenance (petrol. refin.)	ESA	59	899.137-018
Supervisor, Major Appliance Assembly (house. appl.)	RSE	63	827.131-014
Supervisor, Malt House (beverage)	ESR	60	522.132-010
Supervisor, Malted Milk (dairy products)	ERS	59	529.132-070
Supervisor, Manufactured Buildings (mfd. bldgs.; vehicles, n.e.c.)	REI	59	869.131-030
Supervisor, Maple Products (food prep., n.e.c.)	ESA	58	529.137-050
Supervisor, Mapping (petrol. & gas; pipe lines)	ECR	66	018.167-030
Supervisor, Marble (construction)	RES	59	861.131-022
Supervisor, Marina Sales and Service (retail trade)	ERA	59	299.137-026
Supervisor, Marking Room (retail trade)	SEC	54	209.137-026
Supervisor, Matrix (recording)	RES	58	500.134-010
Supervisor, Mattress and Boxsprings (furniture)	RES	55	780.137-010

Title	HOC	Cx	DOT
Supervisor, Melt House (sugar & conf.)	RES	59	522.130-010
Supervisor, Merchant-Mill Rolling and Finishing (steel & rel.)	REI	59	613.130-014
Supervisor, Metal Cans (tinware)	RES	59	703.132-010
Supervisor, Metal Fabricating (any industry)	REI	59	809.130-014
Supervisor, Metal Furniture Assembly (furniture)	ESR	59	709.134-010
Supervisor, Metal Hanging (mfd. bldgs.)	REI	59	809.134-014
Supervisor, Metalizing (any industry)	RES	62	505.130-010
Supervisor, Metallurgical-and-Quality-Control-Testing (profess. & kin.)	IRE	70	011.161-010
Supervisor, Meter Repair Shop (utilities)	ERS	60	710.131-026
Supervisor, Meter Shop (waterworks)	REI	59	710.131-030
Supervisor, Meter-and-Regulator Shop (petrol. refin.; utilities)	SER	60	710.137-014
Supervisor, Microfilm Duplicating Unit (business ser.)	SCE	63	976.131-018
Supervisor, Microwave (radio-tv broad.)	IER	76	003.167-058
Supervisor, Mill (tex. prod., n.e.c.)	RES	58	589.130-026
Supervisor, Mill House (grain-feed mills)	RES	59	529.132-074
Supervisor, Mine (mine & quarry)	REI	63	181.167-018
Supervisor, Mirror Fabrication (glass products)	RES	56	679.137-014
Supervisor, Mirror Manufacturing Department (glass products)	ERS	58	579.131-010
Supervisor, Mixing (tex. prod., n.e.c.)	SIE	56	680.135-010
Supervisor, Mixing (textile)	SRE	59	680.130-014
Supervisor, Mixing Place (construction)	ERS	58	853.137-010
Supervisor, Model Making (clock & watch)	RSE	60	693.130-010
Supervisor, Mold Cleaning and Storage (glass mfg.)	RES	55	579.137-018
Supervisor, Mold Construction (concrete prod.)	SRE	59	860.131-026
Supervisor, Mold Making (glass mfg.)	RES	67	609.131-014
Supervisor, Mold Shop (glass mfg.)	RES	63	609.131-018
Supervisor, Mold Shop (pottery & porc.)	REI	59	777.131-010
Supervisor, Mold Yard (steel & rel.)	RES	59	519.137-010
Supervisor, Mold-Making Plastics Sheets (plastic-synth.)	ERS	55	579.137-022
Supervisor, Money-Room (amuse. & rec.)	CSE	59	211.137-018
Supervisor, Motion-Picture Equipment (motion picture; photo. appar.)	ESR	62	714.131-010
Supervisor, Motor Vehicle Assembly (auto. mfg.)	RSE	65	806.134-010
Supervisor, Motorcycle Repair Shop (automotive ser.)	ERS	60	620.131-018
Supervisor, Natural-Gas Plant (petrol. refin.)	RES	60	542.130-010
Supervisor, Natural-Gas-Field Processing (petrol. & gas; pipe lines)	RSE	61	549.131-010
Supervisor, Net Making (toy-sport equip.)	REI	59	789.132-022
Supervisor, Network Control Operators (any industry)	SEC	65	031.132-010
Supervisor, Nut Processing (can. & preserv.)	RES	58	529.130-026
Supervisor, Nutritional Yeast (food prep., n.e.c.)	RES	60	529.132-078
Supervisor, Open-Hearth Stockyard (steel & rel.)	RES	57	922.137-022
Supervisor, Operations (utilities)	ESI	65	952.137-026
Supervisor, Optical Instruments (inst. & app.)	SEC	59	711.137-010
Supervisor, Order Takers (clerical)	ESC	59	249.137-026

Dictionary of Holland Occupational Codes

Title	HOC	Cx	DOT
Supervisor, Ordnance Truck Installation (ordnance)	SER	59	806.137-014
Supervisor, Ornamental Ironworking (construction)	RSE	59	809.131-014
Supervisor, Ovens (steel & rel.)	ERA	60	542.132-014
Supervisor, Packing (boot & shoe)	RES	59	788.137-010
Supervisor, Packing (sugar & conf.)	RES	58	920.130-010
Supervisor, Packing and Wrapping (any industry)	ERS	58	920.137-026
Supervisor, Packing Room (leather mfg.)	ESA	58	589.137-010
Supervisor, Paint (paint & varnish)	ESR	59	559.132-114
Supervisor, Paint Department (any industry)	ESA	60	749.131-014
Supervisor, Paint Roller Covers (fabrication, n.e.c.)	RES	59	692.130-030
Supervisor, Painting (construction)	ERS	59	840.131-010
Supervisor, Painting Department (pen & pencil)	ERS	57	692.137-010
Supervisor, Painting, Shipyard (ship-boat mfg.)	ESA	59	840.131-014
Supervisor, Paper Coating (paper & pulp; paper goods)	SRE	60	534.132-014
Supervisor, Paper Machine (paper & pulp)	RES	59	539.132-010
Supervisor, Paper Products (paper goods)	REI	59	649.130-010
Supervisor, Paper Testing (paper & pulp; paper goods)	SEC	63	539.134-010
Supervisor, Parachute Manufacturing (tex. prod., n.e.c.)	RIE	58	789.132-026
Supervisor, Parking Lot (automotive ser.)	SER	50	915.133-010
Supervisor, Particle Board (wood prod., n.e.c.)	ERI	58	569.132-010
Supervisor, Paste Mixing (chemical)	RES	58	550.137-014
Supervisor, Paste Plant (steel & rel.)	RSE	58	549.132-026
Supervisor, Pattern Marking (garment)	RSE	59	781.131-010
Supervisor, Payroll (clerical)	ESR	60	215.137-014
Supervisor, Personnel Clerks (clerical)	CSE	62	209.132-010
Supervisor, Phosphatic Fertilizer (chemical)	ESR	61	558.130-010
Supervisor, Phosphoric Acid (chemical)	SRC	60	558.132-014
Supervisor, Phosphorus Processing (chemical)	ERS	59	559.132-118
Supervisor, Photoengraving (print. & pub.)	RSC	59	971.131-010
Supervisor, Picking (tobacco)	ESR	59	521.137-010
Supervisor, Picking Crew (agriculture)	RES	60	409.131-010
Supervisor, Pig-Machine (steel & rel.)	RES	57	514.137-010
Supervisor, Pigment Making (chemical)	ERS	59	559.132-122
Supervisor, Pile Driving (construction)	RES	59	859.137-014
Supervisor, Pipe Finishing (steel & rel.)	RSE	59	619.130-038
Supervisor, Pipe Joints (brick & tile)	RES	60	590.134-010
Supervisor, Pipe Manufacture (fabrication, n.e.c.)	RES	55	739.137-018
Supervisor, Pipeline Maintenance (pipe lines)	RSE	59	869.134-018
Supervisor, Pipelines (petrol. & gas)	REC	59	862.131-022
Supervisor, Pit-and-Auxiliaries (steel & rel.)	RES	56	514.137-014
Supervisor, Plastering (construction)	ERS	59	842.131-018
Supervisor, Plastic Sheets (plastic prod.)	REI	59	557.130-014
Supervisor, Plastics (toy-sport equip.)	RES	59	556.130-014
Supervisor, Plastics Fabrication (boot & shoe; inst. & app.; plastic prod.; plastic-synth.)	RSE	60	556.130-010
Supervisor, Plate Heating, Rolling, and Finishing (steel & rel.)	RES	59	619.132-030
Supervisor, Plating and Point Assembly (pen & pencil)	RES	59	733.130-010
Supervisor, Pleating (tex. prod., n.e.c.)	RES	58	583.137-010
Supervisor, Policy-Change Clerks (insurance)	CSE	62	219.132-010

Title	HOC	Cx	DOT
Supervisor, Pond (chemical)	SRE	59	939.130-010
Supervisor, Poultry Farm (agriculture)	RES	56	411.131-010
Supervisor, Poultry Hatchery (agriculture)	ESR	55	411.137-010
Supervisor, Poultry Processing (meat products)	RES	55	525.134-014
Supervisor, Powdered Metal (nonfer. metal; steel & rel.)	ESR	59	509.130-010
Supervisor, Powdered Sugar (sugar & conf.)	ERS	59	521.130-014
Supervisor, Power-Reactor (chemical)	REI	64	509.130-014
Supervisor, Precast and Prestressed Concrete (concrete prod.)	RES	59	575.131-014
Supervisor, Preparation Department (textile)	RES	61	681.130-010
Supervisor, Preparation Plant (mine & quarry)	EAR	59	549.137-014
Supervisor, Prepress (print. & pub.)	ESR	65	972.137-010
Supervisor, Press Room (print. & pub.)	RES	60	651.130-010
Supervisor, Pressing Department (garment)	ERS	59	583.132-010
Supervisor, Print Line (furniture)	ERS	59	652.132-010
Supervisor, Printed Circuit Board Assembly (electron. comp.)	ERC	60	726.134-010
Supervisor, Printed Circuit Board Testing (electron. comp.)	ERS	60	726.131-018
Supervisor, Printing and Stamping (jewelry-silver.; leather prod.)	RES	56	652.130-014
Supervisor, Printing-Shop (print. & pub.)	RES	60	979.130-014
Supervisor, Processing (chemical)	RES	59	551.130-010
Supervisor, Processing (sugar & conf.)	ECS	59	529.137-082
Supervisor, Product Inspection (textile)	SEA	57	689.134-018
Supervisor, Production (paper goods)	SEA	56	979.137-018
Supervisor, Production (petrol. & gas)	RSE	61	939.131-014
Supervisor, Production (tex. prod., n.e.c.)	SEA	59	589.135-010
Supervisor, Production Clerks (clerical)	CES	66	221.137-014
Supervisor, Production Control (clerical)	ESR	64	221.137-018
Supervisor, Production Department (aircraft mfg.)	ERC	67	806.131-042
Supervisor, Prop-Making (motion picture)	ESR	64	962.137-022
Supervisor, Properties (motion picture)	EAS	64	962.137-026
Supervisor, Protective-Signal Operations (business ser.)	CRE	59	379.137-022
Supervisor, Public Message Service (tel. & tel.)	SEA	60	239.137-026
Supervisor, Publications Production (print. & pub.)	SER	63	979.131-010
Supervisor, Pulp House (sugar & conf.)	RSE	56	529.130-030
Supervisor, Pulp Plant (paper & pulp)	ERS	62	539.132-014
Supervisor, Pumping (smelt. & refin.)	ERS	62	914.131-010
Supervisor, Pumping Station (waterworks)	RES	60	954.130-010
Supervisor, Punch-and-Assembly Department (elec. equip.)	RES	60	619.130-042
Supervisor, Purification (petrol. refin.)	ERS	63	549.132-030
Supervisor, Putty and Caulking (paint & varnish)	ERS	55	559.137-042
Supervisor, Quality Control (furniture)	RSE	59	763.134-010
Supervisor, Quality Control (photofinishing)	SEI	62	976.131-022
Supervisor, Quilting (textile)	RES	57	689.134-022
Supervisor, Radio Interference (electron. comp.)	RSE	63	823.131-022
Supervisor, Rag Room (paper & pulp)	ERS	55	539.137-010

DOT to HOC

From the Dictionary of Occupational Titles Occupations to Holland Codes

Title	HOC	Cx	DOT
Supervisor, Railroad Car Repair (railroad equip.)	RES	60	622.131-010
Supervisor, Reactor Fueling (chemical)	RSE	58	929.132-010
Supervisor, Ready-Mixed Food Preparation (food prep., n.e.c.)	SER	59	529.137-054
Supervisor, Real-Estate Office (real estate)	ECS	65	249.137-030
Supervisor, Receiving and Processing (glass mfg.)	ERS	59	579.137-026
Supervisor, Reclamation (mine & quarry)	ERA	62	850.133-010
Supervisor, Reclamation (wholesale tr.)	ESA	58	621.137-010
Supervisor, Record Press (recording)	RES	59	559.130-018
Supervisor, Refining (chemical)	RES	59	559.132-126
Supervisor, Refining (sugar & conf.)	RES	58	529.130-034
Supervisor, Refractory Products (brick & tile)	ERS	54	579.134-018
Supervisor, Reinforced-Steel-Placing (construction)	RES	59	801.134-010
Supervisor, Repulping (paper & pulp)	ERS	60	539.132-018
Supervisor, Research Dairy Farm (agriculture)	REC	54	410.134-022
Supervisor, Research Kennel (agriculture)	RCI	56	418.137-014
Supervisor, Reverberatory Furnace (smelt. & refin.)	RES	59	519.130-022
Supervisor, Rice Milling (grain-feed mills)	RES	59	521.131-010
Supervisor, Ride Assembly (amuse. & rec.)	RSE	56	801.131-018
Supervisor, Rides (amuse. & rec.)	SEC	59	342.137-010
Supervisor, Rigger (ship-boat mfg.)	RSE	58	806.131-030
Supervisor, Right-of-Way Maintenance (utilities)	RES	59	859.133-010
Supervisor, Riprap Placing (construction)	RES	55	850.137-018
Supervisor, Rocket Propellant Plant (ordnance)	RES	58	559.137-046
Supervisor, Roll Shop (steel & rel.)	RES	59	604.130-010
Supervisor, Roller Printing (textile)	SRE	58	652.130-018
Supervisor, Roller Shop (textile)	RSI	59	979.131-014
Supervisor, Roofing Plant (build. mat., n.e.c.)	RES	62	590.130-018
Supervisor, Rose-Grading (agriculture)	ESR	60	405.137-010
Supervisor, Roundhouse (railroad equip.)	RES	60	622.131-014
Supervisor, Route Sales-Delivery Drivers (retail trade; wholesale tr.)	ESR	59	292.137-014
Supervisor, Roving Department (textile)	RES	59	689.130-026
Supervisor, Rubber Stamps and Dies (pen & pencil)	SEC	60	733.131-010
Supervisor, Rug Cleaning (laundry & rel.)	ESA	56	369.137-014
Supervisor, Safety Deposit (financial)	ESR	58	295.137-010
Supervisor, Salvage (petrol. refin.)	RSE	59	929.131-010
Supervisor, Sample (plastic-synth.)	SER	59	754.137-010
Supervisor, Sample Preparation (textile)	SEA	61	979.137-022
Supervisor, Sandblaster (ship-boat mfg.)	RES	59	503.137-010
Supervisor, Sanding (woodworking)	RSE	60	662.132-010
Supervisor, Sawing and Assembly (furniture)	ERC	59	669.132-010
Supervisor, Sawmill (saw. & plan.)	RSE	59	669.130-026
Supervisor, Scenic Arts (motion picture; radio-tv broad.)	AES	69	149.031-010
Supervisor, Scouring Pads (nonmet. min.)	RSE	59	759.135-010
Supervisor, Scrap Preparation (steel & rel.)	RES	58	519.137-014
Supervisor, Screen Making (textile)	RSE	59	971.131-014
Supervisor, Screen Printing (textile)	SER	62	652.137-014
Supervisor, Securities Vault (financial)	SCE	60	216.132-014

Title	HOC	Cx	DOT
Supervisor, Sewer Maintenance (government ser.)	REI	58	851.137-014
Supervisor, Sewer System (waterworks)	EIR	70	184.167-238
Supervisor, Sewing Department (carpet & rug)	ESR	58	689.137-010
Supervisor, Sewing Room (fabrication, n.e.c.)	EAR	55	787.132-014
Supervisor, Shearing (any industry)	REI	60	615.132-010
Supervisor, Shed Workers (agriculture)	ERS	59	404.131-014
Supervisor, Sheet Manufacturing (smelt. & refin.)	RES	59	500.132-010
Supervisor, Shellfish Farming (fishing & hunt.)	RES	55	446.133-010
Supervisor, Shipfitters (ship-boat mfg.)	RES	59	806.131-034
Supervisor, Shipping (chemical)	SRE	58	550.137-018
Supervisor, Shipping Track (railroad equip.)	ESR	59	806.137-018
Supervisor, Shop (fabrication, n.e.c.)	ERS	56	692.130-042
Supervisor, Shop (petrol. & gas)	RES	59	710.131-034
Supervisor, Show Operations (amuse. & rec.)	ASE	64	969.137-014
Supervisor, Shuttle Fitting (woodworking)	RES	56	669.130-030
Supervisor, Shuttle Preparation (woodworking)	RES	56	669.130-034
Supervisor, Shuttle Veneering (woodworking)	RSC	59	669.130-038
Supervisor, Sign Shop (fabrication, n.e.c.)	AES	60	970.137-010
Supervisor, Silk-Screen Cutting and Printing (any industry)	SRE	59	979.131-018
Supervisor, Silvering Department (glass products)	ESR	56	574.132-014
Supervisor, Sintering Plant (smelt. & refin.)	RES	59	519.130-026
Supervisor, Ski Production (toy-sport equip.)	ERS	54	692.132-018
Supervisor, Slate Splitting (stonework)	SER	54	771.137-010
Supervisor, Slitting-and-Shipping (plastic-synth.)	RES	59	690.130-014
Supervisor, Small Appliance Assembly (house. appl.)	SER	59	723.131-010
Supervisor, Smoke Control (steel & rel.)	ECS	59	861.134-010
Supervisor, Soakers (beverage)	REA	55	529.132-082
Supervisor, Soaking Pits (steel & rel.)	REI	59	509.132-010
Supervisor, Soft Sugar (sugar & conf.)	RES	58	529.130-038
Supervisor, Solder Making (nonfer. metal)	RES	58	519.132-022
Supervisor, Sound Technician (business ser.)	ERS	61	823.131-026
Supervisor, Special Education (education)	SEC	67	094.167-010
Supervisor, Special Services (education)	ESI	67	169.267-026
Supervisor, Specialty Food Products (can. & preserv.; meat products)	RES	60	529.137-062
Supervisor, Specialty Manufacturing (steel & rel.)	REI	59	616.130-014
Supervisor, Specialty Plant (petrol. refin.)	ERS	61	549.137-018
Supervisor, Spinning (textile)	RES	60	682.130-010
Supervisor, Spinning and Winding (plastic-synth.)	RES	59	689.130-038
Supervisor, Split and Drum Room (leather mfg.)	ERS	59	589.132-014
Supervisor, Split Leather Department (leather mfg.)	REI	56	589.130-030
Supervisor, Spray, Lawn and Tree Service (agriculture)	ESR	63	408.131-010
Supervisor, Spring Production (metal prod., n.e.c.)	RES	59	616.130-018
Supervisor, Spring-Up (furniture)	RES	59	780.134-014
Supervisor, Statement Clerks (financial)	SEC	60	214.137-014
Supervisor, Stave Cutting (wood. container)	RCE	55	667.137-010
Supervisor, Steel Division (furniture)	RES	59	616.130-022
Supervisor, Steffen House (sugar & conf.)	REI	59	529.132-086

Title	HOC	Cx	DOT
Supervisor, Steno Pool (clerical)	CES	56	202.132-010
Supervisor, Stitching Department (tex. prod., n.e.c.)	RSE	55	787.132-018
Supervisor, Stock Ranch (agriculture)	RES	55	410.131-022
Supervisor, Structural Rolling-and-Finishing (steel & rel.)	RES	60	613.130-018
Supervisor, Structural-Steel Erection (construction)	RES	59	809.131-018
Supervisor, Sugar House (grain-feed mills)	ESR	58	529.132-090
Supervisor, Sugar Refinery (grain-feed mills)	RES	58	529.132-094
Supervisor, Sulfuric-Acid Plant (chemical)	SCR	60	558.132-018
Supervisor, Surgical Garment Assembly (protective dev.)	ESC	60	712.132-010
Supervisor, Survey Workers (clerical)	SEC	58	205.137-014
Supervisor, Swimming-Pool Maintenance (construction)	REC	59	869.131-038
Supervisor, Syrup Shed (sugar & conf.)	ESR	56	529.137-058
Supervisor, Tan Room (leather mfg.)	ERS	59	582.132-018
Supervisor, Tank Cleaning (paint & varnish)	ESA	55	559.137-050
Supervisor, Tank Cleaning (water trans.)	RES	59	891.137-018
Supervisor, Tank House (meat products)	RES	56	525.132-014
Supervisor, Tank Storage (beverage)	RES	58	529.132-098
Supervisor, Taping (construction)	ESC	58	842.134-010
Supervisor, Tar Distillation (chemical)	ESA	62	542.130-014
Supervisor, Tea and Spice (food prep., n.e.c.)	RES	59	529.132-102
Supervisor, Telecommunicator (government ser.)	ECS	60	379.132-010
Supervisor, Telegraphic-Typewriter Operators (clerical)	CSE	57	203.132-010
Supervisor, Telephone Clerks (tel. & tel.)	ESR	57	239.132-010
Supervisor, Telephone Information (motor trans.)	RES	65	237.137-010
Supervisor, Tellers (utilities)	SEC	62	211.137-022
Supervisor, Terminal Operations (motor trans.)	ESA	61	184.167-242
Supervisor, Terrazzo (construction)	RES	59	861.131-026
Supervisor, Thermostatic Controls (inst. & app.)	RES	59	710.131-042
Supervisor, Threshing Department (tobacco)	ERA	55	521.132-014
Supervisor, Ticket Sales (air trans.)	ESR	59	238.137-022
Supervisor, Tile-and-Mottle (fabrication, n.e.c.)	RES	58	559.130-022
Supervisor, Toilet-and-Laundry Soap (soap & rel.)	ESC	59	559.132-130
Supervisor, Tower (petrol. refin.)	ERS	60	549.130-010
Supervisor, Toy Assembly (toy-sport equip.)	RES	60	731.131-010
Supervisor, Toy Parts Former (toy-sport equip.)	RSE	60	692.130-034
Supervisor, Train Operations (r.r. trans.)	ESR	62	184.167-294
Supervisor, Transcribing Operators (clerical)	CSE	56	203.132-014
Supervisor, Travel-Information Center (government ser.)	ESA	63	237.137-014
Supervisor, Treating and Pumping (petrol. refin.)	ERS	62	549.132-034
Supervisor, Tree-Fruit-and-Nut Farming (agriculture)	REI	60	403.131-010
Supervisor, Tree-Trimming (utilities)	ERS	59	408.137-014
Supervisor, Trust Accounts (financial)	SCE	63	219.132-014
Supervisor, Tubing (textile)	ERS	53	689.137-014
Supervisor, Tufting (carpet & rug)	SRE	59	687.132-010
Supervisor, Tumblers (ordnance)	SER	59	599.132-010
Supervisor, Tumbling and Rolling (clock & watch)	RES	59	715.131-030
Supervisor, Tunnel Heading (construction)	REI	59	859.137-018
Supervisor, Type Photography (machinery mfg.)	ECS	60	976.131-026
Supervisor, Type-Disk Quality Control (machinery mfg.)	ECS	60	979.137-026

DOT to HOC

Title	HOC	Cx	DOT
Supervisor, Typesetting (print. & pub.)	RES	61	650.132-010
Supervisor, Underwriting Clerks (insurance)	CSE	63	219.132-022
Supervisor, Upholstery Department (any industry)	ESR	59	780.131-014
Supervisor, Uranium Processing (smelt. & refin.)	RES	59	519.130-030
Supervisor, Vacuum Metalizing (any industry)	RSE	59	505.130-014
Supervisor, Varnish (paint & varnish)	ERS	59	559.132-134
Supervisor, Vat House (chemical; leather mfg.)	RES	59	582.132-022
Supervisor, Vegetable Farming (agriculture)	RES	56	402.131-010
Supervisor, Vendor Quality (any industry)	EIA	70	012.167-062
Supervisor, Veneer (millwork-plywood)	ERI	58	569.135-010
Supervisor, Vine-Fruit Farming (agriculture)	RES	56	403.131-014
Supervisor, Volunteer Services (profess. & kin.)	ESR	63	187.137-014
Supervisor, Wall Mirror Department (glass products)	ESR	56	739.137-022
Supervisor, Wash House (beverage)	RES	58	529.132-106
Supervisor, Water Softener Service (business ser.)	SEC	60	862.134-014
Supervisor, Water Treatment Plant (waterworks)	EIR	58	954.132-010
Supervisor, Waterproofing (construction)	RCE	57	843.137-010
Supervisor, Waterworks (waterworks)	EIR	70	184.167-246
Supervisor, Weaving (carpet & rug)	RES	58	689.130-030
Supervisor, Webbing (tex. prod., n.e.c.)	RES	59	789.137-014
Supervisor, Welding Equipment Repairer (welding)	ESR	65	626.137-010
Supervisor, Wet End (wood prod., n.e.c.)	ERS	59	539.131-010
Supervisor, Wet Pour (concrete prod.)	ESR	56	575.137-014
Supervisor, Wet Room (paper & pulp)	RES	61	539.130-014
Supervisor, Wheel Shop (railroad equip.)	RES	60	622.131-018
Supervisor, Whipped Topping (dairy products)	RES	58	529.137-066
Supervisor, White Sugar (sugar & conf.)	RES	58	529.130-042
Supervisor, Winding and Twisting Department (textile)	RES	59	681.130-014
Supervisor, Wire-Rope Fabrication (metal prod., n.e.c.)	RES	59	691.130-014
Supervisor, Wood Room (paper & pulp)	RES	58	530.132-018
Supervisor, Wood-Crew (saw. & plan.)	SRE	53	669.137-010
Supervisor, Wool-Shearing (agriculture)	EAI	62	410.134-014
Supervisor, Word Processing (clerical)	CES	63	203.137-010
Supervisor, Yard (beverage)	ERS	62	529.137-070
Supervisor, Yarn Preparation (textile)	ECR	60	689.130-034
Supervisory Wastewater-Treatment-Plant Operator (sanitary ser.)	REI	61	955.130-010
Supplies Packer (any industry)	RSE	47	919.687-022
Supply Clerk (personal ser.)	RES	42	339.687-010
Supply Controller (concrete prod.)	RIE	51	570.382-018
Suppository-Molding-Machine Operator (pharmaceut.)	REC	37	556.686-022
Surface Supervisor (mine & quarry)	RES	62	932.132-014
Surface-Plate Finisher (stonework)	RIS	58	775.281-010
Surfboard Maker (toy-sport equip.)	RCE	45	732.684-126
Surgeon (medical ser.)	IRA	77	070.101-094
Surgical Technician (medical ser.)	ISR	56	079.374-022
Surgical-Dressing Maker (protective dev.)	CRS	40	689.685-130
Surgical-Elastic Knitter, Hand Frame (protective dev.)	RCI	49	685.382-010
Surgical-Forceps Fabricator (inst. & app.)	RCE	48	712.684-054

Title	HOC	Cx	DOT
Surveillance-System Monitor (government ser.)	CSR	49	379.367-010
Survey Worker (clerical)	CSE	48	205.367-054
Surveyor Assistant, Instruments (profess. & kin.)	IER	67	018.167-034
Surveyor Helper (any industry)	RCS	44	869.567-010
Surveyor, Geodetic (profess. & kin.)	IRE	67	018.167-038
Surveyor, Geophysical Prospecting (petrol. & gas)	IER	65	018.167-042
Surveyor, Marine (profess. & kin.)	IER	67	018.167-046
Surveyor, Mine (profess. & kin.)	IRE	69	018.161-010
Surveyor, Oil-Well Directional (petrol. & gas)	RCS	66	010.261-022
Survival Specialist (military ser.)	SRE	54	378.227-018
Survival-Equipment Repairer (government ser.)	RIS	52	739.381-054
Suture Polisher (protective dev.)	RCE	38	712.687-030
Suture Winder, Hand (protective dev.)	CES	38	712.687-034
Swage Tender (ordnance)	CSR	40	617.685-042
Swager Operator (pen & pencil)	RCE	40	616.685-078
Swaging-Machine Adjuster (ordnance)	RES	53	617.360-014
Swaging-Machine Operator (ordnance)	RCE	41	617.585-010
Swatch Checker (textile)	REI	56	683.260-022
Swatch Clerk (garment)	CRS	43	222.587-050
Sweatband Flanger (hat & cap)	REC	39	690.686-058
Sweatband Separator (hat & cap)	RCE	40	585.685-122
Sweatband Shaper (hat & cap)	RCI	37	784.687-090
Sweatband-Cutting-Machine Operator (hat & cap)	REC	40	690.686-062
Swedger (jewelry-silver.)	REC	38	735.687-038
Sweep-Press Operator (clock & watch)	RCE	38	616.685-082
Sweeper-Brush Maker, Machine (fabrication, n.e.c.)	REI	50	692.682-066
Sweeper-Cleaner, Industrial (any industry)	RCE	37	389.683-010
Sweeping-Compound Blender (chemical)	RCS	42	550.685-110
Sweet-Goods-Machine Operator (bakery products)	REC	41	520.685-214
Sweet-Potato Disintegrator (can. & preserv.)	REC	38	521.685-358
Swimming Pool Installer-and-Servicer (construction)	RCI	60	869.463-010
Swimming-Pool Servicer (any industry)	REC	45	891.684-018
Swing-Type-Lathe Operator (woodworking)	RIE	51	664.382-010
Switch Inspector (utilities)	RCI	52	952.381-010
Switch Repairer (r.r. trans.)	RCS	49	622.684-018
Switch Tender (r.r. trans.)	REI	41	910.667-026
Switchboard Operator (chemical)	RIE	56	952.362-038
Switchboard Operator (utilities)	RSI	57	952.362-034
Switchboard Operator Assistant (utilities)	RSE	54	952.367-014
Switchboard Operator, Police District (government ser.)	CRE	48	235.562-014
Switchbox Assembler I (comm. equip.)	RCE	37	722.687-010
Symbol Stamper, Semiconductor Packages (electron. comp.)	RCE	39	652.685-110
Synthetic-Filament Extruder (plastic-synth.)	REC	41	557.565-014
Synthetic-Gem-Press Operator (jewelry-silver.)	CRE	38	575.685-078
Synthetic-Staple Extruder (plastic-synth.)	RCE	45	557.665-010
Syrup Maker (beverage)	REI	51	520.485-026
Syrup Maker (sugar & conf.)	RCE	52	529.482-022
Syrup Mixer (grain-feed mills)	RES	53	529.462-010

Title	HOC	Cx	DOT
Syrup-Mixer Assistant (grain-feed mills)	RES	37	520.687-058
Systems Analyst (profess. & kin.)	IER	69	030.167-014
Systems Programmer (profess. & kin.)	IRC	70	030.162-022
Tab-Card-Press Operator (print. & pub.)	REI	52	651.382-034
Tab-Machine Operator (nonmet. min.)	CER	40	754.685-010
Tabber (paper goods)	CRE	36	794.687-058
Table Hand (tobacco)	RCE	37	521.687-138
Table Operator (nonfer. metal; steel & rel.)	RES	46	613.682-026
Table Tender (smelt. & refin.)	RES	44	511.685-062
Table Worker (boot & shoe)	RCE	40	788.687-142
Table Worker (fabrication, n.e.c.)	RCE	37	739.687-182
Table Worker (leather prod.)	RCE	36	783.687-030
Table-Cover Folder (tex. prod., n.e.c.)	REC	38	920.687-186
Table-Top Tile Setter (brick & tile)	RES	44	763.684-074
Tablet Tester (pharmaceut.)	CER	43	559.667-010
Tablet-Machine Operator (dairy products)	REC	42	529.685-238
Tablet-Making-Machine Operator (paper goods)	RIE	47	649.682-042
Tablet-Making-Machine-Operator Helper (paper goods)	RCI	46	649.685-130
Tack Puller (boot & shoe)	RCE	37	788.687-146
Tack Puller, Machine (boot & shoe)	RCE	37	690.685-410
Tacking-Machine Operator (any industry)	CRE	41	787.685-042
Tacking-Machine Operator (garment)	RCE	40	786.685-034
Tag-Machine Operator (paper goods)	REC	40	649.685-118
Tag-Press Operator (paper goods)	RSE	47	649.682-046
Tailer (mine & quarry)	RES	41	930.666-014
Tailings-Dam Laborer (smelt. & refin.)	REI	40	511.687-026
Tailor Apprentice, Alteration (garment; personal ser.; retail trade)	RIE	58	785.261-018
Tailor Apprentice, Custom (garment; personal ser.; retail trade)	RES	62	785.261-022
Take-Down Sorter (photofinishing)	CSE	44	976.665-010
Take-Up Operator (plastic-synth.)	RCE	41	557.685-034
Taker-Off, Hemp Fiber (tex. prod., n.e.c.)	RES	36	589.686-046
Tallier (clerical)	CSE	47	221.587-030
Tamale-Machine Feeder (food prep., n.e.c.)	RCE	37	520.686-038
Tamping-Machine Operator (construction)	RCE	46	869.683-018
Tank and Amphibian Tractor Operations Chief (military ser.)	ERS	55	620.137-010
Tank Assembler (wood. container)	REC	48	764.684-030
Tank Builder and Erector (construction)	RSI	56	860.381-066
Tank Calibrator (business ser.)	RIC	59	229.387-014
Tank Cleaner (any industry)	REI	41	891.687-022
Tank Cleaner (chemical; plastic-synth.)	REC	38	559.687-062
Tank Cleaner (paint & varnish)	REC	41	559.684-022
Tank Crewmember (military ser.)	REC	44	378.683-018
Tank Erector (construction)	RIS	57	860.381-070
Tank Pumper, Panelboard (beverage)	REC	42	529.685-242
Tank Setter (petrol. & gas)	RCS	52	801.361-022
Tank Tender (smelt. & refin.)	RSE	47	509.685-054

Title	HOC	Cx	DOT
Tank Tender (sugar & conf.)	REC	48	529.585-014
Tank-Car Inspector (chemical)	RSE	44	622.684-022
Tank-Car Inspector (petrol. refin.)	RCS	50	910.384-010
Tank-Farm Attendant (chemical)	RSC	48	559.665-038
Tank-House Operator (smelt. & refin.)	RES	52	519.362-014
Tank-House-Operator Helper (smelt. & refin.)	REC	42	519.565-014
Tank-Setter Helper (petrol. & gas)	RCE	40	801.687-018
Tank-Truck Driver (petrol. refin.; retail trade; wholesale tr.)	REC	45	903.683-018
Tankage Supervisor (construction)	REC	59	869.131-034
Tanker (wood prod., n.e.c.)	RCS	41	561.665-010
Tankroom Tender (plastic-synth.)	RCE	42	559.585-018
Tanner, Rotary Drum, Continuous Process (leather mfg.)	RSI	51	582.482-014
Tanning-Drum Operator (leather mfg.)	RCS	48	582.482-018
Tanning-Solution Maker (chemical)	REI	48	550.682-014
Tap-and-Die-Maker Technician (clock & watch)	RIE	59	601.280-034
Tape Coater (nonmet. min.)	REC	39	692.685-210
Tape Librarian (clerical)	CRS	53	206.367-018
Tape Stringer (garment; knitting)	CRE	38	782.687-054
Tape Transferrer (radio-tv broad.; recording)	RCS	53	194.382-014
Tape-Fastener-Machine Operator (paper goods)	CRE	40	649.685-122
Tape-Folding-Machine Operator (rubber goods; tex. prod., n.e.c.)	RCS	40	689.685-134
Tape-Making-Machine Operator (tex. prod., n.e.c.)	CRE	44	689.685-138
Tape-Recorder Repairer (any industry)	RIE	57	720.281-014
Taper (construction; mfd. bldgs.)	RES	47	842.664-010
Taper Operator (paper goods)	RES	41	649.685-126
Taper, Machine (boot & shoe)	RCE	42	690.685-414
Taper, Machine (fabrication, n.e.c.)	REC	41	692.685-214
Taper, Printed Circuit Layout (electron. comp.)	RCI	42	017.684-010
Tapper (beverage)	RCE	43	529.685-246
Tapper (nonfer. metal; smelt. & refin.)	RES	40	514.664-014
Tapper II (clock & watch)	RCE	41	715.685-062
Tapper Operator (nut & bolt)	REI	49	606.682-022
Tapper Supervisor (smelt. & refin.)	RES	59	514.134-010
Tapper, Balance-Wheel Screw Hole (clock & watch)	REC	46	715.682-022
Tapper, Bit (fabrication, n.e.c.)	RCE	38	739.685-046
Tapper, Hand (ordnance)	RES	35	737.687-134
Tapper, Shank (fabrication, n.e.c.)	RCE	38	739.685-050
Taproom Attendant (amuse. & rec.)	REC	40	312.677-010
Tare Weigher (meat products; sugar & conf.; tobacco)	RES	44	221.587-034
Target Aircraft Technician (military ser.)	RIE	55	378.281-010
Target Trimmer (toy-sport equip.)	RES	38	732.687-078
Targeteer (ordnance)	RCE	44	736.684-042
Tariff Inspector (r.r. trans.)	CSE	58	214.362-034
Tariff Publishing Agent (business ser.)	ESR	61	184.167-250
Tarring-Machine Operator (tex. prod., n.e.c.)	REC	41	584.685-046
Tassel-Making-Machine Operator (tex. prod., n.e.c.)	RCE	38	689.685-142
Taster (food prep., n.e.c.)	SER	59	529.281-010

DOT to HOC

DOT to HOC

Title	HOC	Cx	DOT
Tattoo Artist (personal ser.)	AEC	46	339.571-010
Tax Attorney (profess. & kin.)	ESI	75	110.117-038
Tax Clerk (clerical)	CES	51	219.487-010
Tax Preparer (business ser.)	CES	57	219.362-070
Taxi Driver (motor trans.)	RIE	51	913.463-018
Taxi Servicer (motor trans.)	REC	40	915.687-030
Taxicab Coordinator (motor trans.)	SCE	47	215.367-018
Taxicab Starter (motor trans.)	CES	51	913.367-010
Taxidermist (profess. & kin.)	IRS	64	199.261-010
Taximeter Repairer (automotive ser.)	RIE	57	710.281-038
Teacher (museums)	ESR	66	099.227-038
Teacher Aide I (education)	SCE	58	099.327-010
Teacher Aide II (education)	ESC	54	249.367-074
Teacher, Adult Education (education)	SER	60	099.227-030
Teacher, Adventure Education (education)	SEI	64	099.224-014
Teacher, Art (education)	ASE	66	149.021-010
Teacher, Drama (education)	ASE	65	150.027-014
Teacher, Elementary School (education)	SAE	66	092.227-010
Teacher, Emotionally Impaired (education)	SEC	66	094.227-010
Teacher, Hearing Impaired (education)	SEC	66	094.224-010
Teacher, Home Therapy (social ser.)	SEC	65	195.227-018
Teacher, Industrial Arts (education)	REI	68	091.221-010
Teacher, Kindergarten (education)	SEC	61	092.227-014
Teacher, Learning Disabled (education)	SER	64	094.227-030
Teacher, Mentally Impaired (education)	SEC	66	094.227-022
Teacher, Music (education)	AES	66	152.021-010
Teacher, Physically Impaired (education)	SEC	66	094.224-014
Teacher, Preschool (education)	SAE	62	092.227-018
Teacher, Resource (education)	ESR	69	099.227-042
Teacher, Secondary School, English (education)	ASE	66	091.227-010
Teacher, Secondary School, Home Economics (education)	SAE	66	091.227-010
Teacher, Secondary School, Speech (education)	SAE	66	091.227-010
Teacher, Secondary School, Subject Not Specified (education)	SAE	66	091.227-010
Teacher, Visually Impaired (education)	SEC	66	094.224-018
Teacher, Vocational Training (education)	SEC	65	094.227-026
Teamster (any industry)	RCS	39	919.664-010
Technical Coordinator (government ser.)	ESR	63	209.132-014
Technical Director, Chemical Plant (profess. & kin.)	IER	76	008.167-010
Technical Illustrator (profess. & kin.)	ARI	66	017.281-034
Technical Operator (petrol. & gas)	RIE	63	930.167-010
Technical Support Specialist (profess. & kin.)	SER	67	033.162-018
Technical Testing Engineer (motion picture)	RIE	58	194.381-010
Technical Training Coordinator (education)	ESR	66	166.167-054
Technician, News Gathering (radio-tv broad.)	IRS	60	194.362-022
Technician, Plant and Maintenance (radio-tv broad.)	RIE	58	822.281-030
Technician, Semiconductor Development (profess. & kin.)	IRE	69	003.161-018
Technician, Submarine Cable Equipment (tel. & tel.)	REI	59	822.281-034
Telecine Operator (radio-tv broad.)	RCE	59	194.362-018

Part 3: From Occupational Titles to Holland Codes

From the Dictionary of Occupational Titles Occupations to Holland Codes

Title	HOC	Cx	DOT
Telecommunicator (government ser.)	SIC	58	379.362-018
Telegraph-Plant Maintainer (tel. & tel.)	RSE	57	822.381-022
Telegraph-Service Rater (tel. & tel.)	CSE	45	214.587-010
Telegrapher (r.r. trans.)	CER	54	236.562-010
Telegrapher Agent (r.r. trans.)	CSE	52	236.562-014
Telegraphic-Typewriter Operator (clerical)	CSE	50	203.582-050
Telephone Clerk, Telegraph Office (tel. & tel.)	CSE	52	239.362-010
Telephone Operator (clerical)	CSE	49	235.662-022
Telephone Operator, Chief (clerical)	SEC	59	235.137-010
Telephone Quotation Clerk (financial)	CES	50	237.367-046
Telephone Solicitor (any industry)	ESC	54	299.357-014
Telephone-Answering-Service Operator (business ser.)	CSE	49	235.662-026
Telephone-Directory Deliverer (business ser.)	RSC	36	230.667-014
Telephone-Directory-Distributor Driver (business ser.)	RCE	42	906.683-018
Television Installer (any industry)	RCS	54	823.361-010
Television Technician (radio-tv broad.)	RIA	67	194.062-010
Television-and-Radio Repairer (any industry)	REI	57	720.281-018
Television-Schedule Coordinator (radio-tv broad.)	CSE	57	199.382-010
Teller (financial)	CSE	56	211.362-018
Teller (utilities)	CSE	51	211.462-034
Teller, Head (financial)	ESC	66	211.132-010
Teller, Vault (financial)	CRI	55	211.382-010
Temperature Inspector (meat products)	CRS	44	529.687-202
Temperature Regulator, Pyrometer (foundry)	RES	44	512.667-010
Temperature-Control Inspector (plastic-synth.)	CES	48	559.467-010
Temperer (heat treating)	RIS	48	504.682-026
Template Cutter (cutlery-hrdwr.)	CRE	44	703.684-018
Template Maker (any industry)	RIE	59	601.381-038
Template Maker, Extrusion Die (machine shop)	RIE	60	601.280-038
Template Maker, Track (any industry)	RSC	46	809.484-014
Template Reproduction Technician (aircraft mfg.)	RCI	56	976.381-022
Tennis-Ball Coverer, Hand (toy-sport equip.)	RCE	38	795.687-026
Tennis-Ball-Cover Cementer (toy-sport equip.)	REC	37	795.687-030
Tenoner Operator (wood prod., n.e.c.)	RCE	47	677.682-026
Tenoner Operator (woodworking)	RIS	53	669.382-018
Tensioning-Machine Operator (concrete prod.)	RCE	41	616.665-010
Tenter-Frame Operator (textile)	RCE	44	580.685-066
Terminal Superintendent (r.r. trans.)	ESC	66	184.167-254
Terminal-Makeup Operator (print. & pub.)	CRS	52	208.382-010
Terrazzo Finisher (construction)	RCE	43	861.664-014
Terrazzo Worker (construction)	REI	53	861.381-046
Terrazzo-Tile Maker (brick & tile)	REC	42	575.684-046
Terrazzo-Worker Apprentice (construction)	REI	53	861.381-050
Test Driver I (auto. mfg.)	RES	53	806.283-014
Test Driver II (auto. mfg.)	RIE	58	806.283-010
Test Engineer, Agricultural Equipment (profess. & kin.)	IRE	71	013.061-022
Test Engineer, Marine Equipment (profess. & kin.)	IRE	71	014.061-022
Test Engineer, Mechanical Equipment (profess. & kin.)	REI	70	007.161-034
Test Engineer, Mining-and-Oil-Field Equipment (mine & quarry; petrol. & gas)	IRE	71	010.061-030

Title	HOC	Cx	DOT
Test Engineer, Nuclear Equipment (profess. & kin.)	IRE	71	015.061-022
Test Equipment Mechanic (aircraft mfg.)	RIE	60	710.361-014
Test Fixture Assembler (electron. comp.)	RCI	46	726.684-098
Test Fixture Designer (electron. comp.)	RCI	57	726.364-014
Test Pilot (aircraft mfg.)	RIE	67	196.263-042
Test Preparer (nonfer. metal; steel & rel.)	RCE	46	509.584-010
Test Technician (agric. equip.)	RIS	60	019.261-022
Test Technician (clerical)	CSE	53	249.367-078
Test Technician (profess. & kin.)	IRE	67	019.161-014
Test Technician, Semiconductor Processing Equipment (electron. comp.)	IRC	63	590.262-014
Test Worker (foundry)	RCE	37	519.687-042
Test-Department Helper (comm. equip.; elec. equip.)	RSE	45	729.664-010
Test-Desk Supervisor (tel. & tel.)	ECR	61	822.131-030
Test-Engine Evaluator (petrol. refin.)	RIE	60	010.261-026
Test-Engine Operator (petrol. refin.)	RIE	62	029.261-018
Test-Skein Winder (glass mfg.)	RCE	45	575.685-082
Tester (musical inst.)	RCE	48	730.684-086
Tester (petrol. refin.)	RIE	62	029.261-022
Tester (pottery & porc.)	RCE	40	774.687-026
Tester (profess. & kin.)	RIC	57	011.361-010
Tester (rubber goods)	CRS	43	899.487-010
Tester and Inspector, Lamps (light. fix.)	CRE	39	723.687-014
Tester Operator (nonfer. metal)	RCS	45	614.684-014
Tester, Compressed Gases (chemical)	RIE	53	549.364-010
Tester, Convertible Sofa Bedspring (furniture)	RES	44	780.684-110
Tester, Electrical Continuity (elec. equip.; house. appl.; light. fix.)	CRS	44	729.684-058
Tester, Electronic Scale (office machines)	RES	52	710.381-046
Tester, Food Products (any industry)	ESC	60	199.251-010
Tester, Motors and Controls (elec. equip.)	RIE	57	721.281-030
Tester, Regulator (protective dev.; toy-sport equip.)	REI	49	710.387-010
Tester, Rocket Motor (aircraft mfg.)	RIE	61	806.261-022
Tester, Semiconductor Packages (electron. comp.)	RCI	43	726.685-054
Tester, Semiconductor Wafers (electron. comp.)	RCI	43	726.684-102
Tester, Sound (machinery mfg.)	CRS	50	706.382-014
Tester, Wafer Substrate (electron. comp.)	RCI	49	726.684-106
Tester, Waste Disposal Leakage (house. appl.)	CRE	43	723.687-018
Tester-Operator Helper (nonfer. metal)	RES	38	614.686-014
Testing and Analysis Department Supervisor (can. & preserv.)	SER	60	523.131-010
Testing-and-Regulating Chief (tel. & tel.)	ESA	63	184.167-258
Testing-and-Regulating Technician (tel. & tel.)	RES	58	822.261-026
Testing-Machine Operator (tex. prod., n.e.c.)	RCE	48	586.685-038
Testing-Machine Operator (tinware)	REC	40	703.685-014
Tetryl-Dissolver Operator (chemical)	RCS	43	550.685-114
Tetryl-Screen Operator (chemical)	REC	41	551.685-146
Texturing-Machine Fixer (textile)	RCI	45	628.684-046
Thaw-Shed Heater Tender (steel & rel.)	RCS	41	543.685-022

Title	HOC	Cx	DOT
Thermal Cutter, Hand I (welding)	REI	51	816.464-010
Thermal Cutter, Hand II (welding)	RSE	38	816.684-010
Thermal Molder (rubber goods)	REC	42	553.585-022
Thermal-Cutting-Machine Operator (welding)	RIE	53	816.482-010
Thermal-Surfacing-Machine Operator (stonework)	CRS	40	679.685-018
Thermometer Maker (inst. & app.)	RSE	47	710.681-026
Thermometer Production Worker (inst. & app.)	CRS	40	710.685-014
Thermometer Tester (inst. & app.)	REC	49	710.384-030
Thermoscrew Operator (can. & preserv.)	REI	41	526.685-058
Thermostat Repairer (inst. & app.)	REI	53	710.381-050
Thermostat-Assembly-Machine-Tender, Automatic (inst. & app.)	CRS	42	692.685-218
Thickener Operator (smelt. & refin.)	CRS	47	511.485-014
Thinner (paint & varnish)	RIE	47	550.585-038
Third Dry-Cell-Assembling-Machine Tender (elec. equip.)	RCE	36	692.686-066
Third Helper (steel & rel.)	REI	41	512.687-014
Third-Rail Installer (r.r. trans.)	RCS	49	825.381-038
Thrasher Feeder (paper & pulp)	RCE	38	533.685-030
Thread Cutter (any industry)	RCE	38	789.684-050
Thread Inspector (petrol. & gas)	RIE	57	862.381-038
Thread Inspector (plastic-synth.)	CSR	40	681.687-018
Thread Laster (boot & shoe)	CRE	43	788.684-114
Thread Marker (garment)	RCE	39	782.687-058
Thread Separator (tex. prod., n.e.c.)	RCE	35	789.687-174
Thread Winder, Automatic (textile)	RCE	38	681.685-122
Thread-Cutter Tender (tex. prod., n.e.c.)	CRS	42	689.665-014
Thread-Milling-Machine Set-up Operator (machine shop)	REI	53	605.382-042
Thread-Pulling-Machine Attendant (garment)	REC	38	689.686-046
Threader (knitting)	RCE	47	685.680-010
Threader (tex. prod., n.e.c.)	REC	40	689.687-078
Threading-Machine Feeder, Automatic I (machine shop)	RES	40	604.666-010
Threading-Machine Operator (machine shop)	RES	50	604.682-014
Threading-Machine Operator (ordnance)	RCE	44	604.685-038
Threading-Machine Setter (machine shop)	RIE	55	609.380-014
Threading-Machine Tender (carpet & rug)	CSE	41	683.685-030
Thresher, Broomcorn (agriculture)	RCS	38	429.685-014
Threshing-Machine Operator (tobacco)	RCE	38	521.685-362
Thrill Performer (amuse. & rec.)	ESR	49	159.347-018
Throw-Out Clerk (retail trade)	CSE	54	241.367-030
Thrower (pottery & porc.)	REA	52	774.381-010
Ticket Agent (any industry)	CSE	56	238.367-026
Ticket Broker (amuse. & rec.)	ESA	58	259.357-034
Ticket Marker (wholesale tr.)	CSE	49	216.567-010
Ticket Printer and Tagger (garment)	RCE	40	652.685-094
Ticket Puller (tobacco)	CRE	40	221.687-014
Ticket Scheduler (boot & shoe)	RCE	44	221.587-038
Ticket Seller (clerical)	CES	50	211.467-030
Ticket Taker (amuse. & rec.)	CES	41	344.667-010
Ticket Taker, Ferryboat (water trans.)	REC	46	911.677-010

Title	HOC	Cx	DOT
Ticket Worker (tobacco)	CER	50	221.482-018
Ticket-Chopper Assembler (furniture)	RCE	47	739.684-154
Ticket-Dispenser Changer (amuse. & rec.)	CRS	46	349.680-010
Ticketer (any industry)	CRE	42	652.685-098
Ticketer (textile)	CRE	42	229.587-018
Ticketing Clerk (air trans.)	CSR	54	248.382-010
Tie Binder (garment)	RCE	38	920.687-190
Tie Inspector (saw. & plan.)	RES	41	669.687-026
Tie Presser (knitting)	REC	40	789.687-178
Tie-Up Worker (office machines)	RES	41	710.687-034
Tier (meat products)	RCE	39	525.687-118
Tier-and-Detonator (mine & quarry)	RCE	42	931.664-010
Tightening-Machine Operator (paper goods)	REC	37	640.685-082
Tile Decorator (brick & tile)	RCI	53	773.381-010
Tile Finisher (construction)	RCE	43	861.664-018
Tile Grinder (brick & tile)	CSR	40	679.685-022
Tile Setter (construction)	RSE	54	861.381-054
Tile Setter (mfd. bldgs.)	CRE	43	861.684-018
Tile Setter Apprentice (construction)	RSE	54	861.381-058
Tile Shader (brick & tile)	CRE	51	574.367-010
Tile Sorter (brick & tile)	RES	44	573.687-038
Tile-Conduit Layer (construction)	RCE	50	861.381-062
Tile-Power-Shear Operator (fabrication, n.e.c.)	REC	40	692.685-222
Timber Framer (mine & quarry)	RES	52	869.381-034
Timber Packer (saw. & plan.)	REC	37	922.687-094
Timber-Framer Helper (mine & quarry)	REI	41	869.687-042
Timber-Sizer Operator (saw. & plan.)	RIE	49	665.482-018
Time-Study Engineer (profess. & kin.)	IRE	76	012.167-070
Timekeeper (clerical)	CSE	51	215.362-022
Timing Adjuster (clock & watch)	RES	48	715.681-010
Tin Recovery Worker (smelt. & refin.)	RIE	49	512.382-018
Tin Roller, Hot Mill (steel & rel.)	REI	57	613.360-018
Tin Stacker (tinware)	REC	36	922.687-098
Tin-Container Straightener (tobacco)	RCE	36	709.687-046
Tin-Whiz-Machine Operator (textile)	REI	47	582.685-154
Tinning-Equipment Tender (elec. equip.)	RCS	39	501.685-014
Tinning-Machine Set-up Operator (print. & pub.)	RES	46	653.682-022
Tinsel-Machine Operator (fabrication, n.e.c.)	RCE	40	692.685-226
Tinter (paint & varnish)	RIE	54	550.381-014
Tip Bander (pen & pencil)	REC	38	733.685-030
Tip Finisher (boot & shoe)	CRS	41	690.685-418
Tip Inserter (woodworking)	REI	44	669.682-066
Tip Printer (hat & cap)	CRS	48	651.682-022
Tip Stretcher (hat & cap)	REI	40	580.685-062
Tip-Length Checker (tobacco)	CSR	50	529.467-010
Tip-Out Worker (concrete prod.)	RCI	39	575.687-038
Tipper (print. & pub.)	RCE	42	795.684-022
Tipping-Machine Operator (pen & pencil)	RCE	42	733.685-034
Tipple Operator (saw. & plan.)	REC	42	921.662-026

Title	HOC	Cx	DOT
Tipple Tender (grain-feed mills)	RES	37	521.685-366
Tipple Tender (millwork-plywood)	REC	42	669.685-090
Tire Adjuster (retail trade)	REI	53	241.367-034
Tire Balancer (rubber tire)	CRS	40	750.687-014
Tire Buffer (automotive ser.)	REI	44	690.685-422
Tire Builder (automotive ser.)	REC	42	750.684-022
Tire Builder, Automobile (rubber tire)	RIE	50	750.384-010
Tire Classifier (rubber tire)	RCE	48	750.387-010
Tire Groover (automotive ser.)	RCS	42	750.684-026
Tire Inspector (automotive ser.)	CSR	47	750.687-018
Tire Inspector (rubber tire)	RCE	47	750.684-030
Tire Molder (rubber tire)	RCS	39	553.685-102
Tire Mounter (fabrication, n.e.c.)	REC	38	739.684-158
Tire Recapper (automotive ser.)	RES	43	750.685-014
Tire Repairer (automotive ser.)	REI	41	915.684-010
Tire Repairer (rubber tire)	RCI	45	750.681-010
Tire Setter (toy-sport equip.)	CRE	38	731.685-018
Tire Sorter (rubber tire)	RCS	42	750.687-022
Tire Technician (rubber tire)	REI	53	750.382-010
Tire Trimmer, Hand (rubber tire)	RCS	41	750.684-034
Tire Vulcanizer (automotive ser.)	REC	42	750.684-038
Tire-Bladder Maker (rubber tire)	CRS	42	750.684-042
Tire-Fabric-Impregnating-Range Operator, Chief (tex. prod., n.e.c.)	RES	47	589.662-014
Tire-Regrooving-Machine Operator (automotive ser.)	RSI	46	690.662-010
Tire-Service Supervisor (automotive ser.)	ERS	58	915.134-010
Title Attorney (profess. & kin.)	ESI	73	110.117-042
Title Clerk (petrol. & gas; petrol. refin.; pipe lines)	SEC	62	162.267-010
Title Examiner (profess. & kin.)	CSE	65	119.287-010
Title Searcher (real estate)	CRS	53	209.367-046
Title Supervisor (profess. & kin.)	CSE	68	119.167-018
TNT-Line Supervisor (chemical)	RSE	59	559.131-018
Tobacco Blender (retail trade)	RSC	52	790.381-010
Tobacco Curer (agriculture)	RSE	44	523.682-038
Tobacco-Cloth Reclaimer (tex. prod., n.e.c.)	RES	38	589.686-050
Tobacco-Drier Operator (tobacco)	RCE	42	523.685-118
Tobacco-Packing-Machine Operator (tobacco)	CRE	42	920.685-098
Tobacco-Sample Puller (tobacco)	CRE	41	529.587-022
Tobacco-Warehouse Agent (business ser.)	ESA	51	259.357-038
Toe Former, Stitchdowns (boot & shoe)	RCE	41	690.685-426
Toe Laster, Automatic (boot & shoe)	RCE	42	690.685-430
Toe Puncher (knitting)	RCI	40	689.685-162
Toe-Closing-Machine Tender (knitting)	RCE	40	787.685-046
Toggle-Press Folder-and-Feeder (boot & shoe)	REC	39	690.686-066
Toll Collector (government ser.)	CES	50	211.462-038
Tone Cabinet Assembler (musical inst.)	RES	46	730.684-090
Tone Regulator (musical inst.)	RCS	40	730.684-094
Tongue Presser (boot & shoe)	RCE	38	788.685-022
Tongue-and-Groove-Machine Operator (woodworking)	RSE	47	669.662-018

Title	HOC	Cx	DOT
Tonnage-Compilation Clerk (water trans.)	CRS	56	248.387-014
Tool and Fixture Repairer (auto. mfg.)	RCI	62	601.281-030
Tool Builder (aircraft mfg.)	RIC	62	693.281-030
Tool Design Checker (aircraft mfg.)	IRE	70	007.267-014
Tool Designer (profess. & kin.)	RIS	71	007.061-026
Tool Dresser (any industry)	RES	47	601.682-010
Tool Filer (pottery & porc.)	RCS	46	701.684-030
Tool Grinder I (any industry)	RES	50	701.381-018
Tool Grinder II (any industry)	RSC	39	603.664-010
Tool Maker (machine shop)	RIE	61	601.280-042
Tool Maker, Bench (machine shop)	RIE	58	601.281-026
Tool Planner (any industry)	IRE	70	012.167-074
Tool Programmer, Numerical Control (any industry)	IRE	66	007.167-018
Tool Programmer, Numerical Control (electron. comp.)	RCI	56	609.262-010
Tool Pusher (petrol. & gas)	RES	58	930.130-010
Tool Repairer (smelt. & refin.)	RSE	43	519.684-026
Tool-and-Die Maker (machine shop)	RIE	63	601.260-010
Tool-and-Die Supervisor (machine shop)	RES	63	601.130-010
Tool-and-Die-Maker Apprentice (machine shop)	RIE	63	601.260-014
Tool-and-Equipment-Rental Clerk (business ser.; retail trade)	ESR	54	295.357-014
Tool-Crib Attendant (clerical)	RES	53	222.367-062
Tool-Crib Supervisor (clerical)	ESR	58	222.137-046
Tool-Designer Apprentice (profess. & kin.)	RIS	71	007.061-030
Tool-Grinder Operator (machine shop)	RIE	58	603.280-038
Tool-Machine Set-up Operator (machine shop)	RIE	59	601.280-054
Tool-Maintenance Worker (office machines)	RCE	46	701.384-010
Tool-Maker Apprentice (machine shop)	RIE	61	601.280-058
Tooling Coordinator, Production Engineering (aircraft mfg.)	REI	66	169.167-054
Tooth Clerk (protective dev.)	CSE	47	222.687-038
Tooth Cutter (clock & watch)	CRE	43	605.685-050
Tooth Cutter, Escape Wheel (clock & watch)	RCE	47	605.682-026
Tooth Inspector (protective dev.)	CSE	38	712.687-038
Tooth Polisher (clock & watch)	REC	47	715.682-026
Top Former (boot & shoe)	RCE	38	788.685-026
Top Polisher (stonework)	RES	49	673.662-010
Top Screw (agriculture)	ESR	57	410.137-014
Top-Dyeing-Machine Loader (tex. prod., n.e.c.; textile)	RES	38	582.686-030
Top-Hat-Body Maker (hat & cap)	CRE	42	784.684-074
Top-Precipitator Operator (smelt. & refin.)	RCS	47	511.465-010
Top-Precipitator-Operator Helper (smelt. & refin.)	RCS	41	511.586-010
Topper (knitting)	REC	39	685.687-026
Topstitcher, Lockstitch (garment)	RCE	41	786.682-238
Topstitcher, Zigzag (garment)	RCE	41	786.682-242
Torch-Straightener-and-Heater (any industry)	RIE	45	709.684-086
Torque Tester (clock & watch)	RCE	42	715.685-066
Torsion Spring Coiling Machine Setter (metal prod., n.e.c.)	RIE	59	616.260-022
Touch-Up Carver (fabrication, n.e.c.)	RCI	42	761.684-054

Title	HOC	Cx	DOT
Touch-Up Painter, Hand (any industry)	CSR	38	740.684-026
Touch-Up Screener, Printed Circuit Board Assembly (electron. comp.)	RCE	41	726.684-110
Tourist-Information Assistant (government ser.)	CSE	60	237.367-050
Tow-Truck Operator (automotive ser.)	RES	44	919.663-026
Towel Inspector (textile)	RES	42	652.686-042
Towel-Cabinet Repairer (business ser.)	CRE	46	709.364-014
Tower Attendant (paper & pulp)	RES	40	559.666-010
Tower Erector (construction; utilities)	RES	55	821.361-038
Tower Erector Helper (construction; utilities)	RSC	47	821.684-014
Tower Helper (chemical)	REI	50	558.385-014
Tower Operator (r.r. trans.)	RSE	52	910.362-010
Tower Operator (soap & rel.)	REI	54	559.362-034
Tower-Crane Operator (construction)	CSE	46	921.663-054
Tower-Excavator Operator (construction)	RES	45	850.683-042
Tower-Loader Operator (water trans.)	RCE	48	921.683-074
Town Clerk (government ser.)	ECI	63	243.367-018
Toxicologist (pharmaceut.)	IRC	68	022.081-010
Toy Assembler (retail trade)	CRS	43	731.684-018
Toy Assembler (toy-sport equip.)	CRE	38	731.687-034
Toy-Electric-Train Repairer (retail trade)	REC	46	731.684-022
Tracer (construction; stonework)	RIE	57	779.381-022
Tracer-Bullet-Charging-Machine Operator (ordnance)	RSE	50	694.382-014
Tracer-Bullet-Section Supervisor (ordnance)	ERS	59	694.131-010
Tracer-Powder Blender (chemical)	RIE	48	550.585-042
Track Laminating Machine Tender (inst. & app.)	RCS	39	692.685-290
Track Oiler (r.r. trans.)	RCE	38	910.687-026
Track Repairer (r.r. trans.)	REI	47	910.684-014
Track Supervisor (grain-feed mills)	ESA	52	921.132-010
Track-Laying Supervisor (construction)	RES	60	869.134-022
Track-Moving-Machine Operator (construction; mine & quarry)	RIE	47	910.663-010
Track-Surfacing-Machine Operator (construction)	RIE	46	910.683-018
Trackmobile Operator (any industry)	RCE	44	919.683-026
Tractor Mechanic (automotive ser.)	REI	58	620.281-058
Tractor Operator (any industry)	RCE	46	929.683-014
Tractor-Crane Operator (any industry)	RCS	44	921.663-058
Tractor-Mechanic Helper (automotive ser.)	REI	44	620.684-030
Tractor-Trailer-Truck Driver (any industry)	RIE	50	904.383-010
Trade Marker (fabrication, n.e.c.)	RCS	43	690.685-510
Traffic Agent (air trans.; motor trans.; r.r. trans.; water trans.)	ESR	64	252.257-010
Traffic Checker (government ser.)	ERC	50	205.367-058
Traffic Clerk (business ser.)	CSE	53	221.367-078
Traffic Clerk (clerical)	CRS	50	214.587-014
Traffic Clerk (radio-tv broad.)	CRS	50	209.382-022
Traffic Inspector (motor trans.; r.r. trans.)	ESR	61	184.163-010
Traffic Lieutenant (government ser.)	ESR	61	375.167-046
Traffic Sergeant (government ser.)	RSE	56	375.137-026

DOT to HOC

Title	HOC	Cx	DOT
Traffic Technician (government ser.)	REI	68	199.267-030
Traffic-Maintenance Supervisor (government ser.)	ERI	59	869.137-010
Traffic-Rate Clerk (clerical)	CSE	56	214.362-038
Traffic-Safety Administrator (government ser.)	EAR	67	188.167-102
Trailer Assembler I (auto. mfg.)	RCE	48	806.381-058
Trailer Assembler II (auto. mfg.)	RES	46	806.684-082
Trailer-Rental Clerk (automotive ser.)	ESR	54	295.467-022
Train Clerk (r.r. trans.)	CSR	51	219.462-014
Train Dispatcher (r.r. trans.)	ECS	62	184.167-262
Train Dispatcher, Assistant Chief (r.r. trans.)	ECS	58	910.167-014
Training Representative (education)	SEC	68	166.227-010
Training Technician (can. & preserv.)	RES	50	522.264-010
Transcribing-Machine Operator (clerical)	CSE	50	203.582-058
Transfer Clerk (financial)	CER	53	216.362-046
Transfer Clerk, Head (financial)	ESC	62	216.137-014
Transfer Controller (saw. & plan.)	REI	41	921.682-022
Transfer Operator (paper & pulp)	REC	42	921.685-066
Transfer Operator (print. & pub.)	RCE	50	651.382-038
Transfer-and-Pumphouse Operator, Chief (chemical)	SER	59	559.132-138
Transfer-Car Operator (brick & tile)	RCE	38	921.683-078
Transfer-Car Operator, Drier (nonmet. min.)	RCE	41	921.583-010
Transfer-Machine Operator (knitting; tex. prod., n.e.c.)	RCE	41	659.685-022
Transfer-Machine Operator (machine shop)	RCE	44	609.685-022
Transfer-Table Operator (railroad equip.; r.r. trans.)	REI	45	910.683-022
Transfer-Table Operator Helper (railroad equip.; r.r. trans.)	RES	41	910.667-030
Transferrer (clock & watch)	CRE	44	715.684-190
Transferrer (print. & pub.)	RSE	48	972.381-026
Transformer Assembler I (elec. equip.)	RIE	58	820.381-014
Transformer Assembler II (elec. equip.)	RCS	45	820.684-010
Transformer Assembly Supervisor (elec. equip.)	ERS	63	820.137-010
Transformer Repairer (any industry)	REI	54	724.381-018
Transformer Shop Supervisor (any industry)	ESR	59	724.131-014
Transformer Tester (utilities)	RIS	60	724.281-010
Transformer-Stock Clerk (utilities)	RCS	48	222.587-054
Translator (profess. & kin.)	ISC	71	137.267-018
Transmission Mechanic (automotive ser.)	RES	53	620.281-062
Transmission Tester (auto. mfg.)	RCE	48	806.684-134
Transmission Tester (tel. & tel.)	RIS	57	822.361-026
Transmission-and-Protection Engineer (tel. & tel.)	IRE	76	003.167-066
Transmitter Operator (radio-tv broad.)	RSE	64	193.262-038
Transplant Coordinator (medical ser.)	SEC	68	079.151-010
Transplanter, Orchid (agriculture)	CRE	41	405.687-018
Transportation Agent (air trans.)	ESR	55	912.367-014
Transportation Engineer (profess. & kin.)	ISR	71	005.061-038
Transportation Inspector (motor trans.; r.r. trans.)	SER	60	168.167-082
Transportation-Equipment-Maintenance Worker (museums)	RCE	52	899.384-010
Transportation-Maintenance Supervisor (any industry)	ESR	66	184.167-266
Transporter, Patients (medical ser.)	CER	41	355.677-014
Trapper, Animal (fishing & hunt.)	RES	46	461.684-014

Part 3: From Occupational Titles to Holland Codes

From the Dictionary of Occupational Titles Occupations to Holland Codes

Title	HOC	Cx	DOT
Trapper, Bird (fishing & hunt.)	ECR	45	461.684-018
Travel Agent (business ser.; motor trans.; retail trade)	ECS	60	252.152-010
Travel Clerk (government ser.)	ESC	63	238.167-010
Travel Clerk (hotel & rest.)	ESC	54	238.367-030
Travel Counselor, Automobile Club (nonprofit org.)	SEC	59	238.167-014
Traveler Changer (textile)	REC	40	682.687-010
Traverse-Rod Assembler (furniture)	RCE	39	739.687-186
Trawl Net Maker (tex. prod., n.e.c.)	RES	53	789.381-018
Tray Drier (knitting)	REC	39	581.686-038
Tray Filler (tobacco)	RCE	40	920.686-050
Tray-Casting-Machine Operator (dairy products)	REC	42	520.685-218
Tray-Drier Operator (chemical)	RCE	41	553.665-054
Treasurer (profess. & kin.)	ESR	70	161.117-018
Treasurer, Financial Institution (financial)	ESR	71	186.117-070
Treater (any industry)	RCE	37	582.687-030
Treater (petrol. refin.)	RIA	57	549.362-014
Treater Helper (petrol. refin.)	RCE	44	549.685-030
Treating Engineer (wood prod., n.e.c.)	RES	56	561.362-010
Treating Inspector (wood prod., n.e.c.)	RIE	54	569.367-010
Treating-Engineer Helper (wood prod., n.e.c.)	RCE	40	561.685-010
Treating-Plant Operator (wood prod., n.e.c.)	RIE	48	563.662-010
Treating-Plant Supervisor (wood prod., n.e.c.)	RES	61	561.131-010
Treatment-Plant Mechanic (waterworks)	REI	57	630.281-038
Tree Cutter (agriculture; logging)	RES	41	454.684-026
Tree Driller (boot & shoe)	RCE	42	788.684-118
Tree Planter (forestry)	REC	35	452.687-018
Tree Pruner (agriculture)	RCE	49	408.684-018
Tree Surgeon (agriculture)	REI	56	408.181-010
Tree Trimmer (tel. & tel.; utilities)	RSE	45	408.664-010
Tree-Shear Operator (logging)	RIE	44	454.683-010
Tree-Surgeon Helper II (agriculture)	REC	41	408.687-018
Tree-Trimmer Helper (utilities)	RCS	37	408.667-010
Trim Attacher (cutlery-hrdwr.)	RCE	41	692.685-230
Trim-Machine Adjuster (ordnance)	RES	51	609.280-010
Trim-Machine Operator (ordnance)	REI	41	609.685-026
Trim-Stencil Maker (any industry)	RCE	45	781.684-058
Trimmer (hat & cap)	CRE	40	784.684-078
Trimmer (jewelry-silver.)	RCS	44	705.682-014
Trimmer (mfd. bldgs.)	REC	40	869.684-066
Trimmer (plastic prod.)	RIC	46	690.482-014
Trimmer Helper (saw. & plan.)	RCE	38	667.686-018
Trimmer Operator (nut & bolt)	RES	49	619.462-014
Trimmer Sawyer (saw. & plan.)	RCI	47	667.682-094
Trimmer, Hand (any industry)	RCS	38	781.687-070
Trimmer, Hand (boot & shoe)	RCE	38	788.687-150
Trimmer, Hand (leather mfg.)	REC	39	585.684-010
Trimmer, Hand (paper goods)	CRE	38	794.687-062
Trimmer, Machine (garment; knitting)	RCE	40	781.682-010
Trimmer, Machine (leather mfg.)	RCE	41	585.685-126

Part 3: From Occupational Titles to Holland Codes

From the Dictionary of Occupational Titles Occupations to Holland Codes

Title	HOC	Cx	DOT
Trimmer, Machine I (boot & shoe)	RCE	41	690.685-434
Trimmer, Machine II (boot & shoe)	CRS	45	690.682-086
Trimmer, Meat (meat products)	REC	37	525.684-054
Trimmer, Printed Circuit Board Panels (electron. comp.)	RCI	40	699.685-054
Trimming Assembler (furniture)	REI	46	780.684-114
Trimming Machine Set-up Operator (fabrication, n.e.c.)	RCI	49	664.382-018
Trimming Sewer, Automatic (garment; tex. prod., n.e.c.)	RCE	41	787.685-050
Trimming-Machine Operator (button & notion)	RCS	45	690.682-090
Trimming-Machine Operator (garment; knitting)	RCE	40	583.685-122
Trimming-Machine Operator (toy-sport equip.)	RCE	37	732.685-038
Trip Follower (air trans.)	RCE	54	209.367-050
Tripe Cooker (meat products)	REC	40	526.685-062
Triple-Air-Valve Tester (railroad equip.)	RSE	53	622.382-010
Trolley Cleaner (meat products)	REC	35	529.687-206
Trolley Operator (bakery products)	RCE	39	524.565-010
Trolley-Wire Installer (mine & quarry)	RCE	46	821.684-022
Trombone-Slide Assembler (musical inst.)	RCS	52	730.381-054
Trommel Tender (smelt. & refin.)	REC	42	511.685-066
Trophy Assembler (jewelry-silver.)	RCS	47	735.684-018
Trouble Locator, Test Desk (tel. & tel.)	RCS	54	822.361-030
Trouble Shooter I (utilities)	RES	49	952.364-010
Trouble Shooter II (utilities)	RSE	60	821.261-026
Truck Driver, Heavy (any industry)	RCS	47	905.663-014
Truck Driver, Light (any industry)	RCS	46	906.683-022
Truck Loader, Overhead Crane (nonfer. metal)	RCE	42	921.663-070
Truck Supervisor (motor trans.)	ERS	60	909.137-018
Truck-Body Builder (auto. mfg.; automotive ser.)	RIE	54	807.281-010
Truck-Crane Operator (any industry)	REC	45	921.663-062
Truck-Driver Helper (any industry)	RES	40	905.687-010
Truckload Checker (construction)	REC	52	222.367-066
Truer (metal prod., n.e.c.)	RCE	47	616.484-010
Truer, Pinion and Wheel (clock & watch)	REC	42	715.684-194
Truss Assembler (millwork-plywood)	RSC	46	762.684-062
Trust Officer (financial)	ESR	69	186.117-074
Trust Operations Assistant (financial)	CES	58	219.362-074
Trust-Vault Clerk (financial)	CSE	57	216.367-014
Tubber (jewelry-silver.)	REC	41	599.685-098
Tube Assembler, Cathode Ray (electron. comp.)	REC	42	725.684-022
Tube Assembler, Electron (electron. comp.)	CRE	44	725.384-010
Tube Balancer (rubber tire)	RCS	41	750.684-046
Tube Bender, Brass-Wind Instruments (musical inst.)	RES	49	617.382-010
Tube Bender, Hand I (any industry)	RES	43	709.684-090
Tube Bender, Hand II (any industry)	RCE	40	709.687-050
Tube Builder, Airplane (rubber tire)	CRS	43	750.384-014
Tube Cleaner (any industry)	REC	38	891.687-030
Tube Cleaner (textile)	RCE	37	589.687-042
Tube Coater (metal prod., n.e.c.)	REC	40	599.685-102
Tube Coverer (textile)	REC	37	589.687-046
Tube Drawer (nonfer. metal; steel & rel.)	REI	41	614.685-022

Title	HOC	Cx	DOT
Tube Handler (textile)	REC	39	582.686-034
Tube Molder, Fiberglass (plastic prod.)	RCE	41	690.685-438
Tube Operator (clerical)	CER	45	239.687-014
Tube Rebuilder (electron. comp.)	RIS	58	725.381-010
Tube Repairer (rubber tire)	RCS	41	750.684-050
Tube Sizer-and-Cutter Operator (ordnance)	CRE	44	640.685-086
Tube Sorter (rubber reclaim.)	REC	42	559.687-066
Tube Splicer (rubber tire)	RCE	41	690.685-442
Tube Winder, Hand (nonmet. min.)	RCE	41	692.685-234
Tube-and-Manifold Builder (rubber goods)	RCE	42	759.684-062
Tube-Building-Machine Operator (rubber goods)	REC	39	559.685-174
Tube-Cleaning Operator (foundry)	RCE	38	514.685-026
Tube-Machine Operator (paper goods)	RSE	47	641.662-014
Tube-Machine-Operator Helper (paper goods)	REC	40	641.686-038
Tuber-Machine Cutter (rubber goods; rubber tire)	CRE	41	690.685-446
Tuber-Machine Operator (rubber goods; rubber tire)	RCE	48	690.662-014
Tuber-Machine-Operator Helper (rubber goods; rubber tire)	RES	37	690.686-070
Tubing-Machine Operator (nonfer. metal; steel & rel.)	RES	41	613.685-030
Tubing-Machine Tender (clock & watch)	RCE	41	715.685-070
Tubular-Splitting-Machine Tender (knitting)	RES	41	686.685-070
Tucking-Machine Operator (any industry)	CRE	43	787.682-082
Tuft-Machine Operator (carpet & rug; tex. prod., n.e.c.)	CRS	44	687.682-014
Tufter (furniture)	RCE	43	687.684-014
Tufter, Hand (furniture)	RES	38	780.687-050
Tufting-Machine Operator (carpet & rug; textile)	RCE	47	687.685-018
Tufting-Machine Operator (furniture)	RCE	42	687.685-014
Tufting-Machine Operator, Single-Needle (carpet & rug)	CSE	42	687.685-022
Tugboat Captain (water trans.)	REI	63	197.133-030
Tugboat Mate (water trans.)	REI	59	197.133-034
Tumbler (clock & watch)	RCE	41	599.685-106
Tumbler Operator (any industry)	REC	41	599.685-110
Tumbler Operator (chemical)	REC	38	550.685-118
Tumbler Operator (laundry & rel.)	RES	38	369.685-034
Tumbler Operator (rubber goods)	REC	41	553.585-026
Tumbler Tender (food prep., n.e.c.)	CRE	39	520.685-222
Tumbler Tender (knitting)	REI	40	581.685-062
Tumbler-Machine Operator (rubber goods)	RCE	40	559.685-178
Tumor Registrar (medical ser.)	CES	64	079.362-018
Tune-Up Mechanic (automotive ser.)	REC	58	620.281-066
Tuner, Percussion (musical inst.)	RSE	52	730.381-058
Tungsten Refiner (smelt. & refin.)	RCE	53	511.382-010
Tunnel-Elastic Operator, Chainstitch (garment)	RCE	41	786.682-246
Tunnel-Elastic Operator, Lockstitch (garment)	RCE	41	786.682-250
Tunnel-Elastic Operator, Zigzag (garment)	RCE	41	786.682-254
Tunnel-Kiln Operator (brick & tile)	RES	51	573.382-018
Turbine Attendant (utilities)	RES	50	952.567-010
Turbine Operator (utilities)	RIE	57	952.362-042
Turbine Operator, Head (utilities)	REI	62	952.137-022
Turbine Subassembler (engine-turbine)	REI	53	706.381-042

DOT to HOC

Title	HOC	Cx	DOT
Turbine-Blade Assembler (engine-turbine)	RSE	57	600.380-026
Turkey-Roll Maker (meat products)	RCE	38	525.684-058
Turner (any industry)	REC	39	789.687-182
Turner (can. & preserv.)	REC	39	522.687-038
Turner (fabrication, n.e.c.)	REC	41	669.685-094
Turner (pottery & porc.)	RSE	48	774.684-038
Turner, Machine (clock & watch)	RCE	45	770.685-034
Turning Lathe Tender (furniture)	RCI	40	664.685-034
Turning Machine Set-up Operator (fabrication, n.e.c.)	RCI	50	669.382-026
Turning-and-Beading-Machine Operator (button & notion)	CRE	42	679.685-026
Turning-Machine Operator (tex. prod., n.e.c.)	RCE	40	689.685-146
Turning-Machine Operator (wood. container)	RCE	40	667.685-066
Turning-Machine-Operator Helper (wood. container)	RCS	38	667.686-022
Turning-Sander Tender (woodworking)	REC	41	662.685-038
Turret-Lathe Operator, Tumble Tailstock (clock & watch)	CRS	41	604.685-042
Turret-Lathe Set-up Operator (machine shop)	RIE	59	604.380-026
Turret-Lathe Set-up Operator, Tool (machine shop)	RIE	60	604.280-022
Turret-Punch-Press Operator (any industry)	RIE	54	615.482-038
Turret-Punch-Press Operator, Tape-Control (any industry)	RCE	43	615.685-042
Tutor (education)	SEC	65	099.227-034
Twister (tex. prod., n.e.c.)	CRE	41	681.685-126
Twister Tender (glass mfg.; nonmet. min.; plastic-synth.; textile)	RCE	42	681.685-130
Twister Tender, Paper (tex. prod., n.e.c.)	RCE	41	681.685-134
Twister, Hand (tobacco)	RCE	37	790.687-030
Twisting-Machine Operator (any industry)	REC	41	619.485-014
Twisting-Machine Operator (comm. equip.; elec. equip.)	REC	39	691.686-010
Twisting-Machine Operator (fabrication, n.e.c.)	RCS	49	692.682-070
Twitchell Operator (chemical)	CER	44	558.585-042
Tying-Machine Operator (paper goods; tex. prod., n.e.c.)	RCE	39	929.685-014
Tying-Machine Operator, Lumber (woodworking)	RCE	40	929.685-018
Type Copyist (machinery mfg.)	ASC	57	970.381-042
Type-Casting Machine Operator (print. & pub.)	REI	52	654.582-010
Type-Copy Examiner (machinery mfg.)	CRE	41	979.687-026
Type-Proof Reproducer (machinery mfg.)	RCI	45	652.685-106
Type-Rolling-Machine Operator (office machines)	REI	47	619.382-022
Type-Soldering-Machine Tender (office machines)	RCE	42	706.685-010
Typesetter-Perforator Operator (print. & pub.)	CRE	49	203.582-062
Typesetting-Machine Tender (print. & pub.)	RCE	45	650.685-010
Typing Section Chief (clerical)	ESC	55	203.137-014
Typing-Element-Machine Operator (office machines)	RCI	56	616.382-018
Typist (clerical)	CSE	49	203.582-066
Ultrasonic Tester (any industry)	RCI	57	739.281-014
Ultrasonic Tester (chemical)	RCS	46	709.687-054
Ultrasonic-Seaming-Machine Operator (garment)	CRE	41	786.682-258
Ultrasonic-Seaming-Machine Operator, Semiautomatic (garment)	CRE	39	786.685-038
Ultrasound Technologist (medical ser.)	RSI	61	078.364-010
Umbrella Finisher (fabrication, n.e.c.)	REC	39	739.687-190

DOT to HOC

Part 3: From Occupational Titles to Holland Codes
From the Dictionary of Occupational Titles Occupations to Holland Codes

Title	HOC	Cx	DOT
Umbrella Repairer (any industry)	RCE	44	369.684-018
Umbrella Tipper, Hand (fabrication, n.e.c.)	RCE	40	739.684-162
Umbrella Tipper, Machine (fabrication, n.e.c.)	RCE	37	739.685-054
Umpire (amuse. & rec.)	ESR	63	153.267-018
Unattended-Ground-Sensor Specialist (military ser.)	RIE	59	378.382-018
Unclaimed Property Officer (government ser.)	ERS	65	188.167-106
Undercoater (automotive ser.)	CRE	39	843.684-014
Undercover Operator (retail trade)	SEC	51	376.367-026
Underwater Hunter-Trapper (fishing & hunt.)	REI	51	461.664-010
Underwriter (insurance)	CSE	70	169.267-046
Underwriter, Mortgage Loan (financial)	CRS	69	186.267-026
Underwriting Clerk (insurance)	CSE	54	219.367-038
Unit Clerk (medical ser.)	ECS	54	245.362-014
Unit Operator (chemical)	CES	45	542.685-018
Unleavened-Dough Mixer (bakery products)	REC	40	520.685-226
Unscrambler (can. & preserv.)	RCE	39	921.685-070
Upholsterer (aircraft mfg.)	RCI	54	780.384-014
Upholsterer Helper (any industry)	REI	41	780.687-054
Upholsterer, Assembly Line (furniture)	RCI	41	780.684-134
Upholsterer, Inside (furniture)	RCS	52	780.381-038
Upholsterer, Limousine and Hearse (auto. mfg.)	RES	52	780.381-026
Upholsterer, Outside (furniture)	RCS	46	780.684-118
Upholstery Cleaner (furniture)	RSE	38	780.687-058
Upholstery Repairer (furniture)	RCS	46	780.684-122
Upholstery Sewer (any industry)	CRS	47	780.682-018
Upholstery Trimmer (furniture)	RCE	42	780.684-126
Upper-and-Bottom Lacer, Hand (boot & shoe)	CRE	42	788.684-122
Upper-Leather Sorter (boot & shoe)	RSC	49	788.387-010
Upsetter (forging)	RIS	47	611.662-010
Uptwister Tender (textile)	RCE	41	681.685-138
Urban Planner (profess. & kin.)	ESI	71	199.167-014
Urologist (medical ser.)	IRS	77	070.101-098
Used-Car Renovator (retail trade)	RES	47	620.684-034
User Representative, International Accounting (profess. & kin.)	ESC	72	189.117-038
User Support Analyst (profess. & kin.)	CSI	63	032.262-010
User Support Analyst Supervisor (profess. & kin.)	ESC	66	032.132-010
Usher (amuse. & rec.)	CES	40	344.677-014
Usher, Head (amuse. & rec.)	ESC	53	344.137-010
Utilities Service Investigator (utilities)	EIR	55	821.364-010
Utilities-and-Maintenance Supervisor (any industry)	RES	59	899.131-018
Utility Bag Assembler (leather prod.)	RIE	41	783.684-030
Utility Clerk (utilities)	CER	56	239.367-034
Utility Operator (garment)	REC	44	786.682-262
Utility Operator (saw. & plan.)	RCI	53	669.682-070
Utility Operator I (chemical)	REC	49	559.682-066
Utility Operator II (chemical)	RCS	46	709.684-094
Utility Operator III (chemical)	RCI	41	549.685-042
Utility Supervisor, Boat and Plant (ship-boat mfg.)	RSE	59	899.131-022

Title	HOC	Cx	DOT
Utility Tender, Carding (textile)	RCI	42	689.685-166
Utility Worker (mfd. bldgs.; vehicles, n.e.c.)	RES	49	869.684-074
Utility Worker (sugar & conf.)	REC	38	529.686-086
Utility Worker, Cloth Printing (textile)	RES	41	652.586-010
Utility Worker, Extrusion (nonfer. metal)	REI	43	691.685-030
Utility Worker, Film Processing (photofinishing)	RES	47	976.685-030
Utility Worker, Forge (forging)	RSE	38	612.684-010
Utility Worker, Line Assembly (auto. mfg.)	RES	51	806.367-010
Utility Worker, Merchant Mill (steel & rel.)	RES	45	801.664-014
Utility Worker, Molding (plastic prod.)	RCE	43	559.684-026
Utility Worker, Production (pharmaceut.)	RCI	49	559.684-034
Utility Worker, Roller Shop (textile)	RSE	44	628.684-034
Utility Worker, Woolen Mill (textile)	REI	40	689.686-050
Utility-Tractor Operator (construction)	RIE	44	850.683-046
Utilization Coordinator (radio-tv broad.)	SER	64	169.167-078
Utilization Engineer (utilities)	RCI	71	007.061-034
Utilization-Review Coordinator (medical ser.)	ECS	68	079.267-010
V-Belt Builder (rubber goods)	RCS	45	759.684-066
V-Belt Coverer (rubber goods)	RCE	40	690.685-450
V-Belt Curer (rubber goods)	REC	47	553.682-026
V-Belt Finisher (rubber goods)	RCE	41	690.685-454
V-Belt Skiver (rubber goods)	RCE	41	690.685-458
Vacuum Caster (foundry)	RES	46	514.582-010
Vacuum Cleaner Repairer (any industry)	REI	53	723.381-014
Vacuum Drier Operator (can. & preserv.)	RCE	42	523.685-122
Vacuum Plastic-Forming-Machine Operator (plastic prod.)	CRE	40	556.685-082
Vacuum Tester, Cans (can. & preserv.)	CRE	37	920.687-194
Vacuum-Applicator Operator (fabrication, n.e.c.)	RCE	40	692.685-238
Vacuum-Bottle Assembler (glass products)	CRE	38	739.687-194
Vacuum-Conditioner Operator (tobacco)	RSC	46	522.685-102
Vacuum-Drier Operator (tex. prod., n.e.c.)	RCE	41	581.685-066
Vacuum-Drier Tender (chemical)	RES	44	553.685-106
Vacuum-Metalizer Operator (any industry)	RCE	43	505.685-018
Vacuum-Pan Operator I (chemical)	REC	41	551.685-150
Vacuum-Pan Operator II (chemical)	REC	42	551.685-154
Vacuum-Pan Operator III (chemical)	RCS	45	559.585-022
Vacuum-Tank Tender (textile)	RSE	40	689.665-018
Value Engineer (aircraft mfg.)	IRE	73	002.167-010
Valve Grinder (machine shop)	RES	47	706.684-098
Valve Maker II (musical inst.)	RCE	50	730.681-018
Valve Repairer (chemical)	RSC	52	630.381-030
Valving-Machine Operator (paper goods)	RCE	40	641.685-094
Vamp Creaser (boot & shoe)	RCE	38	788.687-154
Vamp-Strap Ironer (boot & shoe)	RCE	37	788.687-158
Van Driver (motor trans.)	RES	49	905.663-018
Van-Driver Helper (motor trans.)	RES	41	905.687-014
Variety-Saw Operator (woodworking)	RSE	47	667.682-086
Varitype Operator (clerical)	CRE	52	203.382-026
Varnish Inspector (paint & varnish)	RCS	42	559.584-014

Title	HOC	Cx	DOT
Varnish Maker (paint & varnish)	REI	53	553.382-022
Varnish-Maker Helper (paint & varnish)	REC	40	553.686-042
Varnisher (fabrication, n.e.c.)	RCE	37	569.685-070
Varnishing-Machine Operator (print. & pub.)	RCE	41	534.685-030
Varnishing-Unit Operator (ordnance)	CRS	38	737.687-138
Varnishing-Unit Tool Setter (ordnance)	RCS	49	632.380-026
Vault Cashier (business ser.)	ESC	57	222.137-050
Vault Custodian (laundry & rel.)	RES	44	369.587-010
Vault Worker (business ser.)	REI	48	222.587-058
Vector Control Assistant (government ser.)	RIC	55	049.364-014
Vehicle-Fuel-Systems Converter (automotive ser.)	RIE	55	620.281-070
Vending-Machine Assembler (svc. ind. mach.)	RCE	43	706.684-102
Vending-Machine Attendant (hotel & rest.)	SRC	45	319.464-014
Vending-Stand Supervisor (government ser.)	ESI	66	185.167-066
Vendor (amuse. & rec.)	RES	44	291.457-022
Veneer Clipper (millwork-plywood)	RCE	41	663.685-050
Veneer Drier (millwork-plywood)	RCE	40	563.685-022
Veneer Grader (millwork-plywood)	RCS	43	569.687-034
Veneer Jointer (millwork-plywood)	RCS	47	665.682-038
Veneer Matcher (millwork-plywood)	SER	44	769.687-046
Veneer Redrier (millwork-plywood)	RCE	40	563.685-026
Veneer Repairer, Machine (millwork-plywood)	CRE	38	669.685-098
Veneer Stapler (ship-boat mfg.)	RCS	45	869.684-078
Veneer Taper (millwork-plywood)	CRE	41	569.685-074
Veneer-Clipper Helper (millwork-plywood)	RES	39	663.686-030
Veneer-Drier Feeder (millwork-plywood)	REC	36	563.686-014
Veneer-Jointer Helper (millwork-plywood)	CRE	37	665.686-018
Veneer-Jointer Offbearer (millwork-plywood)	RES	38	665.686-022
Veneer-Lathe Operator (millwork-plywood)	RIE	44	664.662-010
Veneer-Slicing-Machine Operator (millwork-plywood)	RSE	44	663.682-018
Veneer-Stock Grader (wood. container)	RCS	38	769.687-050
Veneer-Stock Layer (millwork-plywood)	RES	40	762.687-066
Veneer-Taping-Machine Offbearer (millwork-plywood)	RCI	38	569.686-054
Venetian-Blind Assembler (furniture; retail trade)	REC	43	739.684-166
Venetian-Blind Cleaner and Repairer (any industry)	RES	40	739.687-198
Venetian-Blind Installer (furniture; retail trade)	CRE	48	869.484-018
Ventilation Equipment Tender (any industry)	RCE	48	950.585-010
Ventilator (fabrication, n.e.c.)	REC	47	739.384-022
Ventriloquist (amuse. & rec.)	AES	61	159.044-010
Veterans Contact Representative (nonprofit org.)	ESA	67	187.167-198
Veterinarian (medical ser.)	IRS	73	073.101-010
Veterinarian, Laboratory Animal Care (medical ser.)	IRE	76	073.061-010
Veterinarian, Poultry (agriculture)	IRA	71	073.101-014
Veterinary Anatomist (profess. & kin.)	IRE	73	073.061-014
Veterinary Epidemiologist (profess. & kin.)	IRE	73	073.061-022
Veterinary Livestock Inspector (government ser.)	IRE	67	073.161-010
Veterinary Meat-Inspector (government ser.)	IRE	72	073.264-010
Veterinary Microbiologist (profess. & kin.)	IRE	77	073.061-018
Veterinary Parasitologist (profess. & kin.)	IRE	73	073.061-026

DOT to HOC

Title	HOC	Cx	DOT
Veterinary Pathologist (medical ser.)	IRE	76	073.061-030
Veterinary Pharmacologist (profess. & kin.)	IRE	72	073.061-034
Veterinary Physiologist (profess. & kin.)	IRE	73	073.061-038
Veterinary Technician (medical ser.)	ISR	58	079.361-014
Veterinary Virus-Serum Inspector (government ser.)	SIE	67	073.261-010
Vibrator-Equipment Tester (machinery mfg.)	RCS	56	825.361-014
Vice President (any industry)	ESR	69	189.117-034
Vice President, Financial Institution (financial)	ESR	74	186.117-078
Video Operator (radio-tv broad.)	ISA	63	194.282-010
Videotape Operator (radio-tv broad.)	IRS	53	194.382-018
Vine Pruner (agriculture)	RCE	36	403.687-022
Vinegar Maker (food prep., n.e.c.)	RIE	53	522.382-038
Violin Maker, Hand (musical inst.)	RES	59	730.281-046
Violin Repairer (any industry)	RES	54	730.281-050
Vocational Rehabilitation Consultant (government ser.)	ESR	69	094.117-018
Vocational Rehabilitation Counselor (government ser.)	SEC	66	045.107-042
Voice Pathologist (profess. & kin.)	IER	74	076.104-010
Voltage Tester (utilities)	RSE	57	821.381-014
Votator-Machine Operator (meat products; oils & grease)	REI	41	529.685-250
Voucher Clerk (r.r. trans.)	CSR	57	219.362-066
Vulcan Crewmember (military ser.)	RES	41	378.663-010
Vulcanized-Fiber-Unit Operator (paper goods)	RES	50	539.565-010
Vulcanizer (boot & shoe)	REC	40	690.685-462
Vulcanizing-Press Operator (boot & shoe)	RCE	41	690.685-466
Wad Impregnator (ordnance)	RCE	41	590.685-054
Wad Lubricator (ordnance)	CRE	41	590.685-058
Wad-Blanking-Press Adjuster (ordnance)	RCE	50	690.360-010
Wad-Compressor Operator-Adjuster (ordnance)	REI	51	535.482-010
Wad-Printing-Machine Operator (ordnance)	RCE	40	652.685-102
Wader-Boot-Top Assembler (rubber goods)	CRE	41	795.684-026
Wafer Abrading Machine Tender (electron. comp.)	RCI	41	673.685-102
Wafer Breaker, Semiconductors (electron. comp.)	RCI	39	726.687-046
Wafer Cleaner (electron. comp.)	RCI	42	590.685-102
Wafer Mounter (electron. comp.)	RCI	41	726.685-058
Wafer-Line Worker (elec. equip.)	RCE	38	727.687-082
Wafer-Machine Operator (bakery products)	REC	42	526.685-066
Wafer-Machine Operator (elec. equip.)	RCS	47	692.662-018
Waist Pleater (tex. prod., n.e.c.)	REC	44	583.684-014
Waistband Setter, Lockstitch (garment)	CRE	40	786.682-266
Waistline Joiner, Lockstitch (garment)	RCE	41	786.682-270
Waistline Joiner, Overlock (garment)	RCE	41	786.682-274
Waiter/Waitress (water trans.)	CES	47	350.677-030
Waiter/Waitress, Banquet, Head (hotel & rest.)	ESA	58	311.137-014
Waiter/Waitress, Bar (hotel & rest.)	ESR	49	311.477-018
Waiter/Waitress, Buffet (hotel & rest.)	CRE	44	311.674-018
Waiter/Waitress, Captain (hotel & rest.)	SER	55	311.137-018
Waiter/Waitress, Club (hotel & rest.)	ESC	41	352.677-018
Waiter/Waitress, Dining Car (r.r. trans.)	ECS	49	311.477-022
Waiter/Waitress, Formal (hotel & rest.)	ECS	50	311.477-026

Part 3: From Occupational Titles to Holland Codes

From the Dictionary of Occupational Titles Occupations to Holland Codes

Title	HOC	Cx	DOT
Waiter/Waitress, Head (hotel & rest.)	ESA	59	311.137-022
Waiter/Waitress, Informal (hotel & rest.)	ESC	49	311.477-030
Waiter/Waitress, Room Service (hotel & rest.)	ESR	47	311.477-034
Waiter/Waitress, Take Out (hotel & rest.)	ESR	44	311.477-038
Wallcovering Texturer (paper goods)	ARS	44	749.684-054
Wallpaper Inspector (paper goods)	RSE	43	652.687-042
Wallpaper Inspector and Shipper (paper goods)	CRE	42	652.687-046
Wallpaper Printer I (paper goods)	RSE	47	652.662-014
Wallpaper-Printer Helper (paper goods)	RSE	38	652.687-050
Wardrobe Supervisor (amuse. & rec.)	RES	53	346.361-010
Wardrobe-Specialty Worker (motion picture; radio-tv broad.)	RSE	53	969.381-010
Ware Cleaner (pottery & porc.)	RCE	38	774.687-022
Ware Dresser (pottery & porc.)	RCE	43	774.684-042
Ware Finisher (glass mfg.)	RCS	50	772.381-018
Ware Server (glass mfg.)	RCE	37	652.686-046
Ware Tester (glass mfg.)	REI	55	579.384-018
Warehouse Supervisor (any industry)	ESR	59	929.137-022
Warehouse Supervisor (motor trans.)	ERS	57	929.137-018
Warehouse Traffic Supervisor (wholesale tr.)	ESR	52	922.137-026
Warm-In Worker (glass mfg.)	CRS	39	772.684-018
Warp Coiler (textile)	REI	40	582.686-038
Warp Spooler (narrow fabrics; textile)	RCE	39	681.685-142
Warp-Dyeing-Vat Tender (textile)	REC	46	582.685-158
Warp-Knitting-Machine Operator (knitting)	RCS	47	685.665-018
Warp-Tension Tester (textile)	REC	41	683.687-034
Warp-Tying-Machine Tender (narrow fabrics; textile)	RCE	45	683.685-034
Warp-Yarn Sorter (textile)	CRS	41	681.687-022
Warper (narrow fabrics)	RCS	41	681.685-146
Wash Helper (chemical)	REI	48	559.665-042
Wash Operator (chemical)	RCE	52	559.662-014
Wash-House Worker (beverage)	REI	40	529.685-254
Wash-Mill Operator (chemical)	REC	47	559.485-010
Wash-Oil-Pump Operator (steel & rel.)	RCE	52	549.382-018
Wash-Oil-Pump Operator Helper (steel & rel.)	RCE	41	549.685-034
Wash-Tank Tender (chemical)	RCE	46	559.685-182
Washer (any industry)	REC	40	599.687-030
Washer (clock & watch)	REC	38	715.687-126
Washer (grain-feed mills)	REC	38	529.687-210
Washer (optical goods)	CRE	41	713.684-042
Washer (pen & pencil)	RES	36	733.687-078
Washer (plastic-synth.)	REC	42	582.685-162
Washer Engineer (paper & pulp)	CRS	42	533.685-034
Washer, Agricultural Produce (agriculture; can. & preserv.; sugar & conf.; wholesale tr.)	REC	39	529.685-258
Washer, Carcass (meat products)	REC	36	525.687-122
Washer, Hand (laundry & rel.)	REC	40	361.687-030
Washer, Machine (any industry)	REC	41	599.685-114
Washer, Machine (laundry & rel.)	REI	45	361.665-010

DOT to HOC

Title	HOC	Cx	DOT
Washer-and-Crusher Tender (mine & quarry)	RES	41	939.685-014
Washer-Engineer Helper (paper & pulp)	RCS	38	533.686-014
Washing-and-Screening Plant Supervisor (construction)	REI	57	570.132-018
Washing-Machine Loader-and-Puller (laundry & rel.)	REI	38	361.686-010
Washing-Machine Operator (any industry)	REI	41	599.685-118
Washroom Cleaner (sugar & conf.)	REC	39	529.687-214
Washroom Operator (sugar & conf.)	REC	38	529.665-014
Waste Chopper (tex. prod., n.e.c.)	REC	40	689.686-054
Waste Salvager (garment)	CRS	43	781.684-062
Waste-Disposal Attendant (any industry)	RSE	49	955.383-010
Waste-Machine Offbearer (tex. prod., n.e.c.)	RCS	38	680.686-022
Waste-Machine Tender (tex. prod., n.e.c.; textile)	RCE	39	680.685-114
Waste-Management Engineer, Radioactive Materials (profess. & kin.)	IRC	75	005.061-042
Waste-Paper-Hammermill Operator (paper & pulp)	RCE	36	530.686-018
Waste-Treatment Operator (chemical)	RCS	59	955.382-014
Wastewater-Treatment-Plant Attendant (sanitary ser.)	RIE	47	955.585-010
Wastewater-Treatment-Plant Operator (sanitary ser.)	REI	58	955.362-010
Watch Assembler (clock & watch)	RIE	55	715.381-094
Watch Manufacturing Supervisor (clock & watch)	RCS	59	609.130-026
Watch Repairer (clock & watch)	REI	59	715.281-010
Watch Repairer Apprentice (clock & watch)	REI	59	715.281-014
Watch-and-Clock-Repair Clerk (retail trade)	ERS	55	299.367-018
Watch-Band Assembler (jewelry-silver.)	CRE	42	700.684-082
Watch-Crystal Edge Grinder (glass products)	RCE	44	775.684-062
Watch-Crystal Molder (glass products)	RCE	44	772.684-022
Watcher, Automat (tex. prod., n.e.c.)	CRE	42	689.685-150
Watcher, Pantograph (tex. prod., n.e.c.)	RCE	41	689.685-154
Water Control Supervisor (waterworks)	ESA	66	184.167-270
Water Leak Repairer (auto. mfg.)	CRE	42	807.684-034
Water Regulator and Valve Repairer (waterworks)	REI	47	862.684-030
Water Tender (any industry)	RCS	44	599.685-122
Water-and-Sewer-Systems Supervisor (waterworks)	RES	59	862.137-018
Water-Filter Cleaner (waterworks)	REI	41	954.587-010
Water-Meter Installer (waterworks)	REI	47	954.564-010
Water-Quality Tester (paper & pulp)	REI	55	539.367-014
Water-Service Dispatcher (waterworks)	CRE	51	954.367-010
Water-Softener Servicer-and-Installer (business ser.)	RCE	48	862.684-034
Water-Treatment-Plant Operator (chemical)	RCE	50	551.485-010
Water-Treatment-Plant Operator (waterworks)	REI	53	954.382-014
Water-Truck Driver II (construction; petrol. & gas)	RIE	43	905.683-010
Watershed Tender (waterworks)	REC	49	954.382-018
Waterway Traffic Checker (water trans.)	CRE	52	248.367-030
Wave-Solder Offbearer (electron. comp.)	RCI	41	726.686-010
Wave-Soldering Machine Operator (comm. equip.; electron. comp.; inst. & app.; office machines)	RCS	50	726.362-014
Wax Bleacher (chemical)	RSE	45	551.685-158
Wax Blender (fabrication, n.e.c.)	RSC	45	550.585-046
Wax Molder (foundry; jewelry-silver.)	CRE	41	549.685-038

Dictionary of Holland Occupational Codes

Title	HOC	Cx	DOT
Wax Pourer (chemical)	CRE	40	737.685-018
Wax-Ball Knock-Out Worker (toy-sport equip.)	REC	37	732.687-082
Wax-Machine Operator (textile)	CRE	42	584.685-050
Wax-Pattern Assembler (foundry)	RCE	42	518.684-022
Wax-Pattern Coater (foundry)	RSE	38	518.687-022
Wax-Pattern Repairer (foundry)	RCE	40	518.684-026
Wax-Pot Tender (foundry)	RCE	41	553.685-110
Waxer (glass products)	RCE	37	779.687-038
Waxer, Floor (any industry)	RCS	37	381.687-034
Waxing-Machine Operator (paper goods)	RIE	51	534.482-010
Way Inspector (r.r. trans.)	RCE	52	910.367-030
Weather Clerk (air trans.)	CRS	52	248.362-014
Weather Observer (profess. & kin.)	RIE	61	025.267-014
Weatherstrip-Machine Operator (rubber goods)	RCE	51	690.382-014
Weave-Defect-Charting Clerk (textile)	CRS	42	221.587-042
Weave-Room Supervisor (carpet & rug)	RES	60	683.130-018
Weaver (carpet & rug)	RCE	46	683.682-034
Weaver (fabrication, n.e.c.)	CRE	43	739.684-170
Weaver (nonmet. min.; textile)	RCE	45	683.682-038
Weaver (wood. container)	CRE	44	769.684-054
Weaver Apprentice (nonmet. min.; textile)	RCE	45	683.682-042
Weaver, Axminster (carpet & rug)	RES	41	683.685-038
Weaver, Bench Loom (metal prod., n.e.c.)	RCS	47	616.681-010
Weaver, Hand (narrow fabrics; textile)	CRE	44	782.684-062
Weaver, Hand (personal ser.)	CRS	49	782.381-022
Weaver, Hand Loom (carpet & rug; textile)	RSE	48	683.684-030
Weaver, Narrow Fabrics (narrow fabrics; nonmet. min.)	RCS	46	683.682-046
Weaver, Needle Loom (narrow fabrics)	RCS	45	683.665-010
Weaver, Tire Cord (tex. prod., n.e.c.)	RCS	44	683.682-050
Weaving Inspector (carpet & rug; textile)	RCE	44	683.684-034
Weaving Supervisor (nonmet. min.; textile)	RES	60	683.130-022
Web-Press Operator (print. & pub.)	RIE	57	651.362-030
Web-Press-Operator Apprentice (print. & pub.)	RIE	57	651.362-034
Webbing Tacker (furniture)	RCS	39	780.684-130
Wedding Consultant (retail trade)	AES	60	299.357-018
Wedger, Machine (cutlery-hrdwr.)	RCE	40	701.687-034
Weed Inspector (agriculture)	REC	54	408.381-014
Weeder-Thinner (agriculture)	REC	36	409.687-018
Weft Straightener (textile)	RCE	45	580.682-010
Weigh-Tank Operator (oils & grease)	REI	49	529.485-026
Weigher (toy-sport equip.)	CRE	41	732.687-086
Weigher and Grader (chemical)	RES	44	559.567-014
Weigher and Mixer (chemical)	RSC	41	550.685-122
Weigher Operator (chemical)	RCS	42	559.687-070
Weigher, Alloy (nonfer. metal)	RSC	44	509.687-022
Weigher, Production (any industry)	CRS	42	929.687-062
Weigher-and-Crusher (smelt. & refin.)	RES	45	515.567-010
Weigher-Bulker (chemical)	RIE	50	550.582-014
Weight Analyst (profess. & kin.)	RIS	70	020.167-030

Title	HOC	Cx	DOT
Weight Guesser (amuse. & rec.)	ESA	48	342.357-010
Weight Tester (paper & pulp)	CSE	51	539.485-010
Weight-Reduction Specialist (personal ser.)	SEC	51	359.367-014
Weight-Yardage Checker (textile)	CSE	51	589.487-010
Weld Inspector (elec. equip.)	REC	40	724.685-014
Weld Inspector I (welding)	REI	59	819.281-018
Weld Inspector II (welding)	RES	45	819.687-010
Welder Apprentice, Arc (welding)	RIS	54	810.384-010
Welder Apprentice, Combination (welding)	RES	55	819.384-014
Welder Apprentice, Gas (welding)	RIE	51	811.684-010
Welder Helper (welding)	RES	40	819.687-014
Welder Setter, Electron-Beam Machine (welding)	RIE	57	815.380-010
Welder Setter, Resistance Machine (welding)	RIE	59	812.360-010
Welder, Arc (welding)	RIS	54	810.384-014
Welder, Combination (welding)	RES	55	819.384-010
Welder, Experimental (welding)	RIE	60	819.281-022
Welder, Explosion (welding)	RES	50	814.684-010
Welder, Gas (welding)	REI	51	811.684-014
Welder, Gun (welding)	RCS	42	810.664-010
Welder, Production Line (welding)	RCS	42	819.684-010
Welder, Tack (welding)	RSC	47	810.684-010
Welder-Assembler (machinery mfg.)	RES	53	819.381-010
Welder-Fitter (welding)	RIE	57	819.361-010
Welder-Fitter Apprentice (welding)	RIE	57	819.361-014
Welding Engineer (profess. & kin.)	IRE	76	011.061-026
Welding Supervisor (welding)	RES	61	819.131-014
Welding Technician (profess. & kin.)	RIS	59	011.261-014
Welding-Machine Operator, Arc (welding)	RIE	56	810.382-010
Welding-Machine Operator, Electron Beam (welding)	RIE	57	815.382-010
Welding-Machine Operator, Electroslag (welding)	RIE	51	815.382-014
Welding-Machine Operator, Friction (welding)	REI	52	814.382-010
Welding-Machine Operator, Gas (welding)	REI	52	811.482-010
Welding-Machine Operator, Resistance (welding)	RES	53	812.682-010
Welding-Machine Operator, Thermit (welding)	RIE	52	815.682-014
Welding-Machine Operator, Ultrasonic (welding)	REI	49	814.682-010
Welding-Machine Tender (welding)	RCE	40	819.685-010
Welding-Rod Coater (elec. equip.)	RSE	51	505.382-014
Welfare Director (government ser.)	SEC	69	188.117-126
Well Puller (petrol. & gas)	RIE	53	930.382-030
Well Puller, Head (petrol. & gas)	RES	59	939.131-018
Well-Drill Operator (construction)	RIE	57	859.362-010
Well-Logging Captain, Mud Analysis (petrol. & gas)	RIS	69	010.131-010
Well-Logging Operator, Mud Analysis (petrol. & gas)	RIE	63	010.281-022
Well-Point Pumping Supervisor (construction)	RES	57	862.132-010
Welt Beater (boot & shoe)	RCE	42	690.685-470
Welt Butter, Machine (boot & shoe)	RCE	41	690.685-474
Welt Cutter (boot & shoe)	CRS	42	690.685-478
Welt Wheeler (boot & shoe)	REC	41	690.685-482
Welt-Butter, Hand (boot & shoe)	REC	38	788.687-162

Title	HOC	Cx	DOT
Welt-Trimming-Machine Operator (hat & cap)	RCE	43	686.685-074
Wet Inspector, Optical Glass (optical goods)	RES	45	716.687-034
Wet Mixer (chemical)	CRE	40	550.685-126
Wet-and-Dry-Sugar-Bin Operator (sugar & conf.)	RES	41	529.665-018
Wet-Cotton Feeder (textile)	REC	37	581.686-042
Wet-End Helper (wood prod., n.e.c.)	CRE	42	534.685-034
Wet-End Operator I (plastic-synth.)	RCS	45	559.685-186
Wet-End Operator II (plastic-synth.)	RCE	45	559.685-190
Wet-Machine Tender (paper & pulp)	REC	43	539.685-030
Wet-Mix Operator (chemical)	RSC	49	558.382-058
Wet-Plant Operator (smelt. & refin.)	RCS	47	519.665-018
Wharf Attendant (amuse. & rec.)	REC	45	342.667-010
Wharf Tender (steel & rel.)	RSE	37	542.667-010
Wharf Worker (water trans.)	RES	37	921.667-026
Wharfinger (water trans.)	REC	54	184.387-010
Wharfinger, Chief (water trans.)	ERS	67	184.167-274
Wheat Cleaner (grain-feed mills)	CER	41	529.685-262
Wheel Assembler (mfd. bldgs.; vehicles, n.e.c.)	RES	40	809.684-038
Wheel Cutter (clock & watch)	RCE	47	605.682-030
Wheel Inspector (r.r. trans.)	REC	55	806.387-014
Wheel Lacer and Truer (motor-bicycles)	RCS	42	706.684-106
Wheel-and-Caster Repairer (any industry)	RCE	41	630.684-038
Wheel-Mill Operator (chemical)	RCE	40	555.685-066
Wheel-Press Clerk (railroad equip.)	CRE	42	221.587-046
Wheel-Truing Machine Tender (motor-bicycles)	RCE	42	706.685-014
Wheelwright (automotive ser.)	RES	48	706.381-046
Whipped-Topping Finisher (oils & grease)	REI	51	529.682-034
White-Shoe Ragger (boot & shoe)	RCE	37	788.687-166
Whiting-Machine Operator (wood prod., n.e.c.)	RCE	45	562.485-010
Whizzer (hat & cap)	CRE	40	581.685-070
Wholesaler I (wholesale tr.)	ESA	69	185.167-070
Wholesaler II (wholesale tr.)	ESA	67	185.157-018
Wick-and-Base Assembler (fabrication, n.e.c.)	REC	40	739.687-202
Wicker Worker (furniture)	RES	46	763.684-078
Wicker, Molded Candles (fabrication, n.e.c.)	RCE	42	692.685-242
Width Stripper (boot & shoe)	RCE	42	690.685-486
Wig Dresser (fabrication, n.e.c.; personal ser.)	SEC	52	332.361-010
Wig Maker (fabrication, n.e.c.)	RSE	52	739.381-058
Wildlife Agent, Regional (government ser.)	SER	66	379.137-018
Wildlife Control Agent (government ser.)	RSE	62	379.267-010
Winch Driver (water trans.)	RCE	45	921.683-082
Wind Tunnel Mechanic (aircraft mfg.)	RIE	64	869.261-026
Wind-Generating-Electric-Power Installer (construction; utilities)	RIE	58	821.381-018
Wind-Instrument Repairer (any industry)	RCS	54	730.281-054
Winder (clock & watch)	RCS	42	715.687-130
Winder (toy-sport equip.)	RCE	41	692.685-246
Winder Helper (paper & pulp)	REC	40	539.687-010
Winder Operator (fabrication, n.e.c.)	RSC	42	590.665-018

Title	HOC	Cx	DOT
Winder Operator, Automatic (textile)	RCE	41	681.685-150
Winding Inspector (house. appl.)	REI	51	729.384-022
Winding Inspector and Tester (elec. equip.)	CRS	50	724.364-010
Winding-Lathe Operator (ordnance)	REC	41	619.685-086
Winding-Machine Operator (concrete prod.)	RCE	38	619.665-010
Winding-Rack Operator (tex. prod., n.e.c.)	RCE	42	581.685-074
Window Repairer (any industry)	RCS	43	899.684-042
Window-Shade Cutter and Mounter (furniture)	CRE	41	692.685-250
Window-Shade-Ring Sewer (furniture)	CES	40	692.685-254
Wine Maker (beverage)	EIR	65	183.161-014
Wine Pasteurizer (beverage)	RCE	42	523.685-126
Wine Steward/Stewardess (hotel & rest.)	ESA	56	310.357-010
Winery Worker (beverage)	REC	42	521.685-370
Wing-Mailer-Machine Operator (print. & pub.)	RCE	38	208.685-034
Wink-Cutter Operator (rubber goods)	REC	49	557.382-014
Winterizer (oils & grease)	CRE	40	521.685-374
Wiper (furniture)	RCE	38	742.687-010
Wiper (light. fix.)	RCE	38	723.687-022
Wire Bender (furniture)	RCE	39	709.687-058
Wire Brush Operator (fabrication, n.e.c.)	RCI	40	761.684-058
Wire Charger (elec. equip.)	RES	43	614.586-010
Wire Coiler (house. appl.)	RCS	50	724.362-010
Wire Coiner (button & notion)	RCE	41	616.685-086
Wire Cutter (svc. ind. mach.)	RCE	35	731.687-038
Wire Drawer (clock & watch)	REC	49	614.382-014
Wire Drawer (jewelry-silver.)	REC	42	735.687-042
Wire Drawer (nonfer. metal)	RIE	49	614.382-010
Wire Drawing Machine Operator (inst. & app.; jewelry-silver.)	RCE	49	614.382-018
Wire Harness Assembler (elec. equip.; electron. comp.; office machines)	CSR	42	728.684-010
Wire Inserter (hat & cap)	CRE	40	784.687-082
Wire Preparation Machine Tender (any industry)	RCE	41	728.685-010
Wire Repairer (carpet & rug)	RCE	47	628.684-038
Wire Sawyer (stonework)	REI	47	677.462-014
Wire Setter (glass mfg.)	RCS	40	579.665-018
Wire Threader (clock & watch)	RCE	38	604.686-010
Wire Walker (amuse. & rec.)	AER	52	159.347-022
Wire Weaver, Cloth (metal prod., n.e.c.)	RES	54	616.382-014
Wire-Basket Maker (metal prod., n.e.c.)	RCE	40	709.687-062
Wire-Border Assembler (furniture)	REI	42	780.685-018
Wire-Coating Operator, Metal (galvanizing)	REI	41	501.485-010
Wire-Drawing-Machine Tender (nonfer. metal)	REC	42	614.685-026
Wire-Frame Dipper (button & notion)	REC	40	734.684-026
Wire-Frame Maker (button & notion)	RCE	46	734.481-010
Wire-Frame-Lamp-Shade Maker (fabrication, n.e.c.)	REI	52	709.684-098
Wire-Mesh-Filter Fabricator (metal prod., n.e.c.)	RIE	57	709.381-046
Wire-Photo Operator, News (print. & pub.)	CSE	53	239.382-010
Wire-Rope-Sling Maker (metal prod., n.e.c.)	RES	46	709.684-102

Title	HOC	Cx	DOT
Wire-Transfer Clerk (financial)	CSR	53	203.562-010
Wire-Turning-Machine Operator (wood. container)	RCE	39	692.685-258
Wire-Weaver Helper (metal prod., n.e.c.)	RES	41	616.687-014
Wire-Winding-Machine Operator (wood. container)	RES	38	619.685-090
Wire-Winding-Machine Tender (rubber goods)	REC	40	690.685-490
Wire-Wrapping-Machine Operator (electron. comp.)	RCI	44	726.682-014
Wire-Wrapping-Machine Operator (office machines)	RES	48	692.662-022
Wirer (office machines)	RES	52	729.281-042
Wirer, Cable (comm. equip.; elec. equip.)	RSE	48	729.381-022
Wirer, Street Light (utilities)	CRE	45	821.684-018
Wirer, Subassemblies (office machines)	CRS	46	729.684-062
Wireworker (elec. equip.; electron. comp.)	RCE	41	728.684-022
Wireworker Supervisor (utilities)	RES	62	821.131-026
Wood Caulker (ship-boat mfg.)	REC	44	843.384-010
Wood Grinder Operator (paper & pulp)	REI	47	530.662-014
Wood Grinder, Head (paper & pulp)	REA	55	530.132-022
Wood Hacker (fabrication, n.e.c.; paper & pulp)	RES	41	569.687-026
Wood Handler (paper & pulp)	REC	39	921.687-034
Wood Inspector (paper & pulp)	CRE	41	663.687-010
Wood Scrap Handler (millwork-plywood)	RCI	37	564.686-010
Wood Technologist (profess. & kin.)	IRS	76	040.061-062
Wood-Carving-Machine Operator (woodworking)	RIE	49	665.382-018
Wood-Crew Supervisor (chemical; saw. & plan.)	ERS	59	564.132-010
Wood-Fuel Pelletizer (fabrication, n.e.c.)	RCI	47	569.685-078
Wood-Heel Back-Liner (boot & shoe)	REC	38	662.685-042
Wood-Heel Finisher (boot & shoe)	CRE	39	788.684-126
Wood-Pole Treater (wood prod., n.e.c.)	REC	36	561.687-010
Wood-Turning-Lathe Operator (woodworking)	RIS	49	664.382-014
Wood-Web-Weaving-Machine Operator (furniture)	REI	42	692.685-262
Wooden-Frame Builder (furniture)	RCE	40	762.684-066
Wooden-Shade Hardware Installer (furniture)	CRS	44	739.684-174
Woodenware Assembler (woodworking)	RES	42	762.687-070
Woods Boss (logging)	REI	58	459.137-010
Woodwork-Salvage Inspector (ordnance)	RCE	52	769.387-010
Woodworking-Machine Feeder (woodworking)	REC	40	669.686-030
Woodworking-Machine Offbearer (woodworking)	REC	40	669.686-034
Woodworking-Shop Hand (woodworking)	RES	40	769.687-054
Wool Puller (leather mfg.; meat products)	CRE	42	589.687-050
Wool Sacker (agriculture)	RES	38	920.687-198
Wool Sorter (textile)	RIE	56	589.387-014
Wool-and-Pelt Grader (meat products)	RCS	50	589.387-018
Wool-Fleece Grader (agriculture)	RES	51	589.687-054
Wool-Fleece Sorter (agriculture)	REI	42	410.687-026
Wool-Washing-Machine Operator (textile)	CRE	40	582.685-166
Word Processing Machine Operator (clerical)	CRS	52	203.382-030
Work-Order-Sorting Clerk (utilities)	CSR	52	221.367-082
Work-Study Coordinator, Special Education (education)	SEC	64	094.107-010
Work-Ticket Distributor (knitting)	REC	41	221.667-010
Worm Grower (agriculture)	REI	56	413.161-018

DOT to HOC

Title	HOC	Cx	DOT
Worm Packer (agriculture)	REC	36	920.687-202
Worm Picker (agriculture)	REC	38	413.687-010
Worm-Farm Laborer (agriculture)	REC	36	413.687-014
Wort Extractor (dairy products)	REI	45	526.485-010
Woven-Wood Shade Assembler (furniture)	RCE	43	739.684-178
Wrap Turner (boot & shoe)	RCE	38	788.685-030
Wrapper (metal prod., n.e.c.)	RCE	42	920.685-102
Wrapper Counter (tobacco)	RCE	38	929.687-050
Wrapper Layer (tobacco)	RCE	40	529.685-266
Wrapper Operator (metal prod., n.e.c.)	RES	41	706.684-110
Wrapper Selector (tobacco)	CER	41	529.687-218
Wrapper-Hands Sprayer (tobacco)	REC	41	522.687-042
Wrapper-Layer-and-Examiner, Soft Work (tobacco)	RCE	37	529.685-270
Wrapping Machine Helper (tobacco)	REC	37	529.687-222
Wrapping-Machine Operator (paper goods)	RES	38	641.685-098
Wreath and Garland Maker (fabrication, n.e.c.)	RCE	41	739.684-182
Wreath Machine Tender (button & notion)	REC	40	739.685-058
Wrecking Supervisor (construction)	REA	57	869.137-014
Wringer Operator (chemical)	REC	40	551.685-162
Wringer Operator (tobacco)	REC	40	522.685-106
Wringer-Machine Operator (leather mfg.; tex. prod., n.e.c.)	REC	37	589.685-098
Wrinkle Chaser (boot & shoe)	RCS	38	788.684-130
Writer, Prose, Fiction and Nonfiction (profess. & kin.)	AIE	73	131.067-046
Writer, Technical Publications (profess. & kin.)	IRS	69	131.267-026
Wrong-Address Clerk (retail trade)	CRS	44	209.587-050
X-Ray Inspector (can. & preserv.; tobacco)	CRS	38	529.685-274
X-Ray-Equipment Tester (any industry)	REI	61	729.281-046
Yard Clerk (r.r. trans.)	CSE	50	209.367-054
Yard Coupler (r.r. trans.)	RES	48	910.664-010
Yard Engineer (r.r. trans.)	RIE	52	910.363-018
Yard Inspector (ship-boat mfg.)	RIE	56	869.281-018
Yard Laborer (paper & pulp)	RCE	36	922.687-102
Yard Manager (any industry)	ERS	58	910.137-046
Yard Manager (r.r. trans.)	ESC	61	184.167-278
Yard Supervisor (construction)	ESR	60	229.137-014
Yard Supervisor (forestry)	ERS	55	922.137-030
Yard Supervisor (smelt. & refin.)	ERS	61	929.137-026
Yard Supervisor (woodworking)	RES	59	929.133-010
Yard Supervisor, Building Materials or Lumber (retail trade; wholesale tr.)	ERS	60	929.137-030
Yard Supervisor, Cotton Gin (agriculture)	ERS	58	929.137-034
Yard Worker (agriculture)	RIE	46	929.583-010
Yard Worker (domestic ser.)	RES	42	301.687-018
Yard Worker (ship-boat mfg.)	RCS	43	921.683-086
Yard Worker, Used Building Materials (retail trade)	RCS	46	922.667-010
Yardage Estimator (garment)	REI	55	221.484-010
Yardage-Control Clerk (carpet & rug)	REC	42	221.587-050
Yardage-Control Operator, Forming (glass mfg.)	RES	50	575.662-014
Yarding Engineer (logging)	RES	48	921.663-066

Part 3: From Occupational Titles to Holland Codes

From the Dictionary of Occupational Titles Occupations to Holland Codes

Title	HOC	Cx	DOT
Yarn Cleaner (tex. prod., n.e.c.; textile)	RCE	40	681.687-026
Yarn Examiner (glass mfg.; plastic-synth.; textile)	RSE	42	681.687-030
Yarn Examiner, Skeins (textile)	CRE	42	689.687-082
Yarn Sorter (textile)	RCE	41	689.687-086
Yarn Winder (tex. prod., n.e.c.; textile)	RCE	42	681.685-154
Yarn-Mercerizer Operator I (textile)	CRE	40	584.685-054
Yarn-Mercerizer Operator II (textile)	REC	44	584.685-058
Yarn-Mercerizer-Operator Helper (textile)	REC	37	584.686-010
Yarn-Polishing-Machine Operator (textile)	RCE	40	583.685-126
Yarn-Texturing-Machine Operator (plastic-synth.)	CRE	42	589.685-102
Yarn-Texturing-Machine Operator I (textile)	CRE	41	681.685-158
Yarn-Texturing-Machine Operator II (textile)	CRE	41	689.685-158
Yeast Distiller (beverage)	RCS	53	522.362-010
Yeast Pusher (beverage)	REI	40	522.665-014
Yeast Washer (food prep., n.e.c.)	RCE	48	529.685-278
Yeast-Culture Developer (beverage)	RIS	56	022.381-010
Yeast-Cutting-and-Wrapping-Machine Operator (food prep., n.e.c.)	CRE	40	529.665-022
Yeast-Fermentation Attendant (food prep., n.e.c.)	REC	46	522.685-110
Yield-Loss Inspector (grain-feed mills)	RCS	54	529.367-030
Young-Adult Librarian (library)	AES	64	100.167-034
Zigzag-Machine Operator (garment)	CRE	40	786.682-278
Zinc-Chloride Operator (smelt. & refin.)	REC	50	511.385-010
Zinc-Plating-Machine Operator (electroplating)	REI	50	500.485-010
Zipper Cutter (button & notion)	REC	40	616.685-090
Zipper Setter (any industry)	CRE	43	787.682-086
Zipper Setter, Chainstitch (garment)	RCE	41	786.682-282
Zipper Setter, Lockstitch (garment)	RCE	41	786.682-286
Zipper Trimmer, Hand (button & notion)	CRE	42	734.687-094
Zipper Trimmer, Machine (button & notion)	CRE	40	692.685-266
Zipper-Machine Operator (button & notion)	RCE	45	692.685-270
Zoo Veterinarian (medical ser.)	ISE	76	073.101-018
Zoologist (profess. & kin.)	IRE	78	041.061-090

Note. n.e.c. = not elsewhere classified.

Part 3: From Occupational Titles to Holland Codes

From the Occupational Employment Statistics Occupations to Holland Codes

Title	HOC	Cx	OES
Able Seamen	REC	53	97514
Accountants and Auditors	CEI	70	21114
Actuaries	ISE	72	25313
Adjudicators, Hearings Officers, and Judicial Reviewers	SEC	69	28105
Adjustment Clerks	ESR	58	53123
Administrative Services Managers	ESR	66	13014
Advertising Clerks	CSE	54	53908
Aeronautical and Astronautical Engineers	IRE	76	22102
Agricultural and Food Scientists	IRS	77	24305
Agricultural Engineers	IRE	72	22123
Air Hammer Operators	RCS	38	87702
Aircraft Engine Specialists	RIE	60	85326
Aircraft Mechanics	REI	54	85323
Aircraft Pilots and Flight Engineers	RIE	67	97702
Aircraft Structure, Surfaces, Rigging, and Systems Assemblers, Precision	RIE	58	93102
Airplane Dispatchers and Air Traffic Controllers	SER	64	39002
All Other Agricultural, Forestry, Fishing, and Related Workers	REI	50	79999
All Other Cleaning and Building Service Workers	RES	41	67099
All Other Clerical and Administrative Support Workers	CES	51	59999
All Other Communications Equipment Operators	SEC	54	57199
All Other Communications Equipment Mechanics, Installers, and Repairers	REI	57	85599
All Other Computer Scientists	SRI	64	25199
All Other Construction and Extractive Workers, Except Helpers	RES	40	87999
All Other Construction Trades Workers	RCE	48	87899
All Other Electrical and Electronic Equipment Mechanics, Installers, and Repairers	RIE	59	85799
All Other Engineering and Related Technicians and Technologists	RIE	61	22599
All Other Engineers	IRE	73	22199
All Other Extractive Workers, Except Helpers	RES	45	87989
All Other Financial Specialists	ESI	67	21199
All Other First-Line Supervisors and Managers/Supervisors - Production, Construction, Maintenance, and Related Workers	ESR	59	81099
All Other Food Service Workers	ECS	48	65099
All Other Freight, Stock, and Material Movers, Hand	RES	40	98799
All Other Hand Workers	RCE	41	93999
All Other Health Diagnosing and Treating Practitioners	ISR	66	32199
All Other Health Professionals, Paraprofessionals, and Technicians	RSI	61	32999
All Other Health Service Workers	CRS	49	66099
All Other Helpers, Laborers, and Material Movers, Hand	REC	39	98999
All Other Inspectors, Testers, and Related Workers	RSC	48	83099
All Other Legal Assistants and Technicians, Except Clerical	ESC	66	28399
All Other Lithography and Photoengraving Workers	REI	58	89719

Dictionary of Holland Occupational Codes

Part 3: From Occupational Titles to Holland Codes

From the Occupational Employment Statistics Occupations to Holland Codes

Title	HOC	Cx	OES
All Other Machine Operators and Tenders	RCE	42	92998
All Other Machine Setters and Set-up Operators	REI	50	92997
All Other Machinery Maintenance Mechanics	REI	55	85119
All Other Management Support Workers	ESR	65	21999
All Other Managers and Administrators	ESR	65	19999
All Other Material Recording, Scheduling, and Distributing Workers	CRS	49	58099
All Other Material-Moving Equipment Operators	REC	43	97989
All Other Mathematical Scientists	IRA	73	25319
All Other Mechanics, Installers, and Repairers	RCE	49	85999
All Other Metal and Plastic (cutting, forming, fabricating, or processing) Machine Setters and Set-up Operators	REI	53	92197
All Other Metal and Plastic (cutting, forming, fabricating, or processing) Machine Operators and Tenders	RCE	43	92198
All Other Mining Machine Operators	REC	48	87949
All Other Motor Vehicle Operators	RCE	41	97199
All Other Office Machine Operators	CRS	45	56099
All Other Physical and Life Science Technicians and Technologists	IRE	62	24599
All Other Physical Sciences Teachers, Postsecondary	IRE	74	31209
All Other Physical Scientists	IRE	78	24199
All Other Plant and System Operators	REI	53	95099
All Other Postsecondary Teachers	SEI	74	31299
All Other Precision Assemblers	RES	54	93197
All Other Precision Food and Tobacco Workers	RAS	53	89899
All Other Precision Metal Workers	REI	54	89199
All Other Precision Printing Workers	RIE	55	89799
All Other Precision Textile, Apparel, and Furnishings Workers	RES	53	89599
All Other Precision Woodworkers	RIE	57	89399
All Other Precision Workers	REI	53	89999
All Other Printing Press Setters and Set-up Operators	REI	51	92519
All Other Printing Related Machine Setters and Set-up Operators	REI	50	92529
All Other Printing, Binding, and Related Machine Operators and Tenders	RCE	44	92549
All Other Professional, Paraprofessional, and Technical Workers	ERS	60	39999
All Other Protective Service Workers	SER	50	63099
All Other Rail Vehicle Operators and Controllers	REC	47	97399
All Other Religious Workers	SEA	61	27599
All Other Sales and Related Workers	ERS	54	49999
All Other Sales Representatives and Salespersons, Services	ESA	57	43099
All Other Service Workers	ESR	46	69999
All Other Social Scientists	EIS	69	27199
All Other Supervisors and Managers/Supervisors - Service Workers	ESR	58	61099
All Other Teachers and Instructors	SEA	64	31399
All Other Therapists	SIE	68	32399
All Other Timber Cutting and Related Logging Workers	REC	42	73099

From the Occupational Employment Statistics Occupations to Holland Codes

Title	HOC	Cx	OES
All Other Transportation and Related Workers	RCE	46	97899
Ambulance Drivers and Attendants, Except Emergency Medical Technicians	SRE	47	66023
Amusement and Recreation Attendants	ECS	47	68014
Animal Breeders	RES	58	79015
Animal Caretakers, Except Farm	RES	46	79017
Animal Trainers	SER	56	79016
Announcers, Except Radio and Television	ESR	59	34021
Announcers, Radio and Television	SEC	64	34017
Appraisers, Teal Estate	SCE	67	43011
Architects, Except Landscape and Marine	IAE	74	22302
Art, Drama, and Music Teachers, Postsecondary	ASE	74	31218
Artists and Related Workers	AES	63	34035
Assemblers and Fabricators, Except Machine, Electrical, Electronic, and Precision	RCE	42	93956
Assessors	EIR	62	21917
Athletes, Coaches, Umpires, and Related Workers	ESR	55	34058
Atmospheric and Space Scientists	IRS	70	24108
Audio-Visual Specialists	AES	67	31508
Automotive Body and Related Repairers	REI	50	85305
Automotive Mechanics	RES	52	85302
Auxiliary Equipment Operators, Power	RES	50	95023
Baggage Porters and Bellhops	RES	44	68023
Bailiffs	ESR	45	63023
Bakers, Bread and Pastry	RSA	54	65021
Bakers, Manufacturing	RSE	53	89805
Barbers	ESR	53	68002
Bartenders	ERS	47	65005
Bicycle Repairers	RSC	48	85951
Bill and Account Collectors	ESR	53	53508
Billing, Cost, and Rate Clerks	CSR	55	55344
Billing, Posting, and Calculating Machine Operators	CRS	52	56002
Bindery Machine Operators and Tenders	RCE	44	92546
Bindery Machine Setters and Set-up Operators	REC	49	92525
Biological Scientists	IRS	78	24308
Biological, Agricultural, and Food Technicians and Technologists, Except Health	RIS	57	24502
Blasters and Explosives Workers	RES	52	87905
Boiler Operators and Tenders, Low Pressure	RES	45	92926
Boilermakers	RES	57	89135
Bookbinders	RES	52	89721
Bookkeeping, Accounting, and Auditing Clerks	CSR	56	55338
Brattice Builders	RIS	46	87121
Brickmasons	REC	49	87302
Bridge, Lock, and Lighthouse Tenders	RCS	51	97802
Broadcast News Analysts	EAS	69	34014
Broadcast Technicians	RIS	62	34028
Brokerage Clerks	CSR	55	53128
Brokers, Real Estate	ESC	61	43005

Part 3: From Occupational Titles to Holland Codes

From the Occupational Employment Statistics Occupations to Holland Codes

Title	HOC	Cx	OES
Budget Analysts	ECS	69	21117
Bus and Truck Mechanics and Diesel Engine Specialists	REI	58	85311
Bus Drivers	RSE	49	97108
Bus Drivers, School	RES	50	97111
Butchers and Meat Cutters	RSE	49	65023
Cabinetmakers and Bench Carpenters	RIS	59	89311
Camera and Photographic Equipment Repairers	RCS	61	85914
Camera Operators	RIE	55	89713
Camera Operators, Television and Motion Picture	ARS	62	34026
Cannery Workers	REC	42	93935
Captains, Water Vessel	ERS	60	97502
Cardiology Technologists	ICR	62	32925
Carpenters	RES	53	87102
Carpet Cutters, Diagrammers, and Seamers	RIE	48	93932
Carpet Installers	REI	54	87602
Cashiers	CSE	51	49023
Ceiling Tile Installers and Acoustical Carpenters	RES	56	87105
Cementing and Gluing Machine Operators and Tenders	RCE	41	92956
Central Office and PBX Installers and Repairers	RSE	56	85502
Central Office Operators	CSE	49	57108
Chemical Engineers	IRE	75	22114
Chemical Equipment Controllers and Operators	REI	51	92935
Chemical Equipment Tenders	REC	46	92938
Chemical Plant and System Operators	RCE	54	95008
Chemical Technicians and Technologists, Except Health	IRS	65	24505
Chemistry Teachers, Postsecondary	IRE	74	31204
Chemists, Except Biochemists	IER	72	24105
Child Care Workers	ESA	47	68038
Chiropractors	ISR	67	32113
Choke Setters	RES	37	73005
Civil Engineering Technicians and Technologists	RIC	68	22502
Civil Engineers, Including Traffic	IRS	72	22121
Claims Examiners, Property and Casualty Insurance	SIE	64	21921
Claims Takers, Unemployment Benefits	ESC	55	21502
Cleaning, Washing, and Pickling Equipment Operators and Tenders	REC	42	92958
Clergy	SAE	73	27502
Coating, Painting, and Spraying Machine Setters and Set-up Operators	RCS	48	92951
Coating, Painting, and Spraying Machine Operators and Tenders	REC	44	92953
Coil Winders, Tapers, and Finishers	RCS	47	93908
Coin and Vending Machine Servicers and Repairers	RSE	50	85947
Combination Machine Tool Operators and Tenders, Metal and Plastic	REC	45	91508
Combination Machine Tool Setters and Set-up Operators, Metal and Plastic	RIE	57	91505
Combined Food Preparation and Service Workers	SCR	44	65041
Communications, Transportation, and Utilities Operations Managers	ESR	67	15023

Title	HOC	Cx	OES
Compliance Officers and Enforcement Inspectors, Except Construction	ESR	63	21911
Computer Engineers	IRE	74	22127
Computer Operators, Except Peripheral Equipment	CSR	56	56011
Computer Programmer Aides	IRC	69	25108
Computer Programmers	IRE	68	25105
Computer Science Teachers, Postsecondary	IRE	74	31226
Computer Support Specialists	SCR	63	25104
Concrete and Terrazzo Finishers	REI	51	87311
Construction and Building Inspectors	RIE	63	21908
Construction Managers	ERS	65	15017
Continuous Mining Machine Operators	RSE	47	87941
Conveyor Operators and Tenders	RCE	42	97951
Cooking Machine Operators and Tenders, Food and Tobacco	REC	45	92917
Cooks, Institution or Cafeteria	RES	51	65028
Cooks, Restaurant	RSE	53	65026
Cooks, Short Order	RSE	50	65035
Cooks, Specialty Fast Food	RSE	49	65032
Cooling and Freezing Equipment Operators and Tenders	REC	43	92928
Correction Officers and Jailers	SER	48	63017
Corrective and Manual Arts Therapists	SRI	60	32311
Correspondence Clerks	ECS	54	55317
Cost Estimators	RCE	64	21902
Counter and Rental Clerks	ESR	51	49017
Counter Attendants - Lunchroom, Coffee Shop, or Cafeteria	ECR	44	65017
Court Clerks	CSE	57	53702
Crane and Tower Operators	RCE	45	97944
Credit Analysts	ESC	65	21105
Credit Authorizers	CES	50	53114
Credit Checkers	CSE	52	53117
Criminal Investigators, Public Service	REI	67	63028
Crossing Guards	ECR	44	63044
Crushing, Grinding, Mixing, and Blending Machine Operators and Tenders	REC	44	92965
Curators, Archivists, Museum Technicians, and Restorers	SER	66	31511
Custom Tailors and Sewers	REI	57	89505
Customer Service Representatives, Utilities	CER	54	55335
Cutters and Trimmers, Hand	RCE	41	93926
Cutting and Slicing Machine Operators and Tenders	RCE	41	92944
Cutting and Slicing Machine Setters and Set-up Operators	RCE	48	92941
Dairy Processing Equipment Operators, Including Setters	REI	52	92932
Dancers and Choreographers	AER	64	34053
Data Base Administrators	IRS	71	25103
Data Entry Keyers, Except Composing	CSR	51	56017
Data Keyers, Composing	CRE	52	56021
Data Processing Equipment Repairers	RIS	62	85705
Demonstrators, Promoters, and Models	ESA	50	49032
Dental Assistants	SAI	58	66002
Dental Hygienists	SAI	60	32908

Title	HOC	Cx	OES
Dentists	IRE	75	32105
Derrick Operators, Oil and Gas Extraction	REC	53	87914
Designers, Except Interior Designers	AES	65	34038
Detectives and Investigators, Except Public	ESC	55	63035
Dietetic Technicians	SEI	65	32523
Dietitians and Nutritionists	SIE	69	32521
Dining Room and Cafeteria Attendants and Bartender Helpers	RCE	40	65014
Directors, Religious Activities and Education	SEA	66	27505
Directory Assistance Operators	CER	49	57105
Dispatchers, Except Police, Fire, and Ambulance	ECS	55	58005
Dispatchers, Police, Fire, and Ambulance	SEC	57	58002
Drafters	IRE	66	22514
Dragline Operators	RES	47	97926
Dredge Operators	REC	49	97928
Drilling and Boring Machine Tool Setters and Set-up Operators, Metal and Plastic	RIE	55	91108
Driver/Sales Workers	RES	48	97117
Drywall Installers	RCS	47	87108
Duplicating Machine Operators	REC	44	56005
Earth Drillers, Except Oil and Gas	REI	48	87902
Economists, Including Market Research Analysts	ISA	71	27102
Education Administrators	ESA	68	15005
Electric Home Appliance and Power Tool Repairers	RES	54	85711
Electric Meter Installers and Repairers	REI	56	85911
Electric Motor, Transformer, and Related Repairers	REI	53	85714
Electrical and Electronic Assemblers	RCE	46	93905
Electrical and Electronic Engineers	IRE	74	22126
Electrical and Electronic Engineering Technicians and Technologists	RIE	65	22505
Electrical and Electronic Equipment Assemblers, Precision	REI	54	93114
Electrical Installers and Repairers, Transportation Equipment	RIS	56	85728
Electrical Power-Line Installers and Repairers	RSE	55	85723
Electricians	RES	57	87202
Electrocardiograph Technicians	RCI	54	32926
Electrolytic Plating and Coating Machine Setters and Setup Operators, Metal and Plastic	RIE	57	91917
Electrolytic Plating and Coating Machine Operators and Tenders, Metal and Plastic	REC	47	91921
Electromechanical Equipment Assemblers, Precision	RIE	57	93111
Electromedical and Biomedical Equipment Repairers	REI	61	85908
Electroneurodiagnostic Technologists	RCS	59	32923
Electronic Home Entertainment Equipment Repairers	RSE	56	85708
Electronic Pagination System Operators	CIR	58	89707
Electronic Semiconductor Processors	RCI	48	92902
Electronics Repairers, Commercial and Industrial Equipment	RIC	60	85717
Elevator Installers and Repairers	RIS	59	85932
Elevator Operators	REC	42	67011

Title	HOC	Cx	OES
Embalmers	RIS	61	39014
Emergency Medical Technicians	RIS	59	32508
Employment Interviewers, Private or Public Employment Service	SCE	64	21508
Engineering Teachers, Postsecondary	RIE	74	31222
Engineering, Mathematical, and Natural Sciences Managers	IER	73	13017
English and Foreign Languages Teachers, Postsecondary	AIE	74	31216
Engraving and Printing Workers, Hand	RCE	46	93951
Estimators and Drafters, Utilities	ERI	70	22517
Excavating and Loading Machine Operators	RCS	44	97923
Extruding and Drawing Machine Setters and Set-up Operators, Metal and Plastic	RIE	50	91311
Extruding and Forming Machine Operators and Tenders, Synthetic or Glass Fibers	RCE	42	92708
Extruding, Forming, Pressing, and Compacting Machine Setters and Set-up Operators	REC	49	92968
Extruding, Forming, Pressing, and Compacting Machine Operators and Tenders	REC	43	92971
Fabric and Apparel Patternmakers and Lay-Out Workers	REI	55	89502
Fallers and Buckers	RES	42	73002
Farm and Home Management Advisors	SEC	65	31323
Farm Equipment Mechanics	RES	53	85321
Farm Equipment Operators	REC	44	79021
Farmworkers, Farm and Ranch Animals	REC	43	79858
Farmworkers, Food and Fiber Crops	REC	38	79856
Fence Erectors	RSE	47	87817
File Clerks	CSR	51	55321
Film Editors	AES	62	34032
Financial Analysts, Statistical	CIE	70	25315
Financial Managers	ESR	70	13002
Fire Fighters	RES	50	63008
Fire Fighting and Prevention Supervisors	ERS	62	61002
Fire Inspectors	ERC	57	63002
First-Line Supervisors and Managers/Supervisors - Sales and Related Workers	ESR	62	41002
First-Line Supervisors and Managers/Supervisors - Clerical and Administrative Support Workers	ESC	60	51002
First-Line Supervisors and Managers/Supervisors - Agricultural, Forestry, Fishing, and Related Workers	ERS	58	72002
First-Line Supervisors and Managers/Supervisors - Mechanics, Installers, and Repairers	ERS	61	81002
First-Line Supervisors and Managers/Supervisors - Construction Trades and Extractive Workers	RES	59	81005
First-Line Supervisors and Managers/Supervisors - Productionand Operating Workers	RES	59	81008
First-Line Supervisors and Managers/Supervisors - Transportation and Material-Moving Machine and Vehicle Operators	ERS	59	81011
First-Line Supervisors and Managers/Supervisors - Helpers, Laborers, and Material Movers, Hand	ERS	57	81017

Part 3: From Occupational Titles to Holland Codes

From the Occupational Employment Statistics Occupations to Holland Codes

Title	HOC	Cx	OES
Fish and Game Wardens	RES	63	63041
Fitters, Structural Metal, Precision	REI	57	93108
Flight Attendants	ESR	55	68026
Floor Layers, Except Carpet, Wood, and Hard Tiles	RES	54	87605
Food Batchmakers	RIS	57	89808
Food Preparation Workers	RCE	42	65038
Food Servers, Outside	ERS	45	65011
Food Service and Lodging Managers	ESR	64	15026
Forest and Conservation Workers	REI	39	79002
Forest Fire Inspectors and Prevention Specialists	ESR	56	63005
Foresters and Conservation Scientists	IRS	73	24302
Forging Machine Setters and Set-up Operators, Metal and Plastic	RIS	51	91317
Foundry Mold Assembly and Shake-Out Workers	RCE	39	91914
Frame Wirers, Central Office	REC	51	85505
Funeral Attendants	ESR	42	68041
Funeral Directors and Morticians	ESR	65	39011
Furnace Operators and Tenders	RIS	47	91935
Furnace, Kiln, Oven, Drier, or Kettle Operators and Tenders	RCE	44	92923
Furniture Finishers	RSC	52	89314
Gas Appliance Repairers	RIE	58	85944
Gas Compressor Operators	RSE	57	97921
Gas Plant Operators	RES	54	95005
Gas Pumping Station Operators	REC	54	97917
Gaugers	RCE	56	95017
Gem and Diamond Workers	REC	52	89926
General Managers and Top executives	ESR	69	19005
General Office Clerks	CSE	54	55347
Geologists, Geophysicists, and Oceanographers	IRS	78	24111
Glaziers	RSE	51	87811
Glaziers, Manufacturing	REC	47	93911
Grader, Bulldozer, and Scraper Operators	REI	45	97938
Graders and Sorters, Agricultural Products	REC	47	79011
Graduate Assistants, Teaching	SAE	69	31117
Grinding and Polishing Workers, Hand	RCE	42	93953
Grinding, Lapping, and Buffing Machine Tool Setters and Set-up Operators, Metal and Plastic	RIE	52	91114
Guards and Watch Guards	SEC	46	63047
Guides	ESR	53	68017
Hairdressers, Hairstylists, and Cosmetologists	ESR	54	68005
Hand Compositors and Typesetters	RSC	57	89702
Hand Packers and Packagers	REC	39	98902
Hard Tile Setters	RCS	50	87308
Head Sawyers	RIE	48	92305
Health Specialties Teachers, Postsecondary	ISR	74	31212
Heat Treating, Annealing, and Tempering Machine Operators and Tenders, Metal and Plastic	RIE	47	91932
Heaters, Metal and Plastic	RES	46	91938

OES to HOC

Title	HOC	Cx	OES
Heating Equipment Setters and Set-up Operators, Metal and Plastic	RSI	53	91928
Heating, Air Conditioning, and Refrigeration Mechanics and Installers	RES	56	85902
Helpers, All Other Construction Trades Workers	REC	42	98319
Helpers, Brick and Stonemasons and Hard Tile Setters	REC	41	98311
Helpers, Carpenters and Related Workers	RSC	43	98312
Helpers, Electricians and Power-Line Transmission Installers	RCE	45	98313
Helpers, Extractive Workers	REC	42	98323
Helpers, Mechanics and Repairers	REC	44	98102
Helpers, Painters, Paperhangers, Plasterers, and Stucco Masons	RCE	42	98314
Helpers, Plumbers, Pipefitters, and Steamfitters	RCE	44	98315
Highway Maintenance Workers	RCS	47	87711
Hoist and Winch Operators	REC	44	97941
Home Health Aides	SER	50	66011
Hosts and Hostesses, Restaurant, Lounge, or Coffee Shop	ESR	59	65002
Hotel Desk Clerks	ECS	54	53808
Housekeeping Supervisors	ESR	54	61008
Human Services Workers	SCE	55	27308
Industrial Engineering Technicians and Technologists	RIE	68	22508
Industrial Engineers, Except Safety	IER	72	22128
Industrial Production Managers	ESR	67	15014
Industrial Truck and Tractor Operators	RCE	42	97947
Installers and Repairers, Manufactured Buildings, Mobile Homes, and Travel Trailers	REC	53	85938
Instructional Coordinators	SEI	68	31517
Instructors and Coaches, Sports and Physical Training	SER	61	31321
Instructors, Nonvocational Education	SEA	62	31317
Insulation Workers	RCE	49	87802
Insurance Adjusters, Examiners, and Investigators	ESC	65	53302
Insurance Appraisers, Auto Damage	ERS	58	53305
Insurance Claims Clerks	SEC	55	53311
Insurance Examining Clerks	CES	54	53308
Insurance Policy Processing Clerks	CSR	54	53314
Interior Designers	AES	65	34041
Interviewing Clerks, Except Personnel and Social Welfare	CSE	50	55332
Investigators, Clerical	ECS	58	53505
Janitors and Cleaners, Except Maids and Housekeeping Cleaners	REC	40	67005
Jewelers and Silversmiths	RES	54	89123
Job Printers	RIE	59	89705
Judges and Magistrates	ESI	77	28102
Laborers, Landscaping and Groundskeeping	RCE	45	79041
Landscape Architects	AIR	75	22308
Lathe and Turning Machine Tool Setters and Set-up Operators, Metal and Plastic	RIE	57	91105
Lathers	RCS	52	87114
Laundry and Dry-Cleaning Machine Operators and Tenders, Except Pressing	REC	42	92726

OES to HOC

Part 3: From Occupational Titles to Holland Codes

From the Occupational Employment Statistics Occupations to Holland Codes

Title	HOC	Cx	OES
Law Clerks	SEC	66	28302
Lawn Service Managers	ESR	63	15032
Lawyers	ESI	76	28108
Legal Secretaries	CSE	60	55102
Letterpress Setters and Set-up Operators	RIE	56	92515
Librarians, Professional	SEA	65	31502
Library Assistants and Bookmobile Drivers	CSR	49	53902
License Clerks	SEC	52	53708
Licensed Practical Nurses	SAC	56	32505
Life Sciences Teachers, Postsecondary	IRE	74	31202
Loading Machine Operators, Underground Mining	RIS	47	97932
Loan and Credit Clerks	CSR	56	53121
Loan Interviewers	ESC	57	53111
Loan Officers and Counselors	SCE	68	21108
Locksmiths and Safe Repairers	REC	57	85923
Locomotive Engineers	RES	55	97305
Locomotive Firers	RIE	54	97311
Log Graders and Scalers	REI	50	79008
Log-Handling Equipment Operators	RCS	44	73008
Logging Tractor Operators	REI	44	73011
Longshore Equipment Operators	RIS	47	97902
Machine Assemblers	RCE	46	93902
Machine Builders and Other Precision Machine Assemblers	RES	56	93105
Machine Feeders and Offbearers	REC	39	98502
Machine Forming Operators and Tenders, Metal and Plastic	RCE	44	91321
Machine Tool Cutting Operators and Tenders, Metal and Plastic	RCE	43	91117
Machinery Maintenance Mechanics, Textile Machines	RCS	50	85112
Machinery Maintenance Mechanics, Sewing Machines	RES	57	85113
Machinery Maintenance Mechanics, Marine Equipment	RES	58	85116
Machinery Maintenance Mechanics, Water or Power Generation Plant	REI	59	85118
Machinery Maintenance Workers	RCE	43	85128
Machinists	RIE	60	89108
Maids and Housekeeping Cleaners	RCE	39	67002
Mail Clerks, Except Mail Machine Operators and Postal Service	RCE	49	57302
Mail Machine Operators, Preparation and Handling	REC	44	56008
Main-Line Station Engineers	RCE	53	97914
Maintenance Repairers, General Utility	RIS	59	85132
Management Analysts	ESC	66	21905
Manicurists	SEC	42	68008
Marine Architects	IRE	80	22305
Marine Engineers	IRE	71	22138
Marketing, Advertising, and Public Relations Managers	ESA	67	13011
Marking Clerks	CSR	45	58021
Mates, Ship, Boat, and Barge	ERS	59	97505
Mathematical Sciences Teachers, Postsecondary	IRE	74	31224
Mathematical Technicians	IRC	70	25323

Part 3: From Occupational Titles to Holland Codes

From the Occupational Employment Statistics Occupations to Holland Codes

Title	HOC	Cx	OES
Meat, Poultry, and Fish Cutters and Trimmers, Hand	REC	39	93938
Mechanical Control and Valve Installers and Repairers	REI	54	85928
Mechanical Engineering Technicians and Technologists	RIE	67	22511
Mechanical Engineers	RIE	71	22135
Medical and Clinical Laboratory Technologists	IRE	68	32902
Medical and Clinical Laboratory Technicians	RIE	59	32905
Medical Appliance Makers	RSI	56	89923
Medical Assistants	SRE	54	66005
Medical Records Technicians	CIE	63	32911
Medical Scientists	IRS	78	24311
Medical Secretaries	CES	61	55105
Medicine and Health Services Managers	SEC	71	15008
Menders, Garments, Linens, and Related	CRE	41	85956
Merchandise Displayers and Window Trimmers	RAI	61	34044
Messengers	CER	45	57311
Metal Fabricators, Structural Metal Products	RIC	59	91714
Metal Molding, Coremaking, and Casting Machine Setters and Set-up Operators	RIE	50	91908
Metal Molding, Coremaking, and Casting Machine Operators and Tenders	REC	45	91911
Metal Pourers and Casters, Basic Shapes	RCS	42	93941
Metallurgists and Metallurgical, Ceramic, and Materials Engineers	IRE	75	22105
Meter Readers, Utilities	CSE	50	58014
Milling and Planing Machine Setters and Set-up Operators, Metal and Plastic	RIE	54	91111
Millwrights	RES	62	85123
Mine Cutting and Channeling Machine Operators	RIE	48	87943
Mining Engineers, Including Mine Safety	RIE	72	22108
Mining, Quarrying, and Oil and Gas Well Drilling Managers	ERS	67	15021
Mobile Heavy Equipment Mechanics, Except Engines	REI	57	85314
Molders and Casters, Hand	REC	43	93944
Motion Picture Projectionists	RIC	54	92905
Motorboat Operators	RIE	48	97511
Motorcycle Repairers	RIE	52	85308
Municipal Clerks	ECI	63	53705
Music Directors, Singers, Composers, and Related Workers	AES	70	34047
Musical Instrument Repairers and Tuners	RSC	51	85921
Musicians, Instrumental	ASC	65	34051
New Accounts Clerks	CSE	58	53105
Nonelectrolytic Plating and Coating Machine Setters and Set-up Operators, Metal and Plastic	REI	53	91923
Nonelectrolytic Plating and Coating Machine Operators and Tenders, Metal and Plastic	RCE	44	91926
Nuclear Engineers	IRE	75	22117
Nuclear Medicine Technologists	IRS	68	32914
Nuclear Technicians and Technologists	RCI	59	24508
Numerical Control Machine Tool Operators and Tenders, Metal and Plastic	REI	55	91502

Title	HOC	Cx	OES
Nursery and Greenhouse Managers	ESA	67	15031
Nursing Aides, Orderlies, and Attendants	SER	47	66008
Nursing Instructors, Postsecondary	SIE	71	31114
Occupational Therapists	RIS	69	32305
Occupational Therapy Assistants and Aides	SEC	53	66021
Office Machine and Cash Register Servicers	RES	57	85926
Offset Lithographic Press Setters and Set-up Operators	RCI	57	92512
Oil pumpers, Except Wellhead	RES	56	97908
Operating Engineers	RIS	47	97956
Operations and Systems Researchers and Analysts, Except Computer	IRE	79	25302
Opticians, Dispensing and Measuring	RIS	58	32514
Optometrists	ISE	69	32108
Order Clerks, Materials, Merchandise, and Service	CES	53	55323
Order Fillers, Wholesale and Retail Sales	RCE	51	58026
Ordinary Seamen and Marine Oilers	REI	46	97517
Packaging and Filling Machine Operators and Tenders	RCE	41	92974
Painters and Paperhangers, Construction and Maintenance	RSE	49	87402
Painters,Transportation Equipment	RCE	52	92947
Painting, Coating, and Decorating Workers, Hand	RCE	41	93947
Paper Goods Machine Setters and Set-up Operators	RIE	49	92914
Paralegal Personnel	SEC	66	28305
Parking Enforcement Officers	CES	42	63021
Parking Lot Attendants	CRS	43	97808
Paste-Up Workers	RCA	59	89706
Pattern and Model Makers, Metal	RIE	59	89114
Pattern and Model Makers, Wood	REI	59	89302
Pattern Markers, Wood	RIS	59	89305
Paving, Surfacing, and Tamping Equipment Operators	REC	44	87708
Payroll and Timekeeping Clerks	CSR	56	55341
Peripheral EDP Equipment Operators	CRS	52	56014
Personal and Home Care Aides	SEC	51	68035
Personnel Clerks, Except Payroll and Timekeeping	CSE	54	55314
Personnel, Training, and Labor Relations Managers	ESR	68	13005
Personnel, Training, and Labor Relations Specialists	SER	65	21511
Pest Controllers and Assistants	REC	46	67008
Petroleum Engineers	IRE	75	22111
Petroleum Pump System Operators	RIS	57	95011
Petroleum Refinery and Control Panel Operators	RSE	57	95014
Petroleum Technicians and Technologists	RIE	65	24511
Pharmacists	ISE	75	32517
Pharmacy Aides	SRC	54	66026
Pharmacy Technicians	REC	54	32518
Photoengravers	RIE	57	89712
Photoengraving and Lithographing Machine Operators and Tenders	RES	48	92545
Photographers	RIA	58	34023
Photographic Processing Machine Operators and Tenders	RCE	47	92908
Physical and Corrective Therapy Assistants and Aides	SEC	57	66017

Title	HOC	Cx	OES
Physical Therapists	SIE	67	32308
Physician's Assistants	ISA	66	32511
Physicians and Surgeons	IRS	76	32102
Physicists and Astronomers	IRE	79	24102
Physics Teachers, Postsecondary	IRE	74	31206
Pile-Driver Operators	RIE	49	87705
Pilots, Ship	REI	68	97508
Plasterers and Stucco Masons	REI	54	87317
Plastic Molding and Casting Machine Setters and Set-up Operators	REI	50	91902
Plastic Molding and Casting Machine Operators and Tenders	RCE	42	91905
Platemakers	REI	55	89718
Plumbers, Pipefitters, and Steamfitters	REI	55	87502
Podiatrists	SIR	65	32111
Police and Detective Supervisors	ESR	61	61005
Police Detectives	SER	59	63011
Police Patrol Officers	SER	55	63014
Portable Machine Cutters	RSE	45	93928
Postal Mail Carriers	CSR	52	57305
Postal Service Clerks	SCE	52	57308
Postmasters and Mail Superintendents	ESR	65	15002
Power Distributors and Dispatchers	RSI	56	95028
Power Reactor Operators	RES	61	95026
Power-Generating Plant Operators, Except Auxiliary Equipment Operators	RSE	56	95021
Powerhouse, Substation, and Relay Electricians	RES	60	85721
Precision Dental Laboratory Technicians	REC	56	89921
Precision Detail Design Decorators and Painters	RAC	52	89911
Precision Dyers	RSE	53	89521
Precision Etchers and Engravers, Hand or Machine	REI	55	89128
Precision Foundry Mold and Coremakers	RIC	55	89902
Precision Hand Workers, Jewelry and Related Products	RES	54	89126
Precision Inspectors, Testers, and Graders	REI	57	83002
Precision Instrument Makers	RIE	59	89105
Precision Instrument Repairers	RIE	59	85905
Precision Lay-Out Workers, Metal	RIE	58	89117
Precision Molders, Shapers, Casters, and Carvers, Except Jewelry and Foundry	RIE	55	89905
Precision Optical Goods Workers	REI	55	89917
Precision Patternmakers, Model Makers, Lay-Out Workers, and Cutters	RIE	58	89908
Precision Photographic Process Workers	RCE	53	89914
Press and Press-Brake Machine Setters and Set-up Operators, Metal and Plastic	RSE	51	91305
Pressers, Delicate Fabrics	REC	45	89517
Pressers, Hand	REC	39	93921
Pressing Machine Operators and Tenders, Textile, Garment, and Related Materials	RCE	41	92728
Printing Press Machine Operators and Tenders	RCE	43	92543

Title	HOC	Cx	OES
Procurement Clerks	CSE	52	55326
Producers, Directors, Actors, and Other Entertainers	EAS	59	34056
Production Inspectors, Testers, Graders, Sorters, Samplers, and Weighers	RCE	45	83005
Production, Planning, and Expediting Clerks	CRE	54	58008
Programmers, Numerical Tool and Process Control	RIC	60	25111
Proofreaders and Copy Markers	CSE	53	53911
Property and Real Estate Managers and Administrators	ESR	66	15011
Pruners	RCE	49	79033
Psychiatric Aides	SRE	53	66014
Psychiatric Technicians	SIE	58	32931
Psychologists	ISE	75	27108
Public Administration Chief Executives, Legislators, and General Administrators	SEC	67	19002
Public Relations Specialists and Publicity Writers	AES	68	34008
Pump Operators	RCE	46	97953
Punching Machine Setters and Set-up Operators, Metal and Plastic	RIC	51	91302
Purchasing Agents and Buyers, Farm Products	ESA	66	21305
Purchasing Agents, Except Wholesale, Retail, and Farm Products	ESC	67	21308
Purchasing Managers	ESR	66	13008
Radiation Therapists	RIS	60	32913
Radio Mechanics	RSE	57	85514
Radio Operators	RCE	61	39008
Radiologic Technologists	IRS	66	32919
Rail Car Repairers	RES	55	85317
Rail Yard Engineers, Dinkey Operators, and Hostlers	RIE	48	97308
Rail-Track Laying and Maintenance Equipment Operators	REI	47	87714
Railroad and Transit Police and Special Agents	ESC	56	63038
Railroad Brake, Signal, and Switch Operators	REC	47	97317
Railroad Conductors and Yardmasters	ESC	60	97302
Real Estate Clerks	CSR	58	53914
Receptionists and Information Clerks	CSE	54	55305
Recreation Workers	ESR	62	27311
Recreational Therapists	SAE	66	32317
Refractory Materials Repairers, Except Brickmasons	RES	44	85126
Refuse and Recyclable Material Collectors	RES	36	98705
Registered Nurses	SIE	67	32502
Reinforcing Metal Workers	RES	46	87314
Reporters and Correspondents	ASI	67	34011
Reservation and Transportation Ticket Agents	CES	53	53805
Residential Counselors	SEC	59	27307
Respiratory Therapists	SIR	57	32302
Riggers	RSE	51	85935
Roasting, Baking, and Drying Machine Operators and Tenders, Food and Tobacco	RES	44	92921
Rock Splitters, Quarry	RSC	43	87908
Rolling Machine Setters and Set-up Operators, Metal and Plastic	REI	51	91314

OES to HOC

Title	HOC	Cx	OES
Roof Bolters	RCS	44	87923
Roofers	REC	50	87808
Rotary Drill Operators, Oil and Gas Extraction	REI	54	87911
Roustabouts	RCS	46	87921
Safety Engineers, Except Mining	IES	74	22132
Sales Agents and Placers, Insurance	ESC	63	43002
Sales Agents, Advertising	ESA	59	43023
Sales Agents, Real Estate	ESA	63	43008
Sales Agents, Securities, Commodities, and Financial Services	ESC	65	43014
Sales Agents, Selected Business Services	ESA	61	43017
Sales Engineers	ERI	70	49002
Sales Representatives, Except Retail and Scientific and Related Products and Services	ESA	58	49008
Sales Representatives, Scientific and Related Products and Services, Except Retail	ESR	61	49005
Salespersons, Parts	ESC	56	49014
Salespersons, Retail	ESA	56	49011
Sawing Machine Operators and Tenders	RCE	44	92308
Sawing Machine Setters and Set-up Operators	RCE	47	92302
Sawing Machine Tool Setters and Set-up Operators, Metal and Plastic	RCI	49	91102
Scanner Operators	RES	58	89715
Screen Printing Machine Setters and Set-up Operators	RIS	54	92524
Secretaries, Except legal and Medical	CSE	58	55108
Separating, Filtering, Clarifying, Precipitating, and Still Machine Operators and Tenders	REC	44	92962
Septic Tank Servicers and Sewer Pipe Cleaners	RIE	48	87511
Service Station Attendants	REC	45	97805
Service Unit Operators	RES	59	87917
Sewers, Hand	RCE	42	93923
Sewing Machine Operators, Garment	RCE	41	92717
Sewing Machine Operators, Nongarment	RCE	43	92721
Shampooers	SEA	56	68011
Shear and Slitter Machine Setters and Set-up Operators, Metal and Plastic	RSI	51	91308
Sheet Metal Workers	RIE	58	89132
Sheriffs and Deputy Sheriffs	SER	50	63032
Ship Engineers	RES	59	97521
Shipfitters	RIE	57	89121
Shipping, Receiving, and Traffic Clerks	REC	51	58028
Shoe and Leather Workers and Repairers, Precision	RES	52	89511
Shoe Sewing Machine Operators and Tenders	RCE	43	92723
Shuttle Car Operators	RIE	47	97935
Signal or Track Switch Maintainers	RIS	59	85511
Slaughterers and Butchers	RES	51	89802
Small Engine Specialists	REI	57	85328
Social Sciences Teachers, Postsecondary	SIE	74	31210
Social Workers, Except Medical and Psychiatric	SEC	64	27305

Part 3: From Occupational Titles to Holland Codes

From the Occupational Employment Statistics Occupations to Holland Codes

Title	HOC	Cx	OES
Social Workers, Medical and Psychiatric	SEA	66	27302
Solderers and Brazers	RCI	45	93917
Soldering and Brazing Machine Operators and Tenders	RCI	45	91711
Soldering and Brazing Machine Setters and Set-up Operators	RIE	53	91708
Special Agents, Insurance	ESC	66	21505
Specialty Materials Printing Machine Setters and Set-up Operators	RCS	49	92522
Speech-Language Pathologists and Audiologists	ISR	70	32314
Spotters, Dry-Cleaning	RES	49	89514
Sprayers/Applicators	RIS	47	79036
Statement Clerks	CRS	53	53126
Station Installers and Repairers, Telephone	RIC	59	85726
Stationary Engineers	REI	56	95032
Statistical Clerks	CSR	53	55328
Statisticians	IRE	77	25312
Stenographers and/or Court Reporters	CSE	55	55302
Stevedores, Except Equipment Operators	RES	38	98702
Stock Clerks - Stockroom, Warehouse or Storage Yard	RCE	50	58023
Stock Clerks, Sales Floor	RSE	47	49021
Stonemasons	RES	53	87305
Strippers	REI	56	89717
Structural Metal Workers	REI	54	87814
Subway and Streetcar Operators	REI	49	97314
Surgical Technologists and Technicians	ISR	56	32928
Surveying and Mapping Technicians	IER	65	22521
Surveyors and Mapping Scientists	IRE	68	22311
Switchboard Operators	CSE	50	57102
Systems Analysts, Electronic Data Processing	IRE	69	25102
Tank Car and Truck Loaders	RIC	54	97905
Tapers	RES	47	87111
Tax Examiners, Collectors, and Revenue Agents	ERI	67	21914
Tax Preparers	CES	57	21111
Taxi Drivers and Chauffeurs	REC	45	97114
Teacher Aides and Educational Assistants, Clerical	CES	53	53905
Teacher Aides, Paraprofessional	SCE	58	31521
Teachers and Instructors, Vocational Education and Training	SER	62	31314
Teachers, Elementary School	SEA	66	31305
Teachers, Kindergarten	SEC	61	31304
Teachers, Preschool	SAE	62	31303
Teachers, Secondary School	SER	66	31308
Teachers, Special Education	SEC	66	31311
Technical Assistants, Library	SCR	59	31505
Technical Writers	IRS	69	34005
Telegraph and Teletype Installers and Maintainers	RSE	58	85508
Telegraph and Teletype Operators	CSE	52	57111
Telemarketers, Door-to-Door Sales Workers, News and Street Venders, and Other Related Workers	ESC	48	49026
Telephone and Cable Television Line Installers and Repairers	RIS	58	85702

Title	HOC	Cx	OES
Tellers	CSE	58	53102
Textile Bleaching and Dyeing Machine Operators and Tenders	REC	44	92714
Textile Draw-Out Machine Operators and Tenders	RCE	41	92711
Textile Machine Operators and Tenders, Winding, Twisting, Knitting, Weaving, and Cutting	RCE	42	92705
Textile Machine Setters and Set-up Operators	RES	53	92702
Tire Building Machine Operators	RCI	46	92911
Tire Repairers and Changers	REC	41	85953
Title Examiners and Abstractors	CSE	66	28311
Title Searchers	CRS	53	28308
Tool and Die Makers	RIE	59	89102
Tool Grinders, Filers, Sharpeners, and Other Precision Grinders	REI	55	89111
Traffic Technicians	REI	68	39005
Transit Clerks	CRE	54	53108
Transportation Agents	ERS	55	58011
Transportation Attendants, Except Flight Attendants and Baggage Porters	ECS	46	68028
Transportation Inspectors	RCE	51	83008
Travel Agents	ECS	60	43021
Travel Clerks	ESC	58	53802
Truck Drivers, Heavy or Tractor-Trailer	REI	46	97102
Truck Drivers, Light, Including Delivery and Route Workers	RCE	43	97105
Typesetting and Composing Machine Operators and Tenders	RCI	49	92541
Typists, Including Word Processing	CSR	51	55307
Underground Mine Machinery Mechanics	RIE	57	85117
Underwriters	CSE	70	21102
United States Marshals	SEC	53	63026
Upholsterers	REC	53	89508
Urban and Regional Planners	EIS	71	27105
Ushers, Lobby Attendants, and Ticket Takers	CES	41	68021
Vehicle Washers and Equipment Cleaners	REC	39	98905
Veterinarians and Veterinary Inspectors	IRE	73	32114
Veterinary Assistants	ISR	58	79806
Veterinary Technicians and Technologists	ISR	58	32951
Vocational and Educational Counselors	SEA	69	31514
Waiters and Waitresses	ECS	47	65008
Wardrobe, and Locker and Dressing Room Attendants	ERC	46	68032
Watch, Clock, and Chronometer Assemblers, Adjusters, Calibrators, Precision	RES	52	93117
Watchmakers	REC	53	85917
Water and Liquid Waste Treatment Plant and System Operators	REI	54	95002
Weighers, Measurers, Checkers, and Samplers, Recordkeeping	CRE	47	58017
Welders and Cutters	RIE	51	93914
Welding Machine Operators and Tenders	REI	49	91705
Welding Machine Setters and Set-up Operators	REI	54	91702

Dictionary of Holland Occupational Codes

Part 3: From Occupational Titles to Holland Codes

From the Occupational Employment Statistics Occupations to Holland Codes

Title	HOC	Cx	OES
Welfare Eligibility Workers and Interviewers	SCE	57	53502
Wellhead Pumpers	RES	56	97911
Wholesale and Retail Buyers, Except Garm Products	ESR	63	21302
Wood Machinists	RIE	54	89308
Woodworking Machine Operators and Tenders, Except Sawing	REC	42	92314
Woodworking Machine Setters and Set-up Operators, Except Sawing	RIE	48	92311
Writers and Editors	AES	68	34002

OES to HOC

From the Standard Occupational Classification Occupations to Holland Codes

Title	HOC	Cx	SOC
Accountants and Auditors	CEI	70	1412
Actors and Directors	ESA	64	3240
Actuaries	ISE	72	1732
Administrative Support Occupations, Including Clerical, n.e.c.	CES	53	4799
Administrators—Colleges and Universities	ESA	69	1281
Administrators—Education and Related Fields, n.e.c.	ESR	68	1283
Administrators—Elementary and Secondary Education	SEI	67	1282
Adult Education and Other Teachers, n.e.c.	SER	62	2390
Advertising and Related Sales Occupations	ESA	59	4153
Aerospace Engineers	IRE	76	1622
Agricultural and Food Scientists	IRS	77	1853
Agricultural Engineers	IRE	72	1632
Agriculture Teachers*	IRS	78	2234
Air Hammer Operators	RSC	41	6475
Air Traffic Controllers	SER	64	3920
Aircraft Mechanics (Except Engine Specialists)	RIE	56	6116
Airplane Pilots and Navigators	RIE	67	8250
Animal Caretakers, Except Farm	RES	46	5624
Apparel and Fabric Patternmakers	REI	56	6856
Appraisers and Related Occupations	IRS	64	4440
Architects	IAR	74	1610
Archivists and Curators	SER	66	2520
Art, Drama, and Music Teachers*	ASE	74	2235
Assemblers	RCE	43	7720
Astronomers	IRE	80	1842
Athletes and Related Workers	ESR	55	3400
Atmospheric and Space Scientists	IRS	70	1846
Atmospheric, Earth, Marine, and Space Sciences Teachers*	IRE	74	2212
Attendants, Amusement and Recreation Facilities	ECS	47	5254
Auctioneers	EAS	55	4470
Authors	AES	68	3210
Automobile Mechanics	RES	52	6111
Automotive Body and Related Repairers	REI	50	6115
Baggage Porters and Bellhops	RES	44	5262
Bakers	RSE	53	6872
Bank Tellers	CSE	58	4791
Barbers	ESR	53	5252
Bartenders	ERS	47	5212
Batchmakers (candymakers, cheesemakers, etc.)	RIS	58	6873
Bill and Account Collectors	ESR	53	4786
Billing Clerks	CSR	54	4715
Billing, Posting, and Calculating Machine Operators	CRS	53	4718
Biological Sciences Teachers*	IRE	74	2213
Biological Scientists	IRE	78	1854
Biological Technologists and Technicians, Except Health	RIS	58	3820
Boat and Barge Operators	RES	56	8242
Boiler Operators and Tenders (low pressure)	RES	45	7668
Boilermakers	RES	57	6814

From the Standard Occupational Classification Occupations to Holland Codes

Title	HOC	Cx	SOC
Bookbinders	RES	52	6844
Bookkeepers and Accounting and Auditing Clerks	CSR	56	4712
Brickmasons	REI	50	6412
Bridge, Lock, and Lighthouse Tenders	RCS	51	8245
Bus and Truck Engine, and Diesel Engine Mechanics	RES	58	6112
Bus Drivers	RSE	48	8215
Business and Promotion Agents	ESA	63	1450
Business Service, Except Advertising, Sales Occupations	ESA	61	4152
Business, Commerce, and Marketing Teachers	ESR	67	2233
Butchers and Meat Cutters	RES	50	6871
Buyers, Wholesale and Retail Trade, Except Farm Products	ESR	63	1442
Cabinet Makers and Bench Carpenters	RIS	57	6832
Camera, Watch, and Other Precision Instrument Repairers	RIE	58	6171
Carpenters	REC	53	6422
Carpet and Soft Tile Installers	RES	54	6462
Cartographers	RIE	61	1644
Cartographic Technicians	RIC	65	3734
Cashiers	CSE	51	4364
Cementing and Gluing Machine Operators and Tenders	RCE	41	7661
Chemical Engineers	IRE	75	1626
Chemical Plant Operators	RSE	54	6940
Chemical Technologists and Technicians	IRS	65	3831
Chemistry Teachers*	IRE	74	2214
Chemists, Except Biochemists	IER	73	1845
Chief Communications Operators	SEC	58	4523
Chief Executives and General Administrators	SEC	67	1120
Child Care Workers, Except Private Household	ESA	47	5264
Child Care Workers, Private Household	SEC	43	5060
Civil Engineers	IRS	72	1628
Classified-Ad Clerks	CSE	54	4662
Cleaning and Building Service Occupations, n.e.c.	REC	41	5249
Clergy	SAE	73	2042
Clerks, Social Welfare	SEC	60	4784
Clinical Laboratory Technologists and Technicians	IRE	68	3620
Coating, Painting, and Spraying Machine Operators and Tenders	RCE	44	7669
Communications Equipment Operators, n.e.c.	CSE	53	4739
Communications Equipment Repairers	REI	57	6151
Communications Operations Managers	ESR	66	1341
Compressing and Compacting Machine Setup Operators	RES	48	7467
Compressing and Compacting Machine Operators and Tenders	REC	41	7667
Computer Engineers	IRE	74	1636
Computer Operators	CSR	56	4612
Computer Science Teachers*	IRE	74	2228
Computer Scientists, n.e.c.	IRS	68	1719
Computer Systems Analysts	IRE	70	1712
Concrete and Terrazzo Finishers	REI	51	6463
Construction Inspectors	RIE	63	1472

SOC to HOC

Title	HOC	Cx	SOC
Construction Laborers	RES	41	8710
Construction Managers	ERS	65	1330
Construction Trades, n.e.c.	RCE	47	6479
Cooks, Except Short Order	RSE	52	5214
Cooks, Private Household	RSE	52	5040
Cooling and Freezing Equipment Operators and Tenders	REC	43	7665
Correctional Institution Officers	SER	50	5133
Correspondence Clerks	ECS	54	4663
Cost and Rate Clerks	CSR	55	4716
Counter Clerks	ESR	51	4363
Crane and Tower Operators	RCE	45	8315
Crop, Vegetable, Fruit and Tree Nut Farmers	REI	61	5513
Crossing Guards	ECR	44	5142
Crushing, Grinding and Polishing Machine Operators and Tenders	RCE	43	7677
Crushing, Grinding, and Polishing Machine Setup Operators	REI	47	7477
Dancers	AER	64	3270
Data Entry Keyers	CRE	52	4793
Data Processing Equipment Repairers	REI	56	6154
Day Workers	RES	40	5020
Demonstrators, Promoters, and Models	ESA	51	4450
Dental Assistants	SAI	58	5232
Dental Hygienists	SAI	60	3630
Dental Laboratory Technicians	REC	57	6865
Dentists	IRE	75	2620
Designers	AES	64	3220
Detail Design Painters and Decorators	RCA	52	6863
Dietitians	SIE	69	3020
Dispatchers	ECS	56	4751
Drafting Occupations	IRE	66	3720
Drillers, Earth	REI	48	6474
Drillers, Oil Well	REI	53	6520
Drilling and Boring Machine Operators and Tenders	RCE	43	7518
Drilling and Boring Machine Setup Operators	RIE	55	7318
Driver-Sales Workers	RES	48	8218
Drywall Installers	RCS	49	6424
Duplicating Machine Operators	REC	44	4722
Economics Teachers*	ISA	71	2218
Economists	ISA	71	1912
Editors	AES	68	3312
Education Teachers*	SEI	67	2237
Electric Motor, Transformer, and Related Repairers	REI	53	6152
Electrical and Electronic Engineering Technologists and Technicians	RIE	64	3711
Electrical and Electronic Engineers	IRE	74	1633
Electrical and Electronic Repairers, Commercial and Industrial Equipment	RIS	62	6153
Electrical Power Installers and Repairers	RES	55	6433
Electricians	RES	56	6432

Dictionary of Holland Occupational Codes

Part 3: From Occupational Titles to Holland Codes

From the Standard Occupational Classification Occupations to Holland Codes

Title	HOC	Cx	SOC
Electricity, Gas, Water Supply, and Sanitary Services Managers	ERS	70	1343
Electronic Repairers, Home-Entertainment Equipment	RSE	56	6155
Elementary School Teachers	SAE	66	2320
Elevator Installers and Repairers	RIS	59	6176
Elevator Operators	REC	42	5245
Engineering Teachers*	RIE	74	2226
Engineering Technologists and Technicians, n.e.c.	RIE	62	3719
Engineering Technologists and Technicians	RCI	66	3710
Engineers, n.e.c.	IER	73	1639
English Teachers*	AIE	74	2238
Engravers	REI	55	6823
Excavating and Loading Machine Operators	RES	45	8316
Expediters	CSE	53	4758
Explosive Workers	RES	53	6530
Extractive Occupations, n.e.c.	RES	46	6560
Extruding and Drawing Machine Operators and Tenders	REC	45	7515
Extruding and Drawing Machine Setup Operators	RIE	50	7315
Extruding and Forming Machine Operators and Tenders	REC	43	7663
Extruding and Forming Machine Setup Operators	REC	50	7463
Fabricators, n.e.c.	RCE	39	7740
Farm Equipment Mechanics	RES	53	6118
Farm Machinery Operators	REI	44	5616
Field Crop and Vegetable Farm Workers (hand)	REC	38	5613
File Clerks	CSR	51	4696
Financial Managers	ESR	70	1220
Fire Inspection and Fire Prevention Occupations	ERS	57	5122
Firefighting Occupations	RES	50	5123
Fishers	REC	42	5830
Folding Machine Operators and Tenders	REC	41	7674
Folding Machine Setup Operators	REI	48	7474
Food Counter, Fountain and Related Occupations	ECR	44	5216
Foreign Language Teachers*	AIE	74	2242
Forestry and Conservation Scientists	IRS	72	1852
Forestry Workers, Except Logging	REI	39	5720
Forging Machine Operators and Tenders	REC	44	7519
Forging Machine Setup Operators	RIS	51	7319
Freight, Stock and Material Movers, n.e.c.	RES	40	8726
Furnace, Kiln, and Oven Operators and Tenders	RCE	45	7675
Furniture Finishers	RSE	54	6835
Garage and Service Station Related Occupations	REC	46	8730
Garbage Collectors	RES	36	8722
Gas Plant Operators	RES	54	6920
Gem and Diamond Working Occupations	REC	52	6866
General Farm Workers	RES	43	5612
General Farmers	RIS	63	5512
General Managers and Other Top Executives	ESR	70	1210
General Office Occupations	CSE	53	4630
Geologists	IRS	78	1847

Title	HOC	Cx	SOC
Glaciers	RSE	51	6464
Grader, Dozer, and Scraper Operators	REI	45	8317
Graders and Sorters, Except Agricultural	RCE	43	7850
Graders and Sorters—Agricultural Products	REC	48	5625
Grinding, Abrading, Buffing and Polishing Machine Operators and Tenders	RCE	43	7522
Grinding, Abrading, Buffing, and Polishing Machine Setup Operators	REI	51	7322
Groundskeepers and Gardeners, Except Farm	REC	46	5622
Guards and Police, Except Public Service	ESC	51	5144
Guides	ESR	53	5255
Hairdressers and Cosmetologists	SER	52	5253
Hand Cutting and Trimming Occupations	RCE	42	7753
Hand Rngraving and Printing Occupations	RCE	46	7757
Hand Forming and Shaping Occupations	RCE	43	7755
Hand Grinding and Polishing Occupations	RCE	42	7758
Hand Molding and Casting Occupations	REC	43	7754
Hand Packers and Packagers	REC	39	8761
Hand Painting, Coating and Decorating Occupations	RCE	42	7756
Hand Sewing Occupations	RCE	42	7752
Handlers, Equipment Cleaners and Laborers	RCI	51	8700
Health Aides, Except Nursing	SRC	52	5233
Health Diagnosing and Treating Practitioners, n.e.c.	ISR	66	2890
Health Record Technologists and Technicians	CIE	63	3640
Health Specialties Teachers, n.e.c.	SIE	71	2232
Health Technologists and Technicians, n.e.c.	RIS	60	3690
Heating Equipment Operators and Tenders	RIE	48	7544
Heating Equipment Setup Operators	RSI	53	7344
Heating, Air-Conditioning, and Refrigeration Mechanics	REC	55	6160
Heavy Equipment Mechanics	REI	56	6117
Helpers—Brickmasons, Stonemasons, and Hard Tile Setters	RES	40	8641
Helpers—Carpenters and Related Workers	RSC	43	8642
Helpers—Electrical and Electronic Equipment Repairers	RCE	43	8635
Helpers—Electricians and Power Transmission Installers	RCS	46	8643
Helpers—Extractive Occupations	REC	42	8650
Helpers—Fabricators and Inspectors	REC	41	8620
Helpers—Industrial Machinery Repairers	RCE	45	8633
Helpers—Machine Operators and Tenders, Assorted Materials	REC	40	8618
Helpers—Metal and Plastic Processing Machine Operators and Tenders	RES	40	8614
Helpers—Metalworking and Plastic Working Machine Operators and Tenders	RES	40	8611
Helpers—Miscellaneous Mechanics and Repairers	REC	43	8637
Helpers—Other Construction Trades	RES	41	8648
Helpers—Painters, Paperhangers, and Plasterers	RCE	42	8644
Helpers—Plumbers, Pipefitters and Steamfitters	RCE	43	8645
Helpers—Precision Production Occupations and Setup Operators	REC	43	8619
Helpers—Printing Machine Operators and Tenders	RES	41	8616

SOC to HOC

Part 3: From Occupational Titles to Holland Codes

From the Standard Occupational Classification Occupations to Holland Codes

Title	HOC	Cx	SOC
Helpers—Surveyor's	RSC	45	8646
Helpers—Textile, Apparel and Furnishings Machine Operators and Tenders	RES	39	8617
Helpers—Vehicle and Mobile Equipment Mechanics and Repairers	REC	44	8632
Helpers—Woodworking Machine Operators and Tenders	RES	39	8615
Historians	SEA	66	1913
History Teachers*	SEA	66	2222
Hoist and Winch Operators	REC	44	8314
Home Economics Teachers*	SEA	66	2247
Horticultural Specialty Farmers	RIE	59	5515
Hotel Clerks	ECS	54	4643
Household Appliance and Power Tool Repairers	RSE	54	6156
Housekeepers and Butlers	SER	53	5050
Human Resources Program Administrators	SER	70	1132
Hunters and Trappers	RES	48	5840
Industrial Engineering Technologists and Technicians	IRE	68	3712
Industrial Engineers	IER	72	1634
Industrial Machinery Repairers	REI	55	6130
Industrial Truck and Tractor Equipment Operators	RCE	43	8318
Information Clerks, n.e.c.	CSE	55	4649
Inspectors and Compliance Officers, Except Construction	ESR	63	1473
Inspectors—Agricultural Products	REC	49	5627
Instructional Coordinators	SEA	69	2360
Insulation Workers	RCE	49	6465
Insurance Adjusters, Examiners, and Investigators	ESC	60	4782
Insurance Sales Occupations	ECS	62	4122
Insurance, Securities, Real Estate, and Business Service Sales Occupations	ESC	65	4100
Interviewing Clerks	CSE	52	4642
Investigators and Adjusters, Except Insurance	ESC	56	4783
Irrigation Workers	REC	41	5615
Janitors and Cleaners	REC	40	5244
Judges	SEC	71	2120
Judicial, Public Safety, and Correctional Administrators	ESR	67	1131
Kitchen Workers, Food Preparation	RCS	44	5217
Knitting and Weaving Machine Operators and Tenders	RCS	45	7652
Knitting and Weaving Machine Setup Operators	RES	52	7452
Land Surveyors	IEA	67	1643
Lapping and Honing Machine Setup Operators	RIE	53	7324
Lathe and Turning Machine Operators and Tenders	REC	41	7631
Lathe and Turning Machine Operators and Tenders	RCE	44	7512
Lathe and Turning Machine Setup Operators	RIE	57	7312
Lathe and Turning Machine Setup Operators	RIE	48	7431
Launderers and Ironers	RCE	40	5030
Laundering and Dry Cleaning Machine Operators and Tenders	REC	42	7658
Law Teachers*	ESI	76	2243
Lawyers	ESI	76	2110

Part 3: From Occupational Titles to Holland Codes
From the Standard Occupational Classification Occupations to Holland Codes

Title	HOC	Cx	SOC
Lay-Out Workers	RIE	57	6821
Legal Technicians	SCE	65	3960
Legislators*	ESI	76	1110
Librarians	SEC	64	2510
Library Clerks	CSR	49	4694
License Clerks	SEC	52	4787
Licensed Practical Nurses	SEA	55	3660
Livestock Workers	REC	42	5617
Livestock, Dairy, Poultry and Fish Farmers	REI	58	5514
Loan Officers	SEC	65	1415
Locksmiths and Safe Repairers	REC	57	6173
Locomotive Operating Occupations	RIE	50	8232
Logging Occupations, n.e.c.	REI	44	5790
Longshore Equipment Operators	RIS	47	8313
Machine Feeders and Offbearers	REC	39	8725
Machinery Maintenance Occupations	RCE	43	6140
Machinists	RIE	60	6813
Maids and Housemen	RCE	39	5242
Mail Carriers, Post Office	CSR	52	4743
Mail Clerks, Except Post Office	RCE	49	4744
Mail Preparing and Handling Machine Operators	REC	44	4723
Management Analysts	ESC	65	1420
Management Related Occupations, n.e.c.	ESC	65	1490
Managers—Administrative Services	ESR	66	1370
Managers—Crop, Vegetable, Fruit and Tree Nut Farm	ERI	66	5523
Managers—Engineering, Mathematics, and Natural Sciences	EIR	71	1260
Managers—Entertainment and Recreation Facilities	ESR	63	1352
Managers—Food Serving and Lodging Establishments	ESR	64	1351
Managers—General Farm	ESR	68	5522
Managers—Horticultural Specialty Farm	ESR	66	5525
Managers—Livestock, Dairy, Poultry and Fish Farm	ESR	64	5524
Managers—Marketing, Advertising, and Public Relations	ESA	67	1250
Managers—Medicine and Health	SEC	70	1310
Managers—Membership Organizations	ESA	69	1354
Managers—Mining, Quarrying, Well Drilling, and Similar Operations	ERS	67	1360
Managers—Property and Leasing	ESR	67	1353
Managers—Service Organizations, n.e.c.	ESR	64	1359
Managers—Social Sciences and Related Fields	ESA	67	1270
Manual Occupations, n.e.c.	REC	39	8769
Marine Engineers	RES	59	8244
Marine Engineers and Naval Architects	IRE	72	1637
Marine Life Cultivation Workers	RES	42	5618
Material Recording, Scheduling, and Distributing Clerks, n.e.c.	CRS	48	4759
Mathematical Science Teachers*	IRE	74	2227
Mathematical Scientists, n.e.c.	IRA	73	1739
Mathematical Technicians	IRC	70	3840
Mechanical Controls and Valve Repairers	REC	53	6175

Dictionary of Holland Occupational Codes

Title	HOC	Cx	SOC
Mechanical Engineering Technologists and Technicians	IRE	69	3713
Mechanical Engineers	RIE	71	1635
Mechanics and Repairers	RIC	60	6100
Mechanics and Repairers, n.e.c.	RCE	48	6179
Medical Science Teachers*	ISR	74	2231
Medical Scientists	IRS	78	1855
Messengers	CER	45	4745
Metallurgical and Materials Engineers	IRE	75	1623
Meter Readers	CSE	50	4755
Military Occupations	RES	51	9100
Milling and Planing Machine Setup Operators	RIE	54	7313
Milling and Planning Machine Operators and Tenders	RCE	42	7513
Millwrights	RES	62	6178
Mining Engineers	IRE	71	1624
Mining Machine Operators	REI	47	6540
Miscellaneous Electrical and Electronic Equipment Repairers	RIE	56	6159
Miscellaneous Fabricating Machine Setup Operators	REI	54	7339
Miscellaneous Fabricating Machine Operators and Tenders	RCE	42	7539
Miscellaneous Food and Beverage Preparation Occupations	REC	42	5219
Miscellaneous Hand Working Occupations	RCE	42	7759
Miscellaneous Machine Operators and Tenders, n.e.c.	RCE	43	7679
Miscellaneous Machine Setup Operators	REI	50	7479
Miscellaneous Material Moving Equipment Operators	REC	45	8319
Miscellaneous Metal and Plastic Processing Machine Setup Operators	REC	48	7349
Miscellaneous Metal and Plastic Processing Machine Operators and Tenders	REC	45	7549
Miscellaneous Metalworking and Plastic Working Machine Setup Operators	RIE	54	7329
Miscellaneous Metalworking and Plastic Working Machine Operators and Tenders	RCE	44	7529
Miscellaneous Occupations	EIS	63	9900
Miscellaneous Plant or System Operators	REI	52	6960
Miscellaneous Precision Apparel and Fabric Workers	RES	54	6859
Miscellaneous Precision Food Workers	RAS	53	6879
Miscellaneous Precision Metal Workers	REI	53	6829
Miscellaneous Precision Printing Occupations	RIE	55	6849
Miscellaneous Precision Woodworkers	RIE	57	6839
Miscellaneous Precision Workers, n.e.c.	REI	55	6869
Miscellaneous Printing Machine Setup Operators	REI	51	7449
Miscellaneous Textile Machine Operators and Tenders	RCE	42	7659
Miscellaneous Woodworking Machine Setup Operators	REI	49	7439
Miscellaneous Woodworking Machine Operators and Tenders	RCE	43	7639
Mixing and Blending Machine Operators and Tenders	REC	45	7664
Molding and Casting Machine Operators and Tenders	RCE	44	7542
Molding and Casting Machine Setup Operators	RIE	50	7342
Musical Instrument Repairers and Tuners	RSC	51	6172
Musicians and Composers	AES	69	3230
Nailing and Tacking Machine Operators and Tenders	RCE	39	7636

Title	HOC	Cx	SOC
Natural Resources Program Administrators	ESR	66	1133
Natural Sciences Teachers, n.e.c.*	IRE	74	2216
News Vendors	ESC	45	4365
Nuclear Engineers	IRE	75	1627
Nuclear Technologists and Technicians	RCI	59	3832
Numerical Control Machine Setup Operators	REI	55	7326
Nursery Workers	REC	43	5619
Nursing Aides, Orderlies, and Attendants	SER	48	5236
Occupational Therapists	RIS	69	3032
Office Machine Operators, n.e.c.	CRS	45	4729
Office Machine Repairers	RES	56	6174
Officials and Administrators, Public Administration, n.e.c.	ESR	67	1139
Officials and Administrators—other, n.e.c.	ESC	67	1390
Operating Engineers	RIS	47	8312
Operations Researchers and Analysts	IRE	79	1721
Optical Goods Workers	REI	55	6864
Optometrists	ISE	69	2810
Orchard and Vineyard and Related Workers (hand)	RCE	42	5614
Order Clerks	CES	52	4664
Other Financial Officers	ESC	67	1419
Other Motor Transportation Occupations, n.e.c.	REC	43	8219
Packaging and Filling Machine Operators and Tenders	RCE	41	7662
Packaging and Filling Machine Setup Operators	RCS	50	7462
Painters (Construction and Maintenance)	RES	50	6442
Painters, Sculptors, Craft-Artists, and Artist Printmakers	AES	63	3250
Paperhangers	RSC	47	6443
Parking Lot Attendants	CRS	43	8740
Patternmakers and Model Makers (metal)	RIE	59	6817
Patternmakers and Model Makers, wood	REI	59	6831
Paving, Surfacing, and Tamping Equipment Operators	REC	44	6466
Payroll and Timekeeping Clerks	CSR	56	4713
Performers, n.e.c.	EAS	55	3280
Peripheral Equipment Operators	CRS	52	4613
Personal Service Occupations, n.e.c.	ERS	45	5269
Personnel and Labor Relations Managers	ESI	69	1230
Personnel Clerks, Except Payroll and Timekeeping	CSE	54	4692
Personnel, Training, and Labor Relations Specialists	SEC	65	1430
Pest Control Occupations	REC	46	5246
Petroleum Engineers	IRE	78	1625
Petroleum Plant Operators	RSE	57	6950
Petroleum Technologists and Technicians	RIE	65	3833
Pharmacists	ISE	75	3010
Photoengraving and Lithographing Machine Setup Operators	RIC	52	7444
Photoengraving and Lithographing Machine Operators and Tenders	REC	47	7644
Photographers	ARS	60	3260
Photographic Process Workers	RCE	55	6868
Photographic Processing Machine Operators	RCE	47	7671
Physical Education Teachers*	SER	65	2236

Part 3: From Occupational Titles to Holland Codes

From the Standard Occupational Classification Occupations to Holland Codes

Title	HOC	Cx	SOC
Physical Scientists, n.e.c.	IRE	78	1849
Physical Therapists	SRI	62	3033
Physicians	IRS	76	2610
Physicians Assistants	ISA	66	3040
Physicists	IRE	79	1843
Physics Teachers*	IRE	74	2215
Pile Driving Operators	RIE	49	6476
Plasterers	REI	54	6444
Plating and Coating Machine Operators and Tenders	RCE	44	7543
Plating and Coating Machine Setup Operators	RIE	55	7343
Plumbers, Pipefitters and Steamfitters	REI	55	6450
Podiatrists	SIR	65	2830
Police and Detectives, Public Service	SER	58	5132
Political Science Teachers*	SEI	70	2223
Political Scientists	SEI	70	1914
Postal Clerks, Except Mail Carriers	SCE	52	4742
Postmasters and Mail Superintendents	ESR	65	1344
Power Plant and Systems Operators, Except Stationary Engineers	RES	56	6932
Precision Adjusters and Calibrators	REI	51	6882
Precision Assemblers (metal)	REI	55	6812
Precision Electrical and Electronic Equipment Assemblers	REI	55	6867
Precision Grinders, Filers, and Tool Sharpeners	REI	55	6816
Precision Hand Molders and Shapers (Except jewelers)	REI	56	6861
Precision Hand Molders and Shapers (jewelers)	RES	54	6822
Precision Inspectors, Testers and Graders	REI	57	6881
Precision Laundering, Cleaning, and Dyeing Occupations	RES	51	6855
Precision Lithographers and Photoengravers	RIE	57	6842
Precision Patternmakers, Lay-Out Workers and Cutters	RIE	58	6862
Precision Typesetters	RSI	58	6841
Prekindergarten and Kindergarten Teachers	SEA	62	2310
Press and Brake Machine Operators and Tenders	RCE	43	7517
Press and Brake Machine Setup Operators	RSE	51	7317
Pressing Machine Operators	RCE	41	7657
Printing Machine Operators and Tenders, n.e.c.	RCE	44	7649
Printing Machine Operators and Tenders	RCE	43	7643
Printing Press Setup Operators	RIE	54	7443
Private Household Cleaners and Servants	RSE	43	5070
Private Household Occupations, n.e.c.	SRE	46	5090
Production and Planning Clerks	CRE	54	4752
Production Expediters	REC	49	7870
Production Inspectors, Checkers and Examiners	RCE	46	7820
Production Managers, Industrial	ESR	67	1320
Production Samplers and Weighers	RCE	44	7840
Production Testers	RCE	48	7830
Programmers, Business	IRE	69	3971
Programmers, Numerical, Tool and Process Control	RIC	60	3974
Programmers, Scientific	IRE	79	3972
Proof Readers	CSE	53	4792

SOC to HOC

Part 3: From Occupational Titles to Holland Codes

From the Standard Occupational Classification Occupations to Holland Codes

Title	HOC	Cx	SOC
Protective Service Occupations, n.e.c.	SER	51	5149
Psychologists	ISE	75	1915
Psychology Teachers*	ISE	75	2217
Public Finance, Taxation, and Other Monetary Program Administrators	ESR	70	1135
Public Relations Specialists and Publicity Writers	EAS	66	3320
Public Transportation Attendants	ECS	48	5257
Punching and Shearing Machine Operators and Tenders	RCE	44	7514
Punching and Shearing Machine Setup Operators	RIS	51	7314
Purchasing Agents and Buyers, Farm Products	ESA	66	1443
Purchasing Agents and Buyers, n.e.c.	ESR	67	1449
Purchasing Managers	ESR	66	1240
Radio and Related Operators	RCS	61	3930
Radio, Television, and Other Announcers	SEC	63	3330
Radiologic Technologists and Technicians	IRS	66	3650
Rail and Track Laying Equipment Operators	RIE	46	6467
Rail Vehicle Operators, n.e.c.	REI	47	8239
Railroad Brake, Signal, and Switch Operators	REC	47	8233
Railroad Conductors and Yardmasters	ESR	59	8113
Real Estate Sales Occupations	ESC	64	4123
Receptionists	CSE	52	4645
Record Clerks, n.e.c.	CSE	52	4699
Recreation Workers	SEI	62	2033
Registered Nurses	SIE	67	2900
Religious Workers, n.e.c.	SEA	63	2049
Reporters	AES	69	3313
Reservation Agents and Transportation Clerks	ECS	55	4644
Respiratory Therapists	SIR	57	3031
Riggers	RSE	52	6177
Roasting and Baking Machine Operators and Tenders	RES	44	7672
Roasting and Baking Machine Setup Operators	RES	56	7472
Rolling Machine Operators and Tenders	REC	47	7516
Rolling Machine Setup Operators	REI	51	7316
Roofers	REC	50	6468
Router and Planner Machine Operators and Tenders	RCE	46	7632
Router and Planner Machine Setup Operators	RIE	48	7432
Rural, Urban, and Community Development Program Administrators	ESR	70	1134
Sailors and Deckhands	REI	48	8243
Sales Clerk	SER	49	4362
Sales Engineers	ERI	70	4210
Sales Occupations—other, n.e.c.	RES	52	4490
Sales Occupations—Services, n.e.c.	ESA	57	4369
Sales Representatives, Commercial and Industrial Equipment and Supplies	ESR	59	4242
Sales Representatives, Garments and Related Textile Products	ESA	58	4243
Sales Representatives, Motor Vehicles and Supplies	ESR	61	4244
Sales Representatives—Farm Products and Livestock	ESA	62	4246

Dictionary of Holland Occupational Codes

Title	HOC	Cx	SOC
Sales Representatives—n.e.c.	ESA	57	4249
Sales Representatives—Pulp, Paper and Paper Products	ESA	57	4245
Salespersons—Boats, and Marine Equipment and Supplies	ESA	57	4344
Salespersons—Books, Stamps, Coins, and Stationery	ESA	58	4347
Salespersons—Cosmetics, Toiletries, and Allied Products	ESA	55	4354
Salespersons—Furniture and Home Furnishings	ESA	56	4348
Salespersons—Garments and Textile Products	ESA	55	4346
Salespersons—Hardware	ESA	55	4353
Salespersons—Jewelry and Related Products	ESA	58	4356
Salespersons—Motor Vehicles, Motor Homes and Supplies	ESA	57	4342
Salespersons—Musical Instruments and Supplies	ESR	59	4343
Salespersons—n.e.c.	ESA	55	4359
Salespersons—Parts	ESC	56	4367
Salespersons—Radio, Television, High Fidelity, and Household Appliances	ESA	57	4352
Salespersons—Shoes	ESA	57	4351
Salespersons—Sporting Goods	ESA	57	4345
Samplers	CRS	49	4757
Sanding Machine Operators and Tenders	REC	41	7634
Sanding Machine Setup Operators	REI	46	7434
Sawing Machine Operators and Tenders	RCE	44	7633
Sawing Machine Setup Operators	RCE	47	7433
Science Technologists and Technicians, n.e.c.	RIE	61	3890
Secondary School Teachers	SRE	67	2330
Secretaries	CSE	59	4622
Securities and Financial Services Sales Occupations	ESC	65	4124
Separating and Filtering Machine Operators and Tenders	REC	43	7666
Shaping and Joining Machine Operators and Tenders	REC	41	7635
Shaping and Joining Machine Setup Operators	RIS	49	7435
Sheet Metal Workers	REI	59	6824
Sheetmetal Duct Installers*	RES	58	6472
Sheriffs, Bailiffs, and Other Law Enforcement Officers	ESR	54	5134
Ship Captains and Mates	ERS	64	8241
Shoe Machine Operators and Tenders	RCE	44	7656
Shoemakers and Leather Workers and Repairers	RES	52	6854
Shoppers	ESI	53	4460
Short-Order Cooks	RSE	50	5215
Slicing and Cutting Machine Operators and Tenders	RCE	42	7678
Slicing and Cutting Machine Setup Operators	REC	48	7478
Small Engine Repairers	REI	56	6114
Social Science Teachers, n.e.c.*	SIE	74	2225
Social Scientists, n.e.c.	IRE	69	1919
Social Work Teachers*	SEC	63	2244
Social Workers	SEC	63	2032
Sociologists	IES	71	1916
Sociology Teachers*	IES	71	2224
Solderers and Brazers	RCE	44	7717
Soldering and Brazing Machine Operators and Tenders	RCI	45	7533
Soldering and Brazing Machine Setup Operators	RIE	53	7333

SOC to HOC

Title	HOC	Cx	SOC
Speech Pathologists and Audiologists	ISR	70	3034
Stationary Engineers	REI	57	6931
Statistical Clerks	CSR	53	4794
Statisticians	IRE	77	1733
Stenographers	CSE	55	4623
Stevedores	RES	38	8723
Still, Clarifier and Precipitator Operators and Tenders	REC	47	7676
Still, Clarifying, and Precipitating Machine Setup Operators	RIE	58	7476
Stock and Inventory Clerks	RCE	50	4754
Stock Handlers and Baggers	RES	39	8724
Stonemasons	RES	53	6413
Street Vendors, Door-to-Door Sales Workers, and Related Occupations	ESC	49	4366
Structural Metal Workers	RES	52	6473
Supervisors—Adjusters, Investigators, and Collectors	ESC	61	4528
Supervisors—Brickmasons, Stonemasons, and Hard Tile Setters	RES	59	6312
Supervisors—Carpenters and Related Workers	RES	60	6313
Supervisors—Cleaning and Building Service Workers	ESR	56	5241
Supervisors—Computer and Peripheral Equipment Operators	ESI	67	4512
Supervisors—Correspondence Clerks and Order Clerks	SEC	60	4516
Supervisors—Duplicating, Mail and Other Office Machine Operators	ESR	58	4522
Supervisors—Electricians and Power Transmission Installers	RSE	59	6314
Supervisors—Extractive Occupations	RES	58	6320
Supervisors—Farm Workers	ERS	58	5611
Supervisors—Financial Record Processing Occupations	SEC	63	4521
Supervisors—Firefighting and Fire Prevention Occupations	ERS	62	5111
Supervisors—Food and Beverage Preparation and Service Occupations	ESR	58	5211
Supervisors—Forestry and Logging Workers	ERS	56	5710
Supervisors—General Office Occupations	ESC	64	4511
Supervisors—Guards	ESR	58	5113
Supervisors—Handlers, Equipment Cleaners, Helpers, and Laborers	ERS	56	8500
Supervisors—Information Clerks	ESR	61	4514
Supervisors—Mail and Message Distribution Clerks	SER	58	4524
Supervisors—Material Moving Equipment Operators	ERS	57	8120
Supervisors—Material Recording, Scheduling, and Distribution Clerks	ESR	59	4525
Supervisors—Mechanics and Repairers	RES	61	6000
Supervisors—Miscellaneous Administrative Support Occupations	ESC	62	4529
Supervisors—Motor Vehicle Operators	ESR	60	8111
Supervisors—Other Construction Trades	RES	59	6318
Supervisors—Overall Construction	RES	58	6311
Supervisors—Painters, Paperhangers, and Plasterers	ESR	58	6315
Supervisors—Personal Service Occupations	ESR	58	5251

Title	HOC	Cx	SOC
Supervisors—Plumbers and Pipefitters and Steamfitters	RES	59	6316
Supervisors—Police and Detectives	ESR	61	5112
Supervisors—Precision Production Occupations	RES	60	6700
Supervisors—Production Occupations	ERS	59	7100
Supervisors—Record Clerks	SCE	60	4519
Supervisors—Related Agricultural Workers	RES	59	5621
Supervisors—Sales Occupations, Commodities Except Retail	ESA	63	4020
Supervisors—Sales Occupations, Insurance, Real Estate, and Business Services	ESR	65	4010
Supervisors—Sales Occupations, Retail	ESR	60	4030
Supervisors—Secretaries, Stenographers and Typists	CES	58	4513
Surveying and Mapping Technicians, n.e.c.	IRE	65	3739
Surveying Technicians	IER	67	3733
Surveyors and Mapping Scientists, n.e.c.	IER	69	1649
Tailers and Dressmakers, Hand	REI	57	6852
Taxicab Drivers and Chauffeurs	REC	45	8216
Teacher Aides	CES	53	4795
Teachers, Except Postsecondary Institutions	ESR	69	2300
Teachers—Postsecondary, n.e.c.	SEA	64	2249
Teachers—Special Education	SEC	65	2350
Technical Sales Workers, Agricultural Equipment and Supplies	ESR	59	4233
Technical Sales Workers, Aircraft	ERS	62	4232
Technical Sales Workers, Electronic Equipment	ESR	63	4234
Technical Sales Workers, Industrial Machinery, Equipment, and Supplies	ESR	60	4235
Technical Sales Workers, Medical and Dental Equipment and Supplies	ESR	63	4236
Technical Sales Workers, n.e.c.	ESR	63	4239
Technical Sales Workers—Chemicals and Chemical Products	ESR	58	4237
Technical Writers	IRS	69	3980
Technicians, n.e.c.	RIE	59	3990
Telegraphers	CSE	52	4733
Telephone Installers and Repairers	RIC	59	6158
Telephone Line Installers and Repairers	RSC	57	6157
Telephone Operators	CES	50	4732
Textile Cutting Machine Operators and Tenders	RCE	43	7654
Textile Machine Setup Operators, n.e.c.	RES	54	7459
Textile Sewing Machine Operators and Tenders	RCE	42	7655
Theology Teachers*	SAE	73	2245
Therapists, n.e.c.	SIE	67	3039
Tile Setters, Hard	RCS	50	6414
Timber Cutting and Related Occupations	RES	41	5730
Tool and Die Makers	RIE	59	6811
Trade and Industrial Teachers*	REI	68	2246
Traffic, Shipping, and Receiving Clerks	RCE	51	4753
Transportation Facilities and Operations Managers	ESR	66	1342
Transportation Inspectors	RCE	51	8280
Truck Drivers, Heavy	REI	45	8213

SOC to HOC

Part 3: From Occupational Titles to Holland Codes

From the Standard Occupational Classification Occupations to Holland Codes

Title	HOC	Cx	SOC
Truck Drivers, Light (Including delivery and route drivers)	RCE	44	8214
Truck Drivers, Tractor-Trailer	RIE	48	8212
Typesetting and Composing Machine Operators and Tenders	RCI	49	7642
Typists	CSR	51	4624
Underwriters	CSE	70	1414
Upholsterers	RES	53	6853
Urban and Regional Planners	EIS	71	1920
Ushers	CES	41	5256
Vehicle Washers and Equipment Cleaners	REC	39	8750
Veterinarians	IRE	73	2700
Vocational and Educational Counselors	SEA	69	2400
Waiters and Waitresses	ECS	47	5213
Waiters'/Waitresses' Assistants	RCE	40	5218
Wardrobe and Dressing Room Attendants	ESR	45	5258
Washing, Cleaning and Pickling Equipment Operators and Tenders	REC	42	7673
Water and Sewage Treatment Plant Operators	REI	55	6910
Weighers, Measurers, and Checkers	RCE	48	4756
Welders and Cutters	RIE	50	7714
Welding Machine Operators and Tenders	REC	49	7532
Welding Machine Setup Operators	REI	54	7332
Welfare Service Aides	SEC	51	5263
Winding and Twisting Machine Operators and Tenders	RCE	41	7651
Winding and Twisting Machine Setup Operators	RES	55	7451
Writers, Artists, and Related Workers, n.e.c.	SAE	64	3290

Note. n.e.c. = not elsewhere classified.

* No occupation in the *Dictionary of Occupational Titles* was assigned to this category. The code shown is the code for a closely related category. For example, the code for the SOC psychologist category was applied to psychology teachers in colleges and universities, and the code for the SOC lawyer category was applied to legislator.

SOC to HOC

Part 3: From Occupational Titles to Holland Codes

From the Census Occupational Classification Titles to Holland Codes

Title	HOC	Cx	COC
Accountants and Auditors	CEI	70	023
Actors and Directors	ESA	64	187
Actuaries	ISE	72	066
Adjusters and Calibrators	REI	51	693
Administrative Support Occupations, n.e.c.	CES	53	389
Administrators and Officials, Public Administration	ESR	68	005
Administrators, Education and Related Fields	ESA	68	014
Administrators, Protective Services	ESR	67	006
Advertising and Related Sales Occupations	ESA	59	256
Aerospace Engineers	IRE	76	044
Agricultural and Food Scientists	IRS	77	077
Agricultural Engineers	IRE	72	054
Air Traffic Controllers	SER	64	227
Aircraft Mechanics, Except Engine	RIE	56	515
Airplane Pilots and Navigators	RIE	67	226
Animal Caretakers, Except Farm	RES	46	487
Announcers	SEC	63	198
Architects	IAR	74	043
Archivists and Curators	SER	66	165
Artists, Performers, and Related Workers, n.e.c.	EAS	57	194
Assemblers	RCE	42	785
Athletes	ESR	55	199
Atmospheric and Space Scientists	IRS	70	074
Attendants, Amusement and Recreation Facilities	ECS	47	459
Auctioneers	EAS	55	284
Authors	AES	67	183
Automobile Body and Related Repairers	RES	50	514
Automobile Mechanic Apprentices	RSE	56	506
Automobile Mechanics	REI	52	505
Baggage Porters and Bellhops	RES	44	464
Bakers	RSE	53	687
Bank Tellers	CSE	58	383
Barbers	ESR	53	457
Bartenders	ERS	47	434
Bill and Account Collectors	ESR	53	378
Billing Clerks	CSR	54	339
Billing, Posting, and Calculating Machine Operators	CRS	53	344
Biological and Life Scientists	IRE	78	078
Biological Technicians	RIS	58	223
Boilermakers	RES	57	643
Bookbinders	RES	52	679
Bookkeepers, Accounting and Auditing Clerks	CSR	56	337
Brickmason and Stonemason Apprentices	RIS	56	564
Brickmasons and Stonemasons	RES	51	563
Bridge, Lock, and Lighthouse Tenders	RCS	51	834
Broadcast Equipment Operators	RCI	61	228
Bus Drivers	RES	49	808
Bus, Truck, and Stationary Engine Mechanics	RES	58	507
Business and Promotion Agents	ESA	63	034

COC to HOC

Title	HOC	Cx	COC
Butchers and Meat Cutters	RES	50	686
Buyers, Wholesale and Retail Trade Except Farm Products	ESR	63	029
Cabinet Makers and Bench Carpenters	RIS	57	657
Camera, Watch, and Musical Instrument Repairers	REC	55	535
Captains and Other Officers, Fishing Vessels	REI	61	497
Carpenter Apprentices	RES	57	569
Carpenters	REC	52	567
Carpet Installers	REI	54	566
Cashiers	CSE	51	276
Cementing and Gluing Machine Operators	RCE	41	753
Chemical Engineers	IRE	75	048
Chemical Technicians	IRS	65	224
Chemists, Except Biochemists	IER	73	073
Chief Communications Operators	SEC	58	306
Chief Executives and General Administrators, Public Administrators	SEC	67	004
Child Care Workers, n.e.c.	ESA	47	468
Child Care Workers, Private Household	SEC	43	406
Civil Engineers	IRS	72	053
Classified-Ad Clerks	CSE	54	325
Clergy	SAE	73	176
Clinical Laboratory Technologists and Technicians	IRE	66	203
Communications Equipment Operators, n.e.c.	CSE	53	353
Compressing and Compacting Machine Operators	REC	41	758
Computer Operators	CSR	56	308
Computer Programmers	IRC	68	229
Computer Systems Analysts and Scientists	IRS	67	064
Concrete and Terrazzo Finishers	REI	51	588
Construction Inspectors	RIE	63	035
Construction Laborers	RES	41	869
Construction Trades, n.e.c.	RCE	47	599
Cooks	RSE	52	436
Cooks, Private Household	RSE	52	404
Correctional Institution Officers	SER	50	424
Correspondence Clerks	ECS	54	326
Cost and Rate Clerks	CSR	55	343
Counselors, Educational and Vocational	SEA	69	163
Crane and Tower Operators	RCE	45	849
Crossing Guards	ECR	44	425
Crushing and Grinding Machine Operators	REC	43	768
Dancers	AER	64	193
Data Processing Equipment Repairers	REI	56	525
Data-Entry Keyers	CRE	52	385
Demonstrators, Promoters and Models, Sales	ESA	51	283
Dental Assistants	SAI	58	445
Dental Hygienists	SAI	60	204
Dental Laboratory and Medical Appliance Technicians	REC	57	678
Dentists	IRE	75	085
Designers	AES	64	185

Part 3: From Occupational Titles to Holland Codes
From the Census Occupational Classification Titles to Holland Codes

Title	HOC	Cx	COC
Dietitians	SIE	69	097
Dispatchers	ECS	56	359
Drafting Occupations	IRE	66	217
Dressmakers	REC	54	666
Drillers, Earth	REI	48	598
Drillers, Oil Well	REI	53	614
Drilling and Boring Machine Operators	RCE	47	708
Driver-Sales Workers	RES	48	806
Drywall Installers	RCS	49	573
Duplicating Machine Operators	REC	44	345
Economists	ISA	71	166
Editors and Reporters	AES	68	195
Electrical and Electronic Engineers	IRE	74	055
Electrical and Electronic Equipment Assemblers	REI	55	683
Electrical and Electronic Technicians	RIE	64	213
Electrical Power Installers and Repairers	RES	55	577
Electrician Apprentices	RES	61	576
Electricians	RES	56	575
Electronic Repairers, Communications and Industrial Equipment	RIE	58	523
Elevator Installers and Repairer	RIS	59	543
Elevator Operators	REC	42	454
Eligibility Clerks, Social Welfare	SEC	60	377
Engineering Technicians, n.e.c.	RIE	62	216
Engineers, n.e.c.	IER	73	059
Engravers, Metal	REI	55	649
Excavating and Loading Machine Operators	RES	45	853
Expediters	CSE	53	373
Explosives Workers	RES	53	615
Extruding and Forming Machine Operators	REC	44	755
Fabricating Machine Operators, n.e.c.	REC	46	717
Farm Equipment Mechanics	RES	53	517
Farm Workers	REC	42	479
Farmers, Except Horticultural	REI	60	473
File Clerks	CSR	51	335
Financial Managers	ESR	70	007
Fire Inspection and Fire Prevention Occupations	ERS	57	416
Firefighting Occupations	RES	50	417
Fishers	REC	42	498
Folding Machine Operators	REC	43	765
Food Batchmakers	RSE	55	688
Food Counter, Fountain and Related Occupations	ECR	44	438
Forestry and Conservation Scientists	IRS	72	079
Forestry Workers, Except Logging	REI	39	495
Forging Machine Operators	REI	49	713
Freight, Stock, and Material Handlers, n.e.c.	RES	40	883
Funeral Directors	ESR	65	019
Furnace, Kiln, and Oven Operators, Except Food	RCE	45	766
Furniture and Wood Finishers	RSE	54	658

COC to HOC

Title	HOC	Cx	COC
Garage and Service Station Related Occupations	REC	46	885
Garbage Collectors	RES	36	875
General Office Clerks	CSE	54	379
Geologists and Geodesists	IRS	78	075
Glaziers	RSE	51	589
Grader, Dozer, and Scraper Operators	REI	45	855
Graders and Sorters, Agricultural Products	REC	47	488
Graders and Sorters, Except Agricultural	RCE	43	799
Grinding, Abrading, Buffing, and Polishing Machine Operators	RCE	46	709
Groundskeepers and Gardeners, Except Farm	REC	46	486
Guards and Police, Except Public Service	ESC	51	426
Guides	ESR	53	461
Hairdressers and Cosmetologists	SER	52	458
Hand Cutting and Trimming Occupations	RCE	42	786
Hand Engraving and Printing Occupations	RCE	46	793
Hand Molders and Shapers, Except Jewelers	REI	55	675
Hand Molding, Casting, and Forming Occupations	RCE	43	787
Hand Packers and Packagers	REC	39	888
Hand Painting, Coating, and Decorating Occupations	RCE	42	789
Health Aides, Except Nursing	SRC	52	446
Health Diagnosing Practitioners, n.e.c.	ISR	66	089
Health Record Technologists and Technicians	CIE	63	205
Health Specialties Teachers	SIE	71	134
Health Technologists and Technicians, n.e.c.	RIS	60	208
Heat Treating Equipment Operators	RIE	48	724
Heating, Air Conditioning, and Refrigeration Mechanics	REC	55	534
Heavy Equipment Mechanics	REI	56	516
Helpers, Construction Trades	REC	42	866
Helpers, Extractive Occupations	REC	42	868
Helpers, Mechanics and Repairers	REC	44	865
Helpers, Surveyor	RSC	45	867
Hoist and Winch Operators	REC	44	848
Horticultural Specialty Farmers	RIE	59	474
Hotel Clerks	ECS	54	317
Household Appliance and Power Tool Repairers	RES	54	526
Housekeepers and Butlers	SER	53	405
Hunters and Trappers	RES	48	499
Industrial Engineering Technicians	IRE	68	214
Industrial Engineers	IER	72	056
Industrial Machinery Repairers	REI	55	518
Industrial Truck and Tractor Equipment Operators	RCE	43	856
Information Clerks, n.e.c.	CSE	55	323
Inspectors and Compliance Officers, Except Construction	ESR	63	036
Inspectors, Agricultural Products	REC	49	489
Inspectors, Testers, and Graders	REI	56	689
Insulation Workers	RCE	49	593
Insurance Adjusters, Examiners, and Investigators	ESC	60	375
Insurance Sales Occupations	ECS	62	253

Dictionary of Holland Occupational Codes

Title	HOC	Cx	COC
Interviewers	CSE	52	316
Investigators and Adjusters, Except Insurance	ESC	56	376
Janitors and Cleaners	REC	40	453
Judges	SEC	71	179
Kitchen Workers, Food Preparation	RCS	44	439
Knitting, Looping, Taping, and Weaving Machine Operators	RCE	47	739
Laborers, Except Construction	REC	39	889
Lathe and Turning Machine Operators	RCE	44	704
Lathe and Turning Machine Set-up Operators	RIE	57	703
Launderers and Ironers	RCE	40	403
Laundering and Dry Cleaning Machine Operators	REC	44	748
Lawyers	ESI	76	178
Lay-Out Workers	RIE	57	646
Legal Assistants	SCE	65	234
Librarians	SEC	64	164
Library Clerks	CSR	49	329
Licensed Practical Nurses	SEA	55	207
Locksmiths and Safe Repairers	REC	57	536
Locomotive Operating Occupations	RIE	50	824
Longshore Equipment Operators	RIS	47	845
Machine Feeders and Offbearers	REC	39	878
Machinery Maintenance Occupations	RCE	43	519
Machinist Apprentices	RIE	60	639
Machinists	RIE	60	637
Maids and Housemen	RCE	40	449
Mail Carriers, Postal Service	CSR	52	355
Mail Clerks, Except Postal Service	RCE	49	356
Mail Preparing and Paper Handling Machine Operators	REC	44	346
Management Analysts	ESC	65	026
Management Related Occupations, n.e.c.	ESC	65	037
Managers and Administrators, n.e.c.	ESR	67	022
Managers, Farms, Except Horticultural	ERS	65	475
Managers, Food Serving and Lodging Establishments	ESR	64	017
Managers, Horticultural Specialty Farms	ESR	66	476
Managers, Marketing, Advertising, and Public Relations	ESA	67	013
Managers, Medicine and Health	SEC	70	015
Managers, Properties and Real Estate	ESR	66	018
Managers, Service Organizations, n.e.c.	ESR	65	021
Marine and Naval Architects	IRE	72	058
Marine Engineers	RES	59	833
Marine Life Cultivation Workers	RES	42	483
Material Recording, Scheduling, and Distributing Clerks, n.e.c.	CRS	48	374
Mathematical Scientists, n.e.c.	IRA	73	068
Mechanical Controls and Valve Repairers	REC	53	539
Mechanical Engineering Technicians	RIC	67	215
Mechanical Engineers	RIE	71	057
Medical Scientists	IRS	78	083
Messengers	CER	45	357

Title	HOC	Cx	COC
Metal Plating Machine Operators	RCE	46	723
Metallurgical and Materials Engineers	IRE	74	045
Meter Readers	CSE	50	366
Milling and Planing Machine Operators	RCE	49	705
Millwrights	RES	62	544
Mining Engineers	IRE	71	046
Mining Machine Operators	REI	47	616
Mining Occupations, n.e.c.	RES	46	617
Miscellaneous Electrical and Electronic Equipment Repairers	REI	54	533
Miscellaneous Food Preparation Occupations	REC	42	444
Miscellaneous Hand Working Occupations	RCE	42	795
Miscellaneous Machine Operators, n.e.c.	RCE	44	777
Miscellaneous Material Moving Equipment Operators	REC	45	859
Miscellaneous Metal and Plastic Processing Machine Operators	REC	45	725
Miscellaneous Metal, Plastic, Stone and Glass Working Machine Operators	RCE	47	715
Miscellaneous Plant and System Operators	RES	53	699
Miscellaneous Precision Apparel and Fabric Workers	REC	50	674
Miscellaneous Precision Metal Workers	REI	54	655
Miscellaneous Precision Woodworkers	RIE	56	659
Miscellaneous Precision Workers, n.e.c.	REI	55	684
Miscellaneous Printing Machine Operators	REI	50	737
Miscellaneous Textile Machine Operators	RCE	42	749
Miscellaneous Woodworking Machine Operators	RCE	44	733
Mixing and Blending Machine Operators	REC	45	756
Molding and Casting Machine Operators	REC	45	719
Motion Picture Projectionists	RIE	54	773
Motor Transportation Occupations, n.e.c.	RCE	41	814
Musicians and Composers	AES	69	186
Nailing and Tacking Machine Operators	RCE	39	729
News Vendors	ESC	45	278
Non-Commissioned Officers and Other Enlisted Personnel	REI	50	904
Nuclear Engineers	IRE	75	049
Numerical Control Machine Operators	REI	55	714
Nursery Workers	REC	43	484
Nursing Aides, Orderlies, and Attendants	SER	48	447
Occupational Therapists	RIS	69	099
Office Machine Operators, n.e.c.	CRS	45	347
Office Machine Repairers	RES	56	538
Operating Engineers	RIS	47	844
Operations and Systems Researchers and Analysts	IRE	79	065
Optical Goods Workers	REI	52	677
Optometrists	ISE	69	087
Order Clerks	CES	53	327
Other Financial Officers	ESC	67	025
Packaging and Filling Machine Operators	RCE	42	754
Painters, Construction and Maintenance	RES	50	579

Part 3: From Occupational Titles to Holland Codes

From the Census Occupational Classification Titles to Holland Codes

Title	HOC	Cx	COC
Painters, Sculptors, Craft-Artists, and Artist Printmakers	AES	63	188
Painting and Paint Spraying Machine Operators	RCE	44	759
Paperhangers	RSC	47	583
Parking Lot Attendants	CRS	43	813
Patternmakers and Model Makers, Metal	RIE	60	645
Patternmakers and Model Makers, Wood	REI	59	656
Patternmakers, Lay-Out Workers, and Cutters	RIE	58	676
Paving, Surfacing, and Tamping Equipment Operators	REC	44	594
Payroll and Timekeeping Clerks	CSR	56	338
Peripheral Equipment Operators	CRS	52	309
Personal Service Occupations, n.e.c.	ERS	45	469
Personnel and Labor Relations Managers	ESI	69	008
Personnel Clerks, Except Payroll and Timekeeping	CSE	54	328
Personnel, Training, and Labor Relations Specialists	SEC	65	027
Pest Control Occupations	REC	46	455
Petroleum Engineers	IRE	78	047
Pharmacists	ISE	75	096
Photoengravers and Lithographers	REI	53	735
Photographers	ARS	60	189
Photographic Process Machine Operators	RCE	51	774
Physical Scientists, n.e.c.	IRE	78	076
Physical Therapists	SRI	62	103
Physicians	IRS	76	084
Physicians' Assistants	ISA	66	106
Physicists and Astronomers	IRE	79	069
Plasterers	REI	54	584
Plumber, Pipefitter, and Steamfitter Apprentices	RES	58	587
Plumbers, Pipefitters, and Steamfitters	REI	54	585
Podiatrists	SIR	65	088
Police and Detectives, Public Service	SER	58	418
Postal Clerks, Except Mail Carriers	SCE	52	354
Postmasters and Mail Superintendents	ESR	65	016
Postsecondary Teachers, subject not specified	IRS	74	154
Power Plant Operators	RES	56	695
Precious Stones and Metals Workers (jewelers)	REC	53	647
Precision Assemblers, Metal	REI	55	636
Precision Grinders, Fitters, and Tool Sharpeners	REI	55	644
Pressing Machine Operators	RCE	41	747
Printing Press Operators	RCE	46	734
Private Household Cleaners and Servants	RSE	44	407
Production Coordinators	CRE	54	363
Production Helpers	REC	40	874
Production Inspectors, Checkers, and Examiners	RCE	46	796
Production Samplers and Weighers	RCE	44	798
Production Testers	RCE	48	797
Proofreaders	CSE	54	384
Protective Service Occupations, n.e.c.	SER	51	427
Psychologists	ISE	75	167
Public Relations Specialists	EAS	66	197

Title	HOC	Cx	COC
Public Transportation Attendants	ECS	48	463
Punching and Stamping Press Machine Operators	RCE	46	706
Purchasing Agents and Buyers, n.e.c.	ESR	67	033
Purchasing Agents and Buyers, Farm Products	ESA	66	028
Purchasing Managers	ESR	66	009
Radiologic Technicians	IRS	66	206
Rail Vehicle Operators, n.e.c.	REI	47	826
Railroad Brake, Signal, and Switch Operators	REC	47	825
Railroad Conductors and Yardmasters	ESR	60	823
Real Estate Sales Occupations	ESC	63	254
Receptionists	CSE	52	319
Records Clerks	CSE	52	336
Recreation Workers	ESR	62	175
Registered Nurses	SIE	67	095
Religious Workers, n.e.c.	SEA	63	177
Respiratory Therapists	SIR	57	098
Roasting and Baking Machine Operators, Food	RES	44	763
Rolling Machine Operators	RES	49	707
Roofers	REC	50	595
Sailors and Deckhands	REI	48	829
Sales Counter Clerks	ESR	51	275
Sales Engineers	ERI	70	258
Sales Occupations, Other Business Services	ESA	61	257
Sales Representatives, Mining, Manufacturing, and Wholesale	ESR	59	259
Sales Support Occupations, n.e.c.	ERS	54	285
Sales Workers, Apparel	ESA	55	264
Sales Workers, Furniture and Home Furnishings	ESA	56	266
Sales Workers, Hardware and Building Supplies	ESA	55	268
Sales Workers, Motor Vehicles and Boats	ESA	57	263
Sales Workers, Other Commodities	ESA	55	274
Sales Workers, Parts	ESC	56	269
Sales Workers, Radio, TV, Hi-Fi, and Appliances	ESR	58	267
Sales Workers, Shoes	ESA	57	265
Sawing Machine Operators	RCE	44	727
Science Technicians, n.e.c.	RIE	63	225
Secretaries	CSE	59	313
Securities and Financial Services Sales Occupations	ESC	65	255
Separating, Filtering, and Clarifying Machine Operators	REC	45	757
Shaping and Joining Machine Operators	REC	42	728
Sheet Metal Worker Apprentices	REI	59	654
Sheet Metal Workers	REI	59	653
Sheriffs, Bailiffs, and Other Law Enforcement Officers	ESR	54	423
Ship Captains and Mates, Except Fishing Boats	ERS	59	828
Shoe Machine Operators	RCE	44	745
Shoe Repairers	RES	52	669
Slicing and Cutting Machine Operators	RCE	43	769
Small Engine Repairers	REI	56	509
Social Scientists, n.e.c.	ESI	67	169

COC to HOC

Title	HOC	Cx	COC
Social Workers	SEC	63	174
Sociologists	IES	71	168
Solderers and Brazers	RCI	46	784
Specified Mechanics and Repairers, n.e.c.	RCE	49	547
Speech Therapists	ISR	70	104
Stationary Engineers	RES	51	696
Statistical Clerks	CSR	53	386
Statisticians	IRE	75	067
Stenographers	CSE	55	314
Stevedores	RES	38	876
Stock and Inventory Clerks	RCE	50	365
Stock Handlers and Baggers	RES	39	877
Street and Door-to-Door Sales Workers	ESC	48	277
Structural Metal Workers	RES	52	597
Supervisors and Proprietors, Sales Occupations	ESR	62	243
Supervisors, Carpenters and Related Workers	RES	60	554
Supervisors, Cleaning and Building Service Workers	ESR	56	448
Supervisors, Computer Equipment Operators	ESI	67	304
Supervisors, Distribution, Scheduling and Adjusting Clerks	ESR	59	307
Supervisors, Electricians and Power Transmission Installers	RSE	59	555
Supervisors, Extractive Occupations	RES	58	613
Supervisors, Farm Workers	ERS	58	477
Supervisors, Financial Records Processing	SEC	63	305
Supervisors, Firefighting and Fire Prevention Occupations	ERS	62	413
Supervisors, Food Preparation and Service Occupations	ESR	58	433
Supervisors, Forestry and Logging Workers	ERS	56	494
Supervisors, General Office	ESC	61	303
Supervisors, Guards	ESR	58	415
Supervisors, Handlers, Equipment Cleaners, and Laborers, n.e.c.	ERS	56	864
Supervisors, Material Moving Equipment Operators	ERS	57	843
Supervisors, Mechanics and Repairers	ERS	61	503
Supervisors, Motor Vehicle Operators	ESR	60	803
Supervisors, n.e.c.	RES	59	558
Supervisors, Personal Service Occupations	ESR	58	456
Supervisors, Police and Detectives	ESR	61	414
Supervisors, Production Occupations	ERS	59	628
Supervisors, Related Agricultural Occupations	RES	59	485
Supervisors; Brickmasons, Stonemasons, and Tile Setters	RES	59	553
Supervisors; Painters, Paperhangers and Plasterers	ESR	58	556
Supervisors; Plumbers, Pipefitters and Steamfitters	RES	59	557
Surveying and Mapping Technicians	IRE	66	218
Surveyors and Mapping Scientists	IER	68	063
Tailors	RIE	57	667
Taxicab Drivers and Chauffeurs	REC	45	809
Teachers' Aides	CES	53	387
Teachers, Elementary School	SAE	66	156
Teachers, n.e.c.	SER	63	159
Teachers, Postsecondary, n.e.c.	SEA	64	153

COC to HOC

Part 3: From Occupational Titles to Holland Codes

From the Census Occupational Classification Titles to Holland Codes

Title	HOC	Cx	COC
Teachers, Prekindergarten and Kindergarten	SEA	62	155
Teachers, Secondary School	SRE	67	157
Teachers, Special Education	SEC	66	158
Technical Writers	IRS	69	184
Technicians, n.e.c.	RIE	58	235
Telephone Installers and Repairers	RIC	59	529
Telephone Line Installers and Repairers	RSC	57	527
Telephone Operators	CES	50	348
Textile Cutting Machine Operators	RCE	42	743
Textile Sewing Machine Operators	RCE	42	744
Therapists, n.e.c.	SIE	67	105
Tile Setters, Hard and Soft	RES	52	565
Timber Cutting and Logging Occupations	RES	42	496
Tool and Die Maker Apprentices	RIE	58	635
Tool and Die Makers	RIE	59	634
Tool Programmers, Numerical Control	RIC	61	233
Traffic, Shipping, and Receiving Clerks	RCE	51	364
Transportation Ticket and Reservation Agents	ECS	55	318
Truck Drivers	REI	45	804
Typesetters and Compositors	RCI	53	736
Typists	CSR	51	315
Underwriters	CSE	70	024
Upholsterers	REC	53	668
Urban Planners	EIS	71	173
Ushers	CES	41	462
Vehicle Washers and Equipment Cleaners	REC	39	887
Veterinarians	IRE	73	086
Waiters and Waitresses	ECS	47	435
Waiters'/Waitresses' Assistants	RCE	40	443
Washing, Cleaning, and Pickling Machine Operators	REC	42	764
Water and Sewage Treatment Plant Operators	REI	54	694
Weighers, Measurers, Checkers and Samplers	CRE	48	368
Welders and Cutters	REI	51	783
Welfare Service Aides	SEC	51	465
Winding and Twisting Machine Operators	RCE	41	738
Wood Lathe, Routing, and Planing Machine Operators	REC	45	726

Note. n.e.c. = not elsewhere classified.

Part 3: From Occupational Titles to Holland Codes

From the Classification of Instructional Program Titles to Holland Codes

Title	HOC	CIP
Accounting	CEI	52.0301
Accounting Technician	CSR	52.0302
Acoustics	IRE	40.0809
Acting and Directing	EAS	50.0503
Actuarial Science	ISE	52.0802
Acupuncture and Oriental Medicine	IRS	51.2701
Adapted Physical Education/Therapeutic Recreation	SIR	31.0502
Administration of Special Education	SEC	13.0402
Administrative and Secretarial Services, Other	RCE	52.0499
Administrative Assistant/Secretarial Science, General	CES	52.0401
Adult and Continuing Education Administration	ESR	13.0403
Adult and Continuing Teacher Education	SEA	13.1201
Advertising	ESA	09.0201
Aeronautical and Aerospace Engineering Technology/Technician	RIE	15.0801
Aerospace Medicine Residency	IRS	51.2901
Aerospace, Aeronautical and Astronautical Engineering	IRE	14.0201
African Studies	SEI	05.0101
Afro-American (Black) Studies	SEI	05.0201
Agricultural and Food Products Processing Operations and Management	RES	01.0401
Agricultural Animal Breeding and Genetics	IRS	02.0202
Agricultural Animal Health	IRS	02.0203
Agricultural Animal Husbandry and Production Management	RES	01.0302
Agricultural Animal Nutrition	RIE	02.0204
Agricultural Animal Physiology	IRE	02.0205
Agricultural Business and Management, General	ESR	01.0101
Agricultural Business/Agribusiness Operations	ESR	01.0102
Agricultural Economics	IAS	01.0103
Agricultural Engineering	IRE	14.0301
Agricultural Extension	SEC	02.0102
Agricultural Mechanization, General	REI	01.0201
Agricultural Mechanization, Other	ERS	01.0299
Agricultural Plant Pathology	IRS	02.0406
Agricultural Plant Physiology	IRE	02.0407
Agricultural Power Machinery Operator	RES	01.0204
Agricultural Production Workers and Managers, General	RES	01.0301
Agricultural Supplies Retailing and Wholesaling	ERS	01.0501
Agricultural Teacher Education (Vocational)	SEA	13.1301
Agriculture/Agricultural Sciences, General	IRS	02.0101
Agronomy and Crop Science	IRS	02.0402
Air Traffic Controller	SER	49.0105
Air Transportation Workers, Other	RCI	49.0199
Aircraft Mechanic/Technician, Airframe	REI	47.0607
Aircraft Mechanic/Technician, Powerplant	REI	47.0608
Aircraft Pilot and Navigator (Professional)	RIE	49.0102
Alcohol/Drug Abuse Counseling	SEI	51.1501
Allergies and Immunology Residency	ISE	51.2902

Title	HOC	CIP
American (United States) History	SEI	45.0802
American Government and Politics	SEI	45.1002
American Indian/Native American Studies	SEI	05.0202
American Literature (United States)	ASE	23.0701
American Studies/Civilization	SEI	05.0102
Analytical Chemistry	IRE	40.0502
Anatomy	IRE	26.0601
Anesthesiology Residency	IRS	51.2903
Animal Sciences, General	RIE	02.0201
Animal Trainer	RSE	01.0505
Anthropology	IRE	45.0201
Apparel and Accessories Marketing Operations, General	ESA	08.0101
Apparel and Accessories Marketing Operations, Other	ESA	08.0199
Applied and Resource Economics	ISA	45.0602
Applied Mathematics, General	IRE	27.0301
Aquaculture Operations and Production Management	RES	01.0303
Arabic Language and Literature	AIE	16.1101
Archeology	IRE	45.0301
Architectural Drafting	IRC	48.0102
Architectural Engineering	IRS	14.0401
Architectural Engineering Technology/Technician	RIE	15.0101
Architectural Environmental Design	AIR	04.0401
Architectural Urban Design and Planning	EIS	04.0701
Architecture	IAE	04.0201
Art History, Criticism and Conservation	ERS	50.0703
Art Teacher Education	SAE	13.1302
Art Therapy	SIA	51.2301
Art, General	RES	50.0701
Arts Management	SEC	50.0704
Asian Studies	SEI	05.0103
Asian-American Studies	SEI	05.0206
Astronomy	IRE	40.0201
Astrophysics	IRE	40.0301
Athletic Training and Sports Medicine	SRI	31.0503
Atmospheric Sciences and Meteorology	IRS	40.0401
Auctioneering	EAS	08.0701
Audiology/Hearing Sciences	ISR	51.0202
Auto/Automotive Body Repairer	REC	47.0603
Auto/Automotive Mechanic/Technician	REI	47.0604
Automotive Engineering Technology/Technician	RIE	15.0803
Aviation and Airway Science	RIE	49.0101
Aviation Management	ESR	49.0104
Aviation Systems and Avionics Main. Technologist/Technician	RIE	47.0609
Baker/Pastry Chef	RSE	12.0501
Banking and Financial Support Services	CSE	52.0803
Barber/Hairstylist	ESR	12.0402
Bartender/Mixologist	SEC	12.0502
Basic Medical Sciences, Other	IRS	51.1399

Title	HOC	CIP
Bible/Biblical Studies	SEA	39.0201
Biblical and Other Theological Languages and Literatures	AIE	39.0101
Bicycle Mechanic and Repairer	RSE	47.0610
Bilingual/Bicultural Education	SEA	13.0201
Biochemistry	IRS	26.0202
Bioengineering and Biomedical Engineering	IRE	14.0501
Biological and Physical Sciences	IRE	30.0101
Biological Immunology	IRS	26.0618
Biological Technology/Technician	RIS	41.0101
Biology Teacher Education	SIA	13.1322
Biology, General	IAR	26.0101
Biomedical Engineering-Related Technology/Technician	REI	15.0401
Biometrics	IRE	26.0614
Biophysics	IRS	26.0203
Biopsychology	IRA	30.1001
Biostatistics	IRE	26.0615
Biotechnology Research	IRS	26.0616
Blood Bank Technology/Technician	SCR	51.1001
Blood Banking Residency	IRE	51.2904
Botany, General	IRS	26.0301
Botany, Other	IRS	26.0399
Broadcast Journalism	EAS	09.0402
Building/Property Main. and Manager	RES	46.0401
Business Administration and Management, General	ERS	52.0201
Business and Personal Services Marketing Operations, Other	ESR	08.0299
Business Communications	CSI	52.0501
Business Computer Facilities Operator	SCE	52.1205
Business Computer Programming/Programmer	IRC	52.1202
Business Home Economics	SEI	19.0201
Business Information and Data Processing Services, Other	SRC	52.1299
Business Machine Repairer	REC	47.0102
Business Marketing and Marketing Management	ESR	52.1401
Business Services Marketing Operations	ESR	08.0204
Business Statistics	IRE	52.1302
Business Systems Analysis and Design	ISR	52.1203
Business Systems Networking and Telecommunications	SER	52.1204
Business Teacher Education (Vocational)	SEA	13.1303
Business, General	ERS	52.0101
Business/Managerial Economics	IAS	52.0601
Cabinet Maker and Millworker	REI	48.0703
Canadian Studies	SEI	05.0115
Card Dealer	ESC	12.0203
Cardiology Residency	ISE	51.2905
Cardiovascular Technology/Technician	ISR	51.0901
Carpenter	RES	46.0201
Cartography	IRE	45.0702
Cell Biology	IRA	26.0401
Ceramic Sciences and Engineering	IRE	14.0601

Title	HOC	CIP
Ceramics Arts and Ceramics	REC	50.0711
Chemical and Atomic/Molecular Physics	IRE	40.0802
Chemical Engineering	IRE	14.0701
Chemical Pathology Residency	IRE	51.2906
Chemical Technology/Technician	RIE	41.0301
Chemistry Teacher Education	SIR	13.1323
Chemistry, General	IRE	40.0501
Child Care and Guidance Workers and Managers, General	SEC	20.0201
Child Care Provider/Assistant	SEC	20.0202
Child Care Services Manager	SEA	20.0203
Child Growth, Care and Development Studies	SEC	19.0706
Child Psychiatry Residency	ISA	51.2908
Child/Pediatric Neurology Residency	ISR	51.2907
Chinese Language and Literature	AIE	16.0301
Chiropractic (D.C., D.C.M.)	ISR	51.0101
City/Urban, Community and Regional Planning	EIS	04.0301
Civil Engineering, General	IRE	14.0801
Civil Engineering/Civil Technology/Technician	RIC	15.0201
Civil/Structural Drafting	RIE	48.0103
Classical and Ancient Near Eastern Languages and Literatures	AIE	16.1299
Classics and Classical Languages and Literatures	AIE	16.1201
Clinical and Medical Social Work	SEA	51.1503
Clinical Psychology	SEI	42.0201
Clothing, Apparel and Textile Workers and Managers, General	REC	20.0301
Clothing/Apparel and Textile Studies	ESA	19.0901
Cognitive Psychology and Psycholinguistics	IER	42.0301
College/Postsecondary Student Counseling and . Personnel Services	SEA	13.1102
Colon and Rectal Surgery Residency	IRS	51.2909
Commercial Garment and Apparel Worker	RCE	20.0303
Commercial Photography	RIA	50.0406
Communication Disorders Sciences and Services, Other	ISE	51.0299
Communication Disorders, General	SIE	51.0201
Communication Systems Installer and Repairer	REC	47.0103
Communications, General	ESR	09.0101
Community and Junior College Administration	ESA	13.0407
Community Health Liaison	SEI	51.0301
Community Organization, Resources and Services	SEC	44.0201
Community Psychology (IAE)	SEI	42.0401
Comparative Literature	ASE	23.0301
Computer and Information Sciences, General	IRS	11.0101
Computer Engineering	RIS	14.0901
Computer Engineering Technology/Technician	IRE	15.0301
Computer Installer and Repairer	RIS	47.0104
Computer Main. Technology/Technician	RIE	15.0402
Computer Programming	IRE	11.0201
Computer Science	ICS	11.0701

Part 3: From Occupational Titles to Holland Codes

From the Classification of Instructional Program Titles to Holland Codes

Title	HOC	CIP
Computer Systems Analysis	IRE	11.0501
Computer Teacher Education	SAE	13.1321
Computer Typography and Composition Equipment Operator	CRE	48.0211
Construction and Building Finishers and Managers, Other	RES	46.0499
Construction Equipment Operator	REI	49.0202
Construction Trades, Other	REC	46.9999
Construction/Building Inspector	REI	46.0403
Construction/Building Technology/Technician	REI	15.1001
Consumer Economics and Science	SEI	19.0402
Corrections/Correctional Administration	ESR	43.0102
Cosmetologist	ESR	12.0403
Counseling Psychology	SIE	42.0601
Counselor Education Counseling and Guidance Services	SEI	13.1101
Court Reporter	CSR	52.0405
Crafts, Folk Art and Artisanry	RCS	50.0201
Criminal Justice and Corrections, Other	SER	43.0199
Criminal Justice Studies	IES	43.0104
Criminal Justice/Law Enforcement Administration	ESR	43.0103
Criminology	ISE	45.0401
Critical Care Anesthesiology Residency	IRS	51.2910
Critical Care Medicine Residency	IRS	51.2911
Critical Care Surgery Residency	IRA	51.2912
Crop Production Operations and Management	RES	01.0304
Culinary Arts/Chef Training	ERS	12.0503
Curriculum and Instruction	ESA	13.0301
Custodial, Housekeeping and Home Services Workers and Managers, General	SER	20.0601
Custodian/Caretaker	RES	20.0604
Custom Tailor	RES	20.0305
Cytotechnologist	IRC	51.1002
Dairy Science	IRS	02.0206
Dance	AER	50.0301
Dance Therapy	ASI	51.2302
Data Processing Technology/Technician	SRC	11.0301
Demography/Population Studies	IER	45.0501
Dental Assistant	SAI	51.0601
Dental Clinical Sciences/Graduate Dentistry (M.S., Ph.D.)	IRS	51.0501
Dental Hygienist	SAI	51.0602
Dental Laboratory Technician	REC	51.0603
Dental Public Health Specialty	IRE	51.2802
Dental Residency Programs, Other	IER	51.2899
Dental/Oral Surgery Specialty	IRE	51.2801
Dentistry (D.D.S., D.M.D.)	IRS	51.0401
Dermatology Residency	ISR	51.2913
Dermatopathology Residency	ISR	51.2914
Design and Visual Communications	RIE	50.0401
Desktop Publishing Equipment Operator	CRA	48.0212
Development Economics and International Development	IAS	45.0604

Title	HOC	CIP
Developmental and Child Psychology	IRS	42.0701
Diagnostic Medical Sonography	RIC	51.0910
Diagnostic Radiology Residency	IRS	51.2915
Diesel Engine Mechanic and Repairer	REI	47.0605
Dietetics/Human Nutritional Services	SEI	19.0503
Dietician Assistant	SEC	20.0404
Diver (Professional)	REI	49.0304
Divinity/Ministry (B.D., M. Div.)	SAE	39.0602
Drafting, General	IRE	48.0101
Drama and Dance Teacher Education	SAE	13.1324
Drama/Theater Arts, General	AES	50.0501
Drama/Theater Literature, History and Criticism	ESA	50.0505
Dramatic/Theater Arts and Stagecraft, Other	AEI	50.0599
Drawing	ASE	50.0705
Driver and Safety Teacher Education	SEA	13.1304
Drycleaner and Launderer (Commercial)	RES	20.0309
Earth and Planetary Sciences	IRE	40.0703
East and Southeast Asian Languages and Literatures, Other	AIE	16.0399
East Asian Studies	SEI	05.0104
East European Languages and Literatures, Other	AIE	16.0499
Eastern European Area Studies	SEI	05.0105
Ecology	IRS	26.0603
Econometrics and Quantitative Economics	ISR	45.0603
Economics, General	ISE	45.0601
Economics, Other	IAS	45.0699
Education Administration and Supervision, General	SER	13.0401
Education of the Autistic	SEC	13.1013
Education of the Blind and Visually Handicapped	SEC	13.1009
Education of the Deaf and Hearing Impaired	SEC	13.1003
Education of the Emotionally Handicapped	SEC	13.1005
Education of the Gifted and Talented	SEI	13.1004
Education of the Mentally Handicapped	SEC	13.1006
Education of the Multiple Handicapped	SEC	13.1007
Education of the Physically Handicapped	SEC	13.1008
Education of the Specific Learning Disabled	SEC	13.1011
Education of the Speech Impaired	SEC	13.1012
Education, General	SER	13.0101
Educational Assessment, Testing and Measurement	SEI	13.0604
Educational Evaluation and Research	ESI	13.0601
Educational Psychology	IES	13.0802
Educational Statistics and Research Methods	ESI	13.0603
Educational Supervision	SEA	13.0404
Educational/Instructional Media Design	ESA	13.0501
Educational/Instructional Media Technology/Technician	RCA	10.0101
Elder Care Provider/Companion	SEC	20.0602
Electrical and Electronics Equipment Installer and Repairer, General	RCE	47.0101
Electrical and Electronics Equipment Installer and Repairer, Other	RES	47.0199

Title	HOC	CIP
Electrical and Power Transmission Installer, General	RES	46.0301
Electrical, Electronic and Communications Engin. Technology/Technician	RIE	15.0303
Electrical, Electronics and Communication Engineering	IRE	14.1001
Electrical/Electronics Drafting	IRC	48.0104
Electrician	RES	46.0302
Electrocardiograph Technology/Technician	RIS	51.0902
Electroencephalograph Technology/Technician	RCS	51.0903
Electrolysis Technician	CRE	12.0404
Electromechanical Technology/Technician	RIE	15.0403
Elementary Particle Physics	IRE	40.0804
Elementary Teacher Education	SEA	13.1202
Elementary, Middle and Secondary Education Administration	ESI	13.0405
Emergency Medical Technology/Technician	RSI	51.0904
Emergency Medicine Residency	SRI	51.2916
Endocrinology and Metabolism Residency	IRE	51.2917
Endodontics Specialty	ISE	51.2803
Energy Management and Systems Technology/Technician	RES	15.0503
Engineering Design	RIE	14.2901
Engineering Mechanics	IRE	14.1101
Engineering Physics	IRE	14.1201
Engineering Science	IRE	14.1301
Engineering, General	IRE	14.0101
Engineering-Related Technology/Technician, General	IRE	15.1101
Engineering/Industrial Management	RIE	14.3001
English Composition	ASE	23.0401
English Creative Writing	ASE	23.0501
English Language and Literature, General	ASE	23.0101
English Literature (British and Commonwealth)	ASE	23.0801
English Teacher Education	SAE	13.1305
English Technical and Business Writing	AIS	23.1101
Enterprise Management and Operation, General	ESR	52.0701
Entomology	IRS	26.0702
Entrepreneurship	ESR	08.0301
Environmental and Pollution Control Technology/Technician	RIS	15.0507
Environmental Control Technology/Technicians, Other	RIS	15.0599
Environmental Health	IRE	51.2202
Environmental Science/Studies	IER	03.0102
Environmental/Environmental Health Engineering	IES	14.1401
Epidemiology	IRS	51.2203
Equestrian/Equine Studies, Horse Management and Training	RES	01.0507
European History	SEI	45.0803
European Studies	SEI	05.0106
Evolutionary Biology	IRS	26.0617
Executive Assistant/Secretary	ESC	52.0402
Executive Housekeeper	ESR	20.0605
Exercise Sciences/Physiology and Movement Studies	SIR	31.0505

Title	HOC	CIP
Experimental Psychology	IAE	42.0801
Family and Community Studies	SEI	19.0301
Family and Marriage Counseling	SAE	19.0703
Family Medicine Residency	IRS	51.2918
Farm and Ranch Management	ESR	01.0104
Fashion and Fabric Consultant	ESA	20.0306
Fashion Design and Illustration	AER	50.0407
Fashion Merchandising	ESA	08.0102
Fashion Modeling	AES	08.0103
Fiber, Textile and Weaving Arts	CSE	50.0712
Film-Video Making/Cinematography and Production	ESA	50.0602
Film/Cinema Studies	AES	50.0601
Finance, General	ESC	52.0801
Financial Planning	ESC	52.0804
Financial Services Marketing Operations	ESC	08.0401
Fine/Studio Arts	AES	50.0702
Fire Protection and Safety Technology/Technician	ESR	43.0201
Fire Science/Firefighting	RES	43.0203
Fire Services Administration	ESR	43.0202
Fishing and Fisheries Sciences and Management	RES	03.0301
Fishing Technology/Commercial Fishing	RES	49.0303
Flight Attendant	ESR	49.0106
Floristry Marketing Operations	EAR	08.0503
Food and Beverage/Restaurant Operations Manager	ESR	12.0504
Food Caterer	ESR	20.0405
Food Products Retailing and Wholesaling Operations	ESR	08.0601
Food Sales Operations	SCE	08.0906
Food Sciences and Technology	SIE	02.0301
Food Systems Administration	ESR	19.0505
Foods and Nutrition Science	SIE	19.0502
Foods and Nutrition Studies, General	SEI	19.0501
Foreign Language Interpretation and Translation	SIE	16.0103
Foreign Languages and Literatures, General	ISE	16.0101
Foreign Languages Teacher Education	SAE	13.1306
Forensic Pathology Residency	IRS	51.2919
Forensic Technology/Technician	IRC	43.0106
Forest Harvesting and Production Technology/Technician	ERS	03.0401
Forest Management	IRS	03.0506
Forest Products Technology/Technician	RIE	03.0404
Forestry Sciences	IRS	03.0502
Forestry, General	RIS	03.0501
Franchise Operation	ESR	52.0702
French Language and Literature	AIE	16.0901
French Language Teacher Education	SAE	13.1325
Funeral Services and Mortuary Science	RSE	12.0301
Furniture Designer and Maker	RCS	48.0702
Gastroenterology Residency	IRS	51.2920
General Buying Operations	ESA	08.0704
General Distribution Operations	ESR	08.0709

Title	HOC	CIP
General Marketing Operations	ESR	08.0708
General Office/Clerical and Typing Services	CSE	52.0408
General Retailing Operations	ESA	08.0705
General Selling Skills and Sales Operations	ESA	08.0706
General Studies	***	24.0102
General Surgery Residency	IRA	51.2921
General Teacher Education, Other	SEA	13.1299
Genetics, Plant and Animal	IRS	26.0613
Geochemistry	IRS	40.0602
Geography	IRE	45.0701
Geological Engineering	RIE	14.1501
Geology	IRS	40.0601
Geophysical Engineering	RIE	14.1601
Geophysics and Seismology	IRE	40.0603
Geotechnical Engineering	IRE	14.0802
Geriatric Medicine Residency	IRE	51.2922
German Language and Literature	AIE	16.0501
German Language Teacher Education	SAE	13.1326
Germanic Languages and Literatures, Other	AIE	16.0599
Gerontological Services	SEA	19.0705
Gerontology	IRE	30.1101
Graphic and Printing Equipment Operator, General	REI	48.0201
Graphic and Printing Equipment Operators, Other	REC	48.0299
Graphic Design, Commercial Art and Illustration	RAE	50.0402
Greek Language and Literature (Ancient and Medieval)	AIE	16.1202
Greek Language and Literature (Modern)	AIE	16.0601
Greenhouse Operations and Management	REI	01.0604
Gunsmith	REC	47.0402
Hand Surgery Residency	IRA	51.2923
Health Aide	SER	51.2601
Health and Medical Administrative Services, Other	ESC	51.0799
Health and Medical Assistants, Other	SCR	51.0899
Health and Medical Biostatistics	IRE	51.2204
Health and Medical Diagnostic and Treatment Services, Other	CIR	51.0999
Health and Medical Laboratory Technology/ Technicians, Other	IRC	51.1099
Health and Physical Education, General	SER	31.0501
Health Occupations Teacher Education (Vocational)	SEA	13.1327
Health Physics/Radiologic Health	RIS	51.2205
Health Products and Services Marketing Operations	ESR	08.1301
Health System/Health Services Administration	ESC	51.0701
Health Teacher Education	SAE	13.1307
Health Unit Coordinator/Ward Clerk	ECS	51.0703
Health Unit Manager/Ward Supervisor	ECS	51.0704
Heating, Air Conditioning and Refrigeration Mechanic and Repairer	RES	47.0201
Heating, Air Conditioning and Refrigeration Technology/Technician	RIC	15.0501

CIP to HOC

Title	HOC	CIP
Heavy Equipment Main. and Repairer	REC	47.0302
Hebrew Language and Literature	AIE	16.1102
Hematological Pathology Residency	IRE	51.2925
Hematology Residency	IRE	51.2924
Hematology Technology/Technician	CSE	51.1003
Higher Education Administration	ESR	13.0406
Hispanic-American Studies	SEI	05.0203
Historic Preservation, Conservation and Architectural History	AES	30.1201
History and Philosophy of Science and Technology	SEI	45.0804
History Teacher Education	SAE	13.1328
History, General	ESR	45.0801
Home Economics Communications	SEI	19.0202
Home Economics Teacher Education (Vocational)	SEA	13.1308
Home Economics, General	SEI	19.0101
Home Furnishings and Equipment Installers and Consultants	ERS	20.0501
Home Health Aide	SER	51.1615
Home Products Marketing Operations	ESA	08.0809
Homemaker's Aide	SER	20.0606
Horticulture Science	REI	02.0403
Horticulture Services Operations and Management, General	RES	01.0601
Horticulture Services Operations and Management, Other	RES	01.0699
Hospital/Health Facilities Administration	SER	51.0702
Hospitality and Recreation Marketing Operations, General	ESC	08.0901
Hospitality/Administration Management	ESR	52.0901
Hotel/Motel and Restaurant Management	ESR	52.0902
Hotel/Motel Services Marketing Operations	ESC	08.0902
Housing Studies, General	AES	19.0601
Human Resources Management	SEC	52.1001
Humanities/Humanistic Studies	***	24.0103
Hypnotherapy	SEC	51.2303
Immunopathology Residency	ISE	51.2926
Individual and Family Development Studies, General	SEA	19.0701
Industrial and Organizational Psychology	IES	42.0901
Industrial Design	AER	50.0404
Industrial Electronics Installer and Repairer	RCI	47.0105
Industrial Equipment Main. and Repairers, Other	REI	47.0399
Industrial Machinery Main. and Repairer	REI	47.0303
Industrial Production Technology/Technicians, Other	RES	15.0699
Industrial Radiologic Technology/Technician	RIS	41.0204
Industrial/Manufacturing Engineering	IER	14.1701
Industrial/Manufacturing Technology/Technician	RIE	15.0603
Infectious Disease Residency	IRS	51.2927
Information Processing/Data Entry Technician	CSE	52.0407
Information Sciences and Systems	IRE	11.0401
Inorganic Chemistry	IER	40.0503
Institutional Food Services Administrator	ESR	20.0409
Institutional Food Workers and Administrators, General	ESR	20.0401

Title	HOC	CIP
Instrument Calibration and Repairer	REI	47.0401
Instrumentation Technology/Technician	RIE	15.0404
Insurance and Risk Management	ESC	52.0805
Insurance Marketing Operations	ESC	08.1001
Interior Architecture	RAE	04.0501
Interior Design	AES	50.0408
Interior Environments	AES	19.0603
Intermedia	AER	50.0706
Internal Medicine Residency	IRS	51.2928
International and Comparative Education	SEI	13.0701
International Business	ESI	52.1101
International Business Marketing	ESC	52.1403
International Economics	IAS	45.0605
International Finance	ESI	52.0806
International Relations and Affairs	IES	45.0901
Investments and Securities	ESC	52.0807
Islamic Studies	SEI	05.0204
Italian Language and Literature	AIE	16.0902
Japanese Language and Literature	AIE	16.0302
Jewish/Judaic Studies	SEI	05.0205
Journalism	AES	09.0401
Junior High/Intermediate/Middle School Teacher Education	SAE	13.1203
Juridical Science/Legal Specialization (LL.M., M.C.L., J.S.D./S.J.D.)	ESA	22.0104
Kitchen Personnel/Cook and Assistant Training	RSE	12.0505
Labor/Personnel Relations and Studies	ESR	52.1002
Laboratory Animal Medicine	IRE	51.3006
Laboratory Medicine Residency	IRE	51.2929
Landscape Architecture	AIR	04.0601
Landscaping Operations and Management	REI	01.0605
Laser and Optical Technology/Technician	RIE	15.0304
Latin American Studies	SEI	05.0107
Latin Language and Literature (Ancient and Medieval)	AIE	16.1203
Law (LL.B., J.D.)	ESI	22.0101
Law Enforcement/Police Science	SER	43.0107
Leatherworkers and Upholsterers, Other	RSE	48.0399
Legal Administrative Assistant/Secretary	CSE	52.0403
Liberal Arts and Sciences/Liberal Studies	***	24.0101
Library Assistant	SCE	25.0301
Library Science/Librarianship	SEA	25.0101
Lineworker	RSE	46.0303
Linguistics	IAS	16.0102
Lithographer and Platemaker	RIE	48.0206
Locksmith and Safe Repairer	REC	47.0403
Logging/Timber Harvesting	RES	03.0405
Logistics and Materials Management	ESR	52.0203
Machine Shop Assistant	REI	48.0503
Machinist/Machine Technologist	RIE	48.0501

Part 3: From Occupational Titles to Holland Codes

From the Classification of Instructional Program Titles to Holland Codes

Title	HOC	CIP
Major Appliance Installer and Repairer	RSE	47.0106
Make-Up Artist	AER	12.0406
Management Information Systems and Business Data Processing, General	ISR	52.1201
Management Science	IRE	52.1301
Marine Main. and Ship Repairer	RES	49.0306
Marine Science/Merchant Marine Officer	RES	49.0309
Marine/Aquatic Biology	IRE	26.0607
Marketing Operations Teacher Education/Marketing and Distributive Teacher Education	SAE	13.1310
Marketing Operations/Marketing and Distribution, Other	SEA	08.9999
Marketing Research	IER	52.1402
Mason and Tile Setter	RES	46.0101
Mass Communications	ESA	09.0403
Massage	RES	12.0405
Material Engineering	RIE	14.1801
Materials Science	RIE	14.3101
Mathematical Statistics	IRE	27.0501
Mathematics	IRE	27.0101
Mathematics and Computer Science	IRS	30.0801
Mathematics Teacher Education	SAE	13.1311
Meatcutter	RES	12.0506
Mechanical Drafting	IRE	48.0105
Mechanical Engineering	RIE	14.1901
Mechanical Engineering/Mechanical Technology/Technician	IRE	15.0805
Mechanical Typesetter and Composer	REI	48.0205
Mechanics and Repairers, Other	RIS	47.9999
Medical Administrative Assistant/Secretary	CES	52.0404
Medical Anatomy	IRE	51.1301
Medical Assistant	RSE	51.0801
Medical Biochemistry	IRS	51.1302
Medical Biomathematics and Biometrics	IRE	51.1303
Medical Cell Biology	IRE	51.1305
Medical Clinical Sciences (M.S., Ph.D.)	IRS	51.1401
Medical Dietician	SIE	51.2702
Medical Genetics	IRS	51.1306
Medical Illustrating	AIE	51.2703
Medical Immunology	ISE	51.1307
Medical Laboratory Assistant	CRI	51.0802
Medical Laboratory Technician	IRE	51.1004
Medical Microbiology	IRA	51.1308
Medical Molecular Biology	IRS	51.1309
Medical Neurobiology	IRS	51.1310
Medical Nutrition	ISR	51.1311
Medical Office Management	CSE	51.0705
Medical Pathology	IRS	51.1312
Medical Pharmacology and Pharmaceutical Sciences	IRE	51.2003
Medical Physics/Biophysics	IRS	51.1304
Medical Physiology	IRE	51.1313

Title	HOC	CIP
Medical Radiologic Technology/Technician	IRS	51.0907
Medical Records Administration	SIE	51.0706
Medical Records Technology/Technician	CIS	51.0707
Medical Residency Programs, Other	IRS	51.2999
Medical Technology	ISE	51.1005
Medical Toxicology	IRE	51.1314
Medical Transcription	CSE	51.0708
Medicinal/Pharmaceutical Chemistry	IRE	40.0505
Medicine (M.D.)	IRS	51.1201
Medieval and Renaissance Studies	SIE	30.1301
Mental Health Services, Other	SEC	51.1599
Metal and Jewelry Arts	RES	50.0713
Metallurgical Engineering	IRE	14.2001
Metallurgical Technology/Technician	REI	15.0611
Metallurgy	IRE	40.0701
Microbiology/Bacteriology	IRS	26.0501
Middle Eastern Languages and Literatures, Other	AIE	16.1199
Middle Eastern Studies	SEI	05.0108
Military Technologies	***	29.0101
Mining and Mineral Engineering	RIE	14.2101
Mining Technology/Technician	RIS	15.0901
Miscellaneous Mechanics and Repairers, Other	RCE	47.0499
Missions/Missionary Studies and Evangelism	SEA	39.0301
Molecular Biology	IRS	26.0402
Motorcycle Mechanic and Repairer	REI	47.0611
Movement Therapy	SIE	51.2304
Musculoskeletal Oncology Residency	IRE	51.2930
Museology/Museum Studies	ESR	30.1401
Music - General Performance	AES	50.0903
Music - Piano and Organ Performance	ASC	50.0907
Music - Voice and Choral/Opera Performance	AES	50.0908
Music Business Management and Merchandising	ESA	50.0909
Music Conducting	AES	50.0906
Music History and Literature	AES	50.0902
Music Teacher Education	SAE	13.1312
Music Theory and Composition	ASE	50.0904
Music Therapy	SAE	51.2305
Music, General	AES	50.0901
Musical Instrument Repairer	REC	47.0404
Musicology and Ethnomusicology (IAE)	AIE	50.0905
Natural Resources Conservation, General	IRE	03.0101
Natural Resources Law Enforcement and Protective Services	ERS	03.0203
Natural Resources Management and Policy	EIR	03.0201
Naturopathic Medicine	SIR	51.2704
Naval Architecture and Marine Engineering	IRE	14.2201
Neonatal-Perinatal Medicine Residency	ISR	51.2931
Nephrology Residency	IRE	51.2932
Neurological Surgery/Neurosurgery Residency	IRS	51.2933
Neurology Residency	IRS	51.2934

Title	HOC	CIP
Neuropathology Residency	IRE	51.2935
Neuroscience	IRE	26.0608
Non-Profit and Public Management	ESI	52.0206
Nuclear and Industrial Radiologic Technology/ Technicians, Other	RCI	41.0299
Nuclear Engineering	IRE	14.2301
Nuclear Medical Technology/Technician	IRS	51.0905
Nuclear Medicine Residency	IRS	51.2936
Nuclear Physics	IRE	40.0806
Nuclear Radiology Residency	IRS	51.2937
Nuclear/Nuclear Power Technology/Technician	RSC	41.0205
Nurse Assistant/Aide	SER	51.1614
Nursery Operations and Management	REI	01.0606
Nursing (R.N. Training)	SIE	51.1601
Nursing Administration (Post-R.N.)	SEI	51.1602
Nursing Anesthetist (Post-R.N.)	ISE	51.1604
Nursing Midwifery (Post-R.N.)	SIR	51.1607
Nursing Science (Post-R.N.)	SIE	51.1608
Nursing, Adult Health (Post-R.N.)	SIA	51.1603
Nursing, Family Practice (Post-R.N.)	ISA	51.1605
Nursing, Maternal/Child Health (Post-R.N.)	SIE	51.1606
Nursing, Other	SCR	51.1699
Nursing, Pediatric (Post-R.N.)	SIA	51.1609
Nursing, Psychiatric/Mental Health (Post-R.N.)	SIA	51.1610
Nursing, Public Health (Post-R.N.)	SIE	51.1611
Nursing, Surgical (Post-R.N.)	SIA	51.1612
Nutritional Sciences	ISE	26.0609
Obstetrics and Gynecology Residency	IRS	51.2938
Occupational Health and Industrial Hygiene	ESC	51.2206
Occupational Medicine Residency	ISC	51.2939
Occupational Safety and Health Technology/Technician	RES	15.0701
Occupational Therapy	SRE	51.2306
Occupational Therapy Assistant	SCE	51.0803
Ocean Engineering	RIE	14.2401
Oceanography	IRS	40.0702
Office Products Marketing Operations	ESA	08.0810
Office Supervision and Management	ESC	52.0204
Oncology Residency	IRS	51.2940
Operations Management and Supervision	RES	52.0205
Operations Research	IRE	27.0302
Ophthalmic Medical Assistant	CIS	51.0804
Ophthalmic Medical Technologist	CIS	51.1803
Ophthalmology Residency	ISR	51.2941
Optical Technician/Assistant	REI	51.1802
Opticianry/Dispensing Optician	RIE	51.1801
Optics	IRE	40.0807
Optometric/Ophthalmic Laboratory Technician	REI	51.1006
Optometry (O.D.)	ISE	51.1701
Oral Pathology Specialty	IRE	51.2804

Title	HOC	CIP
Organic Chemistry	IRE	40.0504
Organizational Behavior Studies	ESR	52.1003
Ornamental Horticulture Operations and Management	RES	01.0603
Orthodontics Specialty	IRS	51.2805
Orthopedics/Orthopedic Surgery Residency	IRA	51.2942
Orthoptics	RSI	51.1804
Orthotics/Prosthetics	RSE	51.2307
Osteopathic Medicine (D.O.)	ISR	51.1901
Otolaryngology Residency	IRS	51.2943
Pacific Area Studies	SEI	05.0109
Painter and Wall Coverer	RSE	46.0408
Painting	ASE	50.0708
Paleontology	IRS	40.0604
Paralegal/Legal Assistant	SEC	22.0103
Parasitology	IRS	26.0610
Parks, Recreation and Leisure Facilities Management	ESR	31.0301
Parks, Recreation and Leisure Studies	ESC	31.0101
Pastoral Counseling and Specialized Ministries	SEA	39.0701
Pathology Residency	IRE	51.2944
Pathology, Human and Animal	IRE	26.0704
Peace and Conflict Studies	IAE	30.0501
Pediatric Cardiology Residency	ISE	51.2945
Pediatric Endocrinology Residency	ISE	51.2946
Pediatric Hemato-Oncology Residency	ISE	51.2947
Pediatric Nephrology Residency	ISE	51.2948
Pediatric Orthopedics Residency	IRA	51.2949
Pediatric Surgery Residency	IRA	51.2950
Pediatrics Residency	ISE	51.2951
Pedodontics Specialty	IRE	51.2806
Perfusion Technology/Technician	ISR	51.0906
Periodontics Specialty	IRE	51.2807
Personal Services Marketing Operations	AES	08.0205
Petroleum Engineering	IRE	14.2501
Petroleum Products Retailing Operations	ERC	08.1209
Petroleum Technology/Technician	RIE	15.0903
Pharmacology, Human and Animal	IRS	26.0705
Pharmacy (B. Pharm., Pharm.D.)	IEC	51.2001
Pharmacy Administration and Pharmaceutics	IES	51.2002
Pharmacy Technician/Assistant	RSE	51.0805
Philosophy	AIE	38.0101
Philosophy and Religion	SAE	38.9999
Photographic Technology/Technician	RCE	10.0103
Photography	AES	50.0605
Physical and Rehabilitation Medicine Residency	IRE	51.2952
Physical and Theoretical Chemistry	IRE	40.0506
Physical Education Teaching and Coaching	SEA	13.1314
Physical Science Technology/Technicians, Other	RIE	41.0399
Physical Sciences, General	IRE	40.0101
Physical Therapy	SRI	51.2308

Part 3: From Occupational Titles to Holland Codes

From the Classification of Instructional Program Titles to Holland Codes

Title	HOC	CIP
Physical Therapy Assistant	SRE	51.0806
Physician Assistant	ISA	51.0807
Physics Teacher Education	SIR	13.1329
Physics, General	IRE	40.0801
Physiological Psychology/Psychobiology	IAE	42.1101
Physiology, Human and Animal	IRE	26.0706
Plant Breeding and Genetics	IRS	02.0405
Plant Pathology	IRS	26.0305
Plant Physiology	IRS	26.0307
Plant Protection (Pest Management)	IER	02.0408
Plant Sciences, General	REI	02.0401
Plasma and High-Temperature Physics	IRE	40.0805
Plastic Surgery Residency	IRA	51.2953
Plastics Technology/Technician	REC	15.0607
Playwriting and Screenwriting	ASE	50.0504
Plumber and Pipefitter	REI	46.0501
Podiatry (D.P.M., D.P., Pod.D.)	SIR	51.2101
Political Science and Government, Other	SEI	45.1099
Political Science, General	ESI	45.1001
Polymer Chemistry	IRE	40.0507
Polymer/Plastics Engineering	IRS	14.3201
Portuguese Language and Literature	AIE	16.0904
Poultry Science	RIS	02.0209
Practical Nurse (L.P.N. Training)	SAC	51.1613
Pre-Elementary/Early Childhood/Kindergarten Teacher Education	SEA	13.1204
Pre-Theological/Pre-Ministerial Studies	SAE	39.0605
Precision Metal Workers, Other	REI	48.0599
Precision Production Trades, Other	REI	48.9999
Preventive Medicine Residency	IRS	51.2954
Printing Press Operator	REI	48.0208
Printmaking	AER	50.0710
Prosthodontics Specialty	IRS	51.2808
Protective Services, Other	SER	43.9999
Psychiatric/Mental Health Services Technician	SEI	51.1502
Psychiatry Residency	ISA	51.2955
Psychoanalysis	SIA	51.2705
Psychology, General	ISE	42.0101
Public Administration	ESR	44.0401
Public Finance	ESI	52.0808
Public Health Education and Promotion	SEA	51.2207
Public Health Medicine Residency	IRS	51.2956
Public Health, General	EIS	51.2201
Public Policy Analysis	EIS	44.0501
Public Relations and Organizational Communications	ESA	09.0501
Public/Applied History and Archival Administration	ESR	45.0805
Pulmonary Disease Residency	IRS	51.2957
Purchasing, Procurement and Contracts Management	ESR	52.0202
Quality Control Technology/Technician	RIC	15.0702

Part 3: From Occupational Titles to Holland Codes

From the Classification of Instructional Program Titles to Holland Codes

Title	HOC	CIP
Rabbinical and Talmudic Studies (M.H.L./Rav)	SAE	39.0604
Radiation Biology/Radiobiology	ISR	26.0611
Radiation Oncology Residency	IRS	51.2958
Radio and Television Broadcasting	ESC	09.0701
Radio and Television Broadcasting Technology/Technician	RES	10.0104
Radioisotopic Pathology Residency	IRS	51.2959
Range Science and Management	SER	02.0409
Reading Teacher Education	SAE	13.1315
Real Estate	ESR	52.1501
Receptionist	CES	52.0406
Recreation Products/Services Marketing Operations	ESR	08.0903
Recreational Therapy	SEC	51.2309
Rehabilitation/Therapeutic Services, Other	SIE	51.2399
Religion/Religious Studies	SAE	38.0201
Religious Education	SEA	39.0401
Religious/Sacred Music	ASE	39.0501
Respiratory Therapy Technician	SRI	51.0908
Rheumatology Residency	IRE	51.2960
Robotics Technology/Technician	IRE	15.0405
Romance Languages and Literatures, Other	AIE	16.0999
Russian and Slavic Area Studies	SEI	05.0110
Russian Language and Literature	AIE	16.0402
Scandinavian Area Studies	SEI	05.0111
Scandinavian Languages and Literatures	AIE	16.0502
School Psychology	ISE	42.1701
Science Teacher Education, General	SAE	13.1316
Science, Technology and Society	SIE	30.1501
Sculpture	AER	50.0709
Secondary Teacher Education	SEA	13.1205
Security and Loss Prevention Services	ESC	43.0109
Sheet Metal Worker	RIC	48.0506
Shoe, Boot and Leather Repairer	RCE	48.0304
Sign Language Interpreter	SCE	51.0205
Slavic Languages and Literatures (Other than Russian)	AIE	16.0403
Small Engine Mechanic and Repairer	REI	47.0606
Social and Philosophical Foundations of Education	SIE	13.0901
Social Psychology	IEA	42.1601
Social Science Teacher Education	SAE	13.1317
Social Sciences, General	SIE	45.0101
Social Studies Teacher Education	SAE	13.1318
Social Work	SEC	44.0701
Socio-Psychological Sports Studies	IAE	31.0506
Sociology	IER	45.1101
Soil Sciences	IRS	02.0501
Solar Technology/Technician	RIC	15.0505
Solid State and Low-Temperature Physics	IRE	40.0808
South Asian Languages and Literatures	AIE	16.0703
South Asian Studies	SEI	05.0112
Southeast Asian Studies	SEI	05.0113

Title	HOC	CIP
Spanish Language and Literature	AIE	16.0905
Spanish Language Teacher Education	SAE	13.1330
Special Education, General	SEC	13.1001
Speech and Rhetorical Studies	ASE	23.1001
Speech Teacher Education	SAE	13.1331
Speech-Language Pathology	ISA	51.0203
Speech-Language Pathology and Audiology	ISR	51.0204
Sport and Fitness Administration/Management	ERS	31.0504
Sports Medicine Residency	IRE	51.2961
Stationary Energy Sources Installer and Operator	RES	47.0501
Structural Engineering	IRS	14.0803
Surgical/Operating Room Technician	RIS	51.0909
Surveying	IER	15.1102
Systems Engineering	ERI	14.2701
Taxation	ESC	52.1601
Teacher Assistant/Aide	SEC	13.1501
Teacher Education, Multiple Levels	SEA	13.1206
Teacher Education, Specific Academic and Vocational Programs	SEA	13.1399
Teaching English as a Second Language/Foreign Language	SER	13.1401
Technical Teacher Education (Vocational)	SEA	13.1319
Technical Theater/Theater Design and Stagecraft	AER	50.0502
Technology Teacher Education/Industrial Arts Teacher Education	SAE	13.1309
Textile Sciences and Engineering	IRE	14.2801
Theology/Theological Studies	SAE	39.0601
Theoretical and Mathematical Physics	IRE	40.0810
Theriogenology	IRS	51.3015
Thoracic Surgery Residency	IRA	51.2962
Tool and Die Maker/Technologist	RIE	48.0507
Tourism Promotion Operations	ESC	08.1104
Toxicology	IRE	26.0612
Trade and Industrial Teacher Education (Vocational)	SEA	13.1320
Transportation and Highway Engineering	ISR	14.0804
Travel Services Marketing Operations	ESC	08.1105
Travel-Tourism Management	ESA	52.0903
Truck, Bus and Other Commercial Vehicle Operator	RES	49.0205
Turf Management	REI	01.0607
Umpires and Other Sports Officials	ESR	12.0204
Upholsterer	RCE	48.0303
Urban Affairs/Studies	IES	45.1201
Urology Residency	IRS	51.2963
Vascular Surgery Residency	IRA	51.2964
Vehicle and Equipment Operators, Other	REC	49.0299
Vehicle and Petroleum Products Marketing Operations, Other	ESR	08.1299
Vehicle Marketing Operations	ESR	08.1208
Vehicle Parts and Accessories Marketing Operations	ESR	08.1203
Veterinarian Assistant/Animal Health Technician	SIE	51.0808
Veterinary Anesthesiology	IRS	51.3001

Title	HOC	CIP
Veterinary Clinical Sciences (M.S., Ph.D.)	IRE	51.2501
Veterinary Dentistry	IRS	51.3002
Veterinary Dermatology	IRS	51.3003
Veterinary Emergency and Critical Care Medicine	IRS	51.3004
Veterinary Internal Medicine	IRS	51.3005
Veterinary Medicine (D.V.M.)	IRE	51.2401
Veterinary Microbiology	IRE	51.3007
Veterinary Nutrition	IRS	51.3008
Veterinary Ophthalmology	IRS	51.3009
Veterinary Pathology	IRE	51.3010
Veterinary Practice	IRS	51.3011
Veterinary Preventive Medicine	IRE	51.3012
Veterinary Radiology	IRS	51.3013
Veterinary Surgery	IRS	51.3014
Veterinary Toxicology	IRS	51.3016
Virology	IRA	26.0619
Vocational Rehabilitation Counseling	SER	51.2310
Waiter/Waitress and Dining Room Manager	ESR	12.0507
Watch, Clock and Jewelry Repairer	REC	47.0408
Water Quality and Wastewater Treatment Technology/ Technician	RIE	15.0506
Water Resources Engineering	IRE	14.0805
Water Transportation Workers, Other	RES	49.0399
Welder/Welding Technologist	REI	48.0508
Western European Studies	SEI	05.0114
Wildlife and Wildlands Management	RES	03.0601
Window Treatment Maker and Installer	RCE	20.0502
Women's Studies	SEI	05.0207
Wood Science and Pulp/Paper Technology	RIE	03.0509
Woodworkers, General	REI	48.0701
Woodworkers, Other	RES	48.0799
Zoological Medicine	ISE	51.3017
Zoology, General	IRE	26.0701

*** CIP category is too heterogeneous to classify.

Title	HOC	Cx	GOE
Abstracting, Document Preparation	ESC	67	11.04.04
Accounting	CSR	56	07.02.02
Accounting and Auditing	CEI	70	11.06.01
Administration	ESC	61	07.01.02
Administrative Specialization	ESR	68	11.05.02
Air	RIE	67	05.04.01
Animal Service	RSE	48	03.03.02
Animal Specialization	IRE	76	02.02.01
Animal Training	RES	53	03.03.01
Announcing	ESA	53	01.07.02
Arts and Crafts	REA	57	01.06.02
Barbering	ESR	53	09.02.02
Billing and Rate Computation	CSR	54	07.02.04
Blasting	RES	53	05.10.06
Boat Operation	REI	47	05.08.04
Booking	ESR	64	11.12.03
Bookkeeping and Auditing	CSR	59	07.02.01
Braking, Switching, and Coupling	REI	47	05.12.05
Brokering	ESA	63	11.06.04
Budget and Financial Control	ESR	70	11.06.05
Card and Game Room Services	CES	44	09.05.05
Care of Others	SEC	47	10.03.03
Certifying	SEC	63	07.01.05
Claims Settlement	ESR	66	11.12.01
Cleaning	REC	39	06.04.39
Cleaning and Maintenance	REC	41	05.12.18
Coaching and Instructing	SER	63	12.01.01
Coating and Plating	REI	50	06.02.21
Commercial Art	AES	64	01.02.03
Communications	ESR	66	05.02.04
Company Policy	ESR	59	11.10.05
Composing and Arranging	ASE	70	01.04.02
Computer Operation	CSR	55	07.06.01
Conciliation	ESR	69	11.04.03
Construction	REI	48	05.11.01
Construction and Maintenance	REI	58	05.05.02
Coordinating and Scheduling	ECS	56	07.05.01
Cosmetology	SER	55	09.02.01
Counseling and Social Work	SEI	66	10.01.02
Creative Writing	ASE	68	01.01.02
Critiquing	AES	70	01.01.03
Crushing, Mixing, Separating, and Chipping	REC	42	05.12.07
Custom Sewing, Tailoring, and Upholstering	RES	54	05.05.15
Cutting and Finishing	RCE	45	05.12.13
Data Analysis	IER	72	11.01.02
Data Collection	CIR	58	10.03.01
Data Processing Design	IRE	70	11.01.01
Demonstration and Sales	ESA	56	08.02.05
Dentistry	IRE	75	02.03.02

Part 3: From Occupational Titles to Holland Codes

From the Guide for Occupational Exploration Interest Subgroups to Holland Codes

Title	HOC	Cx	GOE
Design	IRE	73	05.01.07
Detention	SER	49	04.02.01
Doorkeeping Services	ESC	48	09.05.04
Drafting	RIE	64	05.03.02
Drilling and Oil Exploration	REI	52	05.11.03
Driving-Selling	ERS	52	08.02.07
Dyeing	REI	55	05.05.16
Economic	IAS	71	11.03.05
Editing	AES	69	11.08.01
Editing	AES	68	01.01.01
Educational Services	ESA	68	11.07.03
Electrical	RSE	59	05.07.03
Electrical Work	RCE	44	05.12.16
Electrical-Electronic	RIE	58	05.03.05
Electrical-Electronic	REC	53	05.10.03
Electrical-Electronic Equipment Repair	REI	59	05.05.10
Electrical-Electronic Systems Installation and Repair	RES	59	05.05.05
Electricity Generation and Transmission	RES	57	05.06.01
Elevator Services	REC	48	09.05.09
Emergency Responding	RES	53	04.02.04
Entertaining	ESR	45	01.07.03
Environmental	REI	50	05.07.04
Environmental	RES	51	05.10.09
Environmental Control	RSE	60	05.03.08
Environmental Protection	IER	75	05.01.02
Equipment Operation, Assorted materials Processing	REI	50	06.02.18
Equipment Operation, Assorted Materials Processing	RCE	42	06.04.19
Equipment Operation, Chemical Processing	REI	51	06.02.11
Equipment Operation, Chemical Processing	REC	43	06.04.11
Equipment Operation, Clay and Coke Processing	REI	50	06.02.17
Equipment Operation, Clay Processing	REC	41	06.04.17
Equipment Operation, Food Processing	RES	50	06.02.15
Equipment Operation, Food Processing	REC	41	06.04.15
Equipment Operation, Metal Processing	RES	50	06.02.10
Equipment Operation, Metal Processing	RCE	43	06.04.10
Equipment Operation, Paper and Paper Products Processing	REI	49	06.02.14
Equipment Operation, Paper Making	RCE	41	06.04.14
Equipment Operation, Petroleum and Gas Processing	RES	52	06.02.12
Equipment Operation, Petroleum, Gas, and Coal Processing	RCE	44	06.04.12
Equipment Operation, Rubber, Plastics, and Glass Processing	REI	50	06.02.13
Equipment Operation, Rubber, Plastics, and Glass Processing	RCE	41	06.04.13
Equipment Operation, Textile, Fabric, and Leather Processing	RES	49	06.02.16
Equipment Operation, Textile, Fabric and Leather Processing	REC	41	06.04.16
Equipment Operation, Welding, Brazing, and Soldering	REI	51	06.02.19

Title	HOC	Cx	GOE
Equipment Operation, Wood Processing	REC	41	06.04.18
Estimating, Scheduling, and Record Keeping	REC	53	05.09.02
Expediting and Coordinating	SEC	62	05.03.03
Farming	RES	62	03.01.01
Farming	RES	57	03.02.01
Farming	REC	42	03.04.01
Filing	CSR	49	07.07.01
Filling	RCE	40	06.04.36
Finance	ESC	64	11.10.01
Financial Work	CSE	59	07.01.04
Food Preparation	RSE	51	05.10.08
Food Preparation	RCE	41	05.12.17
Food Preparation	SER	60	05.05.17
Food Research	IRS	75	02.02.04
Food Services	ERC	46	09.05.02
Food Services	ESC	56	09.01.03
Food Services	ESC	49	09.04.01
Forestry and Logging	RIS	67	03.01.04
Forestry and Logging	RES	57	03.02.02
Forestry and Logging	RES	42	03.04.02
Fund and Membership Solicitation	ESA	64	11.09.02
Gem Cutting and Finishing	RES	55	05.05.14
General Clerical Work	CES	47	07.07.03
General Engineering	IRE	74	05.01.08
General Wardrobe Services	REC	44	09.05.07
Graphic Arts and Related Crafts	REI	55	01.06.01
Group Transportation	RSE	49	09.03.01
Guide Services	ESC	52	09.01.02
Hand Lettering, Painting, and Decorating	RCE	51	01.06.03
Health and Safety	ESR	63	11.10.03
Health and Safety Services	SEC	70	11.07.02
Health Specialties	ISR	69	02.03.04
Heating and Melting	REC	41	05.12.10
Historical	ESI	69	11.03.03
Hoisting, Conveying	RES	42	05.12.04
Hunting and Fishing	REC	43	03.04.03
Immigration and Customs	SEI	66	11.10.04
Individual Rights	SER	66	11.10.02
Individual Transportation	REI	47	09.03.02
Individualized Services	ERS	45	09.05.06
Industrial and Safety	RIE	65	05.03.06
Information Transmitting and Receiving	ECS	56	07.04.05
Inspecting, Grading, Sorting, Weighing, and Recording	RCE	43	06.03.02
Inspecting, Testing, and Repairing	REC	51	06.03.01
Inspection	REI	56	06.01.05
Instructing and Appraising	AIS	65	01.02.01
Instructing and Choreography	AES	62	01.05.01
Instructing and Directing	AES	67	01.04.01
Instructing and Directing	SEA	64	01.03.01

Title	HOC	Cx	GOE
Instruction and Supervision	ERS	58	09.03.03
Instrumental Performing	ASC	65	01.04.04
Intangible Sales	ESR	62	08.01.02
Interviewing	SEC	62	07.01.01
Interviewing	CSE	53	07.04.01
Investigating	SER	59	04.01.02
Investigating	ERS	62	07.01.06
Justice Administration	SEI	73	11.04.01
Keyboard Machine Operations	CRS	53	07.06.02
Laundering, Dry Cleaning	REC	40	06.04.35
Law and Order	ESR	49	04.02.03
Legal Practice	ESA	74	11.04.02
Library Services	SEC	61	11.02.04
Life Sciences	IRS	61	02.04.02
Loading, Moving	RES	40	05.12.03
Loading, Moving, Hoisting, and Conveying	REC	40	06.04.40
Lodging	ESR	63	11.11.01
Logging and Lumber	REI	50	05.07.06
Lubricating	REC	41	05.12.08
Machine Assembling	RCS	48	06.02.20
Machine Assembling	RCE	40	06.04.20
Machine Set-up	REI	53	06.01.02
Machine Set-up and Operation	RIE	57	06.01.03
Machine Work, Assorted Materials	RCE	48	06.02.09
Machine Work, Assorted Materials	RCE	41	06.04.09
Machine Work, Brushing, Spraying, and Coating	RCE	41	06.04.21
Machine Work, Fabric and Leather	RCE	41	06.04.05
Machine Work, Leather and Fabrics	RCE	43	06.02.05
Machine Work, Metal and Plastics	REC	50	06.02.02
Machine Work, Metal and Plastics	RCE	41	06.04.02
Machine Work, Paper	RES	49	06.02.04
Machine Work, Paper	REC	40	06.04.04
Machine Work, Rubber	REC	48	06.02.07
Machine Work, Rubber	RCE	40	06.0407
Machine Work, Stone, Glass, and Clay	REI	49	06.02.08
Machine Work, Stone, Glass, and Clay	RCE	41	06.04.08
Machine Work, Textiles	RCS	46	06.02.06
Machine Work, Textiles	RCE	40	06.04.06
Machine Work, Wood	REI	47	06.02.03
Machine Work, Wood	RCE	40	06.04.03
Machining	RIE	59	05.05.07
Maintenance and Construction	ERS	63	05.02.02
Management Services: Government	ESR	68	11.05.03
Management Services: Non-Government	ESR	71	11.05.01
Managing	ESR	62	04.01.01
Manual Work, Assembly Large Parts	REC	41	06.04.22
Manual Work, Assembly Large Parts	RCE	49	06.02.22
Manual Work, Assembly Small Parts	RCE	48	06.02.23
Manual Work, Assembly Small Parts	RCE	40	06.04.23

Title	HOC	Cx	GOE
Manual Work, Assorted Materials.	RCE	47	06.02.32
Manual Work, Assorted Materials	RCE	40	06.04.34
Manual Work, Brushing, Spraying, and Coating	RCE	40	06.04.33
Manual Work, Casting and Molding	RCE	41	06.04.32
Manual Work, Food Processing	RES	52	06.02.28
Manual Work, Food Processing	REC	39	06.04.28
Manual Work, Laying Out and Marking	REC	50	06.02.31
Manual Work, Metal and Plastics	RCE	46	06.02.24
Manual Work, Metal and Plastics	RCE	41	06.04.24
Manual Work, Paper	RCE	44	06.02.26
Manual Work, Paper	RCE	40	06.04.26
Manual Work, Rubber	RCE	45	06.02.29
Manual Work, Rubber	RCE	40	06.04.29
Manual Work, Stamping, Marking, Labeling, and Ticketing	RCE	41	06.04.37
Manual Work, Stone, Glass, and Clay	REC	46	06.02.30
Manual Work, Stone, Glass, and Clay	RCE	41	06.04.30
Manual Work, Textile, Fabric and Leather	RCE	46	06.02.27
Manual Work, Textile, Fabric and Leather	RCE	39	06.04.27
Manual Work, Welding and Flame Cutting	RCE	42	06.04.31
Manual Work, Wood	REC	40	06.04.25
Manual Work, Wood	RCE	47	06.02.25
Masonry	REC	40	05.12.09
Masonry, Stone, and Brick Work	RES	54	05.05.01
Materials Handling	REC	46	05.11.04
Materials Handling	ERS	65	05.02.07
Mechanical	RIC	65	05.03.07
Mechanical	RSE	58	05.07.02
Mechanical	RES	53	05.10.02
Mechanical Work	REI	58	05.05.09
Mechanical Work	REC	44	05.12.15
Medicine and Surgery	IRS	76	02.03.01
Metal Fabrication and Repair	REI	56	05.05.06
Mining and Quarrying	REI	49	05.11.02
Mining, Logging, and Petroleum Production	ERS	62	05.02.05
Mining, Quarrying, Drilling	REC	43	05.12.02
Musical Instrument Fabrication and Repair	RES	55	05.05.12
Narrating and Announcing	SEA	64	01.03.03
Nursery and Groundskeeping	RES	60	03.02.03
Nursery and Groundskeeping	REC	45	03.04.04
Nursing	SIE	67	10.02.01
Occupational	SEI	64	11.03.04
Officiating	ESR	52	12.01.02
Oil, Gas, and Water Distribution	RES	57	05.06.03
Order, Complaint, and Claims handling	ESC	56	07.04.02
Packaging and Storing	RIE	60	05.03.09
Packaging-Wrapping	RES	40	09.05.10
Painting, Caulking, and Coating	RCE	43	05.12.14
Painting, Dyeing, and Coating	REC	53	05.10.07
Painting, Plastering, and Paperhanging	RES	56	05.05.04

Part 3: From Occupational Titles to Holland Codes

From the Guide for Occupational Exploration Interest Subgroups to Holland Codes

Title	HOC	Cx	GOE
Patient Care	SRE	53	10.03.02
Paying and Receiving	CES	54	07.03.01
Payroll and Timekeeping	CSR	56	07.02.05
Peddling and Hawking	ESC	45	08.03.01
Performing	RSE	54	12.01.03
Performing	AER	61	01.05.02
Performing	AES	60	01.03.02
Performing	ERA	52	12.02.01
Personal Appearance	AES	45	01.08.01
Petroleum	RIE	64	05.03.04
Petroleum	ERC	55	05.07.05
Physical Conditioning	ESR	44	09.05.01
Physical Sciences	RIE	62	02.04.01
Plant and Animal Specialization	IRE	79	02.02.03
Plant Specialization	IRS	76	02.02.02
Plumbing and Pipefitting	RES	57	05.05.03
Portering and Baggage Services	ERS	45	09.05.03
Precision Hand Work	REI	54	06.01.04
Printing	RIE	56	05.05.13
Processing	REC	58	05.06.04
Processing and Manufacturing	ERS	67	05.02.03
Procurement Negotiations	ESI	66	11.12.04
Promoting	CER	38	08.03.02
Property and People	ERS	49	04.02.02
Psychic Science	AEC	49	01.07.01
Psychological	IES	76	11.03.01
Public Relations	ESA	66	11.09.03
Pumping	REC	43	05.12.06
Purchasing Sales	ESA	63	08.01.03
Rail Vehicle Operation	REI	52	05.08.02
Real Estate	ESA	62	08.02.04
Reception and Information Giving	CES	56	07.04.04
Record Preparation and Maintenance	CSE	54	07.05.03
Record Verification and Proofing	CSE	54	07.05.02
Records Systems Analysis	EAS	66	11.06.02
Recreation and Amusement	ESR	63	11.11.02
Recreation Services	ESR	71	11.07.04
Registration	ECS	53	07.04.03
Religious	SEA	65	10.01.01
Rental and Leasing	ESR	66	11.12.02
Reproduction	RCE	52	05.10.05
Reproduction Services	REC	42	05.12.19
Research	IRE	71	05.01.01
Retail	ESA	57	08.02.02
Risk and Profit Analysis	ESC	66	11.06.03
Routing and Distribution	CSE	52	07.05.04
Safety and Comfort Services	ESC	52	09.01.04
Sales	ESA	65	11.09.01
Sales and Purchasing Management	ESR	67	11.05.04

Title	HOC	Cx	GOE
Sales Engineering	ERI	70	05.01.05
Sales Services	ESC	49	09.04.02
Scientific, Medical, and Technical Equipment Fabrication and Repair	REI	59	05.05.11
Secretarial Work	CSE	60	07.01.03
Services	RES	47	03.04.05
Services	ERS	62	05.02.06
Services	ERC	54	03.02.04
Services	ESR	64	11.11.04
Services	ESA	58	08.02.06
Services Requiring Driving	REC	45	05.08.03
Shipping, Receiving, and Stock Checking	REC	51	05.09.01
Signalling	RCE	43	05.12.20
Social and Recreational Services	ESR	55	09.01.01
Social Services	ESA	67	11.07.01
Sociological	EIS	69	11.03.02
Soliciting-Selling	ESA	54	08.02.08
Sorting and Distribution	CRE	46	07.07.02
Specialized Teaching	SEC	65	10.02.03
Specialty Breeding	RES	59	03.01.02
Specialty Cropping	REI	61	03.01.03
Stationary Engineering	RES	53	05.06.02
Statistical Reporting and Analysis	CSR	59	07.02.03
Structural	RES	51	05.10.01
Structural	REC	54	05.07.01
Structural Work	REC	43	05.12.12
Structural-Mechanical-Electrical-Electronic	RES	52	05.10.04
Studio Art	ASE	62	01.02.02
Supervision	RES	58	06.02.01
Supervision	ERS	58	06.04.01
Supervision	ERS	57	05.12.01
Supervision and Instruction	RES	59	06.01.01
Surveying	IER	66	05.03.01
Switchboard Services	SCE	52	07.04.06
Systems	ERS	68	05.02.01
Systems Design	IRE	75	05.01.03
Teaching and Instructing, General	SER	67	11.02.01
Teaching, Home Economics, Agriculture, and Related	SEC	65	11.02.03
Teaching, Vocational and Industrial	SER	67	11.02.02
Technical Sales	ESR	62	08.01.01
Technology	IER	76	02.01.02
Test Administration	ESC	56	07.01.07
Testing and Quality Control	IRE	72	05.01.04
Theoretical Research	IRE	77	02.01.01
Therapy and Rehabilitation	SIR	64	10.02.02
Ticket Taking, Ushering	CES	44	09.05.08
Translating and Interpreting	SEI	66	11.08.04
Transportation	ESR	64	11.11.03
Truck Driving	REI	48	05.08.01

Part 3: From Occupational Titles to Holland Codes

From the Guide for Occupational Exploration Interest Subgroups to Holland Codes

Title	HOC	Cx	GOE
Verifying, Recording, and Marking	RCE	47	05.09.03
Veterinary Medicine	IRS	68	02.03.03
Vocal Performing	AES	65	01.04.03
Water	REI	61	05.04.02
Welding	RES	40	05.12.11
Wholesale	ESA	58	08.02.01
Wholesale and Retail	ESA	57	08.02.03
Wholesale-Retail	ESR	62	11.11.05
Woodworking	RIE	56	05.05.08
Work Planning and Utilization	IRE	70	05.01.06
Wrapping and Packing	RCE	40	06.04.38
Writing	ISA	66	11.08.02
Writing and Broadcasting	EAS	70	11.08.03

Part 4: Theoretical and Technical Origins

The *Dictionary of Holland Occupational Codes* (DHOC) was developed to make some important but unwieldy sources of occupational information more accessible to clients, counselors, and researchers. Specifically, the voluminous information disseminated by the Department of Labor through its DOT and Supplements will be of more value if it is linked directly to a theory of careers undergirding vocational assistance in schools, colleges, and industry. The largest group of purchasers of the DOT are vocational or career counselors (Miller, Treiman, Cain, & Roos, 1980), most of whom use interest inventories or other forms of vocational assistance based on the Holland occupational classification and theory of careers.

To make this extensive information more available and easier to interpret, an empirically based translation of the DOT information into the Holland classification was required. The following sections provide background on the theory and classification, describe the technical procedures that were used to produce our 1982 translation based on the fourth edition of the DOT (Employment and Training Administration, 1977), and assess the quality of the resulting classification. The following sections also describe some derivatives of the classification research: evidence of the construct validity of the occupational classification; evidence on the distinctions among occupational groups; and information about the distributions of one-, two-, and three-letter occupational codes for DOT occupations. Recent work to revise and extend our initial translation is summarized in Part 5.

Theory and Classification

The occupational classification, like the SDS and associated tools, is the product of a theory of personality types and environmental models (Holland, 1985/1992). Its usefulness depends on the usefulness of the underlying theory. Holland's theory is now the most widely used organizing principle for vocational interest assessment in the world. Although it is not possible to summarize the research evidence here, we evaluate the theory in the following way.

The virtues of the theory are easily summarized: (a) The typologies are easily grasped; (b) it has many virtues of a useful theory—clear definitions, internally consistent structure, broad scope, and formalizations for dealing with personal development and change; (c) it has a broad base of research support from studies of children, adolescents, college students, and adults as old as 70, including both men and women; (d) the theory is easily applied to practical problems—the development of vocational assessment devices, the classification and interpretation of personal and environmental data, and the conduct of vocational counseling; (e) it enables clear predictions of outcomes of person–job interactions; (f) the classification provides a way to incorporate information about new occupations without building a new scale for each occupation.

The weaknesses of the theory are as follows: (a) The hypotheses about work environments are only partially tested and require more exploration; (b) the hypotheses about person–environment congruence have received some support (Gottfredson, 1994; Gottfredson & Holland, 1990; Helms, 1996; Mount & Muchinsky, 1978; Spokane, 1985), but they require more testing with better research; (c) the formulations about personal development and change (Holland, 1985/1992; Holland & Gottfredson, 1976) have received some support (Edwards, Nafziger, & Holland, 1974; Grandy & Stahmann, 1974a, 1974b; Holland, 1973, pp. 53-54; Kelso, 1976), and they are consistent with the persuasive social learning perspective spelled out by Krumboltz (1978), but they should be examined more thoroughly; (d) the classification of occupations and of persons may differ depending on the devices or samples used to assess the types; (e) the evidence about some propositions involving consistency and satisfaction is weak, although it is generally positive (Gottfredson, 1977; Gottfredson & Holland, 1990; Nafziger, Holland, & Gottfredson, 1975; Rounds, Shubsachs, Dawis, & Lofquist, 1978); and (f) important personal and environmental contingencies lie outside the scope of the typology. For example, the distribution of influence or status within a social environment, social class, special advantage or disadvantage, and economic conditions are all important influences on careers that are incorporated in the theory only indirectly. Such conditions must be taken into account in counseling and research applications. Occupational level, especially, should be used as a supplement to the RIASEC system in matching persons with jobs.

One limitation noted earlier was addressed by our research to develop the codes in the first edition of the DHOC (Gottfredson et al., 1982). Alternative identifications (Sokal, 1974) of the occupational classification sometimes differ depending on the method used to derive them. Inventories such as the SDS, VPI, Strong Interest Inventory (SII; Harmon, Hansen, Borgen, & Hammer, 1994), or Career Assessment Inventory (CAI; Johansson, 1982); job analysis data from the Position Analysis Questionnaire (PAQ; McCormick, 1979) or PCI (Gottfredson & Holland, 1991); and different samples of persons or jobs tend to produce similar but not identical codes.

The 1982 DHOC translation used a single source of job analysis data to assign Holland codes for all occupations by a common method. Interest inventory information about an occupation's incumbents was used only indirectly in the resulting classification. In this respect, the DHOC had fewer scientific flaws than earlier classifications that relied on information from divergent sources. At the same time, the use of imperfect job analysis information developed using analysis methods intended for a different purpose meant that our methods were only approximate. The codes presented in the current volume represent a continuing attempt to provide the best and most comprehensive classification possible with available information.

Development

This section summarizes how the 1982 DHOC classification was developed, what data were employed, and how the results support the validity of the classification.

Data

Occupational analysis. The occupational data developed by the Employment and Training Administration (1972, 1974, 1977) to produce the fourth edition of the DOT provided the main source of occupational information used. In producing the DOT, the Department of Labor aimed to analyze all occupations in the U. S. economy. The economy was categorized by industries, and the industries were assigned to occupational analysis field centers around the country. These field centers approached business establishments and other organizations with requests that they be allowed to inventory and analyze the jobs in those firms. If granted permission, the centers proceeded with their job analyses. Miller et al. (1980) have described the methods used to select organizations for examination and some limitations of the sampling. Generally, it appears that established production and other highly structured occupations are covered more extensively than less-structured and newly emerging occupations; and large organizations are over-represented.

Occupations were rated by occupational analysts on the following: three worker functions (Data, People, Things); educational development required in reasoning, mathematics, and language; specific vocational preparation; 11 aptitudes; 10 temperaments; 5 interests; 6 physical demands; and 7 environmental conditions. Table 3 (based on Miller et al., 1980, Tables 7-8 and 7-11) summarizes the ratings made. These ratings were more fully described by the Employment and Training Administration (1972) and by Miller et al. (1980), who also provide extensive information about their factor structure and reliability.

Table 3
Occupational Ratings Made in Producing the DOT

Characteristic	Range	*M*	*SD*
Worker functions (low numbers indicate high ratings)			
Data	0 to 6	4.11	2.09
People	0 to 8	6.83	1.85
Things	0 to 7	4.32	2.31
Education and training			
General educational development	1 to 6	3.00	1.09
Specific vocational preparation	1 to 9	4.46	2.06
Aptitudes (low numbers indicate high ratings)			
Intelligence	1 to 4	3.19	0.72
Verbal aptitude	1 to 5	3.43	0.78
Numerical aptitude	1 to 5	3.63	0.78
Spacial perception	1 to 5	3.47	0.71
Form perception	1 to 5	3.36	0.67
Clerical perception	1 to 5	3.89	0.79
Motor coordination	1 to 5	3.46	0.56
Finger dexterity	1 to 5	3.56	0.61
Manual dexterity	1 to 5	3.21	0.53
Eye-hand-foot coordination	1 to 5	4.67	0.60
Color discrimination	1 to 5	4.52	0.70
Temperaments			
Direction, control, and planning	0 or 1	0.18	0.38
Feelings, ideas, or facts	0 or 1	0.01	0.10
Influencing people	0 or 1	0.04	0.20
Sensory or judgmental criteria	0 or 1	0.17	0.38
Measurable or verifiable criteria	0 or 1	0.39	0.49
Dealing with people	0 or 1	0.23	0.42
Repetitive or continuous processes	0 or 1	0.46	0.50
Performing under stress	0 or 1	0.02	0.16
Set limits, tolerance, or standards	0 or 1	0.60	0.49
Variety and change	0 or 1	0.20	0.40
Bipolar interests (1 = first interest present, 0 = neither, −1 = second interest present)			
Communication of data versus activities with things	−1 to 1	−.57	0.66
Scientific and technical activities versus business contact	−1 to 1	−.12	0.45
Abstract and creative versus routine, concrete activities	−1 to 1	−.47	0.53
Activities involving processes, machines or techniques versus social welfare	−1 to 1	0.62	0.55
Activities resulting in tangible, productive satisfaction versus prestige, esteem	−1 to 1	−.05	0.47
Physical demands			
Lifting, carrying, pulling, pushing	1 to 5	2.39	0.91
Climbing, balancing	0 or 1	0.08	0.27
Stooping, kneeling, crouching, crawling	0 or 1	0.20	0.40
Reaching, handling, fingering, feeling	0 or 1	0.89	0.31
Talking, hearing	0 or 1	0.29	0.45
Seeing	0 or 1	0.57	0.49
Working conditions			
Outside working conditions	1 to 3	1.22	0.56
Extreme cold	0 or 1	0.01	0.08
Extreme heat	0 or 1	0.05	0.21
Wet, humid	0 or 1	0.07	0.25
Noise, vibration	0 or 1	0.29	0.45
Hazardous conditions	0 or 1	0.15	0.35
Fumes, odors, dusts, gasses, poor ventilation	0 or 1	0.12	0.33

Note. From *Work, Jobs, and Occupations* (pp. 165-166, 174-175), by A. R. Miller, D. S. Treiman, P. S. Cain, and P. A. Roos (Eds.), 1980, Washington, DC: National Academy Press.

In a partial simulation of the procedures used to rate Data, People, Things, GED, SVP, one physical demand, and one working condition, Cain and Green (1980), estimated lower-bound reliability coefficients ranging from .25 to .84. These results indicate that the ratings have useful but not high levels of reliability. Similar evidence of reliability was provided by Webb, Shavelson, Shea, and Morello (1981).

Evidence about the construct validity of the DOT ratings is limited. Definitions of some of the variables to be rated are cursory, and few validity studies have been conducted (Miller et al., 1980, chapter 7). Nevertheless, these ratings have been shown to be strongly related to patterns in occupational mobility in much the same way as are the PAQ (McCormick, 1979) dimension scores (Gottfredson, 1982). An inspection of the ratings implies that they appear reasonable and are the most comprehensive source of systematic occupational information available. Equally important, there is no reason to suspect that "women's work" is undervalued relative to "men's work" in the fourth edition of the DOT (Miller et al., 1980, pp. 188-191).

Construction sample. Occupations were selected from the Occupations Finder (Holland, 1978) to represent occupations in each of the six major groups (R, I, A, S, E, and C) approximately equally. We selected occupational titles for which the evidence supporting the code assigned in the Occupations Finder appeared strongest. In all, 189 titles were chosen in this way: 37 Realistic, 35 Investigative, 27 Artistic, 31 Social, 28 Enterprising, and 31 Conventional occupations. This sample is called the construction sample.

Method

Multiple discriminant analysis was used to develop classificatory functions based on occupational analysis data to classify the 189 titles chosen from the Occupations Finder into occupational categories. In a subsequent step, the classificatory functions developed in the construction sample were used to estimate the probability that each of the 12,099 occupations defined in the DOT belonged to each Holland Category.

Specifically, Fisher's linear discriminant functions (Norusis, 1979) were adjusted for estimated prior probabilities of category membership by adding the log of the prior probability to the constants. Estimates of prior probabilities were made judgmentally by directly classifying a random sample of 296 occupations from the DOT.

Each occupation in the DOT was assigned a three-letter Holland code by using the category with the largest classificatory function score (equivalent to the most probable category) to determine the first letter, the function with the second highest score to determine the second letter, and the function with the third highest score to determine the third letter.

Validation

The following subsections review the analyses that were performed to assess the scientific soundness of the classification and to clarify the relation of the classification to the U. S. Department of Labor's GOE categories and the DOT ratings.

Empirical classification versus judgment. To assess the efficiency of the classification, and as a quality control check, Gary Gottfredson and John Holland independently classified a randomly selected validation sample of 289 occupations from the DOT (excluding occupations included in the construction sample). We agreed on the classification of 87.5% of these occupations ($\kappa = .63$), and we resolved disagreements through discussion. The pooled judgment about the classification of validation sample occupations was compared with the classification of these occupations using the new empirical procedure to assess the degree of agreement.

The results of the empirical classification of occupations in the construction sample are shown in Table 4. In general, 87.8% of occupations in the construction sample were correctly classified ($\kappa = .85$). Validation sample results are shown in Table 5. The empirically derived code matched the code based on our pooled judgement 77.4% of the time ($\kappa = .47$). Most disagreements between the empirical and the pooled-judgment codes are for occupations with an empirical code in the Conventional category that were judged to belong to the Realistic category.

Table 4
Concurrent Validity of Classification: Construction Sample

Imputed code	Code listed in Occupations Finder					
	R	I	A	S	E	C
Realistic (R)	**36**	1	1	0	0	2
Investigative (I)	1	**34**	1	0	0	0
Artistic (A)	0	0	**20**	1	1	0
Social (S)	0	0	0	**24**	2	0
Enterprising (E)	0	0	5	5	**25**	2
Conventional (C)	0	0	0	1	0	**27**

Note. Boldface entries show the frequency of occupations for which the imputed code matches the code listed in the Occupations Finder (hits). Hit rate is 87.8%, $\kappa = .85$.

Table 5
Validity of Computer-Generated Codes in a Cross-Validation Sample

Classification based on judgment	Computer-generated classification					
	R	I	A	S	E	C
Realistic (R)	**185**	0	0	5	8	39
Investigative (I)	0	**6**	0	0	1	0
Artistic (A)	1	0	**1**	0	0	0
Social (S)	0	0	0	**6**	3	0
Enterprising (E)	4	0	1	1	**22**	1
Conventional (C)	1	0	0	1	1	**2**

Note. Classification based on judgment is based on independent classifications by the authors with discrepant classifications resolved by discussion. Boldface entries are hits (77.4%), $\kappa = .47$.

Holland and GOE interest categories. The GOE is organized according to "interest areas" based, for the most part, on 11 factors derived from a factor analysis of the items in the U. S. Employment Service Interest Inventory (Droege & Hawk, 1977; Employment and Training Administration, 1979). Of the 12 categories in the GOE, 11 correspond to these 11 interest dimensions; the 12th was added to accommodate a small number of occupations in physical performing that did not seem to fit into the first 11 categories. The assignment of DOT titles to GOE categories by Employment Service Occupational analysts, therefore, forms one method of examining the validity of the present classification. According to the Employment and Training Administration (1979), the GOE categories should map into the Holland categories as shown in Table 6.

Table 6
GOE and Holland Interest Categories

GOE interest group		Holland category
01	Artistic	Artistic
02	Scientific	Investigative
03	Plants and Animals	Realistic
04	Protective	
05	Mechanical	
06	Industrial	
07	Business Detail	Conventional
08	Selling	Enterprising
09	Accommodating[a]	Social
10	Humanitarian	
11	Leading-Influencing[b]	
12	Physical Performing	

Note. From *Guide for Occupational Exploration* (p. 325), by Employment and Training Administration, U. S. Department of Labor, 1979, Washington, DC: U. S. Government Printing Office. [a]Also includes a few occupations included in Holland's Realistic category. [b]Also includes occupations included in Holland's Enterprising and Conventional categories.

A comparison of the Holland category assigned by the empirical formula, and the occupational analysts' judgments about the GOE interest group for the same occupations is shown in Table 7. Overall, 77% of the occupations are classified into the category predicted by the Employment and Training Administration (1979, p. 325). At the same time, the simple rules suggested in the GOE for translating "interest groups" into Holland occupational categories did not always work well. For example, more GOE "artistic" occupations are classified in the present system as Realistic than as Artistic. In addition, substantial numbers of "protective" occupations are classified as Enterprising and Social. Most "accommodating" occupations are classified as Enterprising, and a large proportion of "physical performing" occupations are classified as Enterprising.

Table 7
Holland Category for Occupations Classified in Each GOE Interest Group

GOE interest group		Holland category						n
		R	I	A	S	E	C	
01	Artistic	45.3	1.3	**32.8**	8.4	7.4	4.8	311
02	Scientific	25.4	**69.4**	0.0	1.9	1.4	1.9	209
03	Plants and Animals	**77.7**	0.4	0.0	5.3	13.3	3.4	264
04	Protective	**25.0**	0.0	0.0	25.0	47.3	2.7	112
05	Mechanical	**75.7**	6.2	0.3	2.7	9.1	6.0	2,547
06	Industrial	**80.9**	0.1	0.0	1.1	3.1	14.8	6,936
07	Business Detail	6.3	0.2	0.2	11.4	22.9	**59.1**	589
08	Selling	2.4	0.0	2.4	1.4	**92.4**	1.4	210
09	Accommodating	**15.4**	0.5	0.0	7.4	54.3	22.3	188
10	Humanitarian	6.3	8.0	1.8	**68.8**	14.3	0.9	112
11	Leading-Influencing	2.6	**6.7**	4.8	28.2	54.0	3.6	581
12	Physical Performing	22.5	0.0	7.5	25.0	42.5	2.5	40

Note. Overall, 76.8% of the occupations (*N* = 12,099) fall in the predicted cells. Boldface entries show predicted categories. Table entries display row percentages.

Dictionary of Holland Occupational Codes

These deviations from the predictions notwithstanding, the high degree of correspondence we found lends considerable support both to the GOE classification and to the DOT translation to the Holland classification. Less than perfect correspondence is to be expected because of the judgmental nature of the classification in the GOE, the relatively new interest measures underlying that guide, the limitations of the occupational analysis data used to empirically assign Holland codes in this project, and the sampling and measurement error in the job analysis data.

Sore thumbing. As a final step, John Holland scrutinized the 12,099 empirically derived codes to locate grossly misclassified occupations. This procedure identified 35 occupations for which the empirically derived code did not appear in agreement with common knowledge or interest data. In most other cases, Holland regarded the codes generated by the empirical procedure as sensible.

Some Outcomes of the Development

The research to develop empirical codes produced some helpful information about the classification: the uneven distribution of types of work, the meaning of the environmental classification, and distinctions between occupational categories that are adjacent on the hexagon.

Distribution of occupational codes. The distribution of one-letter codes assigned by the empirical formula is shown in Table 8. Of the 12,099 occupations in the DOT, 66.7% were classified as Realistic—somewhat fewer than estimated by direct judgment or by the census code translation of the random sample. In addition, 13.4% were classified as Conventional—somewhat more than estimated by direct judgment or by the census code translation of the random sample.

Table 8
Distribution of Occupational Titles in the DOT According to Three 1982 Estimates

Occupational category	Method of estimation		
	Judgment % (N = 296)	Census conversion % (N = 295)	Imputation % (N = 12,099)
Realistic	75.7	77.8	66.7
Investigative	6.4	4.7	3.0
Artistic	1.7	1.0	1.2
Social	6.1	6.4	4.6
Enterprising	6.8	6.8	11.1
Conventional	3.4	3.7	13.4

Note. For the judgment method, a random sample of occupations was classified by a judge using the Occupations Finder and a working knowledge of the classification as guides. In the census conversion method, the first census code listed by the Occupational Analysis Branch of the U. S. Department of Labor was recoded to Holland category using the L. S. Gottfredson & Brown (1978) table. One occupation could not be translated using this table. Imputation is based on the classification functions.

Table 9 summarizes the frequency of the results of the empirical classification in another way by showing the number of occupations with each of the six codes appearing somewhere in the three-letter code. As might be expected for occupations in the U. S. economy, most occupations had the letters R or E appearing in their codes, whereas occupations with A in the code were rare (fewer than 5% of titles in the DOT).

Table 9
Number of Occupations With Each Code
Appearing Somewhere in the First Three Letters
in the 1982 DHOC

Code	Number of occupations
Realistic (R)	10,708
Investigative (I)	2,551
Artistic (A)	570
Social (S)	6,064
Enterprising (E)	10,405
Conventional (C)	5,999

Worker functions, aptitudes, and interests. To provide additional insight into the meanings of the Holland categories, selected tables showing occupational analysis information were prepared. These tables describe the job content of typical jobs in each Holland category at GED Levels 5 and 6 and GED Levels 3 and 4. Mean worker function ratings are shown in Table 10. (Recall that the DOT scores worker functions in the reverse direction. A high number means a low complexity of involvement in Data, People, or Things; a low number means a high complexity of involvement.) These ratings generally accord with theoretical expectations. For example, for occupations at GED Levels 5 and 6, Artistic and Investigative occupations are rated as having the most complex involvement with Data. At these GED levels, Social occupations are rated as having the most complex involvement with People, and Realistic and Investigative occupations are rated as having the most complex involvement with Things. For occupations at GED Levels 3 and 4, Artistic and Enterprising occupations are rated as having the most complex involvement with Data, although the involvement is less complex than that of occupations at the higher GED levels. Among occupations at GED Levels 3 and 4, Enterprising and Social occupations are rated as having the most complex involvement with People, and Realistic and Investigative occupations are rated as having the most complex involvement with things. For Realistic occupations, the mean complexity of involvement with Things for GED Levels 3 and 4 is slightly higher than the degree of complexity for GED Levels 5 and 6.

Mean worker aptitude ratings also generally correspond with expectations (see Table 11 for occupations at GED Levels 5 and 6 and Table 12 for occupations at GED Levels 3 and 4). For instance, the higher-level occupations (GED 5 and 6) are rated as requiring greater general intelligence. Among GED Level 5 and 6 occupations, Investigative occupations are rated highest; among GED Level 3 and 4 occupations, Artistic occupations are rated the highest.

Most aptitude ratings relate to cognitive, perceptual, or motor skills. Accordingly, with some exceptions, clear-cut expectations are difficult to specify. One might expect Artistic occupations generally to require more form perception and color discrimination aptitude than other occupations, and they do receive the highest rating in color discrimination. Conventional occupations would certainly be expected to require more clerical aptitude than other categories, and they do receive the highest rating on this aptitude. Finally, Investigative occupations would be expected to require more numeric aptitude than other occupations, and on the average, they are rated the highest. No ratings of interpersonal or social aptitudes are included in the job analysis data.

Table 10
DOT Worker Function Ratings for Occupations by
GED Level and Holland Category

Category	Data		People		Things		n
	M	*SD*	*M*	*SD*	*M*	*SD*	
GED Levels 5 and 6							
Realistic	1.16	.88	6.03	1.26	3.04	2.58	94
Investigative	.79	.81	5.44	2.10	2.90	2.76	340
Artistic	.32	.58	5.11	1.81	4.67	2.91	102
Social	1.21	.56	2.79	2.35	6.50	1.53	227
Enterprising	1.08	.36	4.36	2.30	6.77	1.10	326
Conventional	1.22	.65	5.67	1.28	5.72	2.47	18
GED Levels 3 and 4							
Realistic	3.65	1.80	6.90	1.70	2.45	1.93	4,235
Investigative	3.25	1.42	7.04	1.30	3.08	2.38	24
Artistic	1.96	1.87	5.70	1.59	3.65	2.81	46
Social	2.07	1.49	4.59	2.00	4.75	2.58	315
Enterprising	1.88	1.25	4.54	1.52	5.81	2.20	942
Conventional	4.22	1.51	7.09	1.19	4.27	2.18	695

Note. A *low* number for worker function ratings indicates a *high* degree of involvement.

Because the Holland occupational classification is rooted in the interest measurement tradition, the pattern of DOT interest ratings for occupations classified into each of the six categories is of special importance. The DOT interest ratings are made on bipolar scales that were influenced by Cottle's (1950) factor analysis of the Strong Vocational Interest Blank (Strong, 1943) and other inventories. Although their bipolar nature and the casual method job analysts used to make these ratings limit our analyses, the results shown in Table 13 support many theoretical expectations. For example, Realistic, Investigative, and Conventional occupations are rated, on average, at the scientific end of the scale for "scientific or technical activities versus business contact," and Enterprising occupations are rated, on average, at the other end. Realistic and Conventional occupations are rated, on average, at the machines end of the scale for "activities involving processes, machines, or techniques versus social welfare"; Social and Artistic occupations are rated at the abstract end of the scale for "abstract and creative versus routine, concrete activities"; and Conventional occupations are rated at the other end. In short, the pattern for hexagonally opposite occupational types (Holland, 1985/1992) is reproduced in the pattern of average ratings for these scales.

Table 11
DOT Worker Aptitude Ratings for Occupations at GED Levels 5 and 6 by Holland Category

Aptitude	Realistic		Investigative		Artistic		Social		Enterprising		Conventional	
	M	SD	M	SD	M	SD	M	SD	M	SD	M	SD
Intelligence	4.1	.4	4.5	.5	4.3	.5	4.1	.4	4.1	.4	4.0	.0
Verbal	4.0	.6	4.4	.6	4.3	.6	4.1	.5	4.1	.4	4.2	.4
Numeric	3.9	.6	4.2	.6	3.0	.7	3.2	.6	3.6	.6	3.7	.8
Spatial	3.9	.7	4.0	.7	3.2	1.0	2.4	.7	2.6	.8	3.0	.9
Form perception	3.5	.7	3.8	.7	3.3	.9	2.5	.7	2.6	.7	2.8	.7
Clerical	3.0	.6	3.0	.6	2.7	.7	3.1	.7	3.0	.6	3.8	.4
Motor coordination	2.8	.7	2.8	.7	2.7	.8	2.1	.5	2.0	.4	2.2	.4
Finger dexterity	2.8	.7	3.1	.9	2.8	1.1	2.1	.5	2.0	.4	2.2	.4
Manual dexterity	2.8	.6	3.0	.8	2.6	.8	2.1	.6	2.0	.3	2.2	.4
Eye-hand-foot coordination	1.7	1.0	1.6	.7	1.2	.7	1.2	.6	1.1	.4	1.4	.7
Color discrimination	2.0	.8	2.3	.9	2.3	1.5	1.4	.8	1.3	.6	1.4	.6
n	94		340		102		227		326		18	

Table 12
DOT Worker Aptitude Ratings for Occupations at GED Levels 3 and 4 by Holland Category

Aptitude	Realistic		Investigative		Artistic		Social		Enterprising		Conventional	
	M	SD	M	SD	M	SD	M	SD	M	SD	M	SD
Intelligence	3.0	.3	3.2	.4	3.4	.5	3.1	.4	3.2	.4	3.0	.4
Verbal	2.5	.5	3.0	.6	3.1	.6	3.0	.5	3.2	.5	2.7	.6
Numeric	2.5	.6	3.1	.6	2.5	.7	2.5	.5	2.9	.5	2.5	.6
Spatial	2.9	.6	3.0	.9	3.2	.9	2.4	.6	2.5	.6	2.2	.6
Form perception	2.9	.6	3.2	.7	3.1	.9	2.6	.7	2.6	.6	2.6	.6
Clerical	2.2	.6	2.6	.7	2.1	.7	2.8	.7	2.8	.6	2.9	.9
Motor coordination	2.7	.5	2.9	.6	2.8	.6	2.4	.6	2.3	.5	2.6	.6
Finger dexterity	2.6	.6	2.7	.6	2.9	.8	2.3	.5	2.3	.5	2.7	.6
Manual dexterity	3.0	.4	3.1	.4	2.9	.7	2.5	.6	2.4	.6	2.6	.5
Eye-hand-foot coordination	1.4	.7	1.8	.9	1.6	1.1	1.3	.7	1.3	.6	1.2	.5
Color discrimination	1.6	.7	2.6	1.0	2.7	1.3	1.8	.9	1.6	.7	1.4	.6
n	4,235		24		46		315		942		695	

Table 13
Mean Interest Ratings for Occupations by
GED Level and Holland Category

Category	Data versus things[a]		Science versus business[b]		Creative versus routine[c]		Machines versus social[d]		Production versus prestige[e]		n
	M	SD	M	SD	M	SD	M	SD	M	SD	
GED Levels 5 and 6											
Realistic	−.4	.6	.7	.6	.1	.3	.6	.5	.0	.4	94
Investigative	.0	.6	.8	.4	.1	.4	.2	.7	−.2	.4	340
Artistic	.7	.5	−.3	.6	.7	.5	.0	.3	.0	.9	102
Social	.6	.6	−.2	.8	.5	.2	−.4	.6	−.5	.5	227
Enterprising	.5	.5	−.8	.6	.0	.2	.1	.4	−.8	.4	326
Conventional	.3	.8	.8	.6	−.1	.2	.6	.5	−.3	.5	18
GED Levels 3 and 4											
Realistic	−.8	.4	.0	.4	−.3	.5	.9	.3	.1	.6	4,235
Investigative	−.3	.7	.4	.6	−.2	.5	.6	.6	.1	.3	24
Artistic	.5	.6	−.3	.4	.6	.5	.4	.6	.2	.8	46
Social	.1	.6	−.4	.6	.0	.4	.0	.6	−.2	.6	315
Enterprising	.3	.6	−.8	.4	−.1	.3	.4	.5	−.5	.5	942
Conventional	−.4	.7	−.2	.4	−.8	.4	.5	.5	.0	.2	695

[a]Communication of data versus activities with things. [b]Scientific and technical activities versus business contact. [c]Abstract and creative versus routine, concrete activities. [d]Activities involving processes, machines, or techniques versus social welfare. [e]Activities resulting in tangible, productive satisfaction versus prestige, esteem.

Distinguishing adjacent occupational categories. Some final analyses, using the construction sample, were performed to clarify the distinctions between adjacent types (R and I, I and A, A and S, S and E, E and C, and C and R) in the hexagonal model. Theoretically, the adjacent types are closely related, although they also have some distinguishing characteristics. Earlier accounts (Holland, 1966, 1973) of the differences and similarities among the types were helpful, but more definitive information was needed.

The job analysis ratings that most strongly distinguish between adjacent types are shown in Table 14. The table lists the biggest differences found in an examination of R versus I occupations, I versus A occupations, and so on. It lists up to five occupational analysis variables on which one adjacent type was rated significantly ($p < .05$) higher than the other. In some cases fewer than five ratings were significantly higher for adjacent types, and fewer are shown. In other cases more than five ratings were significantly higher for one adjacent type than another, but only the five biggest differences are shown.

The differences shown in Table 14 are useful in understanding the distinctions between adjacent types. For instance, Investigative work generally requires greater intelligence, more verbal and numerical aptitude, and more education than does Realistic work; but Realistic work requires more strength, stooping, exposure to hazards, and more activity with processes or machines than does Investigative work. Artistic work more often requires a temperament for working with feelings, ideas, or facts, and greater interest in abstract or creative activities than does Investigative work. These, and other distinctions shown in Table 14, are generally consistent with the earlier characterizations of the types (e.g., Holland, 1973).

Table 14
Variables Discriminating Between Adjacent Occupational Types

Realistic versus Investigative (*n* = 72)

Realistic rated higher than Investigative in:	Investigative rated higher than Realistic in:
Strength	Intelligence
Stooping	Verbal aptitude
Hazards	Numerical aptitude
Activities involving processes, machines, or techniques versus social welfare	General educational development
Activities involving tangible, productive satisfaction versus prestige, esteem	Scientific and technical activities versus business contact

Investigative versus Artistic (*n* = 62)

Investigative rated higher than Artistic in:	Artistic rated higher than Investigative in:
Intelligence	Feelings, ideas, or facts
Numerical aptitude	Influencing people
Measurable or verifiable criteria	Talking, hearing
Seeing	Communication of data versus activities with things
Scientific and technical activities versus business contact	Abstract and creative versus routine, concrete activities

Artistic versus Social (*n* = 58)

Artistic rated higher than Social in:	Social rated higher than Artistic in:
Data	People
Spatial perception	Clerical aptitude
Feelings, ideas, or facts	Dealing with people
Abstract and creative versus routine, concrete activities	Variety and change
Activities involving processes, machines, or techniques versus social welfare	Talking, hearing

Social versus Enterprising (*n* = 59)

Social rated higher than Enterprising in:	Enterprising rated higher than social in:
Scientific and technical activities versus business contact	Numerical aptitude
	Activities involving processes, machines, or techniques versus social welfare

Enterprising versus Conventional (*n* = 59)

Enterprising rated higher than Conventional in:	Conventional rated higher than Enterprising in:
Data	Finger dexterity
People	Repetitive or continuous processes
Dealing with people	Set limits, tolerances, or standards
Talking, hearing	Seeing
Abstract and creative versus routine, concrete activities	Scientific and technical activities versus business contact

(continued)

Table 14 (continued)
Variables Discriminating Between Adjacent Occupational Types

Conventional versus Realistic (*n* = 68)

Conventional rated higher than Realistic in:	Realistic rated higher than Conventional in:
Clerical aptitude	Specific Vocational Preparation
Dealing with people	Spatial perception
Repetitive or continuous processes	Measurable or verifiable criteria
Communication of data versus activities with things	Strength
	Stooping

Note. This table shows significant differences ($p < .05$) for up to five variables. When more than five variables significantly discriminate, only the five largest differences are shown.

Discussion

The limitations of the 1982 translation stemmed largely from the quality and comprehensiveness of the job analysis information accumulated during the production of the fourth edition of the DOT. The occupational analysis methods used in producing the DOT are no longer the state-of-the art technology they once were. These methods have remained mostly unchanged over the years, failing to take account of more recent methods of analyzing jobs (Harvey, 1991) or to directly implement the Holland environmental typology (Gottfredson & Holland, 1991). In addition, for most occupations only one or two job analysis schedules were available, and in some cases schedules produced for an earlier edition were used (Miller et al., 1980).

Despite these limitations, the 1982 translation was based on the most comprehensive source of job analysis data available, and the results appeared meaningful and generally in accord with expectations and other occupational information. Other research using these DOT occupational analysis data (Cain & Green, 1980; Gottfredson, 1982; L. Gottfredson, 1980; Miller et al., 1980, chapter 7; Mortimer, 1974; Spaeth, 1979; Spenner, 1977) and numerous practical applications of the occupational information also support the usefulness of the DOT information. Accordingly, the following outcomes are of special interest:

1. The empirical classification of occupations using the DOT job analysis data resulted in many more occupations being designated Conventional than did the judgmental process. We speculate that this outcome was due to a persistent misperception of judges—including ourselves—about the nature of Realistic and Conventional work. Persistent notions that machine operation means "R" may have led to judgmental errors in classification in the past. The empirical translation classified many occupations previously supposed to resemble Realistic work as Conventional. The balance of the evidence now supports the DHOC classification.

2. More insight about the psychological meaning of Enterprising work, and therefore the theoretical category itself, was suggested by our review of the numerous occupations not available earlier in an extensive listing by major category and subcategory. Briefly, Enterprising work—in addition to its obvious involvement in persuasive and manipulative activities—appears also to involve power via the control of information; independent decision making and judgment; responsibility for crucial information with little or no supervision; and social, financial, or physical risk taking. These qualities appear to hold in different combinations and to different degrees for many, perhaps most, Enterprising occupations.

3. The distinctions among occupational types are less marked among lower level occupations. This blurring of categorical distinctions is demonstrated by the low level RC and CR occupations that appear to resemble each other.

4. Some kinds of occupational content are much more common than others. Realistic and Enterprising work is common (see Table 7), whereas Artistic work is rare—about 5% of occupations contain an A anywhere in the three-letter code.

5. The classification based on occupational analysis data, for the most part, closely paralleled (a) the classification based primarily on vocational interest data according to the OF that Holland had prepared earlier, (b) the judgmental classification of occupations, (c) the independently developed classification in the GOE, and (d) the SOC. Accordingly, the construct validity of the classification based on job analysis data was strongly supported.

The classification of occupations using job analysis information, rather than the interests of incumbents, was a basic methodological change. Occupational analysis data may often be more practical to use than interest data. This shift in method provided a procedure for classifying environments that is independent of the assessment of the environment's inhabitants.

Part 5: Revisions and Extensions

With this edition the DHOC has been revised twice to include an increased number of occupations and to provide translations to additional systems. In the 1989 revision, codes were added to cover occupations added to the DOT and Supplements (Employment and Training Administration, 1987) after the first edition of the DHOC was developed.

At that time, the DHOC was extended by providing codes for the 4-digit occupational categories in the SOC and for the census occupations. The revised fourth edition of the DOT (1991) and continuing job analysis activity that was not reflected in published editions of the DOT have made the 1989 edition of the DHOC obsolete.

The most important development since the publication of the 1989 edition of the DHOC is the availability of a translation or "crosswalk" between the DOT classification and the OES classification which is used to make employment projections. This crosswalk (Bureau of Labor Statistics, 1995) shows the relation of each OES grouping with each DOT title.

A second development was the creation of a crosswalk between the DOT and the CIP (National Center for Education Statistics, 1991). The CIP-DOT translation (National Crosswalk Service Center, 1993) was based in part on previous crosswalks for vocational and higher education programs developed by the National Occupational Information Coordinating Committee (NOICC). The CIP-DOT crosswalk was reviewed by representatives of NOICC, the National Crosswalk Service Center, the Office for Educational Research and Improvement, BLS, National Science Foundation, Occupational Analysis Field Centers, State Occupational Information Coordinating Committees, and by a contractor.

A third development has been the changes and updates in occupations in the Employment and Training Administration's designation of occupational titles and job analysis details. The 12,860 titles of the fourth edition DOT and its Supplement were reduced to 12,741 by combining or eliminating excess titles. In some cases the codes for the same title have been changed as a result of changes in the levels assigned in the data-people-things portion of the nine-digit DOT code (digits 4 through 6).

These revisions and our desire to extend the classification to the occupational areas in the OOH (Bureau of Labor Statistics, 1996a; which uses the OES classification) required this third edition of the DHOC.

The methods used to code the 761 occupations added in the 1989 edition of the DHOC were summarized earlier (Gottfredson & Holland, 1989, pp. 561-565). The following sections describe how the revised codes were developed for the present edition.

Empirical Assignment of Codes to DOT Occupations

The Holland codes in the 1982 edition of the DHOC were based on classification equations developed from job analysis data. The same procedure was used as a starting point for the codes in the present volume. A group of 193 DOT occupation classifications in which we had great confidence (multiple data sources supported the first-letter code) were used as a starting point. Multiple discriminant analysis was used to develop classification functions to estimate the probability of assignment of each of the detailed DOT occupations to each of the six Holland categories. Adjustments were made in the constants of the classification functions to take account of the unequal prior probabilities. A number of different sets of functions incorporating different job analysis variables and different adjustments to constants were examined until one that appeared to produce the most satisfactory results was achieved.

Preference for Retaining Existing Codes

At the time the first edition of the DHOC was produced, the job analysis data undergirding the DOT included the Cottle (1950) bipolar interest factors. Each occupation was rated for each factor. In the current DOT data, ratings on these bipolar factors have been replaced by designations of interest areas from the GOE. After exploring the development of alternative classification equations to produce the second edition DHOC (Gottfredson & Holland, 1989), we decided that we were unable to improve upon the original classification equation with new equations without the Cottle bipolar interest data. Accordingly, in preparing the present edition we assumed that existing codes should be given precedence over new codes implied by a new equation, unless there was some compelling information for a different code.

Every nine-digit DOT code that was not present in the second edition DHOC was assigned a three-letter occupation code based on the three Holland categories the classification functions implied were most probable. All nine-digit DOT codes that were present in the second edition DHOC were assigned the second edition three-letter code. Then the listing of codes was reviewed and re-reviewed by the authors in a series of computer assisted inspection and sore-thumbing exercises. First, the lists were reviewed together with lists of occupations for which PCI (Gottfredson & Holland, 1991) data were available, and where job analysis data from this source implied a preference for a code change, the code was provisionally changed.

Then listings of occupations showing second edition and newly derived codes side by side were reviewed to determine whether the second edition code appeared preferable for the titles with both old and new codes. Experience with the 1989 revision taught us to prefer the 1982 classification. Therefore, unless the new codes appeared clearly preferable, the previously applied code was used. In making this examination, DOT definitions were read and discussed and detailed job analysis data were inspected.

Computer assisted sore-thumbing proceeded through additional steps that built on the information available from previous analysts' work to prepare crosswalks between the DOT and other classifications. Specifically, using methods discussed later, we prepared translations of the OES, SOC, and CIP systems to the Holland classification. Following each translation, titles were sorted in RIASEC order and the listings were examined (or sore-thumbed) to identify possible misclassifications of DOT occupations included in the occupational groups. When sore-thumbing suggested a possible misclassification, the list of detailed DOT occupations linked to the higher-level (OES, SOC, or CIP) grouping was examined. Usually this examination revealed that detailed occupations assigned to the higher level grouping supported the computer generated code. In a few cases, however, it led us to revise the code for one or more detailed occupations. Special care also was given to the review of codes for occupations listed in the Occupations Finder (Holland, 1994), the Jobs Finder (Holland, 1995) or the Career Options Finder (Holland, 1990). The final Holland codes that resulted from these multiple inspections are those listed in this volume; they form the basis for the translations to the other systems.

Results for the DOT Translation

A total of 12,756 occupational titles are listed with Holland codes in the classified index for the DOT. This index includes all 12,741 titles in the original DOT data base plus the addition of 15 titles for specific subject areas for secondary and postsecondary faculty. The revised DHOC includes 12,350 specific nine-digit codes that were contained in the second edition (not counting the multiple entries for secondary school and postsecondary faculty). The remainder are titles with revised nine-digit codes or titles of new occupations.

Agreement of 1989 and 1996 classification. Table 15 shows that 98% of the nine-digit occupations in both the second and third editions of the DHOC are classified in the same major category ($\kappa = .96$). Another summary of code changes between the second and third editions is provided by Table 16 which shows the percentage of occupations with the same one-, two-, and three-letter codes in both editions. Changes affected only about 3% of the nine-digit DOT occupations carried over from the second edition.

Table 15
Primary Classification of Occupations in the 2nd Edition of the DHOC by Primary Classification in the 3rd Edition

2nd edition classification	3rd edition classification					
	R	I	A	S	E	C
Realistic (R)	**8,166**	14	3	18	38	23
Investigative (I)	8	**372**	1	3	0	0
Artistic (A)	6	1	**154**	4	4	0
Social (S)	4	2	1	**525**	10	0
Enterprising (E)	12	10	10	12	**1,363**	4
Conventional (C)	11	2	0	12	15	**1,542**

Note. N = 12,350. Includes all nine-digit DOT occupations common to both editions, excluding college or university faculty and secondary school teacher (where the same nine-digit DOT title has multiple entries in the DHOC). Boldface entries indicate occupations with the same first-letter code in both editions (*N* = 12,122, 98%, $\kappa = .96$).

Table 16
Correspondence of Codes for 9-Digit DOT Occupations in Both the 2nd and 3rd Editions of the DHOC

Degree of correspondence	%	N
Same first letter	98	12,122
First two letters the same	98	12,052
All three letters the same	97	12,002

Note. N = 12,350.

Distribution of occupations. The distributions of occupations across the six main categories in the second and third editions are shown in Table 17, and distributions for two-letter subcategories are shown in Table 18. The distribution of occupations across the occupational categories remains essentially unchanged.

Some two- and three-letter combinations are rare, and some do not occur at all. No CA occupations are listed, and very few occupations have both C and A appearing anywhere in the code. Frequencies of all three-letter combinations are shown in Table 19. CA combinations are also rare in interest profiles (Holland, Powell, & Fritzsche, 1994, p. 83).

Table 17
**Distribution of Occupations Among Six Occupational Categories in the
2nd and 3rd Editions of the DHOC**

Category	2nd edition (N = 12,875)		3rd edition (N = 12,756)	
	N	%	N	%
Realistic	8,499	66	8,465	66
Investigative	435	3	426	3
Artistic	178	1	180	1
Social	613	5	581	5
Enterprising	1,476	12	1,449	11
Conventional	1,674	13	1,655	13

Table 18
Distribution of Two-Letter Holland Codes in the 2nd and 3rd Editions of the DHOC

	2nd edition (N = 12,875)		3rd edition (N = 12,756)	
	N	%	N	%
RI	981	7.6	974	7.6
RA	13	.1	15	.1
RS	679	5.3	662	5.2
RE	4,095	31.8	4,027	31.6
RC	2,731	21.2	2,787	21.8
IR	282	2.2	282	2.2
IA	2	.0	6	.0
IS	68	.5	63	.5
IE	76	.6	66	.5
IC	7	.1	9	.1
AR	11	.1	20	.2
AI	6	.0	9	.1
AS	50	.4	46	.4
AE	109	.8	103	.8
AC	2	.0	2	.0
SR	90	.7	75	.6
SI	39	.3	34	.3
SA	15	.1	20	.2
SE	398	3.1	389	3.0
SC	71	.6	63	.5
ER	367	2.9	348	2.7
EI	35	.3	41	.3
EA	38	.3	42	.3
ES	943	7.3	924	7.2
EC	93	.7	94	.7
CR	1,119	8.7	1,117	8.8
CI	3	.0	19	.1
CA	0	.0	0	.0
CS	346	2.7	315	2.5
CE	206	1.6	204	1.6

Table 19
Frequency (f) of Three-Letter Codes in the 3rd Edition DHOC

Code	f	Code	f	Code	f	Code	f	Code	f	Code	f
RIA	6	IRA	3	ARI	6	SRI	8	ERI	37	CRI	15
RIS	144	IRS	72	ARS	5	SRA	0	ERA	12	CRA	2
RIE	767	IRE	163	ARE	9	SRE	51	ERS	266	CRS	423
RIC	57	IRC	44	ARC	0	SRC	16	ERC	33	CRE	677
RAI	1	IAR	1	AIR	2	SIR	9	EIR	18	CIR	6
RAS	3	IAS	3	AIS	2	SIA	4	EIA	4	CIA	1
RAE	10	IAE	2	AIE	5	SIE	18	EIS	13	CIS	8
RAC	1	IAC	0	AIC	0	SIC	3	EIC	6	CIE	4
RSI	53	ISR	26	ASR	6	SAR	0	EAR	4	CAR	0
RSA	2	ISA	5	ASI	7	SAI	5	EAI	7	CAI	0
RSE	468	ISE	25	ASE	28	SAE	14	EAS	30	CAS	0
RSC	140	ISC	7	ASC	5	SAC	1	EAC	1	CAE	0
REI	891	IER	35	AER	17	SER	145	ESR	433	CSR	105
REA	38	IEA	9	AEI	8	SEI	41	ESI	53	CSI	6
RES	1,755	IES	18	AES	74	SEA	51	ESA	232	CSA	0
REC	1,343	IEC	4	AEC	4	SEC	152	ESC	206	CSE	204
RCI	336	ICR	7	ACR	0	SCR	16	ECR	27	CER	83
RCA	5	ICA	0	ACI	0	SCI	2	ECI	5	CEI	3
RCS	622	ICS	2	ACS	2	SCA	1	ECA	0	CEA	0
RCE	1,824	ICE	0	ACE	0	SCE	44	ECS	62	CES	118

Incorporating Occupational Level in the Classification

The earlier editions of the DHOC incorporated occupational level by listing GED level and Specific Vocational Preparation (SVP). Within each three-letter subcategory, occupations were classified in descending order of GED and SVP. The GED level assigned to an occupation was the highest of three ratings of educational development in reasoning, mathematics, and language.

For the present classification, we developed a new index of occupational level that makes greater use of the job analysis data. A factor analysis of the job analysis ratings implied that the largest common factor might be interpreted as cognitive or substantive complexity. A scale was composed by combining standardized scores (z-transformed ratings) for eight items with unit weight: Data, GED Reasoning, GED Mathematics, GED Language, SVP, Intelligence, Verbal Aptitude, and Numerical Aptitude. This composite resembles the factor labeled "substantive complexity" by Miller et al. (1980) in a factor analysis of fourth edition DOT occupational characteristics. The exclusion of items involving clerical perception and complexity of functioning with people implies that "cognitive complexity of work demands" may be a better term for our index of Complexity Level.

Correlations among the eight ratings range from .74 to .81, and α for the scale = .97. The occupational rating with the highest single correlation with Complexity Level is GED Reasoning (corrected $r = .94$). Complexity scores for occupations have been transformed to T scores for occupations ($M = 50$, $SD = 10$).

Table 20 is provided as an aid to users familiar with the GED and SVP levels in previous editions of the DHOC; it shows mean levels of GED and SVP for second edition DHOC titles organized according to scores on Complexity Level.

Table 20
Mean GED and SVP Levels for Complexity Level Intervals

Complexity	GED			SVP			N
	M	*SD*		*M*	*SD*		
≥70	5.2	.8		7.4	1.0		397
65-69.9	4.7	.7		7.1	1.2		718
60-64.9	3.8	1.2		5.7	2.0		793
55-59.9	3.1	1.0		4.7	2.0		2,131
50-54.9	3.0	1.0		4.4	2.0		1,436
45-49.9	2.7	.9		4.1	2.0		1,824
40-44.9	2.6	.9		3.9	1.9		2,961
<40	2.5	.9		3.6	1.8		2,491

Codes for Other Classifications

Codes for the OES, SOC, Census, CIP, and GOE classifications were developed by aggregating information about the Holland classification of nine-digit DOT occupations to the level of the specific classification in question. For example, if 134 DOT occupations had been grouped into a specific OES or SOC category by BLS analysts, then a summary reflecting the classification of those 134 detailed occupations became the code for the grouping.

To produce these Holland codes we began with (a) the three-letter Holland codes for nine-digit DOT occupations, and (b) the OES or other classification codes assigned to each DOT occupation by job analysts. All occupations in the DOT and its Supplements were first assigned scores ranging from 0 to 3 for each Holland category by giving most weight to the first letter of the three-letter Holland code (3), less weight to the second letter of the code (2), and still less weight to the third letter of the code (1). For example, a score of 3 was assigned for R if the occupation's first-letter code was R, 2 was assigned if R was the second letter, 1 was assigned if R was the third letter, and 0 was assigned otherwise. Thus, a DOT occupation coded RES would have a score of 3 for R, 0 for I and A, 1 for S, 2 for E, and 0 for C. Then, the RIASEC scores for the occupations in each four-digit SOC category were summed, and the rank ordering of the resulting means was used to assign a three-letter Holland code for each SOC category. The Holland category with the highest mean became the first letter, the category with the next highest mean became the second letter, and the category with the third highest mean became the third letter.

For each occupational category, a vector of six RIASEC scores was produced so that each element in the vector is the sum of the code-position weights (0 for positions four through six, 1 for third position, 2 for second position, 3 for first position) for R, I, A, S, E, and C letters in the codes for the detailed occupations in the group. For each occupational group, the letter for the Holland category with the largest sum became the first-letter code, the letter for the second highest sum became the second-letter code, and the letter with the third highest sum became the third-letter code.

After an initial classification using this procedure for the OES, SOC, and CIP system, the coding of all occupational or instructional program groups was reviewed to identify possible misclassifications. When necessary, complete listings of the detailed DOT occupations related to each group were reviewed, and DOT definitions and job analysis data for specific occupations were examined. When a review implied that an underlying DOT occupation had been misclassified, its classification was corrected. Following corrections, new aggregations were performed to develop final codes for other classifications.

A few SOC categories were not represented by any occupation in the DOT or its Supplements. Mostly, these categories were college or university teachers in specific fields, and the DOT usually classified occupations in these categories with their respective fields. In the listings in Parts 2 and 3, SOC categories not represented by DOT occupations are marked with asterisks. The Holland code provided for these marked categories is not an aggregation of the empirically derived codes; instead, it is usually a code for a closely related SOC category.

The CIP translation was difficult to implement. The crosswalk of instructional programs with occupations did not appear to be of as high a quality as the crosswalks for other classifications. The CIP crosswalk was also the most difficult for the analysts who prepared the NOICC Master Crosswalk (National Crosswalk Service Center, 1993) because of the complexity of relations among training programs and occupations. In many cases, only one or two occupational titles were linked with an instructional program. In some cases, one of a few titles linked (or the only title) was "Faculty Member, College or University." Earlier we regarded this DOT title as insufficiently detailed and assigned separate codes to faculty occupations in different fields. In preparing aggregations, no weight was given to a linkage with "Faculty Member, College or University." Instead, a code based on occupations we judged to be most related was assigned. In some cases, the occupations assigned as related to an instructional program appear to be poor representatives of the category. Usually, we have followed the relations indicated in the NOICC Master Crosswalk despite reservations about the appropriateness of the resulting code.

Discussion

The present classification, like all previous classifications, is an approximation. Although it is based upon the best and most comprehensive information available, the empirical approximations are subject to error in the underlying data and in our judgments. Users should apply the codes in the context of other information they have available about the occupations or instructional programs. For large applications or for important individual decisions, users should consider supplementing the information about the classification with information derived from direct assessments using the PCI or other sources.

Part 6: Applications

The accessibility of Holland codes for the DOT, OES, SOC, COC, and GOE occupations, and for training areas in the CIP in the present *Dictionary* makes possible many applications of the typology for practice and research. Some applications for research, counseling, and assisting special groups are outlined in the following sections.

Applications in Research

Classifying Occupations

The most popular use of the classification has been the organization and use of occupational information. The translations in this volume of multiple systems used to gather and report occupational and educational information into the Holland classification are intended to improve the organization and use of these diverse systems.

Translations based on indirect and incomplete data will always remain approximate. Therefore we developed the PCI (Gottfredson & Holland, 1991) to directly classify any position or occupation according to the theory. We used the theoretical descriptions of the environmental types together with other job analysis information to write items that represent the demands, rewards, activities, and opportunities to display styles or values characteristic of each environmental model. The PCI enables a user to describe any position or occupation as a profile of resemblances to the six environmental types.

Many users should supplement the occupational codes presented here with direct assessments of occupational environments using the PCI. To illustrate the information produced by a PCI assessment, Figure 3 shows the job analysis profile for "Elementary Teacher." The profile summarizes the regularities in job demands, values and styles reinforced, and the activities involved that explain why the elementary school environment attracts and retains individuals who have Social predispositions and who display characteristic Social values, interests, and behaviors. In short, the environment attracts and fosters individuals resembling the Social personality type.

Describing Other Environments

The typology has been applied to environments other than occupations: organizations, spouses, clients, roommates.

Organizations. One productive application of the environmental classification has been the research on and assessment of (Astin & Holland, 1961) college environments. One example of the power of the classification for understanding college environments is provided by Figure 4. Richards (1975) tabulated the number of faculty representing each environmental type in the 55 agricultural universities of 17 nations. He standardized for size of university by transforming the six Holland scores within nation to standard scores. Richards showed that agricultural universities in countries following a U. S. model (New Zealand, Pakistan, India, U. S., Japan, Trinidad) are characterized by a Realistic–Investigative emphasis, whereas British model agricultural universities (Ghana, Ireland, Australia, Britain, Zimbabwe, Sri Lanka, Nigeria, Canada, and South Africa) have a predominantly Investigative emphasis; in contrast "African" model agricultural universities (Uganda, Malaysia, Botswana, and Sierra Leone) are distinguished by Investigative–Social emphases. These environmental characterizations suggest several hypotheses about the likely outcomes of the divergent models of agricultural education. To perform analyses like those made by Richards, a researcher can now use the codes for the CIP or OES categories to classify the faculties of institutions.

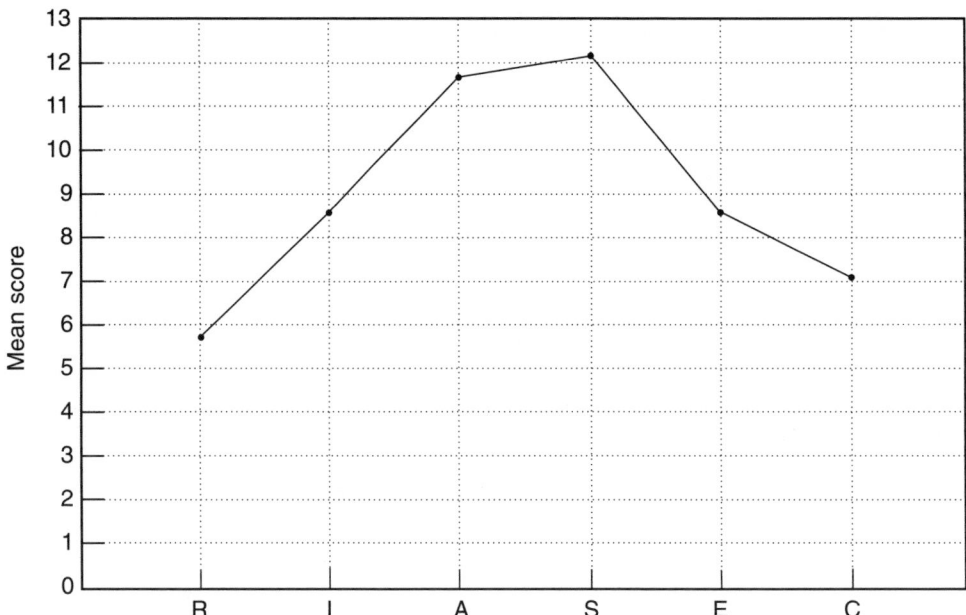

Figure 3. Position Classification Inventory profile, elementary school teacher. Job descriptions were provided by 33 raters. Data are from *Position Classification Inventory professional manual* (p. 49), by G. D. Gottfredson and J. L. Holland, 1991, Odessa, FL: Psychological Assessment Resources, Inc. Copyright 1991 by Psychological Assessment Resources, Inc. Adapted with permission.

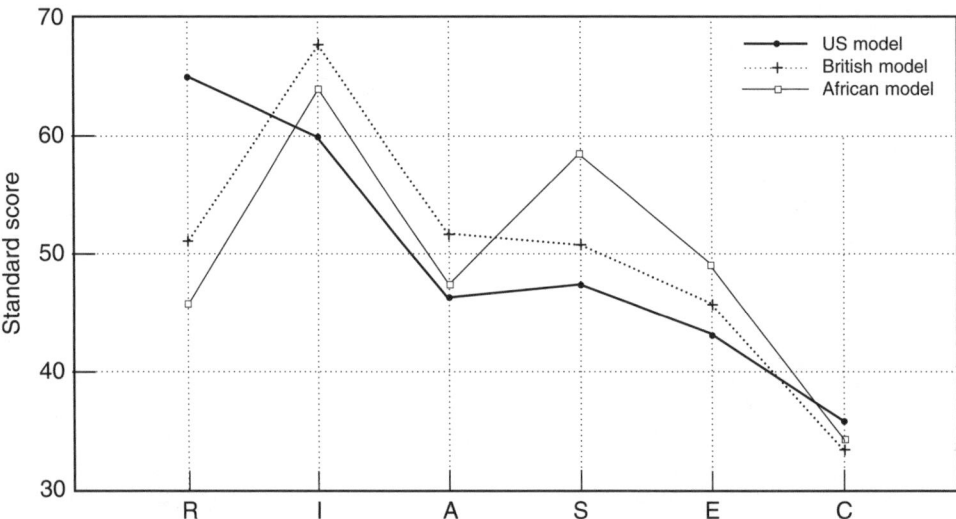

Figure 4. Mean Holland scores for agricultural universities with alternative models. Data are from "Characteristics of U. S., Japanese, and British Commonwealth Universities Offering Education in Agriculture," by J. M. Richards, Jr., 1975, *Research in Higher Education*, *3*, p. 106. Adapted with permission.

The assessment of college environments has been useful in understanding or exploring the influences of these environments. For example, Astin (1965, 1993) showed that college students' career choices come to conform more and more to the dominant or modal career choice in their college environment. Hearn and Moos (1976) showed that the major field composition of a college living unit is related to the social climate of the environment. Richards (1987) examined the environments of predominantly Black colleges and showed that social service environments were over-represented and that technical and managerial environments were under-represented (compared to the U. S. labor force), suggesting that Black college environments may perpetuate the current distribution of occupations of African American workers.

Change and development in an organization. The typology can be used to classify the work done in organizations to examine how they change over time. An illustration comes from an organization where the two authors were once employed—a university-based research and development center. The organization was examined by classifying all of its positions (excluding part-time students). The procedure was straightforward. The positions of all persons employed were listed, then the DHOC was used to assign a one-letter code to each position. The percentage distribution of codes for each environmental type was calculated. The results for this center in 1975 are shown in Figure 5. This appears to be the profile of a traditional, small behavioral science research and development (R&D) center. Investigative positions predominate, followed by Conventional positions (clerical and research support).

The center grew and evolved over time so that by 1991 it resembled the research, development, and dissemination (RD&D) center shown by the darker profile line in Figure 6. The environment was no longer dominated by Investigative work, and a substantial fraction of employees were involved in helping others utilize R&D products through training and dissemination activities. A broader range of individuals could probably find satisfying roles in the organization in 1991 than in the organization of 1975. The demands and rewards of the environment shifted over time: Whereas research, scholarship, and publication in the core scientific journals were the primary position demands and rewarded activities at one time, training, dissemination, and publication in practitioner magazines became an alternate set of demands or rewarded activities.

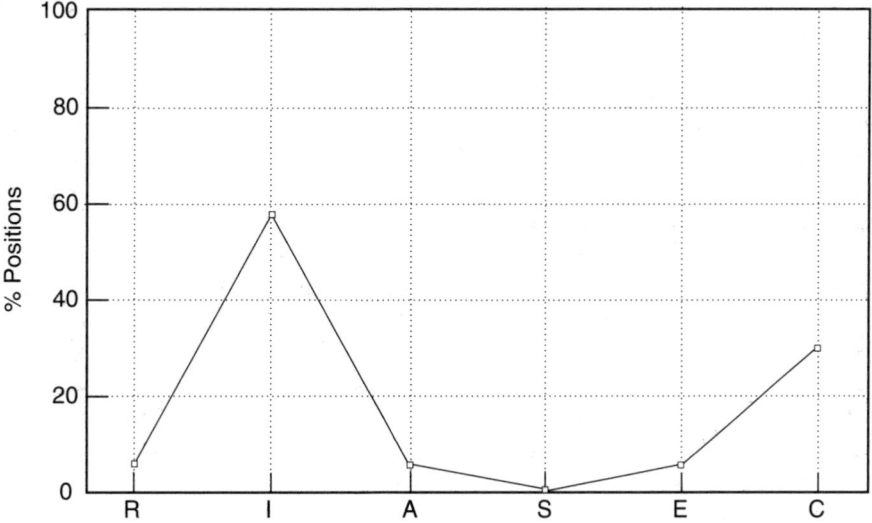

Figure 5. Profile of 23 positions by first letter of Holland Code for an educational research center in 1975. I = 14 positions; C = 6 positions; R,A,E = 1 position.

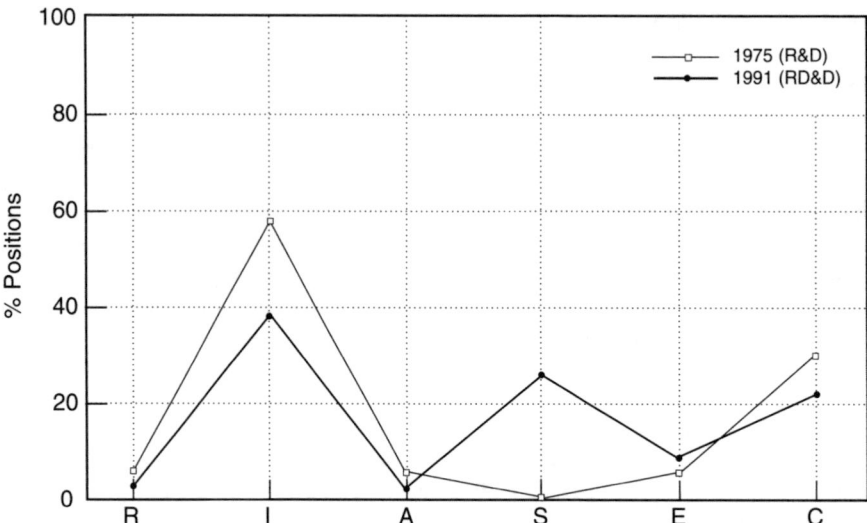

Figure 6. Profile by first letter of Holland Code for an educational research center in 1975 (23 positions) and 1991 (46 positions).

Spouses, roommates, or "natural raters." An interesting possibility is to consider one person as an environment for another (an environment being a source of demands, rewards, opportunities). In this sense, one partner is an environment for another; roommates are environments for each other, a first-grade teacher is an environment for a pupil, and a supervisor is an environment for a worker. These face-to-face relations can be extremely powerful environments because they are proximate sources of rewards, punishments, and clearly communicated demands. In many cases, an individual who is an "environment" in this sense is socially sanctioned as a "natural rater"—a person with the authority to pass judgment on the role performance of the other person (Kellam, Branch, Agrawal, & Ensminger, 1975).

Aspiration and Work Histories

Theoretically, individuals will be attracted to and stay in occupations that are congruent with their personality dispositions. Therefore, one of the most straightforward ways to test the environmental classification is to determine whether it organizes information about the succession of occupations in which individuals are employed. Just as some of the most impressive evidence of the usefulness of Roe's (1954) occupational classification came from a study of occupational mobility (Roe, Hubbard, Hutchinson, & Bateman, 1966), the organization of mobility data according to the Holland occupational classification has provided impressive support for its validity. Roe et al. reasoned that transitions among occupations should most often be shifts from one occupation to another within the same category and that transitions not within the same category should tend to fall in related categories according to her classification and circular ordering of categories. The importance of organizing movement among jobs for the validity of a classification is so compelling that it has been suggested that occupational classifications be built to organize regularities in transitions among occupations on the grounds that this would group occupations making similar demands together (Gottfredson, 1982; Miller et al., 1980, pp. 206-213, 411-418).

The usefulness of the Holland occupational classification for organizing career data to reveal information about adult careers is illustrated by data collected as part of the 1970 population census about the occupations of employed men at T1 and 5 years later (T2). Table 21 (adapted from Gottfredson, 1977) shows that of the 7,571 men employed in Realistic occupations at the beginning of the 5-year period, 7,009 (92%) were employed in a Realistic occupation at T2. The boldface entries in the table show the number of men employed in the same occupational category at the two points in time. The table can be summarized by the percentage agreement—the percentage of men employed in the same category at both points in time (89%) and by coefficient kappa which represents the proportion of greater-than-chance possible agreement that is observed (.82). The same kind of data for a large sample of women is shown in Table 22. For the total sample, 88% of the women were employed in occupations in the same categories at two time points 5 years apart, and the kappa of .84 means that 84% of the greater-than-chance possible agreement in categories at the two points in time was observed. A kappa of 0 would be obtained if the agreement in a 6 X 6 cross classification of occupations at the two points in time were generated by chance alone.

Table 21
Category of Current Occupation by Category of Occupation
5 Years Earlier—Men Aged 41-55

Earlier occupational category	Current occupational category					
	R	I	A	S	E	C
Realistic (R)	7,009	104	9	55	317	77
Investigative (I)	57	699	4	13	49	5
Artistic (A)	6	4	152	1	14	2
Social (S)	37	18	7	600	37	17
Enterprising (E)	180	28	12	32	1,881	58
Conventional (C)	56	12	4	10	54	480

Note. $N = 12,100$. Percentage agreement = 89, κ = .82. Boldface indicates number employed in same category at both points in time. From "Career Stability and Redirection in Adulthood," by G. D. Gottfredson, 1977, *Journal of Applied Psychology, 62*, p. 441. Copyright 1977 by the American Psychological Association. Adapted with permission.

Table 22
Category of Current Occupation by Category of Occupation
5 Years Earlier—Women Aged 41-55

Earlier occupational category	Current occupational category					
	R	I	A	S	E	C
Realistic (R)	1,668	5	1	51	58	121
Investigative (I)	1	62	0	5	2	7
Artistic (A)	0	1	44	2	5	2
Social (S)	32	6	8	1,072	15	42
Enterprising (E)	30	0	0	20	286	46
Conventional (C)	88	6	3	38	75	1,977

Note. $N = 5,779$. Percentage agreement = 88, κ = .84. Boldface indicates number employed in same category at both points in time. From "Career Stability and Redirection in Adulthood," by G. D. Gottfredson, 1977, *Journal of Applied Psychology, 62*, p. 441. Copyright 1977 by the American Psychological Association. Adapted with permission.

Because cross-classification tables are often difficult for readers to interpret, we show the same data organized in a different way in Tables 23 and 24. These tables show the ratio of observed to expected frequencies in each of the 36 cells generated by the 6 (T1) by 6 (T2) occupational categories for the career data for men and women. Table 23 shows, for example, that 11.8 times as many men initially employed in Investigative occupations at T1 were employed in Investigative occupations at T2 as are expected by chance given the marginal distributions of employment at the two points in time. For men employed in Artistic work at T1, 55 times as many are employed in Artistic work 5 years later than would be expected by chance alone. The number of women employed in Realistic occupations at both T1 and T2 is 2.8 times greater than chance expectation.

Table 23
Ratio of Observed to Expected Frequencies for 5-Year
Occupational Transitions—Men Aged 41-55

Earlier occupational category	Current occupational category					
	R	I	A	S	E	C
Realistic (R)	**1.5**	.2	.1	.1	.2	.2
Investigative (I)	.1	**11.8**	.3	.3	.3	.1
Artistic (A)	.1	.3	**54.7**	.1	.4	.2
Social (S)	.1	.4	.6	**14.3**	.3	.4
Enterprising (E)	.1	.2	.4	.2	**4.4**	.5
Conventional (C)	.1	.3	.4	.3	.5	**14.8**

Note. $N = 12,100$. Boldface indicates men employed in same category at both points in time. Calculated from "Career Stability and Redirection in Adulthood," by G. D. Gottfredson, 1977, *Journal of Applied Psychology*, *62*, p. 441. Adapted with permission.

Table 24
Ratio of Observed to Expected Frequencies for 5-Year
Occupational Transitions—Women Aged 41-55

Earlier occupational category	Current occupational category					
	R	I	A	S	E	C
Realistic (R)	**2.8**	.2	.1	.1	.4	.2
Investigative (I)	.0	**58.2**	.0	.3	.3	.2
Artistic (A)	.0	1.3	**84.1**	.2	1.2	.1
Social (S)	.1	.4	.7	**4.4**	.2	.1
Enterprising (E)	.2	.0	.0	.3	**9.8**	.3
Conventional (C)	.1	.2	.1	.1	.4	**2.4**

Note. $N = 5,779$. Boldface indicates women employed in same category at both points in time. Calculated from "Career Stability and Redirection in Adulthood," by G. D. Gottfredson, 1977, *Journal of Applied Psychology*, *62*, p. 441. Adapted with permission.

A byproduct of this test of the classification is the information displayed in Figure 7. The figure displays the kappas summarizing the agreement between category of occupations of men and women separated by 5-year intervals for persons who had attained different ages in 1970. The large samples produce a regularity uncharacteristic of small-sample research, and the unusually smooth graphs for both men and women show increasing stability of careers through age 35, and a high degree of stability thereafter.

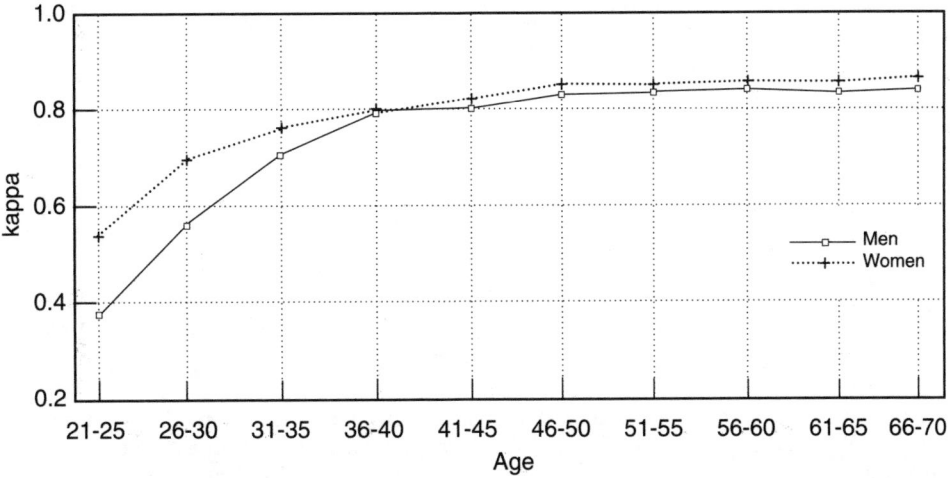

Figure 7. Agreement between occupational category 5 years earlier and current category for employed civilians. *N*s for age-gender subgroups range from 957 to 4,271 except for workers over 65 where *N*s are 781 (men) and 353 (women). Data are from "Career Stability and Redirection in Adulthood," by G. D. Gottfredson, 1977, *Journal of Applied Psychology, 62,* p. 438. Adapted with permission.

The results of a more severe test of the ability of the occupational classification to organize information about career transitions are shown in Figure 8. This figure is limited to employed workers who changed occupations. That is, all persons employed as carpenters (for example) in both years are excluded. The figure shows that when men and women change occupations (not just jobs) they tend to change to other occupations in the same Holland occupational category. The kappas graphically displayed here imply that for women over age 30 about 40% of the greater-than-chance-possible agreement is observed; the corresponding kappas for men imply that about 30% of the greater-than-chance possible agreement is observed. Notice how stability is greater for older (over 30) than for younger workers.

Recall that occupational environments that are adjacent on the hexagon theoretically make similar demands on a person, and occupational environments that are more distant make divergent demands. Accordingly, occupational environments such as IA, which represent closely related environmental models, will make convergent demands on a worker (in this case, occupations would require investigative activities, reward curiosity, and allow expression of an intellectual style). In contrast, an IE occupation would make contrasting or conflicting demands (e.g., requiring both skepticism and persuasiveness). According to the theory, occupations resembling hexagonally related environmental models are expected to lead to stability, whereas occupations resembling hexagonally opposed environmental types are

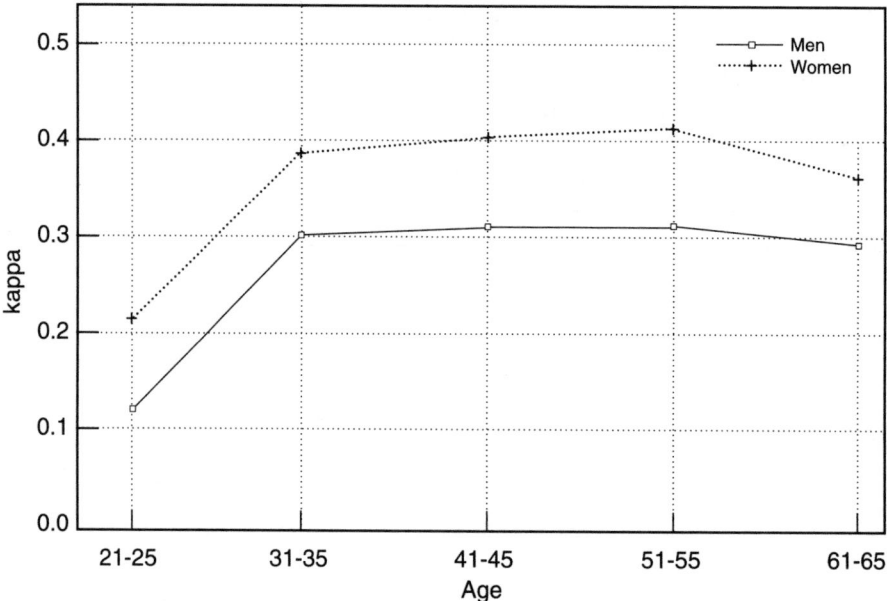

Figure 8. Agreement between category of current job and job 5 years earlier for civilian job changers. *N*s range from 209 to 1,553 for age-gender subgroups. Data are from "Career Stability and Redirection in Adulthood," by G. D. Gottfredson, 1977, *Journal of Applied Psychology, 62,* p. 438. Adapted with permission.

expected to lead to instability or the departure of individuals from the environment as they seek environments that are easier to cope with. Figures 9 (men) and 10 (women) show that inconsistent occupations (RS, IE, AC, SR, EI, CA) result in less career stability according to the classification than do consistent occupations. In every case, men and women initially employed in more consistent occupations show more career stability than those employed in inconsistent occupations (i.e., first two letters of the occupational code representing hexagonally opposite environmental models).

Studying Career Development

The occupational classification has been used as an unobtrusive approach to the study of the influence of employment history and professional accomplishments. Richards (1993) hypothesized that scientific productivity would be positively associated with a history of employment in Investigative positions in a large sample of population scientists. Richards coded employment and other life events according to the classification and found small but significant positive correlations of Investigative experience with measures of scientific productivity and small but significant negative correlations of Social, Enterprising, and Conventional experience with the same productivity measures.

Congruence Research

An important way to test the validity of the environmental classification is to test the theoretical predictions about congruence, because congruence is the heart of any theory of person–environment match (Osipow, 1987). All matching models in vocational psychology, including Holland's theory, assume that if a person's abilities, interests, and personal traits match the requirements, rewards, and opportunities of a work environment, the person will be satisfied and successful. Matching models also imply that congruence between an environment and the workers the environment recruits should lead to a productive and well

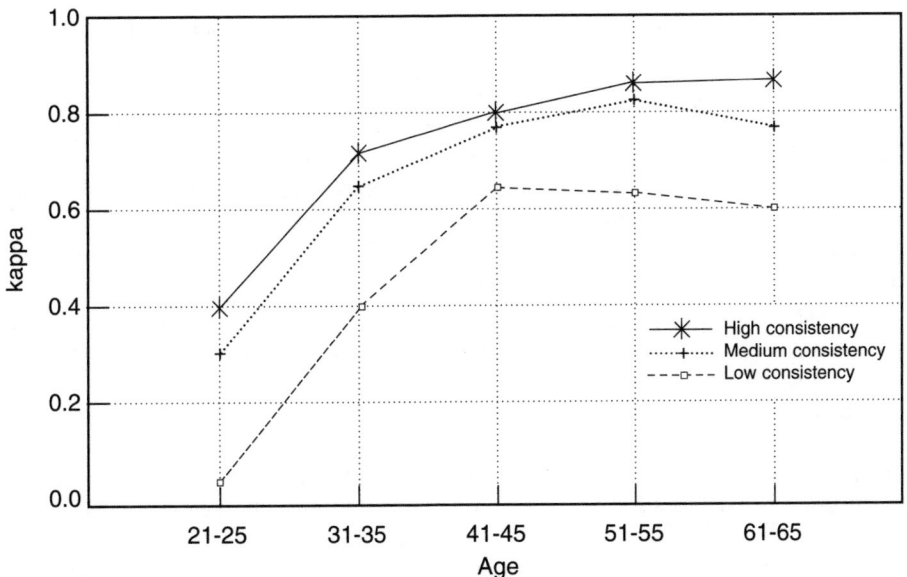

Figure 9. Five-year categorical stability of men whose initial jobs were of low, medium, or high consistency. Age consistency subgroup *N*s range from 201 to 3,166. Data are from "Career Stability and Redirection in Adulthood," by G. D. Gottfredson, 1977, *Journal of Applied Psychology, 62,* p. 440. Adapted with permission.

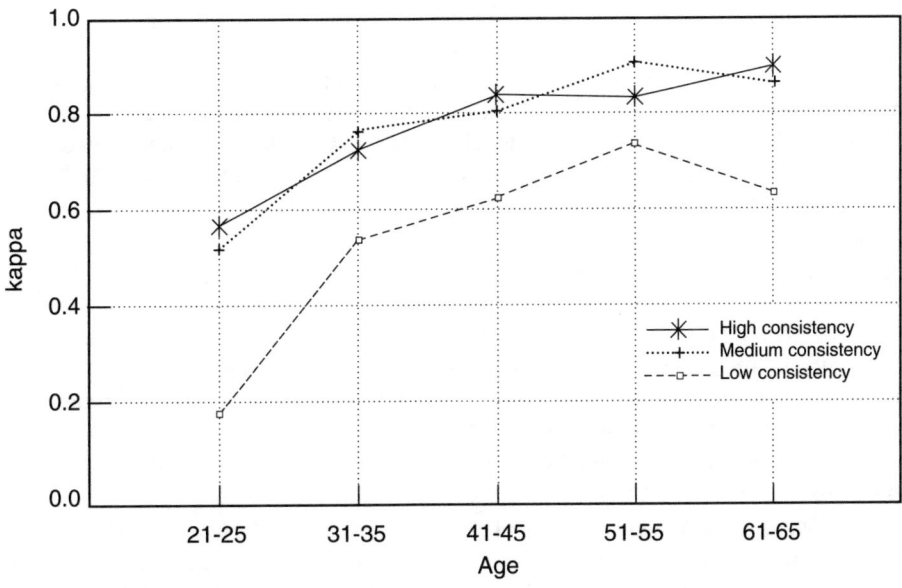

Figure 10. Five-year categorical stability of women whose initial jobs were of low, medium, or high consistency. Age consistency subgroup *N*s range from 128 to 1,040. Data are from "Career Stability and Redirection in Adulthood," by G. D. Gottfredson, 1977, *Journal of Applied Psychology, 62,* p. 440. Adapted with permission.

ordered environment. Schneider (1987a, 1987b) came closest to making this outcome of person–environment match explicit.

The tests of the congruence hypotheses have not always been positive, but they are characterized by generally positive results despite a host of problems with the research (Assouline & Meir, 1987; Borgen, 1986; Gottfredson & Holland, 1990; Holland & Gottfredson, 1990; Spokane, 1985). We illustrate tests of congruence research with a few of the better studies— an outstanding study of simulated work experiences, an important test of congruence hypotheses using a sample of employed workers, and studies taking advantage of naturally occurring interpersonal interaction outside of work environments.

Simulated work experiences. A problem in doing research on person–work environment match is that, as a result of self-selection and selection by others, persons are not randomly distributed across environments. Individuals tend to occupy congruent environments. The obstacles to randomly assigning work representing the six environmental models to individuals representing the six personality types are obvious. Helms (1996) partially overcame this obstacle by experimentally exposing high school students to simulated work environments for brief intervals using Krumboltz's Job Experience Kits (Science Research Associates, 1970). The kit for the Realistic environment was represented by Plumber, Investigative by Medical Technologist, Artistic by Designer, Social by Elementary Teacher, Enterprising by Salesperson, and Conventional by Accountant. Each kit provides a work sample using a form of programmed instruction in which students must solve a characteristic occupational problem.

Helms (1996) exposed 127 boys and 92 girls to the work kits and measured their perceived congruency using a specially devised questionnaire in an elaborate repeated measures design. The Conventional personality type was represented by only 7 boys because there were only 7 boys with high-point codes for C among the 2,933 students initially tested with the SDS to develop the samples for the experiment. For girls, only the I, A, S, and C personality types were represented because there were not enough girls with R and E high-point codes for a meaningful analysis. The results for boys are illustrated in Figure 11. This figure illustrates a complication in research on congruence that it is apparently easy for researchers to overlook. There may be differences in satisfaction levels characteristic of the personality types regardless of environment, and there may be differences in satisfaction (in this case perceived congruence) characterizing the different environments regardless of personality.

Figure 11 is easiest to understand if you search for the highest and lowest scoring person categories within each environmental category. For example, the Realistic individuals perceived the Realistic environment as more congruent than do any other category of individuals. Likewise, the Investigative individuals perceived the Investigative environment as more congruent than do any other category of persons. Figure 12 shows the results for high school girls. Investigative girls perceived the Investigative kit as most congruent; Conventional girls perceived the Conventional environment as most congruent. Notice that all categories of girls perceived the Realistic (plumber) kit as incongruent. This was also true of boys except those classified as Realistic by the SDS.

Studies of employed workers. In one of the most sophisticated studies of the congruence hypothesis, Mount and Muchinsky (1978) found that job satisfaction was related to congruence and also to environment type. In large samples of persons from well defined environments, satisfaction levels differed among environments and personality types, and congruence interacted with environment such that the relation between congruence and satisfaction was stronger—net of personality and environmental type—for certain environmental categories. Their study was an excellent example of an analytical test of the theory, and an antidote for some of the simple-minded tests that ignore the "all other things being equal" provisos. Mount and Muchinsky's results for Job Descriptive Index (JDI; Smith, Kendall, & Hulin, 1969) Total Job Satisfaction are shown in Figure 13.

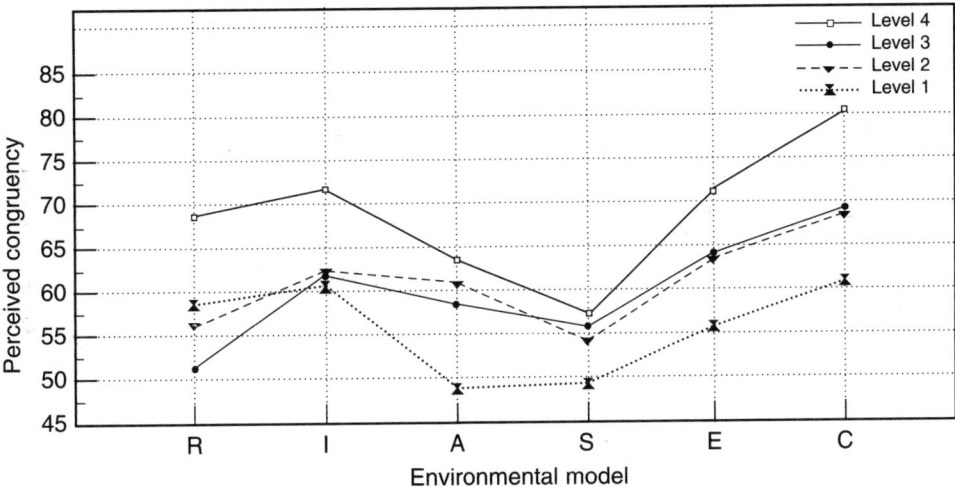

Figure 11. Perceived congruency among 127 high school boys by level of measured congruency. Based on data from "Some Experimental Tests of Holland's Congruency Hypotheses: The Reactions of High School Students to Occupational Simulations," by S. T. Helms, 1996, *Journal of Career Assessment, 4*, p. 263. Copyright 1996 by Psychological Assessment Resources, Inc. Adapted with permission.

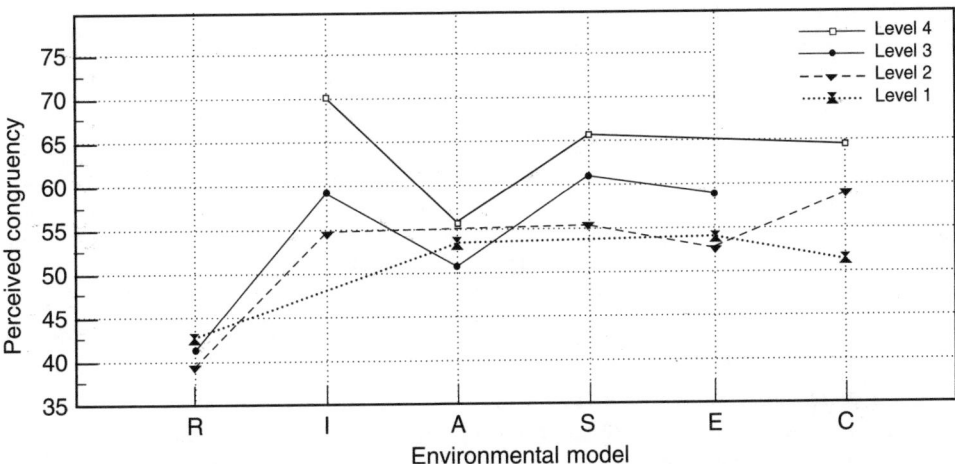

Figure 12. Perceived congruency among 92 high school girls by level of measured congruency. Based on data from "Some Experimental Tests of Holland's Congruency Hypotheses: The Reactions of High School Students to Occupational Simulations" by S. T. Helms, 1996, *Journal of Career Assessment, 4*, p. 263. Copyright 1996 by Psychological Assessment Resources, Inc. Adapted with permission.

Spouses or roommates. A number of investigators have illustrated the usefulness of regarding spouses as environments for each other. Wiggins, Moody and Lederer (1983) found that a marital satisfaction measure correlated .7 with a measure of congruence of spouses' VPI codes. Similarly, Bruch and Skovholt (1985) found that congruence of spouses' Holland types was related to marital satisfaction, and Williams (1967) in an impressive early study found that incongruent roommates provide an environment for each other conducive to conflict. Although we do not expect many replications of correlations as large as that found by

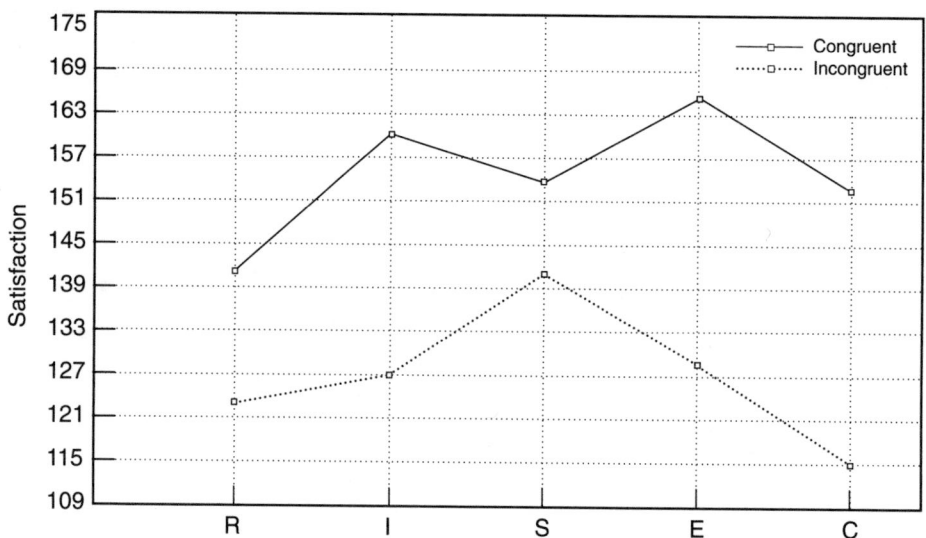

Figure 13. JDI total job satisfaction and congruency for workers in five environments. From "What is Person–Environment Congruence? Supplementary Versus Complementary Models of Fit," by M. K. Mount and P. M. Muchinsky, 1978, *Journal of Vocational Behavior, 31,* p. 268. Copyright 1978 by Academic Press, Inc. Adapted with permission of the author.

Wiggins et al., these results suggest that regarding spouses or roommates as environments for each other and using the classification to predict and understand interactions is a potentially useful application.

Other congruence studies. There are now a large number of studies of congruence between person and environment. For more perspective on congruence and empirical evidence see Assouline & Meir (1987); Gottfredson (1994); Gottfredson and Holland (1990); Helms (1996); Holland (1985/1992); Mount and Muchinsky (1978); Muchinsky and Monahan (1987); Osipow (1987); Rounds, Dawis, and Lofquist, 1987; Spokane (1985); Swaney and Prediger (1985); and Wiggins et al. (1983). An annotated bibliography (Holland & Gottfredson, 1990) provides users with access to research and illustrative applications pertaining to all parts of the theory.

Better congruence research. A flaw in most congruence research is that little care has been given to measuring the work environment. Unlike the exemplary research by Helms (1996) in which the environment was controlled through simulation, most research involves less control. The evidence shows that most occupations are characterized by at least some heterogeneity (Gottfredson & Holland, 1991). Career outcomes such as job satisfaction are influenced by occupational level, personal characteristics, age, and other characteristics of the work environment (Gottfredson, 1994; Gottfredson & Holland, 1990). Better congruence research will assess both persons (e.g., with the SDS) and environments (e.g., with the PCI) and measure or control other influences on the outcomes studied.

Relation to Other Systems

At least seven studies (Gottfredson & Holland, 1989; L. Gottfredson, 1980; Holland, Viernstein, Kuo, Karweit, & Blum, 1972; Hyland & Muchinsky, 1991; Maurer & Tarulli (in press); Rounds et al., 1978; Toenjes & Borgen, 1974) have examined the relation between the occupational classification and other systems for classifying or analyzing jobs. Hyland and Muchinsky examined the ability of the Position Analysis Questionnaire (PAQ)—a structured worker-oriented job analysis inventory developed by E. J. McCormick and his colleagues (McCormick, Jeanneret, & Meacham, 1972)—to distinguish Holland occupational categories according to the DHOC for 86 occupations for which PAQ data were available. Eleven of the 13 overall dimension scores from the PAQ significantly distinguished the Holland occupational categories. Table 25 summarizes some of these results by showing mean scores for the first four dimensions of the PAQ by environmental category. Discriminatory functions correctly classified 69% of the occupations for which PAQ data were available ($\kappa = .62$).

In a similar study as part of the development of this *Dictionary* (see Part 5) we obtained a hit rate of 88% ($\kappa = .85$) for 189 occupations using the U. S. Department of Labor's job analysis system with a more rectangular distribution of environmental types than the distribution used by Hyland and Muchinsky (1991). In a cross-validation of our formula for producing codes against the criterion of our judgmental classification, the formula based on job analysis data agreed with our judgment in 77% of the instances ($\kappa = .47$). Similarly, we found that 77% of occupations were classified by the formula in the expected GOE interest group.

Table 25
Ordering of Environmental Categories on Illustrative
PAQ Dimensions

Dimension and category	M
Decision/communication responsibilities	
Enterprising	.65
Artistic	.52
Investigative	.29
Social	.26
Conventional	−.49
Realistic	−.49
Machine/equipment operation	
Realistic	.59
Artistic	.42
Investigative	−.26
Conventional	−.48
Social	−.49
Enterprising	−.63
Clerical related activities	
Conventional	.28
Artistic	−.19
Investigative	−.53
Realistic	−.66
Social	−.68
Enterprising	−.93
Technical related activities	
Investigative	.99
Artistic	.42
Social	−.05
Enterprising	−.06
Realistic	−.15
Conventional	−.44

Note. Adapted from "Assessment of the Structural Validity of Holland's Model with Job Analysis (PAQ) Information," by A. M. Hyland and P. M. Muchinsky, 1991, *Journal of Applied Psychology, 76*, p. 78. Adapted with permission.

Convergent Validity of the PCI and the DHOC

The classification of occupations using the PCI should generally agree with prior classifications. Information about agreement between codes developed by analyzing jobs using the PCI and those listed in the 1989 DHOC is shown in Table 26. The table shows the classification of occupations according to PCI high-point code and first-letter code in the DHOC. In all, 86% of the 49 occupations were classified in the same major category by the PCI and the DHOC ($\kappa = .83$). Off-diagonal entries are occupations classified in different ways by the two methods. For example, Social Psychologist was classified Artistic according to the 1989 DHOC (probably an incorrect classification) and Investigative according to the PCI. The degree of agreement represented in the table is very high. (The availability of the PCI data led us to revise the code for Social Psychologist for the present *Dictionary*.)

Table 26
Classification of Occupations According to the Highest Scale of
Mean PCI Profile and First-Letter DHOC Code:
Occupations for Which at Least 3 Inventories Were Available

PCI highest scale	DHOC first-letter code					
	R	I	A	S	E	C
Realistic	**8**	0	0	0	0	0
Investigative	0	**8**	1	0	1	0
Artistic	0	0	**6**	0	0	0
Social	0	1	0	**8**	2	1
Enterprising	0	0	0	0	**6**	1
Conventional	0	0	0	0	0	**6**

Note. Agreement = 86%; $\kappa = .83$; N = 49 occupations. Boldface indicates occupations classified in the same category. R = Realistic, I = Investigative, A = Artistic, S = Social, E = Enterprising, C = Conventional. From *Position Classification Inventory professional manual* (p. 44), by G. D. Gottfredson and J. L. Holland, 1991, Odessa, FL: Psychological Assessment Resources, Inc. Copyright 1991 by Psychological Assessment Resources, Inc. Reprinted with permission.

Table 27 shows that as the number of PCI analyses for an occupation increases, so does the agreement between the PCI and the DHOC classification. Very high agreement (88% or 89%, kappa = .86 or .87) was obtained when there were eight or more PCI inventories per occupation. Because relatively few DHOC occupations are based on eight or more job analysis schedules (Miller et al., 1980), we assume that the PCI classification of occupations based on 10 or more inventories will usually be superior to the DHOC classification.

Classification in Practice

In this section we illustrate some applications of the environmental classification in practice. These include organizing occupational information for vocational exploration, career development systems, understanding an individual's career problems, and organizing work or aspiration histories to assist in understanding individuals.

Table 27
Agreement Between PCI High-Point Code and
First-Letter DHOC Code: Occupation-Level Analysis

Number of informants per occupation	% Agreement	κ	Number of occupations
1 or more	72	.66	78
2 or more	82	.79	57
3 or more	86	.83	49
4 or more	86	.84	44
5 or more	86	.83	42
6 or more	86	.83	42
7 or more	88	.85	40
8 or more	89	.87	37
9 or more	88	.86	34

Note. From *Position Classification Inventory professional manual* (p. 44), by G. D. Gottfredson and J. L. Holland, 1991, Odessa, FL: Psychological Assessment Resources, Inc. Copyright 1991 by Psychological Assessment Resources, Inc. Reprinted with permission.

Organizing Information

The most straightforward application of the classification is to organize occupational information for vocational assistance. This application is illustrated in the SDS Occupations Finder which organizes occupational titles according to the major categories and subcategories of the classification so that users can explore related groups of occupations. Many counseling or career services organize occupational exploration materials according to the classification by filing materials by category; the classification is also used to structure computerized occupational search programs.

Clients who have obtained their interest results can use the *Dictionary* to find more suitable occupational alternatives. The availability of long lists of occupations associated with many three-letter codes may, however, cause some clients to focus on a single three-letter code. Clients should be urged to avoid such a narrow search and to explore other permutations of their codes.

The importance of avoiding a narrow search of occupations is underscored by interest measurement results for specific occupations that show a range of interests among persons employed in specific occupations (Holland & Holland, 1977) and some fluctuations in assessment results from sample to sample. Most occupations allow persons with a range of interests to prosper, and most people can thrive in a range of occupational environments. In the same way, job analysis results for specific occupations show a range of results among positions and job analysts (Gottfredson & Holland, 1991; Miller et al., 1980).

Career Development Systems

In some organizations, human resources specialists have established career development programs based on Holland's classification of vocational personalities and work environments. NASA's Career Resource Center (Leibowitz, Farren, & Kaye, 1986) is an example of a career development program structured by the dual classifications. Individuals complete an SDS self-assessment and then search NASA positions, federal jobs, or occupations in the general U. S. economy classified according to Holland category.

Understanding Job Dissatisfaction or Career Problems

One important use of the environmental classification is the assessment of the congruence between a person and his or her current position. For instance, a description of the job based on the PCI may be available and the client may have completed the SDS, VPI, or other inventory intended to measure a person's resemblance to the theoretical personality types.

Interpreting Aspirations

The virtue of the occupational classification is illustrated by its ability to help practitioners organize simple occupational aspirations to predict subsequent vocational choices. It has long been the received view among psychologists that vocational aspirations have limited value in counseling or other applications (e.g., Clark, 1961; Cronbach, 1949; Darley & Hagenah, 1955; Nunally, 1959) compared to inventoried interests. Kuder (1977) wrote, "The facts are that expressed interests in specific occupations appear to be the least stable of the interests of young people, and that measured interests can yield useful suggestions at an earlier age than would otherwise be the case" (p. 2). Kuder's disparaging view of expressed choices extended even to inventoried preferences for occupations.

The received view is in blunt disagreement with the data. Classified occupational aspirations or "daydreams" are more efficient predictors of subsequent vocational choice than any other portion of the SDS (Gottfredson & Holland, 1975), and classified occupational aspirations in combination are far more efficient predictors of later choices than are inventoried interests (Holland & Gottfredson, 1975; Holland, Gottfredson, & Baker, 1990). All that was required to reveal the usefulness of expressed choices in counseling and prediction was a valid occupational classification to organize the data.

Kuder's (1977) dim view of inventoried occupational preferences is also unsupported. Occupational preferences are useful parts of the Strong Interest Inventory (SII; Harmon et al., 1994), and the occupations section of the SDS generates the next most efficient predictions (following classified expressed choices).

The utility of classified occupations is illustrated by an example of a dissatisfied psychologist. Artistic occupations are predominant among her occupational aspirations. Titles she lists include Researcher (current job), Free-lance Writer (A), Pianist (A), Interior Designer (A), Architect (A), Architectural Historian (S/A), English Teacher (A), Librarian (S), Program Service Planner (E), Clinical Psychologist (S), and Editor (A). Her aspiration history provides support for the interpretation that this is an Artistic individual, an interpretation with which she agrees. When she described her job using the PCI, the profile was dominated by Investigative and contained almost no Artistic elements. The incongruence suggests that job redesign may be helpful for her. The streamlined personality assessment made by classifying the psychologist's aspirations was useful in identifying person–job incongruence in this instance.

Applications With Disadvantaged Clients

Most users of the classification have worked with relatively advantaged persons—college students, adults seeking career redirection, and people who can afford a career seminar. Despite the availability of the SDS in Braille and of SDS Form E for the poor reader, the use of the typology with disadvantaged clients has been limited. The availability of the present volume makes possible several experimental applications: (a) Does the present classification provide satisfying occupational exploration for low ability users of the SDS Form E? (b) Can the *Dictionary* be used in conjunction with other job search methods to provide vocational assistance to young people or adults experiencing difficulty finding employment? Can it, for example, be integrated with methods such as the Job Club (Azrin & Besalel, 1980) to supplement the Yellow Pages as a source of job leads? (c) Does limiting the job search for persons with poor work histories or low levels of education to consistent occupations (e.g., RC and CR at modest GED levels) result in greater employment stability as implied by an early study (Gottfredson & Lipstein, 1975)?

Tailoring a Job Search to Local Industries

Because the *Dictionary* provides an industry designation, this volume may help job seekers focus their employment search on occupations found in local industries. Or persons planning their careers may discover that local industries provide limited employment opportunities congruent with their interests; therefore, they should consider jobs outside the local area.

Some Research Questions

Effects on Clients

Never an active field of inquiry, research on the effects of career interventions on clients is in danger of disappearing altogether. We posed the following questions in the 1989 revision of this *Dictionary* to stimulate research. No one was stimulated, but the questions are still important.

The availability of long lists of occupations and the availability of occupations with three-letter codes not present in earlier lists may stimulate research on the process of occupational exploration. Do clients with longer lists search fewer categories? If so, what are the consequences of this? Are clients who obtain rare codes on interest assessments more satisfied with a *Dictionary* that includes entries for more rare codes than does the SDS Occupations Finder? To what extent are the occupational definitions contained in the DOT actually used? What structures would promote their use?

Labor Market Behavior

The comprehensive classification of occupations makes possible many psychological, sociological, and economic investigations of labor markets and career development. Research that examines the theoretical predictions about the divergent talents required in different types of work can now be pursued more easily. Similarly, psychological and economic investigations of the operation of labor markets can be more easily performed. Do internal labor markets more often involve jobs with consistent codes, higher levels of complexity, or a combination of both? To what degree are firms segregated by sex and race according to Holland category? What categories or subcategories of occupations are primarily involved in secondary labor markets, listed by the U. S. Employment Service job banks, or projected for growth and decline in workforce requirement forecasts?

Occupational Classification

The classification of occupations is a complex and error prone process. No single approach to the development of a classification is likely to be flawless. Accordingly, research on the construct validity of the present occupational analysis-based classification is still required. What VPI or SDS profiles characterize samples of workers classified according to occupational analysis data? More evidence about the interest profiles of large samples of computer operators, tractor mechanics, plumbers, midwives, steel workers, mine workers, and various military specialties is needed. Explicit comparisons of large-sample interest profiles for carefully delimited occupations with the codes in this *Dictionary* are required for additional quality control checks on the classification. The accumulation of many tests involving single occupations will prove valuable. For example, the study by Teachout & Hamann (in press) using the PCI with a sample of students preparing to become performance musicians is valuable and reassuring because the three-letter code they obtained matches the code obtained earlier by Gottfredson and Holland (1991) in a sample of employed performance musicians—the code listed in the present *Dictionary*.

Validity Generalization for Personnel Selection Tests

Does the present classification provide a basis for the development of selection or placement batteries that have high probability of predictive validity according to a "synthetic validity" or validity generalization model (Guion, 1976)? Because the present classification is based on comprehensive occupational analysis data, it provides a method to systematize the accumulation of validity evidence with broad applicability in business and industry. Narrow abilities (Carroll, 1992) may be useful in predicting performance in different types of work according to the classification. The persuasive evidence that tests of general ability have predictive validity for nearly all jobs (Schmidt, Ones, & Hunter, 1992), and especially for complex jobs, implies that the index of complexity level in the present *Dictionary* may be useful in identifying work for which general aptitude measures are especially predictive of both performance and time required to become proficient.

Part 7: References

Assouline, M., & Meir, E. I. (1987). Meta-analysis of the relationship between congruence and well-being measures. *Journal of Vocational Behavior, 31*, 319-332.

Astin, A. W. (1965). Effect of different college environments on the vocational choices of high aptitude students. *Journal of Counseling Psychology, 12*, 28-34.

Astin, A. W. (1993). *What matters in college?* San Francisco: Jossey-Bass.

Astin, A. W., & Holland, J. L. (1961). The environmental assessment technique: A way to measure college environments. *Journal of Educational Psychology, 52*, 308-316.

Azrin, N. H., & Besalel, V. A. (1980). *Job counselor's manual: A behavioral approach to vocational counseling*. Baltimore: University Park Press.

Borgen, F. H. (1986). New approaches to the assessment of interests. In W. B. Walsh & S. H. Osipow (Eds.), *Advances in vocational psychology: Vol. I: The assessment of interests* (pp. 83-125). Hillsdale, NJ: Erlbaum.

Bruch, M. A., & Skovholt, T. (1985). Congruence of Holland personality type and marital satisfaction. *Measurement and Evaluation in Counseling and Development, 18*, 100-107.

Bureau of the Census, U. S. Department of Commerce. (1992). *1990 census of population alphabetical index of industries and occupations*. Washington, DC: U. S. Government Printing Office.

Bureau of Labor Statistics. (1995). *blsxw95* [Electronic data file]. Des Moines, IA: National Crosswalk Service Center [Distributor].

Bureau of Labor Statistics. (1996a). *Occupational outlook handbook*. Washington, DC: U. S. Government Printing Office.

Bureau of Labor Statistics. (1996b). *Occupational outlook handbook on CD-ROM*. Chicago: Bureau of Labor Statistics Sales Center.

Cain, P. S., & Green, B. F., Jr. (1980). The rating of DOT worker functions and worker traits. In A. R. Miller, D. J. Treiman, P. S. Cain, & P. A. Roos (Eds.), *Work, jobs, and occupations: A critical review of the Dictionary of Occupational Titles* (pp. 315-335). Washington, DC: National Academy Press.

Carroll, J. B. (1992). Cognitive abilities: The state of the art. *Psychological Science, 3*, 266-270.

Clark, K. E. (1961). *Vocational interests of non-professional men*. Minneapolis, MN: University of Minnesota Press.

Cottle, W. C. (1950). A factorial study of the Multiphasic, Strong, Kuder and Bell inventories using a population of adult males. *Psychometrika, 15*, 25-47.

Cronbach, L. J. (1949). *Essentials of psychological testing*. New York: Harper & Brothers.

Cronbach, L. J. (1984). *Essentials of psychological testing* (4th ed.). New York: Harper and Row.

Darley, J. G., & Hagenah, T. (1955). *Vocational interest measurement*. Minneapolis, MN: University of Minnesota Press.

Droege, R. C., & Hawk, J. (1977). Development of a U. S. Employment Service interest inventory. *Journal of Employment Counseling, 14*, 65-71.

Edwards, K. J., Nafziger, D. H., & Holland, J. L. (1974). Differentiation of occupational perceptions among different age groups. *Journal of Vocational Behavior, 4*, 311-318.

Employment and Training Administration (formerly Manpower Administration), U. S. Department of Labor. (1972). *Handbook for analyzing jobs*. Washington, DC: U. S. Government Printing Office.

Employment and Training Administration, U. S. Department of Labor. (1974). *Definition writer's manual*. Washington, DC: U. S. Government Printing Office.

Employment and Training Administration, U. S. Department of Labor. (1977). *Dictionary of occupational titles* (4th ed.). Washington, DC: U. S. Government Printing Office.

Employment and Training Administration, U. S. Department of Labor. (1979). *Guide for occupational exploration*. Washington, DC: U. S. Government Printing Office.

Employment and Training Administration, U. S. Department of Labor. (1981). *Selected characteristics of occupations defined in the dictionary of occupational titles*. Washington, DC: U. S. Government Printing Office.

Employment and Training Administration, U. S. Department of Labor. (1982). *Dictionary of occupational titles* (4th ed. Suppl., 1982). Washington, DC: U. S. Government Printing Office.

Employment and Training Administration, U. S. Department of Labor. (1986). *Dictionary of occupational titles* (4th ed. Suppl., 1986). Washington, DC: U. S. Government Printing Office.

Employment and Training Administration, U. S. Department of Labor. (1987). *Dictionary of occupational titles* (4th ed. and Suppl., 1986). Arlington, VA: National Technical Information System. (Data tape PB87-194528)

Employment and Training Administration, U. S. Department of Labor. (1991a). *Dictionary of occupational titles* (4th ed., revised, 2 vols.). Washington, DC: U. S. Government Printing Office.

Employment and Training Administration, U. S. Department of Labor. (1991b). *The revised handbook for analyzing jobs*. Washington, DC: U. S. Government Printing Office.

Gottfredson, G. D. (1977). Career stability and redirection in adulthood. *Journal of Applied Psychology*, 62, 436-445.

Gottfredson, G. D. (1982). An assessment of a mobility-based occupational classification for placement and counseling. *Journal of Vocational Behavior*, 21, 71-98.

Gottfredson, G. D. (1994, August). *The person in person–environment interactions*. Paper presented at the annual meeting of the American Psychological Association, Los Angeles.

Gottfredson, G. D., & Holland, J. L. (1975). The vocational choices of men and women: A comparison of predictors from the Self-Directed Search. *Journal of Counseling Psychology*, 22, 28-34.

Gottfredson, G. D., & Holland, J. L. (1989). *Dictionary of Holland occupational codes* (2nd ed.). Odessa, FL: Psychological Assessment Resources.

Gottfredson, G. D., & Holland, J. L. (1990). A longitudinal test of the influence of congruence: Job satisfaction, competency utilization, and counterproductive behavior. *Journal of Counseling Psychology*, 37, 389-398.

Gottfredson, G. D., & Holland, J. L. (1991). *Position Classification Inventory professional manual*. Odessa, FL: Psychological Assessment Resources.

Gottfredson, G. D., Holland, J. L., & Ogawa, D. K. (1982). *Dictionary of Holland occupational codes*. Palo Alto, CA: Consulting Psychologists Press.

Gottfredson, G. D., & Lipstein, D. J. (1975). Using personal characteristics to predict parolee and probationer employment stability. *Journal of Applied Psychology*, 60, 644-648.

Gottfredson, L. S. (1980). Construct validity of Holland's occupational typology in terms of prestige, census, Department of Labor, and other classification systems. *Journal of Applied Psychology*, *65*, 697-714.

Gottfredson, L. S., & Brown, V. C. (1978). Holland codes for the 1960 and 1970 censuses: Detailed occupational titles. *JSAS Catalog of Selected Documents in Psychology*, *8*, 22. (Ms. No. 1660).

Grandy, T. G., & Stahmann, R. F. (1974a). Family influence on college students' vocational choice: Predicting Holland's personality types. *Journal of College Student Personnel*, *15*, 404-409.

Grandy, T. G., & Stahmann, R. F. (1974b). Types produce types: An examination of personality development using Holland's theory. *Journal of Vocational Behavior*, *5*, 231-239.

Guion, R. M. (1976). Recruiting, selection, and job placement. In M. D. Dunnette (Ed.), *Handbook of industrial and organizational psychology* (pp. 777-828). Chicago: Rand McNally.

Harmon, L. W., Hansen, J. C., Borgen, F. H., & Hammer, A. L. (1994). *Strong Interest Inventory applications and technical guide*. Palo Alto, CA: Consulting Psychologists Press.

Harrington, T. F., & O'Shea, A. J. (Eds.). (1984). *Guide for occupational exploration* (2nd ed.). Circle Pines, MN: American Guidance Service. (Distributed for National Forum Foundation; originally published in 1979 by the Employment and Training Administration, U. S. Department of Labor.)

Harvey, R. J. (1991). Job analysis. In M. D. Dunnette & L. M. Hough (Eds.), *Handbook of industrial and organizational psychology* (2nd ed., Vol. 2.). Palo Alto, CA: Consulting Psychologists Press.

Hearn, J. C., & Moos, R. H. (1976). Social climate and major choice: A test of Holland's theory in university student living groups. *Journal of Vocational Behavior*, *8*, 293-305.

Helms, S. T. (1996). Some experimental tests of Holland's congruency hypotheses: The reactions of high school students to occupational simulations. *Journal of Career Assessment*, *4*, 253-268.

Holland, J. L. (1966). A psychological classification scheme for vocations and major fields. *Journal of Counseling Psychology*, *13*, 278-288.

Holland, J. L. (1973). *Making vocational choices*. Englewood Cliffs, NJ: Prentice-Hall.

Holland, J. L. (1978). *Occupations finder*. Palo Alto, CA: Consulting Psychologists Press.

Holland, J. L. (1985). *Manual for the Vocational Preference Inventory*. Odessa, FL: Psychological Assessment Resources.

Holland, J. L. (1990). *Career options finder*. Odessa, FL: Psychological Assessment Resources.

Holland, J. L. (1992). *Making vocational choices: A theory of vocational personalities and work environments*. Odessa, FL: Psychological Assessment Resources. (Original work published 1985).

Holland, J. L. (1994). *The occupations finder*. Odessa, FL: Psychological Assessment Resources.

Holland, J. L. (1995). *The jobs finder*. Odessa, FL: Psychological Assessment Resources.

Holland, J. L., & Gottfredson, G. D. (1975). Predictive value and psychological meaning of vocational aspirations. *Journal of Vocational Behavior*, *6*, 349-363.

Holland, J. L., & Gottfredson, G. D. (1976). Using a typology of persons and environments to explain careers: Some extensions and clarifications. *Counseling Psychologist, 6,* 20-29.

Holland, J. L., & Gottfredson, G. D. (1990). *An annotated bibliography for Holland's theory of vocational personalities and work environments.* Unpublished manuscript, RIASEC International, Ltd., 111 St. Albans Way, Baltimore.

Holland, J. L., Gottfredson, G. D., & Baker, H. G. (1990). Validity of vocational aspirations and interest inventories: Extended, replicated, and reinterpreted. *Journal of Counseling Psychology, 37,* 337-342.

Holland, J. L., & Holland, J. E. (1977). Distributions of personalities within occupations and fields of study. *Vocational Guidance Quarterly, 25,* 226-231.

Holland, J. L., Powell, A. B., & Fritzsche, B. A. (1994). *The Self-Directed Search (SDS) professional user's guide.* Odessa, FL: Psychological Assessment Resources.

Holland, J. L., Viernstein, M. C., Kuo, H., Karweit, N. L., & Blum, Z. D. (1972). A psychological classification of occupations. *Journal Supplement Abstract Service, 2,* 84.

Hyland, A. M., & Muchinsky, P. M. (1991). Assessment of the structural validity of Holland's model with job analysis (PAQ) information. *Journal of Applied Psychology, 76,* 75-80.

Johansson, C. B. (1982). *Manual for Career Assessment Inventory* (2nd ed.). Minneapolis, MN: National Computer Systems.

Kellam, S. G., Branch, J. D., Agrawal, K. C., & Ensminger, M. E. (1975). *Mental health and going to school.* Chicago, IL: University of Chicago Press.

Kelso, G. I. (1976). *Explorations of the developmental antecedents of Holland's occupational types.* Unpublished doctoral dissertation, Johns Hopkins University, Baltimore.

Krumboltz, J. D. (1978). A social learning theory of career selection. In J. M. Whiteley & A. Resnikoff (Eds.), *Career counseling* (pp. 100-127). Monterey, CA: Brooks/Cole.

Kuder, F. (1977). *Activity interests and occupational choice.* Chicago: Science Research Associates.

Leibowitz, Z. B., Farren, C., & Kaye, B. L. (1986). *Designing career development systems.* San Francisco: Jossey-Bass.

Maurer, T. J., & Tarulli, B. A. (in press). Managerial work, job analysis, and Holland's 'RIASEC' vocational environmental dimensions. *Journal of Vocational Behavior.*

McCormick, E. J. (1979). *Job analysis: Methods and applications.* New York: AMACOM.

McCormick, E. J., Jeanneret, P. R., & Mecham, R. C. (1972). A study of job characteristics and job dimensions as based on the Position Analysis Questionnaire (PAQ). *Journal of Applied Psychology Monograph, 56,* 347-368.

Miller, A. R., Treiman, D. J., Cain, P. S., & Roos, P. A. (Eds.). (1980). *Work, jobs, and occupations: A critical review of the Dictionary of Occupational Titles.* Washington, DC: National Academy Press.

Mortimer, J. T. (1974). Patterns of intergenerational occupational movements: A smallest-space analysis. *American Journal of Sociology, 79,* 1278-1299.

Mount, M. K., & Muchinsky, P. M. (1978). Person–environment congruence and employee job satisfaction: A test of Holland's theory. *Journal of Vocational Behavior, 13,* 84-100.

Muchinsky, P. M., & Monahan, C. J. (1987). What is person–environment congruence? Supplementary versus complementary models of fit. *Journal of Vocational Behavior, 31,* 268-277.

Nafziger, D. H., Holland, J. L., & Gottfredson, G. D. (1975). Student–college congruency as a predictor of satisfaction. *Journal of Counseling Psychology, 22,* 132-139.

National Center for Education Statistics, U. S. Department of Education. (1991). *A classification of instructional programs* (1990 edition). Washington, DC: U. S. Government Printing Office.

National Center for Education Statistics, U. S. Department of Education. (1994). *Digest of education statistics, 1994* (NCES 94-115). Washington, DC: U. S. Government Printing Office.

National Crosswalk Service Center. (1993). *NOICC Master Crosswalk, Version 4.0* [Electronic data file and documentation]. Des Moines, IA: Author [Producer and Distributor].

Norusis, M. J. (1979). *SPSS statistical algorithms* (Release 8.0). Chicago: SPSS.

Nunnally, J. C. (1959). *Tests and measurements.* New York: McGraw-Hill.

O'Dowd, D. D., & Beardslee, D. C. (1967). *Development and consistency of student images of occupations* (Cooperative Research Project No. 5-0858). Rochester, MI: Oakland University.

Office of Federal Statistical Policy and Standards, U. S. Department of Commerce. (1980). *Standard occupational classification manual.* Washington, DC: U. S. Government Printing Office.

Osipow, S. H. (1987). Applying person–environment theory to vocational behavior. *Journal of Vocational Behavior, 31,* 333-336.

Richards, J. M., Jr. (1975). Characteristics of U. S., Japanese, and British Commonwealth universities offering education in agriculture. *Research in Higher Education, 3,* 99-109.

Richards, J. M., Jr. (1987). Psychosocial environments of Black colleges: A theory-based assessment. *Population and Environment: Behavioral and Social Issues, 9,* 41-53.

Richards, J. M., Jr. (1993). Career development: A ten-year longitudinal study of population scientists. *Journal of Career Assessment, 2,* 181-192.

Roe, A. (1954). A new classification of occupations. *Journal of Counseling Psychology, 1,* 215-220.

Roe, A., Hubbard, W. D., Hutchinson, T., & Batemen, T. (1966). Studies of occupational history. Part I: Job changes and the classification of occupations. *Journal of Counseling Psychology, 13,* 387-393.

Rounds, J. B., Dawis, R. V., & Lofquist, L. H. (1987). Measurement of person–environment fit and prediction of satisfaction in the theory of work adjustment. *Journal of Vocational Behavior, 31,* 297-318.

Rounds, J. B., Jr., Shubsachs, A. P. W., Dawis, R. V., & Lofquist, L. H. (1978). A test of Holland's environment formulations. *Journal of Applied Psychology, 63,* 609-616.

Schmidt, F. L., Ones, D. S., & Hunter, D. E. (1992). Personnel selection. *Annual Review of Psychology, 43,* 627-670.

Schneider, B. (1987a). The people make the place. *Personnel Psychology, 40,* 437-453.

Schneider, B. (1987b). E = f(P,B): The road to a radical approach to person–environment fit. *Journal of Vocational Behavior, 31,* 353-361.

Science Research Associates. (1970). *Guide to the use of the job experience kits.* Chicago: Author.

Smith, P. C., Kendall, L. M., & Hulin, C. L. (1969). *The measurement of satisfaction in work and retirement.* Chicago: Rand-McNally.

Sokal, R. R. (1974). Classification: Purposes, principles, progress, prospects. *Science, 185,* 1115-1123.

Spaeth, J. L. (1979). Vertical differentiation among occupations. *American Sociological Review, 44,* 746-762.

Spenner, K. I. (1977). *From generation to generation: The transmission of occupation.* Unpublished doctoral dissertation, University of Wisconsin, Madison.

Spokane, A. R. (1985). A review of research on person–environment congruence in Holland's theory of careers [Monograph]. *Journal of Vocational Behavior, 26,* 306-343.

Strong, E. K., Jr. (1943). *Vocational interests of men and women.* Stanford, CA: Stanford University Press.

Swaney, K., & Prediger, D. (1985). The relationship between interest–occupation congruence and job satisfaction. *Journal of Vocational Behavior, 26,* 13-24.

Teachout, D. J., & Hamann, D. L. (in press). A comparison of the environmental models of three types of music classes. *Proceedings of the symposium 95: The sociology of music education—theoretical underpinnings and practical applications.* Norman, OK: GIA Publications.

Toenjes, C. M., & Borgen, F. H. (1974). Validity generalization of Holland's hexagonal model. *Measurement and Evaluation in Guidance, 7,* 79-85.

Viernstein, M. C. (1972). The extension of Holland's occupational classification to all occupations in the Dictionary of Occupational Titles. *Journal of Vocational Behavior, 2,* 107-121.

Webb, N. M., Shavelson, R. J., Shea, J., & Morello, E. (1981). Generalizability of general education development ratings of jobs in the United States. *Journal of Applied Psychology, 66,* 186-192.

Wiggins, J. D., Moody, A. D., & Lederer, D. A. (1983). Personality typologies related to marital satisfaction. *American Mental Health Counselors Association Journal, 6,* 169-178.

Williams, J. E. (1967). *Conflict between freshmen male roommates* (Research Report No. 10-67). College Park, MD: Counseling Center, University of Maryland.